ASIA AND THE PACIFIC

A HANDBOOK

HANDBOOKS TO THE MODERN WORLD

WESTERN EUROPE
THE SOVIET UNION AND EASTERN EUROPE
THE MIDDLE EAST
AFRICA
ASIA AND THE PACIFIC
THE UNITED STATES
CANADA
LATIN AMERICA AND THE CARIBBEAN

HANDBOOKS TO THE MODERN WORLD

ASIA AND THE PACIFIC

Volume 1

Edited by

ROBERT H. TAYLOR

Facts On File
New York • Oxford

ASIA AND THE PACIFIC
Copyright © 1991 by Facts On File Publications

Facts On File, Inc.   Facts On File Limited
460 Park Avenue South   or   Collins Street
New York NY 10016   Oxford OX4 1XJ
USA   United Kingdom

British CIP data available on request from Facts On File.

Facts On File books are available at special discounts when purchased in bulk quantities for businesses, associations, institutions or sales promotion. Please contact the Special Sales Department of our New York office at 212/683-2244 (dial 800/322-8755 except in NY, AK or HI).

Library of Congress Cataloging-in-Publication Data
Asia and the Pacific / edited by Robert H. Taylor.
        p.   cm. — (Handbooks to the modern world)
    Includes bibliographical references.
    1. Asia.   2. Australasia.   3. Islands of the Pacific.   I. Taylor,
Robert H., 1943–   II. Series: Handbooks to the modern world
(Facts on File, Inc.)
DS5.A79 1990
950—dc20   89-23376
    ISBN 0-8160-1826-x (Vol. I)   CIP
    ISBN 0-8160-1827-8 (Vol. II)
    ISBN 0-8160-1622-4 (set)

Composition by Maple-Vail Book Manufacturing Group
Manufactured by Maple-Vail Book Manufacturing Group
Printed in the United States of America

10 9 8 7 6 5 4 3 2 1

This book is printed on acid-free paper.

CONTRIBUTORS

SHIRIN AKINER is lecturer in Central Asian studies at the School of Oriental and African Studies, University of London. Her publications include *Islamic Peoples of the Soviet Union* (1986). She has traveled widely in Soviet Central Asia and western China, and has been a consultant on many films and broadcasts on these regions.

BARBARA WATSON ANDAYA received her doctorate in history from Cornell University and has held positions at the University of Malaya and the Australian National University. She is now senior tutor in the department of history at Auckland University, New Zealand. Her major publications include *Perak, the Abode of Grace: A Study of an Eighteenth Century Malay State* (1979) and *A History of Malaysia* (with Leonard Y. Andaya, 1982).

LEONARD Y. ANDAYA is associate professor of history and director of the Centre for Asian Studies at the University of Auckland, New Zealand. He has taught at the University of Malaya and has been a research fellow in the department of Pacific and Southeast Asian history at the Australian National University. His publications include *The Kingdom of Johor 1641–1728* (1975), *The Heritage of Arung Palakka: A History of South Sulawesi (Celebes) in the Seventeenth Century* (1981) and *A History of Malaysia* (with Barbara Watson Andaya, 1982).

ROBERT F. ASH is lecturer in economics at the School of Oriental and African Studies, University of London, where he is also chairman of the Contemporary China Institute. He has published widely on Chinese agriculture and economy.

HUGH D. R. BAKER is reader in modern Chinese at the University of London, where he teaches Mandarin and Cantonese as well as Chinese social institutions. He has carried out anthropological fieldwork in Hong Kong and China. Publications include *A Chinese Lineage Village: Sheung Shui* (1968), *Ancestral Images: A Hong Kong Album*, 3 vols. (1979–81), *New Peace County: A Chinese Gazetteer of the Hong Kong Region* (with Peter Y. L. Ng, 1983) and *The Overseas Chinese* (1987).

SANJOY BANERJEE is a lecturer in the international relations program at San Francisco State University. He received his doctorate from Yale University in international relations in 1982 and is the author of *Dominant Classes and the State in Development: Theory and the Case of India* (1984). In addition, he has contributed articles to the *International Studies Quarterly* and the *Journal of Conflict Resolution*.

CRAIG BAXTER, professor of the politics and history of Asia at Juniata College, Huntingdon, Pennsylvania, was a U.S. Foreign Service officer from 1956 to 1980 and served in several posts in South Asia, including Dhaka. Among his books are *Bangladesh: A New Nation in an Old Setting* (1984) and *A Historical Dictionary of*

Bangladesh (with Syedur Rahman, forthcoming). He has also written extensively on Pakistan and India.

JAMES R. BRANDON is professor in the department of drama and theater, University of Hawaii, Manoa. His major publications include *Traditional Asian Plays* (1972), *Kabuki: Five Classic Plays* (1975) and *Chushingura: Studies in Kabuki and the Puppet Theater* (1982). Brandon was founding editor of the *Asian Theatre Journal.*

IAN BROWN is lecturer in economic history with reference to Southeast Asia at the School of Oriental and African Studies, University of London. He is the author of *The Elite and the Economy in Siam, c. 1890–1920* (1988) and is editor of and contributor to *The Economics of Africa and Asia in the later-War Depression* (1989).

RICHARD BURGHART was educated at Williams College and the University of London. He has taught at the London School of Economics and the School of Oriental and African Studies, University of London. His present post is at Heidelberg University. He has published widely on Bhutan and Nepal, and has edited works on Hinduism in Great Britain and on Indian religions.

LARRY L. BURMEISTER is assistant professor of sociology at the University of Kentucky and a specialist in international development. His recent publications include *Research, Realpolitik and Development in Korea: The State and the Green Revolution,* and articles in *Pacific Focus, Economic Development* and *Cultural Change.*

TERENCE J. BYRES, founder-editor of the *Journal of Peasant Studies,* is senior lecturer in economics at the School of Oriental and African Studies, University of London. He has written extensively on the Indian economy, especially the agrarian question. Among his works are contributions to *Sharecropping and Sharecroppers* (1983) and *Feudalism and Non-European Societies* (1985).

CHAN HENG CHEE is former head of the department of political science at the National University of Singapore, and is at present director of the Institute of Policy Studies, Singapore. Dr. Chan is the author of many books and articles, including *Singapore: The Politics of Survival, 1965–1967* (1971) and *The Dynamics of One Party Dominance: The PAP at the Grassroots* (1976).

DAVID CHANDLER is research director of Southeast Asian studies at Monash University, Melbourne. Educated at Harvard, Yale and Michigan, he served in the U.S. Foreign Service in Cambodia in the early 1960s. He is the author of numerous publications, including *A History of Cambodia* (1983) and *The Tragedy of Cambodian History* (forthcoming).

EDWARD K. Y. CHEN is director of Asian studies, University of Hong Kong, has held visiting professorships at Yale, Oxford, the East-West Center in Hawaii and the University of California at Davis. He is the author of *Hyper-Growth in Asian Economies* (1979) and *Multinational Corporations: Technology and Employment* (1983).

YANGSUN CHOU is a graduate of National Taiwan University and a doctoral candidate in the department of political science, Columbia University. He is the author and editor of numerous books and articles in Chinese, and teaches political science at National Taiwan University.

STEPHEN P. COHEN, professor of political science in Asian studies at the University of Illinois, has worked on the policy planning staff of the U.S. Department of State (1985–87). He is the author or editor of five books, including *The Pakistan Army* and *The Security of South Asia*. He is cofounder of the Program in Arms Control, Disarmament and International Security at the University of Illinois.

ELISABETH CROLL, a fellow at the School of Oriental and African Studies, University of London, is an anthropologist who has spent over a decade engaged in research on the People's Republic of China. She is the author of numerous books on China, including *Feminism and Socialism in China, The Politics of Marriage in Contemporary China, The Family Rice Bowl: Food and the Domestic Economy in China,* and *Chinese Women since Mao*. She has undertaken several studies and consultancies for the United Nations and other agencies.

BRUCE CUMINGS is professor of East Asian history at the University of Chicago and the author of the two-volume study *The Origins of the Korean War* (1981, 1989) as well as *Industrial Behemoth: The Northeast Asian Political Economy in the 20th Century* (forthcoming). He visited North Korea twice in 1987 with a Thames Television documentary film team.

CHRISTOPHER FINDLAY received his doctorate in economics from the Australian National University, where he subsequently did research on East Asia in the Research School of Pacific Studies. In 1984 he joined the economics department of the University of Adelaide, where he is a visiting senior lecturer. He is also a research associate of the Australia-Japan Research Centre at the Australian National University. Findlay's major publications include *The Political Economy of Manufacturing Protection: Experiences of ASEAN and Australia* (jointly edited with Ross Garnaut, 1986).

DON M. FLOURNOY is associate professor in the school of telecommunications at Ohio University, where he served as dean of University College for 10 years. Educated at Southern Methodist University, University of Texas, Boston University and the University of London, Flournoy has worked as a consultant to the ministries of Education, Information and Science, and Technologies of Indonesia; and he has conducted research on corporate video and the new technologies of telecommunication, especially satellite communications in development.

HARUHIRO FUKUI is a professor in the department of political science, University of California, Santa Barbara. He studied at Tokyo University and received his doctorate from the Australian National University. Fukui's publications include *Party in Power: The Japanese Liberal-Democrats and Policy-Making* (coauthor, 1970), *Managing an Alliance: The Politics of U.S.-Japanese Relations* (1976), *The Textile Wrangle: Conflict in Japanese-American Relations, 1969–1971* (1979) and *Japan and the New Ocean Regime* (1985). He also edited *Political Parties of Asia and the Pacific* (1985) and *Japan and the World* (1988).

SUMIT GANGULY is an assistant professor of political science at Hunter College of the City University of New York. He is the author of *The Origins of War in South Asia: The Indo-Pakistani Conflicts since 1947* (1986) and is at present working on a book that seeks to reassess the origins of the Sino-Indian border war of 1962.

ANTHONY GOLDSTONE is editor for the Far East and Australasia at the Economist Intelligence Unit in London.

SHARON HOFFMAN, who holds a master's degree in public policy from Carnegie-Mellon University, is a research fellow with the Energy Program at the East-West Center in Honolulu, where she supervises research on the Australian and Philippine energy programs as well as the Ocean Thermal Energy Conversion project. She was previously a research fellow at Harvard University and has worked as a consultant for several governments and oil companies. Her publications include *World Synthetic Fuels Production: A Realistic Assessment* (with David T. Isaak, 1983) and *Deregulating Australia's Oil: The Implications for Global and Regional Markets* (with Fereidun Fesharaki, 1987).

CHRISTOPHER HOWE is professor of the economics of Asia at the School of Oriental and African Studies, University of London. He has written widely on the economies of China and Japan.

COLIN A. HUGHES is a graduate of Columbia University and the London School of Economics. He has written extensively about Australian government and politics, and elections in particular. He is professor of government at the University of Queensland and has been professorial fellow in political science at the Institute of Advanced Studies at the Australian National University (1975–84). In 1984–88 he was electoral commissioner of Australia.

GRAHAM HUTCHINGS, a journalist and historian, is China specialist with the London *Daily Telegraph*. He has written on the Republican period in Chinese history for the *China Quarterly*, and has taught modern Chinese history at Hatfield Polytechnic and the City Literary Institute, London.

CHRISTINE INGLIS is senior lecturer in the department of social and policy studies at the University of Sydney. She has conducted research on a variety of educational topics, including ethnic relations in Australia, Southeast Asia and the Pacific, and their relevance to education and economics.

TAKASHI INOGUCHI is associate professor of political science at the University of Tokyo. He received a doctorate at the Massachusetts Institute of Technology, and has worked at Sophia University in Japan, the Graduate Institute of International Studies in Geneva, Harvard University and the Australian National University. Inoguchi has published 10 books in Japanese and in English, his most recent being *State and Societies* (in Japanese) and Vol. 2 of *The Political Economy of Japan: The Changing International Context*, of which he was coeditor (1988). He has also served on the editorial boards of such publications as the *Journal of Japanese Studies* and *International Studies Quarterly*.

GEORGE JOFFE is consulting editor for the Middle East and North Africa for The Economist publications; research associate, Centre of Near and Middle East Studies, School of Oriental and African Studies, University of London; and the author of the articles "Islam in Africa" and "The Maghreb, or Western Arab World: Algeria, Morocco and Tunisia" in companion volumes of the Handbooks to the Modern World series.

CONTRIBUTORS

GAVIN W. JONES is professorial fellow in the department of demography of the Research School of Social Sciences at the Australian National University. He has worked with the Population Council in New York City, and has spent 10 years working with universities and planning agencies in Indonesia, Malaysia, Thailand and Sri Lanka. Dr. Jones has published several books and many articles on population and development issues in Indonesia, Malaysia and Asia generally, as well as on educational planning and population mobility.

AUDREY KAHIN was educated at Nottingham University and Cornell University. She is the editor of Cornell's journal *Indonesia,* as well as of many other publications of the Cornell Southeast Asia Program. Dr. Kahin is the author of articles on the Indonesian revolution, Minangkabau society and the nationalist movement. She has edited *Regional Dynamics of the Indonesian Revolution* (1985), coedited *Interpreting Indonesian Politics* (1982) and translated *Prisoners of Kota Cane* (1986).

FAITH KEENAN, a graduate of Columbia University's School of International Affairs, has worked for the Intergovernmental Committee for Migration at the Philippine Refugee Processing Center (1983) and has covered Indochina and Thailand as a reporter for United Press International's Bangkok bureau (1985). She has traveled extensively in Indochina and has written several articles for Hearst Newspapers on Vietnam, Cambodia and Laos. She is a contributor to *Indochina Issues,* a publication of the Indochina Project in Washington, D.C., and is currently a reporter in the New York bureau of Hearst Newspapers.

SIR EDMUND LEACH, F.B.A. (1910–89), was provost of King's College (1966–79), university reader in social anthropology (1957–72) and professor of social anthropology (1972–78) at the University of Cambridge. He was in Myanmar and eastern India during Worl War II, combining military service with anthropological research. He later did fieldwork in Sarawak and Sri Lanka, and published extensively on the Asia and Pacific region. After taking a first degree from Cambridge in engineering, he received a doctorate in social anthropology from the London School of Economics in 1946.

LEE POH PING received his doctorate from Cornell University in government and teaches in the faculty of economics, University of Malaya, Kuala Lumpur. Dr. Lee has published on the economic and political evolution of Southeast Asia, and on the region's relations with Japan and other extraregional powers.

JOHN A. LENT, who studied in Norway, Mexico, Japan and India, received his doctorate from the University of Iowa. He was a Fulbright Scholar in the Philippines and first coordinator of the pioneering mass communications program in Malaysia, at Universiti Sains Malaysia. He also pioneered in the study of international communications, especially Third World mass media. Lent is a professor at Temple University, Philadelphia, and the founder-director of Third World Media Associates.

R. A. LONGMIRE is editor of *Asian Affairs,* the journal of the Royal Society for Asian Affairs, London. Formerly with the British Foreign Office Research Department as a specialist on Soviet and Southeast Asian affairs, his latest publication is *A Historical Survey of Soviet Relations with South-East Asia* (1988).

CONTRIBUTORS

ERHARD LOUVEN, holder of a doctorate in economics, was until 1981 research fellow in the department of East Asian sciences at Ruhr University Bochum. He is at present senior research fellow at the Institute for Asian Studies, Hamburg. His major works include *Technologietransfer und angepasste Technologien* (1982) and *Perspektiven der Wirtschaftsreform in China* (1987).

JAMES MANOR is professorial fellow and director of research at the Institute of Development Studies, University of Sussex. He has taught at Yale, Harvard and Leicester universities, and since 1980 has edited the *Journal of Commonwealth and Comparative Politics*. His most recent book is *The Excellent Utopian: Bandaranaike and Ceylon* (forthcoming).

THOMAS W. MARETZKI is professor of medical anthropology at the University of Hawaii, Manoa. He has done research on health-related topics in Southeast Asia and in Hawaii and has served as a consultant to government and private agencies in these regions.

BRUCE MATTHEWS is the C. B. Lumsden professor of comparative religion at Acadia University, Nova Scotia. He is the author of *Craving and Salvation: A Study of Buddhist Soteriology* (1983) and numerous articles on religio-cultural and communal problems in South and Southeast Asia.

F. A. MEDIANSKY holds degrees in government from universities in the United States and Australia. He is associate professor and head of the School of Political Science at the University of New South Wales. He has written widely on Pacific security issues and has coedited a major reader on Australian foreign policy.

JUDITH NAGATA was educated at University College, London, and the University of Illinois. She is professor of anthropology at York University, Toronto, where she is conducting research on Southeast Asian immigrants. Dr. Nagata is the author of *Malaysian Mosaic: Perspectives on a Poly-Ethnic Society* (1979) and *The Reflowering of Malaysian Islam: Modern Religious Radicals and Their Roots* (1984), and has also edited *Pluralism in Malaysia: Myth or Reality?* (1975).

ANDREW J. NATHAN, a member of the department of political science at Columbia University, is author of *Chinese Democracy* (1985), coauthor of *Human Rights in Contemporary China* (1986) and coeditor of *Popular Culture in Late Imperial China* (1985).

WILLIAM NESTER received his doctorate in political science from the University of California, Santa Barbara. He teaches politics at St. John's University, New York City. He has done research on marine policy issues in the South Pacific and is the author of two forthcoming books: *Japan's Growing Power over East Asia and the World Economy: Ends and Means*; and *Japan's Modern Political Economy: Continuities, Changes, Challenges*.

URMILA PHADNIS is professor of South Asian studies at Jawaharlal Nehru University, New Delhi. She has written extensively on the politics of South Asia, including *Toward Integration of Indian States* (1968), *Sri Lanka* (1972), *Religion and Politics in Sri Lanka* (1976) and *Maldives: Winds of Change in an Atoll State* (with Indira Malani, 1985).

CONTRIBUTORS

JONATHAN D. POLLACK is head of the political science department of The RAND Corporation, Santa Monica, California. He has published widely on U.S.-Chinese relations, Sino-Soviet affairs, Chinese strategic and technological development, and East Asian security. His recent writings include *Reluctant Warrior: China in the Korean War* (1989) and *Planning for China's Defense: Military R&D in Transition* (1989).

DAVID C. POTTER is senior lecturer in government in the social sciences faculty of the Open University, Great Britain. He is editor of the *Journal of Commonwealth and Comparative Politics*. His research has focused on India's bureaucracy, and his publications include *Government in Rural India* (1964), *Lords, Peasants and Politics* (1974), *The Practice of Comparative Politics* (coeditor, 1978), *Society and the Social Sciences* (coeditor, 1981) and *India's Public Administrators, 1919–1983* (1986).

J. MOHAN RAO, who holds a doctorate in economics from Harvard University, is an assistant professor of economics at Boston University. He has written several articles on the theory of economic development, agrarian relations, agricultural policy and Indian economic history. He has been a consultant to the Food and Agriculture Organization and the World Institute of Development Economics Research.

LINDA K. RICHTER is associate professor of political science at Kansas State University, where she teaches public administration and policy. She is an associate editor of *Annals of Tourism Research,* and the author of two books and many articles on tourism policy. Her most recent volume is *The Politics of Tourism in Asia: A Comparative Policy Perspective* (1989).

WILLIAM L. RICHTER is head of the department of political science at Kansas State University. He has conducted research in India and Pakistan, and has published numerous articles on the South Asian region in such publications as *Asian Survey, Journal of Asian Studies, Pacific Affairs* and *Current History.*

HANS CHRISTOPH RIEGER is research fellow at the South Asia Institute, Heidelberg University. Since 1987 he has been an adviser and visiting fellow of the ASEAN Economic Research Unit of the Institute of Southeast Asian Studies, Singapore, and the representative of the Konrad Adenauer Foundation in Singapore.

ANTHONY ROWLEY was for seven years business editor of the *Far Eastern Economic Review,* and was based in Hong Kong, from where he traveled extensively to study capital market development. He has written for *The Times* of London and has published two books: *Asian Stockmarkets: The Inside Story* and *The Barons of European Industry.* He is at present international finance editor of the *Far Eastern Economic Review* and is based in London.

IRINA RYBACEK is a freelance editor and writer. Since 1980 she has worked on various projects for Scribner's reference department, and she has also edited and written articles for *Worldmark Encyclopedia of the Nations, Lands and Peoples, Academic American Encyclopedia* and *Funk & Wagnalls New Encyclopedia.*

E. F. SCHUMACHER (1911–   ), was born in Bonn and emigrated to England in 1937. He was educated at the universities of Bonn and Berlin, Oxford (as a Rhodes Scholar) and Columbia University. After several years in business, farming and journalism, he joined the British Control Commission for Germany in 1946 as economic adviser. In 1950 he became economic adviser of the National Coal Board, London, and in 1963 director of statistics. In 1955 he was posted to the United Nations as economic adviser to the government of the Union of Burma; and in 1962 he was invited by the government of India to advise the Indian Planning Commission on problems of Indian development policy. Schumacher, who traveled widely in Europe, the United States and Asia, published many articles and several books on economic and philosophical subjects, of which the best known is *Small Is Beautiful: A Study of Economics as if People Mattered* (1973).

HENRY G. SCHWARZ teaches courses on Mongolian history, society and culture, as well as on modern Chinese history at the Center for East Asian Studies of Western Washington University, Bellingham. Over the past 14 years he has spent much time at the Central Nationalities Institute in Beijing and in the border areas of northern China, particularly Inner Mongolia. He has also been a delegate to several conferences of the International Congress of Mongolists in Ulaanbaatar. Professor Schwarz is the director of the Mongolian Summer Program for U.S. students studying Mongolian at Inner Mongolia University.

GERALD SEGAL is editor of the *Pacific Review* and lecturer in politics at the University of Bristol. His publications include *The Great Power Triangle* (1982) and *A Guide to the World Today* (1987); he also edited *The Soviet Union in East Asia* (1984) and *Sino-Soviet Relations after Mao* (1987).

BHABANI SEN GUPTA received his doctorate in comparative politics and international relations from the City University of New York and is research professor at New Delhi's Centre for Policy Research. He has also taught at Jawaharlal Nehru University and at Columbia University. Sen Gupta's numerous articles and 15 books include *The Fulcrum of Asia: Relations among China, India, Pakistan and the USSR* (1968), *Communism in Indian Politics* (1972) and *The Gorbachev Factor in World Politics* (1988).

PHILIP STOTT, a tropical ecologist specializing in Asia, is head of the department of geography and former chairman of the Centre of South East Asian Studies at the School of Oriental and African Studies, University of London. His most recent research has dealt with fire and forestry in Thailand. He is editor of the *Journal of Biogeography* and is a member of the editorial advisory board of *Progress in Physical Geography*. Mr. Stott has written, in addition to other publications, *Historical Plant Geography* (1981), a basic text in the field.

ULF SUNDHAUSSEN has degrees from the Free University, Berlin, and Monash University, Melbourne. He has taught at the University of Papua New Guinea and is now senior lecturer in government at the University of Queensland. He is the author of *The Road to Power: Indonesian Military Politics 1945-1967* and coauthor of *Abdul Haris Nasution: A Political Biography,* and he has written many articles on the military in politics.

DAVID TAYLOR is lecturer in politics with reference to South Asia, and chairman of the Centre of South Asian Studies at the School of Oriental and African Studies, University of London. His field of specialization is the politics of India and Pakistan. He has coedited several volumes, including *Political Identity in South Asia*

(1978) and *Changing South Asia* (1984), and has written numerous articles on India and Pakistan.

ROBERT H. TAYLOR is professor of politics and head of the department of economic and political studies at the School of Oriental and African Studies, University of London. He has taught at the University of Sydney and at Wilberforce University in Ohio. His publications include *The State in Burma* (1987) and he was a contributor to *In Search of Southeast Asia: A Modern History* (edited by David Joel Steinberg, rev. ed. 1987).

M. J. C. TEMPLETON was a New Zealand Foreign Service officer from 1946 to 1984. He served as New Zealand's permanent representative to the United Nations from 1973 to 1978; as leader of the New Zealand delegation to the Law of the Sea Conference, 1978–84; and as deputy secretary of foreign affairs, 1978–84. He was then appointed as the first director of the Institute of Policy Studies at the Victoria University of Wellington, a position he held until 1986. He now coordinates a program of historical research on aspects of the development and conduct of New Zealand's foreign policy.

MARINA THORBORG, an economist who has spent over a decade in research on the People's Republic of China and on Asia, is a fellow at the Center for East and Southeast Asian Studies at the University of Copenhagen. She received her doctorate from the University of Uppsala and has published widely on the subject of women in China and elsewhere in Asia.

CHIEN-CHUNG TSAO is a doctoral candidate in the School of Communication Art and Theater at Temple University, Philadelphia. He holds a master's degree in communication from Western Illinois University (1983). Before he came from Taiwan to the United States, Tsao served as a magazine editor and television producer. He has written several articles in the field of international communications. At present he is an instructor in the department of radio-TV-film at Temple and serves as a research associate for the Third World Media Associates.

WILLIAM S. TURLEY received his doctorate at the University of Washington and is professor of political science at Southern Illinois University. In addition to *The Second Indochina War,* he has written numerous articles and edited volumes on Vietnamese communism and on the third Indochina war. In 1982–84 he was a visiting professor at Chulalongkorn University, Bangkok, under the auspices of the Fulbright Program and the John F. Kennedy Foundation of Thailand.

ANDREW TURTON is senior lecturer in anthropology and chairman of the Centre of South East Asian Studies at the School of Oriental and African Studies, University of London. He has conducted extensive fieldwork in Thailand. His numerous publications include *Production, Power and Participation in Rural Thailand: Experiences of Poor Farmers' Groups* (1987). Turton has also been involved as a consultant in Thailand for various U.N. agencies.

WILFRIDO V. VILLACORTA, who studied at the University of the Philippines and the Catholic University of America, is vice-president of De La Salle University in Manila, where he is also professor of international relations. He is the author of many articles on Philippine politics and affairs, and has been a member of the

Philippines Council for Foreign Relations as well as of the drafting commission of the 1987 Philippine constitution.

ANDREW G. WALDER is professor of sociology at Harvard University. He is the author of *Chang Ch'un-ch'iao and Shanghai's January Revolution* and *Communist Neo-Traditionalism: World and Authority in Chinese Industry.* The latter won the Joseph Levenson prize of the Association of Asian Studies.

MARTIN E. WEINSTEIN holds the Japan chair and is the director of the Japan Program at the Center for Strategic and International Studies in Washington, D.C., while on leave from the University of Illinois. He previously worked at Columbia University, the Brookings Institution and the U.S. Embassy in Tokyo. His numerous publications include *Northeast Asian Security after Vietnam* (1982) and *The Making of Japan's Future Leaders: Portraits of an International Elite.*

JO ANN WHITE, a writer and editor specializing in Third World affairs, holds a master's degree in international relations from New York University. She was managing editor of *Lands and Peoples* and senior social studies editor of *The New Book of Knowledge* and *Academic American Encyclopedia.* Other projects have included work for *Merit Students Encyclopedia, Americana Annual, Worldmark Encyclopedia of the Nations* and *The World and its Peoples.* She is also the author of *Impact: Asian Views of the West and African Views of the West.*

ROBERT WIHTOL, a native of Finland, holds a master's degree from the University of Helsinki and a doctorate from Oxford University. He worked for the International Labor Organization for five years in Asia before taking his present position at the ILO headquarters in Geneva. He is the author of *The Asian Development Bank and Rural Development: Policy and Practice.*

ALAN WOOD is lecturer in Russian history at the University of Lancaster, convenor of the British Universities Siberian Studies Seminar and editor of its journal *SIBIRICA.* Among his most recent publications are *Siberia: Problems and Prospects for Regional Development* (1987), *The Origins of the Russian Revolution 1861–1917* (1987) and *The Development of Siberia: People and Resources* (1989).

M. E. YAPP is professor of the modern history of Western Asia at the School of Oriental and African Studies, University of London. He has studied Afghan history for many years, and in addition to his *Strategies of British India* (1980) has published several articles on the subject. His most recent book is *The Making of the Modern Near East* (1987).

JOSEPH J. ZASLOFF is professor of political science at the University of Pittsburgh. He holds a doctorate in international relations from the Graduate Institute of International Studies at the University of Geneva, and has served as visiting professor at the universities of Saigon, the Philippines and Nice. His most recent publication is *Apprentice Revolutionaries: The Communist Movement in Laos, 1930–1985* (with MacAlister Brown, 1985); and he edited *Postwar Indochina: Old Enemies and New Allies* (1988).

CONTENTS

CONTENTS

CONTENTS

MAPS

PREFACE

The importance of the Asia-Pacific region for the future of the world is obvious. Over half the globe's population lives in the countries discussed in these two volumes. The economic power of the major states of Asia is rapidly overtaking that of the older industrialized nations of Europe and North America. The major wars of the post-World War II era have occurred in Asia. Every one of the world's great religions is represented in Asia. In fact, no complete discussion of any topic of the contemporary period can ignore Asia without leaving out fundamental and growing questions of importance.

The editor of the predecessor to these volumes[1], the late Guy Wint, began his 1965 foreword: "This book is concerned with a huge area containing over half the world's population. In the last half century much of it has undergone great political and social change, and the remainder seems destined for upheaval no less drastic, whether by revolution or by more orderly processes." Wint's description of a quarter century ago could be repeated today; his prediction has come true, and has required an almost complete revision of the Handbook. Only one of the original essays has been reprinted unrevised in this edition[2] and only one other essay has been rewritten by the original author[3]; none of the other authors in the present volumes wrote for the first edition.

In 1965 the decolonization process in postwar Asia was still very much on people's minds. A common concern then was the possible future of Asian states and societies after independence. Framed in the cold war concepts of that time, the simplistic question of whether Asia would "go Communist" or "remain free" seemed to many a real issue. The Vietnam War, itself largely a result of this view of Asia's future, was raging at the time, and it forced most observers to draw conclusions based less on the realities of Asian conditions than on a European and American conception of world politics that very few Asians shared. This conception of reality formed in Washington, Moscow, London and Paris was imposed on governments in Beijing, Jakarta and Delhi. Those governments that accepted it— in Bangkok, Tokyo, Manila and elsewhere—had their own reasons for doing so,

[1] Guy Wint, *Asia: A Handbook* (London: Anthony Blond; New York: Praeger, 1965).
[2] The late E. F. Schumacher's "Buddhist Economics" has been reprinted mainly for its interesting argument and because it inspired his later influential volume *Small Is Beautiful*.
[3] "Minority Groups in Asia," by the late Sir Edmund Leach, F.B.A.

and they were different from those on the basis of which Western governments had constructed the cold war in Asia out of the issues of the cold war in Europe.

Many now foresee the end of the divisions that resulted from the European cold war. Asia has already broken that mold. Bangkok is now allied with Beijing over Cambodia. Jakarta has close ties with Washington. Tokyo has economic interests and, increasingly, political interests that are global and independent of American policy. The major events in Asian politics in the latter part of the 1980s—"people's power" in Manila, elections in Pakistan, revolt in Burma (now Myanmar), economic experimentation in China and Vietnam—are evidence of the fact that external political interests have less impact on Asian affairs now than at any time since before colonization.

Despite the growing political independence of most Asian states, the economic links between Asia and the remainder of the globe are now more interwoven than ever. Asia and the Pacific contain the most dynamic economies in the world, with per capita incomes in some countries equal to or surpassing those of some European countries. The real paradox is that much of the rest of the population of Asia still lives in conditions of extreme poverty and physical deprivation. Whether all of Asia can equal the economic growth rates of Japan, South Korea, Taiwan, Hong Kong and Singapore, or their rapid pursuers, Thailand, Malaysia and others, remains to be seen. If this were to happen, the possibility exists that Europe and the United States would then become more dependent upon Asia than Asia is on the Western economies.

The differences between the perspectives of this Handbook and its predecessor demonstrate the necessity of seeing Asian states and societies from more genuinely independent perspectives than was possible a quarter of a century ago. The overwhelming majority of the authors in this volume, many themselves from Asia and the Pacific, and all specialists on the issues they address, were educated during the postcolonial period that the first Handbook described. Therefore, they bring different approaches and more varied concerns to the topics discussed. The majority of the countries of Asia and the Pacific no longer "exist in the shadow of their colonial past," as Wint wrote. Their immediate past is 30 to 40 years of independent existence, during which, in most of them, new generations of leaders have come to power in political, military, economic and other spheres. The present Handbook attempts to reflect this transition.

Like the first version, this edition also devotes space to considering the relationship of the states of Asia to the remainder of the globe. The essays that form the introduction to Part III provide varying perspectives on these relations. What becomes clear from these brief histories and the related essays that follow is how much more Asian states determine their relations with Europe and America than they did in the 1960s. Equally interesting historically and probably of more significance, however, is the clear perception that emerges that it is the relations of Asian states with each other that is now more important to their existence and potential. The economic, political and military might of India, China and Japan will remain more important to most states of Asia and the Pacific in the future than the balance of power in the North Atlantic and Western Europe.[4]

The essays in these two volumes reveal many things, but one of the most ob-

[4]Of course, barring nuclear war between the United States and the Soviet Union.

vious and important is that the intellectually patronizing attitudes of Europeans and North Americans in the past toward Asia and its civilizations can no longer be tolerated.[5] More is known now about the complexity of the origins of ideas than in previous generations. The artificial boundaries that 19th-century European thought, echoing European colonialism, created between the "stagnant" East and the "dynamic" West, have been shown to be not only racist but sterile. What is now apparent is that the dynamics of Asian civilizations and cultures were often too subtle and complex for most foreigners to grasp. The authors in the present volumes know this, and also know that they are presenting only a small part of the histories, politics and cultures of the countries and regions they are discussing. This humility is not false but genuine and necessary, and it is hoped that readers will be aware of this as they go through the essays. The further suggested readings themselves are only guides to start one on a serious study of the themes raised.

This Handbook on Asia and the Pacific incorporates a great deal more territory and cultures than a discussion primarily concerning Asia as normally conceived entails. Australia, New Zealand and the island states and dependencies of the Pacific are also an integral part of the picture. This is as it should be, for the future of the primarily European settlers of Australia and New Zealand is now, and is increasingly perceived by these people to be, more intimately linked with the future of Asia than with the future of Europe. The smaller island states of the Pacific are also part of the future of Asia, for Asia will determine to a large extent the future of the world's greatest ocean.

Allusion has already been drawn to the intellectual perspectives of the majority of the contributors to these volumes. The quality of their work speaks for itself. As editor, I have given them broad latitude to pursue their topics as they thought most appropriate. I have not tried to force any mold or format upon them, and they have responded by writing in their own idioms and styles. The result should, despite some inevitable overlap, consist of independent essays of merit in themselves. All of the authors have been chosen for their particular scholarly expertise, as well as their depth of understanding of their topics. Others might have written differently, and there are, indeed, contrary arguments presented within the volumes. Despite the paucity of experts on Asia and the Pacific, in contrast to the number of Europeanists and Americanists in the world's universities and learned institutions, as well as in the journalistic world, more is known now about Asia and the Pacific than 25 years ago. Still, not enough is known yet, and more resources need to be devoted to scholarship and research on the region.

Editing these volumes has been a more pleasurable experience than I had expected it to be. The quality of understanding of the purpose of the Handbook, as evinced by the contributions, was reassuring. Many individuals, in addition to the

[5] Wint was doubtless among the most well-intended of authors on Asia, but still he could write that Asia had failed to contribute to the stock of human "ideas" or that "at present only a minority of the people of Asia takes part in politics." The naive notion that a volunteer in the Chinese People's Liberation Army fighting the Japanese or the Chinese Nationalist government, or that Javanese, Burmese, Vietnamese and many other peasant populations did not participate in politics when they rebelled against their colonial rulers before World War II or their "own" governments after independence, does not even stand up to the cold war assumptions of the first edition of the Handbook.

contributors to the volumes, have assisted in its production. I wish to thank the copyeditors and cartographers for their excellent work, as well as the compilers of the basic information that comprises Part I. Janet Marks, secretary of the Department of Economic and Political Studies, School of Oriental and African Studies, provided considerable help. My wife, Joan, as always, helped in more ways than just providing home secretarial assistance. Andrew Kimmens, the handbooks series general editor, was always understanding and enthusiastic. Ultimately, the volume owes any success it may have to the scholarship of the more than 70 contributors, for whose considerable efforts I am most grateful.

Robert H. Taylor

ASIA AND THE PACIFIC

A HANDBOOK

BASIC INFORMATION

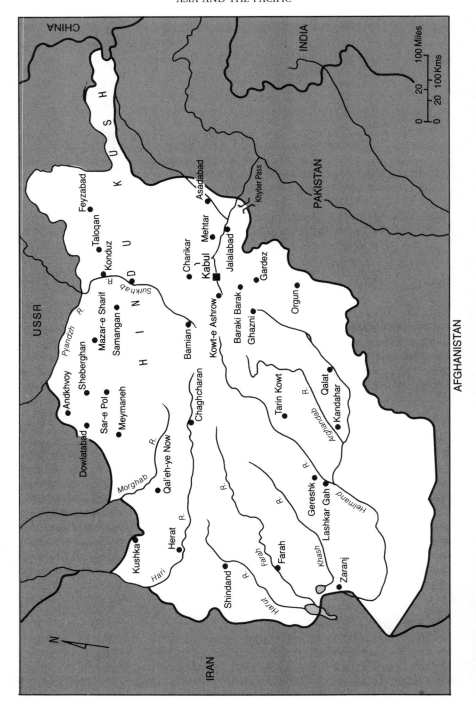

AFGHANISTAN

AFGHANISTAN

Features: Afghanistan, a landlocked country in Southwest Asia, is bordered by the USSR to the north, China to the extreme northeast, Pakistan to the east and south and Iran to the west. The country, which has an average elevation of more than 4,000 ft/1,219 m. above sea level, is divided by a series of high, barren mountain ranges of granite, gneiss, schist and crystalline limestone that extend southwest for some 700 miles/1,127 km. from the Pamir range in the northeast. The highest of these mountain ranges is the Hindu Kush in the northeast, a spur of the Himalaya: Many peaks rise to more than 20,000 ft/6,100 m. above sea level and have permanent snowcovers and glaciers. Thin grasses in the mountain valleys provide seasonal pasturage. The deeply eroded limestone and sandstone southeastern foothills of these mountains, among which the capital of Kabul and many other towns are located, have fertile pockets of alluvial fill and contain most of Afghanistan's remaining forests (which now cover only about 3% of the total land area). It is the most densely settled part of the country and is linked to Pakistan by the Khyber Pass. To the north are the plains of Turan, which contain more than half of the country's agricultural land but are isolated from the rest of Afghanistan by the mountains, where the lowest pass is 9,800 ft/2,987 m. above sea level. Most of southern and western Afghanistan is desert. The most barren and inhospitable areas are the Registan desert region in the south and the Sistan swamps on the Iranian border, where the surface is generally a mixture of gravel, clay, sand and loam, and the water table often lies 200 ft/61 m. below the surface. The southwestern deserts have occasional violent winter storms and are subject to steady, hot and drying winds from the north in summer. These winds cause sandstorms that frequently bury whole villages. Afghanistan's rivers flow outward from the central mountain core. The most important are the Kabul, which flows east to join the Indus in Pakistan; the Helmand, which flows south-southwest to the Iranian border; the Hari Rud, which flows west; and the Kunduz, which flows north to join the Amudar'ya on the northern border. Only the Kabul eventually reaches the sea; the rivers generally disappear soon after reaching the dry plains, but they are very important for irrigation. Most Afghan cities, including Kabul, Kandahar and Herat, are located where rivers leave the mountains. The lack of water limits agriculture more than the quality of the soil; about 6% of the land is cultivated, most of it on irrigated oases. The country is rich in mineral

3

resources, although few deposits have been exploited. Minerals include petroleum, natural gas, iron ore, copper, coal, cement, chrome, lead, zinc, molybdenum, tin, rare earths, gold, barite, celestite, sulfur, asbestos, uranium, talc, magnesite, muscovite and precious stones.

The country has a dry continental climate. Almost all the precipitation falls in winter as snow and in early spring, the mountains receiving by far the greatest amount. Temperatures vary greatly according to the time of day, season and elevation.

Area (est.): 251,733 sq. miles/652,090 sq. km.

Mean max. and min. temperatures: Kabul 32°F/0°C (January); Jalalabad 115°F/46°C (summer).

Mean annual rainfall: 10–12 in/250–300 mm.

POPULATION

Total population (1988 est.): 14,480,863.

Chief towns and populations: KABUL (1989 est., 2,200,000), Kandahar (1984 est., 203,177), Herat (1984 est., 159,804).

Distribution: Afghanistan's location in the heart of Asia has made it a conduit for trade, migration and conquest for centuries. As a result, its people form a mosaic of ethnic, linguistic and regional communities isolated from one another by tradition and geography. Although the country has never had a formal census, the population is estimated to be 52% Pathan (Pushtun), 20% Tadzhik, 9% Uzbek, 9% Hazara, 3% Chahar Amak, 2% Turkmen and 1% Baluch. The Pathan, who live mostly in the southern and eastern part of the country, may have moved into what is now Afghanistan from the Indus River valley in the 11th and 12th centuries. Often called the "true Afghans," they are divided into numerous semiautonomous and sometimes warring tribes. The Tadzhik, of Iranian origin, are mostly settled farmers and urban dwellers who are concentrated in the west around Herat and in the surrounding mountains. North of the Hindu Kush are Turkic Uzbek and Turkmen farmers and herders who are ethnically related to the people of Soviet and Chinese Turkestan. The seminomadic Hazara, of Mongol origin, are believed to have entered the area between the 13th and 15th centuries. They live mostly in the central highlands. The Chahar Amak consist of several tribes living in the western part of the country. The pastoral nomadic Baluch live mostly in the southern desert. Other groups include the Nuristanis in the high mountains of the east, who were known as *kafirs* (infidels) before their forced conversion to Islam in the late 19th century. They may be descended from the first inhabitants of the area.

The last Soviet troops left Afghanistan on February 15, 1989, under the terms of an accord signed in Geneva the previous year. By that time, many Soviet advisers and most foreign diplomats had also left Afghanistan. During the period of Soviet occupation (1979–89), Afghanistan experienced one of the greatest migrations in history. About one-third of the pre-1979

population fled to Pakistan, Iran and other countries. An estimated 3 million Afghans (half of them children) lived in refugee camps in Pakistan's North-West Frontier Province and Baluchistan Province. An estimated 80%–90% of the refugees in Pakistan came from regions near the border, and it was anticipated that they would eventually return home. The 2 million refugees in Iran were integrated into the local population. Within Afghanistan, as many as 2.5 million additional persons were displaced, many of them fleeing from rural to urban areas for safety. During the Soviet occupation, it is believed that at least 12,000 of Afghanistan's 22,000 farming villages were destroyed or abandoned. The population of Kabul swelled from less than 500,000 in the early 1970s to an estimated 2.2 million in 1989. Before the external and internal refugees returned home, it was necessary to remove millions of unexploded mines; provide farmers with draft animals, tools, seed, fertilizer and pesticides; repair destroyed and neglected wells and irrigation canals; rebuild housing; and provide enough food for the population until farmers could again harvest their own crops. The return was to be supervised by the U.N. high commissioner for refugees.

Language: Pashto and Dari (Afghan Persian), both of which belong to the Indo-Iranian language family, are the official languages, with Dari the primary language of literature, government and business. The primary language of about 50% of the population is Pashto; for another 35% it is Dari and for 11% it is various Turkic languages, including Uzbek and Turkmen. Some 30 minor languages are also spoken, and many of the people are bilingual. Arabic has long been taught as part of religious education. In recent years, Russian has been taught in urban schools.

Religion: Most Afghans were converted to Islam in the 7th century. Today, some 74% of the people (including most Pathan, Tadzhik, Uzbek and Turkmen) are Sunni Muslims. Another 25% (mostly Hazara) are Shiite Muslims. There are small numbers of Christians and Sikhs, and adherents of various other Muslim sects. Islam was the official religion until a Communist government came to power in 1978. Official atheism aroused widespread resentment; the government later modified its position, establishing the Department of Islamic Affairs in 1981 to build new mosques and maintain old ones, and declaring itself the protector of Islam in its 1987 constitution.

CONSTITUTIONAL SYSTEM

Constitution: Afghanistan was a constitutional monarchy from 1964 to 1973 and was under military rule from 1973 to 1977, when it was declared a one-party republic with an elected president. In 1978 a Communist government came to power and declared the Democratic Republic of Afghanistan, ruled by a Revolutionary Council headed by a president. The constitution of the present Republic of Afghanistan was adopted in November 1987 by a Loya Jirgah (Grand National Assembly, or traditional gathering of tribal leaders). It provides for a strong president assisted by a prime minister and for an elected Meli Shura (National Council). On February 19, 1989, President Najibullah declared a nationwide state of emergency of unspecified duration. He assumed leadership of a 20-member Military Council named to rule the country during the state of emergency.

Diplomatic efforts to establish a coalition government for Afghanistan prior to the withdrawal of the last of the Soviet forces in 1989 were unsuccessful. By that time about three-fourths of the country was under rebel control, with the government in Kabul controlling urban areas. On February 24, 1989, a Shura (Special Consultative Council) comprised mostly of representatives of the seven Sunni Muslim Afghan rebel groups based in Peshawar, Pakistan, selected an interim government in exile for what they called the "free Muslim state of Afghanistan." This government was recognized as the official government of Afghanistan by the Islamic Conference Organization, but most nations withheld diplomatic recognition pending a resolution of the escalating civil war. The rebel alliance said that it would hold elections for a council to appoint a permanent president. Meanwhile, real leadership of the government in exile remained in the hands of the Supreme Council of the Peshawar-based rebel alliance, whose leadership rotated every six months. It was unclear what role the Shiite Muslim Afghan rebel groups based in Iran (who had boycotted the Shura), traditional tribal and religious leaders and field commanders inside Afghanistan, as well as the exiled former Afghan king, would have in whatever government might ultimately emerge.

Head of state: Najibullah (Republic of Afghanistan); Sibgatullah Mojadedi (interim government in exile).

Executive: Under the constitution of 1987 the executive of the Republic of Afghanistan is a powerful president who also serves as head of the armed forces and is charged with the preservation of Islam. The president, who is elected by the Loya Jirgah, appoints a prime minister and cabinet and four vice-presidents. Prime Minister Mohammed Hassan Sharq (who had held office since May 1988 and was not a member of the Afghan Communist party) resigned on February 20, 1989, and most non-Communist cabinet members have been removed from office.

Legislature: The elected Meli Shura that took office in May 1988 is made up of two houses, the Wolosi Jirgah (Council of Representatives) and the Meshrano Jirgah (Council of Elders). Most of its members are not members of the Communist party, and several seats have been left vacant for rebels. The legislature is responsible to the Loya Jirgah, whose members are indirectly elected.

Political parties: The Afghan Communist party, the People's Democratic party of Afghanistan (PDPA), has an estimated 40,000 to 80,000 members. Since its founding in 1965 it has been divided into two often violently feuding factions, the Khalq (representing rural Pathans) and the less radical Parcham (representing urban Dari-speaking intellectuals). As part of a strategy of national reconciliation, the party redefined itself as nationalistic and Islamic. The party Central Committee (Sazman Iwalia) is headed by a secretary-general; Najibullah was appointed secretary-general in May 1986. The 1988 legislative elections were contested by the PDPA and other "democratic-left" parties grouped under an umbrella organization called the National Front of Afghanistan. The Peshawar-based rebel alliance is comprised of seven parties; refugees in Pakistan had to register with one of these parties to be entitled to food rations. Four of these parties sought the establishment of a fundamentalist Islamic republic in Afghanistan: the Islamic party led by Yunis Khalis, which included several of the most powerful rebel military commanders; the Islamic party led by the militant fundamentalist Gulbuddin Hekmatyar, one of the largest and most controversial groups, which broke with the interim government after the Soviet withdrawal; the Islamic Society, the most pragmatic fundamentalist group and the only one led by a non-Pathan (Burhanuddin Rabbani); and the Islamic Union for the Liberation of Afghanistan, whose leader, Abd-i-Rab Rasoul Sayaf, is prime minister of the interim government in exile. Traditional sources of authority in Afghanistan, such as village and tribal elders, are represented in three groups: the National Islamic Front for Afghanistan, led by hereditary religious leader Sayed Ahmed Gailani; the Afghanistan National Liberation Front, led by Sibgatullah Mojadedi; and the Islamic Revolutionary Movement, led by Mohammad Nabi Mohammadi. Other rebel parties based in Iran represent Afghanistan's Shiite minority.

Local government: In theory, Afghanistan has 29 provinces, including a new province in the north created in 1988, and each is headed by a governor appointed by the president. In fact, the central government has had difficulty finding persons to fill government posts in provinces largely controlled by the rebels and has announced plans to merge several provinces. After the Soviet withdrawal, it also offered local autonomy to rebel commanders willing to end the civil war.

Judicial system: Judges of the Supreme Court and various local and military courts are appointed by the president.

RECENT HISTORY

Although parts of the region now known as Afghanistan were invaded and conquered by many peoples—including Persians, Greeks, Arabs, Turks, Mongols and Moguls—the area did not become a cohesive country until 1747, when Ahmad Shah Sadozai, who had been a military commander under the Persian ruler Nadir Shah, created a Pathan tribal federation in Afghanistan and northern India. His family controlled Afghanistan until Dost Mohammad Khan founded Afghanistan's second dynasty in 1835. Dost and his son, Sher Ali, were defeated by the British in the first and second Anglo-Afghan wars (1838–42 and 1876–80). His grandson, Abdur Rahman Khan (ruled 1880–1901), was a skilled diplomat who gained British support of Afghanistan's position as a buffer between British India and Russia. During his reign the present boundaries of Afghanistan were formally delineated. In 1907 Great Britain and Russia signed an accord guaranteeing Afghan independence under British influence. Afghanistan was neutral during World War I, but in 1919, Afghan forces under Amanullah Khan briefly invaded India in the third Anglo-Afghan war, leading Britain to grant Afghanistan the right to conduct its own foreign policy. Amanullah Khan then launched a program of social and political modernization that was generally unpopular, and he was forced to abdicate in 1929 after an uprising by tribal chiefs. A tribal assembly soon elected Mohammad Nadir Shah as ruler. He was assassinated in 1933 and was succeeded by his son, Mohammad Zahir Shah. Zahir Shah continued his father's more cautious policies of modernization, pacification and neutrality in foreign affairs. After British India gained its independence in 1947, Afghanistan tilted more toward the USSR. It also periodically demanded that Pathan-occupied regions of Pakistan be declared a semiautonomous state. During Zahir Shah's reign, however, the king was generally less powerful than other members of his family who held the post of prime minister. In 1963 Mohammad Daud Khan (brother-in-law of the king, Mohammad Zahir Shah) resigned and was replaced by the country's first civilian prime minister. The following year, a new constitution created a constitutional monarchy. Members of the royal family were forbidden to hold high government posts, and legislative elections were held for the first time the following year. In 1973 Zahir Shah was overthrown in a military coup led by Daud and went into exile in Italy. The authoritarian Daud ruled as a military dictator until 1977, when Afghanistan became a one-party state under a new constitution and the Loya Jirgah elected Daud president.

In April 1978 Daud was killed in a Marxist coup known as the Great Saur Revolution. The imprisoned Communist party general-secretary, Nur Muhammad Taraki, was released and became president of a new, pro-Soviet government. Already close relations with the Soviet Union were strengthened, and the two countries signed a treaty of friendship and cooperation later that year. A main priority of the Communist government was a restructuring of society through a major redistribution of land to landless peasants and an adult literacy program. Its radical reform policies faced widespread opposition, however, from the conservative and deeply religious population. Members of the Communist party also feuded among themselves. Taraki was overthrown and reportedly executed by Hafizullah Amin, who became president and party general-secretary in September 1979 and imposed even more rigorous and unpopular land and social policies. In December, as the Soviet Union began airlifting troops into Afghanistan in support of the government, Amin was killed and Babrak Karmal, the leader of the Parcham faction and a long-time rival of Taraki and Amin, returned from exile in Eastern Europe and took over as president and party leader. The new regime, like its predecessors, failed to win popular support, and resentment of the Soviet military intervention coalesced into a nationwide resistance movement. The rebels, increasingly supplied with sophisticated arms (especially from the United States and China, channeled through Pakistan), maintained control of most of the countryside. Soviet strategy shifted increasingly to a scorched-earth policy involving aerial bombardment of both military and civilian targets in an effort to deprive the guerrillas of sanctuary within Afghanistan. Karmal resigned as party leader in

8

1986 and was replaced by Najibullah, the former head of the Afghan secret police, who later also became head of state. Repeated international diplomatic efforts to resolve the conflict met with little success until April 14, 1988, when under U.N. auspices, Afghanistan and Pakistan signed accords that were guaranteed by the United States and the Soviet Union.

The Geneva accords set up a timetable for the complete withdrawal of the more than 120,000 Soviet soldiers in Afghanistan within nine months; provided for the voluntary return of refugees; and guaranteed the noninterference of Pakistan and Afghanistan in each other's internal affairs. The United States and the Soviet Union retained equal rights to arm their allies. The Najibullah regime attempted to ensure a continuing position in the postwar power structure through diplomatic means and by the launching of a program of national reconciliation. It remained unpopular, however, and only 20,000 of its 150,000-member security force were thought to be reliable. The Soviet withdrawal was completed on schedule on February 15, 1989. By that time more than 1 million Afghans had died and the Soviets had suffered at least 13,000 casualties. The rebels, whose forces were estimated at 130,000, vowed to continue the war until the Najibullah government was ousted. A rebel siege of Jalalabad, however, was unsuccessful, and rebel leaders fought each other as well as the Najibullah regime. By late 1989, the Soviet government had declared that its occupation of Afghanistan had violated Soviet law and international standards of behavior. As Afghanistan was left to sort out its own future, the picture remained bleak. As the United States and Pakistan pushed for a diplomatic solution to the civil war, tribal and ideological divisions seemed likely to continue to divide the country into local fiefdoms, making the rebuilding of the nation's shattered infrastructure and the resettlement of its huge refugee population an almost overwhelming task.

ECONOMY

Background: Afghanistan has a predominantly agricultural economy dependent upon farming and livestock herding. Traditionally, 9% of its limited export earnings came from agricultural products. Despite efforts since the 1930s to modernize the economy, the country had no paved roads when it initiated the first of a series of Five-Year Development Plans in 1957. In that year, with aid supplied largely by the Soviet Union (used primarily in the north) and the United States (used primarily around Kabul), the government launched efforts to modernize the country's infrastructure and thus lay the foundations for future growth. These efforts included the development of air and road transportation, the building of power plants and dams, the improvement of social services, the establishment of fertilizer and food-processing plants, and the exploration and mapping of mineral resources. Foreign aid from the West virtually ceased with the Soviet military intervention, but Soviet development of the north intensified. The first road and rail bridge linking the Soviet Union and Afghanistan across the Amu-dar'ya River was completed in 1982; it helped to further increase trade between the two nations, which had tripled between 1978 and 1982. So-

9

viet investment in Afghanistan's petroleum and natural gas resources has been particularly heavy, and some northern towns have been linked to the Soviet power grid. Although statistics on Afghanistan are notoriously unreliable, the GDP in 1986 was estimated at U.S. $3.08 billion, with a per capita income of $220. In 1987 a government official estimated that 75% of the economic development that had occurred in the previous 50 years had been destroyed by the war. A 1988 study indicated that agricultural production had declined 45%–50% since 1979, and that 50% of all livestock had been destroyed or removed from the country.

Agriculture: Agriculture contributes an estimated 57% of the GDP. Wheat, the leading crop, is cultivated in many parts of the country. Other important crops are cotton, rice and corn. The chief export crops are pistachios, almonds and grapes (raisins). Apricots, cherries, figs, pomegranates, citrus fruit, a variety of root and other vegetables, and sugar beets are also grown. The livestock industry has long been concentrated on the raising of sheep, which provide wool for carpets, karakul pelts for export, and meat and dairy products; but large numbers of cattle and goats are also raised.

Industry: Industry is generally confined to the processing of local raw materials, with traditional handicrafts contributing a larger share of the GDP than modern manufacturing. Handicrafts include carpets, felt and textiles. Modern factories produce textiles, processed fruit, tanned skins and leather goods, cement and refined sugar. Large industries are owned by the government.

Mining: A natural gas pipeline completed in 1967 carries natural gas from northern Afghanistan to the Soviet Union. Natural gas output increased 65% after 1979. Gas, sold to the Soviet Union at well below market prices, was used to offset military aid, but exports have virtually ceased because the Soviets capped most gas wells before withdrawing for fear of sabotage. There are large deposits of petroleum near the Soviet border, and coal, salt, lapis lazuli, barite and chrome are commercially mined. The lapis lazuli deposits are under control of the rebels, who have sold the semiprecious stone to buy armaments. The country contains the world's third-largest iron-ore reserves, but they are located at high altitudes far from world markets. The Soviets are reportedly mining uranium and have aided in the construction of a petroleum refinery, a copper smelter and other projects.

Other industry: About 117,000 tourists visited Afghanistan in 1977, but tourism has been negligible since 1979. All banks are nationalized. The country is heavily dependent upon foreign aid, 97% of which was provided by the Soviet bloc in 1988. The United States and other nations have provided military, food and other humanitarian aid to the Afghan refugees in Pakistan.

Foreign trade: Traditionally, Afghanistan's exports traveled the trade routes to India and Pakistan, but these routes have been disrupted by war, and the overall trade volume has declined since 1979. The Soviet Union became Afghanistan's chief trade partner in the 1950s, and in 1986 took 71% of all exports and provided 39% of all imports. Trade with the Soviet bloc increased from 61% of the total in 1984–85 to 68% in 1986–87; most trade with the Soviet bloc is based on barter rather than hard currency. Traditional exports of handicrafts, karakul pelts, fruit and nuts to Western Europe have declined, but imports of consumer goods from Japan for re-export to Pakistan and Iran have increased. In 1986 Afghanistan's leading exports were natural gas (56%), dried fruit and nuts (17%), carpets (5%) and wool (4%). The chief imports were petroleum products, sugar, textiles and motor vehicles. The Soviet Union imports natural gas, cotton, wool, hides and raisins, and it exports industrial equipment, trucks and petroleum products. The government handles bulk imports, but 45% of foreign trade and most domestic trade remains in private hands.

Employment: In 1985 the settled labor force was estimated at 5.56 million, of which 70% were engaged in agriculture, 15% in manufacturing, and 15% in government and public authorities. There are also about 2.5 million nomadic herders who travel with their animals to mountain pastures in summer.

Price trends: Inflation was estimated at 20%–25% a year between 1980 and 1985. The consumer price index rose an estimated 10% in 1986.

SOCIAL SERVICES

Welfare: Family and tribe are the traditional sources of welfare services.

Health: Health services, never adequate and generally concentrated in urban areas, have been badly disrupted by war. In 1982 the country had an estimated 6,875 hospital beds. There were 1,931 physicians in 1988. Physicians from other nations have attempted to provide some health services to war-ravaged areas on a volunteer basis, but an estimated 60% of all rural health centers have been destroyed since 1979. Life expectancy is among the lowest in the world, and it has declined from 41 years in 1978 to only 38 years in 1985. Infant mortality in 1985—189 deaths per 1,000 live births—was the highest in the world. Only about 20% of the urban population and 3% of the rural population had access to safe water in 1980. Diseases such as malaria and tuberculosis are common, and tens of thousands of people have been maimed for life by war.

Housing: Most people live in rural villages. Houses are often clustered together and surrounded by fortified walls. Much housing has been destroyed by war.

EDUCATION

An estimated 12% of the adult population are literate. Education at all levels is free, and primary education is theoretically compulsory, but few girls and only about 12% of boys attend school. Classes beyond the third grade are taught in Pashto, Dari and Arabic. In 1987 the country had 1,223 schools, with an enrollment of more than 700,000. Although the educational system was greatly expanded between 1950 and 1973, an estimated 2,000 schools have been destroyed since 1979. The country has five universities, the most important of which are the University of Kabul (1946) and the University of Nangarhar at Jalalabad (1963). An estimated 12,000 Afghans are studying at universities and training institutes in the Soviet Union, where many younger children orphaned by war also attend school.

MASS MEDIA

In 1986, Afghanistan had 12 daily newspapers with a total circulation of 106,000. They include *Anis, Hiwad* and *Hagagat Engelab Saur*—all published in Dari and Pashto in Kabul—and the English-language *Kabul News Times*. All newspapers and periodicals are government controlled. There are five radio stations in Kabul, and the government-operated People's Radio and Television Afghanistan in Kabul began television broadcasts in 1978.

BIOGRAPHICAL SKETCHES

Sayed Ahmad Gailani. The most Westernized and powerful of the moderate rebel leaders, Gailani has strong support in the Kandahar area. He heads the Peshawar-based National Islamic Front and served as religious adviser to both King Zahir Shah and President Daud.

Abdul Haq. The young field commander of the underground network in Kabul and the rebel forces surrounding the city, Haq is affiliated with the moderate wing of the fundamentalist Islamic party led by Khalis. He dropped out of school in 1975, at the age of 16, to join an Islamic movement opposing the growing Communist influence in the Afghan government and was imprisoned by Daud after participating in an unsuccessful antigovernment uprising. An outspoken critic of former king Zahir Shah, he has visited the United States several times, and spoke at the United Nations in 1988.

Gulbuddin Hekmatyar. In his forties, Hekmatyar is the most militant of the fundamentalist leaders and head of one of the largest rebel groups. Educated at the University of Kabul, he became active in a fundamentalist student group in the mid-1970s and dropped out of the school of engineering to launch an unsuccessful uprising against Daud. He has received backing from Pakistan and seeks the establishment of a fundamentalist Islamic republic in Afghanistan.

Babrak Karmal. Born about 1929, Karmal was head of the Afghan Communist party and president of Afghanistan from 1979 to 1986. He was educated at the University of Kabul and served as minister of planning from 1957 to 1965 and in parliament from 1965 to 1973. A founder of the Khalq party in 1965 and head of the break-away Parcham party from 1967 to 1977, when the two merged, he served briefly as deputy prime minister and vice-president of the ruling Revolutionary Council after the 1978 revolution. In 1979, following the Soviet invasion, he returned from exile in Eastern Europe to replace Hafizullah Amin as president and party leader. His inability to end party in-fighting and win the civil war led to his ouster as party leader in May 1986; he later resigned his other posts and went into exile in the Soviet Union.

Ahmad Shah Masood. Masood, the most powerful field commander in Afghanistan, is said to control at least five provinces in northern Afghanistan and is affiliated with the Islamic Society. A Tadzhik, he lacks support of the Pathan majority.

Sibgatullah Mojadedi. Head of the rebel Afghanistan National Liberation Front and leader of a respected religious family, Mojadedi was named president of the interim rebel government in exile in 1989. He seeks the establishment of a secular government and has close ties to former king Zahir Shah.

Najibullah (Najib Ahmadzi). Born in 1947 in Paktia Province, Najibullah replaced Babrak Karmal as head of the Afghan Communist party in May 1986 and later replaced him as president. He joined the party in 1965 while studying medicine at the University of Kabul (from which he received his degree in 1975); and he became a member of its Parcham faction despite his Pathan roots. He became head of the party Central Committee in 1977 and served briefly in the ruling Revolutionary Council and as ambassador to Iran after the 1978 coup, before being forced into exile in Eastern Europe by factional struggles within the party. He returned to Afghanistan in 1979 and became head of the secret police. In 1981 he rejoined the powerful party Central Committee and became its secretary in 1985. As president, he launched a campaign of national reconciliation with Soviet backing. Seeking the support of tribal and religious leaders, he offered amnesty to rebels in an effort to build a broad-based government that could end the civil war and survive once Soviet forces had been withdrawn from the country. Late in 1988, however, he admitted that this policy had been unsuccessful, and in 1989 he declared a nationwide state of emergency.

Mohammad Zahir Shah. Born October 15, 1914, and educated at Istiqlal College in Kabul and in France, Zahir Shah became king of Afghanistan in 1933 after the death of his father; he supported the introduction of a constitutional monarchy in 1964. Faced with economic problems and opposition from various ethnic groups, he was overthrown in a bloodless coup by his brother-in-law Mohammad Daud Khan in 1973 and remained in exile in Italy, where he had been when the coup occurred. The former king remains a symbol of national unity for many Afghans and has been suggested for a role in a postwar coalition government by some traditional guerrilla groups and by Najibullah, although he is rejected by fundamentalist rebels seeking the establishment of an Islamic republic.

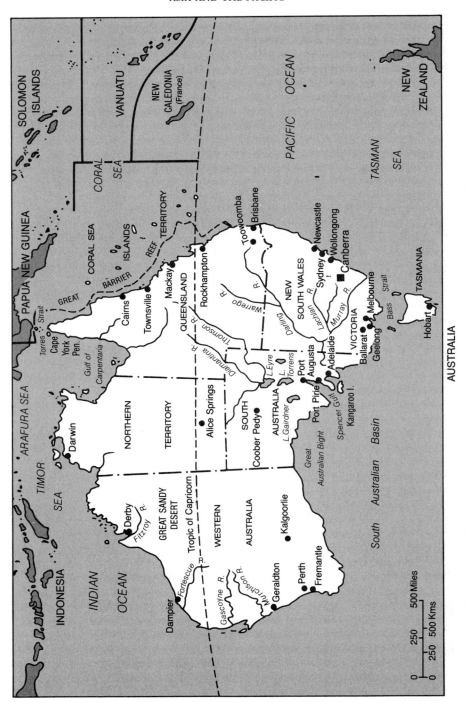

AUSTRALIA

AUSTRALIA

Features: The Commonwealth of Australia is, in terms of land area, the sixth largest country in the world (following the Soviet Union, Canada, China, the United States and Brazil). From its most northern point to its southern extremity (excluding the island of Tasmania) is a distance of 1,946 miles/3,134 km: from east to west is a distance of 2,349 miles/3,782 km. Virtually two-fifths of the Australian land mass lies within the tropics. Australia is one of the flattest land masses on earth; the average elevation is less than 984 ft/300 m. compared with the world's mean of about 2,297 ft/700 m. Only about one-twentieth of the continent is more than 1,969 ft/600 m. above sea level. With the exception of Antarctica, Australia has the lowest rainfall of any continent. The density of population (2.1 inhabitants per sq. km. in mid-1986) is one of the world's lowest national densities. But there are the most marked climatic, topographic and demographic contrasts within Australia—inevitably so, given the country's size—and this makes the use of averages of relatively little value. In the broadest terms. Australia may be divided into three zones. The first, accounting for approximately 70% of the land area, covers the whole of central Australia. About one-third of this zone is desert, of no agricultural value; the remaining two-thirds has only a marginal value for pastoral farming and is almost unpopulated. The second zone, accounting for some 17% of the land area, comprises a broad corridor over 186 miles/300 km. wide, extending from the Eyre Peninsula (to the west of Adelaide), running parallel to the east coast, and across the northern part of Australia to the Kimberley Plateau. This is a zone of considerable climatic and soil variation, but in its temperate areas there is important wheat, sheep and cattle farming; the zone is sparsely populated. The third zone, accounting for approximately 13% of the land area, comprises a coastal corridor that runs from Cairns (in northern Queensland) southward down the length of the east coast, and then westward, embracing the southeast corner of the continent; this zone also includes southwest Western Australia (the region around Perth) as well as a small part of the Northern Territory around Darwin. This zone has a notably broken topography; the Australian Alps in the southeast constitute the continent's highest terrain. But the zone supports the major agricultural production in Australia (beef and lamb, dairy farming, sugar growing); this is also the zone within which Australia's industrial production, urban areas and, of course, population are concentrated. In 1986 the two

15

southeast states of New South Wales and Victoria, comprising 13.4% of Australia's land area, contained 60.8% of the population.

Area: 2,966,151 sq. miles/7,682,300 sq. km.

Mean max. and min. temperatures: Canberra 68.5°F/20.3°C, 41.7°F/5.4°C; Darwin 85.3°F/29.6°C, 77.2°F/25.1°C; Sydney 71.6°F/22.0°C, 53.2°F/11.8°C.

Mean annual rainfall: Canberra 25 in/639 mm.; Darwin 61 in/1,536 mm.; Sydney 48 in/1,215 mm.

POPULATION

Total population (January 1988 est.): 16,250,000.

Chief towns and populations (mid-1985 est.): Sydney (3,391,600), Melbourne (2,916,600), Brisbane (1,157,200), Perth (1,001,000), CANBERRA (273,600).

Distribution: Using the population estimates of mid-1985, 70.4% of the population lived in the 13 principal urban centers; 53.7% of the population lived in Sydney, Melbourne, Brisbane and Perth.

Language: English is in universal use. However, with the official recognition of Australia as a multicultural society, new settlers find no official discouragement of their culture, language and traditions. As a result, a wide variety of European and Asian languages are found in use within those communities.

Religion: In the 1986 census 76.4% of those who stated their religion said that they were Christians: The two principal denominations were Anglican and Roman Catholic. There are substantial Jewish, Muslim and Buddhist communities.

CONSTITUTIONAL SYSTEM

Constitution: The federal constitution that came into force on January 1, 1901, remains in effect.

Head of state: Queen Elizabeth II. *Prime minister:* Robert J. L. Hawke.

Executive: In broad terms, the Commonwealth of Australia has a two-tier system of national government: the federal parliament and government, which have responsibility for all matters of national interest; state governments and legislatures (in New South Wales, Victoria, Queensland, South Australia, Western Australia, Tasmania), which complement the activities of the federal government. At the federal level executive authority is exercised by the cabinet, which comprises just over half the government ministers; legal effect is given to cabinet decisions by the Federal Executive Council, a purely formal body presided over by the governor-general and usually attended by two or three ministers (although all ministers are members). The political party (or coalition of parties) that commands a majority in the House of Representatives becomes the federal government and provides the federal ministers, including the prime minister; all ministers must be members of parliament (either the Senate or the House of Representatives). The administration is collectively responsible to parliament.

Legislature: The federal parliament has two chambers. The House of Representatives has 148 seats, divided among the states on the basis of population (New South Wales, 51; Victoria, 39; Queensland, 24; South Australia, 13; Western Australia, 13; Tasmania, five; Australian Capital Territory, two; Northern Territory, one). Elections for the House of Representatives are held at least every three years. The Senate has 76 members: The six states each provide 12 senators, with a further two senators each being provided by the Australian Capital Territory and the Northern Territory. Senators are popularly elected and serve a six-year term, half the Senate retiring every three years. Each state within the federation has a parliament.

Political parties: Following the July 1987 election there were three political parties with representation in the House of Representatives: the Australian Labor party (founded in 1891), the Liberal party of Australia (founded in 1944) and the National party of Australia (founded in 1916 as the Country party of Australia; it took its present name in 1982). Each party is federal in character, with state organizations that contest state elections and form state administrations.

Local government: There are approximately 900 local government bodies at the city, town, municipal and shire level. The responsibilities of local government vary from state to state, although all are concerned in general terms with the provision of local amenities—road construction; water, sewerage and drainage facilities; public health services; and local recreation facilities.

Judicial system: The judicial power of the Commonwealth of Australia is vested in the High Court of Australia and other courts created by parliament (the Federal Court of Australia and the Family Court of Australia). In addition, the state courts are vested with federal jurisdiction in some areas of law. All the six states, together with Northern Territory, have their own court systems. Under the 1986 Australia Act the final categories of appeal from Australian courts to the Privy Council in London were abolished.

RECENT HISTORY

In the immediate postwar years the Labor administration under the premiership of Joseph Chifley sought an extension of public ownership and an expansion of social services. But by the time of the 1949 general election the mood of the electorate had turned against "socialist controls" (continued consumer austerity and trade union militancy also hurt Labor), and the Liberal party came to power. In coalition with the Country party the Liberals held power until the general election of December 1972—an unbroken span of 23 years. For the major part of that period (1949–66) the government was led by Sir Robert Menzies. On Menzies's retirement from politics he was succeeded by Harold Holt; when the latter died in a drowning accident in late 1967 he was succeeded as premier by John Gorton. Gorton led the Liberal-Country coalition to a narrow electoral victory in 1969 but, following a major internal party dispute, he was replaced by William McMahon in March 1971. The long Liberal domination may be explained by three principal considerations. First, during the 1950s and 1960s Australia enjoyed almost uninterrupted prosperity and a marked rise in living standards, a reflection of the prolonged boom experienced by the Western world in the immediate postwar decades. Second, in 1955 the Labor party suffered a serious split that saw the departure of the right-wing (strongly anti-Communist and predominantly Roman Catholic) interest. This split left the remnant of the Labor party vulnerable to the charge that it was sympathetic to communism, a charge Menzies employed to considerable electoral advantage. This led to the third consideration. Menzies's fierce anticommunism was well attuned to the rhetoric of the cold war years; in particular, the Chinese Communist victory in 1949 and the conflicts in Korea, Malaya and Vietnam fired Australian's long-held fear of invasion from the north. When the 1966 general election was fought principally on the issue of sending conscript Australians to fight in Vietnam, the Liberal-Country coalition was returned with a decisive parliamentary majority.

At the 1972 general election the Labor party, led by Gough Whitlam, finally broke the Liberal domination, on a platform that promised to improve the economic opportunities of all Australians, particularly those who were disadvantaged. Once in office, the party embarked on a high-spending program, an approach that, combined with the oil shocks of 1973–74, created considerable inflationary pressures; the onset of world recession led to a rise in unemployment. The Whitlam government was brought to an end in late 1975 when, following Senate opposition blocking the government's financial legislation, on November 11 the governor-general dismissed the prime minister and dissolved parliament. It was widely held that in taking these actions the governor-general had acted at the very limit of his constitutional authority, and possibly beyond it; there was a strong upsurge in republican sentiment (which, in any event, has considerable support in Australia). In the general election that followed the governor-general's dissolution of parliament, Whitlam's Labor party was heavily defeated by a non-Labor bloc led by the Liberal party under Malcolm Fraser: Whatever the electorate's concern with respect to the constitutional propriety of the governor-general's behavior, there was greater concern over the high-spending policies the Whitlam administration had pursued from 1972. In the 1977 general election he suffered a further clear defeat at the hands of Malcolm Fraser; in December 1977 Whitlam resigned from the leadership of the Labor party, to be succeeded by William Hayden.

Fraser's coalition administration was returned at the 1980 general election, although with a much smaller majority. The government was seriously damaged by internal argument and by economic failures (as inflation and unemployment rose), so that when Fraser called a sudden election in March 1983, in an attempt to reassert his authority, his administration was decisively defeated by the Labor party, now led by Robert Hawke. Labor was again victorious, although less decisively so, at a general election held in December 1984. In July 1987 Hawke led the Labor party to an unprecedented third successive electoral victory. The Labor domination since 1983 was the result in part of disunity within the opposition parties (notably the breakup of the Liberal-National coalition) and the failure of the political opposition—drifting to the right as the Labor party came to occupy the middle ground—to establish a coherent identity. Certainly, the economic policies pursued by the Hawke government, whatever the prospects for long-term success, were damaging to Labor's electoral popularity. Hawke sought to confront Australia's deep-seated economic rigidities (notably its high-cost structures and the "good-life" philosophy of both labor and management) by a deregulation of financial markets, a marked reduction in federal government expenditure, the implementation of wage restraint and the encouragement of corporate Australia—the international expansion of Australian corporations was a very marked feature of the 1980s. Labor's determination to secure a major restructuring of the economy took place against the background of a sharp worsening of Australia's external position, as the terms of trade moved against the country's agricultural and mineral exports. The mid-1980s saw a dramatic fall in the exchange value of the Australian dollar.

At the close of the 1980s Australia had become a remarkably more complex society—in terms, notably, of the fluidity of political loyalties and the range of cultural identities—than that of the immediate postwar years. The crucial influence here was the scale and, more particularly, the changing character of immigration into Australia. The immediate postwar decade saw heavy British immigration; there was substantial Greek and Italian immigration from the 1950s on; more recent years saw immigration from the Middle East and from Asia (including, notably, Vietnam). In the early 1980s less than 70% of the population was of British origin: Over 100 national origins were represented in the Australian population. For a significant proportion of the non-British immigrants, cultural and economic assimilation into an Australian identity has not been easy, in part because the established population has shown some wariness in the face of the culturally and ethnically distinct new waves of settlers. In the mid-1980s there was government recognition of the multicultural diversity of Australia; related to that recognition was an increased awareness of the economic and social plight, as well as cultural distinctiveness, of the aboriginal population, brought into sharper focus in 1988 as Australia celebrated the bicentennial of white settlement.

ECONOMY

Background: The economy of Australia has a moderately high degree of external dependence: In 1986–87 the combined value of commodity exports and imports was equivalent to 31.8% of GDP. The export sector is dominated by food and live animals, crude raw materials, and mineral fuels and lubricants: In 1986–87 these accounted for 70.4% of the total value of commodity exports. Australia is the world's largest producer of fine wools, and is an important world producer of wheat, barley, coal, iron ore, sugar, beef, lamb and mutton. In 1986–87 agriculture, hunting, forestry and fishing contributed 4.5% to GDP; mining contributed 4.7%; manufacturing, 17.4%; construction, 7.8%; wholesale and retail trade, 13.7%; finance, property and business services, 11.2%; public administration and defense, together with other community, social and personal services, 22.1%. In 1986, 5.2% of the labor force was engaged in agriculture and services to agriculture; 1.3% in mining; 15.0% in manufacturing; 6.6% in construction; 18.5% in wholesale and retail trade; 9.3% in finance, property and business services; and 20.6% of the total labor force was employed in public administration and defense, together with community services. During the 1970s the Australian economy experienced only very modest real growth; real GDP per capita grew at an average annual rate of just 1.1% over the period 1972–73 to 1982–83. The later 1980s saw an acceleration—to 2.7% for the years 1982–83 to 1987–88. From the onset of the world recession in the early 1970s Australia experienced strong inflationary pressures and historically high levels of unemployment. In the period 1973–80 the average annual rise in consumer prices was 11.5%; the average annual inflation rate for the period 1981–88 was 8.3%. In 1982 the unemployment rate was 6.7%, rose to 10.0% in the third quarter of 1983 and in mid-1988 stood at 7.4%. The mid-1980s saw a marked deterioration in Australia's external position, with a sharp rise in the current account deficit (as a result of a weakening in the international market for a number of Australia's established primary exports, and, perhaps more notably, a substantial increase in invisible outflows). The Australian dollar, floated in December 1983, fell sharply—from the beginning of 1985—against the currencies of Australia's major trading partners. Hawke's Labor administration sought a major restructuring of the economy along free-market lines: Important here was the deregulation of financial markets and the imposition of notable reductions in federal government expenditure. In 1988 there was a budget surplus for the first time in more than 20 years. The Hawke government sought to bring inflation under control by the establishment (with labor union agreement) of centralized wage determination.

Agriculture: The agricultural sector is dominated by the production of wool (1,346,000 metric tons in 1985–86); beef and veal (1,388,000 metric tons in 1985–86); mutton and lamb (570,000 metric tons in 1985–86); butter and cheese (274,000 metric tons in 1984–85); wheat (17,356,000 metric tons in 1986); barley (3,530,000 metric tons in 1986); and sugar (25,410,000 metric tons in 1986). There is also substantial production of a wide range of fruits (notably apples, pears and citrus fruit) and, increasingly, of wine. During the 1980s there was a shift away from crop production (principally a reflection of the weakening international position of wheat) toward livestock production; in broad terms, agriculture is of declining importance within the domestic economy, although it remains, of course, a crucial source of export earnings. The final removal of trade barriers between Australia and New Zealand in 1990 was expected to lead to considerably stronger competition for Australian agriculture (in particular, dairy farming) in its domestic market. The principal foreign markets for Australia's agricultural exports are: for wool Japan, the Soviet Union, China and the European Community; for beef and veal the United States and Japan; for wheat China, Egypt, the Soviet Union and Japan; for sugar Japan, the United States, Canada, South Korea, Malaysia, China, Singapore and the Soviet Union; for wine Sweden, the United States, Britain, Canada, Japan and New Zealand.

Mining: The mining sector of the economy has expanded markedly from the late 1960s on. The principal minerals exploited include: coal (production in 1986–87 was 182,250,000 metric tons; Australia is the world's most important exporter of coal); iron ore (100,370,000 metric tons in 1986–87; Australia is the second most important exporter of iron ore in the world and the fourth largest producer); bauxite (33,888,000 metric tons in 1986–87; Australia is the most important bauxite producer in the world). There is also substantial production of uranium (Australia possesses about 28% of the Western world's uranium resources), lead, zinc, copper, nickel (Australia is the world's third most important producer of nickel) and gold (production in 1986–87 was 180,492, pounds/81,856 kg.). Australia also produces natural gas (production in 1986–87 was 524,330 million megajoules) and crude petroleum (at the close of the 1980s two-thirds of domestic consumption was met from domestic production).

Manufacturing: In the 1950s the contribution of the manufacturing sector to GDP was about 30%; in 1986–87 it was 17.4%. Part of the explanation for this relative contraction is that from the early 1970s on the high tariffs and strict import quotas that had traditionally protected this sector were considerably eased. The industrial sector is diverse, but particularly important are food processing; the production of chemicals and plastics; the manufacture of electrical machinery, appliances and components; the production of machine tools and engineering plant (oil rigs, power stations, mining equipment); vehicle assembly; the production of iron and steel (prominent here is Australia's biggest company, The Broken Hill Proprietary Company, Limited); and the production of aluminum.

Service sector: At the close of the 1980s the service sector was estimated to account for about 76% of total Australian employment and to contribute about 68% to GDP. The major components of the service sector are the wholesale and retail trades, community services and construction.

Foreign trade: The principal markets for Australia's exports are: Japan (25.4% in 1986–87); the United States (11.7%); New Zealand (5.0%); China (4.4%); Korea (4.2%); and the United Kingdom (3.8%). Australia imports principally from: the United States (21.9% in 1986–87); Japan (20.9%); West Germany (7.5%); and the United Kingdom (7.3%). In the mid-1980s Australia experienced a growing trade deficit; in addition there was a major, and growing, invisible deficit caused principally by the high transport

21

and insurance costs on imports, profit repatriation on foreign investment in Australia, and the costs of Australians traveling overseas. As a result, in the mid-1980s there was a substantial deficit on current account (in 1985–86 the current account deficit was equivalent to 44% of export receipts, although in subsequent years the figure fell); the current account deficit was fully offset by capital inflows in all but two years during the period 1981–87.

Employment: In June 1988 the unemployment rate was 7.4%.

Price trends: The consumer price index (1970 = 100) was 361.3 in 1983; 375.4 in 1984; and 400.8 in 1985.

SOCIAL SERVICES

Welfare: Australia was a pioneer in public welfare, introducing old-age and invalid pensions in 1910 and maternity allowances in 1912. The main components of the present-day public welfare structure are: pensions for the aged, widows, invalids and single parents; unemployment and sickness benefits; and an income-tested family allowance, payable to parents or guardians with one or more children under 16 (or with full-time students aged from 16 to 24). Community service programs—for example, the provision of residential care for the aged and the provision of facilities for the disabled—are maintained by the federal, state and local governments; private organizations and self-help groups are also important in this context.

Health: Australia's public health services have two tiers: Private doctors provide primary medical care; advanced treatment is provided through a comprehensive hospital system, which has both public (state-funded) and private components. A universal health insurance scheme, Medicare, introduced in February 1984, provides Australian residents with protection against hospital costs (excluding private patients) and with medical and optometrical care; under the scheme there is no charge for public hospital accommodation or treatment by hospital doctors, while refunds of at least 85% of government-approved fees charged by other doctors and by optometrists are made to patients. Medicare is partly funded by a 1.25% levy on taxable incomes, with low-income cut-off points.

In 1986 there were approximately 34,600 doctors, of whom about 44% were general practitioners. In 1987 Australia had 1,053 hospitals (excluding mental hospitals, nursing homes and veterans' hospitals), of which 68% were public hospitals. The Royal Flying Doctor Service of Australia, established in 1928, provides medical care for people living in isolated areas.

Housing: Approximately 72% of Australian householders own their homes. The majority of house purchases are made with the assistance of private lending institutions (savings banks, building societies, finance companies). The federal government provides funds to the state governments to assist those with low incomes to rent or to buy accommodations; the federal government also gives eligible first-home buyers assistance of up to A\$6,000 over a five-year period.

EDUCATION

Under Australia's federal structure, the six states and the Northern Territory are responsible for providing education for their own residents. The federal government makes special-purpose financial grants to the states for education: The federal government is responsible for the full financing of higher education. Schooling is compulsory until the age of 15 (16 in Tasmania); education in government primary and secondary schools is free. In 1987 there were 7,575 government schools, with a total enrollment of over 2.19 million. In 1987 there were 21 universities (with a total enrollment of 180,803 students), and 47 colleges of advanced education and institutes of technology (with 212,931 students). Students studying at an approved tertiary institution may receive a government maintenance grant, subject to a means test. The federal government has sought to increase participation in education on the part of disadvantaged and minority groups—aboriginal students, children from non-English-speaking backgrounds, children from economically deprived families.

MASS MEDIA

The press: More than 500 newspapers are published in Australia, including the major dailies, the main Sunday newspapers and more than 350 newspapers published outside the state capitals.

Dailies: The only daily newspapers that may claim a national circulation are: *The Australian,* 138,000, and the *Australian Financial Review,* 78,000. Prominent among the dailies that circulate within one state are: the *Daily Telegraph,* 326,000; *The Sydney Morning Herald,* 266,000; the *Courier-Mail,* 257,000; *The Age,* 236,000; *The West Australian,* 281,000. In recent years there has occurred marked concentration of newspaper ownership; the three principal newspaper groups are: The John Fairfax Group; News, Ltd., owned by Rupert Murdoch; and Consolidated Press Holdings.

Broadcasting: The Australian Broadcasting Corporation (ABC) is a noncommercial statutory organization, funded in large part by the federal parliament. ABC operates 140 radio stations (96 AM, 41 FM and three shortwave), and one national television network of 11 stations. The federal parliament also funds the Special Broadcasting Service, a noncommercial multilingual radio and multicultural television service. Commercial radio and television companies, funded by advertising revenue, operate under licenses granted by the Australian Broadcasting Tribunal, a statutory authority. In January 1983 there were 136 commercial radio stations in operation; in August 1987 there were 51 commercial television stations.

BIOGRAPHICAL SKETCHES

Lionel Bowen. Bowen entered the House of Representatives as the Labor member for Kingsford-Smith in 1969. He held ministerial office in the Whitlam administration between 1972 and 1975. He was deputy leader of the opposition between 1977 and 1983. When Labor returned to power in 1983 Bowen became deputy prime minister and minister assisting the prime minister for commonwealth-state relations; to these posts he added, in 1984, the position of attorney general.

Robert James Lee Hawke. Born in 1929, in Bordertown, South Australia, Hawke was educated at the University of Western Australia, from which he received bachelor's degrees in law and in economics. He won a Rhodes scholarship to Oxford University in 1953, taking a Bachelor of Letters degree there in 1955. Active since 1958 in the Australian Council of Trade Unions as research officer and advocate, he was its president from 1970 to 1980. Concurrently, from 1972 to 1980, he served on the governing body of the International Labor Organization. From 1973 to 1978 Hawke was president of the Australian Labor party, which he joined at age 17. In 1980 he was elected to parliament as representative of the federal electorate of Wills, and later became the party's spokesman for industrial relations, employment and youth affairs. Early in 1983 Hawke was unanimously elected leader of the opposition. Subsequently as Labor candidate for the office of prime minister, he led his party to victory and was sworn in on March 11, 1983. Hawke was reelected prime minister in 1984 and again in 1987 for a record consecutive third term.

Paul Keating. Born January 18, 1944, Keating entered the House of Representatives, as the Labor member for Blaxland, in 1969. In 1975 he was the minister for Northern Australia. With the return of the Labor party to government in 1983, he became party treasurer.

Andrew Peacock. Peacock was born February 13, 1939, and was educated at Melbourne University. He entered the House of Representatives, as the Liberal member for Kooyong, in 1966. He held ministerial office in the closing years of Liberal domination in the late 1960s and early 1970s, and again when the Liberal party regained power in 1975. Between 1975 and 1980 he was minister of foreign affairs. When the Liberal party lost office in 1983, Peacock succeeded Malcolm Fraser as Liberal leader; in 1985 he was removed by John Howard, after a bitter party feud, but in May 1989 returned to the leadership of the Liberal party.

BANGLADESH

GEOGRAPHY

Features: The People's Republic of Bangladesh is located in the northeastern part of the Indian subcontinent. There are two major rivers, the Ganges and the Brahmaputra, flowing into the country from India. These have numerous tributaries and deltas. Most of the country is near sea level, and therefore severe floods frequently ravage the land. The northern and eastern parts of the country are marked by low hills.

Area: 55,598 sq. miles/143,998 sq. km.

Mean max. and min. temperatures: Dacca (23°45'N, 90°29'E; 24 ft/7m.) 86°F/29°C (June), 65°F/17°C (Jan.).

Relative humidity: 59%.

Mean annual rainfall: 52 in/1,320 mm.

POPULATION

Total population (1985 est.): 100,468,000.

Chief towns and populations: DACCA (3,950,000), Chittagong (1,590,000), Khulna (740,000), Rajshahi (300,000).

Distribution: Bangladesh is one of the most densely populated countries in the world, with an average of 1,807 persons per square mile (698 persons/sq. km.). Owing to the high population growth rate, 42% of its people in 1981 were under the age of 15. The urban population was 15.2% of the total in 1981. Ninety-eight percent of the population is Bengali, and 1% is tribal.

Language: The Bengali language is spoken by 98% of Bangladeshis. It is an Indo-Iranian language, also spoken in the Indian state of West Bengal. Urdu, also Indo-Iranian, is spoken by a small number of people but widely understood in the cities. English is known to the educated.

Religion: Muslims constitute 86% of the population, Hindus 12.1%, and Buddhists 0.6%. Bangladesh is a secular state.

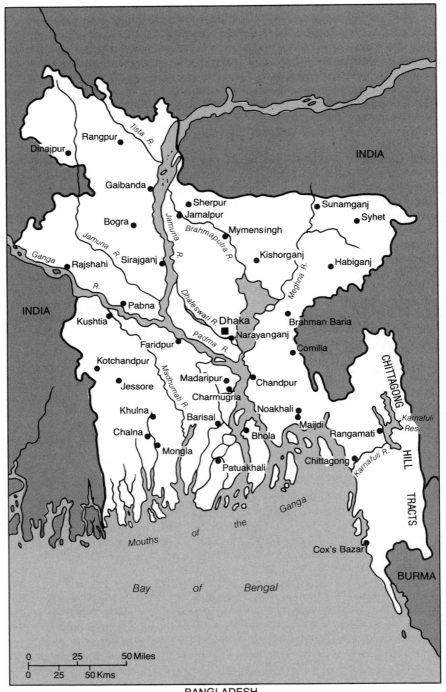

INDIA

Dinajpur

Rangpur

Tista R.

Gaibanda

Sherpur

Sunamganj

Jamalpur

Syhet

Bogra

Jamuna R.

Brahmaputra R.

Mymensingh

Jamuna R. Sirajganj

Ganga

Rajshahi

Kishorganj

Habiganj

Meghna R.

R.

Pabna

Kushtia

INDIA

Dhaleswari R.

Dhaka

Brahman Baria

Padma R.

Narayanganj

Faridpur

Comilla

Kotchandpur

Madaripur

Chandpur

Jessore

Charmugria

Madhumati R.

Khulna

Noakhali

Barisal

Chalna

Maijdi

Rangamati

Karnafuli Res.

Mongla

Bhola

Patuakhali

Chittagong

Karnafuli R.

CHITTAGONG

HILL

TRACTS

Cox's Bazar

BURMA

Ganga

Mouths

of

the

Ganga

Bay   of   Bengal

0   25   50 Miles

0   25   50 Kms

BANGLADESH

BANGLADESH

CONSTITUTIONAL SYSTEM

Bangladesh is effectively a military regime with a democratic facade. The president is H. M. Ershad, who came to power in a military coup. In 1986, Ershad won the office of president in elections boycotted by the major opposition parties. The opposition contends that fair elections have not been held.

Head of state: President Hussain Mohammed Ershad.

Executive and legislature: The formal government is a presidential system with a unicameral parliament. Executive power is concentrated in the presidency. The president is directly elected for a five-year term. He appoints the prime minister and members of the cabinet, up to one-fifth of whom may be from outside the Jatiya Sangsad (National Parliament). The last provision allows experts to serve in the cabinet. Ershad has favored the creation of a national security council as an advisory body. It would include the president, the prime minister and the chiefs of staff of the three armed services. Such a council would give the military a permanent role in government.

Members of parliament are elected by a first-past-the-post rule from 300 constituencies. Thirty appointed seats are reserved for women. The prime minister must retain the confidence of a majority of the parliament.

Judicial system: The Supreme Court has two divisions: Appellate and High Court. The former has only appellate jurisdiction, while the latter has both appellate and original jurisdiction. There are four High Court benches, in different regions of the country. There are district courts, district magistrates, and new *upazilla* courts at lower levels. The legal system is similar to the British, but it incorporates some aspects of Islamic and Hindu personal law as well.

RECENT HISTORY

In the initial period of their hegemony, the British in Bengal acknowledged local Mughal suzerainty. The Mughal attempt to remove the British in 1765 failed, and the British assumed rights of taxation and administration. As they gained power over the region, the British began to handicap the once prosperous and advanced textile industry by coercive methods. At one point the British banned textile production; when weavers continued, they cut off their thumbs. This was the period when the fledgling textile industry in England was expanding. By suppressing the Bengali textile industry, the British were able to create East Indian markets for their own textiles, which initially were inferior in quality and lower in price.

The 19th century was one of British consolidation, repression and expansion. In Bengal, Calcutta emerged as the political and commercial seat of British power. The eastern region, including Dacca (now Dhaka), became peripheral, serving mainly as a supplier of labor, food and raw materials to the small industrial sector that developed in western Bengal. Bengal also

27

became the base from which the British expanded to the rest of the Indian subcontinent. The British exploited the progressive breakdown of the Mughal Empire and the resulting fragmentation and internecine conflict. They recruited Indian soldiers to carry out their expansion. Early attempts at mutiny among the *sepoys* failed, but in 1857 there was a major uprising in northern India that nearly succeeded. Some changes in the imperial structure were made; power was transferred from the East India Company to the British government in London.

The failure of the 1857 uprising did not end subcontinental struggles for freedom. There were continued demands for reform within the imperial system and numerous local uprisings. The British responded with a combination of harsh repressive measures and limited steps toward local rule. Elections based on extremely limited suffrage were introduced in the 1880s. Hindu elites were greater beneficiaries of British reforms in the late 19th century than were Muslim elites. The former became more educated and had greater access to administrative jobs. In 1906 a Muslim delegation met with British authorities and demanded that separate electorates be created for Muslims, Hindus and Sikhs. The British responded favorably to this plan. Also in 1906 a group of Muslims leaders met in Dacca to found the Muslim League. This party asserted that there was a common Muslim interest apart from that of Hindus and other non-Muslims.

In spite of its ideology, the Muslim League initially worked with the Indian National Congress, under the leadership of Mahatma Gandhi and Jawaharlal Nehru, to secure greater freedom for the subcontinent. The Muslim League failed to gain substantial popular support among Muslims until the 1940s. Before then, the league survived on imperial patronage, supported by the British as a counterweight to the Indian National Congress, which had emerged as the leading force in the independence movement.

In 1937 the Muslim League fared poorly in limited-suffrage elections because it failed to gain enough votes in Muslim-majority areas. The Congress party, which included Muslims in prominent positions, claimed that Hindus and Muslims had common interests, and it fared better among Muslim voters in several key areas. Under the leadership of Muhammed Ali Jinnah, the Muslim League asked for a role in a provincial coalition government. When the Congress party refused, the Muslim League demanded a separate state for Muslims of the subcontinent. The Muslim League called the new country they sought Pakistan. It meant "land of the pure" in Urdu and was also an English acronym—Punjab, Afghania, Kashmir, Sind, and Balushi*stan.* Thus, the original concept of Pakistan did not include Bengal. By 1946 support for the Muslim League among the landed and educated Muslim elites in eastern Bengal had grown. There was massive violence between Muslims and Hindus in Calcutta in 1946, when the Muslim League called for "direct action" to create Pakistan. On August 15, 1947, British rule in the Indian subcontinent ended and the independent states India and Pakistan came into being. The nation of Pakistan had two wings separated by 1,500 miles of Indian territory. Bengal itself was partitioned, and the eastern region became East Pakistan. Bengalis constituted 60% of Pakistan's population.

Jinnah died in the year after independence. And the politicians that followed him were not able to form stable governments. Muslim League politicians had sought to impose Urdu as the sole official language. Bengalis protested, demanding parity for Bengali. In Bengal, the League's stand on the language question was its downfall. As the Muslim League disintegrated, the military came to play a greater role in Pakistani politics. But at independence there were hardly any Bengali Muslims in the new Pakistani army.

The language issue mobilized Bengalis who sought to advance their culture; they formed the Awami League. National elections were scheduled for 1959. Owing to the majority of Bengalis in Pakistan, the Awami League was likely to do well in the voting. In 1958 Field Marshall Ayub Khan overthrew the civilian government and declared martial law.

Government expenditures for economic development also favored the western wing of Pakistan. In the 1950s and early '60s the eastern wing generated a majority of the country's exports, primarily jute. But the vast majority of U.S. and other foreign aid went to the western wing. So by the mid-1960s exports from the western wing exceeded those from the eastern. Pakistan's industrialization was almost entirely in the hands of Muslim business houses from the western wing. Even the new industries in the eastern wing were owned by western business elites. The profits from these businesses were transferred back to the western wing, not reinvested in the eastern region.

These conditions led to increasing dissatisfaction among politicians and people in the eastern wing. After the 1965 war with India over Kashmir, the leading Bengali politician, Mujibur Rahman, presented demands to the military for a high degree of autonomy for the two wings and full democratization. The military expressed agreement with most of the demands, wishing only to retain substantial tax authority. In December 1970 national elections were held. Mujibur Rahman's party won an absolute majority in the parliament. However, the leading western-wing politician, Zulfikar Ali Bhutto, objected to the prospect of a Bengali prime minister. The military was also displeased with the results. Mujibur Rahman's ascension to power was delayed, resulting in massive Bengali protests.

In March 1971 the Pakistani military began a campaign of repression in which at least one million Bengali civilians were killed in nine months. Over 10 million refugees fled to India. An armed Bengali independence movement was established with Indian assistance. On March 27, a Bengali officer in the Pakistani army, Ziaur Rahman, declared an independent state. In December 1971 Indian forces invaded East Pakistan and in two weeks defeated the Pakistani garrison of 90,000.

In January 1972 Mujibur Rahman became the first prime minister of Bangladesh. He declared his ideology to be a mixture of nationalism, democracy, socialism and secularism. The problems of economic development proved difficult to solve, however. Furthermore, corruption grew along with public criticism of his policies. In December 1974 a State of Emergency was declared. In the next year, he took further steps that gave his party and himself unrestricted power. In August 1975 Mujibur Rahman was

29

assassinated in a coup led by army majors. In November 1976 the army chief of staff, Ziaur Rahman, became chief martial-law administrator; in 1978 he became president. Ziaur Rahman was widely respected as a progressive leader. He promoted agricultural development and family planning. Nevertheless in May 1981 Ziaur Rahman was assassinated in an army-led conspiracy.

In 1982 H. M. Ershad assumed power in another military coup. He said that the military was the only organization capable of leading the country at that time, and he promised to hold elections. In 1986 he launched a party called the Jatiyo Dal, and won a slim majority in the parliament, in a questionable election. The Awami League, led by Hasina Wajed, and the Bangladesh National party (BNP), led by Ziaur Rahman's daughter, Begum Khaleda Zia, emerged as the major opposition. In October 1986 Ershad won the presidency in an election boycotted by opposition parties.

During 1987 there were a series of extralegal struggles between the government and opposition. An eight-party alliance, led by the Awami League, had participated in the 1986 parliamentary elections and now held 76 of the 300 seats. On opening day of the 1987 session, this alliance staged a noisy walkout. At the same time, a seven-party alliance, led by the BNP, held a street demonstration demanding dissolution of parliament whose election they had boycotted. The opposition factions failed to form a united front against the Ershad government. The BNP consistently demanded dissolution of the parliament. The Awami League came to the view that their participation in the parliament was counterproductive.

In the spring of 1987 the Awami League and its allies sought to undertake joint political action with the BNP. They called a nationwide half-day strike in June that was successful. They protested Ershad's "anti-people budget" and his "autocratic" rule. The strikes spread and intensified. In November Ershad declared a State of Emergency, suspended all fundamental rights and arrested opposition leaders. He explained in a speech to the nation that the opposition's disruptive actions were "planned anarchy" and "planned terrorism." However, in December the president dissolved the parliament and called fresh elections. In March 1988 elections were held. The major opposition parties again boycotted them, and the Jatiyo Dal won 200 of the 300 seats.

ECONOMY

Background: Bangladesh is the most populous country in the world with this level of poverty. Its per-capita gross national product in 1985 was U.S. $150. The two most important goals of successive Bangladeshi governments have been to attain self-sufficiency in food and to reduce population growth. World Bank studies have concluded that rapid industrialization is necessary to improve the standard of living. The government of Mujibur Rahman nationalized the bulk of existing industry and ran it highly inefficiently. The governments of Ziaur Rahman and H. M. Ershad have allowed a mixed economy, combining private and public efforts. Industrial growth has improved in recent years.

Natural disasters have caused considerable harm to the Bangladeshi economy. A tsunami in 1970 killed over 100,000 persons. There was major flooding in 1984 and 1988. During the 1988 floods, over two-thirds of the country's land mass was under water; owing to precautions taken earlier, only 2,000 persons were killed.

Agriculture: Production has grown at 3.0% per year during 1980–1985. In 1984, the Ershad government reduced the maximum area of land a family could own from 33 acres to 20 acres. However, less than 5% of farmers as well as of agricultural land area were affected by this ceiling; the vast majority of farmers own small, fragmented plots. A 1977 agricultural census found that 58.3% of farmers own the land they farm. The average holding is divided into six to nine fragments, since both Muslim and Hindu inheritance laws promote such fragmentation.

Planting of multiple crops is increasing in Bangladesh. Currently, 55% of the land is single-cropped, 38% is double-cropped and 7% is triple-cropped. But multiple cropping requires an efficient irrigation system. As of 1977, 31% of cultivated area was under irrigation, and this percentage has increased since then. Under the Zia government, a food-for-work program was initiated to clear silted irrigation channels. International aid agencies funded the program, which bartered food for labor.

Some high-yielding varieties of wheat and rice have been introduced. These have come mainly from the International Rice Research Institute in the Philippines, as well as from Bangladeshi agricultural research institutions. The progress of such technology has been considerably less than in northwestern India. Successful cultivation of high-yielding varieties requires the coordination of irrigation, planting and fertilizers. Bangladesh is endowed with abundant natural gas, and it has used it to produce nitrogenous fertilizers. But phosphates and potash continue to be imported and animal wastes remain the primary means of fertilization. In 1977, 51% of landholders cultivating 29% of the land used chemical fertilizers.

In Bangladesh, as in India, technology from the green revolution has required transformation of agricultural finance, and this has been a politically sensitive issue. The traditional village moneylenders have been unable to supply adequate credit at low interest rates. New government banks have begun to supply credit. Also, the Ershad government has cut subsidies to urban consumers and raised procurement prices for food grains.

Bangladesh remains dependent on water buffalo and bullocks for ploughing, other agricultural functions, and transport. Buffalo milk is used to produce *ghee* (clarified butter). In 1984, there were 73 million poultry, 22 million head of cattle, 14 million goats, 670,000 sheep, and 570,000 buffaloes. Bengali cooking is distinctive in South Asia for its reliance on freshwater fish. The rivers of Bangladesh contain hundreds of varieties—carp, shad, salmon, pomfret, shrimp and catfish are important catches. In 1983, 750,000 tons of fish were caught. Freshwater fish is exported to India and other neighboring countries, and shrimp and lobster are exported throughout the world. Fishing cooperatives have been established to expand saltwater fishing with modern techniques in the Bay of Bengal. A government fisheries corporation has been set up to promote exports of freshwater fish.

Industry: The industrial and manufacturing sectors of Bangladesh contribute a small proportion to the economy—15% and 9% of gross domestic product (GDP), respectively, in 1986. In both India and Pakistan, industrial production accounts for 26% of GDP. During 1980–1985, industrial growth accelerated, with the leading sectors in labor-intensive exports such as garments, shrimp and leather processing, and in import-substituting chemical fertilizers, basic metals, particularly ship-breaking, and food processing. Slow growth in the traditional jute industry has held down aggregate industrial growth.

A series of reforms introduced in 1981 have promoted industrial growth by reversing the nationalization process and improving credit facilities and import privileges for the private sector.

In 1984–85, there were 69 jute mills producing 520,000 tons of jute products. These mills produced about one-third, in value, of the total output of the manufacturing sector. Cotton was second to jute in value of output. Fifty-eight mills produced three-quarters of textile output, and the hand-loom sector produced the balance. In 1984–85, 105.5 million pounds/ 48 million kg. of yarn and 69 million yards/62 million m. of cloth were produced.

Trade and transport: Manufactured and raw jute constitutes more than half of Bangladesh's exports. Some labor-intensive manufactured exports such as textiles have been on the rise. The United States was the biggest export market in 1984–85, taking 20% of the total; Belgium and Japan import 7% each, and Pakistan, Britain and Iran each import 5%.

Manufactured goods, food grains and petroleum are the major imports. Manufactured goods account for 38% of imports, with 14% from the United States in 1984–85, 12% from Singapore, 11% from Japan and 6% from United Arab Emirates. Bangladesh has run major trade deficits in each year since its independence in 1971. Remittances from Bangladeshi workers in the Arabian Gulf have helped close the gap, as has foreign aid, but substantial borrowing continues to be necessary.

Employment: The 1986 labor force was estimated at 35 million. Of these, 14% are employed in the urban sector and the rest in the rural sector. There is a small but important contingent of Bangladeshis working in the oil-rich Arab states.

SOCIAL SERVICES

The 1972 constitution declares the promotion of social welfare to be a central objective of the state. The Ministry of Social Welfare and Women's Affairs has been established toward that end. However, owing to the country's overall poverty and the political priorities of the current government, funding for this ministry has been scant.

Owing to the country's population density, family planning has been a high priority. The National Population Council and the Ministry of Health have coordinated the effort. In 1984–85, 152 million condoms and 12 million cycles of contraceptive pills were distributed, and half a million persons were voluntarily sterilized. Also, Bangladesh has made considerable progress in coping with floods. In 1988, only about 2,000 people died from floods in spite of their covering more than two-thirds of the country.

Life expectancy in 1985 was 56 years for males and 55 years for females; infant mortality was 110 for every 1,000 live births. There are 760 hospitals, 1,275 dispensaries, 14,154 private physicians and 84,000 other medical personnel.

EDUCATION

The literacy rate in Bangladesh is 30%. In 1985, there were 13.7 million students in primary and secondary schools, and 876,000 in colleges and universities. The language of instruction is Bengali. There are six universities in the country, including the renowned Dacca University. The majority of university students are in disciplines of little direct economic usefulness. The Bangla Academy is a research institute that sponsors the translation of scientific and literary writings into Bengali.

MASS MEDIA

The press: The Ershad government censors the newspapers. President Ziaur Rahman had introduced liberalization after the period of censorship under Mujibur Rahman. There are 37 dailies in the country with a 1986 circulation of 795,800. The largest circulating Bengali papers are *Ittefaq* (225,500), *Azad* (63,000), *Sangbad* (50,000) and *Dainik Bangla* (40,000). The major English newspapers are the *Bangladesh Observer* (50,000) and the *Bangladesh Times* (50,000).

Broadcasting: There are 15 television broadcasting stations covering areas containing 90% of the population. Color television broadcasts commenced in 1980, two years before India. There were 310,508 licensed television sets in 1985. Fifteen radio stations broadcast to 587,000 licensed radios in the country.

BIOGRAPHICAL SKETCHES

Hussain Mohammed Ershad: Born in 1930, president of Bangladesh. Ershad was appointed to the 2nd East Bengal Regiment of the Pakistan Army after finishing Officers' Training School in 1952. He was promoted to Bangladesh Army Chief of Staff in 1978. General Ershad was instrumental in capturing the assassins of President Ziaur Rahman in 1981. In 1982, General Ershad declared martial law and assumed full power. He was elected president in October 1986, in an election boycotted by the major opposition parties.

Begum Khaleda Zia: Born around 1945 (like many Bengalis, she does not know her precise age), the leader of the Bangladesh National party, thus a key opposition leader. Zia is the widow of the assassinated former president, Ziaur Rahman. Upon her husband's death she was chosen as the head of the BNP, which her husband founded. She led the party in boycotting all presidential and parliamentary elections under the Ershad government.

Sheikh Hasina Wajed: Born in 1947, she is the leader of the Awami League and thus an important opposition leader. Wajed led her party in contesting the 1986 parliamentary elections, during which it gained 76 of 300 seats in spite of widespread irregularities in favor of the ruling party. In 1987, she led a walkout of her party and its allies from parliament, and proceeded to call successful strikes in June and November. She has been arrested and released by the Ershad government several times.

BHUTAN

Features: Set in the Himalayas, the Kingdom of Bhutan is an extremely mountainous country. In the south are the foothills of the Himalayas where they adjoin the Brahmaputra River Basin. This is an area of tropical vegetation and agricultural land. Central Bhutan is at a higher elevation, and the northern areas are high in the Himalayas.

Area: 18,000 sq. miles/46,620 sq. km.

Mean max. and min. temperatures: Thimbu (27°33'N, 89°42'E; 5,000 ft./ 1,500 m.) 62°F/17°C (July), 41°F/5°C (Jan.)

Relative humidity: 85%.

Mean annual rainfall: 95 in./2380 mm.

POPULATION

Total population (1988 est.): 1,500,000.

Chief towns and populations: THIMBU (30,000), Phunchsholing (30,000).

Ethnic composition: Sixty percent of the people are indigenous Bhutanese. About 25% are Nepalese immigrants, while the rest are tribal groups originally from India.

Language: Dzongkha, a Tibetan dialect, is the official language and is spoken in western and northern Bhutan. Two other Tibetan dialects, Bumthangka and Sarchapkha, are also spoken. Nepali is used by the Nepalese; Hindi and English are also in use.

Religion: Seventy percent of the Bhutanese are Buddhist, 25% are Hindu, and the remaining 5% are Muslim. The Drupka sect of Buddhism is predominant.

CONSTITUTIONAL SYSTEM

Constitution: Bhutan is a monarchy, in which the king *(Druk Gyalpo)* is assisted by three state organs: the Royal Advisory Council, Central Secretariat, and National Assembly. There is also a system of local administra-

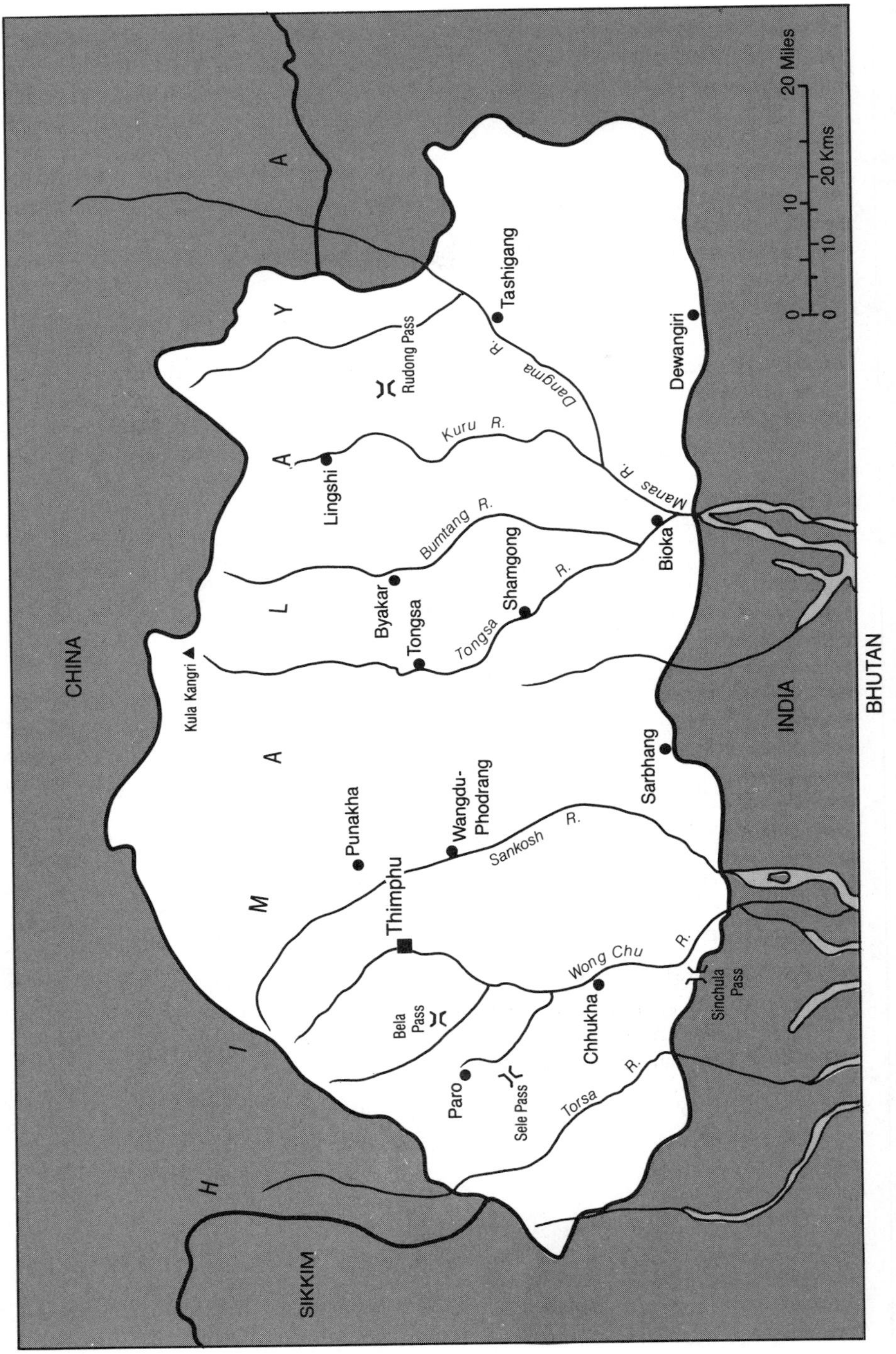
CHINA
SIKKIM
INDIA
BHUTAN
H
I
M
A
L
A
Y
A
Kula Kangri
Punakha
Thimphu
Wangdu-
Phodrang
Sankosh R.
Sarbhang
Paro
Bela Pass
Sele Pass
Chhukha
Torsa R.
Wong Chu R.
Sinchula Pass
Tongsa
Byakar
Tongsa R.
Shamgong
Bumtang R.
Bioka
Lingshi
Kuru R.
Manas R.
Rudong Pass
Dangma R.
Tashigang
Dewangiri
0
10
20 Miles
0
10
20 Kms

tion. If two-thirds of the National Assembly votes to remove the king, he must abdicate in favor of the next person in the hereditary line of monarchical succession. The king cannot veto bills passed by the assembly.

Head of state: King Jigme Singye Wangchuk.

Executive and legislature: The king has sole executive power. He appoints a Council of Ministers, but there is no office of prime minister; all ministers are of equal rank. The Royal Advisory Council is only an advisory body. The Central Secretariat is the administrative arm of the government. The National Assembly has 151 members, 33 of which are appointed by the king, and 106 who are elected by village headmen. The headmen are chosen in elections in which each family has one vote.

Political parties: Political parties are banned in Bhutan. The Bhutanese State Congress, whose leaders are primarily Nepalese, has its headquarters in India.

Judicial system: Village headmen are the lowest rung of the judiciary. Above them are magistrates (*thrimpons*). The next level of appeal is an eight-member High Court. The highest level of appeal is the king.

RECENT HISTORY

Bhutan's relations with the expanding British Empire in India were tense beginning with initial contacts in 1772. Bhutan had refrained from trading with the British, and both sides engaged in border raids. In 1857 Bhutan sympathized with Indian forces in their unsuccessful anti-British rebellion, which only heightened tensions with Britain. In 1864 the British moved to occupy lands near the Assam-Bhutan border. This led to a war in which Bhutan lost the territory. A humiliating treaty was imposed on the Bhutanese and the British began to treat Bhutan as a princely state within British India.

The new relationship with Britain and its empire in India led to a transformation of Bhutan's political structure as the rival factions considered how to balance relations between Tibet (and its ally, China) and British India. Bhutan had strong traditional ties with Tibet, so the dilemma was whether to maintain or break those links. As long as Anglo-Tibetan relations remained placid, the dilemma was avoided, but by the end of the 18th century the British began to assert their power. They demanded suzerainty over Tibet itself and recognition from Tibet and China of British hegemony in the southern Himalayas, including Bhutan. At the beginning of Anglo-Tibetan rivalry, Bhutanese factions sought to avoid choosing between the two powers. But at the end of the 19th century, they were polarized as either pro-British or pro-Tibetan.

In 1903 the British sent the Younghusband Expedition to attack Lhasa, the capital of Tibet. The success of this action led to expansion of British power in the Himalayas. Ugyen Wangchuk and Kazi Ugyen Dorji of Bhutan supported the expedition and helped negotiate the Anglo-Tibetan agreement of 1905. The British then aided Wangchuk in establishing political control over the whole of Bhutan. In December 1907 a gathering of the most important civil and religious officials unanimously proclaimed Ugyen Wangchuk as the *Druk Gyalpo,* or king of Bhutan.

Kazi Ugyen Dorji had been a political ally of Wangchuk since the 1890s. Dorji emerged as Wangchuk's most trusted supporter and was given a wide range of administrative responsibilities in the Wangchuk monarchy. He advised Wangchuk on relations with British India. Dorji's appointments were made hereditary, as long as the incumbent served the Wangchuk family loyally. Dorji cemented his ties to Wangchuk over the success of the Younghusband Expedition. Both men were awarded British titles. In 1908 the Dorji family was given a hereditary claim to the post of prime minister. This established a long alliance between the families, and except for a brief interruption in 1965–1972, the alliance has provided the foundation for political stability in Bhutan.

In 1910 Bhutan agreed to accept British guidance of its foreign relations, while Britain agreed not to interfere in Bhutan's domestic affairs. In 1949 Bhutan signed a treaty with independent India, in which the latter inherited the relationship established with the British. In addition, the 1949 agreement explicitly recognized the sovereignty of Bhutan. The second king of Bhutan, Jigme Wangchuk, died in 1952 and his son, Jigme Dorji Wangchuk, succeeded him. His reign was characterized by reform. In 1953 the king established the national assembly, or *Tshoghdu.*

In 1950 China took control of Tibet and declared it an integral part of the People's Republic. Toward the end of the decade, Tibetan resistance to Chinese rule grew and Beijing instituted severe repression of dissident activity. Because the cultures of Tibet and Bhutan are closely connected, Chinese repression of traditional Tibetan culture was resented by the Bhutanese. As the Sino-Indian border dispute intensified in the late 1950s, Bhutan sympathized with India.

In 1958 Indian Prime Minister Jawaharlal Nehru made his first visit to Bhutan to discuss bilateral relations. Nehru urged the king to permit construction of a road linking India with Bhutan; the road would be of military significance in the context of rising Sino-Indian tensions. Bhutan initially resisted the suggestion, wishing to remain separate from the conflict between its giant neighbors. But in 1959 the Tibetan rebellion and Sino-Indian tensions sharply intensified. Tibetan refugees, some with ties of marriage to prominent Bhutanese families, came into the country. They told of atrocities against Tibetan people and against Buddhist religious institutions. These accounts deeply angered the Bhutanese.

Nehru declared that an attack on Nepal or Bhutan would be regarded as an attack on India. While the Nepalese government expressed some reservations about this declaration, the Bhutanese government did not. Bhutan then agreed to the Indian road-building proposal, and the training of the Bhutanese Army by the Indian army. In 1960 Bhutan imposed a complete ban on trade with Chinese-controlled Tibet. This entailed a great trade loss to the country until the opening of the road to India in 1963, but the action reflected the depth of feeling in Bhutan regarding Chinese actions in Tibet.

In April 1964 Prime Minister Lonchen Jigme Dorji was assassinated in Phunchsholing, near the border with India, by an officer in the Bhutanese army. The king was in Switzerland at the time undergoing treatment for a heart attack but he returned immediately to Bhutan. In all, 41 persons were accused of conspiracy. Among those arrested was the king's uncle, Chabya Nangal Bahadur, the commander of the Bhutanese army. According to authoritative sources, the assassination plot was masterminded by the father of the king's Tibetan mistress.

The assassination disrupted primogeniture in the post of prime minister. Jigme Dorji's youngest brother, Lhendup Dorji, was appointed acting prime minister, and not his eldest son. In late 1964 the king again went to Switzerland for medical treatment. The king's mistress and her father feared that the acting prime minister would take advantage of the ruler's absence to avenge his brother's death. They tried to escape to India but were caught in southern Bhutan. When word reached the king, he sent a strongly worded, but ambiguous note to Lhendup Dorji, which the latter regarded as threatening. The acting prime minister eventually went into exile in Nepal, and the post of prime minister was eliminated.

Though strained, relations between the Dorjis and the Wangchuks were never completely broken. Since the queen was from the Dorji family, the present king is a member of both families. The Dorji and Wangchuk families have been reconciled, but the Dorjis have not been returned to their former political status.

In the late 1960s Bhutan began to expand its participation in international organizations, with a view toward consolidating its status as a sovereign nation. In 1969 Bhutan joined the Universal Postal Union; in 1970 India sponsored Bhutan's application to join the United Nations. Jigme Dorji Wangchuk died in 1972 and his son, Jigme Singye Wangchuk, became King. He continued his father's reformist policies. In 1979 Bhutan proposed a revision of the 1949 treaty with India, but India rejected the demand. Bhutan is a member of the South Asian Association for Regional Cooperation. The king has moved to increase popular participation in economic planning and to increase Bhutan's self-reliance.

ECONOMY

Background: Bhutan's gross national product in 1984 was approximately U.S. $200 million. It is one of the least developed countries in the world, yet its people live in accordance with their traditions and do not experience the hunger and destitution that poor people in more industrialized countries do. The country has an abundance of natural resources, and they remain largely untapped. It has enormous hydroelectric potential and could sell the power to India. Its massive neighbor to the south has played an important role in the development process. Indian aid has gone to a 336 MW hydroelectric dam and to a cement factory that is Bhutan's major source of industrial exports.

Indian assistance to Bhutan's development plans began in 1959. Plan investments have doubled from one five-year plan to the next. An organization to administer development has been built up. In the current plan, 31% of funds are from India and 30% are from the United Nations and other donors. Since the fifth five-year plan, starting in 1981, the government has emphasized national self-reliance and popular participation in the planning process.

Agriculture: About half of Bhutan's gross domestic product (GDP) comes from agriculture. It contains a large subsistence sector. The principal crops are rice, maize, wheat, barley and buckwheat. Animal husbandry is an important part of the subsistence sector. Cattle, chicken and pigs are raised. In higher elevations, sheep and yak are grazed in the alpine grasslands. In addition, forestry contributes 16% of the GDP.

Only 4% of the land is used for permanent agriculture; another 10%– 12% is for seasonal pasture. The western and southern parts of the country have terraced and bunded paddies. The eastern part is dry land. The number of areas under cultivation is expanding, but while this increases production in the short run, it threatens the forest cover. Especially dangerous is the practice of shifting cultivation.

Bhutan produced 62,000 tons of rice in 1985. The country was self-sufficient in food production until recently, when it began small-scale food importation from India. Cereals are the main source of calories and protein in the Bhutanese diet.

There is little multiple-cropping in Bhutan. High-yielding varieties have not been used extensively, since local varieties yield nearly as well. In the 1980s, cash crops have been expanding; potatoes are the most widespread.

Industry: Manufacturing contributes less than 5% of Bhutan's GDP. There are three major factories in the country: the Bhutan Fruit Products Company is in private hands and sells to the domestic market; the Government Welfare Project is a public-sector distillery; and the Penden Cement Authority, built with Indian aid, exports its excess beyond domestic consumption to India. These three plants accounted for two-thirds of the manufacturing output and employment in the early 1980s. All three are profitable and well managed.

The number of small-scale industries has been growing in recent years. These companies manufacture basic consumer goods, including soap, candles, matches, furniture and processed foodstuffs.

A bottleneck in Bhutan's industrialization has been the shortage of industrial entrepreneurship. This is due to the rural nature of the society and the low educational level. In 1979, the National Commission for the Development of Trade and Industry was established to encourage and guide industrialization. Another difficulty facing industry is the shortage of labor.

Petroleum accounts for 60% of the energy produced in Bhutan, while coal and electricity contribute 30% and 10%, respectively. Electrification commenced in 1962. By the middle 1980s, there were six hydroelectric and six diesel electrical power stations in operation. The dams generate 73% of the nation's power supply, while the diesel stations produce the remainder. The Indian-funded 336 MW Chukha Hydroelectric Project was completed in 1987. All the output of the plant in the southwestern region that is not consumed in the country will be exported to India. Installed electrical power capacity is 17,000 kw, and production was 30 million kwh in 1986. The country has no power grid.

Bhutan has a considerable potential for tourism. It possesses magnificent Himalayan scenery and an attractive culture. However, the government has limited the growth of the tourist industry to avoid disruption of traditional life. In 1985, 1,896 tourists brought $1.8 million to Bhutan. The government is planning to expand facilities to accommodate 5,000 tourists a year.

Trade and transport: Prior to 1959, Bhutan's trade had been primarily with Tibet. After absorption of that region into the People's Republic of China, Bhutan ceased trade with Tibet and since then virtually all its trade has been with India. Although the economy functioned virtually autarkically until the 1950s, imports have grown to 40% of GDP and exports to 17%. There is free trade between Bhutan and India. Exports to India consist mostly of agricultural, mineral and forestry products; imports are machinery and equipment, petroleum and metal products, food grains and consumer goods.

Bhutan is a highly mountainous region, and travel and communications are difficult. Bhutan had resisted British offers of road construction in the colonial era, preferring to remain inaccessible. In 1959, the Indian Border Roads Organization began to assist Bhutan in building a road network. In 1985, there were 1,370 miles/2,200 km. of roads and 102 suspension bridges. Much travel continues on foot and by pack animal.

Druk Airlines possesses an 18-seater aircraft that flies between Bhutan's principal airport at Paro Dzong and Calcutta. There are also bus lines connecting Bhutan and India.

Employment: There are 650,000 persons in the labor force and agriculture absorbs over 90%. There is little landlessness in Bhutan, and farmland is equitably distributed. There is an acute shortage of skilled labor, which is overcome by hiring Indian technicians. Bhutan developed a compulsory labor scheme in the mid-1960s for building roads. Currently, each family is required to contribute 23 labor-days per adult member per year. Trade unions are banned.

SOCIAL SERVICES

The family remains the major source of care for the infirm. There is no government social welfare system, however there is a small program for the care of children and mothers.

Life expectancy in Bhutan is 48.6 years for men and 47.1 years for women. In 1985, there were 24 hospitals, 65 clinics and a mobile hospital for the mountainous central region.

EDUCATION

The literacy rate in Bhutan is 12%. In 1985, there were 53,420 students and 1,875 teachers. The educational sequence consists of one year in kindergarten, six years in primary schools, four years in junior school and two years in central school. A college degree takes three years. There is one degree-granting college affiliated with India's Delhi University.

MASS MEDIA

The press: The government publishes a weekly newspaper *Kuensel,* in Dzong-kha, English and Nepalese. It has a circulation of about 5,000.

Broadcasting: There are no radio or television broadcasting services in Bhutan.

BIOGRAPHICAL SKETCHES

Jigme Singye Wangchuk: Born in 1955, the king of Bhutan. As a 17-year-old, he ascended the throne when his father died in 1972. He has followed his father's policies of working with the National Assembly and has moved to increase popular participation in economic planning.

BRUNEI

Features: Brunei Darussalam is situated on the northwest coast of the island of Kalimantan (Borneo). It is bounded on the north by the South China Sea (the state has a coastline of about 100 miles/161 km.) and on all other sides by the Malaysian state of Sarawak, which also divides Brunei into two parts (the eastern territory of Temburong District and the western territory comprising the Brunei-Muara, Tutong and Belait Districts). The major part of the country consists of a low coastal plain: the terrain rises modestly in the interior (the highest point is Bukit Pagon in the Temburong District, which reaches (6,040 ft/1,841 m.). Permanent cultivation is concentrated in the coastal zone; much of the rest of Brunei is covered by dense equatorial forest. Very substantial reserves of petroleum and natural gas are located offshore.

Area: 2,226 sq. miles/5,765 sq. km.

Mean max. and min. temperatures: The daily temperature averages between 73°F/23°C and 89°F/32°C.

Relative humidity: Relative humidity averages between 67% and 91% throughout the year.

Mean annual rainfall: More than 97.5 in/2,500 mm. Precipitation is normally higher in the interior than in the coastal lowland.

Total population (mid-1986 est.): 226,300. Of this total 68.8% were Malay, 18.3% were Chinese. The indigenous races (principally Muruts, Kedayans and Dusuns) comprised 5% of the population.

Chief town and population: BANDAR SERI BEGAWAN (1986 est., 50,500).

Distribution: Approximately 47% of the population are under 20 years of age. The natural increase in the population averages between 2.4% and 2.6% annually.

Language: Malay is the official language, but English, Chinese and a number of native dialects are also spoken.

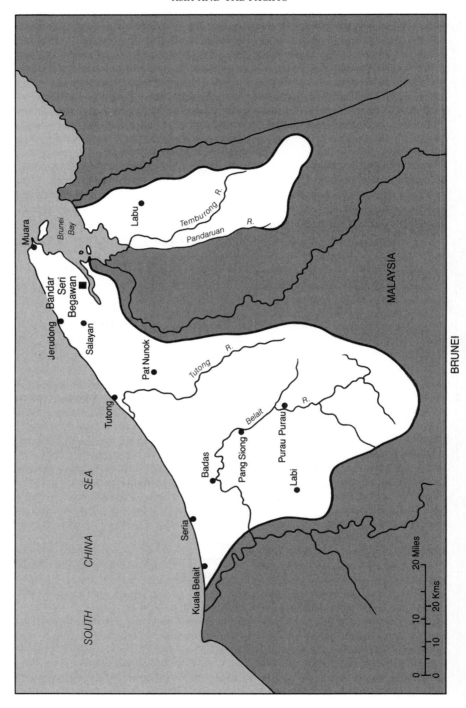

Religion: The official religion is Islam: the sultan is the religious head for all Muslims in the state. The majority of the Malay population are Sunni Muslims. The Chinese are either Buddhist, Confucian, Taoist or Christian. Animist beliefs are widely practiced by the indigenous population.

CONSTITUTIONAL SYSTEM

Constitution: Brunei's first written constitution, promulgated on September 29, 1959, remains in force. However, certain sections have been in abeyance since 1962 and amendments were introduced effective January 1, 1984, reflecting Brunei's status as a fully independent sovereign nation.

Head of state: Paduka Seri Baginda Sultan Hassanal Bolkiah Muizzaddin Waddaulah, who is both sultan and *yang di-pertuan.*

Executive and legislature: Under the constitution, sovereign authority is vested in the sultan and *yang di-pertuan.* He is assisted and advised by four councils: the Council of Cabinet Ministers (over which he presides, and which considers all executive matters); the Privy Council (again over which he presides, and which advises him on the use of the royal prerogative, the amendment of the constitution and the award of ranks, titles and honors); the Religious Council (which offers advice on all Islamic matters and whose members are appointed by the sultan and *yang di-pertuan*); and the Council of Succession (which determines the succession to the throne).

Political parties: Parti Kebang-Saan Demokratik Brunei, or Brunei National Democratic party (PKDB) was formed in July 1985 with the agreement of the sultan (although government employees were forbidden to join). The party sought greater participation by the people of Brunei in government administration, public accountability among civil servants and political democratization. In February 1986 the party split; from it emerged the Parti Perpaduan Kebang-Saan Brunei, or Brunei National United party (PPKB), which sought cooperation with the government and which thus was immediately approved by the sultan. In February 1988 the PKDB was dissolved by government order after it had demanded the resignation of the sultan as head of government, the end of the state of emergency in force from 1962 and the institution of democratic elections. The president and secretary-general of the party were placed under detention.

Local government: Four administrative districts (Brunei-Muara, Tutong, Belait and Temburong) are administered by a district officer; three municipal authorities are located at Bandar Seri Begawan, Kuala Belait and Tutong.

Judicial system: Judicial power is vested in the Supreme Court (consisting of the Court of Appeal and the High Court) and the subordinate courts (consisting of the magistrate's courts). Matters relating to Islam (questions concerning Islamic religion, marriage and divorce) are dealt with by the *Sharia* courts. Appeals from these courts are to the sultan in the Religious Council.

RECENT HISTORY

In the 16th century Brunei was an important power in island Southeast Asia. It was at the center of an empire that embraced the whole of Borneo and extended as far as Java, Melaka and the Philippine archipelago. Brunei's prosperity depended largely on trade with the southern ports of China—an exchange of valuable jungle products (hornbill ivory, edible birds' nests) for silk, stoneware and porcelain. But with the expansion first of European commerce and then of European territorial ambitions in the region, Brunei's importance sharply declined. The decisive intervention occurred at the beginning of the 1840s when Sir James Brooke, an English adventurer, assisted the sultan of Brunei in putting down a major internal revolt in the southern part of his territories: in return for his services, Brooke was appointed rajah (governor) of Sarawak. In the following four decades the Brunei sultanate lost much of its territory to expansionist Sarawak to the south and to ambitious trading interests (British, American, Dutch merchants and from 1881 the British North Borneo Company) in North Borneo (Sabah) to the north. By the 1890s Brunei was reduced in size to little more than 2,120 sq. miles/5,500 sq. km., and the Temburong District was separated (by an extension of Sarawak) from the rest of the sultanate. In 1888 Brunei became a British protectorate; in 1906 a British resident (later designated high commissioner) was appointed to the court to advise on all matters of government except those relating to Malay custom and religion.

Japanese forces occupied Brunei, North Borneo and Sarawak from 1941 to 1945. In 1946 the last two territories became British crown colonies; in 1948 the governor of Sarawak was appointed high commissioner for Brunei. In the 1950s the sultanate began to use its vast petroleum resources (oil was first exploited on a significant commercial scale at the close of the 1920s) to finance development. Particular attention was given to infrastructural investment. In September 1959 agreement between the sultan and the British government gave Brunei its first written constitution. Brunei was given internal self-government; Britain became responsible only for defense and foreign affairs; a resident British high commissioner was appointed to serve on an Executive Council presided over by the sultan; a Legislative Council, an Islamic Religious Council and district councils, elected under universal adult franchise, were established.

In December 1962 a major rebellion broke out in Brunei, launched by the Brunei People's party (BPP) led by A. M. Azahari. The rebels were strongly opposed to the entry of Brunei into the proposed federation of Malayasia. The rebellion was quickly crushed with the assistance of British forces from Singapore, Azahari fled to Malaya, and the BPP was proscribed. At the same time the government declared a state of emergency (which remains in force), certain sections of the 1959 constitution were suspended and the sultan turned to rule by decree. The following year, 1963, the sultan decided against joining the new Malaysian federation. In October 1967 he abdicated in favor of his son, Hassanal Bolkiah. In 1971 a further agreement between the sultanate and the British government left Brunei fully independent internally (the post of British high commissioner became

46

a normal diplomatic position); the United Kingdom remained responsible for defense and foreign relations. A separate agreement led to the location of a battalion of British Gurkhas in Brunei. With assurances from both Malaysia and Indonesia that they would respect the independence of Brunei, in January 1979 Brunei and Britain signed an agreement that would leave Brunei a fully independent sovereign state from January 1, 1984. Under a defense agreement concluded in September 1983, the Gurkhas would remain in Brunei but simply to defend the offshore oil and gas fields.

On independence Brunei became a member of the Association of Southeast Asian Nations (ASEAN), the Commonwealth, the Organization of the Islamic Conference and the United Nations. Political power was, as it had long been, overwhelmingly concentrated in the person of the sultan. In 1984 the sultan established a seven-member cabinet in which he himself was prime minister, minister of finance and minister of home affairs; his father, the former sultan, was minister of defense. In 1985 Hassanal Bolkiah agreed to the formation of a political party, the PKDB, but it was dissolved by government order in February 1988 after it called for the end of the state of emergency and the resignation of the sultan as head of government. The PPKB, formed in 1986 by former members of the PKDB, is progovernment and has the sultan's approval. The fact that Brunei's population enjoys free medical care and schooling, a high quality of public services and high average incomes—all the result of the sultanate's vast oil and gas revenues—undoubtedly makes it difficult for political opposition to the sultan's autocratic rule to gain wide popular support. Despite some resentment among many Bruneians at, notably, the continuing employment of large numbers of expatriates in key positions, the meager progress being made toward political democratization and the severe weakness of administrative accountability, the sultan's position remains firmly secure.

ECONOMY

Background: The economy of Brunei rests on its major reserves of petroleum and natural gas. In 1985 their exploitation accounted for about 72% of GDP and 99% of exports. This heavy dependence on a highly valuable resource has—for a territorially and demographically tiny state—had profound implications for the growth and structure of the economy. Most notably, Brunei has one of the world's highest levels of national income per capita (in 1986 it was estimated that GDP per capita, excluding income derived from the investment overseas of Brunei's substantial official reserves, was $15,000); the growth of the economy has been closely related to the condition of the world energy market (in 1975–79 real GDP increased at an average annual rate of 12.2%; during 1980–84 it grew at only 3.9%); the economy has suffered from acute labor shortages, notably shortages of skilled labor (in 1987 about 37% of the labor force was expatriate). The vast revenues from petroleum and natural gas have allowed the sultan's administration to create a tax-free welfare state and to invest heavily in infrastructural projects (improving water and sewerage facilities and the

47

telecommunications network, and constructing new ports) and in education to reduce the economy's extreme dependence on foreign skills. But those vast revenues have also brought difficulties: They have led to a large income disparity within the population (with wealth being strongly concentrated in the petroleum/natural gas sector); they have produced more investable funds than the nonpetroleum sector of an economy with a very small population could profitably absorb; and they have raised the problem of creating a more diversified economy (again on a tiny territorial and demographic base) against the day when the reserves of petroleum and natural gas are exhausted. Further difficulties have arisen as a result of the sultan's announcement in 1985 that Brunei would become an Islamic state in which the indigenous Malays would receive preferential treatment: Approximately 90% of the ethnic Chinese (some 30% of the population and the dominant local element in the modern economy) were classified as noncitizens. Recent years have seen significant emigration of Bruneian Chinese.

Petroleum and natural gas: The commercial extraction of crude petroleum dates from the close of the 1920s. The early fields were located on land, but from the 1960s on the principal fields have been offshore. Production reached a peak of 254,000 barrels a day in 1979 but declined in the 1980s to 165,000 in 1986. In that last year 30% of production was exported to Japan, 13% to the United States, 34% to the other ASEAN countries and 17% to South Korea. Brunei retains only 3% of production for domestic consumption. It is estimated that petroleum reserves are sufficient to enable production to be maintained at current levels until at least the year 2014. Brunei is the world's second largest exporter of liquefied natural gas. From 1972 on Japan has been the principal, and at times the sole, buyer of Brunei's exports. The natural gas reserves are estimated to be sufficient to meet existing Japanese contracts and to cover domestic needs until around 2022. The extraction of oil is undertaken by the Brunei Shell Petroleum Company, a 50–50 joint venture between the Brunei government and the Royal Dutch-Shell Group. Other interests (notably Société Nationale Elf Aquitaine) have in recent years acquired concessions and undertaken exploration. The processing of natural gas from the offshore fields is undertaken by the Brunei Liquefied Natural Gas Company, a tripartite venture between the Brunei government, the Royal Dutch-Shell Group and the Mitsubishi Corporation of Japan.

Agriculture and fishing: During the oil boom of the 1970s, which created lucrative employment off the land, the area under cultivation fell sharply (from about 8,900 acres/3,600 ha. in 1970 to 4,000 acres/1,600 ha. in 1982). Brunei currently imports about 90% of its food requirements: In 1985 only 25% of rice consumption and 42% of fish requirements were met from domestic production. The government has sought to reduce the dependence on imports—notably by establishing agricultural research facilities and improving marketing structures—but the acute shortage of labor on the land as a result of the existence of more remunerative opportunities elsewhere in the economy makes a marked expansion of food production difficult to achieve. The principal crops are paddy, cassava, bananas, pineapples and vegetables. In addition, cattle and poultry are raised, but on a modest scale.

Industry: Although the government has sought industrial expansion to diversify the economy away from the heavy dependence on petroleum and natural gas, that expansion has been constrained by the smallness of the local market (which has made it necessary to focus in the long-term on export-market industries) and the acute shortage of skilled labor. In 1987, industrial production was mainly connected with the government (the construction sector) or petroleum extraction (the manufacture of offshore platforms, ship repairing and engineering services). Some consideration is being given to the establishment of a microchip and optics industry (using local supplies of high-quality silica sand); but such high technology projects, if successful, will have to overcome serious labor shortages domestically and acute competition externally.

Foreign trade: With the major expansion of petroleum and natural gas exports from the early 1970s on, Brunei has long enjoyed a very substantial trade surplus; with the weakening of the world energy market in the 1980s this has contracted but remains considerable. In mid-1986 the official international reserves were estimated to be $20 billion. In 1985 crude oil and natural gas constituted 97.6% of exports; principal imports were machinery and transport equipment, manufactures and foodstuffs. Brunei's major trading partner is Japan. In 1985 Japan accounted for 61.2% of exports from Brunei.

Employment: Employment is concentrated in the public sector (in 1987 about 48% of the work force was employed in this sector; about three-quarters of economically active Brunei Malays were employed in the civil service) and in the petroleum/natural gas industry (in 1987 the Brunei Shell Petroleum Company was the largest single private-sector employer). Serious labor shortages exist throughout the economy. In 1987 about 37% of the labor force was expatriate.

Price trends: The consumer price index (1977 = 100) was 143.1 in 1984; 146.4 in 1985; and 149.0 in 1986.

SOCIAL SERVICES

Welfare: Brunei's vast oil revenues have made possible the creation of a tax-free welfare state, with free education and medical care, and with the provision of government-subsidized loans for the purchase of houses and cars. A national noncontributory pension scheme has been in operation since 1955, providing monthly pensions and allowances to the aged, the blind, the disabled, lepers and the mentally ill; there were some 7,000 recipients in 1985.

Health services: Free medical and health care is provided through five hospitals (including one owned by Brunei Shell), dozens of clinics and dispensaries and a "flying doctor" service to outlying areas. There are also private clinics, mostly dental.

Housing: The government and Brunei Shell, the largest employers in Brunei, provide their employees with accommodations. In addition, under a government scheme, landless citizens can each own a plot of land and a house at subsidized prices, payable monthly at low rates. A substantial private housing sector constructs luxury houses and high-rise apartment buildings.

EDUCATION

The government provides free education to all Brunei citizens from preprimary level to university study abroad. It also meets the cost of the education of its employees' children who attend nongovernment schools. Three languages of instruction—Malay, Chinese and English—are used, and schools are divided accordingly. All the Malay schools are state-administered; English schools are either state-administered or independent; all Chinese schools are independent and are not assisted by the government. There are also religious schools administered by the Department of Religious Affairs. In 1986 there were 112 preschool classes, 153 primary schools and 18 secondary schools. In addition, there were five vocational/technical schools, two teacher training colleges, one institute of technology, one institute of education and the University of Brunei (founded in 1985). A large number of Bruneians go abroad for higher education at government expense.

MASS MEDIA

The press: One independent newspaper, *Borneo Bulletin,* publishes weekly in English and has a circulation of 35,000. The Department of Broadcasting and Information publishes, in Malay, *Pelita Brunei,* which appears weekly and has a circulation of 45,000; and, in English, *Brunei Darussalam Newsletter,* which appears monthly and has a circulation of 14,000. Both government publications are distributed free of charge.

Broadcasting: The Department of Broadcasting and Information, through its Radio Television Brunei, operates two radio networks (one broadcasting in Malay and local dialects, the other in English, Mandarin and Gurkha) and a color television service transmitting in Malay and English. In 1988 an estimated 82,000 radios and 54,000 televisions were in use.

BIOGRAPHICAL SKETCH

Paduka Seri Baginda Sultan Hassanal Bolkiah Muizzaddin Waddaulah. Born on July 15, 1946, at the Istana Darussalam in Bandar Seri Begawan, he was educated in Brunei and Malaysia. In January 1966 he qualified for admission as an officer cadet at Sandhurst Military Academy in England

50

and was commissioned a captain the following year. He left Sandhurst in October 1967 to succeed his father as sultan, after his father abdicated. When Brunei secured full independence in January 1984, he became prime minister in the new cabinet, as well as minister of finance and minister of home affairs. He remained, as well, sultan and *yang di-pertuan*.

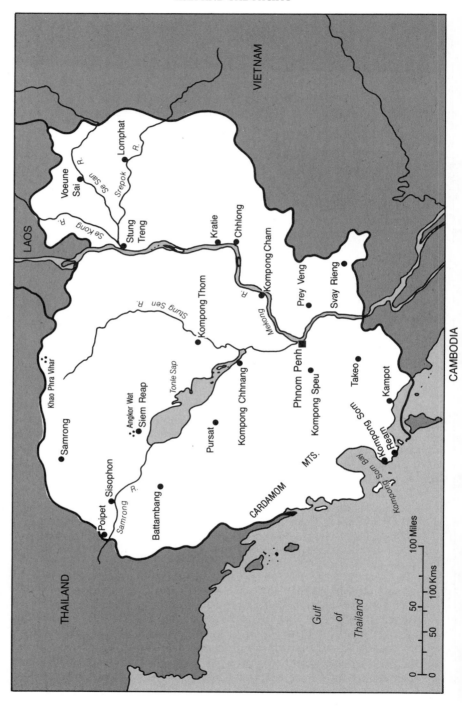

CAMBODIA

Features: The State of Cambodia, located on mainland Southeast Asia, is bordered to the south by the Gulf of Thailand, to the east by Vietnam, to the north by Thailand and Laos and to the west by Thailand. Low plains cover most of the country. The central area consists of a shallow lacustrine basin centered on the Tonle Sap (Great Lake). Many rivers cut across the country, flowing into the Mekong River or the Tonle Sap (often referred to as a large inland sea). During the rainy season (June to October) overflow from the Mekong River causes the flow from the Tonle Sap to reverse direction. The lake expands several times its normal area, silting and fertilizing adjacent river plains. The Mekong averages about 1 mile/1.6 km. in width, and its flow varies widely from season to season. Mountain ranges exist along the northern border and in the southwest. The Cardamom range shuts the interior off from much of its limited southern coastline. The northeast is a forested plateau with an altitude higher than that of the central plain. Cambodia has good alluvial soils and abundant irrigation water, suggesting great potential for the development of agriculture in the future. The Mekong also provides an abundant source of hydroelectric power.

Area: 69,900 sq. miles/181,035 sq. km.

Mean max. and min. temperatures: Phnom Penh (11°33′N/104°55′E) 97°F/ 36°C, 68°F/20°C.

Relative humidity: 75%.

Mean annual rainfall: 80 in/2,000 mm. (lowlands).

Total population (1989 est.): 8,400,000.

Chief towns and population: PHNOM PENH (700,000), Battambang (45,000), Kompang Cham (33,000).

Distribution: Cambodia is predominantly a rural country. Urban population in 1989 was an estimated 12% of the total. Density is 100 people per sq. km. in the heartland, where most people live. More than 80% of the pop-

ulation live in the fertile central plains, where rice is the chief crop cultivated and fishing is rich.

Language: Khmer is the official language. The Khmer people make up 90%
to 95% of the total population. The Islamic Cham, of the Malayo-Polynesian language group, are the most important minority, estimated to number
185,000. Several smaller ethnic groups, linguistically related to the Khmer,
inhabit the northeastern hills and the far west. The current Vietnamese
population was estimated at 200,000–300,000 in 1985.

Religion: The principal religion of Cambodia is Theravada Buddhism, encompassing approximately 90% of the population. Islam and folk religions
are practiced by minorities.

CONSTITUTIONAL SYSTEM

Constitution: The constitution of Cambodia was adopted by its first-sitting,
nonelected National Assembly in June 1981. It states that power belongs
to the people and is exercised through the National Assembly, various organs of state power and popular organizations such as the Front for Construction of the Motherland. The People's Revolutionary party is the leader
in all revolutionary tasks. The state recognizes equality of all ethnic groups.
Freedom of religion, speech and press are declared, but they may not be
used to offend others or disrupt public order or national security.

Head of state: President Heng Samrin. *Head of government:* Prime Minister
Hun Sen.

Executive: The 21-member Council of Ministers is the executive organ chosen by, and responsible to, the National Assembly. In 1982 the National
Assembly passed a law requiring the president of the Council of Ministers
to be a National Assembly member; and a majority of the other members
are to be chosen from the Assembly. The Council drafts laws for submission
to the National Assembly, applies the constitution, formulates economic
progress and the national budget, and works to eliminate "defects of the
old society" and to improve living standards. The Council is responsible
for proper functioning of people's revolutionary committees at all levels.

Legislature: The National Assembly is established as the supreme organ of
state power and the only body entitled to pass laws. Members serve five-
year terms. There are 117 representatives, chosen by province and municipality; the number from each electoral district depends on population. Candidates are nominated jointly by the Front Central Committee, and central
and local-level mass organizations. In each district there are to be more
candidates than the number of representatives to be elected. The National
Assembly amends the constitution and establishes domestic and foreign
policies. It can elect and remove its own officers, as well as those of the
Council of Ministers and of the State Council.

The National Assembly meets twice a year to vote on bills proposed by
the State Council, the Council of Ministers, the Assembly's own commis-

sions, the presidents of the Front, the trade union organizations, the Youth Organization and the Women's Organization. Sessions usually last only a few days, leaving government business in the hands of the State Council and the ministries. The Assembly thus gives formal approval to measures already decided by ministries, the State Council or the party.

The seven-member State Council, an organ of the National Assembly, assumes the Assembly's duties when it is not in session. Its members, who serve for five years, are chosen from the Assembly by the Assembly. The State Council organizes National Assembly elections. It promulgates and interprets laws, reviews judicial proceedings and decides on commutation and reduction of sentences.

Political organizations: The People's Revolutionary party of Kampuchea (the Communist party) is the only political party in Cambodia. The Solidarity Front for the Construction and Defense of the Motherland of Kampuchea was the original organ of Cambodian state power in 1978 (and was then called the National Union Front for the Salvation of Kampuchea). It is a political and administrative organization of the state that serves as a bridge in both directions between the party and the people. Total membership was 120,000 in 1986. It has organizations at all levels, similar to the state administration. Leadership overlaps with that of the state and party.

Local government: The State of Cambodia is divided into 18 provinces *(khet)*, which are divided into 122 districts *(srok)*, 1,325 subdistricts *(khum)* and 9,383 villages *(phum)*. The two municipalities *(krung)*, Phnom Penh and Kompong Som, are divided into wards *(sangkat)* and subdivided into groups *(krom)*. Each division has a people's revolutionary committee. Those at the two lowest levels are chosen by the population in direct elections. At each higher level committees are chosen by members of subordinate-level committees, the Front and mass organizations. Low-level committee members serve three-year terms. Provincial and municipality committees are elected for five years. The committees execute directives of higher-level organs in the interest of carrying out state policies, developing the country and maintaining order.

Judicial system: There are people's courts and military courts in Cambodia. In addition, the State Council may create special courts when necessary. A tribunal includes a judge and "people's councillors." A majority vote by the council determines the outcome of a case. Court proceedings are public and defendants have the right to a defense, conducted either by a lawyer or by themselves. The National Assembly passed bills in 1985 creating a Supreme People's Court and Supreme Public Prosecutor's Department. The National Assembly law does not indicate how court personnel are appointed or what qualifications are required.

RECENT HISTORY

Khmer civilization reached its high point between the 9th and 14th centuries when the Angkor Empire included present-day Cambodia and parts of Thailand, Laos and Vietnam. By the mid-19th century Cambodia had become a semiindependent state subordinate to its rival neighbors. The French made the country a protectorate in 1863. The protectorate was included in the wider French Indochinese Union in 1887.

Little overt opposition to the French existed in the early 20th century; a modern nationalist movement only formed in the late 1930s. The country achieved a short-lived independence in 1945, when King Norodom Sihanouk, then 22 years old, formed a government before the Japanese were defeated. After World War I the French returned to restore their authority. Elections in 1948 and 1951 for a National Assembly were won by the Democratic party, an anti-French, anti-Sihanouk party with links to the nationalists, led by Son Ngoc Thanh. Democratic reforms, however, did not secure Cambodian loyalty, as the French had hoped. Armed resistance developed along with Vietnam's war for independence. In Cambodia the resistance included several groups fighting for independence in the late 1940s: the non-communist Khmer Issarak (Freedom) Committee, with ties to Thailand; and a Vietnam-oriented group that included future prominent Communists such as Son Ngoc Minh. Other groups were founded and fell apart as leaders sorted out their ideological positions and political alliances.

The United Issarak Front (UIF) was established in 1950, unifying revolutionary independence forces under Son Ngoc Minh. Five of its 15 identified leaders were members of the Indochinese Communist party (ICP). The Khmer People's Revolutionary party (KPRP) was founded in 1951 when the ICP split into three national parties. By 1952 the UIF and KPRP forces controlled more than half of the country. Sihanouk dismissed the government in 1953 and assumed personal leadership in an attempt to ensure political stability as he faced increasing criticism from the Khmer Issarak resistance. He then launched a "Royal Crusade for Independence," and some leaders of small Issarak groups joined the royal army. On November 9, 1953, Cambodia was granted independence.

At the same time another revolutionary current was developing among Cambodian students in Paris. This circle included Saloth Sar (Pol Pot), Ieng Sary, their wives Khieu Thirith and Khieu Ponnary, Hou Yuom and Thioun Mum. They all were to become leaders of what was then called Democratic Kampuchea from 1975 to 1978.

After the 1954 Geneva accords revolutionary groups were forced to lay down their arms and reintegrate into Cambodian society under Sihanouk's conservative government. Sihanouk abdicated because the 1947 constitution had limited the political power of the monarchy. As prince, rather than king, he had more opportunity to pursue his political ambitions. He founded the Sangkum Reastr Niyum (Popular Socialist Community), or the Sangkum, a political movement through which he sought to unify all political factions.

At this time many KPRP leaders withdrew to North Vietnam. Others turned from armed to political struggle in order to contest elections. Elections held in 1955, 1958, 1962 and 1966 resulted in total victory for the Sangkum. No non-Sangkum politician sat in the National Assembly during this time. The Sangkum did contain leftists, including Hou Yuom and

Khieu Samphan of the Paris student group, who hoped to move Sihanouk leftward.

Two lines now began to develop within the KPRP. The dominant one, that of the urban intellectuals and the Vietnamese, also hoped to push Sihanouk leftward, realizing that he was too popular to be overthrown. The other line considered Sihanouk the enemy; their primary goal was his overthrow. This was the line adopted by the party under Pol Pot's leadership, and it was popular among rural cadres. Pol Pot became secretary-general of the KPRP in 1963 after the disappearance and presumed murder of Tou Samouth.

Sihanouk continued suppression of the left throughout the 1960s. Leftist ministers in government were forced to resign their positions in 1963. Still, they remained in Phnom Penh to try to work with Sihanouk toward a socialist transformation of society. At that time Sihanouk was becoming increasingly hostile to the United States and to its allies, South Vietnam and Thailand. Although he claimed neutrality Sihanouk broke relations with South Vietnam in 1963 and with the United States in 1965.

Economic conditions in Cambodia deteriorated throughout the 1960s. Banks and industries fell into the hands of Sihanouk's cronies, who treated them as personal fiefs. Conflict between the left and right increased in terms of suppression of leftists and armed attacks by both sides in rural areas. The Pol Pot faction went to the countryside to prepare the rural revolution. Spillover from the Vietnam War, particularly the U.S. bombing of Cambodia, further destabilized the country.

On March 18, 1970, Sihanouk was removed from office while he was out of the country by the right-wing prime minister, Marshal Lon Nol. Sihanouk settled in Beijing and declared his leadership of the leftist revolution—a typical example of shifting alliances and accommodations made in Cambodian politics. Those he allied with were his former enemies. Sihanoukists and the Khmer Rouge formed the National United Front of Cambodia (FUNC) in March 1970, and members of both groups participated in the Royal Government of National Union of Cambodia (GRUNC) in Beijing. The coup and Sihanouk's actions gave full rein to peasant, antiurban tendencies within the Cambodian revolution. The movement became explicitly anti-Vietnamese. The name Cambodia was formally changed to the Khmer Republic in October 1970. Lon Nol declared himself president in March 1972, and led a government marked by factional conflict and corruption until 1975. In the early 1970s Cambodia was heavily bombed by U.S. forces. The Khmer Rouge also led assaults throughout the countryside, but always stopped just short of the capital. Pol Pot's Khmer Rouge forces intensified their assault on Phnom Penh beginning in January 1975, and finally took control of the country on April 17, 1975. Lon Nol had already left for the United States on April 1.

Evacuation of Phnom Penh and other cities immediately ensued as the Khmer Rouge pursued a policy of radical social change with the aim of reducing all citizens to the level of peasants. Poor peasants became the "privileged class," while city people (workers and petit bourgeois) were the lowest and socially most disadvantaged group in the new society. Thousands from the former ruling class were executed; others were submitted to forced labor in rudimentary cooperatives established throughout the land. The country was divided into seven zones, whose leaders represented different backgrounds and political tendencies. Markets and currency were abolished.

Sihanouk became head of state. A constitution promulgated in January 1976 renamed the country Democratic Kampuchea (DK). In April 1976 Sihanouk resigned and was placed under house arrest within the royal palace. GRUNC was dissolved. Khieu Samphan became head of state and Pol Pot became prime minister. The regime was closely allied with China.

The Khmer Rouge had increased purges within the party in 1977–78 as factions protested the continued harsh policies of the Pol Pot clique. Disagreement centered on the country's relationship with Vietnam and on domestic socioeconomic organization. Opponents wanted to maintain cooperation with Vietnam and objected to the extreme communalization policies being carried out. They felt Pol Pot had ignored the revolution's purpose: to improve the standard of living, rather than just to turn the rich into poor peasants. Eastern-zone leaders Heng Samrin and Hun Sen escaped to Vietnam before a purge of their area, and formed the Kampuchean National United Front for National Salvation (KNUFNS). Backed by the Vietnamese army, the rebels returned in December 1978 to overthrow the Khmer Rouge regime. (The Vietnamese army was also responding to DK attacks over the Vietnam-Cambodia border.)

On January 8, 1979, the Khmer People's Revolutionary Council, with Heng Samrin as president, was proclaimed. Penn Sovann was vice-president and Hun Sen held the foreign affairs portfolio. On January 12, the People's Republic of Kampuchea (PRK) was proclaimed. (The Name was changed in early 1989 to the State of Cambodia.) Vietnamese forces numbering an estimated 200,000 remained in the country to prevent the return of the Khmer Rouge.

The regime faced rebuilding a society from scratch. Foreign aid from the Soviet Union, Vietnam and, later, from Western sources prevented starvation in the first year as much of the population, free of DK discipline, abandoned agriculture. Trade was by barter and salaries were paid in kind until a new currency was established in 1980.

Opposition forces retreated to Thailand. They included remnants of the DK array, Sihanouk supporters and the rightist Khmer People's National Liberation Front (KPNLF) under Son Sann. The three factions formed the Coalition Government of Democratic Kampuchea (CGDK) in 1982 with the backing of the United States, China and the Association of Southeast Asian Nations. The United Nations recognized the CGDK as the legitimate government of Cambodia.

As Cambodia rebuilt, defense against the rebel forces was a major concern. China kept the Khmer Rouge steadily supplied with arms. Guerrilla attacks launched from the border area prompted Vietnamese-led dry season offensives up until 1985. Driven from bases within Cambodia, the rebel forces changed their strategy from one of armed attack to political struggle. They attempted to win recruits within the country by using Sihanouk's name. They also continued to launch guerrilla attacks in the interior, even in urban areas.

The political stalemate reached a turning point in July 1988 when the three factions met with the Phnom Penh regime for the first time to begin talks on national reconciliation. The Jakarta Informal Meeting was hailed for bringing the groups together, but it produced no concrete resolutions. Subsequent meetings of the factions, in January 1989 in Jakarta and the following August in Paris, failed to produce a power-sharing agreement. Fighting between rebel armies and Phnom Penh government troops intensified following the final Vietnamese withdrawl in September 1989. Foreign observers predicted the form of Cambodia's future government would be determined on the battlefield.

ECONOMY

Background: The government had to start from scratch in 1979 to rebuild the economy. There had been no currency or markets for four years, and no tax collections for at least nine years. Those factories not deliberately destroyed were in dire need of repair. Many of the skilled workers who did not die from illness or execution between 1975 and 1979 chose to flee the country. Even before 1975 the economy had been disrupted by war. Rubber production had come virtually to a halt. Khmer Rouge activity and U.S. bombing disrupted road and rail communications. Cambodia had reverted to a subsistence economy as public expenditures skyrocketed when the army was increased from 35,000 to 200,000. The country became totally dependent on external aid. By April 1975 there was practically no Cambodian economy.

The government initiated reconstruction by recognizing state, cooperative and private enterprises. The state sector included industry, finance, transport, official foreign commerce and large-scale enterprise. The private sector included retail marketing, handicrafts, repair work, some agriculture and much import trade. The semiprivate/semistate sector controlled a large portion of agriculture and certain urban enterprises. In the late 1980s the country's economy was based almost entirely on agriculture, which made up an estimated 90% of total production. Industry comprised 5%, trade 2%, and construction and transportation made up 1% each. Approximately 2.5 million people were employed in agriculture in 1985. Industry and services, combined, employed an estimated 850,000 people. Cambodia was still not self-sufficient in supplying food, however; the nation relied on U.S. $150 million in annual foreign aid to feed its population.

Agriculture: Rice is Cambodia's main crop. In 1979 some 1.9 million acres/ 774,000 ha. of paddy were planted, increasing to 4.4 million acres/1.8 million ha. by 1986 (compared with 5.9 million acres/2.4 million ha. in 1970). Yield was 1.9 million metric tons in 1983, and reached 2 million tons in 1988. This was still not enough to feed the population, nor could rice be exported (production was over 2 million metric tons in the 1960s). Alternating floods and drought made yields erratic. The 1984 harvest was just over 1 million metric tons. Agricultural expansion was also hindered by lack of draft animals and fertilizer to support high-yield rice varieties.

The growth of other crops, such as maize, beans, kapok and tobacco was still insignificant. Total production fell between 1979 and 1981, but recovered slightly between 1982 and 1985. Rubber plantations yielded 13,300 tons of raw rubber from 48,165 acres/19,500 ha. in 1984.

A fishing program supported by Western assistance increased output threefold between 1980 and 1985. The total catch in 1985 was 65,000 tons, much of which was exported to Vietnam.

Industry: Many of the factories remaining in Phnom Penh in 1979 were looted either by the population returning to the city or by the departing forces, to prevent their future use. By 1984 there were 57 industrial plants in the country, employing 154,000 people. All were under the control of the Ministry of Industry, and most served the agricultural sector. The nation's industries include electricity, vehicular transport, construction, textiles, metal, chemicals, food products, tobacco, soft drinks, soap, paper, tires and manufacture of rubber sandals. Production targets have remained largely unfulfilled due to a lack of raw materials and insufficient power.

Forestry: The area under forestation is about 32 million acres/13.2 million ha., but growth is hampered by poor mechanization, a shortage of fuel, an inadequate road system and a lack of skilled workers. Still, in 1986, log production reached 165,128 cu. yards/126,245 cu. m., an increase of over 100% from 1982.

Foreign aid: Cambodia receives approximately $150 million in foreign aid per year, mostly from the Soviet Union, Vietnam and the socialist bloc. Most aid is given in kind, such as food, cloth, trucks, medicine, school supplies or technical advisers. Several private Western groups have developed assistance projects in medicine, veterinary science and irrigation, among others.

Foreign trade: Reliable foreign trade figures are not readily available. Exports (rubber, beans, timber, kapok and tobacco) were estimated to total $10 million in 1985. Imports (food, fuel, raw materials, equipment and consumer goods) were valued at $120 million the same year, creating a large yearly trade deficit. Cambodia's main trading partners are Vietnam, the Soviet Union and Eastern Europe. A significant amount of unofficial trade also occurs with Thailand and Singapore. International agencies estimated the value of undeclared trade with Singapore to be $2 million in 1985. In March 1986 the Soviet Union and Cambodia signed an agreement on trade and payments, covering the period from 1986 to 1990. Combined with other trade agreements, the volume of trade between the two nations would double compared to the previous five-year period.

Employment: Of an estimated economically active population of 3.3 million in the mid-1980s, some 2.5 million people were employed in agriculture. Industry employed approximately 220,000 and the service sector employed 625,000 people.

SOCIAL SERVICES

Health Services: The ministries of Social Action and Health administer health programs in conjunction with voluntary agencies. Health care is free, but often rudimentary, as much of the professional class—including doctors—was wiped out from 1975 to 1979 or left the country after 1979. There is at least one hospital in every province, and there are clinics containing a few beds in most districts. Phnom Penh has a children's hospital, as well as other specialized hospitals. A traditional medicine research center has been established in Phnom Penh. Emphasis is placed on maternal health and child care. Those suffering the effects of combat, disabled state employees, widows and orphans receive special support from the state. Prosthetic workshops and training are available in several provinces.

EDUCATION

Cambodian education begins at the preschool level. There are two types of preschools for children ages three and older. The first is run by the state; the second type is for children of factory personnel, with teachers paid by the enterprise. Preschools are available only to a minority of the population, however; total enrollment in preschools in 1984 was 30,366. Students enter primary school at age six. Primary and secondary levels comprise a 10-year program divided into three levels: The lowest lasts four years, and the next two are three years each. In 1984 there were 1,542,825 students, enrolled in 3,005 schools with 33,479 teachers. The second level included 146,865 students and 4,329 teachers. Students attending third-level classes numbered 6,969, with 277 teachers. Total enrollment in 1987 was estimated at 1.9 million. Nearly 95% of school-age children were reported to be attending schools, and there were 45,000 teachers. There are few upper-level institutions. A medical college, a teacher training college and a technical college exist in Phnom Penh. All levels suffer from a lack of teachers, buildings and basic supplies.

Housing: When the population came back to Phnom Penh in 1979, some families returned to their former dwellings. Often, however, people were assigned jobs as they returned to the capital and moved into houses near their workplaces without regard to previous ownership. Houses and their contents were considered abandoned, and no effort was made to restore homes to their former owners. Numerous disputes erupted over rightful ownership. The government, faced with more severe problems, refused to mediate the disputes, and left the parties to resolve their own quarrels. Ministers have taken over the dwellings of prewar millionaire businessmen. Others in the hierarchy have smaller quarters. All housing is free. The government has been trying to collect rent for electricity and water services, but with little success.

MASS MEDIA

The KPRP has actively encouraged the news media, but the few existing publications are hampered by distribution difficulties. In the late 1980s there were still no dailies published in Cambodia. All media are run by the government, either under the auspices of the party, the army or the Front. Khiev Kanysrith, a pre-1975 law and economics graduate, is editor of *Kampuchea*. He is one example of a person with a nonrevolutionary background whose talents Cambodia needs and who is willing to work for the country.

The press: Kampuchea, founded in January 1979 with Vietnamese aid, is the oldest paper in Cambodia. It is a weekly run by the Front with a circulation of about 55,000. *Kaset Kangtoap Padivoat* (Kampuchean Revolutionary Army), founded and run by the armed forces, began as a monthly in 1979 and by 1983 was publishing weekly. (No circulation figures are available.) *Pracheachon* (The People), an organ of the KPRP, is published twice a week and has a circulation of about 50,000.

News agency: Saporamean Kampuchea, founded in 1978, is the information service of the Front.

Broadcasting: Samleng Pracheachon Kampuchean (Voice of the Kampuchean People) broadcasts radio transmissions daily in Khmer within Cambodia. It also broadcasts abroad in French, English, Lao, Vietnamese and Thai. The Sihanoukists and the KPNLF established a joint radio station in 1984. Samleng Khmer (Voice of the Khmer) broadcasts three times a day in Khmer. The main television station was established with assistance from the Vietnamese. Cambodian and Soviet programs are broadcast. Kampuchean Television officially opened in December 1984 and broadcasts four times a week. There were about 52,000 television receivers and 200,000 radio receivers in use in 1986.

BIOGRAPHICAL SKETCHES

Heng Samrin. Born in 1934 to a peasant family in Kompong Cham Province, Heng Samrin is currently the president of Cambodia and leader of the KPRP. He had little formal education. In the 1950s he became involved in illicit cattle trading across the Vietnamese border. This marked the beginning of his contact with Vietnamese Communists, and he espoused the revolutionary cause in 1959. He took to the jungle in 1967 as Khmer Communists fled repression in Phnom Penh. He was based in the eastern zone, near the Vietnamese border. In 1978 he joined the pro-Hanoi faction of the party. Samrin fled to Vietnam to escape Pol Pot's purges of cadres in the eastern zone. Shortly thereafter he returned to Cambodia with the Vietnamese invading force and became president of liberated Cambodia in January 1979.

Hun Sen. Born in 1951, Hun Sen is the current prime minister and foreign minister of Cambodia. He joined the resistance in 1967. At the time he was a young student from Wat Tuk La'ak in Phnom Penh. He fled the capital when an older Communist party member, with whom he was secretly working, was arrested and then disappeared. Hun Sen became a courier for the local Communist leader in Memut. Under the DK, he was stationed in the eastern zone where the most effective combat units (trained by the Vietnamese) were based. Sen was one of the leaders forming the KNUFNS on Dec. 2, 1978, in Kompong Cham Province. He was minister of foreign affairs from 1979 to December 1986 and was appointed prime minister in January 1985. He resumed the foreign affairs post in December 1987. Sen met with Prince Norodom Sihanouk in late 1987 in Paris to begin talks on national reconciliation.

Norodom Sihanouk. Born October 31, 1922, son of the late King Norodom Suramarit and Queen Kossamack Nearireath, Sihanouk has been the head of the CGDK—on and off—since it was formed in 1982. He was educated in Saigon and Paris, and in 1941 became king. Because of restrictions on the monarchy's power, he abdicated in 1955 and assumed the positions of prime minister and minister of foreign affairs. He was elected head of state after the death of his father in 1960. His conservative government tried to follow a neutralist path throughout the 1960s to avoid becoming embroiled in the Vietnam conflict. In 1970 Sihanouk was deposed by Marshal Lon Nol and took up residence in Beijing, where he formed the FUNC in alliance with the Khmer Rouge. He was restored as head of state when the Khmer Rouge captured Phnom Penh in 1975, but resigned a year later and spent the remaining four years under house arrest in the capital. In 1982 he became the head of the CGDK. Known for his volatile personality, Sihanouk has since resigned several times. His resignation on January 30, 1988, was interpreted as a ploy to strengthen his position in negotiations with the Phnom Penh government. Sihanouk remains a highly revered figure among the Cambodian population. While he would undoubtedly hold a position in a reconciliation government, it would be that of a figurehead without any real power.

Pol Pot: The notorious leader of the Khmer Rouge was born Saloth Sar on May 19, 1928, in Kompong Thom Province. He was the youngest of seven children in a family that could be classified as "rich peasants." He attended a Catholic primary school in Phnom Penh and Norodom Sihanouk High School in Kompong Cham City. In 1949 he received a scholarship for a two-year technician's course at the Ecole Française de Radioélectricité in Paris. There Pol Pot joined a small group of Cambodian students in the "Marxist Circle." He returned to Phnom Penh in 1953 and later joined the Vietnamese-Khmer UIF cell in the eastern zone. In 1955 he returned to Phnom Penh and became involved with the KPRP. Throughout the 1950s he gained increasing control over the party's activities in the city. After the murder of party leader Tou Samouth in 1962 (perhaps by the Pol Pot faction), he became acting secretary-general of the party. The struggle then returned to the countryside to garner force for the eventual takeover of the country in April 1975. Pol Pot became prime minister of DK in 1976, and his faction orchestrated policies of execution and forced labor from 1975 to 1979. He retreated in 1979 to the Thai border with remaining Khmer Rouge troops, later estimated at 35,000. Though rumored to be ill (he has not appeared in public for years) he and his forces remained the major threat to future stability in Cambodia.

Son Sann. The current leader of the KPNLF was born in 1912. Son Sann comes from a wealthy landowning family of mixed Khmer-Vietnamese ancestry in Travinh. Educated in Paris, Sann graduated with a Diploma of Higher Commercial Studies in 1933. He was appointed governor of Battambang Province in 1935, and of Prey Veng in 1937. He founded the National Bank of Cambodia in 1955 and held various ministerial posts under Sihanouk. He was prime minister in 1967–68. Since 1979 he led the KPNLF in the continuing struggle against the Vietnamese-backed PRK. Sann's guerrilla forces were estimated to number 30,000 in 1985, but Vietnamese attacks and rifts within the organization caused the number to dwindle to an estimated 5,000–10,000.

CHINA

Features: The third-largest country in the world, China stretches from the Himalaya in central Asia east to the Pacific Ocean. In addition to the mainland territory, it includes a number of islands in the East and South China seas, the largest among them being Taiwan, which China continues to claim as part of its territory; and Hainan, east of the Gulf of Tonking. China shares borders with 12 countries and has had a number of territorial conflicts with its neighbors. About one-third of the total area consists of mountain chains, and the relief of China generally slopes from high in the west to low in the east. Topographically, the country can be divided into three major regions: southwestern, northwestern and eastern zones. The southwestern zone rises in the Tibetan plateau, the world's highest mountain massif with the world's largest peak, Mount Everest (29,028 ft/8,848 m.). The plateau occupies about one-fourth of China's territory and most of it lies above 13,000 ft/4,000 m.; it is there that several great rivers, including the Changjiang and Mekong, have their sources. The northwestern zone centers around two basins, the Tarim in the south and the Dzungarian in the north, separated by the Tien Shan mountains. These mountains, which extend into the Soviet Union, contain peaks over 23,000 ft/7,000 m. high and some of the best grazing land in China. One of the world's most barren deserts, the Takla Makan (with an annual precipitation of less than 4 in/100 mm.), lies in the Tarim basin. The basin is connected with the eastern part of China by the Kansu, or Hosi, Corridor, the ancient route of contact between China and Europe. The eastern zone of the country can be further subdivided into several regions. The Northeast plain, also known as the Sung-Liao or Manchurian plain, is drained by the Sunghua (Sungari) River, which flows in a northeasterly direction into the Soviet Union. The loess plateau between the Northeast plain and the western deserts is bounded on the north by the Great Wall of China, a 1,500-mile/2,400-km.-long defensive fortification mostly dating from the 3rd century B.C. The North China plain, a very flat area of about 135,000 sq. miles/350,000 sq. km. along the lower course of the Huanghe (Yellow River), is one of the most densely inhabited parts of the country, with Beijing situated in its northwestern corner. Traditionally it has been the political center of China. Northern China is a major earthquake zone, and the earthquake that struck the city of Tangshan, 90 miles/145 km. east of Beijing, in July 1976 was one of the worst in recorded history: It registered 8.2 on

65

CHINA

the Richter scale and resulted in over 650,000 deaths. The Szechwan basin, also known as Red basin, lies just east of the Tibetan plateau and is surrounded on all sides by mountains, that protect it in winter against cold northern winds. Along the middle and lower Changjiang (Yangtze River) stretches another series of plains, interspersed by a dense network of rivers, canals and lakes. In southeastern China there are several mountain chains, including the Nan Ling mountains and the plain surrounding the delta of the Zhujiang (Pearl River). The promontory of Hong Kong lies on the northern part of this delta.

China's vegetation and animal life, despite the pressures of 4,000 years of human settlement, is extremely rich and varied, and includes the rare gingko and cathaya trees, some 650 to 800 varieties of azalea, 390 varieties of primrose, some 400 varieties of tree peony (which originated in Shandong Province), a golden-haired monkey and the popular giant panda.

The largest river in China is the Changjiang, which flows west-east for 3,900 miles/6,300 km. and has a drainage basin of about 700,000 sq. miles/1,800,000 sq. km. The second-largest river is the 3,400-mile/5,500-km. long Huanghe in the north, while the most important river in the south is the 1,370-mile/2,200-km. long Zhujiang. About 2,000 miles/3,100 km. of the Heilongjiang (Amur River) forms the boundary between China and the Soviet Union in the northeast. Water distribution, however, is regionally very uneven, and about one-third of the total land area is arid. The climate in China is primarily affected by the movement of huge air masses: a dry cold continental air mass from Siberia in winter and a tropical humid Pacific air mass during the summer. The movement of the frontal zone between these masses influences the amount of precipitation in central and northern China and frequently results in either prolonged droughts or heavy rains that lead to flooding. The southeastern coast also suffers from typhoons, which occur mostly between May and September.

Area: 3,646,448 sq. miles/9,444,292 sq. km. (excluding Taiwan).

Mean max. and min. temperatures: Beijing (Peking) (39°55′N, 116°25′E; 146 ft/44 m.) 78°F/25.5°C (July), 23.5°F/ − 4.7°C (Jan.); Tianjin (Tientsin) (39°08′N, 117°12′E; 13 ft/4 m.) 80°F/26.5°C (July), 24°F/ − 4.3°C (Jan.); Shanghai (31°13′N, 121°25′E; 16 ft/5 m.) 81°F/28.2°C (July), 39°F/3.9°C (Jan.); Chongqing (30°37′N, 103°41′E; 655 ft/200 m.) 84°F/28.9°C (July), 39°F/3.9°C (Jan.); Guangzhou (Canton) (23°08′N, 113°20′E; 59 ft/18 m.) 81°F/28.1°C (July), 55°F/13°C (Jan.); Lhasa (29°41′N, 91°10′E; 12,087 ft/3,684 m.) 58°F/14.2°C (July), 29°F/ − 1.5°C (Jan.).

Mean annual rainfall: Beijing 28.4 in/721 mm.; Tianjin 23 in/587 mm.; Shanghai 66 in/1,673 mm.; Chongqing 43 in/1,092 mm.; Guangzhou 67 in/1,706 mm.; Lhasa 21 in/530 mm.

POPULATION

Total population: 1,060,080,000 (1986 official est.); 1,064,147,038 (July 1987 est.); 1,008,180,738 (census of July 1, 1982).

Chief towns and population (1985 est.): Shanghai 6,980,000 (municipality 12,170,000; BEIJING 5,860,000 (municipality 9,600,000); Tianjin 5,380,000 (municipality 8,080,000); Shenyang 4,200,000; Wuhan 3,400,000; Guangzhou 3,290,000.

Distribution: China is the most populous country in the world. It is predominantly rural, with about 70% to 80% of the people living in the countryside, although millions of Chinese are crowded into several huge metropolitan areas. Since much of the western part of China is inhospitable, some 94% of the population live in the eastern half of the country. Population densities range from 4.3 persons per sq. mile/1.7 per sq. km. in Tibet to 5,096 persons per sq. mile/1,968 per sq. km. in Shanghai. The overwhelming majority of the population are Han Chinese; minorities represent only about 7% and include the Zhuang, Hui, Uygur, Yi, Miao and the Tibetans.

Languages: Han Chinese, which belongs to the Sino-Tibetan linguistic family, is the most widely used language. The script, nonphonetic ideograms representing complete words, is uniform throughout China, but the spoken language has a number of dialects and regional variants, some mutually unintelligible. Mandarin Chinese, based on the Beijing dialect, was adopted in 1955 as an official language and is now used or at least understood by more than 90% of the population. In Chinese it is known as *putonghua,* or "common language." Other major dialects are those of the Shanghai and Guangzhou areas. Traditionally, the mastery of Chinese required a familiarity with thousands of characters, but a simplified system of writing (with fewer strokes per character) has been adopted since 1949, and a person who knows 2,000–3,000 characters is now considered functionally literate. In 1979 the Chinese government adopted the Pinyin system for transliteration of Chinese into the Latin alphabet, and the system is taught in schools. The most widely taught foreign language is English.

Religion: Historically, most of the Chinese practiced a blend of three faiths, Confucianism, Buddhism and Taoism, with the first providing a code of ethics and the second and third religious rituals. Muslims live throughout China, and in 1986 they totaled about 14 million. Christianity, which was introduced by missionaries in the 16th century, claimed about 4 million adherents in 1949 (3 million Roman Catholics and almost 1 million Protestants). Reliable current numbers are not available, but a revival of religious practice began in the early 1980s. A distinct religious-national minority are the Tibetans (3.8 million), who follow Lamaism, a form of Mahayana Buddhism. The Buddhist Zhuang, numbering 13 million and the largest ethnic group, live mostly in the Guangxi Zhuangzhu Autonomous Region and are noted for their worship of ancestral spirits.

After the establishment of the Communist regime in 1949 the government embarked on an atheistic course and closed a number of shrines, temples, mosques and churches. During the Cultural Revolution in the late 1960s the antireligious fervor of the Red Guards resulted in widespread destruction of religious objects and persecution of believers. After the mid-

1970s, however, the government increasingly tolerated religious beliefs and activities.

Constitution: China is formally governed under the constitution of 1982 (its fourth constitution since 1949), which restored the position of the state president (head of state) and is much more detailed than the previous three constitutions in listing various legal guarantees of civil rights. Nevertheless, the first general principle proclaims that "China is a socialist state under the people's democratic dictatorship" and that the "sabotage of the socialist system by any organization or individual is prohibited."

Head of state: President Yang Shangkun. *Premier:* Li Peng.

Executive: The State Council is the executive organ of the National People's Congress. It consists of a premier, who is the chief executive of the country, five vice-premiers, and over 50 ministers, councilors and heads of other governmental agencies.

Legislature: The National People's Congress (NPC) is formally the highest organ of the state and the seat of legislative power. It meets annually for about two weeks, and its permanent organ is a Standing Committee, which supervises the executive State Council. Members of the Congress are elected for five-year terms. In the elections held in early 1988 for the seventh NPC, the number of candidates was higher than the number of seats for the first time since 1949. The final number of deputies was 2,978, two-thirds of them members of the Communist party.

Political parties: The actual power in China resides in the Chinese Communist party (CCP), which had been founded in 1921 and in 1949 proclaimed the People's Republic of China. In 1987 the party had 44 million members. From its beginnings until 1976 the CCP was dominated by Mao Zedong (Mao Tse-Tung), who was gradually elevated to a status of virtual infallibility. The most powerful personality of the post-Mao period was Deng Xiaoping (Teng Hsiao-Ping), who dispensed with a major formal position (as of 1989 he was chairman of the Central Military Commission) but was the leading force in a vast modernization drive. The general-secretary of the party in 1987–89 was Zhao Ziyang, a protégé of Deng Xiaoping, but he was replaced by Jiang Zemin in June 1989 following the suppression of the pro-democracy movement. The highest organ of the party is the Central Committee, which had 210 full and 133 alternate members in 1986.

There are nine other political organizations and parties, but none has any real political significance

Local government: China is divided into 26 major local units, which consist of 3 municipalities (Beijing, Tianjin and Shanghai), 21 provinces and 5 autonomous regions; Taiwan is claimed as a 22nd province. Lower units include 165 prefectures, 321 cities, 2,046 counties and 620 urban districts.

Judicial system: During the Cultural Revolution the formal judicial system (modeled on that of the Soviet Union) was virtually destroyed, and it was only in the late 1970s that the government began to reinstate a new legal structure. There are very few schools and institutes for legal training, and in 1987 China had only 26,000 lawyers. The highest judicial organ is the Supreme People's Court, which supervises lower courts. There is no presumption of innocence, and penalties are harsh. In 1986 the courts imposed 624,000 sentences of death or long imprisonment; capital punishment is meted out not only for treason and murder, but also for rape, embezzlement, smuggling, drug dealing, bribery and robbery with violence. Some executions (by firing squad) are public.

RECENT HISTORY

China began the 20th century with an outburst of anti-Christian and anti-foreign upheaval known in the West as the Boxer Rebellion. It was a culmination of an era of foreign encroachment and "unequal treaties," which had started with the Opium War of 1839–42 with Britain and was characterized by the gradual decline of the empire and one defeat after another in economic and military conflicts. Britain, France, Russia, Germany and Japan all gained territories and privileges at China's expense, taking advantage of weak imperial rule and internal strife. In the late 1890s a secret nationalist society called the Boxers (a sardonic Western translation of the society's Chinese name: Righteous Harmony Fists) gathered public support by appealing to a rising antiforeign sentiment, and in June 1900 besieged foreign legations in Beijing. The imperial Manchu court supported the uprising and ordered provincial governors to take part in the conflict. During the following eight weeks several hundred foreigners and many Chinese Christians were murdered, but an international military expedition crushed the uprising in August. The final settlement of the conflict, signed in September 1901, stipulated that huge indemnities (about U.S. $333 million) be paid to the foreign nations, and that permanent guard stations be established by these nations between Beijing and the sea. This was a further humiliation of China and one of the last blows to imperial prestige.

The Manchu dynasty was deposed in an army uprising in 1911–12 and the Chinese republic proclaimed. The leader of the republicans, the Western-educated commoner Sun Zhongshan (Sun Yat-sen), became the first president of the new republic; but because of an increasingly chaotic internal situation he soon relinquished the presidency to an army strongman, Yuan Shikai (Yuan Shih-kai). Despite promises to uphold the fledgling republic, Yuan soon revealed that he intended to establish a new dynasty with himself as emperor, but he died in 1916 before he could implement his ideas. A series of local civil wars during the following decade, known as the Warlord Era, led to a disintegration of central authority and a virtual breakdown of law and order. These years of turmoil witnessed the birth of two political movements that were to shape Chinese history for the rest of the 20th century.

The Nationalist Guomindang (or Kuomintang) originated in an anti-Manchu party and was reconstituted in Guangzhou by Sun Zhongshan in 1919. It took several years for the party to become effective, but by 1923 the Nationalists had been entrenched in southern China. Meanwhile, in May 1919, Beijing students demonstrated against the decisions of the Versailles Treaty to transfer former German rights and possessions in China to Japan. This May Fourth Movement led to the formation of the CCP, originally a group of Marxist intellectuals who supported a revolution against foreign imperialism and Chinese militarism. The CCP was formally set up in 1921 at a meeting in Shanghai of about a dozen Marxists, one of whom was Mao Zedong. At the same time, several Chinese students living in Paris also founded a communist party, and one of these founders was Zhou Enlai (Chou En-lai).

For several years the Nationalists and the Communists were able to cooperate against the warlords in southern China, but a split between the two movements occurred in 1927 when Chiang Kai-shek, Sun Zhongsan's conservative successor, ordered the wholesale massacre of Communists in Shanghai (after they had taken over the government of the city). Within the next few years the Nationalist government became established in Nanjing. In the early 1930s Chiang Kai-shek was distracted from his fight against the Communists by the Japanese invasion of Manchuria, but when that fighting ended in 1933 he again embarked on his anti-Communist campaign. He blockaded and tried to starve into submission the Chinese Soviet Republic that had been set up in Jiangxi Province. The hard-pressed Communists, now led by Mao Zedong, broke out of the encirclement and set out on the famous Long March in October 1934. Within a year they had reached Yan'an (Yenan), in northern Shaanxi Province, after marching for some 6,000 miles/10,000 km. with 100,000 men and their dependents. In January 1935 Mao was elected party chairman. Although the Soviet Communist party had exercised some control over the Chinese Communists in the first period of their existence, by 1935 the CCP was completely emancipated from their tutelage.

During the second Sino-Japanese war, which lasted from 1937 to 1945, both the Nationalists and the Communists fought the Japanese invaders, the former from their capital at Chongqing, in Sichuan Province, and the latter from their bases in the northwest section of the country. When the Japanese surrendered in 1945 and subsequently evacuated China, the Nationalists and the Communists first tried to negotiate a peaceful settlement. It was not long, however, before the numerous limited engagements fought between them for control of the formerly Japanese-held areas turned into a full-scale civil war. The reasons for the eventual victory of the Communists are complex, but at the basis of the CCP triumph was the fact that their movement was a genuine popularly supported revolution. In October 1949 Mao Zedong proclaimed the People's Republic of China, and the Nationalists were driven out to Taiwan. In addition to his post as the chairman of the CCP, Mao also became head of state. The first premier of Communist China was Zhou Enlai, who held this post until his death.

The new regime swiftly embarked on a program of national renewal, and within a short period the wartime disorder was brought under control, the economy began to revive, cities were being restored and a land reform was implemented. The country also received huge grants of economic aid from the Soviet Union for its program of rapid industrialization. In the early 1950s China became involved in the Korean War; because this was the first time that its armies were able to stand up to Western enemies, the prestige of the government was greatly enhanced. At the same time, however, the party fought against "bourgeois" and "rightist" thought, and led a massive campaign of terror against all those who would not bow to the new ideology.

In the 1950s and 1960s Mao's cult was supreme, and he used his position to initiate several campaigns to keep up the revolutionary spirit. In 1956 he gave a speech titled "Let a Hundred Flowers Blossom, Let a Hundred Schools of Thought Contend," which loosened party controls over free expression. When the campaign resulted in sharp criticism of the CCP, however, it was quickly halted. Shortly afterward, Mao launched a crash program of speedy industrial development called the Great Leap Forward, but it proved a failure and instead of leaping forward the country plunged into the "three bitter years" of economic crisis between 1960 and 1962. Then in 1966, concerned about the bureaucratization of the society and the decline of mass activism, Mao proclaimed the Great Proletarian Cultural Revolution. The dramatic upheaval that followed shook the country to its foundations. The Red Guards, consisting mostly of middle-school and university students, took to the streets and, brandishing the Little Red Book of Mao's sayings, attacked teachers, bureaucrats, intellectuals, scientists, technicians and many others accused of being "capitalist roaders." The newly established Cultural Revolution Group in the CCP Central Committee—whose most prominent member was Mao's wife, Jiang Qing—was the chief leader and instigator of the movement. The Communist party almost disintegrated as a national organization, with countless party members forced to undergo humiliating public self-criticism (Deng Xiaoping among them) and sent to prisons, or simply executed on the spot. The only national organization that was not disrupted was the army. When it became clear that the revolution was turning into complete chaos, the Red Guards, at Mao's insistence, were disbanded and sent into the countryside. But the upheaval continued in a fierce intraparty struggle, which crystallized in 1969 into a conflict between Cultural Revolutionaries, headed by Jiang Qing, and "modernizers," led by Zhou Enlai and later the rehabilitated Deng Xiaoping. The final resolution of the conflict came only after the deaths of Zhou Enlai and Mao in 1976. Mao died in September, and in October his widow and her associates were arrested. Branded the Gang of Four, Jiang Qing and her faction were imprisoned for years, then put on trial and sentenced in early 1981 to long terms of imprisonment.

In October 1976 the designated successor of Mao, Hua Guofeng, became chairman of the party, but it was soon apparent that actual political power was wielded by Deng Xiaoping and his group. Deng reemerged after his second fall from grace in 1976; in the spring of 1977 he resumed his previous posts of first vice-premier and chief of the general staff and embarked upon a course of economic modernization, which had been proclaimed by Zhou Enlai in 1975. The third Plenum of the CCP Central Committee, in December 1978, marked the beginning of a new stage in modern Chinese history. Despite the suppression of a short-lived outburst of democratization in late 1978 and early 1979, China was firmly embarked upon a series of reforms that significantly altered the economic as well as the political order. Deng's protégés took over the two most important posts in the country: Zhao Ziyang became the new premier in 1980 and Hu Yaobang the new party chairman in 1981 (the title was changed to general-secretary the following year). Sweeping economic reforms were proclaimed, and both Mao's legacy and the Cultural Revolution were subjected to an ongoing evaluation. By the late 1980s the official verdict was that Mao was about 70% correct and 30% wrong, that he had committed grave mistakes in his later years, and that the Cultural Revolution was an unmitigated disaster. A generational turnover also took place during the 1980s, when many old-guard Communists were forcibly retired and replaced by younger people. The end of the decade was marked by new democratization efforts, with student protests and stirrings among intellectuals. Hu Yaobang fell from grace in January 1987 after student demonstrations for democratic freedoms, and in April 1988 a Soviet-educated conservative technocrat, Li Peng, was confirmed as the new premier. Many delegates to the April 1988 session of the seventh National People's Congress took part in an unprecedented free debate and criticism, which was in turn publicized in the press. A major step backward, however, was taken in June 1989 when army troops killed hundreds of pro-democracy demonstrators in major cities throughout China. The crushing of the demonstrations, which were initially intended to commemorate Hu Yaobang's death in April 1989, was followed by widespread arrests and executions, and by the demotion and disgrace of Zhao Ziyang and the elevation of Jiang Zemin to the party general secretaryship.

China officially recognizes 55 ethnic minorities, and none of them seems to present any problems except one, the Tibetans. After the fall of Manchu dynasty in 1911, Tibet (Xizang) had proclaimed its independence, but in 1950 China invaded the country, asserting the right of sovereignty over the region. For almost a decade Tibet remained under the nominal rule of the Dalai Lama, its temporal and spiritual leader. A violent anti-Chinese uprising in 1959, in which some 87,000 Tibetans were killed (according to recent Chinese sources), led to the flight of the Dalai Lama to India and to an eventual incorporation (in 1965) of Tibet into the People's Republic of China as an autonomous region. The stationing of Chinese forces in Tibet, on the poorly demarcated border with India, also led to a brief Chinese-Indian border war in 1962. Despite steps taken by the Chinese government in the 1980s to revive Tibetan culture—which included the restoration of hundreds of monasteries and shrines, the opening of a Buddhist seminary in Lhasa in 1984, and the establishment of a university in 1985—new anti-Chinese demonstrations began to take place in 1987, and in early 1989 widespread violence led to the imposition of martial law in the region.

International relations: In 1954 China and the Soviet Union signed a treaty of political cooperation, but the relationship began to show strains as early as 1956; and by the early 1960s the break was complete. The main reasons included Moscow's claim to preeminence in the communist world, China's reluctance to denounce Stalinism, and the border disputes. During the 1960s China was turned inward, but as the most violent phase of the Cultural Revolution subsided the country began to play a role in international affairs. After claiming in 1969 that there had been over 4,000 military border clashes with the Soviet Union since 1964, China became interested in some kind of alignment with the West. In 1971 the General Assembly of the United Nations voted 76 to 35 (with 17 abstentions) to replace Taiwan's Nationalist government with the representative of the People's Republic of China; and the following year, in February 1972, U.S. President Richard Nixon made an official visit to China. The famous Shanghai communiqué signed during this visit opened the door to a rapprochement between the two countries and finally led to the establishment of full diplomatic relations in 1979. Fearing Soviet expansionism, particularly in the Third World countries, China pursued anti-Soviet policies during the 1970s. At the end of the decade it briefly invaded Vietnam, a loyal friend of the Soviet Union, as a punitive response to Vietnamese invasion of neighboring Cambodia and the overthrow of the Chinese-supported government of Pol Pot. After short but fierce fighting, with heavy casualties on both sides, the Chinese withdrew, but Beijing continued to oppose the Vietnamese-supported government in Cambodia thereafter. On the other hand, China normalized relations with several East Asian countries, primarily with Japan, which gradually became a major trading partner. A treaty of friendship between the two countries was concluded in 1978 and a new economic treaty was signed in 1988. In early 1988 China reestablished diplomatic relations with Indonesia, which had been broken in 1965 because of alleged Chinese support for a Communist coup attempt against the Indonesian government that year. During the 1980s China also moved to settle the matter of two territories that still belonged to European powers. One was Hong Kong, a British crown colony off the southeast coast of China. It was formally ceded to Great Britain in 1842, and after World War II it developed into a major center of commerce, shipping, industry and banking. According to an agreement of 1984 the territory would revert to China in 1997 but retain its current economic system for a further 50 years, under a formula of "one country, two systems." The same formula was used in the case of Macao, a port just west of Hong Kong; Macao is the oldest European settlement in the Far East and has belonged to Portugal since its founding in 1557. China and Portugal agreed in 1987 that the territory would revert to China in 1999 but that it would also retain its current economic system for another 50 years. The relations between China and

Taiwan, after decades of hostility, began to improve slightly in the late 1980s. When the Nationalists elected their new party chief, Lee Teng-hui, in July 1988, the CCP party chief, Zhao Ziyang, sent him congratulations; and in November 1988 the first mainland Chinese traveled legally to Taiwan.

Soon after Mikhail Gorbachev came to power in the Soviet Union in 1985 the relations between the two Communist powers began to improve. Talks regarding a solution to the Cambodian conflict began in 1986; when Gorbachev announced a reduction of Soviet forces on the Soviet-Chinese border and a withdrawal of three-fourths of Soviet troops from Mongolia, and the Soviet armed forces left Afghanistan in February 1989, the stage was set for a renewal of both party and state relations. These were further improved by President Gorbachev's state visit to China in May 1989.

International outrage at the suppression of the pro-democracy demonstrations in June 1989, however, resulted in the unprecedented condemnation of China by a UN panel in August 1989, and led to a serious setback in China's relations with many foreign countries.

Defense: The People's Liberation Army (PLA) played an important role in Chinese internal politics from the time of the Cultural Revolution until the reorganization of 1985, when the country was divided into seven military regions and the armed forces largely abandoned political involvement for military professionalism. Yet the most powerful political personality of the country, Deng Xiaoping, was the head of the Central Military Commission, which directs and supervises the armed forces. Conscription is selective, and only about one-tenth of potential recruits are called up. Military service lasts three years in the army, four years in the air force and five years in the navy. According to Western estimates the combined strength of the armed forces was 3,200,000 in 1987. In 1964 China exploded its first atomic bomb and in 1980 tested its first long-range intercontinental ballistic missiles.

ECONOMY

Background: When the Communists took power in 1949 the Chinese economy had been completely devastated after more than three decades of internal civil war and Japanese invasion. Land was redistributed to peasants in the early 1950s, and the government succeeded in preventing massive starvation. Industrialization proceeded rapidly as well, with substantial help from the Soviet Union and Eastern European countries. Although the Chinese adopted the Soviet practice of Five-Year-Plans and proclaimed the first such plan in 1953, subsequent economic developments cannot be neatly fitted into these planning periods. A cooperative movement began to gain momentum in the 1950s, and multifunctional communes were soon set up in the countryside, with each commune divided into work brigades and teams. In 1958, in order to speed up growth rates and to increase the economic dynamism of the country at large, Mao Zedong announced his Great Leap Forward program. The communes were declared to be the best form of transition to communism, and he urged the peasants to set up small-scale industrial production in their communes. The useless backyard foundries have from that time became a symbol of the economic absurdity of the campaign. It took several years for the economy to rebound, but the Cultural Revolution of the late 1960s pushed economic considerations into the background. Finally, in the early 1970s, Zhou Enlai began to initiate his economic program of Four Modernizations (of industry, agriculture, defense and science and technology), which actually dated back to 1964. These were launched in 1978. In the later 1970s and the 1980s, under the efficient and pragmatic leadership of Deng Xiaoping, the Chinese economy underwent substantial changes, including a new emphasis on light rather than heavy industry, the dismantling of agricultural communes, the opening up of special economic zones as centers for foreign investment and a loosening of central planning. Economic development, however, was hampered by the lack of a highly skilled labor force, distribution problems, and inefficient and inadequate transport facilities (only 8% of the railroad tracks were electrified in 1985, and the combined length of the tracks was about one-eighth that of the United States, a country of almost the same size).

China has large mineral deposits, particularly coal and iron ore, and since 1973 has also been self-sufficient in petroleum. In 1985 it was the world's sixth-largest producer of oil, with 2.5 million barrels per day and reserves estimated at 18.4 billion barrels. The petroleum industry expanded rapidly, and exports became an important source of foreign exchange, bringing in U.S. $6.79 billion, or one-fourth of the total export value in 1985. Exploration of reserves offshore as well as in mainland China is one of the main areas for joint ventures with foreign companies. Despite these developments, however, three-fourths of the country's energy needs are still met by coal. There are 70 major coal-production centers, the largest being in Shanxi, Shandong and Inner Mongolia. Nuclear power plays a minor role, and only two nuclear power plants were under construction in the late 1980s.

An important part of the modernization drive was the open-door policy. Agreements with foreign firms, mostly Western, about construction of complete industrial plants were first made in the early 1970s, and in 1979 the Foreign Investment Control Commission was established to coordinate foreign investment. Several new codes have been promulgated since that time, and by 1986 the number of equity joint ventures totaled 2,645; there were also 4,075 contractual joint ventures and 130 wholly owned foreign subsidiaries. Four Special Economic Zones (at Shenzhen, Zhuhai and Shantou in southern Guangdong Province and at Xiamen, across the Taiwan Strait from Taiwan) were created and given more autonomy and flexibility in attracting foreign investment; and 14 coastal cities and Hainan Island have been opened to technological imports. In 1986 about 80% of the total foreign investment was from Hong Kong.

The Seventh Five-Year Plan (1986–90), called by Deng Xiaoping the "New Long March," gave priority to expansion of the open-door policy and also envisaged a change from direct to indirect control in many sectors of the economy. A constitutional amendment adopted in April 1988 provided an explicit legal section for private enterprise. One sector to be completely restructured was banking and finance. In 1985 the first foreign joint-venture bank was established, and in 1986 the first stock market opened in Shanghai, followed by stock markets in several other cities. By the late 1980s about 100 foreign banks were operating in China. In 1983 China for the first time published figures on foreign debt—which was at that time $3 billion; according to Western estimates by September 1987 the foreign debt had reached $22–25 billion.

These structural changes brought some new problems, among them inflation, increasing disparities of income and widespread corruption. With the appointment of the conservative Li Peng to the premiership in April 1988 the Chinese leadership had apparently decided it was necessary to reassert control over the economy and slow down the fast pace of development. It was announced in March 1988 that the government would attempt to lower the GNP growth from 9.4% in 1987 to 7.5% in 1988.

Agriculture: Agriculture contributes 42% to the net material product and employs over 60% of the labor force. With 21% of the world's population, China accounts for 20% of the world's production of cereals, 39% of the world's pig population and 38% of the world's rice harvest. After the Communist takeover in 1949 land was first redistributed to peasants and then reorganized into cooperatives, which were in turn grouped into communes. In the modernization program launched in the late 1970s the communes were disbanded, and by the mid-1980s the individual household had become the basic unit of all farming. This profound change led to great increases in agricultural production and peasant's incomes. In 1984 the agricultural output grew by 14.5%, and in 1985 by 13%. The main crops in 1985 were rice (168.6 million tons), sweet potatoes (90 million tons), wheat (85.8 million tons) and corn (63.8 million tons). That year the livestock included 331.4 million pigs, 86.8 million cattle and buffalo, 94.2 million sheep, 61.7 million goats and 1.3 billion chickens. A new constitutional amendment approved in April 1988 legalized the right to buy and sell land, thus invalidating the previous principle that all land should be controlled by the state.

Industry: According to official statistics the gross value of industrial output increased by 13.3% annually between 1950 and 1979. When the Communists came to power in 1949 China had very little industry, most of which was concentrated around the steel-producing Anshan in the northeast, but in 1985 industry accounted for 42% of the GNP. Industrial production has significantly increased since 1978, when the Four Modernizations program was launched, and a greater emphasis was placed on light industry. In 1981 light industry for the first time accounted for more than 50% of the total industrial output. There were 463,200 industrial enterprises in 1985, of which 93,700 were state owned and 367,800 were owned collectively, mostly by rural townships.

Traditionally, the major industry has been steel production: In 1985 China produced 46.8 million tons of steel. Compared to developed nations, however, Chinese steel production is somewhat inefficient, and the quality of steel produced is unequal. The manufacture of textiles has led Chinese industrial development since the late 19th century, and the Chinese cotton textile industry is now the largest in the world. In 1985 China produced 3.53 million tons of cotton yarn and 14.7 billion meters of cotton cloth. Other important industrial products are farm machinery, fertilizers, motor vehicles and various household machines. Production figures for 1985 include 450,000 tractors, 429,554 farm trucks, 437,000 motor vehicles, 32.28 million bicycles (the most popular means of transportation), 8.87 million washing machines and 16.67 million television sets. The electronics industry is another fast-growing field, and China can now produce high-speed computers and specialized electronic instruments.

Foreign trade: Foreign trade plays a relatively small role in the Chinese economy, and total trade value in 1986 represented only 27% of the GNP. Before 1949 China exported primarily agricultural products, and by the mid-1980s these products still accounted for about one-half of all exports. Petroleum and associated products represented 25% of total exports in 1985. Most of the exported manufactured goods consist of clothing and textiles. Food imports, particularly grain, accounted for 16% of the total import value in 1977, but the share decreased to only 3.7% in 1985. That year two-thirds of all imports were machinery, transportation equipment and manufactures. The direction of foreign trade has changed dramatically in recent decades. In the 1950s over two-thirds of all foreign trade was conducted with other Communist countries, with the Soviet Union being the most important trading partner. As Sino-Soviet relations deteriorated and China began its diplomatic offensive in the 1970s, its foreign trade greatly diversified. In 1986, 33% of all exports went to Hong Kong and Macao, 15.3% to Japan, 12.9% to the European Community (EC), 8.5% to the United States and only 4% to the Soviet Union. The origin of imports in 1986 was as follows: Japan, 28.9%; the EC, 18%; Hong Kong and Macao, 13.3%; the United States, 10.8%; and the Soviet Union, only 3.5%. Overall, Japan is the largest trading partner, with 23% of China's total trade volume in 1986. The second major partner is Hong Kong, which continues to serve as a major source of foreign exchange; and the third trade partner is the United States. Statistics released by the Chinese customs administration, which are reportedly closer to international standards than statistics of other government agencies, showed a 29% increase in exports from 1986 to 1987, to $39.92 billion; and a 2.2% increase in imports during the same period, to $43.86 billion.

Employment: According to official Chinese sources the labor force in 1985 was about 499 million. Of this total, 62.5% were engaged in agriculture, forestry and fishing; 16.7% in industry; 4.7% in trade and services; 4.1% in construction; 2.5% in transportation and communications; and 9.5% in other sectors. When the Communist regime took over in 1949 it initially promised job security, or an "iron rice bowl," to everyone, but the formula underwent subsequent changes, and by the 1980s the government admitted that some unemployment might be necessary in order to modernize the economy. It is estimated that unemployment, particularly of young people, amounted to 4.9% in 1980; but the rate decreased to 1.9% in 1985 as some 35 million new urban jobs were created. A small but increasing number of Chinese (13.5 million in 1987, as officially reported) are employed in private businesses.

Prices and wages: Compared to Western standards wages are very low, but the government heavily subsidizes such essentials as housing, transport and staples. According to official sources real wages rose by 5% between 1979 and 1984. The plan to gradually end subsidies and deregulate prices was scrapped in late 1988 because the government became worried about rising inflation. Officially, the inflation in 1988 was over 20%, but in some cities it reached as high as 50%.

SOCIAL SERVICES

Welfare: Large enterprises provide social services to their workers, and state and collective farms administer welfare in rural areas. The retirement age for men is between 55 and 60 and for women five years less, and the state-guaranteed pension amounts to 60%–90% of the employee's last salary. All workers are also entitled to sick leaves and disability pensions.

Since 1949 the government has tried to control population growth, with mixed success. Abortions and various contraceptive techniques are widely available, and monetary incentives have been used to limit the size of the family. There have also been reports about forced sterilizations. Nevertheless, a goal of one child per family is in conflict with traditional values, particularly with the need to produce a male heir, who not only carries the family line but also takes care of his parents in their old age. The economic modernization drive in the 1980s added a further reason to have more children, because the privatization of agriculture makes extra family members economically attractive. It is thus unlikely that the goal of holding the population to 1.2 billion by the year 2000 will be achieved.

Health services: Both Western and Chinese traditional medical care (the latter including acupuncture, cauterization and herbal remedies) is available at low cost in cities. According to Chinese sources there were 1,176 persons per physician in 1985, while the World Bank gave a figure of 1,740 for 1980. Most health services in the countryside are provided by the so-called barefoot doctors, paramedics trained in short courses in the cities. Mass campaigns aimed at improving public health have included programs for the eradication of the "four pests"—rats, sparrows, flies and mosquitoes— and various educational programs on personal hygiene, waste disposal and so on. These campaigns have been only partially successful, but they have led to a substantial increase in life expectancy (68 for men and 71 for women in 1985, against a combined average of 45 years in 1950), and to a reduction in infant mortality from more than 200 per 1,000 live births before 1949 to about 36 in 1985.

Housing: Because of constant population pressure and governmental emphasis on heavy industry, housing has been a great problem since 1949. Agricultural reforms in the mid-1980s led to a rise in housing construction in the countryside.

EDUCATION

It is estimated that before 1949, 85% of the population was illiterate. The Communist government has placed a great emphasis on education, and according to the census of 1982 the illiteracy rate of people over 12 years of age decreased to only 23.5%. The Cultural Revolution of the late 1960s completely disrupted the educational system, particularly at the higher levels. Not only did the students leave school to further the revolution as Red Guards, but many teachers were hounded as counterrevolutionaries, and most university staffs and faculties were disbanded. Some universities remained closed until the early 1970s, and it took several more years before the educational system had recuperated from the upheaval. The Four Modernizations policies launched in 1978 included a new emphasis on education, particularly in technical fields, and an abandonment of ideological criteria in evaluating students' performance. In 1985 an educational reform program began to introduce a compulsory nine-year schooling to replace the existing five-year system. In 1985 there were 832,309 primary schools, with 6.02 million teachers and 133.7 million students; and 104,848 secondary schools, with 4.18 million teachers and 50.93 million students. Colleges and universities in 1985 totaled 1,016, and they had 870,000 teachers and 1.7 million students. Students must pass entrance examinations to be admitted to a university, and they then receive scholarships based on their academic performance. In the 1980s China also began to send students abroad; between 1981 and 1985 over 36,500 Chinese students were studying in more than 60 countries.

MASS MEDIA

All publishing is closely controlled by the Communist party or other political organizations associated with it. In the late 1970s there appeared some unofficial publishing advocating greater democracy, centered around the so-called Democracy Wall, but it was suppressed within a short time; by the late 1980s all media were firmly supervised.

The press

Dailies: In 1985 there were about 700 national and provincial newspapers, with a combined circulation of 191 million copies. The major dailies, with their 1986 circulations, include *Renmin Ribao* (People's Daily), Beijing, CCP, 7 million; *Jiefangjun Bao* (Liberation Army Daily), PLA, Beijing, 100 million; *Wenhui Bao* (Wenhui Daily), Shanghai, 1.3 million; *Jiefang Ribao* (Jiefang Daily), Shanghai, 1 million; *Beijing Ribao* (Beijing Daily), Beijing Municipal Committee of the CCP, 1 million. *China Daily,* founded in 1981, is China's first English-language newspaper; it is published in Beijing and in 1986 its circulation was 120,000.

81

Periodicals: The number of magazines and other periodicals totaled 4,705 in 1985. Those with the largest circulation are *Ban Yue Tan* (Fortnightly Conversations), Beijing, 5 million; *Tiyu Kexue* (Sports Science), (q), Beijing, 1.2 million; *Shichang Zhoubao* (Market Weekly), Shenyang, economic affairs, 1 million. *Beijing Review* (w) is published in English, French, Japanese, Spanish and German, and is distributed abroad. *Renmin Hubao* (China Pictorial) (m), Beijing, appears in Chinese, four minority languages and 15 foreign languages. A number of periodicals on science, technology and economics were founded in the 1980s, including *Chinese Science Abstracts* (m), English, Beijing, founded 1982; *Dianzi yu Diannao* (Electronics and Computers), Beijing, founded 1985; *Guoji Xin Jishu* (New International Technology), Beijing, founded 1984; and *Zhongguo Guanggao* (China's Advertising) (w), Beijing, advertising and marketing, founded 1984.

Broadcasting: In 1985 China had 213 radio-broadcasting stations, the most important of which is Beijing's Central People's Broadcasting Station (CPBS). CPBS broadcasts on six channels in Mandarin Chinese and in eight minority languages or dialects. Television was introduced in 1958, and in 1985 there were 202 television stations. Most of the people, however, do not have a radio or television set: In 1985 there were only 29 television sets per 100 families. There are about 100 million loudspeakers connected to the radio rediffusion system, used by the government for broadcasting.

BIOGRAPHICAL SKETCHES

Deng Xiaoping. Born in 1904 and a member of the Communist party since the early 1920s, Deng Xiaoping emerged as the leading political personality in China in the late 1970s. He was twice purged for his views, first during the Cultural Revolution when he was designated the "number-2 capitalist roader" in 1966 and forced to undergo public self-criticism in 1968; and then in 1976 when he was blamed for public demonstrations in April of that year eulogizing the recently deceased Zhou Enlai. After the defeat of the Gang of Four, Deng returned to the political limelight and thereafter largely shaped Chinese politics, even though he held no major formal position. In 1987 he retired from the politburo of the CCP but retained his post as chairman of the Central Military Commission until November 1989. Diminutive in stature, he has been praised by foreign leaders for his pragmatism, but lost face internationally when in June 1989 he supported the army's massacre of democratic students throughout China, then blatantly lied to the country and the world about what had occurred.

Fang Lizhi. The astrophysicist Fang Lizhi was born in 1937, and his name first became internationally known in early 1987 when he was accused by the Communist party of instigating students' demonstrations for general democratic reforms. Fang was expelled from the party for promoting "bourgeois liberalization," but he retained his academic posts and in January 1988 was promoted from fourth- to second-grade academician of the Chinese Academy of Sciences. Dubbed by some the Chinese Sakharov, Fang does not want to be considered a dissident and believes that China will eventually become democratic. He took refuge along with his wife in the U.S. embassy in Beijing following the army crackdown in June 1989.

Li Peng. Son of a communist writer who had been executed by Chiang Kai-shek in 1930, Li Peng, born in 1928, was adopted at the age of three by Zhou Enlai. He studied engineering in the Soviet Union and is a nuclear expert. He began to rise in the political hierarchy in the late 1970s, and from the early 1980s on served in various ministerial posts. In November 1987 he became acting prime minister, and in April of the following year he was confirmed in this post at the seventh National People's Congress. He is a conservative technocrat and prefers a slower and more cautious approach in the modernization efforts.

Qian Qichen. Born in 1928, Qian studied in the Soviet Union and from the mid-1950s served in various diplomatic positions. Between 1982 and 1988 he was vice-minister of foreign affairs, and in 1988 he became minister of foreign affairs.

Yang Shangkun. A Long March veteran born in 1907, Yang was the second most powerful man in the military and a Politburo member when he was elected by the National People's Congress to the largely ceremonial post of president in April 1988. He is widely considered one of Deng's most trusted supporters.

Zhao Ziyang. Born in 1918, Zhao was in the forefront of the liberalization and modernization efforts in the 1980s. He had been purged during the Cultural Revolution, but in the mid-1970s he distinguished himself by his bold economic modernization in Sichuan Province. He was called to Beijing in the 1980s by Deng Xiaoping and quickly became his foremost associate. Zhao has also vigorously promoted the open-door position to the West and a conciliatory foreign policy. In June 1989, following the military suppression of the pro-democracy student demonstrations, Zhao was demoted from all his positions and denounced for "counterrevolutionary" activities.

Jiang Zemin. Born in 1926, Jiang became Minister of the Electronics Industry in 1983. From 1987 to 1989 he headed the Shanghai municipal party committee and in June 1989 he replaced Zhao Ziyang as party general secretary.

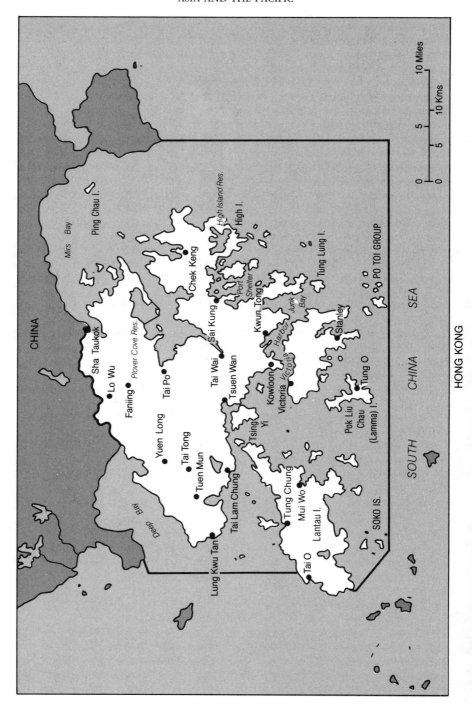

HONG KONG

HONG KONG

Features: The British crown colony of Hong Kong is, with Portuguese Macao, one of the two remaining colonial outposts in China. It is comprised of more than 220 islands off the south coast of China, and a peninsula on the mainland southeast of the city of Guangzhou. Hong Kong is divided into three districts: Hong Kong (30 sq. miles/79 sq. km.), which includes Hong Kong Island and adjacent islands; Kowloon (4 sq. miles/11 sq. km.), a peninsula on the mainland; and the New Territories (377 sq. mi./978 sq. km.), which are partly on the mainland and include Lantau and other islands. The terrain is composed primarily of volcanic rocks. Many of the islands are small, rocky and uninhabited. The mainland is generally rugged and severely eroded, and rises to 3,140 feet/957 m. at Tai Mo Shan, in the New Territories. The coastline is narrow, rugged and deeply indented, with mountains in some places extending to the sea. Productive agricultural land, located almost entirely in the northern and northeastern parts of the New Territories, is scarce. The colony has few minerals, although small quantities of feldspar and kaolin are mined. Its primary resource is Victoria Harbour, the strait separating the Kowloon peninsula and Hong Kong Island, which is one of the world's finest natural deep-water harbors. Due to the extreme shortage of level land suitable for construction, much development (including the runway of the busy Kai Tak international airport) has taken place on land reclaimed from the sea.

Area: 412 sq. miles/1,068 sq. km.

Mean max. and min. temperatures: 82°F/28°C (summer), 59°F/15°C (winter).

Relative humidity: 73%–84%.

Mean annual rainfall: 87.6 in/2,225 mm.

Total population (1988 est.): 5,641,193.

Districts and populations (1986): Hong Kong (1,175,800), Kowloon (2,301,700), New Territories (5,396,000).

Distribution: Hong Kong is 92.5% urban, with urban development centered in areas near the harbor. The colony's population densities in some places are among the highest in the world (up to 380,000 persons per sq. mile, as compared to about 30,000 persons per sq. mile in the average U.S. city). Although the colony has no formally bounded localities, the leading urban areas are Victoria (the administrative center, on Hong Kong Island) and Kowloon. The population of Hong Kong has increased dramatically during this century: a high rate of natural increase coupled with periodic waves of legal and illegal immigration from China. Since the late 1970s numerous Vietnamese refugees have also arrived in Hong Kong. In recent years U.S. citizens have replaced the British as the largest expatriate community in the colony.

Language: Chinese and English are the official languages. Cantonese is spoken by a majority of the inhabitants, 98% of whom are of Chinese origin; Mandarin is understood by many.

Religion: A majority of the population adheres to Buddhism, Taoism and/ or Confucianism. There are smaller numbers of Christians (8.6% in 1987), Hindus and Muslims.

CONSTITUTIONAL SYSTEM

Constitution: As a British colony, Hong Kong has no formal written constitution. Under a 1984 Sino-British agreement to return Hong Kong to Chinese sovereignty on July 1, 1997, Hong Kong will become a special administrative region of China with a basic law that will serve as its post-colonial constitution. The Chinese government created a committee, 23 of whose 59 members were from Hong Kong, to draft this basic law. The first draft, released in 1988, called for a government headed by a powerful appointed governor, with a legislature whose functions would be primarily advisory. It assigned power to interpret the basic law to the Chinese National People's Congress. The 1988 draft aroused some controversy in Hong Kong and a final version was issued in 1990.

Head of state: Queen Elizabeth II. *Governor:* Sir David Wilson.

Executive: The governor, who represents the British monarch, is appointed for an indefinite term by the British government to serve as head of the executive branch. The governor presides over an advisory Executive Council consisting of the chief secretary, the commander of the British forces, the financial secretary, the attorney general and two other appointed official members, plus 11 appointed unofficial members. Although the governor theoretically may reject the advice of the Executive Council on administrative matters, this seldom occurs in practice. The British government has the power to issue mandatory instructions to the governor. The first draft of the basic law preserved the colonial structure in calling for a powerful appointed governor.

Legislature: The Legislative Council consists of the governor, 10 official members, 22 appointed unofficial members and 24 elected members. Half of the elected members are chosen by the district boards and the urban and regional councils; the remainder are selected by representatives of various functional constituencies, such as trade unions, professional organizations and the industrial and commercial sectors. The power of the British Parliament to veto measures passed by the Hong Kong Legislative Council has not been exercised since 1913, and the authority of Parliament to legislate for the colony has generally been applied only in matters pertaining to external affairs. According to the draft basic law the first legislature, which would serve from 1997 to 1999, would be appointed by a committee in Beijing. Thereafter, between 25% and 50% of its members would be directly elected. There have been demands in Hong Kong for the creation of a directly elected legislature before the colony returns to Chinese sovereignty, but the British government has been reluctant to move swiftly on this matter for fear of offending China. Direct elections for 10 seats on the legislative council were scheduled for 1991.

Political parties: Political parties play an insignificant role. Both the Chinese Communist party (known as the Hong Kong and Macau Work Committee, and responsible to Beijing) and the Kuomintang (based in Taiwan) have organizations in Hong Kong, but they do not operate openly as political parties.

Local government: An Urban Council is responsible for overseeing health, recreation and resettlement in the urban area, which is divided into 10 districts. Half of the 30 members of this council are directly elected for three-year terms by persons over 21 years of age who have lived in Hong Kong for seven years. A Regional Council serves a similar function for the New Territories, which are divided into eight districts. Some of the council's 36 members, who also serve three-year terms, are also directly elected. Each district is administered by a management committee made up of area government officials; these committees are assisted by advisory district boards, two-thirds of whose members are directly elected. An elected Advisory Board represents the interests of the indigenous rural inhabitants of the New Territories.

Judicial system: The Hong Kong Supreme Court is comprised of a Court of Appeal and a High Court; the latter has unlimited jurisdiction over civil and criminal cases. There are also four district courts and eight magistrate's courts with more limited jurisdictions. The 1984 Sino-British accord on the future of Hong Kong declared that mainland laws, except those pertaining to foreign affairs and defense, would not apply in Hong Kong. The 1988 draft of the basic law, however, stated that mainland laws concerning "national unity" and "territorial integrity" would apply as well. This raised some question in Hong Kong about the degree of judicial independence it would retain once it came under Chinese sovereignty.

RECENT HISTORY

Great Britain formally declared Hong Kong a crown colony in 1843, but the colony at that time included only Hong Kong Island, which had been occupied by British forces during the first Opium War (1839–42) and was formally ceded to Great Britain "in perpetuity" in 1842 by the Treaty of Nanjing. Henry Pottinger, the first governor, immediately declared Hong Kong a free port. There were further conflicts between British traders and China that erupted into war in 1856. The second Opium War was ended by the 1860 Convention of Beijing, under which the British annexed the Kowloon peninsula and Stonecutters Island. The British demanded further concessions after the Chinese defeat in the First Sino-Japanese War (1894–95), and in 1898 they obtained a 99-year lease on the New Territories and nearby islands, thus greatly increasing the area of the colony. The following year, in violation of the 1898 Convention of Beijing, the British expelled the Chinese magistrates who had been allowed to remain in the old walled city of Kowloon. China protested this expulsion at the time and reasserted its claim to the old walled city in 1933, 1948 and 1962, but its claims were rejected by the Hong Kong courts. Since 1949 the People's Republic of China has repeatedly declared that all three treaties governing Hong Kong were forced upon China and therefore were not binding, although it did not formally abrogate them.

Because of its excellent natural harbor, Hong Kong flourished as a major center for trade between the West and China. Its population increased steadily between 1841, when it stood at 5,000, and 1939, when it numbered more than 1 million. There were major waves of migrants whenever conditions in China were unsettled, particularly during 1911–15, with the overthrow of the Manchu dynasty, and 1937–39, when Japan invaded China. Japanese forces captured Hong Kong in 1941 and occupied it until 1945, when it was returned to British control. During the Japanese occupation most British residents were interned and large numbers of Chinese residents were deported. More than 1 million Chinese fled to Hong Kong after the Chinese Communist victory in 1949, and the British closed the frontier with China in 1950. Since that time China has controlled movement across the border, permitting massive migration only in 1962–65, when the mainland was threatened by famine. Any illegal Chinese migrant who succeeded in reaching the urban area of Hong Kong between 1974 and 1980 was allowed to remain. After that time all illegal arrivals were repatriated by the British colonial authorities, although the colony continues to receive large numbers of legal migrants.

The massive influx of refugees after World War II placed great strains on social services, but it also provided capital, entrepreneurial skills and a vast pool of inexpensive labor. When trade with China was cut off during the Korean War, the colony possessed the talent and infrastructure needed to shift its emphasis from trade to manufacture for export. Political shifts in China affected trade and immigration but were not reflected on the political scene except in 1967, when demonstrations inspired by the Cultural Revolution in China were put down by the British authorities.

The major uncertainty was what would happen when the British lease on the New Territories expired in 1997. Negotiations between Great Britain and China on the future of the colony began in 1982. In 1984 negotiators reached an accord under which the entire colony would be returned to Chinese sovereignty in 1997. Under terms of the accord, Hong Kong would retain its capitalist economic system and life-style for at least 50 years after it was returned to Chinese control, and would be governed by its own inhabitants as a special administrative region of China. The accord was ratified in 1985, and a Sino-British liaison group was established to monitor the accord's provisions.

Although Great Britain had never granted representative government to Hong Kong and the population generally remained politically apathetic, there was increasing pressure after the accord to institute democratic reforms before 1997, in the hopes that such reforms, if in place, would be retained following the transition to Chinese sovereignty. In the face of Chinese objections to any reforms prior to the issuance of or in conflict with the basic law, however, the British moved slowly in this area. In an attempt to answer the concerns of Hong Kong residents who were not British citizens and who would not, as non-Chinese, qualify automatically for Chinese citizenship in 1997, the liaison group announced in 1986 that such residents would be issued special British passports as overseas nationals. These passports would not give their holders the right to live in the United Kingdom and would not be transferable to their descendants. The economy has continued to flourish since the signing of the agreement, although fears for the future have caused over 100,000 skilled and wealthy Chinese to leave the colony at least temporarily (many to Canada, some to the United States and Australia) or to shift some of their business or financial resources elsewhere.

The outflow—and pressures on Britain to loosen restrictions on immigration—increased following the June 1989 crackdown on the pro-democracy movement in China. The movement had inspired unprecedented demonstrations of popular support in Hong Kong, and the Chinese government's hardline attitude provoked new fears about the future under Chinese rule.

Defense: In 1986 Great Britain maintained 8,945 troops in Hong Kong, including one British and four Gurkha infantry battalions. The number of Gurkha battalions was reduced to three in 1987.

ECONOMY

Background: Hong Kong is one of the world's great trading and financial centers, with a freewheeling capitalist economy. It has profited from its location on important East-West trade routes, its fine harbor and its cheap labor, political stability, low taxation and free-port status. During the late 1800s and early 1900s Hong Kong served primarily as an entrepôt between China and the West, and after the Communists came to power in China it turned to manufacturing for export to survive. In recent years trade with China has again become important, and the colony is increasingly becoming a service center for its larger neighbor.

Since 1965 Hong Kong has experienced one of the highest economic growth rates in the world (12% in 1987). Per capita income, less than U.S. $200 in 1948, had risen to more than $7,550 in 1986. The colony provides up to 40% of China's foreign exchange, and offers China a valuable trading outlet and a source of capital and technology to modernize its economy. Because manufacturing costs are much lower in China than in Hong Kong, factories in adjoining Guandong province financed by Hong Kong entrepreneurs produce a variety of goods marketed through Hong Kong. The Chinese have invested in commercial and residential real estate in Hong Kong, and in the colony's tourist and transportation industries. One evidence of China's increasing economic stake in Hong Kong is the 70-story Bank of China building, which opened in 1989; it is the tallest building so far in East Asia. Transportation links between the colony and China are also being expanded. Service on the railroad from Hong Kong to Guangzhou was reestablished in 1979, and a new superhighway linking Guangzhou to Hong Kong and Macao opened in 1985.

A crisis of confidence over the future of the colony led to an economic downturn in the early 1980s, but economic growth resumed after the signing of the 1984 Sino-British accord guaranteeing the continuation of Hong Kong's capitalist system. In the once again booming real estate market, a portion of government revenues for sales and leases extending beyond 1997 was reserved for the government of the Chinese special administrative region. The events of 1989, including China's displeasure at the support of Hong Kong residents for the pro-democracy movement, led to a new fight of capital offshore. After 1997 Hong Kong is to retain its identity as a free port and separate customs territory, and the Hong Kong dollar, whose value is pegged to the U.S. dollar, is to remain a freely convertible currency.

Manufacturing: As Hong Kong's domestic market is small, land is limited, and the supply of capital and skilled labor is abundant, economic development after World War II focused to a large extent on the growth of light industry producing manufactured goods for the export market. The share of the manufacturing sector devoted to heavy industry, including shipbuilding and repair, iron, and steel, has declined steadily. The textile and clothing industry employs 40% of the domestic industrial work force and provides 40% of all domestic exports by value. Electrical and electronics equipment, plastic products (particularly toys, of which Hong Kong is the world's largest exporter), watches and clocks are other important manufactures. The textile industry in particular has been adversely affected by increasing competition from Taiwan, South Korea and other developing nations, and by restrictions on the importation of Hong Kong products in the industrialized world. This has prompted both efforts to diversify the manufacturing sector and the modernization of traditional industries. The textile and clothing industry, for example, has focused increasingly on the production of designer fabrics and high quality apparel, with their larger profit margins. The government has actively encouraged foreign investment in the industrial sector, particularly in high-technology industries. It has also made facilities—including the Tai Po and Yuen Long industrial estates—available to foreign investors through the Hong Kong Industrial Estates Corporation, established in 1977. The United States, Japan, China and the United Kingdom are the leading foreign investors in the colony's manufacturing sector. There are also numerous joint Chinese-Hong Kong ventures, both in Hong Kong and in neighboring Guandong province, where labor costs are lower than in the colony itself. One of the most controversial of such joint ventures is the Daya Bay nuclear power plant in Guandong province. About 70% of the total output of this plant—China's first nuclear power plant, scheduled to begin operation in 1992—is slated for use in Hong Kong. Currently, business and industry consume about 75% of the colony's electrical output (20 billion KWh in 1987).

In October 1989 the government announced plans to build a new international airport and container shipping port off Lantau Island. This ambitious plan, which would not be completed until after China regained control of the colony, was considered a signal of British confidence in Hong Kong's future.

Agriculture and fishing: Agriculture plays a limited role in the economy due to the shortage of arable land; only about 9% of the total land area is under cultivation. Vegetables have replaced rice as the leading crop. Less than 25 acres/10 ha. of land is devoted to rice production, although yields are high due to double cropping and the use of fertilizers. Fruits, nuts and fresh flowers are also cultivated for the surrounding market, and poultry and pigs are raised. A shift to crops producing a much higher return per acre increased the value of agricultural production nearly 700% between 1963 and 1983. About 1% of the population is engaged in fishing. Fish catches from the ocean and from freshwater ponds totaled 177,814 tons in 1986 and provided more than 80% of the colony's domestic consumption. Nevertheless, Hong Kong must import much of its food from China, which also provides at least 25% of its water. The building of reservoirs, including the 1969 conversion of Plover Cove and the recent construction of the world's first seabed reservoir, has increased the domestic water supply and reduced the traditional problem of chronic water shortages.

Finance, communications and tourism: Hong Kong is the world's third largest banking center, with 154 licensed banks (a majority of them incorporated in foreign countries) and an even greater number of deposit-taking institutions in 1987. There is no central bank. Currency is issued by two commercial banks, and banking standards, charges and interest rates on deposits have been regulated by the Hong Kong Association of Banks since 1981. There are also a large number of insurance companies, both foreign and domestic, operating in the colony. Since 1986 Hong Kong has had a unified stock exchange. Excellent domestic and international communications facilities have contributed to Hong Kong's growth as an international financial center. The communications network, with direct links to more than 30 countries, includes three satellite earth-station antennae.

Tourism is Hong Kong's third largest source of foreign exchange. Hong Kong's traditional attraction has been its convenience as a stopover point for travelers, who are able to purchase there a wide range of duty-free goods. The Hong Kong Tourist Association, established in 1957, has attempted to promote longer tourist visits by publicizing Hong Kong's scenic and cultural attractions. More than 5.5 million visitors came to Hong Kong in 1988, an increase of 25% over 1987 and 45% over 1986. The largest numbers of tourists are from Japan and Taiwan, and more than 10% of all visitors are on their way to or from China.

Foreign trade: Hong Kong is the world's third largest shipper, after Japan and Greece, and has one of the world's largest container ports. Some 12% of the world's shipping fleet is registered there. As a free port, the colony has long been a center for the receipt and reexport of goods from all over the world. These goods include textile fibers, textiles, clothing, machinery, electrical and electronics equipment, chemicals (especially dyes), photographic supplies, watches and clocks. Trade between Hong Kong and China tripled between 1980 and 1985, when China replaced the United States as the colony's chief trading partner; it has continued to increase since that time. Of Hong Kong's estimated $47.6 billion worth of exports in 1987, reexports accounted for about $22.9 billion. In 1988, for the first time since the early 1950s, reexports exceeded domestic exports in value. China is the destination of 33% of all reexports and the source of 47% of them. In 1987 imports totaled $47.4 billion. In 1986 the colony's leading exports were clothing and accessories (34%); machinery and transportation equipment (22%); photographic equipment, watches and clocks (8.5%); and textiles and fabrics (7%). The major export destinations were the United States (42%), China (12%), West Germany (7%) and the United Kingdom (6%). The leading imports that same year were machinery and transportation equipment (24%), fabrics (15%), foodstuffs (8%) and chemicals (8%). China provided 30% of imports, Japan 20%, Taiwan 9% and the United States 8%. In 1986 Hong Kong became a full participant in the General Agreement on Tariffs and Trade.

Employment: In 1987 Hong Kong's labor force totaled 2.7 million, of whom 40.2% were in commerce and services, 34.8% in manufacturing, 8.1% in construction, 6.8% in government and public authorities, and 1.6% in agriculture and fishing. In 1986, 15% of the labor force was organized, although unions traditionally have been fragmented and have had little power. Unemployment in 1988 stood at 1.8%.

Price trends: The consumer price index for all items (1980 = 100) rose from 154.9 in 1984 to 169.1 in 1987; there was a rise of about 7.5% in 1988. During these years, however, increases in the consumer price index were generally outpaced by rises in the daily earnings index.

SOCIAL SERVICES

Welfare: Expenditures for social services account for less than 6% of total government spending. The Social Welfare Department is responsible for providing social services, but there is no comprehensive welfare system. The government provides no unemployment benefits, and most social service expenditures have been concentrated on the resettlement of refugee families. Less than 2% of the civil service is comprised of expatriates, although expatriates hold most high-level positions. Existing civil service benefits have been guaranteed by China after 1997.

Health services: In 1986 Hong Kong had an estimated 24,550 hospital beds and 5,150 physicians. Drug addiction is a serious problem in the colony, and treatment is provided in government-owned and aided centers. Tuberculosis is also a problem in squatter areas.

Housing: Serious housing shortages have been a major problem for decades, and overcrowding has led to traffic congestion, air pollution and other urban problems. Construction is hampered by the shortage of buildable land and high real estate prices. Despite a major government resettlement program launched in 1954, almost 400,000 people still live in squatter colonies on land or at sea. The construction and maintenance of public housing is under the supervision of the Hong Kong Housing Authority. More than 40,000 public housing units are being built per year, and public housing units are home to about 50% of the population.

EDUCATION

Education accounts for about 18% of total government expenditures. Approximately 88% of the total adult population is literate. Kindergartens for children between the ages of three and five are privately run, with indirect government assistance. Six years of primary education and three years of secondary education are free and compulsory. In 1985–86 there were 3,546 primary schools with 1,297,818 students. Secondary schools offer both academic and vocational programs, and four government-run colleges of education train primary and secondary school teachers. Higher education is autonomous but receives government subsidies. The colony has two universities (the University of Hong Kong, founded in 1911, and the Chinese University of Hong Kong, founded in 1963) with a joint enrollment of more than 15,000. A new university of science and technology is scheduled to open in 1991. There are also two technical colleges and a Baptist college. The Hong Kong Academy for the Performing Arts, the only such complex in Asia, opened in 1985 and offers programs in both traditional Asian and Western arts. It includes schools of music, dance, drama and the technical arts.

MASS MEDIA

After Japan, Hong Kong has the highest newspaper readership in Asia. There are about 60 daily newspapers, five of which are in English, and about 520 other periodicals.

The press

Dailies: English-language dailies include *South China Morning Post,* 85,000; *Asian Wall Street Week,* 30,000; *Hong Kong Standard,* 17,000. The leading Chinese-language dailies are *Sin Pao Daily News,* 300,000; *Tin Tin Yat*

Pao, 180,000; *Fai Pao,* 160,000; *Wah Kiu Yat Po,* 125,000; *Sing Tao Man Pao,* 122,000; *Ching Pao,* 120,000; *Hong Kong Daily News,* 119,000; *Hong Kong Sheung Po,* 110,000; *Ming Pao,* 110,000; *Ta Kung Pao,* 105,000; *Wen Wei Po,* 100,000.

Periodicals: Major English-language periodicals include the monthly Asia edition of the *Reader's Digest,* 338,000; *Hong Kong Enterprise,* 65,000; *Travelling Magazine,* 61,300; *Asian Business,* 50,000; and the weeklies *Asia Magazine,* 557,000; *Asia Week,* 65,000; *Far Eastern Economic Review,* 62,000. The leading Chinese-language periodicals are the monthly *Reader's Digest,* 300,000, and the weekly news magazine *Sinwen Tienti,* 42,000.

Broadcasting: The government-sponsored Radio Television Hong Kong produces television programming and provides 24-hour radio services on five frequencies in Chinese and English. The British Forces Broadcasting Service broadcasts in English and Nepali; Hong Kong Commercial Broadcasting transmits in English and Chinese on three frequencies. There are two commercial television concerns: Asia Television, Limited, and Hong Kong Television Broadcasts, Limited. Each has two networks and broadcasts in English and Chinese. In 1986 the colony had one radio receiver for every two persons and one television receiver for every four persons.

BIOGRAPHICAL SKETCHES

Sir David Clive Wilson. Born in Great Britain 1935 and educated at Keble College, Oxford, Wilson was knighted and named governor of Hong Kong on January 16, 1987; he assumed office formally as the 27th governor in April 1987, succeeding Sir Edward Youde, who died in his sleep while on a visit to Beijing in December 1986. Formerly assistant under secretary of state at the British Foreign and Commonwealth Office, Wilson was a long-time China scholar. He was deeply involved in the negotiations with China over the future of Hong Kong, and headed the British delegation of the Sino-British liaison group appointed to oversee the transition to Chinese sovereignty.

Xu Jiatun. Born in 1916 in Jiangsu province, Xu became director of the Hong Kong branch of the official Chinese Xinhua news agency in 1983 and is China's chief representative in Hong Kong. Prior to his arrival in Hong Kong in 1983 he held a variety of party and government posts in Jiangsu province. He served as a member of the 11th (1977–82) and 12th (1982–85) central committees, and in 1985 became a member of the Central Advisory Committee. As head of the local branch of the Chinese Communist party (the Hong Kong and Macau Work Committee), he has revamped the party and recruited local businesspeople and professionals. He has served as vice chairman of the committee drafting the basic law for the Hong Kong special administrative region since 1985, and has been an outspoken critic of local demands for democratic reforms.

INDIA

Features: The Republic of India is bounded on the north by the Himalayan mountain range, on the south by the Indian Ocean, on the east by the Bay of Bengal and the plains of the Ganges and the Brahmaputra rivers and on the west by the Arabian Sea, the Thar Desert and the plains of the Indus River. The southern segment of the country is peninsular and is dominated by the Deccan Plateau.

The Himalayas, the highest mountains in the world, are composed of a series of parallel ranges and form a natural barrier separating the subcontinent from North Asia. The average height of the range is in the vicinity of 20,200 feet/6,000 m. Among its many other prominent peaks, such as Mount Godwen Austen, the Himalayan range has the highest peak in the world, Mount Everest. In geologic time, these mountains are relatively new ("young folded mountains"), which explains their great heights. Most of the range is perennially snowcapped. In the summer, some melting takes place, feeding the great river systems of the Ganges, the Brahmaputra and the Indus. The great river systems have given rise to vast alluvial plains, particularly in eastern India. One of the most fertile regions in the world, this part of India is also densely populated. In the extreme eastern portions of the nation, particularly in the states of Assam and Meghalaya, one finds lush, verdant countryside characterized by heavy rainfall and tree-covered mountains. To the west, however, the land is quite arid and the soil is sandy. In fact, a large part of western India, particularly in the state of Rajasthan, are large tracts of desert.

The southern portion of the country is sharply separated from the north by the Vindhya and the Satpura ranges and the Narmada and Tapti rivers. This region is the Deccan Peninsula, which juts outward toward the Indian Ocean. The Deccan is bounded by the mountain ranges of the Eastern and Western Ghats, which run along the coastal areas. The geological composition of the Deccan Peninsula is mostly crystalline rock. It is drained by four major rivers: the Cauvery, the Godavari, the Krishna and the Mahanadi.

Area: 1,269,219 sq. miles/3,287,263 sq. km.

Mean max. and min. temperatures: New Delhi (28°36′N, 77°12′E) 50°–60°F/ 10°–15°C (Dec.), 86°–95°F/30°–35°C (May).

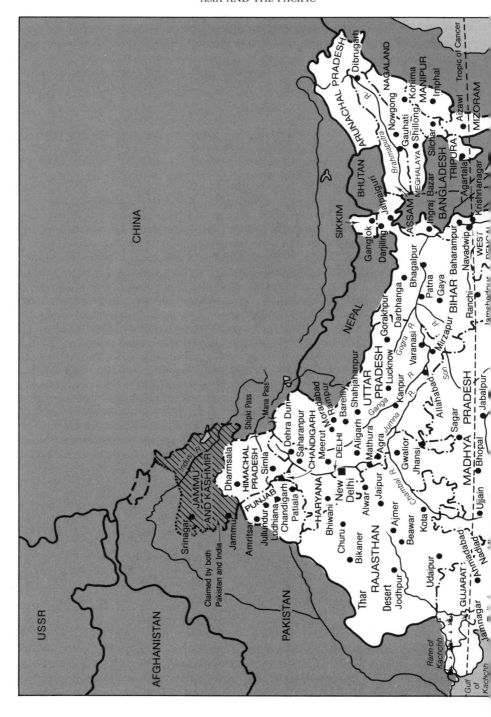

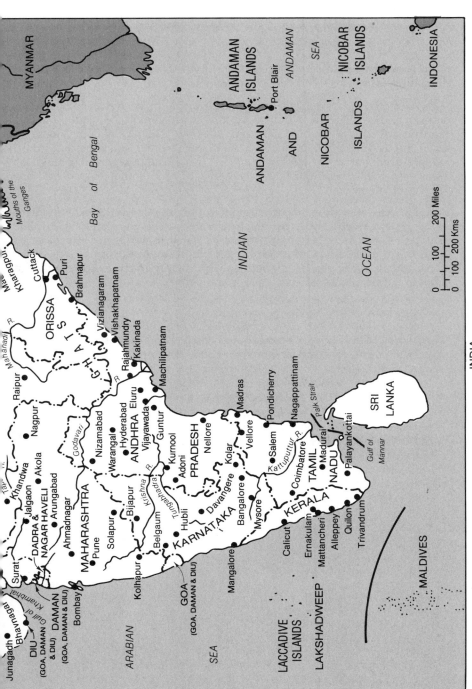

INDIA

POPULATION

Total Population (1988 est.): 816,800,000.

Chief towns and populations: Calcutta (9,194,018), Bombay (8,243,405), Delhi, including NEW DELHI (5,729,283), Madras (4,289,347).

Language: There are two distinct linguistic groups in India: Indo-Iranian and Dravidian. The Indo-Iranian languages are Hindi, Bengali, Marathi, Gujarati, Oriya, Punjabi, Urdu and Assamese. The Dravidian languages are Telugu, Tamil, Kannada and Malayalam. Another language that is also widely used but does not fall into the two broad categories is English. Along with Hindi, English is recognized as one of the two official languages of the nation.

Religion: All the world's major religions are represented in India. Hinduism is the predominant faith. As much as 83% of the population is Hindu. Muslims constitute the single largest religious minority and are close to 11% of the population. Most Muslims in India are of the Sunni sect. Sikhs constitute 1.9% of the population and live mainly in the northern state of Punjab. Christians constitute 2.6%.

CONSTITUTIONAL SYSTEM

Constitution: The Indian Constitution, which went into effect on January 26, 1950, states that the nation is a secular, democratic republic.

Head of state: President R. Venkataraman. *Prime minister:* V. P. Singh.

Executive: The president is the head of state but not the executive head. He is nominally also the commander-in-chief of the Indian Forces. Since India is a parliamentary democracy, his powers are analogous to that of a constitutional monarch—largely ceremonial and consultative. He appoints the cabinet on the advice of the prime minister, who is usually the leader of the majority party in the lower house of Parliament. In the absence of a majority party in the Parliament, or if the majority party is not unified, the president can exercise a degree of discretion in the choice of the individual to form a government. On the advice of the prime minister, the president also makes a range of appointments. For example, he appoints the governors of the states, the justices of the Supreme Court and the state High Courts. He is also responsible for the appointment of the attorney general, the government's legal adviser; and the comptroller and the auditor-general of India, who is responsible for overseeing union and state government expenditures. In addition to these responsibilities, the president is expected to call Parliament into session and on the advice of the prime minister, dissolve Parliament. Under extraordinary circumstances, when Parliament is not in session, again on the advice of the prime minister, the president may pass ordinances. These have the same effect as Acts of Parliament but must be reviewed by Parliament once it reconvenes. Finally, under emergency conditions such as the threat of grave national disorder or foreign aggression, the president can declare a State of Emergency, substantially curbing civil liberties and expanding the powers of the executive branch. This power is only nominally vested in the office of the president, however; a president only invokes these powers at the behest of the prime minister. The presidential term is five years. In the event of the president's death or removal from office, the vice-president assumes the position for a period of no more than six months. During this period a new president must be elected.

For all practical purposes, the powers of the executive are vested in the hands of the prime minister. The prime minister is called to form a government by the president, by virtue of his position of leadership in the majority party of the lower house. The prime minister presides over the Council of Ministers, which is composed of cabinet ministers and ministers of state. Each minister holds one or more "portfolios" (charge of administrative departments), and the prime minister often retains some of the key portfolios, such as Defense or Foreign Affairs.

Legislature: India has a bicameral legislature. The two houses of Parliament are known as the Lok Sabha (House of the People) and the Rajya Sabha (Council of States). The Lok Sabha has 544 members, of whom 542 are elected on the basis of universal adult suffrage. If no Anglo-Indian candidates (people of mixed European and Indian parentage) are elected, the president has the right to nominate two members of that community to those seats. Lok Sabha seats are allocated among the 22 states and 9 union territories (areas of the country directly administered from New Delhi) on the basis of population. In turn, the states are broken down into territorial constituencies.

Members of the Lok Sabha serve a five-year term unless the house is dissolved by the president on the advice of the prime minister. The constitution requires that this body meet at least twice a year with no more than a six-month interval between sessions. The Lok Sabha is the principal arena for the opposition parties to question and debate the government on its policies.

The Rajya Sabha has 250 members, 12 of whom are nominated by the president for their special contributions in the fields of literature, science, art and social service. The remaining 238 seats are allocated among the states on the basis of population. The state legislative assemblies elect the members of the Rajya Sabha for six-year terms. Unlike the Lok Sabha, the Rajya Sabha meets in continuous session and cannot be dissolved. As in other legislative bodies, the terms of the Rajya Sabha members are staggered. Consequently, one-third of the members stand for election every two years. The Rajya Sabha's political role is quite circumscribed and real power is located in the Lok Sabha.

Political parties: Though the Indian Constitution provides for a multiparty political system, and while there is no dearth of political opposition in India, politics since Independence has been dominated by the Indian National Congress. This party has its antecedents in the nationalist movement and was founded as far back as 1885. In 1969, Prime Minister Indira

99

Gandhi split the party to challenge the power of the party bosses, popularly known as the Syndicate. The two parties that emerged from this split were the Congress (R), or "Resolution" Congress, and the Congress (O), or the "Organization" Congress. In subsequent years the Congress (R) changed its name to the Congress (I), which stood for "Indira."

The principal national opposition parties are the Bharatiya Janata party, the Socialist party, the Lok Dal and the two Communist parties—the Communist Party of India and the Communist Party of India (Marxist). In addition to these national parties, there are a range of local and regional parties that seek to represent particular interests. They include the Dravida Munnetra Kazhagam (DMK), or Dravidian Progressive Federation and its offshoot, the All-India Anna DMK in Tamil Nadu, the Akali Dal in Punjab, the National Conference in Kashmir and the Telugu Desam in Andhra Pradesh. A number of these regional parties, particularly the Anna DMK and the Akali Dal, have split into various factions.

Local government: The basic structure of the central government is replicated on a smaller scale at the state level. The nation is divided into 22 states and 9 union territories. Each state has a governor and a chief minister. These positions are analogous to those of the president and the prime minister at the national level. The chief minister is nominally appointed by the governor. Like the prime minister, the chief minister is also the leader of his party in the state Legislative Assembly. The governor of each state is appointed by the president of India on the advice of the prime minister. Like the president, his powers are largely ceremonial. The office assumes considerable power in the event the state government is dissolved and President's Rule is declared. Constitutionally, President's Rule can be declared when the governor makes a determination that a situation has arisen whereby the state government is no longer capable of effectively functioning. In the event of the declaration of President's Rule, the governor and his staff assume the role of the state government for a period of no more than six months. (In particular cases this ordinance may be extended by Parliament for an additional six months.) At the end of the six-month (or year-long, at most) period, new elections must be called.

In addition to the 22 states in the Indian Union, there are 9 union territories. These are administered by a lieutenant governor or a chief commissioner. Again, these appointments are made by the president of India on the advice of the prime minister.

Within each state or union territory the basic administrative unit is the district. The country is divided into some 420 districts. The population and size of these districts vary widely from state to state. Local administration is in the hands of the collector, who is drawn from the elite Indian Administrative Service.

Judicial system: India has an independent judiciary. The highest judicial body in the nation is the Supreme Court. It is the ultimate interpreter of the law of the land and can strike down an Act of Parliament if it fails to conform to the Constitution. The court consists of the chief justice and 17 associate justices. They hold office until the age of 65, when retirement is mandatory. They may be removed from office on grounds of malfeasance as specified in the Constitution. Based on precedent and custom, the senior-most judge of the Supreme Court becomes the chief justice. In the mid-1970s, Indira Gandhi challenged this principle on at least two occasions, leading to charges of political interference.

Below the Supreme Court are the High Courts of the states. The size of the High Courts varies widely among the states based on size and history. Below this level are district and subordinate courts throughout the country.

RECENT HISTORY

British rule: As the Mughal Empire weakened in the 18th century, European entrepreneurs made commercial and political inroads into India. In 1757 the British East India Company defeated the troops of Siraj-ud-Dowlah in West Bengal to obtain a political foothold. One hundred years later, in 1857, when East India Company rule was firmly in place, Hindu and Muslim groups revolted against the British in response to the imposition of Western culture and values. The revolts were effectively and ruthlessly suppressed by the British with the help of Indian collaborators. After the revolt, control of India was taken from the East India Company and transferred to the British Crown. Queen Victoria became empress of India. The nationalism expressed by Indians in the 1857 revolt led to the creation of the Indian National Congress in 1885. From its founding until the beginning of the 20th century, however, it was an organization dominated by Anglicized upper-middle-class Indians. They initially sought reform within the framework of British rule.

The move to independence: The Indian National Congress underwent a fundamental change in the 1920s under the leadership of Mohandas Karamchand Gandhi, popularly known as the Mahatma. At this time, the Congress lost its elitist character and was transformed into a mass-based nationalist movement. The Muslim community, however, had doubted for some time if there was a place for it in the Congress party. Religion had often provided a rallying point for mobilizing Hindu masses, although Congress leaders denied that the party was a "Hindu party." Muslims nonetheless sought to distance themselves and, in 1906, under the leadership of Muhammed Ali Jinnah, the Muslim League was formed to protect the interests of the Muslim minority community.

Pressures from a broadening nationalist movement led the British to pass the Government of India Act in 1935. Under the aegis of this act, elections that offered the possibility of limited self-government were held in 1937. At the beginning of World War II, the British committed India to the war effort without consulting the Indian National Congress. In protest, the Congress ministries resigned. Owing to the nonviolent, noncooperation movement launched by the Congress and led by Gandhi, the British jailed most of its leaders.

Independence and the breakup of the subcontinent: With the end of World War II, the British simply lost the will to hold on to India. The nationalist

101

movement succeeded in winning independence for the subcontinent. However, the possibility of retaining a unified nation after the departure of the British appeared remote. The Congress and the Muslim League were at odds with each other and violent communal clashes became common. Eventually the British decided to partition India and Pakistan on the basis of demographic characteristics and geographic contiguity. The Congress strongly protested the division of India, but the Muslim League actively campaigned for a separate state. India achieved independence on August 15, 1947. States that were predominantly Muslim and adjoined one another became Pakistan, and the remainder went to India. The 562 "princely states" were given the option of joining either India or Pakistan depending on their location and demographic composition. Problems arose over the states of Junagadh, Hyderabad and Kashmir. Junagadh and Hyderabad had Muslim monarchs and Hindu majority populations and were located within areas that would become India. After attempts to persuade the rulers of these two states failed, the Indian authorities used force to integrate them into the Indian Union.

The state of Kashmir posed special problems. It had a Hindu monarch with a predominantly Muslim population. The monarch wanted to have an independent state. Since it had a predominantly Muslim population and was contiguous to Pakistan, a case could be made for a Pakistani claim to Kashmir. As the monarch was hedging, the Pakistani Army attacked portions of northern Kashmir with a view to seizing the state by force. Faced with the invasion, the monarch decided to join India. Indian forces were promptly airlifted into the state to stop the Pakistani advance. A cease-fire was declared shortly thereafter, and on January 1, 1948, India referred the Kashmir case to the United Nations. Various efforts at U.N. mediation were attempted, but they failed to yield concrete results. To this day, both nations continue to claim the entire state. Approximately one-third of Kashmir is in Pakistani hands and two-thirds in Indian hands. The issue of Kashmir has become a symbol for India, in that the Indian government seeks to demonstrate that all minorities can live and thrive under the aegis of a secular polity.

Nation-building: Following the first Kashmir war, the Indian government focused on the problems of nation-building. One of the first issues to be dealt with was a wave of agitation supporting reorganization of the polity on a linguistic basis. Critics of this proposal were afraid it would lead to subnational tendencies. Jawaharlal Nehru, prime minister of the new republic, did not support the creation of states on linguistic lines. He stressed that states were only for administrative purposes. However, in November 1956, the States Reorganization Act was passed by Parliament in recognition of the vast regional sentiment that existed. Fourteen states and six territories were created on the basis of dominant language. Immediately there were challenges to the newly created system. Bombay, which was composed of a majority of Marathi speakers but was dominated by Gujarati wealth, was divided into two separate states: Gujarat and Maharashtra. Sikhs in the Punjab called for a separate Punjabi-speaking state, a communal request masked in linguistic terms. They were granted such a state in 1966. The hill territories of Himachal Pradesh were granted full statehood in 1971. In 1975, Sikkim was extended statehood. Today India is composed of 22 states and 9 territories.

1962 Sino-Indian Border War: The border between India and China had been drawn by Sir Arthur Henry McMahon in 1914, although a treaty was never ratified by China. The border has been in dispute since then, and tensions resulted in armed conflict in 1962. In 1955, Chinese troops crossed into India's Garhwal district in Uttar Pradesh. They were removed after protests from Delhi, but the dispute was firmly in place. In 1959, the Dalai Lama fled to India after his effort to liberate Lhasa failed. In this same year, Indian and Chinese troops clashed in the Aksai Chin region of Ladakh. After failed talks between Nehru and Zhou Enlai in 1960, Nehru ordered Indian troops to take back "our territories" held at that time by Chinese "aggressors." However, Indian troops were no match for the Chinese, who easily advanced over India's northeast frontier. The resounding defeat of Indian forces led to the loss of 14,000 square miles/36,260 sq. km of territory and a reconsideration of foreign policy. Nehru, disheartened by the Chinese failure and lack of Asian unity, died on May 27, 1964, while still in office.

1965 Indo-Pakistani War: Lal Bahadur Shastri was voted the new prime minister on June 9, 1964. Soon after, in 1965, tension again erupted with Pakistan over the state of Kashmir. Initial confrontations took place in a desolate area near the border called the Rann of Kachchh. A cease-fire line was drawn by June 30, 1965, under the auspices of the U.N. Numerous violations by both sides occurred and on September 6, 1965, India launched a massive attack aimed at Lahore. Its sheer size and sophisticated U.S. weaponry enabled India to easily maintain its position in the states of Kashmir and Jammu. A U.N. cease-fire was agreed to by September 23. In early 1966, Soviet Premier Aleksei Kosygin invited both Shastri and Pakistani leader Ayub Khan to Tashkent for a summit meeting. After a week of negotiations, an agreement was signed that attempted to establish better relations. Both sides agreed to withdraw their armed forces to positions held before August 5, 1965, and to "adopt a principle of non-interference in the internal affairs of each other." Prime Minister Shastri died very soon after signing the Tashkent Agreement.

Emergence of Indira Gandhi: After a bitter struggle with Morarji Desai, the Congress party overwhelmingly supported Nehru's daughter Indira Gandhi as the next prime minister. She had the support of the party bosses known as the Syndicate. They were hoping that she would be easily influenced; however, she did not prove malleable at all, and in 1969 was expelled from the party. She went on to form her own branch, the Congress (R), which was later named the Congress (I) for Indira. Her left-wing coalition included the Communist parties and the regional DMK and Akali Dal parties, and it received overwhelming support from the population of India.

1971 Indo-Pakistani War and the creation of Bangladesh: Indira Gandhi won an overwhelming victory in 1971 based upon her campaign slogan of *garibi hatao,* or "abolish poverty." However, in neighboring Pakistan, tension was increasing between the eastern and western wings. Mujibur Rahman's Awami League party had won 160 out of 162 National Assembly seats in East Pakistan, based upon his Six Point Program which called for a near-autonomous eastern wing. Mujib was shortly thereafter imprisoned and the western wing launched a severe crackdown on the citizens of the east. By December 1971, 10 million East Pakistani refugees had drifted into India, placing an enormous strain on India's economy. India engaged in training exercises with East Pakistani rebels known as the Mukhti Bahini. The tension mounted, as West Pakistan accused India of attempting to break up the country. On December 3, 1971, Pakistan attacked 12 Indian airfields in the west. India, with its military superiority, was able to fight a "holding action" in the west while "liberating" much of the east. On December 15, 1971, Pakistan signed a surrender agreement. India declared a cease-fire and the nation of Bangladesh was created.

Imposition of the Emergency: In the years after the 1971 war, Indira Gandhi came under increasing attack for alleged corruption in her administration. In 1974, opposition parties united to form the Janata Morcha (People's Front) in an effort to actively challenge her position. In June of 1975, Indira Gandhi was found guilty of campaign malpractice in connection with her race for a seat in Parliment four years earlier. The Janata Morcha began amassing victories in local elections. In a rapidly deteriorating political environment, Indira Gandhi exercised her constitutional right to proclaim a state of Emergency, and she arrested large numbers of her opponents. Vigorous censorship was imposed upon the press and extremist political parties were banned. A total of 110,806 people were arrested during the two-year duration of the Emergency. There were strict measures giving the executive branch enormous power and denying the Supreme Court judicial review of emergency-enacted legislation. With little advance notice, Indira Gandhi announced in early 1977 that elections would be held in March of that year.

The Janata phase: Over 200 million voters participated in the elections of 1977, and the result was an upset victory for the Janata party, which took a 43% share compared to a 34% share for the Congress. Morarji Desai became India's new prime minister, thus interrupting 30 years of Congress rule. The Janata party was accused of the same kind of corruption that plagued Indira Gandhi in the years before the Emergency—so much so that Indira Gandhi was able to make a successful bid for Parliment only 1½ years later. Morarji Desai stepped down as prime minister after losing the support of his party in 1979. He was replaced by Charan Singh, who lasted for only a few weeks. In January 1979, India's president called for new general elections. The brief rule of the opposition was characterized by an overburdened bureaucracy, corruption, economic exploitation, smuggling, and tax evasion. Meanwhile, Indira Gandhi began to be seen as a figure of political courage in her defeat, and she was earning back the support she lost in 1977.

Indira Gandhi's final phase, 1980–84: Indira Gandhi's Congress (I) party won a two-thirds majority in the 1979 elections. One foreign-policy issue demanding immediate attention was the Soviet invasion of Afghanistan in 1979. Initially, India attempted to justify Soviet intervention. India saw for itself a role in facilitating a solution that would lead to the withdrawal of the troops. Gradually, however, India became more critical of the Soviet Union—but remained equally critical of U.S. military support to Pakistan, an action it feared was immensely destabilizing to the subcontinent.

Domestically, the early 1980s saw the rise of separatism and communalism throughout India. Rioting occurred in Assam and Kashmir. However, the most serious threat to national stability came from Sikh extremists in the Punjab, who mounted a violent secessionist movement for Khalistan. Sikh followers of the extremist leader Jarnail Singh Bhindranwale turned the Sikh holy shrine, the Golden Temple, into a military fortress. Violence between Sikhs and Hindus mounted and hundreds of civilians died in the rioting. Finally, on June 2, 1984, in an effort to quell the Sikh terrorism once and for all, Indira Gandhi ordered Indian troops to storm the Golden Temple in a mission known as Operation Bluestar. Hundreds of people died and much of the temple was desecrated. Moderate and extremist Sikhs alike were outraged at the brutality of the action. Four months later, in October of 1984, in direct response to Operation Bluestar, Indira Gandhi was assassinated by two of her Sikh bodyguards in the garden of her house in Delhi.

Emergence of Rajiv Gandhi: Indira Gandhi's son Rajiv was sworn in as prime minister the day his mother died. Despite his failure to prevent violence against the Sikhs in the aftermath of his mother's assassination, he quickly garnered support, and in December 1984, the Congress party won an overwhelming victory. Rajiv Gandhi was regarded as the representative of a new generation, and he often spoke of bringing India into the 21st century. Gradually, however, the Contress (I) began to lose support at the state level, owing largely to regional communalism. In early 1985, N. T. Rama Rao won in Andhra Pradesh and R. K. Hegde's Janata party won in Karnataka. Rajiv Gandhi's initial reaction was to cooperate with local parties, but Congress (I) support continued to erode at the local level. In 1987, Congress (I) lost Kerala to the Marxists and was not able to maintain any influence in Jammu and Kashmir. As Congress (I) power continued to erode, criticism was soon leveled at the prime minister, charging that he could not deal effectively with caste and communal tensions, especially as separatist movements by the Gurkas in Darjeeling and the tension in the Punjab continued.

India's relations with its neighbors in South Asia have also been met with some ambivalence. While the creation of the South Asian Association for Regional Cooperation has worked to increase cultural understanding among the states of South Asia, the agreement not to bring up bilateral issues has served to limit its role at this time. India continues to deploy the Indian Peacekeeping Force in Sri Lanka, in an effort to mediate between warring Sinhalese and Tamils. Critics accuse India of asserting regional hegemony by intervening in Sri Lanka and, more recently, in 1988, by putting down a coup attempt in the Maldives. With the recent election of Benazir Bhutto in Pakistan, relations between the two traditional adversaries are entering a new phase. Still plagued by charges of corruption in his administration, most recently in 1988 in a case involving alleged defense contractor kickbacks from the Swedish gun manufacturer Bofors, and with elections in India occurring sometime in 1989, it remains to be seen whether Rajiv Gandhi will be successful in retaining the Congress (I) majority.

ECONOMY

Background: From its earliest stages, the aim of Indian economic policy has been to promote economic growth, self-reliance and social justice. In its effort to eradicate poverty, the Directive Principles of State Policy embodied in the constitution called for a more equitable distribution of wealth. Subsequent policymakers interpreted this as a demand for a strong public sector. Some steps toward industrial liberalization were started by Indira Gandhi near the end of her tenure as prime minister, but it has been Rajiv Gandhi who has made steady progress toward economic reform. However, India remains a poor country with a per capita gross national product (GNP) of U.S. $209 and gross domestic product (GDP) of $182.51 billion. Foreign debt is $38,603 million and the account deficit on balance of payments is over 2% of GDP. An estimated 37% (271 million) of the population live below the poverty line, and unemployment in 1987 was 36 million. The mainstay of the economic structure remains agriculture; however, because of India's desire for self-reliance, a strong industrial sector has also been built up. Economic planning is based on a series of five-year plans that outline strategies for national development. India's seventh five-year plan is currently in effect and covers the period 1985–90. Planning has already begun on the eighth five-year plan and a target growth rate of 6% has tentatively been set.

Agriculture: Agriculture accounted for 37% of GDP in 1987–88 and employed slightly over half of the population (51.8%). India is a major producer of rice, wheat, sugarcane, raw cotton and tea, among other things. India's total agricultural production expanded at an average annual rate of just under 2% between the year 1960 and the early 1980s. The volume of output is especially sensitive to the monsoon, and it has been said that Indian economic policy is a gamble on the monsoons. The last serious drought was in 1987–88 and is considered to have been the worst in decades. However, agricultural output fell only 4.9%, a loss much less severe than anticipated and an indication of resilience on the part of the Indian economy. Since a majority of the population depends upon agriculture for its livelihood, and irrigation is available in less than one-third of the country's total cultivated area, a serious drought can have an extremely damaging effect on the entire economy. With the introduction of high-yield seeds and chemical fertilizers in the late 1960s, India experienced a phenomenal agricultural expansion that became known as the "green revolution." As a result, agricultural output has continued to grow at a rate of 2.5%–3% annually, in spite of a marked slowdown in the cultivation of previously vacant fields. Most farms are run by peasants as opposed to large landowners. Fears that mechanization would lead to the displacement of agricultural labor seemed to dissipate as mechanization became more common among peasant farmers.

Industry: Manufacturing accounted for 25% of GDP in 1987–88, and the state plays a large role in manufacturing. There are numerous regulations and constraints on Indian industries, some of which include investment licensing requirements, restrictions on foreign collaboration and limitations on investment by large industrial houses. Indian economic policymakers envisioned the state's guiding investment so that it corresponds with the goals of governmental five-year plans. The result, however, has been the creation of an inefficient bureaucracy and charges of corruption. There has been some measure of economic liberalization under Rajiv Gandhi. In 1987–88, Gandhi introduced reform that allowed additional investment of up to 10% by any company, even those deemed monopolistic under the Monopolies and Restrictive Trade Practices Act. Licensing exemption for investment in backward areas was also introduced. However, Rajiv Gandhi has had to face some political constraints in the implementation of these liberalizing reforms. The measures have met with mixed reactions, even among the large industrial houses who have thus far enjoyed a protected market. The major industries of India are finished steel, cloth, cement, nitrogenous fertilizers and automobiles. In 1986–87, production levels were as follows: finished steel, 9.7 million tons; cloth, 12.988 billion tons; cement, 34.8 million tons; nitrogenous fertilizers, 5.4 million tons; and automobiles, 237,600. Mining is also an important industry in India. For the calendar year 1987, 175.6 million tons of coal, 2.7 million tons of bauxite and 5 million tons of copper ore were extracted. Industry grew 7.7% in 1988 against a 9.1% growth in fiscal year 1987.

Foreign trade: 1988 statistics show that 29% of total imports were capital equipment, 25.3% raw materials and food and 27.2% energy. India's major exports are gems and jewelry, clothing, engineering goods, cotton yarn, fabrics and tea. In 1987, the drought caused India to seek large grain imports from the United States; by mid-1988, India had purchased 2 million tons of wheat. In 1987–88, export earnings in rupees (Rs) rose by 25% against imports of 11%. However, the trade deficit is still a substantial Rs 66 million. Of this, 6.1% of trade was with Japan and 11.9% with the United States. In recent years, India has received substantial remittances from those citizens working in the petroleum industry in the Middle East. In an effort to maintain the level of transfer as the economic activity in this region slows, India has begun to look to the expatriate community of Non-Resident Indians (NRIs), most of whom live in the United States,

Canada and Britain. However, as of May 1988, NRI investment was only Rs 13.1 billion.

Employment: 296 million people were employed in India in 1988. Of these, 51.8% were in agriculture, 19.2% in manufacturing, 12.3% in commerce, 7.3% in construction and 6.6% in government and public administration. Unions represent less than 10 million workers (4% of the labor force), yet there are 25,000 unions in India, most of which are allied to a federation with ties to political parties. The All-India Trade Union Congress is associated with the Communist Party of India and the Bharatiya Mazdoor Sangh with the Bharatiya Janata party. The Indian National Trade Union Congress, the largest of the major trade union federations, is associated with the Congress (I) party.

Education is primarily the responsibility of the state governments. Free primary education is available to all children between the ages of 6 and 11. The sixth five-year plan has set a goal to provide free education for children up to 14 years of age. Elementary education is geared primarily toward teaching basic, socially useful skills such as weaving, gardening, leather working and so on. Secondary education, which is for children between the ages of 14 and 17, usually follows the three-language formula whereby the regional language, Hindi and English all serve as the languages of instruction. Universities are for the most part autonomous. In 1988, India had 129.2 million primary school students, 20.1 million secondary school students, and 3.8 million university students. The literacy rate was 36%.

The press: India has long enjoyed the tradition of a free press. Since independence, it has been a constitutional right embodied in Articles 13 and 19. English-language publications are dominant; however, there is an audience for numerous Indian-language publications as well. Extreme censorship of the press occurred in 1975, during Indira Gandhi's imposed Emergency; for instance, the privilege of reporting parliamentary proceedings, as stated in the Feroz Gandhi Act, was withdrawn. Censorship was declared illegal in 1975, but the Prevention of Publication of Objectionable Matter Act, passed in 1976, continued to greatly restrict the freedom of the press. In 1978, an amendment to the constitution was passed, guaranteeing the right of the press to cover parliamentary proceedings.

The principal dailies are *Hindustan Times* (Delhi), 260,000; *Indian Express* (Bombay), 584,000; *Statesman* (Calcutta), 214,000; *Navbharat Times* (Delhi), 480,000; *Ananda Bazar Patrika* (Calcutta), 409,000.

Up to 66% of India's publications are produced by four large publishing houses, all of which are individually owned. The Times of India Group is controlled by Ashok Jain and family, the Indian Express Group by Ramnath Goenka and family, the Hindustan Times Group by K. K. Birla and family, and the Ananda Bazar Patrika Group by Aveek Sarkar and family.

Periodicals: Some of the more popular periodicals are *India Today* (Delhi), fortnightly in English and Hindi, 348,000; *Grih Shobha* (Delhi), monthly in Hindi, 275,000; *Filmi Duniya* (Delhi), monthly in Hindi, 121,000; *Employment News* (Government of India, New Delhi), weekly in Hindi, Urdu, and English, 325,000.

Broadcasting: Radio broadcasting began in India in 1927. In 1930, it came under government control and remained so until 1978. In 1978, All-India Radio was granted autonomy with Doordarshan India, the commercial television network begun in 1976. The news division of All-India Radio broadcasts 273 bulletins daily, in 24 languages and 36 dialects. Doordarshan India broadcasts 280 hours weekly and reaches approximately 70% of the population, many of whom have access to television through government-sponsored community centers. In 1988, approximately 17 million televisions and 43 million radios were in use.

BIOGRAPHICAL SKETCHES

Rajiv Gandhi. Born August 20, 1944. Grandson of Jawaharlal Nehru and son of Indira Gandhi. Educated at the exclusive Doon School at Dehra Dun in the Himalayan foothills. Studied for three years at Trinity College, Cambridge, and in 1965, obtained a degree in mechanical engineering from London's Imperial College of Science and Technology. Began his career as an airline pilot for the domestic carrier Indian Airlines. Entered politics in 1981, after the death of his brother Sanjay. Became general secretary of the Congress (I) party in 1983 and prime minister after his mother's assassination in 1984.

Ramakrishna Hegde. Born August 29, 1926. Obtained a law degree and was general secretary of the KPCC, 1958–62. Was minister for Development, Panchayati Raj and Co-op in his home state of Karnataka, 1962–65. Was elected to the Karnataka Legislative Assembly in 1983 and 1985. He is currently chief minister of Karnataka and has held that position since 1983.

K. C. Pant. Born August 10, 1931 in the state of Uttar Pradesh. Obtained a master's degree in science and studied in Germany for two years. Was a member of the Lok Sabha from 1962 to 1967 and since 1985. Was a member of the Rajya Sabha from 1978 to 1984. Was minister of finance 1967–69; minister of irrigation and power, 1973–74; minister of energy, electronics and space, 1974–77; and minister of education, 1984–85. Has served as India's minister of defense since 1987.

P. V. Narasimha Rao. Born August 24, 1924, in Rajasthan. Held numerous posts in the Rajasthani provincial government. Was appointed minister of state in the Ministry of Home Affairs, 1970–74; minister of state for defense production, 1974–75. He was deputy chairman of the

Rajya Sabha, 1977–80. Has served as the minister for external affairs since June 1988.

Ramaswami Venkataraman. Born December 4, 1910. Was active in the nationalist movement and was detained by the British from 1942 to 1944. In his long career, he has served as minister of finance, 1980–82; minister of defense, 1982–84; and vice-president of India, 1984–87. Has served as president of India since 1987.

INDONESIA

Features: Indonesia is the world's largest archipelago, extending more than 2,983 miles/4,800 km. from east to west and 1,243 miles/2,000 km. from north to south. It consists of five main islands (Sumatra, Java and Madura, Kalimantan, Sulawesi, and Irian Jaya) and approximately 30 smaller archipelagoes, to give a total of 13,667 islands and islets, of which about 6,000 are inhabited. The islands of Java and Madura, Sumatra, and Kalimantan stand on the Sunda Shelf, an extension of the Asian mainland: Irian Jaya stands on the Sahul Shelf, which links it to Australia. As a result of compressional movements between the shelves, dating from the Tertiary Period, each of the above islands has high mountain ranges facing deep seas along the outer edges of the shelves, and extensive lowland plains facing the shallow inner seas (the Malacca Straits, Java Sea, South China Sea and the Arafura Sea). Between the two shelves lies the main island of Sulawesi and the Nusatenggara and Maluku groups, which rise sharply from deep seas (depths of up to 15,000ft/4,572 m.) and have the most narrow coastal plains. Except in Kalimantan and Irian Jaya, the mountain ranges are volcanic. The archipelago contains some 400 volcanoes, of which approximately 100 are active. The extraordinary richness of the soils in the eastern two-thirds of Java and in Bali reflect generous volcanic replenishment. The archipelago is one of the world's most richly endowed states in terms of its mineral, petroleum and natural gas deposits, and its agricultural capacity.

Area: 735,358 sq. miles/1,904,569 sq. km. (excluding the disputed territory of East Timor). Indonesia is the world's 14th largest territorial unit.

Temperature: The day-time temperature in Jakarta is in the range 82°–93°F/28°–34°C; the night-time temperature is 77°F/25°C.

Average relative humidity: 75%–85%.

Mean Annual rainfall: Pontianak (west coast of Kalimantan) 126 in/3,200 mm.; Surabaya (eastern Java) 68 in/1,735 mm.

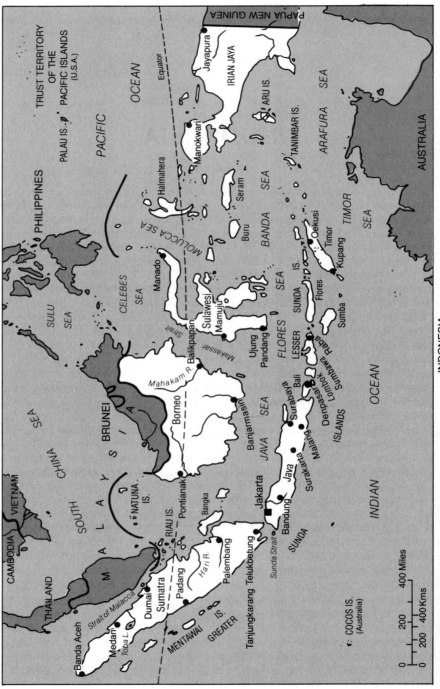

INDONESIA

POPULATION

Total population (October 31, 1985): 163,416,312

Chief towns and populations (official estimates for December 31, 1983): JAKARTA (7,347,800), Surabaya (2,223,600), Medan (1,805,500), Bandung (1,566,700), Semarang (1,205,800).

Distribution: With a population growth rate estimated at just over 2.3% a year, more than half the population is under 20 years of age.

Language: The national language, established since independence, is Bahasa Indonesia, which in its vocabulary and structure is based mainly on Malay. In addition there are 150 to 250 local languages and dialects.

Religion: Indonesia has the largest Muslim population in the world. The Islamic resurgence of the 1970s and 1980s had a limited impact, although fundamentalist thought is strong in certain areas. In 1984 it was estimated that 78% of the population were Muslim. The largest religious minority (11%) are the Christians (there are a number of prominent Indonesian Roman Catholics). The population of Bali is predominantly Hindu. Animist beliefs and mysticism continue to exert a powerful influence.

CONSTITUTIONAL SYSTEM

Constitution: The 1945 constitution, reenacted by presidential decree in 1959, is in force. The preamble includes a statement of Indonesia's fundamental aims and principles *(Pancasila),* including the belief in the one Supreme God, in a just and civilized humanity, in the unity of Indonesia, in democracy guided by consensus and in social justice for all the people of Indonesia.

Head of state: President Suharto.

Executive: The chief executive, in whom authority and responsibility for the conduct of government and administration of the state is concentrated, is the president. Political authority is heavily centralized in his person. The president is elected by the People's Consultative Assembly for a term of five years; he may be reelected. The president's policies and administration must conform to the "guidelines of state policy" as laid down in the decrees of the People's Consultative Assembly. Cabinet ministers are accountable only to the president.

Legislature: The legislative body of the state is the Dewan Perwakilan Rakyat (House of Representatives). It consists of 500 members, 400 of whom are directly elected, the remaining 100 being appointed from the armed forces faction of the Golkar (a political group). The House sits at least once a year, and all legislation requires its approval. The 500 members of the House sit with 500 appointees in the Majelis Permusyawaratan Rakyat (People's Consultative Assembly), the highest political institution in the state. Of the 500 appointees, 147 reflect regional interests, 253 reflect

113

political interests (including members of the armed forces belonging to the Golkar), and the remaining 100 reflect a variety of social groups. The Assembly meets at least once every five years. It sanctions the Indonesian constitution and the guidelines of state policy, and it elects the president and vice-president. Decisions are made on the basis of consensus and unanimity.

Political parties: The April 1987 general election was contested by three parties and groups. The Golkar (Functional Group) was established in 1964 (as Sekber Golkar) and reorganized in 1971. It is the government alliance, representing the interests of functional groups—civil servants, the armed forces, women's organizations, farmers and students. It secured 73.17% of the vote in 1987. The Partai Demokrasi Indonesia (Indonesian Democratic party) was formed in 1973 by the merger of nationalist and Christian parties. It secured 10.87% of the vote in 1987. The Partai Persatuan Pembangunan (United Development party) was also established in 1973 by the merging of four Islamic parties. It secured 15.97% of the vote in 1987.

Local government: The most senior figures in local administration are the governor of the province, the regent, or *bupati,* of the district and the medium-town mayor. They are both agents of the national government and chief executives with respect to their areas. They make local regulations in concurrence with the views of their respective regional representative councils. Governors are appointed by the president on the recommendation of the minister of home affairs from among two or three nominations put forward (through election) by the appropriate level I regional representative council; regents and medium-town mayors are appointed by the minister of home affairs on the recommendation of the governor from among the candidates elected by the appropriate level II regional council. The intermediary level of local administration is the subdistrict *(kecamatan)* and the village administrative unit *(kelurahan):* These are simply subdivisions of the district and medium-town, and have no representative council. At the lowest level is the village *(desa).* The *desa* head is elected by all adults in the village and then appointed by the *bupati* on behalf of the governor. The village council, composed of between nine and 15 prominent members of the *desa,* is a deliberative body, making decisions in concurrence with the village head in a spirit of reciprocal cooperation.

Judicial system: There is a single codified criminal law, which is applied throughout the archipelago. With respect to the civil law, Europeans are subject to the Code of Civil Law published in the State Gazette in 1847; Indonesians are subject to customary law *(hukum adat),* which varies from region to region; "alien Orientals" and Chinese are subject to certain parts of the Code of Civil Law and the Code of Commerce.

RECENT HISTORY

The declaration of Indonesian independence from Dutch rule took place on August 17, 1945, in the political hiatus following Japan's unconditional surrender two days previously. But it was five years before independence was secure: On December 27, 1949, the Netherlands formally transferred sovereignty to the indigenous authority. Those five years were a period of extraordinary complexity, dominated by a powerful Dutch determination to regain control of its colonial possession and by the emergence of the most serious divisions within Indonesian society and its political hierarchy. Those divisions were multifarious: between those who sought armed struggle (prominent were a large number of young, charismatic local leaders who had been politicized and then armed during the Japanese period and who had then been caught up in the euphoria of independence) and those who favored negotiation; between those who sought social revolution (notably in eastern Sumatra and in the north-coast districts of Java) and those elites who opposed it; between the political left and right; between those who drew their inspiration from Islam and those who sought the dominance of secular influences. The opposing forces frequently brought the infant state very close to civil war. Two episodes in 1948 were crucial. First, in May, a Javanese mystic in western Java launched his followers into what became the first regional rebellion against the republic, proclaiming an Indonesian Islamic state (commonly referred to as Darul Islam). Then, in September, local supporters of the Indonesian Communist party (PKI) in the Maduin area attempted a premature coup, which the party leadership hastened to support. The PKI forces were, in the following months, destroyed by pro-government army divisions. The Maduin crisis removed the PKI as a threat to the established republican leadership and, more important, permanently tainted the party as a traitor to the revolution. Only two influences prevented full civil war in this period: a unity in opposition to the Dutch; and the remarkable ability of Sukarno, president of the republic since 1945, to curb opposing elements.

Dutch forces returned to the archipelago in the closing months of 1945, taking control in many areas from Australian, British or Japanese troops. By January 1946 the Dutch reoccupation of Jakarta had proceeded so far as to force the removal of the republic's capital to Yogyakarta. In two "police actions," Dutch forces made shattering advances. The first occurred in July 1947 as Dutch troops occupied much of western Java, Madura and parts of eastern Java. The second took place in December 1948 as the Dutch secured Yogyakarta and captured virtually the entire republican cabinet. Republican forces withdrew into full-scale guerrilla war. But the Dutch position now rapidly weakened as its international standing disintegrated in the face of condemnation by the United Nations and, more particularly, U.S. threats to abandon the reconstruction aid upon which the Dutch economy was then so dependent. A ceasefire was arranged in August 1949; independence negotiations took place in The Hague through to that November, and sovereignty was officially transferred as the year closed. But if independence was now secure, the fundamental divisions of the revolutionary years remained largely unresolved.

In the period 1950–57 Indonesia undertook an abortive experiment in representative parliamentary democracy. That the experiment failed is perhaps not surprising. Indonesia inherited from the preceding Japanese and

Dutch administrations the procedures, assumptions and legal mechanisms of a police state; the largely illiterate Indonesian electorate had yet to free itself from the tradition of authoritarian and paternalistic rule; the political elite was extremely small and had not yet escaped the assumptions of paternalism. Throughout this period the unicameral parliament (the Dewan Perwakilan Rakyat) contained a very large number of political parties—initially 20, but then 28 following parliamentary elections in September 1955. As the cabinet was responsible to parliament, inevitably there were numerous changes of government in this period—each cabinet formed by a realignment of parliamentary pacts, alliances and coalitions. In time the energies and ambitions of Jakarta politicians became increasingly concentrated on parliamentary maneuvering and by the vast opportunities that political and bureaucratic power offered for corruption. The politicking and sheer greed of much of the capital's elite angered and repulsed many influential elements, both in the capital and in important regions beyond. In this period the PKI greatly enhanced its political position, becoming the fourth most powerful party in parliament as a result of the 1955 elections. This was achieved by a concentration on community work and organization at the village level (particularly among nominal Muslim communities), and a relaxation of ideological purity. The PKI had secured a remarkable recovery from Maduin.

While much of the Jakarta elite concentrated on personal advance, the nation came close to disintegration. The period saw a number of serious regional rebellions against central authority, notably in South Sulawesi, in Aceh and in East Sumatra. The rebellions drew part of their initiative from the strong Java-bias of the central administration and in particular from the fact that the economic wealth of the outer islands (notably their foreign-exchange earnings) was being drained away to support an economically stagnant and deficit-ridden Java. The rebellions were also, in many cases, closely linked to internal army politics. This period saw recurrent tension between a central command that sought a rationalization and professionalization of the armed forces, and regional commanders who, not uncommonly, sought to defend their independence and local strength. Many developed local, unorthodox sources of funds to maintain their troops. In late 1956 army commanders in Sumatra took over the civil government; in early 1957 army councils emerged in Kalimantan, North and South Sulawesi, and Maluku, each demanding greater independence from Jakarta. By this time the democratic experiment had clearly failed. The organs of parliamentary rule had proved incapable of establishing stable or effective procedures, corruption was widespread, price inflation was running out of control, territorial unity was under threat, and the economic and social aspirations of Indonesians (heightened by the revolutionary struggle for independence) stood unfulfilled. On March 14, 1957, Sukarno proclaimed martial law.

With the failure of representative parliamentary democracy, Indonesia now entered a period of "guided democracy." This was seen by its proponents, notably Sukarno, as a form of government more suited to the character and traditions of the people than the adversarial structures and procedures found in Western politics. It was based upon a mutual cooperation (*gotong royong*) cabinet, advised by a council of functional groups (youth, workers, peasants, women, intellectuals, and religious and regional interests). At the beginning of this period the single most powerful political force in the country was the army, and its position was further strengthened in December 1957. Following the failure of the United Nations to pass a resolution calling upon the Dutch to negotiate with the Indonesian government over the disputed status of the remaining Dutch territory in the archipelago (Irian), major Dutch businesses were seized and the army was installed to manage them. This gave the army very considerable powers of patronage and funds. Then in February 1958 major rebellions broke out in Sumatra (primarily western Sumatra) and Sulawesi (particularly in the north); they had strong U.S. support, to the extent that in some cases the United States supplied arms to the rebels. The central military command acted decisively, so that by mid-1958 the rebellions were broken, although it took a further three years for them to collapse completely. The army's success secured its domination over all other political forces at this juncture.

The central element in the politics of the guided democracy period was a growing tension between two forces. On the one side was the army, in a position of political, economic and administrative dominance. Ranged against it was Sukarno, increasingly drawn into an alliance with the PKI but also drawing on the support of the air force. Sukarno sought the mobilization of the masses, seeking to sustain the spirit of the revolution. The result was grandiose projects, mass campaigns to secure Irian (transferred from Dutch sovereignty in 1962–63 following U.S. mediation) and against the new Malaysian federation (as of September 1963), and appalling economic mismanagement as well as withdrawal from the international organizations of the capitalist world (United Nations, International Monetary Fund and the World Bank). The PKI, too, sought mass agitation and revolutionary turmoil to sustain its growth. In 1963, excluded from the cabinet by the army's opposition, the PKI sought the political initiative, principally by pushing through the implementation of major land-redistribution programs, particularly in central and eastern Java. The party also urged the creation of a "fifth force," which would involve arming workers and peasants. At the same time the PKI began to infiltrate important army divisions. In late 1964 and early 1965 Indonesia drew itself into a close alliance with the People's Republic of China, which seemed to confirm that the PKI was on the threshold of gaining total dominance. These tensions exploded on the night of September 30–October 1, 1965, when a number of disaffected army divisions with PKI contacts attempted a coup. It was an extraordinarily incompetent—and murderous—attempt, which was rapidly crushed by the central command, Major General Suharto assuming the dominant role.

Suharto immediately pushed forward the opinion that the attempted coup was a PKI plot, a view eagerly taken up by the PKI's many enemies. A ferocious anti-Communist witch hunt swept the country in late 1965 and early 1966, claiming the lives of possibly 500,000 PKI supporters. The party was obilerated. Suharto then moved rapidly to impose economic and political stability—to establish the "new order." Economic discipline was imposed to bring inflation, rampant in the last years of Sukarno's old order, under control: With the return of economic stability and the establishment of competent management of the economy, foreign private investment and international aid was expected to return to Indonesia. In the search for political stability, in March 1967 the People's Consultative Assembly relieved Sukarno of political power (he died in 1970) and appointed Suharto acting president. He became president, without qualification, one year later and was confirmed in this position by the Assembly in 1973, 1978, 1983 and 1988. The position of the new regime was further secured by the transformation of the Sekber Golkar, the army's instrument established in 1964 to organize functional groups of civil servants, students and farmers, into an electoral machine. The Golkar was triumphant in parliamentary elections in 1971 and 1977. Internationally, Suharto sought further stability by ending the confrontation with Malaysia, bringing Indonesia back into the United Nations (1966) and securing the position of Indonesia as a founder-member of ASEAN (1967).

But the stability of the new order could not hide serious tensions. Opposition to the Suharto regime came from Islamic interest, which gained assertiveness from the political resurgence of Islam in the 1970s; from students and intellectuals, concerned by the high degree of intellectual and political repressions exercised by the regime; and from those, found throughout society, who had been angered by the regime's endemic financial corruption (which reached right into the president's inner circle) and the mounting incidence of economic mismanagement.

ECONOMY

Background: By the mid-1960s, after 15 years of acute political instability and serious economic mismanagement, the Indonesian economy had virtually collapsed. The budget deficit approached 50% of government expenditure, the annual rate of inflation was racing above 650%, the foreign-exchange reserves would cover only a few weeks of imports, and the level of external debt was dangerously high. A principal concern of the new-order administration of Suharto was thus to impose economic stability. Government revenue and expenditure were brought into balance, and stringent monetary policies were pursued (together, these actions reduced the annual rate of inflation to approximately 10% by the close of the 1960s); the rupiah was devalued and the complex structure of exchange controls was swept aside; measures were introduced to encourage private foreign investment; the external debt was rescheduled and foreign aid resumed. By the end of the 1960s the Suharto administration's economic strategy moved on to the promotion of growth and development. The latter was sought through a series of Five-Year Plans (known by the acronym *Repelita*), the first of which commenced in 1969. These plans represented primarily guidelines for public-sector investment (focused on agricultural development and infrastructural construction), although they also sought to guide and encourage private investment (focused on industrial growth and the expansion of mining). In the 1970s the Indonesian economy achieved an impressive growth in real GDP (frequently over 7% a year) to an important degree as a consequence of the fourfold increase in oil prices at the beginning of that decade; but the 1980s saw slower growth, significantly a reflection of the effect of lower oil prices on the world market. However, the development task remained an immense one. For two decades since the declaration of independence essential infrastructural rehabilitation, the promotion of agricultural advance and the encouragement of industrial investment had, in effect, been abandoned; and growth, once achieved, would have to race against rapid population growth (well over 2% a year) and an acutely high density of population on the inner islands of Java and Madura and Bali.

Agriculture: Agriculture is the single most important sector of the Indonesian economy, accounting for 23.6% of GDP and 54.7% of employment in 1985. The sector has been the focus of the most intense development effort since the mid-1960s. Within the agricultural sector the most important component (in terms of the creation of income and employment) is the cultivation of food crops for local consumption; within the food-crop sector, rice (cultivated in Java, Bali, southern Sulawesi and parts of Sumatra) is by far the most important. In the early 1960s Indonesia was heavily dependent on imports to make good a serious shortfall in domestic rice production. Under the new order the government placed a very high priority on the expansion of domestic cultivation, through encouraging improvements in farming practices and increased use of (newly available) high-yield seeds and chemical fertilizers, and through heavy investment in irrigation facilities. By 1984 the production of milled rice was more than double the 1969 level, an increase achieved partly through an expansion in harvested area but principally through dramatic improvements in yields. In 1984–85 Indonesia reached self-sufficiency in rice production. However, the financial and economic cost was extremely high, as the government had heavily subsidized both rice production (by establishing a support price to be defended by its food-marketing agency) and the cultivators' yield-increasing inputs. After 1985 the expansion of rice production slowed sharply as the government (under budgetary pressure) reduced its rice-related subsidies.

Indonesia is an important producer of a large number of cash crops for export—tea, sugar, tobacco, copra and, most important, rubber, palm oil and coffee. This sector was largely neglected in the government's development efforts until the late 1970s, when the world oil market (and thus the value of Indonesia's oil revenues) sharply weakened. The 1980s saw a considerable expansion in Indonesian production of palm oil and coffee in particular, although this took place at a time of slipping commodity markets. Timber is also an important production, and it constituted the third most valuable export commodity in the later 1970s. In the early 1980s, concerned about increasing the element of domestic value added in wood exports, the government reduced the export of unsawn logs; export in this form was banned altogether in 1985. The administration also took steps to sharply limit indiscriminate logging, and reforestation was stressed.

119

Petroleum and natural gas: As world petroleum prices soared in the 1970s Indonesia emerged as a major producer (and powerful voice within the Organization of Petroleum Exporting Countries). Since the middle of that decade petroleum and natural gas have dominated the country's export income: Between 1980 and 1985, even as world oil prices slipped, they accounted on average for more than 76% of total export earnings. Exploitation is administered through the state-owned oil company, Pertamina; extraction is undertaken primarily by foreign oil companies as contractors of Pertamina. The principal feature of the exploitation contracts is a provision for the sharing of profits or the sharing of production between the oil company and Pertamina. Under regulations still effective in 1987, 65.91% of production was to be surrendered to Pertamina; the companies' balance of 34.09% remained fully taxable. The early years of the 1980s saw a contraction in exploration and investment, partly a reflection of falling oil prices but also a consequence of the relatively small size of Indonesian oil fields and, in many cases, their geographical remoteness. Indonesian production was, on average, 495 million barrels a year between 1982 and 1985; it had been 615 million barrels in 1977. Recoverable petroleum reserves were estimated to be around 8,300 million barrels; the total reserves were expected to be much higher.

The commercial exploitation of natural gas began in 1977–78, and in the 1980s liquefied natural gas established itself as the country's second most valuable export. Most is exported to Japan, while South Korea and Taiwan are increasingly important customers.

Mining: Indonesia is the world's second-largest exporter of tin, production being undertaken on Bangka, Belitung and Singkep, principally by the state-owned company PT Tambang Timah. Production dwindled in the early 1980s (to 22,414 tons in 1985) as the world tin market remained weak. Indonesia is also an important producer of bauxite, nickel, copper and (particularly in the late 1980s) gold.

Manufacturing: In the mid-1960s Indonesia's manufacturing sector was limited, essentially comprising the production of handicrafts and textiles. It accounted for less than 10% of GDP. The new-order government gave a high priority to industrialization, partly through the establishment of state-owned enterprises but also through encouraging private (domestic and foreign) investment in modern manufacturing. An import-substitution strategy was pursued. This demanded the erection of notably high-tariff and nontariff restrictions against competing imports, and the result too frequently was to maintain inefficiencies and high costs in local industry. In the late 1980s Indonesia's industrial sector embraced the production of food and beverages, textiles, car assembly, electrical goods (this was the private sector, frequently in joint ventures with foreign capital), chemicals, cement, fertilizers and machinery (where the state had a prominent role). Increasingly, emphasis was given to the establishment of processing facilities for raw materials produced locally—rubber, palm oil, woods, petroleum and bauxite. There was also a small but strategically important state-owned high-technology sector.

Foreign trade: With the contraction in the value of Indonesian petroleum and natural gas exports through the 1980s, the trade surplus narrowed, from more than U.S. $7 billion in 1981 to less than $2 billion in 1986. In addition, Indonesia had a consistent invisible deficit, primarily reflecting heavy interest payment on external debt and high profit repatriation by foreign capital. In almost every year of the 1980s Indonesia's current account was in deficit.

Exports are dominated by petroleum and natural gas. Also important are rubber, coffee, tin, palm oil and processed woods. Imports are dominated by capital and intermediate goods; consumer imports (notably of rice and of consumption articles now produced locally) have sharply declined. Japan is the most important trading partner, accounting, in 1986, for 44.9% of Indonesia's exports and 29.2% of its imports. The United States was the second most valuable trading partner. In July 1987 foreign-exchange reserves were $5.3 billion; public external debt in 1987 was estimated at $43 billion, making Indonesia the sixth most indebted of the world's developing states.

Employment: Of an economically active population of 62,457,138 (as of October 31, 1985), 54.7% were employed in agriculture, hunting, forestry and fishing; 9.3% in manufacturing; 15.0% in trade, restaurants and hotels; 13.3% in community, social and personal services. The unemployment rate revealed by that census was given as 0.09%; the level of open and disguised unemployment was clearly much higher.

Price trends: The consumer price index (April 1977–March 1978 = 100) in 1986 was 262.9.

SOCIAL SERVICES

Welfare: In the mid-1980s some 10% of the population (civil servants, their spouses and children) was covered by health insurance financed through a modest salary deduction. There are two social insurance plans run by state corporations: These provide job-related accident insurance and provident funds for pensions. These plans cover employees of private companies employing more than 100 workers, state-owned corporations and banks.

Health services: Basic services are provided through public-health centers (of which there were 5,639 in 1986–87, 80% headed by physicians), sub-health centers (17,302) and mobile health units (3,516). As well as seeking to expand the number of centers and units and the medical and paramedical personnel to staff them, the government has placed emphasis on improving the nutrition of vulnerable groups (through the distribution of vitamins in tablet form) and increasing the provision of clean water (17,000 drilled wells were constructed in 1985–86). In 1986–87 Indonesia had 703 general hospitals (of which 115 were military hospitals and 182 were private hospitals); in the same year there were 705 specialist hospitals (of which no fewer than 558 were private hospitals). In 1985 Indonesia had 295 pharmaceutical plants, and the industry continued to expand.

121

Housing: In relation to Indonesia's vast population and rapidly expanding housing needs, the provision of public housing is modest. During the three years from 1984 to 85, only 38,474 public units were constructed in the whole of Indonesia. Government resources are also committed to village improvement: constructing roads, supplying clean water, providing washing facilities and setting up plants to produce building materials. In 1986–87 housing rehabilitation was carried out in 910 villages in 26 provinces.

EDUCATION

Indonesia is very close to achieving compulsory primary education. In 1986–87, 99.5% of children aged between seven and 12 (that is, 25,150,000 children) were accommodated in primary schools or Islamic primary schools *(madrasah ibtidaiyah)*. The provision of secondary education is notably less extensive. In 1986–87 there were 6,029,000 pupils attending junior high schools and 3,742,000 attending senior high schools (including vocational schools, training colleges and sports-teachers' training colleges). In that same year there were 1,278,400 students in higher education, implying a participation rate (in the 19–24 age-group) of 6.8%. There are 49 state universities and institutions of higher learning, and 637 private ones. The principal universities are the University of Indonesia (Jakarta), the Institute of Technology (Bandung), the Institute of Agriculture (Bogor), Gajah Mada University (Yogyakarta) and Airlangga University (Surabaya).

MASS MEDIA

The press

Dailies: The main dailies include *Kompas,* 415,000; *Pos Kota,* 250,000; *Berita Buana,* 150,000; *Suara Medeka,* 145,000; *Merdeka,* 130,000; *Suara Karya,* 100,000. Each is published in Java and appears in Bahasa Indonesia. The principal English-language dailies are *Indonesia Times,* 35,000; *Jakarta Post,* 16,400.

Periodicals: These include *Buana Minggu* (w), 193,450; *Tempo* (w), 150,000; *Intisari* (m), 141,000; *Femina* (w), 130,000; *Matra* (m), 100,000; *Ekonomi Indonesia* (fortnightly), 20,000; *Indonesia Magazine* (m), 15,000; *Horison* (m), 4,000.

Broadcasting: The state-owned Radio Republic Indonesia (RRI), founded in September 1945, is the largest radio network in the country. As well as having a very extensive domestic service, RRI also provides external broadcasts in Japanese, Thai, German, Spanish, English, French, Arabic, Chinese and Malay. Televisi Republik Indonesia, the state-owned television service, came into full operation in August 1962. National television programs can now be seen in all the provincial capitals and in most district capitals. In 1986–87 there were 6,393,399 registered sets, and the potential audience was about 115 million. In that same year about 80% of the programs were domestically produced. Of the programs broadcast, 28% consisted of news and information, 26% of education and religion, and 44% of entertainment, arts and culture.

General Leonardus Benyamin Murdani. Born in eastern Java on October 2, 1932, Murdani's military career began in the early 1950s. In the late 1960s and early 1970s he had diplomatic postings in Kuala Lumpur and then Seoul; from the mid-1970s he held senior positions in the Indonesian intelligence and security service. In the 1980s he was appointed as commander in chief of the Indonesian armed forces and later as minister of defense and security. Murdani is a Roman Catholic.

Suharto. Born in a village near Yogyakarta, central Java, on June 8, 1921, Suharto underwent his basic military training at cadet schools in the early 1940s. He served in several companies and regiments during the war of independence against the Dutch from 1945 to 1949. During the 1950s and first half of the 1960s Suharto rose through the army command, attaining the rank of major general. He assumed leadership of the army in the immediate aftermath of the September 30, 1965, attempted coup; he was raised to the rank of general in July 1966. With the removal of Sukarno from power in March 1967, Suharto was appointed acting president. He was inaugurated as president on March 27, 1968, and has been reelected to that position in 1973, 1978, 1983 and 1988. He dominated Indonesian political life, essentially unchallenged, throughout that period.

Dr. Johannes Baptista Sumarlin. Born in eastern Java on December 7, 1932, Sumarlin is a technocrat, trained in economics at the University of California (1960) and the University of Pittsburgh (1968). He has held a large number of positions in government, being concurrently minister of state for national development planning and chairman of the National Planning Development Board in the mid-1980s. He was then appointed minister of finance. Sumarlin is a Roman Catholic.

General Try Sutrisno. Born in Surabaya on November 15, 1935, his military career began in the late 1950s, and he subsequently rose through the army command to his position as army chief of staff. With an impeccable Javanese, Muslim and military background, he was widely seen as the most likely successor to Suharto.

NORTH KOREA

SOUTH KOREA

Korea Strait

TSUSHIMA IS.

Kita-Kyushu

Shimonoseki

Fukuoka

Sasebo

Kurume

Nagasaki

Omuta

Kumamoto

KYUSHU

Kagoshima

Miyazaki

Bungo Str.

SHIKOKU

Kochi

Matsuyama

Takamatsu

Himeji

Wakayama

OKI IS.

Matsue

Tottori

Hiroshima

Kure

Okayama

Kobe

Osaka

Sakai

Kyoto

SEA OF JAPAN

Takaoka

Kanazawa

Toyama

Fukui

Nagano

Gifu

Nagoya

Hamamatsu

Shizuoka

Mt. Fuji

Sado I.

Kiso R.

Niigata

Akita

Yamagata

Sendai

Iwaki

Maebashi

Utsunomiya

Hitachi

HONSHU

Arakawa-hosuiro R.

Tokyo

Yokohama

Yokosuka

IZU IS.

Aomori

Morioka

Hachinohe

Kitakami R.

Tsugaru Str.

Hakodate

Muroran

Sapporo

HOKKAIDO

Ishikari R.

Asahikawa

Abashiri

Kushiro

PACIFIC OCEAN

EAST CHINA SEA

TOKARA IS.

AMAMI IS.

OKINAWA IS.

RYUKYU IS.

JAPAN

100 Miles
100 Kms

200 Miles
200 Kms

JAPAN

GEOGRAPHY

Features: Japan is an archipelago consisting of four large islands—Honshu, Hokkaido, Kyushu and Shikoku—and about 3,000 smaller islands. The archipelago forms part of the so-called Circum-Pacific Belt across the Pacific Ocean, which comprises a chain of islands extending from the Aleutian Islands in the north to the Philippines in the south. These islands are geologically very young (from the Tertiary period), which accounts for frequent volcanic activity. In the north, Japan is bounded by the Sea of Okhotsk, where the narrow La Pérouse Strait separates it from the southern tip of the Soviet island, Sakhalin. The Sea of Japan is on the west, and the 120-mile/190-km.-wide Korea Strait lies between South Korea and Japan. To the south extends the East China Sea, and to the east the Pacific Ocean. Several groups of smaller islands, including the islands of Okinawa and Iwo Jima, were occupied by the United States during World War II, but they were returned to Japan in 1968 and 1972, respectively. Several islands just off Hokkaido (Kunashir, Shikotan, Etorofu and the Habomai), forming a southern fringe of the Kuril Islands, have been held by the Soviet Union since 1945, but Japan does not recognize the Soviet claims. Because of this unresolved dispute, Japan and the Soviet Union have not yet signed a peace treaty formally ending World War II.

Over two-thirds of the land area of Japan is mountainous, with the major mountain chains located on central Honshu. These are the Japanese Alps, consisting of the Hida, Kiso and Akaishi mountains. The highest peak, Mount Fuji, east of the Akaishi range, is an extinct volcano; it rises to 12,388 feet/3,776 m. More than 20 other peaks are over 9,800 feet/3,000 m. The forested mountains are extremely rugged, with steep slopes and sharp ridges. The main areas of active volcanoes and thermal springs are in Hokkaido, in northern and central Honshu, and in southern Kyushu. Japan has over 60 active volcanoes; on the average, 1,500 tremors are registered each year. The last major earthquake occurred in 1923, when over half of Tokyo and virtually the whole of Yokohama were destroyed by a series of temblors and resulting fires, and almost 100,000 people perished. There is a multitude of thermal springs; and the rivers are very short and often torrential, carving deep ravines in the slopes. The Shinano River in north-central Honshu, the longest in the archipelago (228 miles/367 km.), flows into the Sea of Japan. A distinct feature of Japanese geography is the scarcity of lowlands, which represent only about 29% of the whole area. Some

125

of them are located between mountain ridges in the interior of the islands, but most are coastal plains formed by river-borne alluvial deposits. In these relatively small areas lives the population of the seventh most populous country in the world; and they are also the location of the world's most sophisticated electronics industry setup. The largest plain, in the Tokyo Bay region on Honshu, covers only about 2,500 sq. miles/6,500 sq. km. (approximately twice the size of the state of Rhode Island), but has a population of some 35 million (1985).

The archipelago lies in the East Asian monsoon climate belt, and therefore the weather is generally mild and very humid. Two ocean currents affect the climatic conditions: the warm Japan Current (Kuroshio) flowing from the south along the Japanese Pacific coast, and the cold Kuril Current (Oyashio) from the north. Their juncture east of Honshu forms a prime fishing area. Winters on the Sea of Japan coastland are characterized by heavy snow, but on the Pacific coast winter temperatures are warmer than in similar latitudes. Variations of temperature also depend on longitude: Winters on Hokkaido are quite cold, while the climate of the southernmost Ryukyu Islands is subtropical. The tropical cyclones, or typhoons, usually arrive in early fall and often cause considerable damage, particularly to the rice harvest.

Area: 145,862 sq. miles/377,781 sq. km.

Mean max. and min. temperatures: Tokyo, Honshu (35°40'N, 139°45'E; 17.4 ft/5.3 m.) 77.4°F/25.2°C (July), 40.5°F/4.7°C (Jan.); Osaka, Honshu (34°40'N, 135°30'E; 75.8 ft/23.1 m.) 80.6°F/27°C (July), 42.1° F/5.6°C (Jan.); Hiroshima, Honshu (34°23'N, 132°27'E; 95.5 ft/29.1 m.), 78°F/25.6°C (July), 39.7°F/4.3°C (Jan.); Kagoshima, Kyushu (31° 37'N, 131°32'E; 13.8 ft/4.2 m) 81°F/27.2°C (July), 44.6°F/7°C (Jan.); Sapporo, Hokkaido (43°05'N, 141°21'E; 56.6 ft/17.2 m.) 68.4°F/20.2°C (July), 23.2°F/−4.9°C (Jan.).

Relative humidity: Tokyo 66%; Osaka 67%; Hiroshima 73%; Kagoshima 75%; Sapporo 73%.

Mean annual rainfall: Tokyo 57.4 in/1,458 mm.; Osaka 47.4 in/1.204 mm.; Hiroshima, 59.2 in/1,503 mm.; Kagoshima 74.3 in/1,887 mm.; Sapporo 44.4 in/1,128 mm.

POPULATION

Total population (1987 est.): 122,264,000; 121,048,923 (census of October 1985).

Major islands and cities: Islands (1985 census): Honshu (96,687,700), Kyushu (13,276,000), Hokkaido (5,679,500), Shikoku (4,227,400). Cities (at October 1, 1986): TOKYO (8,354,615; metropolitan area, 30,000,000), Yokohama (2,992,926), Osaka (2,636,249; metropolitan area, 14,000,000), Nagoya (2,116,381; metropolitan area, 10,000,000), Sapporo (1,542,979),

Kyoto (1,479,218); Kobe (1,410,834), Fukuoka, Kyushu (1,160,440), Kawasaki (1,099,624), Kitakyushu (1,056,402), Hiroshima (1,044,118).

Distribution: The three metropolitan areas, Tokyo, Osaka and Nagoya, account for about 45% of total population. Japan is the most densely inhabited country in Asia, with 832 persons per sq. mile/321 per sq. km.; and if population density is correlated with cultivable land area (15% of the total area), the figures rise to 5,630 persons per sq. mile/2,175 per sq. km. Over three-fourths of the people live in cities and their suburbs; the latter began to develop and grow in the 1960s. Honshu is the most populous island, with about four-fifths of the Japanese living there, while Hokkaido in the north is inhabited by less than 5% of the total population. Hokkaido is also the home of some 20,000 Ainu, a distinct native people whose physiognomy is similar to that of Caucasians. As of December 31, 1986, there were 867,237 foreigners registered in Japan, over three-fourths of whom were Koreans. The number of U.S. citizens living in Japan at that time was 30,695.

Language: Japanese is generally considered a separate language, with some ties to the Malayo-Polynesian language family. Japanese script is based on Chinese ideographs and consists of two systems: *kanji* characters, introduced from China after the 4th century A.D. and adapted to correspond to Japanese pronunciation; and a system of syllabic characters *(kana)*, developed in the 9th century, which are used for foreign words, grammatical inflections and function words. Since the end of World War II, about 2,000 Chinese characters have been standardized and are now generally used. A distinctive feature of the Japanese language is the intricate system of more than 15 personal pronouns and adjectives (corresponding to the English "I, me, my, you, your"), which are used according to the social relationship between the speaker and the person spoken to, their level of intimacy, the formality of the speech, and the age and sex of the speaker. Many Japanese, especially of the younger generation, speak English. The language of the Ainu is virtually extinct.

Religion: Shinto (meaning The Way of the Gods), a polytheistic religion that venerates historical figures, family ancestors, natural phenomena and various spirits, was a state religion between 1868 and 1947, when a complete separation of church and state was instituted. Some 108 million Japanese belong to various Shinto cults. Shintoism is not exclusive and coexists with Buddhism, which had been introduced from Korea in the mid-6th century A.D. The number of Buddhist believers is about 93 million. Roman Catholic missionaries came to Japan in the 16th century; there were over 1.4 million Christians in 1986. Many small religious groups (the so-called new religions) have emerged in the modern period, some apparently as a response to the modernization and Westernization of Japan. The largest of them is the Buddhist-oriented Soka Gakkai (Value Creation Society), which was associated with the Komeito (Clean Government) political party until the 1970 official separation of politics and religion. Historically, Japanese ethics, attitudes and numerous customs have been greatly influenced also by Confucianism.

Japan is governed under the constitution of 1947, which superseded the constitution of 1889 that transformed Japan into a constitutional monarchy. The emperor is the head of state, symbolizing the unity of the people and the Japanese tradition, but he has no governing powers. Inspired by the example of U.S. democracy, the constitution expressly renounces the use of war; provides for the separation of legislative, executive and judicial powers; and guarantees all fundamental human rights.

Head of state: Emperor Akihito. *Prime minister:* Toshiki Kaifu.

Executive: The chief executive is the prime minister, who is selected from the Diet, the bicameral legislative body, and appointed (as a formality) by the emperor. The prime minister selects a cabinet consisting of 20 ministers, at least half of whom must also be members of the Diet. The cabinet is responsible to the Diet and if the House of Representatives passes a no-confidence motion or rejects a confidence motion, all the cabinet members must resign.

Legislature: The legislative branch consists of the Diet, which has two houses: the House of Representatives (512 members) and the House of Councillors (252 members). The former, the lower house—whose members are elected for four-year terms—controls the budget, approves international treaties and has primary overall political power. The upper house, in which the terms are six years (with half of the members elected every three years), replaced the former House of Peers. Suffrage is universal, with the voting age set at 20 and a residency requirement of three months. The voting right of women was codified in the 1947 constitution. An electoral reform, aimed at assuring equal representation for voters, was undertaken in 1986.

Political parties: The Liberal-Democratic party (LDP), which represents the conservative electorate, has held power in Japan since its formation in 1955; and in the elections of 1986 it gained 59% of the seats in the House of Representatives. The characteristic feature of the LDP is its factions. From the early 1970s until 1987 the most powerful of these was the faction led by Kakuei Tanaka, which survived the political misfortunes of its leader (who had been implicated in a bribery scandal) and was displaced from its prominence only after Tanaka became ill in 1985. Other factions at the time of the 1986 election were led by Zenko Suzuki, Yasuhiro Nakasone, Takeo Fukuda and Toshio Komoto. In July 1987 a new faction emerged, led by Noboru Takeshita and consisting mostly of former members of the Tanaka faction.

The largest opposition party is the Japan Socialist party (JSP), which professes classical Marxism and speaks for the working class. In the early 1960s the JSP had won about 30% of the seats in the House of Representatives, but its support gradually declined and in November 1986 the party received only 17% of the votes. Accepting the blame for this defeat, the party leader, Masashi Ishibashi, resigned in the summer of 1986 and was replaced by Takako Doi, the first woman to be chosen a party chairperson in Japanese history. The third largest party in the 1986 elections was the Komeito party, which received 11% of the votes. Two other parties represented in the lower house of the Diet are the Democratic Socialist and Communist parties. Altogether, there are over 10,000 registered political parties in Japan, but most of them are concerned with only local matters.

Local government: Japan is divided into 47 prefectures, each headed by a popularly elected governor. Smaller units include 652 cities, 2,002 towns and 596 villages. Mayors, village heads and representative assemblies in each prefecture, city, town and village are elected by the local electorate. Although local governments supervise schools, taxation, public health, environmental policies and social welfare, the national government exercises central control over the majority of public matters. The police force throughout Japan has been centralized since 1954.

Judicial system: The judicial system consists of a Supreme Court, eight regional higher courts, district prefectural courts and a number of special (such as family and juvenile) and local courts. The chief justice is designated by the cabinet and appointed by the emperor, and the other 14 justices are appointed by the cabinet. All Supreme Court justices have to be confirmed in popular elections, and every 10 years thereafter their appointments must be approved by the electorate. Judges of lower courts are appointed by the cabinet, and the appointments have to be popularly confirmed each 10 years.

RECENT HISTORY

Japan entered into the modern era in 1868 when young members of the military oligarchy dismantled the shogunate system, installed Emperor Meiji on the throne, and launched a vast program of industrialization and modernization. This so-called Meiji Restoration, under the slogan "A rich nation, a strong army," transformed Japan from a feudal state into a major modern power. In 1873 universal military service was established, and several years later the Imperial Council abolished the official status of the samurai—the traditional warrior class. The first constitution, promulgated in 1889, established the bicameral Diet and a civilian cabinet headed by a prime minister.

The Meiji modernizers also did away with the last vestiges of centuries-old Japanese isolationism. It had first been breached as early as 1853, when a squadron of U.S. warships under the command of Commodore Matthew Perry landed in Tokyo Bay and Perry received permission to send a U.S. consul to Japan. Within the next decades Japan opened its doors to Western influences and ideas, imported Western technologies and concluded friendship treaties with such countries as the United States, Britain and the Netherlands. It was Russia and China, however, that were to play a major role in Japanese foreign affairs between the 1890s and 1930s. The first

Sino-Japanese War, over Korea, was fought in 1894–95; the Russo-Japanese war, over Manchuria, followed in 1904–05. Victorious in both these encounters, Japan greatly increased its sphere of influence and gained tremendous military prestige. During World War I, Japan was on the side of the Allies and became their major supplier of ammunition and ships. Its economic development was further enhanced by increasing demand from Asia and Africa, which could no longer rely on British and German exporters. The war also proved beneficial for Japan politically because as an ally of Britain it was asked to destroy German warships protecting German interests in China; this ultimately led to Japan's occupation of the Shantung (now Shandong) province in China. By 1922 Japan had been recognized as a major Asian power and its navy had become the world's third largest, after that of Britain and the United States.

The 1920s were a decade of rapid economic growth and of the rise of *zaibatsu*, large financial and industrial corporations controlled by the descendants of Meiji modernizers. It was during this time that political parties began to be more active. There were numerous antigovernment demonstrations and riots because the economic boom resulted in much hardship as well; most political and economic dissent was ruthlessly suppressed by the police. Nevertheless, an important step in the gradual democratization of Japan was taken in 1925 when the government enacted universal suffrage for males.

Soon after the 1926 ascension to throne of Emperor Hirohito Japan was hit by the worldwide economic depression. The economic dislocations and discontent led to political violence (two prime ministers were assassinated in the early 1930s), to the rise of radical nationalistic groups, and to the reemergence of the military who felt that Japan should become "master of Asia." Without the knowledge of the country's political leaders, the Japanese armed forces took advantage of the political disarray in China and in 1931 invaded Manchuria. Next year the military proclaimed Manchuria an "independent" state named Manchukuo and installed a puppet government. The occupation of Manchuria was just the beginning of a protracted conflict between Japan and China, which escalated into another Sino-Japanese War in 1937 and lasted until 1945.

Meanwhile, Japan found itself embroiled in larger world politics. After signing military pacts with Germany and Italy in 1940, Japanese military leaders already began to plan an attack on the U.S. Pacific Fleet in order to prevent the United States from interfering with Japanese "liberation" of European colonies in East Asia (French Indochina, British Malaya and Burma and the Dutch East Indies). In April 1941 Japan concluded a nonaggression treaty with the Soviet Union to postpone any military encounter with that country. On December 7, 1941, Japanese bombers attacked Pearl Harbor on Hawaii and destroyed or severely damaged most of the U.S. ships and aircraft stationed there. Other U.S. military installations in the Pacific, including two airfields near Manila in the Philippines and bases on Guam, Midway and Wake, were successfully attacked the same day. In January 1942 Japan captured the Philippines, and by the following spring it had conquered a vast area stretching from Malaya eastward to the Pacific islands of Wake and Guam and southward to the Dutch East Indies (present-day Indonesia). The U.S. armed forces, however, soon struck back, and in early May 1942, in the Battle of the Coral Sea off New Guinea, stopped the Japanese expansion. The next three years saw a number of fierce battles (at Midway, Guadalcanal, Leyte Gulf) and a steady American advance. In January 1945 the Philippines were recaptured. Meanwhile, in May 1945, peace in Europe was concluded, and the United States decided to use the newly developed atomic bomb to force Japan to surrender. Two bombs were dropped in August 1945, on Hiroshima and on Nagasaki, causing the death of about 340,000 people. On August 14, 1945, Japan unconditionally surrendered to the Allied powers.

The U.S. military occupation of Japan, headed by Gen. Douglas MacArthur, lasted from 1945 to 1952. It was a period of far-reaching changes in Japanese society, politics and economy. Japan had lost over 3 million people during the war, and when the hostilities ended it was economically devastated, with most of its industry in shambles. The American occupation administration, working through a capable Japanese bureaucracy, set up a course of massive rebuilding of the country. With contributions of huge amounts of American aid and as a result of the Japanese tradition of hard work, the economic recovery was fast and impressive. It was also helped by the Korean War of 1950–52, when Japan became the major base for the United States, providing airfields, harbors, repair and medical services, ships and other matériel. Politically, the aim of the U.S. occupation was the demilitarization and democratization of Japan. After military leaders and others were executed for war crimes and acts of cruelty, the power of the military oligarchy was effectively broken. In 1947 a new constitution was promulgated, renouncing the war, abolishing the divinity of the emperor and proclaiming the sovereignty of the people. With pragmatism, tremendous energy and an admiration for the United States that no one could have imagined a few years earlier, the Japanese started to transform their country. Relations with the West were codified in a peace treaty in 1951. At the same time Japan concluded a bilateral security treaty with the United States, which stipulated that U.S. armed forces would retain military bases in Japan and would assist Japan in case of aggression. The state of war between the Soviet Union and Japan was ended by a mutual agreement, but because of the unresolved dispute over the "Northern Islands" off Hokkaido a peace treaty is yet to be concluded. Japan also normalized relations with its Asian neighbors. In 1965, diplomatic ties with South Korea were established, and in 1972 Japan established full relations with the People's Republic of China. A treaty for economic aid and investment between Japan and China was agreed upon in 1988. Although the 1972 recognition of the People's Republic of China led to termination of formal diplomatic links with Taiwan, economic and cultural ties with the latter country were hardly affected in any negative way. When prime minister Takeshita announced in 1988 that his government would spend U.S. $5 billion in foreign aid over the next five years (and thus become the world's largest donor of foreign aid), it became clear that Japan intends to play a global economic role, as befits a nation with the second largest GNP in the world.

For a short period in 1947 socialists controlled the government, but apart from this postwar Japan has been governed by conservatives. Two leading conservative parties, the Liberals and the Democrats, merged into a single party in 1955 and since that time the LDP has been the predominant political force in Japan. Eisaku Sato, who served as prime minister from 1964 until 1972, was awarded the Nobel Peace Prize in 1974 for his "reconciliation policy that contributed to a stabilization of conditions in the Pacific area." The first Olympic Games to be held in Asia took place in Tokyo in the summer of 1964. Six years later the Japan World Exposition was held in Osaka, and in 1972 Sapporo hosted the Winter Olympics. The thousands of visitors to these events were impressed by the highly developed Japanese technology, especially in transportation.

Kakuei Tanaka, Sato's successor, was in office during the first major oil crisis in 1973, which Japan withstood by making its industry more efficient and less energy-intensive. Politically, however, Tanaka fared worse. He had to resign in 1974; and in 1976 he was charged with and later found guilty of accepting bribes from the Lockheed Corporation. Tanaka was succeeded as prime minister by Takeo Miki, Takeo Fukuda, Masayoshi Ohira, Zenko Suzuki and in 1982 by Yasuhiro Nakasone. Nakasone differed from the previous prime ministers by his forceful, almost flamboyant style, and his great international visibility. He visited the United States, Australia, Southeast Asia and Europe, promoting political and economic ties. Domestically, he concentrated on restructuring government-run enterprises; on fiscal reform, aimed at eliminating the deficit; and on liberalization of the educational system. In 1987, Nakasone stepped down (after an unsuccessful bid for another term) and Noboru Takeshita became the new prime minister. Takeshita introduced a major tax reform that had eluded his predecessor: In 1988, both houses of the Diet approved bills overhauling the entire tax system, including a sales tax on goods and services which was balanced by cuts in personal and corporate income tax rates. Takeshita's political victory was overshadowed, however, by a scandal involving many highly placed politicians and business executives who bought shares in a real estate company before they were publicly traded and thus made huge profits. The scandal eventually led to Takeshita's resignation. He was succeeded briefly by Sosuke Uno, who was himself forced to resign by another scandal. Toshiki Kaifu has been prime minister since August 1989.

Emperor Hirohito died in January 1989, and was succeeded by Crown Prince Akihito. Although the war has not been forgotten and the role of the emperor and the military during the 1930s and 1940s continues to provoke debate, the fact that 163 nations sent delegations to Hirohito's funeral clearly shows that the new Japan has come to be accepted as an important and respected member of the international community.

Defense: Although Article 9 of the 1947 constitution expressly renounces the use of war, Japan established a national reserve force during the Korean

War, at the recommendation of General MacArthur. Renamed the Self-Defense Force in 1954, it numbered 246,000 in 1987. As Japan's economic strength kept rising, the United States began to press the Japanese leaders to increase military spending and to begin participating more fully in the defense of the Pacific. The issue is very sensitive and any hint of militaristic attitude provokes apprehension in Japan's Asian neighbors. Nevertheless, military outlays have increased in recent years; but because the economy has grown as well, they continue to represent only about 1% of the GNP.

ECONOMY

Background: Japan has virtually no mineral resources, but its economy is the most advanced in Asia and the second largest in the Organization for Economic Cooperation and Development. It was the first Asian country in which large-scale industrialization took place, leading to the rise and growth of an urban middle class. During the U.S. occupation (1945–52), Japan completed an agricultural land reform; organized a modern trade union system and paved the way for stable industrial relations between management and workers; introduced the policy of high investment (up to 20% of GNP); adopted new industrial techniques, mostly inspired by U.S. technologies; and greatly enhanced the educational system.

In the 1950s the Japanese miracle began: The real growth rates (adjusted for inflation) were 5% to 12% between 1955 and 1965; and by the early 1970s Japan had become the largest non-Communist power after the United States in total value of GNP. Because of the international oil crisis, the Japanese economy slowed down in 1973–75 (the GNP fell by 1.8% in 1974), which led to a reappraisal of economic policies. Japan eliminated a number of energy-intensive enterprises, greatly increased efficiency and concentrated on energy conservation. The second energy crisis, in the early 1980s, caused some slowing in the rate of growth, but it was smaller than in most other industrial countries. Throughout the 1980s Japan's economy has been characterized by a great surplus of exports over imports. The United States and other Western powers have criticized Japan for its protectionist trade policies, and by 1986 Japan began to react to this pressure by limiting some of its exports and by emphasizing domestic consumption. Other measures intended to decrease Japan's trade surpluses, such as devaluation of the U.S. dollar against the yen, failed to produce the desired results, and as the decade approached its end Japan continued to be the world's greatest net exporter.

Japanese economic development is greatly helped by its modern transportation system. Probably the best known among the transport facilities is the Bullet Train (Shinkansen line), which was opened in 1964 and now runs between Tokyo and Fukuoka at maximum speeds of 130 miles/220 km. per hour. In March 1988 the Seikan train tunnel connecting the islands of Honshu and Hokkaido was opened, after 24 years of construction. It is the world's longest tunnel, with an overall length of 33.4 miles/53.8 km. and an underseas section of 15.4 miles/23.4 km. A month later the

133

Seto Osashi rail and road bridge connecting Honshu and Shikoku was in-augurated, and the four major Japanese islands thus became linked by rail.

Japanese economic success is due to a large number of factors, which include both traditional Japanese attitudes and conscious economic planning. Among the former are the tradition of hard work (it was only in September 1987 that the workweek was reduced from 48 to 40 hours); a high degree of societal consensus, which greatly limits civil friction between various economic groups; and the custom of virtually lifetime permanent employment, both for lower-level workers and for management. Economic planning is mainly done by the powerful Ministry for International Trade and Industry, which coordinates the whole national economy and advises both government and industry leaders. Last but not least, Japanese economy has greatly benefited by the very low rate of defense expenditure.

Agriculture: Although agriculture accounted for only 3.1% of the GDP in 1985 and employed 8.1% of the labor force in 1986, for example, Japan is able to provide over two-thirds of its needed food domestically. The main product is rice, which takes up about 42% of all cultivable land and is mostly grown on mountainside terraces. In 1986, rice output was 11.65 million metric tons, which in terms of value represented about one-third of all agricultural production. The government has traditionally used protectionist policies on rice in order to protect Japanese rice farmers, and imports of rice are prohibited (unless there is a shortage). Recently, however, the protectionist policies have begun to be challenged, both by foreign trading partners and by the domestic food processing sector, because the domestic rice producer price in Japan is much higher than the price of imported rice. The government has started to respond to this pressure by cutting the producer price, first by 5.95% in 1987–88 and then by 4.6% in 1988–89. It was the first decline of this price in 31 years. Furthermore, the policy makers have begun to encourage diversification away from rice to other products.

Modern methods of farming, including fertilizing, hybridization and use of machinery, have led to impressive increases in agricultural yields. Crop cultivation also became much more intensive, and the number of farms decreased from 6.1 million in 1960 to 4.3 million in 1987. Most farms are quite small (about 3 acres/1 hectare) and the majority of farming households supplement their income by other employment. Besides rice the main agricultural products include pulses, potatoes, sugar beets, radishes, Chinese cabbage and fruit, but almost all soybeans, feedstuffs and wheat have to be imported. The livestock sector has grown very quickly in recent decades, and the production of meat products (mainly pork) increased from 1.7 million tons in 1970 to 3 million tons in 1985; but this increase was not sufficient to supply the demand, and meat imports also rose in the same period, from 220,000 tons to 851,000 tons. Food imports are generally increasing because the population is growing and becoming wealthier, and consequently demanding more and better food products. The effect of improved nutrition is most noticeable in the increased average height of the

134

Japanese: The average height of 14-year-olds rose by three and one-half inches between 1958 and 1978.

Although forests cover two-thirds of Japan's land area, they supply only about one-half of the domestic demand for lumber. Much of the forested land is inaccessible, which hampers commercial exploitation; furthermore, forest management policies very strictly regulate tree cutting.

Fishing: Japan is the world's largest fishing nation, with a catch of 12.2 million tons in 1985. Almost half a million people work in the fishing industry, and fish and shellfish supply about 45% of all animal protein in the Japanese diet. The industry has been negatively affected by conflicts with other fishing nations, particularly since 1976 when the 200-mile/370-km. exclusive fishing zones were introduced. By the late 1980s about 80 countries had claimed these zones and the Japanese now have to pay fees in order to be allowed to fish in such waters. Whale meat is considered a delicacy by the Japanese and Japan was one of the last nations to end commercial whaling in 1987. It intends to continue a scientific whaling program, however, despite objections from the International Whaling Commission and environmentalist groups.

Industry: Of the 26 largest industrial companies in the world in 1986, four were Japanese: Toyota Motor, Matsushita Electric, Hitachi and Nissan Motor. For more than a century manufacturing has been the major sector of Japanese economy. Industrialization was one of the main goals of the Meiji Restoration, and from the beginning of the 20th century Japan's industrial development has always been one of the government's top priorities. In the 1930s the emphasis was on heavy industry, which had to supply armaments for military expansion. After World War II manufacturing played a crucial role in the remarkable economic recovery of the country. The textile industry, particularly the production of cotton cloth, was the first to be renovated and redeveloped after the war, but because Japan needed work for millions of skilled workers it soon switched to electronics. The manufacture of Nikon and Canon cameras, rated among the best in the world, was followed by the manufacture of tape recorders, transistors, television sets and stereo systems. The Japanese electronics industry is now the largest in the world: In 1986 Japan produced 64.2 million desktop calculators, 7.7 million telephones, 2.1 million computers, 13.2 million radios, 13.9 million television sets, 17.4 million cameras, and 281.3 million watches and clocks. Japan also conducts high-technology research and has been competing with the United States in developing such products as superconductors. Another electronics field in which Japan leads the world is robotics. Several companies (Fujitsu, IBM Japan and Hitachi) are engaged in developing artificial intelligence, now available in the so-called expert systems. Altogether, production of electrical machinery accounted for about 16.5% of total manufacturing in 1985.

Postwar development of the steel industry was encouraged by the United States, and although Japan has to import most of the iron ore and coal needed for the production of steel, it is one of the world's largest producers. Japanese shipyards and its shipbuilding industry were rebuilt in the late

135

1940s, and the country now leads the world in ship production (despite increasing competition from countries like South Korea and Brazil). More than half of the newly built ships are exported. During the 1970s passenger car production began to increase, and in the early 1980s the Japanese automobile industry became the largest in the world. In 1987 Japan produced 7,891,000 passenger cars and 4,290,000 trucks. About 10 large companies, led by Toyota, Nissan and Honda, dominate this sector.

Japanese industrial development has been affected by the almost complete lack of domestic mineral resources. In 1984, 83.1% of Japanese energy needs had to be covered by imports (compared to the 11.9% dependency rate of the United States). Japanese economic planners are set on reducing the country's dependence on imported oil through increasing the use of hydroelectricity, and the generation of geothermal, solar and nuclear power. In 1986 there were 33 nuclear power stations in Japan, with six more to be added by 1990. In 1987 Japan ranked fourth in nuclear power production, which reached 186.1 billion KWh, or 29% of all electric power.

Foreign trade: The overall value of Japanese foreign trade ranks third in the world, after the United States and West Germany. In 1987 the total value of exports was $229.2 billion, while the imports amounted to $149.5 billion. Japan imports fuel, foodstuffs, raw materials (particularly iron ore and coking coal) and some machinery. Exports are mostly manufactured goods, ranging from ships, passenger cars and various types of engines to tape recorders and other electronics products. The 1980s have been marked by a growing gap between Japanese imports and exports: While in 1980 imports were 8% higher than exports, in 1981 exports overtook imports by 6%, and by 1987 exports exceeded imports by 53%. The United States is Japan's major trade partner: In 1987 it accounted for 36.5% of Japanese exports and 21.1% of its imports. Other trading partners are South Korea, China, the Federal Republic of Germany, Australia and Taiwan. Under international pressure Japan lowered some tariffs, eliminated import quotas on such products as beef and oranges, and introduced some voluntary restraints in exports—which led to a slight decrease in the overall trade surplus; in 1987 it declined by 3.7%, and in 1988 by 2.9%.

Employment: The economically active population in 1987 totaled 59.11 million people; the distribution was as follows: 7.6% in agriculture, forestry and fishing; 0.1% in mining; 9.0% in construction; 24.1% in manufacturing; 6.4% in utilities, transportation and communications; 23.1% in distribution; 4.0% in finance, insurance and real estate; 21.2% in services; 3.3% in government; and 1.1% in other fields. Women constitute about 40% of the total labor force, but the majority of them work in low-paying family businesses. Compared to world standards, the unemployment rate is very low (2.8% in 1987)—mostly in the steel, shipbuilding and coal mining sectors. Family firms are generally small and are run in traditional paternalistic manner. Large companies, which account for a disproportionate part of total output and employment, increasingly use robots in automated tasks: more than 67,300 robots worked on assembly lines in 1983. Unionization of workers decreased in recent decades: Only 28.9% of all

136

workers were unionized in 1986, against 39% in 1955. Unions are typically based in a single enterprise and include workers in different occupations. The strongest are the transportation, teaching and fishing industry unions.

Prices and wages: During the first oil crisis in the early 1970s inflation rose to 26% in 1974, yet within a year it was down to single digits. In 1981 the consumer price index rose by 4.9%, and since 1981 the inflation has never exceeded 3%; in 1987 it was only 0.08%. Wage rises depend on seniority, so that a 50-year-old employee may get twice as large an increase as a 20-year-old worker. Monthly wages rose by 2.7% in 1986, and by 1.9% in 1987.

SOCIAL SERVICES

Welfare: The social insurance system includes health insurance, welfare annuity insurance, unemployment insurance, workers' accident compensation insurance, seamen's insurance, a national government employees' mutual aid association and day workers' health insurance. Workers usually retire at the age of 55 and receive a pension representing, on the average, 40% of their wages or salaries. In 1985 the pension-plan system was reformed to provide basic benefits for all Japanese. The welfare system, based on the Daily Life Security Law of 1946, administers financial aid for livelihood, education, housing, disability and funerals. About 1.5 million persons received these benefits in 1984. Over 1,000 welfare offices are staffed by full-time employees and assisted by volunteers. Since families are generally very close, most elderly people are taken care of by their adult children, and consequently the per capita government expenditure on social security programs is relatively low. In the 1987–88 budget, social security expenditures represented 18% of the total and pension expenditures, 3.3%.

Health Services: Japanese government supervises all clinics and hospitals. In 1985 there were 9,600 hospitals, over 78,000 general clinics and about 44,000 dental clinics. Japan has fewer doctors per capita than most industrialized nations: in 1984 there were about 151 physicians per 100,000 population. (The corresponding figure in the United States was 407.) In addition to standard medical care, the Japanese government recognizes traditional healing practices, such as shiatsu (a form of massage), moxibustion and acupuncture. Some diseases, particularly tuberculosis, have significantly declined in recent decades, but others connected with the stress of modern life, such as cancer and heart disease, have risen. Despite that, Japanese life expectancy is the highest in the world: 75 years for men and 81 for women, as of 1986. The infant mortality rate in 1985 was 5.9 per 1,000 live births one of the lowest in the world (compared with 10.6 in the United States in 1984).

Housing: By 1983 Japan had almost 40 million housing units, that is almost one unit per family. By Western standards, however, the dwellings are often quite small, with sparse furnishings. Housing is very expensive in some of the metropolitan areas, particularly in Tokyo, Nagoya and Osaka, and few people can afford single-family houses. Most live in apartments, either rented or owned as condominiums. In the fiscal year 1987–88, real estate values in Japan went up by 20.2%.

EDUCATION

In 1890 the emperor issued his famous Rescript of Education, which stressed obedience and self-sacrifice as the foremost patriotic duties. During the Meiji Restoration an impressive educational system was established, primary education became compulsory, and all schools were directly or indirectly controlled by the state. After World War II the educational system was reorganized according to the U.S. model, and schools were divided into four levels: six years of primary school, three years of junior high school, three years of high school and four years of college. Education is free and compulsory from the age of six through 14, and all schools are coeducational. There is virtually no illiteracy. Japan, in fact, is known for its high educational standards, especially in sciences and languages. The educational system is characterized by rigorous examinations and intensive competition, particularly for admission to the prestigious Tokyo University. All students entering universities must pass entrance examinations in Japanese, English, mathematics, science and social studies. In 1985 there were 24,982 primary schools, with 10,665,404 students and 454,760 teachers; 11,190 junior high schools, with 6,105,749 students and 289,885 teachers; 5,491 senior high schools, with 5,259,307 students and 270,630 teachers; 62 technological colleges, with 49,174 students and 5,875 teachers; 584 junior colleges, with 396,455 students and 46,580 teachers; and 465 graduate schools and universities, with 1,879,532 students and 192,733 teachers. More than 363,000 students from the high school level upward were receiving some financial aid in the late 1980s. The educational system is centralized, and curricula, textbooks and courses are standardized throughout the country.

MASS MEDIA

The press: In terms of overall newspaper circulation, the Japanese press is the second largest in the world, and in number of copies per person, the largest. There is no censorship and the press is extremely outspoken.

Dailies: The leading dailies, with their 1986 morning circulation, are, in Tokyo: *Yomiuri Shimbun,* 5,429,933; *Asahi Shimbun,* 3,926,657; *Mainichi Shimbun,* 1,760,240; and *Nihon Keizai Shimbun;* in Nagoya: *Chunichi Shimbun,* 2,878,851; in Osaka: *Yomiuri Shimbun,* 2,210,443; *Asahi Shimbun,* 2,180,060. There are also four English-language dailies, all published in Tokyo: *Japan Times,* 60,000; *Asahi Evening News,* 29,000; *Mainichi Daily News; The Daily Yomiuri.*

Periodicals: Weeklies with a circulation of 200,000 or more (all published in Tokyo) are: *Shukan Shincho,* general interest, 800,000; *Shukan Asahi,* general interest, 600,000; *Shukan Bunshun,* general interest, 491,000; *Sunday Mainichi,* general interest, 322,000; and *Asahi Graphic,* pictorial review, 200,000. More specialized Tokyo periodicals with large circulations are *So-en,* fashion monthly, 400,000; *Fujin Koron,* women's literary monthly, 263,000; and *Shukan FM,* biweekly guide to music broadcasts, 200,000.

Broadcasting: The Japan Broadcasting Corporation, partially owned by the state, operated 824 radio stations and about 6,900 television stations in 1984. Almost every home has a radio and a color television set; in 1986 there were an estimated 94.5 million radio receivers and 31.9 licensed television sets. About 270 commercial radio and 6,074 television stations are connected with large newspaper companies.

BIOGRAPHICAL SKETCHES

Shintaro Abe. Born in 1924, Abe has been a member of the House of Representatives since 1958. During the 1970s and 1980s he served in the government, and from 1982 to 1986 was minister of foreign affairs. He leads one faction of the LDP and is the chairman of the General Council of the party.

Akihito. Born in 1933 as the eldest son of Emperor Hirohito and Empress Nagako, Crown Prince Akihito studied marine biology at Jakushuin University. He has traveled widely, knows English and is well versed in Western culture. He assumed imperial duties in September 1988 when his father became ill. On January 7, 1989, upon the latter's death, Akihito became Japan's emperor. He and his wife, the Empress Michiko, were married in 1959; have three children.

Takako Doi. The first woman to head a Japanese political party, Takako Doi replaced Masashi Ishibashi as chairperson of the JSP in September 1986. She was born in 1928, trained as a lawyer and taught constitutional law at Doshisha University until 1969 when she was elected to the House of Representatives. She is very popular and has been labeled the "Japanese Thatcher" by the press.

Yasuhiro Nakasone. Born in 1918, Nakasone served as Japan's prime minister from 1982 until 1987. By Japanese standards, he was an unusual politician because of his flair, eloquence and forcefulness in dealing with foreign leaders. In 1987 he picked Noboru Takeshita as his successor, and he continues to exert political influence as a leader of one faction within the LDP.

Noboru Takeshita. Prime minister of Japan from late 1987 until his resignation in mid-1989, Takeshita comes from the affluent family of a sake brewer in the Shimane prefecture, near the Sea of Japan. He was born in 1924, attended Waseda University in Tokyo and in 1944 took a course in kamikaze pilot training, but before he finished it the war was over. In 1951 he was elected to a seat in the local assembly and in 1958 became an LDP member of the national House of Representatives. Known since his youth for an ability to compromise, Takeshita began to move up in the party hierarchy and held a number of government posts. He was Eisaku Sato's chief cabinet secretary in 1971, and twice he served as minister of finance (from 1979 to 1980 and from 1982 to 1986). In July 1986 Takeshita became secretary-general of the LDP and a year later he formed his own faction, which superseded the Tanaka faction. In October 1987 he was elected the 12th president of the LDP and in November 1987 he became Japan's 17th postwar prime minister.

Sosuke Uno. Born in 1922, Uno became minister of foreign affairs in 1987. He had been elected eight times to the House of Representatives and held a number of government posts. In 1983 he was appointed minister of international trade and industry. He is a close associate of Yasuhiro Nakasone and a member of his faction. He was briefly prime minister in mid-1989 until forced by scandal to resign.

NORTH KOREA

Features: Most of the Korean peninsula is covered with forested mountains dating from the pre-Cambrian period; because of this geological antiquity there are no active volcanoes and earthquakes are extremely rare—in contrast to nearby Japan. The Kaema Plateau, with an average elevation of 3,300 ft/1,000 m., occupies the northeastern part of the country. The highest peak, Mount Paektu (9,003 ft/2,744 mm.) on the Korean-Chinese border, is an extinct volcano. It is believed that a small number of Siberian tigers still live on the slopes of this mountain. Lowlands and plains, which account for about one-fifth of the total area, lie mainly in the southwest. The largest of them, centering around the capital, Pyongyang, is also the most densely populated region of the country. Other western lowlands are the Chaeryong, Anju and Kaesong plains. A series of narrow coastal plains stretches along the eastern shore. The rivers of Korea are short and fast-flowing, and are an important source of hydroelectric power. The longest rivers are the Yalu (known in Korean as Amnok, 491 miles/790 km.) and the Tumen (324 miles/521 km.), the first flowing southwest and the second northeast, from their source on Mount Paektu. Most of the border between North Korea and China is formed by these two rivers. In the southern part of the country the longest rivers are the Taedong (247 miles/397 km.) and the Imjin (158 miles/254 km.), both of which flow southwest and enter the Yellow Sea. In contrast to the generally smooth eastern coast, facing the Sea of Japan, the western Yellow Sea coast is full of deep indentations and has a number of good natural harbors, but it also has an extremely high tide—up to 30 ft/9 m.

In the north the country borders China and, in the farthest northeast, it has a 10-mile/16-km. common border with the Soviet Union. In the south a 13,100-ft/4,000-m. wide demilitarized zone, running roughly along the 38th parallel, separates North Korea from South Korea. Japan lies some 300 miles/500 km. away, across the Sea of Japan.

The climate is influenced by the continental air mass lying over Siberia and Mongolia. This air mass causes very cold winters, particularly in the north, where the temperature drops below the freezing point about 180 days each year. The lowest temperature ever recorded in the peninsula was −46.5°F/−43.6°C, at Chung-gangjin. Although the precipitation in winter is usually not heavy, snow tends to stay on for long periods. Summers

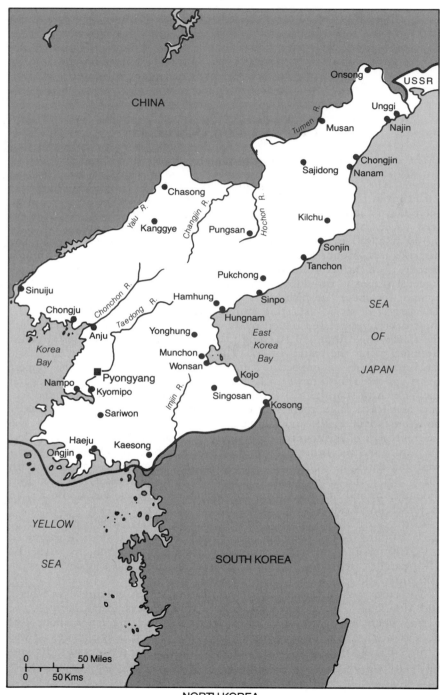

NORTH KOREA

are hot and humid, and most of the rain comes between April and September. Occasional typhoons occur in the early fall.

Area: 46,540 sq. miles/120,538 sq. km., excluding the demilitarized zone, which has an area of 487 sq. miles/1,262 sq. km.

Mean max. and min. temperatures: Pyongyang (39°00'N, 125°47'E; 94 ft/29 m.), 75°F/23.9°C (July), 18°F/−7.8°C (Jan.); Wonsan (39°07'N, 127°26'E), 80°F/27°C (August), 17.6°F/−8°C (Jan.).

Mean annual rainfall: Pyongyang, 37 in/916 mm.

POPULATION

Total population (1986 U.N. est.): 20,883,000.

Chief towns and populations (1986 est.): PYONGYANG (2,000,000), Hamhung-Hungnam (775,000), Chongjin (700,000), Kaesong (240,000), Wonsan (240,000), Sinuiju (200,000).

Distribution: Because of the lack of North Korean statistical information, it is difficult to arrive at meaningful demographic numbers. Estimates of urban population range from 52% to about 64%, against some 18% in 1953, and the discrepancies can be explained by differences in definitions. There are, for example, four "special cities"—Pyongyang, Chongjin, Hamhung and Najin—but all of them include a large rural hinterland.

Languages: The Korean language belongs to the Ural-Altaic linguistic family and is related to such tongues as Turkish, Mongolian and Japanese. Until the 15th century Koreans used Chinese characters, but in 1443 a phonetic Korean alphabet was created. Called Han'gul (or Chosen Muntcha), the alphabet consists of 19 consonants and 21 vowels. There are no ethnic minorities, but some Mandarin Chinese and Russian are spoken along the northern border. English is taught as a compulsory second language from the age of 14.

Religion: Traditionally, most Koreans professed Buddhism and Confucianism, but it has been estimated that by the mid-1980s about 52% of the population was nonreligious and 16% was atheist. About 2% of the people still continue to practice Buddhism, and less than 1% are Christians. An eclectic sect combining Buddhism, Confucianism and Christianity was founded in 1860; it is called Chondokyo (Society of the Heavenly Way) and now claims about 14% of all North Koreans. The remaining 16% of the population are said to practice indigenous shamanism, noted for its rites of exorcism of evil spirits.

CONSTITUTIONAL SYSTEM

Constitution: The present constitution dates from 1972. It describes the Democratic People's Republic of Korea as a socialist state based on the *juch'e* (Chuch'e), or self-reliance, ideology of the Korean Workers' (Communist) party.

Head of state: President Kim Il-sung. *Premier:* Yon Hyong Muk.

Executive: The Central People's Committee combines the executive, legal and judicial powers. It is headed by the president and, in 1987, it had 19 other members. The Administrative Council (cabinet) is headed by the premier; in 1987 it had seven vice-premiers and 35 other members (including ministers, and presidents and directors of various agencies).

Legislature: The unicameral Supreme People's Assembly (SPA) is, theoretically, the highest organ of state power. In 1986 it had 655 members, all of them elected on a single ballot for four-year terms. Elections are favorite regular rituals: Without exception, 100% of the voters cast their votes and all candidates are elected by 100% of the votes. The SPA meets briefly each year to ratify decisions made by the ruling Presidium of the Korean Workers' party (KWP).

Political parties: The KWP was founded in 1946 when two Communist parties, the North Korean Workers' party and the New People's party, decided to merge. In the mid-1980s the membership of the KWP was estimated at 3 million, which represents 15% of the population. The origins of the party date to the 1920s and 1930s, when nationalist and Communist groups were formed in Japan-occupied Korea and among Korean exiles in the Soviet Union and China. After the Japanese troops evacuated Korea in 1945 several Communist groups competed for power, but within a short time the Soviet-backed Kim Il-sung (who had led a group of Communist guerrillas in Manchuria) emerged victorious. He has dominated the party ever since. The highest organ of the KWP is the National Party Congress, which elects the Central People's Committee. This committee, in turn, elects the Politburo. The actual power, however, resides in the three-member Presidium, which consists of Kim Il-sung (general secretary), his son Kim Jong-il (his designated successor) and Vice-Marshal Oh Jin Wu (minister of defense). Ideologically, the party is based on the Korean brand of Marxism, which stresses the *juch'e* idea of self-reliance.

Two non-Communist political parties exist, one connected with the Chondokyo sect and the other a social democratic party, but they do not have any political significance. They unflinchingly support the policies of the KWP.

Local government: The major administrative local units are nine provinces and four cities, and the former are further subdivided into 152 counties. People's assemblies and people's committees are popularly elected to two-year and four-year terms, but actual power is wielded by the KWP.

Judicial system: The highest court is the Central Court (formerly the Supreme Court), which supervises the work of the whole judicial system. Lower organs include provincial courts, courts in cities and counties, martial courts and other special courts. Trials for alleged crimes against the state are conducted in secret, and people convicted of "antistate activities" are sent to "reeducation" camps. According to defectors from North Korea, some 100,000 political prisoners were in such camps in the 1980s.

In 1905 Korea became a Japanese protectorate and in 1910 it was formally annexed by Japan and renamed Chosen. During the following decades political repression went hand in hand with cultural and linguistic repression—the Japanese tried to impose their religion, Shintoism, on the Koreans, and in 1937 even prohibited the use of the Korean language in administration. Japanese occupation did result in some economic benefits—such as the construction of an efficient communications network and the installation of modern industries—but the occupiers were hated by most of the population. The growth of Korean nationalism and anti-Japanese sentiment in the 1920s became almost synonymous with communism, and in 1925 the Korean Communist party was formally inaugurated in Seoul. Other nationalist groups allied with the Communists, but all nationalist activities were harshly suppressed by the Japanese.

After the Japanese capitulated in August 1945 Korea became somewhat arbitrarily divided along the 38th parallel. The Allied High Command decided that the Japanese troops north of the 38th parallel would surrender to the Soviet armed forces, and those south of the parallel to the U.S. forces. A country that had been a unified political entity for more than 1,200 years was thus split into two halves. Several Korean leaders who had lived in exile during World War II returned to Korea in late 1945, and for a short while it seemed that the Allies would together support a gradual establishment of a single independent Korean state. The relationship between the Soviet Union and the Western powers quickly worsened, however, and this worsening was reflected in the internal Korean situation. The Communists became more and more intractable and, with the support of the Soviet Union, tried to establish a national Communist-dominated government. In February 1946 a Provisional People's Committee was set up in the north and recognized as an interim government by the Soviet occupation forces. Shortly after that the United States set up an interim Legislative Assembly in its occupation zone. In September 1947 the United States placed the problem of Korean unification before the United Nations. A Temporary Commission on Korea was set up and charged with organizing elections for the Korean National Assembly, but North Korea, still under Soviet occupation, rejected the U.N. plan. When it became clear that the elections would not be permitted to take place in the north, the commission decided to hold them in South Korea only. The National Assembly was elected in May 1948, and in August the Republic of Korea was proclaimed in Seoul. The northern part of the country responded within a few weeks; on September 9, 1948, Kim Il-sung established the Democratic People's Republic of Korea.

Soviet forces withdrew from North Korea in December 1948 and U.S. forces left South Korea in June 1949, but tension between North and South continued and finally resulted in the Korean War. In June 1950 North

Korean forces, trained by the Russians and vastly superior to the forces of South Korea, crossed the 38th parallel and marched on Seoul, which they captured four days later (on June 29). South Korea requested U.S. assistance and U.S. forces arrived on June 30, to be joined by armed forces from 16 U.N. member-states in September 1950. Gen. Douglas MacArthur led the September amphibious landing near Seoul and then led the U.N. forces north across the 38th parallel up to the border with China. At that point, some 200,000 Chinese troops joined the war and forced the South Korean and U.N. forces to retreat. Peace negotiations started in July 1951, but it took two years to reach an armistice agreement setting the border between the two Koreas roughly along the 38th parallel. This agreement, which was signed in July 1953, has not yet been superseded by a peace treaty. The war was very costly: Not only did it destroy the economy of both the warring parties, but it resulted in the deaths of some 415,000 South Koreans, 23,300 Americans and 3,100 U.N. allies. North Korean casualties were officially given as 50,000, but according to Western estimates they may have reached up to 2 million.

After the war North Korea turned inward. Kim Il-sung purged the Communist party of his opponents, and by the end of the 1950s his *kapsan* (partisan) faction had gained superiority and he had become an undisputed leader surrounded by an increasingly intense cult of personality. The 1960s were marked by concentration on the economy and by the formulation of the *juch'e* ideology based on political autonomy, independence and economic self-reliance. In the international arena the most notable achievement was North Korea's unique ability to stay neutral in the Sino-Soviet dispute. At the same time, hostile anti-South Korean and anti-U.S. propaganda continued unabated, culminating in the seizure of the U.S. navy intelligence ship *Pueblo* in 1968.

The 1970s witnessed an international diplomatic offensive by North Koreans and a brief effort to discuss peaceful reunification of the two Koreas. In 1971 the Red Cross societies of North and South Korea met for the first time, but the talks did not bring any results and were soon suspended and replaced by renewed tension and hostility. About 10 tunnels dug under the demilitarized zone in order to facilitate infiltrations into South Korea were discovered by the U.N. forces in 1974. Meanwhile, in 1973, North Korea became a permanent observer at the United Nations and a member of several U.N. agencies. During the rest of the decade it established diplomatic relations with about 100 countries. No Western developed country has diplomatic relations with North Korea, however, except France, which established semidiplomatic ties in 1980. Internally, the government proclaimed a new constitution in 1972 and in 1974 launched a campaign of "three great revolutions": ideological, technical and cultural. A power struggle within the KWP in the late 1970s was apparently triggered by the naming of Kim Il-sung's son, Kim Jong-il, as heir apparent. The struggle was shrouded in secrecy, but a major purge of Kim Jong-il's opponents reportedly took place. In the early 1980s another family member emerged as Kim Jong-il's adversary—Kim Pyong-il, son of Kim Il-sung and his current wife, Kim Song Ae. Kim Pyong-il was appointed ambassador to Hungary in 1988; this was interpreted by some observers as a demotion.

In the 1980s North Korea became involved in several terrorist acts, particularly the attempted assassination in Canada of South Korean President Chun Doo Hwan in 1982; the killing of 17 South Koreans in Yangon, Myanmar, in a bomb explosion in 1983; and the planting of a bomb on South Korean passenger jetliner KAL 858, which then exploded in midair in November 1987. Although North Korea denied responsibility in all three cases, international consensus blamed the nation for these crimes. The terrorist involvement and ideological rigidity contributed to a certain uneasiness in North Korean relations with the Soviet Union and China. Furthermore, North Korea disapproved of the Soviet invasion of Afghanistan in 1979, while both Moscow and Beijing disapproved of Kim Il-sung's efforts to establish a dynastic rule. Several trips by Kim Il-sung (to Beijing in December 1985, to Moscow in October 1986 and again to Beijing in May 1987) and unconfirmed reports about an attempted coup d'etat in 1986 fueled an international guessing game about the behind-the-scenes developments. Despite the ideological aggressiveness, which always rises to a new crescendo when the annual U.S.-South Korean military maneuvers "Team Spirit" take place in the spring, there are reportedly some moderates in the Korean leadership who would like to see the country embark on a more rational political course.

Talks and contacts between the two Koreas began again in the mid-1980s. The international outcry following the Yangon bombing in 1983 apparently strengthened the hand of the moderates in the North Korean leadership and probably led to the 1984 offer by the North Korean Red Cross to send relief goods to South Korean flood victims. The offer was accepted and shortly after that, in November, the two Koreas held economic talks. During 1985 more comprehensive negotiations took place, but contacts were again suspended in 1985. The approaching Olympic Games caused new friction in the late 1980s. When North Korea demanded the right to cohost part of the games, both South Korea and the International Olympic Committee were willing to reach some accommodation. In January 1988, however, shortly after the confession of two North Korean spies who claimed responsibility for the explosion of the KAL 858 jetliner (despite some discrepancies, the confessions have been accepted by international opinion as basically true), North Korea announced that it would not take part in the Olympic Games. This decision was influenced in part by the fact that the overwhelming majority of the Communist countries accepted invitations to Seoul and thus did not leave North Korea with any leverage.

Later in the year South Korea renewed its overtures to its northern neighbor; President Roh Tae Woo again proposed to meet with Kim Il-sung. This was in line with South Korea's new approach to the Communist nations and with South Korean expansion of economic ties with North Korean allies. The North Korean response seemed mixed: On the one hand, the political realities and atmosphere not only in eastern Asia but throughout the world point away from the bipolarity of the cold-war era, but, on the other hand, the inflexibility of North Korean ideological doctrine has a great momentum. Many observers felt, however, that some kind of political breakthrough in North-South Korean relations was not too far away.

Defense: The North Korean army had an estimated total of 838,000 personnel on active duty in 1987, and was thus one of the largest armies in the world. Military conscription is compulsory for all males between the ages of 17 and 28 for terms of five years in the army or navy and three to four years in the air force. In July 1987 the North Korean government announced that it would reduce its armed forces by 100,000 by the end of the year in a unilateral gesture of goodwill. At the same time, the government continued to assert that because of U.S. and South Korean provocations, "war was imminent."

ECONOMY

Background: After the establishment of the Democratic People's Republic of Korea in 1949 all industry was nationalized and land was distributed among the peasants. The Korean War dealt a new blow to economic reconstruction, but by the end of the 1950s North Korea had achieved an impressive degree of industrialization. The economy continues to be highly centralized and centrally planned; in contrast to most other Communist countries, no economic reforms have been undertaken. One change, however, took place in 1984 when the government promulgated the Joint Venture Act, permitting direct foreign investment for the first time. It was reported in 1987 that about 50 deals with foreign companies had been concluded, but most of them were with Chongryun, a pro-North Korean organization in Japan. The first joint venture with South Korea, agreed upon in early 1989, involved the development of a tourist site around Mount Kumgang.

In the absence of statistical information (the North Korean government has not published comprehensive statistics since 1965), most of the economic data must be estimated. According to some Western estimates the GNP in 1985 was U.S. $24 billion, which would place North Korea well ahead of many developing countries. The per capita income, estimated at $1,180, represented 58% of the corresponding figure for South Korea. South Korean statistics, which are not very reliable either, put the GNP in 1986 at $17.4 billion, which means a per capita income of $860.

Agriculture: The collectivization of agriculture was completed in 1958 when some 1 million North Korean farming families had become members of over 16,000 cooperatives. The cooperatives were later merged into 3,800 units. Farmers are permitted to keep little private plots and to sell the produce raised on these plots at farmers' markets, which are held for short periods during the growing season. The principal crop is rice, and the total production was estimated at 6 million tons in 1986. Other products include corn, potatoes, wheat, barley and millet. Despite claims about grain self-sufficiency, North Korea imported some 100,000 tons of wheat from

India in 1986, and in 1987 it was reported that an economic deal with Thailand provided for imports of 300,000 tons of rice and 500,000 tons of corn annually. Most of the livestock is raised on state farms; the estimates in 1986 included 2,920,000 pigs, 1,122,000 cattle, 352,000 sheep and 19,000,000 poultry. The government has been intensively involved in land reclamation and irrigation projects in order to increase the area of arable land. A dam across the Taedong River, completed in 1986, is allegedly the largest dam in the world. In a way, North Korean agriculture can be considered a success story given the unfavorable natural conditions (very little arable land and inclement weather); but the continuing rationing of food makes this success somewhat questionable.

Mining: The most important minerals are coal and iron ore. Coal is mined at some 40 sites and the annual production is estimated at 50 million tons. Iron ore is extracted at 10 centers, the largest one being Musan, east of Mount Paektu. In 1986 iron ore production was more than 9 million tons. North Korea also has zinc, lead, gold, tungsten and phosphate, and its magnesite deposits are estimated to represent about 40%–50% of the world's total reserves. The mining equipment and facilities however are aging and becoming inefficient because it is increasingly necessary to mine deeper seams; this accounts for recent stagnation of the mining sector.

Industry: The fast pace of industrialization after the end of the Korean War was made possible by the nation's natural endowment with minerals (particularly coal), significant Soviet help and the ideology of self-reliance. Heavy industry predominates; the most important sectors are steel production, machinery, chemicals, textiles and food production. North Korea manufactures two types of jeeps, one make of automobiles, nine types of trucks and a number of lines of construction machinery. The chemical industry has concentrated on the production of fertilizers and synthetic fibers such as vinalon. The largest sector of light industry is the manufacture of textiles (mostly synthetic). This sector, centered in Pyongyang, grew significantly in the 1970s, and the cloth production was officially reported to have increased from 437 million yards/400 million m. of cloth in 1970 to 875 million yards/800 million m. in 1984.

Foreign trade: Foreign trade has played a relatively minor role in the North Korean economy. In the 1950s almost 100% of foreign trade was with the Communist countries, but by the end of the following decade North Korea began to diversify; in 1969 its trade with the West represented 27% of the total. In the late 1980s the Soviet Union and China were the major trading partners, and Japan was the principal connection with the non-Communist world. Since the late 1970s North Korea has also developed its trade with Third World countries. Exports include nonferrous metals, iron, steel, textiles, military equipment and cement; principal imports are machinery and equipment, petroleum, wheat and cotton. In the early 1970s a buying spree in the West, aimed at acquiring modern technology, was supposed to be financed by increased export earnings. When the world prices of minerals went down, however, North Korea suspended payments and in 1976 it became the first (and so far the last) Communist nation to default on its foreign debt. Despite repeated debt rescheduling the problem persisted, and in August 1988 North Korea again was declared in default. Its foreign debt was estimated at $3 billion in 1982.

Employment: In the mid-1980s the economically active population was estimated at 9 million, with 43% of the labor force in agriculture, 30% in industry and 27% in services. Women represent almost half of all workers.

Wages: Monthly wages are mostly in the range of $100–$200, and there are generally small differentials between wages in various occupations and at various levels. Members of the Communist elite, however, enjoy special benefits, such as access to automobiles and to shops with imported goods.

SOCIAL SERVICES

Welfare: North Korea has one of the world's most comprehensive nursery school systems, which cares for children from ages one to five. Medical care is free, and all employees are entitled to retirement pensions, which are about one-half of the last salary earned. The state also provides free vacations to workers, at some 400 recreation centers.

Health services: In 1985 the number of doctors was 51,462—or about one doctor per 370 persons. Infectious diseases have been mostly eliminated, and the leading cause of death is now cancer. According to official figures, life expectancy was 74.3 years in 1985; according to U.N. estimates, however, life expectancy for 1985–90 was 66.2 years for men and 72.7 years for women.

Housing: The Korean War destroyed about one-third of the country's housing, including most houses in the capital. The housing plan for 1978–84 projected 200,000–300,000 new units each year, and the 1987–93 plan aimed at 150,000–200,000 new units annually. High-rise suburbs have grown around many cities, particularly Pyongyang.

EDUCATION

In 1975 the government of North Korea introduced free and compulsory 11-year education. Most children enter nursery schools at a very early age. From nursery schools they move, at the age of five, to kindergartens, and at the age of six to grade one. In 1985 there were 28,538 nursery schools, with 950,000 children in attendance; 19,262 kindergartens, with 715,000 children; 4,792 primary schools, with 1,466,000 pupils; and 4,738 secondary schools, with 2,842,000 students. In addition to Kim Il-sung University in Pyongyang, there are more than 200 other institutions of higher learning. About 95% of all adults are literate.

MASS MEDIA

All communications means are operated and supervised by the state.

The press

Dailies: The mouthpiece of the North Korean leadership is the *Rodong Sinmun* (Labor Daily), published by the Central Committee on the KWP. The presidium of the SPA and the cabinet publish *Minju Choson* (Democratic Korea), and the General Federation of Trade Unions publishes *Rodongja Sinmun* (Workers' Daily). The army also has a daily, *Joson Inmingun* (Korean People's Army); and mass organizations such as the Socialist Working Youth League and the Fatherland Front issue publications as well. In addition, there are provincial newspapers.

Periodicals: The monthly *Kulloja* (Workers), published by the Central Committee of the KWP, has a circulation of about 300,000; and *Jokook Tongil,* a monthly published by the Fatherland Front, has a circulation of 70,000. There are several periodicals published in foreign languages, such as *The Democratic People's Republic of Korea* (m), illustrated news; *Korea Today* (m), current affairs; and the *P'yongyang Times* (w), current affairs.

Broadcasting: In 1984 there were an estimated 1.05 million television sets and 4.1 million radio receivers. More than 1 million public loudspeakers are hooked to the broadcasting system. News also is broadcast in English, Russian, Chinese, Japanese and several other languages.

BIOGRAPHICAL SKETCHES

Kim Dal Hyon. Born about 1933, Kim Dal Hyon is a technocrat who attracted Western attention by his quick rise to power in 1987–88. He first came into public view when he became deputy director of the science academy in 1977. In March 1987 he was appointed to head the Chemical and Light Industry Commission; from February to June 1988 he was deputy premier and chairman of the Planning Commission. After that he was made chairman of the External Economic Affairs Commission; and in October 1988 he replaced Choe Jong Gun as minister of foreign trade.

Kim Il-sung. Born in 1912, Kim Il-sung joined the Communist party in 1927. During World War II he was a guerrilla leader in Manchuria. After the war—and with Soviet support—he prevailed over his opponents from other factions of the party and gradually became a supreme leader, the center of an extreme personality cult. He is extravagantly praised and called the "great leader," the "heaven-sent and talented leader" and so on. He also awarded himself a number of high orders and decorations, such as Hero of the Democratic People's Republic of Korea (two times) and the Order of National Flag First Class (three times). By designating his son as his successor, he is apparently attempting to found a Communist dynasty.

151

Kim Jong-il (Kim Chong Il). Son of Kim Il-sung and his first wife, Kim Jong Suk (who died in 1949), Kim Jong-il studied in Pyongyang, Moscow and Beijing, and since 1973 has been groomed as his father's successor. He was born in 1941, but the year was moved to 1942 so that he and his father (born in 1912) can celebrate their rounded birthdays the same year. The only official position the younger Kim has is membership in the Presidium of the Politburo of the KWP, but he reportedly takes cares of the day-to-day administration of the country. He is said to like Western luxuries, but is a political hardliner very much opposed to any rapprochement with South Korea.

Kim Yong Nam. Born about 1927, he studied in the Soviet Union, and since the 1950s has held various government and party posts. He is North Korea's leading specialist in foreign affairs, and in 1989 was minister of foreign affairs and vice-premier; he is a full member of the Politburo.

Lin Gun Mo. Born in 1924, Lin Gun Mo studied engineering in Leningrad during the Korean War, and then married a cousin of Kim Il-sung. He was deputy premier from 1973–1977 and premier from late 1986 to December 1988, when he stepped down because of ill health. He was succeeded by Yon Hyong Muk in 1989.

Oh Jin Wu (O Jin U; Ok Jin Woo). Born in 1910, Vice-Marshall Oh Jin Wu belongs to the old guard Korean Communists. He was chief of the general staff from 1971 to 1976 and has been minister of the armed forces since 1976. He is third in the party hierarchy after the two Kims.

SOUTH KOREA

GEOGRAPHY

Features: The Republic of Korea (ROK), also known as South Korea, is a small state sharing a peninsula with the Democratic People's Republic of Korea (DPRK), also known as North Korea, its only neighbor. The east coast of the ROK is mountainous, whereas many harbors cut deeply into the western and southern coasts, and there are many islands. Along the east coast run the Taebaek-sanmaek (Taebaek mountains); they and the Sobaek mountains divide the peninsula north to south. In these mountains, none over 5,700 ft/1,737 m. high, all the important rivers originate. Among these are the Kum, Han and Naktong. Along the Han River important hydroelectric plants have been built. Agriculture is predominant in the slender plains that hug South Korea's coasts and the little river valleys that dot the country. Much of the land is forested because of the climate: long hot summers with plenty of rain and long cold winters.

South Korea's arable land is of two kinds: rice paddies (irrigated fields) and dry fields at the higher altitudes. The latter are broken up into very small plots, which are worked generally without the aid of modern farm equipment and are not irrigated. Barley, soybeans, millet and wheat are grown on these higher fields.

Area: 38,291 sq. miles/99,174 sq. km.

Mean max. and min. temperatures: Seoul (37°33′N, 126°58′E) 23°F/−5°C (Jan.), 78°F/25°C (Aug.); Pusan (35°06′N, 129°03′E) 35°F/2°C (Jan.), 78°F/25°C (Aug.).

Mean annual rainfall: Yearly rainfall is 40–55 in/1,020–1,400 mm. In one of the wettest areas of the country, Pusan receives on average 55 inches/1,400 mm. per year; in the least humid area of the country, Taegu receives on average 38 in/960 mm. per year.

POPULATION

Total population (1986 est.): 41,568,640.

Chief towns and populations (1985): SEOUL (9,639,110), Pusan (3,514,798), Taegu (2,029,853), Inchon (1,386,911).

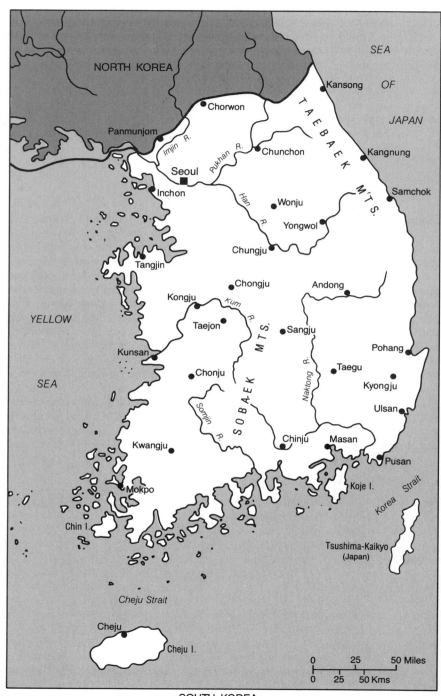

NORTH KOREA

SEA

OF

JAPAN

Kansong

Chorwon

T A E B A E K

Panmunjom

Imjin R.

Pukhan R.

Chunchon

Kangnung

Seoul

Inchon

Han R.

Wonju

M T S .

Samchok

Yongwol

Chungju

Tangjin

Chongju

Andong

YELLOW

Kongju

Kum R.

Taejon

Sangju

Pohang

Kunsan

S O B A E K   M T S .

Naktong R.

Taegu

SEA

Chonju

Kyongju

Ulsan

Somjin R.

Kwangju

Chinju

Masan

Pusan

Mokpo

Koje I.

Korea Strait

Chin I.

Tsushima-Kaikyo
(Japan)

Cheju Strait

Cheju

Cheju I.

| 0 | 25 | 50 Miles |
| 0 | 25 | 50 Kms |

SOUTH KOREA

Ethnic composition: Koreans, who are thought to be mainly Tungusic, a stock related to both the Chinese and the Mongols, make up almost the entire population of the ROK.

Language: Korean is the official language of the country.

Religion: Buddhists make up 37% of the population; Protestants 26% and Roman Catholics 5%. Smaller percentages include Confucian, Daoist and Chondokyo (an indigenous religion) groups.

CONSTITUTIONAL SYSTEM

Constitution: The constitution of the sixth republic established a republican form of government with power centralized in the office of a strong executive, the president. The constitution, which became law on October 29, 1987, was voted into effect through a national referendum held on October 7, 1987.

Head of state: President Roh Tae Woo. *Prime minister:* Lee Hyun Jae.

Executive: At the national level, executive power is answerable to the National Assembly. The government is headed by a president who is elected to one five-tear term; the president cannot be reelected. The president appoints the prime minister (who must be approved by the National Assembly) and various government members.

The State Council (cabinet) and the Board of Audit and Inspection also assist the president in the fulfillment of executive duties.

Legislature: The unicameral National Assembly sits in Seoul. The members are directly elected by universal suffrage and serve four-year terms. The National Assembly is mandated by law to have a membership of at least 200. It meets once a year in a regular session lasting no more than 100 days; extraordinary sessions may be called by the president or by one-fourth of the legislative members. The National Assembly creates the laws and is authorized to call for the impeachment of any government official, including the president.

Political parties: The constitution guarantees the existence and freedom of a multiparty political system. However, the Constitution Court has the power to disband any political party it considers a threat to democracy. In 1987 there were 10 political parties, including the Democratic Justice party—of which President Roh Tae Woo is head—with 1 million members. The two major opposition parties in the 1987 presidential election were the Reunification Democratic party and the Peace and Democracy party.

Local government: The ROK is divided into 13 governmental units. Seoul, Pusan, Taegu and Inchon are cities with special governmental ranking equivalent to that of provinces, of which there are nine. Cities, counties *(kun* or *gun),* and townships *(myon)* are further administrative subdivisions of provinces. Villages *(i* or *ri)* are the smallest administrative units into which provinces are divided.

Judicial system: There is a Constitution Court to decide the constitutionality of laws passed by the National Assembly, if a lower court requests such a decision. The court also considers the impeachment of government officials and matters pertaining to the dissolution of political parties. The judiciary below the Constitution Court consists of the Supreme Court, the highest court in the land, appellate and district courts, courts-martial and a family court.

The chief justice presides over the Supreme Court. There are no more than 14 justices, all of whom, including the chief justice, are appointed by the president with the approval of the National Assembly. They serve six-year terms.

The Supreme Court has jurisdiction over the legality or constitutionality of administrative measures and decrees, is the last court of appeal for the decisions of courts-martial and other lower courts, and deals with cases involving election fraud and similar matters.

RECENT HISTORY

At the end of World War II the Korean situation was decided at the Potsdam Conference in July 1945. Korea, which since 1910 had been annexed by Japan, was to be divided at the 38th parallel into two zones of occupation. Soviet troops began the occupation of Korea north of the 38th parallel on August 10, 1945, and U.S. troops began the occupation of Korea south of that line on September 8, 1945, disrupting the efforts of various Korean groups to unify their country.

After a period of U.S. military trusteeship, variously opposed by Korean political parties, elections were held in South Korea on May 10, 1948, supervised by the U.N. Temporary Commission on Korea. On May 13 the National Assembly met for the first time. In July the former president of the Korean government in exile, Dr. Syngman Rhee, was elected president. On August 15 the military government of Korea ended, and the Republic of Korea was established. The new government was declared the only legitimate government by the U.N.

However, on May 1, 1948, the Soviets helped to establish the Democratic People's Republic of Korea north of the 38th parallel. Both the ROK and the DPRK asserted sovereignty over the whole of Korea. Unlike the U.S. occupation forces—which left behind only about 500 men as a military advisory group to help the South Koreans recruit and train their military forces, and granted only U.S. $10,970,000 for military aid—the Soviet occupation forces provided a long-term scheme whereby the North Koreans were aided in the recruiting and training of their military forces, and were equipped with heavy military hardware after withdrawal of the Soviet occupation forces.

On June 25, 1950, North Korean forces invaded the ROK. The South Korean forces were greatly outnumbered. Even after U.N. forces, principally composed of U.S. troops, entered the field to aid the South Koreans on July 4, 1950, the North Koreans advanced deep into South Korea, eventually occupying Seoul and the rest of the South except for a small area around the southeastern port of Pusan.

The U.N. forces, under the command of Gen. Douglas MacArthur, were eventually able to reoccupy all of South Korea. On October 7 the U.N. General Assembly resolved that the U.N. forces could enter North Korea, and on October 20 the North Korean capital, Pyongyang, was taken by MacArthur. On October 26 the U.N. forces reached the Yalu River, on the border of China.

In November 1950, Chinese Communist forces entered in aid of the routed North Koreans. The 1.2 million Chinese troops in Korea by the end of 1952, under the command of Gen. P'eng Te-hai, forced the retreat of the U.N. forces. On January 4, 1951, the U.N. and South Korean forces withdrew from Seoul. However, by March 31, 1951, the U.N. forces had recovered lost ground and had arrived again at the 38th parallel. At this stage of the conflict MacArthur publicly called for the crossing of the Yalu River and for the U.N. forces to engage the Chinese Communist forces on their own territory because China was a belligerent in the war. President Harry S. Truman thereupon dismissed MacArthur from his commands for challenging the president's role as commander-in-chief of all U.S. troops and for his interference in U.S. foreign policy. After Gen. Matthew B. Ridgway was chosen to replace MacArthur, the U.N. forces essentially maintained their positions along the 38th parallel.

On July 10, 1951, negotiators representing both sides in the conflict began armistice talks at Kaesong in North Korea and later at Panmunjom in South Korea. These negotiations were obstructed by conflicts over three important issues: the Chinese insistence that all foreign military units be removed from Korea; the setting of the postwar boundary between the ROK and the DPRK; and the exchange of prisoners.

With the death of Joseph Stalin and the inauguration of Dwight D. Eisenhower as U.S. president in early 1953, these issues were finally resolved, and an armistice was signed on July 27, 1953. The boundary was the military line between the North and South, which was incorporated into a demilitarized zone (DMZ) under U.N. supervision, not the 38th parallel as the Communists had initially demanded. The U.N. also achieved most of its other demands regarding exchange of prisoners and the continuing presence of U.N. troops in Korea.

The Korean War had lasted three years. During it, South Korean casualties were about 1,313,000 including 1,000,000 civilians and 47,000 troops killed in action. Thirty-three % of South Korea's housing was destroyed, and 43% of its industrial base was ruined.

After World War II Korea had been aided by the United States and to a much lesser extent by the 39-member U.N. Korean Reconstruction Agency (UNKRA). In 1946–48, the military-occupation period, the U.S. Army had supplied $181.2 million for the relief of disease and hunger in the occupation zone. Between 1949 and 1952 the United States had contributed $12.5 million in direct military assistance and $485.6 million in other forms of economic assistance. After the Korean War and until its demise in 1958, UNKRA (of which the United States was the largest single contributor) provided $148.5 million in economic assistance. Between 1946 and 1978 the United States provided economic assistance to South Korea in excess of $5,893,900,000.

From 1948 to 1960 Syngman Rhee ruled South Korea as president. During his autocratic presidency, to which office he was elected four times, a growing opposition formed among diverse political and social groups, including highly vocal student dissidents. After Rhee resigned under pressure and fled to the United States, the South Korean electorate replaced the presidential system of government with a parliamentary system in 1960. However, the second South Korean republic lasted only nine months. On May 16, 1961, the government of Prime Minister Chang Myon was overthrown in a military coup. He had attempted reform but had been blocked by factionalism even among his own followers. After the coup Maj. Gen. Park Chung Hee emerged as the leader of the military junta ruling the country. The Supreme Council for National Reconstruction was created and headed by Park; it controlled the government after the imposition of martial law and the dismissal of the National Assembly.

On October 15, 1963, Park was narrowly elected president of the Third Republic as a candidate of the Democratic Republican party. He was reelected in 1967 and 1971. His presidency was challenged, however by the former president of the Second Republic, Yun Po Sun, by the Civil Rule party, and by students over the issue of constitutional change, among others.

In the election of 1971 Park defeated Kim Dae Jung, candidate of the New Democratic party. This was the third and last four-year term that Park was allowed under terms of the constitution. In October 1972 he began to rule as a dictator, dissolving the National Assembly and suspending the constitution. Park cited the "dangerous uncertainties of the international situation" to justify his actions. In December 1972 the new constitution was announced, allowing the president unlimited six-year terms of office and expanding the power of the presidential office.

Park now created the *yushin* (revitalization or reform) system of government. Under this, a National Conference for Unification, chaired by the president, was organized as the chief organ of government, "to pursue peaceful unification of the fatherland." The 2,000–5,000 members of the conference were elected to six-year terms of office in direct popular elections. The conference controlled the election of the president. In December 1972 and again in December 1978 Park was reelected without opposition through this government scheme.

The Park government instituted highly successful Five-Year Plans for South Korea. Under the third Five-Year Plan (1972–76), South Korea registered an average annual GNP of 11.2%.

On October 26, 1979, however, Park was assassinated by the head of the Korean Central Intelligence Agency (KCIA). Although a liberal atmosphere followed, with Prime Minister Choi Kyu Han serving as acting president until he was elected president in December 1979, the military, under Lt. Gen. Chun Doo Hwan, chief of military intelligence, soon took over the government and reinstated police state conditions similar to those that had existed under Park. Chun was elected president on August 27,

1980. The new constitution that followed his election and establishment of government proclaimed the Fifth Republic. Under this constitution Chun was reelected by a wide margin in February 1981.

Although North Korea made military incursions across the DMZ into South Korea in 1973 and 1974, in July 1972 both the ROK and DPRK had concluded an agreement calling for the eventual peaceful reunification of Korea. In 1985 they cooperated in economic talks. Three years later, however, South Korea faced unrest led by students in 1988 as they fought police during protests demanding the reunification of the country.

In 1983 South Korea became the focus of international tension when a Korean Air Lines plane was shot down over Soviet airspace; all aboard perished. Five years later, with Seoul chosen as the site of the 1988 Olympic Games, foreign visitors thronged the country and international attention became focused on South Korea's great economic progress.

In December 1988 Roh Tae Woo was elected president in national elections after riots opposing President Chun's attempt to appoint his successor as president. Chun backed down and permitted the direct popular election of his successor as well as other constitutional changes.

ECONOMY

Background: The two salient characteristics of the South Korean economy are its central planning and the dominant role of great industrial conglomerates *(chaebol)* that are highly diversified.

Since 1962 South Korea has implemented Five-Year Plans, which have largely been successful in changing the country from an agricultural to an industrial society, and have helped stimulate great economic growth. The World Bank estimated in 1985 that in real terms between 1965 and 1985 South Korea experienced one of the highest national growth rates in the world, an annual average rate of 6.6%.

Although the industrial sector was devastated by the Korean War, subsequent economic aid from the United States and UNKRA, among others, helped the South Koreans to rebuild and advance industry. The South Koreans also borrowed heavily on the world markets, with the country's external debt totaling $33.5 billion at the end of 1987. Economic progress has largely been due to the creation of a dynamic manufacturing sector. From the early 1960s to 1980 the government encouraged large industrial complexes such as oil refineries and fertilizer processing units; however, during this period the textile industry was South Korea's largest industrial employer and its most valuable earner of export revenue. Subsequently, shipbuilding became very important. With its main shipbuilding yards located at Mokpo and Ulsan, South Korea is second only to Japan in the percentage of the world's ships it builds; it is estimated that in 1988 South Korea received 25% of the world's orders for new ships.

During the 1980s the South Korean government aided the diversification of industry into high-technology fields, with the idea that electronics, computers and other high-technology industries would help the country overcome loss of export revenue from declining textile exports occasioned by

159

worldwide import quotas. In 1987, exports of electronics goods represented almost 25% of the value of all South Korean exports that year. The production of semiconductors was, for example, encouraged by a 1 million won investment scheme in 1986.

The assembly of passenger cars and other motor vehicles also became an important industry. In 1987, 5.4% of the value of all exports was achieved by the export of South Korean passenger cars.

Although some 23% of the labor force was employed in the agricultural, fishing and forestry sector in 1986, this sector is not growing. Nevertheless, South Korea is largely self-sufficient in rice; other important crops are wheat, sweet potatoes and barley. South Korea is also one of the leading exporters of fish in the world; its catch is also sufficient to supply the home market, for which fish remains an important source of protein. Lumbering is an important seasonal industry of the farming population of Kyongsang and Kangwon provinces. Although South Korea has few important minerals, it has become one of Asia's most heavily industrialized nations. The chief mineral resources are coal, iron ore, graphite, silver and gold, lead, zinc and tungsten. Recently, the discovery of important fields of natural gas has been reported.

Foreign trade: In 1986 South Korea's exports accounted for 42.2% of the country's GNP. That year, for the first time in 20 years, its merchandise trade account recorded a surplus of $4.206 billion. In 1987 and 1988 South Korea achieved further and greater surpluses, much of these with the United States. This caused the U.S. government to pressure South Korea to open its domestic market to U.S. goods and services and make other efforts to reduce the trade surplus.

South Korea mainly exports to the United States and Japan, where in 1987 it had a trade deficit of $5.2 billion. Of growing importance is the officially unrecognized trade with the People's Republic of China. South Korea is no longer listed as a less-developed country by the United States and the European Community, and in January 1988 it was no longer allowed to export many of its goods and services tariff-free under the generalized system of preferences. In early 1988 South Korea announced that it would allow 445 types of foreign products to be imported into the country without trade constraints.

The nation has been successful in securing overseas construction contracts, primarily in the Middle East. It is estimated that in 1988 the value of these contracts reached $4 billion. They have provided valuable foreign-exchange earnings.

Employment: In 1986 it was estimated that 16,116,000 people over the age of 14 were economically productive in South Korea. Those employed numbered 15,505,000, of whom 23.6% were engaged in the agriculture, fishing and forestry sector; 24.7% in the manufacturing sector; and 51.7% in other sectors, principally services.

In 1985 it was estimated that, on average, a South Korean employed in the nonagricultural sectors worked 52 hours weekly, one of the lengthiest workweeks in the world. The South Korean worker works under highly restrictive conditions, with strikes practically forbidden and the right of collective bargaining highly curtailed.

The most serious labor disputes in South Korea's history took place in 1987. Under terms of the settlement wages were increased, the cost of labor sharply rising (up to an estimated 30%). However, by September 1987 the GNP was estimated to have grown by 12.2%, inflation averaged 3.2% and unemployment stood at 4%.

Standards of living are quite high on average, in comparison with most other Asian countries, including North Korea and the People's Republic of China; but there are substantial differences between the standards of living of South Korean rural agricultural workers and the urban industrial workers. Consumer goods are freely available, of generally good quality and in growing demand.

SOCIAL WELFARE

The South Korean government provides military relief payments to wounded veterans and war widows (132,000 of whom were aided in 1985). Various nongovernmental charitable organizations provide financial aid to orphans, disaster victims and the aged (in 1985, 2,273,000 people were aided by these voluntary programs). The national government has also established a medical and industrial accident insurance scheme; this insures 26% of people who are economically productive and 24% of the total population.

In 1973 the South Korean government approved a scheme to create a national welfare pension plan, which, however, was never realized. In 1986 the government stated that a pension, minimum wage and health insurance scheme would be mandated by legislation in 1988–89.

Health services: Outside the two largest cities, Seoul and Pusan, there are few hospital and health facilities. There were 74,365 hospital beds in 1985, and 29,596 physicians. South Koreans enjoy relatively long lives (with the average life expectancy estimated in 1986 to be 71 for women and 65 for men); in 1986 the rate of infant mortality nationwide was 29 per 1,000 live births. In 1985 potable water was available to 53% of the population; but less than 6% of the population had modern sewage systems.

Housing: Although the annual rate of population growth dropped from 2.7% in 1960–66 to 1.5% during 1973–84, South Korean continues to suffer an acute shortage of housing. The continuing influx of the rural population to the industrial centers of Pusan and Seoul exacerbates the shortage. In 1985, despite the 1981–86 Five-Year Plan's creation of 1,460,000 housing units, there was a shortfall of over 3 million housing units. In that year, 9,588,723 households were housed in 6,274,462 housing units.

EDUCATION

South Korea spends a sizable portion of its national budget on education: In 1986 education accounted for about 2,769,000 won, or 20% of the total. By the terms of the Education Law of 1949 the unified system of

South Korean education comes under the authority of the Ministry of Education. This law also provides six years of free, compulsory primary education; all children between the ages of six and 12 are enrolled in primary schools, after which they can enter secondary schools. The six years of secondary education are divided into two equal stages.

The nearly 7,000 primary schools had 1985 enrollments of 4,856,752 students. Middle school enrollment in 1985 was 2,782,173; vocational and academic high school enrollment was 2,152,802. The 1985 enrollment in universities and colleges was 1,192,172. In the same year there were 11 teacher's colleges and 120 junior vocational colleges, as well as 100 universities and colleges. There were also more than 200 graduate schools. Among the leading universities are the government-run Seoul National University, and the private Chungang, Yonsei, Hanyang, Ewha, Korea and Sung Kyun Kwan universities. All these universities are located in the capital. In 1988, 90% of the appropriately aged population was enrolled in postsecondary studies; this was one of the highest rates in the world.

In 1982 adult literacy stood at 82% of women and 96% of men.

MASS MEDIA

The press

Dailies: Hankook Ilbo, Seoul, independent, 2 million; *Chosun Ilbo,* Seoul, independent, 1.8 million; *Joong-ang Ilbo,* Seoul, 1.6 million; *Dong-A Ilbo* (The Oriental Daily News), Seoul, independent, 1 million; *Ilgan Sports,* Seoul, 500,000; *Sonyou Dong-A,* Seoul, children's 415,000; *Maeil Kyungje Shinmun,* business and economics, 235,000; *The Korean Herald,* Seoul, English, independent, 150,000; *The Korean Times,* Seoul, English, independent, 140,000.

Periodicals: Weekly Chosun (w), 350,000; *Shin Dong-A* (m), general, 335,000; *Yosong Dong-A* (m), women's, 237,000; *Wolgan Mot* (m), fashion, 120,000; *Eumak Dong-A* (m), music, 85,000; *Han Kuk No Chong,* Federation of Korean Trade Unions, 20,000; *Hyundae Munhak,* literature, 20,000.

Broadcasting: South Korean radio and television is controlled by the Korean Broadcasting System (KBS), which is government owned, and the Munhwa Broadcasting Corporation (MBC-TV) Network, which is commercially owned. There is also a U.S. Forces Korea Network. In 1985 there were 81 radio stations broadcasting in the ROK. Besides the KBS, MBC and U.S. Forces Korea networks, there was the Christian Broadcasting System, which had five network-owned stations broadcasting religious programs in Korean. Also in that year there were an estimated 8.2 million television receivers in the ROK. Thirty-six commercial television stations were on the air in 1985.

BIOGRAPHICAL SKETCHES

Kim Dae Jung. Politician of the opposition and president of the Peace and Democracy party from 1987 to 1988, Kim was born in 1924 in Mokpo.

He was captured and incarcerated by the North Korean forces during the Korean War. Later, serving in the National Assembly, he was a member of the Finance Committee in 1960. In 1971 he ran for the presidency as candidate of the Korean Democratic party. In August 1973, because of his opposition to the ROK government then in power, he was kidnapped in Tokyo by ROK agents and confined for three days. In the 1970s he was arrested and imprisoned for opposition activities; and in 1980 he was again arrested. Charged with attempting to overthrow the government, he was sentenced to death, but this was commuted to life imprisonment. Later, this commuted sentence was reduced to 20 years' imprisonment. Released in December 1982, he continued his political activities and was the candidate of the Peace and Democracy party in the 1987 presidential election.

Kim Young Sam. Politician of the opposition and president of the Reunification Democratic party from 1987 to 1988, Kim was born in 1927 in Geoje district, South Kyongsang province. Educated at Seoul National University, Kim served 25 years in the National Assembly. In the 1970s he was twice president of the New Democratic party, in opposition to President Park. He was expelled from the National Assembly in 1979 at the behest of Park, for his opposition to government policies. Under house arrest several times in the 1980s, he also went on a 23-day hunger strike in 1983 to call for more democratic measures in government. Although he was forbidden by the government from taking part in political activity, he helped to organize the New Korea Democratic party, which was very successful in the National Assembly elections of 1985. Kim is the author of several political works and has frequently traveled and lectured in the United States, Southeast Asia, Europe and the Middle East.

Roh Tae Woo. Elected president of the ROK in 1987 and head of the Democratic Justice party, Roh was born in 1932 in Taegu. Educated at the Korean Military Academy and the U.S. Special Warfare School, he fought in the Korean War and rose in the ranks of the Korean Army, becoming commanding general of the 9th Special forces Brigade in 1974, commander of the Capital Security Command in 1979 and commander of the Defense Security Command in 1980. He was made a four-star general in 1981 and retired from the army in July of the same year. In 1981 he entered the cabinet as minister of state for national security and foreign affairs. He was later appointed, in 1982, minister of sports and minister of home affairs. He has held a number of other positions outside the government, including the presidencies of the Seoul Olympic Organizing Committee, the Korean Amateur Sports Association and the Korean Olympic Committee.

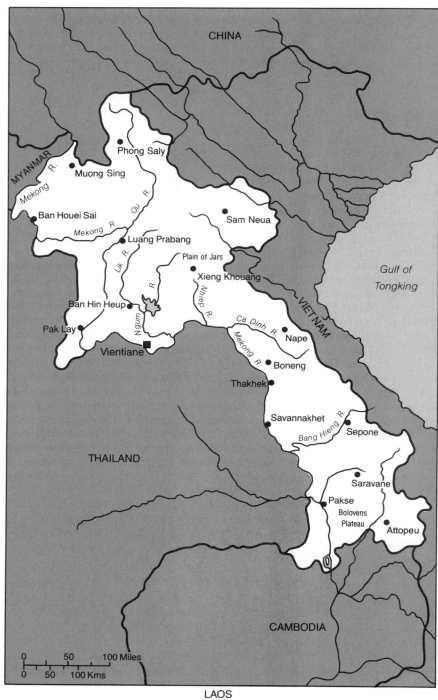

LAOS

LAOS

Features: The Lao People's Democratic Republic (LPDR) is the only land-locked nation in Southeast Asia. It is bordered by China to the north, by Myanmar to the northeast and by Cambodia to the south. The Mekong River forms much of Laos's 1,074 mile/1,730 km. border with Thailand; Vietnam extends along the eastern border for 1,215 miles/1,957 km. The country is long and narrow, extending approximately 620 miles/1,000 km. from north to south, and varying between 124 to 280 miles/200 to 400 km. from east to west. Laos's only easy access to the sea is through the Korat Plateau in northeastern Thailand. It is otherwise blocked by the mountains of southern China to the north, by the Annamese Highlands to the east, and by the Khone and Dangrek ranges along its border with Cambodia. Four series of rapids make the Mekong unnavigable to the sea.

Northern Laos is almost entirely mountainous. The country's highest peak, Phu Bia in Xiengkhuang Province, rises to 9,252 feet/2,820 m. Dense jungle covers mountain slopes throughout the north; rainfall in this area drains into multiple rivers running west and south to the Mekong. The Plain of Jars is a hilly plateau area in Xiengkhuang covered with large earthen "jars" containing burial ashes. Rice plains line the east bank of the Mekong in central Laos, and the forests in the southern and central parts of the country are sparser than those in the north, making them more easily exploitable.

Population groups settled primarily along three navigable stretches of the Mekong: in the north, in Luang Prabang, including Sayaboury Province; in the center, between Vientiane and Savannakhet; and in Champassak, in the south. The country's rugged geography has histori-cally made centralized control difficult and today hampers economic inte-gration.

Area: 91,000 sq. miles/236,000 sq. km.

Mean max. and min. temperatures: Vientiane (18°N, 103°E) 92°F/33.3°C (April), 66°F/18.9°C (Dec.).

Relative humidity: 53%–91%.

Mean annual rainfall: 106.5 in/2,705.1 mm.

POPULATION

Total population (1985 census): 3,584,803.

Chief towns and populations: VIENTIANE (176,637), Savannakhet (50,690), Pakse (44,860), Luang Prabang (44,244).

Distribution: Laos remains a predominately rural country, with only 15% of the population classified as urban. The largest concentrations are found along the Mekong River: in Vientiane, Savannakhet, Champassak and Luang Prabang. The remainder of the population live in some 11,000 villages throughout the country. Average density is 15 inhabitants per sq. km. The Lao Loum, or lowland Lao, constitute approximately 54% of the population; the Lao Theung (midland Lao) make up 34%; and the Lao Soung (upland Lao) account for 9%. Vietnamese, Chinese and Indians make up the remaining 1% of the population. Approximately 310,000 people left Laos as refugees between 1975 and 1985, reducing the population by 10%. Much of the outflow included the former Lao elite and the educated middle class. The heavy loss of trained personnel has set the country back several years in terms of development. The Lao government actively encourages population growth, and birth control devices are unavailable. The 2.9% growth rate is a welcome phenomenon. Nearly half the population is under the age of 15.

Language: Lao is the official language. Since nearly 60 different ethnic groups fall under the lowland, upland and midland designations, many dialects are spoken; these include Hmong, Thai dialects and Lao Theung dialects.

Religion: Theravada Buddhism is the principal religion of the LPDR. Animism is practiced to a lesser extent. Since the mid-14th century Buddhism has provided the framework for the Lao worldview. The Buddhist *wat,* or temple, remains the center of village life, although the Communist leadership has made Buddhism a vehicle to promote socialism. Buddhism is symbolic of what is typically "Lao," and thus encouraged as the Lao attempt to distance themselves from their Vietnamese guarantors. In contemporary Laos, Buddhism and politics are intertwined.

CONSTITUTIONAL SYSTEM

The LPDR has not yet adopted a constitution. A Constitutional Drafting Commission was set up shortly after the Pathet Lao (PL), or "Land of the Lao," came to power in 1975, but it has not yet produced a document. Lao authorities have not explained the delay. Some analysts speculate that profound differences exist between Lao officials and their Vietnamese advisers over what form the constitution should take. Another unresolved question focuses on how the regime will protect the rights of minorities that make up nearly half the country's population. The latest word on progress came in 1986, when the Supreme People's Assembly (SPA) drew up a "fundamental draft" of the constitution and electoral laws.

Since there is no constitution, executive and legislative powers in the

LPDR are not clearly defined. Democratic centralism is the principle underlying the government structure, but actual power is concentrated in the hands of less than a dozen men making up the Lao People's Revolutionary party (LPRP) Politburo and Permanent Secretariat. These men also dominate the Khana Rathaban (Council of Government), or government ministries. Party, executive and legislative branches exist in theory, but with much overlap and in descending order of power.

Head of state: President Phoumi Vongvichit (acting). *Prime minister:* Kaysone Phomvihane.

Political party: The LPRP is the only political party in Laos. The Political Bureau (Politburo) is the center of party power. Kaysone Phomvihane has presided over it since the party's founding in 1955 as the Lao People's party (Phak Pasason Lao). Six other full members, whose average age is 70, have also served since then. Four new full members and two alternate members were elected in November 1986, the first change in the group since 1972. It is not known how often the Politburo meets or how it comes to decisions.

The Central Committee Secretariat is next in the line of power. Nearly all of its nine members also serve in the Politburo. The Secretariat acts for the Central Committee whenever it is not meeting. Since the Central Committee usually meets only once or twice a year, the Secretariat effectively controls the daily affairs of the LPRP. It issues all party decisions and directives, and thus appoints government officials. The Central Committee is elected by the Party Congress, which meets every three or four years, to serve until the next congress. It has no fixed size. After the 1986 Fourth Party Congress there were 41 full members and 19 alternates. Members of the Central Committee are usually veteran Communists and include representatives from most state ministries, party committees and mass organizations.

Executive: The president is the chief of state, and he is assisted by the Khana Rathaban. The government includes 14 ministries and six state committees. There are three levels within the government. At the top are the chairman and five vice-chairmen of the Khana Rathaban, all also members of the Politburo; they make all policy decisions and direct all government activity. Next are 19 ministers and state committee chairmen who are responsible for their own ministries. Below them is a group of approximately 80 vice-ministers and chairmen with specific functions.

Legislature: The Lao Patriotic Front, directed by the LPRP, selected 274 delegates to form a National Congress of People's Representatives (National Assembly) in late 1975. This body then appointed the 46-member SPA, made up of a majority of LPRP members. The SPA was charged with drawing up a constitution. The powers of the body remain unclear, because of the continued lack of a constitution. The SPA ratifies appointments made by the party Secretariat. It adopts the annual political report of the LPRP and ratifies laws it is asked to approve.

Local government: Laos is divided into 16 provinces *(khoueng),* 112 districts *(muong),* 950 subdistricts *(tasseng)* and 11,424 villages *(ban).* Party committees direct local affairs in the provinces. A provincial party secretary holds considerable power within the province and on the national level. Many villages do not yet have a branch of the party since they do not have enough party members (only one or two usually) to form one.

Judicial system: Laws in the LPDR are made by government decree. Until 1980 no one knew the limit of law until he or she was arrested. Those arrested were not tried but sent to reeducation camps. In 1980 a system of socialist justice was instituted, but a written legal code was not publicized. Common crimes at the local level are reviewed by a committee including the local party secretary, local representatives of popular organizations, the head of the village administrative committee (perhaps a monk) and villagers known for their integrity. Political cases are referred to higher levels. Peoples' tribunals exist at the district and provincial levels. The presidents, vice-presidents and judges assisting at these tribunals are government-appointed. At each level two "people's assessors" are elected by the people's assembly at that level.

The Supreme People's Court, established by decree of the SPA in 1983, is the highest court in the land. The SPA elects its president, vice-presidents and judges. It is a court of first instance in important cases, and serves as an appeal court and to determine commutation or remission of sentences. All cases are judged in public except those that threaten national security. Sentences include death, imprisonment, internal exile, confiscation of goods and public rebuke. Periods of punishment are not fixed, but depend on the attitude of the person who has committed the crime. Prisoners must show signs of contrition, which means recognizing the omniscience of the party.

RECENT HISTORY

Laos has been subject to the dominance of its neighbors throughout much of its history. In the mid-19th century the country fell under Siamese control. Siam (now Thailand) ceded Laos to the French in 1893 but retained control of the Korat Plateau of present-day Thailand, with a Lao population three times that of French Laos.

The French ruled Laos with benign indifference; little economic or social development occurred. The Lao monarch was allowed to remain in the palace at Luang Prabang and to exercise limited powers in the northern provinces. It was not until the 1940s that a Lao nationalist movement developed, awakened partly by the Japanese presence in Indochina from 1940 to 1945 and partly by French administrators who purposely promoted Lao nationalism to counter Thai aggression. The new Lao sense of racial and national pride led the Lao to seek freedom from French dominance.

After the Japanese defeat in 1945 the French were determined to maintain their Indochinese empire. Laos then became an independent Associated

State within the French Union, with a constitutional monarchy and an elected National Assembly. The Lao Issara (Free Laos), a group that had declared independence before Japan's defeat, went into exile in Thailand. Prince Souvanna Phouma and his half brother, Prince Souphanouvoung, were Lao Issara leaders. Both were to become significant figures in Lao politics. Souphanouvoung sympathized with the Vietnamese and leaned more to the left than Souvanna Phouma, a firm neutralist. In 1949 the Lao Issara accepted amnesty and returned to Laos.

Resistance also formed along the Laos-Vietnam border under the "Committee of Lao Resistance in the East." Lao and Lao-Vietnamese cadres under the direction of the Indochinese Communist party (ICP) and anti-French tribal chiefs of southern Laos formed the core of this group. Its leaders— Kaysone Phomvihane, Sithon Kommadean and Faydang Lobliayau—later became the most significant leaders of the Lao Communist movement. Another Communist faction included revolutionary members of the traditional Lao elite: Prince Souphanouvoung (after he was expelled from the Lao Issara), Souk Vongsak and Phoumi Vongvichit.

Souphanouvoung formed the first Congress of the People's Representatives or the Lao Resistance Front in August 1950. The Congress formed a resistance government, the PL. Souphanouvoung was prime minister and minister of foreign affairs and Kaysone Phomvihane was minister of defense. These leading resistance figures, backed by the Viet Minh, formed the Lao People's party in March 1955.

Souvanna Phouma formed a rival government in 1951 to work toward national reconciliation. Laos achieved independence on October 22, 1953. After the 1954 Geneva accords, Phong Saly and Sam Neua provinces (along the Vietnamese border) were administered by the PL, which continued to receive advice and military support from the Viet Minh throughout the struggle. The royal Lao government (RLG) under Souvanna Phouma controlled the rest of the country. The next two decades became a struggle between left, right and neutral factions for control of Laos.

An attempt to form a coalition government in 1957 failed due to rightist pressure within the RLG supported by the United States and Thailand. As the fighting continued the United States increased its military aid to the RLG, thus extending its anti-Communist drive from South Vietnam to Laos. When the coalition collapsed in 1958, right-wing leader Phoumi Sananikone came to power.

The American-backed rightist government maintained control through allegedly unfair National Assembly elections in 1960. Any compromise with the PL was now out of the question, leading to assured civil war. An August coup led by Kong Le, a PL paratroop captain, restored a neutral government, with Souvanna Phouma again acting as prime minister. The CIA responded by backing right-wing General Phoumi Nosavan in a military showdown with Kong Le. Phoumi, with U.S. support, marched on Vientiane in late 1960. Kong Le and Souvanna Phouma retreated and established a government on the Plain of Jars. Another government was established in Vientiane, with Boun Oum ana Champassak as prime minister and Phoumi as defense minister. The United States, Great Britain and France backed the Vientiane government, while the Communist bloc and neutralist states backed the Jars government.

Souvanna Phouma (for the neutralists), Boun Oum (rightists) and Souphanouvoung (PL) made another attempt to form a coalition government in 1962. The new government's neutrality was not observed, as Laos was subject to Vietnamese incursions along the Ho Chi Minh Trail, and to U.S. bombing raids attempting to cut Viet Minh supply lines that ran through eastern Laos. The extension of the second Vietnam war to Laos eventually polarized forces there, destroying the neutralists as a political force. The second coalition fell apart, and Souvanna Phouma increasingly moved to the right.

As North Vietnam continued to supply military assistance to the PL, the United States stepped up its bombing of Communist-held areas in Laos in 1964. The United States increased its aid to the Royal Lao Army (RLA) and recruited guerrilla forces from among the Hmong and Yao tribes. The United States dropped more than 2 million tons of bombs on Laos, causing the displacement of 750,000 people, or one-fourth of the population.

Between 1965 and 1973 civil strife between the PL and the RLG continued. Finally, in 1973, the adversaries signed an "Agreement on the Restoration of Peace and Reconciliation in Laos." It called for the cessation of foreign military activity in Laos and for the formation of a provisional government of National Union with a policy-making National Political Consultative Council (NPCC). By this time, an estimated four-fifths of national territory and two-fifths of the population were under PL control. The third coalition government was sworn in in April 1974. The PL and the right had equal representation in the government and on the NPCC. The coalition ran smoothly for the rest of the year, but the collapse of right-wing regimes in Cambodia and Vietnam in April 1975 sped the PL takeover in Laos. Large student- and trade union-organized demonstrations in Vientiane in early May denounced the right wing, causing five ministers to resign and flee with several leading generals. Hundreds more—civil servants, military officers and merchants—followed. PL-backed ministers replaced those who had fled. In August joint military and police forces responsible for assuring the neutrality of Luang Prabang and Vientiane were dissolved, and revolutionary committees took over the two cities. The monarchy, coalition government and the NPCC were abolished in November. The Lao People's Democratic Republic, with political institutions modeled after other Communist states, was proclaimed in December 1975.

RLA police officers and senior civil servants were sent to reeducation camps, effectively stifling opposition to the new regime. The PL's obsession with security created a climate of uncertainty and fear, causing many to leave the country as refugees.

Faced with economic shortages and rising prices, the government nationalized industry. State trading replaced private commerce. Prices skyrocketed and the value of the kip tumbled. Many people were disillusioned by deteriorating economic conditions and tight social controls; nearly 40,000, including much of the professional middle class, left the country in 1976 and 1977. A failed government attempt to collectivize agriculture prompted the flight of an additional 50,000 lowland Lao in 1978.

Economic controls were loosened in 1979 to try to revive the struggling economy. Agricultural taxes were cut to encourage private production. The government placed new emphasis on market socialism, with economic results outweighing ideological orthodoxy. By the end of 1980 food and consumer goods were once again freely available in Vientiane's markets. Rice production increased, foreign trade was liberalized and private investment was permitted. The 40,000 Vietnamese troops stationed in Laos were cut back to 20,000.

Policy changes created dissension within the LPRP between those favoring stricter socialist methods and those supporting liberalization. The latter triumphed for the moment, but the future path of the revolution is still uncertain.

ECONOMY

Background: Debate within the party has centered on the process and pace of socialist transformation. Those favoring a gradual transition endorse a mixed state/private economy. Hard-liners consider this ideological backsliding and favor a rapid transition. After hard-line policies of agricultural collectivization failed dismally in 1976–78, the pragmatists prevailed.

The geography of Laos has resulted in a regionally fragmented economy, which limits the scope for centralist control. Poor transportation retards economic development; merchandise cannot be transported easily and agricultural surpluses cannot be moved to deficit areas. The economy is also hampered by a shortage of trucks, fuel and spare parts.

Subsistence agriculture forms the backbone of the economy, involving 85% of the labor force and accounting for more than 60% of GDP. For that reason, the first Five-Year Plan (1981–85) and the second Five-Year Plan (1986–90) gave priority to agriculture and food security. During the first Plan Laos did attain self-sufficiency in food. However, the bulk of production was for home use rather than for sale, leaving little surplus for capital accumulation by either the individual or the state. Transport and trade accounted for 8% of GDP, and manufacturing and mining 5%—a structure essentially unchanged since 1975. There is no heavy industry in Laos. Estimates of per capita income range from U.S. $98 to $184 per year. The state's share of the agricultural sector is small: When combined with the cooperative sector, the share is 23% of total cultivated land. The public sector dominates industry with its control of electricity and mining.

The Lao economy comprises five organizational forms, existing side by side: (1) the state sector, which includes large industrial farms and banking, and state construction, transport and trading enterprises; (2) the collective economy which is comprised of approximately 3,200 cooperative farms contolling about 444,780 acres/180,000 ha., or 20% of crop land (1984); (3) the individual economy, which includes self-employed farmers, handicraft producers and small traders; (4) the capitalist economy, which is made up of industrial, trading and transport companies owned by private entrepreneurs and only found in larger towns; (5) the state-private economy, which represents joint ventures. These five sectors are likely to coexist for some time as the country forges its path to socialism. Laos's development plans rely heavily on foreign aid, mostly from the Communist bloc. Foreign assistance totaled $80 million in 1985, the bulk coming from Communist countries.

Agriculture: Attempts to collectivize the agricultural sector met with fierce peasant opposition in 1978. The LPRP abandoned the program and introduced sweeping reforms in 1980. A new system of taxation based on average land fertility rather than on output was introduced. Farmers were taxed a fixed amount, leaving them free to dispose of surplus on the open market. This provided incentive to increase yields.

Less than 2.5 million acres/1 million ha. of Laos's total area of 58.3 million acres/23.6 million ha.—or just 4%—is cultivated. Rice accounts for more than 75% of the area planted; another 12 million acres/5 million ha. is potentially cultivable. Rice is still grown by traditional means, with little mechanization and few farmers using fertilizers or organic manure. Irrigation still serves only about 30% of the country's rice land. This results in yields that are among the lowest in the world, at 1.7 tons per hectare for wet rice, 2.0 tons for dry-season crops, and 1.1 tons for upland rice grown by the slash-and-burn method. Yields have improved by about 20% since 1980, mostly due to increases in cultivated land.

Maize, grown on 31,000 acres/12,546 ha. is the second primary cereal crop in Laos. Yields average 1 ton per hectare. Manioc and sweet potatoes, with yields of 8.5 tons per hectare, are cultivated on a total of 27,181–29,652 acres/11,000–12,000 ha. Various vegetables are grown on another 12,355–14,826 acres/5,000–6,000 ha. mostly for home consumption.

Coffee is grown on more than 44,478 acres/18,000 ha. and is the LPDR's principal cash crop. This represents an over 100% increase in the area planted with coffee between 1982 and 1986. Tobacco is grown commerically around Vientiane and supplies the country's single cigarette factory.

Livestock is raised for private slaughter or for use as draft animals. In 1985 there were nearly 1 million buffaloes, 500,000 heads of cattle and flocks of 500,000 to 1.5 million poultry. There are few commercial herds or flocks.

Forestry: Forests cover nearly 50% of the total land area of Laos. Timber is one of the main sources of foreign exchange. Between 7 million acres/3 million ha. and 17 million acres/7 million ha. are being exploited, much for valuable teak and rosewood. Sticklao, benzoin, cardamom, bamboo and rattan are other important forest products. Laos had four sawmills in 1985, with a production capacity of 521,000 tons per year. Only 20% of the capacity is normally used, however, because of shortages of timber (due to lack of transportation and equipment), spare parts and fuel.

Industry and mining: The industrial sector, including electricity and mining, accounts for only 7% of GDP and employs approximately 10,000 people. About 20 factories run by the Ministry of Industry, Handicrafts and Forestry account for 80% of Laos's industrial production. They include rice mills and sawmills as well as factories manufacturing corrugated iron, agricultural tools, industrial gases, plastics, detergents, insecticides, beer and soft drinks, matches, cigarettes, and ceramics. Smaller private factories produce handicrafts, weave cloth, make furniture and retread tires. Production in all areas except electricity is low, and distribution and marketing are inefficient. Small-scale manufacturing and handicraft enterprises located in the provinces comprise the remaining 20% of industrial production. Most are small- and medium-scale, with few employing more than 200 workers.

Output in electricity tripled between 1977 and 1985, when capacity was 167,500 megawatts (MW). About 27,000 MW are consumed locally; the remainder is exported to Thailand. Electricity accounts for 85% of total value of exports, amounting to $25 million annually. Laos's important mineral resources are virtually unexploited but have potential for future development. Gold, copper, lead and manganese have been discovered in small quantities and may provide a potential source of export income in the long term.

Trade: It is difficult to obtain accurate trade figures for Laos since much trade is conducted by the provinces themselves or by private companies and individuals. Also, a certain amount of smuggling between Laos and Thailand occurs across the Mekong. The export of electricity to Thailand accounts for two-thirds of total Lao exports. Other exports include sawn timber, wooden furniture, minerals and coffee. Imports include machinery, vehicles, cement, petroleum products, medicines, tools, spare parts and consumer goods. Because of its heavy need for inputs for economic development Laos suffers a chronic trade deficit. Figures for 1983 showed exports valued at $42.8 million, while imports totaled $135.1 million. Major trading partners are the Soviet Union, Vietnam, Thailand and Japan. Laos's foreign debt is $400 million, $260 million of that being owed to the Communist bloc.

Employment: Eighty-five % of the population are self-sufficient, subsistence-level peasant farmers. The few small factories in Vientiane employ about 15,000 workers. The armed forces account for 54,000 people.

Prices and wages: Salaries for civil servants in 1985 ranged from 150 to 600 kip (400 kip = $1) per month, and were supplemented by coupons used to purchase basic items at state shops at heavily subsidized prices. Rice, for example, sold for three kip per kilo at a state shop, but cost 80 kip per kilo on the open market. Most families grow their own vegetables and raise poultry or pigs. Many people have left government employment because of paltry salaries. A peasant with a stall at the Vientiane market can make 10 to 20 times as much, but must also purchase goods at free-market rates.

EDUCATION

Education for the masses has been a high priority in the LPDR. Primary schools have been set up in most villages and an effort has been made to reduce adult illiteracy. But all education is in Lao, a language many minority people do not speak, let alone read; no provisions have been made for literacy in a minority language. Language is one means by which the government is pursuing national unity.

The education system includes five levels: preschool *(anuban)*, primary school *(pathom)*, middle school *(mathanyom)*, high school *(udom)* and university level of one kind or another *(mahavitanyalay)*. Preschool lasts two years, with the aim being to free working mothers and provide an educational environment for children at an early age. Often, *anuban* are little more than day-care centers, and access is limited. Enrollment in 1985 was an estimated 16,000, only 4% of all children of the ages from four to six. More than 90% of school-age children, approximately 485,000, now attend *pathom*, which lasts for five years (a three-year program exists in some villages). Secondary school is divided into *mathanyom* and *udom*, each lasting three years. Middle schools are located at the subdistrict level, and high schools are located in district capitals. Class sizes tend to be large, and facilities such as science labs and audio-visual equipment are nearly nonexistent. Often, these schools are too far away for many students to attend and there are few boarding facilities. *Mathanyom* enrollment in 1985 was approximately 105,000; *udom* enrollment was 23,000.

Technical secondary schools provide vocational training, usually in agriculture, mechanics and engineering. Students usually live communally at these schools, which are set up in provincial and district towns. Only five college-level institutions exist in Laos, all in Vientiane. They are the Teacher Training College, the School of Civil Engineering, the Medical School, the School of Agriculture and Forestry, and the National Polytechnic Institute. Some students study abroad in Vietnam, the Soviet Union and Eastern Europe.

The quality of education in Laos is low as a result of the lack of qualified teachers. In 1985 there were 18,000 teachers at the primary level, 4,500 at the middle level and 1,400 at the high school level. Many teachers left the country as refugees, and the declining educational standards that ensued caused more to leave to seek opportunities for their children abroad. Schools also lack everything from chalk to pencils to textbooks. Lack of printing facilities and the required ideological orthodoxy have reduced textbook production. Political education is included in the curriculum at all levels, and all teachers are expected to emphasize party policies.

SOCIAL WELFARE

The LPDR emphasizes preventive medicine to improve public health at the local level. Health teams teach methods of simple hygiene to reduce intestinal disease and parasitic infection. Village nurses are trained to use traditional herbal remedies and to dispense elementary health care. All services are free, but there is a charge for Western medicines when available. Basic health education stresses the "three cleans": clean food, clean water and clean houses. In 1985 only 18% of villages had access to fresh, potable water.

174

Women health workers, with a few weeks' training, teach classes in maternal and child health at the village level. Nearly all villages have a "health station," staffed by a part-time public-health worker or nurse. Dispensaries with two to seven beds and staffed by trained nurses exist at the subdistrict level. All of the country's 112 district towns have small hospitals, together containing approximately 3,000 beds. Each provincial capital has a larger hospital. The total number of beds in 1985 was 8,970. In 1984 Laos had 418 doctors (one for every 8,576 people) and 371 auxiliary doctors (with three instead of six years of training)—or one doctor for every 1,700 people. Most medicines are supplied by U.N. agencies or by other humanitarian organizations. Distribution, however, is slow and difficult because of bureaucratic foot-dragging and transportation problems; the use of traditional herbal medicines is thus encouraged.

MASS MEDIA

The State Committee for Propaganda, the Press, Radio and Television (SC) and the Central Propaganda Committee (CPC) are responsible for disseminating information in the LPDR. Both government bodies answer to the party Central Committee. The SC disseminates local, national and international news through the Lao News Agency or Khaosan Pathet Lao (KPL). Daily bulletins are produced in Lao, French and English. Controls on the free flow of information are stringent and effective. The SC is the ideological watchdog for all publications. It can instruct editors to publish a party policy or reprimand them for not doing so.

The press: Pasason (The People), the party journal, 28,000, published six times a week in Lao; *Vientiane May* (New Vientiane), daily party bulletin, 2,500.

Biweeklies: Heng Ngan, organ of the Lao Federation of Trade Unions; *Lao Dong* (Labor), trade union publication, 46,000; *Noum Lao* (Lao Youth), organ of the Youth Union, 6,000.

Periodicals: Meying Lao, women's magazine, 4,000; *Siang Khong Gnaovason Song Thanva* (Voice of the 2nd December Youths); *Vannasin,* magazine of the Ministry of Culture; *Suksa May,* Ministry of Education; *Vasalan Khosana* (Propaganda Journal), organ of the LPRP Central Committee; *Vasalan Pathet Lao,* quarterly of the KPL, 15,000.

Broadcasting: Lao National Radio consists of a station in Vientiane and seven regional stations. Programs are broadcast in Lao, Vietnamese, Khmer, Thai, English and French. Regional stations broadcast programs in minority languages. Chinese radio stations also beam programs to Laos in minority languages.

Television broadcasts under the SC began in 1983. Programs run seven days a week from 7:30 P.M. to 10 P.M. or 11 P.M. Broadcasts include news, folkdancing, children's programs, sports, and Soviet programs. Towns close to the Thai frontier have access to Thai television, which broadcasts for more hours than Lao TV.

Kaysone Phomvihane. Born in 1925, Kaysone has been prime minister since 1975 and is considered the most powerful leader in the Lao Communist movement. He is half Vietnamese, and many attribute his ascendancy to his links with Vietnamese Communists. Kaysone attended secondary school and university in Hanoi and is said to have been taught by the Vietnamese revolutionary, Gen. Vo Nguyen Giap. Kaysone was one of the first Lao to join the Indochinese Communist party in 1946. In 1950 he was named minister of defense in the initial "Resistance Government." Kaysone established the Kommedam Military Training School for future PL officers. He participated in negotiations at the 1954 Geneva Conference and in 1956 with the RLG. Kaysone became the principal PL decision maker in 1960 after many of his colleagues were imprisoned by the RLG in Vientiane. He remained close to Vietnam throughout the PL struggle in the 960s, and became prime minister when the PL took control of the country in 1975.

Nouhak Phongsavan. Born in 1914, Nouhak is considered the number two man in the LPRP. His rise in the party is also attributed to ties to the Viet Minh developed in the 1940s. Nouhak, whose parents were peasants, only completed primary school in Savannakhet. He became a truck driver in 1938, transporting freight and people between Laos and central Vietnam. By 1941 he had developed good contacts with Vietnamese merchants. By the end of World War II he had begun transporting arms to supply the Viet Minh. Nouhak helped establish the Committee of Lao Resistance in the East in 1946, and joined the ICP in 1949. He was minister of finance in the first resistance government. He attended the Geneva Conference as part of the DRV delegation, and negotiated with the RLG in 1955. Nouhak was elected to the coalition government's National Assembly in 1958, but was imprisoned with 16 other PL leaders in 1959. He retreated to the jungle with other PL leaders after the last failed attempt to form a coalition government. From 1975 to 1983 he served as minister of finance. Nouhak yielded his post in a 1983 reshuffle, but as first vice-premier continued to oversee policy matters dealing with the economy.

Phoumi Vongvichit. Born in 1909, Phoumi has been acting president since Souphanouvoung resigned the post in 1986. Phoumi was the son of an official in Xiengkhouang Province, and was educated in French schools. He is referred to as the "intellectual" of the Lao Communist movement. He became governor of Xiengkhouang Province under the French, but later joined the Lao Issara nationalist movement against the colonizers. From 1975 to 1983 Phoumi served as minister of education, sports and religion, as well as deputy prime minister. He gave up the ministerial post in 1983 because of illness, but continued to direct overall policy in the field as vice-premier. Phoumi was appointed acting president in 1986.

Souphanouvoung. Born in 1909 into the Lao royal family, Souphanouvoung became president of the LPDR in 1975. The prince has always enjoyed national prominence because of his royal blood. He received his higher education in Paris, and joined an Indochinese engineering corps in Vietnam upon his return. He began his revolutionary activities in 1944. He was a member of the Lao Issara government that fled to Thailand after World War II, and became chairman of the Lao Resistance Front in 1950. Souphanouvoung was the chief spokesman for the PL and its chief negotiator with the RLG for over two decades. In 1962 he was named deputy prime minister in the second coalition government. After the 1975 takeover he held the president's post until he fell ill in late 1986 and resigned. His actual political power within the PL has often been the subject of debate. Some consider him a figurehead, manipulated by the Vietnamese and their chosen Lao leaders because of his name and traditional status. However, his picture hangs next to that of Kaysone in all public areas in Vientiane.

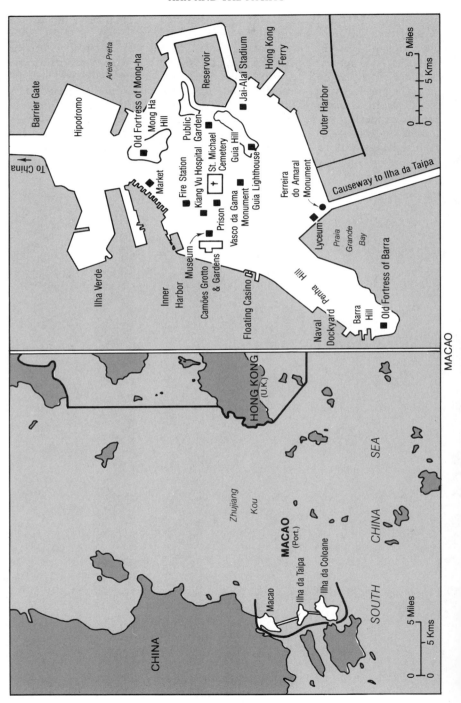

Barrier Gate

Areia Preta

Hipodromo

Old Fortress of Mong-ha

Mong Ha Hill

Reservoir

Jai-Alai Stadium

Hong Kong Ferry

To China

Public Garden

St. Michael Cemetery

Guia Hill

Guia Lighthouse

Outer Harbor

Ilha Verde

Market

Fire Station

Kiang Vu Hospital

Prison

Vasco da Gama Monument

Ferreira do Amaral Monument

Causeway to Ilha da Taipa

Inner Harbor

Museum

Camões Grotto & Gardens

Floating Casino

Penha Hill

Lyceum

Praia Grande Bay

Naval Dockyard

Barra Hill

Old Fortress of Barra

5 Miles

5 Kms

0

0

HONG KONG (U.K.)

Zhujiang Kou

MACAO (Port.)

Macao

Ilha da Taipa

Ilha da Coloane

CHINA

SOUTH CHINA SEA

5 Miles

5 Kms

0

MACAO

MACAO

Features: Macao, a tiny territory under Portuguese administration, is the oldest European colonial outpost in East Asia. It is located on the west side of the Zhu River estuary on the coast of southern China about 40 miles/65 km. southwest of Hong Kong. Macao City, the capital, occupies most of a low-lying peninsula linked to the Chinese mainland by a narrow isthmus. In addition to this peninsula, the territory includes the islands of Taipa (1.5 sq. miles/3.38 sq. km.) and Coloane (2.7 sq. miles/7.16 sq. km.). A causeway links the islands of Coloane and Taipa, and a bridge connects Taipa to the Macao peninsula. The terrain is generally hilly on both the mainland and the islands, but along the coast of the peninsula there are more level areas that have been reclaimed from the sea. Ambitious plans have been made to reclaim additional large areas adjoining the peninsula for urban development. The highest point in the territory, Coloane Hill, rises to 5,305 ft (17,406 m.). Macao has two ports: the Inner Harbor on the west side of the peninsula and the Outer Harbor on the east. Construction of a new deep-water port on the northern shore of Coloane began in 1988 and was scheduled for completion in 1991. This port would permit Macao direct access to oceangoing vessels of up to 10,000 tons, as opposed to the present 2,000-ton limit.

Area: 6.5 sq. miles/16.9 sq. km.

Mean max. and min. temperatures: 84°F/29°C (summer), 68°F/20°C (winter).

Mean annual rainfall: 71 in/1,800 mm.

Total population (1988 est.): 432,232.

Chief town and population (1986 est.): Macao City (416,200).

Distribution: The population is about 97% Chinese, primarily Cantonese refugees from nearby Guandong Province. Most of the remaining 3% are Portuguese or of mixed Chinese-Portuguese descent. Ethnic classification in the territory is based on language, culture and religion, rather than place of birth. Portuguese and locally born people of Portuguese or mixed Portuguese-Chinese descent (known as Macanese) dominate the civil service and hold almost all high-level official posts. Since 1976, illegal migrants from China who are apprehended have been repatriated, but large numbers of legal migrants continue to enter the territory. The population increased by about 65% between the last census (1981) and 1988. Only about 8.5% of the inhabitants live on Coloane and Taipa islands. The territory is 95% urban, and population densities in Macao City are among the highest in the world.

Language: Portuguese, the official language, is spoken by only about 3% of the population. Most of the people speak Chinese (Cantonese and/or Mandarin). The Macanese, many of whom speak both languages, serve as a bridge between the Portuguese administration and the Chinese community, although few of them are able to read and write Chinese. Some English, French and Spanish are also spoken.

Religion: The territory was established in part as a base for Portuguese missionary activity. Roman Catholicism is the official religion, and Macao is a diocese directly responsible to the Holy See. In 1985 there were more than 18,000 Roman Catholics, about half of whom were Chinese. Most Chinese people, however, practice Buddhism.

CONSTITUTIONAL SYSTEM

Constitution: Macao was an overseas province of Portugal from 1951 to 1974, when a military coup in Portugal led to independence for most of its colonies and to political changes in Macao. The colony was declared a Chinese territory under Portuguese administration. Its constitution is embodied in the 1976 Organic Law of Macao, which grants the territory administrative, financial and legislative autonomy. The rights and freedoms of Macao citizens are protected by the Portuguese constitution, which is applied to the territory. Macao sends one delegate to the Portuguese parliament; this representative is elected to a four-year term by universal suffrage. Under the terms of a 1987 accord Portugal will return Macao to Chinese administration in 1999. A commission was appointed by the Chinese government in 1988 to draft a basic law intended to serve as the territory's constitution after 1999, when it will become a special administrative region of China. This committee has 49 members, 19 of whom are from Macao. The representatives from Macao are drawn almost entirely from the business community and are generally considered to be pro-Beijing.

Head of state: Mario Soares (president of Portugal). *Governor:* Carlos Melancia.

Executive: The head of the executive is a governor appointed by the president of Portugal; the president has executive power over foreign matters and can dismiss the governor. The governor is relatively independent of the legislature, with the authority to issue decrees and to veto legislation not passed by a two-thirds legislative majority. Many executive functions are delegated to up to five secretaries-adjunct nominated by the governor and appointed by the president of Portugal. After 1999 the governor will be appointed by the Chinese government on the basis of elections or consultations in Macao.

Legislature: The 17 members of the Legislative Council serve three-year terms; 5 are appointed by the governor, 6 are elected by universal suffrage, and 6 are indirectly elected by various business groups and associations. In 1984, following a dispute between the governor and the legislature over the expansion of the franchise (favored by the governor), the vote was extended to all Macao residents. Previously, Chinese inhabitants needed five years of residence to qualify for the vote. The Legislative Council passes laws proposed by the executive, regulates the civil service and approves the budget. Laws pertaining to civil rights and freedoms, the judiciary and certain economic and commercial statutes must be approved by the government in Portugal. After 1999 the legislature is to have a majority of directly elected members.

Political parties: There are no formal political parties, although a number of civic associations are politically active. They include the Electoral Union, the Pro Macao and Flower of Friendship, and the Development of Macao, all of which are represented in the legislature.

Local government: The territory is divided into two districts (Macao proper and the islands) under the jurisdiction of the Department of Civil Administration in Lisbon. There are five parishes in Macao and one for each of the islands.

Judicial system: The judicial system is administered directly from Portugal. Local special courts handle adminstrative matters and ordinary courts handle criminal and civil cases. Decisions made by local courts may be appealed to higher courts in Portugal.

RECENT HISTORY

Macao was permanently settled by Portuguese traders and missionaries in 1557 and became a center for trade between China and Japan and the West. Although Portugal acknowledged Chinese sovereignty over Macao and paid an annual rent to China until 1849, disputes over jurisdiction developed. Macao and Portuguese Timor were declared a joint overseas province of Portugal under the administration of a governor-general in Goa (Portuguese India) in 1833. In 1849 Portugal unilaterally declared Macao a free port under Portuguese jurisdiction. The first Portuguese governor was appointed in 1860, and Macao became the seat of the Roman Catholic bishopric of China and Japan in 1875. China, however, did not officially recognize the Portuguese occupation and governance of Macao until 1887, when, under the Protocol of Lisbon, Portugal agreed not to turn Macao over to a third party without Chinese consent.

Macao's importance as a trading post declined after Japan closed its doors to the West. Its harbors silted up, and much trade was diverted to Hong Kong. The colony became known for its gambling and as a haven for smugglers. After the Communist victory in China in 1949, the Chinese government renounced all unequal treaties, including the protocol granting Portugal control of Macao. In 1951 the colony was declared an overseas province of Portugal, with the right to elect a representative to the Portuguese legislature.

The colony's worst political crisis occurred in 1967–68, when local leftists staged riots linked to the Cultural Revolution in China. Portugal offered to return Macao to China, but the Chinese government refused. In 1968 the Portuguese administration signed an agreement with Macao's Chinese chamber of commerce agreeing to outlaw political activities by Chinese supporters of the Nationalist regime in Taiwan, to refuse entry to illegal Chinese refugees and to compensate the families of Chinese people killed in the rioting. Since that time, China has exercised de facto control over the affairs of Macao, largely through Chinese business groups sympathetic to Beijing. The Portuguese administration occupies little more than a figurehead role. The last Portuguese troops were withdrawn from the territory in 1976, when Macao was given internal autonomy as a special territory of China under Portuguese administration.

China and Portugal established diplomatic relations in 1979 and Portugal, which had traditionally shown little interest in its distant outpost, again expressed its willingness to return Macao to Chinese administration. The Chinese government refused to discuss the matter, however, until negotiations concerning the future of the economically more significant British colony of Hong Kong had been completed. In 1984 the Chinese inhabitants of Macao were granted the right to vote in legislative elections regardless of how long they had lived in the territory. After elections that year, the legislature for the first time had a majority of ethnic Chinese members.

Formal talks between Portugal and China aimed at restoring to China full sovereignty over Macao began in 1986. An agreement was reached the following year under which Macao would become a special administrative region of China on December 20, 1999. It would be governed by its inhabitants except in matters of defense and foreign policy and would retain its capitalist economy for at least 50 years after the transition. A joint Sino-Portuguese liaison group was formed to oversee the transition. One of its major priorities was to localize the civil service in Macao so as to ensure a smooth transition. The agreement was similar to the 1984 Sino-British accord on Hong Kong, except for its declaration that Portuguese customs and culture would be respected after the transition and that Portuguese, as well as Chinese, people would be members of the future government, legislature and courts. Portugal pledged that after the transition all its citizens in Macao would be able to retain their Portuguese citizenship and pass it along to their descendants; it also announced plans to integrate Portuguese nationals into the Portuguese civil service. (All inhabitants born in Macao before 1980 are automatically Portuguese citizens; after that date, persons desiring such citizenship must have Portuguese parents or demonstrate a familiarity with Portuguese culture.)

In the 1988 legislative elections, voters named independent liberals to three of the six directly elected posts, bypassing representatives of pro-

Beijing and traditional business interests and the Macanese. While this did not change the overall political balance, it apparently reflected a desire on the part of the electorate to influence government policy on such social issues as education, housing, labor and welfare.

Background: Historically a gateway to southern China, Macao is highly dependent on the outside world for consumer goods and industrial raw materials and equipment. Most of its exports and imports are transshipped through Hong Kong. Gold trading was an important activity until 1974, when restrictions on this activity in Hong Kong were lifted. Gambling, which is illegal in nearby Hong Kong, has long been a mainstay of the economy. Manufacturing was limited almost entirely to small quantities of fireworks and matches until the 1970s, when the territory began to develop export-oriented manufacturing in order to survive. Tourism (including the related gambling industry) and manufacturing for export are now the leading sources of revenue. Attempts are being made to diversify the economy through the introduction of new high-technology industries and the expansion of the financial and service sectors. In general, development has been hampered by a shortage of skilled labor and the lack of fresh water, particularly on Coloane and Taipa islands, where development planning has focused. Visible and direct Chinese economic involvement in the territory has steadily increased since the late 1960s, and Macao's purchases of food, water and inexpensive consumer goods provide China with a valuable source of foreign exchange. In 1987 Macao's gross domestic product was valued at U.S. $2.25 billion; per capita income was $5,242. The total external debt in 1984 stood at $796 million.

Manufacturing: Manufacturing contributed 36% of GDP in 1987 and manufactured goods constituted 98% of all exports. About 90% of all goods manufactured in Macao are exported. Factories are generally small, and many of them have been financed by industrialists from Hong Kong seeking to bypass restrictions on the importation of goods from Hong Kong imposed in their traditional markets. As similar restrictive quotas were imposed on goods made in Macao, however, many of these small factories were forced to close. Macao businesspeople have launched joint Macao-Chinese ventures in the neighboring Zhuhai Special Economic Zone of China's Guandong Province. Textiles, toys, plastic flowers, precision instruments, fireworks and furniture are among Macao's manufactured goods. In recent years, the territory has stressed selective industrial development based on modern equipment rather than on skilled labor and water, as the latter are in short supply. The territory consumed 492 million Kwh of electricity in 1985, most of it supplied by China.

Agriculture and fishing: Agriculture is of minor importance in Macao. Some 2% of the land is cultivated, with rice and vegetables the leading crops. There is a small livestock industry consisting of pigs and, increasingly, poultry. Fishing, however, is important. The fishing industry, with a 1985 catch of 13,670 tons/12,400 metric tons, supplies most of the domestic demand and a surplus for export to Hong Kong.

Tourism and other industries: Tourism is a significant part of the overall economy, providing an average of 25% of GDP. Thousands of visitors from Hong Kong arrive each weekend to gamble at the five casinos operated by Macoo Tourism and Amusement Limited, and gambling monies are the leading source of government revenue. Other attractions include many old, colonial-style buildings, a picturesque port, dog racing, horse racing (on Taipa island), jai alai and the annual Macao Grand Prix auto race, held every November. Approximately 5.1 million tourists visited the colony in 1987. Tourist traffic increased by 15% during the first half of 1988, primarily because of an influx of visitors from Taiwan passing through Macao en route to China. The easing of travel restrictions between Taiwan and China has fostered recent Taiwanese investment in Macao's tourist industry, although investment decreased markedly following the 1989 suppression of the pro-democracy movement in China. Large numbers of tourists from South Korea and Japan also visit the territory. Special government tax incentives to developers of the tourist industry have substantially increased Macao's supply of hotel rooms in recent years, and campaigns have been launched to attract visitors for more than the traditional brief stopover. Portugal has proposed building an international airport in Macao, but funding has not yet become available. Meanwhile, frequent shuttle service via ferry, hydrofoil, steamer and jetfoil link Macao to Hong Kong. A ferry service between Macao and Kao-hsiung, in southern Taiwan, began operation in 1987, and a highway through China linking Macao and Hong Kong is under construction.

Macao is also attempting to establish itself as an international financial center. A banking ordinance passed in 1982 opened the financial sector to increased foreign competition, leading to strong growth in the banking industry in recent years. A public corporation, the Issuing Institute of Macao (established in 1980), issues bank notes, regulates the financial markets and advises the government on financial matters. The territory has 23 banks, 14 of which are foreign, and numerous insurance companies. The Macao currency, the pataca, is linked to the Hong Kong dollar and will remain a convertible currency after 1999.

Foreign trade: Exports totaled $1.4 million and imports totaled $1.12 million in 1987. In 1986 exports consisted primarily of textiles and garments (70%), toys (12%), artificial flowers (3%), electronics equipment (4%) and leather goods (2%), destined primarily for the United States (33%), Hong Kong (16%), France (12%), West Germany (11%), Great Britain (7%) and China (4%). Only 1% of all exports went to Portugal. Imports consisted primarily of industrial raw materials (65%), consumer goods (13%), capital goods (10%), foods and beverages (7%) and fuel and lubricants (5%) from Hong Kong (46%), China (20%) and Japan (10%). The territory has had a steadily increasing balance-of-trade surplus since 1983, but this surplus has been due primarily to a decline in imports rather than to an increase in exports. Macao's leading exports, textiles and garments, face both import curbs in European and U.S. markets and competition from other developing nations.

Employment: In 1987 Macao's labor force totaled 190,000, of which 34% were employed in commerce and services (including tourism), 45% in manufacturing, 8% in construction, 7% in government and public authorities and 6% in agriculture and fishing. About 2% of Macao's workers were unemployed in 1986. The importation of foreign workers from China has reduced wages and led to social problems.

Price trends: Consumer prices increased from a 1983 base of 100 to 112.2 in 1984, 115.9 in 1985 and 118.5 in 1986. An increase of 4.7% was forecast for 1987.

SOCIAL SERVICES

Welfare: Macao's first labor law, passed in 1984, banned the use of child labor and prescribed a six-day workweek and minimum annual leave. The territory offers no other worker protection laws or social security, although large companies frequently offer social welfare benefits to their employees. The government supports special homes for children, the aged and the handicapped. No minimum wages or welfare charges are levied on employers. Taxes are low and are imposed on residents and nonresidents alike. Only 4.6% of the 1986 budget was devoted to social welfare and health expenditures.

Health services: Macao has a 400-bed hospital operated by the Medical and Health Department, the 800-bed Kiang Vu Hospital (whose staff has largely trained in China) and several small medical centers. In 1986, some 697 doctors practiced in the territory. Government assistance for health care is provided only in cases of extreme hardship. In 1988 the territory had an infant mortality rate of 12 per 1,000 live births. The leading causes of death are circulatory diseases, cancers and respiratory ailments.

Housing: A total of 133 residential structures with 3,396 units were constructed in 1985 in the private sector. Some government funds—16% of total government investment in 1985—are used for the construction of low-cost housing. About 5% of Macao's inhabitants live on sampans or other floating residences.

EDUCATION

Five years of primary education are officially compulsory between the ages of 6 and 12, and up to 5 years of secondary education are offered. About 61% of the adult population is literate. Most schools are administered by the Chinese with indirect support from the Chinese government. Education accounted for only 4% of government expenditures in 1986, and government schools enroll mainly children of civil servants and wealthy families. In 1985–86 there were 74 primary schools with 31,669 students. There are two teacher-training colleges and numerous evening adult education programs. The University of East Asia, established in 1981 on Taipa, offers courses in business, economics and the liberal arts; it had an enrollment of 1,000 in 1985–86. Most courses are taught in English, and students are primarily of Chinese origin from Southeast Asia.

Professional training centers are being established to upgrade the skills of workers in industry, tourism and education. The government has also instituted programs in Portugal and Macao to train bilingual professionals (a targeted 300 before 1999), some of whom will be groomed for civil service positions. This is an attempt to ensure that there will be a sufficient number of Chinese professionals qualified to take over the top posts in the civil service when the territory comes under the adminstration of China in 1999.

MASS MEDIA

Macao has recently upgraded its telecommunications network. Its telephones have direct-dial access to more than 90 countries. Hong Kong publications are available in addition to those published domestically.

The press: In 1986 the territory had 14 daily newspapers with a circulation of 242,000. Portuguese-language dailies include *Correio de Macau, Gazeta Macanese* and *Jornal de Macau.* There are also biweekly, weekly, and monthly Portuguese-language publications, including the government weekly, *Boletim Oficial,* and the religious monthly, *Boletim Eclesial.* Chinese-language daily newspapers include *Jornal "Va Kio," On Mun lat Pou, Seng Pou, Si Ma Pou, Sing Fon Pou* and *Tai Chung.*

Broadcasting: Teledifusão de Macau (TdM), the territory's television and radio station, broadcasts in both Portuguese and Chinese. It was state owned until 1988, when ownership was transferred to a limited public company; plans to boost its transmission so that broadcasts will reach Hong Kong have been announced. There is also a private Chinese-language radio station, Emissora Vila Verde, and Macao receives transmissions from television stations in Hong Kong.

BIOGRAPHICAL SKETCHES

Joaquim Pinto Machado. Born in 1932, he became the fortieth governor of Macao in April 1986. He was the first civilian to hold the post in 46 years, succeeding Vasco de Almeida e Costa, who resigned in January 1986. A former medical professor at the University of Oporto, Pinto Machado practiced surgery in Angola until 1974. He campaigned for Antonio Ramalho Eanes in the 1980 presidential election in Portugal, but shifted his allegiance to Mario Soares in the 1986 campaign. Pinto Machado participated in the Portuguese-Chinese negotiations on the future of Macao after serving as secretary of state for higher education in Soares's coalition government in 1985. His administration in Macao was plagued by political infighting, and he resigned abruptly on May 30, 1987.

Carlos Melancia. The 59-year-old Melancia was named governor of Macao by Mario Soares on July 3, 1987. He was trained as an electrical engineer and formerly served as a minister in the Portuguese government.

Zhou Ding. On September 21, 1987, Zhou Ding became China's chief representative in Macao when he became head of the newly established Macao branch of China's official Xinhua news agency. He had previously served as deputy mayor and deputy general secretary of the Communist party in the Shenzhen Special Economic Zone. His duties include reporting to the Chinese government on political and economic conditions in Macao and serving as unofficial head of the Chinese Communist party in the colony.

MALAYSIA

Features: Malaysia comprises Peninsular (West) Malaysia (the southern tip of the Asian mainland) and two territories across the South China Sea in northern Kalimantan: Sabah and Sarawak (East Malaysia). In Peninsular Malaysia, a mountainous spine (the Main Range, or Barisan Titiwangsa) runs roughly north-south from the Thai border toward Johor, dividing the peninsula between the comparatively narrow coastal plain draining to the west into the Strait of Malacca and the much more extensive mountainous interior and coastal lowland that drains to the South China Sea. The western coastal plain has been (and still is) far more intensively developed than any other part of the country, for it contains the rich tin deposits that provided the initial impetus for commercial development in the second half of the 19th century and is near the important sea routes that converge in the Strait of Malacca. Sabah is crossed by a series of mountain ranges, of which the most prominent is the Crocker Range (culminating in Gunung Kinabalu, the highest mountain in Southeast Asia), dividing the narrow lowland of the northwest coast from the interior. Sarawak has an extensive coastal lowland and a mountainous interior. Approximately 80% of Malaysia is covered by tropical rain forest.

Area: 127,581 sq. miles/330,434 sq. km. Of this area, Peninsular Malaysia accounts for 50,806 sq. miles/131,587 sq. km; Sarawak, 48,050 sq. miles/ 124,449 sq. km; and Sabah, 28,725 sq. miles/74,398 sq. km.

Mean max. and min. temperatures: Kuala Lumpur 78°F/25.6°C (Nov.–Dec.); 80°F/26.7°C (May).

Relative humidity: The average annual mean relative humidity in the lowlands of West Malaysia is 85%. By day it varies between 55% and 70%, and at night it rises above 95% over almost the entire country.

Mean annual rainfall: Kuala Lumpur, average monthly intensity of rainfall, per rain-day: 0.37 in/9.4 mm. (July), 0.55 in/14.0 mm. (March).

Total population (mid-1985 est): 15,676,813, of whom 12,978,230 live in Peninsular Malaysia; 1,222,198 in Sabah; and 1,476,385 in Sarawak.

189

VIETNAM

Gulf of

Thailand

THAILAND

SOUTH

Kangar
PERLIS
Alur Setar
KEDAH
George
Town
PINANG
Taiping
ANDAMAN
SEA
Kota Baharu

CHINA

Muda R.
Gerik
Perak R.
Kelantan R.
Terengganu R.
Kuala Terengganu

PERAK
KELANTAN
TERENGGANU
Ipoh
Dungun
Cameron Highlands
Cukai
Peninsular

SEA

Lumut
Kampar
Kuala Lipis
Bagan Datuk
Benta Seberang
Teluk Anson
Bentung
PAHANG
Kuantan

Malaysia

Kuala Lumpur
Pahang R.
Pekan
Pelabuhan Kelang
Mentekab
Rompin R.

SELANGOR
Seremban
NEGERI
Tioman I.
SEMBILAN
Melaka
Gemas
Mersing
MELAKA
Muar
JOHOR
Batu Pahat
Johor Baharu
Kota Tinggi

SINGAPORE

INDONESIA

MALAYSIA

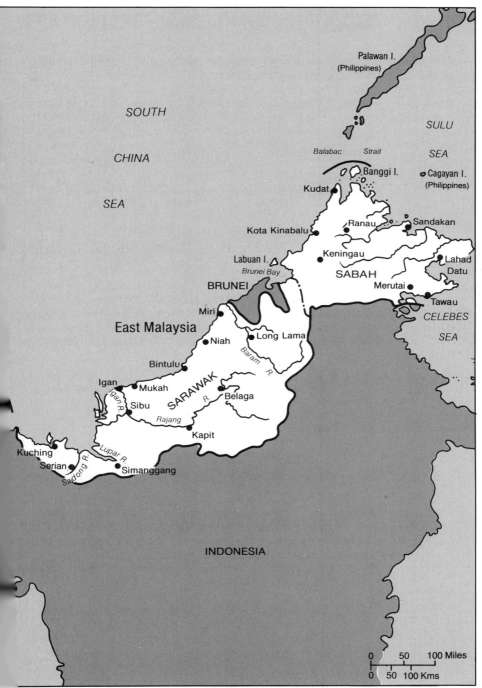

SOUTH

CHINA

SEA

Palawan I.
(Philippines)

SULU

SEA

Balabac *Strait*

Banggi I.

Cagayan I.
(Philippines)

Kudat

Kota Kinabalu

Ranau

Sandakan

Labuan I.

Brunei Bay

Keningau

SABAH

Lahad
Datu

BRUNEI

Merutai

East Malaysia

Miri

Long Lama

Tawau

CELEBES

SEA

Niah

Baram *R.*

Bintulu

SARAWAK

Igan

Mukah

Belaga

Sibu

Rajang

R.

Kapit

Kuching

Lupar R.

Serian

Sadong R.

Simanggang

INDONESIA

0   50   100 Miles

0   50 100 Kms

Chief towns and populations (1984): KUALA LUMPUR (Peninsular Malaysia, 912,610); East Malaysia: Kuching (150,000 est.), Kota Kinabalu (120,000 est.).

Distribution: The 1980 census provided the following estimated percentages of the urban-rural distribution of population.

	Urban	*Rural*
Peninsular Malaysia	37	63
Sabah	21	79
Sarawak	18	82
Malaysia	34	66

Ethnic composition (mid-1985 est): In Peninsular Malaysia the population comprises 7,343,535 Malays, 4,245,052 Chinese, 1,307,038 Indians and 82,605 classified as others.

Language: The national language is Bahasa Malaysia, the language of government administration, education and the market. A number of Chinese dialects and Indian languages are also spoken within those communities. The various peoples of East Malaysia have their own languages. English is widely used.

Religion: According to the constitution, Islam is the religion of the Malaysian federation, but the constitution also guarantees freedom of religious belief. Consequently, Buddhism, Confucianism, Taoism, Hinduism, Sikhism and Christianity are also widely practiced.

CONSTITUTIONAL SYSTEM

Constitution: The independence *(merdeka)* constitution of August 1957, subsequently amended, is still in force.

Head of state: King *(Yang di-pertuan agong)* Mahmood Iskandar ibni al-Marhum. The *yang di-pertuan agong* is elected by the nine hereditary rulers (the Conference of Rulers) from among their own. He holds office for five years. *Prime minister:* Datuk Seri Dr. Mahathir bin Mohammad

Executive: Every act of government derives from the authority of the *yang di-pertuan agong*. The prime minister holds office at the royal pleasure; the *yang di-pertuan agong* may refuse to dissolve parliament against the advice of the prime minister. The head of state (on prime ministerial advice) appoints judges to the Federal Court and the high courts. He is also the supreme commander of the armed forces.

The prime minister must be a Malaysian citizen by operation of law, not by registration or naturalization; and a member of the House of Representatives, not the Senate. The cabinet, headed by the prime minister, consists only of members of the legislature and is collectively responsible to parliament.

Legislature: The legislature has two houses, the Senate (Dewan Negara) and the House of Representatives (Dewan Rakyat). The Dewan Negara has a membership of 69, of whom 26 are elected (each state legislature elects two senators) and 43 are appointed by the *yang di-pertuan agong.* A senator holds office for three years. The Dewan Rakyat has 177 elected members, returned from single-member constituencies on the basis of universal adult franchise. Of the constituencies, 132 are in Peninsular Malaysia, 24 are in Sarawak and 21 are in Sabah. The Dewan Rakyat has a term of five years, although the *yang di-pertuan agong* may dissolve it before the end of its term if the prime minister so advises.

Political parties: The government coalition, the Barisan Nasional (the National Front), is dominated by the United Malays National Organization (UMNO) but also includes, prominently, the Malaysian Chinese Association (MCA); the Malaysian Indian Congress (MIC); the Sarawak United People's party; Parti Pesaka Bumiputera Bersatu (the United Bumiputra party); Berjaya (the Sabah People's Union); and Gerakan Rakyat Malaysia (the Malaysian People's Movement party). The principal opposition parties are the Democratic Action party (DAP), the Pan-Malayan Islamic party and the United Sabah National Organization.

Local government: Malaysia comprises 13 states: 11 in the peninsula, together with Sabah and Sarawak. The heads of four states (Melaka, Penang, Sabah and Sarawak) are each designated *yang di-pertuan negeri;* the heads of the remaining nine states are hereditary rulers who comprise the Conference of Rulers that elects the *yang di-pertuan agong.* Each of the 13 states has its own constitution and legislature, with powers to legislate on matters not reserved for the federal parliament. Each state has an executive council to advise the head of state. These councils are headed by a chief minister (in Melaka, Penang, Sabah and Sarawak) or *menteri besar* (in the remaining states), and are responsible to their respective state legislature. Each state in Peninsular Malaysia is divided into administrative districts; Sabah is divided into four residencies; Sarawak is divided into five divisions.

Judicial system: The court structure in Malaysia comprises the Supreme Court (with the end of appeals to the Privy Council of Great Britain on January 1, 1985, this is now the final court of appeal); high courts; session courts, each consisting of a president—a lawyer—sitting alone; magistrate's courts, consisting of a magistrate sitting alone; juvenile courts; and *penghulu's* courts, the lowest court in West Malaysia, in which cases are usually settled informally. The constitution contains several provisions designed to secure the independence of the judiciary from the direction of either legislature or executive, but recently that independence has been seriously threatened by the executive.

In Peninsular Malaysia there is a separate structure of Islamic courts (courts of the chief *Kathis* and assistant *Kathis*). They hold jurisdiction over

Muslims in such matters as marriage, divorce, separation, maintenance, guardianship of infants and wills. They also have limited criminal jurisdiction with respect to offenses committed by a Muslim against Islam.

RECENT HISTORY

The Federation of Malaysia came into being on September 16, 1963. It comprised the Federation of Malaya (which had achieved independence from British rule on August 31, 1957), Singapore (which had been given internal self-government in 1958), North Borneo (Sabah) and Sarawak—the last two territories having been British crown colonies since 1946. The federation took its present territorial form as of August 9, 1965, with the expulsion of Singapore to become a separate independent state.

This territorial alignment had its immediate origins in the constitutional arrangements sought by the British administration in the later 1940s, following the collapse of Japanese power in August 1945. In the peninsula an important aim of the returning British was to create a unitary state from the disparate constitutional elements (the Federated Malay States, the Unfederated Malay States, and the Straits Settlements of Penang, Malacca and Singapore), which had been in place prior to the war. The first attempt, the Malayan Union of 1946, was abortive, its most lasting impact being the formation in May 1946 of UMNO, created to oppose the British proposals. The second constitutional arrangement, a Federation of Malaya that would embrace all the states of the peninsula, Pinang and Melaka, but which excluded Singapore, was inaugurated in February 1948. These constitutional changes were introduced against a background of considerable labor unrest, largely inspired by a Chinese-dominated communist movement that had borne the major burden of resistance to the Japanese. Following an upsurge in communist violence, on June 18, 1948 the colonial administration declared a state of emergency throughout Malaya. The emergency remained in force until July 1960, although the peak of guerrilla activity had been reached in 1950–51 and the insurgency had been effectively broken by 1954–55. The administration's defeat of the insurgents was achieved in part through a rigorous resettlement of Chinese rural populations into protected villages (to isolate the guerrillas from the support of sympathetic or intimidated communities), and through the offer of a realistic prospect of political independence. In this last regard the British had initially sought the emergence of a noncommunal indigenous political movement to assume the challenge of taking Malaya to independence, but this initiative had faded by 1951. There then emerged from within the indigenous political processes of Malaya an electoral alliance between the three principal communally based parties in the peninsula: UMNO, MCA (established in 1949) and MIC (formed in 1946). This association, in which the parties retained their separate identities but acted as one in determining which candidate from which party would contest a particular seat, was first tested in municipal elections in 1952 and then, on a major scale, in federal elections in 1955. In these last elections, the Alliance (as it was termed) secured 51 of the 52 contested seats and thus established itself beyond doubt as the successor to British authority. The *merdeka* constitution provided that all ethnic groups in Malaya might acquire equal citizenship yet also secured political and administrative privileges for the Malay community.

In May 1961 the first prime minister of the independent Federation of Malaya, Tunku Abdul Rahman, proposed the incorporation of Malaya with Singapore, North Borneo, Sarawak and Brunei in a wider federation. The *tunku's* principal concern was that in 1963 Singapore's transitional constitution would expire and the island could then be expected to achieve full independence. Given the prominence of left-wing elements in Singaporean politics this prospect worried Kuala Lumpur. With Singapore merged with Malaya, those concerns would diminish, and the inclusion of the Borneo territories would restore a balance between Malay and non-Malay populations that would be disturbed by the addition of Singapore's overwhelmingly Chinese population. North Borneo and Sarawak were initially reluctant to join the new federation, for as crown colonies since 1946 their peoples had experienced as limited a political and administrative advance as during the preceding century of rule under a chartered company (North Borneo) and the Brooke family (Sarawak). But concessions were offered, and in state elections in 1963 profederation parties won decisively. The third Bornean state, Brunei, declined to join. The new federation came under strain almost from its creation in September 1963—internally, from the ambitions of Singapore's Lee Kuan Yew to establish political influence over the mainland's Chinese voters; and externally, from the antagonism of the Philippines and Indonesia to this powerful new organism in the region. As part of its opposition, Indonesia launched military raids along the borders of Sabah and Sarawak. The internal threat was ended by the expulsion of Singapore in 1965; the external threat was met by an increased presence of Commonwealth military forces. In mid-1966 the Philippines and Indonesia extended recognition to Malaysia, although the Philippines continued to pursue its claim to Sabah, if intermittently, into the 1980s.

These internal and external threats to the new nation, serious although they were, did have the effect of moderating the domestic demands of the three principal ethnic communities. As the threats receded, ethnic demands, particularly on the crucial issues of education and language, were more openly expressed. At the federal elections in May 1969 interethnic tension exploded into communal violence. The elections reduced the Alliance representation in the Dewan Rakyat from 89 to 66 (thus depriving the Alliance government of the two-thirds majority required to obtain constitutional amendments) and its share of the popular vote from 58.4% to 48.8%. On May 13, the day following the elections, the (essentially Chinese) opposition parties held a victory celebration in Kuala Lumpur. A counter-rally by UMNO supporters then deteriorated into violence. It took four days for order to be restored to the capital city, although intermittent communal violence continued for a further two months. The constitution was suspended and a national emergency declared.

The riots of May 1969—violently exposing the acute distrust running through the ethnic communities—have had a most profound influence on the subsequent history of Malaysia. They led, in brief, to a fundamental shift of political, economic and social authority and assertiveness in favor of the Malay community—to the increasing Malayization of Malaysia. Thus, 1971 saw the introduction of a New Economic Policy (NEP) whose two principal objectives (to be attained by 1990) were a reduction and eventual eradication of poverty, irrespective of ethnic group, and a restructuring of society so that the identification of ethnic group with economic function would be reduced and then eliminated. This second objective implied a major increase in Malay ownership of and participation in the modern sector of the economy, and a major expansion of Malay access to higher education and training. With regard to education, from 1970 on there was a graduated introduction of Malay as the medium of instruction; by the 1980s Malay was used, with very few exceptions, within every university department. Political changes were no less far reaching. After the return of parliamentary rule in February 1971, constitutional amendments were passed that prohibited public discussion of sensitive issues, including the power and position of the Malay rulers, Malay special rights and the status of Islam. Public discussion was considered seditious. In the same year, Prime Minister Tun Abdul Razak (who had succeeded on the resignation of Tunku Abdul Rahman in 1970) greatly expanded the Alliance coalition to form the Barisan Nasional. The new coalition, bringing into government a number of parties that previously had been in opposition, was intended to reduce further open discussion of sensitive issues. In the 1974 federal elections, the Barisan Nasional won 104 of the 124 seats contested. Tun Abdul Razak died in January 1976 and was succeeded by Datuk (later Tun) Hussein Onn.

The 1970s also saw the federal government in Kuala Lumpur seek to draw the East Malaysia states of Sabah and Sarawak into a more integrated relationship with the peninsula. This aim was pursued against the presence of a number of prominent political leaders in East Malaysia who were determined to keep Kuala Lumpur's intervention to a minimum. Most notable here was the chief minister of Sabah, Tun Mustapha, who used the state's vast income from timber concessions to sustain an independent stance. In the mid-1970s Tun Abdul Razak sought to undermine Tun Mustapha's position, in part by accepting the Sabah opposition party, Berjaya, into the Barisan Nasional. In elections in 1976, Berjaya defeated Tun Mustapha's United Sabah National Organization. After a brief interlude, Datuk Harris Saleh was appointed chief minister; in further elections in 1981 he and Berjaya enjoyed a clear victory.

In 1981 Tun Hussein Onn was succeeded as prime minister by Datuk Seri Dr. Mahathir bin Mohammad. The new prime minister has certainly been the most direct, indeed abrasive of Malaysia's leaders; and in the early years of his stewardship that abrasiveness brought an invigorating directness to government administration and policy. In recent years, however, it has brought what many observers see as a dangerous authoritarianism and arrogance, as the government moved swiftly to detain critics and to cow the judiciary. This has been accompanied by the most serious splits within the principal Barisan Nasional parties, first the MCA and then, most damaging of all, within UMNO itself.

Background: The Malaysian economy is strongly export dependent, export earnings being equivalent to more than one-half of GNP in the mid-1980s. The principal exports are natural rubber, crude petroleum, palm oil, timber, tin and a range of manufactures. The heavy export dependence (and specifically the dependence on primary commodity exports) has made Malaysia acutely vulnerable to the international recessions of the 1980s. While in the late 1970s GNP (in constant prices) had risen at an average annual rate of 8.5%, growth in the 1980s was notably slower. In 1981 and 1985 GNP declined in real terms. The 1980s also saw major structural change in the Malaysian economy, in response to the international recession and shifting world market demand. Perhaps most notable has been the sharp relative decline of rubber (by 1986 it accounted for only 8.9% of total export revenues), the emergence of crude petroleum (the single most important source of foreign exchange since 1980) and the rapid growth of the manufacturing sector. In addition, tourism has become an important source of foreign exchange.

The modern sector of the Malaysian economy is heavily concentrated in the west coast states of Peninsular Malaysia. Modern manufacturing is located almost exclusively here; tin mining is strongly concentrated in the western states of Perak and Selangor; and the principal concentrations of rubber and palm oil cultivation are found on the western coastal corridor down to the southern state of Johor. The east coast of the peninsula was left largely unexploited by Western capital during the colonial period and remains relatively undeveloped. The East Malaysia states were actively protected from large-scale commercial penetration (for example, by the major Western rubber companies) during the colonial era. They have yet to experience modern growth comparable to that which has long taken place in the western peninsular states, although recent years have seen a very considerable expansion of forestry operations (in Sabah) and an even more rapid growth of offshore petroleum extraction (principally off Sarawak).

The Malaysian administration pursues an essentially free-market economic ideology. The principal thrust of government economic intervention from the early 1970s, the NEP, has been to secure a major shift in employment structures and capital ownership in favor of the Malay population. This has been pursued largely by legislation (which stipulated minimum levels of Malay employment and ownership) and by acquisition or creation by government of major commercial interests that would be held in trust for the indigenous community.

Agriculture: Agriculture contributed 21.0% of GDP in 1986 and employed 34.3% of the labor force. The principal subsistence crop is rice, Malaysian production meeting just over 80% of domestic requirements in 1986, with imports coming principally from Thailand. Peninsular Malaysia accounted for 85.4% of Malaysian paddy production in 1986.

Rubber: Malaysia is the world's largest producer and exporter of natural rubber, although its share of world production has been declining—from 40% in 1980 to 33.8% in 1985—in the face of increasing cultivation in, notably, Indonesia and Thailand. During the colonial period, rubber was principally a plantation crop; over the last two or three decades, however, there has been considerable plantation disinvestment (as other estate crops offered higher returns than rubber and as difficulties were encountered in recruiting labor), and the industry is now dominated by the smallholding. In a fiercely competitive international market, where cost reduction and productivity increase are imperative, the government—principally in the form of the Federal Land Development Authority (FELDA) and the Rubber Industry Smallholders Development Authority (RISDA)—has provided very considerable support to the rubber smallholder, notably in offering fertilizer subsidies, in assisting large-scale replanting with higher-yielding stock and in making provision for direct purchases of crude rubber. There is also a strong commitment to research and experimentation.

Palm oil: Palm oil cultivation on a major commercial scale took off in the early 1960s as the government sought diversification away from rubber. The crop's expansion has been spectacular. Between 1970 and 1980, production expanded at 19.6% per year, and by the 1980s Malaysia had become the world's largest producer. In 1986 Malaysia accounted for 61.5% of world trade in palm oil. In that year just under half of the total area planted to oil palm was under estate management (many of the oil palm estates being recently converted from rubber): roughly one-third was in FELDA and RISDA schemes, and less than 10% each was under state development schemes and cultivated by smallholders. The depression in world palm oil prices has led to a major Malaysian investment both in replanting and fertilizer provision, and in seed and cultivation research. Labor shortages on the estates have encouraged extensive experimentation with the mechanization of harvesting.

Tin: Together with rubber, tin formed the foundation of the colonial export economy. But it has been severely affected by the recessions of the 1970s and 1980s, not only through the weakness in world demand but also through crises in the operations of the International Tin Council and, notably, the suspension of tin trading on the London Metal Exchange and on the Kuala Lumpur Tin Market in 1985. The industry has also had to face the depletion of ore reserves in its existing areas of exploitation, and rising production costs. There has been large-scale mine closure (and thus a contraction of output) since the mid-1970s. Between 1979 and 1984 Malaysian production of tin-in-concentrates fell by 10.4% per year.

Petroleum: Although Malaysia remains only a very modest world producer of crude petroleum, since 1980 crude petroleum exports have constituted the country's largest single source of foreign exchange. Malaysian output in 1986 averaged 500,900 barrels a day (b/d), compared with an average of just 96,000 b/d in 1975. Of the 1986 production, 52.6% was drawn from peninsular offshore fields, 30.7% from Sarawak and 16.7% from Sabah offshore fields. In the early 1980s Singapore was the principal buyer of Malaysian crude, but was replaced by Japan in the middle of the decade— the latter taking 37% of Malaysian exports of crude petroleum in 1986. The very rapid expansion of crude petroleum extraction since the mid-1970s has been accompanied, as elsewhere in the world, by a comparable expansion of natural gas exploitation.

Industry: In the early 1970s Malaysian industrial development strategy shifted from import substitution to one of export expansion, drawing largely on the local resources of rubber, timber and palm oil as well as emphasizing production of electronic goods and textiles. Despite international recession and domestic market contraction in the 1980s, the expansion of the modern industrial sector has been very substantial. Manufacturing production contributed 19.1% of GDP in 1985; in the same year, manufactured goods accounted for 32.1% of total gross exports. There has been a particularly rapid growth in exports of electrical machinery and products; in 1986 these constituted 53.3% of total manufactured exports. Industrial expansion has relied heavily on foreign investment, notably by the Japanese. Manufacturing production is strongly concentrated in the peninsular states of Perak and Selangor.

Foreign trade: Malaysia's principal trading partner is Japan, the latter accounting for 22% of Malaysia's total foreign trade in 1986. Malaysia maintains a substantial trade surplus with Japan, although exports to that country consist principally of primary commodities. The United States is a major importer of Malaysian electrical goods and textiles; that trade would be seriously threatened by American protectionism. In general, Malaysia has maintained a clear surplus in balance of payments; a trade surplus is secured primarily because import demand is highly sensitive to changes in export earnings (through fluctuations in the level of domestic demand), and Malaysia attracts very substantial capital inflows.

Employment: In 1985 the total labor force was estimated at 5.468 million, of whom 35.7% were in agriculture, forestry and fishing; 15.1% in manufacturing; 15.0% in government service; and just 1.1% in mining and quarrying. In the same year, the unemployment rate was 7.6%.

Cost of living: The cost of living index for Peninsular Malaysia in 1985 (1980 = 100) was 125.5.

SOCIAL SERVICES

Welfare: Although Malaysia is not a welfare state in the sense of there being a uniform or comprehensive system of social welfare, the government does provide a wide range of social services that are available to all, irrespective of income. The Ministry of Welfare Services is responsible at the federal level for family and child care services, social development programs and rehabilitation services for the disabled. In addition, there is a substantial body of legislation ensuring protection for workers against sickness, accident and arbitrary dismissal. Important welfare services are also provided by a large number of private charitable and voluntary organizations.

Health services: The Ministry of Health provides a comprehensive health service, although there is also an extensive private sector offering sophisticated medical treatment for those who can afford it. In 1984 there were 90 government general and district hospitals, and eight government special medical institutions; in the same year there were 121 private hospitals, nursing and maternity homes, (of which 108 were in Peninsular Malaysia). In 1984 there were 4,505 registered doctors in government and private practice (of whom 4,111, or 91.25%, were in Peninsular Malaysia).

Housing: A Ministry of Housing and Local Government was created in 1978 to increase construction of low-cost houses. In 1984, 59 low-cost housing projects, requiring an investment of almost 70 million Malaysian dollars, were approved. In addition, a Housing Loan Division provides loans for low-income families to build their own houses. To the end of 1984, over M$13.5 million had been allocated in this way.

EDUCATION

The Ministry of Education provides a comprehensive education structure from primary school to university level. It regulates syllabi, controls national examinations and in general supervises educational development. In 1985 there were 6,629 primary schools and 1,178 secondary schools. There are six fully established national universities. The medium of instruction throughout the education structure (with the very minimum of exceptions) is Bahasa Malaysia. There is also a substantial private education sector, the establishment of a private school requiring the authorization of the Ministry of Education. The private sector is obliged to conform to national education requirements. Recent decades have seen a major expansion of private colleges, a number being joint ventures with foreign universities. These colleges seek to provide an opening into higher education (through either external degrees or secure access to foreign universities) to those non-Malays who, because of the preferential treatment granted to Malays, find it difficult to gain admission to Malaysia's own universities.

MASS MEDIA

The press: The press is very strictly regulated by the government. Newspaper publishers are required to hold two documents: a license to use a printing press and a permit authorizing the printing and publication of a newspaper. Both documents are renewable annually. The minister of home affairs has, and uses, the power to refuse, suspend or revoke the annual license. In addition, newspapers are bound by the 1971 Sedition Act, which prohibits public discussion of the sensitive issues of Malay rights, the status of Bahasa Malaysia, citizenship and the authority of the Malay rulers.

In 1986 there were 79 newspapers (daily, twice weekly and weekly) published in Malaysia. Of these, 14 were published in Bahasa Malaysia, 18 in English, 35 in Chinese, seven in Tamil, two in Punjabi, one in Malayalam and two in English/Bahasa Malaysia/Kadazan.

Dailies: The main daily newspapers published in Peninsular Malaysia include: *Utusan Malaysia,* Bahasa Malaysia, 244,000; *Berita Harian,* Bahasa Malaysia, 133,220; *New Straits Times,* English, 201,200; *The Star,* English, 127,000; *Nanyang Siang Pau,* Chinese, 143,000; *Sin Chew Jit Poh,* Chinese, 115,000; *Tamil Nesan,* Tamil, 21,500.

Periodicals: Dewan Masyarakat (m), Malay, current affairs, 65,000.

Broadcasting: Radio and Television Malaysia (RTM) is a government body, responsible to the Ministry of Information, and as such devotes a high proportion of airtime to presenting government programs and policies, promoting national unity, encouraging cultural and religious awareness, and developing civic values. Entertainment shows, conversely, receive less emphasis. In line with this format, RTM aims to limit the foreign content of radio and television programs to 40%. RTM operates two television channels. A private television network has been transmitting since 1984. There are five domestic radio networks.

BIOGRAPHICAL SKETCHES

Encik Anwar Ibrahim. Born in 1947, Anwar Ibrahim was an active student leader at the University of Malaya. In 1974 he became leader of the Malaysian Muslim Youth Movement, but in the same year he was detained under the Internal Security Act for alleged involvement in a student demonstration; he was released in 1976. In 1982 he joined UMNO, was elected leader of the UMNO Youth and entered parliament in the federal elections. He became minister of agriculture in 1984 and subsequently minister of education. Anwar Ibrahim is widely seen as a successor to Dr. Mahathir, if the latter can influence the succession.

Lim Kit Siang. Born in 1941, he entered parliament as a result of the federal elections of 1969, but was detained under the Internal Security Act from May 1969 to October 1970. While in detention Lim began law studies as an external student at London University. He graduated in 1976 and completed his British bar finals the following year. As secretary-general of the DAP, Lim has been the most persistent parliamentary critic of government over the last decade. He was again detained under the Internal Security Act in late 1987.

Datuk Seri Dr. Mahathir bin Mohammad. Dr. Mahathir has served successively as prime minister, minister of home affairs and minister of justice (October 1987). Born in 1925, he received a medical degree from the University of Malaya, Singapore, in the early 1950s and then began practice. He entered parliament after the 1964 federal election, but lost his seat in the election of 1969. In the aftermath of the May 1969 riots, Dr. Mahathir led the campaign within UMNO to force the resignation of Tunku Abdul Rahman; he was expelled from UMNO for breach of party discipline. Dr.

Mahathir was soon restored to the party and returned to parliament in 1974. He became one of the three vice-presidents of UMNO in 1975, and deputy prime minister in March 1976. He was elected president of the party in June 1981 and became prime minister the following month.

Datuk Musa bin Hitam: Born in 1934, Musa bin Hitam was educated at the University of Malaya and the University of Sussex. He entered parliament as a result of a by-election in 1969, but was almost immediately expelled from UMNO for his part in the postriot criticism of Tunku Abdul Rahman. He soon returned to the party, however, becoming deputy minister of trade and industry in 1972, minister of primary industries in 1974 and minister of education in 1978. He was elected deputy president of UMNO in June 1981, and became deputy prime minister the following month. A close working relationship with the prime minister, Dr. Mahathir, in the early 1980s had seriously deteriorated by the middle of the decade; and in February 1986 he resigned from the cabinet, citing "irreconcilable differences" with Mahathir. Musa bin Hitam remained deputy president of UMNO until successfully challenged at party elections in April 1987.

Tengku Razaleigh Hamzah. Born in 1937, into the Kelantan royal family, Razaleigh Hamzah was educated at the Malay College in Kuala Kangsar and then at Queen's University in Belfast. In 1966 he became executive director of the newly opened Bank Bumiputra. He entered parliament in the 1969 federal election. In 1974 he was appointed an UMNO vice-president. He became finance minister under Hussein Onn in 1976, a post he held until 1984 when he became minister of trade and industry. He twice bid unsuccessfully for the UMNO deputy presidency—in 1981 and 1984. His relations with Dr. Mahathir severely worsened in the mid-1980s, and he challenged the prime minister for the UMNO presidency (and thus in effect for the premiership) in April 1987. Razaliegh Hamzah lost, but only very narrowly; he then resigned from the cabinet. In early 1988 he was denied membership in the new UMNO.

MALDIVES

Features: The Republic of Maldives, an island nation in the Indian Ocean southwest of India and Sri Lanka, is the smallest country in Asia. The more than 1,200 islands of the Maldives archipelago, administered as 19 atolls, extend for about 510 miles/820 km. north and south across the equator. Even the largest of the low-lying coral islands (which seldom rise to more than 6 ft/1.8 m. above sea level) have areas of less than 5 sq. miles/13 sq. km., and most of them are much smaller. The highest point in the country, on Wilingili island in Male Atoll, is only 80 ft/24 m. above sea level. The islands have formed above an underwater ridge that may be of volcanic origin. New islands are constantly being created, while others are washing away. The northeastern and southeastern islands are the most fertile, but soils are generally alkaline and sandy loam with poor moisture-retaining capacity; only about 10% of the total land area is suitable for agriculture. Most of the islands are covered with dense, low-growing tropical scrub and grasses; some have groves of coconut palms and fruit trees. The climate is hot and humid throughout the year, with often violent rainstorms occurring during the southwest monsoon (June to August). The country's major resources are its rich fishing grounds; its sheltered harbors in many of the atolls; its strategic location astride major sea lanes in the Indian Ocean; and its tropical climate, clear blue waters, colorful reefs and white sandy beaches that have made Maldives a popular tourist resort. Because the country's ecosystem is very delicate and its scenic beauty is a major economic asset, the government has been greatly concerned with environmental issues. Of special importance are the safe disposal of garbage associated with increased tourism and the even more critical threat of a worldwide rise in ocean levels. Although the islands are removed from cyclone paths and protected by reefs, they saw unusual tidal wave activity in the late 1980s, particularly in 1987. Most of the islands would be submerged by a large storm swell or by a rise of only 6.5 ft/2 m. in the mean sea level.

Area: 115 sq. miles/298 sq. km.

Mean max. and min. temperatures: 80°F/27°C year round.

Relative humidity: 80%.

Mean annual rainfall: 100 in/2,540 mm. in the north; 150 in/3,800 mm. in the south.

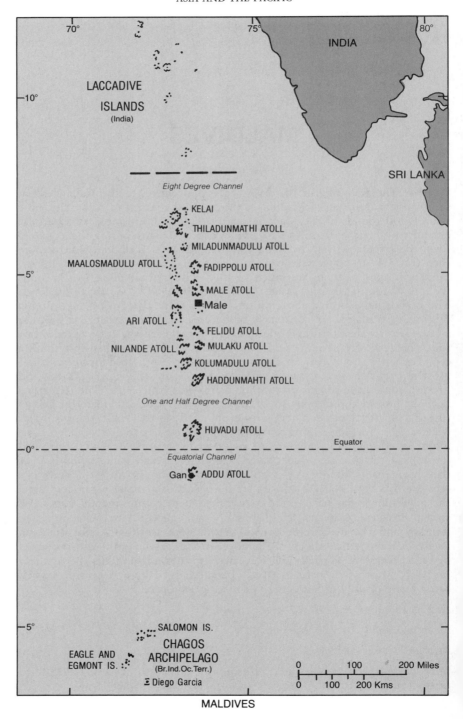

MALDIVES

POPULATION

Total population (1988 est.): 208,187.

Chief town and population (1985): MALE (46,334).

Distribution: Settlement on most islands is limited by a lack of fresh water and arable land. Only about 200 of the islands are inhabited, with the populations of individual islands ranging from about 100 to more than 45,000 persons. Since 1972 a number of resort hotels have been built on previously uninhabited islands. Some 25% of the total population is crowded onto Male, the capital island and only urban center, which has an area of about 1 sq. mile/2.6 sq. km. In 1986 Male's area was increased by nearly 50% upon the completion of a major land reclamation project. The rate of natural population increase (4.07% in 1985) is more than twice the world average. Most of the inhabitants are descended from the south Indian and Sinhalese migrants who first settled the islands; their descendants later intermarried with Arab traders and black African slaves.

Language: The official language, Divehi, is related to ancient Sinhalese and incorporates elements of Arabic and Urdu. About 3% of the population—mostly government officials—speak English.

Religion: The people of Maldives were once adherents of Buddhism; in the 12th century they were converted to Islam which is the country's official religion. Virtually all of the people are Sunni Muslims, and citizenship is restricted to this group. No pork or alcohol, which are forbidden to Muslims, may be imported into Maldives, and the legal system is based on Islamic law. Although the propagation of any religion other than Islam is forbidden, the Maldivians are not fundamentalists. Women, for example, do not wear veils and have equal opportunities in education and employment.

CONSTITUTIONAL SYSTEM

Constitution: Maldives was declared a republic on November 11, 1968, with the approval of 80% of its citizens, as indicated in a nationwide referendum in March of that year. The constitution of 1968, which has been revised several times in subsequent years, provides for executive, legislative and judicial branches of government and vests considerable power in the president. The rights of freedom of "life movement," speech and development are guaranteed to all citizens within the provisions of Islam.

Head of State: President Maumoon Abdul Gayoom. *Prime Minister:* Office abolished 1975.

Executive: The president, who also serves as minister of defense and national security, has full executive power. The members of the cabinet are appointed by the president and are responsible individually to the legislature. An appointed special consultative council advises the president on economic affairs. The president, who is nominated by the legislature but must win popular endorsement in a national referendum, may serve unlimited five-year terms. All citizens over 21 years of age have the right to vote.

Legislature: The unicameral legislature, known as the Majlis (Citizens' Council), has 48 members; eight are appointed by the president and 40 are elected (two from each of the 19 atolls and two from Male). Elections are held to fill a seat whenever one becomes vacant, and each member serves a five-year term from the date of election. Most members of the legislature also hold ministerial or civil service posts. Legislation is drafted by the Majlis but requires presidential approval to become law. In addition to the Majlis, Maldives has a special council made up of the members of the legislature, the cabinet ministers and an additional 48 members (two from each atoll and two from Male who are directly elected and eight who are appointed by the president). This special council deals with matters related to the constitution, economic activities, individual rights, changes in administrative structure and the leasing of land to foreigners. The speaker of the legislature also chairs the special council.

Judicial system: Sharia (Islamic) law guides the judiciary. There is a High Court, as well as lower courts. Judges are appointed by the president.

RECENT HISTORY

The Maldive Islands were probably first settled by people from southern India and Sri Lanka; Buddhist ruins dating to the 2nd or 3rd century B.C. have been found there. Arab traders reached the islands in the 9th century, and the population was converted to Islam in 1153, when a sultanate form of government was established. In the 14th century the famous Arab geographer and traveler Ibn Batuta, who lived in Maldives for several years and married the daughter of a government official, described the islands in his writings. The first European to visit Maldives, the Portuguese explorer Dom Lourenço de Alameida, arrived in 1507. The Portuguese maintained a garrison there intermittently, and the islands were forced to pay tribute to Goa in Portuguese India until 1573. In that year the Portuguese were driven out by Sultan Muhammad Thakurafaani al-Azam, who introduced a monetary system and established a standing army. Due to its geographic isolation, Maldives escaped other European colonization, although the sultan paid a tribute to the Dutch government on Sri Lanka in exchange for its protection until 1796, when the British took over colonial responsibility for that country. During this period, in 1752, the Maldivian throne was seized by Malabari pirates, but the invaders were soon driven out of the country.

Maldives was formally declared a British protectorate with internal self-government in 1887. The protectorate arrangement continued under a new agreement after Sri Lanka gained its independence in 1948. The powers of the sultan were restricted by a constitution adopted in 1932, and the islands were briefly declared a republic under President Muhammad Amin

Didi in 1953, but the sultanate was restored in 1954. The islands gained full independence on July 26, 1965.

One of the most controversial issues in the years immediately before and after independence was the British military presence on the southern island of Gan, in Addu Atoll. The island had been a British base during World War II, and in 1956 the government agreed to allow the reconstruction of the air base at Gan. There was widespread opposition to the British military presence in the northern and central parts of the country, and the three southern atolls who most benefited economically from the base seceded from Maldives in 1959 and declared themselves the United Suvadivian Republic. The central government, which accused the British of supporting the rebels, crushed the rebellion in 1960. It then signed an agreement granting the British free use of the base for 30 years in exchange for development aid, the right to handle most of its own foreign affairs and a British pledge of assistance in reconciling the government and the dissident southerners. Anti-British feelings continued, however, and the British formally evacuated the base in 1976. Several subsequent offers by other nations to lease the base, including one from the USSR in 1977, were rejected by the government, which said it would never again allow a foreign power to occupy the island. The closing of the base adversely affected the economy of the southern islands, although an international airport and a business and industrial complex have since been established on Gan.

The public outcry over the issue of the base forced the first prime minister of the newly independent nation, Ibrahim Ali Didi, to resign in 1957. He was succeeded by Amin Ibrahim Nasir, who gradually assumed more and more of the powers originally held by the sultan, Muhammad Amin Didi. The country officially became a republic in 1968, with Nasir as president; he won a second presidential term in 1973. Nasir dismissed Prime Minister Ahmed Zaki in 1975 and abolished the post. Unexpectedly, he declined to run for a third term, and in 1978 he was succeeded as president by Maumoon Abdul Gayoom. Gayoom survived an attempted coup in 1980; Nasir, who had been charged in absentia with misappropriation of government funds, denied from his home in Singapore government allegations that he had been involved in the attempt. Gayoom was reelected in 1983 and 1988 with increasing percentages of the popular vote, particularly from inhabitants of the outer islands.

In 1988 there was another attempt to overthrow the government. The attackers, later identified as Sri Lankan Tamil mercenaries apparently recruited by Maldivian opponents of Gayoom, landed on Male on November 3 and stormed the presidential palace and other key installations. The coup was quickly crushed when, at Gayoom's request, the Indian government sent paratroopers and warships to Maldives. About 20 Maldivians died in the attack; there were no Indian casualties. In the aftermath of the coup the government decided to increase the size of its small security force and purchase more sophisticated weapons. A small contingent of Indian soldiers remained in Maldives to train the local security force. Ties with India, already strengthened by the establishment in 1985 of the South Asian Association for Regional Cooperation (SAARC), grew even closer. A number of foreign workers from Sri Lanka were ordered to leave the country after the attempted coup, but relations between Sri Lanka and Maldives generally remained cordial.

Maldives has consistently followed a nonaligned foreign policy and has expressed concern over environmental issues. It has been especially vocal in pushing for the declaration of a nuclear-free zone in the Indian Ocean and has sought to create greater international awareness of the special problems facing small island-states.

ECONOMY

Background: Until the late 1980s Maldives was relatively self-sustaining in economic terms. The growth in the tourist industry and the mechanization of the traditional economic mainstay, fishing, led to an average economic growth rate of 8.9% between 1976 and 1986, when GDP was U.S. $9 billion. Per capita income increased from $160 in 1978 to $458 in 1987. Much of the initial economic growth, however, almost entirely benefited those directly involved in the modern sector, leading to a disproportionate concentration of wealth on Male and nearby islands, and undermining the traditional economic and social structure. In the 1980s the government placed great emphasis on extending social services and development projects to the outer islands; projects combining health and educational services, infrastructure and industry were developed for most of the atolls. There was also special concern about the deterioration of the fragile environment, upon which the nation's leading industries—tourism and fishing—depend: The government threatened to shut down tourist resorts that did not install adequate garbage-disposal facilities; spearfishing around Maldivian reefs was outlawed; the export of live tropical fish was strictly controlled; and foreign trawlers fishing illegally in Maldivian waters were confiscated.

Fishing: The fishing industry, the mainstay of the economy, was modernized rapidly in the late 1980s. Traditionally, the nation's chief export was "Maldive fish" (tuna sliced, boiled and smoked over coconut-wood fires) exported to Sri Lanka, where it is considered a delicacy. When this traditional market virtually dried up in the 1970s, processing methods and markets changed. Fish canning plants, modern cold storage facilities and refrigeration plants were constructed to process skipjack and tuna, the leading catches. Some 61,925 U.S. tons/55,290 metric tons of fish were caught in 1986; the following year fish exports provided 17% of all government revenue. About half of the catch is consumed domestically. Since 1985 the government has issued fishing licenses to foreign countries, allowing them to harvest specified quantities of tuna in exchange for a 10% royalty on the catch. By 1988 about 200 modern fishing vessels had been constructed with government funding and sold to local fishermen on easy credit terms. While the mechanization of the fishing fleet has increased catches, it has also increased the nation's dependence on imported fuel. The government is funding research programs on marine resources and fishing techniques.

Tourism: Tourism (developed since about 1973) contributed 18% of government revenues in 1987, when 131,000 tourists visited the islands (up from 1,799 visitors in 1972). The expansion of this industry is overseen by a tourist advisory board established in 1981, when the completion of an international airport on Male Atoll gave the country a direct link to the outside world. There are now three international and two regional airports. Tourist facilities are being expanded and upgraded to attract wealthier visitors. By 1986 there were 56 resorts with more than 5,500 hotel beds; that number has since increased. Traditionally, visitors to Maldives first stopped in Sri Lanka and spent time in both countries. This linkage worked to the disadvantage of Maldives when violence erupted in Sri Lanka in the 1980s. Today about 90% of all visitors come from Western Europe and Japan, many of them via India—with December being the peak month. In addition to the country's climate and scenic beauty, Male's free-port status attracts shoppers.

Agriculture: Agriculture, which accounts for about 12% of GDP, is generally a supplementary source of income. Crops are irrigated with natural rainfall. Coconuts, long the leading commercial crop, now barely provide for local needs due to neglect of the coconut plantations and to population growth. The government is attempting, however, to rehabilitate the islands' coconut plantations and hopes to resume copra exports. Millet, sweet potatoes and cassava are also grown, particularly in the south; and varieties of local tropical fruits include mangoes, bananas and pineapples. Rice, which is a staple food, must be imported.

Banking and finance: The nation's central bank, the Maldives Monetary Authority, was established in 1981. It issues currency, supervises the banking industry and advises the government on banking matters. The national currency, the Maldivian rupee, was renamed the rufiyaa that same year. In 1982 the Bank of Maldives Limited, the country's first commercial bank, was founded; there are now five commercial banks. In 1985 Maldives had an outstanding foreign debt of $52.1 million.

Other industries: The government-owned shipping line, Maldives National Ship Management, was established in 1958 and operates a fleet of about 25 vessels. It suffered substantial losses during much of the 1980s due to a recession in international shipping, but returned to profitability in 1987. The shipping industry was also adversely affected by international restrictions imposed on third-country carriers in 1983, since third-country trade accounts for more than 90% of the Maldivian fleet's cargo. The opening of a new commercial harbor at Male in 1986, however, increased the port's cargo-handling capacity by more than 500%. In an effort to diversify the economy, part of the former British military facility on Gan island has been converted to business and industrial use—especially garment manufacturing. Cottage industries supplying the small domestic market include handicrafts (lace, lacquer ware and woven mats), boat building and the weaving of coir rope and yarn from coconut fibers. Both coir weaving and the gathering of cowrie shells (exported for use as ornaments) are activities performed exclusively by women. In general, the development of manufacturing for export has been hampered by a shortage of skilled labor and inadequate infrastructure. The government also gets some revenue from the sale of postage stamps.

Foreign aid: More than 20% of government revenue comes from foreign aid. Maldives receives aid from a variety of sources, including other Islamic countries and various international organizations such as SAARC.

Foreign trade: In 1987 exports totaled $29 million and imports totaled $58 million. Fresh and processed fish and fish products constitute by far the bulk of all exports, followed by clothing and accessories. Small quantities of coir yarn, shells and handicrafts also are exported. The leading export destinations in 1985 were Thailand (29%), the United States (24%), Sri Lanka (20%), Japan (10%) and Canada (8%). Imports in 1985 consisted primarily of foodstuffs (including rice, wheat flour and sugar), beverages and tobacco (29% by value), machinery and transportation equipment (18%), petroleum products (15%), textiles (13%) and chemicals (6%). In 1983 about 63% of the nation's imports came from Singapore, 11% from Japan, 8% from Sri Lanka and 4.5% from India. Fresh fish exports are controlled by the State Trading Organization. Although exports of frozen fish have declined, overall fish exports are up due to increased shipments of canned and salted fish and fish meal.

Employment: The salaried labor force in 1987 consisted of 99,000 workers. In 1986 some 41% were employed in the fishing industry; 23% in manufacturing, construction and utilities; 20% in government and services (including tourism); and 16% in agriculture.

SOCIAL SERVICES

Welfare: Maldives has no organized social welfare system; by tradition assistance is provided through the extended family. The delivery of social services is complicated by the fact that the country is divided geographically into small, isolated communities.

Health services: Health expenditures consumed 6.7% of the government budget in 1985. That same year the country had 23 doctors, 74 nurses and 312 midwives, and 121 government-supported hospital beds. The largest hospital, in Male, has 86 beds. In addition there are three smaller regional hospitals and government-sponsored medical rescue services on the outlying islands. The government also provides assistance for medical care abroad for the seriously ill. Most Maldivians, however, receive medical care from *hakims*, who follow traditional Islamic practice. In 1987 the infant mortality rate was 57.5 per 1,000 live births, down from 77 per 1,000 in 1983. Malaria, long a problem on all of the islands except Male, has been brought under control but not eradicated, and waterborne diseases such as cholera remain common; Male suffered a serious cholera epidemic as recently as

1982. A long-planned water supply and sewage program on Male was completed in 1988, but only about 8% of the rural population has access to safe water.

Housing: Most of the inhabitants live in houses with walls of coconut wood or coral; roofs are tiled or made of corrugated iron. The extreme concentration of population on Male has led to serious housing shortages there, and the government is attempting to discourage migration to the capital through development projects on the outer islands.

EDUCATION

Maldives has three types of schools: traditional Islamic schools teaching reading, writing and simple arithmetic as well as providing religious training; modern government-funded Divehi-language primary schools on the outer islands; and English-language primary and secondary schools, first established on Male in 1961. In general, primary education lasts for five years and secondary education for up to seven years. In 1986 there were 243 primary schools, with an enrollment of nearly 42,000; and nine secondary schools, with more than 3,500 students. Those seeking higher education must study abroad. Although education is not compulsory, adult literacy increased from 82% in 1977 to 93.2% in 1986; the country has one of the highest literacy rates in the Third World. This is largely due to an ambitious government-sponsored adult education program and to the expansion of educational facilities on the outer islands. As recently as 1976 there were only 16 government-operated schools, all of them on Male. U.N. assistance has contributed to the expansion of the educational system since that time. Special emphasis has been placed on programs designed to train the skilled workers required for development projects, particularly in the fishing industry. There are several vocational training centers, and Male has a science education center.

MASS MEDIA

Since 1977 a satellite earth station has facilitated international communications. A network of high-frequency transceivers links the various atolls, and direct-dial telephones are being installed. Walkie-talkies are the common means of communication between islands and with boats.

The press: In 1985 Maldives had two daily newspapers, *Aafathis* and *Haveeru,* both published on Male in English and Divehi. The biweekly *Spectrum* and *Maldives News Bulletin* are published in English. Divehi-language publications include the weekly official religious publication *Dheenuge Magu,* and the monthly cultural magazine *Faiythoors.* The monthly business-oriented *Trade Information News Sheet* is published in English and Divehi.

Broadcasting: In 1987 the country had 4.1 television receivers and 22 radio receivers per 1,000 persons. The government-operated local radio station

(Voice of Maldives) and the local television station (TV Maldives) transmit in both Divehi and English.

BIOGRAPHICAL SKETCHES

Maumoon Abdul Gayoom. Born in Maldives in 1937, Gayoom became the nation's president in 1978 and was reelected in 1983 and 1988. He is considered an Islamic scholar, and was educated at Cairo's al-Azhar University before serving as a research assistant in Islamic history at the American University of Cairo (1967–69). After his return to Maldives he served as minister of transportation and permanent representative of Maldives to the United Nations in the administration of Amin Ibrahim Nasir. As president, Gayoom has worked to diversify and modernize the economy, and has given high priority to improving the standard of living outside the capital. His extensive travels and active participation in numerous international forums have increased the nation's profile on the international scene.

Amin Ibrahim Nasir. Born on Male in 1926 and schooled in Colombo, Nasir worked for an automotive firm as a young man. He became the first president of the independent Republic of Maldives in 1968. He had served as prime minister under Sultan Muhammad Amin Didi from 1957 to 1968, when the sultanate was abolished for the second time. Nasir eliminated the post of prime minister in 1975 and strengthened his powers; the following year he signed an agreement formally terminating the British military presence on the islands. After Nasir declined to stand for reelection in 1978, he left the country. He was later charged in absentia with misappropriation of government funds.

MONGOLIA

GEOGRAPHY

Features: The Mongolian People's Republic (MPR) is located in east-central Asia, wedged between the People's Republic of China and the Soviet Union— a factor that has had much influence on the country's development. It shares a 2,800-mile/4,670-km. border with China to the south, east and west, while an 1,800-mile/3,000-km. border is shared with the Soviet Union to the north. Much of the western and northern areas of Mongolia are mountainous, and many large rivers originate in these regions, emptying into the Arctic or the Pacific Ocean. A continental watershed divides Mongolia, with smaller rivers in the south draining into lakes or being lost in the ground. Snow-covered peaks reaching to over 13,120 ft/4,000 m. above sea level dominate the Altay area in the west. The Hangayn-Hentiyn mountains in the north-central region surround the Selenge-Tuul basin, a fertile agricultural region in which remnants of early settlements in the northern steppes of Mongolia can be found. Eastern Mongolia is the sight of a great depression, with fresh- and saltwater lakes throughout. Some, such as Uvs Lake (1,290 sq. miles/3,350 sq. km.) and Hovsgol Lake (1,010 sq. miles/2,620 sq. km.) are considerably large and can be important for navigation. Further east lies the plateau region that stretches to the Chinese border. The Gobi desert covers the country's southern and eastern stretches, or fully one-third of Mongolia's territory. The Gobi is not actually a sandy desert but a stony plain with sparse vegetation. Mongolia is subject to severe earthquakes, especially in the mountainous regions, but damage is usually limited because the population is so widely scattered.

Area: 604,250 sq. miles/1,565,000 sq. km.

Mean max. and min. temperatures: Ulaanbaatar (47°55'N, 106°53'E) 61° F/16.5°C (July), −8°F/−22.5°C (Jan.).

Mean annual rainfall: Ulaanbaatar 12 in/312 mm.

POPULATION

Total population: 1,595,000 (1979 census); 1,965,000 (1987 est.).

Chief towns and populations (1986 est.): ULAANBAATAR (500,200), Darkhan (74,000), Erdenet (45,400).

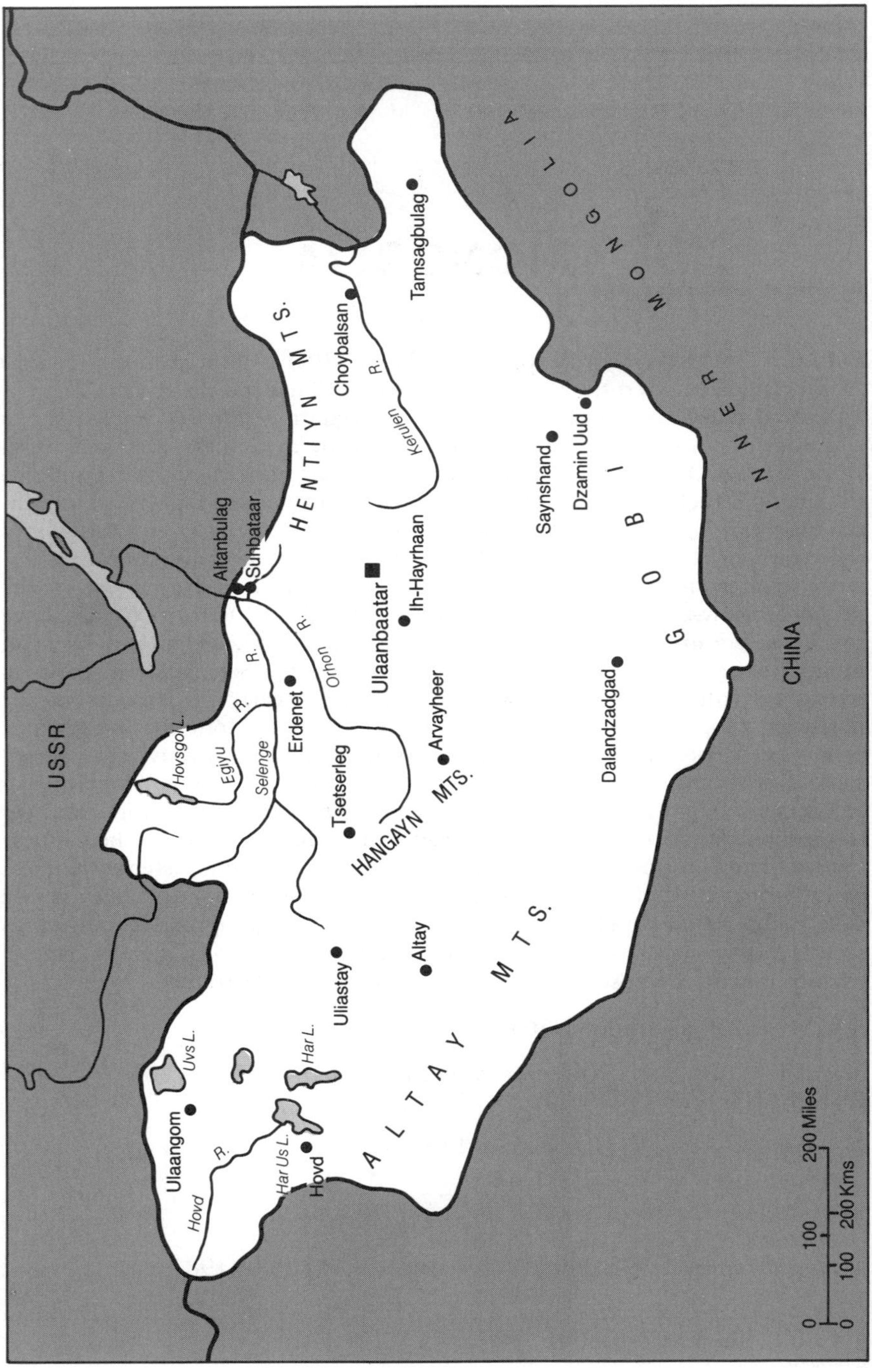

USSR

MONGOLIA

CHINA

INNER MONGOLIA

HENTIYN MTS.

Tamsagbulag

Choybalsan

Kerulen R.

Altanbulag
Suhbaatar

Saynshand

Dzamin Uud

Ih-Hayrhaan

Ulaanbaatar

Orhon R.

Erdenet

Arvayheer

Hovsgol L.

Egiyu R.

Selenge R.

Tsetserleg

HANGAYN MTS.

G O B I

Dalandzadgad

Altay

Uliastay

ALTAY MTS.

Uvs L.

Har L.

Ulaangom

Hovd R.

Har Us L.

Hovd

200 Miles

200 Kms

0   100   200

0   100   200

Distribution: Mongolia is sparsely inhabited, with a density of just over one person per sq. km. Fully one-quarter of the population lives in the capital, Ulaanbaatar. Nearly half live in towns. A national policy encouraging settlement of rural areas through capital investment in construction has created about 300 settlements that house 22% of the population. Mongolia's population growth rate was 2.6% in 1985, down from 3.3% in 1960. The population grew steadily in the 1970s and 1980s, increasing 75% between 1963 and 1983. The country has a very young population as a result: The 1979 census showed that two-thirds of the population was under 30 years old. A current labor shortage has led to official promotion of population growth to fulfill plans for long-term development of new industry. Abortion is illegal.

The population is relatively homogeneous. Approximately 87% are Mongols, mostly belonging to the Khalkha (Halh) group. The Kazakhs, a Turkic-speaking people, are the only other significant ethnic group, comprising roughly 5% of the total population.

Language: The official language is Mongol, which shares some aspects of Turkish, Korean and Japanese. Today it is written in an adaptation of the Cyrillic script. Khalkha is the dominant dialect, but several other Mongol dialects are also spoken. In the Kazakh province of Bayan-olgiy, Kazakh is the first language, with most people being bilingual in Mongol.

Religion: The government's Council of Religious Affairs of the Council of Ministers technically controls religious affairs in the MPR, but little is known about its activities. The Lamaist (Mahayana Buddhist) sect was practically wiped out by 1940. The 1960 constitution, however, guarantees freedom of religion and separation of church and state. Freedom of religion also implies freedom to disseminate antireligious propaganda, although authorities issued public warnings in 1984 against the smuggling of Bibles and religious literature into Mongolia, saying this would cause "ideological harm" to the population. Of the few Mongolians who practice religion, most are Lamaists. The only active monastery is in Ulaanbaatar, with about 100 lamas and a small seminary; by contrast, in 1921 there were several hundred monasteries with tens of thousands of lamas. The Kazakhs of western Mongolia are nominally Sunni Muslims, but their mosques are inactive.

CONSTITUTIONAL SYSTEM

Constitution: Mongolia's third constitution, adopted on July 6, 1960, proclaims the MPR to be a sovereign democratic state of working people. The state owns all land, natural resources, factories, transport and banking institutions. Citizens have cooperative ownership of public enterprises, especially in livestock herding. Workers exercise state power through their locally elected *hurals* (assemblies), according to the constitution. Some private ownership is permitted.

Head of state: Jambyn Batmonh. *Prime minister:* Dumaagiyn Sodnom.

Executive: The Council of Ministers is the highest executive power. Members include the chairman, the first vice-chairman, five vice-chairmen, 18 ministries and 12 state committees, including the State Bank and the Academy of Sciences. The Council directs the ministries and state economic planning. It generally directs foreign relations and defense policy, and is responsible for internal security as well. In 1986 half the Council's members were also members of the party Central Committee, and nearly all the rest were candidates, indicating party overlap and thus dominance in all branches of government.

Legislature: The People's Great Assembly is the supreme state power. It normally convenes once a year. In the June 1986 elections 370 unopposed deputies were elected to the Assembly to serve five-year terms. The number of deputies was fixed in 1981. Of those elected in 1981 and 1986, 93% were party members or candidates. The head of state, who is also the general secretary of the Mongolian People's Revolutionary party (MPRP), serves as chairman of the Assembly Presidium. The Assembly has the power to amend the constitution by a two-thirds majority vote, to adopt laws, to formulate policy, and to approve the state budget and economic plans. The Presidium—which includes the chairman, a vice-chairman, a secretary and five members—interprets legislation and issues decrees, ratifies treaties and appoints or dismisses members of the Council of Ministers (with Assembly approval).

Political parties: The MPRP is the only political party permitted in Mongolia. According to the constitution, it is "the guiding and directing force of society and the state in the MPR . . . which is guided in its activity by all-conquering Marxist-Leninist theory." The Party Congress, which meets every five years, is the supreme body of the MPRP. The Congress elects the party's Central Committee, which meets at least twice a year. The Central Committee elects the Political Bureau, or Politburo (Uls Toriyn Tovchoo) to conduct party work between Central Committee plenums. The Central Committee also elects the Secretariat, which oversees implementation of party resolutions and the selection of cadres. In 1986 it had 88,000 members.

Local government: Hurals and their executive committees at provincial *(aymag)* and subprovincial *(sum-negdel)* levels comprise the local government structure. There are 18 provinces and 299 counties *(somons)* combining "administrative and economic primary levels under a single managerial organization." Ulaanbaatar has special status and its own representative on the Council of Ministers. The city is divided into four *rayons* and subdivided into 44 *horoo.* Darkhan and Erdenet are separate municipalities also, divided into districts. In rural areas there are 22 *horoo*—mostly small industrial or transport centers. State power at all levels lies with the assemblies of people's deputies, which elect administrations of seven to 11 persons. They are responsible for directing "economic and cultural, political construction" and enforcing laws. Local elections are held every three years.

Judiciary: The judicial system includes the Supreme Court, the City Court of Ulaanbaatar, 18 provincial courts and local courts. The Supreme Court has 14 members and 80 "people's assessors." There are also procurators and courts at provincial and town level. The People's Great Assembly elects the chairman and members of the Supreme Court, as well as the procurator of the republic, for five-year terms. Local assemblies elect other judges for three-year terms.

RECENT HISTORY

There is no consensus on the meaning of the word "Mongol," but it was perhaps the name of a single tribe of the region before it came to denote the entire nation. Genghis Khan, perhaps the most noted Mongol, was from the Borjigin clan. By 1194 he had conquered and unified other Mongolian tribes into a state. Conquests by his successors extended the Mongol empire from Dalmatia to Java by the end of the 13th century.

What is today Mongolia (previously Northern or Outer Mongolia) came under Manchu dominance, partly through complicity and partly through conquest, as the Manchus expanded outward from China in the late 17th century. The Manchus administered Outer Mongolia as a separate state from Inner Mongolia. Khalkha was considered another Mongol princedom, and a fourth was created in 1725. They were renamed leagues shortly thereafter, and Mongol league heads appointed by the Chinese government replaced tribal princes. The real power of the Mongol khans was destroyed and the Lamaist religion became the focus of Mongolian identity. The territory was divided into about 100 banners (military districts) and several temple territories, a state structure that survived the fall of the Manchus in 1911 and lasted until 1924, when the MPR was founded.

With the fall of the Manchus Mongolia broke its association with China (the Mongols mostly considered themselves allies of the Manchus) and, with aid from Russia, proclaimed an independent monarchy. A 1913 Russo-Chinese treaty, however, made Outer Mongolia an autonomous state under Chinese suzerainty. The territory then included what is today Mongolia, plus Dariganga in the southeast, which was acquired by China in 1921. Autonomous Mongolia was a theocratic monarchy that did very little to change the country during its short reign. Russian advisers helped modernize the army and organize the fiscal system, making Mongolia in fact a Russian protectorate. But the collapse of czarist Russia and the outbreak of revolution paved the way for a return of Chinese dominance to Mongolia.

In 1920 the Mongol People's party (MPP) was formed to counter the Chinese. The party included men from various social backgrounds who sought independence from the Chinese, an elective government, internal administrative reforms, social justice, and the consolidation of the Buddhist faith and sect. They sought advice and support from the USSR. Their bargaining power was weakened, however, when a White Russian army ousted the Chinese and restored the Mongol king to the throne while they negotiated in the Soviet Union. They were thus forced to make concessions to the Soviet government for its help in countering the government at home backed by White Russians.

A provisional revolutionary government was set up in 1921 at the first MPP congress, which was held on Soviet territory. Backed by Soviet forces, they ousted the White Russians and proclaimed a new government in July 1921. The monarchy was retained but in name only. Dogsomyn Bodoo was appointed the country's first prime minister and foreign minister. Damdiny Sühbaatar became commander in chief and minister of war, and Horloogiyn Choybalsan was appointed minister of finance. Bodoo was executed in 1922 by a pro-Soviet faction after being implicated in counter-revolutionary plots. Sühbaatar died of illness in 1923. The MPP was renamed the MPRP, and a people's republic modeled after the Soviet Union was proclaimed in 1924.

The new government was saddled with severe underdevelopment, a church that commanded deep loyalty from the people, and local separatism. It suffered a large population loss as disillusioned herdsmen emigrated to China. There was no currency, no banking system, no industry and no modern medical service. With little capacity for independent action, the regime relied more and more on its stronger Soviet neighbor, and Mongolia's development closely followed that of Stalin's Soviet Union. Rightists were dismissed from leadership positions in 1928 and Mongolia entered a long period of isolation. It ended all foreign contact except with the Soviet Union. A poorly planned collectivization program between 1929 and 1932 caused many Mongols to turn against the MPRP, which resulted in uprisings and mass emigration. The party then adopted a more moderate line, allowing private ownership of cattle and private trade.

Harsh policies returned in 1936 under the dictatorship of Marshal Choybalsan, whose methods mirrored those of Stalin. Much of the revolutionary guard was liquidated and the Lamaist sect was just about destroyed. Choybalsan's protégés moved into government positions to lead the country to socialism, and many remain in those posts today.

Modernization, however, did not really begin until after World War II, when Mongolia's first Five-Year Plan (1948–52) was introduced. Mongolia's isolation began to erode in the postwar years as it established diplomatic relations with much of the Eastern bloc as well as with some nonaligned states. Mongolia was admitted to the United Nations in 1961. Nevertheless, it remained closely aligned with the USSR; and the country's political structure, educational system and economic programs still closely resemble those of the Soviet Union. For decades it maintained a sharp anti-Beijing line and justified the presence of Soviet troops on its soil as a counter to Chinese "great-power" expansion.

However, as the Sino-Soviet dispute began to thaw in the mid-1980s, Mongolia's relationship with its two neighbors changed. In 1986 relations between Mongolia and China improved significantly with the signing of a treaty establishing consular relations. Mikhail Gorbachev offered to withdraw some Soviet troops from Mongolia to encourage diplomatic relations between Moscow and Beijing. A partial withdrawal (about 20% of the 75,000 Soviet troops stationed there, according to Western estimates) was completed by June 1987. In that year, also, the United States established diplomatic relations with Mongolia.

Internally, Mongolia imitated the partial thaw initiated by Nikita Khrushchev in the 1950s and 1960s. Mongolian nationalism, which had been repressed for 20 years, reemerged. The school curriculum was modified to include teachings in Mongolian culture and literature, subjects that had been ignored since 1936, although communist ideas were still emphasized. Mongolia has occasionally been rebuffed by the Soviet Union for asserting its national identity too enthusiastically at the expense of proletarian internationalism.

Party shuffling throughout the 1980s placed Jambyn Batmonh in the main seat of power.

Background: Since 1948 the Mongolian economy has developed with much assistance from the Communist bloc. Successive Five-Year Plans begun in the postwar years have completed the country's transition to a socialist system of production. The agriculture and government-service sectors together employ over 600,000 members of the estimated 773,000-strong work force; industry accounts for the remainder. In 1985, 34% of the population were engaged in agriculture and forestry, and nearly 19% in industry. Mongolia's estimated GDP in 1985 was U.S. $1.67 billion. Per capita income was $880.

Herding is the mainstay of the economy. It remained a private enterprise until a second collectivization effort launched in the 1950s succeeded in collectivizing all but a small portion of herdsmen by the end of the decade. Propaganda and economic expulsion were the main methods used to encourage herdsmen to join. State loans were granted to newly formed cooperatives, and individuals who owned large herds were forced to pay higher taxes. The industrial sector, mostly developed since World War II, is divided between cooperative and state ownership. The cooperative sector mainly produces items for domestic use. The principal "industrial" areas are located in the central region, at Ulaanbaatar and Darkhan, the areas of densest population in the country. However, Mongolia has no single major industry and continues to rely on imports for capital and consumer goods. Trade is still conducted almost entirely with the socialist bloc; Mongolia became a member of the Council of Mutual Economic Aid (Comecon or CMEA) in 1962. From 1965 to 1985 Soviet economic aid to Mongolia grew tenfold, and national income grew almost fourfold.

Agriculture: Herding, with its related products such as milk, wool, hides and skins, dominates Mongolia's agricultural sector. Herding cooperatives were organized in the 1950s according to the Soviet collective farm model. The 255 cooperatives are economic units as well as units of local administration. Families are allowed to keep a certain number of private animals, and the state purchases the produce. Cooperatives are divided into brigades, each with its own territory and special tasks. Livestock production suffered continuous declines during the 1970s due to harsh winters. At the end of 1977 alone, 2.6 million animals had died from cold, starvation, thirst and neglect. Numbers declined again by 13% in the period 1981–85 due to disease and neglect. In 1985 sheep numbered 13,249,000—down from 14,955,000 in 1982. The number of goats dropped from 4,802,000 to 4,299,000 in 1985. Horses, cattle, camels, pigs and poultry are also raised.

Mongolia has developed large-scale agriculture, increasing the number of state farms from 10 in 1940 to 60 in 1980. Annual grain production averages 400,000 to 600,000 metric tons, produced from 2.5 million acres/ 1 million ha. of land. In 1985 Mongolia reportedly set a record in grain production, producing 889,000 tons—enough to satisfy internal requirements. The principal crops produced are cereals, potatoes and vegetables.

Industry: Mongolia's industrial growth could not have been achieved without foreign aid. In the 1950s China and the Soviet Union vied to win Mongolian support through economic assistance: Moscow provided rubles and Beijing contributed laborers. In 1960 several thousand Chinese were building apartments, laying roads and constructing irrigation systems in Mongolia. By the mid-1960s, however, the Sino-Soviet rift had widened, and Mongolia came to depend more on Moscow. Industrial centers at Ulaanbaatar and Darkhan, between the capital and the Soviet border, account for most of the country's production of electrical power, cement, bricks and consumer goods such as food, drink, leather, sweets and soap. A cement and lime factory, a joint Soviet-Mongol project, was inaugurated in January 1986. The complex was expected to meet the country's requirements for both materials: 100,000 metric tons of lime and 500,000 tons of cement per year. In 1986 cement output was 425,000 metric tons, up from 150,000 the year before. A joint Soviet-Mongol venture is also exploiting copper and molybdenum deposits at Erdenet. In 1983 the food industry accounted for 18% of the gross industrial output; timber and woodworking, 11%; textiles, 10.6%; leather, fur and footwear, 9.4%; electricity generation and heating, 9.2%; clothing, 6.5%; and building materials, 6.2%.

Foreign trade: Virtually all of Mongolia's foreign trade is conducted with socialist countries. Exports are mostly primary products including hides, furs and wool. These accounted for 30% of exports in 1980. By 1985, however, mineral raw materials comprised 43% of exports. Export-quality goods such as carpets, leather and sheepskin coats and cashmere sweaters are becoming more widely available for export. Raw foodstuffs and food products, including meat and meat products, made up another 13% of exports. Main imports are machinery and equipment, consumer goods and fuels, minerals and metals. In 1985 Mongolia's exports to the USSR amounted to 410 million rubles, while imports were valued at 1,138 million rubles. The country signed its first long-term trade agreement with China in 1986, under the terms of which China exports silk and light industrial products while Mongolia exports timber and animal products.

Employment: Of an economically active population estimated at 773,000, 308,000 are employed in agriculture, 303,000 in services, and 162,000 in industry. All belong to trade unions. For most industrial and office workers the workday is eight hours six days a week, and six hours on Sundays and public holidays. Basic annual leave is 15 working days, plus eight public holidays. Little information is available on real income, wages or prices.

SOCIAL SERVICES

The state social fund covers costs for education and public health, as well as assistance in the form of pensions for the aged and disabled. In 1983 nearly 60% of disposable national income went into this fund. Workers receive payments and allowances from the social consumption funds in the form of social insurance payments, pensions, grants to students, free education and free medical services, and expenditure on kindergartens and nurseries. Parents receive allowances according to the number of their children. Under regulations in force since 1970 the minimum old-age pension was U.S. $45 and the maximum about $225, calculated according to monthly wage. Income tax is payable on incomes over $140, to a maximum of 5%. Enterprises and institutions are largely responsible for housing their workers, but the role of local government in supervising and improving housing is being extended. Only half of the capital's population live in apartments. The rest, and many in most other towns, live in shacks or yurts in fenced compounds. Electricity and piped water are available to urban yurt dwellers, but most lack sewage. The number of physicians in 1985 was 4,595, or 24 per 10,000 of the population; women comprised 65.6% of this number. There were also 3,807 physician assistants, 8,504 nurses and 112 hospitals with 21,227 beds in 1985. Each province has at least two hospitals, and each cooperative and state farm has a medical station.

EDUCATION

The Ministry of Education and the State Committee for Higher Special Secondary and Technical-Vocational Education run Mongolia's educational system. Education is mandatory, free, secular and coeducational, according to a 1982 education law. There are eight-year general schools and 10-year general schools (with fewer pupils in grades nine and 10), and 11-year secondary schools for agricultural and industrial specialists. An 11th year of compulsory education was also added to general schools during the 1988–89 academic year. Ten-year schools include four years of elementary education, four years of secondary education and two years of "upper" education. Children begin school at eight years of age. There were 587 general education schools during the 1985–86 school year, with 412,600 students—and with more than 17,000 teachers in general education and 1,500 in higher education. There are also special schools for the mentally and physically handicapped, and orphanage schools. Women make up 67% of the teachers in general education schools. Many of the schools have two shifts. Children of herdsmen attend boarding schools. Twenty-five special secondary schools and 40 technical-vocational schools train personnel for the service industries, and drivers and machine operators for industry and agriculture. In the 1985–86 term 46,000 pupils studied at these schools. Seven tertiary institutions, including Mongolia State University, had a total of 24,500 students in 1985–86. There are also special colleges for party cadres and army officers, and a teacher training college. In 1985–86 approximately 11,000 Mongolian students were studying abroad, mostly at universities and technical colleges in the USSR.

MASS MEDIA

The press: All newspapers and periodicals are published by a government body. Most ministries publish a periodical addressing their appropriate fields. There are 19 provincial newspapers, most published biweekly by provincial MPRP and executive committees. Nalayh, Erdenet and Darkhan also have their own newspapers.

Major government papers and periodicals published in Ulaanbaatar include the following: *Ardyn Tor* (People's Power), (q), People's Great Assembly (11,000); *Dzaluuchuudyn Unen* (Young People's Truth), (m), Central Committee of the Revolutionary Youth League; *Hodolmor* (Labor), (m), Central Council of Trade Unions; *Huuhdyn Humuujil* (Children's Education), six times a year, Ministry of People's Education (23,400); *Namyn Am'dral* (Party Life), (m), MPRP Central Committee (28,000); *Nayramdlyn Dzam* (Road of Friendship), twice weekly, Mongolian Railway Authority; *Pionyeriyn Unen* (Pioneers' Truth), 84 times a year, Central Council of the D. Sühbaatar Pioneers' Organization of the Central Committee of the Revolutionary Youth League (175,000); *Shine Hodoo* (New Countryside), (w), Ministry of Agriculture; *Sportyn Medee* (Sports News), (w), MPR State Committee of Physical Culture and Sports; *Surgan Humuujuulegch* (Educator), six times a year, Ministry of People's Education; *Tonshuul* (Woodpecker), 18 times a year, satirical, MPRP Central Committee; *Uhuulagch* (Agitator), 18 times a year, MPRP Central Committee (34,000); *Ulaan Od* (Red Star), twice weekly, ministries of Defense and Public Security; *Unen* (Truth), six days a week, MPRP Central Committee and MPR Council of Ministers (170,000); and *Utga Dzohiol Urlag* (Literature and Art), (w), Writers' Union and the Ministry of Culture.

Broadcasting: The State Committee for Information, Radio and Television controls the airwaves. There were 193,500 loudspeakers, 200,700 radio receivers and 88,100 television receivers in Mongolia in 1985. Ulaanbaatar Radio broadcasts programs in Mongolian, Russian, Chinese, English, French and Kazakh. Mongoltelevidz is the television station that provides daily transmission of either local material or Soviet programs via the Molniya satellite and the Orbita ground station. Television reaches about 60 percent of the population.

BIOGRAPHICAL SKETCHES

Jambyn Batmonh. Born March 10, 1926, the current MPRP general-secretary and MPR president (chairman of the Presidium of the People's Great

Assembly), came to both posts at the retirement of Yumjaagiyn Tsedenbal in 1984. Batmonh was educated at Mongolia State University and at the Soviet Union's Academy of Social Sciences. From 1951 to 1973 he served in various positions at Mongolia State University, advancing from lecturer to rector. In 1973 he became head of the Science and Education Department of the MPRP Central Committee. He was appointed chairman of the Council of Ministers a year later, a position he held until 1984. He assumed the posts of president and general-secretary of the MPRP when Tsedenbal was effectively retired. Batmonh is credited with reviving party life since Tsedenbal's departure, and pressing for a restructuring of leadership and the intensive development of the Mongolian economy.

Dumaagiyn Sodnom. The current chairman of the MPR Council of Ministers was born about 1933. Sodnom has a strong financial and economics background, having been educated at the School of Finance and Economics in Ulaanbaatar, and at the Higher School of Finance and Economics in the USSR. He served from 1950 to 1969 in the Ministry of Finance, ending his stint there as minister of finance. He then transferred to the State Planning Commission, where he was first deputy chairman from 1969 to 1972. From 1972 until 1984 he was chairman of the State Planning Commission. He became chairman of the Council of Ministers upon Tsedenbal's departure from the political forefront in 1984, when Batmonh left the position to take up the chairmanship of the assembly.

Yumjaagiyn Tsedenbal. Born September 17, 1916, Tsedenbal stepped down from his position as general-secretary of the MPRP in 1984 after a 35-year career in Mongolian government. Educated at the Institute of Finance and Economics in the USSR, he became deputy minister, then minister of finance in 1940. From 1941 to 1945 he was deputy commander in chief of the Mongolian People's Army, then chairman of the State Planning Commission from 1945 until 1948. He became deputy chairman of the Council of Ministers, being appointed premier, or chairman, in 1952. He held that post until 1974, when he became chairman of the Presidium of the People's Great Assembly. From 1981 until 1984 he was also general-secretary of the party. Tsedenbal attained the military rank of marshal in 1979, a rank rarely awarded in Mongolian history. He was removed from his posts in 1984 "on account of his health and with his agreement," according to the party. Many assumed his autocratic ways triggered his downfall.

CHINA

BHUTAN

INDIA

CHINA

BANGLADESH

Putao

Makaw

Myitkyina

Chindwin R.

Katha

Bhamo

Kindat

Mawlaik

Yeu

Namtu

Falam

Shwebo

Hsipaw

Lashio

Sagaing

Monywa

Maymyo

Myinmu

Mandalay

Kehsi Mansam

Pakokku

Myingyan

Irrawaddy R.

Kengtung

Meiktila

Taung-gyi

LAOS

Minbu

Magwe

Yamethin

Sittwe

Pyinmana

Salween R.

ARAKAN YOMA

Kyaukpyu

Allanmyo

Loikaw

Thayetmyo

Cheduba I.

Toungoo

Sandoway

Prome

Bay

Myanaung

Paungde

Sittang R.

Henzada

Tharrawaddy

Shwegyin

of

Pegu

Kyaikto

Yangon

Bengal

Bassein

Maubin

Syriam

Thaton

Myaungmya

Kawkareik

Pyapon

Gulf of

Moulmein

THAILAND

Mouths of the Irrawaddy

Martaban

Ye

Preparis North Channel

Preparis I.

Preparis South Channel

Coco Channel

ANDAMAN

Tavoy

ANDAMAN

ISLANDS

(India)

SEA

MERGUI

Mergui

Gulf

ARCHIPELAGO

of

Siam

0   50   100 Miles

Isthmus

0   50 100 Kms

Kawthaung

of

Kra

MYANMAR (BURMA)

MYANMAR

Features: The Union of Myanmar (formerly Burma) divides structurally into three clear divisions. On the west is a series of mountain ranges running from north to south, apparently a continuation of the eastern Himalayan series. Toward the northern end the peaks may exceed 11,976 ft/3,650 m.; in the most southern portion the height decreases to under 4,922 ft/1,500 m. Throughout its length this formation, consisting of densely forested, fever-infested ridges, is a formidable natural barrier between Myanmar and the Indian subcontinent. On the east is another series of mountain ranges again running from north to south, at first as a continuation of the Yunnan Plateau but then extending through the Shan and Karenni plateaus into the modest ranges that divide Tenasserim and peninsular Thailand. In the far north of the country the western and eastern mountain ranges join. Lying within these ranges is the third structural division, a vast central trough. Its southern portion contains a great alluvial lowland, drained principally by the Irrawaddy River; the northern portion, at a higher elevation, comprises the dry zone. In contrast to the rich agricultural capacity of the alluvial lowland and the dense monsoon forest cover of the mountain ranges, the dry zone is largely covered by thorny scrub. The alluvial lowland of central Myanmar and in particular the huge delta area of the Irrawaddy, constitutes one of the world's great rice-producing regions; it is now the economic and demographic center of the country. In the eastern plateaus are substantial deposits of silver, lead, zinc and tungsten. In the lower mountain slopes that encircle central Myanmar lie the world's richest reserves of teak. In the middle Irrawaddy lowlands are considerable reserves of petroleum and natural gas.

Area: 261,218 sq. miles/676,552 sq. km.

Mean max. and min. temperatures: In the Irrawaddy delta, Arakan and Tenasserim mean annual temperatures are about 81°F/27°C. The dry zone experiences a relatively wide seasonal range of temperatures: Mandalay, 70°F/21°C (Jan.), 90°F/32°C (April). Temperatures on the Shan and Karenni plateaus are substantially below those experienced in the lowlands.

Relative humidity: Yangon, 73%; Mandalay, 61%.

Mean annual rainfall: Myanmar receives by far the major part of its rainfall on the southwest monsoon. Those parts of the country that face that mon-

225

soon and are backed by high ranges, notably Arakan and Tenasserim, experience extremely high rainfall. Thus Akyab receives 204 in/5,180 mm.; Amherst receives 196 in/4,980 mm. The Irrawaddy delta receives rainfall of about 99 in/2,500 mm. In the interior of the dry zone—a rain-shadow area relative to the southwest monsoon—the rainfall is less than 33 in/ 1,000 mm. In some districts in the dry zone it is less than 25 in/640 mm.

POPULATION

Total population (September 1987 est.): 38,595,000.

Chief towns and populations (1983 est.): YANGON (Rangoon) (2,458,712), Mandalay (532,895), Bassein (335,000), Moulmein (219,991).

Distribution: In the 1983 census 23.98% of the population was classified as urban.

Language: Burmese is the official language of the state, the language of instruction at all levels of education (although there has been an extending restoration of English since the beginning of the 1980s) and the national lingua franca. A number of local languages are spoken among approximately 25% of the population, who define themselves as members of minority ethnic groups.

Religion: Freedom of religion is guaranteed by the state. About 85% of the population are Buddhists, 5% are animists, 4% are Muslims, 4% are Hindus and 2% are Christians.

CONSTITUTIONAL SYSTEM

Constitution: The most recent constitution was the one that came into force on January 3, 1974. This constitution was suspended following the army coup of September 18, 1988.

Head of government: Gen. Saw Maung.

Executive and legislature: The leaders of the 1988 army coup became the members of a State Council for the Restoration of Law and Order. This body has unqualified executive, legislative and judicial authority. The executive and legislative institutions established under the 1974 constitution (notably the People's Assembly, the State Council and the Council of Ministers) were swept aside.

Political parties: Under the 1974 constitution, the sole legal political party was the Burmese Socialist Program party (BSPP), founded in 1962 by the Revolutionary Council following the coup that took place in March of that year. Until the early 1970s it was a "cadre" party. It then became the party of the masses and claimed a membership of about 1.5 million in 1981. In early September 1988, following weeks of severe popular unrest and political turmoil, President Maung Maung announced the abrogation of the article in the 1974 constitution that made the BSPP the sole legal party. The State Council for the Restoration of Law and Order later confirmed the return to multiparty politics. On September 27, 1988, it issued legislation for the registration of political parties. By early January 1989 there were said to be 161 registered parties; most of the prominent ones were led by politicians who last experienced active political life in the 1950s. On September 26, 1988, the BSPP was renamed the National Unity party. Multiparty elections were to take place in 1989, but were postponed.

Local government: Under the 1974 constitution local government was exercised through elected people's councils, each responsible for economic and social conditions, the administration of justice, security and defense and the maintenance of law and order in their locality. The State Council for the Restoration of Law and Order has created new state and divisional administrative institutions composed mainly of military officers. Township groups comprise a defense service officer as chairperson, the deputy head of the state or divisional general department, the deputy commander of the relevant police force and a secretary. This structure is very similar to that of the security and administration committees established after the March 1962 coup.

Judicial system: On September 26, 1988, the State Council for the Restoration of Law and Order established by decree a new judicial structure under a Supreme Court of one chief judge and no more than five other judges. Subordinate state, divisional and township courts, manned by judicial officers, were established by the Supreme Court on September 29, 1988. Under the 1974 constitution the highest judicial organ beneath the Council of State was the Council of People's Justices, composed of three members of the People's Assembly. Below this council were state, divisional, township, ward and village tract courts, composed of members of the appropriate local people's council.

RECENT HISTORY

In the early months of 1942 the British administration in Myanmar collapsed before the invading Japanese, leaving the several hundred thousand Britons and Indians who had dominated the government and economic structures of the colony to trek toward the Indian border. With the support of the Japanese, Dr. Ba Maw (a noted prewar Burmese leader) and a number of prominent members of the *thakin* (master) movement, established a central government under which, in August 1943, the country was granted nominal independence. Leftist elements in the *thakin* movement refused to collaborate with the Japanese and began to organize resistance through the Burmese Communist party. In 1944 the Communists sought alliance with those members of the collaborationist administration who had become severely disillusioned by the harshness of Japanese overlordship (prominent here was Aung San). In August 1944 the Anti-Fascist Organization, later to be renamed the Anti-Fascist People's Freedom League (AFPFL), was formed with the aim of driving out the Japanese in alliance with the British—and then securing the country's independence from Britain. As British forces reconquered the country in the early months of 1945, they received considerable assistance from the AFPFL. The AFPFL cooperated with the British military administration that assumed authority after the Japanese surrender.

The first postwar governor, Reginald Dorman-Smith (who had been the last prewar governor), refused to acknowledge the obvious political popularity of the AFPFL and, indeed, sought to restore the prewar economic structure dominated by Indian and British interests. The AFPFL organized effective demonstrations and strikes, and in July 1946 Dorman-Smith was replaced by the notably less rigid Hubert Rance. The new governor, recognizing the strength of the AFPFL, offered Aung San and other non-Communist members of the league the majority of positions on the Executive Council; Aung San became, in effect, premier. The exclusion of the Communists led to their separation from the AFPFL. The latter now entered into negotiations with the British, and in January 1947 agreement was reached to hold elections for a constituent assembly that would have the task of drafting an independence constitution. In April 1947 the AFPFL won 171 of the 182 seats in the assembly. Work then began on the independence constitution. It was an extraordinarily difficult task because a structure had to be found that would incorporate the interests of a large variety of ethnolinguistic communities, which had remained outside the independence struggle and had never been integrated into the modern sector of the country's economy. On July 19, 1947, Aung San and a number of his associates were assassinated (apparently at the behest of a former premier, U Saw). Aung San was succeeded by the vice-president of the AFPFL, U Nu, and it was under his premiership that the country moved to independence, outside the Commonwealth, on January 4, 1948.

Three months later (March 1948) the Communists began an open revolt, and in July a major faction of the AFPFL joined the insurrection. At the end of 1948 the Karen National Union embarked on rebellion. Other ethnic groups, believing that their interests had not been effectively recognized in the new state, also entered the open conflict with the central government. In 1949 central authority extended to only a few urban centers. Gradually, however, the government was able to assert control, in part because the various rebellious interests could not combine against Yangon (Rangoon). Although the government survived, it did not defeat its ideological and ethnic rebels; indeed, the latter continue to defy the authority of the central state.

In the first postindependence elections, held in 1951–52, the AFPFL and its affiliates won 200 of the 239 seats contested. The economy continued to stagnate as the insurrections drained resources and authority from the government, and the position of the AFPFL was eroded. In the 1956 elections the AFPFL and its affiliates won 173 of the 230 seats, but only 48% of the vote. In 1958 the AFPFL split. The faction headed by U Nu remained in power, although now it was dependent on the support of former opposition parties. The problems of ethnic and ideological factionalism, however, coupled with bureaucratic and economic paralysis, threatened the political structure. In October 1958 U Nu handed over power to

228

the army commander, Gen. Ne Win. This caretaker administration was to hold power until early 1960 as preparations were made for new elections. U Nu's faction secured a substantial majority at the elections in February 1960 and the former premier resumed office. But crisis again threatened to overwhelm the political structure; religious, ethnic and ideological divisions could no longer be held in check. On March 2, 1962, the army, under Gen. Ne Win, launched a successful coup against the government. The constitution was suspended and an army-led Revolutionary Council, under the chairmanship of Ne Win, began to rule by decree.

The new administration rapidly dismantled the existing constitutional structures and practices, imposing a centralized, dictatorial authority. In July 1962 the Revolutionary Council established its own political party, the BSPP. In 1964 the BSPP was declared the sole legal party. By the early 1970s it became the party of the masses, and by 1981 it had 1.5 million members, which represented about 5% of the population. The economic policies of the new regime were developed from a statement of ideology, *The Burmese Way to Socialism,* published in April 1962, which combined Marxist analytical categories with the basic principles of Buddhist thought. In practical terms, in the 1960s the government nationalized all foreign and the larger indigenous businesses; all internal trade in essential goods (notably rice) became a government monopoly; and both domestic and foreign trade were brought under government control. The economy experienced minimal growth in the 1960s.

Military rule, imposed by a coup on March 2, 1962, formally ended on March 2, 1974. A new constitution, promulgated the previous January, then came into force. It established a one-party socialist state, with the BSPP as the sole legal party. Although the constitution declared that the state was a federal organization, in practice it was a unitary structure. Local administration was in the hands of elected people's councils charged with carrying out the policies of the central administration. Land was formally state-owned and agriculture was largely under state control. Ne Win, who had retired from the army in April 1972, was elected chairman of the Council of State and thereby became the first president under the new constitution. He remained by far the country's dominant political figure until the breakdown of the established order toward the end of the 1980s.

From the time it seized power in 1962 the army under Ne Win sought above all the maintenance of political stability in the face of a startling range of ethnically and ideologically disparate elements. In 1981 the army was said to have faced four major and 11 minor armed insurrectionist groups; prominent among them were the Burmese Communist party, the Karen National Liberation Army and the Kachin Independence Army. In its foreign relations the army regime followed the strict nonalignment that had been pursued almost from the time of independence. In 1979 the country withdrew from the Nonaligned Movement on the grounds that certain members (for example, the Philippines) could hardly be said to qualify for membership. Indeed, in its external political and economic relations, the country has been close to xenophobic. The major multinationals have not been permitted to invest locally; scholarly, technological and educational exchange with the outside world has been slight. It is partly for this reason, but also because of the rigidly bureaucratic control of the economy (and, on occasions, simple economic mismanagement) that the economy has failed to overcome the serious stagnation and shortages that have been its dominant feature since independence. In 1974–75 there were serious riots over food shortages and maldistribution. The ostentatious wealth displayed by the politically powerful has made it yet more difficult for the government to persuade the people to accept the decline in economic conditions. General discontent has also been provoked by the suppression of political and intellectual freedoms under the army's rule. Students in particular have sought to voice their frustration, notably in 1974 when the body of U Thant, the former U.N. secretary-general, was returned home. The long stifling of intellectual creativity, the suppression of political opinion in a one-party state, unrelieved economic hardship and some four decades of essential isolation from the international community brought Myanmar to a state of political and social crisis at the end of the 1980s.

ECONOMY

Background: With a GNP per head of only U.S. $200 in the mid-1980s, Myanmar can be classified as one of the least-developed countries in the world. Certainly, since independence the country's economic growth has fallen far behind that achieved by most of its Southeast Asian neighbors and far below the level that its abundant natural and human resources would permit. At the same time, the incidence of severe poverty is quite small, partly because the prices of food and other essentials are kept low (although it must be added that in 1988 the urban population suffered serious food shortages) and partly because there exists a very substantial informal economy that lies beyond the official statistics of income, production and trade. It is believed that the volume of trade handled through the black market is at least equal to the official volume of internal transactions.

Since independence, but most forcefully in the period from the military coup of March 1962, the government has pursued four principal economic objectives, outlined in the policy document *The Burmese Way to Socialism.* Those objectives were to eliminate foreign control of the economy; to reduce dependence on foreign markets; to reduce dependence on primary production and increase the importance of the industrial sector; to centralize economic power and economic decision making in the hands of the state. The result was the creation of an essentially autarkic economy, severely neglecting the primary exports of rice, teak and petroleum that had been the foundation of the preindependence economy; excluding multinational investment and accepting only limited government and international agency aid; shunning the development of a major tourism trade. It was an economy in which the state closely planned and minutely regulated, although major areas of production and domestic trade remained in private ownership. Myanmar has a far smaller degree of collective ownership than is found in the socialist economies of Eastern Europe.

GDP rose by only 2.7% per year in the period from 1962 to 1972. The economy's growth was hampered primarily by the government's failure to provide essential infrastructural and technical support for the dominant agricultural sector (indeed, in the interests of urban consumers, the state may well have seriously discouraged rice production by setting its purchase price too low); by serious bureaucratic mismanagement of state enterprises; and by almost exclusive dependence on domestic sources for capital investment. From the mid-1970s the economy experienced notably more rapid growth as government policy objectives and economic administration underwent adjustment. Important here was a firm commitment to raising agricultural (notably rice) productivity, a partial return to the world trading community and an increased, but still comparatively small reliance on international aid. GDP rose by 4.8% per year between 1974–75 and 1977–78, and by 6.6% per year between 1978–79 and 1981–82. In the closing years of the 1980s it was clear that the autarkic, statist policies pursued since 1962 were being dismantled. In 1987 the government announced that the economy would in the future be more open to domestic and international market forces. In September of that year the government abandoned its long-established control of rice and other basic commodity prices (although the immediate effect of deregulation was to ignite a serious inflation that fueled the political crisis of mid-1988).

Agriculture: Myanmar remains predominantly an agricultural country. In 1987–88 agriculture, livestock and fisheries, and forestry accounted for 37% of GDP and no less than 65% of employment. In the decade that followed independence, the recovery of agriculture from war, occupation and civil war was distressingly slow. For example, it was not until 1964 that the area used for growing rice, by far the most important crop, returned to the level achieved immediately prior to World War II. In the 1960s agriculture received low priority in the government's economic ambitions. Increases in agricultural production were modest and were achieved largely through an expansion in the area under cultivation. From the mid-1970s, however, the agricultural sector has been a major focus of the government's development effort, with particular attention being paid to raising productivity through the use of high-yield seeds, the utilization of fertilizers and pesticides (in 1987 Myanmar had three urea plants that had more than doubled production between 1981–82 and 1985–86), and the expansion of irrigation facilities. Agricultural production increased at an average annual rate of 6.6% over the period from 1973 to 1983, and 4.7% from 1983 to 1986.

In 1985–86 rice paddy accounted for 46% of all land under cultivation. Improvement in seed varieties and increased use of chemical inputs have been very important in the rice sector, roughly doubling yields from the mid-1970s, although they remain low by international standards. Rice accounted for 46% of total export value in 1981, but the value of rice exports declined sharply from the mid-1980s (leaving a major contraction of total export earnings). In 1987 rice accounted for 27% of total foreign earnings. Despite the major expansion in rice production in recent years—from a production of 8.4 million tons in 1964–65 to one of 14.5 million tons in

1985–86—increasing local consumption at the end of the 1980s left relatively little for export: of a production of 13.72 million tons in 1987–88, only 3.1% was exported. Burmese rice has a poor international reputation, in part because the run-down condition of the country's rice mills means that the rice entering the market contains a high proportion of broken grain.

Approximately 48% of Myanmar's land area is covered with forest, of which as much as one-half consists of teak and other hardwoods. It is estimated that about 75% of the world's teak reserves are Burmese. The teak industry was severely disrupted by the war and the insurgency and grew relatively slowly in the 1950s and 1960s; it has expanded markedly since the early 1970s. Teak production reached a postwar peak of 436,000 tons in 1981–82; and as rice exports declined in the mid-1980s, teak became the principal export. In 1986 it accounted for 49% of total export earnings.

Petroleum and Mining: Prior to World War II petroleum was the country's second most important export. The industry was almost completely destroyed during the occupation and recovered only very slowly after independence. Even in the 1970s the country required petroleum imports. Rising investment and important injections of foreign technology beginning in the mid-1970s, however, increased production substantially, to 11 million barrels in 1985–86. Myanmar became self-sufficient in oil and petroleum products in 1977 and even briefly exported oil to Japan in 1980. But self-sufficiency has been maintained only by the severe restriction of domestic consumption; thus, there is a thriving black market in petroleum. The late 1970s and early 1980s saw a major increase in natural gas production, rising to 32.6 million cubic feet in 1985–86. Massive onshore and offshore reserves have been located, but large-scale exploitation has been discouraged by a weakening of the world energy market and by high development costs. Myanmar is an important producer of tin, gypsum, jade, silver and copper.

Manufacturing: The manufacturing sector accounted for 9.9% of GDP in 1987–88. As a result of the nationalization of all major industries after the 1962 coup, the state plays a dominant role in this sector: in 1985–86 the state controlled about 80% of industrial output, while the private sector was responsible for 19%. Yet in terms of the number of establishments and employment, the private sector is dominant: of the 41,658 factories and establishments operating in 1987–88, some 94% were privately owned (although of the 650 factories employing 50 or more workers, only 2% were in private ownership). Manufacturing is dominated by food processing, textile manufacture and (in the state sector) the production of industrial raw materials. The 1980s saw the establishment of major industrial projects (a cement factory, fertilizer plant and rubber products factory) in conjunction with Japanese, German and Czechoslovakian firms, respectively.

Foreign trade: From the early 1970s, in a significant shift away from the rigid autarky of the 1960s, the government sought to increase the tradi-

232

tional primary exports of rice and teak. In 1987 they accounted for 70% of total export value; pulses accounted for a further 9%. Minerals and gems were also important exports. The principal markets for Myanmar's exports are Southeast Asia (notably Indonesia and Singapore), the European Community, Japan and India. Imports consist primarily of capital goods and industrial raw materials; in 1985–86 consumer goods accounted for only 8% of official imports. Japan and West Germany were the principal importing partners. In the 1980s the country ran a large trade deficit as well as a notable adverse balance on current account. The above description reflects the official statistics; there was, however, a very high volume of illegal foreign trade, with both exports and imports entering the black market.

Employment: In 1987–88, of a total labor force of 15.8 million, 9.9 million workers were in agriculture, 1.4 million were in manufacturing and 1.6 million were in trade. There are no statistics available for unemployment and underemployment, but partial surveys indicate that both are widespread in urban and rural areas in certain seasons. In the state sector, job security is high.

Price trends: The Yangon consumer price index (1978 = 100) was 178.11 in 1987. This index is based primarily on prices in the official state- and cooperative-run retail outlets; black market prices may differ substantially.

SOCIAL SERVICES

Welfare: The government provides three principal forms of nonmedical social welfare service. There were 60 labor employment exchanges in 1984–85, with 258,009 persons registered who were seeking employment; only about 10% of those registered found employment through this service. The Social Security Service insurance system takes its contributions from employers, employees and the state, and provides insurance for sickness, maternity benefits, death and disability. In 1986–87 the number of persons covered by the system rose to 400,000. The state also provides limited residential facilities for orphans, the blind and hearing impaired, the physically handicapped, and recovering drug addicts.

Health services: Since 1962 the government has sought to make medical facilities more readily available to all sections of the population. Perhaps in consequence, the crude death rate per thousand fell from 18.4 in 1961 to 8.4 in 1987; the infant mortality rate per thousand live births fell from 129.9 in 1961 to 44.3 in 1987. These figures, however, are only for the urban areas. No statistical data are available to indicate the effectiveness of the government's expansion of medical services in the rural and remote parts of the country. In 1986–87 there were an estimated 636 hospitals, 1,372 rural health centers, 10,579 doctors, 714 dentists, 7,895 nurses and 8,372 midwives. This is a modest level of medical care for a population approaching 40 million. Provisional estimates suggest that in 1986–87 for every 10,000 persons there were 6.83 hospital beds, 2.79 doctors and 2.09

nurses. Fewer than half the doctors are in the public sector; the remainder are in cooperative and private practice.

Housing: The Housing Department of the Ministry of Construction is engaged in a modest number of public housing projects. In 1986–87 just 410 dwelling units were completed.

EDUCATION

The principal emphasis in government education policy is on the provision of primary education. Attendance at primary school (for children aged five to nine) has been compulsory since 1975. It was estimated in 1983 that 91% of appropriately aged children attended primary schools. In 1986–87 there were 33,499 state primary schools, with a total student enrollment of 5.05 million. The provision of secondary education is notably less extensive. In 1986–87 there were 1,772 lower secondary schools (10–13 age group), with an enrollment of 1.126 million; and 750 upper secondary schools (14–19 age group), with an enrollment of 238,000. In 1983 it was estimated that only 23% of children of secondary school age attended school. The provision of tertiary education is even less extensive. In 1983 it was estimated that only 5% of the appropriate age group attended higher education institutions. In 1986–87 the total number of students attending teacher training, agricultural, vocational and technical institutes was a mere 27,723; the number of students at Myanmar's two universities and 33 colleges was 211,493. In the 1960s and 1970s there was an appreciable deterioration in the country's educational standards, in part because it avoided open contact with the outside world. Perhaps the most notable manifestation of that disengagement was the abandonment of English in favor of Burmese as the medium of instruction. In the early 1980s English was reintroduced into the curriculum from the primary level upward, and, increasingly, English was used in instruction at the university level. In the same period a greater emphasis was placed on the teaching of science at all levels. In addition, a small, but increasing, number of Burmese graduates were sent abroad for postgraduate training.

MASS MEDIA

Dailies: Prior to July 1988 there were five Burmese-language daily newspapers and two English-language dailies. Each was state owned and therefore subject to considerable censorship. Each was published and printed in Yangon and circulated almost exclusively in the capital. The main Burmese-language dailies were: *Botahtaung Daily,* 140,000; *Kyemon Daily,* 140,000; *Loktha Phyithu Nezin,* 140,000. The principal English-language daily newspaper was *Working People's Daily,* 20,000. After July 1988 only *Loktha Phyithu Nezin* and *Working People's Daily* appeared; it was the government's intention to have the other daily newspapers reappear under private ownership.

234

Periodicals: Do Kyaung Tha, 100,000; *Teza*, 60,100; *Aurora*, 50,000; *Guardian Magazine*, 50,000. Each of these periodicals appears monthly.

Broadcasting: The Burma Broadcasting Service was formed in 1946. Its radio network now broadcasts in Burmese, Arakanese, Mon, Shan, Karen, Chin, Kachin, Kayah and English to approximately 1.6 million licensed radios (and many unlicensed receivers). A television service began in 1980, originally from Yangon and Mandalay transmitters. The number of broadcast hours and the geographical range of transmission are being extended.

BIOGRAPHICAL SKETCHES

Aung San Suu Kyi: Born on June 19, 1945, she is the daughter of the national independence leader, Aung San. She was educated in Myanmar and India and then attended the University of Oxford. Aung San Suu Kyi settled in England but in April 1988 returned home (to attend her ailing mother) and became publicly identified with the student protest of mid-1988. In early 1989 she was secretary-general of the National League for Democracy.

U Ne Win: Born on May 14, 1911, Ne Win has been by far the dominant figure in the political life of independent Myanmar. He was chief of the armed forces from 1948, deputy prime minister from 1948 to 1950, prime minister from 1958 to 1960, chairman of the Revolutionary Council from 1962 to 1974, president from 1974 to 1981 and chairman of the Burmese Socialist Program party from 1962 to 1988. Ne Win has a retiring, self-effacing public persona; paradoxically, he exerts a most powerful charisma. It is widely believed that Ne Win has corruptly acquired vast wealth. It was that belief, allied to severely deteriorating economic conditions, that fueled the unrest in mid-1988, which drove Ne Win to resign as chairman of the BSPP on July 23. He remains a powerful figure, and it is thought that he was the major guiding hand behind the army coup of September 18, 1988.

Gen. Saw Maung: Born on December 5, 1928, Saw Maung began his military career after 1945, rising through the ranks to become head of the Southwest Command in the early 1980s. He became minister of defense in 1988 and led the September 1988 army coup. He subsequently became head of the government.

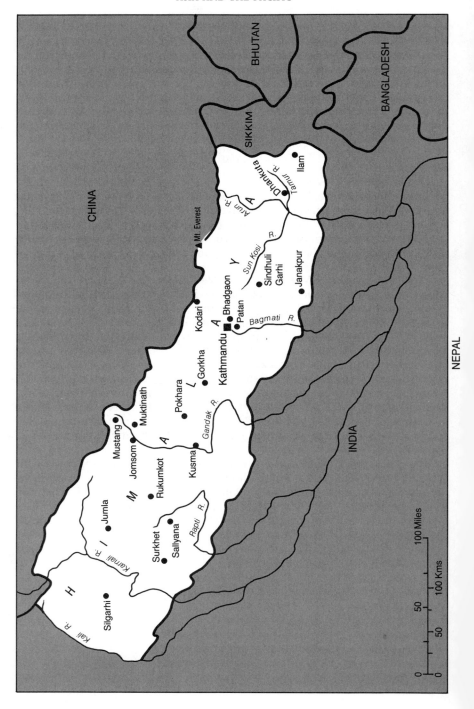

NEPAL

Features: The Kingdom of Nepal lies in the Himalayas between India and China. The southern region of the country, called the Tarai, borders the Ganges plain. This area is densely forested and highly fertile. The middle part of the country is the hill regions, or foothills of the Himalayas. The northern region is in the high Himalayas and includes Mount Everest, the world's highest mountain at 29,028 feet/8,848 m. Nepal has a greater diversity of terrain than any other country of comparable small size; the distance from the top of Mount Everest to the low-lying tropical forests of the Tarai is only 100 miles/161 km.

There are numerous streams and rivers flowing south from the mountains, across the Tarai and into India. The population is concentrated along the major rivers and their tributaries. Nearly the whole country is drained by three large river systems: the Kosi, the Narayani, and the Karnali.

Area: 54,463 sq. miles/141,059 sq. km.

Mean max. and min. temperatures: Katmandu (27°42'N, 85°20'E), 62°F/17°C, 36°F/2°C (Jan.), 84°F/29°C (July).

Relative humidity: 60%.

Mean annual rainfall: 60 in/1500 mm.

POPULATION

Total population (1987 est.): 17,663,000.

Chief towns and populations: KATMANDU (422,000), Patan (195,000), Bhaktapur (140,000). The hill districts contain two-thirds of the population. The urban population is 8% of the total.

Ethnic composition: There are two major racial groups in Nepal: Indo-Nepali and Tibeto-Nepali, with the former making up about 80% of the population. The Paharis are a group of Indo-Nepali castes that constitute half of the nation's population. The royal family is of Indo-Nepali extraction, whereas the famous Gurkha regiments of the British and Indian armies have recruited Tibeto-Nepalis. The Sherpa, a small but well-known group living at higher elevations, have acted as guides for mountain climbers; Tenzing

Norkay was a Sherpa who guided Sir Edmund Hillary in the first successful expedition to the top of Mount Everest.

Language: Nepali, the official language, is spoken by 60% of the population. Maithili and Bhojpuri, two dialects of Hindi, are spoken by 11% and 8%, respectively. A total of 16 northern Indian and Tibeto-Burman languages are spoken in the country.

Religion: Hindus constitute 90% of the society. In Nepal, Hindu beliefs contain substantial elements of Buddhist ritual and thought. Three percent of the population is Muslim.

CONSTITUTIONAL SYSTEM

Constitution: Nepal is a monarchy. There is a national assembly, called the Rashtriya Panchayat, but it has no legislative authority. The king rules as a full sovereign, while a Central Secretariat carries out governmental activities. In practice, the elected representatives of the people have very limited influence over the workings and structure of government. At present, the majority of Rashtriya Panchayat members are opposed to the monarch-dominated panchayat system but are unable to effect change. In 1980, King Birendra held a referendum on whether to promulgate a reformed version of the partyless panchayat system or to move to a multiparty system; 55 percent of the voters chose the reformed panchayat system.

Head of state: King Birendra Bir Bikram Shah Dev.

Executive and legislatures: The king holds exclusive sovereign power. The royal family gained its status in 1769, when its armies occupied the region of Katmandu. In 1846, it was forced into a subsidiary role by the Rana family, but the Shah dynasty regained power in 1951 and King Tribhuvan was the first monarch in the new era. His son and grandson, King Mahendra and King Birendra, respectively, have been his successors.

The king appoints the Council of Ministers from the members of the Rashtriya Panchayat. The ministers are answerable both to the king and to the Panchayat. The ministers hold authority over the Central Secretariat. In practice, senior bureaucrats have been transferred frequently to assure monarchical control. King Birendra has enhanced the role of his Palace Secretariat. As crown prince, he assembled a team of technocrats to advise him on economic planning and administration. Upon coronation, the young king brought those advisers into the Palace Secretariat and moved to dismiss senior officials in the Central Secretariat. Policymaking functions were transferred to the Palace Secretariat, while the palace-controlled press criticized direct contacts between members of the Rashtriya Panchayat and bureaucrats of the Central Secretariat.

The Rashtriya Panchayat is the apex of a hierarchy of councils. It is a unicameral body with 140 members. Elections based on universal adult suffrage select 112 members, and the remaining 28 are appointed by the king. The Rashtriya Panchayat elects a prime minister, who heads the Council of Ministers, however the king retains the right to dismiss any minister.

The nation is divided into 14 zones, which are subdivided into 75 districts. The districts have 11-member panchayats, and these provide members for the zonal panchayats, the latter functioning as executive bodies. At the lowest level, each village and town has its own panchayat. Candidates for panchayat elections must run as individuals.

Political parties: Under the 1962 constitution, all political parties are banned, however informal political groups do exist. The Nepali Congress party, formed in 1946, is the most popular and most prominent group. It had been the ruling party during the brief democratic period of 1951–1960, and in 1959 it formed Nepal's only democratically elected government. The party promoted a social democratic ideology and opposed the monarchy-panchayat system. Its philosophy is similar to that of the Indian Congress party, and it has received support from India at various points.

The Nepali Communist party is divided into two factions aligned with either the USSR or China. However, the party won 16 seats in the 1986 Rashtriya Panchayat elections, including the constituency of Katmandu.

Judicial system: In each district there are a court of first instance and an appeals court. There is also a higher court in each zone. At the next level, there are five regional courts. The king appoints the chief justice to the Supreme Court in Katmandu, plus six other judges and seven additional judges in reserve.

RECENT HISTORY

The independence movement in India contributed to the collapse of the powerful extended Rana family which had ruled Nepal for a century. Because of Rana dependence on the British, many Nepalis believed that the departure of the British from India would also weaken the Ranas. Thus many anti-Rana Nepalis backed India's independence movement. King Tribhuvan supported the anti-Rana movement, and he gave encouragement and covert financial support to the activists. After World War II, the movement grew in strength. The new Nepali Congress party, formed in India, began its political activity with civil disobedience (*satyagraha*) against the government in support of a strike that had been suppressed by the Ranas. In exchange for a withdrawal of the *satyagraha*, Prime minister Padma Shamsher agreed to establish a committee to study Nepali political reform. In 1948 the committee promulgated a liberal constitution. This led the more conservative Ranas, headed by Mohan Shamsher, to force Padma Shamsher from office, seize power, declare the Congress party illegal and block implementation of the new constitution.

India grew alarmed at the events in Nepal and the Chinese revolution of 1949 and occupation of Tibet in 1950 intensified this concern. Jawaharlal Nehru sent a warning to the Ranas that failure to reform could lead to more radical uprisings later. The Nepali government agreed to some changes, but proceeded slowly in their implementation. In November 1950 Tribhuvan was implicated in a Congress party conspiracy but escaped through the Indian Embassy in Katmandu. A nationwide rebellion erupted, coordinated by the Congress party, but the government suppressed it within a month. In December armed rebellion resumed and many government troops began to desert. Forty Ranas resigned from high offices, demanding that India's conditions be met. Mohan Shamsher was forced to accept the return of the king and the expansion of royal authority.

Tribhuvan reigned from 1950 to 1955 as head of a constitutional monarchy. Nepal's democratic constitution was modeled after the Indian constitution but reflected the desires of Nepali political leaders. The King was authorized to appoint interim cabinets until national elections could be held, so he chose a cabinet of Congress party politicians. Tribhuvan emerged as the most important political figure in Nepal. His courageous role in the anti-Rana movement led to his being regarded as a national hero. The appointed politicians were weak, so the king became directly involved in political decisions, and the Indian government enhanced the king's powers by giving him political support. The monarchy established treaty relations with India that gave the latter certain prerogatives regarding Nepal's foreign and defense policies. Nepal also accepted India's concept of nonalignment.

Tribhuvan died in 1955 and his son Mahendra succeeded him. Mahendra objected to the strong influence that the political parties had and he hoped to increase the power of the monarchy. He opposed the social democratic measures of the Congress party as well as the limitation of his powers under the constitution. Political parties agitated for elections, and in 1959 voting for a national parliament was held. Surprisingly, the Congress party won 74 of the 109 seats. After some hesitation, Mahendra appointed the leader of the Congress party, B. P. Koirala, as prime minister. But in December 1960 the king invoked his constitutional emergency powers and used the army to overthrow the Koirala government.

The royal coup was supported by elements associated with the Ranas. Mahendra had married a daughter of the Rana family, in spite of Tribhuvan's objections. Many army leaders involved in the coup were members of the Rana family. And conservative political groups allied with the Ranas were involved in the civil violence that formed the pretext for the royal takeover.

In 1962 Mahendra introduced the panchayat system. A partyless national assembly was assembled from popularly elected village panchayat heads and from members of professional and social class organizations. Mahendra appointed as ministers disaffected former party activists; these persons could mobilize some popular support for the panchayat system without reviving political parties. The panchayat system was designed to ensure the creation of a royalist political elite. Since elections to a panchayat above the village level were open only to panchayat members at lower levels, members of the higher-level panchayats were likely to be loyal to the system. In spite of a variety of royal controls over the panchayats, the king faced difficulties in retaining compliance from the representatives. In the early 1960s, Mahendra replaced his more independent ministers with weaker figures.

Under Mahendra the role of the bureaucracy was expanded under his control. In 1961 he screened all officials and dismissed all deemed loyal to the earlier Congress party government, taking steps to ensure that no challenge to his authority arose from the administrative ranks. Officials were frequently transferred so that they could not develop independent bases of support. Local authority was further divided between district officers and local panchayat members. The king also cultivated the loyalty of his army. He expanded it from 6,000 to 10,000, and awarded loyal officers with agricultural land in the Tarai. Mahendra was careful to keep the officers oriented toward technical tasks and out of politics. Mahendra came to the throne at a time of rising Sino-Indian hostility, so he redefined nonalignment as neutrality between India and China. The king moved to reduce Nepal's trade dependence on India while seeking increased economic aid from China.

In 1972, upon the death of his father, Birendra ascended to the throne. As prince he had gathered around him a circle of technocratic advisers with whom he developed a strategy for his future reign. After Birendra's coronation, these advisers began to implement their plans. Unlike his father, Birendra did not often seek the advice of established political figures in the country. Advisers restricted the access of politicians and citizens to the king, allowing only those contacts they deemed appropriate. Birendra introduced several measures designed to upgrade administrative performance and reduce the autonomy of bureaucrats or their power to alter royal policies. Individual performance superseded evaluations by immediate superiors as the criteria for promotion. Thus young administrators were motivated to adhere to royal policies rather than to the goals of their bureaucratic superiors. In addition, greater decision-making powers were granted to district officers, leading to greater local authority.

In 1974 Birendra began to consider reform of the panchayat system. He initiated discussions with former party leaders and granted amnesty to some jailed or exiled party workers. They were encouraged to run for office, without party organization. In 1975 the king created a back-to-the-village campaign whose goal was to recruit new loyal monarchists into the panchayat system and to enhance central control over the panchayat representatives. The king held a referendum in 1980 on whether Nepal should have a partyless panchayat system or a multiparty system. The panchayat system received 54.7% support, and was modified by referendum to allow direct election of panchayat representatives through adult suffrage. It also permitted the Rashtriya Panchayat to elect a prime minister. The king still retained sovereign power.

Birendra continued his father's efforts at increasing Nepal's independence from India. In 1973 he announced his desire to have Nepal declared a "zone of peace." Implementation of this proposal would have required abrogation of Indo-Nepali agreements concluded in the 1950s. While China, Pakistan and Bangladesh endorsed the "zone of peace" proposal, India did not. Through the 1980s Indo-Nepali relations remained stable. Nepal is a member of the South Asian Association for Regional Cooperation. However, there has been slow progress in agreements with India for economic cooperation, especially in the development of Nepal's enormous hydroelectric potential.

241

Rashtriya Panchayat elections were held in 1986. Though there were complaints about election procedures, many who complained won seats and an antimonarchist majority emerged. The king appointed an ex-Communist, Marich Man Singh Shrestha, as prime minister. However, owing to the inherent weakness of the Rashtriya Panchayat, the majority is not able to change Nepal's political system.

ECONOMY

Background: Nepal's per-capita income in 1985 was U.S. $160, making it the fifth poorest country in the world. (Bangladesh is the only South Asian country poorer.) Real gross domestic product (GDP) has grown at the rate of 2.6% during the two decades ending in 1985.

Nonagricultural production has grown at 4.4% in 1965–1985. Agricultural production has grown at only 1.6%, below the rate of population growth. This stagnation has occurred in spite of a steady rise in investment in agriculture. While there was virtually no irrigated land in Nepal in the middle 1960s, by the middle 1980s, 13% of land area had been brought under irrigation. Investment in irrigation has gone from one-tenth of total development expenditure in the middle 1960s to one-third in the middle 1980s.

Nepal's foreign debt in 1987 was estimated at $925 million, or one-third of its GDP. However, the bulk of the debt is noncommercial, with interest rates of 1%–6%. Thus, the ratio of debt service payments to exports was at a relatively favorable 12% in 1987.

Agriculture: During the democratic period in the 1950s there was an intensive effort at land reform; however, the campaign was not very successful. Landowners evicted many tenants before government officials could record the tenants' claims. The resulting redistribution was as much among different ethnic groups as from the rich to the poor.

In the 1960s, the new monarchical government switched to a more technological strategy oriented toward promoting a green revolution. However, this strategy could not succeed in the hill regions and in the 1970s, a more cash-crop and export-oriented strategy was promulgated in the hill areas.

In the 1960s, migrants from the hill areas settled and cleared forested areas, thereby increasing Nepal's arable land by 10 percent. This process was facilitated by the government's program to eradicate malaria in the forested areas as well as by the expansion of the road system. The seventh Five-Year Plan, covering 1985–1990, recognizes that pressures from rising population call for an integrated strategy, covering all regions of the country, to increase food production.

Animal husbandry is central to the economy. Oxen and donkeys are the principal work animals, though sheep and goats serve as pack animals in the mountainous regions. Yaks, cows, sheep, and goats are grazed in valleys and hill regions. In 1985, there were 7 million cattle, 4.5 million water buffalo, 2.7 million goats, 2.5 million sheep and 400,000 hogs.

Industry: Industrial production increased 58% in 1978–1984. The principal industries are jute goods, sugar, cigarettes, cement and leather. Of these, the fastest-growing sectors have been leather, cigarettes and cement, which have more than doubled production in 1978–1984.

Nepal's industrial growth is closely linked with its trade with India. In 1950, Nepal entered into an agreement with India that made the country an extension of India's protected industrial market. There was free trade between the two countries, but not between Nepal and other countries. Nepali industrialists were at a major disadvantage when competing with Indians and as a result, there was little industrialization in the 1950s.

A new agreement between Nepal and India was signed in 1960, enabling Nepal to protect its domestic industries from Indian competition. Foreign aid helped launch a public-sector import-substituting industrialization program in which sugar, cigarettes, shoes and agricultural tools were the focus. Furthermore, the government encouraged Indian industrialists to establish factories in Nepal, to import goods from the advanced countries and to export products to the protected Indian market at an enormous profit. These policies spurred Nepali industrialization.

In the 1970s, Nepal grew increasingly concerned with the influence of Indian industrialists in its economy. In 1974, it promulgated regulations limiting Indian investment, but in 1978, the country commenced a policy of closer economic cooperation with India. Talks resumed on the exploitation of Nepal's vast hydroelectric potential, which is estimated to be greater than the entire installed capacity in North America. However, little progress has been made to date.

Foreign trade: Nepal has had advantageous trade relations with India and Tibet since ancient times. Until the early part of the 20th century, Nepal served as the principal trade route between India and China and Tibet. The principal exports to Tibet in the last century had been copper, brass, bronze and other metal goods, as well as some Indian manufactures. The main imports were wool and woolen goods, musk, salt, cattle, borax, mercury and gold bullion. Some of these imports were then exported to India. In earlier centuries, Nepal imported scrap metals, precious stones, spices, tobacco and various luxury goods from India, while it exported to India rice, timber, hides, honey, wax, clarified butter, artistic metal wares and some Tibetan products. But in the early 20th century, alternative routes between India and China were found, and the Nepali trade routes declined in importance.

Since the 1950s, a very large but declining percentage of Nepal's trade has been with India. In the fifties, trade with India constituted over 90%; by 1984, it had fallen to 58%. Since then, Nepal has run persistent trade deficits owing to its low industrial base and to rising construction and development efforts for its growing population. The trade deficit with India is less pronounced than with other countries. In spite of these deficits, the country has maintained surpluses in its balance of payments. Remittances from Nepalis working in India and Britain, notably including Gurkha sol-

243

diers, have enabled Nepal to maintain a high level of imports. Tourism and foreign aid have also been important sources of revenues.

Nepal has concentrated on exporting primary products. Food, live animals and crude materials (nonfuels) have constituted the majority; however, manufactured goods have risen to constitute over 40% of total exports. Among imports, manufactured goods, machinery and transport equipment, and chemicals and pharmaceuticals account for over 70%.

Employment: In 1985, the Nepali labor force totaled 4.1 million, with agriculture absorbing 93% of manpower. Independent trade unions are banned. The Nepal Labor Organization, created by the government, has the authority to call strikes and mediate labor disputes.

SOCIAL SERVICES

The government has established a system of social services for villages. The village development workers assist villagers in meeting their minimum needs of food, housing, health care, clothing and education. There is a vigorous family-planning program. During 1965–1976 the percentage of married women using contraceptives climbed from 1% to 17%. However, a study in 1978 discovered that 65% of women who begin using contraceptives cease to do so within a year.

Gastrointestinal diseases, in combination with malnutrition, constitute the major health threat. Life expectancy in 1985 was 47 years for men and 45 years for women. The 1985 infant mortality rate was 139 per 1,000 live births. As of 1986, Nepal had 89 hospitals and clinics, 692 physicians and 1,573 nurses and midwives. A training hospital was opened in Tribhuvan University in 1985.

EDUCATION

In 1986, there were 1.75 million primary school students and 454,000 secondary school students. The literacy rate in 1985 was 20%. The majority of young children are enrolled in school. There are three educational streams: an English-language school system modeled on English-language schools in India; a traditional system focusing on Nepali-language education; and a Buddhist religious system that trains males to become priests and monks. A government system with a standardized curriculum has been promulgated.

Tribhuvan University is the only institution of higher education in the country. It has 48,000 students, 75% of whom are in liberal arts and sciences; the remainder are in engineering, commerce, law, forestry and education. More than one-fifth of the students are women.

The current Five-Year Plan emphasizes the expansion of literacy; the upgrading of teaching staff, textbooks, and curriculum; the improvement of school buildings; education of girls and women; and vocational training. Education accounted for 7.5% of the government budget in 1984–85.

MASS MEDIA

The press: In 1985, there were 58 daily newspapers. Each must be licensed by the government. While the constitution guarantees freedom of the press, in practice licenses have been revoked and journalists and other press figures arrested for criticism of the political system or for expressing support for political parties. The largest dailies are the Nepali *Gorkha Patra,* (35,000), the English *Rising Nepal* (20,000) and the Hindi-language *Hindi Nepali* (12,000).

Broadcasting: The government-controlled Radio Nepal is the only radio broadcasting organization; it produces Nepali and English programs in short and medium wavelengths. A television broadcast facility for the Katmandu valley was established in 1985. The seventh Five-Year Plan calls for expansion of radio coverage to ensure clear reception in the eastern and western border areas.

BIOGRAPHICAL SKETCHES

Birendra Bir Bikram Shah Dev. Born in 1945, crowned as King of Nepal in 1972. He received his schooling in St. Joseph's public school in India and Eton in England. Birendra received his higher education at the University of Tokyo and Harvard. As crown prince he established a group of technocratic advisers called the *Janch-Bujh Kendra.* After ascension to the throne he moved toward a more technocratic and administrative style than his father had followed. In 1979, there were student riots protesting the panchayat system. In response, King Birendra called a referendum and a reformed version of the panchayat system received majority support. However, opposition to the monarchy has continued. King Birendra finds himself increasingly isolated in South Asia as an advocate of nondemocratic government.

Marich Man Singh Shrestha. Born in 1942, selected by King Birendra to be prime minister in 1986. Shrestha was born an illegitimate child in a low-caste family of the Newar clan. At one time he was a member of the Nepali Communist party. Before winning an uncontested election to the Rashtriya Panchayat, he was a high school headmaster.

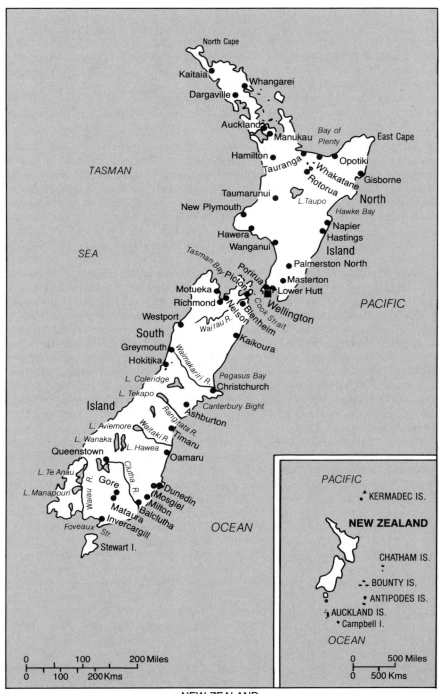

North Cape

Kaitaia

Whangarei

Dargaville

Auckland

Manukau

Bay of Plenty

East Cape

Hamilton

Opotiki

Tauranga

Whakatane

Gisborne

Rotorua

TASMAN

Taumarunui

L.Taupo

North

New Plymouth

Hawke Bay

Napier

Hawera

Hastings

Wanganui

Island

SEA

Tasman Bay

Porirua

Palmerston North

Picton

Masterton

Motueka

Lower Hutt

Richmond

Nelson

Wellington

Westport

Blenheim

Cook Strait

PACIFIC

Wairau R.

South

Kaikoura

Greymouth

Waimakariri R.

Hokitika

L. Coleridge

Pegasus Bay

L. Tekapo

Christchurch

Island

Canterbury Bight

Ashburton

Rangitata R.

L. Aviemore

Waitaki R.

Timaru

L. Wanaka

L. Hawea

Queenstown

Oamaru

L. Te Anau

Waiau R.

Gore

Clutha R.

L. Manapouri

Dunedin

Mosgiel

Mataura

Milton

Balclutha

Foveaux

Invercargill

OCEAN

Str.

Stewart I.

PACIFIC

KERMADEC IS.

NEW ZEALAND

CHATHAM IS.

BOUNTY IS.

ANTIPODES IS.

AUCKLAND IS.

Campbell I.

OCEAN

0	100	200 Miles

0	100	200 Kms

0	500 Miles

0	500 Kms

NEW ZEALAND

NEW ZEALAND

GEOGRAPHY

Features: New Zealand is situated in the southwest Pacific, lying some 1,000 miles/1,600 km. southeast of Australia. It comprises two main islands (North Island and South Island) with a third, considerably smaller island (Stewart Island) lying immediately south of the South Island; there are also a number of minor islands. Both the North and South islands are long (the distance from the northern extremity of the North Island to the southern tip of the South Island is 1,100 miles/1,770 km.) and narrow (no inland area is more than 68 miles/110 km. from the sea). New Zealand is a mountainous country. More than three-quarters of the land stands over 660 feet/200 m. above sea level. On the North Island, the higher mountains (those above 4,125 feet/1,250 m.) occupy approximately one-tenth of the surface; the South Island is considerably more mountainous than the North Island, with a major mountain chain (the Southern Alps) running along almost its entire length. New Zealand forms part of the geologically unstable Pacific ring of fire: there is considerable volcanic activity (notably in the central plateau of the North Island) and associated hot springs and geysers; the country experiences a moderate level of seismic activity. There is a substantial glacial system on the South island. Despite its predominantly mountainous character, New Zealand also possesses extensive plains: on the east coast of the South Island (Canterbury and Southland) and on the North Island, northeast of Wellington (Manawatu), south of Auckland (Waikato) and in the western region (Taranaki).

Area: 103,883 sq. miles/269,057 sq. km.

Mean max. and min. temperatures: Wellington (41°18'N, 174°46'E) 68°F/ 20°C (Jan.), 43°F/6°C (July).

Relative humidity: In coastal areas, 70%–80%; 10% lower in inland areas.

Mean annual rainfall: Wellington 50 in/1,271 mm.

POPULATION

Total population (1988 est.): 3,347,300.

Chief towns and populations (1987 est.): WELLINGTON (351,400), Auckland (899,200), Christchurch (333,200), Hamilton (169,000), Dunedin (113,300).

247

Distribution: Approximately 54% of the population live in the seven urban centers (Auckland, Wellington, Christchurch, Dunedin, Hamilton, Palmerston North, Tauranga). Nearly three-quarters of the population live on the North Island; over half live in and around Auckland.

Language: Almost all New Zealanders speak and use English. A considerable effort is being made to halt the decline in the number of Maori-speakers.

Religion: Of the total 1981 population, 25.7% were recorded as Anglicans, 16.7% as Presbyterians and 14.3% as Roman Catholics; 23.5% were of no religion, objected to stating their religious preference or did not specify any religion.

CONSTITUTIONAL SYSTEM

Constitution: New Zealand has no written constitution. Constitutional practice is determined by parliamentary statutes, judicial rulings and administrative precedent and tradition.

Head of state: Queen Elizabeth II. *Prime minister:* Geoffrey Palmer.

Executive: The parliamentary leader of the political party with a majority in the House of Representatives becomes prime minister, on the appointment of the governor-general. The prime minister advises the governor-general on the appointment of the remaining ministers who will form the cabinet, each of whom must be a member of parliament. Ministers are responsible to parliament.

Legislature: Parliament consists of one chamber—the House of Representatives—which has 97 members, each representing a single constituency; four members are elected from Maori seats, while the remaining 93 are elected from general electoral districts. Parliament can be dissolved by the governor-general or expires by efflux of time after three years.

Political parties: In New Zealand's modern history, government has alternated between just two political parties: the National party and the Labour party. In the August 1987 general election those parties secured all 97 seats in the House of Representatives and 90.2% of the votes cast. The Labour party, established in 1916, traditionally has advocated a pronounced measure of state economic regulation; however, in office from 1984 it has strongly pursued deregulation and privatization. The National party, formed in 1936, has traditionally advocated support of private enterprise.

Local government: There are three forms of local government in New Zealand: territorial authorities—councils administering counties, boroughs and districts—that provide local services such as drainage and sewerage, garbage collection and public transportation; special agencies charged with a particular task in a given area, for example, the management of reservoirs, hospitals or electricity generation; and regional administration, developed recently to carry out regional economic planning and civil defense.

248

Judicial system: The judiciary comprises a Court of Appeal, a High Court and district courts (all of which have both civil and criminal jurisdiction), and other courts, notably the Maori Land Court and the Labour Court, which have special jurisdiction. The highest organ of judicial appeal is the Judicial Committee of the Privy Council, in the United Kingdom.

RECENT HISTORY

Having secured a narrow victory in the first postwar election, held in November 1945, the Labour party saw its electoral position weaken, principally as a result of poor economic conditions, popular unease against the high level of bureaucratic regulation and anger at the introduction of compulsory military training during peacetime. In the 1949 election the National party led by Sir Sidney Holland, won a clear victory. Despite considerable concern over the state of the economy (there were strong inflationary pressures in the early 1950s) and the government's handling of industrial unrest (troops were used to break a strike by dock workers), the National party was returned to power at elections held in 1951 and 1954, but it lost narrowly to the Labour party under Walter Nash in the 1957 election. However, the new administration faced severe economic problems, occasioned principally by falling international prices for meat and dairy products. It was forced to impose import licensing and exchange controls and to sharply raise the tax rates on beer, spirits, tobacco and petroleum. In the 1960 election, under the leadership of Sir Keith Holyoake, the National party was returned to office and retained power through the 1963, 1966 and 1969 elections. In the 1972 election the Labour party, led by Norman Kirk, won a decisive victory; when Kirk died in August 1974 he was succeeded by Sir Wallace Rowling. The Labour party lost office at the November 1975 election, decisively beaten by the National party now led by Sir Robert Muldoon, and retained its position through the 1978 and 1981 elections. Then the July 1984 election returned the Labour party, now led by David Lange, to office. The Labour party won the August 1987 election, partly as a result of disarray in the opposition National party, and this was the first occasion since the war that the Labour party had won two consecutive general elections.

The economic policies pursued by the Labour administration of David Lange have in important respects marked a decisive break with Labour's traditionally interventionist philosophy. In essence, Labour has sought to confront New Zealand's recurrent inflationary pressures and balance-of-payments difficulties by restructuring the economy along free-market lines. In practical terms this has involved reform of certain state-owned enterprises to make them more responsive to commercial considerations as well as a marked reduction in price-support subsidies for agriculture. Whatever the prospects for long-term success, the immediate impact of deregulation and reduced government expenditure has been to provoke a marked rise in unemployment; the agricultural sector has faced a particularly painful period of readjustment.

Even if the Lange government's economic policies have been electorally unpopular, there has been wide popular approval of Labour's antinuclear defense strategy. In the early 1970s the Kirk administration sought to disrupt French atmospheric tests in French Polynesia by sending a New Zealand frigate into the testing zone; in the 1980s the Lange administration imposed a ban on the entry of nuclear-powered or nuclear-armed vessels into New Zealand ports; in June 1987 that ban became law, with the passing of the New Zealand Nuclear Free Zone, Disarmament and Arms Control Bill. The antinuclear strategy strained relations with the United States, the latter arguing that it voids security arrangements established under the ANZUS defense treaty of 1952. In August 1986 the United States suspended the security guarantees made to New Zealand under ANZUS arrangements. During this period the Lange administration sought to evolve a new defense strategy, based on increased military self-reliance, closer cooperation with Australia and greater involvement in the geopolitics of the South Pacific.

The 1980s Labour administration under David Lange also attempted to defuse long-standing Maori grievances that arise, essentially, from their dispossession by the original waves of European settlers in the 19th century. In 1985 the government appointed the Waitangi Tribunal to consider those grievances, and a large number of Maori claims were submitted; in many cases the tribunal ruled in favor of the appellant. The movement to preserve Maori cultural forms, beliefs and language, which became more forceful in the 1980s, was not fully welcomed by all sections of the white population; indeed, a marked level of white resentment was apparent. Full reconciliation of Maori and European interests and ambitions seemed still some way from being secured.

ECONOMY

Background: The economy of New Zealand has a high degree of external dependence; in 1986–87 the combined value of commodity exports and imports was equivalent to 42.2% of gross domestic product (GDP). The export sector is dominated by wool, dairy produce, lamb and beef; in 1986–87 these accounted for 44.0% of total commodity exports. Yet agriculture, hunting, forestry and fishing contributed only 8.1% to GDP in 1986–87; in February 1984 that sector accounted for only 11.2% of total civilian employment. Manufacturing contributed 21.0% to GDP in 1986–87; in February 1984 it accounted for 23.6% of total civilian employment. The service sector (trade, restaurants and hotels; transport, storage and communications; finance, insurance, real estate and business services; community, social and personal services) contributed 60.5% to GDP; in February 1984 it accounted for 57.0% of total civilian employment.

In recent years the New Zealand economy has performed relatively poorly, partly because of external constraints (the long international recession, adverse movement in the terms of trade and constriction of important foreign markets for New Zealand's agricultural exports) but also because of internal economic rigidities that have made adjustment difficult. Between 1975 and 1982 there was virtually no growth in real GDP; in 1986–87 GDP grew, in real terms, by just 1.6%. From the late 1970s on there was a marked rise in unemployment; in mid-1988 it stood at 8.5% of the labor force. In the same period there were strong inflationary pressures, persistent deficits on the balance-of-payments current account, budgetary deficits and increased recourse to foreign borrowing. The Labour administration under David Lange, in power from July 1984, sought to tackle the internal economic weakness with a major program of deregulation, seeking to restructure the economy along free-market lines: important here was the more intensive intervention of commercial considerations ("corporatization") in the management of state-owned enterprises, and the privatization of major state concerns (Bank of New Zealand, Petroleum Corporation of New Zealand, Air New Zealand); delicensing of the internal transport system and the meat-packing industry; discontinuation of farm subsidies; major tax reform, including a reduction in corporate taxes and institution of a single-rate income tax; major dismantling of import licensing; and a floating New Zealand dollar.

Agriculture: New Zealand's mild climate, with an even distribution of rainfall and abundant sunshine, is highly suited to sheep and dairy farming, but the terrain and soil conditions (a relatively small proportion of the land is naturally arable and soil fertility generally is low) have required both advanced agricultural management and heavy investment: establishment of controlled grazing schedules and efficient stock administration, major investment in stock breeding programs and use of phosphate fertilizers. As a result, farming in New Zealand is highly efficient. The principal products—strongly orientated to export markets—are wool (production in 1986–87 was 350,200 metric tons), beef (548,300 metric tons), mutton (199,000 metric tons), lamb (407,400 metric tons), liquid milk (17 million gallons/68.5 million l.), butter (248,300 metric tons), cheese (113,300 metric tons) and preserved milk (348,300 metric tons). New Zealand is the world's largest exporter of lamb and mutton. In 1987 the country had 8 million cattle (including 2 million dairy cows) and over 64 million sheep. In recent years this extremely important sector of the economy has been vulnerable not only to price fluctuations, which are an integral feature of primary markets, but also to threatened restrictions in traditional markets, notably the European Community and the United States. Abandonment of support prices has substantially reduced real farm income.

Industry: Processing of agricultural exports (notably wool yarn, woollen and worsted piece goods, and processed dairy products) accounts for approximately one-fifth of manufacturing production, with the rest of the sector concerned with production of a wide range of items for the domestic market (although increasing attention is being paid to development of export markets for local manufactures). There is important domestic production of steel (with New Zealand Steel using indigenous ironsands and Pacific Steel using scrap) and aluminum; vehicle assembly; woollen milling (including the production of carpets); production of industrial electrical goods, household appliances and food and beverage products. In the mid-1980s manufactured exports accounted for about 30% of total export income.

251

Energy: In the late 1980s approximately 10% of New Zealand's total energy needs were met through imported petroleum. Increasingly, energy requirements are being met by indigenous resources: natural gas, hydroelectricity and geothermal steam.

Services: In terms of its contribution to GDP (60.5% in 1986–87) and to employment (57.0% in February 1984), services clearly represent the major economic sector. The most important elements are public-sector employment in health, education and administration; wholesale and retail trades; transport and communications; and finance, insurance, real estate and business services. Tourism is of growing importance. In 1987–88 it became the largest single source of foreign exchange; in 1986–87 there were 763,200 visitors to New Zealand, of whom 36% were from Australia, 21% from the United States and 9% from Japan.

Foreign trade: In 1986–87 the principal markets for New Zealand's exports were the United States (16.3%), Japan (15.1%), Australia (14.9%) and the United Kingdom (9.3%). In the same year New Zealand imported principally from Japan (20.7%), Australia (18.0%), the United States (16.1%) and the United Kingdom (9.8%). The principal imports are automobiles, iron and steel, crude petroleum, commercial vehicles, chemicals and miscellaneous manufactures. The main exports are beef, lamb, mutton, dairy products and wool. In 1985 and 1986 New Zealand had a modest trade surplus; it became more substantial in 1987. But in those three years there was also a substantial deficit on invisibles, the result being a major deficit on current account; indeed, despite the growing trade surplus between 1985 and 1987, the current account deficit worsened.

Employment: In March 1987 the total labor force (including the unemployed was 1.6 million. The unemployment rate was 4.1% (3.7% for males, 4.7% for females).

Price trends: The consumer price index (December quarter 1983 = 100) was 108.1 in 1985 (March year average); 124.6 in 1986; and 142.8 in 1987.

SOCIAL SERVICES

Welfare: New Zealanders have long enjoyed comprehensive social welfare provision. The Labour administration, which took office in 1935, established a social security system that provided comprehensive medical, hospital and pharmaceutical services; improved old-age and sickness pensions; established a 40-hour working week and began an extensive state-financed home-building program to provide low-rent housing. The present social welfare system is financed from general taxation. Benefits universally applied without regard to other income are national superannuation (paid to persons aged 60 or over), family benefit (paid with respect to each child until that child reaches 16 years) and medical benefits. The wide range of other provisions—including widows' benefits, invalids' benefits, sickness benefits, unemployment payments and orphans' benefits—are income tested.

Health services: Most medicines, prenatal and maternity services, and public hospital treatment are provided free. In addition the government assists private hospitals by lending money for buildings and equipment, while patients in private hospitals receive a daily subsidy from the government. There is free dental provision for children and adolescents: for dependent adolescents, dental care by private dentists is paid for by the government. In 1987 there were approximately 8,000 medical practitioners and over 1,000 dentists in New Zealand.

Housing: Seventy percent of houses in New Zealand are owner-occupied. The government-owned Housing Corporation supplies mortages at moderate rates of interest; house purchase may also be financed through banks, insurance companies, cooperative building societies and legal trusts. Subsidies and incentives are provided by the state to assist first-home buyers. The Housing Corporation and some local authorities build houses, renting them to families with low incomes.

EDUCATION

Education is compulsory for all children between six and 15 years and free until the age of 19. In 1987 there were approximately 2,300 state primary schools and 60 private primary schools; in the same year there were 315 state secondary schools and 15 private secondary schools. New Zealand has six universities (Auckland, Waikato, Massey, Victoria, Canterbury, Otago) and an agricultural college (Lincoln College). The state provides approximately 80% of the universities' funds; it also provides bursaries for students. Approximately 12% of secondary school graduates go on to university. Considerable attention is paid to meeting the distinct educational needs of children in remote rural areas. There is also concern to increase educational opportunities for Maori children, and there has been a substantial growth in Maori-language teaching in schools and in Maori Studies courses in teacher training colleges and universities.

MASS MEDIA

The press

Dailies: The main dailies include the *New Zealand Herald* (243,000), *Auckland Star* (111,000), *Evening Post* (83,000), *The Press* (85,500) and *The Dominion* (73,000). In the four main urban areas there are seven daily newspapers, with a combined circulation of more than 700,000; in the smaller urban centers there are 23 daily newspapers, with a total circulation of around 350,000.

Weeklies: The main weeklies include *New Zealand Truth* (125,000), *The Dominion Sunday Times* (89,000), *Weekend Star* (36,000) and *Mercantile Gazette of New Zealand* (24,000). Also published are a large number of magazines and specialist periodicals.

Broadcasting: The Broadcasting Corporation of New Zealand, which was established in 1977, is a public corporation responsible to parliament. It operates Radio New Zealand, which runs three national radio networks, one of them commercial. In addition, there are 13 private commercial radio stations. The Broadcasting Corporation of New Zealand also operates Television New Zealand, which runs two nationwide television networks. The income for public broadcasting comes from advertising (on television, on radio and in the corporation's publication the *Listener*) and from a public broadcasting fee.

BIOGRAPHICAL SKETCHES

David Lange. Born in Auckland in 1942 he graduated in law from the University of Auckland in 1966. He practiced as a lawyer, was a tutor at the University of Auckland and completed a postgraduate degree in law. David Lange entered parliament at a by-election in 1977; he became deputy-leader of the Labour party, then in opposition, in November 1979; he became leader of the party on February 3, 1983, upon the resignation of Sir Wallace Rowling. He became prime minister following Labour's victory in the July 1984 election, New Zealand's youngest prime minister in this century. He stepped down as premier in mid-1989.

Michael Moore. Born in Whakatane in 1949, Moore entered the House of Representatives at the 1972 election, lost his seat in 1975 but returned in 1978. In November 1988 he was the third-ranking member of the government; as minister of overseas trade and marketing, he led a large number of trade missions (notably to the Asian countries, the Middle East and Latin America) to develop markets for New Zealand's agricultural exports.

Geoffrey Palmer. Born in Nelson in 1942, he was educated at the Victoria University of Wellington (B.A. in Political Science in 1964; LL.B. in 1965) and the University of Chicago (Doctor of Laws in 1967). Before entering parliament, Geoffrey Palmer practiced as a solicitor and taught at Victoria University, the University of Iowa and the University of Virginia. He entered the House of Representatives at a by-election in August 1979 and became deputy-leader of the Labour party in February 1983. In November 1988 he was deputy prime minister, minister of justice, attorney general and minister for the environment. Palmer became prime minister in mid-1989.

THE PACIFIC ISLANDS

AMERICAN SAMOA

AMERICAN Samoa comprises seven islands (Tutuila, Aunuu, Tau, Ofu, Olosega, Rose and Swains) lying in the south central Pacific. Their total area is 76.1 sq. miles/194.8 sq. km. The average temperature ranges from 70°F/21°C to 90°F/32°C; humidity averages 80%; the annual rainfall (at Pago Pago) is around 197 in/5,000 mm. At the 1980 census the total population was 32,297, of whom 30,124 lived on the principal island of Tutuila; in mid-1986 the total population was estimated at 36,000. The capital is Pago Pago (situated on Tutuila); at the 1980 census it had a population of 3,075. The indigenous language is Samoan but most American Samoans also speak English. Christianity is widely practiced: More than half of the population are members of the Christian Congregational Church and about 19% are Roman Catholics.

The territory now known as American Samoa was first located by Western navigators in the 1720s. In the early 19th century it became a refuge for runaway sailors and escaped convicts; in the 1830s missionaries from the London Missionary Society settled there. Toward the close of the 19th century, the United States, Germany and Great Britain each sought advantages in the Samoa group. In 1872 an American naval commander negotiated a treaty with the local ruler of the Pago Pago area that gave the United States the exclusive right to build a naval station there in return for U.S. protection. That treaty was not ratified, but in 1878 certain harbor lands in Pago Pago were transferred to the United States to establish a coaling depot. In 1899 the three Western powers agreed to settle their conflicting ambitions in the islands: Germany annexed what became Western Samoa; the United States secured the eastern islands (Eastern Samoa) into what became American Samoa; and the British withdrew (in return for German concessions elsewhere).

Until 1951 the administration of American Samoa was the responsibility of the U.S. Department of the Navy. From 1951 to 1978 American Samoa was administered by a governor appointed by the U.S. Department of the Interior, and a legislature comprising a Senate and House of Representatives. The 1960s saw the governor attempt to force the pace of economic development in the territory, principally through a major program of infrastructural investment. In the early part of the 1970s Washington sought to persuade the population to elect their own governor; this proposal was repeatedly defeated in referenda. But the fourth referendum produced a

255

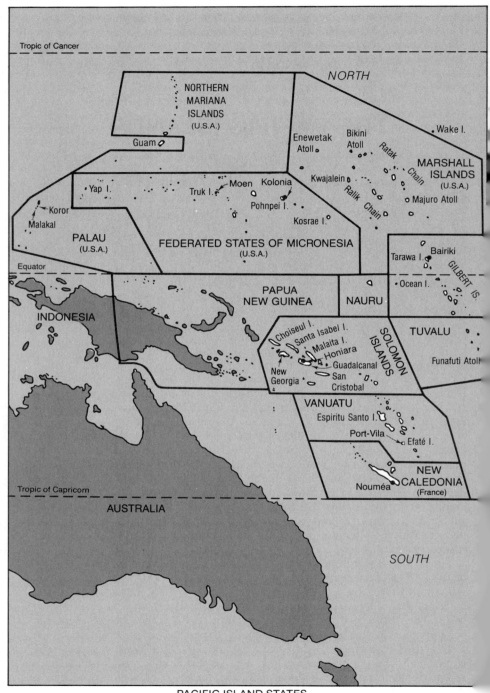

Tropic of Cancer

NORTH

NORTHERN
MARIANA
ISLANDS
(U.S.A.)

Guam

Enewetak
Atoll

Bikini
Atoll

Wake I.

Ratak Chain

MARSHALL
ISLANDS
(U.S.A.)

Kwajalein

Yap I.

Truk I.

Moen

Kolonia

Ralik Chain

Pohnpei I.

Majuro Atoll

Koror

Malakal

Kosrae I.

PALAU
(U.S.A.)

FEDERATED STATES OF MICRONESIA
(U.S.A.)

Bairiki

Tarawa I.

GILBERT IS.

Equator

Ocean I.

PAPUA
NEW GUINEA

NAURU

INDONESIA

TUVALU

Choiseul I.

Santa Isabel I.

Malaita I.

SOLOMON
ISLANDS

Funafuti Atoll

Honiara

New
Georgia

Guadalcanal

San
Cristobal

VANUATU

Espiritu Santo I.

Port-Vila

Efaté I.

NEW
CALEDONIA
(France)

Nouméa

Tropic of Capricorn

AUSTRALIA

SOUTH

PACIFIC ISLAND STATES

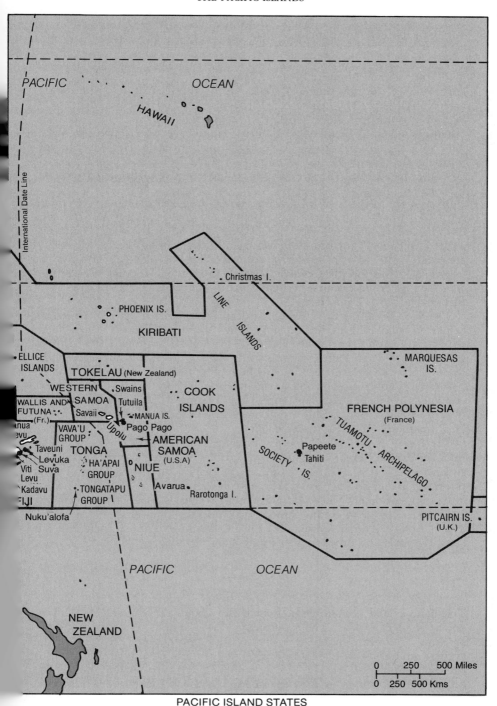

PACIFIC ISLAND STATES

vote in favor. In November 1977 Peter Tali Coleman became the first popularly elected governor of American Samoa; he took office in January 1978.

The executive consists of the governor and lieutenant governor (both of whom are popularly elected), and departmental and office heads (who are appointed by the governor and confirmed by the legislature). The legislature is bicameral: The Senate has 18 members, elected in accordance with Samoan custom from local chiefs for a four-year term; the House of Representatives has 20 members, elected by popular vote for a two-year term. American Samoa sends to the U.S. House of Representatives one non-voting delegate, popularly elected every two years. In October 1988 the governor was A. P. Lutali; the lieutenant governor was Faleomavaega Eni Hunkin.

The two principal sectors of the economy are government service (which accounted for 40.3% of the employed labor force in 1981) and the tuna canning industry (21.6% of the employed labor force in 1981). The latter, located at Pago Pago, processes fish from U.S., Taiwanese and South Korean vessels. In 1984, canned tuna accounted for 98% of total export value, largely destined for the mainland American market; imports (which substantially exceeded exports) consisted mainly of fuel, food and cans. Tourism is of growing importance.

The U.S. Social Security Administration maintains an office in American Samoa to handle all matters relating to the payment of social security benefits. There is one general hospital (The Lyndon B. Johnson Tropical Medical Center at Pago Pago); dispensary services are available throughout the territory. In 1984 there were four public high schools, 24 elementary schools, 130 early childhood centers, a special education school, eight private schools and one college (The Samoa Community College). Under a Government of American Samoa scholarship program, many able Samoans proceed to the U.S. mainland for tertiary education.

The Samoa News, 4,500, publishes three times a week in English and Samoan; *Samoa Journal and Advertiser,* 3,000, publishes weekly in English and Samoan; *News Bulletin,* 1,800, is published by the Office of Public Information and appears daily Monday through Friday in English. There is one radio station, WVUV, formerly administered by the government but as of 1975 leased to Radio Samoa; it broadcasts in English and Samoan. There is one television station, KVZK, which is government owned; it has three channels and broadcasts in English and Samoan.

COOK ISLANDS

The Cook Islands comprise 15 islands lying in the south central Pacific: The main island is Rarotonga, which lies about 1,860 miles/3,000 km. northeast of Auckland. The total area of the islands is 91.5 sq. miles/237 sq. km. The mean annual temperature in Rarotonga is 75°F/23.9°C; the average annual rainfall is 80 in/2,030 mm. At the December 1986 census the total population was 17,185, of whom 9,281 lived on Rarotonga. The capital (on Rarotonga) is Avarua. Most of the Cook Islanders are bilingual, speaking their own Polynesian dialect and English. Approximately 70% of the population belong to the Cook Islands (Congregational) Christian Church; some 15% are Roman Catholic.

Prior to the arrival of European authority, the islands that comprise the present-day Cook Islands were essentially separate entities. In the early 1820s most of the islands came under the spiritual and, to a major extent, the administrative control of missionaries from the London Missionary Society, who were stationed on Rarotonga. The 1880s saw increasing concern over possible French involvement in the group, consequently, in 1888 a British protectorate was declared on Rarotonga. In June 1901, the Cook Islands were annexed by New Zealand. In 1946 a Legislative Council was established, in 1957 a Legislative Assembly and in 1962 an advisory Executive Committee of the Legislative Assembly. In 1964 the Executive Committee became a fully responsible cabinet. In April 1965 the Cook Islands party won a substantial majority in the first general election for the Legislative Assembly. On August 4, 1965, the Cook Islands became a self-governing territory in free association with New Zealand; the latter retained responsibility for the external affairs and defense of the territory and undertook to provide financial support for the Cook Islands. The islanders remained citizens of New Zealand, with unrestricted right of entry into that country: Over the last three or four decades a significant proportion of the population has exercised that right. The Cook Islands party was reelected in 1968, 1971, 1974 and 1978. An inquiry into alleged electoral malpractice overturned that last "victory" and brought to power the Democratic party. The following general election, held in March 1983, brought in a protracted period of parliamentary instability, coalition realignments and party defection.

Executive government lies with a cabinet comprising the prime minister and six ministers; the cabinet is collectively responsible to parliament. The parliament of the Cook Islands, which has a term of five years, consists of 24 members elected by universal suffrage; one member is elected by Cook Islanders living in New Zealand. The principal political organizations with parliamentary representation are the Cook Islands party (formed in 1965) and the Democratic party (formed in 1971). The House of Ariki, consisting of up to 15 *ariki* (hereditary chiefs), can advise the administration on traditional issues and matters of custom, but it has no legislative power. Each of the main islands, except Rarotonga, has an island council. In November 1988 the Queen's representative was Sir Tangaroa Tangaroa; the New Zealand representative was Adrian Sincock; the prime minister was Dr. Pupuke Robati.

The Cook Islands run a severe trade deficit (in 1986 the total value of commodity imports was over eight times the total value of commodity exports), a deficit that may be covered by substantial aid from New Zealand (NZ$420 million in 1988) and by remittances sent back to the islands by the substantial Cook Islander population overseas. The principal exports are fresh fruit and vegetables (encouraged by the establishment of airfreight services), copra and clothing (there are two clothing factories on the islands). Agriculture, commerce and government are the major employers.

259

Perhaps the most severe barrier to the economic expansion of the Cook Islands in recent decades has been the very heavy emigration of Cook Islanders, particularly the young and those with skills; in 1988 there were 40,000 Cook Islanders living in New Zealand, more than double the population of the islands themselves.

Many civil servants have retained membership in the New Zealand Public Service Superannuation Scheme. There is an old age and destitute persons scheme as well as provision for payment of child benefits. Cook Islanders receive free medical and surgical treatment; there is a general hospital on Rarotonga and cottage hospitals and dispensaries on the other inhabited islands. Those patients needing specialist care are sent to New Zealand. Education is free and compulsory for children aged between six and 15. Schools, which numbered 36 in 1985, are operated by the government, the Roman Catholic mission and the Seventh-Day Adventist mission. The New Zealand administration offers scholarships that enable young islanders to pursue secondary and tertiary education in New Zealand, Australia or on other islands in the Pacific.

Cook Islands News, 2,000, is government owned and is published daily except Sunday in English and Maori; the Cook Islands party publishes a weekly, *Akatauira*. There are two radio stations, the government-owned Radio Cook Islands (IZC)—broadcasting in English and Maori—and Radio Ikurangi.

FIJI

Fiji comprises approximately 800 islands, of which about 150 are inhabited. The main islands are Viti Levu, Vanua Levu, Taveuni and Kadavu. The group is located in the south central Pacific. The total area of the islands is 7,095 sq. miles/18,376 sq. km. During the cool season (May–October) temperatures are in the range 68°–79°F/20°–26°C; for the rest of the year (November–April) temperatures are in the range 75°–86°F/24°–30°C. The humidity in Suva (the capital, on Viti Levu) can be as high as 95%; the average annual rainfall in Suva is 128 in/3,251 mm. There is considerable geographical variation in temperature, humidity and precipitation. At a census taken in August 1986 the total population was 715,375, of whom 48.7% were Indians and 46.1% were Fijians. Suva had a population (provisionally calculated) of 69,481 at the 1986 census. The official language is English; the most widely used of the Fijian languages is the Bau dialect; Hindustani is spoken by the majority of the Indian population. Most ethnic Fijians are Christian—principally Methodist, although there is also a substantial Roman Catholic community; the Indians are principally Hindu, although there are also substantial Muslim and Sikh communities.

The modern history of Fiji may conveniently be dated from 1858: In that year, a prominent local ruler, Cakobau, claiming to possess full and exclusive sovereignty in the islands, offered to cede them to Great Britain provided that the latter would settle a substantial financial claim being made against him by various American interests. The British government refused the offer; but through the 1860s and early 1870s the pressure for

260

British intervention increased, partly as a result of mounting imperial rivalries in the area but also because there occurred considerable settlement of Britons from Australia and New Zealand in anticipation of annexation. In 1874 Britain accepted the offer of cession: On October 10 a Deed of Cession was signed at Levuka by Cakobau and the principal chiefs; and Fiji became a British Crown Colony. With the establishment of British administration, Fiji rapidly emerged as an important world producer of sugar. The principal initiative here lay with the Colonial Sugar Refining Company of Australia, which moved into Fiji in 1881. Cane sugar cultivation required the importation of indentured Indian labor, the first ship of migrants reaching Fiji in May 1879. After serving 10 years under contract each Indian laborer could elect to remain in Fiji, and it was in this way that the Indian community in the islands soon grew to challenge the indigenous population numerically. Crucially, however, British colonial administration consistently favored the interests of the ethnic Fijians against those of the Indians. Thus, notably, the indigenous community had its own administrative and judicial structures, and its land could not be alienated. Here were the principal origins of the racial divisions that have been the dominant theme in Fiji's history since independence.

Fiji became an independent state on October 10, 1970. From independence until 1987 the ruling party was the Alliance party (under Ratu Sir Kamisese Mara), which was supported principally by indigenous Fijians. In elections held in April 1977 the Indian-led opposition won a majority; but its leaders were uncertain whether Fijians would be willing to accept an Indian political leader and Mara was reappointed prime minister. In the July 1982 elections the Alliance party, emphasizing Fijian values and interests, won a relatively narrow victory over the National Federation party, which derived its support mainly from the Indian community. In the April 1987 elections victory went to a coalition of the National Federation party and the Fiji Labour party; the new prime minister was Dr. Timoci Bavadra. For the first time the ruling party (or parties) and the cabinet were dominated by ethnic Indians. On May 14, 1987, the government was removed by a military coup led by Lt. Col. Sitiveni Rabuka. Rabuka formed an interim ruling council. The governor-general, refusing to recognize this administration, declared a state of emergency. There followed several months of widespread racial violence and political maneuvring: On the one side there was powerful pressure for constitutional restructuring that would secure the political dominance of ethnic Fijians, on the other an insistence that the Indian community must have adequate political representation. By late September there was agreement between the factions for the establishment of an interim bipartisan administration that would attempt to resolve the political/constitutional crisis. On September 25, 1987, Rabuka launched a second coup; on October 1, 1987, the independence constitution was formally revoked and Queen Elizabeth II was deposed as head of state. On October 7 Rabuka installed an interim council of ministers and in December Mara was reappointed prime minister. In September 1988 a new draft constitution was approved by the interim government: The constitution would guarantee ethnic Fijian domination of the political structure. In November the head of state was Ratu Sir Penaia Ganilau, the prime minister Ratu Sir Kamisese Mara. Maj. Gen. Sitiveni Rabuka was minister of home affairs, National Youth Service and Auxiliary Army Services.

The mainstay of the Fijian economy has long been sugar. In 1985 sugar-cane production was 3,042,000 metric tons; in 1986 sugar accounted for 47.7% of the total value of commodity exports; in 1981 the cultivation and processing of sugar employed about 42,000 people. In the late 19th and early 20th century the crop was grown on large estates, using inden-tured Indian labor; but following the ending of indentured migration in 1916 the estates were gradually broken up and the present structure, where sugar is grown on smallholdings by tenant farmers, emerged. The large majority of sugar farmers are of Indian origin. During the colonial period and up to the early 1970s the milling of sugarcane was predominantly (and latterly, exclusively) in the hands of the Colonial Sugar Refining Company of Australia. But at the close of the 1960s that company announced that it was withdrawing from Fiji; in 1973 its interests were bought out by the Fiji government and established as the Fiji Sugar Corporation. Following nationalization the company embarked on an extensive modernization of its milling facilities. In more recent years the Fijian sugar industry has faced a number of serious difficulties: Notable here has been a long-term insta-bility in the international sugar market; severe hurricane damage; and the political/constitutional crisis from 1987, for in that year the mainly Indian sugar smallholders refused to cut the cane crop in protest against the re-moval of the elected government. Fiji also exports coconut products, fish, wood products and gold. The principal markets for Fijian exports are Aus-tralia, New Zealand and the United Kingdom. Fiji imports a wide range of capital and consumer goods: In 1986 machinery, electrical goods and transport equipment accounted for 23.4% of the total value of commodity imports; petroleum products accounted for 16.0%. Fiji runs a persistent, substantial trade deficit. From the late 1960s on tourism grew into a major industry; indeed, as of 1982 it became the largest source of foreign-exchange earnings. In 1986 there were 257,824 foreign tourist arrivals, but the political instability and communal violence that occurred the fol-lowing year caused a sharp contraction in tourist arrivals.

Social security is provided through the Fiji National Provident Fund, established in 1966, which pays members upon retirement either a lump sum, a pension or a combination of the two; from 1971 on an insurance scheme has been included in the fund, and from 1976 on the government has offered housing finance for fund members. The contribution is 12% of the employee's wages, half being paid by the employer, half by the em-ployee. The Fiji National Provident Fund had 72,856 contributors in May 1980. Most of the medical care facilities in Fiji are provided by govern-ment; in 1982 there were 25 hospitals, 49 health centers and 89 nursing stations operating in both rural and urban areas. Medical treatment is free to all children under 15 years of age; adults are required to pay a nominal fee when they receive medical or dental treatment at government hospitals and clinics. In 1984 the total number of physicians in Fiji was 444, which implied a doctor/medical assistant to population ratio of 1:1,553. Fiji is widely said to have a population that enjoys relatively good health condition, with an average life expectation of nearly 70 years, and notably low infant morality and crude death rates. Recent years, however, have seen increasing concern expressed over the rapidly rising levels of alcoholism, malnutrition and venereal disease (the latter being frequently linked to the tourist explosion). The central government commits a major part of its resources to education. In 1984 educational expenditure represented 22.5% of total spending. Primary education is free; in 1984 nearly 100% of children of primary-school age attended school; in the same year there were 672 primary schools. Complete or partial remission of fees is provided for poor children attending secondary school; in 1984 there were 139 secondary schools. With respect to tertiary education, in 1984 there were three teacher training colleges and 36 vocational and technical institutions. The University of the South Pacific, established in 1968 at Laucala Bay, Suva, draws students not only from Fiji but from many other of the Pacific states. In 1983 it was attended by approximately 2,300 students.

Fiji possesses an extensive press. The principal newspapers include: *Fiji Times,* 27,000, which appears daily in English; *Fiji Royal Gazette,* the official gazette of the Fiji government, which appears weekly in English; *Jagriti,* 5,500, which appears three times a week in Hindi; *Nai Lalakai,* 18,000, which appears weekly in Fijian. Sunday newspapers have not been published since the September 1987 military coup. The Fiji Broadcasting Commission (Radio Fiji) broadcasts in English, Fijian and Hindustani. In 1985 a contract to establish and operate a commercial television service was awarded to Pacific Television Pty., Ltd., a subsidiary of an Australian television company. All broadcasts have been subject to government control since the coup of September 1987.

FRENCH POLYNESIA

French Polynesia, an overseas territory of France situated in the southeast Pacific, contains some 130 islands, comprising five main groups. The total land area is 1,622 sq. miles/4,200 sq. km. The average temperature is 81°F/27°C, but falls to 70°F/21°C during July and August and rises as high as 90°F/32°C in January and February; humidity is generally high, particularly in the wet season; the average annual rainfall in the capital, Papeete, is 69 in/1,750 mm. The total population was officially estimated on December 31, 1985, at 176,543. Papeete, on the island of Tahiti, had an estimated population of 23,496 in 1983. The official languages are French and Tahitian. Approximately 55% of the population are Protestants, a little over 30% are Roman Catholics; virtually all the Protestants are Polynesians, the Roman Catholics being found among the French and the Polynesians in two of the main island groups.

European interest in the islands that now comprise French Polynesia began to emerge firmly in the second half of the 18th century, with the visits from, notably, Lt. James Cook and Lt. William Bligh. At the close of the century missionaries from the London Missionary Society were landed at Tahiti; from around 1815 the missionary effort rapidly began to secure converts throughout many of the islands. By the late 1830s there was a growing French interest in the islands, as France sought a settlement in the eastern Pacific that could service its whalers, gunboats and merchantmen. In 1842 a French protectorate was declared over Tahiti; in 1880 Tahiti was ceded to France and thereby became a French colony. In the remaining years of the 19th century the other island groups of what is now French Polynesia were annexed by France. From 1885 to 1957 the islands were governed from the metropole. In August 1957 the islands, reconstituted as French Polynesia, became an overseas territory of France; the legislative authority of its Territorial Assembly was considerably extended, and a Council of Government was created in which local political figures would hold ministerial positions (the appointed governor was ex-officio president of the Council). In 1977 Paris agreed to the creation of a fully elected local executive; in 1984 the local administration was given greater powers, and the Council of Government was replaced by a Council of Ministers whose president was to be elected by the Territorial Assembly from among its members.

From at least the end of the 1950s there has been a substantial (if minority and occasionally silenced) voice within the Polynesian community that would seek to sever the territory's relationship with France; in a referendum held in 1959, 36% of the people of French Polynesia voted for independence. A major part of the desire for independence is derived from the widely felt concern over France's use of the territory to test nuclear devices: The first tests took place in 1966. But there is also the view that a French withdrawal (which would imply the removal of the extensive French military establishment in French Polynesia) would bring economic ruin to the territory; and it is that view that secures the widest support among the population, although it is coupled with a desire for a greater measure of internal self-government. The ruling party, Tahoeraa Huiraatira/Rassemblement pour la République, which secured 24 of the 41 seats in the Territorial Assembly at elections held in March 1986, is committed precisely to maintaining the relationship with France while allowing a greater measure of internal autonomy. In November 1988 the high commissioner was Jean Montpezat; the president of the Council of Ministers was Alexandre Leontieff.

The modern economy of French Polynesia rests primarily upon the large French military establishment (engaged principally on the testing of nuclear devices) and upon tourism. In 1987 there were 142,820 visitors (excluding cruise passengers and excursionists), of whom almost half were from the United States. The growth of tourism has been inhibited, however, by the nuclear-testing program and by insufficient investment in tourist facilities (primarily hotel rooms). French Polynesia's principal exports are coconut oil (which accounted for 3.6% of the total value of commodity exports in 1987) and cultured pearls (which accounted for 24.8%). The principal markets are metropolitan France and the United States. French Polynesia runs a massive trade deficit (covered by French aid and military establishment payments): In 1987 the total value of imports was over nine times the total value of exports.

Social benefits, including accident compensation, are financed through a payroll tax paid into a social security fund. Medical facilities are well provided: In the mid-1980s there were more than 50 doctors at the service of the civilian population in Tahiti (with specialist military personnel available in emergencies); in each group of the outer islands there is a small general hospital as well as a structure of dispensaries attended by traveling doctors. Education is compulsory for children aged six to 14 years. Government schooling is free. In 1982–83 there were 223 government and 16 private primary schools, and 24 government and 10 private secondary schools. There is a structure of government financed technical schools. The metropolitan government provides tertiary-level scholarships to allow French Polynesians to continue their education in France. The University of the Pacific, with its administrative center in Papeete, was established in 1987.

There are three French-language daily newspapers: *La Dépêche de Tahiti,* 15,000; *Le Journal de Tahiti;* and *Les Nouvelles.* The *Tahiti Bulletin* publishes daily in French and English. *Te Ve'a Porotetani* is published monthly, in French and Tahitian, by the Evangelical church. Radio-Télé-Tahiti is government controlled and operated by Société Nationale de Radio-Télévision Française d'Outre-Mer; broadcasts are in French and Tahitian. In 1985 there were an estimated 80,000 radio receivers and 26,000 televisions in use.

KIRIBATI

Kiribati (pronounced Kiribas) comprises 33 islands, in three main groups (Gilbert Islands, Phoenix Islands, Line Islands), lying astride the equator. The total land area is 332 sq. miles/861 sq. km. The temperature ranges between 79°F/26°C and 90°F/32°C; rainfall varies considerably not only between the islands but also year by year (in an average year, the precipitation on the main island of Tarawa will be in excess of 59 in/1,500 mm.). At a census held in May 1985 the total population was 63,883, of whom 21,393 lived on Tarawa. The administrative center is Bairiki, on Tarawa. The population speaks a Micronesian dialect and English, and is Christian—the principal groups being the Roman Catholic church and the Kiribati Protestant church.

The establishment of formal European authority in the territory now known as Kiribati came at the close of the 19th century. In 1892 Great Britain established a protectorate over the Gilbert Islands; in the same year a British protectorate was declared over the Ellice Islands to the south (present-day Tuvalu). In 1900 Britain annexed Ocean Island (now known as Banaba), following the discovery there of rich deposits of phosphate. In 1915, having secured the formal approval of the indigenous governments, Britain annexed the Gilbert Islands and the Ellice Islands; as of January 12, 1916, the two island groups became the Gilbert and Ellice Islands Colony (GEIC). Other islands were subsequently incorporated in the new colony, notably Ocean Island (1916), Christmas Island, now Kiritimati (1919), Phoenix Islands (1937). The Gilbert Islands were occupied by the Japanese in 1942–43: The main island of Tarawa saw fierce fighting between Japanese and U.S. forces.

Constitutional reform, establishing and later extending the involvement of the local population in government, began effectively in the early 1960s. An Executive Council and an Advisory Council, with members nominated by the resident commissioner, were created in 1963; in 1967 the Advisory Council was replaced by a (partially elected) House of Representatives and in 1971 the House of Representatives was replaced by a (partially elected) Legislative Council; in 1974 the Legislative Council was replaced by an elected House of Assembly, which then elected from within its number a chief minister. Later in 1974 the people of the Ellice Islands voted clearly in a referendum to secede from the colony; the separation took place on October 1, 1975. The Gilbert Islands (as the remainder of the GEIC was now known) obtained internal self-government on January 1, 1977; on July 12, 1979, the territory became an independent republic, within the Commonwealth, and took the name Kiribati. In the final years of colonial administration, the people of Banaba (Ocean Island) pressed for secession. This movement had its origins in the fact that from the time of annexation in 1900 the island had been the focus of large-scale phosphate extraction by the British Phosphate Commission. In early 1975 the Banabans took legal action in the High Court in London against the commission and the British Government, claiming royalty payments on phosphate exports and recompense for environmental damage. Their claim for royalties was dismissed, that for damages was upheld. But the Banabans failed to persuade either the British government or the rest of the territory to allow them to secede: Banaba remains part of Kiribati, although the independence constitution makes special provisions for the Banabans.

The legislature, Maneaba ni Maungatabu, is a unicameral body, with 39 elected members and one nominated representative of the Banaban community. Executive authority rests with the cabinet, which is directly responsible to the Maneaba ni Maungatabu. There is one political organization, the Christian Democratic party, formed in 1985 to oppose the granting of fishing rights to Soviet vessels. In November 1988 the president (who is head of state and head of the government, presiding over the cabinet) was Ieremia T. Tabai.

During the colonial period the economy of the territory rested heavily on phosphate extraction, which took place on Banaba. Phosphate mining ceased at the end of 1979, with devastating effects on export earnings and taxation revenue. In 1987 an Australian consortium was given permission to undertake a feasibility study on Banaba, with the prospect of there being a resumption of phosphate mining using new techniques. Kiribati's only significant exports are copra and fish; the territory has a massive trade deficit and thus relies heavily on aid, notably from Britain but also from Australia, New Zealand and Japan. Most of the people of Kiribati are fully engaged in the subsistence economy.

In the mid-1980s there were two major hospitals on Tarawa, supported by 22 dispensaries and 39 medical clinics distributed throughout the islands. In 1986 there were 112 primary schools (almost all of which were operated by the government) and six secondary schools (maintained either by the government or the church missions). The government also supports

266

a teacher training college, a technical institute and a marine training school. Kiribati participates in the University of the South Pacific, which is based in Fiji.

The Broadcasting and Publications Authority, a statutory body established in 1979, publishes a weekly newspaper, *Te Uekera,* which has articles and items in both English and I-Kiribati; it has a circulation of 1,500. The Roman Catholic church produces a monthly newsletter, *Te Itoi ni Kiribati,* 2,000; the Protestant churches produce a quarterly newsletter, *Te Kaotan te Ota,* 1,700. The Broadcasting and Publications Authority also operates Radio Kiribati, broadcasting in English and I-Kiribati. In 1985 there were an estimated 10,000 radio sets in use.

MARSHALL ISLANDS

The Republic of the Marshall Islands comprises a double chain of coral atolls (the Ratak Chain to the east and the Ralik Chain to the west) located in the central Pacific. The total land area is 69.5 sq. miles/180 sq. km. The northern islands of the territory are cooler and receive far less rainfall than the southern atolls; there is little seasonal variation in rainfall or temperature. At a census taken in 1980 the total population was 30,873; in 1986 the estimated population was 35,000. The administrative center of the Marshall Islands is Majuro Atoll, which had an estimated population of 12,800 in 1986. A local dialect within the Malayo-Polynesian language family is spoken; but English is widely understood. The population is predominantly Christian; most Marshallese are Protestant.

Visited by American whalers seeking food and water beginning in the 1820s, and the focus of American missionary interest from the 1860s, in 1885 the Marshall Islands became a German protectorate. German administration lasted until 1914 when, with the outbreak of war in Europe, the islands were occupied by the Japanese. In 1920 the Marshall Islands were mandated to Japan by the League of Nations. In 1944–45 U.S. military forces captured the islands from the Japanese; and in 1947 the Marshall Islands became part of the Trust Territory of the Pacific Islands, established by the United Nations, under U.S. administration. From the mid-1960s there were increasing demands for local autonomy, and in a plebiscite held in July 1978 the population of the Marshall Islands chose to separate from the other components of the Trust Territory. The following year the electorate approved a separate constitution for the islands; in April 1979 a Marshall Islands government was formed. In October 1982 the United States signed a Compact of Free Association with the Marshall Islands, under which the latter would be responsible for its internal and foreign affairs, while the United States would be responsible for defense and security; in addition, the United States would retain its military bases in the island group for at least 15 years in return for an annual aid payment. The compact was approved in a plebiscite held in September 1983; following U.N. endorsement, the compact came into effect in October 1986. At the heart of the relationship between the Marshall Islands and the United States has been the use of the territory as an area for the testing of American

267

nuclear devices and intercontinental missiles. In 1946 the United States used Bikini Atoll for tests; nuclear testing continued through to the early 1960s. In the Bikini and Eniwetok atolls a high degree of radioactive contamination has occurred; the American administration has had to meet substantial financial claims in respect of those whose lives and livelihood were seriously disturbed by the testing, and has had to undertake extensive programs of decontamination.

Under the 1979 constitution legislative authority is vested in a 33-member body, the Nitijela; the latter elects the president of the Marshall Islands from among its own members. In November 1988 the president was Amata Kabua.

The economy of the Marshall Islands is heavily dependent on American payments; annual financial assistance is secured under the Compact of Free Association; the U.S. military bases, notably the Kwajalein missile range, provide substantial wages for Marshallese workers and substantial compensation payments for islanders evicted from their homes. Copra is the only significant export; there is, as well, a substantial income from Japanese tuna-fishing vessels, securing rights to fish in the islands' waters, and a very modest tourist industry. Many of the islanders are engaged in subsistence farming and fishing. Education is compulsory up to the eighth grade.

There are two news publications: *Marshall Islands Gazette,* a government publication; and *Marshall Islands Journal,* a weekly publication with a circulation of 3,000. The radio station, Station WSZO–Radio Marshalls, broadcasts in both English and the local dialect.

FEDERATED STATES OF MICRONESIA

The Federated States of Micronesia, comprising the four states of Yap, Truk, Pohnpei (formerly Ponape) and Kosrae, is situated in the west central Pacific. Together with the Republic of Palau, it forms the archipelago of the Caroline Islands. At its longitudinal extremities (from the island of Yap in the west to Kosrae in the east), it stretches over 1,553 miles/2,500 km. The total land area is 271.6 sq. miles/700.8 sq. km. The average annual temperature is 80.6°F/27°C; the whole territory experiences heavy rainfall, although precipitation decreases from east to west. At a census taken in 1980 the total population was 73,160; the estimated population in 1987 was 85,200. The central government administration is located in Kolonia, on Pohnpei. A variety of local dialects within the Malayo-Polynesian language family are spoken through the territory; English is widely understood. The population is predominantly Christian. There is substantial adherence to the Roman Catholic church, but the people of Kosrae are mainly Protestant.

During the 1870s the Caroline Islands (the present-day Federated States of Micronesia together with the Republic of Palau) became the focus of increasing commercial and territorial rivalry between Spain and Germany. In 1885 both European powers agreed to place their conflicting claims before the Pope for arbitration: The Pope suggested that sovereignty should rest with Spain but that Germany have the freedom to trade in the archipelago and to establish coaling stations and settlements there. Following

Spain's defeat in its war with the United States in 1898, it sold the Caroline Islands to Germany: A German-Spanish treaty in early 1899 secured the transfer of sovereignty. With the outbreak of war in Europe in August 1914, Japanese forces occupied the Carolines. In 1921 the territory was mandated to Japan by the League of Nations; early in 1944 U.S. forces attacked Truk, a key Japanese military installation—although by the time the Japanese surrendered in August 1945, the Americans had taken only one atoll in the archipelago. In 1947 the Caroline Islands became part of the Trust Territory of the Pacific Islands, established by the United Nations, under U.S. administration; the territory was divided into four districts—Palau, Yap, Truk and Ponape (Pohnpei), of which Kosrae was (until 1977) a subdistrict. In a plebiscite held in July 1978 the population of Palau chose to separate from the other components of the Trust Territory of the Pacific Islands; a few months later Yap, Truk, Pohnpei and Kosrae came together as the Federated States of Micronesia. The electorate then approved a locally drafted constitution, and on May 10, 1979, constitutional government was installed. In October 1982 the United States signed a Compact of Free Association with the Federated States of Micronesia, under which the latter would be responsible for its internal and foreign affairs, while the United States would be responsible for defense and security; in addition the United States would undertake to provide regular economic assistance to the territory. The compact was approved in a plebiscite held in June 1983; following U.N. endorsement, the compact came into effect in November 1986.

Under the 1979 constitution, each of the constituent states of the federation has a locally elected governor and legislature. The central government, located at Kolonia, has as its legislative body the National Congress of the Federated States of Micronesia; the Congress elects the president and the vice-president from among its senior members. In November 1988 the president was Yapese John Haglelgam.

The principal sources of income for the Federated States of Micronesia are U.S. aid (there has also been economic assistance from Japan), tourism and the issue of licenses to foreign vessels, permitting them to fish within the territory's 200-nautical mile exclusive economic zone. The principal commodity export is copra. The principal employer in the modern sector of the economy is government, but many of the islanders remain in the subsistence sector.

There are two news publications: *The National Union,* which appears twice a month and has a circulation of 5,000; and *Truk News Chronicle.* Each of the four constituent states of the federation has its own radio station, broadcasting in the local dialect and in English. There are two television stations, one on Pohnpei and one on Moen (Truk). In 1984 an estimated 15,800 radios were in use; in 1987 an estimated 1,125 televisions were in use.

NAURU

The Republic of Nauru is a single island in the central Pacific: It lies some 2,485 miles/4,000 km. northeast of Sydney and 2,583 miles/4,160 km.

southwest of Hawaii. The area of the island is 8.2 sq. miles/21.3 sq. km. Located just south of the equator, Nauru experiences no seasonal variation in temperature. There is a westerly monsoon from November to February; precipitation varies greatly from year to year. At a census taken on May 13, 1983, the total population was 8,042, of whom 4,964 were Nauruan and 2,134 were from other islands in the Pacific. The national language is Nauruan, but English is widely spoken. The population is predominantly Christian—adherents to either the Nauru Congregational church or the Roman Catholic church.

The island of Nauru came under European administration in October 1888, when it was declared a German protectorate. At the turn of the century it became clear (essentially as a result of investigations conducted by the Pacific Islands Company, Sydney) that Nauru contained vast deposits of phosphate; after negotiation with the German administration it was agreed that those deposits would be exploited under joint British-German arrangements, and in 1905 the Pacific Phosphate Company (which had grown out of the Pacific Islands Company) was established. Within two years there was a major export of phosphate to Australia. With the outbreak of war in Europe in 1914, Nauru was taken by Australian forces; in 1920 a mandate for the administration of the island was conferred jointly on Great Britain, Australia and New Zealand by the League of Nations, although, for reasons of convenience, Australia continued in sole administrative control. Also in 1920 the British Phosphate Commissioners, controlled by the three mandated governments, bought out all rights to the deposits: Their exploitation was now a government monopoly. The industry brought little benefit and much distress to the local population. Right through to the mid-1960s the islanders received only minuscule royalty payments on phosphate shipped, while the foreign laborers brought to Nauru to work the deposits introduced many diseases (dysentery, polio, pneumonia) that cut through the ranks of the indigenous people.

Nauru was occupied by the Japanese in August 1942, and retaken by Australian forces in September 1945. In November 1947 the island became a U.N. trust territory, with Australia, Britain and New Zealand as the trust powers (although, again, Australia held sole administrative control). In 1951 an elected Nauru Local Government Council was established. In 1964 the Nauruans rejected an Australian offer that they be settled on Curtis Island, off the coast of Queensland—an offer made in anticipation of the eventual exhaustion of the phosphate deposits. In January 1966, with the creation of legislative and executive councils, Nauru achieved a considerable measure of self-government. On January 31, 1968, Nauru became an independent republic. The previous year the trust governments had agreed that the Nauruans could buy out the British Phosphate Commissioners: In 1970 the phosphate industry was transferred to the Nauru Phosphate Corporation.

Under the independence constitution, which came into force on January 31, 1968, the territory is governed by the Nauruan parliament, comprising 18 members elected by common roll every three years. In elections held in January 1987 all members were elected as independents; the following month, however, saw the establishment of the Democratic party of Nauru, which sought to curtail the extension of presidential power and to promote democracy. The president is elected by the Nauruan parliament from among its members; the cabinet is chosen by the president. The Nauru Local Government Council is an important component in the island's administration: It has responsibility, for example, for the operation of Nauru's shipping line. At the end of 1988 the president of Nauru was Hammer DeRoburt. In mid-1989 he was replaced by Kenas Aroi.

The economy of Nauru rests upon the mining of the phosphate deposits, said to be the purest grade of phosphate found anywhere in the world. Approximately two million tons are exported each year, primarily to Australia and New Zealand where, as an outstanding fertilizer (after treatment with sulfuric acid), it finds a major market. It is anticipated that the phosphate deposits will be exhausted by the mid-1990s, and it is suggested that at that point Nauru's income might be derived from its shipping and airline services or from a proposed status as a tax haven for international business. In the meantime, the Nauru government has been investing some 60% of the income from the phosphate industry in long-term trust funds that are intended to provide for the future economic security of the people. The revenues from the industry are sufficient to ensure free education up to the age of 16, free medical and dental services in the government hospital, and free electricity and housing; there is no income tax. The per capita income of Nauruans is said to be the highest in the world.

There is one news publication: *Nauru Bulletin,* which appears weekly in Nauruan and English and has a circulation of 750. The government-owned Nauru Broadcasting Service broadcasts in English and Nauruan. In 1984 there were an estimated 5,500 radio receivers in use.

NEW CALEDONIA

New Caledonia comprises one large island (approximately 249 miles/400 km. long and 31 miles/50 km. across) and several smaller islands, situated in the southwest Pacific. The total land area is 7, 376 sq. miles/19,103 sq. km. The average annual temperature is 73°F/23°C, with little monthly variation. The east coast of the New Caledonia mainland receives an average annual rainfall of 79 in/2,000 mm.; the west coast receives half that figure. At a census taken in April 1983 the total population was 145,368: of these, 42.6% were Melanesians, 37.1% were Europeans. The capital is Nouméa (which at the time of the 1983 census had a population of 60,112). The official language is French; many indigenous languages, reflecting the varied ethnic origins of the people, are spoken throughout the territory, however. The population is almost exclusively Christian. Approximately 65% of the people are Roman Catholic and there is a substantial Protestant community.

The focus of increasing attention from European navigators, traders, runaway seamen and escaped convicts beginning in the final decades of the 18th century, New Caledonia was annexed by France in 1853. From then until 1884 the territory was administered by military governors, but in

1885 a civilian governor was installed, assisted by an elected advisory council. In these early decades of French rule, New Caledonia's principal value to the colonial power was as a penal settlement (the transportation of convicts ended only in 1897); the 1860s saw the discovery of nickel ore; and the French settler population, many of whom were convicts who had served their time or were the descendants of convicts, acquired substantial landholdings (principally for cattle grazing), frequently to the disadvantage of the Melanesians (Kanaks). During World War II New Caledonia became a major U.S. military base.

In the mid-1950s New Caledonia achieved a modest degree of self-government: In 1956 an Assemblée Territoriale was created, its 30 members being elected by universal adult suffrage. In recent years (and most notably since the late 1970s) the constitutional status of the territory has become the cause of the most bitter conflict within New Caledonia, as well as between certain interests in New Caledonia and the metropolitan administration. At one end of the political range are those who seek either to maintain the status quo (whereby New Caledonia is an overseas territory of France, with executive authority in the hands of a French political appointee) or to weld the territory more effectively to France (by making New Caledonia a department of the country. The principal political organization here is the Rassemblement pour la Calédonie dans la République. Others, the Fédération pour une Nouvelle Société Calédonienne, seek internal autonomy. At the other end of the political range are those—the Front de Libération Nationale Kanake Socialiste (FLNKS)—who seek independence from France. A settlement of these conflicting views has been extremely difficult to achieve, principally because the Melanesian community, which seeks independence, is outnumbered by the French and other settler populations. It appears to be almost inevitable that any test of local opinion in which all inhabitants of New Caledonia were eligible to participate would have an inbuilt antiindependence majority; and it has been for this reason that FLNKS has sought to confine participation in referenda to the indigenous (Melanesian) community; it also explains the very high level of Melanesian abstention from tests of opinion. During the later 1980s the level of political violence has been extremely high: There have been a number of political murders; civil unrest has been common, and French troops have been brought into the territory to maintain order. At the end of 1988 political power was temporarily transferred to metropolitan France as part of a proposed settlement that includes a referendum on self-determination, to be held in 1998. In November 1988 the high commissioner was Bernard Grasset.

The modern sector of the New Caledonian economy is dominated by nickel. The territory possesses the world's largest known deposits of that ore, representing approximately 30% of the world's known reserves. New Caledonia is the world's third most important producer of nickel (after the USSR and Canada): In 1984 exports of ferro-nickel, nickel ore and nickel matte accounted for 97% of export income, the principal markets being France and Japan. This very high dependence on nickel implies a considerable economic vulnerability; weakness in the world nickel market (as in the early 1970s) and internal industrial unrest (as in the mid-1980s) have brought severe hardship to the economy as a whole, and have encouraged the French administration to think seriously about promoting economic diversification (notably to increase rice and fruit production, and to revive the potentially important tourist industry). Metropolitan France has long provided substantial financial aid to the territory.

The social service administration, CAFAT, is responsible for a social security provision under which employees receive benefits (including pre-natal and maternity leave, and child endowment), the cost of which is secured through a payroll tax of about 25%, paid by employers. The provision of government health services is in the hands of military personnel, in order to ensure that the interior districts (where most of the Melanesian population lives) are adequately covered. There is very substantial private provision, concentrated in the towns. Schools are operated by both the state and the church, under the supervision of the Department of Education. The French government finances the state primary and secondary school structure. In 1986 there were 271 primary schools, 45 secondary schools, and 34 technical and higher institutions, with a total enrollment of 51,648. In 1987 the University of the Pacific was founded, with a center in Nouméa.

The daily newspapers include: *Les Nouvelles Calédoniennes*, 18,000; and *La Presse Calédonienne*, 8,000. *Le Journal Calédonien* appears weekly; *Le Devenir Calédonien* appears monthly, containing social, cultural and economic news. The principal radio station and the television station (Télé Nouméa) are French government controlled and are operated through Radiodiffusion Française d'Outre-Mer. All programs are in French. In 1985 there were an estimated 80,000 radio sets and 32,000 television sets in use.

NIUE

Niue is a coral island situated in the south central Pacific. It has an area of 100 sq. miles/259 sq. km. The mean annual temperature is 76.5°F/24.7°C, and the average annual rainfall is 86 in/2,177 mm. At a census taken in September 1986 the population was 2,531; at a census taken previously, in September 1981, it had been 3,281. The administrative center is Alofi. The indigenous language is closely related to Tongan and Samoan; English is in universal use, however. Approximately 75% of the population belongs to the Ekalesia Niue, a church that has evolved from initial contact with the London Missionary Society; the population also includes adherents to the Roman Catholic church and the Church of Latter-Day Saints (Mormon).

Throughout the 19th century Niue was the focus of missionary activity. In 1900 the island was declared a British protectorate. The following year it was formally annexed to New Zealand as part of the Cook Islands; in 1904 it was granted a separate administration, with its own resident commissioner and island council. In 1960 the first Niue Assembly was established, with an elected representative from each of the island's villages under the presidency of the resident commissioner. Further constitutional advances were put in place in the latter 1960s and the early 1970s. On

October 19, 1974, Niue became a self-governing Commonwealth country in free association with New Zealand; the latter remained constitutionally responsible for Niue's defense and external relations, and undertook to provide budgetary support and development assistance. Executive authority is in the hands of the premier, assisted by three ministers; the Assembly has 20 members (14 of whom are village representatives, the remaining six being elected on a common roll). There is only one political organization, the Niue People's Action party, founded in 1987: Its principal concern has been to draw attention to the government's alleged economic mismanagement. In November 1988 the premier of Niue was Sir Robert Rex: He had been the island's political leader since the early 1950s.

Niue exports limes, passion fruit, copra, papaw and honey—overwhelmingly to New Zealand. The value of commodity imports (food products, manufactures, fuel) exceeds the value of commodity exports by over four times. More than 80% of the labor force works in the government sector, funded by grants-in-aid from New Zealand. The economy has suffered a serious drain of population in recent decades: Far more Niueans reside in New Zealand than in Niue. almost all the families on the island are self-sufficient in food.

A social security scheme, introduced by the Niue government in 1974, now provides a modest pension for Niueans from the age of 60. All medical and dental treatment, including hospitalization, is provided without charge, as those services are subsidized by the New Zealand administration. There is a hospital at Alofi and clinics in three of the large villages. Education is free and compulsory between the ages of six and 14. In 1987 there were seven primary schools (with a total of 392 pupils) and one secondary school (with 310 pupils). Instruction is in Niuean and English. For tertiary education, Niuean school graduates seek opportunities elsewhere in the Pacific or (to a smaller extent) in New Zealand.

The island has a weekly newspaper, *Tohi Tala Niue,* which is published in English and Niuean by Information and Broadcasting Services, Central Office, Government of Niue. Information and Broadcasting Services also operates Radio Sunshine Niue, broadcasting in Niuean and English. In 1984 there were an estimated 900 radio sets in use.

PALAU

The Republic of Palau (or Belau) consists of more than 340 islands, in a chain (lying roughly northeast/southwest) about 404 miles/650 km. long. It is situated in the west central Pacific, and together with the Federated States of Micronesia forms the archipelago of the Caroline Islands. The total land area is 191 sq. miles/494 sq. km. The average annual temperature on the principal island of Koror is 81°F/27.2°C, with only a slight monthly variation; the average annual rainfall on Koror is 147 in/3,729 mm., with substantial seasonal variation. The total population at a census taken in 1980 was 12,116; in 1987 it was estimated to be approximately 14,000. Most of the population lives on the island of Koror, on which the capital is located. A number of local dialects within the Malayo-Polynesian language family are spoken through the territory; English is almost universally spoken. The population is predominantly Christian, mainly adherents of the Roman Catholic church.

The modern history of Palau up to 1978 is most effectively read as the history of the present-day Federated States of Micronesia: the establishment of Spanish sovereignty in the mid-1880s; German purchase in 1899; Japanese occupation from 1914; the creation of the Trust Territory of the Pacific Islands, under U.S. administration, in 1947. In 1978 the population of Palau chose to separate from the other components of the Trust Territory of the Pacific Islands. A locally drafted constitution, prepared in early 1979, incorporated provisions for the banning of nuclear materials from Palau. This constitution was overwhelmingly approved by Palauans in a referendum held in July 1979—and approved again in referenda held in October 1979 and in July 1980. In August 1982 the United States signed a Compact of Free Association with the Republic of Palau, under which the latter would be responsible for its internal and foreign affairs, while the United States would be responsible for defense and security; in addition, the United States would undertake to provide regular economic assistance to the territory. Crucially, the compact would have given the United States tax-free military use of one-third of Palau's territory: The American determination to establish a major military presence (a possible alternative to the bases in the Philippines, should the Philippine administration demand their removal) is clearly in conflict with Palau's nuclear-free constitution. Further referenda, court writs, alleged physical intimidation on the part of pronuclear Palauans, a campaign of arson and bombing, the reduction of U. S. financial assistance to the Palau government in an attempt to instigate a payroll crisis failed to resolve the conflict. The locally drafted constitution prepared in early 1979 came into effect on January 1, 1981. But as of late 1988 the Republic of Palau was the only remaining component of the Trust Territory of the Pacific Islands. In November 1988 the high commissioner (appointed by the president of the United States with the consent and approval of the U.S. Senate; and retaining only that authority necessary to carry out the obligations and responsibilities required of the United States under the terms of the 1947 trusteeship agreement) was Janet McCoy; the president was Ngiratkel Eptison.

The long delay in implementing the Compact of Free Association (and the prospect that it may never be implemented) has caused a grave financial crisis for Palau, as it has made the territory ineligible for the substantial American payments that were contingent upon that status. The Palauan administration found itself unable to repay a major debt to a consortium of foreign banks, incurred in the construction of a power station; faced with legal action, in 1986 the government arranged repayment through the issue of tax-exempt bonds. Budget deficits have been consistently incurred since the early 1980s, as the government has increased expenditure (there has been a notable rise in the pay scales for government employees) without securing new sources of revenue. A number of American companies have withdrawn from the territory (including Van Camp, which had operated a cannery on Malakal); but Japanese companies have moved in, particular attention being paid to the development of tourist facilities for a mass Japanese market. Japanese industrial interests have also sought to create a major installation for transferring and storing oil from supertankers coming from the Middle East; strong local resistance has halted the proposal, although a settlement of the compact dispute with the United States might signal its revival.

There are two news publications: *Rengel Belau,* a biweekly with a circulation of 2,000; and *The Palau Weekly,* which has a circulation of 1,000. There is one radio station (WSZB), which broadcasts American, Japanese and Micronesian music; and there is one television station (WALU).

SOLOMON ISLANDS

The Solomon Islands comprises six principal islands (Choiseul, Santa Isabel, New Georgia, Malaita, Guadalcanal, San Cristobal) and numerous small ones, located in the southwest Pacific. The total land area is 10,639 sq. miles/27,556 sq. km. Daytime temperatures are usually above 79°F/26°C; average annual rainfall in the capital, Honiara (on Guadalcanal), is 89in/ 2,250 mm., but it reaches as high as 315 in/8,000 mm. in some parts of the territory. At a census taken in November 1986 the total population (provisionally enumerated) was 285,796; Honiara, on the island of Guadalcanal, had a provisionally estimated population of 30,499. The official language is English; some 87 different vernacular forms are also to be found through the territory. More than 95% of the population is Christian: According to the 1976 census, some 34% of the population belonged to the Anglican Diocese of Melanesia; 19% were Roman Catholics; and 17% belonged to the South Seas Evangelical church.

In the second half of the 19th century, the Solomon Islands attracted the attention of traders, whalers, missionaries and labor recruiters (seeking workers for plantations in Fiji and Queensland). It was the evils of that labor trade that caused Great Britain to declare a protectorate over the southern Solomon Islands in 1893. In 1898 and 1899 outlying islands to the south were added to the protectorate; and in 1900 several islands in the northern Solomon Islands (which had been a German protectorate since 1885) were ceded to Britain (in exchange for Britain's withdrawal from Western Samoa). The territory was now known as the British Solomon Islands Protectorate. The islands were invaded by Japanese forces in 1942 but, after fierce fighting, were recaptured by the Americans the following year. After the war the returning British administration reestablished and expanded the Advisory Council, which consisted of the resident commissioner as president and a number of nominated members. In 1960 the Advisory council was replaced by a Legislative Council and an Executive Council. Initially, all members were appointed, but from 1964 on the Legislative Council included an increasingly large elective element. A new constitution was adopted in April 1974: It instituted a single Legislative Assembly, which chose a chief minister, who appointed a council of ministers. The territory was officially renamed the Solomon Islands in June 1975; on January 2, 1976, it became internally self-governing; on July 7, 1978, the Solomon Islands became independent.

Under the 1978 independence constitution, legislative power is vested in the unicameral National Parliament, composed of 38 members elected by universal adult suffrage; executive power is held by the cabinet, which is responsible to the National Parliament; the prime minister is elected by and from the members of the National Parliament; cabinet ministers are appointed by the governor-general, on the recommendation of the prime minister, from members of the National Parliament. In November 1988 the cabinet comprised a coalition of the United party, the Nationalist Front for Progress and a number of independents; the prime minister was Ezekiel Alebua (of the United party); the governor-general was Sir George Lepping. The head of state is Queen Elizabeth II.

The established export of the Solomon Islands has long been copra, but from the 1960s on a substantial measure of export diversification has been achieved. In 1986 fish accounted for 46% of the total value of commodity exports, timber for 31%, cacao for 6%, palm oil and kernels for 5%, copra for 5%. In 1986 the Solomon Islands had a modest trade surplus. The agricultural development of the territory has been seriously hampered by its poor transportation network: Development plans have given priority to infrastructural investment. The Solomon Islands has received considerable development aid, notably from Great Britain, Australia, New Zealand, the World Bank, the Asian Development Bank and Japan; some concern has been expressed over the territory's aid dependence and its high level of external debt. Approximately 90% of the population depends on subsistence agriculture (and, to a lesser extent, subsistence fishing). In June 1985 the total number of wage earners was just 24,796.

Social security legislation provides for the payment of compensation for accidents at work; there is a National Provident Fund. In June 1982 there were eight hospitals (six were government hospitals, two were church owned), 122 clinics, four health centers, and 31 health and village aid posts; there were 38 doctors and 851 nurses and aides. Approximately two-thirds of children of school age receive formal schooling, mainly in government schools. In 1987 there were 462 primary schools (with a total enrollment of 42,374 pupils) and 20 secondary schools (with a total enrollment of 5,604 pupils). There are two teacher training colleges and a technical institute; in 1977 the Solomon Islands Centre of the University of the Pacific was opened in Honiara.

The news publications include: *Island Reporter,* 2,000, weekly; *Solomon Nius,* a weekly published by the government information service, with a circulation of 4,000; *Solomon Star,* 3,000 weekly; and *Solomons Toktok,* a weekly published in Pidgin, with a circulation of 3,000. The Solomon Islands Broadcasting Corporation, an independent statutory body, operates a radio service in English and Pidgin. In 1987 there were an estimated 40,500 radio sets in use.

TONGA

Tonga comprises 172 islands (of which only 36 are permanently inhabited), divided into three groups (Vava'u, Ha'apai, Tongatapu) located in the south central Pacific. The total land area is 289 sq. miles/748 sq. km. The average temperature in the capital, Nuku'alofa on the island of Tongatapu, is 70°F/21°C. The average annual rainfall on Tongatapu is 59 in/1,500 mm.; mean humidity is about 77%; temperatures are higher and rainfall heavier in the northern part of the territory. At a census taken in November 1986 the total population was 94,535, of whom 63,614 lived on the island of Tongatapu. At the November 1986 census Nuku'alofa had a population of 28,899. The people of Tonga speak a local dialect within the Polynesian language family and, usually, English. Almost the entire population is Christian. The Free Wesleyan church of Tonga (founded in 1826), with 36,500 adherents, has had a profound influence; there are also substantial communities of Anglicans, Roman Catholics and Mormons.

Many centuries before Europeans intruded into Tonga the indigenous society had established an enduring lineage of paramount rulers, designated "kings" by the early European visitors. In November 1875 King Siaosi (George) Tupou introduced a constitution that guaranteed rights to life, property and worship, and defined the form of government in ways that set limits to monarchical power. Toward the end of the century Tonga experienced serious civil unrest—due in large part to an excessive exercise of political authority on the part of the Rev. Shirley Baker, who had come to Tonga as a Wesleyan missionary and who became premier in 1879 under the aging King George Tupou. The unrest prompted British fears that another European power might intervene in the territory; consequently, in 1900 a treaty was negotiated whereby Tonga agreed not to conclude agreements with other powers, and to transact its foreign relations through the British agent and consul. Queen Salote Tupou III succeeded to the throne in 1918 and ruled Tonga until her death in 1965. In 1967 Tonga secured increased control over its internal affairs; it became fully independent, within the Commonwealth, on June 4, 1970.

The constitution is based on that granted in 1875 by King George Tupou: Within it the monarch exercises considerable power. The government structure consists of the sovereign; the Privy Council, which is appointed by the sovereign and consists of the sovereign and the cabinet; the cabinet; and a Legislative Assembly, which consists of the speaker, the members of the cabinet, nine nobles elected by the 33 nobles of Tonga, and nine representatives elected by all Tongans aged 21 and over. The Legislative Assembly must meet at least once every year. In November 1988 the sovereign was King Taufa'ahau Tupou IV, who had succeeded to the throne on December 15, 1965; the prime minister was Prince Fatafehi Tu'ipelehake.

In the financial year 1984–85, agriculture, forestry and fishing accounted for 40.5% of GDP. The two principal crops have for some time been coconuts and bananas, but recently vanilla has emerged as an important item of cultivation and export. By far the major export is coconut oil; 1986 also saw substantial export of watermelons and vanilla. The principal export markets are New Zealand and Australia. Tonga runs a substantial trade deficit: In 1986 the total value of commodity imports was almost seven times the total value of commodity exports. The visible trade deficit is, however, offset by earnings from tourism (there were 81,199 visitors in 1985) and remittances from Tongans working overseas. The high level of unemployment—estimated to affect some 20% of the work force in 1984—has encouraged a striking volume of temporary emigration, notably to New Zealand. Tonga has received substantial foreign aid, the principal donors being the United Kingdom, New Zealand, Australia, West Germany, Japan and the Asian Development Bank.

Legislation for the provision of social security benefits was being planned by the administration in 1983; the government and some of the statutory bodies already provided retirement benefits for their employees. In the early 1980s there were four general hospitals, 12 health centers and 30 public health nurse clinics; there was, however, a general shortage of trained medical staff. Free state schooling is compulsory for children between the ages of six and 14. In 1985 there were 100 government primary schools and 12 church primary schools—with a total of 17,019 pupils; and four government secondary schools, 49 church secondary schools and one private secondary school—with a total of 14,655 pupils. In addition, there were 10 technical and vocational colleges (with a total of 430 students) and a teacher training college (with 126 students).

The news publications include: *Kele'a,* which focuses on economic and political issues and has a circulation of 10,000; and *Tonga Chronicle/Kalonikali Tonga,* a government-sponsored weekly with a circulation of 6,000 (Tongan) and 1,200 (English). The Tonga Broadcasting Commission, an independent statutory body, provides radio broadcasts in Tongan and English. In 1986 there were an estimated 55,000 radio sets in use in the territory.

TUVALU

Tuvalu (prior to October 1975 known as the Ellice Islands) comprises nine small atolls, situated in the central Pacific. The total land area is 10 sq. miles/26 sq. km. The mean annual temperature is 86°F/30°C; the average annual rainfall is 138 in/3,500 mm. At a minicensus held in June 1985 the total population was 8,229; the capital, on Funafuti Atoll, had a population of 2,810. The indigenous language is a member of the Polynesian family, closely related to Samoan. Virtually the entire population are adherents of the Church of Tuvalu (Ekalesia Tuvalu), founded in 1861 and derived from the Congregationalist foundation of the London Missionary Society.

From the early 1860s on the islands that now comprise Tuvalu were the focus of attention from labor recruiters/slave traders and from missionaries. In 1892 a British protectorate was declared over the territory; it was administratively tied to the Gilbert Islands (present-day Kiribati) to the north. In 1915, having secured the formal approval of the indigenous governments, Great Britain annexed the Gilbert Islands and the Ellice Islands; as of January 12, 1916, the two island groups became the Gilbert and Ellice Islands Colony (GEIC). During the war in the Pacific the Ellice Islands remained outside the immediate zone of hostilities, although the Americans established a base on Funafuti in 1942. Constitutional reform, establishing and later extending the involvement of the population of the GEIC in government, began effectively in the early 1960s. (This process is described above in the section on Kiribati.) But as Great Britain began to prepare the territory for self-government there was increasing pressure within the Ellice Islands for secession: The core influence here was the Ellice Islanders' anxiety over their minority position as Polynesians in a colony dominated by the Micronesians of the Gilbert Islands. In a referendum held in 1974, over 90% of the population of the Ellice Islands voted for separation; on October 1, 1975, the Ellice Islands (taking the name Tuvalu) became a separate British colony. On October 1, 1978, Tuvalu became an independent state.

Under the independence constitution of 1978 parliament is composed of 12 members, elected by universal adult suffrage for four years (subject to dissolution). The cabinet, directly responsible to parliament, consists of the prime minister and the other ministers. The prime minister is elected by parliament; up to four other ministers are appointed by the governor-general from among the members of parliament, after consultation with the prime minister. There are no political parties. In November 1988 the governor-general was Sir Tupua Leupena; the prime minister was Dr. Tomasi Puapua. The head of state is Queen Elizabeth II. In mid-1989, Bikenibeu Paeniu became prime minister.

In 1983 the GDP of Tuvalu, at $A3.8 million, was the smallest of any independent state; in 1986 Tuvalu was placed on the U.N. list of least-developed countries. The only significant export is copra; copra production in the early 1980s averaged just over 240 metric tons per year. There is the prospect of income from the licensing of foreign (notably American) fishing vessels that wish to operate within Tuvalu's exclusive waters; the sale of Tuvalu postage stamps, however, an important source of foreign exchange in the early 1980s, has recently contracted. In 1983 the value of commodity imports was more than double GDP and approximately 20 times the value of commodity exports. Britain provided substantial budgetary aid in the years following independence, but by the close of the 1980s this was being phased out (with British contributions to capital projects continuing). Tuvalu receives development aid from Britain, New Zealand, Australia, Canada, Japan, West Germany, the United States and North Korea. Most of the population supports itself by subsistence cultivation; in 1979, of the 4,952 inhabitants aged 15 years and over, 3,456 were engaged in village economy.

A general hospital at Funafuti was opened in 1978; each island has a state-registered nurse and a maternity child-health nurse. In 1984 there were 11 primary schools (with a total of 1,349 pupils) and one secondary school (with 243 pupils); for further and higher education, Tuvaluans must leave the islands.

The principal news publication is *Sikuleo o Tuvalu* (in Tuvaluan)/*Tuvalu Echoes* (in English); it is published fortnightly by the Broadcasting and Information Division, and has a circulation of 150 in Tuvaluan and 250 in English. Radio Tuvalu broadcasts in Tuvaluan and English. In 1985 there were an estimated 2,500 radio sets in use through the territory.

280

VANUATU

The Republic of Vanuatu (prior to July 1980 known as the New Hebrides) comprises some 80 islands, situated in the southwest Pacific. It has a total land area of 4,707 sq. miles/12,190 sq. km. At the capital, Port-Vila on the main island of Efaté, the average year-round humidity is 83%; the average annual rainfall is approximately 91 in/2,300 mm. In mid-1986 the total population was officially estimated at 140,154. Port-Vila had an officially estimated population of 14,184 in January 1986. A variety of Melanesian dialects are spoken throughout the territory; the national language is Bislama and the official languages are Bislama, English and French; the principal languages of instruction are English and French. According to a census taken in 1979, over 80% of the population were Christians; the largest number of whom were Presbyterians, followed by Anglicans and then Roman Catholics.

From the mid-19th century on the islands that now constitute Vanuatu were the focus of increasing attention from missionaries, labor recruiters, traders and settlers. In the closing decades of the century both British and French interests were represented in the island group; in 1886–88 Great Britain and France created a Joint Naval Commission to safeguard order in Vanuatu. In 1906 an Anglo-French condominium was established to govern the territory. During the period of the condominium, the administration had three elements—the British structure, the French structure and the condominium (joint) departments: In practice this implied two official languages, two police forces, three public administrations, three courts of law, three currencies, three national budgets, two resident commissioners, and two district commissioners in each district of the New Hebrides. During the war in the Pacific the territory became an important U.S. military installation. In the postwar period native movements (notably a messianic cause, the John Frum movement) and indigenous modern political organization began to emerge; important here was Na-Griamel, which from the late 1960s began to campaign against the alienation of land and then for independence. In 1974–75 a representative assembly (with 42 members, of whom 29 were directly elected) was established, but this did not quell local aspirations. A measure of self-government was introduced early in 1978; independence was achieved on July 30, 1980.

The closing years of condominium rule and the following years of political independence constituted a period of considerable political instability and, on occasions, of open political violence. Among the contributory influences were divisions between the departing colonial powers (and allegations of attempted French intervention in the affairs of the independent state), and serious separationist ambitions on the part of the island of Espiritu Santo (allegedly encouraged by French colons and assisted by private American business interests). The independent government sought to establish diplomatic relations with the Soviet Union and with Libya; it provided continued support for the Kanak National Liberation Front in its efforts to secure independence for New Caledonia.

281

Under the independence constitution of 1980, legislative authority rests with a single-chamber parliament, which has 46 members elected on the basis of universal franchise through an electoral mechanism that includes an element of proportional representation. Executive power rests with the Council of Ministers, which consists of the prime minister (elected by parliament from among its members) and other ministers (appointed by the prime minister from among the members of parliament). At the general election held in November 1987 the Vanuaaku Pati, advocating "Melanesian socialism," won 26 of the 46 seats and thus remained the ruling party; the Union of Moderate Parties picked up the remaining 20 seats. In November 1988 the president was Ati George Sokomanu; the prime minister was Father Walter Hayde Lini.

Vanuatu's principal exports are copra (accounting for 25% of the total value of commodity exports in 1986), fish (20%), cacao (11%), and meat and meat products (8%). The South Pacific Fishing Company, a Japanese-controlled concern, receives tuna caught in local waters for freezing at its storage plant on Espiritu Santo; meat export consists of beef, shipped from the abattoir on Espiritu Santo. Tourism has emerged as an important source of foreign earnings (there were 17,500 visitors in 1986), and Port-Vila has developed as a financial center, with facilities as a tax haven and provision for ship registration under a flag of convenience. Vanuatu has had a persistent, substantial trade deficit throughout the 1980s. There have been a number of devaluations of the vatu since mid-1985. Approximately 80% of the population are engaged in subsistence agriculture.

In the mid-1980s there were 11 hospitals; clinics and dispensaries offer basic medical facilities in the more remote districts. In 1982 there were 224 English-language primary schools (with 12,836 pupils) and 105 French-language primary schools (with 9,894 pupils); there were eight secondary schools with English as the medium of instruction (with a total enrollment of 1,085 pupils) and three French-language secondary schools (with 867 pupils). In the mid-1980s the Vanuatu Technical Institute had 293 students; the Vanuatu Teachers College had 58 students in 1982. In 1987 there were plans for the construction of a University of the South Pacific center in Port-Vila, construction to be financed by the New Zealand government.

Vanuatu Weekly, which appears in Bislama, English and French, has a circulation of 1,700. The government-owned Radio Vanuatu broadcasts in English, French and Bislama. In 1986 there were an estimated 18,000 radio receivers in the territory.

WESTERN SAMOA

Western Samoa comprises two large islands (Savaii and Upolu) and seven small ones (of which five are uninhabited), situated in the south central Pacific. The total land area is 1,093 sq. miles/2,831 sq. km. The average annual rainfall for the capital, Apia, on the northern coast of the island of Upolu, is 118 in/3,000 mm.; the south and southeast areas receive from

197 in/5,000 mm. to 276 in/7,000 mm. each year. At a census taken in 1986 the total population was 158,940, of whom 114,815 lived on Upolu and the adjacent small islands. Apia had a population of 33,170 at a census taken in 1981. The Samoan language belongs to the Polynesian family; English is widely spoken and is used in government departments and in commerce. Almost the entire population professes Christianity. More than 60% of the people are Protestant; there are substantial Anglican and Roman Catholic communities.

From the mid-19th century the Samoan Islands were the focus of increasingly tense commercial and strategic rivalry between Germany, Great Britain and the United States. In 1899 the three powers reached an agreement whereby Germany was permitted to annex Western Samoa, the United States would exercise sovereignty over Eastern Samoa (now American Samoa) and Britain would renounce all ambitions in the area (in return for advantages elsewhere). With the outbreak of war in Europe in 1914, Western Samoa was taken from German administration by a New Zealand force. In 1920 the League of Nations granted a mandate over the territory to New Zealand. During the interwar decades there was considerable political tension: The Samoan traditional leaders simply did not accept the need for foreign administration, while the New Zealand mandate (led by military officers) appeared to be unprepared and ill suited for the exercise of authority in the culturally and politically sensitive circumstances of Western Samoa. In 1946 the United Nations, through its Trusteeship Council, assumed responsibility for the territory, with New Zealand as the administering power. In the mid-1950s an increasing measure of internal self-government was introduced. By late 1960 a draft independence constitution had been approved by the Samoan Constitutional Convention; a U.N.-supervised plebiscite in May 1961 demonstrated strong popular approval of the constitution and of the prospect of immediate independence. Western Samoa became an independent state on January 1, 1962.

Under the independence constitution of 1962, legislative authority rests with the Fono (Legislative Assembly). The Fono has 47 members; two members are elected by universal adult suffrage; the remaining 45 members are chosen by the *matai* (elected clan leaders/village chiefs) in 41 traditional constituencies. At a general election held in February 1988 the Human Rights Protection party, Western Samoa's first formal political party, won 24 of the 47 seats; the Christian Democratic party coalition, together with the Va'ai Kolone body of independents, won the remaining 23 seats. Executive power rests with the cabinet, consisting of the prime minister (who must have the support of the majority in the Fono) and eight ministers chosen by the prime minister. The decisions of the cabinet are subject to review by the Executive Council, which comprises the head of state and the cabinet. In November 1988 the head of state (O le Ao o le Malo) was Malietoa Tanumafili II; the prime minister was Tofilau Eti Alesana.

Approximately 90% of Western Samoa's export income comes from agricultural production, notably the cultivation of coconuts, cacao, taro and bananas but also coffee and timber. A substantial external income is provided by the remittances of Western Samoans working overseas (principally in New Zealand); there is also a modest tourism income (in 1983 Western Samoa had 36,717 visitors). In the 1980s the territory had to face a serious debt-servicing problem and severe shortages of foreign exchange; International Monetary Fund assistance in 1983–84 required the imposition of limits on government expenditure, import restriction and devaluation of the tala. There has been considerable investment (in part financed through international grants-in-aid) in the development of hydroelectric power; in addition there has been an emphasis on developing timber extraction, exploitation of the local waters for tuna and development of the coconut oil milling sector. Perhaps a majority of the population are engaged in subsistence agriculture.

The National Provident Fund provides social security payments (principally a lump sum payment and pension payments on retirement); contributions to the fund come from employers (who may recoup part of the contribution from employees earning above a minimum wage). In early 1982 there were eight hospitals, nine health centers and 14 subcenters in Western Samoa; there were 55 doctors. The education system of Western Samoa is based on the New Zealand system; at the primary level instruction is in Samoan, with a strong program in English; instruction at the intermediate and secondary levels is in English. The National University of Samoa was to open in mid-1987.

The news publications include: *The Samoa Observer,* weekly, 4,500; *The Samoa Times,* weekly, 3,000; and *Samoa Weekly,* 4,500. Each paper publishes in English and Samoan. *Savali,* a government publication, appears fortnightly; the Samoan edition has a circulation of 10,000, the English edition a circulation of 1,000. The government-owned Western Samoa Broadcasting Service, established in 1948, broadcasts in English and Samoan. In 1984 there were an estimated 70,000 radio receivers in the territory. The American Samoan television channel KVZK-TV is widely received in Western Samoa. In 1981 there were an estimated 2,500 television sets in use in Western Samoa.

PAKISTAN

Features: Pakistan is bounded on the west, northwest and north by Afghanistan and Iran. A tiny piece of Afghan territory called the Wakhan Corridor separates Pakistan from the Soviet Union. The northern highlands contain some of the world's most massive mountain ranges, most notably the Himalayas. The Himalayas merge with the Karakoram Mountain Range and the Pamirs in the northwest, while west of the Pamirs are the mountains of the Hindu Kush. Numerous passes run through these mountains, including the well-known Khyber Pass. Most elevations in this area are above 15,000 feet (50,000 m) and close to 70 peaks are above 22,000 feet (73,000 m). The Baluchistan Plateau is defined by the western ranges on the border of Afghanistan and stands approximately 3,000 to 4,000 feet (10,000–13,300 m). Pakistan borders the People's Republic of China on the northeast and India on the east. It is bounded on the south by the Arabian Sea. The Indus River enters Pakistan through the Baltistan Agency and flows southwest for a 1,000 miles (3,300 m) until it reaches the Arabian Sea. All of Pakistan's major rivers flow into the Indus. They are the Kabul, Jhelum, Chenab, Ravi, and Sutlej. The Thar Desert stretches along the India-Pakistan border southward to a desolate area of dispute known as the Rann of Kachchh.

Area: 310,403 sq. miles/803,943 sq. km.

Mean max. and min. temperatures: Lahore (31°35'N; 74°18'E) 54°F/12°C (Jan.) 88°F/31°C (May); Karachi (24°52'N; 67°03'E) 65°F/18°C (Jan.), 85°F/29°C (May).

Mean annual rainfall: 17 in/440 mm in the plains; up to 44 in/1,750 mm in northern hills.

Total population (1988): 103.8 million.

Chief towns and populations: Lahore (3 million, est.), Karachi (9 million, est.), ISLAMABAD (250,000, est.).

Distribution: The average growth in 1980–87 was 2.9%. The urban population constitutes 28% of the total; 43% of the population is under 15

285

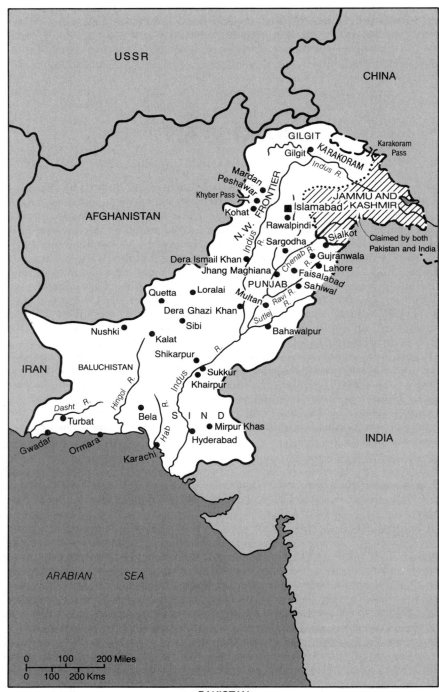

USSR

CHINA

GILGIT

Karakoram
Pass

Gilgit

KARAKORAM

Indus R.

AFGHANISTAN

Mardan
Peshawar

N. W. FRONTIER

Khyber Pass

JAMMU AND
KASHMIR

Kohat

Islamabad

Indus R.

Rawalpindi

Claimed by both
Pakistan and India

Sargodha

Sialkot

Chenab R.

Gujranwala

Dera Ismail Khan

Lahore

Jhang Maghiana

Faisalabad

Quetta

Loralai

PUNJAB

Sahiwal

Multan

Ravi R.

Dera Ghazi Khan

Sutlej R.

Sibi

Nushki

Bahawalpur

Kalat

Shikarpur

Indus R.

BALUCHISTAN

Hingol R.

Sukkur

Khairpur

Dasht R.

Hab R.

S I N D

Bela

Mirpur Khas

Turbat

Hyderabad

INDIA

Gwadar

Ormara

Karachi

IRAN

ARABIAN   SEA

| 0 | 100 | 200 Miles |
| 0 | 100 | 200 Kms |

PAKISTAN

years of age. The Punjab and Sind are the most populous provinces, containing close to 80% of the population.

Language: The official languages are Urdu and English. About 8% of the population claims Urdu as its native tongue, although close to 80% can understand Urdu. Of the total population, 63% speak Punjabi; 16% speak either Baluchi, Pashto, or Brahui; and 12% speak Sindhi.

Religion: Pakistan was proclaimed an Islamic Republic in 1956. About 97% of the population is Muslim, with the majority belonging to the Sunni sect and approximately 10% belong to the Shiite sect. Also, 1.3% are Christian and 1.6% Hindu.

CONSTITUTIONAL SYSTEM

Constitution: The constitution of 1973 has been amended many times to reflect the dominance of Pakistan's previous military rule. Many of the democratic rights guaranteed to citizens were suspended following the 1977 imposition of martial law. The constitution states that Pakistan is an Islamic republic and that Muslims are able to live their lives "in accordance with the teachings and writings of Islam, as set out in the Holy Qur'an and Sunnah."

Head of state: Acting president Ghulam Ishaq Khan. *Prime minister:* Ghulam Mustafa Jatuj.

Executive: The president is bound to act on the advice of the prime minister and is elected for a five-year term in a joint session of the legislature. He must be at least 45 years old and Muslim. Presidential orders, if countersigned by the prime minister, may declare a state of emergency, dissolve the National Assembly, appoint the chief justice and other justices to the Supreme Court and appoint provincial governors, among other things. The prime minister is the chief executive officer of the central government, elected by a majority of the total membership of the National Assembly. If no such majority exists, the president may invite a member of the party that carries the most seats to form a government. The prime minister appoints ministers of state and federal ministers from among the members of Parliament. He or she is responsible for both domestic and foreign affairs.

Legislature: Pakistan has a bicameral legislature. The lower house is called the National Assembly, and has 207 members who are elected directly and serve five-year terms. Twenty seats in the National Assembly are allocated to women and 10 to minorities. The upper house, called the Senate, has 87 members who serve six-year terms. The Senate acts largely in an advisory capacity, but reserves the right to send back to the National Assembly any legislation with which it disagrees. In 1982 the Majlis-i-Shura was established as a consultative committee to ensure that the democratic system evolves in accordance with the tenets of Islam. At this point, its role is strictly advisory.

Political parties: Political activity has been restricted periodically since the creation of Pakistan. Following the imposition of martial law in 1977, all political parties were suspended and then subsequently banned in 1979. In the spring of 1988, President Zia announced "partyless" elections for November. After his death in August of that year, acting president Ghulam Ishaq Khan referred the issue to the courts, which declared that prohibition of parties in elections was unconstitutional. In the November 1988 elections, the Pakistan People's party (PPP) won 93 seats and named Benazir Bhutto as prime minister. The Islamic Democratic Alliance won 55 seats, the Muhajir Qaumi Movement won 13 seats and independents accounted for 27 seats.

Local government: Pakistan is composed of four provinces: Sind, North-West Frontier, Punjab and Baluchistan, each with its own provincial assembly. Government on the provincial level is similar to that on the federal level. A governor is appointed by the president of Pakistan. He must act on the advice of the chief minister of the province, who is elected by a majority of the provincial assembly. Members of the provincial assembly are elected for a term of five years. The 1973 constitution stipulates the size of each provincial assembly, which is as follows: Baluchistan 40, North-West Frontier 80, Punjab 240, Sind 100.

Judicial system: The Supreme Court is the highest court in Pakistan, and its juridistictions are original, appellate and advisory in civil and criminal cases as well as in mediation between the central government and provincial governments or between provincial governments. The provincial High Courts have original and appellate jurisdiction in certain criminal cases. Conciliation courts at the village level mediate minor disputes. Constitutional amendments have restricted the effectiveness of the court system in Pakistan. A 1979 amendment established the supremacy of military courts and denied the High Courts the ability to overrule any judgment handed down by a military court. Article 199 denied the courts the ability to question any of the government's actions during the administration of martial law.

RECENT HISTORY

The two-nation theory: Pakistan came into being on August 14, 1947, created out of the Muslim majority areas of British India. These were the provinces of East Bengal, Baluchistan, Sind, North-West Frontier, and a divided Punjab. The creation of two separate nations when the British departed has its roots in the nationalist movements of the early 20th century. The Muslim League had been founded in 1906, in an effort to further the interests of the Indian Muslim community over and above those of the Indian National Congress, an organization many Muslims believed was only serving the interests of Hindus. In his 1930 presidential address to the Muslim League, Sir Muhammad Iqbal first articulated the idea of a separate state for Muslims. It was not until 1940, however, that the Muslim League, led by Muhammad Ali Jinnah, formally adopted the notion at a conference held in Lahore. The Lahore Resolution stated that the areas of Muslim majority in the northeast and northwest of India should be constituted to form autonomous and sovereign independent states.

Forming a nation: At the time of independence, no one could have foreseen the tragedy that would come with the migration of Hindus and Muslims to India and Pakistan. Approximately 8 million refugees, who came to be known as *muhajirs,* came to Pakistan, while close to 6 million left Pakistan for India. Widespread rioting occurred during partition and as many as 250,000 people were killed. In addition to the chaos of partition, there was the issue of accession of princely states to either India or Pakistan. These princely states had retained limited autonomy under British rule, and at time of partition were allowed to choose whether to join India or Pakistan. Pakistan peacefully acquired the princely states of Dir, Chitral, Swat, Amb and Hunza. However, the state of Jammu and Kashmir proved more difficult. It had a Hindu ruler and a majority Muslim population. The Hindu ruler vacillated and finally an uprising by North-West Frontier tribesmen occurred. The ruler eventually acceded to India, which saw this disturbance as an opportunity to move in and restore order. Muhammad Ali Jinnah, now governor-general of Pakistan, refused to acknowledge India's claim to the territory and initiated a military response. The first Indo-Pakistani war was temporarily resolved in January 1949 by a U.N. cease-fire. Under the terms, 38% of Jammu and Kashmir remained under Pakistani control.

In the late forties, Pakistan was confronted with the task of creating a government bureaucracy. Muhammad Ali Jinnah, the head of the Pakistan nationalist movement and known as "Quaid-e-Azam" (the Great Leader), became the governor-general, thus combining the ceremonial duties of a head of state with the effective power of a chief executive. Jinnah also was the president of the constituent assembly. He was not able to institutionalize the Pakistani polity owing to his untimely death in September 1948. The duties embodied in the position of governor-general were divided among his three successors. Khivaja Nazimuddin, chief minister of East Pakistan, became governor-general, and Liaquat Ali Khan became the first prime minister. Maulvi Tamizuddin was elected president of the constituent assembly. Liaquat Ali Khan was assassinated in 1951, allegedly by a group in the military that may have felt the government was not aggressive enough on the issue of Kashmir. Subsequent shifting of various political personalities to various positions soon brought allegations of corruption, smuggling and tax evasion while the 1953 imposition of martial law in Punjab brought political unrest. In 1955, the second constituent assembly enacted the West Pakistan Bill, which declared Pakistan a state of two equal units: the eastern wing and a united western wing. This caused tremendous unrest among the East Pakistanis, who constituted a larger proportion of the population than the West Pakistanis. They saw this as a direct effort by the West to dominate and exploit the East. The declining political situation caused the president, General Iskander Mirza, to declare martial law in October of

1956. The initial support of the army enabled Mirza to carry out his order, however the army eventually exiled him and General Ayub Khan was able to assume power.

The Ayub Khan Era, 1958–68: General Ayub Khan had been commander-in-chief of the army since 1951. His assumption of power in 1958 was justified by the need for stability. He immediately created a highly centralized form of government and implemented controls on the press, trade organizations and political parties. In 1959, he instituted the Basic Democratic Order, which was intended to promote economic development and social welfare through a hierarchy of locally elected councils. In 1962, he promulgated a new constitution that vested enormous power in the office of president. The president controlled the legislature, had protection from impeachment, controlled the budget, and had the ability to enact special emergency powers. He was to be elected by an electoral college of 80,000 "Basic Democrats." At this time, there was a ban on political parties and many of the "Basic Democrats" were implicit supporters of Ayub. In late 1962, the ban was lifted and a powerful opposition, headed by Muhammad Ali Jinnah's sister Fatima Jinnah, emerged. In preparation for the elections of 1965, Ayub Khan became president of a faction of the Muslim League and Fatima Jinnah represented a united opposition that supported complete restoration of parliamentary democracy. Ultimately, Ayub Khan won the election with an overall majority of 63%, although he was only able to obtain 53.1% of the vote in the eastern wing.

1965 Indo-Pakistani War: The Kashmiri issue of the late 1940s had reached only a temporary conclusion in the minds of many Pakistanis. Skirmishes along the U.N. cease-fire line broke out in 1965, and full-fledged conflict erupted in a wasteland along the Indo-Pakistani border known as the Rann of Kachchh. Neither India nor Pakistan were militarily or economically capable of carrying on a prolonged war, especially since economic and military aid was cut off by many Western nations with the advent of war. This was especially difficult for Pakistan, since the country depended on such aid to a greater extent than did India. A U.N. cease-fire was again declared in September 1965. In January 1966, President Ayub Khan and Indian Prime Minister Lal Bahadur Shastri agreed to meet in Tashkent, at the invitation of Soviet Premier Aleksei Kosygin. The Pakistanis did not expect Ayub to agree to continued Indian posession of the disputed territories and were angered and surprised when they learned that he had signed the Tashkent Agreement. The backlash resulted in rioting throughout Pakistan. The economic toll the war had taken, the unfavorable results of Tashkent, as well as the memory of Ayub's narrow victory in 1965 spurred Ayub's political opponents. In 1968, the two most prominent opponents were Zulfikar Ali Bhutto, who had formed the Pakistan People's party (PPP) in the West, and Mujibur Rahman (Mujib), leader of the Awami League in the East. Mujib first advanced his six-point program for increased autonomy of the eastern wing in 1968, and Bhutto capitalized on poor economic performance in the West in order to gain support. The two leaders were unable to reach a compromise in order to present a unified opposition, and in the light of increasing political polarization, the military stepped in to declare martial law in March of 1969. Ayub Khan was forced to resign and General Yahya Khan was declared the new president.

Yahya Khan Era and creation of Bangladesh: Yahya Khan moved quickly to militarize politics, yet paradoxically arranged for elections. He abolished the "one unit" concept of West Pakistan and reverted back to a system of four separate provinces. Elections for the National Assembly were scheduled for October 1970 on a one man—one vote system, thus granting East Pakistan an electoral majority. Elections were held in December of 1970, and Mujibur Rahman emerged with a mandate from the East for autonomy while Zulfikar Ali Bhutto came out with a victory in the West based upon a platform that encouraged socialism. Because of the vast differences between Bhutto and Mujib, as well as Mujib's undisputed majority, Bhutto boycotted the National Assembly meeting scheduled for March 1971. This caused outrage in the Eastern wing, and despite numerous talks among Yahya Khan, Bhutto and Mujib, a solution could not be found and Mujib called for a completely separate state of Bangladesh. India helped train the Bangladeshi rebel army, known as the Mukhti Bahini, and formally entered into war with Pakistan on December 4, 1971. Pakistan surrendered on December 16, when the city of Dacca fell and the nation of Bangladesh was created. Zulfikar Ali Bhutto became the president of a truncated Pakistan on December 20, 1971.

Zulfikar Bhutto Era, 1971–1977: Bhutto's primary aim as prime minister remained the restructuring of the Pakistan economy and increased dominance of the public sector. He also faced the challenge of restoring civilian and military morale to a country that had been bitterly defeated. A third constitution went into effect on August 14, 1973. It created a bicameral legislature in an effort to reassure the smaller provinces, which were afraid of Punjabi dominance, an effective voice in government. As Bhutto's administration progressed, it became clear that he wanted Pakistan to become a one-party state. An amendment to the constitution gave the executive the power to declare illegal any political party found "operating in manner prejudicial to the sovereignty or integrity of the country." Bhutto used this amendment to justify the dismantling of the Baluchi provincial government, which was in opposition to the PPP. In 1977, Bhutto declared that elections would be held, and a united opposition composed of both liberal and conservative parties quickly mobilized against him. The Pakistan National Alliance (PNA), had a large following and was expected to do well in the elections. When the returns came in and the PNA had won only 36 out of 192 seats, riots erupted and the election was declared rigged. The violence that ensued caused the army to intervene, and Bhutto was forced out of power on July 5, 1977, by General Zia ul-Haq. Investigations into Bhutto's administration were launched and he was eventually found guilty of orchestrating the murder of a political opponent. He was hanged on April 4, 1979.

Zia ul-Haq Era, 1979–88: General Zia initially promised new elections, stressing that the new political order would have to include a move to

291

greater Islamization in Pakistan. Zia initiated this move in February of 1979 by reinstating Islamic penal laws and imposing a *zakat* (poor tax) and *ushr* (tax on agricultural produce). He also implemented interest-free banking in accordance with the laws of Islam. In May 1980, a federal *Sharia* court replaced Shariat benches of High Courts. Citing the political instability that democratic campaigning was creating, Zia imposed martial law on October 16, 1979, and postponed elections indefinitely. Martial law was strengthened in May of 1980 by the imposition of Article 199, which amended the constitution to debar High Courts from ruling on the validity of martial-law regulations. In response to increased repression, nine opposition parties, including the PPP, united to form the Movement for the Restoration of Democracy. The group had limited success in garnering support, owing largely to internal disagreements. In December 1984, General Zia announced that a referendum would be held to seek popular approval of his process of Islamization and a five-year presidential term for himself. Running principally on the issue of Islam, Zia was able to gain widespread support in rural areas. Official results stated that of the 64% of the population who voted, 97% were in favor of his continued rule. Bolstered by this supposed show of support, Zia allowed national and provincial assembly elections on a nonparty basis in February 1985. In March 1985, Zia was sworn in as president and appointed Muhammad Khan Junejo as prime minister. Martial law was to be lifted by the end of the year, and in preparation, the 8th Amendment was passed, indemnifying all acts of the martial-law regime. Martial law was indeed lifted on December 30, 1985, and opposition parties were nominally allowed to operate. Benazir Bhutto, the daughter of Zulfikar Ali Bhutto and new leader of the PPP, returned to Pakistan from exile in April 1986.

Events took a surprising turn on May 29, 1988, when General Zia unexpectedly dismissed Prime Minister Junejo and dissolved the national and provincial assemblies. Zia justified these actions by citing incidences of corruption and a slowdown in the Islamization process. Observers cite Junejo's increasing exertion of political independence at the expense of Zia's programs. His plans to reprimand the military for the Ojhi ammunition-dump disaster, in which hundreds of people died, caused serious disagreement with General Zia. Zia promised elections within 90 days, but they were inevitably postponed until November. Benazir Bhutto began actively campaigning for the PPP and started to develop a large following. Events took an even more surprising turn on August 17, 1988, when the C-130 transport plane carrying General Zia, the U.S. ambassador and numerous Pakistani military officers mysteriously crashed, killing all aboard.

Rise of Benazir Bhutto: Immediately after Zia's death, Ghulam Ishaq Khan, president of the Senate, became acting president of Pakistan. Elections were to proceed on schedule and political parties were allowed to participate. Benazir Bhutto's challenge came in trying to reassure the military and political elite that a return of the PPP would not result in a return to socialist policies. She also needed to reassure the general population that she would bring a welcome change from the status quo. The *ulama* (religious leadership), which had flourished under Zia, needed to be convinced of her piety as a Muslim. She agreed to an arranged marriage and was careful to appear veiled before crowds, in an effort to counter the image of a person influenced by Western mores and attitudes, with little understanding of Islamic values. On election day the PPP won 93 seats. Since no party had an absolute majority, the president was required to select the prime minister. On November 31, 1988, Ishaq Khan invited Benazir Bhutto to form a government. At 35, Benazir Bhutto became one of the youngest leaders of any country, and the first woman to lead an Islamic state. The constraints upon her appear enormous, and it remains to be seen what shape her administration will take.

ECONOMY

Background: Since its inception in 1947, Pakistan has focused on building a nation that has a sound industrial base and shifting the economic emphasis from agriculture to manufacturing. Early economic planners sought to achieve growth through a private-sector economy. There was a brief directional interlude during the administration of Zulfikar Ali Bhutto (1972–78) when, in an effort to more equitably distribute income, increased attention was given to the public sector. Unfortunately, owing to a number of factors, the growth of the gross domestic product (GDP) declined from a high of 6.7% in the 1960s to 3.7% between 1970 and 1977. The decline can be attributed in part to a tapering off of the dramatic increases in agricultural output during the "green revolution" of the late 1960s. Bhutto's nationalization of some industries also discouraged private investors. With the return of a military government, the GDP resumed a high growth rate of 6.2% between 1978 and 1983. In 1987–88, GDP growth was 5.7%. Per capita gross national product (GNP) was U.S. $390. Foreign debt is currently $1.3 billion, and the account deficit on balance of payments is $1.07 billion. In the early 1980s, the Pakistani economy was affected by General Zia ul-Haq's general move toward Islamization. Most banks carry interest-free deposit accounts, and since 1980, the *zakat* has been imposed on the wealthy in order to provide for the poor. The newly elected government of Benazir Bhutto has stated it will not move toward greater nationalization. With a population increasing at an annual rate of roughly 3% and gradually declining GDP growth, as well as prospects for cuts in civilian and military aid as the war in Afghanistan ends, the economy of Pakistan is currently in a state of transition.

Agriculture: In 1987–88, agriculture contributed 24.8% to the GDP and employed approximately half the population. Of a total land area of 198 million acres/80 million ha., 48 million acres/19.4 million ha. are cultivated. The major crops in 1987–88 were wheat (12.65 million tons), rice (3.27 million tons), cotton (8.9 million bales) and sugarcane (31.24 million tons). The annual rate of agricultural growth from 1973 to 1983 was 3.4%. The political administrations of this period attempted to stimulate output in various ways. In the mid-1970s, Zulfikar Bhutto implemented

293

land reforms in a scheme designed to take land out of the hands of large landlords and redistribute it to smaller farmers. The state also extended subsidized credit and price-support programs during this time. In the 1980s, General Zia moved away from this strategy and restored the natural price of such items as fertilizers and pesticides. The Indus River provides Pakistan with an irrigation system that enables it to cultivate much land that would not otherwise be farmable. An agreement signed with India gives Pakistan access to the western tributaries of the Indus—the Jhelum and Chenab rivers. Punjab and Sind, the provinces adjacent to the Indus River basin, are the most agriculturally productive.

Industry: At independence in 1947, Pakistan had virtually no industrial base. Today, industry accounts for 20% of the GDP and is enjoying a steady rate of growth. In 1987–88, Pakistan's major industries were cotton cloth (335 million sq. yards/281 million sq. m.), cotton yarn (1,500 million pounds/685.5 million kg.), cement (7.072 million tons), and vegetable ghee (685,000 tons). About 90% of industry is concentrated in the provinces of Punjab and Sind. In the late 1960s, the private sector was dominant, and a large concentration of wealth and power was in the hands of 22 families. These 22 families, it was discovered, owned 22% of industrial capital, 80% of banking and 97% of insurance. The administration of Zulfikar Bhutto called for the nationalization of 10 major companies, including iron and steel, metals, chemicals and cement. Industrial output during this time fell from 7% in the late 1960s to 2.3% between 1970 and 1977, owing largely to the failure of public investment to compensate for the sudden lack of private investment. The military government of General Zia aimed to return to the predominant private-sector system by offering fiscal and financial incentives. Some of the industries nationalized under Bhutto, such as cement, were returned to the private sector. Others, such as banking, however, remain under state control. Prime Minister Benazir Bhutto has not given any indication as to whether she will continue the trend toward denationalization implemented by General Zia.

Foreign trade: In 1987–88, foreign trade accounted for 28.1% of the GDP. The principal commodities exported were cotton textiles ($235.3 million), cotton yarn ($331.2 million), rice ($210 million) and carpets ($140 million). As a result of the recession in the early 1980s, many of Pakistan's exports are to other developing nations. Asia and the Middle East are its primary trading partners. About 32% of Pakistan's imports are oil and petroleum products from the Middle East ($1.6 billion in 1987–88). Other imports for 1987–88 were plants and machinery ($632.3 million), transport equipment and vehicles ($363 million), and iron and steel manufactures ($192.6 million). The projected trade deficit for 1988 is close to $1.07 billion.

Employment: In 1987–88, Pakistan had a total work force of 30.5 million. Of this group, 50% was employed in agriculture, 33% in services and 13% in mining and manufacturing. There is extensive export of labor to petroleum-producing countries in the Middle East, and Pakistan has benefited from the remittances sent home by these workers.

EDUCATION

In 1986, Pakistan had 8.1 million primary school students, 3.1 million secondary school students and 550,000 university students. The literacy rate in 1988 was 22%, and 10% of the budget was allocated to education. The educational structure consists of five years in primary school, three years in middle school and four years in high school. Students are promoted to higher levels by successful completion of government-controlled examinations. A large number of students are enrolled in private schools. In 1983, 50% of high school students attended private school. Education is largely reserved for boys, and less than 35% of the population of primary, secondary and postsecondary institutions is composed of girls. The literacy rate among females is 12.2%.

MASS MEDIA

The press: The press in Pakistan is heavily influenced by the government despite the easing of censorship in 1985, when martial law was lifted. The Urdu press accounts for close to 800 newspapers. Many publications of importance are printed in English although they are accessible to only 2% of the population.

In 1986, there were 106 daily newspapers with an aggregate circulation of 1.689 million. Seventy are published in Urdu and 22 in English. The main dailies are *Jang* (750,000), with editions published in Quetta, Rawalpindi, Lahore and London; *Nawa-i-Waqt* (250,000), published in Lahore; *Mashriq* (160,000), published in Lahore; *Dawn* (70,000), published in Karachi. Several regional-language newspapers are printed in smaller cities throughout Pakistan.

Periodicals: The weeklies include *Akhbar-e-Jehan* (138,000), an Urdu family magazine published in Karachi; *Akhbar-e-Khawateen* (40,000), a women's magazine published in Karachi. There are also numerous periodicals published for the Pakistani population living abroad.

Broadcasting: Radio broadcasting is controlled by the state-owned Pakistan Broadcasting Corporation. It offers a variety of programs for over 800 hours a week. Television broadcasting is controlled by a public company, the Pakistan Television Corporation, and the Pakistani government is the major shareholder. Programs are broadcast for 105 hours a week. In 1988, there were close to 1.5 million television receivers in Pakistan.

BIOGRAPHICAL SKETCHES

Gen. Mirza Aslam Beq. Appointed chief of army staff in 1985, he has had a long and illustrious military career. He joined the Pakistan Military Academy in 1949, became a brigadier general in 1974 and was subsequently the chief instructor of armed forces at the National Defense College. He commanded an infantry battalion on the Lahore front in the 1971 war with India.

Benazir Bhutto. Born June 21, 1953, she was graduated from Radcliffe College in 1969 and obtained a master's degree from Oxford University in 1976. Benazir Bhutto is the daughter of former Pakistan Prime Minister Zulfikar Ali Bhutto, who was executed in 1979. With her mother, Begum Nusrat, Benazir Bhutto assumed the leadership of the PPP. She returned to Pakistan from exile in 1986 and became prime minister in December 1988.

Ghulam Ishaq Khan. Born January 20, 1915, he attended Punjab University and served in the North-West Frontier civil service from 1940 to 1947. He was finance secretary from 1966 to 1970, and was elected chairman of the Senate in 1985 and reelected to the position in 1988. He assumed the position of acting president in August 1988, after the death of General Zia ul-Haq.

PAPUA NEW GUINEA

GEOGRAPHY

Features: Papua New Guinea is situated east of Indonesia and north of the northeastern extremity of Australia. It comprises the eastern half of the New Guinea mainland (the Indonesian territory of Irian Jaya occupies the western half); the Bismarck Archipelago (the main islands of which are Manus, New Ireland and New Britain); the northernmost Solomon Islands of Bougainville and Buka; and the groups of islands lying immediately to the east of the New Guinea mainland (including Trobriand and the D'Entrecasteaux Islands). The central spine of the New Guinea mainland consists of a massive mountain chain, running west-east for 1,553 miles/2,500 km. from one end of the island to the other. In the Papua New Guinea territory the highest peaks are well over 13,124 ft/4,000 m. A large number of rivers drain from the central mountain chain, both to the north and to the south. Within the interior there is a series of wide, well-watered valleys on both sides of the mountain divide: these valleys, with an average elevation of over 5,250 ft/1,600 m., are clear of jungle and possess a cool climate. The major rivers (notably the Fly and the Sepik) flow to the sea through vast areas of permanent inland swamp: Mangrove swamps occur all along the coasts of the mainland. The islands of New Britain, New Ireland and Bougainville also possess central mountain chains, although on a far more modest scale than that on the mainland. A volcanic range (only very rarely showing signs of activity) stretches along the northern coast of the mainland, through the north coast of New Britain to Bougainville; most of the islands in the D'Entrecasteaux Islands are of volcanic origin.

Area: 178,704 sq. miles/462,840 sq. km.

Mean max. and min. temperatures: Average daily coastal temperature: minimum 70°F/21°C; maximum 90°F/32°C. In the highland areas of the interior average temperatures are significantly lower.

Relative humidity: 70%–85%.

Mean annual rainfall: About 79 in/2,000 mm., but there are wide regional variations (47 in/1,195 mm. in Port Moresby; 200 in/5,080 mm. at Kikori).

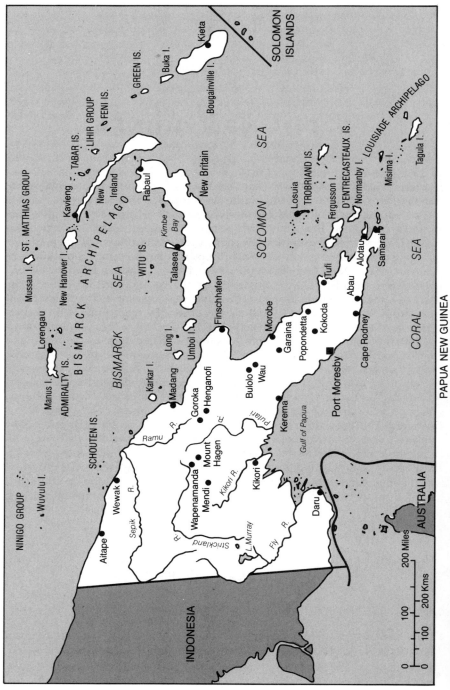

PAPUA NEW GUINEA

POPULATION

Total population (January 1, 1987 est): 3,479,400.

Chief town and population: PORT MORESBY (145,300, 1987 est).

Distribution: According to the 1980 census 13% of the population was settled in urban centers.

Language: It is estimated that about 700 to 800 languages are in use in Papua New Guinea. The principal languages are Pidgin, English and Police Motu. There is a high level of illiteracy.

Religion: A belief in the efficacy of magic or sorcery is almost universal, even among those who have accepted Christianity. Christian missions were established before the imposition of colonial rule and during the colonial period they played a very important social and educational role. A high proportion of the population (93% in 1966) declare themselves to be Christian.

CONSTITUTIONAL SYSTEM

Constitution: The independence constitution, which came into effect on September 16, 1975, remains in force.

Head of state: Queen Elizabeth II. *Governor-general:* Sir Kingsford Dibela. *Prime minister:* Rabbie Namaliu.

Executive: The National Executive Council, comprising all government ministers, with the prime minister acting as chairman, is responsible for the executive government of Papua New Guinea. The prime minister is appointed and dismissed by the head of state on the proposal of the National Parliament; ministers are appointed and dismissed by the head of state on the proposal of the prime minister.

Legislature: The National Parliament is a single-chamber legislature. It has 109 members elected by universal adult suffrage: 89 members represent open constituencies and 20 represent provincial constituencies. The normal term of office is five years. The speaker and deputy speaker are members of the National Parliament, elected to those positions by the National Parliament.

Political parties: In November 1988 the National Executive Council was a coalition in which the following parties were represented: Pangu Pati, Melanesian Alliance, People's Action party, National party, Papua party and League for National Advancement.

Local government: There are 19 fully elected provincial governments, with the authority to impose provincial taxes; geographic, linguistic and ethnic distinctions have required the central government to concede a relatively high degree of administrative decentralization.

Judicial system: The highest judicial authority is the Supreme Court, which considers all matters that involve the interpretation of the constitution and appeals from the National Court. The latter has unlimited jurisdiction in both civil and criminal matters. District courts are responsible for civil cases involving compensation, some indictable offenses and the more serious summary offenses. Local courts deal with minor offenses. Village courts deal with customary matters (except those involving land, which are considered in district and local land courts) at the village level and are expected to provide more understandable justice for village communities; warden's courts have jurisdiction over all mining matters. The chief justice is appointed and dismissed by the head of state on the proposal of the National Executive Council.

RECENT HISTORY

The territory presently occupied by Papua New Guinea first came under colonial rule in 1884 when a German protectorate was proclaimed over northeast New Guinea and the Bismarck Archipelago (New Britain, New Ireland, Admiralty Islands and the adjoining smaller islands), and a British protectorate was proclaimed over southeast New Guinea and the adjoining islands. German New Guinea was formally annexed in 1885, British New Guinea in 1888. With the outbreak of war in Europe in 1914, Australian troops occupied German New Guinea; the territory remained under Australian military administration until 1921. In 1920 a mandate for the administration of German New Guinea was given to Australia by the League of Nations (the mandate became effective in May 1921). During World War II the territory was occupied by the Japanese from early 1942 on, but following the Japanese defeat it was returned to Australian administration under U.N. trusteeship arrangements. With respect to British New Guinea, from the time of annexation in 1888 administrative responsibility was at first shared between Great Britain and Queensland (acting on behalf of all the Australian colonies). Following the creation of the Australian federal government in 1901, Australia agreed to assume full responsibility for the territory: In 1905–06 British New Guinea became a territory of Australia and was renamed Papua. This constitutional structure remained in place, except for the years of the Japanese occupation, until 1949.

Thus, in the interwar decades the Australian Territory of Papua and the mandated Territory of New Guinea were administered (by Australia) as two separate entities. But it had become clear by the end of the war in the Pacific—indeed, largely as a result of the creation of the Australian New Guinea Administrative Unit in late 1942 to assume administrative responsibility as areas were cleared of Japanese forces—that there were considerable advantages to be secured by administering Papua and New Guinea jointly. In March 1949 the Australian parliament passed legislation that effected the administrative merger of the territories, now referred to as the Territory of Papua and New Guinea. The 1950s and early 1960s saw the Australian administration become increasingly intent to draw the indigenous populations into the modern world. A Legislative Council of Papua and New Guinea was inaugurated in 1951; it was reconstituted and enlarged in 1961, but it had little authority and afforded only limited representation for the local people. Significant political advance came in 1964 with the establishment of a House of Assembly, in which there were 10 official members, 44 members elected from open electorates and 10 members from reserved electorates for which only nonindigenes could stand. There was universal adult suffrage. The House of Assembly was enlarged in 1968 and again in 1972—by which time it had 100 elected members; 82 from open electorates and 18 from regional electorates where candidates were required to have specified educational qualifications. Ministerial members were appointed from 1968 on; and beginning in 1972 ministers began to exercise real constitutional power. Papua New Guinea (as the territory became known in 1971) achieved self-government on December 1, 1973 and then full independence on September 16, 1975. The independence government initially comprised a coalition of three main political parties under Prime Minister Michael Somare of the Pangu Pati. Somare remained in office until March 1980; subsequently, the 1980s saw a succession of prime ministers (Somare himself returned to power in mid-1982 but was again replaced in November 1985) at the head of shifting coalitions.

The principal political problem faced by independent Papua New Guinea has been the need to create a national identity in a territory where clan, tribal and district loyalties remain extremely powerful and where internal communications remain difficult. There have been strong secession instincts among many groups (perhaps most strongly on Bougainville); and the frequent removal of government coalitions through parliamentary votes of no confidence may be said to reflect in large part the difficulties experienced by all prime ministers in reconciling diverse domestic interests. The devolution of administrative responsibility to provincial governments—executed in the second half of the 1970s—has done much to curb centrifugal forces, although a number of provincial administrations have been seriously weakened by internal political conflict and economic mismanagement.

ECONOMY

Background: Prior to World War II, modern economic growth was very modest in the mandated territory (it centered on the export of copra and gold) and virtually non-existent in Papua. The postwar decades saw considerable modern economic development; but even at the close of the 1980s around 80% of the population was employed to some extent in the subsistence, nonmonetized sector of the economy, meeting almost all their basic requirements of food, shelter and clothing. Particularly since independence a powerful effort has been made to expand the modern sector of the economy: Papua New Guinea has received a substantial volume of long-term loans from the Asian Development Bank and the World Bank, while Australia has long supplied very substantial budgetary support. But modern economic growth has clearly been more difficult to achieve in a territory where internal communications remain poor, where the population is small and widely scattered, and where (after decades of serious neglect) educational and training levels among the local population remain poor. Estimates based on the 1980 census suggest that 77% of the economically active population is engaged in agriculture, hunting, forestry and fishing (this figure excludes those solely engaged in the subsistence sector); 2% in manufacturing; 10% in community, social and personal services (in part a reflection of the large size of the bureaucracy—a legacy of the Australian period); and 0.6% in mining and quarrying.

Agriculture: The most important agricultural exports are copra and copra oil (which accounted for 2.8% of total export value in 1987), palm oil (2.2%), cacao beans (5.3%), and coffee (12.7%). There is also a modest timber export industry; in 1987, logs, wood chips and lumber accounted for 10.5% of total export value. There is substantial production of food plants (notably sweet potatoes but also yams, sago palms and sugarcane) for domestic consumption. Papua New Guinea imports a significant part of its food requirements: In 1986 food and live animals accounted for 18% of total import value.

Mining: By far the most important export, accounting for 48.8% of total export value in 1987, is copper ore and concentrates. The principal extraction takes place at Panguna on the island of Bougainville, where Bougainville Copper, Ltd., a subsidiary of Conzinc Rio Tinto, went into production in 1972. Copper is also mined at Ok Tedi on the mainland, close to the border with Irian Jaya. Extraction here is in the hands of Ok Tedi Mining, Ltd., a largely private consortium with a minority government investment. Production began in the mid-1980s. Both Panguna and Ok Tedi also produce a substantial volume of gold; indeed, the expansion of mining of the latter was expected to make Papua New Guinea the world's third most important gold-producing country (after South Africa and the USSR). In 1986 total production of gold was 96,983 lb/43,983 kg. and the total estimated production of copper concentrates was 173,900 metric tons.

Foreign trade: From the early 1970s on the rapid expansion of copper exports and increased income from agricultural exports secured a substantial recurrent trade surplus. As primary commodity prices weakened in the early 1980s the trade balance moved into deficit; in the mid-1980s it returned to surplus. In 1986 Australia accounted for 40.4% of the total value of imports into Papua New Guinea, Japan for 17.7%. The principal categories of imports were machinery and transport equipment, basic manufactures, and food and live animals. The principal markets for Papua New Guinea exports in the mid-1980s were the Federal Republic of Germany and Japan.

Employment: There is no comprehensive, reliable series of wage-employment data or consistent data on changes in unemployment and underemployment. Partial evidence and random observation suggest that there exists a relatively high level of disguised unemployment in the urban areas. In 1987 there was an estimated labor force of 1.5 million persons; the public sector was the largest formal employer, accounting for almost one-third of identifiable employment.

Price trends: The consumer price index—average for urban areas—1977 = 100, was 1985 = 170.0; 1986 = 179.5; 1987 = 185.8.

SOCIAL SERVICES

Welfare: A National Provident Fund was established in mid-1981 covering most private-sector firms. Those firms with more than 25 workers were required to contribute 7% of an employee's wage to the fund, the employee contribution being 5%.

Health services: The Department of Health provides hospitals, dispensaries and public health facilities for the whole country; in addition, the various Christian organizations provide hospitals, nursing staff and medical officers. There are four government base hospitals that provide specialist services for the four geographical divisions of Papua New Guinea; and there are district hospitals in those provinces that do not have a base hospital. In addition, there are a large number of rural health centers, maternal and child health clinics, and dispensaries. In January 1983 there were 184 health centers, 236 subcenters and 2,201 aid posts. Hospital charges are based on ability to pay: Most people are treated free or for only a nominal sum.

Housing: A national housing authority, the National Housing Commission, was established in 1968 to build houses for sale and rent; the bulk of this government housing has been heavily subsidized.

EDUCATION

Education is administered through the Department of Education, with the Christian missions and churches playing an important part in educational provision, particularly at the primary level. The first level of schooling, which takes place in community schools, lasts from the ages of seven to 13; an average of 58% of children of primary-school age attend school, although the proportion is much higher in the urban areas and far lower in the interior districts. At the age of 13 children go on to provincial high schools (there were 94 in 1983) for three years; and at 16 they may move on to one of the national high schools (there were four in 1983) to prepare for entry to tertiary education. There are a substantial number of technical, vocational and teacher training colleges; there are also two universities: the University of Papua New Guinea and the University of Technology. Originally school education was free, but in recent years fees and charges for equipment have been introduced. Although educational provision has in general improved markedly in the years since independence (particularly in the urban areas), there is concern that children in many of the more remote districts remain seriously disadvantaged.

MASS MEDIA

The press

Dailies: Niugini Nius, Monday–Saturday, English, 20,000; *Papua New Guinea Post-Courier,* English, 32,000.

Periodicals (weeklies): The Times of Papua New Guinea, English, 13,000; *Wantok,* Pidgin (for a mainly rural readership), 15,000. There are also many news-sheets, periodicals and magazines produced by government departments, statutory bodies and Christian missions, among others.

Broadcasting: The National Broadcasting Commission of Papua New Guinea, formed in December 1973, provides radio services in English, Melanesian, Pidgin, Motu and 30 vernacular languages. It operates 19 provincial stations (which focus on local interests, using languages suited to the village audience in their locality) and three networks (provincial, national and commercial). In 1984 there were an estimated 220,000 radio receivers in use. Television has recently been introduced, in the form of Niugini Television Network (formed in 1987 and 50% owned by the Australian company PBL Pacific Television) and Em TV (formed in 1988).

BIOGRAPHICAL SKETCHES

Rabbie Namaliu. Born in April 1947 in Raluana Village (Gazelle Peninsula, east New Britain), Namaliu was educated at the University of Papua New Guinea and the University of Victoria, British Columbia. In 1974 he became a member of the Pangu Pati executive and principal private secretary to the chief minister, Michael Somare. Namaliu was elected chairman of the east New Britain Constituent Assembly in March 1976; in the 1982 general elections he was the successful Pangu Pati candidate for Kokopo. Namaliu was appointed minister for foreign affairs and trade in August 1982 and minister for primary industry in December 1984. In March 1985 he was elected deputy leader of the Pangu Pati, became leader in May 1988 and on July 4, 1988 became prime minister.

Michael Somare. Somare was born in April 1936 in Rabaul, Gazelle Peninsula, east New Britain. He began his career as a teacher, information officer and radio announcer. He was a founding member of the Pangu Pati in 1967, and the following year won the East Sepik provincial seat in the House of Assembly. Somare has successfully defended that seat at all subsequent national elections. Michael Somare became the first chief minister of the self-governing Territory of Papua New Guinea in 1973 and the first prime minister upon the declaration of independence in September 1975. He remained as prime minister until March 1980, then went into opposition and returned as prime minister following the 1982 general elections. He retained that position until November 1985. Somare was leader of the Pangu Pati until June 1988 when he was succeeded by Rabbie Namaliu. Somare became minister for foreign affairs in July 1988 in the Namaliu administration.

Paias Wingti. Born in February 1951 in Moika Village, Mount Hagen, Western Highlands Province, Wingti enrolled at the University of Papua New Guinea in 1974 but left in 1977 to enter politics; he won the Mount Hagen open seat in the National Parliament that year. Wingti was minister of transport and civil aviation from August 1978 to March 1980 in the Somare administration. In opposition from 1980 to 1982, he became deputy prime minister in August 1982 when Somare returned to power. Wingti left the Somare administration in March 1985. The following month, having left the Pangu Pati, he founded the People's Democratic Movement. On November 21, 1985, following a parliamentary vote of no confidence in the Somare government, Paias Wingti became prime minister; he retained that position until July 1988.

BATAN IS.

Luzon   Strait

PACIFIC

Babuyan   Channel

Laoag

Tuguegarao   Aparri

SOUTH

Vigan   Bontoc

Ilagan

Cagayan R.

San Fernando   Baguio

PHILIPPINE

Dagupan   Bayombong

Lingayen   **Luzon**

SEA

CHINA   *Tarlac R.*   Tarlac

Iba   Cabanatuan

OCEAN

Olongapo   Quezon
City

POLILLO
IS.

Manila   *Lamon Bay*

Laguno de Bay

Tagaytay City   San Pablo   Daet

Batangas   Naga   Catanduanes I.

Calapan   Boac   Oas   Sorsogon

SEA   **Mindoro**   *SIBUYAN*   Irosin

Masbate   Samar

CALAMIAN
GROUP   *SEA*   Catbalogan

Mindoro Strait   Roxas   *VISAYAN*   Tacloban

SAMAR SEA

CUYO   **Panay**   *SEA*   *Leyte*
IS.   Iloilo   *Gulf*

Bacolod   *Leyte*   Dinagat I.

Cebu   Pilar I.

Negros   Cebu   Bohol   *Surigao Strait*   Surigao

Puerto Princesa   *BOHOL*   Dumaguete   *SEA*

Palawan   Butuan

Dipolog   Cagayan
de Oro   *Agusan R.*

SULU   Ozamis   *Lake Lanao*

Pagadian   **Mindanao**

Balabac I.   SEA   Datu Piang   *Mindanao R.*   Davao

Balabac Strait   *Davao*
Gulf

Zamboanga   *Moro*
Gulf

Cagayan Sulu I.   Basilan I.

Jolo   SARANGANI IS.

CELEBES SEA

MALAYSIA   *SULU ARCHIPELAGO*

0		100		200 Miles

0	100	200 Kms

PHILIPPINES

PHILIPPINES

Features: The Philippines is an archipelago of approximately 7,100 islands scattered over a distance of 1,110 miles/1,850 km. from north to south and 580 miles/965 km. from east to west. The islands lie on the western rim of the Pacific Ocean, north of the equator and about 620 miles/1,000 km. from the Asian mainland. Tawi-Tawi, the southernmost island group, is only 14 miles/24 km. from Borneo. The Batan Islands, the northernmost part of the chain, is 96 miles/160 km. south of Taiwan. The island chain is bordered on the east by the Pacific Ocean, on the west by the South China Sea, and on the south and southwest by the Celebes and Sulu seas, respectively. The Philippine Deep, a trench in the ocean floor off the east coast of Mindanao (the large, southeasternmost island) is, at 34,580 ft/10,540 m., the world's second deepest sounding.

The Philippines is divided into three island groups: Luzon in the north, the Visayas in the center and Mindanao in the south. Luzon is the largest island with an area of 40,420 sq. miles/104,688 sq. km., followed by Mindanao (35,537 sq. miles/94,630 sq. km.) and Samar (5,050 sq. miles/13,080 sq. km.). The other major islands, in decreasing order of size are Negros, Palawan, Panay, Mindoro, Leyte, Bohol and Masbate. Luzon and Mindanao account for 66% of the country's territory. They, with the nine next largest islands, make up more than 90% of the country's total land area. Approximately 880 islands are inhabited. The Philippines is a mountainous country with a dozen still active volcanos. The highest mountain is Mount Apo (9,690 ft/2,954 m.) on Mindanao. The two best-known volcanos are Mayon and Tsal, both on Luzon. The country's highly volcanic soil and abundant rainfall provide fertile ground to some 10,000 plant species.

Nearly all the larger islands have interior mountain ranges, with typical altitudes of 3,937–7,875 ft/1,200–2,400 m. Few have extensive lowlands, except for narrow strips of coastal plain. This is the country's greatest natural liability. Luzon, the exception, has for this reason played a dominant role in the agricultural and economic life of the country.

Area: 115,600 sq. miles/299,400 sq. km.

Mean max. and min. temperatures: Manila (14°35'N, 121°00'E; 49 ft/15 m.) 91°F/33°C (June), 75°F/24°C (January).

Relative humidity: 80%.

Mean annual rainfall: 100 in/2,500 mm, but varies widely.

POPULATION

Total population (1986 est.): 56,900,000. The last census was taken in May, 1980, and recorded 48,098,460.

Chief towns and populations: Metro MANILA (10,000,000 est.). According to the 1980 census: Davao City (610,375), Cebu City (490,281), Zamboanga City (343,722).

Distribution: The shortage of lowlands in the Philippines means that a large part of the population is concentrated in a relatively small area. The resultant pressure is a serious problem, particularly in central Luzon. The 2.4% per year growth rate is likely to aggravate the problem. Average population density is 415 per sq. mile/160 per sq. km., nearly double the Southeast Asian average, and exceeded only by northern Vietnam and Singapore. Density ranges from 15.9 per sq. km. on Palawan to 1,529 per sq. km. in Rizal Province, east of Manila.

Language: More than 100 linguistic, cultural and racial groups in the Philippines speak a total of about 87 dialects. An effort has been made in recent decades to develop Tagalog, the language of central Luzon, as the national language—called Pilipino. English is widely spoken and understood, and is used particularly among the largely mestizo elite. English is also still the language of instruction in schools. Arabic is also spoken by an Islamic minority on Mindanao.

Religion: Approximately 90% of the Philippine population is Roman Catholic, a result of the Spanish colonial missionary influence. Muslim Moros inhabit the southern and southwestern peripheries and form about 5% of the total population. Islam was introduced in the south during the 14th century as a result of the expansion of Arab trade in Southeast Asia. It has undergone substantial cultural assimilation since. Protestantism was introduced in 1899, and various sects encompass approximately 5% of the population today. Two Filipino independent churches, the Aglipay (Philippine Independent Church) and Iglesia Ni Kristo (Church of Christ) were established at the turn of the century. The latter has greatly expanded, and the distinctive architecture of its churches make it a conspicuous presence in almost all major cities and important towns.

CONSTITUTIONAL SYSTEM

Constitution: A new Philippine constitution was ratified in a national plebiscite on February 2, 1987, and proclaimed effective by President Corazon C. Aquino on February 11. It superseded the temporary "Freedom Constitution" adopted a year earlier when Aquino assumed the presidency after a "People's Revolution" forced the departure of then President Ferdinand Marcos for the United States. The new constitution reflects the constitutional form that operated from 1935 to 1973 (except during World War II), with a United States–style bicameral legislature and an executive presidency. It emphasizes a commitment to democracy, social justice, human rights and honesty in government. Education, the arts, sport, private enterprise, and agrarian and urban reforms are also promoted. It extends the term of the Presidential Commission on Good Government, whose purpose is to recover large quantities of Marcos wealth accumulated at government expense.

Head of state: President Corazon Cohuangco Aquino. *Vice-president:* Salvador Laurel.

Executive: Executive power is vested in the president, limited to one six-year term. Vice-presidents are limited to two successive six-year terms. Candidates are elected to both posts by direct universal suffrage granted to all citizens over 18 years of age. Candidates must be natural-born citizens, literate, at least 40 years old, registered voters and resident in the Philippines for at least 10 years before election. The president signs bills approved by Congress. A presidential veto can be overridden by a two-thirds majority of members of Congress. The president is commander in chief of the armed forces and may place the republic under martial law for a period not exceeding 60 days when, in the president's opinion, public safety demands it. The vice-president becomes president if the president dies in office.

Legislature: The Senate and the House of Representatives, with a total of 274 members, form the legislative branch. All members must disclose their financial and business interests upon taking office. The Senate has 24 members, elected for six years (the 1987 constitution provided for the first Senate to serve for a five-year term). Senators must be natural-born citizens, at least 35 years old, literate and registered voters in their districts. They must be resident for at least two years before election. A maximum of 250 representatives may sit in the House of Representatives. Members are elected for three years and may not serve more than three consecutive terms. They must be natural-born citizens, literate and at least 25 years old. Of the total House of Representative membership, 200 are elected by direct vote. The president appoints the remaining 50 from listed candidates and opposition groups. Half of these must be from indigenous, but not religious-affiliated, minority groups (the urban poor, peasantry, women and youth). Both houses have an Electoral Tribunal that judges the outcome of congressional elections. Each tribunal has nine members, three belonging to the Supreme Court. The remaining six are members of either house and are selected on a proportional basis from the political parties represented.

Political parties: Political parties were banned in the Philippines under martial law between 1972 and 1978. In 1978 National Assembly elections, the Kilusan Bagong Lipunan (KBL—New Society Movement, founded by Marcos), Lakas ng Bayan (People's Power) and Pusyon Visaya party (based in the Visayas) took part. All political parties took part in 1984 elections after martial law was lifted in 1981. The new constitution recognizes parties registered by the Commission on Elections. They are Alliance for New Politics (ANP), a coalition of three leftist organizations advocating social change and land reform; Bandila (pro-Acquino, centrist); Grand Alliance for Democracy (—anti-government and anti-Communist, wants to keep U.S. military bases in the Philippines); Kababaihan Para Sa Inang Bayan (Women for the Mother Country, first all-women's party, militant); Labor party (labor and agrarian groups); Lakas ng Bansa (People's Struggle, pro-Aquino); Mindanao Alliance (for economic development of Mindanao); Partido Nacionalist ng Pilipinas (Nationalist party of former KBL members); Partido ng Bayan (New Patriotic Alliance, militant nationalist group founded by the former head of the Communist party); United Nationalist Democratic Organization (UNIDO—coalition of seven anti-Marcos parties: Liberal party, Nacionalista party, National Union for Christian Democracy, National Union for Liberation, PDP-Laban party, Pusyon Visaya party and Social Democratic party). Groups in conflict with the government include the Moro National Liberation Front (MNLF), which seeks autonomy for Muslim communities in Mindanao and other southern islands. It has an estimated force of 5,000 full-time soldiers and 12,000 reserves, and includes the Moro Islamic Liberation Front (supported by Egypt) and the Bangsa Moro National Liberation Front (supported by Saudi Arabia). The National Democratic Front (NDF) is a left-wing alliance with 13 member groups, including the Partido Kommunist ng Pilipinas (PKP, Communist party of the Philippines) and the New People's Army (NPA), military wing of the PKP based in central Luzon with an estimated force of 25,000–30,000.

Local government: The Philippines is divided into provinces, cities, municipalities and *barangays*. Each unit enjoys a large measure of local autonomy to make local government officials more responsive to the needs of their constituents. There are two autonomous regions—in Muslim Mindanao and the Cordillera region of Luzon. Defense and security in these areas remain the responsibility of the national government.

Judicial system: A chief justice and 14 associate justices comprise the Supreme Court. Justices may sit en banc or in divisions of three, five or seven members. The president appoints justices for four-year terms. The Commission of Appointments, consisting of 12 senators and 12 congresspeople, must approve nominations. Justices must be citizens, at least 40 years old, and must have been judges of the lower courts or engaged in law practice in the Philippines for at least 15 years. Other courts include the Court of Appeals, regional trial courts, metropolitan trial courts, municipal courts in cities, municipal courts and municipal circuit trial courts. Islamic *Sharia* courts were established in the southern Philippines in July 1985 under a 1977 presidential decree. Three district magistrates and six circuit judges preside over these courts.

RECENT HISTORY

The Philippines was the first area in Southeast Asia to be colonized by a European power. The first Spanish settlement in the archipelago was established in Cebu in 1565, and by the early 1570s Spanish control extended over Cebu, Leyte, Panay, Mindoro, and central Luzon. The fragmented political nature of the islands made coordinated native resistance impossible. Roman Catholicism is the potent enduring legacy of the Spanish period.

During the 1890s the writings of José Rizal exposed the repression of the Spanish. A revolt against the colonial power erupted in 1896 under Andres Bonifacio. Although Rizal played no part in the revolt, he was executed. The event sparked Filipino revolutionary fervor. Spain ceded the Philippines to the United States in December 1898 as part of the Treaty of Paris that ended the Spanish-American War. The Philippine Republic was declared on January 23, 1899, and Emilio Aguinaldo, a revolutionary and member of the provincial elite, became its first president. Skirmishes developed between natives and the U.S. occupying forces. In March 1901 Aguinaldo was captured and pledged his allegiance to the United States. The United States did little to advance agricultural practices, and the Philippines became heavily dependent on agricultural exports throughout the early 20th century. The Filipino elite occupied much of the lower echelons of the U.S. colonial administration, reinforcing their dominance of society. The rural masses were increasingly exploited as the elite collaborated with the Americans. Pushed by opposition to colonialism at home and by hard times brought on by the Depression, U.S. President Franklin D. Roosevelt signed the Tydings-McDuffie Act on March 24, 1934, which called for a 10-year transitional period of Philippine self-government to be followed by independence on July 4, 1946. Manuel Quezon became the first president of the Philippine Commonwealth on November 15, 1935. Revolts by increasingly dispossessed peasants led to the formation of peasant unions and the founding of the PKP in 1930. Quezon's attempted rural reforms were largely ineffective because they encroached on the power of the elite who dominated both local administration and national politics.

World War II put class tensions on hold. Japanese occupation of the Philippines, however, gave rise to the Hukbalahap (People's Army Against Japan) in 1942. Disenchanted militant peasants dominated the movement. The U.S. military returned in 1944 and their advance was prepared by guerrilla groups led by the Huks. Thus, the Huks expected prominent positions in any postwar government for their contribution to Japanese resistance; they were to be disappointed. The U.S. administration and the Philippine elite attempted to suppress the Communist-influenced movement as the war came to a close.

In April 1946 Manuel Roxas became president in the first postwar election. The United States still dominated the country's economy through laws controlling imports and exports. In March 1947 the United States and the Philippine Republic concluded an agreement granting the United States a lease on 23 military bases in the island. The agreement spurred controversy, and the two nations negotiated an agreement to take effect once the lease on two major bases (Subic Bay naval base and Clark Air Base) expired in 1991.

On March 6, 1948, Roxas declared the Hukbalahap to be an illegal organization and launched a fierce campaign against the movement. Elpidio Quirino became president after Roxas's death in April 1948 and was re-elected in 1949 as the Liberal candidate. As the economy worsened in the late 1940s the Huks continued their insurgency. Ramon Magsaysay became minister of national defense, and his reforms of the corrupt armed forces, combined with the government's more constructive response to rural griev-ances that fueled the revolt, resulted in elimination of the Huks as a polit-ical and military entity. As the Nacionalista candidate against Quirino, Magsaysay was elected president in 1953. He reinforced the Philippines' relationship with the United States, and instituted agricultural and land reform programs before his death in a plane crash in 1957. He was suc-ceeded by his vice-president, Carlos P. García, who won the presidential election later that year. Garcia's government was characterized by a policy of economic nationalism, but was rife with corruption and graft. He was defeated in the 1961 election by the Liberal party candidate, Diosdado Macapagal. The latter instituted far-reaching economic reforms, including the abolition of foreign-exchange control and measures to stimulate export production. He established the Philippine claim to Sabah, causing the country to sever diplomatic relations with Malaysia.

Nacionalista candidate Ferdinand E. Marcos defeated Macapagal in the 1965 elections. By the beginning of Marcos's second term in 1969, eco-nomic disparities began to fuel conflict that dominated Philippine politics for the next two decades. Student activism emerged in the early 1970s, and clashes between government forces and the NPA (the military wing of the Communist party) increased. The MNLF continued to challenge central authority on Mindanao. Private armies under the control of political figures increased their acts of political intimidation and violence. As the political and social fabric of the country disintegrated, the country became split between those who wanted Marcos to leave office in 1973 and those who supported him.

Marcos declared martial law in September 1972 and arrested opponents of the right and left. A new constitution ratified in 1973 conferred the offices of president and prime minister on Marcos. Martial law continued, and in national elections in 1978 and local elections in 1980 the ruling KBL triumphed, albeit amid accusations of widespread electoral fraud. Leading opposition figure Benigno B. Aquino was released from prison in May 1980 and allowed to travel to the United States for medical treatment. Martial law was lifted in January 1981, but Marcos still dominated the political scene. Economic policies under Marcos emphasized an expansion in exports, a reduction of tariffs, an increase in foreign investment and the suppression of labor organizations. A worldwide recession in the early 1980s, however, sharply reduced Philippine export earnings and produced chronic balance-of-payments crises. As a result, the Philippines became deeply in-debted to the World Bank and International Monetary Fund (IMF).

Aquino returned to Manila in 1983 and was immediately assassinated on the airport tarmac after disembarking from his plane. Military guards then shot the alleged assassin, Rolando Galman. A major political crisis ensued, marked by large-scale street demonstrations and labor strikes. The resignation of Marcos was demanded. An independent commission appointed to investigate the assassination ruled in October 1984 that Galman was not the assassin, but that Aquino had been the victim of a military conspiracy. It indicted 25 military officers, including the chief of staff, Gen. Fabian Ver. This marked the beginning of the end of the Marcos regime. Many Filipinos believed that Marcos and his widely disliked wife, Imelda, were implicated in Aquino's death. Rumors about the Marcos's extravagances and dishonestly accrued personal wealth began to circulate widely. A population once fearful of publicly criticizing the government opened up.

At the same time, the economy began to collapse. Political instability caused foreign creditors to suspend short-term loans that had sustained the economy since the late 1970s. Capital fled the country and new investment fell off. The United States strongly urged Marcos to submit the failing regime to elections. The next presidential election, scheduled for May 1987, was moved up to February 7, 1986. In the months preceding the election Marcos's chances of retaining his post seemed favorable as the opposition was split into multiple factions. Cardinal Jaime Sin, archbishop of Manila, and the U.S. Embassy there urged the groups to unite. In late November 1985 the groups compromised. Corazon Aquino, widow of Benigno Aquino, became the presidential candidate of the UNIDO party, and Salvador Laurel, president of the party, hesitantly agreed to be the vice-presidential candidate. Amid allegations of widespread voting fraud and much confusion surrounding the vote count, Marcos was declared the winner. The Roman Catholic church issued a pastoral letter on February 14 claiming the election had been "a fraud unparalleled in history." Aquino then announced a campaign of nonviolent civil disobedience to protest the outcome. On February 22 Juan Ponce Enrile, minister of defense, and Lt.-Gen. Fidel Ramos, deputy chief of staff of the armed forces, withdrew their support of Marcos. Responding to an appeal by Cardinal Sin, thousands of Filipinos flooded the streets, effectively blocking the path of Marcos's troops and protecting the defectors holed up in Camp Aguinaldo. The United States declared its support for Enrile and Ramos on February 24. The strength of the People's Revolution rendered Marcos's troops helpless. On February 26 he fled the country on a U.S. Air Force plane and remained in exile in Hawaii, where he died in late 1989.

Aquino was inaugurated as president on February 25. Enrile remained minister of defense and Ramos became the armed forces chief of staff. The coalition government, though united in their opposition to Marcos, was divided on many other issues. Many were concerned about growing NPA insurgency and Aquino's virtually dictatorial powers. She had abolished the legislature under an interim constitution, demanded the resignations of several Supreme Court judges and dismissed local officials. A 50-member constitutional commission was convened to draft a new constitution. Rumors of impending coups led by Marcos supporters put the capital on edge. Many wondered how Aquino would resolve the disparate positions within her administration.

Some of her initial moves included releasing more than 500 political detainees, restoring the right of habeas corpus, abolishing censorship of the media and retiring pro-Marcos military officers. She began negotiations for a ceasefire with the NPA. She also sought to end the MNLF's 16-year secessionist war. The group agreed to a truce, and the government promised it would grant legal and judicial autonomy to four predominantly Muslim provinces on Mindanao.

A July 1986 coup attempt staged by Marcos supporters was put down by the army. In November an ill-planned uprising by officers at several military camps in and around the capital resulted in the dismissal of Enrile as minister of defense and the dissolution of the cabinet. Aquino made new appointments with the aim of eliminating financial corruption.

Civil unrest intensified during the days preceding the February 2, 1987, plebiscite to ratify the constitution. Demonstrations were put down by force, and troops attacked military and civilian targets in Manila. Troops loyal to Aquino put down the insurrection. The approval of the new constitution considerably strengthened Aquino's position. Elections were scheduled for May 11. When the NDF rejected an amnesty offer at the end of a 60-day cease-fire, the armed forces resumed their campaign against the NPA with major offensives. By June, about 4,000 insurgents had surrendered, but the NPA was still active in more than 60 of the country's 74 provinces. In April government forces overcame another abortive coup engineered by rebel soldiers.

The May 11 elections resulted in an overwhelming majority for Aquino's PDP-Laban candidates, who gained 22 of the 24 senatorial seats. The elections effectively concluded the interim revolutionary government. However, violence and tension continued to escalate in Manila, and a fifth abortive coup took place on August 28. Led by Col. Gregorio Honasan, a former chief of security under Enrile, the coup was the most serious attempt to overthrow the Aquino government since it came to power. The rebels bombarded the presidential palace and took over a radio station, but they were overwhelmed after 20 hours of fighting. Dissension continued to plague the administration, and tension rose. In mid-October Laurel announced that he and Enrile had formed an anti-Aquino alliance and that they would lead the country in the aftermath of a successful military-backed coup. With his power steadily dwindling, Laurel completely broke with Aquino in a critical letter to her on August 13, 1988. Many saw the move as a feeble attempt by Laurel to bolster his influence. He remained vice-president, but the two were as estranged as ever.

The first local elections since 1980 were held in January 1988. The parochial feuding, score-settling and hometown rivalries that surrounded them were characteristic of Philippine patron-client politics. Aquino supporters won in an overwhelming majority of districts, leading observers to believe that she might finally have stabilized her government and that opponents were looking ahead to the 1992 elections.

ECONOMY

Background: The Philippine economy was formerly dominated by agriculture, forestry and fishing, which provided one-third of GDP, generated 60% of total export earnings and accounted for half of the labor force. The agricultural sector continued to employ half the labor force in 1986, but it contributed 29% of GDP and export earnings had dropped to about 16%. Since independence in 1946, the economy has suffered from poor export organization, an inequitable distribution of wealth, and a tendency for wealth to be accumulated through monopoly privileges derived through patronage rather than through improved productivity. Government policies between 1970 and 1985 that favored Marcos's cronies perpetuated these structural flaws. The economy expanded throughout the 1970s, with an annual increase in real GDP averaging 6.6%. By 1980, however, the pace had slowed due to high inflation, restrictions on the availability of credit, and the increasing burdens of fuel imports and foreign debt. GNP expanded in real terms in 1982 and 1983 but declined by 7.1% in 1984 and 4.2% in 1985. By then the economy was in a severe state of recession, with per capita income no higher than in 1975. Real wages stagnated and fell thereafter. The assassination of opposition leader Benigno Aquino in 1983 resulted in lost credibility for the government and a lack of business confidence, which culminated in a balance-of-payments crisis and a devaluation of the peso by 21.4% in relation to the U.S. dollar. Capital flight preceded the devaluation.

When Corazon Aquino took office in 1986 her government assured foreign creditors it would fully repay the country's $28.2 billion debt. In October 1986 agreements were signed with the IMF and World Bank to provide funds to continue structural adjustment begun under an austerity program initiated in 1984. The government's Medium-Term Development Plan (1987–92) aimed to reduce the government's role in the economy and to pursue demand-led, employment-oriented and rural-based development strategies. The plan envisaged an annual GNP growth rate of 6.5%. The economy registered GNP creation projects. The government began to dismantle the monopolies of Marcos cronies, but real per capita income continued to decline by 2.2%. In 1987 domestic investment began to increase but foreign investment continued to fall. New investment was essential to the Aquino government's strategy for economic growth. However, continuing divisions within the armed forces, intensified labor unrest, opposition to the government and persistent poverty continued to destabilize the economic climate. The government's budget deficit exceeded 28 billion pesos ($1.4 billion) in 1986—45% of GNP. External debt was an estimated $28 billion. Interest payments on the external debt were 82.8% of total export earnings in 1986, or 46.5% of budgetary expenditure. In 1986 the government reached an agreement with the IMF to reschedule debt payments. Under the agreement, $2.4 billion (40% of the national budget) was to be paid per year in debt servicing. In 1987 foreign government creditors agreed to reschedule $870 million of loans due in 1987 and 1988. The agreement allowed a five-year grace period, with payments to begin in 1993. An agreement was also reached with commercial bank creditors to reschedule loans totaling $13 billion.

Agriculture: The country's major food-producing area is the central lowland of Luzon. Rice is the most important crop, but on some islands maize is the leading crop. Coconuts, sugar, bananas and pineapples also are major agricultural commodities. Rice occupies about 38% of total cultivated area of 23.9 million acres/8.7 million ha. Coconut palm takes up 5.7 million acres/2.8 million ha. (29%), and maize 5 million acres/2 million ha. (21%). In 1986 more than half of the country's population depended on agriculture for their livelihood; and this sector, with forestry and fishing, contributed 29% of GDP.

The sector expanded by an average 5% throughout the 1970s, partly due to the introduction of high-yield rice varieties. The country became self-sufficient in the crop in 1978. However, high production costs and poor weather conditions caused growth to slow in the 1980s, registering a decline of 2.1% in 1983. In 1984 and 1985 the country had to import 300,000 and 390,000 metric tons of rice, respectively. By 1986 production had increased by 2.4%, but this was still below the projected rate of 4%. Sugar and coconut sectors suffered because of low world prices and excessive export taxes, while marketing monopolies kept wholesale prices for produce low. Approximately 68% of the sugar-growing land is concentrated on Negros. The sector provides employment for some 500,000 workers, albeit at one of the lowest wage levels in the country. Annual output had declined from 2.6 million tons in 1983 to an estimated 1.5 million tons in 1986. The level of exports for coconut products in 1984 was the lowest for 20 years. Exports increased in 1986 because of governmental reforms that included removing export taxes on agricultural products, dismantling trade monopolies, and maintaining price supports for rice and maize. The overall objective was to enhance small farmers' incomes while increasing productivity.

In February 1987 the government introduced a land reform program. It was a four-part plan aiming to turn 400,000 tenants working 1,375,790 acres/557,000 ha. of rice- and maize-growing land into landowners; to divide about 2.4 million acres/1 million ha. of expropriated land and waste land among 670,000 people; to redistribute some 3.7 million acres/1.5 million ha. of mainly sugar and coconut plantations; and to regularize access and tenancy rights on public lands. The plan, signed into law on June 10, 1988, was directed at improving the standard of living of farmers, thus diluting their support for the Communist insurgency.

Industry: Between 1971 and 1980 industrial production, mainly of textile products and electronic components, increased at an average annual rate of 8%. This was partly due to the establishment of export-processing zones, which provided for 100% foreign ownership to promote foreign investment, and allowed companies to pay employees less than the legal minimum wage. By 1983 these products accounted for nearly 50% of total exports. Still, 85% of Philippine industry was heavily protected, relatively inefficient and oriented toward the home market. Manufacturing output had declined by 7.1% in 1984 and 7.3% in 1985. The domestic market declined because of reductions in real income. Annual automobile production (assembled from imported parts) fell from 19,000 in 1983 to 6,000 in 1985. The sector began to recover in 1986, recording 1.2% growth. The government projected annual growth of 7.6% through 1992.

Mining: The Philippines has extensive deposits of gold, silver, copper, nickel, iron, lead, manganese, limestone and chromium. The government gave high priority to development of mining in the 1970s, resulting in rapid growth; but low world prices for minerals adversely affected the sector between 1980 and 1985. Of the country's 62 large- and medium-scale mining concerns, 27 were closed during that period. Eight of the country's 14 leading mining companies registered losses in 1985. Production declined after 1983.

Employment: In 1986 an estimated 10.4 million people were employed in agriculture, forestry and fishing. Manufacturing accounted for 1.9 million workers; trade restaurants and hotels employed 2.9 million; and community, social and personal services employed 3.6 million. Of a total work force of 21.5 million people, the government estimated that 11.8% were unemployed and 35.2% were underemployed. Independent estimates placed the unemployment figure at 20%. Between 1983 and 1985, about 500,000–600,000 new entrants to the labor force were seeking a shrinking number of jobs. The government aimed to reduce unemployment to 4.9% by 1992, through the creation of 1 million jobs per year. A community employment and development program was launched in 1986 to work toward this goal; by year end, the program had produced 362,541 jobs, or 68.7% of the 618,000 target.

Wages and prices: Real wages have fallen steadily since the early 1970s. In 1986 they were at least 30% below the 1972 level. The consumer price index for all items (1978 = 100) rose to 355.3 in 1986, compared to 286.4 in 1984.

Foreign trade: Export performance has been erratic because of fluctuations in international prices for the country's export commodities. Dependence on petroleum imports produced substantial trade deficits for the years 1974–84. Debt-rescheduling negotiations forced the government to limit imports beginning in 1984. By 1985 imports had fallen to $5.2 billion (from $7.9 billion in 1983), but exports, adversely affected by price drops, also fell to $4.5 billion from $6.3 billion in 1984. Since the early 1970s the country has expanded nontraditional exports such as nickel, electronics, bananas, clothing and handicrafts. The depreciation of the peso and consistent demand from the United States (the country's principal trading partner) have enabled these exports to maintain their growth. Export revenue from traditional exports such as sugar, copper, coconut and timber fluctuates depending on prevailing market prices. The fall of international prices and the rising trend of manufactured exports have caused the relative importance of these exports to fall. Coconut products, copper, sugar and wood together contributed 41% of total export earnings in 1980. By 1984 they contributed only 25%.

Mineral fuels account for approximately one-third of the Philippines' total imports. Nonelectric machinery, transport equipment and base metals are also major imports. In 1981 purchases of crude petroleum accounted for 26% of the import bill. By 1985 reduced prices and demand (due to economic uncertainty) resulted in lower import costs.

The United States and Japan are the country's main trading partners. Imports from the United States totaled $1.3 billion in 1986; from Japan they totaled $868 million. Exports to the United States totaled $1.7 billion; to Japan, $851 million. Members of the Association of Southeast Asian Nations account for less than 5% of total trade.

SOCIAL SERVICES

Welfare: The social security system established in 1957 provides mandatory coverage for all wage and salary workers. The Philippine government insurance system covers all public servants. Benefits include compensation for work-related injuries, pensions, and death benefits for widows and orphans. The Philippine Medicare system pays hospital and surgical expenses for covered workers. The Social Welfare Administration administers public welfare programs in conjunction with private relief agencies in providing services for the needy.

Health services: In 1980 some 3.5% of the national budget ($3.70 per capita) was allocated to public health. The country had 1,416 hospitals with 93,744 beds at that time. Of the hospitals, 25% were run by the state and 75% by private, nonprofit enterprises.

Housing: A national housing program to help low-income families was established in 1972. (In 1978 the National Housing Authority was incorporated into the Ministry of Human Settlements, under the direction of Imelda Marcos). By the end of 1983, however, only 171,600 homes had been built, fewer than 41,000 others were upgraded, and 36,000 lots had been made available for uprooted slum families. There were still shortages of nearly 2 million units in 1985. The poor state of the economy and continuing population growth exacerbated the problem.

EDUCATION

The government, according to the 1987 constitution, provides free elementary and high school education. Elementary education is compulsory. Public and private (sectarian and nonsectarian) schools exist in the Philippines. The educational system is divided into four stages: preschool (from the age of three), elementary school (lasting six years), secondary or high school (four years) and higher education (normally four years). A common general curriculum is provided for all students in the first and second years of high school. The curriculum is more varied during the last two years, leading to either college or technical-vocational courses. Instruction is in English and Pilipino. In 1985 there were 2,334 preschools, with 4,522 teachers and 177,593 students. Elementary schools numbered 32,809, with 284,337 teachers and 8,794,000 students. There were 5,430 secondary schools, with 99,468 teachers and 3,323,000 students. Universities, colleges and vocational schools numbered 1,157, with 57,000 teachers and 1,504,000 students.

All print and broadcast facilities were closed in the Philippines when martial law was declared in 1972. At the time the Philippine press had a reputation for being the freest in Asia, but had become sensationalist. Publications that resumed under martial law were pro-Marcos, sycophantic papers owned by friends and relatives of the first family. After the Aquino assassination in 1983 the press again began to criticize government policies, opposition publications increased.

Freedom of press and speech were guaranteed under the 1987 constitution. Privately owned newspapers proliferated after the Aquino government took power. Aquino, however, closed three radio stations after the August 1987 attempted coup, in order to prevent "dissemination of panic through rumors of future coup attempts." The government sequestered papers suspected of being owned by Marcos cronies. Some believe the most serious threat to the press, however, is the press itself as new publications use sensationalism and gossip to compete for circulation and fame. The National Telecommunications Commission supervises and controls all private and public telecommunications services.

The Manila press (there are also several regional publications)

Dailies: Ang Pahayagang Malaya (English, 165,000); *Balita* (Pilipino, 137,000); *Daily Tribune* (English and Pilipino, 35,000); *Manila Bulletin* (English, 245,000); *Manila Evening Post* (English, 90,000); *Manila Standard* (left-wing, English); *Manila Times* (English); *News Herald* (English, 175,000); *Observer* (English and Pilipino, 60,000); *The Orient News* (English and Chinese, 26,000); *People Tonight* (English and Pilipino, 500,000); *People's Journal* (English and Pilipino, 508,000); *Philippine Daily Inquirer* (English, 285,000); *Philippine Herald-Tribune* (Christian); *Tempo* (English and Pilipino, 129,000); *United Daily News* (English and Chinese, 24,000).

Weeklies: Bannawag (Ilocano, 48,820); *Bisaya* (Cebu-Visayan, 55,000); *Focus Philippines* (English, 70,000); *Liwayway* (Pilipino, 159,000); *Philippine Panorama* (English, 260,000); *The Rizal Chronicle; Weekend; Woman's Home Companion* (English, 97,000); *Women's Journal* (English, 80,000).

Monthlies: Asia Mining (English, 14,000); *Farming Today* (English, 20,000); *National Observer; Philippine Law Gazette.*

Broadcasting: About 270 radio stations (commercial and noncommercial) and five major television networks operate in the Philippines. The principal radio networks are Banshaw Broadcasting Corp. (14 stations); Far East Broadcasting Co. (21 stations, operating a home service and an overseas service in 63 languages); Manila Broadcasting Co. (10 stations); Nation Broadcasting Corp. (25 stations); Newsounds Broadcasting Network (10 stations); Office of Media Affairs Radio Network (21 stations); Philippines

Broadcasting Service (largest, owned by the government); Philippine Federation of Catholic Broadcasters (19 stations); Radio Mindanao Network Inc. (37 stations); Radio Philippines Network; Radio Veritas Asia; Republic Broadcasting System Inc. The principal television networks are Banshaw; GMA Radio Television Arts; Inter-Island Broadcasting Corp.; Kanlaon Broadcasting System; Maharlika Broadcasting System; Radio Philippines Network.

BIOGRAPHICAL SKETCHES

Corazon Cohuangco Aquino. Born January 25, 1933, President Aquino had little formal political experience before taking office. She earned a bachelor of arts degree at Mount Saint Vincent College in New York in 1953. She married Benigno ("Ninoy") Aquino, a journalist and law student, in October 1954. When he was imprisoned in 1972 after martial law was declared, she served as his liaison with the opposition until 1980. She first emerged in political life in 1978 during the 1978 National Assembly elections, when Ninoy ran for assemblyman from prison. Her husband was released in 1980 and allowed to seek medical help in the United States. From 1980 to 1983 they lived in Newton, Mass. Upon their return to Philippines on August 21, 1983, Ninoy Aquino was assassinated. Corazon Aquino became the key figure in many opposition rallies, and in May 1984 supported the opposition candidates in parliamentary elections. In October 1985 she agreed to lead a unified opposition as their candidate for president. Following allegations of fraud in the February 7 election, she waged a civil disobedience campaign. On February 25 she took the oath of office as president. The next day, after Marcos fled for the United States, she formed a government.

Salvador Laurel. The vice-president of the Philippines was born November 18, 1928, in Manila into a family with a long history in Philippine politics. He received his B.A. from the University of the Philippines in 1952 and a master of laws degree and a doctorate of juridical science from Yale University. He was a professor of law and jurisprudence and founded the Legal Aid Society of the Philippines. Laurel was elected a senator in 1967 and became a member of the interim National Assembly in 1978. He has been active in opposition politics since 1982, and became leader of UNIDO in 1981. At the urging of Cardinal Jaime Sin he reluctantly ceded his party leadership to Aquino to unify the opposition for the 1985 presidential election. He became vice-president in February 1986 and continued to hold that office although his own political ambition caused him to break with Aquino.

Ferdinand Marcos. Born on September 11, 1917, the former president of the Philippines was ousted from power by a "People's Revolution" in February 1986. He was educated at the University of the Philippines and served as a captain in the Philippine Army and in the U.S. Forces in the Far East during World War II. From 1946 to 1947 he was special assistant to President Manuel Roxas. Marcos served as a member of the House of Representatives from 1949 to 1959 and of the Senate from 1959 to 1966.

He was elected president in 1965 and reelected in 1969. He imposed martial law in 1972 as worsening economic conditions led to widespread violence. Repressive rule continued until 1981, when martial law was lifted and Marcos was again reelected in reportedly fraudulent elections. He and his wife, Imelda, have been accused of hoarding government funds for their own personal use to the detriment of the Philippine economy. The government's credibility was destroyed after opposition leader Benigno Aquino was assassinated in 1983. Overt opposition culminated in the People's Revolution, which forced the end of the Marcos regime and the reinstitution of democracy in the Philippines. The Marcos family fled to Hawaii, living in comfortable exile. Marcos died there in late 1989.

Lt.-Gen. Fidel Ramos. The secretary of defense, born on March 18, 1928, is perhaps President Aquino's most loyal supporter. He graduated from the U.S. Military Academy at West Point in 1950 and earned a master's degree in civil engineering from the University of Illinois in 1951. He also possesses other military degrees. Ramos ascended through the military ranks of the Philippine army to become chief of the Philippine constabulary in 1972. He became vice chief of staff of the army in 1981 and chief of staff in 1986. He loyally supported Aquino against attempted coups and was widely considered an honest and disciplined military man, though not one without presidential ambitions. He was appointed secretary of defense in January 1988 after the resignation of Rafael Ileto.

SINGAPORE

SINGAPORE

Features: The Republic of Singapore is located immediately south of the Malay Peninsula, to which it has been joined by a causeway, ¾ mile/1.2 km. in length. The republic consists of the main island of Singapore and over 50 small islands and reefs (of which about half are of little importance). The main island is 26 miles/41.8 km. in length from west to east, and 14 miles/22.9 km. in breadth from north to south. The central core of the island, formed of granite and other igneous rocks, contains a number of modest peaks rising to over 328 feet/100 m. (the highest is Bukit Timah, 541 feet/165 m.). To the west and southwest are a number of narrow ridges (of which perhaps the most prominent is the ridge of Mount Faber. The first colonial settlement (and subsequently the commercial and administrative center of the island) was located in the south-central extremity, on the firmer ground adjacent to the Mount Faber ridge. To the east the surface is intersected by small streams and gulleys. The coastline of the island is, except in very few places, flat. Considerable stretches of it have been substantially modified by reclamation work; particularly important here has been the reclamation, since the early 1960s, of a vast expanse of mangrove swamp on the west of the island to provide land for the Jurong industrial estate.

Area: 240 sq. miles/621.7 sq. km.

Mean max. and min. temperatures: 87.3°F/30.7°C–73.4°F/23°C. The period from November to January is generally cooler.

Relative humidity: Relative humidity often exceeds 90% at night and in the early hours of the morning before sunrise. On dry afternoons it is usually about 65%–70%.

Average annual rainfall: 92 in/2,367 mm.

Total population (June 1987 est.): 2,612,800. Of this number, Chinese constituted 76.1%, Malays 15.1%, Indians 6.5% and others 2.3%.

Distribution: People aged below 15 years comprise 23.4% of the population: those above 60 years comprise 8.1%.

Language: The official languages are Malay, Chinese, Tamil and English. Malay is the national language and English the language of administration. Mandarin is increasingly being used by the Chinese in place of the main dialects—Hokkien, Teochew, Cantonese, Hakka, Hainanese, Foochow. Among the Indians, Malayalam, Punjabi, Telugu, Hindi and Bengali are spoken as well as Tamil.

Religion: Freedom of religious belief is guaranteed by the constitution. The 1980 census recorded that 56% of the population aged 10 years and over were Buddhists and Taoists, 16% were Muslims, 10% were Christians and 4% were Hindus. There were also a number of smaller religious groups: Sikhs, Jews, Jains and Zoroastrians.

CONSTITUTIONAL SYSTEM

Constitution: The constitution that came into force on June 3, 1959, as Singapore attained internal self-government—amended in 1963 and 1965 (as a consequence of Singapore's entry into and separation from Malaysia)—remains in force. On March 31, 1980, a reprint of the constitution was published, incorporating those provisions in the Malaysian constitution that continued to apply to Singapore after its separation from Malaysia.

Head of state: President Wee Kim Wee. *Prime minister:* Lee Kuan Yew.

Executive: The president, elected by parliament for a term of four years, normally acts on the advice of the cabinet. The cabinet is led by the prime minister, who is appointed by the President as the member of parliament who commands the confidence of the majority of the members of parliament. The president also appoints the remaining cabinet ministers, on the advice of the prime minister. The cabinet is charged with the administration of the country: it is collectively responsible to parliament.

Legislature: The legislature consists of the president and a parliament of 79 members. Parliament is unicameral and elected by universal adult suffrage in single-member constituencies. It has a maximum legal life of five years but may be dissolved earlier, in which case a general election must be held within three months. Parliament is presided over by the speaker, who may be elected by parliament from among its members who are not ministers or parliamentary secretaries, or from among qualified persons who are not members of parliament.

Political parties: The People's Action party (PAP), founded in 1954, has been continuously in power since 1959. In the four parliamentary elections up to and including that of 1980, the PAP won every seat, but in the 1980s two seats went to opposition parties and the PAP share of the vote fell (to below 63% in the 1984 election). However, the PAP remains overwhelmingly the dominant political organization on the island. The opposition parties that, between them, won two parliamentary seats in the early 1980s were the Workers' party (founded in 1957), which seeks the establishment of a democratic socialist government, and the Singapore Democratic party (founded in 1980). The Barisan Sosialis, formed in 1961 by former members of the PAP, advocates in its left-wing platform the abolition of military service and the liberalization of the citizenship laws. The PAP government is barely tolerant of—and frequently actively hostile to—these opposition parties.

Judicial system: Judicial power is vested in the Supreme Court (consisting of the High Court, the Court of Appeal and the Court of Criminal Appeal) and in the subordinate courts (consisting of district courts, magistrate's courts, juvenile courts, coroner's courts and small claims tribunals). The chief justice and the other judges of the Supreme Court are appointed by the president, acting on the advice of the prime minister. District judges, magistrates, coroners and small claims referees are appointed by the president on the recommendation of the chief justice. Appeals from the Court of Appeal and the Court of Criminal Appeal lie to the Judicial Committee of the Privy Council in London, which is the final appellate court of Singapore.

RECENT HISTORY

The modern history of Singapore dates from 1819 when Sir Stamford Raffles, an official in the East India Company, secured permission from the local sultan and chief to establish a trading settlement on the island, then occupied by only a few Malay fishing families. In 1824 the Malay rulers ceded the island in perpetuity to the East India Company. Two years later the company joined Singapore with its other possessions on the west coast of the Malay Peninsula—Penang (acquired in 1786) and Melaka (finally acquired from the Dutch in 1824)—to form the Straits Settlements. These territories were administered by the East India Company until 1858 when the company was abolished. They then came under the India Office but in 1867 were transferred to the authority of the Colonial Office. The Straits Settlements remained under that authority until the Japanese occupation. In terms of commercial importance, Singapore emerged as the dominant settlement by the middle decades of the 19th century. Indeed, by that time it was established as by far the principal trading center in Southeast Asia and as one of the world's great ports. In this period it drew trade in two directions. It gathered to itself the vast range and volume of primary production cultivated and mined in its hinterland, sorted and part-processed it and then shipped it to the consuming markets of the industrial world; in the opposite direction, it imported cheap manufactures from the industrial world, frequently repackaged them and then distributed them through its Southeast Asia hinterland. Singapore's commercial dominance was due primarily to its superb geographical position (at the focal point for intra- and extraregional trade), its fiercely defended free trade tradition and the acute business acumen of its largely Chinese immigrant population. But there also emerged in the colonial period a serious tension between Singapore and its neighbors. That tension derived in part from Singapore's character as a Chinese outpost at the center of the Malay world, but also from the commercial dependence of the Southeast Asia hinterland (notably the Malay States and the Netherlands East Indies) on Singapore. This tension was maintained into the recent past and continues to shape fundamentally Singapore's present.

Following the Japanese surrender in August 1945 the returning British administration sought a major constitutional restructuring of their Malayan possessions. This was eventually achieved in 1948 with the creation of the Federation of Malaya, which comprised all the states of the peninsula, together with Penang and Melaka. Singapore was separated from its former partners, partly because of its special position as a free port and its great importance to the British as a military base, but also because it was difficult to see how this Chinese city could be integrated into a Federation of Malaya that would now move toward independence as a Malay-dominated polity. Singapore itself cautiously moved toward self-government. In 1948 elections were held for a limited number of positions on the Legislative Council but there was little popular enthusiasm for this initiative. And there was considerable repression of indigenous radical political activity during the most tense period of the "emergency" in the late 1940s and early 1950s. A new constitution introduced in 1955 contained provision for a Legislative Assembly in which 25 of the 32 members were elected; the leader of the largest party would, as chief minister, form a Council of Ministers responsible to the Assembly. The Assembly elections of 1955 saw the domination of two left-wing parties, the PAP, led by Lee Kuan Yew, and the Labour Front, led by David Marshall. Marshall formed a minority government. The Communists now made a bid for power through the trade union movement and Chinese middle schools: for a short period they gained control of the Central Executive Committee of the PAP. The Marshall administration used emergency powers to imprison prominent Communists. Marshall resigned in 1956, having failed to negotiate immediate self-government. But in 1957 the terms for full internal self-government were agreed, and at elections held in 1959, which would give effect to this, the PAP won a massive majority (43 out of 51 seats). The PAP under Lee Kuan Yew has remained in power since that time.

A central concern of Lee Kuan Yew as he took office was to achieve full independence for Singapore through merger with the Federation of Malaya, which itself had achieved independence in 1957. The prospect of merger with the strongly anti-Communist Federation severely angered radical elements in the PAP, and in July 1961 they attempted to bring down the Lee Kuan Yew government. When they failed, these elements left the PAP to form a socialist front in opposition—the Barisan Sosialis. Ironically, this left-wing challenge brought merger closer, for the anti-Communist administration in Kuala Lumpur now saw more clearly the need to bring the potentially left-dominated Singapore under its control. A public referendum in Singapore in 1962 endorsed merger with the Federation of Malaya and with the Borneo territories of Sabah and Sarawak; the Federation of Malaysia came into being on September 16, 1963. The merger failed. Indonesia's forceful opposition to the new formation seriously damaged Singapore's trade, and Kuala Lumpur was sharply angered by what it saw as

Singapore's unwarranted intervention in the internal politics of the peninsula—notably when the PAP sought to contest seats in the 1964 general election and subsequently when Lee Kuan Yew attempted to unite all Malaysian opposition parties. On August 9, 1965, Singapore was forced out of the Federation of Malaysia and became a separate independent state.

It was widely feared that Singapore—of tiny geographical extent, very high population density and no natural resources, and dependent almost exclusively on its external trade and commercial relationships—could not survive in that form. A further blow came in 1966 when the United Kingdom decided to withdraw its military forces from the island (the withdrawal was completed in 1971). The decision, of course, had important defense implications for the infant state and necessitated the introduction of compulsory military service, but the economic implications were, if anything, more serious. The Lee administration responded to these challenges with extraordinary creative determination. Crucial to its response was an acceptance that the economy of the island must now discard its entrepôt focus; emphasis was now given to the creation of a strongly export-oriented industrial economy, notably attractive to foreign investment (made attractive in large part by the pressure of a highly disciplined and technologically trained work force and by the existence of tough labor legislation that severely regulated union activity). Toward the end of the 1970s strong emphasis was given to the development of high-technology export industries. The administration sought no less radical a restructuring of the social environment, including heavy investment in the provision of education and medical facilities and a major program of housing renewal that by 1987 saw some 84% of the population living in public housing (the majority as owner-occupiers). Finally, following separation in 1965, the Lee government rapidly stabilized the new state's external relations: A generally cooperative relationship was established with Malaysia, and Singapore was a founder-member of the Association of Southeast Asian Nations (ASEAN) in 1967. In the longer term Singapore has sought friendly relations with all states, irrespective of ideology.

Singapore's remarkable economic success has secured striking electoral support for the PAP: In the four parliamentary elections up to and including that of 1980 it won every single seat. But the 1980s saw a marginal erosion of its position, as the opposition Workers' party (in 1981) and the Singapore Democratic party (in 1984) won parliamentary seats, and as the PAP's share of the vote (nearly 78% in 1980) dropped toward 60%. The reasons for this erosion are complex; important considerations include the arrival of a generation of voters who did not witness Singapore's early struggles and were thus perhaps less appreciative of the PAP's achievements; an increasingly widespread irritation with the PAP's excessively paternalistic, arrogant and censorious attitude toward the people of the island; possibly an unease at the government's ruthless opposition to dissident beliefs; and, arguably, the failure (thus far) of the independence-generation leadership of the PAP to bring forth a second-generation of leaders to whom power could confidently be transferred.

ECONOMY

Background: By the time Singapore attained internal self-government in 1959 it was widely recognized that the island could no longer depend (as it had for some 140 years) on the entrepôt trade for economic survival; the hinterland economies (prominently Malaysia and Indonesia) would as independent states now seek to develop direct trade with their markets and suppliers beyond the region. Toward the end of the 1960s a further, long-established foundation of the economy was dismantled as the British military facilities (which at that time created 16% of Singapore's employment and generated 20% of GDP) were rapidly withdrawn. From the introduction of Singapore's first Development Plan in 1961, therefore, the administration has sought a fundamental (and continuing) restructuring of the economy, primarily in the direction of extensive industrialization. In the 1960s the emphasis was on the development of labor-intensive industries (notably textile and clothing manufacture, and electronics assembly), reflecting the fear that rapid population growth (due to a high rate of natural increase and unrestricted immigration in the 1950s) was leading to unacceptably high levels of unemployment. Until the late 1960s this form of industrialization was directed primarily toward import-substitution; in the 1970s it was redirected toward export expansion. The close of the 1970s, with full employment effectively restored, saw a further major shift in emphasis toward capital-intensive, high-technology and high value-added industries (although again strongly directed toward export markets). Indeed, in this last period, the government pursued a "high wage" policy in part to induce productivity growth through increased capitalization. Also, from the late 1970s on the government placed strong emphasis on the expansion of the service sector; on the development of Singapore as a regional financial, insurance and tourism center (again involving investment in capital-intensive, high-technology systems); and on the expansion of transportation and warehouse facilities. A central element in the government's economic strategy was the need to attract substantial foreign investment into the rapidly expanding industrial and service sectors. This was done by the enactment of tough union legislation that virtually eliminated militant unionism and industrial unrest, the provision of generous tax incentives, the creation of an increasingly skilled and highly disciplined work force, and the existence of firm prospects of political stability. Despite the image of Singapore as having a free-wheeling, laissez-faire economy, the government is highly interventionist: Through some 80 statutory bodies (notably, for example, the Jurong Town Corp.) the government has imposed policies for industrial development; there is substantial state involvement in individual companies; the government invests heavily in the economic and transport infrastructure of the island; there is a powerful emphasis on high-technology training for the work force. Singapore has achieved impressive economic growth: from 1964 to 1968 GDP expanded, in real terms, at an average annual rate of 10%; from 1969 to 1979 at 9.4%; from 1980 to 1984 at 8.2%. But in 1985 real GDP fell by 1.8%; it rose by 1.9% in 1986 and by 8.8% in 1987. The recession in the mid-1980s primarily reflected worsening external conditions (although internal factors, notably a sharp contraction in construction activity, also played an important part). Strongly oriented toward export markets to absorb its production of manufactures and services, Singapore remained highly vulnerable to changes in the regional and world economy.

Agriculture: In 1986 agriculture, hunting, forestry and fishing accounted for 0.84% of employment; agriculture and fishing accounted for 0.71% of GDP at factor cost. The principal items of production are poultry, eggs, pigs (although pig farming is soon to cease), vegetables and fish. Singapore relies on imports for most of its basic food needs.

Manufacturing: In 1986 manufacturing accounted for 25.25% of employment and 27.17% of GDP at factor cost. In the 1980s this sector became dominated by capital-intensive plants producing high-technology products. Of particular importance here is the electronics industry (producing microchips, complex printed computer circuit boards and computer peripherals), which in 1987 employed about 84,000 workers and accounted for about one-third of the total value-added in manufacturing. Also important are the electrical industry (precision motors, generators, switchgears, power switches); the transport equipment industry (concentrating on ship repairs and maintenance); the machinery and machine tools industry; the garment industry; publishing; and the food, beverage and tobacco industry. Singapore is the third largest oil-refining center in the world after Rotterdam and Houston, importing some 44 million tons of oil in 1986 (of which only 10% was for local consumption). But as Singapore's traditional overseas customers establish their own refining plants, this sector faces difficulties. Chemical production expanded; a new petrochemical complex began to supply local pharmaceutical and specialized chemical plants. The growth of Singapore's manufacturing sector has depended heavily on foreign investment: in 1987, foreign investment commitments accounted for 83% of total commitments. More than two-thirds of foreign investment came from Japan, the United States and Europe. Japan has recently become the single most important source of foreign capital, accounting for 34% of total investment commitments in 1986 (heavily concentrated in the electrical and electronics components and office equipment fields). Singapore's manufacturing sector is located primarily in a vast industrial estate in Jurong, on the west of the island.

Construction: In 1986 construction accounted for 8.66% of employment and 8.53% of GDP at factor cost. A high proportion of the labor employed in construction is immigrant. This sector has been supported largely by a major program of public housing and urban renewal, the construction of the Mass Rapid Transit project, and substantial private investment in commercial and industrial property and hotels.

The service sector: Singapore is now established as the financial and insurance center of Southeast Asia. It has arrived at this position partly because of its traditional function as a commercial and trading center but also because the government's economic strategy has strongly emphasized the expansion of this sector. Important here has been the liberalization of exchange regulations, the provision of tax incentives, the development of training facilities for local personnel, the removal of restrictive practices to encourage competition and growth in the banking and financial system. Singapore's development as an international financial center has been built on the Asian Dollar Market, established in the late 1960s. The principal suppliers of funds come from Europe, the Middle East and the United States, while the users include the ASEAN states, Hong Kong and Japan. The Asian Dollar Market is, after Japan, the largest external currency market in Asia. In 1986 financing, insurance, real estate and business services accounted for 8.7% of employment; finance and business services accounted for 23.15% of GDP at factor cost. Reference must also be made to the tourist industry. In 1987 there were 3.7 million visitor arrivals in Singapore; tourism is the third largest earner of foreign exchange.

Foreign trade: In 1986 the total value of Singapore's foreign trade was U.S.$45 billion, almost as large as that of China. Approximately two-thirds of exports were domestically produced, one-third were reexports: The principal exports were machinery and transport equipment (including electric and electronic goods) at 38.6%; petroleum products at 20.5%; basic manufactures (including textile yarn and fabrics) at 7.4%. Also in 1986 the principal export markets were the United States (23.4%), Malaysia (14.8%) and Japan (8.6%). The principal sources of imports were Japan (19.9%), the United States (15.0%) and Malaysia (13.3%). The main imports are food, mineral fuels, machinery and equipment, and miscellaneous manufactures. In recent years Singapore has regularly experienced a deficit on merchandise trade, partly offset by earnings from services; but the current account steadily improved during the first half of the 1980s to move into a surplus in 1986 as the trade deficit was more than offset by a services surplus. Official foreign reserves at the end of 1986 totaled almost $13 billion, sufficient to finance about eight months' retained imports.

Employment: In the 1960s and early 1970s government economic policy focused on the need to create employment opportunities to absorb a rapidly expanding labor force: Unemployment stood at 9.2% in 1966 and 10.4% in 1970. The government's industrialization strategy has reduced that figure substantially, to 2.7% in 1984. Indeed, labor shortages have appeared, particularly in the industrial and construction sectors; these have been relieved by importing labor from Malaysia, Indonesia, Thailand, the Philippines, India and Sri Lanka. In 1984 there were about 150,000 foreign workers (11% of the total labor force). The government intends to eliminate the need for unskilled foreign workers by 1991.

Price trends: In the 1960s the average annual increase in consumer prices was modest. But Singapore was strongly affected by the worldwide inflation of the mid-1970s (the consumer price index rose by 34.6% in 1973). In 1980 it rose by 8.5%. By 1986 inflation had stabilized at around 1.2% per year. The rate of increase in the consumer price index has been held in check in recent years by the strength of the Singapore dollar and the weakness of world petroleum prices.

Welfare: The Central Provident Fund (CPF), established in 1955, is a compulsory national social security savings scheme that seeks to meet the basic needs of Singaporeans in the provision of financial security in retirement, in housing and in health care. The rate of contribution from April 1986 was 35% of the employee's wages, the employer contributing 10% and the employee 25%. Since March 1986 the government has been paying a market-based interest rate on CPF savings: The rate for January 1988 was 3.19% per year. At the end of 1987 the CPF had 1.9 million members.

Health services: Singaporeans enjoy a high standard of health. In 1986 the average life expectancy at birth was 73.6 years; the infant mortality rate was 9.4 per thousand live births. Government health services are heavily subsidized to bring health care within the reach of all, and a substantial private sector exists. Singaporeans may pay their hospitalization bills through the Medisave scheme, implemented in April 1984. Every CPF contributor has 6% of monthly income credited to a Medisave account. There are nine government hospitals (7,717 beds) and 12 private hospitals (2,076 beds). Primary health care is provided through an extensive network of community, maternal, child and elderly health services. Polyclinics are situated in the major housing estates. The government vigorously pursues public campaigns to promote a more healthy life-style for Singaporeans (the campaign "Towards a Nation of Non-Smokers" was launched in 1986). In addition there is an intensive health education program on AIDS; screening for AIDS carriers among blood donors is routinely carried out.

Housing. Since 1960 the Housing and Development Board (HDB) has carried out a major national housing program—clearing land for redevelopment, constructing apartments, administering the sale and rental of public and middle-income housing, undertaking the management of new towns and housing estates, resettling people displaced by urban renewal. Under the Home Ownership for the People scheme introduced in 1964, almost 450,000 units of HDB apartments have been sold to the public; more than 86% of the population enjoy subsidized housing. CPF savings are usually used in house or apartment purchase. From the late 1960s on considerable emphasis was placed on the renewal of the island's urban center (which included the large-scale demolition of slums) and the construction of major housing estates in satellite towns (a notable early example was Ang Mo Kio).

Singapore has invested heavily in education, recognizing that the skills of its people are by far its most valuable resource. Every child is assured a place in the education system. In June 1986 there were 236 primary schools (with 268,820 pupils) and 157 secondary schools (with 203,088 pupils). English, the language of technology and international business, is the language of instruction. All pupils also study one of the other official languages (Chinese, Malay or Tamil); there are also opportunities to learn French, German or Japanese. In 1980 streaming procedures were inserted at a number of stages in primary and secondary education, in recognition of the different needs and abilities of pupils. An extensive structure of further and higher education included, in June 1986, 16 technical and vocational institutes (20,873 students) and five universities and colleges (42,007 students). Pupils and students in Singapore face intense pressures from both family and the state for examination achievement; academic qualification is widely seen as the only route to a secure, well-paid occupation.

MASS MEDIA

The press: Since 1974 the government has supervised all newspaper management. All newspapers exercise a high degree of self-censorship and are clearly responsive to the government's views. Legislation passed in 1986 empowered the government to restrict the circulation in Singapore of foreign periodicals that, in the view of the authorities, exert influence over readers on domestic political issues. Action has been taken against *Time* (lifted in July 1987), the *Far Eastern Economic Review, Asiaweek* and the *Asian Wall Street Journal*.

Dailies: Daily newspapers in English include the *Straits Times*, 276,829; *Business Times*, 18,000. In Chinese there are *Lian He Zao Bao*, 190,000; *Shin Min Daily News*, 107,000; *Lian He Wan Bao*, 80,000. A Malay daily is *Berita Harian*, 42,352; in Tamil, *Tamil Murasu*, 8,500. Except for the *Business Times* all publish seven days a week. With the exception of *Tamil Murasu*, all are owned and printed by the Singapore Press Holdings Ltd., a group comprising the Singapore News and Publications Ltd., the Straits Times Press Ltd. and Times Publishing Company.

Weeklies and Periodicals: Also owned by the Singapore Press Holdings Ltd. are the two weeklies, *The Sunday Times*, 308,747, and *Berita Minggu*, 55,353. Periodicals include *Singapore Business* (monthly), 10,000.

Broadcasting: The Singapore Broadcasting Corp. (SBC) operates five radio channels (one each in English, Malay, Mandarin and Tamil, with the fifth channel devoted to classical/traditional music and cultural programs presented in English and Mandarin); and three television channels (broadcasting in English, Malay, Chinese and Tamil). Radio broadcasting dates from 1935 (when it was operated by the British Malaya Broadcasting Corp.); the television service began in 1963, with color being introduced in 1974. In all its services the SBC seeks to maintain a balance between informational/educational and entertainment programs. It derives revenues from radio and television license fees and from commercial advertising. In 1987 some 531,215 TV and 109,453 radio licenses were issued.

BIOGRAPHICAL SKETCHES

Goh Chok Tong. Born in Singapore in 1941, Goh Chok Tong was educated at Raffles Institution, the University of Singapore and Williams College in the United States. He joined the Singapore Administrative Service in 1964; in 1969 he was transferred to Neptune Orient Lines, Singapore's national shipping line, and became its managing director in 1973. In 1977 he left the company to become senior minister of state, finance. He was first elected to parliament in 1976. Since the late 1970s he has held a variety of cabinet posts of increasing importance. In October 1987 he held the position of first deputy prime minister and minister of defense. Goh Chok Tong is perhaps the outstanding figure in Singapore's second generation of leaders.

Brig.-Gen. Lee Hsien Loong (retd.). Born in 1955, Lee Hsien Loong is the eldest son of the prime minister. He graduated from the University of Cambridge with first class honors and distinction in mathematics. On graduation he entered the Singapore armed forces, rising on retirement to the rank of brigadier-general. He subsequently entered parliament and embarked on a political career. In October 1987 he held the positions of minister of trade and industry and second minister of defense. He is widely seen as a successor to his father.

Lee Kuan Yew. Born in Singapore on September 16, 1923, Lee Kuan Yew was educated at Raffles College, Cambridge University (double first in law with star for special distinction) and the Middle Temple, London. In the early 1950s he was legal adviser to a number of trade unions in Singapore. He helped found the PAP in 1954 and was elected to parliament in 1955. He has been prime minister of Singapore since 1959. Lee Kuan Yew is widely recognized both within and outside Singapore as a man of outstanding intelligence, political skill and vision, but he is also seen as a man of ruthless determination who has found it increasingly difficult to tolerate opposition to his views. He remains the dominant figure in the political life of Singapore and one of Asia's most well-known political figures.

Sinnathamby Rajaratnam. Rajaratnam, born in Sri Lanka on February 23, 1915, was educated at Victoria Institution in Kuala Lumpur, Raffles Institution and King's College in London. In the early 1950s he was a journalist with the *Straits Times*. He was a founder-member of the PAP in 1954. In 1959 he abandoned journalism to concentrate solely on politics; he was elected to the Legislative Assembly in that year. With Singapore's separation from Malaysia in 1965, Rajaratnam became minister of foreign affairs, a position he held until 1980. In October 1987 he held the position of senior minister, prime minister's office.

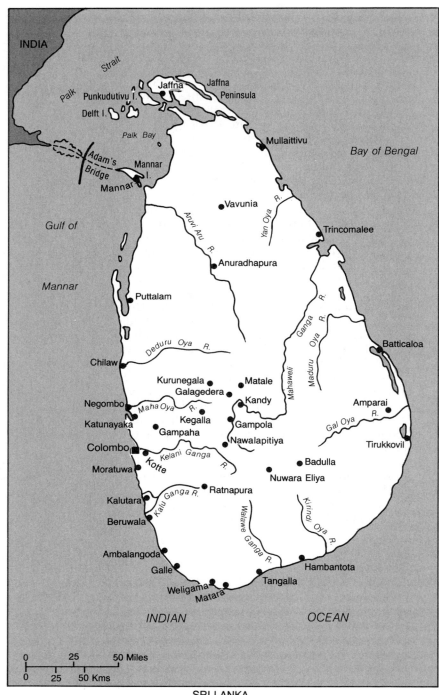

INDIA

Palk Strait

Punkudutivu I.

Delft I.

Jaffna

Jaffna Peninsula

Palk Bay

Adam's Bridge

Mannar I.

Mannar

Mullaittivu

Bay of Bengal

Gulf of

Mannar

Aruvi Aru R.

Vavunia

Yan Oya R.

Trincomalee

Anuradhapura

Puttalam

Deduru Oya R.

Ganga R.

Maduru Oya R.

Batticaloa

Chilaw

Kurunegala

Galagedera

Matale

Kandy

Mahaweli

Amparai

R.

Negombo

Maha Oya R.

Kegalla

Gampola

Gal Oya

Katunayaka

Gampaha

Nawalapitiya

Tirukkovil

Colombo

Kotte

Kelani Ganga R.

Badulla

Moratuwa

Nuwara Eliya

Kalutara

Kalu Ganga R.

Ratnapura

Beruwala

Walawe Ganga R.

Kirindi Oya R.

Ambalangoda

Galle

Hambantota

Weligama

Matara

Tangalla

INDIAN   OCEAN

0   25   50 Miles

0   25   50 Kms

SRI LANKA

SRI LANKA

Features: The Democratic Socialist Republic of Sri Lanka is a pear-shaped island of crystalline rock south of India. The coastal regions are at low elevation, while the highest elevation is found in the south-central part of the island. There are several rivers flowing from the high elevations to the sea in all directions. The longest river is Mahaweli Ganga, which flows to the northeast.

Area: 25,332 sq. miles/65,610 sq. km.

Mean max. and min. temperatures: Colombo (6°56'N, 79°51'E; 22 ft/7m.) 83°F/28°C (May), 80°F/27°C (Jan.).

Relative humidity: 75%.

Mean annual rainfall: 50 in/1,300 mm. in the dry zone, 200 in/1,300 mm. in the wet zone.

POPULATION

Total population (1985 est.): 15,837,000.

Chief town and populations: COLOMBO (643,000), Dehiwala-Mount Lavinia (184,000), Moratuwa (138,000), Jaffna (133,000), Kandy (120,000).

Distribution: There are two principal groups of Sri Lankan nationals: Sinhalese, who constitute 74% of the population and Sri Lankan Tamils, who make up 12%. The Sinhalese have inhabited the island since antiquity, but large-scale migration by Tamils from southern India added to their numbers in medieval times. The Sri Lankan Tamils are concentrated in the northern and eastern provinces, and the major Tamil town is Jaffna. Indian Tamils, commonly called Moors because of their Arab origins, migrated to the central region in the 19th century and make up 6% of the population. There has been substantial conflict between Sinhalese and Tamils, especially Sri Lankan Tamils, since independence in 1948.

Language: Sinhala, an Indo-Iranian language, previously was the sole official language and is spoken by the Sinhalese majority. Tamil is spoken by 18% of the population. Since 1987, English and Tamil have also been recognized as official languages.

335

Religion: Sinhalese Buddhists constitute 69% of the population, with the Hinayana sect predominating. Tamil Hindus total 16%, Muslims 8%, and Christians 7.5% of the population.

CONSTITUTIONAL SYSTEM

Constitution: The 1978 Constitution makes Sri Lanka a presidential democracy with power concentrated in the presidency. The system is modeled after that of France, with a weaker prime minister appointed by the president with the approval of Parliament. Parliament is elected by proportional representation; important issues can be submitted to a national referendum.

Head of state: President Ranasinghe Premadasa.

Executive and legislature: The president may declare war, grant pardons and execute the orders of the legislative branch and the Supreme Court. The president has the power to appoint and dismiss members of the Supreme Court. He can also dismiss members of his own party from the legislature. The executive is authorized to dissolve Parliament and to call new elections at any time.

Parliament has the power to impeach the president with the consent of the Supreme Court, but given presidential control over both these institutions, impeachment is virtually impossible. There is a strict separation between government and opposition in the Parliament, and legislatures are forbidden from crossing over between government and opposition. Strict party discipline is maintained in the legislature. The majority party must approve the president's choice of prime minister.

Local government: The 1987 Indo–Sri Lankan accord provided for creation of provincial councils. The bill establishing these councils was narrowly passed by Parliament in late 1987, but it was an important step in the decentralization of government, granting the Tamil regions a degree of political autonomy.

Judiciary: Sri Lankan civil law is based on Roman-Dutch law dating back to the Dutch colonialist period. Criminal law is structured along British lines. The Supreme Court has a chief justice and 6 to 10 associate justices, all of whom are appointed and may be removed by the president. There is also a Court of Appeal, a High Court, and Courts of First Instance. Below these are district courts, magistrates' courts, and civil and rural courts.

Political parties: The two major parties are the United National Party (UNP) and the Sri Lanka Freedom Party (SLFP). Though both have ruled Sri Lanka at various points since independence, the UNP is the party currently in power. The major Tamil political party is the Tamil United Liberation Front (TULF).

RECENT HISTORY

In the 1830s the British commenced administrative reforms that shaped the development of Sri Lankan society and economy for the next century.

The reforms had the impact of expanding plantation agriculture especially for tea, creating a legal system based on European methods that practiced racial discrimination against Sri Lankans, expanding the network of roads to connect the central and coastal parts of the island and creating a Western-educated elite. A serious labor shortage developed on the plantations. Peasants cultivating the paddies had far higher status than landless laborers and made more than the low wages offered by plantation owners, thus peasants were not attracted to plantation work. Further, the peak period for the coffee harvest coincided with the rice harvest. Under these circumstances, the British began to import Tamil laborers from India, who had been living in even greater poverty than the Sri Lankans. The colonial government of Sri Lanka in the 19th century has been described as an "appendage of the estates." All its efforts at economic development were focused on British-owned plantations; no attempt was made to improve the welfare of Sri Lankans or the productivity of Sri Lankan farms.

At the beginning of the 20th century, professional and upper-middle-class Sri Lankans began agitating for political reform. A Buddhist revivalist movement, formed in the 1880s to protest the Christian bias of missionary education, continued to grow. These two groups created the foundation of the independence movement to come. The colonial governor had opposed the demands of the educated elites for constitutional reform, but in 1910 the colonial office agreed that one educated Sri Lankan could be elected to the legislative council through restricted suffrage. However, the desire for freedom continued to grow among the Sri Lankans and the Indian independence movement encouraged them further. In the 1920s representation in the council was expanded on a regional and communal basis. Members would be elected to represent the Sinhalese, the Tamils, the Europeans and others. This official division of society along ethnic lines served the colonial strategy of divide-and-rule, thus discouraging any Sri Lankan national identity that could unite the various ethnic groups. In 1931 a new constitution was adopted that allowed universal adult suffrage, but the elected assembly had little influence over the executive. Colonial authorities retained actual control over the government.

During World War II the British began to fear the rising anti-British feeling in Sri Lanka. To maintain quiescence they promised independence after the war. And during the war, the powers available to elected representatives were increased. On February 4, 1948, independence was granted to Sri Lanka. In the 1947 elections the United National Party (UNP) gained a majority of parliamentary seats and D. S. Senanayke became the first prime minister; there were some Tamil members in the UNP. But there was considerable hostility among Sinhalese toward the Indian Tamil plantation workers, and in 1949 steps were taken to limit their franchise. All "Indians and Pakistanis" in Sri Lanka were required to register as Sri Lankan citizens before gaining the right to vote; the Supreme Court held that the government had discretionary power to withhold such citizenship. In 1951 S. W. R. D. Bandaranaike left the UNP and founded the Sri Lanka Freedom Party (SLFP).

The Korean War caused an increase in the price of rubber, and Sri Lanka benefitted in the years preceding the 1952 elections. The UNP won those elections; however, the SLFP continued to organize and began to appeal to Sinhalese communal sentiments. In 1956 Buddhist organizations campaigned to upgrade the status of Buddhism in the country. They demanded official patronage of the religion. The UNP resisted some of the demands, seeking to maintain a degree of secularism. If elected, Bandaranaike offered to accept the principal demands of the Buddhist communal organizations. He also proposed establishment of Sinhalese as the official language and offered a socialist economic policy. In foreign affairs, Bandaranaike sought nonalignment and the abrogation of military agreements with Britain. The SLFP won the elections.

One of the early acts of Bandaranaike's government was to make Sinhalese the sole official language. Bandaranaike had moderated his language-policy declarations by saying that "reasonable use" of Tamil and English would continue. However, implementation of the "Sinhalese Only" policy touched off riots between Tamils and Sinhalese. In the 1956 elections, the Tamils had voted almost exclusively for the Federalist party, which advocated establishment of a federal system. The Tamil-dominated Federalists planned civil disobedience to protest the new language policy. Bandaranaike agreed to allow the use of the Tamil language in the predominantly Tamil northern and eastern provinces. Plans for civil disobedience were cancelled, but while negotiations continued, tensions between Tamils and Sinhalese mounted. In March 1958 Bandaranaike and Federalist leaders announced an agreement for the "reasonable use" of Tamil. This led Sinhalese radicals to denounce Bandaranaike. Under pressure, Bandaranaike repudiated his agreement with the Federalists.

In May 1958, 500 Sinhalese militants attacked members of the Federalist party who were boarding trains to go to their party convention. Violence throughout the country led to hundreds of deaths. A State of Emergency was declared and arrangements were made for Tamils stranded in the Colombo area to sail to Tamil regions. Order was restored by March 1959, and the State of Emergency was rescinded. In August the reasonable use of Tamil in the context of Sinhalese as the sole official language was enacted. In spite of his promotion of the Sinhalese communalist cause, Bandaranaike was not acceptable to Sinhalese extremists. On September 25, 1959, a Buddhist monk shot and killed him.

The Federalists continued to hope that the new law would be implemented; however, Sinhalese opinion turned strongly against Bandaranaike's agreement with the Federalists. In the 1960 general elections, neither the UNP nor the SLFP won a clear majority. The Federalist party held the balance of power. The SLFP, led by the assassinated prime minister's widow, Sirimavo Bandaranaike, entered into negotiations with the Federalists and agreed to implement the language accord. Instead of calling upon the SLFP and the Federalists to form a coalition government, however, the governor-general dissolved parliament and called new elections. The SLFP won an overwhelming majority and abrogated its earlier agreement with the Federalist party.

The SLFP government, under criticism from the UNP and Sinhalese

Buddhist militants for its earlier agreement with the Federalists on a coalition government, implemented an extreme version of the "Sinhalese Only" policy. Sinhalese was made the sole official language, even in Tamil areas. The Federalist party launched a civil-disobedience campaign that effectively shut down administration in the Tamil areas. In an act of defiance, the Federalists established a separate postal system in Tamil areas, and the SLFP responded by arresting Federalist leaders, banning the party and sending the army into Jaffna. A State of Emergency was imposed in April 1961 and lasted over two years. During this time the SLFP pursued economic development and the "Sinhalization" of the country. Tamil government employees who did not become proficient in Sinhalese were denied salary increments or were forced to retire.

The capitalist-oriented UNP fell 10 seats short of a majority in the 1965 elections. Instead, it formed a coalition government with the Federalist party and the Tamil Congress. The new government drafted a law providing for Tamil use in the northern and eastern provinces for the "transaction of all government and public business and for the maintainance of public records." Sinhalese militants accused the UNP of granting "parity of status" to the Tamil language, of enabling Tamils to exploit the wealth of Sri Lanka and of opening the possibility of an eventual Tamil takeover of the country. As implementation of the new language law began, Tamils cooperated with the government in the expansion of Sinhalese use in Tamil areas. Tamil public servants took Sinhalese language instruction and accepted Sinhalese as the national language.

The Sri Lankan government followed a policy of settling ethnic Sinhalese in predominantly Tamil areas, thereby converting them to Sinhalese areas. The Tamils bitterly resented this but the district councils had no power to halt such settlements in their areas. To assuage the fears of many Sinhalese, the SLFP enacted a new constitution in 1972 after it came to power. It included the statement that "it shall be the duty of the state to protect and foster Buddhism." It also eliminated a clause that read "Parliament has no right to enact legislation that would confer an undue advantage to a race, religion, or community." This had been an important protection for Tamils. In 1972 previously divided Tamil parties united to form the Tamil United Front (TUF) which demanded a federal state.

While economic conditions had deteriorated throughout the country, Tamils faced especially acute unemployment because of discriminatory government policy. This led to rising militancy among Tamil youths and ultimately to demands for a separate state they called Eelam. In May 1973 over 100 Tamil youths were arrested for staging a demonstration to protest the visit of SLFP cabinet ministers to Jaffna. Militants succeeded in inducing Tamil students to boycott classes. In response to the rising youth militancy, the TUF increased its own militancy. In May 1973 it "resolved upon a separate state of Tamil Eelam as its goal," and renamed itself the Tamil United Liberation Front (TULF). At this point, the Ceylon Workers Congress withdrew from the coalition. Representing the descendants of 19th-century immigrant Indian Tamils in central Sri Lanka, the party had a different perspective from the Sri Lankan Tamils whose ancestors had lived on the island for centuries. The TULF remained committed to using non-violent methods for the establishment of Eelam; however, it issued appeals for support from the Indian government and from Tamils in the Indian state of Tamil Nadu.

The Tamil youth movement, on the other hand, began to take up arms in pursuit of secession. In January 1974, the fourth annual World Conference of Tamil Language and Tamil Culture was held in Jaffna. Police charged into the nonviolent crowd and killed nine people. The Sri Lankan government ordered no inquiry and offered no apology. After this point the militants staged a series of robberies and attacks on police and soldiers. In 1975 the mayor of Jaffna, who was a Tamil member of the SLFP, was assassinated by Tamil militants.

In the 1977 national elections, the UNP returned to power, while the TULF won majorities in both the northern and eastern provinces. The TULF still hoped to work out a peaceful settlement with the government. In April 1978 a group ambushed a Tamil police inspector and claimed responsibility for the action under the name of the Liberation Tigers of Tamil Eelam (LTTE). The government sought to fight the Tigers by issuing an order that effectively permitted security forces to torture detainees.

In 1978 another constitution was established giving Sri Lanka a presidential system. The constitution concentrated enormous power in the hands of the president. Junius Richard Jayewardene, head of the UNP, was elected the first president and he pursued a carrot-and-stick policy toward the Tamils. In the election campaign, Jayewardene had conceded that some Tamil demands were justified. As president, he "was persuaded that means could—and indeed must—be found to bring a real measure of decentralization without risking partition." Negotiations proceeded between the TULF and the government by way of a presidential commission. The parties agreed to set up popularly elected district development councils in the 24 districts. The TULF contested the Jaffna district elections in June 1981, while the Tamil militants sought to sabotage them. The TULF won 80% of votes and all the seats in the Jaffna district elections.

After December 1982 there was an intensification of violence. Tamil militants attacked security forces, and the latter attacked Tamil civilians and militants. In July 1983 security personnel massacred 51 people in the Jaffna peninsula. The LTTE retaliated by killing 13 soldiers. This triggered a round of riots that proved an important turning point in Sri Lankan politics. Over 800 Tamils were killed in Colombo, 53 Tamil prisoners in Welikade Prison were killed by Sinhalese inmates, and naval personnel killed several Tamil civilians in the eastern port of Trincomalee. The riots were organized by a powerful trade union that was highly influential in the government. At this point there began an exodus of Tamil refugees to India and Europe; in 1983, an estimated 30,000 Sri Lankan Tamils were in refugee camps in Tamil Nadu, while more than 10,000 went to Europe.

The Indian government began involving itself in the negotiations. The Sri Lankan government charged that India was supporting Tamil militants with money, training and arms. While there is no doubt that Tamil militants received training on Indian soil, the extent of government involve-

340

ment is difficult to ascertain. Subsequent events suggest that it was not very great. But, while India is a predominantly Hindu society and is about 7% Tamil, it was clear that the government sought to secure some fundamental rights for Tamils in a united Sri Lanka. India was itself wracked with ethnic and communal conflict, and the principle of secularism is paramount to the Indian state. The partition of Sri Lanka along linguistic and religious lines would have set a bad precedent. Furthermore, India sought to avoid any involvement by Western countries in Sri Lankan affairs.

Indian prime minister Indira Gandhi dispatched a special envoy, G. Parthasarathy, to mediate between the Tamils and the Sri Lankan government. Parthasarathy persuaded President Jayewardene to call an all-party conference to negotiate an end to the conflict, but the talks broke down in 1984. In the next year, India persuaded Tamil militants and the Sri Lankan government to set a ceasefire and begin peace talks in Thimbu, the capital of Bhutan. But by 1986 these talks also collapsed and the Sri Lankan government planned a military solution to the conflict.

The next year there were more dramatic changes in the political alignment of Sri Lanka. At the start, the Colombo government sustained its campaign against the LTTE and the Sri Lankan army trapped the Tigers in the Jaffna peninsula. By spring there was a long siege and essential supplies became increasingly scarce. In May, the Indian government sent boats with supplies to Jaffna, but the Sri Lankan navy turned the boats back. Prime Minister Rajiv Gandhi responded by sending five transport planes, accompanied by fighter planes, to parachute the supplies into Jaffna. This action drew protests from Colombo and all other South Asian nations. There was a brief increase in Colombo-Delhi tensions, but in July the two nations concluded a treaty that granted a measure of autonomy to the Tamil areas while pledging Indian assistance in maintaining order in Tamil areas and, indirectly, in guaranteeing the integrity of Sri Lanka. A small Indian peacekeeping force was sent to the Tamil area in the hope that the Tigers would accept a nonviolent political role. But they did not. The Tigers began a fierce guerrilla campaign against the peace-keeping force and continued killing Sinhalese civilians. At the same time, a radical Sinhalese group (JVP) commenced violence against the Sri Lankan government.

In 1988 the level of Tiger violence against the Indian peacekeeping force declined, although attacks on Sinhalese civilians continued. Jayewardene announced his retirement from the presidency and Ranasinghe Premadasa won the election. The JVP had opposed the elections and threatened to kill candidates, party workers and voters. But Premadasa, who had opposed the Indo-Sri Lankan accord when it was concluded, gave qualified support to it during his campaign. His narrow victory, as well as a good voter turnout, signaled a major defeat for the JVP. Shortly after the election, some units of the Indian peacekeeping force were withdrawn.

ECONOMY

Background: In 1985, Sri Lanka's per-capita gross national product (GNP) of U.S. $386 placed it among the poorest countries in the world. However,

341

the Physical Quality of Life Index, which is based on infant mortality, life expectancy and literacy, ranks the country between upper-middle and high-income groups of countries. The socialist policies of the SLFP have enabled a highly egalitarian distribution of income.

When the island-republic gained independence it was one of the most fortunate in South Asia. Its British-owned plantations had generated a high volume of exports. At present, one-third of Sri Lanka's national income is derived from the export of tea, rubber and coconut products. The overall economy is mainly agricultural, a sector that employs 49% of the labor force and accounts for 24% of the 1985 GNP of $5.8 billion. The economy experienced a real growth rate of 5% in 1985.

Under the SLFP government during 1973–1977, social welfare expenditures boosted the quality of life but not the GNP. Under the UNP government during 1978–1981, the economy grew at a real rate of 6% per annum. Unemployment fell but inflation rose. Since 1986, the rising cost of the civil war and the decline of export prices has devastated the Sri Lankan economy.

Agriculture: Seventy-five percent of persons employed in agriculture work in tea, rubber and coconut production. Total agricultural production in 1985 was worth $1.2 billion. These crops account for 60% of areas under cultivation. The tea crop in 1984 was 458 million pounds/208 million kg. on 563,076 acres/227,874 hectares, compared with 394 million pounds/179 million kg. in the previous year. The 1984 rubber crop was 312 million pounds/142 million kg. on 508,010 acres/205,589 hectares. The coconut crop of that year was 1.9 billion nuts from plantations covering 1 million acres/416,423 hectares.

Traditional paddy cultivation in the dry zone is based on the use of water tanks for irrigation, thus the intensity of cultivation declines with distance from a water tank. Agricultural techniques remain backward on most farms. As in the rest of the subcontinent, there is a heavy reliance on bullock for plowing and other draft work.

The wet zone in the southeastern part of the island has different patterns of cultivation. Water tanks are unnecessary because of greater rainfall. Peasants cultivate paddies and fruit and timber trees.

Industry: Sri Lankan industry is relatively underdeveloped and accounts for only 17% of GNP. The UNP government has succeeded in spurring industrial growth since 1977, with its market-oriented policies. Private entrepreneurs have focused on textiles, wood products, food and beverages, plastics and rubber products, and other consumer goods. Public-sector enterprise continues to dominate heavy and large-scale industries such as oil refining, chemicals, paper and plywood, cement, fertilizers and ceramics. In 1985, Sri Lanka produced 603,140 tons of fuel oil, 364,150 tons of diesel and 116,181 tons of gasoline. In that year the country also produced 396,633 tires and tubes, 397,545 tons of cement, 72 million square feet/6.7 million sq. m. of plywood and 19,501 tons of refined sugar.

In attempting to develop a variety of manufacturing industries, Sri Lanka has faced a range of difficulties. These include a small domestic market,

SRI LANKA

shortage of skilled personnel and lack of capital. Furthermore, the status of industry has been the object of considerable political struggle between the leftist SLFP and the rightist UNP.

Trade and transport: Sri Lanka's principal exports have been tea, rubber and coconut products. In recent years textile exports have risen above the levels for rubber and coconut products. The share of manufactures in exports has risen steadily. Imports have focused on input for industry. Intermediate goods accounted for nearly 50% of imports in 1984. Sri Lanka has run persistent trade deficits since 1974. Its principal export markets are the United States, West Germany, Japan and Britain. Its main import sources are Japan, Iran, the United States and Britain.

Employment: The 1985 labor force totaled 5.5 million, with 46% in agriculture, 29% in industry and 19% in services. In 1985, 770,000 persons, or 14% of the labor force, were unemployed. There were 1.6 million workers in labor unions in that year.

SOCIAL SERVICES

Sri Lanka has the most developed social-service program in South Asia. In spite of the country's low per capita income, its system of social welfare has enabled the population to have 87% literacy for persons above the age of 10, a life expectancy of 68 years for men and 71 years for women, and an infant mortality rate of 34 per 1,000 live births. These figures are almost as good as those of the advanced countries.

The government pays a monthly stipend to the elderly, infirm, destitute widows and wives of imprisoned and disabled men. In 1984, 199,009 persons received monthly public allowances totaling approximately $3 million. In 1985, the country had 2,151 physicians, 9,567 medical assistants, 8,091 nurses and 402 hospitals with 44,206 beds. In 1981, there were 2,813,844 housing units. Between 1970 and 1975, 28,000 to 30,000 houses per year were built.

EDUCATION

All education, from kindergarden through university, is free. In 1985, there were 3.6 million pupils and 147,680 teachers in the public schools. There were nine universities in 1984, with 18,217 students and 1,942 teachers.

MASS MEDIA

The press: There is no official press censorship in Sri Lanka; however, the government-appointed Press Council exercises substantial control. In 1985, the major Sinhalese newspapers were *Dinamina* (140,000), *Dawasa* (117,000) and *Lankadipa* (65,000); the major Tamil newspapers were *Dinapathi* (41,200), *Virakesari* (35,000), and *Eelanadu* (20,000); the major English papers were the *Daily News* (65,000), and *The Sun* (56,360).

343

Broadcasting: In 1986, four government-controlled television stations were functioning in the country. State-controlled radio programming is in Sinhalese, Tamil and English. In 1985, there were 1,268,321 licensed radios; in 1983, there were 162,024 licensed television sets.

BIOGRAPHICAL SKETCHES

Ranasinghe Premadasa. Born in 1924, was elected president of Sri Lanka in 1988. Educated in Colombo, he joined the UNP in 1956. In 1977, he became the prime minister. Premadasa took a strongly Sinhalese chauvinist stand and criticized former president Jayewardene for his accord with Indian prime minister Rajiv Gandhi. In his presidential campaign he promised to oust the Indian peace-keeping force that entered the country under the accord. However, as president he has pursued a moderate course. Some Indian military units have been withdrawn, but the process of Indian withdrawal has been gradual.

Junius Richard Jayewardene. Born in 1906, elected the first president of Sri Lanka in 1978 and reelected in 1982. He has led the country through the most difficult period of its postindependence. He pursued a carrot-and-stick policy toward Tamil moderates and militants until 1987. Under his rule military forces committed brutal atrocities against Tamil civilians. In 1987, in a remarkable change of policy, he signed an agreement with Indian prime minister Rajiv Gandhi, in which the Tamils were allowed a degree of regional autonomy and India effectively committed itself to maintain the unity of Sri Lanka. Jayewardene declined to seek a third term in 1988.

Sirimavo Bandaranaike. Born in 1916, became the world's first female prime minister in 1960. She was the wife of the founder of the Sri Lanka Freedom Party, S. W. R. D. Bandaranaike. He had been the prime minister from 1956 until his assassination in 1959. His widow took over leadership of the party, then as prime minister she vigorously pursued a policy of socialist economics and Sinhalese domination of culture and politics. She ran against Premadasa in the 1988 presidential elections and lost.

TAIWAN

Features: Taiwan (Formosa) is located in the western Pacific Ocean off the southeastern coast of mainland China, from which it is separated by the 80–120-mile/130–190-km.-wide Taiwan Strait. Both the Kuomintang (Nationalist) government on Taiwan (Republic of China) and the Communist government on the mainland (People's Republic of China) consider Taiwan a province of China and seek, on different terms, its reunification with the mainland. In addition to the main island, the Taiwan group includes several other tiny islands. The P'eng-hu (Pescadores) islands to the west are also considered part of Taiwan Province. The Quemoy (Chin-Men) and Matsu island groups just off the mainland are part of the province of Fujian but are held by the Kuomintang government. Taiwan also claims the Spratly Islands; the main island of this group, T'ai-ping, has been occupied since 1946 by a Kuomintang marine battalion. This claim is disputed by the People's Republic of China, Malaysia, the Philippines and Vietnam.

Taiwan island is a tilted fault block sloping to the west from the mountainous east; frequent earthquakes indicate that the faulting process continues. The eastern two-thirds of the island is rugged and mountainous and drops precipitously to the sea. More than 30 peaks exceed 10,000 ft/3,050 m., with the highest, Yu Shan, rising to 13,113 ft/3,997 m. The sea is shallower along the western coastal plain, where there are wide tidal flats created by erosion and floods. Only about 15% of the land could be considered flat. Both the coastal plain and the adjoining terraced hillsides are intensively farmed; about 60% of all agricultural land is irrigated to permit the cultivation of two or three crops per year. The soils suitable for agriculture, found mostly in the southwest, are alluvial and highly fertile. Northern soils are mostly shales and sandstone. The island has small deposits of coal (the most economically important mineral), gold, sulfur, copper, marble, limestone, petroleum and natural gas, and salt is extracted from seawater. Rivers are short and flow rapidly from the central mountains to the coasts. Only the Tan-shui River, on which the capital city of T'ai-pei is located, is navigable, but many rivers have been harnessed for hydroelectric power generation. To further reduce the dependence on imported petroleum the government has also constructed three nuclear power plants that provide more than half of Taiwan's electricity. The construction of a fourth nuclear plant has been slowed by environmental protests. Tai-

345

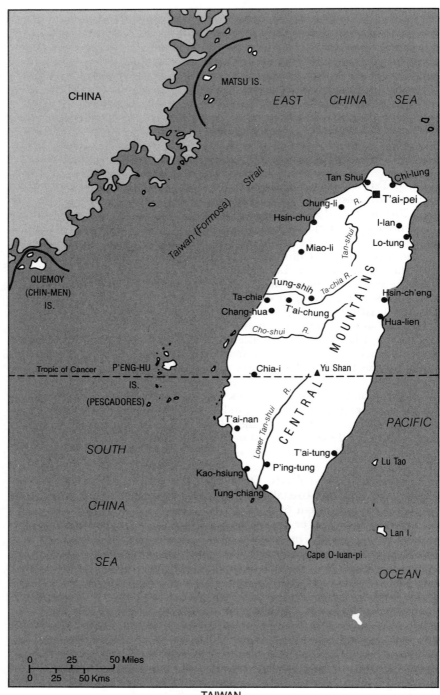

CHINA

MATSU IS.

EAST CHINA SEA

Taiwan (Formosa) Strait

QUEMOY
(CHIN-MEN)
IS.

Tan Shui

Chi-lung

Chung-li

T'ai-pei

Hsin-chu

I-lan

Lo-tung

Miao-li

Tung-shih

Ta-chia R.

Hsin-ch'eng

Ta-chia

Chang-hua

T'ai-chung

Hua-lien

Cho-shui R.

Tan-shui R.

Tropic of Cancer

P'ENG-HU

IS.

(PESCADORES)

Chia-i

Yu Shan

CENTRAL MOUNTAINS

PACIFIC

SOUTH

T'ai-nan

Lower Tan-shui R.

Lu Tao

T'ai-tung

CHINA

Kao-hsiung

P'ing-tung

Tung-chiang

Lan I.

SEA

Cape O-luan-pi

OCEAN

0   25   50 Miles
0   25   50 Kms

TAIWAN

wan has four major harbors: Chi-lung in the north, Kao-hsiung in the south, T'ai-chung in the west and Hua-lien in the east. All of these ports are being modernized and expanded. There are international airports at Kao-hsiung and T'ao-yuan.

Located on the Tropic of Capricorn at about the same latitude as Cuba, Taiwan has a tropical monsoon climate in the south and a subtropical monsoon climate in the north. Climate patterns are modified by topography and by the warm Japan Current that flows around the island. Rain is abundant during the northeast monsoon (October to March), which is characterized by strong winds, and during the southwest monsoon (May to September); the northern mountains receive some of the heaviest rainfall in the world. Typhoons are common, especially from July to September.

Area: 13,900 sq. miles/36,000 sq. km.

Mean max. and min. temperatures: 82°F/28°C (summer), 59°F/15°C (winter).

Mean annual rainfall: 102 in/2,590 mm.

POPULATION

Total population (1989 est.): 20,040,146.

Chief cities and populations (1987 est.): T'AI-PEI (2,575,180), Kao-hsiung (1,320,552), T'ai-chung (695,562), T'ai-nan (646,298).

Distribution: Taiwan is densely populated, especially in the western plains, where population densities often exceed 2,700 persons per sq. mile/1,040 per sq. km. Some 67% of the inhabitants live in urban areas, up from about 30% in 1963 due to the growth of industry. The population, which numbered only about 25,000 in 1624, increased to about 2 million by 1895, to 6.6 million by 1943, and to 10.5 million by 1960. Much of this increase was due to successive waves of migration from the Chinese mainland. The natural rate of increase declined from 3.5% in the 1950s to only 1.1% in the 1980s. The high rate of literacy, rapid urbanization and a high per capita income have contributed to smaller families and a growing elderly population. Some 84% of the people are native Taiwanese descended from earlier Chinese immigrants from Fujian and Guangdong provinces. Another 14% are mainland Chinese supporters of the Kuomintang government who migrated to Taiwan after the Communist victory on the mainland in 1949. The mainlanders, who have been slow to assimilate with the Taiwanese, live mostly in urban areas, while many of the earlier Chinese immigrants and their descendants (mainly Hoklos and Hakka) live in the foothills and western plains. Unassimilated aborigines, who comprise about 2% of the total population, have been pushed into remote areas in the eastern and central mountains by the later Chinese arrivals. They are of Indonesian and Malaysian descent, mostly members of the Ami, Tyal and Paiwan tribes.

Language: Mandarin Chinese is the official language. It is still transliterated into English according to the Wade-Giles system, rather than by the Pinyin system now used on the mainland. Other Chinese dialects, particularly Minnan, are widely spoken. Many older residents can speak Japanese, which they learned when Taiwan was under Japanese rule (1895–1945). Tribal peoples speak various unwritten dialects of Malayo-Polynesian origin.

Religion: There is no official religion. Nearly half of the inhabitants follow various Chinese folk religions that may include elements of Buddhism, ancestor worship and the veneration of local deities. Most of the remainder are Buddhists and Taoists. About 7% are Christians who adhere to various Protestant denominations and to Roman Catholicism. There is a tiny Muslim minority.

CONSTITUTIONAL SYSTEM

Constitution: Taiwan continues to be governed under the 1947 constitution of the Republic of China. A powerful president serves as head of state, and a National Assembly exercises political powers on behalf of the people. There are five *yuans* (governing bodies, or councils). The Legislative Council is the highest legislative body, and the Executive Council (cabinet) is responsible to it. The Judicial Council interprets national laws and the constitution. The Control Council has the power to impeach public officials; and the Examination Council appoints, classifies, promotes, transfers and retires government personnel. The Examination Council is based upon the traditional Chinese civil service examination system formally adopted in A.D. 132. The Kuomintang government effectively controls only Taiwan and has been unable to hold elections on the mainland since 1949. To support its continuing claim to be the legitimate government of all China, it has extended the terms of delegates elected to represent mainland constituencies for life. Although some vacant seats have been filled by appointment and some new seats have been created, the overall number of elected representatives has been drastically reduced by attrition. Taiwan was under martial law from 1949 to 1987; since the lifting of martial law the military no longer occupies a direct role in governing and punishing civilians, although a controversial new national security law still limits political activities.

Head of state: President Lee Teng-hui. *Prime minister:* Lee Huan.

Executive: The president, who is elected to a six-year term by the National Assembly, serves as head of the executive. The president is commander in chief of the armed forces and has the authority to promulgate laws, declare war, impose martial law, make treaties, handle foreign affairs and issue certain emergency orders to preserve national security. Under the constitution the president can serve two terms. (The two-term limit was suspended in 1960, permitting Chiang Kai-shek, then president, to remain in office until his death in 1975.) If the president is unable to fulfill an entire term, succession passes automatically to the vice-president until the next scheduled election. The Executive Council, or cabinet, is headed by a prime minister. It includes a vice-premier, a secretary-general, full ministers (of interior, foreign affairs, national defense, finance, education, economic affairs and communications), and several ministers without portfolio. In a major cabinet shake-up in 1988 the average age of cabinet members was greatly reduced. Most of the new members were considered reform-minded technocrats.

Legislature: The National Assembly, whose members are theoretically elected to six-year terms to represent various occupational and regional constituencies on the Chinese mainland, has the power to elect and recall the president and vice-president, and to amend the constitution and vote on constitutional amendments proposed by the Legislative Council. The last full elections for the National Assembly were held in 1947, when it had 2,961 members. In 1987 only 84 of its remaining 957 members had been elected on Taiwan; another 343 had been appointed to fill vacant life-term mainland seats. Most members (elected and appointed) of the Legislative Council also have lifetime terms. Although elections for supplementary seats are held every three years, only 73 of its remaining 320 members were elected in 1986.

Political parties: The Kuomintang (Nationalist party), founded on the mainland by Sun Yat-sen, is the ruling political party in Taiwan and claims to be the legitimate ruling party of all China. One of the basic aims of the Kuomintang is the overthrow of the Communist government on the mainland and the reunification of China. During the period of martial law (1949–87) the formation of new political parties was illegal. Opposition candidates did run as independents *(tangwai)* in legislative elections, however, and two smaller parties—the China Democratic Socialist party and the Young China party—founded before 1949 remained active. In 1986 a number of opposition leaders formed the technically illegal Democratic Progress party. The government tolerated this party's existence and permitted it to field candidates in the 1986 elections, in which it captured 25% of the popular vote. The principal demands of the Democratic Progress party, which is split into various factions that hinder its ability to serve as an effective opposition, are self-determination for the people of Taiwan, and improved trade and travel links with the mainland. It also pushed for an end to martial law and continues to oppose restrictions on civil liberties and political activity.

Local government: The provincial government, with its capital at T'ai-chung, is headed by a governor nominated by the prime minister and appointed to an indefinite term by the president. A 21-member council appointed by the Executive Council has the power to set provincial policy provided it does not conflict with the laws of the national government. The locally elected provincial legislature (whose members serve six-year terms) has broad legislative powers, but it can be dissolved by the Executive Council if it is determined that the legislature is acting contrary to national policy. For administrative purposes the province of Taiwan is divided into 16 counties, five municipalities administered by the provincial government and two self-governing municipalities (T'ai-pei and Kao-hsiung), each with its own elected assembly. All citizens over the age of 20 may vote in local elections, and most local offices are held by native Taiwanese.

Judicial system: The Judicial Council consists of grand justices who are appointed by the president for nine-year terms. It has the power to interpret the constitution and other laws and to discipline public officials. The Judicial Council supervises the district courts, the high courts and the Supreme Court—the highest court in Taiwan. Supreme Court justices are appointed for life. There is also an Administrative Court to handle final appeals in cases brought against government agencies.

RECENT HISTORY

The name "Taiwan" was first used in official Chinese sources during the time of the Ming dynasty (1368–1644). The indigenous inhabitants were joined by immigrants from Fujian and (later) Guangdong provinces beginning in the latter part of the 16th century. At about this time the Portuguese became the first Europeans to sight Taiwan, which they called Ilha Formosa (Beautiful Isle). The Dutch captured the P'eng-hu (Pescadores) islands in 1622, but withdrew two years later when they signed a treaty with the Chinese government giving them the right to establish trading posts on Taiwan. The Japanese, who had long occupied the northern tip of the island, voluntarily withdrew in 1628. The Dutch consolidated their control by driving out Spanish settlers in the north in 1642 and putting down a Chinese uprising in 1656. In 1662, however, they were forced out by the Chinese leader Cheng Ch'eng-kung (Koxinga), a Ming Dynasty loyalist who formed an independent kingdom that served as a center of anti-Manchu activity, and encouraged immigration from Fujian and Guangdong. In 1683 Taiwan was brought under Manchu control and made a prefecture of Fujian. Under Manchu rule, immigration and shipping to the island were severely restricted, hampering development. Several Taiwanese ports were finally opened to the West in the 1860s, and Japanese forces landed on the southern part of the island in 1874. In 1886 Taiwan was made a separate province of China. Nine years later, in 1895, after China's defeat in the First Sino-Japanese War, Taiwan was ceded to Japan under the Treaty of Shimonoseki. It was not returned to China until 1945, after Japan's defeat in World War II. Japan formally renounced all claims to Taiwan and the P'eng-hu islands in a 1951 treaty, although the document did not formally cede Taiwan to China. During this interim period (in 1947), the Taiwanese staged a massive uprising to protest corrupt Chinese rule. This resulted in a series of administrative reforms.

In 1949 the Kuomintang government, led by Chiang Kai-shek, retreated from the mainland to Taiwan. Since that time mainlanders have dominated the central government, the army and the upper levels of the educational system. The Communist government on the mainland and the Kuomintang government on Taiwan continue to claim sovereignty over all of China. After the outbreak of the Korean War in 1950 the United States provided military and economic aid to the Kuomintang. In 1954 Taiwan and the United States signed a mutual defense treaty under the terms of which the United States promised to protect Taiwan and the P'eng-hu Islands. The Quemoy (Chin-Men) and Matsu islands, which had repeatedly been shelled by the Communist government, were added to the treaty in 1955. The Kuomintang government (a charter member) continued to represent China at the United Nations until 1971, when it was replaced by the People's Republic of China. The first legislative elections since 1947 were held in Taiwan in 1972.

Chiang Kai-shek died in 1975 and was succeeded as president by vice-president Yen Chia-kan. Real power, however, rested with Chiang Kai-shek's son, Chiang Ching-kuo, who held the post of prime minister and succeeded his father as leader of the Kuomintang. Chiang was named president in 1978. The following year the United States established diplomatic relations with the People's Republic of China and recognized it as the sole legal government of China, although unofficial U.S. ties to the Kuomintang government continued through various nongovernmental organizations. The U.S. defense treaty with the Republic of China was abrogated later in 1979, although the United States agreed to furnish Taiwan with the arms necessary for its self-defense under terms of the 1979 Taiwan Relations Act. After the 1982 signing of the U.S.-Sino Shanghai Communique calling for a gradual reduction in government-to-government arms sales, arms transfers from the United States to Taiwan continued on a commercial basis in order to supply the Kuomintang armed forces, which numbered 405,500 active members in 1988. (In 1987 defense expenditures consumed 7.33% of GNP.) Chiang Ching-kuo was elected to a second presidential term in 1984. Although the technically illegal Democratic Progressive party was successful in the 1986 legislative elections, the legislature remained dominated by mainlanders. In 1987 Chiang acceded to public pressure and lifted martial law everywhere except the Quemoy and Matsu islands. Restrictions on travel to the mainland by Taiwanese residents were eased that same year; in 1988 indirect trade with the mainland received official approval. Chiang Ching-kuo died in January 1988, ending 60 years of rule by the Chiang family. Under their rule the foundations of Taiwan's spectacular economic growth had been laid. In addition, a cautious policy of democratic reform and a relaxation of Taiwan's attitude toward the People's Republic of China was begun in 1986. Lee Teng-hui, the former vice-president, succeeded Chiang to become the first native-born Taiwanese head of state; he was confirmed as head of the Kuomintang later that year, despite some conservative opposition. Lee continued Chiang's policy of cautious reform. The July 1988 Kuomintang party congress, for example, was the first in which delegates were elected by local party members rather than appointed from the top, and a primary system for choosing party candidates for electoral posts was introduced in 1989. The powerful party Central Standing Committee was restructured so as to have a Taiwanese majority for the first time, and reformist party general secretary Lee Huan replaced conservative Yu Kuo-hua as prime minister in 1989. Although Lee gradually consolidated his power, he faced recurrent demonstrations by workers, students and farmers seeking to hasten the pace of social and political change. Conservatives, strengthened by events on the mainland in 1989, feared that political reforms would weaken efforts to restore Kuomintang rule over a reunified China, and there was some indication that the moderate middle class felt that too-rapid change would disrupt Taiwan's economic and political stability. Taiwan's future position in the international community remained unclear—by 1988 only 22 nations still had formal diplomatic relations with the government. Since 1981 the People's Republic of China has repeatedly sought the reunification of Taiwan with the mainland by diplomatic means, offering it an arrangement similar to the 1984 Sino-British accord on Hong Kong; Taiwan would become a special administrative region of China with a high degree of political and economic autonomy. There appeared to be as little support for this plan on Taiwan (particularly after the suppression of the pro-democracy movement on the mainland in June 1989) as there was backing in Beijing for the concept of dual recognition.

ECONOMY

Background: During the period of Japanese occupation, agriculture and infrastructure expanded as Taiwan was developed as a supplier of rice, sugarcane and fruit for the Japanese market. Some industry also was established there after 1937. Real economic growth, however, began in 1950 with land reform and agricultural investment that increased production and released farm labor for industrial expansion. Attention then turned to the manufacture of goods—particularly textiles—for export. Industrial goods constituted only 8% of all exports in 1952; by 1985 they constituted nearly 94%. The per capita income, only U.S.$48 in 1952, had risen to $6,053 by 1988. The GNP ($119.66 billion in 1988) rose an average 10.2% per year between 1982 and 1987, giving Taiwan one of the highest economic growth rates in the world. In recent years, faced with protectionist pressures in traditional markets, increased competition from developing nations and rising labor costs, emphasis has shifted increasingly to capital-intensive and high-technology products. Despite Taiwan's diplomatic isolation it continues to maintain strong economic links with the outside world. In 1987 it had foreign exchange reserves of $76.7 billion (the highest in the world except for Japan) and an outstanding foreign debt of only $1.9 billion.

Manufacturing: Industry, which generates 43.5% of GDP, is dominated by small and medium-sized manufacturers, although much heavy industry is under government control. The leading manufactured goods are textiles and clothing, chemicals, electronics equipment, processed foods, footwear, toys, plywood, cement, ships, refined petroleum and traditional handicrafts (ceramics, silk and objects made of bamboo and paper). Textiles provided 32% of export earnings in 1970, but that percentage has since declined; many Taiwanese industrialists have shifted production of labor-intensive goods to Southeast Asia and mainland China. There have also been efforts to develop new markets in Eastern Europe, Africa and Southeast Asia, and to produce higher-quality goods for specialty markets. The government has invested heavily in the chemical and steel industries, and in research projects in such high-technology fields as digital communications equipment, electronics and automation. A science-based industrial park at Hsin-chu and several export-processing zones have been established to encourage foreign investment.

Agriculture, forestry and fishing: Agriculture now constitutes only about 5.3% of GDP. Taiwanese farms are small, averaging only 2–3 acres/0.8–1.2 ha. in size. Almost all of the arable land is cultivated, and yields are high due to heavy use of fertilizer, irrigation and double or triple cropping. The principal crops are rice (grown on about half of the cultivated land), sweet potatoes, sugarcane, bananas, pineapples and citrus fruits. The government is encouraging mechanization and the cultivation of specialty crops (such as tea, asparagus and mushrooms) for export. Hogs, poultry and water buffalo also are raised. Many of Taiwan's forests, which cover some 55% of the main island, are inaccessible for commercial exploitation. Forest products include bamboo, camphor, lumber, paper and plywood. The fishing industry, concentrated on the west coast, had a total 1985 fish catch of 1,143,891 U.S. tons/1,037,721 metric tons. Ocean species included tuna, mackerel, sardines and shellfish; pond-raised species such as carp and eels constituted 24% of the total catch.

Other industries: The oil and natural gas industries are government operated; the sizable petrochemical industry is heavily dependent on imported petroleum. Half of Taiwan's 130 coal mines were closed in the mid-1980s after a series of mine disasters, and coal now provides only about 4% of the total energy output. In 1987 some 1.76 million tourists visited Taiwan, spending an estimated $1.6 billion. Efforts to develop Taiwan as an offshore banking center have been hampered by antiquated and restrictive banking and financial regulations. Taiwan has 59 banks, including 35 branches of foreign banks. Revenues from Taiwanese-owned shipping vessels and remittances from overseas Chinese are important to the economy. The chief sources of foreign investment in 1986 were Japan (33%), the United States (18%) and overseas Chinese (8%). Direct U.S. economic aid ceased in 1965, although some military aid continued.

Foreign trade: Foreign trade increased more than tenfold between 1964 and 1974, and continued to expand rapidly into the 1980s, although the linkage of Taiwan's currency (the New Taiwan dollar) to the U.S. dollar made Taiwanese products less competitive in Japan and Europe. Its huge trade surplus with the United States led to increasing pressure on Taiwan to open its markets to U.S. goods and financial institutions. In 1987 exports totaled $52.04 billion, of which textiles (20.5%), electrical machinery (18.8%), general machinery and equipment (9%), telecommunications equipment (9%), basic metals and metal products (7.4%) and foodstuffs (5.4%) were the most important. The leading export destinations in 1986 were the United States (48%), Japan (11%), Hong Kong (7%), Canada (3%) and West

353

Germany (3%). Imports (an estimated $50.5 billion in 1988) included plant and capital equipment (29%), raw materials and foodstuffs (62%) and energy (9%). The chief import sources in 1986 were Japan (34%), the United States (22%), West Germany (5%), Saudi Arabia (4%), Australia (4%) and Canada (2%). In 1986 clandestine trade with mainland China was estimated at $140 million in imports and $950 million in exports, the latter consisting primarily of consumer goods, appliances, electrical equipment and motorcycles. Regulations adopted in 1987 permit imports of herbal medicines, food, cigarettes, liquor and nonpolitical literature.

Employment: In 1988 Taiwan had a labor force of 8.2 million, many of whom belonged to occupational or trade organizations. The unemployment rate in 1988 was 1.7%. In 1986 34% of the employed labor force was engaged in manufacturing, 18% in trade, 17% in agriculture and fishing, 16% in government and public authorities, 7% in construction, 5% in transportation and communications and 3% in finance.

Price trends: The consumer price index, which stood at 86.0 in 1980, rose to 104.4 in 1983 and 104.9 in 1986. It rose another 1.8 from 1986 to 1988. Overall, the monthly earnings index outpaced the consumer price index during the 1980s, rising from 84.2 in 1980 to 145.4 in 1986.

SOCIAL SERVICES

Welfare: Some 16% of total government expenditures in 1986 were devoted to social welfare and relief. More than half of the labor force is covered by a labor insurance program initiated in 1957. This program, 80% of which is employer financed, pays medical, disability and other benefits. A separate benefit program covers government employees, and the government provides direct aid to poor children, disaster victims and mainland refugees.

Health services: In 1985 Taiwan had nearly 17,000 physicians and more than 70,800 hospital beds. The infant mortality rate in 1987 was 6.9 per 1,000 live births—the lowest in Asia outside of Japan. The leading causes of death are circulatory diseases, cancer, accidents and suicide.

Housing: The government constructed nearly 400,000 units of public housing between 1949 and 1986, primarily to house the large numbers of mainland refugees. Recent government programs have focused on slum clearance and the construction of low-cost housing in urban areas.

EDUCATION

In 1987, when 92.2% of the adult population was literate, 12.8% of government expenditures was devoted to education. Six years of primary education and three years of secondary education are compulsory for all children. Teachers' salaries are paid by local governments, and school facilities are used after hours for extensive supplementary adult education programs. Although preschool education is optional, Taiwan had more than 2,200 preschools in 1985–86, and in 1988 there were 2,478 primary schools with 2.4 million students and 851 secondary schools with 1.3 million students. There are also 212 vocational schools and 109 institutions of higher learning, including 16 universities with a total enrollment of nearly 465,000 in 1987. The largest universities are the government-run National Taiwan University (established in 1928) in T'ai-pei, the privately controlled Feng Chia University (1961) in T'ai-chung, and Fu-Jen Catholic University (1961) and Tamkang University (1950) in T'ai-pei—all of which have enrollments exceeding 15,000.

MASS MEDIA

After Japan, Taiwan has the most highly developed communications system in Asia. This government-operated system includes extensive microwave transmission links, two INTELSAT ground stations and submarine cable links to Okinawa, the Philippines, Guam, Singapore, Hong Kong, Indonesia, Australia, the Middle East and Western Europe. Printed matter is not censored prior to publication, but it can be seized or banned after publication if found objectionable by government security officers. The media frequently are used to promote an appreciation of traditional Chinese culture.

The press

Dailies: In 1984 there were 31 daily newspapers in Taiwan with a total circulation of 4,917,000 (one for every 259 persons). The largest newspapers, all published in T'ai-pei, are the *United Daily News,* 1,300,000; the *China Times,* 1,205,523; the *Central Daily News,* 530,000; the *China Post,* 80,000. The largest provincial newspapers are the southern edition of the *China Daily News* (T'ai-nan), the *Min Chung Daily News* (Kao-hsiung), the *Taiwan Daily News* (T'ai-chung) and the *Taiwan Times* (Kao-hsiung).

Periodicals: Nearly 3,000 magazines are published in Taiwan. Popular weeklies include *Agri-week,* the English-language news magazine *Free China Journal* and the Chinese-language news magazine *Sinwen Tienti.* Monthly publications include *Artist Magazine, Information and Computer, Issues and Standards* (international affairs); *National Palace Museum Monthly, Sinorama* (cultural); *Tiensia* (business); and *Unitas* (literary).

Broadcasting: In 1986 Taiwan had about 100 radio broadcasting stations owned by 33 companies, as well as three television networks. The leading radio corporations were the Broadcasting Corporation of China, with 44 domestic and external stations providing services in 14 languages and dialects; the Fu Shing Broadcasting Corporation, with 27 stations; and the Cheng Sheng Broadcasting Corporation, with 9 stations. The three television networks are Taiwan Television Enterprise Limited, China Television Company and Chinese Television Service. Both the Chinese Television Service and the Educational Broadcasting Station are operated by the government; they offer cultural and educational programs. Most radio stations are privately owned, but all of them are supervised by the government.

BIOGRAPHICAL SKETCHES

Lee Huan. Born in 1917, Lee Huan was sworn in as Taiwan's 13th prime minister on May 30, 1989. He graduated from National Cheng Chi University and Columbia University, headed various party youth organizations, and taught at the university level before becoming (1979–84) president of Sun Yat-sen University. A moderate and a long-time associate of Chiang Ching-kuo, he was considered a possible heir-apparent before losing power to party rivals in the late 1970s, but he regained political prominence after being appointed minister of education in 1984. He was named to the Kuomintang Central Standing Committee in 1986 and became party general secretary in July 1987, gaining widespread popular support as an advocate of political reform. James Soong replaced him as party general secretary in 1989.

Lee Teng-hui. Born in 1923, Lee became the first native-born president of Taiwan in 1988. Educated in Japan, Taiwan and the United States, he received a Ph.D. in agricultural economics from Cornell University in 1968 and entered government service in 1972. He served as mayor of T'ai-pei from 1978 to 1981 and as governor of Taiwan Province from 1981 to 1984, when he was named vice-president. He automatically succeeded to the balance of Chiang Ching-kuo's term (until 1990), and he was confirmed as chairman of the ruling Kuomintang party in July 1988.

Soong Mei-ling (Madam Chiang Kai-shek). Born about 1897 in Shanghai, Soong Mei-ling was a member of the wealthy and influential Soong family. She was trained in sociology at Wellesley College in the United States and was married to Chiang Kai-shek from 1927 until his death in 1975. Her son Chiang Ching-kuo (1910–88) succeeded his father as head of the Kuomintang regime. Although she held few official posts she served as her husband's adviser and became internationally known while traveling widely seeking support for the Kuomintang cause. In 1988 she joined other conservative mainlanders in an unsuccessful attempt to block Lee Teng-hui's confirmation as head of the Kuomintang.

Sun Yun-hsuan. Born in 1930 in Shantung Province, he succeeded Chiang Ching-kuo as prime minister in 1978. Trained as an engineer at Harbin Polytechnic Institute, he worked at power plants in China, the United States, Nigeria and Taiwan, where he was president of the Taiwan Power Company from 1962 to 1964. He served in the cabinet as minister of communications (1967–69) and economic affairs (1969–78) before becoming prime minister. He retired in 1984 after suffering a stroke.

Yu Kuo-hwa. Born in 1914 in Zhejiang Province, Yu became personal secretary to Chiang Kai-shek in 1936. He held a succession of important financial posts in the Kuomintang and the government before replacing Sun Yun-hsuan as prime minister in 1984. His economic advice to the government is considered to have contributed to Taiwan's spectacular economic growth, and he served as leader of Taiwan's conservative bloc. His popularity declined as pressures for political reform increased, however, and he resigned as prime minister in May 1989.

THAILAND

GEOGRAPHY

Features: The Kingdom of Thailand, formerly Siam, is situated in the center of the Southeast Asian mainland. It is bordered by Burma (Myanmar) to the west, Laos and Cambodia to the north and east, and Malaysia to the south. Much of the country's territory lies to the north of the Bight of Bangkok and is removed from the main shipping routes across the South China Sea and the Gulf of Thailand. The southern Thailand peninsula that extends to the Malaysian border has a 576-mile/960-km. coastline along the Gulf of Thailand and a shorter one on the western side facing the Andaman Sea. The peninsula consists mainly of narrow coastal lowlands backed by low and wooded mountain ranges. The rest of the country consists of four main upland tracts in the west, north, northeast and southeast that surround a large central plain. The Chao Phraya River drains the central plain. The western hills are formed by a series of north-south ridges, thickly covered by tropical forest with much bamboo. Summits average 1,970–2,950 ft/600–900 m., but the ridge-and-furrow pattern makes the area generally uninhabitable. Altitudes in the north are higher, reaching 4,920 ft/1,500 m. Much of this area is forested. The Ping, Wang, Yom and Nan rivers flow through this area, converging further south to form the Chao Phraya and creating broad lowlands used for rice cultivation. The Korat Plateau in the northeast is generally lower than areas in the north and west. Its mostly low surface drains eastward, to the Mekong River that flows along its northern and eastern edge. The central plain is the most important region in the country because of its fertile soils and well-developed system of natural waterways. The highest densities of rural population occur in this area.

Area: 198,115 sq. miles/513,115 sq. km.

Mean max. and min. temperatures: Bangkok (13°45′N, 100°31′E; 7 ft/2m.) 97°F/36°C (May), 62°F/16°C (Dec.); Chieng Mai (18°47′N, 98°59′E; 1,030 ft/351 m.) 89°F/32°C (April), 68°F/20°C (Dec.).

Relative humidity: 60%–90%.

Mean annual rainfall: 60 in/1500 mm.

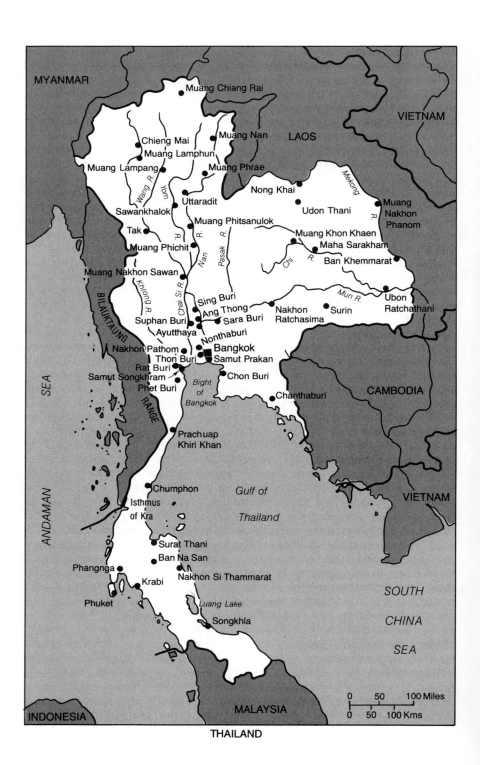

MYANMAR

Muang Chiang Rai

Chieng Mai
Muang Lamphun
Muang Lampang

Muang Nan

LAOS

VIETNAM

Muang Phrae

Wang R.
Yom
Nong Khai

Udon Thani

Muang Nakhon Phanom

Sawankhalok
Uttaradit

Tak
Muang Phitsanulok

Muang Phichit

Muang Khon Khaen
Maha Sarakham
Ban Khemmarat

Nan R.
Pasak R.
Chi R.

Muang Nakhon Sawan

Khlong R.
Chai Si R.

Mun R.
Ubon Ratchathani

Sing Buri
Ang Thong
Suphan Buri
Sara Buri
Ayutthaya
Nonthaburi
Nakhon Pathom
Bangkok
Thon Buri
Samut Prakan
Rat Buri
Samut Songkhram
Chon Buri
Phet Buri

Nakhon Ratchasima
Surin

BILAUKTAUNG

SEA

RANGE

Bight of Bangkok

Chanthaburi

CAMBODIA

Prachuap Khiri Khan

VIETNAM

ANDAMAN

Chumphon

Isthmus of Kra

Gulf of Thailand

Surat Thani
Ban Na San
Phangnga
Krabi
Nakhon Si Thammarat

Phuket

Luang Lake

Songkhla

SOUTH

CHINA

SEA

| 0 | 50 | 100 Miles |
| 0 | 50 | 100 Kms |

INDONESIA

MALAYSIA

THAILAND

POPULATION

Total population (1987 est.): 53,605,000; 44,824,540 according to the last census taken in 1980.

Chief towns and populations: BANGKOK (5,468,915, est., 4,697,071 in 1980), Songkhla (172,604, 1980), Chon Buri (115,250, 1980), Nakhon Si Thammarat (102,123, 1980), Chieng Mai (101,594, 1980).

Distribution: Average population density is 104.5 per sq. km., but average densities fall to between one-quarter and one-half that in the sparsely populated west and north. The population, however, is not as unevenly distributed as in other Southeast Asian countries. Virtually the entire indigenous population belongs to the Thai ethnic group (including the Shan and Lao). Ethnic minorities include an estimated 700,000 Muslim Malays in the far south, a smaller number of Cambodians along the eastern border, and about 300,000 hill-tribe people, including the Meo, Lahu, Yao, Lisu, Lawa, Lolo and Karen, living mainly in the northwest. The northeastern population tends to be linguistically closer to the Lao populations on the other side of the Mekong than to the people of central Thailand. The Chinese form another large ethnic minority, but estimates of their numbers are difficult to determine because many have assimilated into Thai culture.

Language: Thai is the official national language and the native tongue of 90% of the population. The language has four dialectical forms: Central Thai, Lao, Kham Muang, and Southern Thai (Tamprue). Tribal groups speak their own dialects.

Religion: Theravada Buddhism is the dominant religion in Thailand, professed by more than 95% of the population. The ethnic Malay population in the south (4% of the total) is Muslim. Most of the Chinese are Confucians. Christians number less than 300,000, and of these 75% are Roman Catholic. Hindus and Sikhs number about 65,000.

CONSTITUTIONAL SYSTEM

Constitution: The latest Thai constitution, the 12th since 1932, was promulgated on December 22, 1978. It declares the king to be head of state and head of the armed forces. The king is sacred and shall not be violated, accused or sued in any way. He exercises power through the legislative, executive and judicial branches, namely the Council of Ministers, the National Assembly and the courts. The king may issue emergency decrees when there is an urgent necessity to maintain national or public safety or to avert public calamity. The decree must be submitted to the National Assembly as soon as possible. If approved, it will continue in force; if not, it will lapse. In fact, however, the king is primarily a figurehead, and real power lies with the prime minister, often a member of the Thai military. Thailand has been called a de jure constitutional monarchy but a de facto military dictatorship. The king's approval gives legitimacy to the government, but his influence on its composition and its policies is limited.

Head of state: King Bhumibol Adulyadej (Rama IX).

Head of government: Prime Minister Chatichai Choonhavan.

Executive: The Council of Ministers, headed by the prime minister, is the executive body, and the most powerful branch of the Thai government. The most important government office is that of the prime minister, who supervises the office of the royal household, commands one branch of the armed forces under military governments, countersigns all laws and royal decrees, controls the agenda of cabinet meetings, and exercises unlimited powers over national security and the economy in emergency situations. The prime minister also heads the National Economic Development Board, the National Security Council and the National Research Council. The cabinet also includes two deputy prime ministers and 12 ministers. The executive branch may overrule unfavorable actions of legislative committees.

Legislature: The National Assembly is the least powerful organ of government and is subordinate to the executive branch. It consists of a Senate and a House of Representatives. The Senate has 268 members appointed by the king on the recommendation of the prime minister. The 357 members of the House are elected by the people. Senators must be Thai citizens by birth, at least 35 years old and unaffiliated with any political party. They serve six-year terms. Representatives must be Thai nationals by birth, at least 25 years old and members of a political party. They serve for four years. The king is empowered to dissolve the House for new elections. The National Assembly considers and approves bills. The government is assured of a majority in the National Assembly because joint meetings of the two houses are required to pass appropriations bills and important legislation. Bills submitted must also be approved by the Extraordinary Commission to Study Bills; half of its members are appointed by the cabinet.

Political parties: The military's dominance of the Thai polity has not eliminated politics per se. Political parties exist, often representing particular business interests rather than ideologies. The main parties are Chart Thai (Thai Nation, right-wing); Community Action party (CAP); Kij Prachakhorn (liberal democratic); Democrat party (Prachatipat, liberal); Democratic Labor party (Raen Ngam Pracha Tippatai, liberal and socialist); Liberal party (Seriniyom); Mass party (Maunchon); National Democracy party (Chart Pracha Tippatai, right-wing); New Force party (Palang Mai, left of center, social-democratic); Prachakhorn Thai (Thai Citizens' party, right-wing, monarchist); Progress party (Koa Nar, or Revolutionary party, right-wing); Puangchon Chao Thai; Rak Thai (Love Thai party); Rassadorn (Citizens' party, conservative); Raum Thai (Thai Unity party); Social Action party (SAP, conservative); United Democratic party (Saha Pracha Tippatai, promotes business and commercial interests). None has the power to challenge the bureaucracy.

Local government: Seven administrative levels comprise local government. There are 72 *changwad* (the largest units in provinces), 565 *amphoe* (districts), 34 *king amphoe* (subdistricts), 5,036 *tambon* (communes), 44,606 *muban* (villages), 82 *muang* (towns) and three *nakhon* (cities). The divisions are only units of national government and have little autonomy, except below the district level, where there are no central government officials. Commune heads are chosen by village headmen, who in turn are chosen by villagers for five-year terms. However, they tend to serve until death or retirement.

Judicial system: The Thai judicial system has three levels. The lowest level consists of courts of first instance. These include provincial and urban civil and criminal courts, magistrate's courts, juvenile courts and a labor court. Provincial courts exercise unlimited jurisdiction in all civil and criminal matters within their own districts; two judges form a quorum. In southern Thailand, where the majority of the population are Muslims, Muslim judges administer *Sharia* (Islamic law). Magistrate's courts adjudicate in minor cases with minimum formality and one judge; in Bangkok courts two judges form a quorum. The Central Labor Court has jurisdiction in labor cases throughout the country. Central juvenile courts have jurisdiction over juvenile delinquency and matters affecting children; two judges and two associates (one of whom must be a woman) form a quorum. Appeals from all courts of first instance except for the Central Labor Court are taken to the Court of Appeals (Sarn Uthorn); two judges form a quorum. The Supreme Court (Sarn Dika), which has six justices, is the final court of appeal in all civil, bankruptcy, labor, juvenile and criminal cases; three justices form a quorum.

RECENT HISTORY

Thailand as it exists at present is the culmination of centuries of shifting borders between rival kingdoms of Southeast Asia. Bangkok became the capital in 1782 under the Chakri dynasty. Chakri kings pressed Siamese authority over Laos, western Cambodia and the northern Malay states. As the European powers established colonies in neighboring states, Thailand under Kings Mongkut (Rama IV, 1851–68) and Chulalongkorn (Rama V, 1868–1910) was able to maintain independence. However, it had to cede to France its claims to Laos and western Cambodia, and to Great Britain its claims over the Malay states of Kedah, Perlis, Kelantan and Trengganu. Siam accepted European and American advisers in key governmental posts to improve its expertise and to finance economic and administrative modernization. Siam prospered with the development of the international rice trade, and Bangkok became a major trading center.

The influences of Western ideas and modern education led young army officers to attempt to overthrow King Wachirawut (Rama VI, 1910–25) in favor of a republic. A rift between royal authority and the new bureaucratic elite was apparent. The king responded by equating royalty with nationalism in the slogan "Nation, Religion, King." This became and remains the central patriotic slogan of the country. The royal symbol was preserved, but not royal power. Tension between royal and bureaucratic authority erupted in 1932 after the collapse of the international rice market. A bloodless coup ended the absolute rule of King Prajadhipok (Rama

VII, 1925–35). Power has since lain in the hands of the bureaucratic elite, dominated by the armed forces.

A conservative constitutionalist regime was established under Col. Phahon Phonphayuhasena in 1933; but Maj. Phibun Songkhram, minister of defense, held real power. Communism was declared illegal, political parties were banned and press censorship was instituted. Power increasingly rested with the army. Politics became a struggle for office and patronage by elite bureaucrats. Phibun replaced Phahon as prime minister in 1938 and initiated an anti-Chinese, anti-Western campaign, playing on popular resentment toward the Chinese because of their dominant economic role. In his attempt to modernize society, he changed the country's name to Thailand in 1939, and imposed modes of dress he considered more in keeping with the times. He set out to reacquire lands lost to the French and British and in 1940 attacked Indochina. In a Japanese-sponsored settlement, Thailand acquired Laotian lands west of the Mekong, and the northwestern provinces of Cambodia. Thailand allied with Japan during World War II, declaring war on Britain and the United States in 1942. Some prominent Thais, however, opposed the Japanese alignment. Seni Pramoj, ambassador to the United States, and Pridi Phanomyang, former leader of the 1932 "revolution," established the Free Thai movement, an anti-Japanese resistance. Phibun was deposed in 1944 and replaced by moderate Khuang Aphaiwong. Seni Pramoj was appointed prime minister in September 1945, accomplishing a shift to a democratic government supporting the Allies.

Political turmoil characterized the postwar years. Political parties were legalized but were unable to agree on a common course the government should take. Pridi became prime minister in March 1946 but gave no more legitimacy to the struggling democracy. King Ananda died mysteriously in June 1946, and Phibun assigned the blame to Pridi, who was forced to resign. After a succession of weak civil governments the army seized power in November 1947. Phibun returned to power, dissolved the National Assembly and abrogated the constitution in 1951 after suppressing a naval revolt. Political parties were banned, radical leaders were imprisoned or executed and dissent was stifled. Thailand followed a new foreign policy allied with the United States against communism and received considerable U.S. aid. Phibun's second dictatorship was the first of military-political factions that were to mark Thailand's subsequent rule. As his power waned in 1955, Phibun restored free speech, legalized political parties and announced elections in 1957. His efforts were not enough to secure his position, however, as the vote was blatantly rigged and the government discredited. Gen. Sarit Thanarat, head of the Bangkok army, seized power and assumed leadership in October 1958.

Sarit called for a restoration of traditional values, but accompanied it with rapid economic modernization. U.S. involvement in Vietnam provided conditions for an economic boom. Thailand provided the United States with military bases and supplies, and Bangkok became a rest and recreation center for U.S. troops. U.S.-funded road building rapidly increased communications and transport, and peasants became increasingly involved in the money economy. As the old social structures weakened, rural resentment awakened and was encouraged by Chinese, Vietnamese and Pathet Lao rebel groups. A China-based Thai Patriotic Front proclaimed a "war of national liberation" in 1965 and commanded strong influence in provinces outside the central plain by 1970. In 1968 military leaders (Sarit had died in 1963) moved toward democracy, promulgating a constitution establishing an assembly and holding elections in 1969. This was seen as a reaction to uncertainties about the country's economic and foreign policies. In 1971, after much criticism, the military again seized full power. Student demonstrations against the regime began in 1972, and army leaders gradually withdrew their support from Gen. Thanom Kittikachorn and Gen. Praphat Charusathien. The king withdrew his support, depriving them of any legitimacy, and in October 1973, the military regime collapsed. Thanom and Praphat went into exile.

Student demonstrations marked only the beginning of three years of turbulent public participation. Students worked to organize peasants and laborers against economic exploitation. Peasants began to form farmers' associations, and workers in Bangkok's numerous textile mills began to strike, protesting low pay and hard working conditions. The formerly apolitical Buddhist monkhood called for social justice and sided with peasants in presenting their claims. Though the government allowed free play to these sentiments, it did little to satisfy demands. Sany Thammasak, a university rector, presided over an interim regime until elections were held in January 1975. A coalition government was then formed under Kukrit Pramoj and his SAP. His regime lasted less than a year. In 1976 Kukrit's brother, Seni, and the Democratic party came to power in a center-right coalition. The civilian government was unable to maintain order in society, and a return to military rule became increasingly popular among the urban middle class who preferred authoritarianism to paralysis and disorder. A military-dominated reform council took over in October 1976, banning political parties, dissolving the National Assembly and setting up a right-wing government. Supreme Court judge Thanin Kraivichien headed the new government. Labor unions, left-wing parties and farmers' associations were suppressed and dissent was silenced. Many students—offspring of the ruling elite—fled to the jungle to join Communist forces. Thanin's unstable government was overthrown in October 1977 by a military coalition headed by commander in chief Gen. Kriangsak Chomanan. He reduced censorship, released detainees and permitted the resumption of party activity. Disunity plagued his government, effectively smothering policy initiatives. In March 1980 Kriangsak was replaced as prime minister by retired Gen. Prem Tinsulanonda, the army commander in chief and defense minister. Center-right politicians dominated his government but ultimate power lay with the armed forces. Still, the coalition was at odds over how to realize their goals, and Prem's indecisive government was threatened by unsuccessful coups in April 1981 and September 1985.

In the international arena Vietnam's invasion of Cambodia threatened Thailand with further Vietnamese expansionism. However, the resulting breach between Vietnam and China reduced China's support for the Thai Communist insurgency, as Thailand and China were now on the same side.

Although refugees streaming into Thailand burdened government resources, they provided further testimony of the dark side of Communist
rule. Bangkok has refused to compromise with Vietnam over Cambodia
and was rewarded by Beijing's withdrawal of support for the Thai insurgency. Disillusioned students accepted amnesty and returned quietly to the
cities. By early 1983 many of the demoralized rank-and-file members of
the Communist insurgency also accepted amnesty, effectively ending the
rebellion.

The encampment of Cambodian rebel groups on Thai territory led to
occasional skirmishes between Thai and Vietnamese troops, especially during the 1984–85 dry season offensive, when Vietnam drove the rebels from
their bases inside Cambodia. Clashes also occurred with Laos over refugees
and border disputes. Thailand quietly restored U.S. military aid projects
and training schemes; in January 1987, for example, the two countries
signed an agreement providing for a U.S. weapons stockpile in Thailand.
The stockpile was intended to defend Thailand against attacks from Cambodia. Thailand sustained its firm resolve not to seek a compromise with
Cambodia's Heng Samrin regime, due in part to political immobilism, to
historical rivalry with Vietnam, to the profitability of smuggling and to
the involvement of major powers in the conflict.

Thailand experienced a surge in economic development in the early 1980s,
largely fueled by Japanese investment. Light manufacturing, particularly of
textiles, for the first time comprised a significant portion of export. Thailand was regarded as the most dynamic economy in Southeast Asia in the
mid-1980s, as the economies of Singapore and Malaysia waned. Banking,
manufacturing and agribusiness interests began to play an important role
in politics, breaking up the old patron-client relationships. Constitutional
changes in 1983 greatly reduced the power of the nominated Senate and
banned the appointment of civil servants (including military officers) to the
Council of Ministers. Both senior and younger officers objected to the reforms. Gen. Arthit Kamlang-ek, supreme commander of the armed forces
and commander in chief of the army, formed an alliance with the young
officers, or "Young Turks." Their opposition led to the aborted coup of
September 1985. Arthit was dismissed from his military posts in 1986 and
replaced by Gen. Chaovalit Yongchaiyut, one of Prem's closest advisers.
Chaovalit also moved to strengthen the army at the expense of the state.

Prem dissolved the parliament in May 1988 to ward off a no-confidence
motion. In general elections held in July 1988 the vote was splintered,
with the Chart Thai party taking the most seats (87) in the House of
Representatives. It was widely believed that Prem would continue as prime
minister, but he declined renomination to a fourth term. Chatichai Choonhavan, former deputy prime minister and leader of Chart Thai, became
prime minister of the five-party coalition government. The change was viewed
as another step toward fuller democracy, but also raised concerns about
party conflicts and subsequent instability. Some doubted that Chatichai
could duplicate Prem's ability to balance interests of the bureaucracy and
the armed forces.

ECONOMY

Background: Throughout the 1960s and early 1970s Thailand's free-market economy was largely developed with infusions of U.S. aid related to the Vietnam War. Between 1961 and 1980 GDP increased at an average annual rate of 6.6%, but the rate was slower after 1970. Growth averaged 4.9% between 1979 and 1986, reaching a low of 3.2% in 1985. The economy rebounded in 1986 and 1987. GDP increased 4% in 1986 and 6.6% in 1987; the balance on payments moved into surplus on current account; and the supply of foreign exchange sharply increased. However, a fall in world prices for major export commodities such as rice, sugar, rubber, maize and tin reduced income for a majority of the Thai population after 1982. Gains were concentrated in Bangkok and the Central Plain area, while the northeast had a per capita income of less than half the national average. Income disparities widened steadily from the early 1960s on.

The Economic Development Plan of 1982–86 emphasized a reduction in state involvement in the economy in favor of stimulating the private sector. Heavy industry in particular was targeted. The plan aimed to reduce rural poverty, improve the balance of payments and reduce the budget deficit by increasing government revenue. Results, however, did not meet targets. Because of increases in rural poverty, the next plan (1987–91) emphasized the rural sector. The plan envisaged economic growth of 5% per year and the creation of more than 3.9 million jobs.

Thailand's economy remains dependent on export commodities that are subject to price fluctuations and unreliable production levels.

Agriculture: Agriculture accounts for about two-thirds of the Thai labor force, or 26 million people in 1985. It was the largest single contributor to GDP and export earnings until that year. In 1986 the sector comprised 16.7% of GDP (down from 40% in 1960). Increases in yields were largely accomplished through expansion in cultivated area. This caused serious problems of land shortage and soil erosion in parts of the north and northeast. The slow development of irrigation outside the central plain inhibited the development of more intensive and sophisticated production. Sugar cane, cassava, rice and maize are the principal cultivated crops. Production in 1985 included 25.6 million metric tons of sugar cane, 20 million metric tons of cassava, 19.5 million metric tons of rice and 4.6 million metric tons of maize. The area planted each year varies considerably because of unreliable rainfall. Rice exports have averaged over 3 million tons per year since 1978, reaching a high of 4.6 million tons in 1986. Thailand has been the world's largest rice exporter since 1981, and provided about 40% of world rice exports in 1985. Falling prices, however, have decreased rice revenues. Thailand's cassava crop is almost entirely exported, in the form of tapioca pellets for cattle food, to members of the European Community (EC). Cassava exports reached a record 7.8 million tons in 1982, but fell to 5 million tons in 1983 when the EC imposed a 5-million-ton import

365

quota. Exports jumped back to 7 million tons in 1985 as new markets in Israel, Portugal and Taiwan opened. A 1986 agreement with the EC guaranteed Thailand a market for 21 million tons during 1987–90. Sugar production varies according to climate conditions and international price levels (75%–90% is exported). A collapse of prices in 1982 reduced production from 30.3 million tons of cane to 22 million tons. Refined sugar fell from 2.9 tons to 2.1 tons. Production slightly increased in 1986 to 24 million tons of cane and 2.37 million tons of refined sugar. Sugar's share of export earnings fell from 9.7% in 1982 to 3.2% in 1985. A slight rise in prices reversed the trend in 1986. Until the 1970s rubber was Thailand's second most important export earner. Rubber production has increased at an annual rate of nearly 6% since 1971, making Thailand the world's third largest producer—representing 15% of world rubber production in 1984. Exports have steadily increased, but price declines have caused revenues to drop. In 1987 rubber production was 840,000 tons, with 92% destined for export. Fresh fruit, soybeans, groundnuts and mung beans are also grown for export.

Mining: Tin dominates the mining sector and has accounted for more than 60% of the value of Thailand's mineral production. However, production declined from 46,547 tons in 1980 to 23,298 tons in 1986. The collapse of the international tin market in 1985 caused export earnings to decline by 46% in 1986. Tungsten, lead, antimony, manganese, copper and zinc are produced in small quantities. Only lead and zinc are not declining. Production of zinc has increased from 262,000 tons in 1985 to 340,000 tons in 1986. The precious-stone sector has revived since 1983 as new markets in Japan, the United States and the EC have opened and the Thai jewelry industry has rapidly developed. Thailand is a rich source of sapphires, rubies, zircons, garnets, quartz and jade. Exports totaled U.S. $313 million in 1986, or 3% of export earnings.

Industry: This sector has expanded steadily since 1960, increasing its share of GDP from 6.8% in 1960 to 20.6% in 1986. The sector employs an estimated 3 million people. Labor statistics are unreliable, however, because of widespread underregistration of small operations in order to avoid compliance with safety and minimum wage regulations as well as taxes. Growth of this sector may therefore be much larger. Small-scale plants that process primary products dominate the sector. Traditional agricultural processes such as rice milling, tapioca chipping and running sawmills still attract the greatest amount of new investment. Industries are mostly under family control. Textile production has grown steadily since the 1960s; by 1983 textiles comprised 25.8% of industrial production and employed 30% of the industrial labor force. The sector passed rice as the largest export earner, contributing 12.7% in 1986. Tariffs and quotas in the EC and United States have since slowed expansion. A new five-year Multi-Fiber Arrangement (MFA) that took effect in August 1986 guarantees that exports will be allowed to expand at a minimum of 6% per year.

Construction has grown slowly since 1983, and represented only 4.6% of GDP in 1985. Reductions in government spending, stringent credit

controls, high interest rates, and increased prices of imported equipment
and raw materials led to a recession in this sector. Large foreign companies
have also increased competition. The development of basic industry is still
limited. Steel producers can satisfy only about one-third of domestic demand; the country's three petroleum refineries are inadequate; and production of fertilizers also falls short of demand. Thailand remains heavily dependent on petroleum imports to satisfy its energy needs. In 1980 petroleum
imports represented 31.1% of the total import bill. The fall in prices,
however, reduced petroleum's share of the import bill to 15% in 1986.

Foreign trade: An adverse balance of payments has been a consistent feature
of the economy. Exports have failed to keep pace with imports of consumer
goods, raw materials, machinery and petroleum. The deficit on the current
account of the balance of payments reached a record 7.7% of GDP in 1979,
declined to a low of 2.7% ($1 billion) in 1982, increased to 7.2% ($2.9
billion in 1983) and dropped again to 4% ($1.5 billion) in 1985. The drop
was achieved through an increase in the volume of several exports, a devaluation of the baht in 1984 and a decline in petroleum imports. During
1986 export earnings increased by 22.9%, while imports fell by 0.7%. For
the first time since 1956, there was a slight surplus on the current account
of the balance of payments. Of the deficit, 75% was financed by foreign
loans. Between 1970 and 1985 foreign debt increased from 5.4% of GNP
to 40%. Total debt rose from $5 billion in 1981 to $16 billion in 1986.
Exports such as tin, rice, rubber and teak, which accounted for 50% of
export earnings in 1969, comprised only 16.8% in 1986. They were replaced by maize and cassava and, to a lesser extent, by manufactured goods
and earnings from tourism. In 1985 and 1986 the main source of foreign
exchange was tourism ($1.2 billion in 1985). Manufactured goods exceeded
50% of total export earnings. Japan and the United States remain Thailand's main trading partners. But increasing protectionism has caused Thailand to search for new markets in Eastern Europe, Africa and the Middle
East. Previous uncertainty over Thailand's political future had curtailed
foreign investment. Investment prospects, however, are now being reeval-
uated because of increasing instability in other parts of the region.

Employment: Total employment in 1985 was 37,733,500. Of that number,
25,963,000 were in agriculture, forestry or fishing; 3,666,900 were employed in the service sector; 3,623,900 in commerce; and 2,988,500 in
manufacturing—with the rest divided among mining, construction, public
works, and transportation and communication. Official unemployment in
1985 was 1.7 million, or 6.3% of the total labor force. Although this rate
is low compared to Southeast Asian and world standards, closures and re-
trenchments in such sectors as textiles, construction and electrical appliances were expected to increase the unemployment level, while the labor
force continues to grow at a 3% annual rate. Some 700,000 persons enter
the job market every year. Unemployment is especially high among university graduates.

Prices and wages: Increases in minimum wage rates have generally been well
below the level of inflation. An increase of 6% in 1985 was the first since

367

1982. Low wages and increasing unemployment have led to renewed labor unrest and public protests. The consumer price index for all items (1976 = 100) was 197.7, up from 194.1 in 1985.

Welfare: Social welfare expenditures comprise 1.3% of the national budget. The Department of Public Welfare, with the assistance of the International Committee for the Red Cross, the Catholic Association and other nongovernmental organizations, coordinates welfare activities. Thailand has no social security system, but a plan is under study and being promoted by the country's 500 labor unions. The workers' draft proposed compensation for general health care, childbirth and death expenses. Workers would also contribute to a pool of funds (including contributions from the government and employers) to provide welfare for the unemployed. Families with many children receive special state assistance.

Health services: Health expenditures constituted 4.2% of the national budget in 1982, or $5.70 per capita. Availability of health care, however, is heavily weighted toward Bangkok. In 1980, of 6,803 physicians in the country, 3,425 were based in the capital. In 1980 the country had 615 hospitals with 71,858 beds, 1,084 dentists and 10,118 nursing personnel. Nearly half of the country's administrative districts had no full-time doctors. The state runs 77% of hospitals, private for-profit agencies run 20% and non-profit agencies run 3%.

Housing: In 1975 the government allocated $175 million per year to build housing units for the estimated 2 million squatters living in Bangkok. The low-income housing system run by the National Housing Authority included sites built at or near the workplace, and temporary dwellings of wood usually on government land. Efforts were mostly remedial, leaving most people to depend on their own resources to provide their own shelter. Beginning in 1985 the government moved away from subsidized housing to embrace the concept of new towns where shelter and employment were supplied through the creation of entire social and industrial communities.

Education in Thailand is free and compulsory for six years. All schools are state controlled and four types exist: (1) government schools established and maintained by government funds; (2) local schools, which are usually financed by the government (if they are founded by people of a district, collected district funds may support the school); (3) municipal schools, a type of primary school financed and supervised by the municipality; and (4) private schools set up and owned by private individuals. There are four levels of education. Preschool (nursery and kindergarten) is not compulsory. The next level is elementary education, which begins at age seven and lasts six years. In 1983 some 7.3 million students were enrolled in elementary schools. Secondary education is divided into two levels, each lasting three years. The lower level covers a range of academic and vocational subjects. The upper level prepares students directly for specific occupations. Secondary students numbered 2.1 million in 1983. Fourteen universities and technical institutes in Thailand in 1985 offered undergraduate and graduate courses in all fields. Total enrollment at all levels of education in 1985 was 10.4 million; there were 37,210 institutions and 554,370 teachers.

MASS MEDIA

The press in Thailand is mostly privately owned. Although there is no prepublication censorship, the media generally follow a form of self-censorship that conforms to government-established guidelines. Lively criticism of government policies within the regulations occurs, and the media are given wide latitude in nonpolitical news. Under Prem, Thailand's vernacular press played an increasingly important role as "watchdog" of government. Nothing can be aired or published that offends the king or contributes to the growth of communism. The government can still close papers and revoke licenses of editors who publish stories deemed to be libelous or contrary to national security interests.

The press

Dailies (Thai language): *Ban Muang* (70,000); *Chao Thai; Daily Mirror* (60,000); *Daily News* (450,000); *Daily Times; Dao Siam* (140,000); *Khao Panich* (30,000); *Matichon* (55,000); *Matupoom* (21,000); *Naew Na* (50,000); *Palangchon; Sai Klang; Siam Rath* (120,000); *Siam Times; Siang Puang Chon* (93,000); *Tavan Siam* (90,000); *Thai; Thai Rath* (800,000); *Thailand Times* (30,000). English language dailies include: the *Bangkok Post* (40,000) and *The Nation* (37,000). The Chinese-language dailies are *New Chinese Daily News* (25,000); *Sing Sian Yit Pao Daily News* (90,000); *Srinakorn* (80,000); *Thai Shang Yig Pao* (100,000); *Tong Hua Daily News* (50,000); *Universal Daily News* (25,000).

Weeklies: Thai-language publications include *Bangkok Weekly; Mathichon Weekly Review; Stri Sarn; See Ros; Siam Rath Weekly Review;* and *Skul Thai. Business Times* is published in English.

Monthlies: Chao Krung; The Dharmachaksu (Buddhism, 5,000); *Grand Prix; The Investor* (business, industry, economics, 6,000); *Kasikorn* (agriculture); *The Lady; Look East; Satawa Liang; Villa Wina Magazine.*

Broadcasting: The state maintains a monopoly on radio broadcasting. Most of the 39 radio stations are owned by the government directly or indirectly through the Royal Thai Army, the office of the prime minister, the minister of education, the National Police Department or the Royal Household. The army owns one television network, and Television of Thailand is also government-owned. The Thai Television Company is a commercial concern with state participation.

BIOGRAPHICAL SKETCHES

King Bhumibol Adulyadej (Rama IX). Born December 5, 1927, Rama IX of the Chakri Dynasty is Thailand's longest-reigning monarch; he was crowned May 5, 1950. He spent much of his young life in Switzerland, where he was educated at the Ecole Miremont in Lausanne and the Ecole Nouvelle de la Suisse Romande. He succeeded his elder brother, Ananda Mahidol, on June 9, 1946, after Ananda was found dead in the palace from a gunshot wound. Whether the death was an accident, suicide or murder has never been determined. The king is highly respected not only because of his title but because of his unending defense of and assistance to Thailand's rural poor.

Prem Tinsulanonda. Born August 26, 1920, Prem was a career military man before serving as prime minister from 1980 to 1988. He was educated at Chulachomklao Royal Military Academy in Bangkok and began his military career as a sublieutenant in 1941. He became the commander of cavalry headquarters in 1968, then assistant commander in chief of the Royal Thai Army in 1977. In 1977 he was appointed minister of interior and in 1979 minister of defense. Prem began his tenure as prime minister in 1980 and served the longest of any civilian prime minister before he declined to accept a fourth term after general elections in July 1988. He retired from the army before heading the government, thus acting as a civilian, nonpartisan leader. The balance he struck between the political parties and the military enabled him to sustain a fragile democracy throughout his tenure. He thwarted two coup attempts—in 1981 and 1985—thus diluting the military's influence on mainstream politics.

Chatichai Choonhavan. Born in 1922, Chatichai became prime minister in late July 1988 when former Prime Minister Prem Tinsulanonda declined a fourth term. Chatichai's colorful life-style, which has earned him the title "playboy minister" contrasts sharply to that of the mild-mannered Prem. Chatichai was a former army major general, serving in Indochina in 1940–41 and as part of the first Thai expeditionary force to Korea in 1950–52. His army service abruptly ended in 1958 when the regime, of which his father was deputy prime minister, was toppled in a military coup. For the next 15 years Chatichai served in various ambassadorial postings in Latin America and Europe. In 1973 he returned to Bangkok to serve as deputy foreign minister and has held senior government posts since. He became deputy premier under Prem but was not expected to be able to exert the same degree of influence over the military as his predecessor.

VIETNAM

Features: The Socialist Republic of Vietnam (SRV) is the easternmost country of mainland Southeast Asia. It is bordered by the People's Republic of China to the north, by Laos to the west, by Cambodia to the southwest and by the South China Sea to the east. The shape of the country has been likened to two rice baskets suspended from a connecting pole. The (Hong) Red River delta in the north and the Mekong delta in the south are linked by the narrow, mountainous central region. Land in the north is much more rugged than that in the south. The largely inhospitable upland is a southward extension of the Yunnan and adjacent plateau of southwestern China. The Annamese Highlands extends these uplands to within 90 miles/ 150 km. of the Mekong delta. The mountain chain exceeds 4,920 ft/1,500 m. in altitude at many points, and effectively separates Laos and Cambodia from the coast. The northern delta comprises about 5,600 sq. miles/14,500 sq. km., while the southern is nearly three times that, measuring 14,290 sq. miles/37,800 sq. km. Most of the country experiences a tropical monsoon climate, but the north, exposed to cold northern air, has a cool season from December to March. Rainfall is erratic in the northern and central regions, which are subject to frequent typhoons during the wet season. The Mekong delta is therefore the most favorable region for wet-rice agriculture.

Area: 127,250 sq. miles/329,570 sq. km.

Mean max. and min. temperatures: Hanoi (12°02'N, 107°36'E; 59 ft/18 m.) 62°F/17°C (Jan.), 81°F/27°C (Aug.); Ho Chi Minh City (10°45'N, 106°40'E; 33 ft/10 m.) 78°F/26°C (Jan.), 84°F/29°C (April).

Relative humidity: 75%–80%.

Mean annual rainfall: 73 in/1,900 mm.

Total population (1988 est.): 62,000,000 (52,741,766 according to 1979 census).

Chief towns and populations: Ho Chi Minh City (1979 census: 3,429,978), HANOI (1983 est.: 2,674,400), Haiphong (1979 census: 1,279,067), Da Nang (1979 census: 492,194).

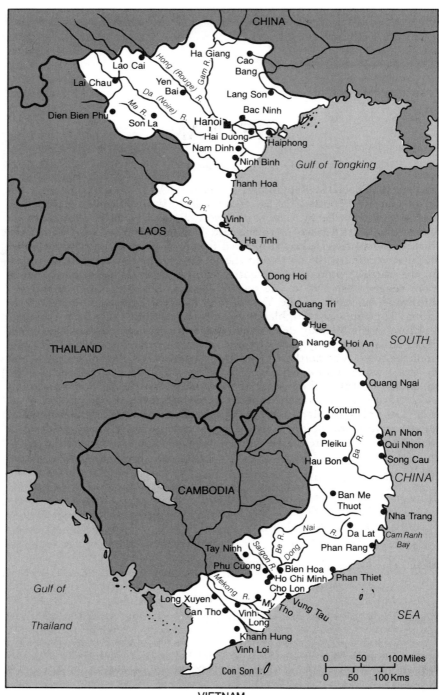

CHINA

Ha Giang

Lao Cai

Cao
Bang

Lai Chau

Yen
Bai

Lang Son

Dien Bien Phu

Son La

Bac Ninh

Hanoi

Hai Duong

Haiphong

Nam Dinh

Ninh Binh

Gulf of Tongking

Thanh Hoa

Ca R.

LAOS

Vinh

Ha Tinh

Dong Hoi

Quang Tri

THAILAND

Hue

Da Nang

Hoi An

SOUTH

Quang Ngai

Kontum

An Nhon

Pleiku

Qui Nhon

Hau Bon

Song Cau

CHINA

CAMBODIA

Ban Me
Thuot

Nha Trang

Da Lat

*Cam Ranh
Bay*

Tay Ninh

Phan Rang

Phu Cuong

Bien Hoa

Ho Chi Minh

Phan Thiet

Cho Lon

Gulf of

Long Xuyen

My
Tho

Vung Tau

SEA

Can Tho

Vinh
Long

Thailand

Khanh Hung

Vinh Loi

0   50   100 Miles

0   50   100 Kms

Con Son I.

VIETNAM

Distribution: The average population density of 181.2 per sq. km. is misleading, because the majority of the population lives within the lowlands, an area that comprises one-third of southern Vietnam and barely one-sixth of the northern area. The Red River delta in the north and the Mekong delta in the south account for 60% of the population, but possess only 23% of the total land. In 1987, 57% of the population was under 19 years of age. Densities in the Mekong delta vary from 40 to 200 per sq. km., but they are between four and five times that in the Red River delta. Vietnam is trying to reduce its annual growth rate of 2.2% with family planning programs and incentives. That figure is down from nearly 3% in 1983. The population-growth target for 1990 was 1.5% and for the year 2000, 1.1%. The high growth rate places strains on the economy in the areas of food production and employment. The Fifth Party Congress therefore set up a national Family Planning Program in 1982 to try to limit population growth. To encourage families to have two children instead of the average five, the state provided allowances for the first two children only. More births would incur higher maternity clinic charges. Payments for undergoing sterilization after the birth of a second child were offered. The permissible marriage age was set at 22 for women and 24 for men. The Family Planning Program was more successful in urban than in rural areas, where families wanted more children and failed to understand the intent of the program. The government has tried to resettle up to 1.4 million people a year, mostly from overcrowded cities, in new economic zones (NEZs).

Language: Vietnamese is the official language. The Viet ethnic group (also known as Kinh) forms 80% of the population. Vietnam is home to 54 minority groups. The largest are the Tai in the north (2 million), the Hmong (750,000), and smaller groups in the central highlands, known as montagnards, who together number about 1 million. An estimated 600,000 Cambodians live along the southwestern border, and an estimated 600,000 Chinese live in Cholon, the Chinese section of Ho Chi Minh City (formerly Saigon). Hundreds of thousands of Chinese fled the country as refugees, but many believe their population is back to its pre-1975 size.

Religion: Popular religions include Mahayana Buddhism, ancestor worship, Hoa Hao (a fundamentalist Buddhist sect of 1.5 million), Caodaism (an attempt to synthesize Buddhism, Confucianism and Catholicism, with 2 million adherents) and Catholicism.

CONSTITUTIONAL SYSTEM

Constitution: The current constitution is the third since the founding of the Democratic Republic of Vietnam in the north in 1945. Promulgated in 1980, it affirms the primary role of the Vietnamese Communist party (VCP) in leading the country to socialism. The constitution describes the Socialist Republic of Vietnam, formed in 1976, as "a state of proletarian dictatorship." The office of the presidency was replaced by the Council of State, considered a collective presidency. The most important positions in the

373

party and state are kept separate to emphasize collective leadership. The prime minister's office and the chairmanship of the National Assembly Secretariat are the most powerful posts within the state apparatus. However, the party is intertwined with state affairs, concerning itself with day-to-day management of the government. Party cadres play an important role at all levels of government.

Head of party: Secretary-General Nguyen Van Linh. *Head of state (Chairman of the Council of State):* Vo Chi Cong. *Chairman of the Council of Ministers (prime minister):* Do Muoi.

Party: The Central Committee is at the top of the Communist party structure and usually decides major changes in policy direction. In 1987 it consisted of 124 members and 49 alternates. The Central Committee elects a Political Bureau as its executive body. This includes the secretary general and a number of other senior party leaders. Current membership is 13 full members and one alternate. The Political Bureau is the most powerful party organ, since the Central Committee only meets once or twice a year. The Political Bureau initiates legislation and has the power, independent of the formal government apparatus, to issue decrees that have the force of law. At the next level are provincial and municipal organizations. Next come district committees (or wards in urban areas), then local party cells of usually three to 10 members. Party committees at each level are elected by party congresses comprising delegates elected by the level below. Growth in party membership is about 2% annually. Economic crises of the 1980s led to drives to eliminate bureaucratism, arrogance and corruption, and to revitalize confidence in the leadership. Total membership was 1.8 million in 1986. The party holds a National Congress every five years. The congress is a culmination of the political process, since it usually meets to ratify decisions already made by the Political Bureau and Central Committee.

Executive: The Council of Ministers is the highest executive body of the state. It is elected by the National Assembly and is responsible to it, but members need not be Assembly deputies. The Council currently consists of a chairman, nine vice-chairmen, a secretary-general, 23 ministers, seven chairmen of state commissions, and the director-general of the state bank. A minister may hold more than one title. The Council is the equivalent of a Western cabinet, but some powers overlap those of the State Council

Legislature: The general responsibility for governing resides in the National Assembly, which had 496 members in 1987. Deputies are elected to serve five-year terms. The Council of State is the supreme body of the National Assembly and is the collective presidency of Vietnam. The Council presides over National Assembly elections, promulgates laws, interprets the constitution, supervises the activities of people's councils, receives diplomats and has the power to declare war when the Assembly is not in session. The Council of State had 15 members in 1987. The Assembly is empowered to make and amend laws, to elect and remove members of the Council of State and Council of Ministers, to institute or dissolve ministries or state commissions, to levy or repeal taxes, to decide on matters of war and peace, and to ratify treaties. In reality, the Assembly is a rubber stamp for decisions made at a higher level, usually by the Political Bureau. The Assembly usually meets twice a year for one week at a time. One deputy represents 100,000 voters.

Local government: Vietnam is divided into 36 provinces, three municipalities (Hanoi, Haiphong, and Ho Chi Minh City) and one special zone (Vung Tau-Con Dao). These are subdivided into 443 districts, which are further divided into villages and townships. The local population elects members of the appropriate people's council, which oversees economic and cultural development in their area. These councils have the power to draw up budgets and plans. Members of the people's councils at the provincial level are elected for four years; council members at all other levels serve two years. The people's committees are the executive bodies of the people's councils.

Judicial system: The Supreme People's Court, the local people's courts and military tribunals are the juridical bodies of Vietnam; the National Assembly or Council of State may establish special tribunals for special purposes. Judges at all levels are elected. Supreme People's Court justices, elected by the National Assembly, serve for five years; provincial court justices serve for four years; and lower court justices serve for two years. People's assessors are also elected to the Supreme People's Court and to the lower courts for terms of 2½ years and 2 years, respectively. They have the same power as judges, but it is not clear how many of each category preside over a trial. Judgments and sentencing are by majority decision.

Political participation: Citizens participate in political life through four channels: through mass organizations (trade unions, peasant associations, women's unions, youth unions, or religious bodies), which were established to bring most of the population under the national united front; through electing National Assembly deputies; through joining the Communist party; and through writing letters to newspapers. The mass organizations are the liaison between the party and the people. The Fatherland Front (Mat Tran To Quoc) is the most broadly based mass organization.

RECENT HISTORY

France established its first Asian colony in southern Vietnam in 1867. Cochinchina included Saigon and the Mekong delta area. By 1883 France had extended its control to central and northern Vietnam, which became the protectorates of Annam and Tonkin, respectively. Vietnamese rebellions during the 1880s and 1890s were subdued by the French, who by 1902 had established direct rule over the entire country. Opposition to the French continued, however, and gave rise to Vietnamese nationalist movements in the early 20th century and the eventual Communist triumph. Intellectuals like Phan Chu Trinh and Phan Boi Chau were the most influential nationalist figures of the 1920s. The Viet Nam Quoc Dan Dang (VNQDD) was founded in 1927, but this nationalist party was destroyed after a failed uprising in 1930. Ho Chi Minh (born Nguyen Ai Quoc) came to prominence after 1925 as leader of the Communist opposition to the French. Ho recognized the need to harness the power of the peasants for revolution, whereas the nationalists did not have the organizational means to carry out modernization programs. The Communist party emerged as the strongest anticolonial force due to its mass appeal and a political vision based on the understanding of domestic and international forces affecting Vietnam.

In Canton, Communist revolutionaries formed the Association of Vietnamese Revolutionary Youth to train activists in political theory and organization. The Vietnamese Communist party (Dang Cong San Viet Nam) was formed in 1930 in Hong Kong with the support of the Comintern; February 3, 1930, is considered the founding date of the party. In October the name was changed to the Indochinese Communist party (ICP), to stress internationalization of the class struggle. Massive Communist-led rebellions in 1930 were subdued by the French a year later, and many ICP leaders were either killed or imprisoned, while the party's activities were temporarily put on hold. After a leftist Popular Front government came to power in France in 1936, a more liberal policy on Vietnam enabled the Communists to work within the confines of the legal and administrative system. But renewed repression was experienced in 1939, as a southern insurrection was put down by force and important southern leaders were imprisoned, including Pham Van Dong and Le Duan.

The Vietnam Independence League (Viet Nam Doc Lap Dong Minh Hoi, or Viet Minh) was formed in 1941 to lead the struggle for national liberation. The party headquarters was moved to Hanoi. France retained administrative control over the region, but Japanese troops exercised real power during World War II. They eventually overthrew the French in March 1945 and installed Bao Dai, the last of the Nguyen emperors, as head of an independent Vietnamese government. By this time the revolutionary army had been strengthened and units were consolidated into the Vietnamese Liberation Army. The army controlled an area covering all or part of 10 northern provinces. After the Japanese surrender, the Viet Minh filled the power vacuum that was left and established the Democratic Republic of Vietnam (DRV) on September 2, 1945. In an attempt to prevent war with the returned French, Ho Chi Minh signed an agreement in February 1946, which recognized Vietnam as a free state within the French Union and Indochinese Federation (this did not include Cochinchina). The French government did not ratify the treaty, however, and the French again assumed colonial control. Fighting broke out in late 1946 and did not end until the Viet Minh had decisively defeated the French at Dien Bien Phu in 1954, despite U.S. support for the French effort. The 1954 Geneva Conference, convened to settle the dispute, only set the stage for 20 more years of fighting. Participants included the United States, Great Britain, France, the Soviet Union, China and the DRV. China exerted a strong influence over a settlement that was unfavorable to the DRV and the United States. The DRV was given control of northern Vietnam, but a French-dominated "associated state" gained control over southern Vietnam. Elections were to be held two years later to form a unified government. The country was split at the 17th parallel. Approximately 1 million people, mostly Roman Catholics, moved south at the time, while a few hundred thousand Viet Minh troops and supporters traveled north.

The United States, which had supplied Bao Dai's government with economic aid since 1951, persuaded him to appoint the anti-French Ngo Dinh Diem as prime minister in the south. France was thus pressured to leave the country by the middle of 1955, and abrogated its responsibility to ensure elections would be held in 1956. Diem, supported by the United States, deposed Bao Dai in October 1955 and established the Republic of Vietnam (RVN), with himself as president. Diem and his brother, Ngo Dinh Nhu, who headed the internal security forces, followed a policy of repression against all opposition until Diem was deposed in 1963. Secrecy, brutality and arbitrariness were endemic to the regime. Such repression, combined with land-reform measures that placed tracts in the hands of military officers supporting Diem, only deepened opposition (especially in rural areas) to the regime. Backed by the United States, Diem refused to hold elections, fearful that Ho Chi Minh would be elected premier. Party leaders in the south countered repression with assassinations of local officials and village headmen, and other armed activities. The DRV encouraged southern cadres to focus on political struggle and did not provide military assistance at this time, as it concentrated on construction and economic development. In 1959 the DRV began to play a more active role and formed the National Front for the Liberation of South Vietnam (NLF) in December 1960. The NLF was able to enforce rent reductions and land-reform measure over large areas of the country, thus winning the support of the peasants. The RVN, in retaliation, created the policy of "strategic hamlets" in 1962, and by 1963 it had moved an estimated 8 million people, usually by force and often to a considerable distance from their homes. The policy aimed to separate peasants from the NLF, but it only increased their support for the opposition.

Diem and Nhu were assassinated by the U.S.-backed military on November 1, 1963. Military regimes of the next two years did little to solve the problems of the previous government. The NLF increased its pressure, and the RVN military was geared more toward political advancement than military combat. Political office brought wealth, and military leaders vied for power. The administration of President Lyndon B. Johnson introduced the Tonkin Gulf Resolution to justify sending more U.S. troops to back the fumbling southern regime, and the escalation peaked in 1968, when over 500,000 U.S. troops were in Vietnam. Total U.S., RVN and Southeast Asia Treaty Organization troops numbered 1.5 million in that year, compared to less than 400,000 for the NLF/PAVN forces. An air war was launched against northern Vietnam, as U.S. planes bombed the main industrial areas and communications facilities of the DRV under Operation Rolling Thunder. Twice as much tonnage was dropped on northern Vietnam as was used during World War II. The bombing strengthened anti-American sentiment and increased popular commitment to evict the "foreign invader." A U.S. attempt to cut supplies flowing from north to south along the Ho Chi Minh Trail failed, and the flow actually increased between 1965 and 1968. The U.S. troops' use of defoliants further disrupted rural life, creating far greater social upheaval than at any stage under French domination.

The Tet Offensive of 1968 marked a turning point in the war. Though it was considered a military victory for the south, it was a psychological blow to U.S./ARVN troops. In planning the offensive, the Communist party had hoped that a general uprising in southern cities would cause the collapse of the Nguyen Van Thieu regime. City populations, however, did not rise up in revolt, and U.S. forces squelched the offensive, but not until after Hue and the U.S. embassy in Saigon (later Ho Chi Minh City) had been temporarily taken over by NLF troops. The NLF lost many soldiers, wounded or captured, and the rest suffered from low morale, since a quick end to the war was not achieved; they went on the defensive from 1969–1972. The Tet Offensive did prove that RVN forces could not survive without U.S. backing, and it showed the United States the futility of its escalation policy. The United States began to feel the effects of the war at home, both in terms of the economy and public opinion. Military expenditures had skyrocketed from nearly $6 billion in 1965–66 to over $25 billion in 1967–68. Foreign governments began to lose faith in the dollar and converted their reserves to gold, thereby depleting U.S. reserves. Americans were no longer convinced that there "was light at the end of the tunnel," and the antiwar movement became stronger and more vociferous during the 1968 election year. The United States began to look for newer and less costly ways to achieve its goals in Vietnam.

When Richard Nixon took office in 1969, he continued the troop demobilization begun under Johnson, and instituted a policy of "Vietnamization," which aimed to make the ARVN responsible for fighting its own war. Peace negotiations began in 1969, but both sides continued fighting, each wanting to negotiate from a position of strength. The secret U.S. bombing of Cambodia began at this time in another effort to stop the flow of supplies along the Ho Chi Minh Trail, which ran through Laos and Cambodia. The ARVN invaded Cambodia in March 1970, and U.S. support troops followed in April. The new escalation in Cambodia diluted ARVN troop concentration elsewhere, opening doors for the NLF and further inflaming antiwar sentiment in the United States. As the United States began to withdraw its troops, the weakness of the ARVN became apparent.

As Nixon and U.S. National Security Adviser (later Secretary of State) Henry Kissinger made some progress on the diplomatic front, the United States resumed its bombing of Hanoi and Haiphong in the spring of 1972. The U.S.-DRV agreement reached in October 1972 provided for a cease-fire followed by complete withdrawal of U.S. troops within two months and a political settlement to be worked out later. The pact allowed the United States to pull out while buying time for the ARVN. The DRV was convinced the Thieu regime could not endure without U.S. backing. Nixon, however, refused to sign the cease-fire agreement and after winning a second term in office pushed for more concessions. Bombing of the north continued, but when a new agreement was reached in January 1973, it contained little that was different from the earlier one. The last U.S. combat troops were withdrawn by March 1973. As the Thieu regime became increasingly corrupt and an economic recession began to shroud the country, large segments of the apolitical society in the south began to call for an end to the war. Many felt that the only way to restore peace and stability was for the NLF to take power. A Communist offensive in early 1975 forced ARVN withdrawal from the central highlands. Panic took over in the south. Troops deserted to save their families. Ban Me Thuot and Hue fell, and Thieu left the country on April 22, when Saigon was surrounded. The city fell on April 30, 1975, and the war was over.

Reunification of the country was accomplished by July 1976. The year's delay was attributed to debate within the Hanoi leadership over how best to deal with the south. The victory came earlier than expected, and no plans had been formed for socialization of the south. The regime began a rapid transition to socialism in 1977, causing hundreds of thousands of predominantly ethnic Chinese who controlled the business establishment to flee the country as what were called boat people. A rapid collectivization of agriculture proved disastrous for the southern economy, and a 1979 border war with China further contributed to the flow of refugees from 1978 until 1980. The party initiated reforms in 1979 and extended them following major self-criticism in 1986. The Sixth National Congress, held in December of that year, introduced liberal economic reforms. A certain amount of private enterprise was condoned, and a new law on foreign investment, passed in late 1987, attempted to lure foreign capital to revive the stagnant economy.

A major strain on the economy was the Vietnamese army's occupation of Cambodia from 1978. Responding to Khmer Rouge attacks on its territory, Vietnam invaded Cambodia in December 1978 and pushed out the Khmer Rouge leadership by January 1979. A pro-Hanoi government was installed, and nearly 200,000 Vietnamese troops remained in Cambodia to provide the decimated country with defense and to prevent the return of the previous regime. As a result, the United States maintained its economic embargo of Vietnam and continued to pressure its allies to follow suit.

Vietnam gradually began to withdraw troops from Cambodia in 1982. The final 50,000 left in September 1989, earlier than the 1990 deadline. Vietnam expected the move to break down the U.S.-imposed barrier to Western economic aid, but the change was slow in occurring.

ECONOMY

Background: The main problem the regime faced in 1975 was how to integrate the southern capitalist system into the northern socialist framework, where most peasants were members of cooperatives and industrial plants were owned by the state. Debate over the speed of socialization dominated the party. In 1976 the regime began a quick transformation to the south, inciting much resistance and causing many to leave the country. NEZs were formed to boost the areas under production and to relieve the population pressure on already overburdened cities. GDP improved slightly in the late 1970s, at an average of 0.4% a year. Between 1981 and 1983 it averaged 6.4% a year but slowed to 3.6% a year between 1984 and 1985. Years of low productivity inspired economic reform in 1979: Enterprises were allowed to obtain their own raw materials rather than rely on state supplies, and they could sell their products on the open market. Years of economic stagnation continued nevertheless, caused by poor harvests, corruption and mismanagement, and lack of foreign aid ensued. Vietnam instituted new, sweeping economic reforms at the Sixth Party Congress in December 1986 to revive the devastated economy. More liberal economic reformers moved in to try to save the country from skyrocketing inflation, unemployment and, in some cases, starvation. The reforms emphasized production of food and consumer goods, and exports. Producers were given more independence to boost efficiency. State investment was channeled away from urban industry toward these sectors. Private enterprise was encouraged. Businesses were given tax breaks; some companies obtained bank loans and were allowed to set their own prices. The Central Committee called for an end to discrimination against private capitalists, and for reduced central planning. Moonlighting was legalized, and bonuses to reward hard workers were approved. Guidelines for foreign investment were loosened in December 1987. Foreigners could now provide up to 99% of the investment (up from 49%) in joint ventures and 100% in foreign-owned ventures. Still, economic problems plagued the nation. Distribution and circulation of goods continued to be problems, and prices continued to soar. Vietnam's external debt in convertible currencies was $1.46 billion out of a total $5 billion. An estimated 40% of the state budget was spent on defense. Yearly inflation was 700%. A U.S.-led economic embargo of Vietnam denied the country much-needed Western aid, forcing it to rely more heavily on the Eastern bloc. Most aid from multilateral agencies was aimed at humanitarian efforts, Sweden, for example providing about $100 million per year in development aid. Soviet aid was estimated to be $2 billion a year, including $1 billion in military aid. In early 1989, however, Hanoi adopted a new package of economic measures proposed by the International Monetary Fund. The dong was devalued, subsidies were cut, and interest rates were increased to encourage savings. These measures curtailed inflation, but at the cost of increased unemployment.

Agriculture: Agriculture forms the foundation of the Vietnamese economy, contributing about 51% of GDP and employing about 70% of the country's labor force. Total cultivable land was estimated at 14.6 million acres/ 5.9 million ha. in 1983. The area slowly expanded as a result of the establishment of NEZs in the Mekong delta and central highlands, where the main crops are rice, tea, coffee, oil palm and rubber. Rice was grown on 14 million acres/5.67 million ha. in 1984; half of that land is double-cropped. In parts of central Vietnam three crops per year are grown. In the late 1980s average yield was 2.66 metric tons per hectare in the north and more than 4 tons per hectare in the south. Secondary food crops such as maize, sweet potatoes and cassava are also cultivated. Because rice production is emphasized, the output of these secondary crops fell from 2.6 metric tons in 1980 to 2.14 metric tons per hectare in 1983. Higher procurement prices offered for paddies caused food output to increase to 16.98 metric tons per hectare in 1983 and to 17.9 metric tons per hectare in 1984, with further slight increases in 1985 and 1986. This allowed the country to achieve self-sufficiency, although at a very low level—about 661 pounds/ 300 kg. per capita. However, poor weather conditions adversely affected agricultural production in 1987–88, forcing the government to appeal for emergency food aid. Certain areas of the north reported near famine conditions. Output per head dropped to 617 pounds/280 kg. in the entire country and below 551 pounds/250 kg. in the Red River delta. Lack of technical inputs such as irrigation, fertilizers, water pumps and mechanization of land preparation further hindered agricultural expansion. Reforms introduced in March 1988 gave cooperatives independence from district administrators, promoted the family economy and set up an Agricultural Development Bank to stimulate production. New policies and favorable harvests made Vietnam a rice exporter in 1989. Fish is an important food source and export commodity, but the estimated 545,000-ton catch in 1984 was just half that of 1973. Rubber production reached a high of 60,000 tons in 1987, up from just over 40,000 tons in 1979.

Mining: Vietnam's most important mining activity is centered on its coal deposits. Coal is Vietnam's main source of energy, and reserves are estimated at 130 million metric tons. Coal mines had originally been developed in the north by the French. Output expanded in the early 1970s but fell back beginning in 1977, a trend attributed to the withdrawal of Chinese laborers after the Sino-Vietnamese dispute of 1978–79. Yearly production now averages 5 million metric tons. Vietnam began to exploit its petroleum reserves in the South China Sea in 1986 through a joint agreement with the Soviet Union. By mid-1987 the Bach Ho oil field was producing 5,000 barrels per day. Lacking domestic refineries, Vietnam exports the petroleum to Japan. Reserves are estimated at 20 million barrels. Foreign companies have invested $250 million in offshore oil and gas exploration, an amount equal to more than half of all foreign investment since laws were liberalized in late 1987.

Industry: Since 1979 emphasis has been placed on light- and consumer-goods industries and on export industries in order to reduce the burgeoning trade deficit. The industrial sector by 1988 accounted for 28% of national income and employed 11% of the labor force. Reforms divided state industry into two sectors to improve efficiency while maintaining state influence over important industries. One sector, made up of consumer-goods factories and light industry, no longer receives quantity output targets from the state but is only responsible for meeting a set level of payments to the state budget. Factories do not receive supplies through the state planning system but develop commercial relations with suppliers and customers. The state maintains control over 30 to 40 key enterprises, including coal, electricity, steel, chemicals and fertilizers, transport and communications, textiles, paper, and electronic products. Ho Chi Minh City produces about half the total national industrial output. Production increased at an annual rate of 9.5% in 1981–85, but progress was uneven. Locally run, privately owned industries increased 15.2% and handicrafts 19.7%, but large-scale state industries witnessed only a 3.2% increase in output. Many factories work at 40%–50% of capacity due to power shortages, outdated equipment, shortage of raw materials and poor management. Growth slowed sharply in the first half of 1988. Factories producing textiles, motorcycles, motors, cosmetics, rubber, paint, clothing and appliances did not meet planned targets. Official reports attributed the slowdown to changes in financing, prices of materials and production costs, and uneven supplies. Industrial output grew by 8% in 1987. Production figures for 1986 were as follows: oil and natural gas, 40,500 tons; electricity, 5.2 million KWh; steel, 62,000 tons; cement, 1.4 million tons; cotton fabrics, 439 million sq. yards/367 million sq. m.; paper 79,000 tons; fish sauce, 46 million gallons/174 million liters; coal, 5.4 million tons.

Foreign trade: The 1979 reforms permitted most cities and provinces to trade directly with foreign countries. Exports grew at an annual rate of 7% through 1985, while imports grew at only 3% a year. Despite the Western trade embargo, exports to the West increased at 33% per year. Exports in 1985 covered 45% of total imports, up from 37% in 1979. Southern cities and provinces were the main sources of export, with agricultural, forestry and marine products and crude oil the top export items. Most of Vietnam's trade was conducted with Eastern Europe. In 1984 the Soviet Union accounted for about 60% of the country's total foreign trade. Vietnam attempted to lessen its dependence on the Eastern bloc, and in 1984 the country reported $120 million of trade with Singapore, $165 million with Japan and $125 million with Hong Kong. Japan is the major market for Vietnam's coal and fish exports. Singapore's principal export to Vietnam is mineral fuels. A continuing trade deficit led to a serious shortage of foreign exchange; emphasis was thus placed on developing exports. Imports totaled $2 billion in 1985, while exports were only valued at $945 million, leaving a deficit of $1.1 billion. The figure rose to $1.3 billion in 1987.

Employment and wages: Unemployment in 1987 was reported to be 1.6 million. One-third of the national budget went to subsidizing food prices in 1987. Moonlighting was sanctioned by the reforms of 1986, and many people must hold two or three jobs to support their families. Government employees experienced a 13-fold wage increase in October 1987, in an attempt to keep up with runaway inflation. Basic wages remained around 5,000 dongs–10,000 dongs (U.S. $2–$4, according to the Import-Export Association exchange rate) per month. The free-market price of rice had risen to D1,000 (40 cents) per kilogram. The official exchange rate is about D800 = $1, but the black market rate can be as high as D3,000–D4,000 = $1.

SOCIAL SERVICES

After reunification the regime was faced with hundreds of thousands of people affected by the legacies of war: invalids, orphans, widows, prosti-

tutes and drug addicts. The SRV adopted an approach based on rehabilitation and job training for these people, whom it considered to be victims
of war neocolonialism. Two renowned rehabilitation programs were the
treatment of drug addicts (about 100,000) and the rehabilitation of prostitutes. The drug-treatment program used acupuncture to relieve withdrawal symptoms. Physical education, political education and the learning
of handicraft skills were introduced in later stages. Prostitutes underwent
medical treatment, political education and training in handicraft techniques. They were returned to their communities after finishing their course,
with the idea that social pressure would prohibit them from returning to
their former ways. These programs, though successful, heavily drained scarce
medical resources and government finances. Other areas that affect health,
such as the provision of water and sewage, electricity and housing, are
long-term projects that must rely on economic development. Overall, the
health situation remains poor. Malaria and malnutrition have returned, and
the system of village clinics cannot cope with the load of maladies without
Western medicine. Hospitals are understaffed and lack facilities. In addition, many doctors left the country in 1975. In 1982 the SRV had 2,282
hospitals and treatment centers, and 10,000 village health stations with a
total of 208,400 beds. The ratio of physicians to inhabitants is 1 to 1,200.
Each district has a health center in charge of 50 to 100 beds. Each provincial center has one or more hospitals, with 300 to 500 beds. There are
specialized hospitals (for gynecology, endocrinology, surgery) in urban centers.

<h2 style="text-align:center">EDUCATION</h2>

Education has been a priority of the SRV as well as the DRV since 1945.
In 1975 a literacy campaign was launched among the estimated 1.4 million
illiterates of working age in the south. By 1978 the government claimed
that 94% could read and write. Since then, however, the United Nations
has reported a sharp decline in the literacy rate, mainly because teachers
are poorly paid and must often hold additional jobs. The number of students in the general education system in the DRV was 4.7 million in
1970. That number had more than doubled, to 11.7 million, by 1986.
The system was overhauled, however, in 1979, shifting the focus from
theoretical and classical subjects to training that could give students technical competence in future careers. The more vocationally oriented curriculum aimed to match student aptitudes with the possibilities of employment.

Until 1982 education was compulsory for 10 years. A new 12-year cycle
was instituted after the 1981–82 school year. Children enter the primary
level at age six and follow a standard curriculum for nine years. About
30% of those who finish the primary cycle are admitted, based on examination results, to the three-year secondary cycle. Others are directed to
technical schools, study-cum-work schools or to production jobs. University admissions are also determined by examination results. Enrollment levels in 1985 included 1.6 million preprimary students, with 57,600 teach-

ers; 7.9 million primary students, with 204,100 teachers; 3.8 million secondary students, with 149,000 teachers; and 114,700 students enrolled in higher education, with 17,400 teachers. There were 93 universities and colleges and 287 vocational schools. Some tertiary institutions fall under the Ministry of Higher and Vocational Education, while others are supervised by related ministries. Between 1981 and 1986, approximately 10,000 students studied abroad, mostly in Eastern Europe. Private schools were disenfranchised in the south after 1975 but were reportedly allowed to reopen in early 1988.

MASS MEDIA

The Ministry of Information was established in 1987 as an organ of the Council of Ministers. It exercises uniform state management over newspapers, news agencies, publications, radio and television. Newspaper reform followed general reform measures sweeping the country; papers began to publish critical editorials and addressed serious problems facing the country. The constitution guarantees freedom of the press, but anything that opposes government policies is not allowed.

The press

Dailies: Hanoi Moi (New Hanoi), Hanoi committee of the VCP; *Nhan Dan* (The People), VCP, 300,000; Quan Doi Nhan Dan (People's Army), 200,000; *Saigon Giai Phong* (Liberated Saigon), Ho Chi Minh City Committee of the VCP, 45,000; *Giai Phong Nhat Bao,* Fatherland Front, Chinese; *Tuoi Tre* (Youth Paper), 70,000.

Weeklies: Phu Nu, Women's Union; *Lao Dong,* Trade Unions Federation; *Tien Phong,* Youth Union; *Dai Doan Ket,* Fatherland Front; *Van Nghe,* art and literature; *Doc Lap* (Independence), Democratic party; *Thieu Nien Tien Phong,* Young Pioneers.

BIOGRAPHICAL SKETCHES

Vo Chi Cong. The number-three man in the hierarchy, behind Linh and Muoi, was born Vo Dan on August 7, 1913, in central Vietnam. He took part in the Communist Youth Movement from 1930 until 1934 and joined the ICP in 1935. He was arrested by the French for his revolutionary activities and imprisoned between 1943 and 1945. He continued his revolutionary activities in the central region after World War II. In 1955 he became deputy party secretary. In 1962 he became representative of the party in the NLF. He was elected to the National Assembly in 1976 and appointed vice-chairman of the Council of Ministers. He joined the Political Bureau in 1976 and became minister of agriculture in 1978. In June 1987 he was appointed chairman of the State Council. Cong was long an opponent of decentralization but became converted to reform. Some believe political pragmatism prompted the move.

Le Quang Dao. The chairman of the National Assembly was born Nguyen

VIETNAM

Duc Nguyen on August 8, 1921, in Ha Bac Province. He joined the Democratic Youth Union in 1938 and the CPV in 1940. In 1945 he was nominated secretary of the party committee of Haiphong and in 1948 of Hanoi. He was deputy commissar of the 1954 Dien Bien Phu campaign and served in the army as a major general from 1958 until 1974, when he became a lieutenant general. He was an alternate member of the party Central Committee from 1960 until 1972 and became a full member in 1972. Since 1984 he has headed the Central Committee's Commission for Science and Education.

Nguyen Van Linh. Born Nguyen Van Cuc on July 1, 1915, Nguyen Van Linh was elected secretary-general of the CPV in 1986. He joined the students' union of the Vietnam Revolutionary Youth Association in 1929 and was imprisoned in 1930 by the French for his resistance activities. He joined the ICP upon his release from prison in 1936, and founded a provisional party organization and many party bases in Haiphong. He was arrested again in 1941 after conducting revolutionary activities in central Vietnam. After his release in 1945 he became secretary of the Saigon Party Committee and led the resistance against the French. From 1957 until 1960 he was acting secretary of the Central Party Commission for the South. In 1960 he was elected to the party Central Committee. Linh's party positions made him a major leader in southern resistance to the U.S.-backed regimes. He was appointed secretary of the Ho Chi Minh City Party Committee after reunification. He was reelected to the party Central Committee and appointed to the Political Bureau. Though originally a northerner, Linh has spent much time in the south and many attribute his dedication to reform to capitalist influences there.

Do Muoi. The prime minister, appointed in June 1988, was born in 1917. He joined the ICP in 1939 and held key party and government posts during the struggles against the French and then against the Americans and South Vietnamese. After Vietnam was united in 1975 Muoi served in several high economic posts and helped forge the strict Marxist policies that the party later said led to economic ruin. He has a reputation for being a party organizer and disciplinarian, leading many to believe he was appointed prime minister to bring law and order to the economy.

Nguyen Co Thach. The foreign minister and deputy chairman of the Council of Ministers was born on May 15, 1923. He began his anti-French resistance activities in 1937 and participated in the 1945 insurrection that led to the establishment of the DRV. He was appointed consul general in New Delhi in 1956 and became vice-minister for foreign affairs in 1960. Thach took part in the Paris peace talks between the United States and North Vietnam and was elected to the CPV's Central Committee in 1976. He was appointed minister for foreign affairs in 1980, and became a full member of the Political Bureau in 1986 and deputy chairman of the Council of Ministers in 1987. Thach is regarded as an economic reformer. He headed the commission for economic relations with foreign countries, formed in early 1987, which gave him considerable power over deciding Vietnam's economic relations with Western investors and traders.

COMPARATIVE
STATISTICS

COMPARATIVE STATISTICS

AREA AND POPULATION

Country	Area (sq. km.)	Population mid-1986 estimate (millions)
Afghanistan	652,225	14.92
Australia	7,682,300	15.97
Bangladesh	143,998	102.86
Bhutan	46,500	1.45
Brunei	5,765	0.224 [1985]
Burma	676,552	37.85
Cambodia*	181,035	7.49
China	9,571,300	1,072.2
Cook Islands	237	0.017
Fiji	18,376	0.714
Hong Kong	1,071	5.53
India	3,287,263	766.1
Indonesia	1,904,569	168.66
Japan	377,815	121.49
Korea, North	120,538	20.88
Korea, South	99,222	41.57
Laos	236,800	3.7
Macao*	16.92	0.434 [Dec. 1987]
Malaysia*	329,758	16.109
Maldives	298	0.182
Mongolia	1,565,000	1.94
Nepal	147,181	17.13
New Zealand	269,057	3.25
Pakistan	803,943	99.16
Papua New Guinea	462,840	3.4
Philippines	300,000	56.00
Singapore	622.6	2.59
Solomon Islands	27,556	0.285
Sri Lanka	64,453.6	16.12
Taiwan*	36,000	19.455 [Dec. 1986]
Thailand	513,115	52.65
Tonga	748	0.100
Vanuatu	12,190	0.140
Vietnam	329,566	60.92

Sources:
All the figures for area, and the population estimates for Cambodia, Macao, Malaysia and Taiwan (marked*) are taken from Europa Publications, *The Far East and Australasia 1989*. The remaining population estimates are from United Nations, *Statistical Yearbook for Asia and the Pacific 1986–1987*.

GNP PER CAPITA

Country	U.S. dollars (1986)	Average annual growth rate (percent) (1965–86)
Australia	11,920	1.7
Bangladesh	160	0.4
Bhutan	150	—
Brunei	15,400	—
Burma	200	2.3
China	300	5.1
Fiji	1,810	2.7
Hong Kong	6,910	6.2
India	290	1.8
Indonesia	490	4.6
Japan	12,840	4.3
Korea, South	2,370	6.7
Malaysia	1,830	4.3
Maldives	310	1.8
Nepal	150	1.9
New Zealand	7,460	1.5
Pakistan	350	2.4
Papua New Guinea	720	0.5
Philippines	560	1.9
Singapore	7,410	7.6
Solomon Islands	530	—
Sri Lanka	400	2.9
Thailand	810	4.0
Tonga	740	—
Western Samoa	680	—

Source:
The World Bank, *World Development Report 1988.*

ECONOMICALLY ACTIVE POPULATION:
PROPORTION IN AGRICULTURE, 1987

Country	Economically active population (thousands)	Percent in agriculture
Afghanistan	5,440	56.6
Australia	7,595	5.5
Bangladesh	30,585	70.5
Bhutan	657	91.3
Burma	17,330	48.8
Cambodia	3,663	71.3
China	641,995	69.5
Fiji	239	41.0
Hong Kong	2,963	1.4
India	304,730	67.5
Indonesia	66,473	51.0
Japan	60,787	7.6
Korea, North	9,615	36.2
Korea, South	17,515	27.8
Laos	2,101	72.8
Malaysia	6,516	34.8
Mongolia	946	33.1
Nepal	7,200	92.1
New Zealand	1,462	9.7
Pakistan	31,299	51.1
Papua New Guinea	1,755	69.9
Philippines	20,875	48.2
Singapore	1,253	1.1
Sri Lanka	6,095	52.2
Thailand	27,770	66.3
Vietnam	30,352	62.6

Source:
Food and Agriculture Organization of the United Nations, *FAO Production Yearbook 1987.*

URBANIZATION

Country	Urban population as percentage of total population (1985)	Average growth rate of urban population (1980–85)	Average growth rate of rural population (1980–85)
Afghanistan	18.5	3.92	−0.13
Australia	85.5	1.25	1.74
Bangladesh	11.9	5.35	2.41
Bhutan	4.5	4.95	1.90
Burma	23.9	1.94	1.94
China	20.6	1.44	1.18
Hong Kong	92.4	2.12	−0.26
India	25.5	3.64	1.39
Indonesia	25.3	4.59	1.13
Japan	76.5	0.74	0.41
Korea, South	65.4	4.36	−2.80
Laos	15.9	5.52	1.66
Malaysia	38.2	4.65	1.20
Mongolia	50.7	2.61	2.88
Nepal	7.7	6.95	1.99
New Zealand	83.7	1.02	0.44
Pakistan	29.8	4.25	2.57
Papua New Guinea	14.2	4.35	2.30
Philippines	39.6	3.59	1.67
Singapore	100.0	1.16	—
Sri Lanka	21.1	1.35	1.91
Thailand	19.8	4.67	1.39
Vietnam	20.3	2.98	1.69

Source:
United Nations, Economic and Social Commission for Asia and the Pacific,
Economic and Social Survey of Asia and the Pacific 1987.

LAND USE, 1986
(1,000 Ha.)

Country	Land area	Arable land	Permanent crops	Permanent pasture	Forest and woodland	Other land
Afghanistan	64,750	7,910	144	30,000	1,900	24,796
Australia	761,793	48,360	176	436,808	106,000	170,449
Bangladesh	13,391	8,895	269	600	2,119	1,508
Bhutan	4,700	95	7	218	3,295	1,085
Brunei	527	3	4	6	265	249
Burma	65,774	9,596	477	362	32,228	23,111
Cambodia	17,652	2,910	146	580	13,372	644
China	932,641	94,458	3,320	319,080	116,865	398,918
Fiji	1,827	152	88	60	1,185	342
Hong Kong	99	7	1	1	12	78
India	297,319	165,350	3,420	12,070	67,270	49,209
Indonesia	181,157	15,800	5,420	11,800	121,494	26,643
Japan	37,643	4,194	538	626	25,198	7,087
Kiribati	71	—	37	—	2	32
Korea, North	12,041	2,300	92	50	8,970	629
Korea, South	9,819	1,991	150	84	6,505	1,089
Laos	23,080	880	20	800	13,100	8,280
Macao	2	—	—	—	—	2
Malaysia	32,855	1,040	3,335	27	19,820	8,633
Maldives	30	3	—	1	1	25
Mongolia	156,500	1,307	—	123,225	15,178	16,790
Nepal	13,680	2,292	29	1,985	2,308	7,066
New Zealand	26,867	500	21	13,881	7,200	5,265
Pakistan	77,088	20,269	431	5,000	3,150	48,238
Papua New Guinea	45,171	30	355	86	38,270	6,430
Philippines	29,817	4,530	3,400	1,180	11,150	9,557
Samoa	283	55	67	1	134	26
Singapore	57	2	2	—	3	50
Solomon Islands	2,754	40	15	39	2,560	100
Sri Lanka	6,474	912	975	439	1,747	2,40
Thailand	51,177	17,693	2,170	740	14,800	15,77
Tonga	67	17	37	4	8	
Vanuatu	1,476	20	125	25	16	1,29
Vietnam	32,536	6,200	600	272	13,000	12,46

Source:
Food and Agriculture Organization of the United Nations, *FAO Production Yea* *book 1987.*

AGRICULTURE: PRODUCTION INDEXES—
PER PERSON
(1979–81 = 100)

Country	1977	1987
Afghanistan	97.17	93.54
Australia	97.50	99.50
Bangladesh	102.45	90.86
Bhutan	98.80	122.41
Burma	91.96	120.74
Cambodia	139.82	138.50
China	86.66	131.02
Fiji	86.07	87.44
Hong Kong	110.45	9.07
India	103.80	99.26
Indonesia	87.80	114.18
Japan	115.23	101.24
Korea, North	99.33	109.94
Korea, South	110.35	95.39
Laos	74.96	118.84
Malaysia	100.90	98.68
Mongolia	97.63	99.54
Nepal	101.78	97.38
New Zealand	96.20	103.67
Pakistan	96.28	108.53
Papua New Guinea	99.51	91.74
Philippines	97.60	90.88
Singapore	124.78	83.15
Solomon Islands	101.43	94.71
Sri Lanka	83.43	79.68
Thailand	94.24	101.19
Tonga	104.10	88.99
Vanuatu	110.04	84.84
Vietnam	90.02	114.58

Source:
Food and Agriculture Organization of the United
Nations, *FAO Production Yearbook 1987.*

FOOD: PRODUCTION INDEXES—
PER PERSON
(1979–81 = 100)

Country	1977	1987
Afghanistan	94.26	94.27
Australia	96.99	94.84
Bangladesh	101.73	92.13
Bhutan	98.91	122.29
Burma	91.71	122.03
Cambodia	137.80	135.77
China	86.92	129.83
Fiji	85.22	87.48
Hong Kong	110.45	9.07
India	103.98	99.86
Indonesia	88.29	116.06
Japan	115.21	102.42
Korea, North	99.32	109.70
Korea, South	109.00	95.94
Laos	73.78	118.30
Malaysia	96.43	103.56
Mongolia	97.31	102.99
Nepal	102.30	97.93
New Zealand	99.14	106.92
Pakistan	97.13	105.65
Papua New Guinea	102.63	92.73
Philippines	97.94	90.64
Singapore	124.56	83.50
Solomon Islands	101.43	94.76
Sri Lanka	77.30	75.23
Thailand	94.37	99.81
Tonga	104.10	88.99
Vanuatu	110.69	85.14
Vietnam	89.82	114.44

Source:
Food and Agriculture Organization of the United Nations, *FAO Production Yearbook 1987*.

INDEXES OF MANUFACTURING PRODUCTION
(1980 = 100)

Country	1985	1986	1987
Australia	98	96	—
Bangladesh	100	109	105
Fiji	98	118	102
India	137	153	—
Indonesia	132	141	—
Japan	119	118	122
Korea, South	167	203	242
Malaysia, West	121	130	146
Pakistan	154	164	—
Philippines	241	291	333
Singapore	107	116	—

Source:
United Nations, *Monthly Bulletin of Statistics,* March 1989.

DISTRIBUTION OF MANUFACTURING VALUE
ADDED, 1985
(Percent: Current Prices)

Country	Food and agriculture	Textiles and clothing	Machinery and transport equipment	Chemicals	Other
Australia	17	7	23	7	46
Bangladesh	26	36	6	17	15
China	13	13	26	10	38
Hong Kong	5	39	21	2	33
India	11	16	26	15	32
Indonesia	23	11	10	10	47
Japan	10	6	37	9	38
Korea, South	16	17	23	9	36
Malaysia	21	6	23	10	40
New Zealand	27	10	17	6	41
Pakistan	34	21	8	12	25
Papua New Guinea	52	1	10	3	35
Philippines	34	10	11	11	34
Singapore	6	4	49	8	33
Thailand	30	17	13	6	34

Source:
The World Bank, *World Development Report 1988.*

INDEXES OF MINING PRODUCTION
(1980 = 100)

Country	1985	1986	1987
Bangladesh	184	209	252
Fiji	241	369	370
India	168	180	—
Indonesia	84	87	—
Japan	94	94	85
Korea, South	115	124	125
Malaysia, West	163	189	194
Philippines	85	71	87

Source:
United Nations, *Monthly Bulletin of Statistics,* March 1989.

EXCHANGE RATES AND CURRENCIES
(National currency per U.S. dollar)

Country and currency	End of period		
	1986	1987	Nov. 1988
Afghanistan (afghanis)	50.600	50.600	50.600
Australia (dollars)	1.504	1.384	1.139
Bangladesh (taka)	30.800	31.200	32.270
Brunei (dollars)*	—	(June 30, 1988)	2.047
Burma (kyats)	7.039	6.110	6.284
Cambodia (riels)*	—	(June 30, 1988)	100.00
China (yuan renminbi)	3.722	3.722	3.722
Fiji (dollars)	1.145	1.441	1.372
Hong Kong (dollars)	7.795	7.760	7.806
India (rupees)	13.122	12.877	14.969
Indonesia (rupiahs)	1,641.000	1,650.000	1,721.000
Japan (yen)	159.100	123.500	121.750
Kiribati (dollars)	1.504	1.384	1.139
Korea, North (won)*	—	(June 30, 1988)	2.128
Korea, South (won)	861.400	792.300	687.500
Laos (new kips)	95.000	95.000	—
Macao (patacas)*	—	(June 30, 1988)	8.037
Malaysia (ringgit)	2.603	2.493	2.675
Maldives (rufiyaa)	7.244	9.395	8.663
Mongolia (tughrik)	3.000	2.840	3.000
Nepal (rupees)	22.000	21.600	25.200
New Zealand (dollars)	1.910	1.521	1.527
Pakistan (rupees)	17.250	17.450	18.000
Papua New Guinea (kina)	0.961	0.878	0.816
Philippines (pesos)	20.530	20.800	21.379
Singapore (dollars)	2.175	1.998	1.943
Solomon Islands (dollars)	1.986	1.974	2.091
Sri Lanka (rupees)	28.520	30.763	32.973
Taiwan (dollars)*	—	(June 30, 1988)	28.890
Thailand (baht)	26.130	25.070	25.060
Tonga (pa'anga)	1.504	1.384	1.140
Vanuatu (vatu)	116.240	100.560	103.850
Vietnam (dong)	18.000	18.000	18.000

Sources:
United Nations, *Monthly Bulletin of Statistics,* February 1989.
*Europa Publications, *The Far East and Australasia 1989.*

EXPORTS
(Millions of U.S. Dollars)

Country	1985	1986	1987
Afghanistan	719.43	708.93	791.39
Australia	22,611.00	22,541.00	26,510.00
Bangladesh	998.80	888.90	1,076.80
Brunei	2,934.40	1,797.50	1,796.20
Burma	518.60	517.38	520.40
China	27,329.00	31,367.00	39,464.00
Fiji	229.84	239.47	280.44
Hong Kong	30,182.00	35,420.00	48,473.00
India	10,211,00	10,516.00	12,430.00
Indonesia	18,580.00	11,071.00	16,548.00
Japan	177,189.00	211,735.00	231,332.00
Korea, North	640.40	684.30	783.10
Korea, South	30,289.00	34,732.00	47,301.00
Laos	18.37	14.39	23.71
Macao	907.09	1,033.55	1,396.53
Malaysia	15,408.00	13,977.00	17,934.00
Maldives	24.00	29.10	23.70
Nepal	138.20	146.20	166.60
New Caledonia	271.93	208.44	223.99
New Zealand	5,714.30	5,920.80	7,158.40
Pakistan	2,738.40	3,383.00	4,168.30
Papua New Guinea	917.60	1,047.50	1,172.10
Philippines	4,614.00	4,806.70	5,696.00
Singapore	22,812.00	22,497.00	28,596.00
Solomon Islands	69.82	65.35	62.69
Sri Lanka	1,264.90	1,162.70	1,363.50
Thailand	7,122.00	8,863.90	11,301.50
Tonga	5.00	5.82	6.09
Vanuatu	36.06	30.38	31.70
Vietnam	331.90	324.20	403.20
Western Samoa	27.26	10.49	11.08

Source:
International Monetary Fund, *Direction of Trade Statistics,* 1988.

IMPORTS
(Millions of U.S. Dollars)

Country	1985	1986	1987
Afghanistan	857.22	1,054.13	1,189.75
Australia	23,499.00	23,916.00	27,007.00
Bangladesh	2,526.20	2,550.40	2,730.30
Brunei	605.70	653.30	1,296.90
Burma	655.74	675.66	679.23
China	42,480.00	43,247.00	43,222.00
Fiji	441.47	378.04	314.71
Hong Kong	29,701.00	35,360.00	48,463.00
India	17,769.00	18,996.00	20,683.00
Indonesia	10,214.00	10,724.00	10,234.00
Japan	130,516.00	127,660.00	150,926.00
Korea, North	834.50	827.10	1,093.90
Korea, South	31,058.00	31,588.00	41,019.00
Laos	64.82	70.33	89.44
Macao	775.68	874.31	1,111.58
Malaysia	12,301.00	10,828.00	12,701.00
Maldives	71.10	79.20	99.40
Nepal	297.20	320.60	493.30
New Caledonia	346.75	531.27	623.54
New Zealand	5,943.50	5,996.60	7,262.90
Pakistan	5,888.60	5,367.30	5,818.80
Papua New Guinea	788.20	844.30	1,054.50
Philippines	5,351.40	5,211.00	6,936.80
Singapore	26,237.00	25,513.00	32,498.00
Solomon Islands	69.22	60.93	67.17
Sri Lanka	1,831.80	1,829.40	2,123.60
Thailand	9,259.50	9,165.50	13,002.60
Tonga	41.55	39.85	42.04
Vanuatu	65.81	70.55	95.44
Vietnam	642.90	634.20	640.20
Western Samoa	54.15	48.50	62.94

Source:
International Monetary Fund, *Direction of Trade Statistics,* 1988.

RATIO OF EXPORTS AND IMPORTS TO GDP
(PERCENT), 1986

Country	Exports	Imports
Afghanistan	15.9 (1980)	20.0 (1980)
Australia	13.7	15.8
Bangladesh	5.8	16.4
Burma	3.8	3.8
China	13.6	18.9
Fiji	20.8	33.2
Hong Kong	92.2	92.0
India	4.1	6.6
Indonesia	19.7	14.3
Japan	10.8	6.5
Korea, South	35.3	32.1
Malaysia	49.9	39.0
Maldives	27.4 (1985)	62.7 (1985)
Nepal	6.0	19.5
New Zealand	21.1	21.7
Pakistan	10.3	16.4
Papua New Guinea	40.6	42.0
Philippines	15.4	17.4
Singapore	128.4	145.6
Solomon Islands	53.8 (1985)	63.8 (1985)
Sri Lanka	19.0	29.0
Thailand	21.1	22.0
Tonga	9.0 (1985)	73.7 (1985)
Vanuatu	25.0 (1985)	58.3 (1985)
Western Samoa	11.7	52.4

Source:
International Monetary Fund, *International Financial Statistics: Supplement on Trade Statistics,* 1988.

CENTRAL GOVERNMENT EXPENDITURE
BY FUNCTION, 1985
(As Percent of Total Expenditure)

Country	Defense	Social security and welfare	Education	Health
Australia	9.14	27.63	7.25	9.54
Bangladesh	10.03	9.84	10.59	4.97
Bhutan (1984)	—	1.40	11.39	5.55
Burma	18.84	5.27	11.74	7.71
Fiji	4.56	8.58	23.22	8.96
India	18.49	—	1.87	2.11
Indonesia	10.61	—	10.42	2.50
Korea, South	29.67	5.65	18.44	1.44
Malaysia (1981)	15.05	3.95	15.88	4.39
Maldives	—	3.69	11.98	5.78
Nepal	6.19	0.72	12.07	4.97
New Zealand	4.67	30.31	10.90	12.50
Pakistan	33.92	6.20	3.16	1.00
Papua New Guinea	4.52	0.40	17.01	9.62
Philippines	11.88	—	20.12	5.95
Singapore	22.48	1.58	21.59	6.47
Solomon Islands	—	0.87	18.99	9.13
Sri Lanka	8.52	9.04	8.22	3.86
Thailand	20.19	2.97	19.53	5.69
Vanuatu	—	1.12	22.65	12.03
Western Samoa (1984)	—	—	13.84	9.31

Source:
International Monetary Fund, *Government Finance Statistics Yearbook 1988.*

DISTRIBUTION OF GROSS DOMESTIC PRODUCT
(PERCENT), 1986

Country	Agriculture	Industry	(Manufacturing)	Services
Australia	5	34	17	62
Bangladesh	47	14	8	39
Burma	48	13	10	39
China	31	46	34	23
Hong Kong	0	29	21	71
India	32	29	19	39
Indonesia	26	32	14	42
Japan	3	41	30	56
Korea, South	12	42	30	45
Malaysia (1965)	28	25	9	47
Nepal (1965)	65	11	3	23
New Zealand	11	33	—	56
Pakistan	24	28	17	47
Papua New Guinea	34	26	9	40
Philippines	26	32	25	42
Singapore	1	38	27	62
Sri Lanka	26	27	15	47
Thailand	17	30	21	53

Source:
The World Bank, *World Development Report 1988.*

DISTRIBUTION OF GROSS DOMESTIC PRODUCT
(PERCENT), 1986

Country	General government consumption	Private consumption	Gross domestic savings
Australia	19	61	21
Bangladesh	8	90	2
Burma	14	74	12
China	14	50	36
Hong Kong	8	65	27
India	12	67	21
Indonesia	12	64	24
Japan	10	58	32
Korea, South	10	55	35
Malaysia	17	51	32
Nepal	8	84	9
New Zealand	16	60	24
Pakistan	12	81	7
Papua New Guinea	22	63	15
Philippines	8	73	19
Singapore	12	48	40
Sri Lanka	9	78	13
Thailand	13	62	25

Source:
The World Bank, *World Development Report 1988.*

PRICES: GENERAL INDEXES
(1980 = 100)

Country	1985	1986	1987
Australia	148.9	162.4	176.3
Bangladesh (Dhaka)	163.3	182.3	199.3
Brunei	123.9	126.1	—
Burma (Rangoon)	123.6	135.0	166.7
China	122.6	131.2	142.8
Cook Islands (Rarotonga) [1981 = 100]	152.4	202.4	224.3
Fiji [1985 = 100]	100.0	101.8	107.6
Hong Kong	154.7	159.2	168.0
India (Delhi)	151.9	167.1	184.4
Indonesia	158.9	168.2	183.8
Japan	114.5	115.2	115.3
Kiribati (Tarawa)	130.9	—	—
Korea, South	141.0	144.2	148.8
Malaysia	125.1	125.8	126.8
Nepal	155.0	184.5	204.3
New Zealand	176.3	199.7	231.0
Pakistan	145.8	151.3	159.5
Papua New Guinea	137.1	144.6	149.4
Philippines	253.9	255.8	265.4
Samoa	202.6	213.1	—
Singapore	117.3	115.7	116.3
Solomon Islands (Honiara) [1985 = 100]	100.0	113.6	126.1
Sri Lanka (Colombo)	176.4	190.4	205.0
Thailand (Bangkok)	128.4	130.7	134.1
Tonga	167.4	203.7	213.2
Tuvalu (Funafuti)	142.1	—	—
Vanuatu [1981 = 100]	115.0	121.1	139.7

Source:
International Labor Organization, *Year Book of Labor Statistics 1988.*

DEBT-SERVICE RATIOS

Country	Total long-term debt service as percentage of exports of goods and services	
	1970	1986
Bangladesh	—	25.1
Burma	12.2	55.4
China	—	7.8
India	27.3	24.6
Indonesia	13.9	33.1
Korea, South	20.4	24.4
Malaysia	4.5	20.0
Nepal	3.1	9.4
Pakistan	23.7	27.2
Papua New Guinea	29.1	35.8
Philippines	23.0	21.3
Sri Lanka	10.9	18.4
Thailand	13.9	25.4

Source:
The World Bank, *World Development Report 1988.*

ENERGY PRODUCTION, 1985

Country	Electricity (million kilowatt hours)	Crude petroleum (thousand metric tons)	Hard coal (thousand metric tons)
Afghanistan	1,060	—	151
Australia	118,969	23,393	130,182
Bangladesh	4,870	22	—
Bhutan	30	—	—
Brunei	949	7,901	—
Burma	1,756	1,640	40
Cambodia	80	—	—
China	410,700	124,895	810,000
Cook Islands	10	—	—
Fiji	395	—	—
Hong Kong	19,235	—	—
India	188,479	29,860	149,710
Indonesia	27,797	67,710	1,492
Japan	673,412	530	16,382
Kiribati	6	—	—
Korea, North	48,000	—	39,000
Korea, South	62,716	—	22,543
Laos	1,350	—	—
Malaysia	14,915	21,752	—
Maldives	11	—	—
Mongolia	2,788	—	480
Nauru	28	—	—
Nepal	408	—	—
New Zealand	26,764	843	2,182
Niue	3	—	—
Pakistan	25,732	1,271	2,162
Papua New Guinea	1,565	—	—
Philippines	21,018	561	1,223
Samoa	42	—	—
Singapore	9,876	—	—
Solomon Islands	29	—	—
Sri Lanka	2,464	—	—
Thailand	24,179	1,158	2
Tonga	12	—	—
Vanuatu	25	—	—
Vietnam	5,000	—	5,300

Source:
United Nations, *Statistical Yearbook for Asia and the Pacific, 1986–1987.*

8

CRUDE PETROLEUM: IMPORTS AND EXPORTS, 1985
(Thousand metric tons)

Country	Imports	Exports
Australia	6,273	900
Bangladesh	992	—
Brunei	—	8,176
China	250	30,030
India	14,811	2,044
Indonesia	3,321	40,000
Japan	164,596	—
Korea, North	2,600	—
Korea, South	27,092	—
Malaysia	2,257	16,998
New Zealand	833	—
Pakistan	4,207	—
Philippines	7,911	—
Singapore	35,754	398
Sri Lanka	1,657	—
Thailand	6,745	—

Source:
United Nations, *Statistical Yearbook for Asia and the Pacific, 1986–1987.*

TELEPHONES, TELEVISION RECEIVERS AND
RADIO RECEIVERS
(Thousands)

Country	Telephones	Televisions	Radios
Afghanistan (1982)	23.7	50.0	1,350.0
Australia (1982)	8,055.0	6,500.0	17,600.0
Bangladesh (1982)	122.0	83.0	750.0
Brunei (1982)	26.8	29.0	49.0
Burma (1979)	37.0	—	700.0
China (1982)	4,712.0	6,000.0	65,000.0
Cook Islands (1981)	1.7	—	8.0
Fiji (1982)	47.0	—	320.0
Hong Kong (1982)	1,947.0	1,200.0	2,650.0
India (1983)	3,462.0	2,780.0	40,000.0
Indonesia (1983)	718.0	3,600.0	22,000.0
Japan (1982)	62,804.0	66,342.0	82,400.0
Kiribati (1981)	0.8	—	—
Korea, South (1983)	6,036.0	7,000.0	18,000.0
Laos (1982)	—	—	390.0
Malaysia (1983)	976.0	1,425.0	6,100.0
Maldives (1980)	1.1	—	7.0
Mongolia (1982)	42.9	10.0	175.0
Nauru (1979)	1.6	—	—
Nepal (1983)	—	—	390.0
New Zealand (1983)	2,011.0	922.0	2,850.0
Niue (1983)	0.4	—	1.0
Pakistan (1983)	445.0	1,116.0	7,000.0
Papua New Guinea (1982)	51.0	—	210.0
Philippines (1982)	658.4	1,250.0	2,180.0
Samoa (1983)	6.2	3.5	70.0
Singapore (1985)	1,074.0	500.0	720.0
Solomon Islands (1983)	3.2	—	24.0
Sri Lanka (1981)	109.9	45.0	1,600.0
Thailand (1983)	623.0	840.0	7,350.0
Tonga (1982)	3.5	—	22.0
Vanuatu (1985)	—	—	30.0

Source:
United Nations, *Statistical Yearbook for Asia and the Pacific, 1986–1987.*

MOTOR VEHICLES IN USE
(Thousands)

Country	Passenger cars	Commercial vehicles
Afghanistan (1982)	32.5	31.7
Australia (1984)	6,636.0	1,751.0
Bangladesh (1981)	43.8	38.2
Brunei (1984)	71.5	10.2
Burma (1982)	47.8	47.2
China (1980)	237.8	1,436.2
Fiji (1986)	33.6	23.7
Hong Kong (1985)	184.7	90.4
India (1982)	1,351.2	984.1
Indonesia (1985)	987.1	1,076.8
Japan (1984)	27,144.0	16,477.0
Korea, South (1985)	556.7	541.0
Malaysia, East (1983)	175.5	62.3
Malaysia, West (1986)	1,209.7	265.5
Maldives (1984)	0.4	0.1
New Zealand (1986)	1,558.0	318.0
Niue (1982)	0.3	0.1
Pakistan (1984)	404.4	127.4
Philippines (1984)	360.5	534.3
Samoa (1984)	1.8	2.5
Singapore (1986)	234.6	114.3
Solomon Islands (1982)	1.1	1.7
Sri Lanka (1984)	141.7	121.8
Thailand (1979)	388.8	451.3
Tonga (1980)	1.0	1.3
Vanuatu (1979)	3.3	1.2

Source:
United Nations, *Statistical Yearbook for Asia and the Pacific, 1986–1987.*

RAILWAYS

Country	Length of railways (km.)	Passenger-kilometers (millions)	Net ton-kilometers (millions)
Australia (1983)	39,065	—	34,494
Bangladesh (1984)	2,892	6,284	779
Burma (1986)	—	3,792	576
China (1985)	52,100	242,000	813,000
Hong Kong (1982)	34	407	64
India (1982)	61,385	226,900	174,400
Indonesia (1982)	6,637	6,105	885
Japan (1985)	22,461	328,500	22,100
Korea, South (1985)	3,121	22,595	12,086
Malaysia, East (1984)	—	0.209	0.190
Malaysia, West (1984)	2,075	1,512	1,080
Mongolia (1984)	—	420	5,121
New Zealand (1983)	4,273	458	3,165
Pakistan (1985)	8,775	17,807	7,203
Philippines (1982)	1,059	284	21
Sri Lanka (1985)	1,453	2,101	229
Thailand (1985)	3,735	9,141	2,718
Vietnam (1982)	—	3,107	661

Source:
United Nations, *Statistical Yearbook for Asia and the Pacific, 1986–1987.*

HEALTH SERVICES

Country	Physicians	Population per physician	Hospitals	Population per hospital bed
Afghanistan (1982)	1,160	12,172	83	2,054
Australia (1981)	28,500	524	1,142	157
Bangladesh (1985)	14,944	6,723	760	3,634
Brunei (1983)	116	1,793	8	239
Burma (1982)	8,381	4,285	614	1,140
China (1984)	597,000	1,758	67,000	485
Cook Islands (1981)	19	916	8	115
Fiji (1980)	284	2,232	27	355
Hong Kong (1985)	4,887	1,117	90	222
India (1984)	297.200	2,476	29,200	1,203
Indonesia (1983)	17,647	8,958	1,244	1,529
Japan (1984)	181,100	663	9,574	82
Kiribati (1980)	30	1,953	32	198
Korea, South (1985)	29,596	1,387	500	557
Malaysia, East (1984)	442	5,917	35	461
Malaysia, West (1984)	4,111	3,077	173	390
Maldives (1984)	20	8,652	—	—
Mongolia (1983)	4,234	425	112	118
Nepal (1986)	734	23,338	89	4,547
New Zealand (1982)	5,201	606	370	99
Niue (1980)	2	1,650	1	71
Pakistan (1986)	46,494	2,133	4,111	1,718
Papua New Guinea (1980)	192	15,625	390	236
Philippines (1985)	8,524	6,413	1,814	643
Samoa (1981)	63	2,476	16	229
Singapore (1985)	2,631	973	22	318
Solomon Islands (1983)	34	7,412	8	353
Sri Lanka (1985)	2,151	7,197	402	350
Thailand (1985)	8,650	5,975	856	645
Tonga (1982)	41	2,310	9	283
Vanuatu (1980)	22	5,345	21	165
Vietnam (1982)	14,200	3,972	2,407	430

Source:
United Nations, *Statistical Yearbook for Asia and the Pacific, 1986–1987*.

FOOD SUPPLY: CALORIES PER PERSON PER DAY

Country	1961–63	1984–86
Australia	3,071	3,326
Bangladesh	1,952	1,922
Brunei	2,081	2,850
Burma	1,778	2,592
China	1,654	2,628
Fiji	2,592	2,901
Hong Kong	2,486	2,778
India	2,049	2,204
Indonesia	1,758	2,513
Japan	2,536	2,858
Kiribati	1,874	2,936
Korea, North	2,295	3,199
Korea, South	2,045	2,875
Macao	2,131	2,205
Malaysia	2,266	2,723
Mongolia	2,486	2,829
Nepal	1,868	2,050
New Zealand	3,260	3,407
Pakistan	1,721	2,244
Philippines	1,828	2,353
Samoa	1,852	2,462
Singapore	2,251	2,854
Solomon Islands	2,170	2,163
Sri Lanka	2,078	2,436
Thailand	1,925	2,328
Tonga	2,427	2,942
Vanuatu	2,481	2,344

Source:
Food and Agriculture Organization of the United Nations, *FAO Production Yearbook 1987.*

LITERACY RATE, 1985*

Country	Male	Female
Afghanistan	38.9	7.8
Bangladesh	43.3	22.2
Burma	80.5	59.3
China	82.4	55.5
Hong Kong	94.7	80.9
India	57.2	28.9
Indonesia	83.0	65.4
Laos	92.0	75.8
Malaysia	80.9	66.0
Nepal	38.7	11.9
Pakistan	39.9	18.6
Papua New Guinea	54.8	35.3
Philippines	86.0	85.4
Singapore	93.4	78.6
Sri Lanka	91.2	82.7
Thailand	94.2	87.8

*Literacy rate calculated on the basis of population of age 15 years and over.
Source:
United Nations, Economic and Social Commission for Asia and the Pacific, *Economic and Social Survey of Asia and the Pacific 1986.*

EDUCATION: NUMBER OF INSTITUTIONS
BY TYPE

Country	First level[1]	Second level[2]	Third level[3]
Afghanistan (1982)	4,016	632	—
Australia (1984)	8,443	3,141	65
Bangladesh (1985)	44,423	9,314	373
Bhutan (1985)	145	—	—
Brunei (1984)	178	34	—
Burma (1985)	31,499	2,524	35
China (1984)	853,700	97,000	900
Fiji (1981)	656	—	—
Hong Kong (1985)	769	515	36
India (1984)	510,700	—	—
Indonesia (1984)	158,590	—	—
Japan (1986)	25,000	16,800	1,000
Kiribati (1986)	112	—	—
Korea, South (1985)	6,519	4,088	456
Laos (1984)	7,470	—	—
Malaysia (1985)	6,229	—	—
Nepal (1985)	11,783	4,899	—
New Zealand (1982)	2,483	411	—
Pakistan (1985)	86,142	11,392	604
Papua New Guinea (1982)	2,197	—	—
Philippines (1984)	33,074	5,388	1,178
Singapore (1986)	236	178	5
Solomon Islands (1984)	423	—	—
Sri Lanka (1985)	9,634	—	8
Thailand (1984)	33,086	3,761	30
Tonga (1985)	112	—	—
Vanuatu (1983)	244	—	—
Vietnam (1985)	12,511	—	—

[1] First level: elementary school, primary school.
[2] Second level: middle school, secondary school, high school, vocational school, teacher training school.
[3] Third level: university, teachers college, higher professional school.
Source:
United Nations, *Statistical Yearbook for Asia and the Pacific, 1986–1987.*

EDUCATION: NUMBER OF STUDENTS
BY LEVEL
(Thousands)

Country	First level[1]	Second level[2]	Third level[3]
Afghanistan (1982)	1,198.4	157.7	13.7
Australia (1984)	1,747	2,087	366
Bangladesh (1985)	9,914	2,599	424
Bhutan (1984)	44.275	5.872	—
Brunei (1984)	34.373	19.904	0.607
Burma (1985)	5,021.1	1,322.5	184.4
China (1985)	133,702	50,926	1,779
Cook Islands (1983)	3.998	1.542	—
Fiji (1981)	116.318	48.608	2.003
Hong Kong (1984)	541.2	501.8	76.8
India (1984)	83,933	—	—
Indonesia (1983)	29,109	7,446	832
Japan (1986)	10,665	11,365	2,403 (1984)
Kiribati (1986)	13.331	2.306	—
Korea, South (1986)	4,798	4,864	1,515
Laos (1983)	485.741	105.012	4.792
Malaysia (1985)	2,192	1,295	93
Maldives (1983)	5.060	2.756	—
Nepal (1985)	1,812.1	496.8	54.4
New Zealand (1984)	465.353	231.657	95.754
Pakistan (1983)	6,860	2,744	560
Papua New Guinea (1982)	313.790	50.353	—
Philippines (1985)	8,926	3,214	1,973
Samoa (1983)	31.447	21.055	0.137
Singapore (1986)	268.820	223.961	42.007
Solomon Islands (1983)	34.953	5.837	—
Sri Lanka (1984)	3,539.2	—	18.217
Thailand (1985)	7,151	2,240	715
Tonga (1985)	17.019	15.232	—
Vanuatu (1983)	22.244	2.904	—
Vietnam (1985)	8,125.8	—	—

[1] First level: elementary school, primary school.
[2] Second level: middle school, secondary school, high school, vocational school, teacher training school.
[3] Third level: university, teachers college, higher professional school.
Source:
United Nations, *Statistical Yearbook for Asia and the Pacific, 1986–1987.*

417

EDUCATION: PUPIL/TEACHER RATIOS

Country	First level [1]	Second level [2]	Third level [3]
Afghanistan	30 [a]	18 [b]	11 [a]
Bangladesh	47 [c]	26 [c]	26 [d]
Bhutan	39 [c]	10 [c]	9 [b]
Brunei	16 [a]	12 [e]	3 [d]
Burma	48 [a]	30 [a]	27 [f]
China	25 [c]	17 [c]	4 [d]
Cook Islands	17 [d]	—	9 [b]
Fiji	28 [e]	18 [e]	—
Hong Kong	28 [d]	26 [d]	13 [a]
India	43 [c]	—	19 [g]
Indonesia	29 [a]	16 [e]	8 [a]
Kiribati	28 [c]	15 [d]	—
Korea, South	40 [c]	35 [c]	37 [c]
Laos	27 [d]	19 [b]	12 [d]
Malaysia	26 [d]	21 [d]	10 [b]
Mongolia	32 [a]	23 [g]	16 [e]
Nepal	43 [d]	26 [d]	13 [b]
Pakistan	31 [d]	18 [e]	22 [g]
Papua New Guinea	31 [a]	21 [a]	8 [b]
Philippines	32 [a]	34 [a]	30 [e]
Samoa	21 [d]	—	15 [d]
Singapore	29 [d]	20 [d]	11 [d]
Solomon Islands	25 [g]	16 [b]	—
Sri Lanka	32 [c]	—	11 [d]
Thailand	22 [e]	27 [g]	26 [e]
Tonga	20 [d]	—	11 [e]
Vanuatu	24 [d]	13 [e]	—
Vietnam	39 [b]	—	7 [b]

[1] First level: elementary school, primary school.
[2] Second level: middle school, secondary school, high school, vocational school, teacher training school.
[3] Third level: university, teachers college, higher professional school.
[a] 1982. [b] 1980. [c] 1984. [d] 1983. [e] 1981. [f] 1975. [g] 1979.
Source:
United Nations, Economic and Social Commission for Asia and the Pacific, *Economic and Social Survey of Asia and the Pacific 1986.*

PART ONE

THE COUNTRIES OF ASIA
AND THE PACIFIC

AFGHANISTAN

M. E. YAPP

BACKGROUND

Historical introduction

BEFORE the middle of the 18th century Afghanistan was no more than a geographical expression, a mountainous region interposed between the Iranian plateau in the west, the Indian subcontinent in the south and Turkestan in the north. Its usual fate was to be disputed by regimes based in these neighboring regions; occasionally Afghanistan itself served as a base for dynasties that went forth to conquer, mainly in northern India. At the same time the remote valleys of Afghanistan afforded refuges wherein a variety of ethnic and religious groups hid from their enemies and from government. There was no concept of an Afghanistan in either a political or a cultural sense; allegiances were to clan, religion and locality and the term "Afghan" was applied only to speakers of Pashto.

During the second half of the 18th century Afghanistan became the center of the Durrani empire, a political structure resting on the military power of the Afghan tribes and sustained by loot from conquests in Turkestan, Iran and, especially, India. This empire collapsed at the beginning of the 19th century; its dependencies broke away and Afghanistan itself became divided among a number of petty states. The transformation of this political debris into the state of Afghanistan took place during the 19th century and was the product of two factors. The first was the skill of a number of ruthless Afghan rulers, including the emirs Dost Mohammed, who first unified the country during the middle years of the 19th century, and Abdur Rahman, who hammered it into a firmer mold at the end of the century. For state building they employed a number of devices of tribal management, using marriage alliances, hostages and patronage and setting one tribe against another. The process was legitimized by appeals to Islam, for which purpose they bought the services of religious figures. And it was supported by the development of a small, detribalized, Persian-speaking bureaucracy and a paid, disciplined army. For the maintenance of this last, vital element of the state rulers of Afghanistan were able to use a British subsidy, paid to them for much of the period. The second factor was international. In the course of adjusting their Asian rivalries, Great Britain and Russia found it convenient to leave Afghanistan as a nominally independent state separating their territories. Britain and Russia defined the frontiers of

Afghanistan; those frontiers were not the choice of the people of the country.

During the first half of the 20th century there were few notable outward changes in Afghanistan. In 1921, following the third Anglo-Afghan war, Afghanistan obtained its independence, freed itself from British control of its foreign relations and established diplomatic links with other states. Nevertheless, until the British departure from India in 1947 Afghanistan's freedom of maneuver was closely restricted by the overwhelming presence of its two great neighbors. Efforts to modernize the internal structures of Afghanistan continued, but they had only limited success; the ambitious projects of Shah Amanullah (r. 1919–1929) ended in civil war and his successors were content to proceed with caution. More rapid change came only in the second half of the 20th century, but before considering the nature of that change it may be useful to summarize the situation of Afghanistan on the eve of its recent revolutions.

The economic, social and political structures of traditional Afghanistan
Afghanistan was predominantly an agricultural and pastoral country. Almost 90 percent of the population was dependent for its livelihood on these two sectors. About 20 percent were nomads and seminomads, who produced meat, skins and dairy products and provided most of the animals that sustained Afghanistan's transport system. There were no railways. The building of paved roads began only in the 1930s and the principal towns were not adequately linked until a major road construction program was completed during the early 1960s. The agricultural population was largely concerned with the production of cereals for subsistence or local consumption; the difficulties of moving bulk commodities were so great as to make Afghanistan constantly prone to regional famines. Manufactures were few and consisted mainly of handicrafts produced in the towns and in rural areas. The best-known product was the so-called Bukhara carpet produced in northern Afghanistan. Apart from handicrafts and a few more modern industries concerned with food processing and textile manufacture, the towns provided some services connected with government, religion, education and health, and functioned as markets for the exchange of goods internally and externally. Afghanistan's foreign trade was small, consisting largely of the export of fruit, nuts, skins, cotton, and a few specialized products such as lapis lazuli, and the import of manufactured goods, sugar and fuel. Natural-gas resources were not exploited until the end of the 1960s although they quickly came to dominate Afghanistan's export trade as well as serving as the foundation for the establishment of new industries, such as chemical fertilizer production in the north. The development of natural gas had the effect of further emphasizing the economic importance of the seven northern provinces, which also produced most of Afghanistan's cotton, its valuable karakul skins and its carpets.

Socially, Afghanistan consisted of a number of kinship groups ranging from the family to the tribe, linked to each other through various networks. Ties of blood and marriage were overwhelmingly the most important; ethnic and religious links were of less significance in daily life. Ethnically, Afghanistan was divided. About half the population spoke Pashto and more than one-third spoke dialects of Persian (Dari). The remainder spoke many languages, of which the most notable were the Turkic languages of northern Afghanistan. So long as the linguistic division was roughly reflected in geographical division, with the Pathans in the south and east, Persian speakers in a belt through central Afghanistan from northeast to west, and Turkic speakers in the north, friction was limited. Persian was the language of the towns and the government and the lingua franca of the country. The emigration of Pathans to the north from the late 19th century onward, the mixing of language groups in the towns, the spread of literacy and the competition for government jobs all conspired to give ethnic divisions greater prominence as the 20th century wore on.

After the forcible conversion of the people of Nuristan at the end of the 19th century, Afghanistan was overwhelmingly Muslim. Eighty percent were Sunni and about 20 percent Shiite, mainly Imami but including some Ismailis. Sunni-Shiite rivalries were often fierce, but the Shiites did not challenge Sunni dominance and endeavored to avoid conflict. The principal victims were the Persian-speaking Shiite Hazaras of central Afghanistan, who were crushed as heretics in brutal wars at the end of the 19th century and thereafter remained an oppressed minority, whether in their poverty-stricken mountains or as laborers in the towns. As an institution, Islam functioned in various ways. From the point of view of government, the hierarchy paid by the central government to serve as judges, administrators, etc., gave religious sanction to the actions of the regime; from the point of view of the urban ulama, government was a means by which a purer Islam could supplant the mass of superstition and tribal customs that reigned in the countryside. Both shared a view of Islam as an antidote to anarchy and as the basis of law and education. In the rural areas the perception was different. There, local religious figures served as articulators of popular grievances, as arbiters between groups in conflict and as providers of a modicum of education. Their educational successes were very slight; even by a generous measure of literacy not more than 2 percent of the people of Afghanistan could read and write in the middle of the 20th century.

Politically, Afghanistan was characterized by minimal government. The state took a very small part of the national income in taxation and imposed a modest burden of conscription. In return it provided some measure of peace, law and order and a few public works. For the most part people were left to their own devices and power was distributed among local notables, tribal chiefs and landowners who provided economic services, settled disputes and bargained with government. One should not fall into the trap of seeing the Afghan state as the enemy of society, however; rather it was perceived by some groups as an ally in their relations with others. The state was an important element in the bargaining that characterized Afghan politics at all levels and that was a necessary feature in a situation where no power had a monopoly on violence.

Since 1747 Afghanistan had been a monarchy, although for half of that time the rulers had not aspired to the title of shah, and the paraphernalia of the Persian tradition of kingship had never established itself in Afghanistan. Nor had any clear pattern of succession established itself among the Durrani rulers; power belonged to him who could seize and keep it. The Afghan political tradition was an extremely violent one. Leaving aside foreign wars, there were three major civil wars—1809–26, 1863–68 and 1928–29—and of 20 Afghan rulers between 1747 and 1987 only four died in office of natural causes. Eight were deposed and eight more died violently as rulers or immediately after their deposition. Add to this the bloodthirsty purges that followed unsuccessful coups, the wars that established the state and the endemic violence between groups, and one has a picture of a situation in which resort to violence was a normal way of settling political conflicts. In this sense there is nothing very new about the events of recent years.

The principal traditional political institution of Afghanistan was the *jirga,* or council, which functioned at every level from that of the family to the state. At the lower levels was a meeting, weighted in favor of age and power, of all those who had a right to be consulted about a decision. At the national level was the *loya jirga,* a gathering of notables usually called to ratify some major state decision concerned with foreign policy, the succession or the inauguration of a major departure in domestic policy, such as the introduction of a radical reform or a new constitution. Commonly, it served as a rubber stamp to legitimize the actions of the state. The new constitutions from the 1920s onward introduced a different type of institution, the representative assembly. The two most important modernizing institutions introduced during the 19th century were the army and the bureaucracy.

The bulk of the traditional Afghan army had been recruited on a tribal basis, tribal leaders being given rent-free land grants in return for supplying troops, usually cavalry. This force, the mainstay of the Durrani empire, was politically unreliable as well as militarily ineffective against disciplined troops equipped with artillery, and it had first been supplemented and eventually replaced by a standing force trained and disciplined on the model of European forces and equipped, insofar as Afghanistan could afford them, with similar weapons. This force was recruited and organized on a nontribal basis and generally proved a reliable weapon of state power against tribal forces. Its collapse in the civil war of 1928–29 may have been due to economies that had temporarily reduced its effectiveness. Against foreign enemies it was ineffective. It is interesting to observe that in the three wars against Britain, Afghan successes were almost all achieved by tribal forces, the regular army having quickly collapsed; only the battle of Maiwand (1880) is a partial exception. Supplemented by police and gendarmerie forces, however, the army (and air force) had, by the middle of the 20th century, begun to alter the balance of political forces in Afghanistan decidedly in favor of the state. Further, its officer corps, drawn largely from Pathans, constituted an educated, modernizing force impatient of the constraints imposed by the traditional structure and resentful of the power of old notables.

The bureaucracy had been recruited especially from the detribalized population of Kabul, including the Persian-speaking Shi-i Qizilbash. Its loyalties were to the state and, more than any group except possibly the army, to the idea of Afghanistan. It was among the bureaucrats of the early 20th century that the first ideas of Afghan nationalism appeared. The bureaucracy also became the spearhead of modernization, evolving programs of economic development centering on ambitious schemes of road building, industrialization and agricultural development, of social change founded on educational expansion and the development of the press and publication, and of political reconstruction around a constitution. In the reign of Amanullah these schemes had led to disaster. But the idea of reform had not been lost within the bureaucracy and bureaucrats still formed the most important component of the small intelligentsia of Kabul that existed in the mid-20th century.

In the second half of the 20th century Afghanistan was offered four models of change: autocratic modernization, constitutional development, Islamic revolution and leftist revolution. The conflicts between the proponents of these different models plunged Afghanistan into civil war and opened the way to foreign intervention.

Autocratic modernization
The model of autocratic modernization developed from the path pursued by the Afghan state during the 19th and the first half of the 20th century; modernization was extended from the political and military to the economic and social areas. The development of the army and the bureaucracy and the prospect of foreign aid reduced the need for the state to bargain with other groups and enabled it to rely more on coercion. The most prominent exponent of this approach during the second half of the 20th century was Muhammad Daud, prime minister of Afghanistan, 1953–63, and ruler of Afghanistan, 1973–78. Daud launched the first Five-Year Plan in 1955, inaugurated an extensive road-building program with Soviet and U.S. aid, developed industry, and increased school building and teacher training. He also forced through social changes including the banning of the veil (1959). He espoused a nationalist policy reflected in his strong support for the creation of an independent Pashtunistan (or Pathanistan) to be carved out of Pakistan's North-West Frontier Province and Baluchistan. This last endeavor led to disputes with Pakistan, the closing of the Pakistan border and severe economic difficulties only partially remedied by the expansion of trade with and through the Soviet Union. The difficulties contributed to Daud's fall from power in 1963. Daud retained strong support within the army, however, and it was with military support that he overthrew the monarchy in 1973 and established the Republic of Afghanistan. As president, Daud planned a major program of industrialization (including the construction of a railway to exploit Afghanistan's iron resources), nationalized the principal private bank, began land reform and remodeled the political system. But he could not find adequate external financing for his

425

ambitious economic projects, and he alienated other groups by the great increase in taxation for which he was responsible and by the manner in which he and his cronies monopolized political power. He became dependent on the army to crush opposition, but the army overthrew him in April 1978.

Constitutional development
The constitutional model of change was the project especially favored by the higher bureaucrats, who hoped thereby to reduce the power of the royal family, conciliate the newly emerging Afghan intellectuals and win broader support for a program of modernization. The centerpiece of their endeavor was the new constitution of October 1964, which provided for an elected lower chamber and a partially elected upper chamber of parliament to replace the ineffectual assemblies that had existed under the preceding constitutions of 1923 and 1931. Elections, in which women voted for the first time, were held in 1965.

The parliamentary system did not work well. The first parliament was dominated, at least vocally, by a tiny group of left-wing radicals supported by students outside parliament, and the second parliament, elected in 1969, fell under the control of conservative provincial notables who opposed all reforms. A liberal press law led to the appearance of a host of newspapers and periodicals expressing the views of many political groups. These groups, however, were not allowed to form into official political parties, which remained illegal. Nor did the intended extension of democracy to local government take place. Nevertheless, the constitutional system did bring into high government office many nonroyal figures, and it began to familiarize Afghans with parliamentary processes. But any hopes that Afghanistan might eventually settle on the path of constitutional development were finally destroyed by economic disaster. The severe famines of the early 1970's led to widespread criticism of the government and paved the way for the virtually bloodless military coup of Daud in 1973. No parliament met during the reign of Daud, and the constitutionalists were thrust from power.

The Islamic revolution
The so-called fundamentalist movement in Afghanistan is closely related in its character and aims to the Muslim Brotherhood in Egypt. It began not among the traditional ulama but among teachers of theology, some of whom had studied in Egypt. These teachers attracted a following among students (especially students of scientific and engineering subjects) in Kabul during the 1960s. Their objectives were similar to those of the Muslim Brotherhood. They emphasized education and social work and they advocated a program of economic modernization. They insisted, however, that all should be based upon the strict application of the *Sharia*. They opposed the monarchy, the constitutional government and the leftists, and during the Daud regime they began armed resistance. Their attempt to launch a major uprising in 1975 failed, however; they found little support in the traditional rural society and were crushed by government forces. Some of their leaders were killed or executed, some were imprisoned, and others fled to Pakistan

in search of sanctuary and support. Among them were some of the men who became the leaders of the fundamentalist resistance groups that came to prominence in 1979. The Soviet invasion was for them the great opportunity to obtain outside support and to present themselves to the people of Afghanistan as the standard-bearers of an authentic Afghan and Muslim resistance to foreign intervention and an atheist government. In fact their program was as revolutionary in its own way as the program of their opponents; the roles they proposed for Islam and for government were wholly different from those of traditional Afghanistan.

Leftist revolution

The revolution of April 1978 was essentially a military coup carried out by a group of discontented and frightened army officers. Partly through inclination and partly for want of an obvious alternative, they handed over power to the leaders of the People's Democratic party of Afghanistan (PDPA) who had recently been imprisoned by Daud. The PDPA had been founded on January 1, 1965, by a group of mainly young urban intellectuals. In 1967 it had divided into two wings, known as Parcham and Khalq (after their newspapers), and had reunited in 1977. In its 1965 program it had set as its aim the execution of a national democratic revolution, that is to say, a moderate, broad-based program of change intended to eliminate what was called feudalism and imperialism. This program remained that of the Parcham group (which cooperated with Daud in 1973); but a substantial part of the larger Khalq wing, which had a strong following among Pathan army officers and humble but educated Pathans, advocated a more radical program of change after 1978. The leader of this group, Hafizullah Amin, proclaimed that the Afghan revolution was a proletarian revolution and the regime was a working-class dictatorship. It did not matter that there was no proletariat to speak of in Afghanistan; the PDPA had become a proletarian party by osmosis, acquiring its character through contact with parties outside Afghanistan. In practice this ideological position was translated into the monopolization of power by the Khalq, the brutal destruction of opposition and the inauguration of radical reforms, including a drive against illiteracy, and, especially, land reform.

Land reform was intended to liquidate feudalism, establish a worker-peasant alliance and increase agricultural output. A very low ceiling on landholdings, of 15 acres 6 ha. of best land per family, was imposed and the surplus was to be confiscated and redistributed to landless and other poor peasants. Land reform failed miserably to achieve its ends. It was based on poor information that misrepresented the existing distribution of land, the role of landlords in the economy and society, and the nature of the Afghan family. There was no bureaucratic machinery adequate to the task, and the young Khalqi volunteers sent into the countryside took the opportunity to feather their own nests and those of their families and friends. No provision was made for supplying water, seed, credit and implements to the beneficiaries of land grants. Land reform was a major factor (although not the only one) in the disturbances that began in the latter part of 1978 and in 1979 turned into a real threat to the existence of the regime.

427

The overthrow of the Khalq regime was accomplished not by the rebels but by the Soviet Union, which invaded Afghanistan at Christmas 1979. There is no good evidence that the USSR had any hand in the 1978 coup, but from the first it had supported the PDPA regime with military and economic aid and with praise for its achievements. However, it is clear that Soviet advisers became increasingly concerned about the radical direction that the Khalq had taken and the hostility their activities had aroused. The USSR pressed for more moderate policies and a broadening of the government to include prominent figures from the preceding regimes. But it was the radicals who won the internal struggle in Afghanistan. The Parcham faction was driven out in the summer of 1978, and in September 1979 Amin completed his victory by removing his Khalqi opponents, including the PDPA leader, Nur Muhammad Taraki, who was murdered in October 1979. When further efforts failed to persuade Amin to change direction the Soviet Union sent in forces to replace him with a Parchami-dominated government under Babrak Karmal. Amin was killed.

The new PDPA regime reinstated the doctrine of the national democratic revolution. In practice this meant an attempt to broaden the government by introducing nonparty men into minor posts and moderating the pace of reform. At the same time the PDPA maintained its monopoly of power (and the rewards that flowed from that position) and endeavored to preserve as much as possible of the revolution. The hope was to persuade part of the opposition to give up armed resistance and to defeat the remainder with Soviet help. Between 1981 and 1988 the PDPA pursued this policy without success despite the offer of greater and greater concessions to the opposition, culminating in the national reconciliation policy introduced at the end of 1986. This policy involved the virtual abandonment of land reform, the offer of all but a handful of key government posts to the opposition, the declaration of a unilateral cease-fire, and the introduction of a new constitution in November 1987 and a multiparty system. The term "Democratic" was dropped from the name of the state, The Democratic Republic of Afghanistan (DRA), Islam was given a prominent position in the new constitution, the state role in the economy was reduced, and a new emphasis was given to private industry.

The failure, despite its many concessions, of the PDPA to end the rebellion and to consolidate its position may be attributed to several factors. First, factional rivalries continued within the party—partly ideological as between Parchamis and Khalqis, partly ethnic, and partly personal and clan disputes. Mounting criticism of Babrak Karmal and his faction led to the replacement of Karmal by Najibullah as general secretary of the party in April 1986. In November 1987 Najibullah became president of the republic. A second factor was the weakness of the bureaucracy, bereft of its old constitutionalist leaders and bloated by young, inefficient placemen. A third factor was the weakness of the army. Purges, desertions and evasion of conscription reduced both the strength and morale of the army and the gendarmerie (Sarandoy). The regime was obliged to rely more and more on some 120,000 Soviet troops and air support for operations against the resistance.

The resistance, the war and negotiations
The resistance was gaining increasing strength. The early resistance had
been conducted largely by local groups within Afghanistan, dependent upon
their own resources for supplies. As the war continued after 1980, groups
outside Afghanistan became more important, partly because they were able
to enlist followers from the flood of refugees who found their way into
Pakistan and Iran, and partly because they were able to secure support from
foreign Muslim sources and from the United States. Their control of supplies of weapons became the key to the extension of the influence of the
outside groups over the local groups within Afghanistan. Under the pressure of Soviet-DRA attacks on the villages in which they found refuge and
supplies, the local resistance became more dependent upon assistance from
outside. The resistance groups in Pakistan and Iran also began to coalesce.
After several abortive attempts, a seven-party alliance of the leading groups
based in Peshawar was formed in 1985, and greater coordination of political and military activities began. Within this alliance the dominant groups
were the so-called Islamic fundamentalist groups, who were able to impose
upon the alliance their own goal of the creation of an Islamic state in
Afghanistan. They rejected any outside control over their affairs, refusing
any compromise with the PDPA regime and demanding only an unconditional Soviet withdrawal. In Iran an alliance of the mainly Shiite-controlled
groups was formed with similar objectives.

The war went through several phases. In the beginning it took the form
of the exclusion of government authority from certain areas and the effort
of government to recover control. Subsequently, resistance bands began to
concentrate their attacks upon government and party property and personnel, and upon collaborators. Schools and schoolteachers (often PDPA supporters), factories and government buildings became obvious targets, but
the main attacks were delivered against power lines, communications and
convoys. Elaborate defenses were created by the Soviet-DRA regime to protect convoys, and mass attacks were made upon resistance base areas such
as those in the Panjshir valley commanding the main road to the USSR
north of Kabul. As the resistance became more dependent upon outside
supplies, the regime focused its efforts on reducing traffic across the Pakistan frontier by patrols, mining and attempting to win over the border
tribes. The one great advantage possessed by the regime in all its operations
was air power. This enabled it to supply isolated garrisons, hit resistance-
controlled areas at will, and move troops rapidly by helicopter to strategic
and tactical locations. By 1986 the measures adopted by the regime, combined with the rebuilding of the regime's military forces, notably the gendarmerie, were beginning to have some success; resistance activity in several areas of Afghanistan was diminished and concentrated in areas adjacent
to the Pakistan and Iran borders. The acquisition by the resistance, from
1986, of better weapons, particularly Blowpipe and Stinger ground-to-air
missiles, tipped the balance of advantage back toward the resistance.

The effects of the revolution and the war upon Afghanistan were considerable. The old political elite was extinguished and new young men dominated the PDPA and the resistance; 60 percent of the PDPA was under

30. In more remote rural areas, however, older groups came to power; the traditional ulama recovered an influence long ago lost to government, and former networks were restored. Economic losses were great: Agricultural production fell heavily and there was damage to industrial plant. The demographic changes were most drastic of all. Of a population of about 15 million, nearly one-third became refugees in Pakistan (3 million) and Iran (1.5 million). More than half a million people left the countryside and went to Kabul, and a similar number are estimated to have perished. Some areas were almost depopulated; in others, the ethnic balance was drastically altered, especially in the central and northern areas from which Pathans withdrew. Pathans accused the Parchami leaders of partiality toward the minorities.

Many commentators sought to discern in Soviet policy in Afghanistan a long-term plan to convert the country into a secure Soviet base from which the USSR could try to dominate the Arab/Persian Gulf and the Indian Ocean. It is doubtful whether such calculations had any prominent part in Soviet thinking. Soviet aims appear to have been defensive, seeking to prevent the establishment of a hostile regime on their southern borders and to preserve in power an ideologically congenial government. Even these modest aims were called into question by the cost of the Afghanistan war measured in extensive military and economic aid, the commitment of 120,000 troops and the adverse political consequences for Soviet relations with other countries. From 1980 the USSR began to look for a way out by negotiation. Indirect talks between Pakistan and the DRA began in 1983 at Geneva, and an agreement covering the international aspects of the dispute was reached in April 1988. The agreement had four elements: an end to outside help to the resistance; an international guarantee (by the Soviet Union and the United States) that it would not be resumed; arrangements for the return of the refugees; and a Soviet withdrawal to be completed in nine months. Efforts to reach agreement on the future government of Afghanistan failed, however; the PDPA was willing to share power but demanded a leading position, while the resistance was reluctant to share power at all with the PDPA. The United States refused to stop supplying weapons to the resistance so long as the USSR supplied the regime, and Pakistan continued to assist the resistance in a variety of ways. Iran took no part in the Geneva negotiations and publicly supported the stance of the fundamentalist resistance groups. So the civil war continued. The Soviet withdrawal was completed by February 15, 1989; the regime abandoned some areas; and the resistance put the major cities, including Kabul, under siege. The resistance failed, however, to establish a united front; differences between Sunni and Shiite groups, between moderates and fundamentalists, and between those outside Afghanistan and commanders inside persisted, hindering united action and making it difficult to establish any plausible alternative government. The regime was also divided between those who supported the continuation and extension of the national reconciliation policy, and those who looked primarily to a military solution.

At one level the great and violent changes of the past 20 years in Afghanistan may be represented as the conflict of ideologies: traditional, democratic, socialist and Islamic. At another level the conflict may be seen as reflecting older divisions, of clan, sect, region and ethnic group. Neither of these perceptions seems sufficient in itself, however. At the heart of the changes is a generational conflict; rapid population increase and educational development produced a young, impatient generation for which both ideologies and traditional links were mere devices to be employed in their struggle to wrest the fruits of power from older men. The involvement of outside powers ensured that the struggle would be a long and bloody one.

FURTHER READING

Arnold, Anthony. *Afghanistan's Two-Party Communism: Parcham and Khalq*. Stanford, California: Hoover Institution Press, 1983.

Bradsher, Henry S. *Afghanistan and the Soviet Union*. Durham, North Carolina: Duke University Press, 1983.

Dupree, Louis. *Afghanistan*. Princeton, New Jersey: Princeton University Press, 1973.

Fraser-Tytler, W. K. *Afghanistan: A Study of Political Developments in Central and Southern Asia*. 3rd ed. London and New York: Oxford University Press, 1967.

Fry, Maxwell J. *The Afghan Economy: Money, Finance, and the Critical Constraints to Economic Development*. Leiden: E. J. Brill, 1974.

Girardet, Edward R. *Afghanistan*. London and New York: Croom Helm, 1985.

Gregorian, Vartan. *The Emergence of Modern Afghanistan: Politics of Reform and Modernization*. Stanford, California: Stanford University Press, 1969.

Hammond, Thomas T. *Red Flag Over Afghanistan: The Communist Coup, the Soviet Invasion, and the Consequences*. Boulder, Colorado: Westview Press, 1984.

Roy, Olivier. *Islam and Resistance in Afghanistan*. Cambridge and New York: Cambridge University Press, 1986.

Yapp, M. E. *Strategies of British India: Britain, Iran, and Afghanistan, 1798–1850*. Oxford: Clarendon Press; New York: Oxford University Press, 1980.

431

AUSTRALIA

COLIN A. HUGHES

WHILE the stereotypical Australian is an extrovert to a fault, there has always been a verbal minority of introverts who dissect the national character and brood over national destiny—prickly patriots who are at the same time debunkers of most national institutions. The bicentennial of European settlement in 1988 and its attendant celebrations provided the occasion for a monumental bout of introspection and speculation, which this chapter attempts to record. The order of the subjects covered here is conventional: the environment, society, the economy and polity, although each of the first three eventually leads to politics. Such an account of Australia is necessarily fragmentary: few of the commentators and critics selected have grand schemes of their own. It is fragmentary also because the separation of an Australian identity from the older, larger, English-speaking Anglo-American conglomerate is still not fully accomplished. Consequently, a sharp eye is needed to distinguish phenomena that are to any extent peculiarly Australian from those that are local performances of scripts written elsewhere for other actors and other audiences.

THE ENVIRONMENT

If to begin with the environment means to ask how today's Australians regard their physical surroundings, then painting might be the best medium to start with. After an initial misconceived attempt to see and reproduce an extraordinary landscape and unusual vegetation through European eyes, by the latter part of the 19th century the best Australian artists had recognized that uniqueness and painted it accurately. Among the plastic arts painting has always been dominant, and for painters landscapes have always held pride of place. Popular enthusiasm for art is not overly nationalistic, so that a good exhibition of paintings from overseas collections draws crowds of the same scale as showings of the best-known local artists, but those who have chosen to paint native trees, flowers, animals and the wilderness hold a special place in the national esteem. This is evidenced by inflated prices for Australian-scene paintings; national pictures are seen as good investments.

Better roads, more reliable automobiles, air-conditioned buses and relatively cheaper air travel have all given more coastal Australians direct knowledge of the country's inhospitable interior. The conversion of Ayers Rock, the enormous monolith at the continent's center, into a place of mass tourist pilgrimage is the clearest manifestation of this. The site's significance as a popular symbol of national identity was intensified when it became the backdrop for Australia's most sensational murder trial.

The interior has always had almost mythic significance as the place where the Australian ideal of mateship had been formed as a defense against the harsh environment as well as the economic power of the wealthy settlers who had seized ownership of it. In addition it is the source of the economy-sustaining exports of minerals, wool and beef. But Australian historians point to the falsity of the myth. Only a tiny proportion of the total population ever settled away from the coast. Australia's "pioneering" mode of suburban domesticity in the 19th century created the national character that prevails today, not the male world of itinerant shearers and cane cutters. Only a small share of the work force actually engaged in the export industries involving minerals, wool and beef once the peak of the gold rush was over.

Drought and economic difficulties in the 1890s started a drift of the small interior population back to the coast and into the cities. That trend continued until the 1970s, by which time populations of five million each were being predicted for Sydney and Melbourne by the end of the 20th century. Canberra, with a population of 250,000, has remained the only inland city of any size, and its population projections have decreased from the heady days of bureaucratic expansion in the 1960s and early 1970s. The rest of coastal Australia outside the six state capitals unexpectedly began to hold its own in the mid-1970s. Occupational and residential mobility, originally dependent on public transportation and subsequently on privately owned automobiles, that had created the first suburbs and then later problems of urban sprawl in built-up areas, now scattered population growth farther away. Growth in Queensland, Western Australia and the Northern Territory, compared with that in southeastern Australia, started talk of a "sun belt" movement. In particular, the long coast of New South Wales and the even longer coast of Queensland, outside of Sydney and Brisbane, respectively, began to attract older and wealthier retirees.

In the early 1970s there had been widespread concern with the problems created by rapid urban sprawl and the failure of basic services to keep pace with population needs. Although the worst deficiencies of physical infrastructure were remedied by the public sector's provision of more paved roads and sewerage systems, and the private sector's construction of regional shopping centers, social problems remain. Limited local employment opportunities left new arrivals in the outer suburbs dependent on only partially rehabilitated public transportation systems or else having to meet the rising costs of private transportation. Cheaper housing in decayed inner-city areas or in underserviced outer suburbs attracted the newest immigrants, whose language difficulties and educational deficiencies restricted job opportunities. Such areas also attracted increasing numbers of impoverished one-parent families.

Increased areas of spreading cities means longer traveling times and higher

433

costs even for the relatively affluent. This led, on a limited scale, to the gentrification of the first rings of inner suburbs. A brief period of highway development in the areas around central business districts was brought to an abrupt halt, due to urban "community politics," and rapid rises in land acquisition and construction costs. On the other hand, expansion in white-collar employment in central business districts, coupled with property speculation financed in part by overseas capital, routed the few feeble attempts by local and state governments to curb overdevelopment of these areas. While urban conservation groups are able for the most part to block public-sector programs in existing urban areas, attacks by the private sector are almost invariably successful.

It is in the countryside that conservationists are more successful; consideration of why this happens provides some insight into the Australian political process. One possible explanation is that the urban scene has less meaning or attraction for the average citizen. Old buildings are for the most part Victorian or post-World War I, while the few elegant colonial Georgian-style structures that have survived earlier periods of rebuilding are sufficiently small and rare to be saved and rehabilitated without much inconvenience or loss of profit. Another explanation is the rural myth that portrays the people in the countryside and the outback as Australia's heroic figures. Conservation campaigns in the cities frequently become matters of trying to stop people who live in the country from doing what they want to do with local flora, fauna or landscape, on the grounds that native nature is not theirs alone but belongs to all Australians, indeed to all humans. Exotic trees, and softwood conifer plantations in particular, are regarded as abominations because they interfere with native species of plants and animals. Imported livestock with hard hooves permanently damage fragile vegetation. Damming rivers for hydroelectric schemes floods native forests and archaeological sites. "Development," which had motivated government policies for a century, has come under attack, nowhere more so than in the peripheral parts of Australia trying to catch up with the benefits ruthlessly secured by the southeast in the 19th century.

In many respects Australian conservationists are part of an international network (or conspiracy according to their opponents) of like-minded persons and nonprofit groups, just as mine owners and timber cutters are part of another. Television shapes popular perceptions, and thus determines the outcome of many of the conservation battles. The small platoons of Australians who actually hike and camp in the remote corners of the country where development has still to come are often reinforced by armies who have done no more than watch sandy beaches, lush rain forests, foaming wild rivers or storybook marsupials on television. These groups are so numerous that a tiny proportion ready to take reprisals at the ballot box is sufficent to put the fear of nature into political parties whose electorates are mainly city based. When the tourist industry started to develop, first as a prosperous part of the domestic economy and then as a source of earnings overseas, only a government with a steady nerve and a narrow electoral base could resist conservationist demands.

A DIVERSE SOCIETY

The celebration of 200 years of European colonization inevitably reopened the long and sad story of relations with the continent's original settlers, the aborigines. Conservationists, somewhat erroneously in light of prehistorical evidence, praised aborigines as careful custodians of the natural environment. A 1968 constitutional amendment to delete obsolete and vaguely discriminatory provisions relating to the aborigines was carried by an unusual popular majority. It had been hoped that the amendment would mark a new era of social, economic and political progress for the 300,000 aborigines, but improvement in many areas has proved frustratingly slow. Health and housing conditions are still deplorable; educational achievements are still minimal; and relations with law enforcement authorities are still hostile. Some aborigines remain close to traditional lifestyles in remote parts of the interior and the north. Others continue as they have for decades in fringe settlements adjacent to country towns. Many more than previously have moved into the coastal cities, mainly in inner city or outer suburban sections where they add to an especially disadvantaged portion of the population that already had ample problems. Substantial bureaucratic structures have been created to administer welfare and development programs for aborigines, but these are largely staffed by civil servants of European ancestry. A handful of aborigines have been elected, including one federal senator and one who is a minister in Western Australia; but only in the Northern Territory are there electoral districts where aboriginal voters have the numbers to determine the outcome. Money has been committed on a large scale, but few aborigines enter the middle class, which increasingly characterizes Australia. Worse still, a large part of what had earlier seemed genuine enthusiasm for aboriginal causes, whether motivated by feelings of guilt for past wrongs or as an extension of the national expectation of a "fair go" to those most obviously in need, appears to have dissipated in the face of intractable aboriginal problems. Thus, new proposals to restrict mining activities in remote areas or to place land with any potential for economic use under aboriginal control now face strong opposition from rural interests and right-wing ideologues, while receiving diminished support from liberal and leftist groups on whom aborigines could previously have counted. More militant aboriginal spokesmen condemned the bicentennial as a commemoration of the invasion and conquest of their country, and were not appreciative of suggestions that they should be thought of as the first in a series of settlers.

Two centuries of immigration have supplied another set of questions for national debate. Following World War II Australia sought and accepted two million new immigrants. Those coming from the British Isles were a minority for the first time but Australia's nearest continental neighbor, Asia, accounted for only one-quarter of a million of the total. In the latter part of the 19th century Australia became alarmed at the possibility of Asian, particularly Chinese but to a lesser extent Japanese and Indian, immigrants flooding into thinly populated areas. The defense against that fear

435

was embodied in the "White Australia" policy that as recently as the early 1960s kept Asian immigration down to 200 to 300 a year at a time when hundreds of thousands were coming from Europe. The first steps to ease restrictions were taken under the Harold Holt and Gough Whitlam governments. Thereafter, Asian immigration rose to about 25,000 people a year, or 25 to 30 percent of the total. Although half of that number came from western Asia, mainly Lebanon and Turkey, it was the appearance of refugees from Indochina that set off a new reaction, which briefly threatened the revival of old attitudes. The arrival of boat people was virtually uncontrollable short of returning them to the hazards of the sea. The so-called domino theory that had been used to justify the commitment of Australian troops to the war in Vietnam had been largely forgotten, but the circumstances of the Indochinese refugees reopened divisions created by involvement in that war as an ally of the United States. This latest wave of immigrants was ethnically identifiable. The Vietnamese concentrated in a few urban areas, more so than many other (but not all) postwar settlers had done, and they quickly achieved well-publicized educational and economic successes. For a time it appeared that public debate would reopen old wounds, but no significant sections of the major political parties picked up the opportunity. The boat people phenomenon ended, and new, tightly controlled processes for the selection of immigrants quieted public concern.

What remains is the question of just what multiculturalism is supposed to mean in contemporary Australia. One manifestation is to be found in the government-owned and operated sector of the "ethnic" media, where radio and television programs are presented in "community languages." For radio this means mainly local productions and consequently some political problems with the selection of factions from divided communities. For television this means mainly imported programs that, it is alleged by critics, are watched by the "Anglo-Celtic" (another Australianism reflecting the substantial Irish component of 19th-century immigration) upper middle class and ignored by more recent immigrants who prefer American programs on the commercial channels.

For many new Australians the strongest demands are for the preservation of their languages in the schools but ready access to English instruction as a means of integration into the work force. Ethnic groups are numerous and widely scattered, and so are usually brought under semiofficial umbrella organizations for consultations and funding of their modest activities. However, political parties involve new immigrants in special bodies in the party machinery. In a few inner-urban areas there are sufficient concentrations of immigrants of a single national origin to secure de facto control of the local Australian Labor party (ALP) branch, and to influence the selection of local candidates. But the mixing of nationalities has been so complete, and the movement from the localities of first settlement so rapid, that the remarkable volume of postwar immigration (second only to Israel) has had no significant impact on political parties or on their competion for power. The first generation of East European refugees was strongly anti-communist and avoided the ALP because of its mild socialist flavor. Immigrants from southern Europe were more likely to adopt the ALP, perhaps because they worked at first in relatively unskilled manual jobs. The government has retitled bureaucratic offices from "immigration" to "ethnic affairs," meaning that it now focuses on the special problems of immigrants once they are in Australia. In comparison with the total population, a disproportionately small percentage of members of the federal and state legislatures was born outside Australia, and among this small group those born in English-speaking countries is more numerous than the rest. The handicap of the non-English-speaking immigrant appears to lie in the processes that select candidates as well as in the volunteering behavior of party activists, the group from which candidates are almost entirely drawn. There is no evidence from voting statistics that birth outside Australia or descent from recent immigrants is a handicap at the ballot box.

SOCIAL ISSUES

Compared with the aboriginal and immigration issues, crime and political corruption are relatively new social phenomena in Australia. Historians have been able to trace aspects of organized crime back to the interwar period in Sydney and Melbourne, but on its present scale the problem is largely a matter of the 1970s and 1980s. The traditional mainstays of Australian crime had been betting and prostitution, with narcotics a minor and variable feature. Law enforcement, it was thought, had been generally free from corruption. With the arrival of a new school of investigative journalism, concern with the increase in narcotics trafficking and the health problems that follow, as well as exposés of corruption at high levels of law enforcement and government have shattered the prevailing complacency. Previously, corruption in public life had been thought to concern regulation of land use and thus primarily a local government issue that could be kept under control by dismissing elected councils from time to time. Now the names of senior public officials, police officers, cabinet ministers and even one premier, and several judges have been bandied about as allies of extensive criminal conspiracies. The government has responded with new means to assemble information and to coordinate responses to criminal activities that cut across state and national boundaries. Concerns for the civil liberties of suspects and those accused are matched by demands from law enforcement authorities for more invasive procedures to intercept information, seize the proceeds of criminal transactions and interdict imports of dangerous drugs. Evidence of criminal activities in the police and prisons of some states has intensified public concern as to how far the process has already gone.

EDUCATION

At the end of World War II Australian universities were still few in number and small in enrollment. Entrance standards reflected Scottish rather than English models, while the postgraduate sector was confined almost entirely to the natural sciences. Provision for returning servicemen brought

437

the federal government for the first time into what had been the states' responsibility; and from the mid-1950s through the 1970s rapid growth was driven by federal funds. Uniform national standards were set for pay and teaching conditions, a factor that worked to the advantage of weaker institutions in the smaller states. Federal policy also compelled the development of a dual system of universities and colleges; the latter soon sought to diminish the vocational commitments for which they had been created. At the beginning of the period of expansion New South Wales was the only state with a university outside its capital city; and despite more than doubling the number of universities in the country only five provincial cities have ever acquired one. Colleges of advanced education are, however, scattered widely in response to regional pressures for the economic stimulus they bring. In some instances their creation has involved little more than transferring control of the local teachers' college to more autonomous management, but such institutions have remained vulnerable to merger or closure when the period of expansion has ended. Partly because of their location, universities continue to draw students disproportionately from the urban middle class, despite the abolition of fees in the early 1970s. By the late 1980s women students were as numerous as men, but long-standing gender differences still distinguish the predominantly male science and applied science faculties from the predominantly female social science and humanities faculties, with some professional faculties like law and medicine more evenly split.

The improving quality of tertiary institutions and their proximity to Southeast and East Asia has begun to attract English-speaking students from Hong Kong, Singapore and Malaysia. Some have come on scholarships provided by Australia or their own governments, but many are financed by their families. As regional prosperity grew the possibility of "exporting education" was recognized by both traditional universities and colleges, and a new breed of commercially founded and operated tertiary institutions tried to enter the market. Appearance of the latter reopened the question of free tertiary education for Australian students, although first suggestions that fees be charged again in public-sector tertiary institutions fell before the political onslaught of teachers, students and incensed middle-class parents.

The decades of growth for the social sciences and humanities have at least been marked by two analogous but largely separate questions: What should be the Australian content or bias of such disciplines? What should be the mix of European and Asian content? In the period of rapid growth (1955–75) academic staff was in short supply. Many were recruited from Britain and the United States, very few from anywhere else. During that period Australian graduates, pursuing for the first time and in large numbers postgraduate studies, set off for British and American universities. Yet it was in this period that a variety of disciplines began to take on a more distinctively Australian flavor. Textbooks were written by local scholars and printed by local publishers; teachers were promoted for writing them (though perhaps promoted faster if the books were published overseas according to some critics); and with the combination of the worldwide demand for rel-

438

evance and an upsurge in nationalistic sentiment, students sought Australian courses and Australian research topics. By the time the Robert Hawke government appointed an advisory committee, the battle had been won by institutions that claimed to be part of a wider world of ideas.

Getting the Asian connection right was more difficult. The Joseph Chifley government established the Australian National University (ANU) in Canberra to direct research in neglected fields such as astronomy and demography, to promote postgraduate studies in Australia, to help staff other universities and to "call home" distinguished Australian scholars. One of the original four research schools at ANU had been for Pacific studies—covering Southeast and East Asia and the Pacific islands. When that research unit merged with the undergraduate Canberra University College, the latter developed a faculty of Asian studies and extended the curriculum to cover South Asia. Although all three levels of activity—undergraduate, graduate and research—meet high international standards, the number of students in the programs remains small and the whole enterprise is regarded as somewhat esoteric by the larger university and public communities. In other Australian universities there are likely to be small departments teaching Chinese, Japanese, Indonesian and Malay language courses. The departments of history and political science offer a few courses dealing primarily with Asian content. And if there is a department of anthropology its students study a variety of cultures of the Pacific Basin. If there is an attached nondegree center for teaching modern languages, Arabic, Thai or Vietnamese might be added to the other Asian languages available; but many of the students will be the children or spouses of immigrants seeking a smattering of the language as an act of cultural piety rather than Anglo-Celtic Australians acquiring a useful skill.

If there is any agreement on what is wrong, it is that the limited teaching of languages in secondary schools is most at fault. The three-year pass degree that most students take cannot cope with the addition of new language instruction, particularly languages as demanding as Asian languages may seem. French, and to a lesser extent German, still dominate the secondary school curriculum. Indeed, immigrants from the rest of Europe are equally critical of the difficulties of getting Italian, Spanish, Greek or Serbo-Croatian into the secondary or tertiary curriculum. Alarmingly, the number of graduates who have not studied any language continues to rise, influenced to some extent by the universities' general abandonment of language requirements. One of the first steps in the federal government's secondary school policy has been the provision of funds for language laboratories. But implementing such a policy and ensuring its acceptance by the community is not always easy.

THE ECONOMY

In a radio interview in 1986 the federal treasurer, Paul Keating, warned that unless Australian economic performance improved there were real dangers of the country slipping to the level of a "banana republic." When author Donald Horne years earlier had entitled his savage critique of na-

439

tional failings *The Lucky Country,* the label was taken by many readers to refer to the inevitability of national good fortune rather than the narrowness of the margin for survival. At first Keating's remark was considered to be a serious lapse of political judgment. Normally the government painted both the present and future in the rosiest of colors, and any opposition spokesperson who uttered even the mildest word of caution was immediately criticized as mean-spirited and lacking faith in the country.

Australia has long relied on exports of commodities to pay for imported manufactures and capital, although over the years (and particularly under the pressure of two world wars) a modest manufacturing sector has been raised behind a tariff wall that was criticized only by the farmers and occasional economists. Traditional markets were lost upon Britain's entry into the European Community (EC), but the simultaneous expansion of the Japanese domestic market provided a ready substitute that quieted anxieties. When the 1973 oil shock rolled around the world its local manifestations were attributed by many Australians to economic mismanagement by the Whitlam government. More positively, the development of domestic supplies of oil for the first time and the creation of a major new export trade in coal appeared to promise continuation of prosperity, with Australia now an "energy-rich" nation. What went unnoticed was that the turmoil of the late 1970s and early 1980s had weakened and nearly destroyed the manufacturing sector. Economic difficulties in the mid-1980s combined continuing problems concerning agricultural exports (buffeted by rough competition from the EC and the United States) with a general slowdown in world economic activity that ultimately reduced demands for mineral and energy exports.

The final days of the Malcolm Fraser government coincided with drought in rural areas. No sooner had there been a change of government than the drought broke, prospects brightened and the former prime minister was held to have been unlucky in calling the election early. The Hawke government proceeded cautiously, fearing repetition of the mistakes attributed to the Whitlam government or at least identification with the riskiness of its breakneck pace. Simultaneously, the retirement of Fraser as Liberal party leader and of two main figures in the National party allowed the coalition, once it was in opposition, to lean away from pragmatism and toward a commitment to what might have been thought to be its true ideological position. In addition to these developments the appearance of Australian advocates of New Right principles (as they had developed in Britain and the United States) changed the nature of the economic debate. Hawke, whose previous public career had been in the trade union movement, at first espoused political consensus and economic corporatism. West Germany and Austria were praised as suitable models for Australia. Hawke was reinforced in this approach by the arrival at the Australian Council of Trade Unions of a new generation of leaders who were less inclined to press wage claims whatever the economic circumstances and more interested in promoting economic growth even though benefits might accrue to capitalists.

The first shift in economic policy, and the most remarkable in light of

440

traditional ALP attitudes, was substantial deregulation of the banking industry and abandonment of remaining exchange controls. An enduring monument of the ALP's first golden age under the Andrew Fisher government before World War I was the creation of a state-owned bank, the Commonwealth Bank, to compete with private banks in the financial world. One of the ALP's worst defeats had been the collapse at the outset of the Great Depression of the government led by James Scullin, an affair in which local and international bankers played key roles. A second ALP defeat was caused by the rejection by the federal High Court of an attempt to nationalize private banks by the Chifley government after World War II. This was followed by that government's defeat at the polls and 23 years in the political wilderness for the ALP. Thus to admit overseas banks, even if somewhat restricted in number, to Australia, and to extend the range of financial institutions that could operate in the banking sphere, with no more than a bit of grumbling within the party, was an enormous achievement and proof of the authority that Hawke and Keating, and the right-wing faction they led, had acquired in the ALP.

An even more spectacular exercise in deregulation was conducted subsequently in the mass media, like the banks also suspected by ALP stalwarts. Although the print media is largely outside the legislative powers of the federal government, the attractions of television channel ownership and the scope for profit for print proprietors ensure that rules intended to keep the two media separate in ownership will have an impact on newspapers as much as on television. For many years newspaper ownership had been divided among four (subsequently only three) groups that had been allowed limited involvement with radio and television. Changed rules removed one of the three players and curtailed the influence of another, leaving Rupert Murdoch's News Limited with unprecedented dominance in the press. But the changes also brought new players from other business sectors into television and radio, so that it was possible to argue that media ownership had in fact been diversified by government action rather than concentrated.

Other ALP shibboleths were harder to alter despite their attractions to the economic rationalists who carried great weight in the cabinet. The party allowed only minor concessions for trade benefits to be obtained from exporting uranium, and proved cool to suggestions of privatizing state enterprises in transportation, communications and banking. Reductions in income tax levels were more generous to those in the upper brackets, but this regressive development was offset by some enhancement of welfare schemes, including a major new benefit designed to reduce the incidence of child poverty.

In its 1983 election campaign the ALP used a television commercial that showed Australia walking backward down the economic up escalator while other members of the Organization for Economic Cooperation and Development went up. Greater economic progress in other countries, first in western and southern Europe, then in selected countries of East Asia, unsettled Australians. Another popular phrase, which did not grab the attention of Keating's banana republic remark but was equally meaningful because of both its extravagance and its slightly racist overtones, pointed to

441

the danger of Australians becoming "the poor white trash of Asia." Australians who traveled overseas began to notice the fall in value of their currency. The increase in Japanese investment in Australia, including purchase of both business and residential real property, as well as the increase in Japanese tourism in cities and resort areas brought the lesson home to an even wider audience. Domestic political considerations could still set limits to what would be allowed to happen, yet investment in domestic housing was quickly cut off when it threatened electoral repercussions in the politically crucial Sydney area. The days when "buying back the farm" was a popular slogan were ended by balance-of-trade figures that required a steady stream of foreign investment to permit the volume of imports of consumer goods to which the public had become addicted and capital goods on which the economy relied.

POLITICS

Australia has been described as the frozen continent in constitutional matters because of the minimal changes that have taken place since the federal constitution came into effect in 1901. It might be similarly described with respect to its party system, which took shape between 1890 and 1910. The ALP is the oldest, but all three of the major parties—the ALP and the permanent coalition of the Liberal and National parties—reflect aspects of the political regime under which they developed. In the immediate pre- and postfederation years, local and state politics were the predominant focus of interest. National politics was less significant for the average voter. As a consequence each major party has preserved strong local and state structures for control of the selection of parliamentary candidates and thus ultimate control of parliamentary behavior. Similarly, each of the parties reflects the democratic tenor of the formative period with constitutions that pay lip service at least to rank-and-file democracy, and to varying degrees give the extraparliamentary wing some power over the parliamentary. Each of the states constitutes close to a microcosm of the national party system, with the only substantial variation being the National party's relative weakness in some states and dominance over its Liberal partner in one, Queensland. However, party federalism shows some signs of eroding in practical ways during national elections. The spotlight is on the parties' federal leaders and a few front-benchers. In addition, campaigning is organized through the national mass media by the parties' federal secretariats and ad hoc campaign structures, and with modification of state delegations in party councils and assemblies. Approximately 90 percent of voters support one of the three major parties, with the ALP and the coalition remarkably evenly balanced, so that in each of the last four national elections (1980, 1983, 1984 and 1987) a shift of only a few thousand votes in an electorate of 10 million could have changed the outcome.

What might be called substantial minor parties have usually arisen from schisms within the major ones. In the postwar period a predominantly Roman Catholic segment of the ALP's right wing broke away to form the Democratic Labor party. For almost 20 years it kept the ALP out of office

442

by assigning to the coalition its second preferences under the alternative vote system that has prevailed since the National (then Country) party was formed after World War I, and has allowed coalition partners to coexist in reasonable peace. After almost 20 years the Democratic Labor party declined to a point of no return; it was replaced by a new party emerging primarily from the left wing of the Liberal party, the Australian Democrats. The federal Senate adopted a form of proportional representation in 1948; for 30 of the last 40 years minor parties and occasional independent legislators with sufficent personal support have been able to hold the balance of power in the Senate. Given the equal status the Senate shares with the House of Representatives in most matters, this situation provides ample occasion to limit and frustrate the government despite its majority in the lower house. The only power the government has over an obstructive Senate is the dissolution of both chambers. The ensuing election is then for the whole membership of the Senate rather than the half that usually faces the electorate, and requires only half the usual percentage of votes for candidates to secure election. Such a threat is unlikely to intimidate minor parties. The Communist party of Australia was never a significant electoral force, but derived much notoriety and some influence from its involvement in trade union affairs. In the post-Stalin period it fragmented into an assortment of Marxist groups, all of which are even further from electoral success. The organizations espousing causes that occupy political space to the left of the ALP and the Australian Democrats or to the right of the coalition usually participate in electoral politics through advertising their views and endorsing or condemning candidates of the major parties rather than by nominating their own. When they do, direct support is minimal.

Party machinery and procedures have been innovative in Australia, or at least were so in the formative period. Political debate, on the other hand, is derivative, drawn almost entirely from the North Atlantic rim. In the closing days of World War II and the immediate postwar period the predominant style was interventionist and welfare oriented. Little remains of that period except a nostalgia for better days in the history of the ALP among its followers. The next two decades were dominated by the virtuoso performance of Robert Menzies as prime minister (1949–66) as he presided over an era of good feelings in which the economy appeared to grow steadily, the middle class expanded rapidly and memories of the Great Depression were forgotten. Menzies's three successors, Harold Holt, John Gorton and William McMahon (1966–72), were less fortunate. A reformist ALP government led by Gough Whitlam (1972–75) was elected, only to come apart when economic conditions deteriorated and internal difficulties were revealed. Lack of control of the Senate finally brought about the government's dismissal by the governor-general it had appointed.

The ideological flavor of the 1950s and 1960s was mainly lip service to market and federal principles while those in office proceeded in completely pragmatic ways to reconcile competing interest groups with a minimum of public friction. The second half of the 1970s and the early 1980s, with Malcolm Fraser as prime minister, reverted to the old mixture of market and federalism in supposed reaction to intervention and centralism under

Whitlam; but the reasserted weight of political forces was still hostile to too much implementation of principles. As already noted, once the ALP was back (in 1983) with Robert Hawke as prime minister the brief flirtation with corporatism was quickly succeeded by a period of applying market doctrines on a scale never attempted by the coalition. Federalism was slower to be altered.

Twice before, from a royal commission in 1929 and from a joint select committee of the federal parliament in 1959, there had been proposals for a general revision of the federal constitution. None had come near implementation. In the early 1970s, discontent at the state level with the allocation of financial responsibilities—most revenue accrues to the federal government, much expenditure has to be undertaken by the states, and so the reallocation of money from the first level to the second is a perennial battle—led to the resurrection of the conventions that had negotiated the constitutional settlement of the 1890s. This time, however, representatives of the states were joined by representatives from the federal and local levels. Although the successive sessions generated useful studies of what was wrong and interesting proposals for improvement, the immediate impact on the text of the constitution was minimal. The Hawke government eventually created a constitutional commission that devised a package of proposals voted on by referendum in 1988 as part of the bicentennial celebrations.

Although the federal constitution has successfully resisted reform, the machinery of government has been subject to almost constant tinkering. In recent years significant developments have included the steady growth in the size of both federal and state ministries; separation of a smaller cabinet from the larger ministry at the federal level; identification of new portfolios to symbolize commitments to current issues and values promoted by government; consolidation of the prime minister's department as the powerbase of administration at the expense of the traditionally dominant treasury-finance bureaucracy; and in 1987, at the federal level, a completely tidy political machine with all functions shared by a set of megadepartments, matching equally heroic efforts by a majority of the states to bring order to their ramshackle administrative systems. More pioneering still has been the development of administrative law at both federal and state levels. Ombudsmen have become virtually universal and fairly effective. At the federal level and in Victoria freedom of information legislation has been introduced and administrative appeals courts have been set up to provide an overview of administration and to alleviate the procedural defects of the common law remedies. Once ALP and governments held office in a majority of the states and at the federal level, modest steps were taken to introduce industrial democracy and equal opportunity in employment in the public services. However, the concern with equity issues that characterized talk about reforming public administration from the beginning of the 1970s wilted in the harsher economic climate of the mid-1980s, when concerns of efficiency, privatization of state enterprises, the cutting back of their own affairs and resources, and the elimination of excessive numbers of public servants, all became the dominant policy.

444

FOREIGN AFFAIRS

While Australia's geographic isolation might suggest remoteness from danger, traditionally it has suggested remoteness from help when danger has come. Such fears at the end of the 19th century contributed to the formation of a federal union in a period when the world was being divided by imperial powers. It seemed then that a sufficiently determined European power could deliver military force almost anywhere in the world, and that Japan, a power that was partly European in its development, could deliver in its own neighborhood. Prime Minister William Hughes, who held office during most of World War I, sought to contain the second possibility through postwar negotiations. The experience of World War II, when Japanese forces approached the northern edge of continental Australia, proved his point.

For a quarter of a century after the end of World War II Australian strategists and ordinary citizens worried about two developments. One was the diminution of British power that had led to the withdrawal from east of Suez and had forced Australian dependence on the United States for great power protection. America's capacity to provide a shield for the western rim of the Pacific had been recognized by Australia before World War I and proven during World War II, but U.S. economic and political ties to Australia were weaker than Britain's had been and appeared to need more deliberate cultivation. The second development was that there were now in eastern Asia three major powers that had the economic and population resources to move southward and invade Australia. Japan, occupied by Allied forces and devastated by war, would need a while to recover. Japan's needs for natural resources and living space still suggested a powerful case for expansion, however. The other two powers, the Soviet Union and China, were controlled by Communist regimes that maintained huge postwar military forces, and were driven by an ideology that posited world domination. Communist parties were at work in the countries separating Australia from the Communist powers—in Indochina, India, Malaya and Indonesia. Thus either successful civil wars or invasions by the Soviet Union and China could install Communist governments close to Australia's unpopulated northern coastline.

In such a context the war in Korea was for Australians a popular and unifying experience. Australian troops fought alongside those of the United States and Britain. The war in Vietnam, by contrast, was unpopular and divisive. By the mid-1970s, as the war wound down, apart from the three nations of Indochina, the threat of communist subversion in the countries between China and Australia had subsided. India remained democratic, and if there was a threat to Indian democracy it did not come from the Communists. Malaysia had overcome its insurgent Communists with British help and was a successful democracy. Even Indonesia, which at one point had threatened to embroil Australia in a regional war in defense of Malaysia, had purged its Communists and shed signs of expansionism that had caused concern in the mid-1960s. Finally, Papua New Guinea's and the

445

Pacific islands' decolonization proceeded slowly but steadily, with good will on the part of most concerned. Australia's regional threats had diminished at the same time that the predominance of the American nuclear deterrent began to instill confidence. Domestically, the fragmentation of the Communist party into small and impotent fragments deprived all but the most paranoid of the threat of a fifth column.

Menzies had been enthusiastic for the British Empire and the Commonwealth of Nations until its membership became too broad for his liking. There was revived interest in the Commonwealth under Fraser, which withered again under Hawke. The generalized concern for the problems of the Third World has been kept on a tight rein by budgetary constraints. The farther shores of the Indian and Pacific Oceans are largely ignored, and news of Africa and Latin America only seems to show political and economic instability. The focus of national attention is limited to Southeast and East Asia and the Pacific islands, mixing military threats with trading prospects.

Within that region there are three possible choices for a national defense strategy. In the tradition of the two world wars and the conflicts in Korea, Malaya and Vietnam, Australian forces can be prepared to fight elsewhere, of necessity in company with the forces of a major power, thereby keeping trouble from Australian shores. The American failure in Vietnam and Richard Nixon's Guam Doctrine make this option the least attractive. The limited domestic capacity for weapons manufacture, however, may push the Australian armed forces toward compatible weapons systems purchased from allies such as the United States. The other two choices posit defense of the Australian continent on a substantial capacity to intercept enemy forces at some distance, or emphasize resistance in the immediate vicinity of Australia.

More controversial than the policies of Australia's armed forces is the presence in Australia of several U.S. installations and the degree of mystery about their current functions, including potential involvement in a nuclear exchange between the Soviet Union and the United States. Opposition to their continuation has been confined to the left wing of the ALP, the Australian Democrats and other groups, but it is possible that an international crisis in which Australia's interests were not directly at stake could spark new criticism. The Hawke government's cooperation with a U.S. missile launching experiment was abandoned with some loss of face, and the days when an Australian prime minister (Harold Holt) could win an election by adopting a slogan like "All the Way with LBJ" have probably gone forever. The Fraser government's attempt to concern the Australian electorate with the Soviet move into Afghanistan ran into opposition from those who nevertheless wanted Australia to participate in the Moscow Olympics.

Closer to home, Australian relations with Indonesia, Papua New Guinea, New Zealand and the Pacific island countries display wide variation. Strongest by far are the links to New Zealand. Proximity, the personal ties of many families, and economic complementarity in bilateral trade and shared interests in world trade, all encourage economic connections but leave talk of political union little more than idle speculation. Next are the ties to Papua

446

New Guinea, scene of Australia's one experience as a colonial power, an experience that ended peacefully, and remains the source of mild self-congratulation for those Australians who think about it at all. Australia is the principal and very necessary source of aid; and while Papua New Guinea politics is robustly democratic, with urban crime and ministerial instability the only blemishes, there is little Australian concern or interest. The multiplicity of identities and problems of the small Pacific island countries are even further below the threshold of Australian public attention. A natural disaster or a political coup may produce a momentary spasm of reporting, while the growth of tourism in the region does familiarize some Australians with their near neighbors, but that is all. Despite its size and potential importance Indonesia is by far the least known neighbor. Fear of Indonesia as a threat to Australia, or at least to Papua New Guinea, has subsided; trade contacts are limited, and the provision of military and civil aid is restricted. Outside the tourist enclave of Bali, few Australians are interested in the country. When Indonesian fishing boats are turned back or arrested off the northern coast, it is fear of animal or human diseases they may carry rather than of military adventures they might presage that makes the news. A handful of major political figures are known by name to the best-informed Australians, but a long-standing tension between Indonesian authorities and the Australian news media, attributable both to particular incidents and to widely different views of the correct role of journalists in political life, keeps the flow of information to a minimum.

FURTHER READING

Crowley, Frank. *Tough Times: Australia in the Seventies.* Melbourne: Heinemann, 1986.
Grabaud, Stephen R., ed. *Australia: The Daedalus Symposium.* Sydney: Angus & Robertson, 1985.
Horne, Donald. *The Lucky Country.* 2nd ed. Melbourne: Penguin, 1967.
Kahn, Herman, and Pepper, Thomas. *Will She Be Right? The Future of Australia.* St. Lucia, Queensland: University of Queensland Press, 1980.
Scutt, Jocelynne A., ed. *Poor Nation of the Pacific: Australia's Future?* Sydney and Boston: Allen & Unwin, 1985.
Walsh, Maximilian. *Poor Little Rich Country: The Path to the Eighties.* Melbourne: Penguin, 1979.

BANGLADESH

CRAIG BAXTER

BANGLADESH is one of the newer entrants to the ranks of independent states in the Asia-Pacific area. It became independent on December 16, 1971, following a bitter civil war in the eastern wing of Pakistan and with the assistance of Indian military personnel.[1] It is also one of the poorest nations in the world, with a per capita annual income of about U.S. $150 (1985). With its population of about 100 million, it has been described as the world's largest poorest country, although there are several poorer and seven larger in terms of population. At independence, a senior American official grimly called it an "international basket case."

Measurable progress in some areas, such as production of food grains, has been diminished in per capita terms by the rapid growth of the population. Industry has expanded only minimally in a country with few natural resources and an as yet largely unskilled labor force. Most notable, however, is the lack of development of open and stable political institutions: Bangladesh has been under military or civilian authoritarian regimes for more than half its period of independence, even if one discounts regimes that have the trappings of a parliamentary democracy but are dominated by military leaders turned civilians.[2]

THE LAND AND ITS PEOPLE

The dominant and most important feature of Bangladesh is water, and it can be both a blessing and a curse. During the monsoon this country of numerous intertwined rivers appears, from an aerial view, to be an immense lake with scattered islands. The annual monsoon is one key to agri-

[1] Bangladesh was known as East Pakistan from 1955 until 1971 and as East Bengal from 1947 to 1955. For the purposes of this essay, what is now referred to as Bangladesh will be called "eastern Bengal" for the period preceding 1947 when it was a part of India.

[2] For convenience, the political history of independent Bangladesh can be divided as follows: (1) the Sheikh Mujibur Rahman period, January 1972–August 1975; (2) the Khondakar Mushtaque Ahmad interregnum, August 1975–November 1975; (3) the Ziaur Rahman period, November 1975–May 1981; (4) the Abdus Sattar interregnum, May 1981–March 1982; and (5) the Hussain Mohammed Ershad period, since March 1982.

cultural production: If it is too abundant, crops, animals and people can be washed away; if it is too sparse, such key crops as rice and jute suffer low output. In 1987 and 1988 Bangladesh (and eastern India) experienced two of the most devastating floods in modern times. Flooding is often exacerbated by the failure to dredge the shallow and silt-filled rivers, a task for which funds and management are usually lacking. On the other hand, the rivers deposit silt in the flood plains and replenish the natural fertility of the soil.

The rivers both divide and unite the country. The major streams, the Ganges, the Brahmaputra and the Meghna (which rises inside Bangladesh), are difficult to cross with bridges, pipelines and power lines because of their width and their tendency to migrate. Bangladesh is now undertaking a major project to cross the Jamuna (as the Ganges is known in Bangladesh) with gas and electric transmission lines to bring the benefits of natural gas and hydroelectricity to the southwestern quarter of the country. The rivers and their almost countless tributaries, however, provide routes for water-borne transportation of people and goods, routes that could be made more extensive and stable if dredging operations were expanded.

The land itself is largely alluvial plain. Only in the northeast and east are there hilly areas. There is only one hydroelectric station in Bangladesh, at Karnaphuli on the border between the Chittagong Hill Tracts and the rest of Bangladesh. While the country has not yet discovered any commercially useful petroleum deposits, there is a sizable quantity of natural gas. This is used for industrial (especially the manufacture of nitrogenous fertilizer) and residential purposes as well as for electricity generation. Proposals to export liquefied natural gas have so far been unsuccessful.

The people of Bangladesh represent the most easterly extension of the Indo-Aryans who migrated to the Indian subcontinent in the second millennium B.C. When the Bang (or Vanga) tribe arrived and gave their name to the region, they presumably met Dravidian groups already present and probably Mongoloid peoples as well. The darker skin and shorter stature of the Bengalis are usually attributed to their mixture of these three groups. Mongoloid features are more discernible among those who live in the eastern parts of Bangladesh.

Nonetheless, the Bengali language or its antecedents took root in the region to the extent that Bangladesh is, for all practical purposes, the only unilingual state in South Asia. The name of the country means, literally, "land of the Bengalis." About one-third of Bengali speakers, however, live in India, mainly in the state of West Bengal. The principal Bengali city of Calcutta in West Bengal was the cultural center of Bengal in the years before independence, as well as the capital of British India until 1911. Bengali has a rich literary tradition exemplified best by Rabindranath Tagore, the Nobelist in literature in 1913. His works and those of the Muslim poet Nazrul Islam are highly honored in Bangladesh. Tagore is the author of "Sonar Bangla," the Bangladesh national anthem, and he also wrote the words to India's national anthem, perhaps the only person to whom is attributed the anthems of two countries.

About 85 percent of the Bangladeshis are Muslims, almost all of them

Sunnis. Islam is an important aspect of the lives of most Bengali Muslims. However, Bangladeshi Islam tends to be a personal matter in which individuals themselves take responsibility for performance of their religious duties. Bangladesh, therefore, has not yet been caught up in a wave of fundamentalism demanding state enforcement of Islamic injunctions, as has been the case with its former partner, Pakistan. For example, in Dhaka, the capital, many restaurants remain open in the daytime during Ramadan (the Islamic month of fasting), and there is no legal prohibition on alcoholic beverages.

Fundamentalist movements, however, do exist and exercise some influence on parts of the population. In elections, these groups have done poorly. A greater influence is seen in the popularity of various shrines to Muslim leaders of the past and the loyalty given to the *pirs* who run these shrines. The influence, however, is much more religious than political.

Most of the remaining 15 percent of the people are Hindus. With the partition of India in 1947, the transfer of populations in eastern India was much less complete than it was in the north and northwest. By comparison, Pakistan's population is about 97 percent Muslim and very few Hindus remain there. There were substantial migrations of Hindus from the territory that is now Bangladesh in the early 1950s and again during the civil war of 1971. In the latter period, India wanted a full return of all refugees, both Hindu and Muslim, to Bangladesh but it is clear not all Hindus did return. These two migrations were made up primarily of caste Hindus. Consequently, most of the Hindus in Bangladesh today are members of the group described legally as the Scheduled Castes (formerly known as "Untouchables," or, in the terms of Mahatma Gandhi, Harijans or children of God). There are, of course, many exceptions to this and Hindus (both caste and Scheduled Caste) have been represented in the cabinet, parliament, government services, education and the professions in independent Bangladesh. There are no legal impediments for Hindus and indeed their principal religious festivals, like those of the Muslims and Christians, are legal holidays.

The remainder of the population is Christian or Buddhist. Many Christians are from tribal groups in the northern part of the country. These tribes are usually southern extensions of tribes whose principal residence is in the Indian state of Meghalaya. There are also nontribal Christians, most of them living in the major cities such as Dhaka and many of Eurasian background. Christian missions, educational and medical, have been important since the early 19th century. Foreign contributions to their work are controlled by the government, but the institutions continue to provide services and to prosper even if conversions are rare.

The Buddhists are concentrated in the Chittagong Hill Tracts where the tribals are either Buddhist or animist. The Hill Tracts were set aside by the British as an area reserved for tribals. Since the independence of Pakistan in 1947, there has been increasing movement of "flatlanders" into the hills and increasing resistance to the central government by tribals. This has developed into an endemic insurgency in the tracts that has provoked military operations by the army against some sections of the tribes. The independent Bangladesh government has not been rigid in enforcing laws against settlement in the tracts. The level of violence varies from time to time, but usually the entry of foreigners into the tracts is prohibited.

Women play a mixed role in Bangladesh. The rate of women's literacy, for example, is much lower than that of men, 13 percent compared to 26 percent (1981). In rural areas, women are members of the family farming team and are expected to perform chores assigned to them in agriculture as well as household work and the rearing of children. In urban areas, most women who are employed are in menial and often physically taxing jobs such as construction. On the other hand, opportunities for women at the higher educational levels may be greater than they are in many other Muslim countries. There are a fair number of women doctors, lawyers and teachers in higher education. The leaders of the two principal opposition parties are women, one the daughter and the other the widow of previous leaders.

Efforts to control the growth rate of the population are now emphasizing the importance of women workers reaching out to the women of society. Earlier programs directed at males have proved unsuccessful. The growth rate is 2.3 percent, indicating a projected population of 141 million in the year 2000. President Ershad has put family planning at the top of his agenda along with increased agricultural production, expansion of industrial output, improvement of education and better health-delivery capabilities.

ECONOMY

Both the economic and social aspects of Ershad's agenda are critical if the standard of living for Bangladeshis is to be raised. The economy is heavily dependent on agriculture, which accounts for 50 percent of the GNP. For domestic consumption the key crop is rice; for export, it is jute. Considerable investment has been made in the rural sector since independence. However, small farm size has made greater efficiency more difficult. The average landholding was 3.5 acres in 1977, but when the almost one-sixth of families who are landless are factored into the calculation the average family holding is only 2.3 acres. In addition, owing to Muslim and Hindu inheritance patterns, the holdings are often fragmented into many segments.

Domestic cereal production has increased by more than half, from about 10 million tons a year just before independence to more than 15 million tons in 1982–83. This has been accomplished through several methods. Improved strains of rice have been imported from the International Rice Research Institute in the Philippines and developed locally. During the Zia regime under the "food for work" program, many small irrigation works such as tanks (or man-made ponds) were begun. There was an increase in land under double- or triple-cropping. More chemical fertilizers were used. The Ershad government has also addressed the question of prices, raising the government procurement price in an effort to stimulate increased production. Yield, nonetheless, remains low by comparison with other major

451

rice producers in East Asia. And the output can be, and often is, affected by the vagaries of the weather and the water flow.

In addition to domestically produced rice, Bangladesh must import rice and wheat to have enough to feed its population even at the low nutritional levels that prevail. Most imported wheat enters under grants from the United States, the European Community and other international donors; most imported rice is purchased. It has been said, with no solid statistical data but with a believable ring of truth, that more than half of the Bangladeshis are underfed and undernourished. Protein deficiency among lower-income persons appears to be acute. While output of meat and poultry has increased since independence, that of fish, a key element of the Bengali diet, has declined, as has the primary source of vegetable protein, pulses.

Jute, a natural fiber used for burlap sacking, carpet backing and rope, has seen its market decline against the competition of artificial fibers. Before 1947 it was grown mainly in eastern Bengal but processed in Calcutta. Afterward, India diverted some land from rice to supply the mills in Calcutta while East Pakistan built mills, both actions coming as demand declined. The Adamjee jute mill at Narayanganj near Dhaka is the largest in the world. Jute, both raw and processed, remains the single largest export, but the volume has declined about 10 percent since Bangladeshi independence.

Other agricultural exports include tea and shrimp. Tea is grown in the Sylhet region and accounts for almost 6 percent of exports. The tea, however, is considered inferior to that grown in India and Sri Lanka and it is not expected that the volume sent abroad will expand. Fish and shellfish constitute about 7.5 percent of total exports.

During the Zia regime, the World Bank stated: "Rapid industrial growth is a necessary condition for the eventual solution of Bangladesh's problems of slow GNP growth, mass poverty and heavy dependence on foreign investment resources."[3] In the years following independence several factors inhibited industrial development. Not the least of these was the dogmatic insistence on socialism, i.e., state ownership of industrial, commercial and financial operations, during the regime of Mujibur Rahman. Much of the industrial sector had been owned by West Pakistanis whose property was declared "abandoned" and taken over by the state. But property owned by Bangladeshis was also nationalized. The present writer has commented elsewhere that these government enterprises had a "common thread . . . inefficiency, overemployment, underproductivity and regular losses."[4]

By 1987 the situation had improved somewhat. Liberalization on a limited scale began during the Zia regime when investment in the private sector was encouraged to a degree. Under Ershad, there has been an emphasis on investment coupled with denationalization of many industrial units and even a tentative reversal of the nationalization of banking and

---

[3] *Bangladesh: Current Trends and Development Issues* (Washington, D.C.: International Bank for Reconstruction and Development, March 1979), 41.
[4] Craig Baxter, *Bangladesh: A New Nation in an Old Setting* (Boulder, Colo.: Westview Press, 1984), 84–85.

other financial institutions. Ershad has also liberalized rules for foreign investment, although there has been little result from this so far.

There are difficulties with investment in Bangladesh. One of these is the endemic instability of the political system, which will be discussed below. Another is the lack of raw materials; for example, the textile industry must be substantially fueled by imported raw cotton. A third is the shortage of trained labor, which ties into the critical need for the expansion of the educational system and its extension into what in the West would be called vocational training. Bangladesh has also exported many skilled workers to the Middle East, with remittances of the overseas workers amounting to about half a billion dollars annually. Declines in world oil prices and consequent declines in investment in the Arab/Persian Gulf have caused the number of overseas workers and the amount of the remittances to decline.

In recent years, most foreign assistance to Bangladesh has been in the form of grants rather than loans. This is true especially for food assistance but has also been the case, for example, with American aid to such infrastructure areas as health delivery. Consequently, Bangladesh's debt-service ratio of 16.7 percent in 1985 of exports of goods and services is not unduly high in raw numbers but could cause difficulty as the possibilities for expansion of exports are limited.[5]

EARLY HISTORY

The word "Bengal" is presumably derived from "Vanga," the name of the first Indo-Aryan tribe believed to have penetrated eastward to the lower reaches of the Ganges valley. A noted historian of the subcontinent has said: "No definite affirmation of any kind can be made about specific events in . . . Bengal before 300 B.C."[6] There are references to Bengal in the edicts and inscriptions of the Maurya emperor Asoka (ruled c. 273–232 B.C.) and one inscription has been located at Pundra in Bogra district. It was from Bengal that Asoka's son carried the message of Buddhism by sea to Ceylon (Sri Lanka). After the decline of the Mauryas, Bengal was left very much on its own until the Gupta empire in northern India drew tribute from the area in the 4th and 5th centuries A.D. The short-lived empire of Harsha (606–47) also exacted tribute, but Bengal was a backwater as far as the empires based in Uttar Pradesh and Bihar in present-day India were concerned.

In the 8th century a local dynasty, the Palas, gained control of Bengal and extended their rule into the upper Gangetic plain. But as the Palas

[5] Predictions of the future debt-service burden are difficult to make. Although exports seem unlikely to expand significantly, this is offset by the provision of much economic assistance on a grant basis, as, for example, in the case of the United States and most countries of the Organization for Economic Cooperation and Development. Borrowing is largely from international agencies such as the Asian Development Bank and organs of the Islamic countries. There is also little international borrowing by private-sector firms.
[6] Vincent A. Smith, *The Oxford History of India* (Oxford: Clarendon Press, 1958), 71.

moved westward, their center of power also moved to Monghyr, in today's Bihar in India. The Palas were ardent Buddhists and did much to spread that religion in Bengal. By 1150 the dynasty had weakened and was replaced by a new group, the Senas. The Senas were orthodox Brahmanic Hindus who reinstated the caste system with its disabling restrictions for the lower levels of that hierarchical structure of society. The resentment thus caused may have contributed to the rapid acceptance of Islam by the mass of Bengalis at the beginning of the 13th century.

In 1202 the last major Sena ruler was defeated at his capital, Nadia (now in West Bengal), by a general representing the Muslim rulers of Afghanistan and the Punjab, the Ghurids. With the establishment of the Delhi sultanate in 1206, Bengal passed under the rule of Delhi (first the sultanate and then the Moghul empire), a legal status that would remain until the British began to exercise effective control after 1757.

Although eastern Bengal would not be under native rulers until 1971, there were frequent challenges to the nominal allegiance owed to the rulers in Delhi. The decline of the Tughluq dynasty of Delhi in the 14th century resulted in an all but independent Bengal from 1336 to 1539. In the latter year, a rebel dynasty led by the Afghan Sher Shah Suri who had displaced the second Moghul emperor, Humayun, conquered Bengal. The Afghans, although losing power in Delhi in 1555 to a returning Humayun, retained their hold in Bengal until 1576. In that year, forces under the "Great Moghul" Akbar reincorporated Bengal into the empire.

During this period the city of Dhaka (formerly spelled Dacca) was developed as the capital of Bengal. A neighboring site, Vikrampur, had for a time been the seat of the Pala dynasty. The name is perhaps derived from the goddess Dhakeshwari, whose temple still stands in the city. Dhaka flourished as a seat of government and a center of small manufacturing, especially of the famed diaphanous Dhaka muslin. In 1704 the seat of the Moghul governors was transferred to Murshidabad, now in West Bengal, and under the British to Calcutta. Dhaka began to lose its importance, despite a temporary revival from 1905 to 1912, as the capital of a short-lived province of Eastern Bengal and Assam. Bengal commercial and intellectual life centered instead on Calcutta.

UNDER THE BRITISH

The first Europeans to set up stations in Bengal were the Portuguese, who arrived in Chittagong in 1517. They were followed by the Danes, the Dutch, the French and the British. The last arrived in Bengal in 1650 and founded their major base at Calcutta in 1686. The stations were under the control of trading companies (of which the British East India Company was the most noted) but they operated under permission granted by the Moghul emperors and their governors in Bengal. As the power of the Moghuls declined owing both to foreign pressure and internal Indian power struggles, the role of the governor increased.

In 1756 the then governor, Sirajuddaulah, attacked Calcutta and precipitated the Black Hole incident. The British under Robert Clive defeated

Sirajuddaulah at the battle of Plassey in 1757, in part through the action of the governor's relative, Mir Jafar, whose name remains a symbol of treachery in the subcontinent. British rule in northern India is usually dated from that battle. The British used their base for expansion up the Ganges valley as well as eastward. They also obtained the *diwani* from the Moghul emperor, which gave them the right to collect and expend taxes.

Taxation would be a key in gaining control. Calcutta was made the leading British city in India when the governor, Warren Hastings, was designated governor-general in 1773. One of his successors, Lord Cornwallis, introduced the "permanent settlement" in 1793. This act transformed the tax collectors (*zamindars*) into landowners. Most of these were Hindu; most of the farmers in eastern Bengal were Muslims. This system of primarily Hindu *zamindars* would last until land-reform legislation was passed after the independence of Pakistan. It was opposed by some Muslim political leaders, most notably Fazlul Haq, about whom more below. As many of the *zamindars* were absentee landlords living in Calcutta, the effect on the agriculture of eastern Bengal was profound.

The Bengalis were also adversely affected by the aftermath of the Sepoy Mutiny of 1857–58, which was limited to the Bengal army; the Madras and Bombay armies did not participate. Britain was aided by the Punjabis (Sikh and Muslim) in putting down the rebellion. The British afterward decreed that members of "nonmartial races" would no longer be recruited into the army; these included the Bengalis. The "martial races" included, among others, the Punjabi Muslims. The system continued well past the independence of Pakistan and the almost complete absence of East Bengali Muslims from the Pakistani army would be one of the grievances leading to the breakup of Pakistan in 1971.

The mutiny also saw the winding up of the British East India Company, already limited in its operation by a series of acts by the British Parliament. Power was transferred to the crown. Over the next 90 years there would be a series of acts that would increase the Indian role in the governance of India, leading to independence and partition in 1947. Some of these need to be noted.

The 1909 Government of India Act instituted the system of separate electorates for Muslims and "others," i.e., primarily Hindus. As changes took place leading toward an electoral arrangement for Indians participating in government, the Muslims feared that they would be a permanent minority and would be subjected to a Hindu raj. Earlier, an important Muslim educationist, Sir Syed Ahmad Khan, had declared that there were sufficient differences between the Muslims and the Hindus of India to warrant treatment as separate nations, the "two nations theory," that would reach its culmination in partition of India in 1947. A group of Muslims met the viceroy, Lord Minto, in 1906 and convinced him that Muslim interests could only be satisfied if Muslims elected their own representatives. In the system of separate electorates (later extended to Sikhs, Christians and other groups), Muslims would vote for Muslims, "others" (then primarily Hindus) for "others." In the same year, 1906, the Muslim League was founded in Dhaka to represent Muslims in politics. The league asserted that the Indian National Congress (founded in 1885) represented only Hindus.

In 1905 the viceroy, Lord Curzon, determined that the large province of Bengal (then including Bihar and Orissa as well) was too unwieldy to manage. He partitioned Bengal into two sections: Eastern Bengal and Assam, with a Muslim majority; and Western Bengal, Bihar and Orissa, with a Hindu majority. While this delighted the Muslims, the Hindus objected, often with violence. The British yielded to the Hindu demands and nullified partition in 1911. Bengal would be united, Assam would be separated and a new province of Bihar and Orissa was created (to be split in 1919). The capital of India was moved from Calcutta to New Delhi.

An act in 1919 set up a system of dual rule (diarchy) under which some departments of provincial government were placed under Indian ministers. This evolved to full provincial autonomy under the Government of India Act of 1935. Elections were held in 1937 and resulted in a provincial government under Fazlul Haq and his Krishak Praja party (farmers' and people's party) in coalition with the Muslim League. Haq had championed the cause of the Muslim peasant, but many of them were not eligible to vote under the restricted franchise. His party finished slightly behind the league in the Muslim seats but he emerged as the leader of the whole assembly. Haq served until 1943, although his coalition with the league ended in 1941. In 1943 Khiraja Nazimuddin of the league succeeded Haq. After the 1947 elections, Husain Shahid Suhrawardy became the Muslim League premier. Suhrawardy would later form the Awami League, a spokesman for the rural mass as well as for the urban. These three men, whose views and backgrounds were very different, were the principal leaders of eastern Bengal before and after independence. Despite their differences, the state has honored them by having them buried in adjacent graves on the *maidan* (park) in Dhaka.

Bengal voted heavily for the Muslim League in 1946, giving it a greater share of its Muslim votes than any of the provinces in the west that were included in Pakistan. Fazlul Haq and other Bengalis also had strongly supported the Lahore resolution (often called "Pakistan resolution") of March 23, 1940. In that document the Muslim League stated that if conditions for Muslims did not improve there would be no alternative to the partition of the country. Bengal gave its support to this in 1946.

A PROVINCE OF PAKISTAN

Support for partition soon diminished. Bengalis believed that they were being treated as second-class citizens by the ruling group largely drawn from the west and from refugees from India. A key issue was the matter of the national language of Pakistan. Governor-General Muhammad Ali Jinnah, who had led Pakistan to independence, stated that Urdu would be the sole national language. Bengalis reacted with demonstrations, the heaviest in February 1952, demanding that Bengali be given equal status with Urdu. The demand was eventually conceded but the legacy of discontent remained.

Other issues included the small number of Bengalis in the civil and military services, the expenditure in West Pakistan of much of the foreign exchange earned by East Pakistan from jute and the uneven economic development of the eastern province. When provincial elections were held in 1954, the Muslim League was trounced by a United Front headed by the Krishak Sramik party (farmers' and laborers' party) of Fazlul Haq and the Awami League led by Suhrawardy. With universal franchise in effect for the first time, these parties that articulated the grievances of Bengalis could now gain the support of the population. The outcome was not as effective. Central government intervention—the parliamentary system in East Pakistan was suspended until 1956—and the breakup of the United Front led to tussles between the KSP and the Awami League that disrupted the government in East Pakistan. At the center and in West Pakistan government also failed, culminating in the takeover by the military led by Gen. Mohammad Ayub Khan in October 1958.

The Ayub government, it may be fairly said, tried to redress some of the problems that concerned the Bengalis, but it did so in a regime (called "basic democracy" by Ayub) that abandoned the parliamentary system for one with a strong presidency. Bengali opposition was most strongly expressed by Sheikh Mujibur Rahman ("Mujib"), who succeeded Suhrawardy as the leader of the Awami League when Suhrawardy died in 1963. Mujib stated the Bengali demands succinctly in January 1966 in his Six Points: (1) a federal parliamentary system; (2) federal government to control only foreign affairs and defense; (3) separate fiscal systems for each province; (4) taxation only at the provincial level with provinces granting funds for federal operations; (5) separate foreign trade arrangements; and (6) provincial militias.

When in March 1969 Ayub fell from power as a result of widespread demonstrations by the opposition, the new president, Gen. Yahya Khan, declared that elections would be held and the elected body would frame a new constitution. Mujib and the Awami League ran on the platform of the Six Points in the December 1970 poll. Although the party won no seats in West Pakistan, it won 160 of 162 seats in East Pakistan, giving Mujib and his followers a clear majority in the new assembly, which had 300 directly elected seats.

Negotiations toward a compromise on the Six Points failed, due to a number of factors. The military under Yahya clearly expected the election results to be inconclusive, anticipating neither the extremely successful result for the Awami League in East Pakistan nor the majority gained by the Pakistan People's party of Zulfikar Ali Bhutto in West Pakistan. In addition, West Pakistani sentiments, expressed especially by Bhutto (who proclaimed that there were "two majorities" in Pakistan), opposed both a leadership of Pakistan headed by an East Pakistani (Mujib) and Mujib's growing insistence that his Six Points form the basis of a new constitution. West Pakistanis, both military and civilian, objected especially to the fourth point which, if enacted, would place the central government (and the military) at the mercy of the fiscal generosity of the provincial governments. Mujib has been quoted, perhaps apocryphally, as saying that the province of East

Pakistan would contribute funds to defense in the same ratio as its share of military personnel, 6 percent. Yahya's delay in calling the constituent assembly to meet led to increased pressure on Mujib from more radical elements in the Awami League to declare independence unilaterally. Meanwhile, violence increased in East Pakistan.[7]

In March 1971 the Pakistani army went into action against the Bengalis. In a bitter conflict, the Bangladeshis with the strong assistance of India forced a Pakistani surrender on December 16, 1971. Bangladesh became independent, the first country since World War II to secede successfully, though at great cost.

INDEPENDENT BANGLADESH

Mujib, who had been in jail in West Pakistan, was released and returned to Bangladesh to become prime minister in January 1972. By the end of the year Bangladesh had a constitution embodying a parliamentary system. It also enshrined the principles of *Mujibbad* (Mujibism): nationalism, secularism, democracy and socialism. The cost of rehabilitating the country after the terrible destruction of the civil war was high, but international assistance was available from many quarters.

Despite the American tilt toward Pakistan during the civil war, which provoked anger in Bangladesh, the principal source of funds for rehabilitation was the United States. The largest amount came from American government funds, but many American private groups joined European and other private organizations in providing assistance. Funds were also provided from European, Canadian, Australian, Japanese and other governments.[8] The Soviet Union, for example, aided in clearing the Chittagong harbor, but then stayed too long, an event that contributed to the cooling of Bangladeshi-Soviet relations. The Islamic countries and China, however, continued to support the Pakistani position that Bangladesh was still legally part of Pakistan and should not be accorded international recognition. Pakistan invoked its version of the West German Hallstein Doctrine and began to break diplomatic relations with countries establishing relations with Bangladesh, as West Germany once did with nations recognizing East Germany. When the major powers recognized Bangladesh, this policy was

[7] For additional information on this period see David Dunbar (pseudonym for Craig Baxter), "Pakistan: The Failure of Political Negotiations," *Asian Survey* 12 (May 1972): 5; and Craig Baxter, "Pakistan and Bangladesh," in *Ethnic Separatism and World Politics,* ed. Frederick L. Shiels (Lanham, Maryland: University Press of America). The latter also discusses the American tilt toward Pakistan mentioned later in this essay.

[8] In recent years, in the post-rehabilitation period, the largest donors and lenders have been the United States and Japan. In fiscal year 1983–84 the donors or lenders that committed $100 million or more were the International Development Association ($340 million), Japan ($210 million), the Asian Development Bank ($198 million), Canada ($142 million) and the United States ($125 million). The total for the year was $1.7 billion, as listed in the *1984–85 Statistical Yearbook of Bangladesh.*

458

dropped, but the admission of Bangladesh to the Commonwealth did result in Pakistan's withdrawal from that group, an absence the Pakistanis reversed only after Benazir Bhutto became prime minister.

It should be noted that Mujib rewarded Indian assistance in the civil war by concluding a 25-year treaty of friendship with India in 1972. This followed India's treaty of 1971 with the Soviet Union and in the eyes of many Bangladeshis indirectly tied Bangladesh to the Soviet Union. Relations between India and Bangladesh soon soured. Indian forces remained in Bangladesh, especially in the Chittagong Hill Tracts, much longer than most Bangladeshis considered necessary. India also assumed custody of Pakistani prisoners and confiscated much of the military equipment captured from the Pakistani forces. In addition, the Farraka dispute (see below) soon became critical to Bangladesh.

Mujib's administration was neither strong nor effective. Mismanagement and corruption caused increasing opposition. He responded by creating a strong and authoritarian presidential system in January 1975 and a single-party state in June of that year. In August, in a coup led by field grade military officers, he was assassinated.

After a period of turmoil lasting through early November, a military regime dominated by Maj. Gen. Ziaur Rahman ("Zia") was established. Zia gradually opened both the political and economic system. He allowed political parties to resume activities and held a presidential election in June 1978, which he won. Parliamentary elections followed in February 1979, and Zia's party, the Bangladesh Nationalist party (BNP), won about two-thirds of the seats. There were, as has been mentioned, steps to widen economic as well as political participation. Zia put forward a program for development that emphasized agriculture, family planning and health delivery. Nonetheless, opposition to his system went beyond parliamentary and peaceful opposition. On May 30, 1981, Zia was assassinated by disgruntled military officers.

Zia's legal successor, the civilian Abdus Sattar, was unable to resist military demands for a constitutional role in the government, and he was overthrown in a peaceful coup by Lt. Gen. Hussain Mohammed Ershad on March 24, 1982. Ershad has not been able to develop the charismatic leadership displayed by Zia. He has, however, continued Zia's development programs, modifying them somewhat to suit his own ideas. The economic system has been opened up, although, as noted above, the effect of the changes cannot yet be measured. In the political arena he has been less successful. Although parliamentary and presidential elections have been held, there is a widespread feeling that the announced results do not accurately reflect the opinion of the voters. The government in office is headed by Prime Minister Kazi Zafar Ahmad, but ultimate power is held by the president—and behind him is the military.

In November and December 1987 widespread demonstration, accompanied by rioting and violence, against Ershad and his government broke in Dhaka and other cities. These were led by Sheikh Hasina Wajed (the daughter of Mujib) of the Awami League and Begum Khaleda Zia (Zia's widow) of the BNP. The key demands were the resignation of Ershad, his replacement by an acceptable president (at that time under the Bangladesh constitution the president appointed the vice-president, who would become acting president if the president resigned) and the holding of new presidential and parliamentary elections. Ershad met the demonstrations with police power and refused the demands. The future of his regime is at best questionable; what may follow should he be ousted is even more questionable.

In international relations, the honeymoon between India and Bangladesh soon ended. Bangladesh has several problems with India, the most important of which is the division of the waters of the Ganges during the low flow season (April–June). This results from the building by India of a barrage at Farraka, just upstream from the border. The barrage is intended to divert water to Calcutta, but it also diverts water from southwestern Bangladesh. On the other hand, Bangladesh has done much to rebuild relations with Pakistan, and on such issues as Afghanistan the views of the former partners are almost identical. Under Zia, Bangladesh took the lead in promoting regional cooperation. Although it occurred after Zia's death, the signing of the formal agreement to create the South Asian Association for Regional Cooperation is a monument to him.

Despite the American tilt toward Pakistan in 1971, relations between the United States and Bangladesh have been close and productive. And despite China's several early vetoes on Bangladeshi membership in the United Nations, relations between Bangladesh and China have also been warm. Relations with the Soviet Union, close during the early Mujib period, can now best be termed correct. Bangladesh is an active and important member of the Organization of the Islamic Conference.

THE FUTURE

If the future of Bangladesh is reflective of its first decades as an independent state, the prospect is not promising. The country has been most often governed by authoritarian civil or military regimes. Even when popular regimes have governed, such as the early period of Mujib's rule and the bulk of the rule of Zia, the opposition has rarely accepted its status and served as a "loyal opposition." Changes of government have been extraconstitutional and occasionally violent, as in August and November 1975 and May 1981. The prospect for future changes being conducted in a constitutional manner through the electoral process is very questionable. Further, the likelihood that any such constitutional change might prevail is also very questionable. This record alone inhibits long-term investment in Bangladesh, as does the potential for wide swings in economic policy.

Since economic and social development in the country are linked with political development, their future is also unclear. As the World Bank stated, industrialization is needed to alleviate the rural and urban poverty of the nation, but that of course is easier to prescribe than to implement. Although the weak natural-resource base cannot be improved, the educational and health levels can, but only with a government that is legitimate and does not have to constantly fend off opposition challenges.

Bangladesh is thus a nation that is still in the early stages of political development, has severe limitations in economic development and is restricted in social development by the instability of the political system and the weakness of the economy. It is, therefore, a country that will require the assistance of the international community for many years to come.

FURTHER READING

Baxter, Craig. *Bangladesh: A New Nation in an Old Setting.* Boulder, Colorado: Westview Press, 1984.

———, and Rahman, Syedur. *Historical Dictionary of Bangladesh.* Metuchen, New Jersey: Scarecrow Press, 1989.

Faaland, Just, ed. *Aid and Influence: The Case of Bangladesh.* London: Macmillan, 1981.

———, and Parkinson, J. R. *Bangladesh: The Test Case of Development.* Dhaka: University Press; London: C. Hurst, 1976.

Franda, Marcus. *Bangladesh: The First Decade.* New Delhi: South Asian Publishers; Hanover, New Hampshire: Universities Field Staff International, 1982.

Jahan, Rounaq. *Bangladesh Politics: Problems and Issues.* Dhaka: University Press, 1980.

Jannuzi, F. Tomasson, and Peach, James T. *The Agrarian Structure of Bangladesh: An Impediment to Development.* Boulder, Colorado: Westview Press, 1980.

Johnson, Basil Leonard Clyde. *Bangladesh.* 2nd ed. London: Heinemann; New York: Barnes and Noble, 1982.

Khan, Zillur R. *Leadership in the Least Developed Nation, Bangladesh.* Syracuse, New York: Maxwell School of Citizenship and Public Affairs, 1983.

Maniruzzaman, Talukder. *The Bangladesh Revolution and its Aftermath.* Dhaka: Bangladesh Books, 1980.

———. *Group Interests and Political Change: Studies of Pakistan and Bangladesh.* New Delhi: South Asian Publishers, 1982.

BRUNEI

BARBARA WATSON ANDAYA

INTERNATIONAL attention only rarely focuses on the tiny state of Brunei, for its evolution over the last 80 years has proceeded relatively uneventfully. Yet, on several counts, Brunei merits closer attention. It may be among the world's smallest nations, but it is distinguished from other microstates by its enormous wealth, based on extensive oil and natural gas deposits. Brunei's annual GDP is reckoned at an average of U.S.$15,000 per capita, excluding income from investment of its foreign assets estimated at $20 billion. It is also unusual in that political power lies not with elected representatives but with a monarch, Sultan Sir Hassanal Bolkiah, who is twenty-ninth in a line that stretches back to the 15th century. And although the honorific, *Darussalam* (Abode of Peace), proclaims Brunei's independent Islamic status, it was not until 1984 that ties with Britain were formally severed.

THE ORIGINS OF BRUNEI

The distinctive features of modern Brunei are readily understood in terms of its historical experience. During the early times, Brunei's position on the northwest coast of the island of Borneo meant it was somewhat isolated from the principal Southeast Asian trading routes. From the 15th century, however, links with the Malay world were strengthened with the rise of a major entrepôt, Melaka, on the west coast of the Malay Peninsula. Here Brunei traders brought highly valued products from Borneo's seas and jungles, notably camphor, to exchange for such items as Indian cloth. Brunei, though a month's sail from the peninsula, thus became a redistribution point in a Melaka-centered trading network.

It is impossible to overestimate the importance of this association in Brunei's development. The unparalleled success of Melaka and its reputation as a center of Islam led to an equivalent rise in the prestige of Malay language and culture. Brunei, like so many states in the area, strove to emulate Melaka's example. Royal protocol and the organization of trade alike were modeled after Melaka, and Brunei's rulers adopted Islam about 1515. The Malay-Islamic culture of the Brunei court quickly assumed an aura that raised it above that of neighboring non-Muslim peoples. During the 16th century, active proselytization by Brunei spread Islam into the

462

southern Philippines, and Brunei extended its overlordship northward to Luzon and down Borneo's northwest coast to incorporate most of modern-day Sarawak.

The cultural influence of Melaka was so great that when the first Europeans arrived in Brunei, at the beginning of the 16th century, they saw it as a typical Malay port. But in Brunei the non-Muslim, non-Malay interior groups were far more numerous than in most Malay kingdoms. The seacoast and jungle-covered hinterlands of Borneo were home to a variety of peoples, from the fierce seagoing Bajau to small hunting-gathering bands like the Punan and shifting agriculturalists such as the Iban and Melanau. As collectors of local products, they were an essential part of the economy. They also contributed to the ruler's prestige by providing labor and services. The legacy of this profitable relationship between a Malayo-Muslim court and a uniquely Bornean environment is apparent in legends of Brunei's founding that trace the royal line from a marriage between a Malay princess and a mythical local hero who subsequently adopted Islam and became "Malay."

To some outsiders this experience may appear to have occurred in a very distant past, but in contemporary Brunei it retains a particular relevance. The strength of the state, Bruneis believe, lay in its ability to draw together a vast area inhabited by peoples who may have differed widely in customs and language but who were linked by allegiance to the ruler and the blend of Malay-Islamic and local culture he upheld. Its wealth was then so great that in 1578 the Spanish attempted to take control; their withdrawal two years later is regarded as a victory for Brunei "nationalism." There are still some who see in 16th-century society an ideal toward which modern Brunei should strive.

Memories of Brunei's "golden age" are also important because its trade declined in the 17th century and it was eclipsed by a former vassal, Sulu, located in the southern Philippines. With Sulu's expansion, Brunei lost not only considerable territory along the northern tip of Borneo, it also lost people—notably the Bajau, whose fighting skills had been so important in maintaining Bruneian dominance of the region.

Through the 18th century continued incursions by Sulu raiders, combined with weakness at the center, further depleted Brunei's strength. The result was a clear shift in its self-perception. Brunei's rulers now began to see their state as weak and in need of assistance. From the 1770s on, overtures were made to the British in the hope that they would establish a post in Brunei that would offer protection against Sulu raiding. But British interest in the proposals waned in the face of financial losses, and northwest Borneo was not sufficiently prosperous to attract any other European commitment.

Brunei's willingness to seek outside assistance assumed importance in the mid-19th century when the court faced a rebellion by chiefs in the Sarawak district, nominally under Brunei control. An offer of help from a British adventurer, James Brooke, was readily accepted, and, with his support, order was restored. In return, Brooke, in 1841, was made raja of Sarawak. His ambition, however, did not stop there. For the next 40 years, backed by their fighting force of Ibans, Brooke and, later, his nephew Charles steadily extended Sarawak, purchasing or leasing large tracts of Brunei territory from the impecunious court or from semi-independent chiefs.

In 1881, a further threat to Brunei appeared in the form of the British North Borneo Chartered Company, which began to expand along the northern coast, often using questionable means to acquire river districts from the Brunei ruler or his nobles. In the hope of gaining support, in 1888 the sultan ceded the island of Labuan to the British government and agreed to accept the "protection" of the British crown. Unfortunately, this did not have the desired result. In 1890, Charles Brooke seized the Limbang River, Brunei's last remaining territory of importance. By so doing, he divided the state into two separate enclaves, a division that Brunei has still not accepted.

Unofficially, Westminster continued to favor an absorption of Brunei by one of its neighbors until 1904, when a British envoy to Brunei realized the depth of resentment this would arouse. At the same time, Britain was anxious to ensure that northwest Borneo remain a British sphere of interest. In 1906, therefore, London appointed a resident whose advice had to be "asked and acted upon" in all matters except those relating to Islam. In essence, the British took over the government of Brunei.

THE BRITISH RESIDENCY

The willingness of the Brunei ruler to agree to the protectorate agreement must be seen in context. By 1906, Brunei had shrunk to the four river systems that today make up its four districts—Tutong, Belait, Brunei and Temburong. Continued opposition to the agreement by Charles Brooke, even after 1906, left Brunei rulers with a deep suspicion of Sarawak's intentions, and to some extent that attitude has been transferred to modern Malaysia. The sense of beleaguerment also strengthened a consciousness of being "Brunei" and a wariness of any suggested association with the other Borneo territories. On a number of occasions Britain proposed a greater Borneo union, but Bruneis only favored this if it meant a reconstitution of the old Brunei sultanate.

Against this background of hostility toward both Sarawak and northern Borneo, Britain came to be perceived as a protector. At the beginning of the 20th century, there seemed little reason to oppose the British presence. First, Brunei had been rescued from its predatory neighbors. Second, there was minimal British interference with the existing social structure. Because governmental decrees were issued from the Sultan in Council, most Bruneis did not realize that this council rarely met and that the resident had complete control. If anything, the formal position of the ruler was enhanced because the British made a point of emphasizing his dignity and privileges vis-à-vis his chiefs and nobles. The latter were a potential source of opposition, but rumblings of discontent were blunted by the inclusion of several in the council and the continuing importance placed on rank and hierarchy.

Third, the social and economic changes that normally come in the wake of a colonial administration were not evident in Brunei for several decades.

464

The main reason for this was financial. The new administration was set in place with a loan from the Federated Malay States (see the article on Malaysia by Ian Brown in this Handbook), but although revenue after 1910 always exceeded expenditure, there was little to spare for development. Outside investors could not be attracted because everything Brunei produced could be obtained more cheaply in the Malay Peninsula. Some experiments were conducted in cash crops, but settled agriculture had never been a feature of the Brunei economy. In the capital, the British residents found it impossible to persuade people to abandon their traditional homes, which were built out over the water, and move to land, and it was difficult to woo interior groups away from subsistence agriculture to wet rice cultivation. Lack of manpower was also an obstacle to economic development, and with customs duties the chief source of income, careful management was needed to avoid further indebtedness.

British residents, therefore, could hope to achieve little more than financial stability, limited social services and a basic administrative system. In itself, this was an achievement, but during the process, Brunei, like Malaya, took on many of the characteristics of a plural society. The Chinese population, 736 in 1911, had doubled by 1921, and they established themselves as the dominant commercial class, displacing local Malay traders. The British considered the Malays more suited to administration, and set up schools to train Malay boys as district officers and for minor posts in government service. In this Malay-Chinese division, there was no clear role for the non-Muslim indigenous people. Most remained in their traditional occupations as shifting agriculturalists, fishermen or collectors of jungle products.

THE DISCOVERY OF OIL

In view of Brunei's then relative poverty, the discovery of oil in viable quantities at Seria in 1929 by the newly formed British Malayan Petroleum Company (BMPC; owned by Royal Dutch Shell) must be seen as a watershed. Although the first commercial exports began in 1932, there was no dramatic increase in expenditure. Rather, the immediate concern was to pay off loans, since the extent of the oil was unknown. By 1936, however, Brunei was out of debt and its oil-producing future appeared more certain. Cautious advances were made, therefore, in the provision of social services—sanitation, medical clinics, schools. But it was in the Belait area where the real effects of oil exploration could be found. Here a government within a government was created, with the BMPC constructing its own roads and providing housing and medical facilities for its workers. Here, too, clustered a new society of immigrant Europeans, Indians and Chinese, the nucleus of what was later to be dubbed the "Shellfare State."

Localized though it was, the development of oil made Brunei part of an international commercial network. Improved communications brought a growing awareness of rising nationalism in Asia and an increasing opposition to colonial rule. With no trade unions and with limited educational institutions, Brunei lacked obvious breeding grounds for even incipient

465

nationalism. In 1938, however, the Barisan Pemuda Brunei (Brunei Youth Movement) was formed, the aims of which were to "foster loyalty to the Sultan and the country and to obtain certain democratic advances."

THE JAPANESE OCCUPATION AND EARLY NATIONALISM

The first stirrings of the notion of "Brunei for Bruneis" were encouraged by Japan's victory over British forces during World War II. Japanese troops landed at Kuala Belait in December 1941 and made their immediate goal the rehabilitation of the oil fields destroyed by the retreating Allies. At the same time, the Japanese were also intent on fostering anti-European sentiment by singling out promising nationalist leaders. One of their protégés was a Labuan, Sheikh Ahmad Azahari, who was sent to Indonesia for further training. The effects of this were to be felt in Brunei nearly two decades later.

If the Japanese occupation was not the milestone in Brunei history that it was elsewhere in Southeast Asia, it did nonetheless encourage a questioning of the status quo and of the British presence, which did not disappear with the end of hostilities. If anything, the comparatively rapid return to normalcy and the recovery of the oil industry fed an impatience among some Bruneis for greater control over their country. Oil production between 1947 and 1955 trebled to 5,109,000 tons, and Brunei's income reached 102,669,000 Brunei dollars. Gradually, tangible benefits in the form of improved social services did begin to flow down into Brunei society, but there was still a perceptible gap between the life-style of those living in the "Shellfare State" and those in the rest of Brunei.

The anachronism of any colonial association in the postwar world, the aspirations of many Bruneis and the country's growing wealth made the end of protectorate status inevitable. The question, then as now, was how much and how quickly should change be introduced. A group of younger Bruneis under the banner of the Partai Rakyat, led by the charismatic Sheikh Ahmad Azahari, demanded a constitutional monarchy, a target date for independence and free elections. They gained a considerable following because of their adamant opposition to any union with Malaya and their cry for a restoration of Brunei's former territory in North Borneo. This militant nationalism had a particular appeal for Malays and indigenous groups, and in 1955 the Partai Rakyat claimed to have 16,000 members.

But opposition to rapid change had advocates in high places. The sultan, Sir Omar Ali Saifuddin, supported by the British resident, felt that Brunei was not ready for self-government. Regardless of popular opinion, it was they who held effective power. Accordingly, in 1959, a written constitution was promulgated giving Brunei complete internal autonomy but leaving control of defense and foreign affairs in Britain's hands. The resident was replaced by a high commissioner, most of whose powers were transferred to the sultan. The sultan was to be assisted by several advisory bodies, the most important being the Legislative Council, which was to consist of 33 members, with 16 indirectly elected.

466

THE 1962 REBELLION AND ITS AFTERMATH

Even this limited move toward democracy received a major blow following the elections of August 1962. The Partai Rakyat gained 98 percent of the vote, but it was soon clear that it would not be permitted to dominate the administration. In December, Azahari announced a rebellion, and 3,000 adherents began to attack police stations and government installations.

Although the rebellion was quickly put down by British troops, its effects were long-lasting. The aftermath of the election fed an apprehension among the ruling elite in Brunei that "democracy" could prove disruptive to the existing social and political order. Because of the support the rebels had received from within Indonesia, the Philippines and Malaya, long-standing suspicions concerning the ambitions of Brunei's neighbors appeared confirmed. The rebellion strengthened the sultan's conviction that a continued British military presence was vital for Brunei's security; and even when arrangements for complete independence were finally concluded in 1979, it was with the understanding that a Gurkha battalion, financed by Brunei, should remain.

In 1962, the greater security offered by inclusion in a larger political unit persuaded the sultan to consider joining the new Federation of Malaysia, despite widespread feeling against such a move. A telling argument was the question of Brunei's future when oil supplies were depleted, especially given the declining production of the Seria fields. But reaching agreement on the terms of Brunei's entry proved difficult, and negotiations came to an abrupt end in 1963, when promising new offshore yields were discovered. The sultan then decided to stand alone and refused to become part of Malaysia.

Four years later, Sir Omar abdicated in favor of his son, the 22-year-old Sir Hassanal Bolkiah, who had been educated at Sandhurst, in England. The older man, however, retained effective power, steadily resisting efforts to expand political representation and tenaciously holding to the British connection. The annexation of Portuguese Timor by Indonesia and the continuing tensions with Malaysia remained persistent reminders of Brunei's vulnerability, even though Britain's Labour party, coming to power in 1974, was anxious to cut the links with Brunei. It was not until 1979 that a Treaty of Friendship and Cooperation between Brunei and Britain was concluded, ushering in a five-year transition period to prepare for the transfer of complete sovereignty.

THE CONTEMPORARY SCENE

On January 1, 1984, Brunei officially assumed control of its own affairs once again. In many respects its future looks more secure than it has for more than a century. In the first place, its financial position is enviable. Brunei is regarded internationally as a reliable and safe source of oil, and even cautious projections see production continuing at the present level of about 150,000 barrels a day well beyond the end of the century. Since 1973, oil production has been augmented by the annual export of 5.03

million metric tons of liquid natural gas, sold mainly to Japan. Although known oil reserves will be exhausted in about 30 years, by then Brunei will have $40 billion in foreign reserves and should be able to live comfortably off the investment income.

Nor is a takeover by a neighboring power likely. Since 1978 both Indonesia and Malaysia have reiterated that they have no designs on Brunei, and it has received significant moral and practical support from Singapore, which has a vested interest in Brunei's survival. In recent years, Brunei has gained added security by involvement in a number of international associations, including the United Nations, the British Commonwealth, the Islamic Conference and, most importantly, ASEAN (the Association of Southeast Asian Nations). An indication of Brunei's determination to maintain its independence is the growing strength of the Royal Brunei Malay Regiment, which receives one-third of the government budget, numbers about 4,000 men and is equipped with the very latest technology.

Given Brunei's continued existence as an independent state, other questions arise. A major one is the degree to which the government will open up to democratic participation. Elections were suspended in 1969, but a considerable increase in government spending on public welfare has helped mute opposition to the sultan's paramount authority. Yet it is impossible to ignore the underlying tension between the desire to create a modern state and the concentration of so much power in the sultan. The traditional respect in which Malays hold their king is also under strain because of the obvious inequities in the distribution of Brunei's wealth. Ripples have already been caused by accusations of corruption and concerns about the opulent life-style of the royal family, especially when it is alleged that the average employee makes less than $300 a month. The real shock waves, however are probably yet to come. Brunei's population should double in another generation, and younger, less traditional and more educated citizens will almost certainly make louder calls for a greater share in governing the country.

Sir Hassanal Bolkiah, the present ruler, is reputed to be more liberal than was his father, although he has shown no great eagerness to hasten the pace of political change. A cabinet form of government replaced the Legislative Council in 1984, but in 1986, following the death of his father, Sir Hassanal increased the membership of the Council of Ministers from seven to 11. At the same time, ministerial responsibilities were divided so that aristocrats and commoners now outnumber the sultan and his relatives in the highest organ of state. Nonetheless, government continues to operate in secrecy, and there has been little encouragement of greater popular participation. In May 1985, a new political party, the Brunei National Democratic party (PKDB), was formed to press for a liberalization of democracy and an eventual constitutional monarchy. It also insisted that Brunei should assume greater control of Brunei Shell Petroleum (BSP), at present a fifty-fifty venture between Shell and the Brunei government. However, even though civil servants (about 40 percent of the 80,000-member labor force) were not allowed to join, the sultan apparently considered the existence of even this small party a threat to internal harmony, and in early 1988 it was abolished. No public outcry greeted this move, and without elections or opinion polls, it is difficult to gauge the extent of criticism of the existing form of government.

A second concern is the training of Bruneis to take over the positions held by expatriates in key areas. The process of indigenization has encountered difficulties in the skilled and technical areas, a major problem being the lack of educated local people. Numbers of young Bruneis have been sent overseas for further training, while at home education receives a hefty portion of the budget. Stress is placed on mastering English starting in primary school, and in 1985 a university was established. BSP is taking on more Brunei Malays at senior staff level, and Bruneis are also replacing expatriates in managing the country's finances, particularly overseas reserves. Nonetheless, in a small population there is inevitable competition for able, educated employees, and the demand from both government and the private sector will continue to outstrip the supply for many years.

A third consideration is the preparation for the eventual day when oil reserves run dry. In a time of falling oil prices, the government is very conscious that currently oil makes up 70 percent of the GDP and, with natural gas, 99 percent of exports. Much of Brunei's food is imported, but there remain hopes that in the future it may become less reliant on outside supplies. The expansion of agriculture has been a principal concern of the five development plans to date, although it is not easy to encourage wide-scale participation in rice growing, cattle rearing or commercial fishing. The security and higher remuneration of wage labor are a real deterrent to farmers; and although tracts around the capital have been cleared, about 70 percent of the land is still covered with jungle or unsuitable for development.

Renewed attention is also being given to economic diversification, and suggestions have been made for future projects such as building up a specialist glass industry with Brunei's extensive silica deposits. An ongoing difficulty with this and other proposals is the chronic shortage of labor, especially as local Malays prefer to move into government positions rather than blue-collar jobs. Despite some unemployment among locals, about 37 percent of the work force is foreign, mainly from India, Pakistan, the Philippines and Malaysia. Any increase in this number would bring undesirable social consequences. It is hoped that the Twenty-Year Development Plan now being formulated will make concrete proposals to resolve these problems.

A less tangible but ultimately more important question is the creation of a *bangsa Brunei,* a Brunei race. The espoused ideal is to create a "unified and prosperous society which will operate in the interests of all, regardless of race and origin," but the core of this society will be Islamic-Malay culture. Ideally, as many as possible of Brunei's population should be brought within this fold, and official categories have been redefined to reflect that aspiration. The definition of "Malayness" has already been widened to include "indigenous people of the Malay race" like the Kedayan, and there is an active Islamization program that aims to bring social mores closer to Koranic teaching. Sir Hassanal has warned against fundamentalist Islam,

469

but the importance of the Muslim faith as an element of the Brunei identity is symbolized by the magnificent Omar Ali Saiffudin mosque, a focal point of Bandar Seri Begawan, the capital of Brunei.

Malaysia has provided an obvious model for strengthening Malay-Islamic culture, although stress is also placed on Brunei's separate identity. At the same time, the widening rifts in Malaysian society have pointed up the inherent difficulties of advocating Malay-Islamic dominance in a multiethnic society. In Brunei, the Chinese community comprises a quarter of the population but dominates the commercial and private non-oil sectors. Although there is rarely any outward display of racial tension, the Chinese do have real grievances. They are eligible for Brunei citizenship only if they have lived in the country for a minimum of 21 years, can pass a stringent language test and indicate their willingness to live in an Islamic-Malay environment. About 90 percent still fail to satisfy these requirements, and as noncitizens they do not qualify for the free education and medical treatment available for Bruneis.

The sultan shows no intention of relaxing these regulations, and many Chinese feel their position has become more uncertain since 1984. Prior to this they were entitled to a Brunei British passport, but now they must be content with an International Certificate of Identity, which, in effect, renders them stateless. The number of younger Chinese applying to migrate to Canada or Australia suggests that many no longer see financial rewards as sufficient compensation for exclusion from full citizenship. For those who remain, the uncertainty of their future, especially if Brunei's Islamic mood should grow more demanding, cannot fail to affect their commitment to the state.

Brunei may continue to remain out of the glare of the international spotlight, but the manner in which these issues are resolved will be decisive in determining the way the country develops. The generation of Bruneis reaching adulthood in the 1990s has a greater chance of living longer, healthier, more prosperous lives than at any other period in the country's history. It remains to be seen if the pragmatism that has helped Brunei survive past changes in its fortunes can be combined with the tolerance and vision that will be necessary to meet the challenges of the 21st century.

FURTHER READING

Andaya, Barbara Watson and Andaya, Leonard Y. *A History of Malaysia*. London: Macmillan, 1982.
Bedlington, Stanley S. *Malaysia and Singapore: The Building of New States*. Ithaca, New York: Cornell University Press, 1978.
Brown, D. E., *Brunei. The Structure and History of a Bornean Malay Sultanate*. Monograph of the *Brunei Museum Journal*, vol. 2, no. 2, 1970.
Horton, A. V. M. *The British Residency in Brunei, 1906–1959*. Occasional Paper No. 6. Hull: Centre for Southeast Asian Studies, 1984.
Leifer, Michael. "Decolonization and International Status, the Experience of Brunei." *International Affairs* (April 1978) 240–52.
Tarling, Nicholas. *Britain, the Brookes and Brunei*. Kuala Lumpur and New York: Oxford University Press, 1971.

Southeast Asian Affairs, published annually since 1974 by the Institute of Southeast Asian Studies, Singapore, and *Far Eastern Economic Review Yearbook,* also published annually, provide valuable interpretations of the contemporary scene in Brunei.

CAMBODIA

DAVID CHANDLER

THE State of Cambodia, a socialist state in Southeast Asia, covers approximately 69,498 sq. miles/180,000 sq. km. It is bordered on the east by Vietnam, on the north by Laos and on the west by Thailand. Its population of 7.2 million people (1984) is predominantly agricultural. Principal crops are rice, corn, pepper and tobacco. The capital, Phnom Penh, contains about 700,000 people. Devastated by foreign invasions, mismanagement and civil war since 1970, Cambodia's export economy has not yet recovered its vitality. Development has also been hampered by the country's diplomatic isolation, which followed the establishment of the present government, aided by an invasion from Vietnam in 1978–79 and by insurgency, particularly in the normally productive northwestern sector of the country. The government of the State of Cambodia, closely allied with Vietnam, has devoted its energies to rebuilding the country's infrastructure, educating its children and combating guerrilla forces affiliated with the previous regime.

HISTORY

The territory that constitutes present-day Cambodia has been inhabited for at least 5,000 years, and probably longer; a cave in the northwestern part of the country indicates that a pottery-making people lived there about 4000 B.C. Where these people came from, what they looked like and what languages they spoke are still debated by scholars, but it is likely that well before the beginning of the Christian era the inhabitants of Cambodia spoke languages related to present-day Khmer, itself related to minority languages in Thailand, Vietnam, Laos, Malaysia and Burma (now Myanmar).

These early people, according to scattered archaeological evidence, knew about bronze casting. They domesticated pigs, dogs and water buffalos. In certain areas, they lived in walled villages, in houses raised on stilts. Their diet contained a good deal of fish, and they practiced slash-and-burn agriculture, as many minority populations of Southeast Asia continue to do. Their religion was probably a mixture of reverence for ancestors and reverence for the spirits of certain sites.

About the beginning of the Christian era, a process known as Indianization, which had been going on for centuries, intensified in Cambodia and

472

elsewhere in Southeast Asia, as merchants, holy men and scholars from the Indian subcontinent fanned out across the region, partly to trade directly, partly in response to requests from local chiefs and partly to set up port cities through which to carry out trade between India and China. While the early stages are unrecorded, it is clear that Indianization was not a one-way process. Interaction took place between Indian ideas and local ones, particularly in the religious sphere. Here, the Cambodian idea of ancestor spirits, which resembles those of Vietnam and southern China, blended with the Indian cult of Siva, and the Indian cult of Vishnu blended with those attached to local chiefs.

In the early years of the Christian era a prosperous trading port developed on the southern coast of Cambodia, near the present-day village of Oc Eo. The city, and the hinterland behind it, were known to Chinese writers as Funan, and until recently this "state" was considered to be a forerunner of later Cambodian ones. It now seems likely that no such state existed, and that the port was one of such small port kingdoms strung along the southern coast of Southeast Asia. The city was abandoned around the 5th century A.D., and soon afterward the first dated stone inscriptions, in Sanskrit and Khmer, appear on Cambodian soil. Before the 9th century, however, inscriptions and Chinese-language evidence fail to prove the existence of large, unified kingdoms. Thus, the belief that a strong kingdom known as Chenla succeeded Funan is no longer given much credit by scholars. The evidence points instead to scattered, small kingdoms, each with an absolute ruler, often warring and trading with each other and occasionally allied. Society was stratified—the majority of the population was classified as slaves—but the Hindu caste system per se never took root. Hinduism, in fact, often existed side by side with Buddhism and older local cults.

Angkor civilization
In the 8th century, Cambodia became politically coherent. What brought this about is still debated, and was probably a combination of a series of military victories by a strong leader (later known as King Jayavarman II), demographic growth and improvements in agricultural technology that privileged the area to the north of Cambodia's Great Lake, the Tonle Sap. It was here, in the vicinity of the modern city of Siemreap, that the so-called civilization of Angkor (A.D. c.802–c.1350) developed. In its heyday, this kingdom, known in its own inscriptions as Kambuja-desa, was the most powerful on the mainland of Southeast Asia. It was able to extract tribute from populations as far away as peninsular Malaya, northern Laos, central Thailand and Vietnam.

Because several hundred stone inscriptions, in Sanskrit and Khmer, have survived from Angkor, many of them precisely dated, it is possible to re-create the chronological framework of the kingdom. (No literary evidence has survived.) Hundreds of stone temples, including the world's largest surviving religious monument, Angkor Wat (built in the 12th century), attest to the religious fervor of the Angkorean elite, the skill of its artisans and the material prosperity of the kingdom. Extensive irrigation works in the temple area not only served the rice fields but also were waterways to

473

transport building materials to construction sites and further evidence of a given monarch's grandeur. The temples themselves were often built to serve, eventually, as royal mausoleums. Smaller ones were for elite or priestly families. Inscriptions indicate that many temples had annexes, built in perishable materials, housing monks, scholars, dancers, servants and artisans. Angkor was a dense conglomeration of villages rather than a city along Mediterranean lines. In the 12th century, however, it probably encompassed more people than any city in the Western world.

The inscriptions are concerned with elite behavior but also include information about individual temples. The bas-reliefs of several temples, notably the Bayon (13th century), show scenes of village life not markedly different from that of the French colonial era in the 1860s. Although the temple sites were abandoned more or less definitively in the 15th century, several "Angkorean" relationships lingered on into post-Angkorean times and influenced Cambodian behavior. These traditions, of course, were widespread in Hinduized and Buddhist Southeast Asia. They included the notion that an individual king, endowed with extraordinary merit, resided (however incompetent he might be) at the apex of the kingdom, while those below owed him service, allegiance and respect. The relationship of master/servant and patron/client repeated itself along the chain of human relationships in courts, villages and families. Thus, in traditional Cambodia, one's position in the chain, in theory at least, determined one's freedom of movement.

Ideally, such a system should have kept the kingdom in balance. In practice, Cambodian politics have always been dominated by rivalries, factions and violence and by the tensions inherent between familial and village obligations and sociability on the one hand and deference and service owed to higher authorities on the other. Because of the grandeur of Angkorean civilization, "discovered" by the French in the 1850s, and because of the contrast it formed, materially at least, with most subsequent Cambodian cultures, Cambodia, other than Zimbabwe, is the only country in the world to feature a ruin on its successive national flags.

The temples of Angkor Wat and the complex known as Angkor Thom (literally, "Big City") were built in the 12th and 13th centuries, during the height of the Angkor Empire. Angkor Wat, dedicated to Vishnu, was the mausoleum for Suryavarman II and took over 20 years to build. Its bas-reliefs, depicting warfare, kingly processions and scenes from the Indian epic known as the *Ramayana,* cover over 2½ miles/4 km. of wall. Recent scholarship has shown that the dimensions of the temple were keyed, numerologically, to astronomical calculations. The ruler responsible for Angkor Thom, Jayavarman VII (r. 1178–c. 1220), unlike most of his predecessors, was a Buddhist, who came to power after ruinous wars with Cambodia's neighbor to the east, the Hindu kingdom of Champa. For the remainder of the 12th century, Jayavarman supervised the most extensive building program of any Cambodian king.

During his reign, or soon afterward, many Cambodians converted to Buddhism. Interestingly, they did not choose the variety espoused by Jayavarman—the so-called Mahayana, or Great Vehicle, still practiced in

474

northern Asia and Vietnam—but the Theravada (also called Hinayana, or Lesser Vehicle), now practiced in Laos, Thailand, Myanmar and Sri Lanka. It seems likely, in fact, that Theravada missionaries came to Cambodia from what are now Thailand and Burma, as well as from Sri Lanka. This sect paid less attention to the divine or semidivine attributes of kingship, stressed by Jayavarman, and more to individual salvation.

In the 13th and 14th centuries, as these changes were taking place, Angkor was subjected to attacks from former tributary states to the west, which by the mid-13th century had consolidated into the Thai kingdom of Ayudhya, the forerunner of present-day Thailand. At Angkor, temple building slowed, and inscriptions were carved less frequently. By 1431, when Thai forces invaded Angkor for the last time, most Cambodians who had inhabited the area had either been taken off to Thailand as prisoners of war or had moved southeastward, to the vicinity of Phnom Penh, where the Cambodian capital has been located ever since.

The "fall" of Angkor was a protracted process, with many causes, and it is poorly documented. The substitution of Phnom Penh for Angkor probably reflected a conscious choice among the Khmer elite to move to a region that was more accessible to international trade, less easy for the Thai to invade and less dependent on intensive agriculture.

Beginnings of the modern state
From the 15th century until the 1780s, Cambodia was a small but prosperous kingdom, able to withstand occasional Thai attacks and feed its people while maintaining a rich literary and cultural tradition. It played a minor role in European colonization of Southeast Asia, welcoming trade delegations from the Philippines and the Netherlands Indies. These conditions changed sharply in the 1760s, when Ayudhya fell to a Burmese invasion. The new Thai monarch, Taksin, who sought to rebuild Thai prestige after the Burmese had left, did so in part by renewing attacks on Cambodia, by this stage in no position to offer much resistance. By the late 1770s, a massive social upheaval in Vietnam, known as the Tay Son movement, had spilled over into Cambodia. Also, Vietnam's "march to the south" in the 17th century had meant that many Khmer-speaking parts of southern Vietnam, nominally under the control of Cambodian kings, passed into Vietnamese hands. This series of events, and the loss of Cambodian sovereignty involved, have remained a bone of contention between the two countries ever since.

By 1782, a new dynasty took power in Bangkok. Cambodia was temporarily without a king, and its people were liable to attacks from Thailand and Vietnam. In the 1790s, the Thai placed a young Cambodian prince, named Eng, on the Cambodian throne and offered him their protection. Thai suzerainty persisted until about 1811, when Eng's son, Chan, chose to throw off Thai patronage in exchange for protection from Vietnam. The Thai attempt to overthrow Chan with a military invasion in 1833 was defeated, and the Vietnamese imposed a protectorate of Cambodia, in some respects foreshadowing the one their descendants established in 1979. However, a widespread popular rebellion, followed by another Thai invasion, led, in 1848, to the retreat of the Vietnamese and the reestablishment of Thai protection.

French colonialism

By the late 1850s, the French had established a colonial presence in southern Vietnam. Hopeful that the unmapped Mekong River would lead them to the riches of China, they established a protectorate over Cambodia in 1863. It seems likely that the Cambodian king, Norodom, thought he could use French protection to extract concessions from the Thai. In fact, by the end of the 1860s, Thai influence in Cambodia had been replaced by French control, which intensified over the remainder of the 19th century, particularly after an anti-French rebellion was crushed in the 1880s. When Norodom died in 1904, he was succeeded by his brother, Sisowath, long a favorite of the French.

The French colonial era brought several benefits to Cambodia. The most important of these was that it provided a breathing space after nearly a century of domination by Vietnam, Thailand or both. The French also restored many of the ruins at Angkor, and French scholars worked out the chronological outlines of early Cambodian history. Jayavarman VII, long forgotten, became a powerful symbol of Cambodia's past. Finally, by constructing a network of roads, by establishing rubber plantations and by linking Cambodia to international markets for its agricultural products, the French brought the Cambodian people into a world larger than their villages and larger than Southeast Asia.

At the same time, however, French expenditures on education were minimal. At the beginning of World War II, when there were over 3 million Cambodians, the country had fewer than half a dozen university graduates, and only one functioning high school. Political institutions were also neglected, and so was industry. Thus, most of Cambodia's social institutions remained unchanged, and the French, deliberately, did nothing to prepare Cambodia for the strains and benefits of the modern world. Finally, by linking Cambodia administratively with their other possessions in Indochina, the French strengthened links between Cambodia and Vietnam in ways that few if any Cambodians, including members of the royal family, approved.

Independence

In 1941, Japanese troops, with the consent of the French authorities, occupied several key locations in Cambodia, but the French remained in administrative control until March 1945, when the Japanese, fearing Allied landings in Indochina, imprisoned all French citizens. For several months, Cambodia enjoyed a period of semi-independence, led by their recently crowned king, Norodom Sihanouk (b. 1922). When the French returned to Indochina at the end of 1945, they were obliged to negotiate with the Cambodians to retain their political and economic interests. This meant that Cambodia was allowed to have a constitution and political parties. The constitution, unsurprisingly, resembled that of the recently established Fourth Republic in France.

476

The most powerful political party, the Democrats, urged independence from France with more fervor than young King Sihanouk was able to muster. Armed resistance to the French throughout Indochina was directed to a large extent by the Vietnamese Communist party, aided in Cambodia by local guerrillas known as the Khmer Issarak. By 1953, however, with French encouragement, Sihanouk dissolved the National Assembly, dominated by the Democrats, and then surprised the French by demanding independence himself. When the king threatened to mobilize hundreds of thousands of young Cambodians into an anti-French militia, the French caved in and gave Cambodia nearly total independence. The remaining components followed the Geneva Accords of 1954. The Communists, who had done so much to force the French from Indochina, gained little in Cambodia.

In 1955, Sihanouk moved against the Democrats, and against local Communists as well, by founding a political movement, the Sangkum Reastr Niyum, or Popular Socialist Community, opposed in principal to all political parties. Just before the elections, Sihanouk abdicated as king and, as a private citizen, led the Sangkum in the legislative elections. The Sangkum gained all the seats in the Assembly, eliminating the Democrats as a force in Cambodian life and forcing local Communists underground. Sangkum candidates also won all the seats in elections held in 1958, 1962 and 1966. Indeed, throughout this period, Sihanouk dominated the Cambodian media and every aspect of Cambodian political life. Internationally, he chose to follow a neutralist foreign policy, distancing himself from South Vietnam and Thailand, whose regimes were allied with the United States. At the same time, between 1955 and 1963, Sihanouk accepted over $400 million worth of U.S. aid, much of it for his army. When he rejected further aid in 1963, he called it "humiliating," but no other power ever provided him with as much assistance.

In fact, as the 1960s wore on, discontent in Cambodia intensified, and Vietnamese insurgents began to carve out sanctuaries in Cambodian territory. The indigenous Cambodian Communists, a small clandestine group led after 1962 by Saloth Sar, a schoolteacher who had studied in France, took advantage of these conditions to recruit followers, and by 1968 had launched a widespread but not particularly effective armed resistance to Sihanouk's regime. Sihanouk's response was to renew diplomatic relations with the United States (broken off in 1965), to allow U.S. bombing of Vietnamese sanctuaries on Cambodian soil and to cede a good deal of political power to conservative politicians, such as General Lon Nol, the commander of the army. At this stage, he feared that a Communist victory in Vietnam, which he had long predicted, would lead to his overthrow as chief of state. Like many other observers, he overestimated the loyalty of Cambodian Communists for their Vietnamese colleagues.

Coup and Vietnamese domination
In March 1970, while Sihanouk was traveling in Europe, he was deposed by the National Assembly. Pressure to overthrow him came from Cambodia's merchant elite, from discontented right wing and centrist politicians, from members of the army humiliated by Vietnamese Communist occupa-

tion of Cambodian territory and, in Phnom Penh, from the majority of young, educated Khmer. In his final years of power, Sihanouk had allowed his entourage to amass large fortunes, while he himself, increasingly absorbed in filmmaking, had seemed to lose touch with the Cambodian people. U.S. involvement in the coup was widely suspected at the time but never proved, and it is doubtful that the coup served long- or even short-term American political interests.

From Beijing, Sihanouk declared a government-in-exile, allying himself with the Cambodian Communists against whom, only a month before, his government had been waging war. The alliance meant that his government-in-exile could count on support from China, North Korea and North Vietnam, and also that Vietnamese Communist troops could now occupy even larger portions of Cambodia. A U.S. military incursion in May–June 1970 had the effect of pushing these forces out of their frontier bases, westward into Cambodia. Lon Nol's army, untrained, often badly led and poorly equipped, offered little systematic resistance. By the end of July, Vietnamese troops had overrun the border areas, several provincial capitals and large parts of the interior. With the exception of a couple of provincial capitals, retaken at enormous cost, these areas never returned to the control of Lon Nol's government.

In Phnom Penh, that government retained its popularity for about a year. In October 1970, it declared itself a republic, ostensibly bringing to an end over 1,200 years of monarchy in Cambodia. The move was welcomed by the urban elite, but made the chances for a compromise settlement with Sihanouk even more remote. Lon Nol and his colleagues squandered their popularity by a series of disastrous military campaigns, rigged elections and monumental corruption, particularly among the officer corps. More able administrators, like In Tam and Sisowath Sirik Matak, were brushed aside and others were exported as ambassadors.

In the countryside, Cambodian Communist troops gradually took on more of the burdens of combat. In liberated zones, after 1973, these forces— who called themselves *angkar,* or "The Organization"—had introduced collectivization, partly in response to devastating U.S. air bombardment (halted at the insistence of the U.S. Congress in August 1973) and partly to demonstrate that they were no longer taking orders from the Vietnamese.

U.S. involvement in Cambodia meant propping up the Lon Nol regime, largely by pouring in hundreds of millions of dollars of military aid. By 1974, military activity had slowed down, the republican government had lost its credibility and over 2 million refugees had sought shelter, under appalling conditions, in Phnom Penh, Battambang and other cities that remained under republican control. The U.S. government, meanwhile, was enmeshed in the Watergate scandal, and presidential efforts to increase aid to Cambodia as the Vietnam War wound down encountered congressional resistance. In April 1975, three weeks before the fall of Saigon, Cambodian Communist troops entered Phnom Penh, in the name of Sihanouk's united front government, and brought the republican period to an end. Many survivors now claim that these troops were welcomed by a population weary with war and longing for a more honest regime than what Lon Nol and his colleagues had been able or willing to provide.

Over the next few days, these hopes were dashed, for everyone in the city (and within a week, everyone in other republican towns) was driven into the countryside, walking in some cases for weeks on end, before being allowed to settle in rural districts and become "poor peasants." These refugees were called "new people" by the regime. Almost overnight, everything in Cambodia was transformed. Money, markets, postal communications, personal property, formal education and religious activity—to name only a few—were abolished. Western medical practices, by and large, were forbidden; so were foreign languages, Western-style clothing, jewelry and sports. Under the clandestine guidance of the Communist Party of Kampuchea (which still called itself The Organization) everyone in Cambodia was mobilized over the next few months in a breakneck, utopian effort to "build and defend" the country, Cambodia's "2,000 years of history" were deemed to have ended on April 17, 1975, when Phnom Penh had come into Communist hands. A new era had begun, and radio broadcasts promised that Cambodia would move beyond socialism to communism faster than any other country in the world. The major decisions over the next three years were made by a handful of veteran Communists, led by Saloth Sar, who now called himself Pol Pot. Others included Nuon Chea, Ieng Sary, Son Sen and Vorn Vet.

The costs of imposing their all-inclusive vision on a poorly equipped, conservative and exhausted population were enormous, particularly since vengeful and uneducated cadres were encouraged to hate and destroy all vestiges of nonrevolutionary life. Parallels can be found to the Cultural Revolution in China, but the Cambodian experience, in terms of violence, was more severe. Over the next three years, at least 1 million Cambodians (one in eight of the population) died of causes directly related to the regime. Some estimates run higher. Beginning in 1976, deaths from starvation, assassination, beatings, executions, overwork, and misdiagnosed diseases were supplemented by killings of "traitors" to the Communist party. Surviving records indicate that at least 40,000 of these men, women and children were interrogated, tortured and put to death in 1976–78. The actual number is probably higher. These included many who had served the party in the united front period, others who came home from abroad to join the revolution after April 1975 and still others who had belonged to the party in its pro-Vietnamese phase in the 1950s. Prince Sihanouk, brought back to Cambodia from China in 1976, spent these two years in Phnom Penh, out of touch with the leaders of the regime, but under relatively comfortable conditions.

In 1977, sporadic fighting along the border with Vietnam, in most cases instigated by the Cambodians, erupted into warfare and culminated in a Vietnamese invasion in January 1978. By this time, probably responding to pressure from China, itself at odds with Vietnam, the Communist Party of Kampuchea (CPK) had at last admitted its existence and had taken all the credit for Cambodia's transformation. As conditions worsened with

Vietnam, the regime made belated efforts to seek diplomatic support outside the Communist bloc. In October 1978, it announced an amnesty of the population, abolishing the category of "new people."

By that time, a revolt and widespread purges had devastated much of eastern Cambodia. People who had sought refuge in Vietnam, or had been herded there by Vietnamese troops, were formed by the Vietnamese into a resistance movement. In December 1978, allegedly acting in support of this movement, Vietnamese forces invaded Cambodia, overran Cambodian defenses and within 10 days had captured Phnom Penh. Pol Pot and his advisers fled to bases in the northwest. Prince Sihanouk, flown out of Cambodia at the last minute, pleaded Cambodia's cause before the United Nations and then took up residence in China. Over the next 12 months, while the Vietnamese consolidated their client regime—soon known as the People's Republic of Kampuchea (PRK)—in Phnom Penh, their forces drove most of Pol Pot's army across the border into Thailand.

The new government moved cautiously at first, allowing people far more freedom than they had enjoyed for several years. Hundred of thousands took to the roads, searching for lost relatives, trying to return to former homes or seeking refuge in Thailand, where the United Nations had set up refugee camps along the border. In 1979–1983, nearly 1 million Cambodians passed through these camps on their way to residence abroad. About 400,000 more sought refuge in other camps along the Thai-Cambodian border, where they were exploited by the Thai, shelled by the Vietnamese and recruited by Cambodian resistance forces. The strongest of these was made up of remnants of Pol Pot's army, fed by the Thai and rearmed, with Thai permission, by the Chinese.

After 1981, the PRK introduced a new constitution and held elections for a representative assembly. The Kampuchean People's Revolutionary party, under Vietnamese guidance, took political control of the country. Its members were drawn at first from the ranks of Cambodian Communists who had spent the 1960s and 1970s in North Vietnam or from former Democratic Kampuchea (DK) cadres who had fled to Vietnam in 1977 and 1978. The latter group included the president of the PRK, Heng Samrin, and the prime minister, Hun Sen. After 1985, membership in the party was opened up to people who had never been members of any Communist faction.

Resistance to the PRK was slow to develop. To an extent, this was due to the horrific reputation which Pol Pot's regime had earned. Exhausted survivors were unwilling or unable to take up arms. The CPK, attempting to improve its image, formally dissolved in 1981, but none of its leaders was dismissed, and it seems likely that the clandestine, central apparatus of the party remained intact. In the same year, a reequipped Communist army had begun guerrilla operations from its bases along the Thai border against the Vietnamese. Under pressure from China, the United States and the ASEAN powers, Prince Sihanouk, who had played no important role in postwar Cambodian politics, was persuaded in 1981 to join a coalition consisting of himself and his supporters, the Pol Pot faction and a faction led by Son Sann, an elderly former Cambodian prime minister, long in exile in France. This coalition "government," which controlled no significant territory inside Cambodia, was recognized by most members of the United Nations, in deference to China and the United States. It was the only government-in-exile to receive this kind of recognition. The PRK, on the other hand, was recognized diplomatically only by India, the socialist bloc and some left-leaning Third World regimes.

For several years, the stalemate continued. In 1988, however, international pressure and a convergence of national interests began to produce some changes. Encouraged to do so by the USSR, the Vietnamese withdrew over 50,000 of their remaining troops from Cambodia, placed the remaining ones under tactical PRK command and promised to complete their withdrawal by 1990. In fact, the last troops were withdrawn before the end of 1989. Fighting diminished as the resistance forces maneuvered for political advantage. In mid-1989, many observers were confident that some sort of settlement might be worked out between the three factions of the coalition government on the one hand and the PRK and the Vietnamese on the other. Sihanouk, a key figure in Cambodian political life for nearly half a century, was expected to play an important role in these developments. Other observers, however, were worried by the recalcitrant, and heavily armed, DK faction. Some feared the reimposition of the terror of the 1970s. Others doubted that these hardened fighters had the faith in a compromise solution that is so essential to the survival, or the reemergence, of a recognizable Cambodian state.

ECONOMY

When the French established their protectorate in 1863, Cambodia's economy was based on subsistence agriculture, with exports limited to dried fish, spices and forest products. Under the French, Cambodia became a rice-exporting country, and after the 1920s, when rubber plantations were established in the eastern part of the country, a producer of high-grade rubber as well. Other exports in the colonial era included pepper, cattle, corn, timber and kapok. The French used revenue from export taxes primarily to pay for public works; the roads that soon crisscrossed Cambodia and the railroad between Battambang and Phnom Penh aided the process of urbanization and helped Cambodians to transport their goods to market.

The First Indochina War disrupted Cambodia's exports, as well as the collection of taxes levied on land. With independence, increased expenditures on education, new military expenditures and a vastly expanded civil service forced the Cambodian government to operate at a deficit, which was "balanced" by injections of foreign aid. The principal donor between 1955 and 1963 was the United States, which provided over $400 million of assistance to public works, agriculture, teacher education and the police, as well as paying for military equipment and the salaries for the Cambodian army.

Other powers, particularly from the Communist bloc, provided Cambodia with a fragile industrial base. Factories were established, for example, to manufacture cotton textiles, tires, glass, plywood and cement. For the most part, however, the factories were mismanaged, and industrialization never proceeded very far, although light industry, especially enterprises connected with rice milling and timber, flourished in those years. One hopeful development in the 1950s was the opening of Cambodia's deep-water port at Kompong Som (renamed Sihanoukville), which freed the country from its commercial dependence on Vietnam.

In 1963, Sihanouk broke off U.S. aid and sought to balance the loss with aid from other countries, particularly China, but the same amounts were not forthcoming. At the same time, Sihanouk nationalized Cambodia's import-export trade and the banking system in an effort to wrest their control from "foreign" (i.e., French and ethnic Chinese) interests; Cambodia's valuable rubber plantations, however, remained for the most part under French control. Sihanouk's moves were popular at first, because they seemed to demonstrate Cambodian independence, but mismanagement of state enterprises, in several cases by members of Sihanouk's entourage, soon alienated the commercial elite.

By 1966–67, when the war in Vietnam was at its height, clandestine trade in rice between Cambodian farmers and the Communist insurgents, accounting for 40 percent of the export crop, deprived the government of earnings and alienated even more members of the elite from Sihanouk's regime. Under the Khmer Republic, foreign invasions, bombings and civil war tore Cambodia apart. The years of Communist control, in commercial terms, were even worse. By 1988, Cambodia had still not regained its export capacity or its commercial infrastructure. Always one of the poorest countries in Southeast Asia, Cambodia had at least been self-sufficient in food before the 1970s. In the 1980s, however, the disruptions of war, the Vietnamese occupation, pressures from abroad and local inexperience frequently led to food shortages, while the absence of entrepreneurs and a run-down infrastructure meant that Cambodians had to learn the art of marketing their products, domestically and overseas, from the ground up. Because of Cambodia's diplomatic isolation, imposed by China and the United States, government-to-government foreign aid was confined to the Communist bloc, plus India, and such nongovernmental aid as could be funneled into the country via church groups and others. Through 1988, ASEAN, China and the United States continued to aid the coalition government, in its camps in Thailand, thus forestalling a political settlement.

PROSPECTS

In the summer of 1989, spirited negotiations got under way regarding Cambodia's fate. They were spurred on by a growing willingness on the part of China and the Soviet Union to resolve outstanding differences. One of these had been, since 1979, the Vietnamese occupation of Cambodia, China's former client. Vietnamese troop withdrawals began, and the coalition government-in-exile began talks with the PRK regime, encouraged to do so by the Vietnamese and the Soviet Union. The armed forces affiliated with DK, perhaps 35,000 strong, and the fact that the leaders of DK were the same ones who had presided over the deaths of so many Khmer in

482

1975–79, posed difficulties to the negotiators, and so did long-standing mutual distrust. The Vietnamese pledge to withdraw all their troops by 1990 added some urgency to the negotiations, shared by the ASEAN states, which had, throughout the 1980s, been more concerned with "punishing" Vietnam. It was hoped that growing cooperation among larger powers, and pressure from the Cambodians themselves, would dislodge the Cambodian Communists as a force in Cambodian politics; but the Communists showed no willingness to be removed, considering themselves the rightful rulers of the country; no one seemed willing to take up arms against them. This combination of factors meant that one prospect awaiting Cambodia after the Vietnamese withdrawal was a protracted civil war, of the sort that the country has endured, with brief respites, since 1970.

FURTHER READING

Becker, Elizabeth. *When the War Was Over: Cambodia's Revolution and the Voices of its People.* New York: Simon & Schuster, 1986.

Chandler, David P. *A History of Cambodia.* Boulder, Colorado: Westview Press, 1983.

———, and Kiernan, Ben, eds. *Revolution and its Aftermath in Kampuchea: Eight Essays.* New Haven, Connecticut: Yale University Press, 1983.

Kiernan, Ben. *How Pol Pot Came to Power: A History of Communism in Kampuchea, 1938–1975.* London: Verso, 1985.

Ponchaud, François. *Cambodia: Year Zero.* New York: Holt, Rinehart & Winston, 1978.

Vickery, Michael, *Cambodia, 1975–1982.* Boston: South End Press, 1984.

———. *Kampuchea.* London: F. Pinter, 1986.

CHINA

ANDREW G. WALDER

INTRODUCTION

THE establishment of the People's Republic of China punctuated a historical experience different from that of China's Asian neighbors. It was never colonized outright, like India or Vietnam. Yet unlike Japan, it saw its isolation and territorial integrity rapidly erode after the Opium War of the 1840s. A once-proud empire and civilization, already in the beginning stages of the political decline of the Ch'ing (or Manchu) dynasty, began a downward spiral into chaos that culminated in the warlord period of the late 1910s through mid-1930s, and then the Japanese invasion and occupation of the mid-1930s to mid-1940s. Only four years after the defeat of Japan, Mao Zedong in October 1949 would declare the establishment of the People's Republic—the only enduringly unified government that China has known in the 20th century.

Much about this historical experience explains the victory of the Communist party in 1949. China was never colonized and subject to the kind of stable foreign administration that the British, French and others lent to their colonial dependencies. Instead, the Ch'ing dynasty lost a series of small wars against imperialist powers, starting with the British in the 1840s. Under the guise of "free trade," the British militarily battered the Chinese for daring to interdict the importation of opium, seizing the island of Hong Kong and forcing China to grant it special trading privileges in several coastal cities. There would be a series of humiliating defeats into the early 1900s by the British, French, Germans, Russians, Japanese and others. By the turn of the 20th century, these foreign powers had carved out districts in many coastal and inland ports, "foreign concessions" subject not to Chinese but to foreign law. They claimed special trading rights; they issued their own currency; and their armed forces patrolled Chinese waters and territory to protect their interests. This slow political and economic dismemberment, occurring in a proud but decaying empire where a Chinese dynasty still technically was sovereign, would fuel Chinese nationalism and make territorial integrity a principle of paramount importance for China's future revolutionaries.

The counterpart to this decline in Chinese sovereignty over its own soil was a decline in the central government's ability to exert control over various regions of the country. The trend began shortly after the Opium War.

484

The Taiping Rebellion of the 1850s was one of the most disastrous civil wars in human history. Tens of millions died; cities were laid waste and the inhabitants massacred. For a number of years the rebels held huge areas of southern and central China and almost succeeded in toppling the emperor, who was hastily propped up by imperialist powers at the end. The rebels were defeated, but only by expanding the military powers of regional governments, who would play an expanded role in guarding against the smaller regional rebellions that persisted for the rest of the century, and growing social banditry in the hinterlands. While dramatic in its own right, the history of rebellion and regional militarization served to undermine central Chinese government control and strengthen regional officials and military commanders. When the Ch'ing dynasty finally fell in 1911, China quickly descended into a collection of local civilian and military powers, or "warlords."

National unity and territorial integrity thus became the two supreme values for China's 20th-century revolutionaries. The Nationalist party, at first allied with the Communists, made the first serious effort at national unification in its Northern Expedition of 1926–27. Moving north from Canton, they confronted warlords with their armed forces, while fomenting peasant uprisings and general strikes in the rear. After a massive general strike and the conquest of Shanghai in 1927, however, Chiang Kai-shek suddenly expelled Communists from the alliance and systematically imprisoned and executed all party members he could find. From that time forward, the Communists would concentrate on an independent rural strategy of revolution. The Nationalists' subsequent unification of the rest of China would take place not through military conquest coupled with revolutionary social agitation, but through alliances and political deals with the remaining regional warlords.

The Nationalists' attempt to rule a unified China in the "Nanking Decade" (1927–37) was troubled from the beginning. From the outset, it was less a unitary central government than a federation based on alliances with regional warlords. Growing Japanese militarism resulted in the occupation and annexation of Manchuria in the early to mid-1930s, and increasing pressures elsewhere in north and east China. The Communists were beginning to develop viable rural bases, at first in south and central China, and were able to survive a concerted series of "extermination campaigns" in the early 1930s, finally escaping through the "Long March" to establish its famous northern base area and later wartime capital of Yenan (Yan'an). Generals who headed armies from the areas occupied by the Japanese, and students throughout China, protested the Nationalists' perceived failure to confront Japanese aggression. Finally, the full-scale subsequent Japanese invasion of 1937, the first violent phase of what would later become the war in the Pacific, forced the Nationalists to evacuate most of China and retreat to Chongqing.

Historians now debate whether the rapid Communist victory after the Pacific war was the result more of Nationalist failure than of Communist success. The Nationalists never successfully reestablished control after the Japanese surrender. Their increasingly harsh police repression of dissidents alienated many urban educated and business classes; the evident corruption of their local officials offended both peasants and urbanites; and runaway inflation devastated the economy.

However historians may weigh Nationalist ineptitude versus Communist competence in explaining the outcome of 1949, there is general agreement that the Communists, unlike the Nationalists, molded an effectively disciplined and highly motivated fighting force, one that enjoyed considerable logistical support from rural areas. This tradition of political organization and discipline, developed over more than a decade of rural party experience, would greatly shape the regime that followed from its victory. Communist revolutionary cadres were intensely indoctrinated, selected for their single-minded commitment to the cause and expected to display unswerving obedience to the party's current revolutionary line. The party official of the military unit or a territory was the law within his jurisdiction. Those who displayed the most unerring loyalty would embark upon careers in a growing national political apparatus.

This conception of the political cadre—of loyalty, discipline and obedience to the dictates of the supreme leaders and their doctrine—effectively molded a revolutionary fighting force. Naturally, the Communists translated this fighting force into a form of government administration after 1949. They created a national party apparatus, a "parallel government" stretching from the capital to the grass roots. Every government office, factory, school and village was placed under the leadership of a party committee and its ranking member, a party secretary. Hundreds of thousands of revolutionary officers were transferred to these powerful civilian posts. The secretaries were the supreme authority in their jurisdictions, deciding all major questions, making staffing and career decisions and allocating housing, opportunities for schooling and many other things. Their actions were restrained not by a civilian legal system but only by the discipline of their superiors in the regional and national party organization. The party integrated and disciplined the nation, and was to serve as the engine for the massive social transformations planned by the Communist party. But as the Communists translated this conception into subsequent government practice, they would witness, along with the dreamed-for national unity and territorial integrity, a number of tragic consequences.

CHINA'S POSTREVOLUTION HISTORY

Today's China is the product of two starkly opposed periods of its recent history. Two dominating leaders headed the country during these years. They used their powers in very different ways and toward very different ends. In the first period, Mao Zedong's fundamentalist radicalism, which began to emerge on the Chinese stage in the late 1950s, erupted in China's disastrous Great Leap Forward of 1958 to 1960 and the tragic Cultural Revolution of 1966 to 1969, and cast a heavy shadow over the country until the old revolutionary's death in September 1976. In the second period, Deng Xiaoping reemerged from political limbo after Mao's death and, in a spirit of flexible and moderate reformism, proceeded to push a startling series of economic and political changes that by the mid-1980s appeared to have undone much of Mao's legacy. In the process, China, once one of the most xenophobic, inaccessible, rigidly Leninist and economically backward of Communist regimes, became one of the more cosmopolitan, open, ideologically flexible and economically dynamic.

In different ways, both Mao and Deng were radicals who sought far-reaching changes in their party and nation, while seeking to offer a new vision of socialism. Yet their styles of doing so, and their relative success, provide a study in sharp contrasts. Mao, despite his occasional and unconvincing disclaimers, styled himself a genius and visionary worthy of emulation and worship, largely removing himself from practical matters but periodically intervening in Chinese life in destructive political campaigns. He fostered a harshly repressive regime of political intolerance and thought control, and closed China's borders to the influence of foreign ideas and life-styles, largely destroying China's educational system and persecuting intellectuals in an effort literally to remake human nature so as to fit the requirements of a Communist utopia. In this quest, Mao found little to learn from the other Socialist countries, much less from the capitalist ones. From the relatively conservative Soviets to the more progressive Czech and Yugoslav reformers, Mao's China declared the other Socialist regimes "revisionists" who had taken the capitalist road. Only the xenophobic regimes of Albania, Korea and Vietnam would retain China's approval.

Deng Xiaoping, while himself brooking no opposition to his guidance of China's future from 1978 to the end of the 1980s, had no pretensions as a theorist or political visionary, and had a tough-mindedness and acerbic wit implicitly skeptical of all such claims, including Mao's. Deng involved himself in practical political and economic questions, aiming to remake China into a modern and prosperous Socialist country. Deng's dogmatism was more restrained: while firmly believing in the fundamentals of party dictatorship and a planned economy, he was more willing to allow experimentation that may on the surface contradict these fundamentals, but in the long run strengthen the economy and party. Deng sought stability and economic rationality, ending the mass political campaigns of his predecessor.

While no champion of liberalism, he sought to unshackle China's intelligentsia, rebuild the educational system and revive its managerial elite. He opened China's borders not only to foreign ideas and influences, but to extensive foreign trade and even foreign capital investment. Under him, China's intolerant disdain for foreign economic models, both capitalist and socialist, turned into an eager quest to learn from the experiences of Japan, the United States, Eastern Europe and any other country that might contribute to a new and relatively open-ended search to define "Chinese-style socialism."

While the terms "conservative" and "liberal," "left" and "right," do not fit Chinese politics very well, there is no doubt that Mao's China and Deng's occupy different ends of the political spectrum. For this reason, the nature of each leader's respective post-1949 "revolution" is best appreciated in relation to the other. Mao's China was the product of a doctrinaire effort to forestall the kind of stable reformism that Deng would come to champion in the 1980s. Deng's China emerged from an effort to repair the extensive damage wrought by the failures of Mao's Cultural Revolution. To understand the emergence of Deng's China, one therefore needs to understand the legacy of the Cultural Revolution; and to understand this, in turn, one needs to understand what the Cultural Revolution was and how it emerged out of the decade after 1956.

THE ORIGINS OF MAO'S CULTURAL REVOLUTION

In some ways, one can trace the origins of Cultural Revolution Maoism to the Chinese Communist party's experience in leading a guerrilla war against the Japanese and the Nationalists. In a way that was not true of the Soviet Communist party, the Chinese party grew to a large disciplined force, administering vast territories more than a decade before it ruled the entire nation. It was able to use Marxist-Leninist doctrine and intensive monitoring of its troops and members as the primary means of integrating its far-flung forces. Doctrinal purity and strict adherence to it in thought and deed were crucial to the party's effective functioning, survival and eventual success.[1]

This was not true of the Soviet Communist party, which seized power in a coup and had little mass base outside the labor movement in Moscow and Leningrad and the radical intelligentsia. Their Red Army would not be formed until afterward, in their civil war. By the time their power was consolidated, and Stalin's drive for collectivization and rapid industrialization began at the very end of the 1920s, the party did not have a tradition of doctrinal purity and discipline—indeed the party was still in the midst of its first great burst of growth. Moreover, the party's formative period was precisely in the midst of the great industrial transformation of the 1930s, leading Stalin to shape doctrine to the requirements of industrial development from the outset.

Given these different histories, there was bound to be tension between the Chinese and Soviet understanding of the role of Marxist-Leninist doctrine and of party leadership in the building of a socialist society. And this tension was bound to be heightened as the Chinese, isolated by U.S. and Nationalist trade and diplomatic boycotts, became more dependent on the Soviet Union. That being the case, the Chinese sought to make their practices conform to the Soviet model with the help of Soviet advisers and aid in the 1950s.

The tension, however, might have remained dormant were it not for the changes in the Soviet Union and Eastern Europe that followed Stalin's death in 1953. These changes created friction between China and the Soviet bloc

[1] See Franz Schurmann, *Ideology and Organization in Communist China* (Berkeley: University of California Press, 1968), ch. 1; and John W. Lewis, *Leadership in Communist China* (Ithaca: Cornell University Press, 1963), ch. 1.

that caused the tension suppressed during the great period of Sino-Soviet friendship to erupt in the 1960s.

While the Chinese had adapted Marxism-Leninism in their own distinctive ways in the 1930s and 1940s, the Marxism that they absorbed came to them in a Stalinist incarnation and had a great impact on the policies they pursued in the early to mid-1950s. This variety of Marxism-Leninism stressed the unbridgeable differences between socialist and imperialist camps locked in a life-and-death struggle; a corresponding necessity to struggle against the conspiracies of class enemies and traitors within the country who would sell the country out to capitalism and imperialism; an undying hostility to markets, private enterprise and profit motives as remnants of capitalism; and a devotion to collectivized and nationalized property, and centralized planning and distribution, as the harbingers of the new socialist society. This is how the Chinese understood the basic tenets of socialism and the task that faced them in the 1950s.

The death of Stalin and the rise of a reform-minded Khrushchev disrupted the Sino-Soviet relationship and brought these hidden tensions to the surface. This occurred with an event that sent shock waves throughout the Communist bloc: Khrushchev's "secret speech" to the 1956 Soviet Party Congress in which he denounced Stalin's crimes.

These criticisms were heard with alarm in many communist capitals. Khrushchev accused Stalin of intensifying a contrived "class struggle" in which he used his security services to search out and liquidate tens of thousand of imaginary "enemies of the people." He criticized Stalin for excessively rapid collectivization by force, which would cripple Soviet agriculture for decades, and for a forced-pace industrialization that would extract excessive sacrifice from citizens. And he denounced Stalin for surrounding himself with an aura of infallibility, for attacking those who challenged him as traitors and for fostering a "cult of the individual" by glorifying himself in statues and billboard portraits, as well as naming cities after himself.

As these and related criticisms were repeated and expanded upon by Soviet writers in the ensuing months, they implicitly called into question the ideological credentials of many leaders who had conformed to the Stalinist mold. Mao had already begun a personality cult of his own in the 1940s, and had even had himself named as a "great Marxist-Leninist" in the same breath with Marx, Lenin and Stalin in the party constitution (a description quickly deleted—not surprisingly—from the new 1956 constitution). He had pushed forward collectivization of agriculture and nationalization of industry much faster than the party originally planned, completing them in 1955 and 1956. And he had already promoted a series of persecution campaigns that sought to eradicate old class enemies, expunge capitalist influences among intellectuals and exercise doctrinaire control over cultural and artistic circles.

In other words, the Soviet Union under Khrushchev began to move in a different direction, leaving many Communist leaders, including Mao, in an awkward position, exposed to international and domestic criticism. Mao

489

and other Communist leaders began to conform to the new Soviet line, at least outwardly, in 1956, but there were other factors that prevented the emerging differences between the Soviets and Chinese from being papered over.

The first was the abrupt manner in which Khrushchev denounced Stalin. Neither the Chinese nor other Communist leaders were consulted or even notified beforehand. Given the explosive and potentially damaging nature of Khrushchev's attack, the failure to notify and consult was perceived as lacking in the spirit of comradely cooperation, if not an unfriendly act. In China, whose Communist party, unlike those of Eastern Europe, did not owe its power to the Soviet army, this was taken as an affront to the Chinese leadership and to Chinese national pride.

This disregard for Chinese sensibilities, in retrospect, must certainly have been made more galling by the fact that Mao himself was a genuine revolutionary, enjoying a status in his own country that matched that of both Lenin and Stalin in the Soviet Union. Khrushchev, on the other hand, was a Stalinist bureaucrat, an administrator—not a revolutionary. Mao's later emphasis on revolutionary tradition and his expressed contempt for bureaucrats may well have reflected his resentment.

Foreign policy issues were also involved. Mao had fostered a revolutionary nationalist policy in foreign relations, supporting and urging revolutions to roll back imperialism throughout the Third World. He had also supported, at a staggering cost of Chinese lives, the North Korean army, and China was already involved in backing North Vietnam. This hard line toward imperialism was connected in the Chinese mind with the recovery of Taiwan. Khrushchev, on the other hand, began to reduce tensions, seek arms reduction and hold forth the prospect of peaceful coexistence. Chinese leaders must have felt that their revolutionary and nationalist aspirations were being sold out by the Soviets.

Finally, and certainly not of least importance, was the reaction in Eastern Europe to Khrushchev's portended de-Stalinization. Leaders of many of the smaller Eastern bloc countries were under attack for their Stalinist policies. In Poland, urban unrest led to the institution of a more moderate leadership, a rollback of collectivization and a removal of older Stalinists. A Soviet invasion of Poland was barely averted. In Hungary, a similar pattern of leadership upheaval and political ferment led unexpectedly and suddenly to a full-scale revolution against Soviet domination and Communist party leadership, necessitating a massive Soviet invasion. Both events highlighted for the Chinese the potential instability that de-Stalinization might bring in its wake.[2]

The Chinese reacted to these events, and to Khrushchev's new line, conservatively. While admitting that Stalin had made certain "mistakes," they stressed that he was a great revolutionary, that he had built the first socialist country and defined the correct model for socialism. They warned

[2] See Roderick MacFarquhar, *The Origins of the Cultural Revolution,* vol. 1, *Contradictions among the People, 1956–1957* (New York: Columbia University Press, 1974), chs. 4, 6, 8, 9, 12.

that talk of de-Stalinization would only strengthen the hand of the imperialists and hidden antisocialist forces within the socialist camp. The term, they argued, gave the mistaken impression that there was something fundamentally wrong with the socialist system, rather than a few mistakes in implementation. The Chinese position was that Stalin's mistakes could be avoided by making sure that the party adhered to the correct revolutionary line, maintained a proper style of leadership and was properly disciplined in accord with its policy. In other words, Mao's leadership minimized Stalin's crimes and sought to ensure that these crimes were not identified with the socialist system that Stalin created.

To show by example the kind of remedial action through which a party might avoid Stalinism's excesses while keeping the system that created them intact, Mao pushed through an innovative policy of "blooming and contending." In early 1957, Mao proclaimed the party's desire to "let a hundred flowers blossom, let a hundred schools of thought contend." In other words, instead of forcing strict ideological conformity, he would allow criticisms of orthodox Marxism-Leninism and of the party's policies and leadership styles. He apparently felt that in this competition the correctness of the party's policies and of Marxism-Leninism would shine through, and that at the same time the party would receive criticisms that would help it in its work and sharpen its ideological positions.

But this is not what occurred. After a long period of hesitancy due to mistrust of Communist intentions, China's intellectuals, students, workers and others began to express ever more damning criticisms of the party. Moreover, local party officials began to exhibit both demoralization and disorientation, leaving the field open for ever bolder criticisms. And young party members and students who were members of the Communist Youth League joined in with the harsh critics in an idealistic effort to rectify the party's dictatorial and bureaucratic tendencies. Before long, students and workers began to organize petition drives and strikes, and local party offices even began to echo criticisms that seemed to go beyond those sanctioned in Beijing. It began to appear to some leaders that a potential "Hungarian uprising" was in the making.

The fear that these developments generated in the party can be seen in the harshness of its reaction. In June 1957, after only a couple of months of the "hundred flowers," a strong antirightist campaign completely reversed party policy. Now the hunt was on for critics who expressed doubts about the party, showing that they were in reality antisocialist elements. Tens of thousands of students and workers, many of them loyal party members, were given sentences that ranged from terms in labor camps to expulsion from the party to execution. Severe censorship and punishment for criticism were reinstituted. Marxism-Leninism became an even more aggressively enforced orthodoxy.[3]

As the purges were still sweeping across China at the end of 1957, Mao launched China's Great Leap Forward. Another of Mao's efforts to force

[3] See Mu Fusheng, *The Wilting of the Hundred Flowers* (New York: Praeger, 1962); and MacFarquhar, *The Origins of the Cultural Revolution,* chs. 15–18.

through his own vision, despite changes in the Soviets' view of things, the Great Leap sought to mobilize citizens for a massive industrialization drive that would simultaneously push China toward full communism. Small agricultural collectives were rapidly amalgamated into huge communes with collective meal halls and free supplies of food. Schools, offices and collective farms were ordered to smelt their own steel from scrap metal that they found. Thousands of small factories were organized quickly with little planning and minimal investment, and some 15 million peasants moved into the cities to work in them in 1958 alone. Existing factories were ordered to double or triple current output by any means, hiring new workers and directing their work forces to stay for double shifts, often resulting in workers eating and sleeping in the workshops. Technical specifications, safety regulations and quality controls were thrust aside by ambitious party secretaries who viewed them as "bourgeois superstitions" that held back the intrinsic creativity of the aroused masses.

Before the end of 1958 it became apparent that the Great Leap Forward could not be sustained. Neglect of safety regulations and technical standards led to an upsurge of industrial accidents, costly damage to equipment and industrial plants and the production of badly flawed or unusable products that in the end only wasted scarce supplies and fuel. The initial upsurge of production that resulted from massive speedups and overtime quickly exhausted stores of supplies and parts throughout the country. The metal produced in the "backyard steel furnaces" was little better than scrap metal. Despite all this, party secretaries under severe political pressures to report great successes to their superiors continued to do so. The foundation was slowly being laid for a man-made industrial depression.

In agriculture, these practices had more ominous consequences. Fair weather led to rich harvests in 1958 and encouraged even greater pressures to increase output beyond realistic limits. Party officials, declaring that communism was imminent, freely supplied food to peasants in collective mess halls but neglected to build up reserves. They also forced through irrational practices designed to increase output: for example, planting rice stalks closer together, vastly increasing the application of fertilizers, diverting large amounts of labor for new construction projects, quickly harvesting only the biggest root crops and leaving the smaller tubers to rot. By 1959 these unwise practices, combined with poor weather in some areas, led to serious crop failures in vast stretches of the country and the depletion of grain reserves. Meanwhile, the state continued to procure and remove from the countryside large amounts of grain, based on targets premised on inflated crop estimates. The Great Leap Forward was laying the groundwork for a great man-made famine.[4]

By 1959, what was already evident to ordinary citizens was becoming obvious to many party leaders: The Greap Leap Forward threatened disastrous consequences. Peng Dehuai, leader of China's armed forces, reported these problems to Mao at a party meeting in late 1959, and was purged as

[4] See Thomas Bernstein, "Stalinism, Famine, and Chinese Peasants," *Theory and Society* 13 (May 1984), pp. 1–38.

a result. Moreover, the "anti-right-wing elements" campaign swept over the country and purged ordinary party members and officials who had dared to express doubts about the Great Leap. Having thus blinded itself, Mao's party machine lumbered on to disaster.[5]

By 1960 industry was in a shambles. Supplies of basic raw materials and fuel were exhausted. The work force was dispirited and suffering from overwork and emerging food shortages. Vast amounts of hastily manufactured products were useless and contributed to the shortage of inputs. From 1960 to 1962, almost 20 million workers were fired and sent back to the countryside. Severe shortages of most consumer goods plagued citizens for many years, and a draconian rationing system for almost all basic foodstuffs and consumer items, of the kind usually seen in time of war, was instituted.

More seriously, by 1960 the country was in the grip of one of the worst famines in its history. Between 20 and 30 million people died of malnutrition between 1959 and 1961. Entire villages in the countryside were wiped out. Food supplies in cities were severely curtailed. Urbanites stripped the bark and leaves off the trees. Beriberi and other diseases were endemic, and in the general torpor of malnutrition, work almost ground to a halt. By 1960, the Maoists had no choice but to call a halt to the Great Leap, blaming its results on the 1959 pullout of Soviet advisers, bad weather and the excessive zeal of local party officials.[6]

After a few years of concessions to limited reform policies that restored agriculture and industry to good health, by 1963 the Maoists had regrouped their political forces and were once again on the attack. Khrushchev had renewed his condemnations of Stalinism in 1961, which must have stung Mao to the quick in the wake of his recent policies and their disastrous outcome. Moreover, there were stirrings of criticism and dissent, often wrapped within historical allegory in fiction and drama, expressing dissatisfaction with Mao and his policies.

Still unwilling to back down from his defense of Stalinism, Mao began to assert it even more militantly. But there emerged in these years a new wrinkle to his old position, one that would soon have more grave consequences for the nation. In 1964, Mao declared that the Soviet Union had succumbed to revisionism. It had so departed from the revolutionary line of the Stalin years—declaring the end of class struggle, advocating peaceful coexistence with imperialism and showing a willingness to experiment with markets and profit motives to make central planning work better—that it was no longer a socialist country. The privileged Soviet bureaucratic class had turned into a new bourgeoisie, and their ideology of de-Stalinization and reform expressed their class interests.

To this picture of international betrayal Mao linked a new variety of the old Stalinist vision of domestic subversion. China, he claimed, was at a

[5] See Roderick MacFarquhar, *The Origins of the Cultural Revolution*, vol. 2, *The Great Leap Forward, 1958–1960* (New York: Columbia University Press, 1983), chs. 7, 8, 10.
[6] See Judith Banister, *China's Changing Population* (Stanford: Stanford University Press, 1987), pp. 85–89.

crossroads. It could continue to take the socialist road, or it too could succumb to revisionism. To remain socialist, he claimed, China had to uncover and purge the hidden traitors who sought to steer the country back toward capitalism. There could no longer be any loyal opposition, no permissible dissent. The only question was whether or not a person had enthusiastically greeted Mao's revolutionary doctrine, or whether the person had expressed vacillation or doubt, responding with insufficient enthusiasm. These people and other hidden traitors had to be exposed. The only question was how. The stage was set for the Cultural Revolution, a political and social disaster that matched the economic and demographic one of the Great Leap Forward.

The Cultural Revolution began in the spring of 1966 with an attack against a famous Chinese playwright and some newspaper editors for writing disguised anti-Mao satires. This in itself was not an unprecedented event in Mao's China. But the purge did not stop with the writers and editors. It extended to several officials in the Beijing city government responsible for culture and propaganda and eventually to the mayor himself. They were said to form an "antiparty clique." Clearly, something more was afoot.[7]

Mao declared that China was riddled with revisionists and traitors who needed to be rooted out. Shortly thereafter the party organized "work teams" of ordinary party officials who were to go to factories, schools and offices to investigate the backgrounds and activities of individuals and look for signs of their "antiparty" nature. These officials examined the political dossiers that are kept on all urban citizens in China and interviewed people in the locality, encouraging letters of accusation. In large measure, however, they accused the habitual targets of China's past persecution campaigns: those who had foreign educations or relatives overseas or those who had been punished as "rightists" in previous campaigns.

During this period, the Red Guards made their first appearance. These were groups of students who were most trusted by the party—active members of the Communist Youth League, with parents who were party officials, workers or poor peasants. They were told by work teams and the party officials of their schools that they were the pure revolutionary elements of society and their task was to smash all the remnants of China's old feudal culture and old exploiting classes along with its semicolonial past. On their campuses, they attacked teachers who had been educated overseas or in missionary schools or who affected bourgeois airs by showing too great an appreciation for foreign cultures, books or ideas. They raided their campus libraries, and the homes of their teachers, confiscating and burning anything published before 1949 or outside China. They made forays into the streets of their cities, defacing foreign-style buildings in the business districts and attacking ancient temples and their works of art.

[7] See Edward Rice, *Mao's Way* (Berkeley: University of California Press, 1972), for a readable narrative of the Cultural Revolution.

They raided large homes, tearing up floorboards and breaking through walls, allegedly searching for hidden gold or antiparty materials; often they beat or imprisoned the residents. And they would confront people on the streets who wore Western styles of dress or grooming, cutting their clothing into strips or shearing off their hair.

But the wheels of intrigue continued to turn among the top party leadership. By the fall of 1966 it was clear that two of the top leaders of the country, Liu Shaoqi and Deng Xiaoping, would be purged as China's top two revisionists, the former being declared "China's Khrushchev." Moreover, they were charged with using the work teams and the Red Guards to protect party leaders throughout the country, turning the attack away from them onto other convenient targets. Now all students—not just those who had "revolutionary" parentage—and white- and blue-collar workers as well, were exhorted to organize their own groups of "revolutionary rebels" and to "drag out" the revisionists hidden in the party leadership of their organizations and local governments.

The stage was now set for the most chaotic and violent period of the Cultural Revolution. Schools and workplaces throughout the country saw two, three or more rebel factions rise up and contend for the right to "seize power." Each claimed to be the most loyal to Chairman Mao, accusing their opponents of being reactionaries or dupes of the revisionists. The groups engaged in a deadly competition to see who could prove their revolutionary mettle by imprisoning, torturing and extracting the most sensational confessions out of their captives. Some preferred to kidnap former capitalists, nationalists or "reactionary academic authorities" with foreign degrees. Others preferred party secretaries with heretofore impeccable careers. Local party leaders and their public security forces, confused by political developments and afraid of being accused of "suppressing the revolutionary masses," did little to stem the growing lawlessness.

From the end of 1966 through much of 1967, China's cities and towns were trapped in an escalating spiral of violence. The unfortunate targets of rebel groups were beaten and forced to sign confessions in makeshift cells, often kept in darkness and isolation for months, and when paraded on the streets or presented for public humiliation at staged "struggle sessions," were often beaten with clubs or forced to kneel on broken glass.

Many committed suicide under the pressures and some murders were made to look like suicides. Others were simply tortured to death or bound and pushed from buildings or dumped into rivers. The different rebel factions broke into caches of arms and began to fight one another for turf in the streets. Local military forces covertly aided one side or another, fanning the flames. Many local governments and party offices had already ceased to function, their leaders either imprisoned or too paralyzed to act. By the summer of 1967 China verged on full-scale civil war.[8]

Mao finally consented to the use of the army, China's only intact orga-

---

[8]See Gao Yuan, *Born Red* (Stanford: Stanford University Press, 1986), and Stanley Rosen, *Red Guard Radicalism and the Cultural Revolution in Guangzhou* (Boulder, Colo.: Praeger, 1982).

nization, to restore order. As troops moved into every school, office and factory, they crushed armed resistance from active rebels, who were now declared "counterrevolutionaries" and executed or given long prison terms. Workers were intimidated into returning to work "for loyalty to Mao." Schools were formally closed and most students sent to the countryside for an undefined term of farming. Government officials and teachers were sent to "cadre schools" that were barely disguised labor camps for intellectuals. Engineers and white-collar workers were required to perform manual labor on the shop floor. Soldiers appointed new leaders for organizations and enforced a strict regime of Mao worship. For most of 1968, 1969 and even into 1970, they conducted a series of persecution campaigns of their own, "cleansing the class ranks" by rooting out entire categories of people with suspicious backgrounds or those who had engaged in disapproved Cultural Revolution activities. Not until the mysterious death in 1971 of Lin Biao, who was Mao's newly chosen successor and head of the People's Liberation Army, did these persecution campaigns abate and the troops begin to withdraw from their dictatorship over the civilian sector.

While the chaos and violence of the Cultural Revolution had largely subsided by the end of the 1960s, it laid a heavy burden on the Chinese psyche in the 1970s. It is impossible to gauge the numbers killed or wounded—perhaps a million, perhaps more. But the numbers permanently scarred by their experiences must have been far greater. It was rare for an urban Chinese not to have had a close relative or friend who was tortured, killed or arrested, or transferred indefinitely to the countryside. Vast numbers of Chinese youth, if they did not kill with their own hands, participated in or witnessed activities that resulted in the death of respected members of their schools. Few of those who participated in these struggles did not in the end feel betrayed or used.

Moreover, China's educational system and intellectual life were delivered a staggering blow from which it would take more than a decade to recover. Universities were simply closed until 1972, and then operated only with demoralized teaching staffs and impoverished libraries and curricula, taking in students who were selected not for aptitude (the entrance exams were abolished) but for their "revolutionary" heritage and political loyalty. Only a few periodicals continued to publish; few new works of drama or literature were produced. Factories and offices institutionalized the denigration of intellectual aptitude. Trained personnel, after a few years of work at manual labor, were allowed to return to their offices under politically loyal but incompetent officials. New technical innovations and designs were neither encouraged nor rewarded.

Finally, the political movement that began by encouraging the masses to rise up against authority ended by introducing even more arbitrary and dictatorial exercise of power by local officials. Citizens endured a heightened fear of political campaigns, and this encouraged more pronounced ritualism and hypocrisy in public life. New and surviving officials wielded unbridled power to brand the people under them political enemies. The Cultural Revolution ushered in an era of official lawlessness and public cruelty.

THE LEGACY OF THE CULTURAL REVOLUTION

For much of the 1970s, China's top leaders were divided over whether or not to restore different policies and practices that had been destroyed by the Cultural Revolution. For example, Deng Xiaoping was brought back into the leadership in 1973 to help rebuild China's shattered economy, only to be purged again in early 1976 for seeking to reverse too many of the Cultural Revolution policies. While leadership intrigues continued, pressing social and economic problems went unattended, leaving China, upon Mao's death in 1976, with a difficult legacy to overcome.

Technological progress, for example, had almost come to a standstill. Factories were using outmoded designs from the 1950s, and engineering departments, still crippled by the Cultural Revolution, could do little more than reproduce old designs with minor improvements. Imports of new technology had virtually slowed to a halt. Spare parts were nowhere to be had. Every factory sought to create its own toolmaking and machinery shop in order to keep its outdated capital equipment in running condition.

Industrial waste was a growing problem. Since the late 1950s, China had reinvested huge proportions of its annual surplus (as was the case in Stalin's great industrial drive), between 25 and 33 percent. Yet the return on this investment was dwindling to a mere fraction of the amounts of the 1950s. The Cultural Revolution, by forestalling economic reforms, had done nothing to overcome the characteristic inefficiencies of Society-style central planning. The entire system operated inefficiently because the political upheaval had so destroyed planning and technical capacity. Greater amounts of scarce capital had to be invested in order to get the same amount of output as before. The country was running a losing race against waste and inefficiency.

In agriculture, meanwhile, output was barely keeping pace with population growth. By bringing new acreage into production, through the careful application of fertilizers and through the development of new seed strains in the 1970s, China was able to double agricultural yield in the two decades after 1957. However, the population doubled during the same period. Centralized administration of agriculture had led to unwise cropping decisions, and the collective work point system, in which private plots were forbidden and all were paid shares of the collective profits, weakened the incentive to work.[9]

Living standards, moreover, had stagnated since 1957. Over the succeeding two decades, average per capita grain consumption fell somewhat in rural areas, leaving Chinese peasants in 1978 with a diet somewhat worse than the average Indonesian's, but somewhat better than the average Bangladeshi's. Rural incomes had fallen further behind those in the cities in the same period. By 1978, one-fourth of China's peasants lived in a state of perpetual hunger, just at or below official subsistence minimums.

[9] See Nicholas Lardy, *Agriculture in China's Modern Economic Development* (Cambridge: Cambridge University Press, 1983); and Carl Riskin, *China's Political Economy* (New York: Oxford University Press, 1987), pp. 261–68.

Urban citizens also suffered from stagnating living standards. The entire range of products from staple foods and cotton cloth to such consumer durables as transistor radios, watches and bicycles remained in short supply and were still under the draconian rationing system imposed after the Great Leap Forward. Even the purchase of such necessities as matches and toilet paper could be a major problem. With greater amounts of investment required to keep the heavy industrial system operating, light industry was neglected, wages were depressed and investment in such areas of nonproductive construction as housing, transportation, road building, hospitals and telecommunications was well below social needs. The average real industrial wage fell by 20 percent from 1957 to 1976. The housing stock was increasingly inadequate and in dilapidated condition. Average housing space per person declined 20 percent in the cities from 1952 to 1977. Toilet facilities, modern heating and plumbing were rare. Public transportation was frighteningly overcrowded, as was the intercity rail system. The country still did not have a modern network of paved highways. Telephones were largely restricted to government offices. Because of the suppression of private marketing and services, fresh vegetables were notoriously difficult to buy, and finding someone to repair a bicycle or a pair of shoes was a trying affair.[10]

The denigration of China's educated experts, and the destruction of the educational system, meant that factories, schools and offices were increasingly in the hands of incompetents. These people were loath to take responsibility or initiative, and given the poor incentives for doing so and the threatening political environment, even the well trained were unwilling to take action on even the smallest matter. The reading of newspapers became one of the most time-consuming activities in Chinese offices. Work in Chinese organizations became mired in staggeringly inefficient bureaucracy for which the country has become famous.

White-collar sloth and evasion of responsibility were only one side of an increasingly appalling lack of incentive to work. Wages had been frozen since before the Cultural Revolution. All bonuses, piecework and other incentive pay were also abolished, and it was virtually impossible to be dismissed even for the most flagrant abuse of work discipline or sick leave. Poor housing and the scarcity of even the simplest daily necessities also took their toll on worker motivation. The quality and intensity of work effort fell to minimal levels. Managers knew what was going on, but they were either powerless to stop it or were indifferent. This in turn helped exacerbate the wastefulness of investment in physical plant, which operated well below capacity.[11] For such a poor country, the situation was appalling.

The sad fact was that China was steadily falling behind the rest of the world, most strikingly the surging economies of nearby Japan, Taiwan, South Korea and Hong Kong. Mainland Chinese cityscapes in the late 1970s

[10] See Andrew G. Walder, *Communist Neo-Traditionalism: Work and Authority in Chinese Industry* (Berkeley: University of California Press, 1986), ch. 6; and Carl Riskin, *China's Political Economy*, ch. 11.
[11] Walder, *Communist Neo-Traditionalism*, ch. 6.

were monotonous reproductions of Chinese cities of the 1950s. Bicycles were the primary means of transport. Clothing was drab and functional. Private shops and restaurants were almost nonexistent. Outdoor privies were still common in the city centers. When (some years after Mao's death) Chinese citizens were finally allowed—with a purpose—to see television footage of the futuristic skylines of such cities as Tokyo, Hong Kong and Houston, most were shocked and stunned by a sudden awareness of how backward China had become. The average citizen was now fully aware of what many in the Chinese leadership had been conscious of for some years: Maoist China was a stagnant, irrational society.

The final legacy of the Cultural Revolution led, oddly enough, directly to its undoing—the thorough discrediting of Mao's version of Marxism-Leninism and a considerable erosion of the appeal of orthodox Marxism. This was especially true among the youth, who would soon become enamored of Western-style Marxism and various kinds of liberalism. After years of senseless political campaigns that had exhausted the nation and led to no good end, people were sick of politics and cynical about their leaders. Nothing could have done more to discredit Marxism than the calamities of the Cultural Revolution and the poverty and decay that followed. Within a few years of Mao's death, party organs talked openly of a "crisis of confidence" in the party, and in socialism, and were casting about for answers.

DENG'S REFORMS

Within weeks after Mao's death, a broad coalition of Chinese leaders arrested Mao's wife and several other top leaders who had helped to launch the Cultural Revolution and who, if they had been able to take control of the country, would have continued the policies of that era. After a few years of jockeying for power, Deng Xiaoping emerged at the end of 1978 as China's premier leader, and he immediately set about to launch a vigorous program to rejuvenate and reinvigorate the country.

Deng's first step was to declare an end to the mass campaigns and contrived "class struggles" of the past. He oversaw a complete reassessment of China's history since 1949, and officially downgraded Mao for his gradual loss of a sense of Chinese realities and increasingly serious errors after 1956. China was a backward country, Deng declared, and it could ill afford to waste effort on anything but the task of building it into a modern, powerful country. Peaceful nation building was the main task of the party, and in this effort all citizens would be welcome to contribute on an equal basis. Moreover, intellectuals were declared to be a part of the working class, not class enemies, and so long as they were quietly loyal to the regime, every step would be taken to reward their contributions and aid them in their work.

Rebuilding the educational system was the cornerstone of this effort. The curriculum was modernized, graduate schools re-established and provincial academies of science and social science established for the first time, and provided with resources and personnel. Elite schools and the tracking system, with its highly competitive examinations beginning after elementary

499

school, were restored. Foreign textbooks were translated and put into use by the hundreds. Foreign scientists and professors, especially from developed Western countries, were invited to lecture at Chinese universities, reestablishing long-neglected disciplines and specialties. Collaborative research with foreigners also became common. Tens of thousands of Chinese were sent abroad as graduate students or postdoctoral scholars in the leading academic programs of the United States, Japan, England, West Germany and other nations.

Deng also began, and continued to carry out well into the 1980s, an effort to install younger, better trained and more capable leaders, from provincial factory executives up to the nation's Central Committee. Maximum ages and minimum educational levels were set for different offices, and all new appointments had to conform to them. Older and ill-educated officials were gradually lured into retirement with full salaries, honorary titles and fringe benefits. By the mid-1980s, the effort had made a major impact. Factory directors, who in the mid-1970s had averaged 55 to 60 years of age with less than high school education, now averaged 35 to 40 years with a few years of college. Provincial and national party leaderships were similarly transformed. By the 13th Party Congress in 1987 the Central Committee had been changed from an aging collection of old revolutionaries and bureaucrats with primary school educations to a group dominated by 60-year-old college graduates with engineering and professional degrees.

The most audacious and successful of Deng's reforms was the dismantling of the commune system of collective agriculture. Within a two-year period after 1978, collective farms were pulled apart and their assets, smaller enterprises and land leased out to peasant households. State procurement prices for basic crops were raised. Prohibitions against private marketing of produce were abolished. The result was an explosion of peasant productivity. Within six years, agricultural output had doubled without any increase in state investment; half of this increase was due solely to greater labor productivity in these family enterprises and farms. Peasant household income doubled, and peasants poured their savings into new housing construction that was visible wherever one traveled in the Chinese countryside.[12] Farmers' markets sprang up in cities, and a surge of supplies of fresh vegetables, meat and a complete variety of other produce finally relieved the urban consumer's plight.

Similar although less successful reforms were later begun in urban industry. State-owned enterprises, instead of turning over their profits to the state, were allowed to keep all of their after-tax profits for investment or the wage bill. Factories often could no longer count on having all of their production automatically procured by state commercial organs. They had to find customers, produce to their satisfaction and absorb the losses caused by poor quality. Managers and productive workers were once again given incentive pay. Bonuses and piece rates grew to some 20 percent of the wage bill. Basic salaries were raised continuously; by 1986 they had finally sur-

[12] Riskin, *China's Political Economy*, ch. 12.

passed in real terms the average wage of 1957. While the effect that this had on worker productivity was nothing like that in rural areas, there was clear movement away from the pattern of the past.

These changes were accompanied by a virtual consumers' revolution in urban as well as rural areas. The state built as much new housing for urbanites from 1977 to 1984 as it had in the entire previous history of the People's Republic. The housing shortage, still severe, had eased to the point that people were now somewhat better off than they were in even the best years of the 1950s. Light industry grew twice as fast as heavy industry after 1976 and resulted in a wide variety of new types of consumer goods. Rationing for most items was finally ended. Imports of Japanese and other foreign consumer items surged. By the mid-1980s, the best domestic brands of wristwatches, radios, bicycles and sewing machines were no longer the most prestigious items. Color television sets (especially those jointly produced within China by Hitachi), washing machines, refrigerators and even motorbikes proliferated. The slogans and propaganda billboards that dominated Chinese cities into the late 1970s were replaced by advertisements for Seiko watches, Jeep Cherokees and Sony tape decks. Commercials became a fixture on Chinese television as well. The gray, olive green and navy blue that clothed the Chinese masses in the late 1970s gave way to a profusion of bright colors and Western fashions.

The legalization of private trade and services also led to the rapid reemergence of the kind of small-scale private sector that so dominates Chinese cities outside the mainland. Small private restaurants, antique and furniture shops, bicycle, watch, camera and other kinds of repair shops, flea markets, dentists' offices and beauty salons sprang up along city streets.

In the midst of all of these startling changes, perhaps the most striking was the total reversal of Mao's policy of strict isolation from the outside world. China has become wide open to foreign influences, foreign fashions, foreign imports and even foreign investment. Western Marxism and liberal political and economic thought have become very popular among young Chinese and for a while were openly in vogue among leading party theorists. Foreign fashions have penetrated the country to such an extent that in the larger cities it is not always possible to tell the natives from the overseas Chinese. Disco and ballroom dancing has been a craze for much of the 1980s. Hotels for foreign tourists and businessmen have been the biggest single growth industry. The Japanese automobile now far outnumbers all others, the domestic sedan car industry having disappeared as a result of foreign competition. Provinces now invite joint ventures, coproduction agreements and even wholly owned foreign enterprises on Chinese soil. It is probably fair to assume that even in his wildest nightmares, Chairman Mao never thought that China's "revisionists" would go this far. Had it not been for his Cultural Revolution, they probably never would have.

MAO'S CHINA AND DENG'S: AN ASSESSMENT

While the successes and transformations of the 1980s have been impressive, the Deng era is not without serious difficulties of its own. The bureaucracy is still greatly overstaffed and inefficient. Official corruption, which grew during the privations and lawlessness of the Cultural Revolution, has grown to even greater proportions now that there is a lucrative and burgeoning economy on which to prey. Potential foreign investors are often driven away by this inefficiency and bureaucratic avarice.

Moreover, the reforms in industry, which is where the heart of China's economic inefficiencies lie, have not yet made decisive headway. Industrial productivity has only recently begun to improve significantly. The price system still badly needs to be realigned, and a labyrinth of hidden industrial subsidies has yet to be attacked. Price inflation for foodstuffs and consumer goods has been a serious problem, reaching 30 percent by the late 1980s, and this eats into the salaries of urban citizens. Economic planners have found that once they give freedom to managers to invest their profits, the managers tend to overinvest in redundant plant capacity that is inefficient from a macroeconomic perspective, or spend excessive amounts on housing or wages. So far, there has been no consensus about how to handle these intractable problems. A decisive attack on them would risk some economic dislocations, further inflation and unemployment. As yet, the political will is lacking to take the rigorous measures that some of China's leading economists deem necessary.

Moreover, many of China's intellectuals and college students appear to have had their expectations for thorough political reform disappointed by the slow pace of change. While the scope of sanctioned expression has expanded, there are still clear if shifting lines beyond which criticism and protest may not go. The party still is able to intervene extensively in intellectual life, and political change in China has lagged far behind that in Eastern Europe. Waves of student demonstrations at the end of 1986 and the beginning of 1987 and, most notably, in mid-1989 dramatized the frustrations of many who are eager for more than cosmetic changes.

Throughout the 1980s, this unrest, coupled with the upsurge of foreign influence, especially among college students and intellectuals within the party, led to resistance from the more conservative elder party leaders. Two campaigns, against "spiritual pollution" in 1983 and against "bourgeois liberalization" in 1987, sought to stem the tide of westernization and bourgeois influences. These same forces were at work in the brutal crackdown against the democracy movement in 1989. While these conservative forces have not been able to reverse Deng's program of reform, they have certainly served to moderate it. (In 1987 they were able to have removed the liberal-minded party general secretary, Hu Yaobang, who had sponsored a progressive liberalization of artistic and intellectual life, and who had talked of more far-reaching democratic reform.) After the June 1989 crackdown, they have waged a battle to reverse some of the political and economic reforms of the 1980s. For these reasons, it remains to be seen just how far-reaching, and how successful, China's reforms will be.

Despite these problems, it now appears that Deng has been a more successful "revolutionary" than Mao was from the late 1950s through the 1970s. China made great strides in many fields in the early 1950s, after decades of civil war and foreign invasion. But in his ill-conceived Great Leap Forward, and his destructive Cultural Revolution, Mao not only failed to accomplish what he set out to do, but he also threw away the gains of the early period and caused widespread suffering. At his death, China was an exhausted and cynical society, eager to cast off the suffocating oppression and poverty of the chairman's last years.

Despite his political failures of the late 1980s, and his personal responsibility for the Beijing massacre, Deng Xiaoping could still claim to have accomplished more than he initially thought possible. He reinvigorated the economy and educational system and revolutionized the agricultural sector. He ushered in an era of prosperity and growth unequaled in China's modern history. Without trumpeting his own genius or declaring his intention to do so, he helped to redefine the meaning of socialism not only for China but for the entire Communist world. Mao had tried passionately to do this and had failed. In fact, his failures provided Deng and other Chinese leaders with the determination to remake China into a country removed as far as possible from Mao's vision. But Deng's own vision, as demonstrated so brutally in June 1989, was tragically limited in the end. As China entered the 1990s, it was far from clear what Deng's legacy would be.

FURTHER READING

Harding, Harry. *China's Second Revolution: Reform after Mao.* Washington, D.C.: Brookings Institution, 1987.
Gao Yuan. *Born Red.* Stanford, California: Stanford University Press, 1986.
Lee, Hong Yung. *The Chinese Cultural Revolution.* Berkeley: University of California Press, 1978.
Liu, Guokai. *A Brief Analysis of the Cultural Revolution.* Armonk, New York: M. E. Sharpe, 1987.
MacFarquhar, Roderick. *The Origins of the Cultural Revolution.* 2 vols. New York: Columbia University Press, 1974, 1983.
Nathan, Andrew J. *Chinese Democracy.* New York: Knopf, 1985.
Riskin, Carl. *China's Political Economy: The Quest for Development Since 1949.* Oxford and New York: Oxford University Press, 1987.
Tsou, Tang. *The Cultural Revolution and Post-Mao Reforms: A Historical Perspective.* Chicago: University of Chicago Press, 1986.
Walder, Andrew G. *Communist Neo-Traditionalism: Work and Authority in Chinese Industry.* Berkeley: University of California Press, 1986.
Yue, Daiyun. *To the Storm: The Odyssey of a Revolutionary Chinese Woman.* Berkeley: University of California Press, 1985.

HONG KONG

HUGH D. R. BAKER

UNTIL the mid-19th century the small area that is now known as Hong Kong was a sparsely populated, economically and politically unimportant fragment of south China's neglected coastline. The island of Hong Kong itself went unmarked on many of the Chinese maps.

China was an isolationist nation, uninterested in the sea and maritime trade. Its enemies had always appeared from the north and northwest, so that where China had reluctantly recognized the need to deal with the outside world it had been at its land borders. It was not simply culture shock that traumatized China when the Western adventurers, traders, missionaries and soldiers sailed out of the southern seas: China was literally caught off balance. The entire country was organized around and from the north, and the south had neither sufficient arms nor enough administrators to deal with the Westerners. Making a virtue out of imbalance, the emperors responded to demands for trade by banishing it to the city of Canton (now known as Guangzhou), a port as far removed from the capital at Peking (now Beijing) as could physically be found. These ostrich-type tactics were of no avail: the Westerners did not go away, and their demands became more pressing.

The British, in pursuit of trade, found themselves in 1840 at war with China. Their base had been in Macao, a Portuguese colony at the mouth of Canton's Pearl River, but Chinese pressure forced them out. The British then sailed across the estuary and anchored for the duration in the deep and sheltered waters between the island of Hong Kong and the mainland. It was the beginning. When the Opium War was over they claimed the island as one of the spoils, and in the 1842 Treaty of Nanking it was ceded to Great Britain in perpetuity. In 1860, after a second war, China also ceded forever the small peninsula of Kowloon, which faced Hong Kong across the harbor. The British Crown Colony of Hong Kong was completed in 1898 when China leased for 99 years (without rent) a large area of hinterland, known originally as the New Territory and later as the New Territories.

The island of Hong Kong has an area of 29 sq. miles/75 sq. km.; Kowloon, less than 4 sq. miles/10 sq. km.; and the New Territories (including a large number of islands), 365 sq. miles/ 1,100 sq. km. Most of the land area is taken up by barren hills. Only about 12 percent of the land is cultivable, virtually all of it in the New Territories, and traditionally it was given over to wet rice farming.

POPULATION

The population of Hong Kong island in 1842 was very small indeed—perhaps no more than a few hundred land dwellers and a larger number of boat people at semipermanent anchorages here and there. Kowloon, at the time it was ceded, was largely agricultural, but very few people actually lived there. Once Britain had acquired these areas, however, there was a complete change. Land became valuable not for agriculture but for building. A steady stream of people moved in, both Chinese and Westerners. The focus of activity was the harbor, a natural asset that was totally ignored and unvalued before the British arrival.

In contrast, the New Territories were quite heavily populated before 1898, with more than 80,000 farmers and fishermen eking out a meager but stable living there. When the lease was announced these inhabitants became very concerned; and in April 1899, at the time of the official flag-raising, they fought a pitched battle with British troops. This attempt at resistance to the takeover was put down within three or four days with little loss of life, but the governor of Hong Kong felt constrained to issue a proclamation in an effort to reassure the populace. He promised them that "your commercial and landed interests will be safeguarded," and that "your usages and good customs will not in any way be interfered with." For half a century this promise was honored so closely that the New Territories became almost a living museum of imperial Chinese rural life.

Thus, up until the Japanese occupation in 1941, there was a clear difference between Hong Kong and Kowloon on the one hand and the New Territories on the other. The former underwent rapid development into urban settlements of migrated and transient people whose activities were dependent upon the harbor and shipping. The latter remained the preserve of the indigenous subsistence farmers and fishermen, with any marketing activity directed not toward the harbor but northward to China. During this time the total population of the colony had risen to well over a million people.

By 1945, when the defeated Japanese left, fewer than 600,000 people remained in Hong Kong. Almost immediately the numbers began to rise, not least because of the gathering momentum of the civil war in China. As the Communists drove the Nationalists southward, they pushed ahead of them a wave of refugees, many of whom fled to Hong Kong. Nor did refugees stop pouring into the colony after the 1949 triumph of the Communists in China; successive political movements and natural disasters generated further waves. In 1961, when Hong Kong held a census, the population was more than 3 million, and 25 years later nearly 5.4 million (96 percent of them Chinese) were crammed into the less than 400 sq. miles/ 1036 sq. km.

The vast majority of the migrants headed for Hong Kong and Kowloon, partly because that was where they might find work and partly in the belief that if they made it to ceded (and therefore perpetually British) territory they would have reached a safer refuge than that afforded by the merely leased New Territories, from which they might be deported back to China. The Hong Kong government denials that there was any meaningful distinction between the different parts of the colony rang somewhat hollow when in 1980 it publicly announced that the "Reached Base Policy" would no longer apply and that any person found anywhere without proper papers was liable to be deported.

Long before 1980, however, the integration of the New Territories with the rest of Hong Kong had begun. The closing of the border with China after 1949, and the embargo on trade with China after the outbreak of the Korean War in 1950, had turned the New Territories toward the urban areas. The growing of rice ceased to be profitable as cheaper grades from Thailand undercut the local product. The men in the New Territories abandoned their fields and either commuted to the city to work or, armed with the British passports to which their birth in British territory entitled them, left the colony for the countries of Western Europe where the restaurant trade was to make many of them wealthy. Then came a backwash of people out to the New Territories. Living conditions in the cities often were appalling, and the rural areas offered the only reasonable alternative. Recent immigrants with farming skills rented the abandoned land and grew the vegetables that the swollen city populations demanded. Men with capital salvaged from Shanghai and other industrial regions of China bought up available New Territories land to build factories, and labor from the cities then was attracted to the new jobs they created. The communications system slowly was improved in order to service this trend.

A major shift in population distribution was under way. The small village of Tsuen Wan to the west of Kowloon was the first to experience change. Textile factories were built there in the early 1950s. The government then created new housing and other amenities, and by 1988 Tsuen Wan had a population of about 700,000. Next came the lush agricultural Sha Tin valley, to the north of Kowloon and separated from it by a rugged hill chain. Road tunnels were driven through the hills, massive land reclamation was undertaken, concrete began to pour, and people moved in. By 1988 more than 400,000 people lived there, and by the mid-1990s it was planned to increase this figure to about 750,000. The mid-1990s should also see the small fishing port of Tuen Mun in the western part of the New Territories transformed into a city of over half a million inhabitants. Another five large new cities are currently growing from old settlements. About 35 percent of Hong Kong's population now lives in the New Territories.

THE PEOPLE

Permanent settlement of the Hong Kong area by Chinese people seems to date from less than 1,000 years ago. Before that, such resident population as there was consisted of non-Chinese slash-and-burn agricultural people, notably the Yao. Chinese settlers gradually pushed down into the region in response to pressure from the north, in particular to the southward sweep of Kublai Khan's victorious Mongol armies in the late 13th century. It seems likely that those Yao who were not annihilated were absorbed into the Chinese population.

The ancestors of the majority of New Territories farmers were Cantonese-speaking people. They occupied the small alluvial plains in the west and north, and turned them into rice fields, raising two and occasionally three crops a year. In 1662 the entire region was forcibly abandoned when the Kangxi emperor implemented a scorched-earth policy to combat coastal piracy. Return to the region was permitted seven years later, but there were too few survivors and new settlers were encouraged. This time Hakka-speaking Chinese moved in and took up the remaining land, settling per-force on the eastern side where agriculture was much more onerous than in the fertile plains that the Cantonese had monopolized. Until urban reloca-tion began in the 1950s, the Cantonese and the Hakka made up the bulk of the New Territories people. The languages are distinct and mutually unintelligible forms of Chinese; the two groups have different customs; and there are differences in dress, architecture and work patterns. In neighbor-ing Guangdong Province during the 19th century there were some bloody wars fought between the two groups, but in the Hong Kong area mutual distrust and dislike did not progress that far; indeed, in some parts, vil-lages were actually shared, with a compromise language spoken for inter-communication.

The "water-surface people," as the boat dwellers style themselves, some-times are called by others the Tanka, a name that they reject as derogatory. They live at various recognized anchorages around the coast, either on moored houseboats or on working boats engaged in fishing or lighterage. They speak Cantonese and differ from the land dwellers only in ways that may be attributed to their waterborne life-style. A second, much smaller, group of water people are the Hoklo. Their name means "Men of Fujian," and their speech betrays the fact that they have in the past migrated down the coast from Fujian Province.

The migrants who have come to Hong Kong since its founding in 1842 up to the present have been overwhelmingly Cantonese-speaking people from the nearby counties of the Pearl River delta region. The refugees of the civil war period included a sizable number of Chinese from other prov-inces, but the Cantonese still predominated, and the Cantonese language has all along been the lingua franca of the Chinese community. As new generations grow up in close proximity in the cities, and as the urbaniza-tion of the New Territories proceeds, education and intermarriage have if anything strengthened the position of Cantonese. Putonghua (Mandarin) is now seriously advanced as the language of the future for Hong Kong, but there has been no rush to learn it. Evidence from Cantonese-speaking areas in China suggests that even after nearly 40 years of official encouragement, Putonghua is making only slow progress there.

Nearly 4 percent of the population of Hong Kong are non-Chinese. They include Americans, British, Indians, Japanese, Filipinos, Portuguese and many other nationalities. The common language among this expatriot community is English. Chinese and English are the joint official languages of Hong Kong.

Hong Kong's superlative harbor was a major reason for its founding and success, but its geographical position was also important. For sailing ships, it was ideally placed as a landfall when traders came up to the China coast on the summer southwesterlies. It was convenient for trade with Canton and as a transshipment point for commerce with all East and Southeast Asia. For the first hundred years it was from the entrepôt trade that Hong Kong made its living.

When the United Nations imposed an embargo on trade with China during the Korean War it destroyed at a stroke the colony's only means of livelihood. However, the simultaneous huge influx of people was not composed entirely of the impoverished. Those with capital seized the opportunity to make use of so much labor, and Hong Kong very rapidly switched from entrepot into manufacture. Soon the world was presented with massive quantities of cheap (and often very low-grade) textiles. When tariff barriers were raised against them, Hong Kong's manufacturers diversified into other lines—plastics, wigs, toys, transistor radios, watches and clocks. When other developing countries began to compete at the bottom end of the market, Hong Kong moved up-market into haute couture, computers, electronics, aircraft engineering and so on. A flexible and comparatively well-educated work force, only lightly organized into trade unions, has been a key feature of industrial development.

About 90 percent of Hong Kong's output is exported, and once again geographical position has proved its worth. Although trade with China had fallen off, the harbor remained important for receiving raw materials and shipping end products. In 1978 China's leader Deng Xiaoping announced the "open-door policy," paving the way for increased trade with the outside world, and Hong Kong regained its status as the transshipment port for large quantities of goods passing in and out. When containerization came in, Hong Kong responded to the challenge by building a major terminal near the new city of Tsuen Wan. In 1988 Hong Kong overtook Rotterdam to become the largest container port in the world.

The harbor, however, is not the only feature benefiting from geography. The international airport derives the same advantages from its position both at the convergence of East and Southeast Asian air routes and on the direct line of round-the-world east-to-west flights. As manufacturing has changed to lighter, higher-value goods, so it has become more economical to airfreight them; some 25 percent (by value) of Hong Kong's exports now pass through Kai Tak Airport. The airport also plays a key role in the large and lucrative tourist industry. More than 3.5 million tourists a year pass through the airport to spend dollars, yen and other currencies on the sights, services, food and duty-free luxury goods of Hong Kong. A concentration of high-class hotels and the largest convention and exhibition center in Asia also draw organizers of international conferences to consider Hong Kong.

In addition, the combination of geographical convenience and free money exchange status has, in recent years, made Hong Kong into a major financial center for banks, pension funds and insurance companies from all over the world. A very active stock exchange, a futures exchange, and gold and silver exchanges add to Hong Kong's financial importance. Its flourishing economy is now based on four principal foundation stones—industry, commerce, finance and tourism; all but the first of these are directly influenced by geography.

Few would dispute that Hong Kong's hallmark is free enterprise. Restrictions on trading practice have been minimal; taxation has always been very light; duty on incoming goods has been confined to alcohol, tobacco and petroleum products; and all currencies change freely and legally. Yet the Hong Kong government has not been idle. Deriving its major revenues from land sales, the government has committed the greater part of these revenues to building up the infrastructure that has permitted the private sector to operate so fluently. Some 49 percent of the population lives in public housing. Government-backed engineering schemes have provided roads, tunnels, the airport, waterworks, an underground railway system, a modernized double-track electric railway link with China, and new sites for building development. The provision of educational facilities has been shared with the private sector, but the government has assumed an increasingly important role in ensuring better standards and in raising the level of compulsory schooling. Tourism and trade are promoted worldwide through semiautonomous bodies set up by the government.

Hong Kong has no natural resources either of fuel or minerals. There is insufficient water and no possibility of feeding the inflated population from its own scarce lands. Hong Kong also is at the mercy of every wind that blows through the world of international finance and commerce. The one great asset of Hong Kong has been its people—their abundance, their industriousness and their combined wits. On this apparently slender foundation has been built a prosperous society that enjoys one of the highest standards of living in Asia.

THE FAMILY

The New Territories in the 19th century were dominated by kinship groups of considerable size, with some clans having several thousand members. Five major surnames between them controlled the greater part of the most fertile land. A clan ran its affairs almost as an independent city-state, each with its own territory, leadership, income, laws and punishments, religion, army and foreign policy. Disputes with neighboring clans frequently resulted in battles, and a state of feud was normal. Overall social order was dependent more on a rude balance of power struck by alliances between clans than on the remote and ineffectual authority of the central government.

British rule from 1899 onward gradually tamed the worst excesses of the clans, but the landholdings that provided the income to finance clan activity remained a powerful cohesive force. Even in the late 1980s the wealth and influence of the major clans have not been entirely dissipated. When employment opportunities arose in the restaurants of Western Europe, it was not unusual for the clans to dip into their communal funds to finance their members' ventures abroad. One clan ran its own air charter flights to Britain for several years. Most damaging to clan strength have been the drain of members settling abroad, the compulsory purchase by the government of clan lands required for development projects and the swamping effect of the huge numbers of urban newcomers moving to the rural areas.

In the 19th century the inhabitants of Hong Kong island and Kowloon were all newcomers. Since many of them were single men or men who had left their families in China while they sought their fortune in Hong Kong, not only were there no clans, but there were at first comparatively few families. Before long, however, this frontier-town period was over and families blossomed. On a smaller scale, urban Hong Kong stressed the importance of kin unity and loyalty quite as much as did the rural areas.

To a considerable extent, that commitment to the elderly, care of the young and concern for the group is still in evidence in Hong Kong today. When the Great Proletarian Cultural Revolution in China reached a stage where children were being encouraged to report their parents for misdemeanors and to criticize and abuse them publicly, the press and people of Hong Kong were outraged; such conduct was considered almost subhuman. Of course, family loyalty is not quite as tight as it once was. For example, modern economic realities tend not to permit the family business to employ a family member who is obviously incompetent; indeed, know-how is rapidly replacing know-who as a qualification for employment.

LIFE-STYLE

For 40 years the citizens of the People's Republic of China have looked over the border at Hong Kong with feelings of both revulsion and attraction. For many of them, the glow in the sky at night that they can see from miles away seems to come from the gold with which the streets must be paved. Would-be immigrants have attempted the crossing into Hong Kong by walking, swimming, speedboating, stowing away, bribery and bluff, and it has taken a triple fence, army and police patrols, helicopters and constant vigilance to keep illegal entry under any kind of control. Those who succeed in making the crossing either legally or illegally quickly find that Hong Kong works very hard indeed for its riches.

Many people in the construction industry, small factories, shops and traditional businesses work a seven-day week with time off on a casual basis when required. For others, the six-day workweek is now the norm, although some white-collar workers have only a five-and-a-half-day week, but for almost everyone the working day is very long. Most workers also have long waits for crowded transport to and from home. Hong Kong has one of the most densely used road systems in the world, with 223 vehicles for each of its 839 miles/1,350 km. Four major road tunnels (including two across the harbor between Hong Kong and Kowloon) and more than 550 overpasses and bridges have been built, others are planned, and a very efficient modern underground railway system (the Mass Transit Railway) has been dug. But the confines of space and the continuous growth of population and economic activity have ensured that any amelioration of traffic congestion and commuter crowding is usually only temporary. Transportation of all kinds swarms through the seas, lands and airspace of Hong Kong, typifying in its frenetic activity the life of the people. Helicopters, light aircraft and jumbo jets are seldom not in view in the air; on the water are rowing, sailing and motorized craft of all types, including hydrofoils, jetfoils, hovercraft, triple-decked ferries, warships, tramp steamers, luxury cruise liners and gigantic container ships; on land there are cars, minibuses, huge double-deck buses, trams, taxis, trucks, cablecars, underground trains, light railway trains, fast main-line electric trains and the world's largest concentration of Rolls-Royce cars.

When work is done, recreational activities are undertaken with no less fervor. For many people the most important activity is eating; it would not be wrong to call it the national sport. Food shoppers at all income levels are knowledgeable, insisting on freshness, cooking with flair and eating with dedication and joy. Practically everyone is a gourmet. Perhaps because of the extraordinary price of land and housing and the consequent minute size of most people's living accommodation, entertaining is rarely done at home. Hong Kong has a vast number of restaurants. They serve many different kinds of Chinese and exotic cuisine, go in and out of fashion with great rapidity and provide a constant topic of serious conversation for rich and poor alike. On Sundays the restaurants are crammed with family parties who build their day around a meal.

In 1961 Hong Kong's film industry produced more titles than any country in the world other than Japan. There are more than 100 movie theaters in the territory, and on average every man, woman and child attends 12 times a year—a figure that has been constant for some years. The level of attendance was even higher when theaters were almost the only air-conditioned buildings, before crime had risen to levels that made some people fear to be out on the streets at night, and before the advent of universal color television. Television is now the most popular pastime: well over 90 percent of households own a set, and there are two English-language and two Chinese-language channels. The catchphrases of comedians and soap-opera stars permeate everyday language.

Active pastimes include swimming, soccer, walking, bowling, basketball and table tennis. The many beaches are packed throughout the summer months, and more than 20 public swimming pools cater to those who want only water, not sand and litter. Some 40 percent of the territory's land area now is designated country park, and weekend hiking and camping have captured the imagination and interest of the young in particular. Soccer is a very popular spectator sport.

Nightlife is rich and colorful. There are night markets, concerts, traditional Chinese operas, discotheques, expensive nightclubs, dance halls, open-air restaurants on land and sea, pubs and "girlie bars." For the more serious residents, there are well-attended adult education classes.

If eating is the national sport, gambling is the national vice. Horse racing takes place twice a week from September to May, drawing capacity crowds, and providing the government with Hong Kong $1 billion in tax income a year. In addition, the Royal Hong Kong Jockey Club annually donates some HK $100 million to charity. The two racetracks and official off-course betting shops are the only legalized places for gambling. Many people regularly travel 40 miles/64 km. across the estuary to Portuguese Macao where there are casinos, a dog-racing track and a trotting track, and where all forms of gambling are legal. One form of gambling that has no season, does not require sea transport and has fascinated the Chinese for centuries is Mah-Jongg. The game is enjoyed in the privacy of homes or in private rooms upstairs in restaurants, and it is seldom played without heavy betting.

What today marks life in Hong Kong—and has marked it since its founding—is the short-term outlook of its people. Very few Westerners make it their permanent home; for most of them, three or perhaps five years is the limit of their stay. Even expatriots working a full career for the Hong Kong government usually retire at age 55 and leave the scene of their labors. For the Chinese who first were attracted to the possibilities of a better life in the new colony, it was only a place from which to send money back to their true homes in China. For those who did eventually settle, a life of constant hard work replaced the slow pace and confidence in a long future over many generations that they had enjoyed in their rural villages. Since the Japanese invasion in December 1941 there has been no long period of calm and certainty in Hong Kong. First there was the civil war in China, then the Korean War, water shortages, the riots of the Great Proletarian Cultural Revolution, typhoons, problems over rights to British nationality, oil crises, stock market booms and crashes, negotiations over the future of the territory, an influx of Vietnamese refugees and now a terminal date for British rule: people, nature and accidents have all contributed to making today seem more important than tomorrow.

The people of Hong Kong live hard, work hard and play hard. They have achieved a remarkable level of economic life and created a unique society, and they are proud of what they have done.

THE FUTURE

Since Hong Kong grew in three stages, theoretically it could also shrink in stages. The island and Kowloon were ceded to Britain in perpetuity and the treaties that ceded them are there to prove it. Of course, the New Territories were only leased for 99 years and the lease expires in 1997. Couldn't the other two parts then revert to the separate existence they had before 1898?

The trouble with this theory is that things are no longer the same as they were in the 19th century. Hong Kong island and Kowloon essentially were created by Britain. Artificially isolated from the landmass of China, they were nurtured by the sea, existed for the sea and were otherwise self-contained. Since the war in the Pacific, however, they have not been truly independent. Inexorably their existence has been entwined with the New

Territories: the economy operates on a territorywide basis. The capital that finances the factories of the planted cities in the New Territories is raised in the financial center of Hong Kong island. Some of the electricity generators that power the elevators and computers of the stock exchanges are located in the New Territories, as is the airport through which pass the tourists, the business executive going to the exhibition halls of the Hong Kong Trade Development Council on the island, and the New Territories farmers heading for Amsterdam, Frankfurt or London to become restaurateurs. The road system, the Mass Transit Railway, water storage and distribution facilities are all integral. The people live in one area and work in another. Education, broadcasting, language, life-style and government system are homogeneous. The government has spent 15 years encouraging the people to "think Hong Kong," to identify as one with a unitary whole. In short, the New Territories and the older ceded areas have been stitched together so tightly that they cannot now be separated; they are one territory. (In 1976, at Chinese government insistence, Hong Kong was taken off the U.N. list of "colonies," and has since been known simply as a "territory.")

In 1982 the British and Chinese governments began negotiations to decide the future of Hong Kong, and in December 1984 the Joint Declaration was signed in Beijing. It was decided that the total territory will be treated as one unit, and that British rule over all of it will terminate on June 30, 1997 (which is the date when the New Territories lease expires). For 50 years thereafter the Special Administrative Region of Hong Kong will be a highly autonomous unit within the Chinese state, with its own currency, its own laws, its own economy, its own capitalist system and its own (largely elected) government. It will be dependent on China for defense and foreign policy. By the year 2047 the two systems are expected to be aligned closely enough so that Hong Kong can be fully reintegrated with the rest of China. This solution recognizes at once the impossibility of treating the three parts of Hong Kong as anything other than a single unit, and, at the same time, offers a means of continuing the prosperity and identity that have been built up with such great effort.

The people of Hong Kong reacted to the uncertainties of the negotiation period with much fear. The stock market fell, as did the Hong Kong dollar and the price of housing. Equally volatile was the way the news of the agreement was received: optimism returned and so did business confidence. The breathing period of 50 years is designed to maintain that confidence. In 1988 the economy raced ahead, trade figures soared, and the tonnage of goods moving in and out of Hong Kong broke new records. Optimists say that this will remain the pattern through 1997 and into the future. Pessimists, however, see this frenzied trading as another manifestation of the short-term outlook: an attempt to get rich quickly in the 10 years that are left. They also point to the lines for immigrant visas to the United States, Canada, Australia and other countries, and to the social composition of the majority of successful applicants—professional people, business people with capital to invest and skilled workers—just the kind of people needed in Hong Kong if it is to remain prosperous. Reactions in Hong Kong to the severe Chinese crackdown of mid-1989 were fearful and apprehensive, and showed how fragile business confidence is.

Thus, the future of Hong Kong is an uncertain one. Many of the people who have obtained their foreign passports return to the territory to enjoy and profit by the frenzy and excitement of this most vital place. They are secure in the knowledge that, should confidence and the economy collapse, they can escape to their new countries. It might well be their collective judgment that will determine whether Hong Kong survives as a viable society beyond the British era; by their actions they will be able to create, as well as respond to, a crisis of confidence.

FURTHER READING

Baker, Hugh D. R. *A Chinese Lineage Village: Sheung Shui.* London: Frank Cass, 1968.
Birch, Alan, Jao, Y. C., and Sinn, Elizabeth. *Research Materials for Hong Kong Studies.* University of Hong Kong: Centre of Asian Studies, 1984.
China Quarterly. *Hong Kong Briefing.* London: Contemporary China Institute, 1983.
A Draft Agreement between the Government of the United Kingdom of Great Britain and Northern Ireland and the Government of the People's Republic of China on the Future of Hong Kong. Hong Kong: Government Printing Office, 1984.
Eitel, E. J. *Europe in China.* Hong Kong, 1895. Repr. by Oxford University Press, Hong Kong, 1983.
Lethbridge, Henry. *Hong Kong: Stability and Change.* London and Hong Kong: Oxford University Press, 1978.
Wesley-Smith, Peter. *Unequal Treaty, 1898–1997: China, Great Britain and Hong Kong's New Territories.* London and Hong Kong: Oxford University Press, 1980.

INDIA

DAVID TAYLOR

INDIA has always evoked divergent images in the minds of its citizens and of the outside world. Thirty or so years ago, a decade after independence in 1947, the prevalent perceptions were, on the one hand, of poverty on a massive scale, and on the other, of a welfare-oriented parliamentary democracy. Both images persist but are in need of major qualification if they are to serve as reflections of reality in the last years of the 20th century. The poverty has been offset by the rapid development of a modern urban sector and by the impact in some parts of the country of new agricultural technology. India's economic development, although slow and ponderous, has begun to deliver real benefits to an increasingly large and vocal middle class, as well as reducing to some extent and in some areas the level of real poverty. At the same time, India's constitutional and political fabric is now under greater strain than ever before. The violence arising from the complex Punjab crisis that has claimed the lives not just of Prime Minister Indira Gandhi but of thousands of ordinary people has been paralleled by incidents between religious groups, between rival castes and simply between local factions. The roots of the violence are to be found partly in the economic progress that has been made and partly in the decline of earlier norms of political life. And yet, despite the increased level of political violence, the decline of many earlier political institutions and the rise of groups demanding mutually irreconcilable redefinitions of what it is to be Indian, the country's internal unity seems to survive. Since independence India has also developed a distinct position for itself in world affairs.

In 1988 the population of India was estimated at around 800 million. Although there has been considerable growth of the main urban centers, so that Bombay, Calcutta and New Delhi are among the world's largest cities, more than three-quarters of the population still lives in the villages and is for the most part dependent on agriculture. The country today occupies the major part of the Indian subcontinent, which is bounded on three sides by the Indian Ocean and on the north by the Himalaya. The immediately preceding British Indian empire had wider frontiers, but in 1947 the transfer of power was to not one but two states. The Muslim-majority areas in the northwest and in the east demanded and obtained the separate state of Pakistan. Before 1947, however, one must look at the whole of the subcontinent.

INDIA BEFORE COLONIAL RULE

The first urban culture recorded in the Indian subcontinent was the Harappan, or Indus Valley, civilization, of which impressive archaeological remains are the only evidence available. Many details remain vague, not least the language that was used, but scholars argue that some elements of Hinduism are to be found in it. The civilization declined in the latter part of the second millennium B.C., at the same time that large-scale movements into India of tribes speaking Indo-European languages were taking place. The interaction of these tribes with the indigenous population provided the setting for the development of "classical" Indian civilization.

What is now thought of as classical Indian civilization in fact emerged over a period of more than a thousand years. The earliest written source for it is the *Rig-Veda,* dating in its present form from the early first millennium B.C. This collection contains a series of hymns to the gods, which recognize the mysteries of nature and creation and prescribe forms of worship and sacrifice. Only later on was the metaphysical basis of Hinduism elaborated. Eventually, six canonical schools of thought emerged. So too did the elaborate mythology and epics that are the basis of so much of Indian art. Alongside the development of Hinduism (never called that by its practitioners until the name was borrowed from the outside in the 19th century) went the crystallization of a form of social organization based on a religiously sanctioned stratification. This caste system, which still plays an enormous part in the organization of Indian society, operates at two levels. At one, the population falls neatly into five general categories, with the Brahmans at the top and the Untouchables (who technically are excluded from the system) at the bottom. At the second level, which counts for much more in everyday life, people are organized into thousands of separate groups, sometimes called subcastes, membership in which determines whom they may marry and, in traditional settings, with whom they may eat.

From very early on some aspects of orthodox Hinduism, especially the inflexibility of the caste system, provoked social and religious protest movements. The most important of these was Buddhism, which was established in the 6th century B.C. Its opposition to the rigidity of the caste system and rejection of priestly authority gained it a large following. It was in fact Buddhism that became associated with the first ruler to dominate most of the subcontinent. This was the emperor Asoka in the 3rd century B.C., who used his authority to patronize and encourage the teachings of the Buddha, although it is not clear if he himself became a formal adherent. After Asoka, the Gupta dynasty in the 4th and 5th centuries A.D. and the emperor Harsha in the 6th century held sway over large areas and acted as patrons of orthodox Hinduism. Thereafter, India was dominated politically by a series of regional rulers.

In south India, Hindu dynasties continued to dominate until the 16th century, but from the 12th and 13th centuries on most of north India came under the sway of Muslim invaders from central Asia who came via the northwest passes. Numerically, these groups were rather small and most were motivated mainly by dynastic ambition. Nor did they generally engage in forced conversion. Nevertheless, the Muslim population of the subcontinent grew until by the 19th century it was perhaps one-quarter of the total. What happened was that in certain areas, particularly those where orthodox Hinduism was weakest, intinerant Muslim saints, or *pirs,* were able to attract large followings from among the lower strata of society and gradually drew them to the more egalitarian teachings of Islam. At the same time, the converts retained many of their earlier religious beliefs. These converts were to be found in all areas, but particularly in Bengal and the northwest.

The most successful of the Muslim dynasties was the Moghul, whose founder, Babur, arrived in India at the beginning of the 16th century. Within 50 years, his grandson Akbar had extended Moghul sway over the whole of the subcontinent except for the extreme south. In the process they displaced both earlier Muslim groups and a number of Hindu rulers. The latter were, however, in many cases not eliminated altogether but absorbed into subordinate positions within Akbar's overall scheme. Deliberate efforts were made to diminish the social distance between Hindu and Muslim elites. While this attitude did not totally vanish, in the 17th century Akbar's successors found themselves faced with a series of regional revolts, notably in western India and the Punjab. In such a situation the tolerance of Akbar's court could not last.

THE BRITISH PERIOD AND NATIONALIST RESPONSE

The 18th century in India was a period of considerable confusion that has often been written off by historians as simply a prelude to European expansion. This view ignores the fact that several of the regional powers that emerged at this point might have had the capacity to absorb Western technology and ideas on their own account. Such possibilities were, however, aborted by the rapid spread of the power of contending European forces, notably the French and British. It was in the end the British, in the guise of the East India Company, that prevailed. By the late 18th century the British were in firm command of Bengal and very quickly extended their hold elsewhere, so that by the 1820s the company exercised its control over most of the subcontinent.

The so-called Indian (or Sepoy) Mutiny of 1857 (in India often called the "First War of Independence," or perhaps most aptly the "Great Rebellion") represents in several ways a turning point in the history of colonial rule. For Indians it was clear that after a century of colonial presence it would not be possible to reconstruct an Indian polity based on past forms of rule. At the same time it was clear to the British that the old form of government that it had employed, derived from 18th-century Britain, would no longer work. Immediately after the suppression of the rebellion, East India Company control gave way to direct rule by the crown. This in turn was followed by the introduction of new legal codes, competitive examinations for the senior ranks of the civil service and the expansion of communications, particularly the railways, which were introduced a few years before 1857. All was justified in terms of an ethic of imperial service.

Alongside the expansion of colonial government went a transformation in the economic relationship between Britain and India. Whereas the East India Company had seen India as a source of luxury goods to supply the European market, or of opium to exchange for tea from China, in the latter half of the 19th century India became a market for the products of the Lancashire cotton industry, a source of selected raw materials such as indigo or a recipient for British capital. The power of the state was used to ensure favorable conditions for British interests, often at the expense of local ones, for example by guaranteeing the return on private railway investment or by manipulation of excise duties. From the 1860s on, Indian intellectuals claimed that Britain was in fact draining India of its wealth, a debate that continues today in the form of arguments over whether India benefited more from the imposition of stable, centralized government under the British or lost from the unequal and distorted exploitation of its resources. In a sense the exact figures are not of great importance. What mattered, but is less easy to quantify, is the general legacy of attitudes, institutions and economic relationships that were in place at independence in 1947. These derived in part, for example, from the emphasis on law and order rather than development, but also from the insistence by the leaders of the nationalist movement that independence must be accompanied by economic transformation.

The nationalist movement in India (as opposed to the initial resistance encountered by the British from the existing rulers of the country) acquired a formal shape with the establishment of the Indian National Congress in 1885, but more local groups had preceded it by several decades in the major cities of India. As part of the process of coming to terms with the significance of what had happened, intellectuals in these places took advantage of the English education that was available to a few and also of the new employment opportunities, either as subordinate government officials or as lawyers and other professionals. From these new vantage points they turned their attention either to the question of social reform within India or to questions of political reform, or in many cases to both. The Indian National Congress likewise concerned itself with both categories of activity. It was of course very moderate in its demands, confining itself in the early years to issues such as conditions for the admission of Indians into the higher ranks of the civil service. Within a decade of its founding, however, some of its members, notably B. G. Tilak, began to explore the possibility of more militant methods and of linking those methods to a reassertion of Hindu pride. In the early years of the 20th century young men in Bengal, outraged by Lord Curzon's decision to divide their province on what appeared to be religious lines, formed secret societies and followed a campaign of assassination of officials.

World War I had a major impact on political activity in India, particularly as a consequence of the unprovoked massacre of protesters at Jallianwala Bagh in Amritsar in April 1919 in which approximately 400 people were killed and many more injured. The fact that the massacre was condoned by most sections of British public opinion, as well as the event itself, infuriated the Indians. The immediate result, however, was not a further upsurge in secret-society activity but the consolidation of the position of Mohandas K. Gandhi. Gandhi had established a reputation for himself as a leader of the Indian community in South Africa, where he had gone as a young man after qualifying as a barrister in London. There he had developed the idea of nonviolent resistance as a morally superior as well as more effective form of struggle. He had also begun to experiment with a series of ideas on life-style that challenged traditional Hindu norms, for example, on the position of the lowest, or "Untouchable," castes.

After his return to India in 1915 Gandhi initiated some local movements in which he followed through the same ideas, and in 1919 he was ready to apply them to the national question of freedom from colonial rule. There were some in Congress who resisted his arrival, and many more who were distinctly lukewarm, but his charismatic authority and his demonstrable ability to bring into the movement for the first time significant sections of the rural population enabled him to put his stamp on Congress and to lead it into the noncooperation movement (1920–22) and the civil disobedience movement (1930–33). During these movements people engaged in activities designed to undermine the position of the government, ranging from the boycott of British goods to the nonpayment of taxes. At the same time, Gandhi's followers were instructed to work for the reform of Indian society through the promotion of temperance, the elimination of Untouchability and the improvement of the economic conditions of the villages. One notable feature of these movements was the involvement of women on a large scale.

The government's response to the Gandhian Congress was very much carrot and stick. Some aspects of the campaign were put down firmly, for example, by the confiscation of the land of those who refused to pay the land revenue. At the same time, constitutional measures were proposed that were designed both to encourage the non-Congress political forces in the country and to wean away from Congress its more "moderate" elements. There was also a compelling financial motive for these policies, as the expenses of the Indian government were high and decentralization offered a possible solution. The culmination of these measures was the Government of India Act of 1935, which was intended to establish a federation in which the various provinces of British India would be given elected ministries with control over most aspects of administration, with a central government in which the British would retain ultimate control. It also provided an opportunity to balance the Hindu-dominated Congress with two key groups that remained largely outside it, the Muslim population and the rulers of the princely states. This continued a much earlier policy of using these groups as counterweights to Congress, which inevitably drew most of its support from the Hindu majority. In the eyes of nationalist opinion, the British sought to divide and rule.

In the end, however, only the provincial part of the 1935 act was actually put into effect. The other parts were overtaken by events, notably the outbreak of World War II. Domestic pressure in Britain, American hostility to the idea of formal empire and the large-scale agitational campaign led by Congress in 1942 combined to make it clear that after the end of the war effective independence would have to be given to India. If this could be done smoothly, it was felt, then some part of Britain's economic and strategic interests in Asia could be maintained. The problem was, however, to find a formula that would meet the demands not only of Congress but of the numerous other politically organized groups then in existence which had the capacity to obstruct the transfer of power.

The most significant of these groups was the Muslim community under the leadership of Muhammad Ali Jinnah and the Muslim League. It had until then been very difficult for any leader to create a solid political force out of the Muslims, who were divided along class, linguistic and indeed religious lines. Some sections had in fact explored the possibility of cooperation with Congress, notably during the noncooperation movement, but these attempts had petered out. Indeed, the 1920s had seen an upsurge of intercommunity violence. As soon as it became clear that there was to be a major transfer of power at the national level, many of the local Muslim leaders saw the need for a national-level Muslim organization. Especially prominent were the professional and property-owning Muslim groups in the areas where they were in a numerical minority and anxious about their position in an independent state. The Muslim League, which had been founded in 1906 but had latterly been moribund, was the most appropriate vehicle, once Jinnah could be induced to return from London where he had retired to practice as a lawyer. This was achieved in 1935, and thereafter Jinnah used his considerable organizational and tactical skills to build up the league's support. In March 1940 the league officially declared its aim to be the achievement of independent states for those areas of India in which Muslims were in a majority. Thereafter, as the negotiations for independence proceeded, Jinnah had only to stand firm on his demand for it to be eventually granted, although it has been argued that his real aim was a guaranteed share of power in an undivided India.

INDEPENDENCE AND THE ASCENDANCY OF NEHRU

India obtained its independence at midnight on August 14, 1947, the same day that the country was partitioned. Gandhi in fact refused to attend the independence celebrations, so discouraged was he both by the fact of partition on religious grounds and by the degree of violence that accompanied it. The violence reached to Gandhi himself, who was assassinated on January 30, 1948, by a Hindu who believed he had sold out by not opposing Muslim demands more vigorously. The immediate consequence of partition was the large-scale movement of refugees across the border between India and the western half of Pakistan. Up to 10 million in all made the journey in one direction or the other, and many thousands were killed. The partition also raised tricky questions about boundaries. Most of these were settled, albeit not to the entire satisfaction of either side, by the Radcliffe Award, made by a British lawyer, but the fate of the princely states was left to their rulers. While in most cases the rulers were faced with a Hobson's choice, things were not always so simple. The state where greatest difficulty arose was Jammu and Kashmir, whose territory fell between the two new countries. The ruler of the state was Hindu, his population largely but not exclusively Muslim. For both sides it was a test case—for India of the idea of noncommunal secularism and for Pakistan of the idea of religious solidarity. The maharaja chose India, but Pakistan refused to accept his decision, and in 1948 a war was fought in Kashmir that was ended only with a U.N.-sponsored cease-fire in January 1949.

There was, however, no doubt as to who should be the new country's prime minister and which its ruling party. Congress had demonstrated its capacity to lead large-scale campaigns of civil disobedience and to win electoral support, most recently at elections in 1945 and 1946. Its acknowledged leader was Jawaharlal Nehru, who, despite differences of outlook on India's future, had always had a close relationship with Gandhi and clearly had more widespread support than any of his close colleagues. The period immediately after independence was overshadowed by the consequences of partition and the war over Kashmir, but the basic framework of government remained intact. It was therefore possible to make a start on building up the India that Nehru and Congress had fought for.

The immediate task in 1947 was for the Constituent Assembly, which doubled as parliament and had been elected in 1946, to frame a constitution. The final document was adopted by the assembly on November 26, 1949, and came into effect on January 26, 1950, the anniversary of Congress's decision in 1930 to commit itself to full independence as its goal, and a day that remains the most important public holiday in India. Although the assembly was dominated by Congress, Nehru went out of his way to seek a national consensus. In fact the principal draftsman of the constitution was Dr. B. R. Ambedkar, who before independence had been one of the most outspoken opponents of Gandhi. The constitution, which has been amended a number of times but which still retains its basic structure, is based on a parliamentary system derived from British experience. The judiciary is given a more explicit role to play, although this has been interpreted in several different ways over the years. To accommodate the size and cultural diversity of the country, government is divided between the Union, or central government, in New Delhi and a number of states, currently 25. The residual powers of the central government, which include the power to alter the boundaries of the states, are such, however, as to make India at most a quasi-federation. The presidency of India has been a largely ceremonial post, although there has been discussion among lawyers and politicians of what the president's powers would be in a situation of constitutional breakdown. For the most part the Indian constitution provides a framework for the development of liberal democratic institutions based on universal suffrage and competitive political parties. It includes a chapter on fundamental rights, which are subject to judicial review, and one on "directive principles of state policy," including the creation of a more equal society, which are not.

Underlying the constitution was Nehru's vision that India's future was as a democratic socialist state—the leader of Asia and a major world power.

In economic terms this meant that India was to be a mixed economy, but with the public sector taking pride of place. Through science and technology, and with an educated population, India would evolve into a modern state on its own terms. While this attractive vision was shared by many senior politicians and officials and by many intellectuals, Gandhi himself had his doubts about its implications for the quality of life in India. He favored a village-oriented approach in which Western-style politics would be replaced by decentralized, consensus-oriented institutions. After his assassination his ideas were developed by such men as Vinoba Bhave and Jayaprakash Narayan. Nehru was also challenged from the Left by Socialists and Communists who thought that he was prepared to make too many concessions to vested economic interests. Their criticism was fairly muted, however, and they were prepared to engage in dialogue with Nehru on the best way forward. Another challenge came from those who expected India to be not a secular but a Hindu state. Their initial position was seriously compromised by the fact that it was a member of an extremist Hindu organization who had assassinated Gandhi, and the organization concerned, the RSS, was banned for some time. In 1951 the Jana Sangh was founded to put forward similar views, and it proved able to tap a section of opinion that found neither the Marxist nor the Fabian versions of socialism attractive.

In order to achieve the goals laid out in the directive principles, Nehru and his advisers were convinced that India must follow the path of economic planning, using the techniques that had been pioneered in the Soviet Union but within a democratic framework. There was remarkably little opposition to this decision from the business community. In 1944, toward the end of World War II, a committee of leading Indian businessmen had in fact drawn up what was called the "Bombay plan," which argued for major roles for the public sector in industry and for the government in allocating scarce resources. In 1950, therefore, Nehru established the Planning Commission, with himself as chairman. Although it has no constitutional status, the Planning Commission has been one of the most important institutions of Indian government. It has operated on the one hand by drawing up a series of five-year plans—the seventh plan runs from 1985 to 1990—and on the other by vetting and approving major investment projects from other government agencies at central and state level to ensure that they conform to plan priorities, and setting guidelines for other parts of the economy.

The first Five-Year Plan, from 1951 to 1956, was a modest affair that essentially sought to tidy up after the disruption of World War II. The second, by contrast, embodied a clear strategy of economic development through building up a basic goods capacity in the pubic sector, notably in steel, machine tools and heavy electrical equipment. To achieve these goals, import and other controls were imposed in order to direct scarce resources into the priority areas, and a massive effort was made to build up further resources both domestically through the tax system and internationally through aid from both East and West. Two areas were relatively neglected or given low priority: agriculture, where it was hoped that institutional reform, particularly through land redistribution, would lead to substantial improvements in productivity at little cost; and employment, where it was thought that once the economy began to grow rapidly jobs would be created in both the urban and the rural sectors.

The plans were primarily economic in intent, but they did of course express a political will to implement the Congress commitment to increased welfare for all. The message that the party was actively concerned to achieve these goals was reinforced by its adoption in 1955 of the aim of a "socialistic pattern of society." At the same time as Nehru insisted on the Congress goals of economic progress, secularism, and national unity and strength, the party base was expanded to incorporate a much wider range of social groups than had been politically active before independence. Any group of significant size that could demonstrate its willingness to support Congress at election time was given the opportunity to join the party and thereby to derive benefits for itself collectively and for its leaders, who gained the opportunity to compete for positions as elected officials at the local level or as members of the state legislative assemblies or parliament.

This expansion of the Congress base was matched and reinforced by legislation to bring about institutional change. A series of land-reform measures were introduced that were intended to impose land ceilings and to control tenancy arrangements. After some earlier experimentation, the whole structure of local government was radically altered from 1959 onward by the creation of the Panchayati Raj system of local councils. Drawing on Gandhian admiration for the traditional self-governing village, this system was meant to place local development schemes under the control of directly elected local bodies (*panchayats*). Another area of change was in the provision of special facilities for members of the Untouchable (renamed Scheduled) castes. A number of seats in elected bodies at all levels were reserved for them, and a program of scholarships and job quotas was established. Another important development was the reorganization, primarily in 1956, of state boundaries along linguistic lines. This reorganization, with certain difficulties resolved at a later stage, satisfied the strong local feelings that were expressed in many areas and at the same time removed a source of potential opposition to Congress.

As will be seen later, many of the policies and programs of the Nehru era failed to achieve their stated goals or became distorted, but in the 1950s the full extent of these problems had yet to become apparent. The planning process appeared to be succeeding in expanding the country's industrial base, while Congress had no difficulty in winning elections. Turnout increased from 51.6 percent in 1952 to 54.8 percent in 1962, despite the illiteracy of the majority of the electorate. Congress itself gained 45 percent of the vote in 1952, 47.8 percent in 1957 and 46 percent in 1962. Although not an overall majority, this represented more than four times the vote of the next largest party. In the first two general elections this was the Socialist party, itself an outgrowth of Congress; in 1962 the Communist party of India, by this stage firmly committed to a peaceful transition to socialism, occupied second place.

It was during the Nehru era too that the main lines of the country's foreign policy were established, based on the principles of nonalignment. Along with Egypt and Yugoslavia, India was one of the founders of the nonaligned movement. Although sharply critical of Britain over the Suez episode, India retained its membership in the Commonwealth. As far as possible within the confines of the cold war, it maintained economic and political links with both the superpowers and also tried to develop a special relationship with China, the other major continental power in Asia.

Nehru died in May 1964, having already seen the collapse of his hopes for Indo-Chinese friendship in the 1962 war. But it was only a couple of years after his death that the full extent of India's crisis became clear. The political system that had been constructed by Nehru and his senior colleagues in the Congress party was coming under increasing strain as the new groups that had been recruited to the party became overly demanding. Increased factionalism and infighting was the result, and in the 1967 election Congress saw its share of the national vote significantly reduced to a bare 40 percent. Worse still, immediately after the election it lost control either through electoral defeat or through internal defection of many of the larger states. On the economic front, it was becoming clear in the early 1960s that the planning strategy of the second and third plans was failing to deliver the expected results. Although the core sectors continued to develop, albeit at a lower level of efficiency than had been hoped, there was no sign of a breakthrough to a new level of industrial growth. More urgent was the problem of agriculture, where the low growth in output was inadequate to deal with the increasing demands of the industrial sector for food, let alone generate a substantial volume of investable resources. Poor monsoons in 1965 and 1966 led to an acute crisis that could only be overcome by large-scale imports of food grains from the United States under the PL420 program.

It was in the midst of these crises that Indira Gandhi, Nehru's only child (and the widow of a back-bench Congress MP, Feroze Gandhi) emerged as prime minister. Nehru's immediate successor had been Lal Bahadur Shastri, a respected figure from the nationalist period, who had been the preferred candidate of Nehru's senior colleagues. Shastri had died suddenly in Tashkent, where he had gone in January 1966 to negotiate a settlement with Pakistan over the Kashmir issue. The same senior figures then saw to the succession of Indira Gandhi, whom they considered more pliable than the main alternative, Morarji Desai. Whether Nehru had seen his daughter as a future prime minister is unclear. He had made her his confidante and given her some political experience, but had not so arranged things as to make her the only possible choice. It would indeed have been difficult to have done so in the atmosphere at that time.

In her first year in power, Indira Gandhi was feeling her way. She was forced, however, to respond to the economic crisis by devaluing the rupee, a decision she later felt had been pushed on her by an alliance of officials and outside aid donors. After the 1967 elections she was again elected prime minister by the Congress MPs and could turn her attention to the problem of political direction. During the next five years Gandhi transformed the face of the political system. Initially, she aimed to strengthen her position within the party by encouraging new groups to challenge the old guard and undermine the non-Congress governments, an enterprise in which she was assisted by the internal weaknesses of the coalitions that had taken power in many of the states. By 1969 Gandhi was ready to make a radical break with the past. This she did by engineering a split in the party, following which most of the old guard left. By making the casus belli a set of apparently radical measures, including for example the nationalization of the banks and the removal of the special privileges then enjoyed by the former princely rulers, Gandhi prepared the way for the next stage. This was the holding in March 1971, a year ahead of schedule, of parliamentary elections which she fought on a platform of *garibi hatao*—abolish poverty. The program put forward and Gandhi's personal campaigning style were in stark contrast to earlier elections. In social terms, Gandhi sought to bring in to the center of the Congress support base groups that had previously been given only a subordinate position. These included particularly the Scheduled castes. The results were dramatic. Gandhi's Congress by itself won 43.7 percent of the vote, which was sufficient, given the extreme fragmentation of the opposition, to net it 352 out of 518 seats.

During the remainder of 1971, while implementing the program she had put forward, Gandhi had to cope with the crisis that had blown up in East Pakistan. The virtual civil war that erupted there had sent millions of refugees into India, leaving a heavy burden of caring for these numbers. There was great sympathy in India as well as internationally for the plight of the Bengalis and therefore little opposition to the decision to intervene militarily. As it turned out, the army won an easy victory and Bangladesh duly came into existence in December under Indian auspices. Gandhi's personal prestige at home and abroad reached a new peak, reflected politically in continuing electoral victories, this time in the state elections held in March 1972.

Despite the successes of the early 1970s, the political and economic situation rapidly deteriorated. On the economic front, the oil price rise of 1973, poor harvests following monsoon failures over much of the country and budgetary pressures in the wake of the Bangladesh crisis all contributed to a sharp upswing in the rate of inflation, which had hitherto been contained. During 1973 it reached 24 percent. More seriously, however, the political strategy that Gandhi had pursued began to come apart. An attempt to bring the wholesale trade in wheat into the public sector had been a failure. Charges of corruption began to be made against Congress ministries in several of the states. The enthusiasm that had been generated in the elections was not converted into stable political structures. Instead, Gandhi tried to make all political officeholders beholden to her personally.

At the end of 1973 a minor political crisis developed in the state of Gujarat, and it began to escalate in the face of a movement led by the widely respected Congress veteran and Gandhian, Jayaprakash Narayan. In February 1974 the Congress ministry was forced to resign, and in the meantime the JP movement, as it was known, spread to other areas. A year later Gandhi chose to respond to a judgment against her on an alleged electoral offense by declaring an internal state of emergency. It is tempting to see the Emergency, which remains a traumatic event for India's population, especially the elite, as a purely passive response to a situation gone out of control. It may also be, however, that Gandhi had in mind a more long-term reconstruction of Indian politics. The populist experiment of the early 1970s having failed to produce a stable political result, it was necessary to investigate other possibilities, notably the introduction of a presidential system to replace the parliamentary one.

The Emergency was declared on the night of June 25, 1975 (in circumstances that some declared to have been strictly outside the constitution). Almost all the leading opposition political leaders, and one or two of the more outspoken Congress people, were detained, and strict press censorship was imposed. Once Gandhi had succeeded in her immediate aim of repressing all opposition, she moved on three fronts. First, a range of new policies was put forward that continued the populist tone but laid greater stress on increasing productivity and in general increasing the level of social discipline. In pursuit of the latter, strikes were effectively banned and efforts made to remove squatter settlements from the center of the capital. Above all, the Emergency became identified with measures to control population growth that infringed on the individual's liberty to choose. Second, constitutional changes were introduced that strengthened the position of Gandhi in particular and of the prime minister's post in general. The most important of these amendments, passed in December 1976, placed considerable restrictions on the role of the judiciary. It did not, however, introduce a presidential system, although there was considerable support in Congress circles for this to be done. Third, the Congress party itself was remodeled in such a way as to give Gandhi's younger son, Sanjay, the opportunity to establish himself as her vice-gerent within the party. There seemed little doubt that the long-term plan was for him to succeed to power. Sanjay's own vehicle was the Youth Congress, through which a new generation of party members, more loyal to the Gandhi family than to the Congress movement, was recruited.

The initial response to the Emergency, which was essentially, perhaps, one of passive acceptance, can be interpreted in several ways. In the eyes of some power-oriented elites it appeared to suggest that the ordinary Indian was not overly concerned with elections and would readily accept a government that promised effective action. For others, the sheer scale of the repression had evoked only a temporary stunned silence. Overt resistance to the Emergency in fact remained at a level easily managed by the government. The press, which had initially found ingenious ways to make its points, gradually lapsed into a dull mediocrity. In early 1977 Gandhi decided to hold elections, assuming undoubtedly that she would safely be returned to power. She could then claim that she enjoyed the support of the masses and perhaps have proceeded to introduce a presidential form of government. The elections were announced on January 18, and the Emergency was suspended. The opposition leaders, putting aside their usual quarrels, managed to forge a viable coalition, while Indian public opinion discovered through a reborn press the magnitude of the events. In the early stages of the campaign, Gandhi suffered a wholly unexpected blow when one of her most senior ministers and the undisputed representative within Congress of Scheduled Caste interests, Jagjivan Ram, defected to the opposition. It is generally thought that he did so out of anxiety for his own position once Sanjay was installed as heir apparent. During the campaign it also became clear that Congress had lost the support of the Muslim population, which had come to see itself as particularly hard hit by the Emergency policies.

Even setting aside these two groups as special cases, the results were a stunning defeat for the Congress and for Gandhi personally. In the northern heartland the party could win not a single seat, and Gandhi herself lost her seat by a humiliatingly large margin. Although Congress remained strong in some of the southern states, the opposition coalition, which after the elections became the Janata party, had no difficulty in forming a government. The results suggest that the attempt by Gandhi and her son to give a new orientation to Congress, in which the emphasis was to be on centralization rather than sharing of power and on power as command rather than negotiation, had alienated the Indian voter both in terms of immediate self-interest and of perceptions of India's democratic norms.

The Janata government, however, proved incompetent to handle the task of governing India, and within two and a half years the optimism of March 1977 had completely evaporated. The internal strains within the party were beyond the capacity of the rival leaders to resolve. The initial choice of leader had been handled by the arbitration of Jayaprakash Narayan. He had nominated Morarji Desai, who had less grass-roots support than his rivals but longer experience in government. The unsuccessful contenders, notably Charan Singh, a powerful peasant leader from northern India, were not content to accept the verdict and used every opportunity to attack his authority. Inevitably this impinged very quickly on the authority of the government and on its cohesion. Meanwhile, Gandhi had with great political courage been rebuilding her political support and capitalizing on any sign of weakness and division in the Janata party. In the middle of 1979 Morarji Desai was ousted and Charan Singh took over, but he in turn was unable to muster a parliamentary majority. In the ensuing elections at the beginning of 1980 Congress was returned to power.

The Janata phase in Indian politics is important because it demonstrated that there is room within Indian democracy for alternation of parties in power at the national level. In some areas of policy—for example, the balance between agriculture and industry—there were efforts to introduce new policy initiatives. At the same time, the failure at the political level illustrated the extent to which the mainstream non-Congress parties mirrored Congress in terms of factionalism and personal ambition, but without a single dominant leader to maintain stability.

INDIA IN THE 1980S

Indira Gandhi's second period in office seemed to show that there had been little rethinking of political strategy. The same traits that had emerged in the 1970s became even more marked. Politics became largely a matter of manipulation. Economic and social policies hovered between populist measures designed to maintain the party's hold on the poor and a new emphasis on liberalization of the economy, which mainly benefited the middle class. Sanjay Gandhi, who had also been elected to parliament along with a number of his personal supporters, was killed in July 1980 in a plane crash. It soon became clear that Indira Gandhi was taking steps to groom Sanjay's brother, Rajiv, as her intended successor, although he had previously remained out of the political limelight.

Although the economy responded to the measures taken by the government, with GNP growing at 7.7 percent in 1983–84, the political situation became increasingly unresponsive to the measures taken by Indira Gandhi. In 1983 the two states that had remained loyal to her during the darkest days of 1977, Karnataka and Andhra Pradesh, threw out their Congress governments and replaced them with much more regionally oriented parties or coalitions. But it was the rapidly escalating crisis in the Punjab that began to dominate the political scene. The Sikhs, a religious group closely linked to Hinduism but in the 20th century increasingly insistent on the things that distinguished it, had chafed at the limitations imposed by India's federal system, especially after the prosperity that agricultural development had brought. The crisis was also intimately bound up, however, with the short-term political calculations of Congress and the main Sikh communal party, the Akali Dal. The emergence onto the political scene of Sant Jarnail Singh Bhindranwale, a fundamentalist preacher, was no accident but in fact a stage-managed affair, designed by individuals within Congress to divide the Sikh parties. The consequences, however, were to limit the degree of maneuverability enjoyed by the Akali leaders and to produce an extremist wing willing to use violence in the pursuit of a vision of a theocratic state that went far beyond anything envisaged by previous Sikh political leaders.

The crisis came to a head in 1983–84. A steadily increasing level of violence, directed apparently from headquarters in the Golden Temple (the Sikh sanctum in Amritsar), and the unwillingness of the central government to make sufficient concessions to bring about a negotiated solution set the scene for the military action in June 1984 in which the Golden Temple complex was stormed, with the loss of many lives on both sides, including that of Bhindranwale himself. On October 31, 1984, Indira Gandhi was assassinated by two Sikh members of her bodyguard whom she had insisted on retaining as a mark of confidence in the community. Her death was followed by an outbreak of violence against the Sikh community, especially in the capital, Delhi, in which many hundreds died.

Gandhi was succeeded immediately by her elder son. It was perhaps a measure of the extent of the decay in the party that there was no other possible candidate. Rajiv Gandhi was able, however, to win a record majority in the elections that were held on schedule at the end of 1984. There was indeed a sympathy factor at work, and Rajiv Gandhi did little to prevent an anti-Sikh element in the Congress campaign that appealed to atavistic communal feelings among the Hindu population. But at the same time there was a strong feeling that Rajiv belonged to a new, postindependence generation, and that he and his advisers would be able to bring the country into a new phase of its history. Although this was particularly strong in the urban areas, it was not confined to them. Rajiv Gandhi responded after the election by bringing in a new set of advisers with technocratic backgrounds. His finance minister, V. P. Singh, introduced a budget that went far beyond any previous attempts to liberalize the economic regime. Rajiv Gandhi also succeeded in achieving what appeared to be a settlement in the Punjab, and another in Assam, where there had been a less acute but no less intractable confrontation between New Delhi and a local movement. A year after the election, Rajiv seemed to be on the verge of a breakthrough in Indian politics after the difficulties of the previous 20 years. He celebrated with a speech to the Congress party that suggested that he was about to take on the power brokers within it.

In retrospect, December 1985 will probably come to be seen as a watershed. In the next two years virtually everything that seemed to have been achieved came apart, and new problems emerged that demanded the government's resources and energy. Because of short-term political obstacles, the Punjab accord was not fully implemented, and before long the extremists had regained the offensive. In 1987 the central government dismissed the Akali ministry that had been elected in 1985, on the grounds of its inability to control terrorism. Thereafter, however, the level of violence continued to rise. Although the government continues to speak in optimistic terms, it seems likely that the Punjab issue will remain unresolved for some years. While the Assam agreement remains in force at the time of writing, it is too early to say that the underlying tensions have been resolved. Meanwhile, new areas of ethnic and regional difficulty have arisen— for example, the demand by Nepali-speaking groups in northern Bengal for their own "Gurkhaland." In addition, the economy was badly hit by a succession of poor monsoons. On the one hand, the extension of irrigation and other technical changes in the past decades meant that a crisis did not turn into a catastrophe, but on the other, the buoyant growth rates that had been achieved in the early 1980s declined.

The government's response to the increased level of political and economic difficulties after 1985 was initially to backtrack on many of its earlier commitments to open up institutions and structures. Within the Congress party, the promised organizational elections were postponed and some of the earlier leaders who had been sidelined were brought back into prominence. Conversely, others were demoted or pushed out altogether. Most notably, V. P. Singh, who had been responsible for the liberalization program, was ousted, reportedly because he had upset powerful vested interests. The liberalization program itself, although not reversed, was slowed down, and Rajiv Gandhi's rhetoric began to include references to the traditional Congress themes of socialism. Like his mother, Rajiv seemed to have decided that the only safe way to rule India is to maintain firm control of all the levers of power, both at the center, where the key institutions have become the prime minister's secretariat and the cabinet secretariat, and in the states.

For the 1989 elections, the opposition parties endeavored to put together a new coalition more durable than its Janata predecessor and to exploit the charges of corruption against members of Congress, particularly in connection with large arms purchases from abroad. The main thrust of their program was the importance of redefining the relationship between the center and the states in such a way as to guarantee the latter control over their own affairs. Leadership and orientation toward urban or rural interests remained serious obstacles to their success. After a particularly violent five days of voting, Congress emerged as the largest party, but lost hundreds of seats and its overall majority. V. P. Singh, leading a varied coalition of opposition parties, took over the prime ministership from Rajiv Gandhi in December 1989.

FUTURE PROSPECTS AND PROBLEMS

In the longer term, whichever combination of forces should come to power, a number of critical questions must be resolved. Perhaps the most fundamental is that posed by one of India's leading intellectuals, Rajni Kothari, who asked in his recent book *State against Democracy* (1988) whether the way India's state has evolved is not in fact fundamentally hostile to the development of democratic institutions. There has been, he argues, a steady erosion of institutional autonomy in recent years, in which the survival of the government has taken priority over all other considerations. The rapid growth in the size of the paramilitary forces, the politicization of bureaucratic appointments at all levels, the increasingly blatant use of development programs for patronage purposes, the manipulation of local elections to suit short-term political needs, could all in their various ways be seen as evidence of this trend. At the same time, not enough is being done to ensure that the benefits of development reach the mass of the population. At present, India has a large urban middle class, many of whom have benefited directly from the economic policies of the 1980s that have allowed rapid growth of consumer-oriented industries and of imported technology. There is also a substantial class of richer farmers who have benefited much more than have subsistence farmers from the new agricultural technology, and who have entrenched themselves politically at the state level. Each class in its own sphere has erected effective barriers, against drastic land reform, for example.

Although a number of programs have been instituted to deal with the most acute manifestations of poverty, and although the state has taken good care in the past couple of decades to develop the police and military capacity to deal with most direct challenges to its authority, the tensions that flow from inequality are likely to pose a serious threat to India's future. It is in fact not so much the direct clashes between rich and poor that are likely to be difficult to handle, but rather areas of conflict in which growing disparities are an indirect cause. For example, in the 1980s there have been violent conflicts between caste groups over access to special privileges in employment and education. Intended originally for the Scheduled Castes, these special reservations have been extended to any group large

530

enough to be able to press its case with the government. Similar rivalries appear to lie behind some of the Hindu-Muslim clashes that have taken place in a number of cities.

Dissatisfaction with the results of economic development also lie behind the demands for greater regional autonomy mentioned above. In the substantial number of states ruled by parties with strong regional orientations, demands for a fairer deal from the central government are frequently heard. In some cases, direct pressure is also brought to bear on those perceived as nonlocals to leave or accept a diminished status.

One aspect of India's present position that has recently been brought under greater scrutiny is the state of the environment. The issue of deforestation, for example, has attracted particular attention, not only from urban intellectuals but also from local pressure groups concerned about the threat to traditional ways of life. As environmental problems come to be seen as a hindrance to further development, they may be given more priority on the political agenda. Issues concerning the relative position of women in society may also achieve greater prominence. Here, too, the development path followed so far has had deleterious results, as working women have been displaced by technological change.

Educational policy is yet another area about which concern has been expressed. Literacy is still far from universal, although the levels vary widely—from the high rates of 60 percent or more achieved in the major cities and in the southern state of Kerala, to the low of 25 percent or so in parts of northern India. Although primary education is intended to be compulsory, the facilities available at the village level are often meager. At the other end of the scale, India has an enormous tertiary sector, but the quality of many of the colleges leaves much to be desired, and learning is often too much by rote. What in fact has happened in both schools and colleges is the emergence of a two-tier system, with high-quality institutions available for a minority—generally from the urban middle class—on a competitive basis or for payment, and poorer-quality ones for the rest. One major problem still to be resolved is that of language. Should education be in the local language or in English? For political as well as educational reasons there are strong arguments in favor of using the local tongue, but to do so on a thoroughgoing basis would mean massive investment in new facilities and a head-on confrontation with the vested interests of most of the existing elite, including the principal policymakers in Delhi. So far, there has been an uneasy compromise.

But if this seems a formidable agenda, and one whose outcome may appear uncertain, it must be remembered that India has built up considerable reserves over the past few decades. Its overall economic performance has been modestly impressive, with growth in GNP at between 3 percent and 4 percent a year. This has comfortably exceeded population growth, which has now declined to a little over 2 percent a year. India's cautious approach to overseas borrowing means that it has no major debt problem. One should also note the extent to which the structure of the economy has been, if not transformed, then substantially altered. The country is no longer overwhelmingly dependent on agriculture. Although the bulk of employment is still in the rural sector, there is a large and varied manufacturing sector, both private and public. India is still often dependent on foreign suppliers for the most advanced technology, but the country's own huge pool of scientific and engineering personnel is such that it can absorb and develop that technology to meet its own needs. In agriculture, the so-called Green Revolution, which was initiated in the late 1960s to bring in new seeds and other improved inputs in a limited area of the country, is now spreading widely, and India is within sight of its target of permanent self-sufficiency in food.

Less tangible than these economic advances but of equal importance are the political factors. India's rulers do not have to fear arbitrary military intervention in politics. The army has carefully maintained its internal norms of political neutrality in return for adequate salaries and access to high-quality technology. The civil service, although under increasing strain in some areas of the country and in some aspects of its activities, has the capacity to implement new strategies of development. While many of the opposition political parties seek radical changes in one or another aspect of the Indian polity, most political leaders remain committed, often passionately so, to the basic idea of Indian unity and strength. This is buttressed by a press that, like the opposition parties, exerts its very real freedom both to criticize and expose and to support the general orientation of the political system. There is thus a substantial margin within which Rajiv or his successors can operate. The question is whether or not it will be used constructively.

INDIA AS A REGIONAL POWER

Under Nehru, India had developed a distinctive foreign policy based on leadership of the newly defined nonaligned world. This stance, however, was not seen as precluding the pursuit of national interests, and under Indira Gandhi these interests became more pronounced. After the successful conclusion of the war with Pakistan over the issue of Bangladesh India was in a position to move forward on the world stage, not merely as a leader of the nonaligned movement but as the dominant force in South Asia and thus a potential major power. It has, however, had to face criticism from its immediate neighbors who have expressed increasing concern about what they see as Indian hegemony.

After the surrender of the Pakistani forces in Bangladesh in 1971, Gandhi and the Pakistani leader, Zulfikar Ali Bhutto, negotiated a settlement at Simla in July 1972 that provided for the bilateral settlement of all outstanding issues between the two countries. In practice, this meant that the de facto division of Kashmir was recognized. After the Simla agreement relations between the two countries slowly began to improve. In the 1980s, however, this process was reversed and on several occasions the countries came close to war. From India's perspective, the problems focused first on what was seen as Pakistan's active assistance to Sikh terrorists in the Punjab, although the evidence was far from decisive. Second, India was extremely concerned by Pakistan's obvious efforts to develop a nuclear-weapons capability through the covert importation of material and technology from abroad. This was linked to continuing concern over supplies of the most advanced U.S. arms to Pakistan. There were also minor clashes along the undemarcated border in the northern part of Kashmir.

In 1987 there were dramatic developments in India's relations with Sri Lanka. After the civil war in that country a stream of Tamil refugees fled to India. Political pressures for India to ensure fair treatment for the Tamil minority in Sri Lanka were strong, particularly among the population of Tamil Nadu in South India. India's initial efforts at promoting a negotiated settlement failed. Under what was undoubtedly considerable pressure from India, the Sri Lankan government of J. R. Jayewardene eventually agreed to an arrangement in July 1987, whereby the Indian army would come in as the guarantor of a peace agreement worked out with Indian help. An important addendum to the agreement provided that the Sri Lankan government would eschew any attempt to bring in other countries and would not provide facilities to any outside power at the major naval base of Trincomalee. While India thus established its right to a privileged position in Sri Lanka, it soon found itself embroiled in an armed struggle not with the Sinhalese majority but with the main Tamil guerrilla group, the Tamil Tigers, who felt that their demand for complete independence had been ignored. India is likely to have to pay a high price for its presence in the island.

With its other neighbors, Bangladesh and Nepal, India's relations have been less frenetic, but there have nonetheless been issues on which marked differences of opinion exist. With Bangladesh, for example, India's construction of a barrage on the Ganges River just before it crosses the Bangladesh border has created a long-standing dispute; and there have been sharp differences over allegations of large-scale illegal migration of Bangladeshis into Assam.

Bangladesh in fact took the initiative in 1980 in suggesting that the time was right for a regional organization of the seven South Asian states. India's initial response was cautious, but in 1985 the South Asian Association for Regional Cooperation (SAARC) was formally inaugurated. It has been careful to confine itself to noncontentious issues and has made little progress, for example, in increasing intraregional trade, which currently stands at a very low level.

One reason that India has not seen SAARC as a major forum for itself is that its own ambitions are to negotiate with the world's other major powers on an equal footing. In pursuit of this goal it would like to exclude all outside naval forces from the Indian Ocean. It has, however, had little success in this field and has had to content itself with building up its own naval forces as a counterweight to the growing U.S. and Soviet presence in the area. Diplomatically, India has developed a special relationship with the Soviet Union, which was enshrined in a 20-year treaty signed during the Bangladesh crisis of 1971. Even before that India had come to regard the Soviet Union as supportive of its ambitions in the field of public-sector industry and as more understanding of its regional aspirations. India has repaid Soviet support with a sympathetic response to the latter's policies in

Afghanistan and Southeast Asia. At the same time, there are limits to the identity of interest. India has resolutely refused to endorse the Soviet Union's plans for an Asian security system or to sign the nuclear nonproliferation treaty.

India's differences with the United States have been more open, often stridently so. It has accused the United States of siding with Pakistan and of being primarily responsible for the intrusion of outside powers into the Indian Ocean, as well as of a lack of sympathy for its economic policies. Here, it is tempting to ignore the very real links that do exist between the two countries. The United States has been a major supplier of aid and technology and, in the past, of food. Many Indian professionals have migrated to the United States in the past few years. There is something of an India lobby in the U.S. Congress, and it would be perfectly possible to envisage a situation in which the United States reoriented its whole policy toward South Asia to recognize India's regional hegemony. Much will depend on the future course of events in Afghanistan and elsewhere in Asia. India's relations with China will also affect its other links. Until now there has been only very gradual improvement since the 1962 war, but the old antagonism has been blunted.

India is thus plausibly on the verge of taking on a much more prominent role in world affairs in the next few decades. It retains its important position within the nonaligned movement and also plays a prominent role within the Commonwealth, while at the same time seeking to build on its regional preeminence to play an individual part. The problem may be, however, that Indian political leaders will seek to place too great an emphasis on foreign affairs in order to distract public opinion from domestic difficulties or to build up easy popularity.

FURTHER READING

Bardhan, Pranab. *The Political Economy of Development in India*. Oxford and New York: Basil Blackwell, 1984.

Frankel, Francine. *India's Political Economy, 1947–1977: The Gradual Revolution*. Princeton, New Jersey: Princeton University Press, 1978.

Jeffrey, Robin. *What's Happening to India? Punjab, Ethnic Conflict, Mrs Gandhi's Death and the Test for Federalism*. London: Macmillan, 1986.

Kohli, Atul, ed. *India's Democracy: An Analysis of Changing State-Society Relations*. Princeton, New Jersey: Princeton University Press, 1988.

Kothari, Rajni. *State against Democracy: In Search of Humane Governance*. New Delhi: Ajanta, 1988.

Morris-Jones, W.H. *Government and Politics of India*. 4th rev. ed. London: Eothen Press, 1987.

Singhal, Damodar P. *A History of the Indian People*. London: Methuen, 1983.

INDONESIA

AUDREY KAHIN

INTRODUCTION

Some of the cultural characteristics of present-day Indonesia were already present before Indian influences penetrated the Malay Archipelago. Communities in several coastal regions had developed irrigated rice cultivation and were living in political groupings larger than family-based units. At that time, as still today, there was a basic cultural division between the coastal peoples and the upland interior groups (such as the Bataks of Sumatra and the Dayaks of Kalimantan), who until just recently depended on shifting, slash-and-burn agriculture.

In the early centuries of the Christian era, trading ships from India began to ply the Malacca Strait, and it was perhaps two centuries later that direct trade began between the western archipelago and China. Indian culture, in particular, exerted a powerful influence on the character of the states that developed in the Indonesian region. By the 7th century there were two principal types of political units in the archipelago: the maritime trading states along the coasts of Sumatra, North Java, Kalimantan (Borneo), Sulawesi and some of the other eastern islands and the rice-based inland kingdoms, particularly of East and Central Java.

The greatest maritime empire was Sri Vijaya, a Mahayana Buddhist kingdom on Sumatra's southeast coast, which, by the late 7th century, was a center of trade with India and for several centuries monopolized much of the trade of the Malacca Strait and the western archipelago with China. This extensive empire has left few traces.

In contrast, the interior, rice-based Hindu-Buddhist kingdoms that developed in Java between the 8th and 14th centuries have left extensive remains in the form of temples, buildings and inscriptions. These bear witness to the extent of Indian cultural influences on the religion and state organization of the kingdoms. A Hindu kingdom of Mataram, which flourished on Central Java's Dieng Plateau in the early 8th century, was followed by a Mahayana Buddhist kingdom on the nearby Kedu Plain, which left as a memorial the massive Buddhist temple Borobudur, built in the mid-9th century. Close by, the extensive Sivaite monuments of Prambanan bear witness to the stronger Hindu nature of a near-contemporary kingdom. During the succeeding centuries, the center of power shifted to East Java, and the kingdoms that developed there—under Sindok (r. 929–47)

535

and later under Airlangga (r. 1014–49)—united with Bali and relied more on trade with the outside world. By the 13th century, the kingdom of Singasari, under the Tantric Buddhist king Kertanagara (r. 1268–92), was asserting its ascendancy over areas of Sumatra formerly controlled by Sri Vijaya.

Kertanagara was killed in Kublai Khan's attack on Java in 1292, but his successor, Vijaya, expelled the Mongols and founded the greatest of the Javanese empires, Majapahit, in 1293, which claimed sovereignty over much of present-day Indonesia and parts of the Malay Peninsula.

Before the end of the 13th century, merchants from South India and Gujarat were successfully propagating Islam among some of north Sumatra's coastal trading states. (The earliest grave of a Muslim ruler, that of the sultan of Pasai, is dated 1297.) Until the rise of Melaka in the early 15th century, however, Islam spread only gradually throughout the archipelago.

The entrepôt of Melaka on the west coast of the Malay Peninsula dominated the strait and thus the trade route between the Spice Islands of the eastern archipelago and India. By 1436, Melaka had become the major emporium for the spice trade that had grown up in response to the rising European demand for spices, and was at the same time the major center for the spread of Islam. The Melaka sultanate developed close ties with the North Javanese kingdoms of Tuban and Gresik, and many Javanese came to Melaka, converted to Islam and organized the trade between Melaka and North Javanese ports. Strengthened by this trade, these coastal states exerted commercial and military pressure on the Javanese kingdom of Majapahit, contributing to its virtual disappearance by the early 16th century.

WESTERN INTRUSION AND THE COLONIAL STATE

From the early 16th century, the trading states of island Southeast Asia faced growing pressure from the Portuguese, British, Spaniards and Dutch, all seeking to profit from the European demand for spices. Portugal and Spain also saw the region as a field of religious endeavor.

The Portuguese made a major effort to wrest the spice trade (especially the cloves and nutmeg of the eastern archipelago) from the local Islamic states, seeing Melaka as the key to gaining a monopoly of the trade. They conquered that sultanate in 1511, and from there attempted to exclude all competitors from the trade to Europe. In response, the local powers strove to establish alternative trading routes. The most powerful of the competing trading states was Aceh in northern Sumatra, which controlled the pepper ports down Sumatra's west coast and ultimately extended its influence to some of the sultanates on the Malay Peninsula. Strong Islamic states also emerged: Makassar, Bantam in West Java and Islamic Mataram in Central Java, which grew in importance in the second half of the 16th century. Under Sultan Agung (1614–45), Mataram absorbed many of Java's maritime principalities, and its influence spread to the island of Madura and to Banjarmasin on the southern coast of Borneo.

With the founding of the Netherlands' United East India Company (VOC) in 1602, the Dutch soon replaced the Portuguese as the dominant outside power in the region. Jan Pieterszoon Coen established a base in Sunda Kelapa on the northwest coast of Java, which he named Batavia, and moved to isolate the archipelago's interisland network from international commerce. After capturing Melaka from the Portuguese in 1641, the Dutch also attempted to impose a monopoly on the spice trade, to this end restricting cultivation of cloves to Ambon and of nutmeg and mace to the Banda Islands.

Over the next century, although continuing to dominate the trade of the eastern archipelago, the Dutch shifted their attention from the Spice Islands to Java. They introduced coffee and other export crops to the island, forcing the peasantry to cultivate them under very harsh conditions. In extracting these exports the Dutch worked with amenable local aristocrats and collaborators from among the growing numbers of Chinese they encouraged to immigrate to Java. In other parts of the archipelago, however, the VOC played an exceedingly limited role, with the major part of the trade of Kalimantan and particularly of Sumatra outside its control. The company's finances declined during the second half of the 18th century and in 1798 it collapsed, with the Dutch government then assuming direct responsibility for administration of its possessions in the East Indies.

In the Napoleonic Wars, Dutch areas of the archipelago came under a brief British interregnum (1811–16), during which T. S. Raffles attempted to centralize and reform the administration of Java. Shortly after their resumption of power, the Dutch were forced to expend massive sums in suppressing a rebellion (1825–30) led by the Javanese prince Diponegoro. They then annexed extensive areas of Central Java, and in 1830 Governor-General Johannes van den Bosch instituted the "Cultivation System" (Cultuurstelsel), whereby peasants had to devote a percentage of their land (officially one-fifth but usually far more) to cultivating government-designated export crops instead of rice. Although extremely profitable for the Dutch, the system was partly responsible for the widespread famine that swept parts of Java in the 1840s and 1850s.

Concurrently, Dutch power was spreading over other parts of the archipelago. Their forces intervened in West Sumatra against the reformist Muslim Padri movement, finally defeating and exiling its leader, Tuanku Imam Bonjol, in 1837. In the 1850s they annexed Sumatra's northeast coast principalities and the tin-mining island of Billiton. Finally, after 30 years of warfare, the Dutch subdued Aceh and Bali in 1908 and 1909 and continued to bring regions of Sulawesi, the Moluccas, the Lesser Sundas and most of Kalimantan under firmer control.

A bitter campaign by Dutch liberals against the Cultivation System had succeeded by the 1870s in removing some of its harsher aspects, though forced deliveries of coffee continued until 1919. Oil, tin and rubber, coming mostly from the newly acquired areas of Sumatra and Kalimantan, began to replace coffee, sugar and tobacco as the main exports to Europe. As further response to criticisms in the Netherlands leveled against the colonial government, but also as a means of training a local work force to help run the expanding state bureaucracy, the Dutch at the beginning of the 20th century, introduced their "Ethical Policy." They expanded the infrastructure of the archipelago through development of railways, roads and interisland shipping and provided some health and educational services for the local people.

Although this change had very limited results, with only a few thousand Indonesians receiving even a secondary-level Western education, the policy did help create two new social elements in the archipelago: a small Western-educated intelligentsia, particularly on Java, which served the colonial regime (mostly in clerical roles) and an even smaller group of entrepreneurs and smallholders on some other islands, who began to compete with a still predominantly Chinese commercial class. In time, both elements became resentful of a colonial structure that denied them a role commensurate with their education and abilities.

It was the local entrepreneurs who formed the basis of the first major anti-Dutch nationalist movement, a mass-based organization that for a while embraced most of the archipelago. The Sarekat Islam (SI; Islamic Union), established in 1912, grew out of an association of batik merchants to contain the competition of Chinese entrepreneurs and claimed a membership of more than 2 million by 1918, with branches throughout the Netherlands East Indies. The Dutch response to the Union's calls for self-government was initially conciliatory though limited. The colonial government established a Volksraad (People's Council) in 1916, where selected representatives of major population groups were able to offer advice, and at the end of the World War I, the Dutch governor-general promised wider freedoms. Within three years, however, the colonial government was again emphasizing repression rather than reform.

Other organizations questioning the Dutch right to control the archipelago also developed during the 1910s, the strongest being the Indies Social Democratic Association (ISDV), made up largely of intellectuals—Dutch, Eurasian and Indonesian—who saw socialist teachings as directly relevant to the colonial situation they faced in the Indies. At that time, it was possible to hold membership in more than one party, so these radicals also constituted an influential component of the SI. In 1920, the ISDV became the Indonesian Communist party (PKI) and thereafter conflict grew between the Communist and the Islamic streams within the Sarekat Islam, until the Communists were expelled from all branches of the party in 1923. That struggle severely weakened the Sarekat Islam, which never regained its coherence, size and unity. Nor were the Communists able to retain great strength, for a deep schism developed within the party, and an effort to mount a nationwide anticolonial revolution, planned for 1926, resulted in only a few scattered outbreaks, mainly in Banten and West Sumatra. The Dutch easily suppressed these and then took harsh steps to eradicate the influence of the Communists and other anticolonial groups from the Indies.

From then on the anti-Dutch political movement in Indonesia was headed by leaders who were not identified closely with either communism or Islam. Sukarno, Mohammad Hatta and Sutan Sjahrir emerged as the foremost leaders of the nationalist movement. Sukarno founded the Indonesian National Party (PNI) in 1927, an organization that demanded complete independence from the Dutch. In October 1928 a youth congress articulated Indonesian aspirations in the slogan "Indonesia, one people, one language, one motherland," and adopted Indonesian as the national language.

The strength and outspokenness of the PNI alarmed the Dutch, and at the end of 1929 they arrested Sukarno and seven other party leaders. The leaders who took over from Sukarno dissolved the old PNI and adopted more cautious policies. Although Sukarno was released from jail in 1931, the Dutch rearrested him two years later, sending him into exile until he was released by the Japanese in 1942.

Mohammad Hatta and Sutan Sjahrir, two leaders of the other principal nationalist organization, saw Sukarno's 1929 arrest as proof of their contention that mass parties such as the PNI "and the charismatic leadership upon which they depended" were very vulnerable to the Dutch counterattack. They sought instead to train a small cadre of potential leaders in many parts of Indonesia. Their strategy, however, was no more successful than that of the PNI, for both Hatta and Sjahrir were arrested in 1934 and remained in exile until the eve of the Japanese occupation.

Although the Dutch accompanied their widespread arrests of nationalist leaders with a ban on noncooperating parties, by this time the anticolonial movement had developed an ongoing momentum. During the 1930s more adequate leaders and parties emerged with programs based on cooperation with the Dutch and gradual achievement of self-government, but these attracted only small followings. The Netherlands government rejected such moderate proposals as the Volksraad's request for an Indonesian parliament and the Soetardjo petition (mid-1936), calling for evolutionary development toward self-government. Only in 1941, after Germany overran the Netherlands, did the Dutch queen promise some postwar devolution of political authority.

REMOVAL OF THE DUTCH

Dutch hopes of retaining power after the war were undercut by their humiliating defeat by the Japanese in early 1942. Three and a half years of Japanese occupation of the Indies dismantled the Dutch power structure and divided the archipelago into three separate military administrations. Of these, the Japanese regime on Java was most sympathetic to the Indonesian nationalists, encouraging use of the Indonesian language and allowing Sukarno, Hatta and other prewar leaders contact with mass audiences. The Japanese military authorities elsewhere were extremely repressive, permitting the nationalists no more latitude than had the Dutch.

From September 1943, the Japanese established "volunteer" militias in Java, Bali and Sumatra to help repel expected Allied landings. Two years later these same militias would form the nucleus of Indonesia's postwar independence army. In October 1944, in an effort to muster support against what were believed to be imminent Allied attacks, the Japanese promised independence to Indonesia and partially relaxed controls over the nationalist leaders' activities on Java; but prior to their surrender to the Allies on

August 15, 1945, they paid little more than lip service to their promise of self-government.

On August 17, 1945, Sukarno and Hatta proclaimed Indonesia's independence, and the following day, members of a Japanese-sponsored preparatory committee for independence elected them president and vice president of the new Republic of Indonesia. By late September, when British forces on behalf of the Allied command began to land in Java and Sumatra to accept the Japanese surrender, a functioning republican administration already existed in much of Java and Sumatra. When the British attempted to take over on behalf of the Dutch, they met with fierce resistance in many parts of Java and Sumatra, and the severe losses they sustained on Java influenced their future actions and policies. Before the Japanese surrender, Australian forces had already established themselves in New Guinea and parts of Kalimantan, however, and they were able to restore Dutch authority with relative ease to most of the eastern archipelago. The relative strength of the republic and the Dutch in these areas was reluctantly acknowledged by both sides in the Linggajati agreement, which the British, before their withdrawal in November 1946, persuaded the Dutch to initial with the republic. It recognized the de facto authority of the republic in only Java and Sumatra and planned establishment of a federal system for the whole of Indonesia.

Departure of the British precipitated a direct military and diplomatic struggle between the republic and the Dutch. From 1946, in the areas they controlled, the Dutch began to set up autonomous territories that were to form part of a projected Federal State of Indonesia that would have strong ties with the Netherlands. Twice the Dutch attempted to reimpose their rule over republican-controlled areas through major military operations, in July 1947 and December 1948. In the second of these they overran the republican capital at Yogyakarta and arrested most of its top leaders, including Sukarno and Hatta, but the vigor of republican guerrilla resistance and pressure from the international community forced them toward accommodation.

After preliminary talks in June 1949, a conference was convened in The Hague among the Netherlands, the Dutch-sponsored states and the republic. The Netherlands government agreed to transfer sovereignty over all Indonesia at the end of 1949, with the exception of West Irian (western New Guinea)—whose status was to be defined in further negotiations—to a federal Republic of the United States of Indonesia (RUSI), which would consist of the republic and the Dutch-sponsored states.

The tarnishing of the idea of a federal state through its identification with a Dutch divide-and-rule policy was a major factor in the demands for merger of the Dutch-sponsored territories with the republic, and by August 1950, a Unitary State of Indonesia had replaced the RUSI. This sparked a brief revolt first in southern Sulawesi and then on Ambon for a South Moluccan Republic (RMS). In September, the Indonesian National Army (TNI) launched a campaign that after three months suppressed these rebellions, with many of the rebel soldiers fleeing with their families to the Netherlands.

The ambiguous compromise reached at the roundtable talks on West Irian—that after a year its future would be decided by negotiation between the Dutch and the Indonesians—festered during most of the following decade. The Dutch refusal either to negotiate the Indonesian claim to the territory bilaterally or to permit the dispute to be addressed in the United Nations, sparked in 1957 a move by Indonesian workers and the armed forces, encouraged by Sukarno, to take over Dutch-owned enterprises. In line with Sukarno's "active and independent foreign policy," Indonesia soon embarked on a more openly military confrontation with the Dutch over West Irian, beginning an arms buildup and dropping paratroopers into the territory. Under U.S. pressure an agreement was finally reached in 1962, whereby the United Nations took over administration of West Irian until May 1963, when the territory was handed over to Indonesia. For its part, Indonesia agreed to provide the Irianese with the opportunity to express through an "act of self-determination" before 1969 whether or not they wished Indonesian rule to continue.

SUKARNO'S INDONESIA

Indonesia's new government, launched in January 1950, immediately encountered immense problems as it attempted to create a viable state out of the archipelago's disparate peoples and cultures. The Dutch bequeathed it not only an enormous debt ($1.13 billion) but also a poorly educated population, with many of the small components of educated civilians discredited by their identification with the colonial administration. Furthermore, an economic and political imbalance existed between Java, where two-thirds of Indonesia's people lived, with its wet rice agriculture, hierarchical political tradition and syncretic religion, and the other major islands of the archipelago, with their rich economic resources, relatively autonomous rural communities and usually more Islamic societies.

The inheritance left by Indonesia's revolutionary experience did not augur well for the new state once the cohesive power of the confrontation with the Dutch had been removed. In a sense the republican government had derived much of its appeal in the regions from its very physical weakness, for republican leaders at the center had been in no position to impose their views of government on nationalists in the other islands. Instead, they had been compelled to appeal to local ideals of independence and local visions of the form an independent Indonesia would assume.

A federal system of government would have been better adapted to the variety of these visions and to the myriad cultures and societies that made up an extensive archipelago whose limits had been defined by arbitrary colonial boundaries. But because of the way the federal idea had been manipulated by the Dutch in their attempts to retain power, it was impossible for such a system to be acceptable after the transfer of sovereignty. Instead, within a year, Indonesia emerged as a unitary state, centered and with its capital on Java and with a form of government that was ill-suited to political and economic realities and likely to feed outer-island fears of Javanese dominance.

These fears were exacerbated by the fact that the republic's leaders had rejected the idea that Islam should play any major political role in the new state. In 1945, the formateurs of the constitution had come down on the side of the "Five Principles" or "Pancasila"—nationalism, internationalism (humanitarianism), representative government, social justice, belief in God—as the ideology on which the state would rest. This lack of a specifically Islamic religious orientation created dissatisfaction, particularly in the more Islamic areas of the outer islands and West Java. This led to serious rebellions, soon after the transfer of sovereignty, by the Darul Islam (State of Islam) forces, particularly in West Java, Aceh and south Sulawesi.

Indonesia also emerged from the revolution with a rift between its military and civilian sectors. Largely born to military service through the paramilitary training they received from the Japanese, most army officers believed they had played a crucial role in winning Indonesia's independence, particularly at a time when they saw the civilian leaders as willing to endanger the ideals of the revolution through a negotiated compromise. Their contempt for the civilian politicians was only increased by the faction-torn, ineffective and often corrupt governments that ruled from Jakarta during the early 1950s.

Disappointment with the new government was shared by other groups in the society, but there was also widespread hope that the factionalism and economic woes that characterized Indonesia's first years as a unitary state would end when nationwide elections were finally held in late 1955. The elections, however, resolved nothing. In the elected parliament no single party held a majority and only one, the modernist Islamic Masjumi, had a major following outside Java. Just as before, parliamentary government was seen as ineffective and corrupt, with few ties to the regions it was supposed to represent.

Outer-island disillusionment with the political scene in Jakarta was strengthened by both Java's political dominance and the insufficient funds allocated to economic development of the other islands, despite their providing most of the country's export earnings. Responding to this dissatisfaction, regional military commanders, particularly in north Sumatra and north Sulawesi, began large-scale smuggling in copra and rubber, using the profits for themselves, their soldiers and their regions. Subsequently, in a series of largely bloodless coups (December 1956–March 1957) army-led councils seized power from the local civilian authorities in several regions of Sumatra and Sulawesi.

At the center, Sukarno faced the crisis of confidence in Indonesia's post-revolutionary government by calling for an overhaul of the party system, a return to the 1945 constitution and the "liberal democracy" of the West to be replaced by "Guided Democracy." Under Guided Democracy, the president's powers would be expanded and functional representation in parliament would be added to that of the parties.

Fearing that Guided Democracy would lead to an authoritarian state, several top Masjumi party leaders joined the rebel army commanders on Sumatra. Emboldened by support from these civilian political leaders, as well as from regional military commanders on Sulawesi and other parts of

Sumatra, West Sumatran commander Ahmad Husein challenged the central government in Jakarta by proclaiming a competing Revolutionary Government of the Republic of Indonesia (PRRI) on February 15, 1958.

Despite arms and covert paramilitary assistance to the insurgents from the United States and Taiwan, Jakarta's army soon defeated the major rebel forces on Sumatra, though it took longer for government troops to gain the upper hand in Sulawesi. Guerrilla activity against the central government continued on both islands until 1961.

Guided Democracy replaced parliamentary democracy in 1959. Under the new form of government President Sukarno worked to bring into being his concept of Nasakom (nationalism, religion, communism), a fusion of what he viewed as the major streams making up Indonesia's political culture. At the same time he was attempting to provide a balance between the two strongest competing forces in the society, the army and the Communist party.

COUP OF 1965

In the early 1960s, as the power of both the army and the Communists grew, so did the tensions between them. Indonesia's economy fell further into chaos, with the budget deficit growing and inflation reaching 134 percent by 1964. At the same time, Sukarno was hardening his anti-Western stance. U.S. support of the outer-island rebellions convinced Sukarno of American involvement in assassination attempts against him and confirmed his belief that the United States intended to oust him. He renounced Western aid, criticized American actions in Vietnam, withdrew Indonesia from the United Nations and proposed establishment of an anti-imperialist axis stretching from Beijing to Jakarta. Together with the Indonesian army he opposed Britain's incorporation of its Borneo colonies (Sarawak and Sabah), fronting on Indonesian Kalimantan, into the new British-sponsored state of Malaysia. This "confrontation" of Malaysia culminated in late 1963 in two years of sporadic Indonesian attacks, mostly into Sarawak.

By the summer of 1965, there were widespread rumors of a "Generals' Council," allegedly supported by the U.S. Central Intelligence Agency (CIA), plotting to overthrow Sukarno. In early August these rumors intensified and intermingled with warnings of Sukarno's imminent demise as he suffered the resurgence of a kidney complaint. The period of rumor and uncertainty broke on September 30, 1965, when that night Lieutenant Colonel Untung of Sukarno's palace guard led an action in which six top generals were kidnapped and brutally murdered. Among the dead were General Achmad Yani, army commander, and most members of the small group of high-ranking officers surrounding and supporting him. The plotters also targeted Yani's predecessor as army commander, Minister of Defense General A. H. Nasution, but he escaped, although his young daughter and one of his aides were killed.

The dynamics and real instigators of this so-called "abortive coup," or

Gestapu[1] have remained obscure and subjects of intense controversy. Members of the group that carried out the killings and proclaimed the takeover of the government declared they were acting to protect Sukarno from the CIA-supported "Council of Generals." In contrast, General Suharto, head of the army's Strategic Reserve (Kostrad), and his supporters, who emerged as victors in the power struggle, charged that the PKI was the instigator of the so-called coup. Clearly, some PKI elements were involved, but the actions of top PKI leaders, including Party Chairman Aidit, were those of men ignorant of what in fact was going on; nor, except belatedly in Yogyakarta, were the PKI mass organizations mobilized to support actions in the capital, an essential move if the party hoped to prevail against any military counterattack. It would also seem unreasonable for the PKI to target Yani and other left-leaning generals in the high command who were willing to work with Sukarno.

It is tempting to look for the perpetrators of the coup among those who actually rode it to power. Evidence supporting their involvement can be found in the fact that Suharto, who, as head of the army's Jakarta-based strategic command, should have been the plotters' most obvious target, was in fact bypassed[2] and that on the eve of the kidnappings he met with Colonel Latief, one of the principal conspirators. Also pertinent is the fact that Suharto's close associates, Ali Murtopo and Benny Moerdani, were then negotiating with British and American agents in an effort to end the confrontation with Malaysia. The most effective way of achieving this goal would have been removal of the strongest forces promoting the policy, namely Sukarno, the PKI and the elements in the army led by General Yani who were cooperating with them; and once their power was broken, General Suharto did, indeed, bring an end to that confrontation.

Whatever the case, Suharto successfully crushed the Untung forces, took control of the army and eventually maneuvered Sukarno into surrendering effective presidential power to him on March 11, 1966. The army alleged PKI responsibility in the Gestapu, and, despite Sukarno's efforts to prevent

[1] "Gestapu" is an acronym for Gerakan September Tiga Puluh (or the September 30th Movement). Actually the correct Indonesian would be Gerakan Tiga Puluh September, a fact that Benedict Anderson and Ruth McVey have used to argue against this being home-grown terminology. See their letter, "What Happened in Indonesia," *The New York Review of Books,* June 1, 1978.
[2] Crouch's view of the reason for this is: "Suharto . . . may have been regarded as a potential friend of the movement. Suharto had not been given to speech-making and his taciturn manner had made it difficult for outsiders to know his political views. The plotters probably considered him to be an essentially apolitical general who would be unlikely to move to save Yani and Nasution once the action against them had been endorsed by the president. . . . Further, Suharto was known to be on bad terms with Nasution since his dismissal as Diponegoro commander in 1959 and he had apparently quarreled with Yani over the role of Kostrad in 1963." Harold Crouch, *The Army and Politics in Indonesia* (Ithaca, N.Y.: Cornell University Press, 1978), pp. 124–25. This antagonism against Yani and Nasution could, on the other hand, explain why both top generals were targeted, a puzzling factor in alternative scenarios for the course of events that night.

the bloodshed, during late 1965, army units together with some Muslim organizations and others launched massacres, particularly in the country-side, of Communists and supporters of their mass organizations (estimates of the dead range between 300,000 and 1 million).

The PKI was banned on March 13, 1966, and the army arrested hundreds of thousands of people accused of having ties with the party. More than 1,000 of the detainees were tried and sentenced either to death or to periods of imprisonment ranging from 15 years to life. Tens of thousands were held without formal trial in jail or on the island of Buru for over a decade.

<h2 style="text-align:center">NEW ORDER INDONESIA</h2>

In his moves to replace the Guided Democracy government of Sukarno, Suharto dealt cautiously with the former president, a policy that contrasted markedly with the brutality of his military strategy in the countryside of Java, Bali, and parts of Sumatra. He initiated some basic changes in the government's ideological and political orientation and in its economic policies. At the same time, using remnants of the colonial law still on the books and the authoritarian legislation that accompanied the introduction of Guided Democracy, he gradually imposed a militarily enforced "bureaucratic authoritarian regime"[3] that has gained power and coherence over the ensuing years.

The task faced by the "New Order" government in the late 1960s was formidable; Sukarno had dominated the political arena since independence and his vision had largely defined the Indonesian nation and the parameters of political debate. Suharto and his colleagues abandoned Sukarno's concepts of everlasting revolution and Nasakom at home and of neutrality and alliance with the "New Emerging Forces" abroad. They deemphasized party politics, emphasizing instead economic rehabilitation; "development" became the slogan of the New Order, a development that, in contrast to the Sukarno regime, welcomed foreign capital and was "primarily oriented toward the interests of the elite and the white-collar middle class"[4] as well as of the military. Their pursuit of these economic policies in conjunction with a generally pro-Western foreign policy, together with the discovery of vast new oil fields, enabled them to attract huge influxes of Western capital.

Pancasila, one of Sukarno's central concepts was, however, not abandoned, and "Pancasila democracy" was formulated and elaborated to describe the major characteristic of the government with which Suharto replaced Guided Democracy. Ideally viewed as government through consensus rather than political competition, the character of "Pancasila democracy"

---

[3] See Dwight Y. King, "Indonesia's New Order as a Bureaucratic Polity, a Neopatrimonial Regime or a Bureaucratic-Authoritarian Regime: What Difference Does It Make?" in *Interpreting Indonesian Politics: Thirteen Contributions to the Debate,* ed. Benedict Anderson and Audrey Kahin (Ithaca, N.Y.: Cornell University Modern Indonesia Project, 1982), pp. 104–16.
[4] Crouch, *The Army and Politics in Indonesia,* p. 273.

has become increasingly authoritarian. Attempts to establish it as the sole state ideology entered a new phase in 1982, when Suharto asserted that all organizations, particularly political parties, had to affirm that their "sole foundation" *(azas tunggal)* is Pancasila. For many Muslims, it seemed that this demand was specifically targeted against Islamic parties and organizations.

The new government's initial caution vis-à-vis its rival aspirants for political leadership was dictated by the weakness of Suharto's claims to power and the need to establish legitimacy. Having destroyed the PKI and maneuvered Sukarno into handing over effective power in 1966, Suharto still faced the daunting task of restoring political stability and creating his New Order. In 1969 he and his closest advisers embarked on a two-pronged strategy aimed at strengthening and consolidating their control over Indonesia and its peoples. In the political arena they resuscitated Sekber Golkar, an alliance of functional groups founded in the early 1960s, to supplant the old political parties; and in the military sphere, they consolidated Indonesia's military forces under firm central control, using them to suppress any potential regional dissidence.

Economic strengths and weaknesses
Suharto's success in consolidating his control over the country owes much to his economic policies. In appealing for economic support from the Western powers in the aftermath of his seizure of power, he brought into his government a number of American-trained economists, the so-called "Berkely Mafia," headed by Widjojo Nitisastro. These technocrats established a number of priorities in 1966, notably ending hyperinflation, overcoming the balance of payments problem and, especially, restoring export production.[5] At their urging, the following year the Inter-Governmental Group for Indonesia (IGGI), consisting of Japan, the United States, the Netherlands and 12 other Western nations, was set up to provide economic support and advice to the Indonesian government. Working in conjunction with the International Monetary Fund and the World Bank, this aid consortium provided during Suharto's early years more than 75 percent of all his development expenditures. The massive influx of Western grants and loans made it possible to decrease Indonesia's inflation rate from 764 percent in 1966 to 85 percent in 1968 and 22 percent for the years 1969–72.

The government's first five-year development plan (Repelita 1), introduced in 1969, had as its main goal rice self-sufficiency, with an industrial expansion focused principally on the agricultural sector. To help achieve its aims, the government opened the country to foreign investment, which was first directed to the extractive sectors of oil, mining and timber and over the years to manufacturing areas.

The government's economic success was not only a result of the support it received from outside financial institutions. Of critical importance were new discoveries of oil and the dramatic surge in oil prices during the 1970s. This bonanza was soon threatened by the crisis in the state-owned oil en-

[5] Hamish McDonald, *Suharto's Indonesia* (Blackburn, Victoria: Fontana Books, 1980), p. 78.

terprise Pertamina headed by General Ibnu Sutowo, a close friend and ally of Suharto. When, in 1975, Pertamina was unable to meet repayments of debts amounting to $10.5 billion, the crisis threatened Indonesia's financial structure. Only through project cancellations, renegotiation of loans and further help from Japan, the United States and other Western governments, was Jakarta, by late 1977, able to salvage the situation. The rise in oil prices (from $2.50 per barrel in 1973 to $36.15 in 1982) aided recovery from this debacle. By the early 1980s, oil was providing at least 65 percent of Indonesia's exports and over 61 percent of the government's total revenues.[6]

The Indonesian economy was hit hard by the collapse in oil prices in the mid-1980s, when the spot price of oil fell from $27 a barrel in 1985 to $14 in 1986.[7] Indonesia's net oil and natural gas export earnings fell from about $6.0 billion in fiscal 1986 (April 1985–March 1986) to about $2.4 billion in fiscal 1987. In response, the government inaugurated an austerity program and devalued the rupiah by 31 percent in the fall of 1986, hoping to preempt speculative capital outflows and boost exports. It also attempted to diversify Indonesia's exports and increase its non-oil domestic revenues. (These had decreased from over 50 percent of total revenues in 1969–70 to about 25 percent in 1981–82.[8]) There was a surge in the value of non-oil exports (such as wood products, vegetable oils, rubber) in the first half of 1987, although some of this increase was due to the devaluation of the rupiah.[9] Oil and liquid natural gas, which constituted 73 percent of the total value of Indonesian exports in 1984, formed only 51.7 percent in January–September 1987, with agricultural, industrial and mining exports making up the remaining 48.3 percent.[10]

The effect of the lower oil prices on personal income and employment has been severe, and Indonesia's economic future remains clouded in large part because of the country's huge debt, which in early 1988 totaled U.S. $43.2 billion, by far the largest in Southeast Asia. Debt servicing in 1988 accounted for 37 percent of all government expenditure, and was estimated to total about $6.3 billion for the year.[11] With such a huge debt, and with the Jakarta government still depending on petroleum exports for such a sizable proportion of its revenues, the World Bank estimates that Indonesia is exposed to major uncertainty even if oil prices recover somewhat.

Control of the political arena
To establish its legitimacy in the late 1960s, the Suharto government urgently needed a popular mandate for governing Indonesia, as well as to fulfill the expectations of donor nations. To obtain these credentials, it

[6] See Richard Robison, *Indonesia: The Rise of Capital* (Sydney: Allen & Unwin, 1986), p. 171.
[7] *The World Bank Annual Report 1987* (Washington D.C., 1987), p. 46.
[8] Robison, *Indonesia: The Rise of Capital,* p. 172.
[9] Anne Booth, "Survey of Recent Developments," *Bulletin of Indonesian Economic Studies* (henceforth *BIES*) 24, 1 (April 1988): 15.
[10] Based on tables in Ross Muir, "Survey of Recent Developments," *BIES* 22, 2 (August 1986): 13, and Booth, "Survey, *BIES,* 24, 1 (April 1988): 16.
[11] *The Asian Wall Street Journal Weekly,* June 13, 1988, p. 22.

believed it was necessary to hold parliamentary general elections. Suharto and his colleagues, however, were reluctant to allow any elections to take place until they were confident of ensuring a satisfactory outcome. In 1966 the military leadership first considered allying with one of the existing political parties, but it rejected this route and over the next three years moved instead to weaken the parties and finally discredit and overwhelm them. By 1969 Suharto had decided to use the General Secretariat of Functional Groups (Sekber Golkar) as his principal instrument in dominating the political process, and the army increasingly threw its support behind the Golkar.

In conjunction with efforts to strengthen Golkar in the general elections, finally held in July 1971, the army took steps to establish its control over not only the secular parties but more particularly the Muslim forces that initially supported the new government. Suharto saw dangers in both the Muslim and nationalist streams of Indonesian politics. He was convinced that the Nahdatul Ulama (NU) and other Muslim groups were still aiming to create an Islamic state, while he viewed the Mathaenism of the PNI as "Marxism applied to Indonesian conditions." [12]

To ensure that the military would control the conduct and outcome of the elections, the State Intelligence Coordinating Body (Bakin) and the Operational Command for Restoration of Security and Order (Kopkamtib)—set up on November 1, 1965 under Suharto's leadership to eradicate those accused of supporting the Gestapu—monitored electoral preparations, and military personnel were introduced at all levels of the electoral administration. Such military control was justified as necessary to maintain public order and prevent Communist elements from taking advantage of the electoral process. Nine political parties, together with Golkar, were eventually accepted as eligible to participate in the 1971 elections. Golkar emerged with 62.8 percent of the vote, gaining 236 seats in the People's Representative Council (DPR). A hundred additional seats in the 460-member body were reserved for the armed forces.

Golkar's success in this and subsequent elections is, in fact, guaranteed, for not only do all government employees, including teachers, have to vote for Golkar, but it also controls voter registration and supervises voting and (as it is officially not a party) is the only contender allowed to organize at the village level. These electoral charades, it should be observed, are more attuned to impressing outside audiences than the Indonesians themselves.

Immediately after the elections Suharto moved to consolidate the eight surviving political parties into two groupings, which eventually became the Partai Demokrasi Indonesia (PDI), incorporating the old PNI, Parkindo

---

[12] David Jenkins, *Suharto and His Generals: Indonesian Military Politics 1975–1983* (Ithaca, N.Y.: Cornell University Modern Indonesia Project, 1984), p. 34. Mathaenism was a political philosophy elaborated by Sukarno, which emphasized the importance not only of the proletariat but of all the "destitute people of Indonesia." See Sukarno, *Nationalism, Islam and Marxism* (Ithaca, N.Y.: Cornell University Modern Indonesia Project Translation Series, 1960).

and the Catholic party, and the Partai Persatuan Pembangunan (PPP), incorporating the Islamic parties NU, Parmusi, PSSI and Perti.

The elections of 1977, 1982 and 1987 followed the pattern established in 1971, with Golkar's share of the vote remaining stable in the first two (62.1 percent in 1977 and 64.3 percent in 1982), then leaping to 73.2 percent in 1987 as the emasculation of the opposition was completed. By this time, Suharto had effectively changed the political parties to non-oppositional bodies.

In the early years of his regime Suharto worked to sever ties between the political parties and their former adherents. Party leaders, handpicked by the central government, now owed their positions to the regime and not to their party members and constituents. The stronger of the two "opposition" parties, the Muslim PPP, was the particular focus of government manipulation. In its early years, the PPP had to cut all connections with the earlier powerful Masjumi party, for the authorities refused to allow any Masjumi members to be nominated to leadership positions in the PPP. By 1987, after the party and all its component social organizations had been obliged to accept Pancasila rather than Islam as their *azas tunggal* (sole foundation), the nominally Muslim party lost its final raison d'etre. Signaling this, the NU, the traditional Islamic organization with major strength in rural Java, seeing that its religious aims could better be pursued outside the political process, withdrew from the PPP.

In the 1987 elections the PPP's share of the popular vote dropped to 16 percent (from a high of 29.3 percent in 1977), not significantly more than the 11 percent achieved by the secular PDI. With its 73 percent majority in these elections, Golkar garnered 299 seats in the new house as against 61 for the PPP and 40 for the PDI. Eighty percent of the 100 seats allotted to the army in the new assembly were occupied by active officers. With these elections the political parties seemed to lose even the insignificant role they had hitherto played in the governing process.

Although Suharto's government has been successful in eliminating any challenge in the political arena, particularly from Islamic organizations, a danger still remains. Lacking a legitimate spokesman, critics of the regime, such as devout Muslims, students, intellectuals and other alienated groups in society, have little option but to oppose the government in less legitimate ways. Eruptions of discontent have surfaced periodically throughout the New Order. The following are a few of the most notable.

Protests against foreign economic domination, unemployment and poverty gained strength in 1973 and finally broke out in violent riots in Jakarta during the visit of Japanese Prime Minister Kakuei Tanaka in 1974. These riots, which came to be known as the Malari Affair, resulted in several deaths and nearly 900 arrests, although most detainees were soon released.

Two years later, in September 1976, the government announced that it had foiled a "dark conspiracy to replace the president." An extraordinary and articulate ex-official of the Agriculture Department, Sawito Kartowibowo, turned out to be the prime mover in this strange affair. He had enlisted the support of a group of prominent political, military and religious figures who had joined him in signing a document criticizing the Suharto government and calling on it to resign. After a sensational trial that drew nationwide attention, Sawito was sentenced and imprisoned for five years. [13]

A more recent major eruption of discontent spanned a six-month period from early September 1984 to mid-March 1985. It followed the acceptance by the only Muslim party (the PPP) of Pancasila as its "sole foundation." Many Muslims saw this as a betrayal, and a series of incidents at the Jakarta port of Tanjung Priok between local Muslims and security forces led to escalating violence, with bomb attacks against Chinese-owned banks and other targets. There were widespread arrests, and more than 100 people, mostly Muslim activists, were brought to trial, many receiving sentences of 10 to 20 years in jail.

The most prominent of the detainees was a retired lieutenant general, H. R. Dharsono, who initially had been a strong supporter of Suharto but had become an outspoken critic of the government. Dharsono had been allied with a group of retired officers and influential civilians known as the Petition of 50 group. These prominent figures had presented a Statement of Concern to parliament in May 1980 protesting Suharto's use of Pancasila "as a tool to attack his political enemies, whereas the founders of the Republic had intended it as a tool to unite the nation." [14] Although General Dharsono had not signed the statement, he was believed to have been involved in drafting it. He was arrested in November 1984 in connection with the Tanjung Priok outbreaks on charges of subversion and inciting violence, and in January 1986 he was sentenced to 10 years' imprisonment. [15]

Combating regionalism by militarization and centralization

Postindependence Indonesia has been plagued by disaffection in the regions outside Java, which has frequently fueled regional movements for greater autonomy. In confronting problems of national integration, Suharto's strategy has differed from that of his predecessor. From the time of his accession to power he has undercut threats posed by movements for regional autonomy through a policy of militarization and centralization.

The first steps were taken in 1969 with a major structural reorganization of the armed forces, wherein control was centralized within the Department of Defense and Security and a new system of regional commands was created that ensured greater subordination to the center. Through the army's territorial structure, which corresponded to the various levels of the civilian bureaucracy, the regime was able to exert political pressure at every level

[13] For a full account of this affair, see David Bourchier, *Dynamics of Dissent in Indonesia: Sawito and the Phantom Coup* (Ithaca, N.Y.: Cornell University Modern Indonesia Project, 1984).
[14] See Jenkins, *Suharto and His Generals,* p. 162.
[15] For an account of the Tanjung Priok incident and the trials of the Muslim leaders, see Amnesty International, *Indonesia: Muslim Prisoners of Conscience* (London: Amnesty International Publications, 1986).

of society, for the army was able not only to exercise its military functions at every level but also to monitor and largely control political and social developments.[16] The concept of the army's dual function, or *dwi-fungsi,* originally developed by Nasution in the 1950s, was much expanded under the Suharto regime. This doctrine asserted not only the army's right but its duty to participate as a "social-political force" throughout the society, with its commanding role legitimized in the civilian as well as military arena.

To prevent the warlordism of the 1950s from reemerging in the regions, throughout the 1970s no territorial command outside Java was held by a native son, and Javanese dominated all top echelons of the army hierarchy.[17] The firmness of central military control was successful in preventing a serious challenge to Jakarta from any of the previously volatile regional commands, nor during the past two decades has militant Islamic opposition in any region posed more than a minor problem.

But the government has faced real challenges in two principal territories—East Timor and Irian Jaya, formerly West Irian. Claiming it was combating a leftist threat within the archipelago, Jakarta, on December 7, 1975, invaded the former Portuguese colony of East Timor, less than two weeks after one of the contending groups, Fretilin, had declared it an independent nation. Indonesian forces met fierce resistance from the Fretilin troops and carried out a long, drawn-out, bloody and brutal war in which perhaps a third of East Timor's population (which numbered 650,000 prior to the invasion) have died. In 1976, after a show of consultation with selected leaders, Jakarta officially incorporated East Timor as Indonesia's twenty-seventh province, and the Suharto regime defied repeated U.N. resolutions calling for the withdrawal of Indonesian forces. Some 20,000 Indonesian soldiers were reportedly still engaged in a war that had become a running sore for Indonesia's relations with the outside world. Although the intensity of the guerrilla fighting gradually wound down, as late as October 1987, more than a decade after the initial invasion, Fretilin probably still had about 3,000 soldiers in the field and there seemed little likelihood that the war would peter out.[18]

The other major armed opposition has been in Irian Jaya (West Irian), which was finally relinquished by the Dutch and, via the United Nations, turned over to Indonesia in mid-1963. Subsequently, "Indonesia's secret war" has been waged against stubborn resistance from a number of Papuan groups, the largest being the Organization for a Free Papua (OPM), which are disorganized but persistent, and often able to find haven across the border in Papua New Guinea.

[16] For a table of the parallel military and civilian bureaucracies and their interaction, see Jenkins, *Suharto and His Generals,* p. 46.

[17] Javanese consistently constituted between 74 and 80 percent of the office holders listed in the "Current Data on the Indonesian Military Elite" prepared by the editors of the journal *Indonesia.* See, for example, *Indonesia* 26 (October 1978), 161, and 29 (April 1980), 157.

[18] See Raymond Bonner, "A Reporter at Large: The New Order—II," *The New Yorker,* June 13, 1988.

In attempting to strengthen its grip on the archipelago, Jakarta has utilized one of the major components of Indonesia's development policy, the transmigration program, under which people are transferred from densely populated provinces of Central and East Java and Bali to some 250 sites in the more sparsely populated provinces of the outer islands. The transmigrants have been settled in Sumatra (primarily the Lampung area of South Sumatra), Kalimantan and Sulawesi, as well as in East Timor and Irian Jaya. The transmigration policy has helped Jakarta strengthen its control over dissident and potentially dissident areas, but it also has increased fears of Javanese colonization. The indigenous inhabitants resent the intrusion and encroachment of the Javanese settlers on their land and the fact that the Javanese are usually given privileged access to jobs, housing and education. Some 750,000 families were involved in the Suharto regime's third Five-Year Plan (Repelita 3, 1978–83), bringing to over a million those reported as having been resettled since 1969.

In recent years, the ecological damage inflicted by many of these transmigrant settlements has strengthened opposition to the policy and led to international criticism. Originally a strong proponent of transmigration, the World Bank has urged that the rate of sponsored settlement be eased and major emphasis shifted to the consolidation and development of existing sites. After the fall in oil prices in 1986, the transmigration budget was reduced by 42 percent.

Leadership and succession

At this writing, Suharto's position at the apex of government remains unchallenged. In March 1988, at the age of 66, he was elected to his fifth, and what many believe will be his final, five-year term as president. The steps that preceded and accompanied this reassertion of his dominance demonstrate the skills he has employed to maintain and strengthen his position over the previous two decades. But the latest maneuvers left the scene no clearer as to how power will be transferred from Suharto to a successor government or who his successor as president might be.

During his fourth presidential term (1983–88), Suharto became more isolated. Two of his closest colleagues since he seized power, Ali Murtopo and Sudjono Humardani, died, leaving him with few close contemporaries on whose counsel he could rely. He also became vulnerable to ever-increasing public criticism of the greed and corruption of his family. His wife has long been notorious for her business activities, but her greed has now been surpassed by that of their children, as they have used their privileged position to build their own business empires. As the *Wall Street Journal* reported in November 1986: "The growing power and importance of the Suharto family and its friends in Indonesia's economy has tarnished the president's reputation as a shrewd and pragmatic leader." [19]

Public criticism of the president's family and of his unwillingness to restrain their rapacity also spread to the armed forces. This probably influenced the events of early 1988 when Suharto replaced Army Commander

[19] See the *Asian Wall Street Journal*, November 24, 25, 26, 1986.

Benny Moerdani with Try Sutrisno and there was unprecedented dissension over the election of the vice president.

The government party Golkar nominated 61-year-old Lieutenant General Sudharmono, formerly state secretary and general chairman of Golkar for the vice-presidency. The army leadership, however, was unwilling to join Golkar in putting Sudharmono's name into nomination, and its unhappiness with the choice was dramatized when a member of the military faction in parliament grabbed the microphone to protest the mode of selection. And even before Sudharmono's name was officially proposed, the PPP had nominated its own chairman, Naro, who withdrew only at the last moment when Suharto made it clear that Sudharmono was his personal choice. Although Sudharmono was finally unanimously elected by the MPR (People's Consultative Assembly), such public contention over the vice-presidency was unprecedented; previous holders of the position (the sultan of Yogyakarta, Adam Malik, and Umar Wirahadikusuma) had been unopposed. And whether the strife was real or contrived—possibly as an indication to Sudharmono not to presume on an automatic succession—it underscored the uncertainty surrounding Indonesia's post-Suharto leadership.

It was in late February 1988 that the president precipitately removed Benny Moerdani from his position as commander-in-chief of the armed forces and announced his replacement by the former army chief of staff, Try Sutrisno, who had several years earlier served as Suharto's aide. Although, after a period of uncertainty regarding Moerdani's fate, Suharto ultimately included him in his new cabinet as minister of defense, the abruptness of Moerdani's dismissal seemed to signal the president's determination to assert his own dominance vis-à-vis the army. Moerdani, however, appears to have retained much of his support within the armed forces. Although the Ministry of Defense lost considerable authority during Moerdani's tenure as commander-in-chief, it is probably not beyond his abilities to resuscitate it. As of June 1988 he still had not been officially removed as head of the Security and Order Command, Kopkamtib, although it had been announced that Kopkamtib would be reorganized and a new head appointed.

It is not beyond the realm of possibility that the sudden surge of rumors in the spring of 1988 that former PKI members were posing a renewed danger could be part of a power play to justify maintaining Kopkamtib in existence. Moerdani also retains many of his protégés and intelligence subordinates in key positions under the new commander-in-chief, Try Sutrisno, and it is unclear whether Try, who does not have a reputation as a strong leader, will be able either to replace them with his own people or win their loyalty. For the time being, it appears that Try, generally viewed as Suharto's preferred heir, and Moerdani are making at least a public show of cooperation, and Moerdani still appears to be much the stronger.

Although technically in line to succeed Suharto, Vice President Sudharmono is not viewed as Suharto's likely successor, probably not even by Suharto himself and certainly not by the army, and it is generally assumed that even if Suharto were to die in office the vice president would be in no position to take over. The events of the early months of 1988 demonstrated that Suharto himself intends for at least the next five years to control the political scene, ensuring that no potential successor is in a position to accumulate too much power. The president's brusqueness and shrewdness in his manipulation of the competitors for office demonstrate a notable self-confidence and a clear determination that even those officials wielding most power under him should realize that they serve at his pleasure.

FURTHER READING

Anderson, Benedict. *Mythology and the Tolerance of the Javanese.* Ithaca, New York: Cornell Modern Indonesia Project, 1965.

————, and Kahin, Audrey, eds. *Interpreting Indonesian Politics: Thirteen Contributions to the Debate, 1964–1981.* Ithaca, New York: Cornell Modern Indonesia Project, 1982.

————, and McVey, Ruth. *A Preliminary Analysis of the October 1, 1965 Coup in Indonesia.* Ithaca, New York: Cornell Modern Indonesia Project, 1971.

Bourchier, David. *Dynamics of Dissent in Indonesia: Sawito and the Phantom Coup.* Ithaca, New York: Cornell Modern Indonesia Project, 1984.

Crouch, Harold. *The Army and Politics in Indonesia.* 2nd ed. Ithaca, New York: Cornell University Press, 1988.

Feith, Herbert. *The Decline of Constitutional Democracy in Indonesia.* Ithaca, New York: Cornell University Press, 1962.

Geertz, Clifford. *The Religion of Java.* Glencoe, New York: Free Press, 1960.

Jenkins, David. *Suharto and His Generals: Indonesia's Military Politics, 1975–1983.* Ithaca, New York: Cornell Modern Indonesia Project, 1984.

Kahin, Audrey R., ed. *Regional Dynamics of the Indonesian Revolution: Unity From Diversity.* Honolulu: University of Hawaii Press, 1985.

Kahin, George McT. *Nationalism and Revolution in Indonesia.* Ithaca, New York: Cornell University Press, 1952.

Legge, J. D. *Indonesia.* Englewood Cliffs, New Jersey: Prentice-Hall, 1964.

McDonald, Hamish. *Suharto's Indonesia.* Blackburn, Victoria, Australia: Fontana, 1980.

Mortimer, Rex. *Indonesian Communism Under Sukarno: Ideology and Politics, 1959–1965.* Ithaca, New York: Cornell University Press, 1974.

Robison, Richard. *Indonesia: The Rise of Capital.* Sydney: Allen & Unwin, 1986.

JAPAN

HARUHIRO FUKUI

INTRODUCTION

To most casual, and many not so casual, observers, Japan is a miracle. Despite its modest physical size, its peripheral geographical position and its lack of natural resources vital to a modern industrial economy, it has attained one of the highest standards of living in the world, as measured by per capita GNP, life expectancy at birth and education. Moreover, this has been accomplished with minimal social dislocations, as measured by the incidences of labor disputes, violent crimes, divorces, etc.[1] It has done so not only with remarkable rapidity—in fact, within one century since it abandoned feudalism and self-imposed isolation and began consciously and systematically to modernize itself, and half a century since its devastating defeat in World War II—but also with rare political peace and stability. Nothing testifies to the extraordinary degree of political stability in postwar Japan more eloquently than the fact that the conservatives—the Liberal Democratic party since 1955—were in power for years without interruption since 1948.

A number of eminent scholars[2] attribute the success of the Japanese (and also their failure) mainly to their "national character," which emphasizes the virtues of learning, industry, self-discipline, loyalty, cooperation, consensus-based decision-making, social harmony, collective achievement and, above all, strong national identity and cohesiveness. The combination of these qualities makes Japan, according to these observers, unique among the countries of the world.

To borrow the language and categories developed nearly two decades ago by erstwhile modernization theorists,[3] Japan thus appears to have resolved its "crises of development"—i.e., crises of identity, legitimacy, participa-

---

[1] Keizai Koho Center, *Japan 1988: An International Comparison* (Tokyo: Keizai Koho Center, 1987), pp. 8, 10–11, 92–93.

[2] Ruth Benedict, *The Chrysanthemum and the Sword* (Boston: Houghton Mifflin Co., 1946); Chie Nakane, *Japanese Society* (Berkeley: University of California Press, 1970); Ezra F. Vogel, *Japan as No. 1: Lessons for America* (Cambridge, Mass.: Harvard University Press, 1979).

[3] Leonard Binder et al., *Crises and Sequences in Political Development* (Princeton, N.J.: Princeton University Press, 1971).

tion, penetration and distribution—with great finesse and resounding success. To use another term that was also once popular with those modernization theorists, Japan's nation-building process appears to have been singularly smooth and effective. These impressions are in fact well-founded as far as the majority of its male population is concerned, but, as will be seen later, not as far as some of its minorities and women are concerned.

This essay first briefly reviews the processes of the developmental crises—or rather "problems," as one of the principal architects of the original analytical model preferred to call them at the time[4]—from the perspective of the male majority, characterized as the "mainstream," and then examines them in greater detail from the perspective of the minorities and women, referred to as the "sidestreams." In so doing, the temporal sequence of the several types of problems assumed by the modernization theorists is ignored, and the discussion begins with penetration and proceeds to identity, participation and distribution in that order, without specifically dealing with legitimacy, which is of a somewhat different order and has to do with each of the four problems mentioned.[5]

Throughout the discussion, penetration is taken to mean the extension of central government authority and control into geographical areas or population groups formerly not under such control. Identity means the sense of belonging to a group, i.e., acceptance of membership in a group, in this case the Japanese state. Participation refers to active involvement in the political process—whether peaceful and orderly, as in the case of voting in an election, or disorderly and violent, as in the case of a politically inspired riot. Finally, distribution is defined as allocation of goods, services or opportunities among various segments of a population.

POLITICAL DEVELOPMENT IN MAINSTREAM JAPAN

Penetration
The earliest unified state of Japan, known as Yamato, emerged apparently in and around what is now Nara prefecture by the 4th century A.D., as one influential clan among dozens established hegemonic rule over the others either by force or by suasion. Within the next few centuries the embryonic state ruled by the clan claiming a divine right to rulership (thus known as the Emperor Clan) successfully extended its effective power southwestward as far as the southern end of Kyushu, though not without some fierce resistance from local tribal groups. Northeastward, Yamato's authority expanded fairly quickly and easily as far as the Kanto Plain at roughly midpoint in Honshu. By the early 8th century the imperial government seated in Nara thus ruled, more or less effectively, the southwestern half of what is Japanese territory today, with a population estimated at six to seven

[4] See Sidney Verba, "Sequences and Development," in Binder, *Crises and Sequences,* p. 299.
[5] See Raymond Grew, ed., *Crises of Political Development in Europe and the United States* (Princeton, N.J.: Princeton University Press, 1978), 28.

million.[6] Farther up beyond the bend of the bow-shaped Honshu island, however, the penetration by the Yamato state and its successors encountered far more determined and effective resistance among the aboriginal population, known as the Ezo or Emishi and probably ethnically identical with the Ainu in Hokkaido. It took the central state authority until the early 10th century to conquer and penetrate the northernmost parts of Honshu, and until the 19th century even to begin to bring Hokkaido under its effective rule.

The early Yamato rulers relied mainly on ideological and legal means to extend their control over alien and hostile groups and territories. The two extensive codes of laws enacted in the early 8th century by imperial order *(Taiho ritsuryo;* 701 and *Yoro ritsuryo;* 757) and the two official records of imperial acts and related events compiled during the same period, also by imperial order *(Kojiki;* 712 and *Nihongi;* ca. 720), typify the use of such means.

Emperors did not personally rule the state very long. They were replaced in the early 10th century by their aristocratic advisers and regents, who were in turn replaced by warrior (samurai) rulers in the late 12th century. This was followed by nearly four centuries of chronic political instability and intermittent civil war; while leading warrior clans battled each other for temporary advantage and hegemony, armed Buddhist orders, bands of disgruntled lower samurai and mobs of impoverished peasants revolted against the precarious central and local government authority.

Effective central authority was reestablished, and the country, which now extended from the northern end of Honshu to the southern end of Kyushu, was reunified in the 1580s by the last successful warrior ruler, or shogun, of pre-Tokugawa Japan, Toyotomi Hideyoshi. He did two things that none of his predecessors had ever done to ensure the effective penetration of his government and its firm grip on the country and its population, estimated to be about 18 million. First, he undertook a series of systematic land surveys throughout the country, with a view to better controlling the peasant population and stabilizing tax revenue. Second, he made it illegal for peasants to possess arms (swords) and thus ensured the monopoly of force by members of the warrior class. These two measures vastly expanded the scope of effective central government authority over the territory and population of what was then Japan.

Tokugawa Ieyasu, who founded a new shogunate in 1603, and his heirs (the Tokugawa), who maintained the regime for the next two-and-a-half centuries (1603–1867), built on Toyotomi's legacies, further extending and consolidating the power of the central government over nearly 300 local lords (daimyo) and their domains, with a total population of about 30 million in the early 19th century. An effective method used by the Tokugawa to achieve that end was the initially informal requirement for all daimyo to visit and stay in the country's new capital, Edo (contemporary Tokyo), every other year. Referred to as *sankin kotai,* or alternate-year at-

[6] This figure and all the others hereafter cited for pre–19th-century periods are the best estimates available and not hard and fast numbers.

tendance, the system kept the Tokugawa shogunate's potential rivals not only under constant surveillance but also economically weakened by forcing them to travel considerable distances between their home domains and the capital as often as every second year, and then requiring their stay in the capital for a year, in appropriate style and with a large number of retainers.

Another and even more important means by which the Tokugawa shogunate kept the country under control for so long was the ban on travel abroad by Japanese and on visits to Japan by all foreigners except a small number of Chinese, Korean and Dutch merchants. Principally intended to prevent the spread of Christianity—a religion believed to be fundamentally hostile and inimical to the shogunate—the policy also helped the central government to maintain a virtual trading monopoly by preventing potentially anti-Tokugawa daimyo in southwestern domains from freely engaging in lucrative deals with foreign merchants.

Both the alternate-year attendance system and the travel and trade ban were maintained until the Tokugawa shogunate was overthrown in the restoration of imperial rule (the Meiji Restoration) in the mid-19th century. By then Japan had successfully resolved a substantial part of its penetration problem, with, however, a few important exceptions, which will be discussed further on.

Identity

The consciousness of distinctive national character, and the assertion of national identity and independence developed early in the history of the Japanese state. The name Yamato was written in contemporary Chinese records with a character meaning deference or obedience, and in all likelihood with dismissive overtones. By the late 7th century, however, the Japanese had replaced this character with a combination of two, meaning a place where the sun rises. Increasingly it was pronounced Nihon rather than Yamato, until the mid-19th century when the Meiji government decreed that it be pronounced Nippon.

By the early 8th century an elaborate myth about the divine creation of the country was current among the ruling elite, though probably not among the common people until a few centuries later, as the official history book, *Nihongi,* attests.[7] Japanese national identity was thus born in defiance of mighty imperial China, and was wrapped in the mythology of divine conception and protection of the island empire. This national identity in turn nurtured fundamentally defensive, deliberately mystical and often fanatical nationalism, especially as the country was subjected to repeated invasion attempts by foreign forces after the late 10th century.

Particularly significant in this regard were the assaults by Mongolian forces in the late 13th century. Kublai Khan's flotillas were twice stopped and destroyed—off the Kyushu coast in 1274 and off the southwestern tip of Honshu seven years later—not by Japanese naval forces or garrisons onshore but by powerful typhoons. The typhoons were quickly interpreted as

[7] Murayama Shuichi, *Shinbutsu shugo shiso* [The ideology of Shinto-Buddhist syncretism] (Kyoto: Heirakuji shoten, 1957), 95–101.

"divine winds," and the "miracle" was subsequently related with much exaggeration in countless popular stories, adding enormously to the credibility of the old myth about the divine origin and the sacred and invincible character of the country among the elite and the masses alike. The popularity of the myth subsequently had tragic consequences for many people, especially during World War II.

Scholars and publicists played a critical role in identity-building among Japanese. During the Tokugawa period, two groups of scholars were particularly influential in formulating, or reformulating, and disseminating nationalistic ideas and sentiments. One was the large and heterogeneous group of neo-Confucianist scholars who subscribed to many of the doctrines developed by the Chinese philosopher, Zhuxi (Chu Hsi), in the late 12th century; they were thus collectively known as the Zhuxi school. They preached the duty of a subject to be absolutely loyal and obedient to his lord, a child to his or her parents and a wife to her husband. They also fought against the traditional Chinese ideology that held China to be the center of human civilization (the "Middle Kingdom") and the rest of the world, including Japan, to be barbarian; and they developed a counterideology of essential equality between China and Japan, though not between the two and the rest of the world.

The other, and somewhat more cohesive, group, known as the national-learning *(kokugaku)* school, was interested in clarifying the origins and essential character of the Japanese state and its culture. Politically, the most potent of their efforts was to restore Shinto in its unadulterated form—as it had presumably been before contact with and contamination by Buddhism and Confucianism, both imported from abroad. This provided an ideological justification for the Meiji Restoration in the mid-19th century and the designation of Shinto as the state religion by the new government. Some members of the school also emphasized the ethnic homogeneity of the Japanese people and argued for equality among all Japanese regardless of class differences. Perhaps for this reason, the majority of their students were common farmers and townspeople rather than samurai.

Tokugawa Japan, however, (and pre-Tokugawa Japan, too) was ideologically no more homogeneous or monolithic than post-Meiji Japan.[8] Neither neo-Confucianists nor national-learning scholars ever monopolized the attention and support of the entire elite or, especially, of the common people. Many scholars deliberately attempted to integrate Shinto and Confucianist ideas. Among the masses, Shinto and Buddhist beliefs and rites were not only almost totally mixed up but often inspired open and violent revolts against the authorities, contrary to and in defiance of the orthodox ideology of loyalty and obedience. The so-called new religions of the late Tokugawa and early Meiji period, such as the Kurozumi, Konko, Tenri, Maruyama and Omoto sects, all tended in the beginning to be antiestablishment, reformist and antinationalist, until they apostatized under government pressure and invariably became fervently nationalistic.

[8] For perceptive comments, see Carol Gluck, *Japan's Modern Myths: Ideology in the Late Meiji Period* (Princeton, N.J.: Princeton University Press, 1985).

Despite the ideological diversity suggested above, a set of core values was preached by virtually all ideologues and publicists, and accepted nearly universally both among the elite and the masses of Tokugawa and post-Tokugawa Japan. These values were honesty, industry, thrift, filial piety and communal harmony, all of which became integral ingredients of modern Japanese national identity, often in combination with the belief in the divinity of the country. They were inculcated into the masses by Shinto, Buddhist and, especially, Confucian and neo-Confucian scholars, not only at congregations of the faithful but, even more important, at secular schools.

The earliest Tokugawa-era schools that began to appear in the second quarter of the 17th century, called "domain schools" (hangaku), were run by domain governments for the benefit of youth from samurai families. The schools taught fairly sophisticated subjects, including Chinese classics, Shinto theology and, increasingly, Western sciences such as medicine, geography, astronomy and mathematics. This type of school multiplied in the 18th century, and about 280 were set up in all major urban centers of the country by the end of the Tokugawa period. These official schools were joined by private and far more modest "temple schools" (teragoya) for children from commoner families. Typically, volunteer Shinto priests, Buddhist monks and samurai taught the Japanese alphabet (syllabary), simpler Chinese characters, arithmetic (often including the use of abacus) and morals at some 10,000 establishments of this kind that dotted the map of Tokugawa Japan.

Education provided by these various schools played a critical role in the crystallization of Japanese national identity. First of all, it significantly raised the general level of literacy. The first letters Japanese ever learned, probably in the late 3rd century A.D., were Chinese ideographs, which, however, they pronounced as Japanese words rather than Chinese. By the late 9th century this bastardization had gone so far as to give rise to creation of a new and totally distinctive alphabet of 47 (later 48) phonetic symbols (kana or hiragana), derived from so many Chinese characters, and then further to a second alphabet with the same number of letters but with each letter written slightly differently (katakana). This Japanization of Chinese characters had revolutionary significance in the development of Japanese identity: it brought literacy within the reach not only of the privileged few but also of many common people.

An elegant and easier way to learn the alphabet was invented probably by a very literate Buddhist monk around A.D. 1000—a 47-letter poem that used every letter in the alphabet once and only once. It went "i-ro-ha ni-ho-he-to, chi-ri-nu-ru-wo, wa-ka-yo ta-re-so tsu-ne-na-ra-mu, u-i no o-ku-ya-ma ke-hu ko-e-te, a-sa-ki yu-me mi-si, e-hi mo se-su" or, to translate roughly, "Even while fragrance still lingers, [flowers] are now gone. But who in this world of ours can ever be permanent? I passed through the remote mountain of impermanence today, dreaming a faint dream while not even drunk." Subsequent generations of children—and vastly increased numbers of them after the 17th century, when domain and temple schools were introduced, and virtually all after the turn of the 20th century, when compulsory universal primary education became a practice as well as theory under the Meiji government—owe their literacy to the inspirational, if not entirely coherent, poem.

The dreariness of learning arithmetic was no doubt considerably reduced by a similar method. Children learned numbers by singing "hi-hu-mi-yo, i-mu-na, . . ." (one-two-three-four, five-six-seven, . . .), much as American children do with their numbers. Since at least the 16th century Japanese children have learned multiplication as well by chanting "ni-ichi-ga-ni, ni-ni-ga-shi, ni-san-ga-roku . . ., ku-shichi-rokujusan, ku-ha-shichiju-ni, ku-ku-hachijuichi" (two by one is two, two by two is four, two by three is six, . . . nine by seven is sixty-three, nine by eight is seventy-two, and nine by nine is eighty-one).[9]

It was with the help of these pedagogical devices of premodern origin, as well as the schools of more recent vintage, that the standards of literacy and numeracy among Japanese were vastly improved during the Tokugawa period. The spread of literacy and numeracy in turn helped popularize the beliefs and values of neo-Confucian and national-learning scholars among the masses. A series of popular moral texts by the neo-Confucianist Kaibara Ekiken became best-sellers in the late 17th century. Girls from samurai families, and even from some commoner families after the late 17th century, were increasingly taught at schools and with textbooks not only the special skills expected of women—cooking, washing, child-rearing, sewing, weaving, etc.—but also special morals for women, above all, obedience and faithfulness to husbands and in-laws.

For most Japanese, then, a sense of national identity, anchored on a set of myths about the country's unique origin and character and beliefs about correct social order and proper individual behavior, was well developed by the mid-Tokugawa period. In the last half of that period and the first 70 years after the Meiji Restoration, up until the end of World War II, that identity, and its mythological, ideological and moral foundations, were subjected to occasional criticisms both within Japan and abroad but were never seriously threatened. The Japanese had thus become "the most thoroughly unified and culturally homogeneous large bloc of people in the whole world, with the possible exception of the North Chinese."[10] This observation by no means applies to all members of Japanese society.

Participation
There was little in the political traditions of premodern and early modern Japan that encouraged participatory government in the contemporary sense of the term. Nonetheless, there was some political participation by certain segments of the ruled: Farmers and townspeople participated in local administration, and peasants frequently petitioned or protested to local authorities, often with violence, for a variety of grievances. This limited experience helped to prepare many Japanese for the introduction of representative

[9] Yokoi Kiyoshi, *Gekokujo no bunka* [The culture of the lower ranks dominating the upper ranks] (Tokyo: Tokyo daigaku shuppankai, 1980), 203–10.
[10] Edwin O. Reischauer, *The Japanese* (Cambridge, Mass: Harvard University Press, 1977), 34.

and electoral government after the Meiji Restoration. Some groups, notably women, however, were almost totally excluded from any form of political participation until after World War II.

The Tokugawa shogunate was a remarkably durable military dictatorship with a rigidly hierarchical power structure and an equally rigid system of social stratification. The country's population was neatly divided into two general classes—samurai (the rulers) and nonsamurai. The latter were further divided into two subclasses—peasants and townspeople—one living off the land and the other involved in business. The underclass were the outcaste, known as *eta* (unclean multitudes, or untouchables) or *hinin* (nonhumans).

The Tokugawa owed the moral inspiration and justification for their rule to the same neo-Confucian and national-learning scholars and ideologues who, as already seen, helped mold national identity in pre-Meiji Japan. The early Tokugawa neo-Confucianist Hayashi Razan, for example, told readers of his popular moral text *A Summary of Three Virtues (Santokusho)* that relations between a lord and his subjects, father and children, husband and wife, brothers, and friends were set for eternity and could not be changed. Significantly, most Japanese students of Zhuxi-school neo-Confucianism, unlike their Chinese counterparts, rejected revolution as a legitimate means of political change. National-learning scholars, such as Kamo no Mabuchi and Motoori Norinaga, too, preached the subject's duty to respect and obey his lord under any and all circumstances.

As important in providing moral justification for the centralized power structure of the Tokugawa regime was the conception of "family" (fictitious and highly patriarchal) that had evolved since the 14th century. According to this conception a family was not primarily a kinship group but a quasi-corporate entity whose members may not necessarily be related to each other by blood and whose essential rationale is to perpetuate itself, with its name, crest, property, trade and reputation. It could thus survive the deaths of its members, even of its head, by adopting new members to replace them. This model of corporate family easily lent itself to the view that a village, a domain and, ultimately, the nation were all a kind of family; each daimyo domain was a large "family" and the nation was the largest, the shogun being its patriarch.

The Tokugawa owed the physical conditions of their rule to their immediate predecessor, Toyotomi Hideyoshi, who had reunified the war-torn country and separated the ruling class from the ruled by totally disarming the latter. Members of the ruling class, which accounted for no more than about 7 percent of the total population,[11] were subdivided into a number of ranks, each with its own duties and tasks to perform in national, i.e., shogunal, interest.

With the help of the sympathetic ideologues and publicists, and a cleverly contrived system of social stratification, the Tokugawa shogunate ruled the country almost unchallenged. They owned one-fourth of Japan's agri-

[11] Sekiyama Naotaro, *Kinsei nihon no jinko kozo* [The population structure of early modern Japan] (Tokyo: Yoshikawa kobunkan, 1957), 312.

cultural land, controlled all major cities and mines, monopolized effective military power and dictated to everybody else, including the most powerful among the rival lords, the imperial court in Kyoto, and venerable Shinto and Buddhist establishments throughout the country.[12] Except within their own domain (called *tenryo*, i.e., the heaven's domain) scattered throughout the country, Tokugawa's power was exercised indirectly by the lords and officials of nearly 300 domain *(han)* governments. The latter in turn directed the headmen of villages in their domains to administer the day-to-day local affairs and, most importantly, collect and deliver taxes promptly and in exactly prescribed amounts.

Even this seemingly watertight system, however, left some space for limited popular participation in political processes. Affairs within a village, including, for example, the assessment and collection of taxes from farm families, were managed normally by a village government made up, typically, of three kinds of officials: the headman *(nanushi,* or *shoya),* who acted as the agent of the domainal lord; several vice-headmen *(kumigashira, otona-byakusho,* or *toshiyori),* often each representing a particular hamlet in the village; and a farmers' representative *(hyakushodai).* Often these village officials were elected by taxpaying farmers, usually by consensus. Poorer peasants did not pay taxes and did not participate in village administration.

The neo-Confucianist and national-learning scholars' admonition about proper relationships between the ruler and the ruled was occasionally challenged by an older tradition of popular uprisings. Since the earliest recorded period in Japanese history, one messianic belief or another had periodically led normally silent, obedient and law-abiding people, often in large itinerant groups, into collective frenzy and orgies, ostensibly to celebrate the alleged or expected arrival of an era of universal happiness and abundance. They would enter the houses of wealthy farmers or merchants, help themselves to food, wine, furniture, etc., and dance and sing, oblivious to the normal codes of behavior that governed their daily lives. This tradition was combined with another stream of traditional popular belief, probably dating back at least to the early 13th century, which held that those of lower station (the ruled) might rightfully rebel against and dominate those of higher station (the rulers) under certain circumstances—as when the latter acted in an obviously unreasonable way.

The series of peasant revolts that rocked the Tokugawa regime was at least partially a product of the coming together of the two old traditions in the life and culture of the Japanese peasant. Throughout the Tokugawa period, and with increasing frequency and intensity as time passed, hordes of disgruntled peasants, armed with sickles, hoes and other handy "weapons," attacked local government offices and officials' dwellings to vent their grievances over high taxes, blocked access to water or the village commons, wrongdoing by officials, etc. These revolts were nearly always started by a collective decision of the villagers, not by individuals. In the last half of

---

[12] For a general survey of the politics of the period, see Conrad Totman, *Politics in the Tokugawa Bakufu, 1600–1843* (Cambridge, Mass.: Harvard University Press, 1967).

the Tokugawa period, moreover, revolts were often planned and led by village headmen against domain policy and/or officials, and tended to spread quickly from one village to another until the whole domain was engulfed in the turmoil. Some even spread over two or more domains.

According to one study there were 3,200 such revolts recorded during the Tokugawa period, or slightly more than one per month; according to another study there were 3,711 of them between 1590 and 1877. As a comparison of these two sets of statistics suggests, rural revolts continued after the Meiji Restoration, until the last rebels were brought to their knees by the newly created Western-style army. Thereafter, mob-style political participation was gradually replaced by a better controlled and more orderly form, represented by political party and electoral institutions. The old-style revolts, however, never completely disappeared, because the trappings of modern representative government introduced by the Meiji leaders—a national legislature, i.e., the Imperial Diet, and prefectural and local assemblies, set up by 1890—by no means opened avenues of orderly and effective political participation for all Japanese. Franchise was initially limited to the wealthy men (those who paid prescribed amounts of taxes) in both national and local elections, and it was not until 1925 that this "property requirement" was removed and the franchise was extended to all male adults. Even then, women remained categorically excluded from formal political participation.

Distribution

While one tends to focus on the rapid growth of the Japanese economy in the post—World War II period, it had actually been growing at a steady pace for centuries before the war. During the Tokugawa period, in particular, both the rural and urban sectors of the economy expanded significantly. Extensive development of new agricultural land added millions of new acres to the country's total stock of farmland. This was done both at individual farmers' initiative and under national or local government auspices and with the use of increasingly sophisticated irrigation and drainage systems. According to one estimate, farmland acreage doubled from about 3.7 million at the end of the 16th century to 7.3 million by the early 18th century, and further increased to about 10.8 million by 1880.[13] Agricultural technology made substantial progress, too, resulting in the increasing use of improved seeds, fertilizer and farming implements, while a variety of cash crops, such as cotton, mulberry (for sericulture), tobacco, tea and indigo, were planted in many parts of the country.

The urban sector of the economy expanded even faster. By 1800 the country's major cities had larger populations than most of their European counterparts: Tokyo had well over a million people, and Kyoto and Osaka both had over one-third of a million, while a dozen other cities had 100,000 or more.[14] These populations included growing ranks of artisans, mer-

---

[13] Egashira Tsuneharu, *Nihon kokumin keizai shi* [A history of the Japanese national economy] (Tokyo: Minerva shobo, 1970), 320.
[14] Ibid., pp. 338–39.

chants and fledgling manufacturers. Pottery, metallurgy, papermaking, and silk reeling and weaving, in particular, developed quickly, partly spurred by the introduction of a wide array of new Western technology.

Despite all the progress made during the Tokugawa period, however, the prevailing standard of living in Japan at the beginning of its modern economic development was considerably lower than that in any of today's advanced industrial states at a comparable stage of economic history. For example, according to one set of estimates, Japan's per capita GNP in 1886 was equal to U.S. $136 in 1965 (in 1965 dollars), as compared to the United States' $474 (1834–43), Great Britain's $227 (1765–85), Germany's $302 (1850–59), France's $242 (1831–40) and Italy's $261 (1861–69). In the first few years of the 1870s Japan's per capita GNP was about one-fourth that of Britain's and one-third that of the United States'.[15] Steady progress in the next half-century raised the Japanese standard of living by the late 1930s to a rank "halfway between the 'elite' nations of the West and the populations of Asia still ridden with grinding poverty, malnutrition, and disease."[16]

World War II caused Japan catastrophic losses both in human lives and in material wealth. The war left some three million Japanese dead, missing or seriously wounded and reduced Japan's national wealth by one-quarter, or an amount equal to that accumulated during the preceding decade, 1935–45. At the end of 1945 not only were there some 13 million jobless but those fortunate enough to be employed at that time were paid real wages equal to about 10 percent or less of the 1934–36 national average. Annual manufacturing and mining production in 1946 was about 30 percent of the 1934–36 average. Japan lay in ruins both economically and spiritually.

How the Japanese not only survived the postwar crisis but achieved in the next 40 years the highest rate of sustained economic growth in modern world history, to emerge as an economic superpower, is a story already told countless times. With changes in the yen/dollar exchange rate, the Japanese now enjoy the highest nominal per capita GNP of the advanced industrial nations. The material affluence brought about by this "miracle" of economic growth has significantly changed Japanese social structure and lifestyle. In particular, it has substantially eased the distribution problem; no longer are there visible pockets of destitution and poverty anywhere in the country, nor are there conspicuous inequalities either across social classes or geographical regions. In fact, Japan's pattern of income distribution in the mid-1980s is one of the most egalitarian in the world.[17] As will be seen later, however, the distribution problem was salient and serious until

[15] Minami Ryoshin, *Nihon no keizai hatten* [Economic development in Japan] (Tokyo: Toyo keizai shinposha, 1981), 3. Cf. Simon Kuznets, *Economic Growth of Nations: Total Output and Production Structure* (Cambridge, Mass.: Harvard University Press, 1971), 22, 24–26.

[16] William W. Lockwood, "The Scale of Economic Growth in Japan, 1868–1938," in Simon Kuznets, Wilbert E. Moore, and Joseph J. Spengler, eds., *Economic Growth: Brazil, India, Japan* (Durham, N.C.: Duke University Press, 1955), 131.

[17] See, for example, The World Bank, *World Development Report 1987* (New York: Oxford University Press, 1987), 252–53, table 26.

very recently in Japanese history and remains a problem, if in a much attenuated form.

Economic growth, social harmony and political stability, significant as they are, do not adequately summarize either Japanese historical experience or the nature of contemporary Japanese society. The country has a long history of widespread material and spiritual poverty, institutionalized discrimination against segments of its population and chronic social conflict—a history that continues to cast its long shadow over the affluent economic superpower. The Ainu, outcastes (*burakumin*) and Koreans are the most obvious examples of victimized groups, but some others, such as Okinawans and women, have also suffered.

The penetration of the Ezo/Ainu territory

As suggested earlier, the penetration and subjugation of the Ezo (Ainu) territory in northern Honshu and Hokkaido by the Japanese state proved a difficult and expensive enterprise, beginning in the 7th century and ending in the 19th century. It required a succession of military assaults both by land and sea, construction of a chain of fortified garrison outposts and enclosed settlements, capture and enslavement of the nomadic hunter-gatherers, their forced conversion to settled agricultural life and their gradual assimilation and/or extermination in one frontier community after another. In this protracted process of conquest, leaders of a few native Ezo clans, such as the Abe, Kiyohara and Fujiwara, managed not only to maintain but even substantially expand their local rule during the 11th and 12th centuries. Their triumph, however, was only temporary and did not survive the continuous and relentless northward advance of Japanese power and presence spearheaded by the Matsumaes, who were ensconced as the rulers of the region in the mid-15th century.

The Japanese invasion of Hokkaido thus began under the pre-Tokugawa rule of the local daimyo, the Matsumaes, who chartered Japanese fishermen and traders to fish and to barter-trade with Ainu in designated parts of the island and for designated periods of time, in exchange for fees. As in many parts of Honshu, the arrival of the Japanese and their ruthlessly exploitative attitudes provoked a number of violent outbursts among the local Ainu, as, for example, the battles of Koshamain in the 15th century and of Shakushain in the 17th century, both recorded in the few surviving old Ainu epics (*yukar*). Throughout the Tokugawa period, sporadic battles continued between Japanese invaders and local Ainu until, in 1769, the shogunate placed the bulk of the Ainu territory—which ambiguously extended beyond Hokkaido to parts of the Sakhalin and Kurile islands—under the central government's direct rule, and appointed the head of the Matsumae clan as the Tokugawa's representative and local administrator. This move was inspired primarily by strategic rather than economic calculations in light of the growing indications of Russian interest in the region.

The Tokugawa shogunate handed the authority to rule Hokkaido back to the Matsumaes in 1821, for financial reasons; but, as the Russian southward advance down the coasts of the Sea of Okhotsk intensified, they reclaimed it in 1855. As will be seen later, this marked an important shift in official Japanese policy toward the Ainu: from the simple physical conquest, occupation and exploitation of their territory, labor and resources to the assimilation of the population—that is, from penetration to Japanization. The Tokugawa government's expanded policy goals were inherited by the Meiji government, which launched a far more systematic development of Hokkaido almost as soon as it replaced the 250-year-old warrior state in 1868.

By the time the penetration of the Ainu territory finally came to an end around the turn of the 20th century, Japanese had successfully colonized and populated the northeastern half of Honshu and Hokkaido. In the latter alone, the immigrant population had risen to about 800,000, including about 40,000 farmers and would-be farmers brought in under a subsidized immigration program launched in 1873. The entire undertaking cost the Japanese state and its citizens not only a great deal of money but also labor. If the penetration of the Ainu territory was a problem for the invaders, to the Ezo/Ainu it was a crisis. Their estimated population in Hokkaido dropped from over 26,000 in the early 19th century to less than 19,000 by the middle of the century and to slightly over 15,000 by 1920. While the Ainu population appears to have recovered somewhat since then—to about 17,000 by the mid-1970s—the Ainu have been culturally, as well as physically, conquered and marginalized in their own country in the name of the development and security of the Japanese state.

The penetration of the Ryukyu islands
The southward expansion of the Yamato state proceeded quickly to the southern tip of Kyushu and nearby offshore islands. Until the early 8th century it had encountered sporadic but violent resistance among the aboriginal population known as either Kumaso or Hayato and, according to some sources, ethnically identified as Malay. However, the Japanese state's relationship with the people inhabiting the island chain more than 300 miles/483 km. farther to the south remained far more tenuous and ambiguous until the early 17th century (and psychologically until the late 20th century).

Ethnically as fully Japanese as Yamato, Ryukyu islanders traded with Kyushu merchants informally but actively as early as the 7th century, and with the formal approval of authorities on both sides by the early 15th century. Meanwhile, they developed just as close a commercial relationship with the Chinese. Moreover, after the late 14th century the Ryukyu court not only maintained an official tributary relationship with the Ming imperial court but frequently used immigrant Chinese as official advisers. In 1609 the southernmost daimyo domain in Kyushu, Satsuma (today's Kagoshima prefecture), annexed the islands by force, established formal political control over them and then proceeded to purge their capital and royal court of pro-Chinese officials. In its desire, however, not to jeopardize lucrative trade with China by offending the Ming court, Satsuma, and at its behest the Ryukyu court as well, not only did not inform the Chinese of the nature of their changed relationship but even behaved as if nothing had happened. The Ryukyu court thus continued to send tributary missions to Beijing every two years, and Ryukyu kings continued to be crowned by Chinese emperors under the policy characterized as one of "dual affiliation" by the Ryukyu king, Shokei, in the early 18th century.

Japan's sovereignty in the Ryukyu islands was officially recognized by the Chinese government only in 1871, following an armed attack on Taiwan by a Satsuma force to revenge the murder of stranded Ryukyuan sailors by islanders. A year later the island group ceased to be a kingdom and became the newest Tokugawa-style feudal domain under the administrative control of the Japanese Ministry of Foreign Affairs. In 1874 it came under the Ministry of Home Affairs' jurisdiction, and the next year it was renamed Okinawa prefecture. The legal status of the island group, however, had not yet been finally settled at this point; in 1880 the Japanese government consented to a scheme proposed by a former president of the United States, Ulysses S. Grant, on behalf of the Chinese government, which would have separated the two southernmost islands in the group, Miyako and Yaeyama, from the rest of the prefecture and reestablished the semiautonomous kingdom in those islands, a scheme eventually aborted by opposition in China.

The apparent ambivalence in the Meiji government's treatment of the Ryukyu islands and their inhabitants was more than matched by the ambivalence in the islanders' response to the deepening Japanese penetration, and eventual destruction, of their once autonomous kingdom. This was inevitable, considering that the whole process was initiated and completed unilaterally by Japanese and with the use, or threat of use, of a considerable amount of military force. That was the case when Satsuma annexed the islands in the early 17th century, and so it was when Tokyo divested the local ruler of his royal title and nationalized his kingdom in the late 19th century. When the island domain was turned into a prefecture in 1875, a unit of the brand-new imperial army's southern (Kumamoto) division was stationed there despite strong local opposition; that 500-man unit joined the Japanese police four years later when the royal palace in the old Ryukyu capital, Shuri, was cleared of its traditional occupants and their possessions converted into a local administrative office of the Meiji state.

Such display of force, however, did not persuade recalcitrant islanders to give up their resistance against the Japanese takeover as quickly as Tokyo hoped. In a series of incidents, those regarded as pro-Japanese met violent reprisals by anti-Japanese local officials and villagers, as in the well-publicized "Sanshi" incident. (*Sanshi* was a local version of the Japanese word "sansei," i.e., approval, of Japanese rule.) In this incident an employee of a police substation on Miyako island was lynched and murdered by a mob for his alleged Japanese sympathy, and members of his family were expelled to another island. Some escaped to China rather than stay in the islands under Japanese rule. Among those who stayed, opponents of Japan, known as the "obstinate" (*gankoha*), were both more numerous and more influential than friends of Japan, known as the "progressives" *(kaikato)*, until Japan defeated China in the 1894–95 war.

Unlike the Ezo/Ainu in northern Japan, Ryukyu islanders were not decimated, at least until the last years of World War II. To many islanders, especially members of the traditional elite, Japanese penetration was nonetheless a disaster of crisis proportions. The experience has had a profound and continuing effect on the islanders' self-image and identity.

National identity among the minority groups

As has been seen, the Japanese penetration and conquest of the northern parts of the country, especially Hokkaido, before and during the Tokugawa period resulted in the decimation and virtual cultural extermination of the Ainu. This was a result, first, of the view of the Matsumae domain government that the Ainu were not only an alien race but should not be allowed to become Japanese or treated like Japanese. They were thus forbidden to speak Japanese until, in the early 19th century, the Tokugawa shogunate temporarily took away from the Matsumaes the administrative authority over the entire Ainu country. After the central government took direct control of the territory for the second and last time in 1854, the Ainu were culturally further deprived—ironically, by the new policy of rapid assimilation and Japanization.

In its effort to make sparsely populated Hokkaido and its indigenous population look like an integral part of the country, the Meiji government now ordered the Ainu, in 1876, to give up their native names in favor of more Japanese-sounding names, their native language in favor of Japanese, and such native customs as the disposition by funerary burning of the dwelling of a deceased person, the wearing of earrings by men and the tattooing of women. In order to ensure the success of the Japanization program, the government then proceeded not only to build schools (as many as 21 by 1909) in larger Ainu villages but even brought some three dozen selected Ainu students to Tokyo to train as future teachers at Ainu schools, an exercise that proved to be a near-total disaster. Equally unsuccessful was the attempt to force the Ainu to give up their highly mobile hunter-gatherer pattern of life and settle down as farmers. As late as 1935 no more than 56 percent of the Ainu were identified as farmers in a survey conducted by the Hokkaido prefectural government. Japanese identity was thus clearly unwanted by most Ainu, not surprising in light of the blatant discrimination to which they continued to be subjected.

The evolution of Japanese policy toward the Ryukyu islands and their inhabitants was somewhat similar to the policy toward the Ainu. The Satsuma domain government viewed the islanders essentially as aliens and treated them as such; in the early 17th century it forbade islanders' use of Japanese names and Japanese-style clothing or hairdos, as well as Japanese visits to the islands without official permission. When a group of islanders went to the Paris exposition in 1867, with Satsuma's permission, members of the group wore a pin identifying them as representatives, not of Japan, but of a "Satsuma-Ryukyu Kingdom"; when the group of stranded Ryukyu sailors were murdered by Taiwanese in 1871, senior Japanese officials argued that the king of the Ryukyu islands was a Ryukyuan and not to be confused with the Japanese nobility; and when the Ryukyu domain was renamed Okinawa prefecture in 1875, the senior secretary of home affairs in the Tokyo government compared Ryukyu "natives" to American Indians.

On the islanders' part, it was not until after the Sino-Japanese War (1894–95) that the majority began to identify themselves as Japanese rather than as either Ryukyuan or Chinese, and not until after the Russo-Japanese War (1904–5) that a few began to adopt Japanese names. Thereafter, however, Japanese identity was not only accepted but even eagerly sought by an increasing number of islanders. Editors of the first local newspaper published in the islands, the *Ryukyu Shinpo*, repeatedly urged their readers to become "exactly like [people in] other prefectures in ways both good and bad."[18] By the early 1930s there were a number of groups, apparently organized with the blessing and support of the prefectural government, that campaigned for the abolition of Ryukyu dialects and wider use of Japanese names. This seemingly voluntary conversion of islanders to Japanese national identity probably reflected their desperate desire to free themselves from persistent discrimination among people in other prefectures, rather than their love of those people's ways. A "theory of ancestral identity between Japanese and Ryukyuans" *(Nichi-ryu doso ron)*, as it was called, was developed by one of the best known Okinawan scholars, the linguist Iha Fuyu; this theory held that Okinawans' ancestors were Japanese, and was explicitly motivated by the same sentiment.

This shift in the local attitude is graphically shown in the enrollment statistics at local public, i.e., Japanese, schools. The percentage of children attending such schools rose from about 2.5 in 1884 to 7.8 in 1888, 31.2 in 1896 and 90.1 in 1906.[19] Discrimination based on differences in speech was particularly widespread and devastating in the armed services. The pre–World War II Japanese conscription system required all normal and healthy boys from the islands as well as other parts of the country to serve in the military for prescribed lengths of time. At least some from every prefecture of the country hated the military and tried to evade the draft, but apparently substantially more from the islands did so to escape the institutionalized practices of discrimination for which the services were notorious. Draft evasion, however, was widely condemned as unpatriotic and dishonorable by both the authorities and the local public and was soon stopped. By the time World War II broke out, patriotism, whether genuine or feigned, swept the islands as powerfully and destructively as it did the rest of the country.

The case of Korean immigrants was far more complicated for at least two reasons. First, they were an ethnically distinct group, with their own old and well-defined national identity. Second, many of them were brought to

[18] Ota Masahide, *Kindai Okinawa no seiji kozo* [The political structure of modern Okinawa] (Tokyo: Keiso shobo, 1972), 122–23.
[19] Arakawa Akira, *Izoku to tenno no kokka* [Aliens and the emperor state] (Tokyo: Nigatsusha, 1973), 91.

Japan against their will and often by force. As a result, Koreans would have been far more resistant to assimilation than the Ainu or Okinawans even if the Japanese had seriously tried to force them to assimilate, which they not only did not try to do but deliberately discouraged.

While a small Korean student community had formed in Tokyo by the beginning of the 20th century, it was after Japan formally annexed the peninsula in 1910 that substantial numbers of Koreans began to migrate to Japan. To a large extent this was a direct result of harshly exploitative Japanese colonial policy, especially expropriation of farms and transfer of their titles to Japanese immigrant farmers, that devastated the economic life of many Korean peasants. Despite the quotas on Korean immigrants that the Japanese maintained between 1925 and 1939, the number of Korean residents in Japan exceeded one million by the latter year, when the quotas were removed in a total reversal of policy in Tokyo. During the next several years, hundreds of thousands of Koreans were literally collected in their towns and villages and shipped to Japan to fill the ranks of Japanese workers badly depleted by the vastly accelerated military draft. By the war's end the Korean population in Japan had doubled to over two million. Treated with indifference and condescension at best and with open contempt and violence at worst by the Japanese authorities, and almost universally shunned by the general public, Koreans in Japan began to build "Korean hamlets" (chosenjin buraku), first around the ports of their entry, Moji (on Kyushu) and Shimonoseki (on Honshu), and later in most major urban centers, including Tokyo, Osaka and Kyoto.

For the greater part of the period when they had colonial control of Korea (1910–45), the Japanese were never as seriously interested in Japanizing Koreans as they were in Japanizing the Ainu and Okinawans. A 1924 survey of Korean workers in Osaka prefecture showed that only 21 percent had finished primary school and more than half were illiterate in Japanese.[20] The illiteracy rate among all Koreans in Japan in 1944 was even higher, at 77 percent. A survey of schools and students in Korea conducted in 1942 showed that, in the colony with a de facto segregated population of some 25,525,000 native Koreans and 753,000 resident Japanese, and an equally segregated school system, about 99,000 Japanese children attended 532 Japanese primary schools, while over 1,876,000 Korean children attended 3,110 Korean primary schools.[21] In other words, Koreans in their own country, with 34 times as large a population as Japanese, had 5.8 times as many primary schools enrolling 19 times as many pupils.

Only as Japan began to prepare itself for war in the late 1930s, under the slogan "One hundred million people with one mind," did the Tokyo

[20] Chosen sotokufu shomubu chosaka [The Government-General of Korea, Department of General Affairs, Research Section], "Chosenjin rodosha no kyoiku shisetsu" [Educational facilities for Korean workers], in Ozawa Yusaku, ed., Kindai minshu no kiroku [Records of the masses in the modern period] (Tokyo: Shin jinbutsu oraisha, 1978), 315–16.
[21] Chosenjin kyoiku taisaku iinkai [Committee on educational policy for Koreans], in Ozawa Yusaku, ed., Kindai minshu no kiroku, p. 364.

government change its own mind and launch a concerted, though short-lived, campaign aimed at wholesale Japanization of Koreans as well as all the other minorities. A special semigovernmental organization called the Central Association for Harmony (chuo kyowakai) was founded in 1938 to promote the new cause; characteristically, school education received special attention in its program. A Japanese reader edited by the organization in 1940 for use in Korean primary schools (both in Japan and in the colony) thus devoted the bulk of its space to the explanation of national holidays, major events and characters in Japanese history and mythology, and the neo-Confucian and Shinto dogmas, especially the status and role of the emperor in Japanese government. Koreans were now required not only to use Japanese as their "mother tongue" but also, like the Ainu and Okinawans before them, to adopt Japanese names. By 1944, Korean youth in Korea became subject to military draft. In the remaining months of the war 187,000 joined the imperial army and 22,000 joined the imperial navy.[22] This contrived wartime effort to turn Koreans into loyal and patriotic Japanese workers and soldiers sowed the seeds of one of the most complex legal/political issues in post–World War II Japan; it remains still unresolved.

Following the Japanese surrender in August 1945 and the independence of all Japanese colonies, roughly one-half of the approximately two million Koreans in Japan returned to Korea. The nationality and citizenship status of those who chose to stay in Japan at the time, and those born to them since, remains uncertain and controversial. Under the rules in effect in the 1970s and 1980s, children born to a Japanese parent married to a Korean automatically acquire Japanese citizenship, but all other Korean residents in Japan were aliens who were allowed to become naturalized only if they had independent means of livelihood, possessed special knowledge or skills, had not been involved in activities against Japanese government policy and had no criminal record. A modest number—about 50,000 by 1970—have met these requirements and been naturalized, while another 100,000 or so have been granted permanent-resident status under special provisions made in the 1965 treaty between Japan and South Korea that normalized diplomatic relations between the two countries.[23] This still leaves about half a million Koreans who legally have alien status and are eligible for only temporary residence in Japan, but who are de facto permanent residents.

An acute identity problem thus exists, particularly for young Koreans, an overwhelming majority of whom have been born in Japan, have Japanese names, attend or have attended Japanese schools and speak little or no Korean. To all intents and purposes, they look, sound and behave like Japanese. Yet they may be unable to become legally Japanese due, principally, to historical and contemporary Japanese policy and attitude, and also

---

[22] Rimujun O, *Zainichi chosenjin* [Koreans in Japan] (Tokyo: Ushio shuppansha, 1971), 227.

[23] Lee In-jik, "Sabetsu no kabe wo tsukiyaburu tame ni wa" [How to break through the barriers of discrimination], in Sato, Katsumi, ed., *Zainichi chosenjin no shomondai* [Problems of Koreans in Japan] (Tokyo: Doseisha, 1972), 129–30.

partly to pressures exerted by nationalistic Korean organizations, such as the pro-North Korean General Federation of Korean Residents in Japan, which runs a chain of Korean schools. The Korean community remains an important source of identity-related conflicts in contemporary Japan.

Women and political participation
Prejudice and discrimination against women have been, and still remain, an integral part of Japanese political culture. Confucianism, Buddhism and, less consistently, Shinto have all contributed to the perpetuation, if not the creation, of the prejudice. Important exceptions in this regard are the several newer Shinto sects that built considerable popular followings in the late Tokugawa and early Meiji period, such as the Fujiko, Maruyama, Konko, Tenri and Omoto sects, the last two of which were founded by women.[24] They were all egalitarian and, at least initially, antiauthoritarian in their basic doctrinal orientation and not only preached but practiced equal treatment for men and women.

Despite the nonconformist practices of the "new" religions, and despite the legal recognition of certain social and economic rights of women—e.g., a married woman's right to dispose of her dowry, a widow's right to inherit family property and to remarry—male chauvinism prevailed in both theory and practice in Tokugawa Japan. A married woman was expected to defer to and obey not only her husband but also her in-laws and even her own sons; upon her husband's death, the family property was inherited by her oldest surviving son or, in the absence of a son, by her oldest daughter, and by her only if there was no surviving child; she could be divorced only by her husband's or father-in-law's decision, not by her own. This system left no room for women's political participation. Nor was there any recorded organized movement before the Meiji Restoration, among either men or women, for changing the status quo to permit women even minimal political participation.

The first Japanese women since the advent of the Tokugawa shogunate to play a significant political role were involved in the Restoration move-

[24] The Fujiko sect of worshippers of Mount Fuji was founded by an early 16th-century ascetic but thrived in the late Tokugawa period. The Maruyama sect was founded in 1873 as a subsect of the Fujiko. The Konko sect emerged in the late Tokugawa period but it was not officially recognized as a Shinto sect until 1900. The Tenri sect was founded in 1838 by a peasant woman, Nakayama Miki, and became one of the largest and most successful religious organizations after the turn of the century, especially after World War II. The Omoto sect was founded by a widow around the turn of the century and, like the Tenri, has considerably expanded its following since World War II. On their views of and attitudes toward women, see Hirota Masaki, "Bunmei kaika to josei kaiho ron" [The civilization and enlightenment movement and the liberation of women], in Joseishi sogo kenkyukai [Association for comprehensive research in the history of women], ed., *Nihon joseishi* [A history of Japanese women], vol. 4: *Kindai* [The modern period] (Tokyo: Tokyo daigaku shuppankai, 1982), 32–37; Miyata Noboru, "Josei to minkan shinko" [Women and popular religions], in Joseishi sogo kenkyukai, *Nihon joseishi,* vol. 3, pp. 247–54.

ment and came from well-to-do farm or merchant families. Most of these 12 women acted as personal helpers to one or another male anti-Tokugawa revolutionary, but it was essentially a clandestine role, and probably illegitimate in the eyes of all but themselves and the handful of revolutionaries who employed their services. The first important public advocacy of equality for women came from the early Meiji male publicist, Fukuzawa Yukichi, who spearheaded the civilization and enlightenment (i.e., Westernization-cum-modernization) movement of the period and who published a series of newspaper and magazine articles on women's rights. Similar articles by other Japanese publicists and translations of works by Western authors, such as John Stuart Mill and Ann Garlin Spencer, soon followed; by the early 1890s explicitly political women's groups had been formed in various parts of the country and a suffragist movement was born. In the next half-century, however, the movement achieved little in winning either legal equality or political rights for women. In fact, it lost more than it gained.

For example, the civil code enacted in 1898 not only reaffirmed the Tokugawa concept and practice of the patriarchal family but, for the first time and contrary to tradition, legally required all married women to adopt their husbands' family names rather than choose to retain their maiden names. Politically even more devastating was a provision in the Peace and Police Law, enacted in 1900, that categorically prohibited all types of political activity by women. In the period following the Russo-Japanese War, especially in the early 1910s, there was a flurry of suffragist agitation in the liberal media; but it was not until 1922 that the controversial provision of the Peace and Police Law was revised to allow "political discussions" by women. Another flurry of activities occurred in the late 1920s, following the formation of a national suffragist organization in 1924, but without any tangible results before the country plunged into war. The participation problem for women was finally addressed directly and effectively by the Allied occupation after World War II. For the first time, Japanese women were granted the vote and equal rights. This has revolutionized their status and role in countless ways. In practice, however, they have not won anything like complete equality.

The distribution problem for minorities and women
In a society with as enduring a tradition of respect for stratification and hierarchy as Japan, it is tempting to argue that all have suffered from inequalities in a variety of ways, and women and minorities are not exceptions. Japanese women have no doubt always worked as hard as men, if not harder, but within a much narrower range of jobs and at much lower rates of remuneration. Many women from nonsamurai urban and rural families worked outside their homes. In medieval Kyoto, women hawkers selling candies and dried fish in crowded streets were a common sight. In Tokugawa-era Edo (today's Tokyo) and Osaka, some women from merchant families ran their own businesses, perhaps to help supplement meager family incomes and pay taxes rather than to enrich themselves. In villages, women routinely worked in the fields alongside men. Many also sought jobs as

housemaids or laundry women at landlords' houses, shrines, temples, etc., and a substantial and increasing number found employment in the rapidly expanding silk industry. Some women from the poorest families, including outcaste families, worked in brothels, which were operated under government license within designated neighborhoods in Kyoto, Edo and other major cities in medieval and modern Japan, from the 1190s to the late 1950s. These and a few other odd jobs, however, exhausted the range of paid employment available to most women in pre-Tokugawa and Tokugawa Japan.

Reliable wage statistics for pre-Meiji periods are rare, but fragmentary information suggests that women were paid at most two-thirds of what men were paid for comparable jobs. According to one study, for example, a housemaid was typically paid about half as much as a male servant in the 18th century and about two-thirds as much in the 19th century.[25] Licensed prostitution exploited human labor, economically as well as morally. Judging by a case studied in the 1920s, three-quarters of an average prostitute's income went to the brothel owner as rent, and 60 percent of the remainder went to the brothel owner as repayment of the advance the woman had been given at the beginning of her employment, leaving 10 percent for her wages. Out of that, she would then pay for her clothes, cosmetics, hairdo, public bathhouse charge, doctor's fee, lunch, sweets for clients, soap, etc. Once employed by a brothel, a woman was thus trapped virtually for life by a large and growing debt.

The fact that there were nearly 50,000 prostitutes employed by about 550 licensed and over 10,000 unlicensed brothels around the beginning of the 20th century testifies to the desperate economic conditions of the poor in general and of poor women in particular in late Meiji Japan. At that time, even for women from more well-to-do families, outside job opportunities remained confined largely to silk reeling, cotton spinning, teaching, nursing and midwifery. In the following decade an increasing number of white-collar jobs did become available to able and willing women—as telephone operators, post office clerks, bank tellers, photographers, stenographers and newspaper reporters. The number of women holding blue-collar jobs grew even more rapidly, until they accounted for over half of Japan's total industrial labor force, and over 80 percent of labor in the textile industry, by the end of the 1920s.[26]

The ranks of women white-collar and blue-collar workers have indeed increased, and prostitution has been illegal since 1958. And yet, in the mid-1980s the average female employee in the private sector was only paid about 48 percent of what the average male employee was paid. The final battle of the Japanese woman for equal rights was yet to be fought.

The Ainu were conquered by the Japanese not only through the outright occupation of their territory, decimation of their population and suppres-

[25] Sugano Noriko, "Noson josei no rodo to seikatsu" [The rural woman's work and life], in Joseishi sogo kenkyukai, *Nihon joseishi,* vol. 3, pp. 82–87.
[26] Yasukawa Junnosuke, "Hisabetsu buraku to josei" [The outcaste hamlets and women], in Joseishi sogo kenkyukai, *Nihon joseishi,* vol. 4, p. 199.

sion of their culture, but also through seemingly peaceful and voluntary trade. During the pre-Tokugawa and Tokugawa periods Japanese traded rice, rice wine, pottery, tobacco, cutlery and cotton goods for the Ainu's hawks and eagles (for hunting), salmon, hides and skins (bear, seal, sea lion, etc.), whale oil, seaweeds, etc. Rather than leading to prosperity, however, this trade led to steady impoverishment of the Ainu communities involved, as the recurrent anti-Japanese insurrections indicated. The Meiji government publicly admitted this, especially in the 1899 Law for the Protection of Former Native People in Hokkaido. Under the terms of that law, the Ainu were "granted" pieces of farmland in their own territory, as well as schools, but in many instances the land turned out to be unsuitable for farming and 15 years later it was returned to the Japanese government and then sold to Japanese ranchers.

By the early 19th century Japanese pressure began to force the Ainu to abandon their traditional hunting-and-gathering life and to work for the Japanese. Men found jobs in increasing numbers with Japanese fishing firms, which by then controlled many of the best salmon rivers, and at Japanese-operated quarries; women worked as housemaids or cooks. Many women served as their employers' mistresses, contracted venereal disease and became sterile, a circumstance responsible, along with the smallpox epidemic that was also brought by the Japanese, for the rapid decline of the Ainu population in the first half of the 19th century. The Japanese government subsequently implemented a series of programs to reverse the population trend, including free vaccination, encouragement of intra-Ainu marriages and childbearing, and maternity protection. Today, however, the Ainu population still hovers around 17,000, a level only marginally higher than the bottom reached around 1920.[27] The Ainu may have lost forever both the physical and mental energy to rebound and fight another battle for equality and justice in Japanese society.

The distribution problem faced by Okinawans has been quite different from that of the Ainu. The Okinawans had an old monarchy of their own. Before it was formally incorporated into the Meiji state in 1871, the kingdom was an authoritarian and corrupt regime ruled by a hereditary elite of some 50 individuals and supported by ruthlessly exploited and chronically impoverished peasantry. Many islanders were therefore probably eager to identify themselves with the no less authoritarian, but perhaps less corrupt, Japanese regime, at least after the Sino-Japanese War. Incorporation into and identification with Japan, however, brought neither significant improvement in the Okinawan peasant's economic life nor obvious distributive justice.

Intended or otherwise, the Okinawan standard of living remained consistently and conspicuously lower than that in the rest of Japan. A report presented around 1920 by an official of the prefectural government to the

[27] Takakura Shin'ichiro, *Shinpan Ainu seisakushi* [A revised history of Ainu policy] (Tokyo: San'ichi shobo, 1972), 291–92, 300–11, 340–47; Shinya Gyo, *Ainu shizoku to tennosei kokka* [Ainu tribes and the emperor state] (Tokyo: San'ichi shobo, 1977), 291–92, 300–11, 340–47.

Japanese minister of finance showed that the average Okinawan farm family had an annual income slightly over one-third the annual income of its counterpart in the rest of the country. After nearly 40 years, interrupted by a devastating war and a foreign military occupation, another survey by the Okinawan teachers' union showed that the average Okinawan farm family still had an annual income of slightly less than 40 percent of the national average. Even more obviously discriminatory was the Japanese government's refusal to establish a single institution of higher education in Okinawa before World War II, despite repeated requests by the prefectural government. (On the other hand, the Japanese government set up a fully government-supported "imperial" university in the capital of each of its two major colonies, Korea and Taiwan, respectively in 1924 and 1928, as well as in seven major cities in Japan proper.) The first university in Okinawa was founded by Americans after the war.

The most controversial and emotional issue related to the problem of distribution, broadly defined, was the disproportionately large sacrifices demanded of and made by Okinawans during and after World War II. During the last year-and-a-half of the war, most major Japanese cities were subjected to and destroyed by repeated air raids by American bombers. Many lives were lost, along with a staggering amount of material wealth. No Japanese prefecture except Okinawa, however, was invaded and occupied by enemy forces, and none lost as high a proportion of its civilian population. Altogether, the war claimed the lives of about 1.5 million Japanese soldiers and 300,000 civilians; in the battle of Okinawa about 90,000 soldiers, most of whom came from other parts of Japan, and 160,000 civilians, overwhelmingly Okinawan, died.[28] Some of those civilians were deliberately killed by Japanese soldiers as they had allegedly interfered with the last-ditch military operations against the invading American forces. The numbers are extraordinary on two counts. First, Japan as a whole lost five times as many combatants' lives as civilians', while Okinawa lost 1.8 times as many civilian lives as combatants'. Second, Japan as a whole lost about 0.4 percent of its total population (about 73 million), while Okinawa lost more than one-third of its population (about 460,000). Whether intentionally or not, Okinawans were made to pay a grossly disproportionate price for the war started by the government in Tokyo.

As outrageous from the Okinawan point of view is the fact that, following the postwar occupation by the Allied powers, Japan regained independence in 1952 by signing a peace treaty providing for, among other things, the continued administrative control of Okinawa and a few other islands in its vicinity by the United States under the U.N. strategic trusteeship system. In other words, Japan won its independence by unilaterally signing away Okinawa. Moreover, during the next two decades, until the islands and their people were finally "returned" to Japan in 1972, it was the Okinawans who initiated and sustained the reversion movement rather than the

---

[28] See Takafusa Nakamura, *The Postwar Japanese Economy: Its Development and Structure* (Tokyo: University of Tokyo Press, 1981), 14; Ota, *Kindai Okinawa*, pp. 382–83.

Japanese. To this day, Okinawans commemorate April 28, the date on which the peace treaty was signed in 1952, as a "day of humiliation." And to this day, Okinawa remains the poorest of the 47 Japanese prefectures in terms of per capita GNP. Distributive justice thus remains an important ongoing issue for Okinawans.

The same applies even more acutely to the outcaste people who number over one million, an overwhelming majority of whom still live in about 4,400 outcaste communities, or hamlets, scattered over about 1,000 towns and villages.[29] Their ancestry may be traced to the poorer peasants in the late 16th and early 17th centuries, who were gradually segregated from the community of more fortunate villagers and began to form their own hamlets on the outskirts of villages, often on dry riverbeds. Soon these hamlets and their inhabitants began to be associated with the particular types of work, commonly shunned by others, that the "riverbed dwellers" were probably forced to do in order to survive—disposal of dead human bodies and animals, tanning, butchery, gravedigging, assisting executioners, singing and dancing, and begging. By the early 18th century they became officially designated untouchables or nonhumans. Their population substantially increased during the remainder of the Tokugawa period, as a large number of convicts and homeless people were added to their ranks. At the same time, their lives became increasingly regulated in minute detail by both the central and domain governments—from place of residence, travel and type of work to clothing, hairstyle and footwear.

The Meiji government nominally "liberated" all outcaste communities in 1871 by renaming them "new commoners" (shin-heimin) and expunging the older terms eta and hinin from all official documents. In practice, however, neither the official announcement nor the well-intentioned efforts of some private groups to help had much immediate impact, and the hamlets and their inhabitants remained as isolated, impoverished and ignored as before. This led to some violent, but invariably futile, riots by the victims. During and after the 1910s, several moderately reformist organizations were formed, along with one radical group called National Levelers' Association (Zenkoku suiheisha) and its women's and youth auxiliaries, which campaigned for improvement of economic and social conditions in outcaste communities. Due to their efforts, and even more to the growing needs of the economy undergoing rapid industrialization, employment opportunities for outcaste people gradually expanded. According to one estimate, about 60 percent of the miners employed by the largest coal mines in Kyushu in the early 1920s and about 80 percent of those hired by the smaller mines in the same region came from outcaste communities. These included a large number of women—nearly 46,000; but all outcaste miners shared the smallest and most dingy sleeping quarters and bathtubs, which they often shared with horses as well.[30]

The situation has drastically changed since the end of World War II.

[29] Buraku kaiho kenkyujo [Hamlet liberation research institute], Buraku kaiho nenkan: 1980/81-nen ban (Osaka: Buraku kaiho kenkyujo, 1983), 2–3.
[30] Yasukawa, "Hisabetsu buraku," pp. 198, 209–10.

Inspired and driven by the occupation-authored democratic constitution, both the succession of central and prefectural governments and nongovernmental organizations, especially the (Outcaste) Hamlet Liberation League (Buraku kaiho domei) founded in 1946, have invested substantial and increasing amounts of effort and money in combating centuries-old public prejudice and discrimination against the outcaste population. Notable progress has been made in some areas. For example, communities with exclusively outcaste population had virtually ceased to exist by the end of the 1960s, and on the average about 40 percent of the inhabitants of so-called outcaste hamlets was nonoutcaste by 1970. More fragmentary evidence suggests also that intercaste marriages have slowly but steadily increased in most regions, although nearly two-thirds of the newlyweds in 23 representative outcaste communities in 1977 were outcaste couples.[31] Nor has progress in some economic areas been negligible. According to a study of outcaste communities in Kyoto, the percentage of outcaste people holding white-collar jobs, as opposed to blue-collar or primary-sector jobs, increased from 2.2 in 1937 to 8.9 in 1970 and 10.8 in 1977.[32]

As important as these improvements are, they do not suggest that social and economic equality has been achieved. On the contrary, large gaps remain, and are likely to remain for a long time to come. One indicator of the magnitude of such gaps is the proportion of families poor enough to be exempted from the payment of local resident taxes. In 1975, for example, 20.5 percent of families in outcaste communities were exempted from such taxes, as compared to 7.0 percent of families in nonoutcaste communities. In the same year, twice as high a percentage of outcaste families as nonoutcaste families paid resident taxes at the minimum flat rates.[33] Moreover, in 1980, 57.1 percent of families in outcaste communities received public assistance under the livelihood protection law, as compared to 12.3 percent in the country as a whole. These statistics clearly indicate considerable income differences between the average Japanese family and the typical outcaste family. The results of a 1979 poll conducted in Nagano prefecture showed that a clear majority (57.6 percent) of respondents believed, and only 27.3 percent did not believe, that discrimination against outcaste people still existed in the prefecture—one of the most integrated of the country's 47 prefectures in which the average outcaste family had a considerably higher income than the average outcaste family in the nation at large.[34]

[31] Buraku mondai kenkyujo [Hamlet problem research institute], *Sengo buraku no genjo gyosei no kenkyu* [A study of the conditions and administration of outcaste hamlets in the postwar period] (Kyoto: Buraku mondai kenkyujo shuppankai, 1980), 126–40.
[32] Buraku kaiho kenkyujo [Hamlet liberation research institute]; *Buraku mondai: Shiryo to kaisetsu* [The outcaste hamlet problem: Documents and comments] (Osaka: Kaiho shuppansha, 1981), 57.
[33] Buraku kaiho kenkyujo, *Buraku kaiho nenkan*, pp. 16, 47.
[34] Naikaku soridaijin kanbo kohoshitsu [The Office of the Prime Minister, Office of Public Information], *Showa 55-nen ban: Seron chosa nenkan* [Public opinion yearbook: 1980 edition] (Tokyo: Okurasho insatsukyoku, 1981): 303; Buraku kaiho kenkyujo, *Buraku kaiho nenkan*, pp. 8, 17.

As suggested earlier, however, the most complicated and intractable distribution problem concerns Koreans in Japan, whether they have acquired Japanese citizenship or remain resident aliens. The majority of the approximately two million Koreans who lived in Japan at the end of World War II had either come of their own free will or been born of those who had done so. A significant minority—715,000, or 36 percent, according to one source—[35] however, had been brought to Japan under duress under the wartime government-sponsored labor recruitment program. They were assigned, essentially as corvée labor, to mines, factories and construction sites in various parts of Japan.

At the end of World War II the Japanese government, faced with prospects of mass starvation, and a spate of riots by Koreans, quickly reversed its wartime policy and attempted to ship back Koreans as quickly as possible. Ironically, however, the partition of Korea, and unsettled political and economic conditions in both halves of the peninsula discouraged many from returning; about half a million, or one-quarter of the total at the end of the war, remained in Japan. By 1970 the number had increased to about 710,000, including approximately 100,000 children with Japanese fathers or mothers who had automatically acquired Japanese citizenship. Of the remainder, slightly more than half had South Korean, and the rest North Korean, nationality.[36]

Data on the average Korean's economic and social life in contemporary Japan are hard to find, but fragmentary and anecdotal evidence suggests that, by and large, Koreans are economically substantially better off than outcaste people but are subjected to persistent social discrimination. For example, nearly twice as high a percentage of Koreans as outcaste people (15.7 percent in 1969 as against 8.6 percent in 1971) held white-collar jobs around 1970, although the Korean figure was considerably lower than the national average of 24.6 percent in 1970.[37] Meanwhile, Koreans apparently continue to face ruthless and blatant discrimination in all spheres of their social life: education, employment, marriage and application for insurance policies.

The more fundamental problem for Koreans is legal and political rather than economic or social. As suggested above, their citizenship and alien resident status, and conditions for the acquisition and/or maintenance of either status, remain an unresolved and bitterly controversial issue. Under the terms of the 1965 Japan–South Korea treaty, those Koreans who had lived in Japan before the end of World War II, their children born in Japan before January 1971 and their grandchildren may become permanent residents. Issues yet to be settled include the status of the children of the last mentioned, referred to as "third-generation Koreans in Japan," and the fingerprinting requirement and other indignities that Koreans suffer, along

[35] O, *Zainichi chosenjin*, p. 105.
[36] Nomura Hiroshi, "Zainichi chosenjin no zairyu jokyo to kokuseki mondai" [The living conditions of Koreans in Japan and the citizenship problem], in Sato Katsumi, ed., *Zainichi chosenjin* p. 219.
[37] Ibid., p. 226; Buraku kaiho kenkyujo, *Buraku mondai*, p. 57.

with other alien residents in Japan. Given the checkered history of relations between the two countries since the 1910 annexation, and especially during World War II, the Korean issue is bound to remain a particularly troublesome problem for both Japanese and Koreans.

CONCLUSION

The foregoing discussion has shown that Japan has had and continues to have serious and complicated problems of penetration, identity, participation and distribution. In this respect it is not very different from most other advanced industrial countries. In fact, Japan's problems may have been relatively mild by international standards, especially in the post–World War II period. It is obviously absurd to claim, as many Japanese and others have done, that the Japanese are ethnically and culturally homogeneous, that national unity and social harmony have been the distinguishing marks of their society and that contemporary Japan is an exceptionally if not uniquely egalitarian society. The fact is that heterogeneity, conflict and inequalities have been integral and enduring features of Japanese national life.

On the other hand, it would be equally absurd to argue that the Japanese have totally failed to resolve the problems. Except for the Ainu, all the minorities discussed above, and women, today face far less outright discrimination, oppression and exploitation, and enjoy far more rights and opportunities, than they did before World War II or even as recently as two decades ago. Even if the major impetus for the change came not from the Japanese themselves but from the American reformers who occupied the country after World War II, it is important to note that the Japanese have built on and extended these legacies of democratic reform. The postwar generation of Japanese is increasingly free from the kind of blatantly ethnocentric and chauvinist prejudices that the earlier generations so thoroughly embraced. Education has been a key agent of this change.[38]

The main question that should be addressed today is thus not whether progress has been made toward resolution of these problems but how fast the progress has been. In at least some areas, especially in that of distribution, it has clearly been too slow for all the groups discussed above. This keeps many Japanese in a state of tension that can occasionally be detected through the veil of rising national confidence born of their globally recognized and acclaimed economic success.

FURTHER READING

Borton, Hugh. *Japan's Modern Century: From Perry to 1970.* 2nd ed. New York: Ronald Press, 1970.

DeVos, George, and Wagatsuma, Hiroshi. *Japan's Invisible Race: Caste in Culture and Personality.* Berkeley: University of California Press, 1966.

Gluck, Carol. *Japan's Modern Myths: Ideology in the Late Meiji Period.* Princeton, New Jersey: Princeton University Press, 1985.

[38] William K. Cummings, *Education and Equality in Japan* (Princeton, N.J.: Princeton University Press, 1980).

Hane, Mikiso. *Peasants, Rebels, and Outcastes: The Underside of Modern Japan.* New York: Pantheon, 1982.

Krauss, Ellis S., Rohlen, Thomas P., and Steinhoff, Patricia G., eds. *Conflict in Japan.* Honolulu: University of Hawaii Press, 1984.

Reischauer, Edwin O. *The Japanese.* Cambridge, Massachusetts and London: Belknap Press, 1977.

————. *The Japanese Today: Change and Continuity.* Cambridge, Massachusetts and London: Belknap Press, 1988.

Sansom, George B. *Japan: A Short Cultural History.* Rev. ed. New York: Appleton-Century-Crofts, 1962.

Totman, Conrad. *Japan before Perry: A Short History.* Berkeley: University of California Press, 1981.

NORTH KOREA

BRUCE CUMINGS

INTRODUCTION

THE Democratic People's Republic of Korea (DPRK), or North Korea, is a singular and puzzling nation that resists easy description. Because its leadership is secretive and unyielding to foreign attention, many basic facts about the country are unknown; thus pundits are able to project equally unyielding stereotypes onto it (a Stalinist attempt at recreating *1984,* a socialist basket case, a Confucian/Communist monarchy, Joan Robinson's economic miracle, Che Guevara's idea of what Cuba should eventually look like). In the night of our ignorance, "North Korea" confirms all stereotypes. But closer familiarity confounds simple expectations.

For example, a British film crew, visiting in 1987, expected Pyongyang to be something like Tehran in the 1980s; they had heard this was a "terrorist" nation, and so assumed that cars filled with "revolutionary guards" would careen through the streets, machine-guns dangling out the windows. (The film crew had requested and received the equivalent of combat pay from their employer.) Or they thought it would be a poorer version of China, the gathered masses pedaling to work on phalanxes of bicycles, clad in drab blue work clothes. They dreaded that services could only be worse than in Moscow, through which they had recently suffered. They were ill-prepared for the wide, tree-lined boulevards of Pyongyang, swept squeaky clean and traversed by determined, disciplined crowds of urban commuters held in close check by female traffic guards in tight uniforms, pirouetting with military discipline and a smile atop platforms at each intersection. They had not expected a population living in modern high-rises, hustling out in the morning like Japan's "salarymen" to a waiting subway or electric bus. They were suddenly enamored of the polite waitresses who served ample portions of tasty Korean and Western food at hotels and restaurants.

Pyongyang is, with Singapore, the most efficient, best-run city in Asia. Older, utilitarian, Soviet-style apartment houses and state office buildings mingle with grand, new, monumental architecture, topped off with traditional Korean curved roofs. About 2 million people live there, or 10 percent of the population. If the pickings are predictably slim among consumer goods, daily necessities seem ample and the traveler observes few lines. Well-tended parks dot all sections of the city, through which two rivers flow along willow-lined banks.

583

Smaller cities are less pleasing; many are unrelievedly ugly in their mimicry of Soviet proletarian architecture, the apartments all stamped from the same mold, sitting akilter along jolting, potholed roads. But then most of them have been built since the Korean War (1950–53), when nearly every urban building of note was razed by American bombing. And always there is color, whether affixed self-consciously to storefronts or leaping out from the ever-present political billboards.

North Korean villages are spartan, plain and clean; they bring back the bucolic atmosphere of the Korean past so lacking in the capital. They are linked by a network of hardpack dirt roads, in contrast to the extensive railways connecting cities. Residents plant vegetables raised for home consumption or the small private market on every square meter of land. Electric wires run to all peasant homes, but television aerials are much less ubiquitous than in the cities. As in South Korea, thatched roofs have given way to tile, signifying modernity; modernization is also evident in the rice paddies, which as a result of widespread use of chemical fertilizer no longer give off the peculiar odor of human manure. Signs urge self-reliance ("regeneration through one's own efforts") on the locals, no doubt a reflection of state priorities that emphasize heavy industry, military preparedness and the city.

In city, town and village there is Kim Il sung; everywhere there is Kim Il-sung, staring down from a billboard or in the subway or on an apartment wall: offering here a maxim for industry, there, one for agriculture ("rice is communism"), or simply averring (in the National Folk Museum) that "Koreans can hardly be Korean if they don't eat *toenjang*" (fermented bean paste). In the spring of 1988 the regime pointed to the fact that the native flower, kimilsungia, a type of orchid, now grows all over the country. (In utterly predictable DPRK fashion, there is also now kimjongilia, a new and different flower.[1]) No leader in the 20th century has stamped a nation with his presence more than Kim, born on the day the *Titanic* sank (April 15, 1912) and now in power more than four decades. But because of that, there has been unusual continuity from the early days of the regime.

REGIME FORMATION

In the late 1940s the regime emerged from within the Russian Red Army occupation, and thus took its administrative and industrial structure from Soviet models (as did every socialist state in the period). The DPRK was proclaimed on September 9, 1948, but much of it was in place within a year after Japan's colonial rule ended in 1945. Kim Il-sung's rise to power is still murky in the literature, but it is now established that he was a guerrilla leader in Manchuria from 1932 on, fighting Japanese imperialism in league with many Chinese allies.[2] His own Korean guerrilla partners

[1] Korean Central News Agency, April 11, 20, 1988.
[2] See Robert Scalapino and Chong-sik Lee, *Communism in Korea,* 2 vols. (Berkeley: University of California Press, 1972); they lay to rest the South Korean myth that Kim was an impostor who stole the name of a famous patriot.

eventually structured the core or commanding heights of the regime; and now, as they pass on, they grace a stunning cemetery atop a mountain outside Pyongyang, each person's exploits memorialized with a stone and a life-size bronze bust.

Thus the Soviet experience has commingled with two others: resistance to the Japanese and close cooperation with China. Resentment of Japan is still so prominent that one would think the war had just ended. Many signs exhort citizens to "live in the way of the anti-Japanese guerrillas," and most young people go on camping trips that retrace the paths of the guerrillas. In the 1930s, then again in the Chinese Civil War (in which tens of thousands of Koreans took part in the period 1947–49), Korean guerrillas fought with Chinese comrades, and, of course, China later sent many divisions to the Korean War. This explains basic DPRK foreign policy; since 1950 it has based its strategy on close relations with and backing from China, while tilting toward Moscow from time to time for tactical reasons.

Politically the DPRK has always been unique in the socialist world for its top-down leadership principle and its corporate organizational doctrine.[3] The Koreans have never challenged the principle that leadership and Communist "consciousness" coincide at the top, although they have leavened this principle with attention to Chinese-style "mass line" politics. Their publications for 40 years have trumpeted the critical role of Kim Il-sung, fount of all "good ideas." It is a doctrine more Hegelian than Marxist, emphasizing willpower, the triumph of ideas over material obstacles. The leader, in turn, is seen as the father of a body politic embracing the Korean masses.

The mass line usage was not much different from that of Mao Zedong; the same phrases ("from the masses, to the masses") and the same practices (sending cadres down to lower levels, small group-criticism/self-criticism sessions) were to be found. Like China, North Korea had a mostly peasant population in the 1940s, and the party enrolled millions of poor peasants, seeking to make proletarians out of them.

What was different in Korea was the peculiar organizational aspect of mass politics. The Korean Workers's party (KWP), from the beginning in 1946, was designated a "mass party of a new type," not a typical small vanguard unit. Of any Marxist-Leninist regime, Korea has always had the highest percentage of the population enrolled in the party, fluctuating between 12 percent and 14 percent. (If China followed suit, the Chinese Communist party (CCP) would have about 120 million to 140 million members, instead of its current 40 million.) Kim Il-sung argued that almost anyone should be able to join the party, as long as they were patriots who put the nation and the revolution first. Young people not eligible for the party and the 70 percent to 75 percent of the adult population not in the party were recruited by extensive mass organizations of youths, work-

[3] For elaboration see Cumings, "Corporatism in North Korea," *Journal of Korean Studies*, no. 4 (1986).

ers, women and peasants that made it virtually obligatory for everyone to join something.

The unique symbol of the KWP places a writing brush across the hammer and sickle, acknowledging an inclusive policy toward intellectuals and experts. In contrast to Maoist China, Kim has rarely if ever denigrated them, and has explicitly authorized their widespread introduction into positions of authority. The Koreans also established a vague category, *samuwon,* meaning clerks, petit bourgeois traders, bureaucrats, professors and so on. This category served two purposes. For the regime it retained educated people and experts who might otherwise have fled south, and for large numbers of Koreans it provided a category within which to hide "bad" class background.

Thus the Korean revolution, far from polarizing the population exclusively into good and bad classes, pursued an inclusive, all-encompassing mass politics. The Koreans have envisioned their society as a mass, the gathered-together "people," rather than a class-based and class-divided society. The union of the three classes—peasant, worker, *samuwon*—excluded few but the landlords of the old period, who, after all, were much stronger in southern than in northern Korea. Probably the key factors explaining this would be the relatively industrialized character of the North, an inheritance from the heavy Japanese investment there from 1935 to 1945, the opportunity for many capitalists and landlords to flee to the South, and chronic labor shortages, especially among skilled experts.

The Koreans also adapted typical post-colonial Third World policies to their indigenous political culture and to Soviet-style socialism: an economic program of rapid industrialization and a philosophy of subjecting nature to human will; Lenin's notion of national liberation; Stalin's autarky of socialism-in-one-country (to become in Korea socialism-in-one-half-a-country, and now, as one wit remarked, socialism-in-one-family). Autarky fit Korea's "Hermit Kingdom" past, and answered the need for closure from the world economy after decades of opening under Japanese imperial auspices. What was unusable was dispatched as soon as possible: above all the "socialist internationalism," including a transnational division of labor that the Soviets wanted and that Korea successfully resisted, beginning in the late 1950s. Traces of foreign lingo, such as in *puroretariatu* and *Makussu chuui* (proletariat and Marxism), have not been so much eliminated as overwhelmed by the indigenous doctrine of *chuche* (juche). In the arts, socialist realism has been muted as traditional art forms reassert themselves, including family-theme soap operas that seem dominant in North Korea today.

NORTH KOREAN CORPORATISM

Over time, a unique political system has evolved within the Marxist-Leninist crucible and is fully in place today. It can best be compared to varieties of corporatism, and might be called socialist corporatism.[4] It is a

---

[4] The term grows out of the Iberian and Latin American experience, and refers to a political system that seeks inclusion and absorption of everyone, with little space for intermediate or alternative organization.

tightly held, total politics with undoubted repressive capacity and many political victims—although no one really knows how repressive it is, how many political prisoners there are, and the like, because of the exclusionism and secrecy of the regime. Some reports suggest as many as 100,000 people may be held in prisons and reform-through-labor camps.

Central to the political system is the position of Kim Il-sung and what many observers call the personality cult surrounding him. With its absurdly inflated hero worship and its endless repetition, the North Korean political rhetoric seems to know no bounds; it is repellent to a person accustomed to a liberal political system. Every book or article must begin with quotes from Kim's work, everyone tells the foreigner that all successes owe to "the beloved and respected leader," or, these days, to his rotund heir-apparent.[5] It seems impossible that anyone actually reads the mind-numbing prose that flows out in the millions of words. Consider an example from the party newspaper:

> Only a man of great heart . . . possessed of rare grit and magnaminity and noble human love can create a great history. . . . His conception of speed and time cannot be measured or assessed by established common sense and mathematical calculation. . . . The grit to break through, even if the Heavens fall, and cleave the way through the sea and curtail the century [is his]. . . . His heart is a traction power attracting the hearts of all people and a centripetal force uniting them as one. . . . His love for people—this is, indeed, a kindred king of human love. . . . No age, no one has ever seen such a great man with a warm love. . . . Kim Il-sung is the great sun and great man. . . . Thanks to this great heart national independence is firmly guaranteed.
>
> As there is this great heart, the heart of our Party is great. As the heart of our Party is great, the victory of the cause of Juche is fimly guaranteed . . . and the entire people [are] rallied in one mind and thought.

This peculiar form of socialist corporatism might be briefly summarized as follows:

THE LEADER: functions as a father figure, head of the Korean family, also as a charismatic source of legitimacy and ideology and as the "head and heart" of the body politic.

THE FAMILY: core unit of society, for which the leader's family is the model and the historical extension symbolizing the great chain linking past and present; metaphor for the nation; interpenetrates the state.

THE COLLECTIVE: social organizations mediating between party and family; the model also is the family; pools state and family property.

THE PARTY: the core of the body politic; itself a living organism, it also provides the sinews linking the nation together and represents the blood ties linking ruler and ruled. Metaphorical images are blood relations and concentric circles of organization. Now termed the "mother party."

THE IDEA: *Juche (chuche),* the symbol of the nation and its place in the world; its source is the leader's thought. It is the metaphor for the people acting as one mind.

[5] The stories are many but the evidence slim on the son's ways; among other things, he enjoys a huge library of Western films, according to two people in the film industry who recently defected.

THE GUIDE: the leader's progeny; symbolizes the transition to power and thus the future. Thus Kim Jong-il is called "the dear guide."

THE REVOLUTION: the leader's biography, stretching back half a century through him and a century through his family; model for how to apply *chuche*.

THE WORLD: structured by national solipsism, according to which the sun (the leader) is the center; the sun spreads its rays outward; the world tends toward the sun.

The first principle is that the leader is the center and the source of all good ideas. Second, the leader surrounds himself with a core, or nucleus *(haeksim)*. Third, the critical core group is the leader's family: it is virtuous (i.e., revolutionary), it is exemplary (all the relatives were virtuous), and it is a chain linking past with present and future (e.g., Kim's great-grandfather supposedly led the first blows struck at U.S. imperialism, in 1866). Fourth, the core holds all effective political power. From the 1930s until the 1980s, that core has consisted of Kim, his family and relatives, and those Manchurian guerrillas who either fought with him or quickly united with him after liberation. Fifth, the leader spreads love and benevolence (the classic Confucian virtues), and the followers respond with loyalty, devotion and fulsome accolades designed to enchance the leader's stature.

If all this seems odd, at least it helps the reader of North Korean newspapers. The Confucian resonance is obvious, fashioning the state and even international relations on the model of the well-ordered family. Kim's rhetoric rings with Confucian virtues of love, morality, beneficence, solicitude—except where the enemy is concerned, of course. It also harks back to Japanese interwar rhetoric, especially the old *Nippon kokutai* doctrine, another kind of corporatism. If familial succession is strange to Marxists, it is not unusual in East Asia: Chiang Kai-shek prepared the way for Chiang Ching-kuo in similar fashion.

The idea, *chuche,* seems at first glance to be readily understandable. Meaning self-reliance and independence in politics, economics, defense and ideology, it first emerged in 1955 as Pyongyang drew away from Moscow, and then appeared full-blown in the mid-1960s as Kim sought a stance independent of both Moscow and Beijing. On closer inspection, however, the term's meaning is less accessible. The North Koreans say things like "everyone must have *chuche* firm in mind and spirit"; "only when *chuche* is firmly implanted can we be happy"; *"chuche* must not only be firmly established in mind but perfectly realized in practice"; and so on. The closer one gets to its meaning, the more the meaning recedes. It is the opaque core of Korean national solipsism. Few would have much guidance for how to get up every morning and "perfectly realize" *chuche.* Its real meaning might best be translated as "Put Korean things first, always"—a type of nationalism, in other words.

A socialist corporatism also appeals to a people with a very strong extended-family system, high consciousness of lineage ("the great chain"), major cottage industries that put out genealogies, and the Confucian background that justifies and reinforces it all. The hierarchical language, with verb endings and even grammatical markers differing according to the stations of the speaker and the listener, is deeply embedded in Korean family practices, so much so that, surprisingly, the North Koreans have not done much to eliminate it. There is even a high and a low form of the term "comrade." The DPRK constitution defines the family as the core unit of society. Furthermore, marriages apparently are still arranged in the North, family themes are exalted in the arts, and the regime has never sought to break up the family unit. For these and other reasons, North Korea often impresses foreign visitors precisely in its cultural conservatism; a Japanese visitor old enough to remember prewar Japan remarked on the similarities he found, and noted the "antiquarian atmosphere" in North Korea.

THE SUCCESSION TO KIM JONG-IL

In 1980 there was a "blessed event" in North Korea. Kim's son by his first marriage, Kim Jong-il, was publicly named at the Sixth Congress of the KWP to the Presidium of the Politburo, the Secretariat of the Central Committee, and the Military Commission. In other words, he was designated successor to his father. Kim was reportedly born in 1941 in the Manchurian fastness; his mother, Kim Jong-suk, died in the late 1940s. His rank is now second, behind his father and ahead of his father's old comrade-in-arms, Oh Jin Wu.

The ground was carefully laid for this succession throughout the 1970s: Jong-il was immersed in party organizational work, and in a key campaign ("the Three Revolutions") at the grass-roots level. His rise to power was carefully coordinated with party control. For years he was referred to as "the party center" (*dang chungang*), then "the glorious party center." When the glorious party center began visiting factories, external observers realized it was a person. People began displaying pictures of the son alongside the father in their homes. A few years ago there were rumors that some generals tried to run over Jong-il with a truck and injured him; he did drop out of view in 1977 and 1978. Over the past decade, however, the move toward familial succession has been inexorable.

The basic line is that the revolution, "started by the Father Marshal," must be carried through to completion "generation after generation." Editorials on "the glorious party" asserted that the KWP "can have no traditions except those established by the Leader," and that this tradition must be "brilliantly inherited" and passed on to future generations. At the leader's birthday in 1980 (the big event every year), editorials called for "reliable succession" so that the Korean people will never forget Kim's "profound benevolence" generation after generation. A Soviet diplomat in Pyongyang asked if the succession would be disruptive, replied no; a new generation is tied to Kim Jong-il's inheritance, and it will go smoothly. "Come back in the year 2020 and see *his* son inherit power."

THE CHUCHE IDEA AND NORTH KOREAN FOREIGN POLICY

Self-reliance is not a matter of mere rhetoric. North Korea is the supreme example in the postcolonial developing world of conscious withdrawal from the capitalist world system. Unlike Albania in the socialist world and Burma (now Myanmar) in the free world—two countries that have withdrawn but to no apparent purpose as their economies idle along—North Korea never idled but always raced. This is withdrawal with development, withdrawal for development. It has been more successful than generally realized in its aggregate totals, not just in industry—which might be expected, given Japanese industrialization of northern Korea—but also in agriculture (the North stands somewhere between Taiwan and Japan in its per hectare grain production).

According to a published Central Intelligence Agency (CIA) report, North Korea's per capita GNP was the same as South Korea's in 1976.[6] It probably kept pace through 1983, in part because of South Korea's 6 percent loss of GNP in 1980. Since 1983 the South has forged ahead, but not nearly as far ahead as its backers claim. A reasonable figure for per capita income in the North today would be U.S. $1,500; for the South, $2,300. DPRK industrial growth boomed along at 25 percent per year in the decade after the Korean War, and about 14 percent from 1965 to 1978.[7] Its total production of electricity, coal, fertilizer, machine tools and steel was comparable to or higher than South Korean totals in the early 1980s, despite having half the population of the South. Such figures do not indicate the quality of production, however, which is lower in the North; also, several zero or negative growth rates have marred the past decade, as the North reaps diminished returns from an industrial system badly needing new infusions of technology. Still, one critic of DPRK economic performance puts its annual average industrial growth rate for 1978–84 at 12.2 percent, while noting how far North Korea fell short of its own planning targets.[8]

Both Koreas now have an agrarian sector no larger than 30 percent of the population and 20 percent or less of GNP. The CIA in 1978 reported that "North Korean agriculture is quite highly mechanized, fertilizer application is probably among the highest in the world, and irrigation projects are extensive." It thought that DPRK agricultural growth in the 1970s was higher than the South's despite the South's heightened investment in the agrarian sector; kilograms per capita of all grains have generally been higher in the North.[9] The hard data for such conclusions are not available, however, and accounts from travelers say that a great deal of rice is exported, with much of the population left to eat coarser grains like millet and barley.

Some ambitious machinery purchases in the mid-1970s created for North Korea a foreign debt problem from which it has yet to emerge; in 1987 North Korea was temporarily declared in default on part of its external

[6] U.S. Central Intelligence Agency, "Korea: The Economic Race Between North and South," (Washington, D.C.: CIA, 1978).

[7] Ibid.

[8] Joseph Chung, "North Korea's Economic Development and Capabilities," *Asian Perspective* 11, no. 1 (Spring-Summer 1987): 45–74.

[9] CIA, "Korea: The Economic Race."

burden, the total of which is estimated at about $2.5 billion. Its dogged pursuit of relative autarky has clearly hurt industrial growth, sacrificing economies of scale and closing the country off to the more developed capitalist economies (although it should be remembered that the United States has mounted an economic blockade against North Korea since 1950). But one unqualified success for self-reliance is DPRK energy policy, which has one of the lowest world rates for dependence on petroleum. The DPRK has substituted hydroelectric power and coal for oil, using petroleum products primarily for its military.[10]

Few countries have a more unfortunate geopolitical position than the DPRK: jammed cheek-by-jowl against two feuding Socialist giants, and with an always-tense confrontation with the United States and South Korea along the DMZ. The combination of external geopolitical pressure and internal ethnic homogeneity is almost enough to predict a tight little polity. Defense expenditures account for 13–15 percent of the state budget officially, 20–25 percent according to American figures. In recent years the South has been outspending the North on defense.

From 1976 through 1983, DPRK foreign policy sought a breakthrough in relations with the United States, hoping to be the Korean beneficiary of Sino-American detente. Kim Il-sung referred to President Jimmy Carter as "a man of justice" while indirectly denouncing the Soviets as "dominationists." For several years China sought to bring the United States and the DPRK together for talks. This policy came to a head in October 1983, when the Rangoon bombing took out much of the South Korean cabinet and demolished a Chinese diplomatic demarche on Korea. A Burmese court determined that North Korean terrorists were behind the bombing.

From 1983 to 1987 Pyongyang tilted toward the Soviet Union. Relations warmed markedly, and Kim visited Moscow twice—his first visits in a quarter century. The Soviets upgraded the North Korean Air Force with MIG23s, jet fighters that nonetheless reflected early-1960s technology. The advent of Mikhail Gorbachev, however, seems to have put a damper on this warming trend, as the Soviets appear to have pressured Pyongyang to use Soviet aid more wisely and have given little support to the North's increasingly hard line against the United States and South Korea.

In 1988 DPRK foreign policy was in trouble. The South had energetically reached out to North Korea's socialist allies. Its indirect trade with China in 1988 will be higher than the DPRK's, and it succeeded in attracting China, the USSR, and the East European socialist countries to the Seoul Olympics. Only Cuba followed the North's demand for a boycott. It is likely that this South Korean policy will only deepen in years to come, further isolating North Korea. Although Pyongyang has opened its doors a crack to joint ventures with capitalist firms and to Western tourism (a French company has put up an international hotel, and the English and Australians have organized tours), it has not really begun the arduous process of knocking down its socialist/mercantilist barriers to international

[10] "North Korea," *Asia Pacific Annual Review 1980* (London: World of Information, 1981).

commerce, and in this respect remains where China was more than a decade ago.

Nothing suggests that the DPRK will soon depart from its long-standing policies of corporate politics and heavy-industry-first economics at home, and self-reliance and Sino-Soviet tilting abroad. And yet the world at the end of the 1980s seemed more inhospitable to such policies than at any point since 1948. North Korea faced a leadership transition, with Kim Il-sung entering his late seventies. A national nervous breakdown may attend his death, given his extraordinary role for over forty years.

The Pacific Basin is becoming the center of the world economy, and economic forces are running roughshod over previously impervious political and strategic boundaries. North Korea remains dangerously outside this developing economic sphere, which its major ally, China, has joined. It seems doggedly committed to domestic policies that worked several decades ago, but not now. However, an enlightened diplomacy, especially by the United States, which bears much more responsibility for the continuing volatility of the Korean peninsula than any other power, might help defuse the building pressures and bring the DPRK into the world on a new basis.

FURTHER READING

Chung, Joseph S., *The North Korean Economy: Structure and Development*. Stanford, California: Hoover Institution Press, 1974.

Cumings, Bruce, ed. *Child of Conflict: The Korean-American Relationship, 1943–1953*. Seattle: University of Washington Press, 1983.

————. *The Origins of the Korean War*. 2 vols. Princeton, New Jersey: Princeton University Press, 1981, 1989.

Henderson, Gregory. *Korea: The Politics of the Vortex*. Cambridge, Massachusetts: Harvard University Press, 1968.

Lee, Chong-sik, *The Korean Worker's Party: A Short History*. Stanford, California: Hoover Institution Press, 1978.

North Korea: A Country Study. American University Foreign Area Studies. 3rd ed. Washington, D.C.: Government Printing Office, 1981.

Scalapino, Robert, and Lee, Chong-sik. *Communism in Korea*. 2 vols. Berkeley: University of California Press, 1972.

Suh, Dae-sook. *The Korean Communist Movement, 1918–1948*. Princeton, New Jersey: Princeton University Press, 1967.

SOUTH KOREA

LARRY L. BURMEISTER

THE YI DYNASTY LEGACY

KOREA, unlike so many former colonial territories granted formal independence in the post–World War II era, entered the 20th century as a linguistically and culturally unified nation. This exceptional degree of sociocultural unity made it easier for both Koreas to mobilize their populations for interstate and international competition after the division of the peninsula into two separate states.

Korean national identity was solidified during the long-lived Yi dynasty. During this period of Korean history, the Confucian ideals of scholarship, moral virtue and public service were adopted and refashioned in a way that made educational achievement (knowledge of the Confucian classics) a key determinant of high social status and the social criterion for holding government office. In Korea, the scholar-official status was not based exclusively on merit. As a result of both political dictates and family economic resources, access to the state examinations for public office was confined principally to an aristocratic *yangban* class of landholding notables. Thus social stratification in Yi dynasty Korea was determined through ascriptive ties (the kinship and locality attributes of *yangban* lineage) as well as through the merit examination system. Both group affiliation—now often extended from ascriptive primary groups (kin and locality) to cliques within secondary associations such as the schools—and education still greatly influence social relationships in contemporary Korea.

Yi dynasty Korea had the formal trappings of a centralized agrarian bureaucracy. A royal house commanded a centralized bureaucratic staff of government ministers, headquartered in the capital city of Seoul, and an ancillary provincial officialdom. However, a censorate of scholar-officials steeped in the Confucian classics of ideal governance had significant authority to monitor court decision making, thus limiting the monarch's executive prerogatives. In addition, this same body of scholar-officials was responsible for educating the royal family. Heirs to the throne were trained to respect the authority of scholar-officials to question, redefine and perhaps even countermand royal edicts. As a result of this institutional constraint on royal authority, relations between a theoretically absolute monarchy and a theoretically subservient bureaucratic staff often approximated a balance-of-power standoff between the royal family and the scholar-officialdom.

Although Yi dynasty political institutions did not facilitate an effective central bureaucracy, neither did they encourage the buildup of countervailing local centers of autonomous power in the countryside that challenged central government authority in Seoul. *Yangban* energies were diverted away from provincial politics by the competition among the elite for the most prized bureaucratic positions in the capital. The concentration of political and economic resources at the center (i.e., in Seoul) continues to characterize Korean society.

Yi dynasty politics, in effect, became a stylized contest between the royal court, bureaucratic scholar-officials and *yangban* lineages over who had the moral authority to rule. Factional struggles for position took precedence over substantive policy concerns. This scramble for position was inimical to serious nation-building efforts in the economic and military spheres. The politically debilitating features of this elite standoff became painfully obvious during the era of great-power colonial expansionism in the late 19th century, when China and Korea became targets of external aggression. Historically, Korea's vassal status under the Chinese Empire had provided the shield of the "mandate of Heaven," a shield supposedly impervious to threats from culturally and morally inferior outsiders. As China crumbled under the combined weight of external colonial advances and internal decay, Yi dynasty Korea became extremely vulnerable to external threats. Although a group of "modernizers" did finally emerge, they drew intellectual sustenance from alien traditions—Western social philosophy and Christian religion—and were thus unable to mount a sustained sociopolitical challenge to the ruling elite. Neither a strong royal court nor a dynamic dominant class was able to mobilize the social resources necessary to confront effectively Japanese colonial designs. Korean independence was formally ended by Japanese annexation in 1910.

Korea continues to face difficulties in achieving a culturally acceptable level of national independence. Early dependence on China gave way first to the wrenching period of Japanese colonial annexation, followed by the North-South division and unacceptable degrees of obeisance to superpower "protectors." A self-deprecating interpretation of Korean history as *sadae-chuuei* (big-power subservience) is often evoked in internal political conflicts and in external posturing in both Koreas.

THE JAPANESE COLONIAL PERIOD (1910–45)

From the outset, Japanese colonial policy was aimed at integrating Korea into the imperial production and exchange network, albeit with economic activities and terms of trade established for the benefit of the Japanese metropole. Japanese colonists fanned out into the occupied territories, established economic enterprises and provided a visible constituency for economic development policies that were territorially comprehensive, rather unlike the enclave-oriented economic policies often associated with European colonization. Not only extractive primary product exports, but industrial and staple food grain production activities were encouraged. The end result was the development of a complex physical and governmental infrastructure (e.g., public utilities, roads, bureaucratic organizations) and the establishment of agro-industrial linkages with the colonies.

The first major economic push in colonial Korea was in the agricultural sector. Following the rice riots in Japan in 1918, Japanese policymakers sought new sources of cheap rice for the growing urban proletariat. Rice exports from the colonies became the solution. Ecological similiarities between physically proximate Japan and Korea facilitated the direct introduction of improved Japanese rice production technology in Korea. The production potential of the new rice varieties depended heavily on inputs of water and fertilizer. Colonial agricultural policies promoted the improvement of irrigation infrastructure in prime rice-growing regions. Fertilizer production capacity was given priority attention in nascent colonial industrialization plans. Many peasants obtained knowledge of and access to science-based agricultural production techniques and inputs for the most important staple food grains.

The great majority of Korean peasants, however, did not benefit from the Japanese upgrading of Korean agriculture. The colonial government's cadastral survey effectively dispossessed many Korean peasants and made them tenants who could be exploited by those who obtained "legal" title to the land. The beneficiaries were Japanese landholders and Korean landlords who retained their landholding rights. The Japanese colonial administration's ultimate objective was to generate agro-industrial exchanges within the Greater East Asian Co-Prosperity Sphere, providing direct support for the economic and military buildup in Japan. In Korea, rice was obtained from peasants through harsh rental terms and confiscatory marketing arrangements. This squeeze on the peasantry led to a dramatic decline in living standards in rural Korea. As a consequence, many peasants were politically radicalized, and in the 1930s clandestine "Red peasant unions" emerged to challenge colonial authority in the countryside.

The extraction of an agricultural surplus against the will of Korean peasant producers required a penetrating agrobureaucracy. During the Yi dynasty, central authorities tapped the agrarian surplus in a haphazard, ineffective manner. Local government magistrates did not oversee an effective government organization; rather, they depended on tax-farming intermediaries who often struck self-serving bargains with the villagers and local officials. The inability to appropriate systematically the agrarian surplus was revealed in the constant fiscal crises that plagued the central government in the Yi dynasty's waning years.

By contrast, the Japanese colonial agrobureaucracy was an effective extractive agency. Colonial economic mobilization efforts were coordinated and enforced through local agents of a central Ministry of the Interior. A tradition of central government control of agricultural-sector marketing, credit allocation, input distribution and technology diffusion was established and retained in the South in the postindependence era, as the Japanese agrobureaucratic structure was quickly reinstituted there as a means of maintaining control.

As Japan became more dependent on labor and natural resources in the colonies to support its imperial designs, Korea was targeted for significant industrial development. The northern region received the most intensive industrial investment due to the relative abundance of minerals and hydroelectric power potential. Koreans, however, played minor roles in the ownership and management of this new industrial infrastructure. Ownership of the bulk of the facilities remained in the hands of Japanese nationals or the colonial government. Korean business enterprises were confined primarily to small retail outlets and traditional handicraft industries. However, some Korean landed elites were able to secure a foothold in "modern" entrepreneurial ventures such as publishing, food processing and retail merchandising. A sizable contingent of Korean peasants was drawn from marginal, often poverty-stricken, economic conditions in the countryside into the growing industrial sector as laborers. This employment experience spread industrial work skills, factory discipline and an acquaintance with industrial management techniques among a growing proletariat. Japanese colonial economic policy fostered a degree of human-capital formation that was often absent in agro-export colonial enclaves.

In political terms, Japanese colonial rule fostered a reactive nationalism. The March 1st Movement, a spontaneous national uprising in 1919 against Japanese rule, provided the catalyst for more repressive Japanese measures of social control. During the 1930s attempts were made to Japanize Korean culture through such draconian measures as mandating the Japanese language as the sole medium of instruction in the school system and forcing Korean families to adopt Japanese surnames. This severe counterreaction to an emergent Korean nationalism increased the likelihood of organized resistance to Japanese rule. The authorities instituted a systematic crackdown on all opposition groups. A dense network of infiltrators and spies (often Koreans) was employed to ferret out clandestine anticolonial political activity. Opposition forces either went underground or into exile. The end result was the splintering of the nationalist opposition into physically isolated and ideologically distinct subgroups. Elements of the nationalist movement sought exile in Shanghai and the United States. Only the Communists managed to evade entrapment through their organizational system of self-contained, underground party cells that were relatively impervious to detection. The Communists' presence in Korea as the only active guerrilla force throughout the colonial occupation stood them in good stead in the postindependence era, as they were able to claim the mantle of the true nationalist partisans. On the whole, the Japanese repression of dissent managed to fragment the nationalist movement, complicating postliberation political settlements.

PENINSULAR DIVISION AND THE KOREAN WAR (1945–53)

Japan's surrender in August 1945 did not free the Korean peninsula from great-power interference. Disposition of colonial territories was a topic of the Allied summits from 1943 to the end of the war. The Korean question, however, was never resolved, and Koreans were presented with a fait accompli at the time of the Japanese surrender. The Soviet Union, which officially entered the Pacific theater of the war just one week before Japan surrendered, was poised with military forces at the Sino-Korean border. A quick decision was made in the U.S. State Department to divide the Korean peninsula into Soviet and American "trusteeships" at the 38th parallel. The Soviet Union acquiesced, setting in motion three years of sporadic, unproductive unification talks before separate, independent states—the Republic of Korea (South) and the Democratic People's Republic of Korea (North)—were proclaimed in 1948.

The partition of the peninsula set the stage for the U.S. military occupation of South Korea from September 1945 to August 1948. Amid the chaos of the Japanese surrender, indigenous political forces had established a peninsula-wide network of local governing committees operating under the auspices of an interim governing authority, the Korean People's Republic (KPR). The KPR coalition, a loose grouping of self-proclaimed provisional government leaders representing a wide spectrum of political opinion with an important "radical-left" element, commandeered the colonial government bureaucratic apparatus left behind by the Japanese, and proceeded to organize citizens at the local level to take control of Japanese property and to redistribute seized assets to workers' committees and peasants. High on the list of activities of the "people's committees" was the criminal prosecution (via "people's courts") and seizure of property of Koreans singled out as collaborators. In effect, indigenous forces advocating revolutionary change seized the political moment in the South before the U.S. military occupation forces arrived a month later in September 1945.

The usurping KPR governing apparatus posed a grave threat to the social power of members of the traditional Korean landed aristocracy (especially those who had forged pragmatic accommodations with the colonial regime) and those Koreans who had served in colonial administrative capacities as lower-echelon officials. These groups realized that an alliance with the incoming U.S. military occupation forces offered the only hope of avoiding retribution from Koreans wishing to transform the social order. In Korea as in Western Europe, the American fear of radical (i.e., Communist) political movements led to alliances of convenience between American occupation authorities, politically discredited conservatives and collaborators, and émigrés from Communist-controlled regions whose recent experience with revolutionary upheaval predisposed them against accommodations with left-leaning political factions. In South Korea, this alliance was consummated with the abrogation of the provisional government's (KPR) authority, the dismantling of the local-level-affiliated people's committees, and the reinstallation of the colonial governmental machinery to regain administrative control (replete with many of the same personnel who had served in the colonial period). Particularly galling to many Koreans was the retention of the bulk of the colonial Korean police contingent, a group widely vilified by the populace. The American military occupation authorities opted to roll back, if possible, the popular redistributionist programs of the KPR. They lacked the personnel to do the job themselves, so they had to reinstitute the social control mechanisms of the colonial period.

U.S. commitment to a long trusteeship in South Korea was lukewarm at best. Attempts were made early after the arrival of U.S. military occupation authorities to identify conservative or moderate nationalists, untainted by a collaborationist past, who could lead an indigenous national political movement consonant with American political and economic ideals. Waiting in the wings were the leaders of the exiled opposition who viewed themselves as rightful heirs to political control of postliberation Korea. The problem of leadership in the South became more acute with the failure of the United States and the Soviet Union to come to any agreement on a peninsular reunification formula. The United States became eager to identify and recognize an independent government in the South.

To the later consternation of many U.S. officials, the obstreperous Syngman Rhee became the only viable conservative presidential candidate. Rhee's solid nationalist credentials enabled him to piece together political alliances of the moment and mount a successful campaign for the South Korean presidency in 1948. Rhee's early political moves included the promulgation of anticommunism and Korean reunification as penultimate policy rationales; the systematic persecution of leftist opponents, leading eventually to the political "sanitization" of the South; temporary accommodations with the "collaborationist" landlord-entrepreneurial elite; and the promulgation of a thorough land reform that effectively dispossessed the old *yangban* landed aristocracy from the countryside.

The outbreak of the Korean War in June 1950 halted any momentum toward economic reconstruction and political normalcy. Leaders in the North and the South had built their political followings on campaigns for reunification, by force if necessary. Belligerent threats and sporadic episodes of military confrontation along the demilitarized zone (DMZ) preceded the outbreak of the war. Regardless of one's interpretation of the war's final causes (and there are many divergent views among historians), the war's effect on the South was profound. Massive physical destruction produced further social leveling that complemented land reform measures promulgated by Rhee. In the course of 50 years, the highly stratified Yi dynasty society gave way to unprecedented social fluidity. Massive destruction made the postwar Republic of Korea abjectly dependent on infusions of U.S. food aid, military support and financial assistance. Korean society was militarized in a previously unparalleled way; this militarization, coupled with the retention of the colonial structure of bureaucratic centralism, combined to lay the foundations for postwar authoritarian politics in the South. Acquiescence to an authoritarian mode of governance based on national security justifications was legitimated, in part, by the experiences of refugees from the North and of exposure in the South to Communist control during the early part of the war, when Southern forces and their U.S. allies were pushed back to the Pusan perimeter.

THE POSTWAR PATRIMONY OF SYNGMAN RHEE (1953–61)

Perhaps the most enduring economic legacy of the Rhee years was land reform. Rhee was not personally predisposed to a radical land redistribution program, but continued peasant unrest in the countryside over land tenure conditions forced his hand. The example of land redistribution in the North in 1946 sparked agitation for an equivalent formula in the South. Advisers cautioned Rhee that his political survival hinged on a resolution to the problem of peasant landlessness that had been a lightning rod for radical political mobilization since the 1930s.

The 3-hectare ceiling on rice paddy acreage encoded in the land reform statute transformed the agrarian structure of the South into a mini-farm, owner-operated configuration. After a short, disastrous experiment with decontrolled markets in the early period of U.S. occupation, pressures on the domestic food supply forced the reimposition of tight government control over agricultural pricing and marketing of strategic food commodities. Government intervention has been a fixture of agricultural development policy ever since. The division of the countryside into tiny, mini-farm units proved to be quite conducive to centralized administrative control of agriculture in the service of national development objectives.

Foreign aid proved to be the fulcrum of Rhee's post–Korean War reconstruction strategy. Counterpart funds—funds generated by the sale of goods and services provided through U.S. foreign aid channels—provided a substantial portion of South Korea's recurrent budgetary expenditures during the 1950s. Food commodities distributed under the Public Law 480 Food for Peace program and sold or rationed by the government were used to generate government revenues and pay the salaries of government officials. Within the government bureaucracy, the concern for maximizing foreign assistance mitigated against dynamic economic policy initiatives. Rhee's lack of interest in self-sustaining economic development programs is evidenced by the fact that formal government economic planning capacity was not activated until 1958, only two years before the "student revolution" toppled his regime.

The government's tight control of lucrative import concessions, military contracts and highly overvalued foreign exchange engendered "political" rather than "entrepreneurial" capitalism. Business activity degenerated into a scramble for access to the government-controlled rations. Often, entrepreneurial success in these ventures depended on political contacts and payoffs, thus providing the Rhee political machine with a readily accessible campaign war chest. A few of the former landed elites did manage to retain footholds secured during the colonial period in such modern economic enterprises as the manufacturing of light consumer goods, food processing and publishing. Some of these assets were later parlayed into the big-business combines that currently dominate the South Korean economic landscape.

Rhee's political posturing focused on the immediate goal of North-South reunification. Given the aforementioned economic complementarity of the North and the South, Rhee argued that an aggressive industrialization program aimed at economic self-sufficiency in the South amounted to tacit acceptance of the status quo of a divided Korea—that is, admission that reunification would not occur soon. Rhee refused to accept this reality, and instead claimed that impending reunification would solve the peninsula's economic development problems. In addition, Rhee's ardent nationalism precluded the reestablishment of diplomatic relations with Japan, blocking opportunities for economic expansion through trade with one of Korea's most logical trading partners. U.S. attempts to encourage a more dynamic economic development program met with little success. Rhee was content with aid dependency, and he knew that the United States was not going to pull the economic plug, given the symbolic and military importance of Korea as a geopolitical linchpin in the global containment policy that activated the United States' costly Korean War intervention.

Along with the land reform initiative, Rhee's policy legacy was the implementation of a nationwide system of primary education. As a result, South Korea entered the 1960s with an unusually high literacy rate, given its low per capita income. The Korean prospensity toward investment in education was revealed further in the extraordinary willingness of families to invest their savings in postprimary education for their children, as advanced schooling was not supported by public funds. Rhee's education initiative, combined with the cultural predisposition toward education (a significant part of the Confucian legacy), provided an important human-capital base for South Korea's subsequent "economic miracle."

Paradoxically for the education-minded Rhee, a growing cohort of college and university students provided the demographic base for an effective political challenge to his decaying regime. Suspected electoral fraud in the 1960 presidential election was the immediate catalyst for tumultuous anti-Rhee street demonstrations orchestrated by student leaders, which brought down the regime. During the course of Rhee's 12-year presidential tenure, he had failed to institutionalize effective means for political decision making and regime change. He bullied the National Assembly into reneging on a constitutional provision prohibiting a third presidential term in 1956; he used a divide-and-conquer strategy to retain political support within the military; and he filled the coffers of his Liberal party political machine with bribes and payoffs solicited for access to government-controlled economic privileges. Rhee's advanced age and his unyielding temperament, coupled with a stagnating economy and a soaring unemployment rate, made his rule increasingly untenable. When students took to the streets to protest rigged elections, the security forces were unwilling to use force to quell the disorder, and Rhee was forced into exile.

The Rhee legacy of political nondevelopment did not bode well for Chang Myon's successor parliamentary government (1960–61). The post-Rhee political parties were not effective, disciplined organizations capable of routine decision making and problem solving. Factional infighting within the National Assembly quickly overtook substantive policy concerns—a disastrous show of political ineptitude given the country's deteriorating economic situation. The politicians were especially eager to purge the allegedly corrupt "Rhee generals" from the military and, in the course of this campaign, they managed to threaten the military's institutional power base. The military had, in fact, emerged as the most powerful social institution in post-Rhee Korea. Uncertainties within the military about future power prerogatives, the emergence of a group of discontented middle-level officers whose career paths were blocked by the politically discredited Rhee generals, and military worries over an increasingly vocal radical-left critique of anticommunist and conservative reunification dogma instigated the military coup that brought Gen. Park Chung Hee to power in May 1961.

ECONOMIC DYNAMISM AND POLITICAL RETROGRESSION: THE PARK AND CHUN YEARS (1961–88)

Public disgust with political chaos, and continued economic stagnation during the Chang Myon interregnum diffused overt opposition to the military coup. The ruling junta committee justified its intervention with a scathing critique of aid dependence during the Rhee era, a message that coincided with the economic nationalism expressed by those opposing Rhee's rule. Military concerns about the national security risks embodied in "leftist" proposals to engage the North in unconditional reunification talks also found sympathy among a wary population who feared and distrusted the North.

The relative economic progress of the North vis-à-vis the South worried Park and his key advisers. Taking a more realistic view of the prospects for reunification, Park focused his political energies on organizing the South for more effective competition in an economic "war of development" and an international "war of recognition" with the North. Long-term prospects for peninsular reunification on terms acceptable to the South would depend ultimately on the relative economic capabilities of the divided Koreas. Park surmised that the South was presently losing the battle that counted most, the economic contest.

From the outset, national economic development became a policy issue of the highest priority for Park. The superministerial Economic Planning Board (EPB) was organized as a direct staff appendage to the executive office, with the EPB director holding a high-profile deputy prime minister cabinet portfolio. The personnel of the functional ministries were replaced or resocialized to ensure that economic policy implementation goals would be served. A dual career track was established within the government bureaucracy, with the lateral movement of former military officers directly into high-ranking positions—providing the executive and his staff with surveillance capabilities and watchdog operatives who guarded against bureaucratic slippage in high-priority economic development initiatives. Civilian recruitment patterns were altered to secure a cadre of technocrats, often educated abroad, thus diluting the influence of career bureaucrats whose recruitment paths predisposed them to traditional political management rather than technical skills.

Park's conscious restructuring of government/civil society relations in the direction of executive-bureaucratic dominance was seen early in his tenure. Not only was the state bureaucracy overhauled to respond more expeditiously to executive dictates, but those political organs theoretically responsive to the interests of civil society, the National Assembly and local government jurisdictions, were emasculated. Legislative initiatives and budgetary authority were concentrated within the executive branch to the degree that the National Assembly could only ratify or reject government-sponsored proposals. The minimal local government autonomy during the Rhee years was completely eviscerated during the Park era. All local government jurisdictions were controlled directly by the central Ministry of Home Affairs (MHA). Provincial governors were directly appointed by the president; all local officials were appointed through MHA channels. Local government offices became agencies of the central administration in Seoul, charged with the implementation and administration of programs formulated within and passed down from the central ministries.

Economic development programs were based on a hybrid import control–export industrialization policy mix. Korean economic planners, and their American advisers, saw the need for viable export industries as a way to address the chronic balance-of-payments deficits that required constant infusions of U.S. aid. The traditional prescription for agrarian economies, development of agricultural primary product exports, did not fit the factor endowment of densely populated, resource-poor Korea. In fact, the colonial rice export economy proved to be a misleading historical analogue. In the 1960s, South Korea was in a food deficit as well as a balance-of-payments bind. Policymakers deduced that Korea's competitive economic advantage resided in a relatively well-educated, cheap, underemployed labor force. Export potential was asserted to exist in light-industry consumer goods (e.g., textiles, footwear, leather goods, simple electronic products). And even these labor-intensive manufacturing activities depended on the import of constituent raw materials and manufactured components.

Selected export industries were targeted for government-supplied production incentives such as subsidized credit, low tariffs on raw material and component intermediate imports, access to lucrative import concessions, and tax breaks for export production. Early on, Park enlisted the private sector in the export industrialization drive. The "speculative" entrepreneurs of the Rhee era were first threatened with confiscation of wealth as punishment for alleged illegal wealth accumulation, but, in fact, were given the option of following government directives to invest in priority economic sectors. A complex system of incentives—financial and political—was constructed by the government to encourage private-sector participation in targeted export activities.

The success of the early phase of the South Korean export industrialization drive was due in no small measure to an expansionary world economy in the 1960s. In addition, Korea's strategic position in U.S. geopolitical calculations paid economic dividends in terms of preferential treatment of Korean exports in the huge U.S. market, ready access to international loans from U.S. banks and U.S.-influenced public lenders (e.g., the World Bank), and minimal pressure on Korea to open its own markets to competitors. In addition, Park was able to weather serious political opposition to the normalization of relations with Japan in 1965. Economic linkages were quickly established, giving Korea some access to appropriate technology and sunset industries that the Japanese wished to farm out. Asian markets expanded even further with Korean involvement in the Vietnam War. Lucrative economic contracts for the provision of goods and services for the Allied forces in Vietnam proved a boon to fledgling Korean manufacturers.

The ability of the South Korean government to segment markets is an important, often underemphasized, dimension of Korean development pol-

602

icy. Selected markets were chosen for export penetration. Foreign exchange rates were realigned to more realistic levels, and prices in export markets were pegged to meet or undercut competitors. However, many domestic markets, including markets for the same exported products, remained protected from foreign competition by a complex system of tariff and nontariff barriers. Market segmentation gave exporting firms a profit cushion in domestic markets, enabling them to absorb initial losses in export product lines in attempts to gain market shares. Protected markets allowed the government to promote strategic backward and forward infant industry linkages. Promotion of higher degrees of industrial integration was designed to avoid South Korea's entrapment as a low-wage assembler of imported industrial components and as a finisher of imported raw materials. In the early phase of industrialization, these labor-intensive, import-dependent enterprises were courted and encouraged, but on the underlying rationale that they served as technology and labor skill transfer conduits. The ultimate objective of the Korean economic bureaucracy was to develop world-class industrial capabilities.

State intervention occurred at many critical stages in the national industrialization process. Strict control was placed on the inflow of direct foreign investment. Projects were carefully screened by the economic bureaucracy and were approved only if they met technology diffusion, labor training and labor intensity standards. Most direct foreign investment was approved only on conditions of joint venture participation by a Korean partner, either private or public. In fact, direct foreign investment played a relatively minor role in the first two decades of industrialization. Foreign capital flows have fueled expansion, but these flows have been portfolio rather than direct investments (i.e., loans from foreign banks and multilateral public lending agencies). Foreign borrowing often flowed directly into the state-controlled banking system. Credit was then allocated by the government on a priority basis, assuring a significant government influence over investment strategies and facilitating the attainment of government development targets. The government, through the banking system, kept a tight rein on the sale and allocation of scarce foreign exchange. Imports were closely monitored by government agencies to assure that priority technology, and intermediate goods' import needs consonant with industrialization plans, were being served. The diversion of foreign exchange into luxury consumption expenditures was, to a degree, controlled and discouraged. Finally, the government was willing to take the role of entrepreneur in sectors where risks, profitability, or economic scale made private investment problematic. Public utilities, the Pohang Iron and Steel Company, parts of the petrochemical industry, most sectors of the fledgling defense industry and other ventures remain under full or partial government ownership.

The emphasis on light-industry consumer goods in the 1960s gave way to a heavy industrialization push in the 1970s. While textiles, footwear and electronics remain key industrial sectors, rapid growth of the petrochemical, steel, automobile, shipbuilding and industrial machinery sectors has occurred during the last two decades. Huge investments were channeled by the government to heavy industry during the last years of Park's

603

rule, as he feared gradual U.S. disengagement from past defense commitments and sought to promote self-sufficiency in weapons production for national security reasons. Many of these ventures remain economically problematic. Recently both private and public funds have been invested in the computer industry, as plans to move further up the industrial technology ladder are activated. Again, the government is playing an instrumental role in industrial restructuring to upgrade the national industrial plant for international competition in the 21st century—that is, firms are merged, credit is secured and allocated, and research and development efforts are stimulated under the not-so-invisible hand of government guidance and government-controlled resource allocation incentives.

At the outset of the Park era, South Korea was still predominantly agricultural. A massive flow of labor from the countryside to urban areas has occurred during the past three decades. Farmers now comprise approximately one-quarter of the work force. Agriculture retains its mini-farm structure, but farm operations are now more integrated into national markets for commodities and production inputs. The agricultural development strategy pursued during the Park era illustrates how the government attempted to build agro-industrial linkages by organizing and protecting markets for key agricultural commodities (e.g., rice, barley, livestock) and production inputs (e.g., fertilizer). Agriculture was drawn into the national economy in a way that increased agricultural productivity while at the same time releasing surplus rural labor for industrial expansion.

Park's initial "agriculture first" policy promise to increase commodity prices and reduce onerous farm debt was only partially honored, with government action concentrated on some relief from the latter problem. Economic stabilization problems forced the government to continue a low commodity pricing policy to keep inflation under control. As during the Rhee years, low agricultural commodity prices were maintained through South Korea's access to surplus U.S. food commodities under the P.L. 480 program. In effect, these surpluses were dumped on the Korean domestic market, thus depressing prices for Korean-produced staple food commodities. During the 1960s, Park's main emphasis was on improving production infrastructure—upgrading irrigation systems, reorganizing the research and extension services, and investing in agricultural production input industries (fertilizer, agrochemicals and farm machinery).

Decreasing access to P.L. 480 food grants in the 1970s and sharp price increases in the international commodity markets forced the government to embark on a crash import-substitution program in agriculture, centered on the goal of self-sufficiency with respect to the most important food staple, rice. New high-yielding rice varieties were developed and diffused by the national agricultural research and extension system; product and input prices were realigned to increase production incentives and encourage new technology adoption; and the parastatal National Agricultural Cooperatives Federation was enlisted to serve as the central marketing agency for the new varieties and their production inputs, as well as to provide credit for investment in more intensive agro-industrial farming methods. During the 1970s agricultural production increased, farm incomes rose and foreign exchange expenditures for food imports were dampened as a result of the government's agricultural development mobilization efforts. Agriculture was harnessed to support the national industrialization project in a way that increased agro-industrial linkages and increased the ability of farm families to purchase both consumer goods and production inputs, while at the same time rural families released labor to industry. The relative farm boom in the 1970s was short-lived. The Chun regime (1980–88) had to start dealing with agricultural adjustment problems that threaten the long-term viability of mini-farm agriculture. During the 1980s, rural household incomes began to decline once again in comparison with urban household incomes.

The Rhee era was marked by sporadic episodes of political repression, in particular the periodic purges against regime-threatening opponents. An organized leftist opposition was, for all practical purposes, removed from the scene at the conclusion of the Korean War. The extant political party system—Rhee's conservative Liberal party and the conservative-to-moderate opposition—congealed around personalities, not pragmatic programs or ideological platforms. During elections and legislative deliberations, formal political rights were often disregarded, as the Rhee political machine cowed opponents when democratic procedures would not produce desired results. With the advent of post-coup politics, formal legal rights were gradually eroded further and systematic repression increased. Particularly significant indicators of the new hardline position were increasing censorship in the mass media and the frequent classification of perceived antiregime activities (e.g., union organization and discussion of alternative perspectives on North-South reunification) as crimes against the state.

Exclusionist political tendencies were a natural outgrowth of the fusion of the national security apparatus and the formal political machinery brought about by the military's predominant position in the post-coup polity. General-turned-President Park had a particularly jaundiced view of democratic politics (or at least what had passed for democratic politics during the Rhee tenure) as self-indulgent, profligate, corrupt means of conducting affairs of state. Obviously, obeisance to outward democratic forms was required for domestic political legitimation and international public relations reasons. Thus Park's decision to continue to serve as president required "civilianization" of the polity in 1963. But the hard military core of the regime mitigated against any relaxation of the authoritarian relationship of the government toward the people.

Political organization during the Park regime is illustrated by the ruling group's formation of a "civilian" political party, the Democratic-Republican party (DRP), to contest the 1963 presidential election. When Park decided to run as a civilian candidate for the presidency, he asked Kim Jong Pil—a coup coconspirator and subsequent organizer and chief of the Korean Central Intelligence Agency (KCIA)—to organize a political party. Using the resources of the intelligence service and other government connections, Kim mobilized a nationwide network of DRP cadres and amassed a sizable campaign war chest. Thus Park, in effect, directly organized the party machinery from the presidential office, using the covert and overt political power at his disposal. The fact that the coterie of ex-military officers and former government officials that formed the core of the DRP and its successor political party during the Chun era was (and still is) referred to as the "ruling camp," connotes the tenor of military-government fusion that constitutes politics in post-coup Korean society.

Opposition parties, on the other hand, lacked programmatic focus and a strategic resource base. To a considerable extent, a moderate-populist opposition was suffered for cosmetic reasons and was easily manipulated by DRP opponents. Increased government control of the mass media, government manipulation of electoral rules and the elections themselves, the narrowing of acceptable political discourse and the ability of the government to intimidate potential financial donors to opposition organizational efforts combined to produce an ineffectual countervailing political force. When a charismatic threat to the DRP's electoral plurality appeared in 1971 in the person of Kim Dae Jung, he was removed forcibly from the political scene and eventually charged with treason.

The 1970s ushered in an era of increasingly rigid authoritarian rule that eventually proved fatal to President Park. Early in the decade, Park had maneuvered to secure lifetime presidential tenure through the abrogation of all meaningful mechanisms of political accountability. The *yushin* (revitalizing) constitution, in effect, subjugated all political institutions to executive direction and gave the president carte blanche to rule by decree. Two sources of potential organized opposition, the students and a growing urban proletariat, were singled out as subversive threats. Their actions were closely monitored, mobilization attempts were crushed, and many student and labor activists were imprisoned. Charges of torture and disrespect for any semblance of legal due process accompanied the crackdowns on vocal regime opponents. In the United States, the Carter administration's initial foreign policy emphasis on human rights targeted South Korea as a perpetrator of serious violations. The publicity caused much grumbling among U.S. politicians about continued military and economic support for the South, and enraged the Park inner circle, who interpreted the initiative as blatant interference in the South's domestic affairs. This international blacklisting seemed to stiffen Park's resolve to deal mercilessly with suspected regime opponents. Finally, internal opposition to Park's intransigence boiled over into civil disorder in the spring of 1979. Conflicts about how to handle the growing rebellion divided Park's narrowing inner circle of confidants. In October 1979 Park was assassinated by the head of the KCIA, an act the perpetrator claimed was a desperate effort to save the country from impending self-destruction.

Park's death was welcomed by many as an opportunity to extricate the country from two decades of repressive, authoritarian, military rule. In the ensuing political interregnum, the voices of democratization quickly surfaced. The press, suddenly unfettered, expressed a wide range of opinion about the shape of a new democratic South Korea. The three Kims—Kim Dae Jung; opposition Assemblyman Kim Young Sam, whose support of striking women garment workers garnered widespread publicity; and former DRP operative Kim Jong Pil—started to position themselves as presidential candidates. The military, however, was not willing to risk a wide-open political contest that would surely decrease their institutional power as well as open up possibilities for purges in the military in the event that the "radical" opposition (i.e., Kim Dae Jung) won a contested election. The "window of democratic opportunity" became a "window of vulnerability" for the military. In December 1979 Gen. Chun Doo Hwan engineered an internal coup within the military. Chun gradually gained control over key military and government posts and blocked a democratic electoral transition. A rebellion against Chun's usurpation of power occurred in May 1980 in the opposition stronghold of Kwangju (the home region of Kim Dae Jung). To suppress this week-long revolt against central authority, Chun finally called in special military units, whose brutal suppression of the uprising resulted in significant loss of life. Chun's leadership position was fundamentally compromised by this incident. Despite some impressive accomplishments during his seven-year tenure—continued national economic growth, increased international status as a formidable industrial power, widely acknowledged victory in the North-South war for international recognition, the successful campaign to host the 1988 Olympics and, perhaps most importantly, a peaceful transition to a successor regime in 1988—Chun's presidency is widely perceived as an illegitimate interlude in Korean history. The considerable accomplishments of the Chun regime, it seems, will always be overshadowed by the "Kwangju massacre."

Politics in Chun's Fifth Republic was organized in the Park tradition. A successor party to the DRP, the Democratic Justice party (DJP), was formed in much the same way—that is, through top-down mobilization by the executive and his staff. Influential members of the DJP ranks were drawn from the same core of ex-military officers and ex-government officials as in Park's DRP. Opposition forces remained organizationally and programmatically weak and thus were easily manipulated by the ruling camp. In an attempt to ease debilitating speculation about his long-term intentions, Chun promised the nation that he would relinquish the presidency upon the completion of one seven-year term and further promised that he would be the first president of the Republic of Korea to oversee a peaceful transfer of power. The method of succession was, however, not detailed. Chun's declaration did not bring about a significant political honeymoon. From the start, opposition forces, especially students and activist church groups, challenged the government's suppression of political dissent. Antigovernment protests on university campuses became everyday occurrences in 1986, and a full-scale riot in the port city of Inchon signaled a level of social discontent that was no longer confined to the universities. The designation of Chun's heir apparent, ex-general and cabinet officer Roh Tae Woo, along with the reported torture death of an alleged student activist detained by the police, brought an unparalleled explosion of mass street demonstrations throughout the country in the spring of 1987. These demonstrations were joined, for the first time, by large numbers of the middle and working classes—housewives, white-collar workers and factory workers—pressing demands for political liberalization and the popular election of a presidential successor.

607

Unlike the last years of the Park regime, the ruling camp, represented in public by DJP-selected presidential candidate Roh, acceded to opposition demands for direct elections and promised to heed the public's strong demand for fundamental political reforms. Opposition leaders Kim Dae Jung and Kim Young Sam were released from virtual house arrest, and agreement was reached on an election format. In December 1987 the first meaningful (i.e., competitive) election in 16 years was held, with Roh winning a plurality of the vote (37 percent) in a crowded four-candidate field. Once again, personal rivalries between the two Kims had seemingly thwarted opposition victory, although speculation continues about electoral irregularities and about how the military would have reacted in the advent of Roh's electoral defeat.

The high political drama in 1987 and the apparent changes in the Korean political landscape tell much about changes in the social structure that have occurred in South Korea during the past three decades. The society is now highly urbanized, with approximately 65 percent of the population living in cities and 25 percent of the nation's citizens now residing in the Seoul metropolitan area. Physical concentration, in and of itself, has made it easier for the opposition to mobilize effectively and press its demands on an obstreperous government.

The benefits of a three-decade-long national economic boom have trickled down rather effectively. Increases in per capita income, a relatively egalitarian income distribution, the satisfaction of basic nutritional needs, high educational achievement, low infant mortality rates and increases in expected lifespan—to name only a few of the most salient social welfare indicators—place the South in an extraordinarily favorable economic light vis-à-vis comparable late-developing societies. Broad-based social welfare gains have occurred. Political repression during the Park and Chun years was tolerated, in part, because of public recognition of substantial economic progress. Park, in fact, made no secret of his equation of Korean economic success with "Korean-style democracy."

These economic successes, engendered by rapid industrialization, produced a social transformation. The premodern, bipolar class division of scholar-officials and peasants has been replaced by a variegated class structure incorporating new classes—industrial and finance capitalists, middle-class professional functionaries in both the public and private sectors, and factory workers. The rapid expansion of the middle class and an unusually well-educated working class, as well as an ever-expanding cohort of politically active college students, have generated political tensions that forced ruling-camp accomodations in 1987. Big businesses in Korea have profited enormously from a government support system that has fueled their expansion. Although some business sectors may, in fact, favor a liberal capitalist sociopolitical order, business criticism has been muted given the symbiotic relationship between the business sector and the Park and Chun governments. But the numerically ascendant middle and working classes have vowed that economic advance without political development is an unacceptable status quo. Increasingly strident demands for political voice in

608

public affairs and in the workplace are now difficult to suppress in light of the new class demographics.

SOUTH KOREA: FUTURE PROSPECTS

Prospects for future democratization in South Korea are, of course, contingent on significant changes in civil-military relations. "Olympics politics" undoubtedly played a major role in the ruling camp's decision to accommodate public demands for the direct election of a successor regime. The successful completion of the 1988 Olympics—the international showcasing of South Korea's emergence as a major industrial power—was foremost among outgoing President Chun's political priorities. Continued civil disorder posed severe risks for the games. How will continuing demands for political liberalization be met in the post-Olympics period when the Roh political honeymoon is over? Is Roh committed to fundamental reforms, and if so, will he command sufficient political resources to implement substantive change in civil-military relations? With Roh's election, the ruling bloc of military–government bureaucracy–big business remains intact. Internal bargaining over power shares within this coalition will determine post-Olympic presidential and DJP political initiatives.

The external threat from the North remains the legitimating fulcrum of the military's role in South Korean politics. Questions about leadership change in the North, and sporadic terrorist attacks against the South (e.g., the Rangoon bombing in 1983 and the alleged North Korean orchestration of the 1983 Korean Air Lines disaster) keep the issue of unpredictable Northern aggression in the forefront of South Korean political life. However, the demographics of age may be mitigating the political potency of arguments about external threats for a military-dominated polity. A substantial majority of South Korea's 40 million citizens have been born since the Korean War; they have no direct experience with the war or North Korean occupation. In addition, the cohort of émigrés from the North is aging, and their control over South Korean politics is fading. The legitimation of heavy-handed military involvement in politics by constant reference to the external threat from the North is likely to become more threadbare with the passage of time.

Economic factors also enter the democratization equation, specifically the regional concentration of economic activities and the structure of industry. Concentrated investment in the Seoul-Inchon corridor, the Taegu industrial belt and the Pusan coastal strip have contributed to growing regional income inequalities that complicate the democratization process. The Kim Dae Jung–Kim Young Sam split, based on personal ties and regional loyalties, revealed an alarming degree of regional political polarization that has been exacerbated by the previously discussed regional economic inequalities (along with the Kwangju incident). In addition, the government has nurtured the expansion of a few big-business conglomerates, the largely family-held *chaebols* that, in effect, wield oligopolistic power over the Korean economy. While this degree of business concentration may be benefi-

609

cial in international economic competition—for example, South Korea is one of the few late-developing Third World countries that has generated homegrown national firms that are marketing products under their own brand names on a worldwide scale—it represents a degree of concentrated social power that is hard to square with the power dispersion requisites of democratic politics. The *chaebols'* control of such a large proportion of GNP and export production makes them an effective veto group within government councils. Democratization is hindered by *chaebol* economic predominance, and yet continued national economic growth depends on satisfactory *chaebol* performance.

South Korea's economic successes have taken some of the political pressure off past authoritarian regimes. Continued high national economic growth rates will certainly ease inevitable political tensions accompanying liberalization, especially the expected labor offensive. However, South Korea's sudden multibillion dollar trade surplus with the United States is clouding future rapid economic growth prospects. Restricted access to markets in the advanced industrial world (especially the absorptive U.S. market) would undoubtedly make the democratization process more difficult. A severe test of stated commitments by President Roh to increase industrial wages, rein in the *chaebols* and encourage interest-group politics would occur in the event of a substantial international economic downturn or significant changes in the international trade regime.

FURTHER READING

Ban, Sung Hwan, Moon, Pal Yong and Perkins, Dwight H. *Rural Development.* Cambridge, Massachusetts: Harvard University Press, 1980.
Burmeister, Larry L. *Research, Realpolitik, and Development in Korea: The State and the Green Revolution.* Boulder, Colorado: Westview Press, 1988.
Cumings, Bruce. *The Origins of the Korean War.* 2 vols. Princeton, New Jersey: Princeton University Press, 1981, 1989.
Jones, Leroy P., and Sakong, Il. *Government, Business and Entrepreneurship in Economic Development: The Korean Case.* Cambridge, Massachusetts: Harvard University Press, 1980.
Jones, Leroy P. *Public Enterprise and Economic Development: The Korean Case.* Seoul: Korea Development Institute, 1975.
Kihl, Young Hwan. *Politics and Policies in Divided Korea: Regimes in Contest.* Boulder, Colorado: Westview Press, 1984.
Kim, Se-Jin. *The Politics of Military Revolution in Korea.* Chapel Hill: University of North Carolina Press, 1971.
Luedde-Neurath, Richard. *Import Controls and Export-Oriented Development: A Reassessment of the South Korean Case.* Boulder, Colorado: Westview Press, 1986.
Myers, Ramon, and Peattie, Mark R., eds. *The Japanese Colonial Empire.* Seattle: University of Washington Press, 1984.
Palais, James B. *Politics and Policy in Traditional Korea.* Cambridge, Massachusetts: Harvard University Press, 1975.
Wade, Robert, and White, Gordon, eds. *Development States in East Asia: Capitalist and Socialist.* Bulletin No. 15. Brighton, Sussex: Institute of Development Studies, 1984.

LAOS

JOSEPH J. ZASLOFF

Land and People

LAOS, a small, mountainous, landlocked country, is among the least developed of Southeast Asian nations. Surrounded by Vietnam, Cambodia, Thailand, Myanmar and China, its people, estimated at 3.5 million in 1985, live in an area with a population density of only 15 inhabitants per square kilometer. Laos, therefore, has not experienced either the land hunger or the urban poverty felt by so many of its Asian neighbors. Rather, the country has had the problem of achieving unity and coherence, owing primarily to communication difficulties among its dispersed, ethnically diverse peoples. The French colonial power built only a small road network, with few roads penetrating the rugged mountains. No bridge was ever built to span the Mekong River to Thailand, nor were railroad tracks ever laid down in Laos.

More than two-thirds of Laos is mountainous. The remaining third—the central plain—has been carved by the Mekong River, which runs from Myanmar through the center and northern half of Laos, and then runs south, forming the boundary between Laos and Thailand for approximately 620 miles/1,000 km.

The various ethnic groups in Laos may be classified according to the altitude at which they live: (1) the lowland Lao (Lao Loum), (2) the Lao of the mountain slopes (Lao Theung), and (3) the Lao of the mountain summits (Lao Soung). By linguistic classification, the Lao Loum are Thai-speaking, as are a group of upland tribal Thai who make up to 10% to 20% of the population. These tribal Thai are composed of Thai Dam (Black Thai), Thai Deng (Red Thai) and Thai Khao (White Thai), named for the colors of the women's dress. The Lao Theung, estimated at 20% to 30% of the population, include a variety of groups who speak Mon-Khmer languages. (The Lao Theung are still frequently referred to by the pejorative term *kha*, meaning "slave.") The Lao Soung, composed primarily of the Hmong (still sometimes referred to as Meo) and Yao, speak Tibeto-Burman languages. In addition, Vietnamese, Chinese and a small number of Indians came to Laotian towns during the French colonial period and engaged in commerce. Many of these commercial minorities fled following the Communist takeover in 1975.

The people of Laos traditionally have been self-sufficient farmers. Plains dwellers use wet-rice methods, while those on the mountain slopes make their living from dry-rice, slash-and-burn cultivation. People on the mountain tops have long grown opium, which in earlier years entered world trade through networks controlled by the French colonial government and via smuggling channels into China and Thailand. Fish taken from the Mekong River and its tributaries supplement farm animals as the major source of protein. The forests are commercially logged. Laos appears to be endowed with rich deposits of iron ore, potash, gypsum and other minerals, but few mineral surveys have been made and little commercial mining has been developed. The current chief export is electricity, sold to Thailand, which is generated by the Nam Ngum Dam, a hydroelectric plant built in the 1970s with financial assistance from Western states and Japan and organized, in part, by the World Bank.

Pre-colonial history
The state of Laos is said to have had its origins in 1353, when Prince Fa Ngoum created Lan Xang, or the Kingdom of the Million Elephants. Fa Ngoum had spent his childhood in the Hindu culture of the Khmer Empire, whose capital was at Angkor (in modern Cambodia). In earlier centuries the Thai peoples, forerunners of the ethnic Lao, had emigrated to the river valleys of present-day Laos from southern China. They came under the administration of the Khmer Empire and met with Theravada Buddhism, which was taking root in the region. Fa Ngoum established his government at Luang Prabang, and he launched the institutions, ceremonies and practices that would persist under the tutelage of a Lao monarchy for some 600 years, until the overthrow of the kingdom in 1975. With Khmer assistance, Fa Ngoum conquered many of the surrounding principalities and expanded his rule over the Korat Plateau to the west of the Mekong, eastward to the Annamite mountain watershed and south to the frontier of the Khmer and Cham civilizations. Fa Ngoum promoted Buddhism, and the Lao monarchs who followed him continued in this practice, stimulating the construction of *wats* (temples) and Buddhist schools that became the heart of social life among the lowland Laotians. Nevertheless, Buddhism was not fully embraced by the non-Laotian peoples of the kingdom, many of whom continue to this day the worship of spirits *(phi)*.

In 1563, the capital of Lan Xang was moved south to Vientiane in order to provide better defense against the Burmese. There was an interlude of Burmese domination, followed by a "golden age" from 1637 to 1694, during the reign of King Souligna-Vongsa. Vietnam profited when a succession crisis helped make Souligna's nephew the monarch in 1700, and it achieved suzerainty over Vientiane. In 1707 Souligna's grandson escaped to Luang Prabang and proclaimed independence from Vietnam. In 1713 Champassak, a principality in the south, also separated from the kingdom, with the assistance of Siam. This established the rivalry between Siam (modern Thailand) and Vietnam for control of Laos, a pattern that persists to the present.

In 1828, following an abortive military expedition launched by the king

612

of Vientiane against Siam, the Siamese retaliated by sacking Vientiane, depopulating the region and forcing the inhabitants of the Mekong's left bank to the other side of the river. Assisted by Vietnam and Siam, the chiefs of the principalities in the region continued to battle until the late 1880s. At that time the French, who had established control of Vietnam by the mid-1800s and then expanded their colonial reach to Cambodia, also extended their domination to Laos.

French colonial rule

The French ruled Laos from the late 1880s until 1954. It was almost as if, as colonial administrators of Vietnam, the French had absorbed the historic Vietnamese aspiration for control of adjacent western territories. They succeeded in pushing the Siamese in Laos to the right bank of the Mekong, pressuring them to renounce their claim to the left bank and confirming the Lao-Siamese boundaries in the Franco-Siamese Treaty of October 1893. The Siamese made further concessions to the French in treaties signed in 1904 and 1907, in which they gave up some provinces in Cambodia as well as the Laotian provinces of Bassac and Sayaboury on the Mekong's right bank. (In border disputes with Laos during the 1980s, the Thai have claimed that these were unfair treaties, imposed upon Siam by a more powerful Western nation.)

French colonial rule did consolidate the contemporary state of Laos, but its modernization of the economy was modest. At Luang Prabang, the French provided protection to a king and a viceroy *(maha oupahat)*, under whose aegis they brought in the defunct kingdoms of Vientiane, Xieng Khouang and Champassak, as well as the northern territories of Nam Tha and Phong Saly. The new kingdom was organized into 14 provinces *(khoueng)*, subdivided into cantons *(muong)* and administered by French *résidents* through Laotian governors at both levels. Overall direction was provided by a French *résident supérieur* situated in Vientiane, the administrative capital. A few thousand Frenchmen conducted the French colonial government, with the aim of making their rule self-sufficient. Their minimal expenditures were met largely from local sources, through head taxes. Unpaid corvée labor was mobilized to build roads and perform other public works. The French created a small primary educational system and an even smaller secondary system, of which the Lycée Pavie in Vientiane was the cornerstone, training the children of French administrators, selected members of the urban Vietnamese and sons of prominent Laotian families. The French also made some improvements in the public health system.

There was little economic development during French colonial rule. A limited road network linked Laos to Vietnam, which remained the center of French colonial interests. The French exploited small deposits of tin, largely in the Bolovens Plateau; they also helped create a small handicrafts industry, engaged in limited timber exploitation and made some improvements in agriculture.

French rule encouraged the Vietnamese to emigrate to Laos, and Vietnamese filled a significant number of posts in the colonial administration, just below those held by the French. Vietnamese artisans and merchants also moved to Laos and, along with the Chinese and Indians, were more numerous than ethnic Laotians in the major towns. Despite the importance of the Vietnamese in the administrative ranks and in urban commerce, prominent Laotian families retained their social importance in traditional society.

Rise of nationalism

Although many of the Laotian elite looked upon the French as protectors from the country's more powerful neighbors Vietnam and Thailand, and they accepted patronage from the French, they were not immune to the stirrings of nationalism that affected other colonized peoples in Asia. These feelings were stimulated by the growth of the Viet Minh nationalist movement among the Vietnamese living in Laotian towns. Many Laotians feared that if the Viet Minh were successful in forcing the French to depart, the Vietnamese simply would replace the French as the rulers of Indochina. A nationalist movement named Lao Issara (Free Laos) took root among members of the Laotian elite in Vientiane following World War II. First calling for increased autonomy for Laos, the Lao Issara later demanded independence. Simultaneously, another Laotian nationalist group, the Resistance Committee of Eastern Laos, was nurtured in eastern Laos under the tutelage of the Viet Minh. In 1946, facing a French refusal to grant greater autonomy, the Lao Issara, under the leadership of Prince Pethsarath, went into exile in Thailand. Both the Lao Issara and the Resistance Committee of Eastern Laos fought skirmishes against the French colonial administration.

In 1949, the French, through a Laotian faction already cooperating with the colonial administration, invited Laotian nationalists to return, offering a measure of greater political autonomy. Most members of the Lao Issara government in exile accepted the invitation, but the eastern faction shunned the offer and castigated those who returned. These events created a split in Laotian political leadership that was to endure until the Communist victory in 1975. The faction that returned to Vientiane in 1949, under the leadership of Prince Souvanna Phouma, cooperated with the French and, after the termination of French rule in 1954, aligned with the West. The eastern faction, whose leaders included Kaysone Phomvihane, Nouhak Phongsavan and Prince Souphanouvoung, came to be known as the Pathet Lao (Land of the Lao), and remained linked to the Vietnamese revolutionaries in the ensuing revolutionary war.

Laos after the Geneva Agreement, 1954–75

The Geneva Agreement of 1954 marked the end of French rule in Indochina. The Viet Minh had inflicted such heavy losses upon the French that, following a severe defeat at Dien Bien Phu, the French decided to withdraw. Although the major powers at the Geneva Conference agreed that all of Laos should come under the rule of the royal government and should not undergo partition (as did Vietnam), they provided for two "regroupment zones" in the provinces of Sam Neua and Phong Saly for the Pathet Lao forces to assemble. These provinces, which were adjacent to North Vietnam, remained under de facto control of the Laotian Communists. Peace in Laos was short-lived following the Geneva Agreement, with hostilities breaking out between the left and right factions in 1959. Another Geneva Conference was convened in May 1961, culminating in an agreement in July 1962 that called for neutralization of Laos and formation of a tripartite government. The new government was composed of factions from the left (the Pathet Lao who were linked to North Vietnam), the right (linked to Thailand and the United States) and neutrals (led by Prince Souvanna Phouma). Once again the cease-fire was short-lived. The coalition split apart by 1964 and a war larger in scale than the preceding hostilities engulfed Laos, following the rhythm of the war in Vietnam. During this larger war, Laos, like Cambodia, was viewed as a sideshow by the major protagonists. The Paris Agreement of 1973, signed by the United States and North Vietnam, called for a cease-fire in each of the three Indochinese countries. Only in Laos did peace actually occur. In February 1973, just a month following the Paris Agreement, the Laotian factions signed the Vientiane Agreement, which provided for a cease-fire and yet another coalition government composed of factions from the left and right, presided over by Prime Minister Souvanna Phouma. As the balance tipped toward the Communists in Vietnam, the Pathet Lao gained political ascendancy in Laos. When the Communists marched into Saigon and Phnom Penh, the right-wing forces lost heart and most of their leaders fled, permitting a bloodless takeover by Laotian Communists in mid-1975. In December 1975 the Laotian Communists proclaimed an end to the 600-year-old monarchy, with the establishment of the Lao Peoples Democratic Republic.

THE LAO PEOPLE'S DEMOCRATIC REPUBLIC

Government and politics

Guiding the politics of the Lao People's Democratic Republic (LPDR) is the Lao People's Revolutionary Party (LPRP), the ruling Communist party of Laos. Its 13-member Politburo is still dominated by the stalwart, cohesive band of revolutionaries that founded the party in 1955. Their remarkable record of continuity is equaled by few regimes in the contemporary world.

These Laotian leaders have had a long and intimate relationship with their Vietnamese allies. Prior to founding the LPRP they had been members of the Vietnamese-led Indochina Communist party. Most speak Vietnamese and some have family ties with Vietnam. The party's general secretary, Kaysone Phomvihane, had a Vietnamese father; second-ranked Nouhak Phongsavan and third-ranked Prince Souphanouvoung have Vietnamese wives. Their world view has been shaped by their common revolutionary struggle with Vietnam. Moreover, the Vietnamese have numerous channels—party, military and economic—through which they directly convey their influence. Thus, the LPDR is intimately linked to Vietnam and closely follows its policy line. Notwithstanding their dependence upon Vietnam, the Laotian Communist leaders exercise control over the major part of day-to-day activities. The Vietnamese are discreet in the exercise of their influence, and the Laotian leaders understand well the limits within which they can make decisions. They have operated so many years in tandem with Vietnam that they seem to have almost a sixth sense of what is acceptable to the Vietnamese. Indeed, it is difficult to find areas in which Laotian leaders define their interests as separate from those of their Vietnamese senior partners.

The LPDR has been functioning without a constitution since its establishment in 1975. General Secretary Kaysone announced the appointment of a drafting committee for a constitution at the Third Party Congress in 1982, and he assigned the task a high priority, but by mid-1988 there was still no announcement of the completed draft. Even in the absence of a formal constitution, the LPDR's governmental and political organs have evolved. The party membership reached 40,000 in 1982, according to a government announcement. As in Communist systems elsewhere, the party assigns cadres to key positions in the principal institutions of the society, exerting its control through them. Unlike most other Communist parties, except for the top party leaders, party members are not publicly acknowledged—thus the system retains some of the secrecy that characterized the revolutionary struggle.

At the apex of state power is the Supreme People's Assembly (SPA). The role of the SPA is largely honorific, with members convened semiannually to listen to the speeches of key party leaders. With prominent members of various ethnic groups, regional political leaders, chairmen of mass organizations, several women activists, a few "patriotic neutralists" and a handful of personalities formerly associated with the royal government, the SPA is supposed to symbolize unity among the different elements of Laotian society.

The government of the LPDR, like the SPA, was proclaimed by the founding congress on December 2, 1975, and is guided by a Council of Ministers, led by a chairman, party chief Kaysone. The government was restructured by a basic law, dated July 10, 1982, which formed three levels of government. At the top level, the chairman of the Council of Ministers and five vice-chairmen are charged with policymaking and coordination of major sectors of national life. At the second level are the ministries, which have technical functions. At the third level are about 80 deputy ministers, who include a sizable proportion of technically trained personnel.

The system gives power to party leaders and assigns little importance to citizens rights. In the early years of the LPDR, party authorities arbitrarily sent what they labeled as social deviants ("prostitutes, addicts, gamblers, hippies, thieves and lost children") to "reeducation" centers. Political opponents associated with the former royal government—perhaps as many as 30,000—were also confined to these centers. By 1988 many, although not all, of these reeducation camps had been closed. Some former inmates of the camps—Amnesty International has estimated 5,000 of them in 1986—were assigned to labor in construction units and on collective farms near the camps.

LPDR authorities govern with little popular support, but most Laotians simply incline to its authority, since they have little alternative. Even though it is difficult to find a segment of society that is enthusiastic about the new regime, when compared to other Communist regimes in the early stages of power the LPDR's policies cannot be judged as harsh. Laotian Buddhist gentleness combined with ineptitude in deploying Communist political and economic policies help modulate the efforts of even Vietnamese-inspired revolutionaries. Moreover, if the pressure for revolutionary change were to be seen as too onerous, there would be an escape route across the Mekong River, a reality that the rulers of Laos must keep in mind.

Although active resistance has little appeal for most Laotians, there remains a low-level insurgency in the countryside. It is small, fragmented and poorly led, and it receives little outside support. The resistance constitutes a minimal threat to the government; however, former officers of the royal army can find some recruits among restless young men in the refugee camps in Thailand. They draw some support from local Thai commanders, who want intelligence from Laos and who also judge it useful to harrass the Laotian Communists and their Vietnamese mentors. These are some Hmong and other highland dissident bands who gain recruits from the refugee camps and join the few highlanders who have regrouped to fight in the mountains. The government of China denies that it gives any support to insurgency in Laos, but the Chinese are not averse to creating anxiety about their potential to cause trouble.

Economy

Laos remains one of the world's poorest and most economically backward countries. Per capita income has increased since 1975 but remains pitifully low, with estimates ranging (in 1986) between U.S. $120 and $150 annually. Health problems are severe, with malaria still rampant. The average life expectancy is 43 years, and the national infant mortality rate is 184 deaths for 1,000 babies born.

A U.N. study estimates that only about 1.9 million acres/800,000 ha. of the land, or 3.4% of the total land surface, is worked each year. Approximately the same area is used for animal pasturage. Fruit trees, coffee, tea and other plantation crops cover less than 49,000 acres/20,000 ha. Rice paddies occupy more than 90% of land devoted to yearly crops, producing a crop that accounts for more than 70% of the caloric value of the Laotian diet.

During the LPDR's first five years (1975–80) the economy suffered from the termination of U.S. aid; the flight of tens of thousands (almost 10% of the population), including a large proportion of those with education and technical skills; and the imposition of measures aimed at collectivizing agriculture and socializing commerce. These latter measures were modified beginning in 1980, following similar reforms in Vietnam, which eased the level of social control, slowed agricultural collectivization, reduced the intensity of tax collection and permitted some market incentives. By 1988 there were signs of economic stabilization and, in some sectors, even an improvement in the quality of life. The most encouraging economic sign was that Laotian farmers were producing enough rice to satisfy the country's needs, albeit at a low level; but they were still hindered by a poor transportation system that hampered distribution to areas in short supply.

617

External relations

The fundamental factor that shaped the foreign policy of Laos· is its dependence upon Vietnam. The guiding principle of Laotian foreign policy is that it must be compatible with the vital interests of Hanoi. The formal tie between the two countries was regularized in a 25-year treaty of friendship signed in 1977, and both sides use the term "special relationship" to describe this link. An integral element of the special relationship is the concept of solidarity among the three former Indochinese nations.

The Soviet Union ranks second only to Vietnam in the LPDR's official expressions of dedication. On state occasions Laotian leaders first celebrate their "special solidarity, militant alliance and all-round cooperation with Vietnam," and next praise the "close solidarity and all-round cooperation with the Soviet Union." LPDR spokesmen give obeisance to the Soviet Union as leader of the socialist bloc and as the leading proponent of world peace, and LPDR diplomats unfailingly support the Soviet Union at the United Nations and other official forums. The Soviet Union is the LPDR's principal donor. Estimates in the mid-1980s put contributions from the Soviet Union and its Eastern European allies at more than 50% of Laos' external assistance. In addition to economic assistance the Soviets provide some military aid, giving particular support to the Lao Air Force.

Laos follows the Vietnamese line in its relations with China. Its relations with China had been good until tensions between Vietnam and China resulted in the Chinese punitive strike against Vietnam in February 1979. Afterwards, the LPDR officially called for the Chinese to terminate their road-building projects in Laos and to withdraw their personnel in March 1979; three months later they obliged the Chinese embassy to reduce its personnel to 12. Not until Vietnam alters its hostile relationship with China will the LPDR have the option of significantly modifying its own ties with China.

Although there is a serious political cleavage between the Communist government of Laos and the conservative royal government of Thailand, strong ties bind the two peoples. The people of Laos and Thailand are both Theravada Buddhists. The Lao and Thai languages are sufficiently similar for the peoples to understand each other. A lowland, wet-rice culture provides the foundation of the rural economy and society on both sides of the Mekong River, making the traditional life-styles similar. Many Laotians have relatives living in northeastern Thailand, and family visits in both directions have long been commonplace. Although the Mekong River forms a large segment of the political boundary between the two countries, its valley constitutes an environment with common seasonal rhythms and an active commerce that unites the two peoples.

Despite these close ties, however, there are tensions. Many Laotians see the large numbers of Laotian people living in northeast Thailand as a reminder that the Thai have a historic tendency to aggrandize their own kingdom at the expense of Laos. Thai leaders regard Laos' stridency against Thailand as manipulation by Vietnam. Laotian leaders see Bangkok as a government that collaborated with the imperialist United States to fight against the Laotian revolution, and that now has linked itself to China.

618

Within the context of this tension there were a variety of minor border incidents in the 1980s that added to the tension and, in several cases, escalated to the point of restrained military clashes.

Laotian relations with the United States, as with other countries, are derivative of the policies of Vietnam. Vietnamese leaders—isolated from the Association of Southeast Asian Nations and from much of the Western world because of its occupation of Cambodia, disturbed by the rattling of Chinese sabers on their northern border and groaning under a dismal economy—would like to improve relations with the United States and the West without compromising their fundamental security interests in Cambodia. Within this context, the Laotian government agreed with the Reagan administration to bring about a modest improvement in relations, principally by assisting in accounting for U.S. servicemen missing in action (MIA). A series of U.S. delegations to discuss the MIA issue visited Vientiane between 1983 and 1987, and Laos authorized, in February 1985 and February 1986, joint Laotian-U.S. teams to excavate sites where U.S. planes had crashed.

On its side, the United States gave support for loans to Laos by the Asian Development Bank (the United States had previously abstained on such loans), and dispatched two shipments of emergency medical assistance and a contribution of emergency food through an international agency in 1984, in response to a plea that bad weather had reduced the rice harvest. Furthermore, the U.S. Congress, in December 1985, deleted Laos from a list of countries prohibited from receiving most forms of U.S. assistance. Despite these positive signs, however, it appeared unlikely that there would be a substantial amelioration of relations between Laos and the United States until such improvement developed between Vietnam and the United States.

FURTHER READING

Brown, MacAlister, and Zasloff, Joseph J. *Apprentice Revolutionaries: The Communist Movement in Laos, 1930–1985.* Stanford, California: Hoover Institution Press, 1986.
Dommen, Arthur J. *Conflict in Laos: The Politics of Neutralization.* New York: Praeger, 1971.
———. *Laos: Keystone of Indochina.* Boulder, Colorado: Westview Press, 1985.
Langer, Paul F., and Zasloff, Joseph J. *North Vietnam and the Pathet Lao: Partners in the Struggle for Laos.* Cambridge, Massachusetts: Harvard University Press, 1970.
Stuart-Fox, Martin, *Contemporary Laos: Studies in Politics and Society of the Lao People's Democratic Republic.* St. Lucia, Australia: University of Queensland Press; New York: St. Martin's, 1982.
———. *Laos: Politics, Economics and Society.* London: F. Pinter; Boulder, Colorado: Lynne Rienner, 1986.
Toye, Hugh. *Laos: Buffer State or Battleground.* London: Oxford University Press, 1968.
Zasloff, Joseph J., *The Pathet Lao: Leadership and Organization.* Lexington, Massachusetts: Lexington Books, 1973.

MACAO

HUGH D. R. BAKER

FOR well over 400 years this tiny peninsular and island territory on the south coast of China has been in the hands of Portugal, and for a good half of that time Macao has been politically and economically almost as insignificant as its size would indicate. For two centuries it has been a place with a past, not much present and little realistic hope of a future. It is history that makes Macao.

HISTORY

The Portuguese reached the south China coast in 1513, and in 1557 they were allowed to settle at Macao as a reward for assisting local Chinese officials clear up piracy. In later years a ground rent of 500 taels of silver was paid to the county magistrate, but it is uncertain whether this was a condition of the tenancy originally or whether it developed as a perquisite to maintain Macao's dubious status. From this base Portuguese ships traded up to Canton, down to Manila and across to Japan, and exotic goods and surplus profits found their way back over the long ocean routes to Goa and Lisbon. In 1586 Macao was christened Cidade do Nome de Deos na China (The City of the Name of God in China), in recognition of its other major role as a center for Christian missionary effort in the Far East.

Macao prospered, and others began to look enviously at its riches. An all-out Dutch attack in 1622 was decisively repulsed by the tiny amateur garrison bolstered by slaves and Jesuit priests, but it marked the beginning of the slow eclipse of Macao as new international factors came into play. In 1638 the profitable trade with Nagasaki ended when Japan entered the Tokugawa era of isolationism. Two years later Spain and Portugal parted company, making Macao's trade with Manila far less easy. In 1641 the Dutch seized Melaka and cut Macao's link with Goa. The tiny territory was still the main center for what remained of the China trade, but in the next hundred years the wealth and the glory drained away.

By the mid-18th century other nations, especially the British, were trading with China through Canton. The only nearby base was Macao, and the foreign merchants began to settle there and bring in their families. The opium trade benefited the British because of their control over the poppy-growing areas of India, and the British benefited Macao because they brought

620

back trading activity; but they also brought an arrogance that led them to lord it over their Portuguese hosts and ultimately, in 1808, to occupy Macao by force. The Chinese government had tolerated a weak Portuguese presence, but could not stand by in the face of this aggression; it put sufficient pressure on the British that they withdrew.

Meanwhile, Macao harbor, never deep and growing shallower with silt, was proving inadequate to cope with the larger vessels involved in the China trade. When the British were forced to decamp during the Opium War, they sailed across the mouth of the Pearl River and came upon the natural deep-water harbor of Hong Kong. And when Hong Kong became British in 1842, Macao's brief resurgence of trade and importance came to an end.

From 1842 to the present day Macao's story is one of weakness and desperate survival. The assassination of a governor in 1849, the signing of a treaty with China in 1887 giving Portugal perpetual rule over the territory, the involvement in the infamous coolie trade at the end of the 19th century, the wresting of power from the Portuguese authorities by the Red Guards during the Great Proletarian Cultural Revolution in 1967, China's refusal to accede to Portuguese offers to abandon Macao in 1974—there have been incidents, but they have had no great impact on the world, much as they may have affected the people of Macao.

PEOPLE

In 1563 the population consisted of some 900 Portuguese, plus several thousand Melakans, Indians and African slaves. Chinese were at first forbidden by their government to reside in Macao, but the inconvenience of commuting over the border to work was too great, and before long there were Chinese residents too. By 1700 the territory had a population of over 19,000, by 1874 over 68,000, and by 1927 over 157,000. During the Japanese invasion and occupation of China refugees swelled the population to about one-quarter of a million, and with the civil war and later political movements in China more and more people fled. By the mid-1980s the population figure was given as "over 400,000," but this was based by guesswork on the figure of 276,000 from the 1980 census, in which many people had refused to be enumerated. The vast majority of the present population live on the small peninsula of Macao itself, making it one of the world's most densely populated areas.

Nearly 97 percent of the population is said to be of Chinese descent, the majority from the neighboring county of Zhongshan (formerly called Xiang Shan). Portuguese and other nationalities make up the remaining 3.5 percent of the official figure, but it is likely that, owing to the underreporting of illegal immigrants from China, the true percentage of non-Chinese is smaller. Many of the Portuguese may in fact be "Macanese" (also known as "Macaense"), people of mixed Portuguese and other blood. They figure largely in such literature as there is about Macao, and their language is a patois of Portuguese unknown elsewhere.

LIVELIHOOD

Macao's prosperous early years were the result of entrepôt activities. Later, opium revived Macao's fortunes temporarily, but before that, and after trade followed the British across the Pearl River estuary, Macao had almost nothing left but fishing.

In 1850 gambling licenses were issued, the beginning of a lucrative tax revenue for the government. By 1901 the revenue from gambling was running at nearly 1 million patacas a year. Large as this amount was, recent years have dwarfed it, even when allowing for inflation. In 1975 the syndicate running the gambling concession paid nearly 7 million patacas in tax, and only nine years later, in 1984, the figure had risen to 806 million. This was nearly 60 percent of Macao's total public revenue.

Gambling is a vital ingredient in Macao's economy and the main tourist attraction. Other attractions are restaurants and a fairly relaxed attitude toward prostitution. (The *Almanac of Macau's Economy 1983* gives without comment the number of Thai residents as 747, composed of 33 men and 714 women.) Since 1984 the number of tourists entering Macao from Hong Kong has exceeded 4 million a year, over 85 percent being Hong Kong residents. More than 130 hotels, inns and boardinghouses cater to the ever-growing influx, but average occupancy rates are low (around 60 percent), because although on the weekends gamblers compete for rooms, the rest of the week sees comparatively few visitors.

Light industry has been the other mainstay of the Macao economy since the end of the war in the Pacific. Wages are considerably lower than in Hong Kong, allowing a competitive edge that has only partly been offset by Macao's higher electricity prices and less favorable transport situation. Until the 1980s textiles and garments accounted for the bulk of exports (nearly 90 percent in 1979), but in recent years there has been diversification, and other products such as toys, artificial flowers, leather goods and electronics now provide more than 30 percent of export income. The United States is by far the largest customer, with Hong Kong, France and West Germany some way behind. Portugal takes only 1 percent of Macao's exports.

LIFE

For much of Macao's early history the secular government and the Roman Catholic church vied for power. The government won, but was rarely convincingly in control. In recent times the government can ignore neither the massive influence of the gambling syndicate, the Sociedade do Turismo e Diversoes de Macau (STDM), nor the looming presence of China. Its weak position is not bolstered by any recourse to military power, the Portuguese army being only nominally represented in the territory. The governor is appointed by the president of Portugal, but the rest of the government (Consultative Council and Legislative Assembly) is locally appointed and in a few cases elected. With the exception of the 8,000 civil servants the people of Macao are not much troubled with government.

Some 30,000 Roman Catholics live in the territory, ministered to by a bishop whose mightier predecessors' diocese covered all of China and Japan as well. Many Catholic churches and missions, schools, orphanages and charitable institutions are still active in Macao. Protestant churches are little represented. For the majority of the population Christianity has little meaning, but the many Chinese temples and shrines are much used. The A-Ma Temple to the goddess Tin Hau is thought to have given rise to the name Macao. It is heavily patronized by local people and tourists alike, as is the even older Goddess of Mercy Temple. In a society with as little security as Macao the need to seek nontemporal aid is common to most people, and gamblers in particular resort to prayer at temples as well as observance of customs that are thought to bring good fortune. Many gamblers believe that the doorways of the main casino have swords embedded in the lintels to "cut the luck" of customers entering, and they try to go in by the employees' entrances to avoid the danger.

Casinos, churches and hotels are much in evidence in Macao, and so are pawnshops whose neon signs glow 24 hours a day to suck in the watches, cigarette lighters and jewelry of those whom no amount of prayer or ritual behavior can save from gambling disaster. Newer landmarks are the long bridge that now links Macao with the island of Taipa, and the modern buildings of the University of East Asia—an institution designed to take in some of the many from East and Southeast Asia who cannot get places in the older, established and much sought-after universities of the region.

Macao used to be renowned for its quiet, its cobbled streets, its pink-washed Mediterranean-style buildings, its sleaziness, its position as a mysterious link in international gold smuggling, its hospitality to those who for one reason or another could not find haven elsewhere. (Many remember with gratitude Macao's open doors when Hong Kong was occupied by Japan during the Pacific war.) To some extent these images persist. It is not an unhappy place, and people mostly are cheerful and warm. There are still cobblestones, there are still color-washed buildings, there is still gambling and those who feed off the gamblers in ways legal or vicious, and there is still a measure of sleepiness and quiet in comparison with neighboring Hong Kong's constant bustle. Most of all there is an atmosphere of end-of-the-road, of survival rather than ambition, of impotent submission to fate.

THE FUTURE

During 1987 the Portuguese and Chinese governments signed an agreement on the future of Macao. With the already existing agreement on Hong Kong as a model, it has been decided that Macao will revert fully to China in December 1999, and like Hong Kong will enjoy 50 years of near autonomy before merging fully with the mainland.

Meanwhile there are plans for expansion of trade, for the building of a deep-sea terminal off the island of Coloane, even for an international airport to serve Macao. Few are optimistic that these plans will ever be put into effect, and realists query the necessity for such facilities. In 1924 Francisco

Monteiro published *The Renascence of Macao* in which he writes of "the great Harbour Improvement Scheme now in operation." The scheme was costing $6.5 million and was to provide, among other things, for the docking of ocean-going vessels up to 25 ft. draft. "Upon completion of the works now in hand, about the year 1926, the Harbour Works Department contemplates embarking upon other extensive undertakings . . ." More than 60 years later there is still no sign of the works Monteiro describes, but contemplation goes on. Many find that Macao's peculiar charm lies in just such an unhurried attitude.

FURTHER READING

Boxer, C. R. *Fidalgos in the Far East, 1550–1770.* Reprint of 1948 ed. London and Hong Kong: Oxford University Press, 1967.

Braga, J. M., *Macau: A Short Handbook.* Macao: n.p., 1970.

Coates, Austin. *City of Broken Promises.* London: Muller, 1967.

————. *A Macao Narrative.* London and Hong Kong: Heinemann, 1978.

Cremer, R. D., ed. *Macau: City of Commerce and Culture.* Hong Kong: University of East Asia Press, 1987.

Governo de Macau. *Anuario Estatistico* (Yearbook of Statistics). Macao: annual.

Guillen-Nuñez, César. *Macau.* London and Hong Kong: Oxford University Press, 1984.

Jones, P. H. M. *Golden Guide to Hongkong and Macao.* Hong Kong: Far Eastern Economic Review, 1969.

Montalto de Jesus, C. A. *Historic Macao.* (1902), Reprint of 1902 ed. London and Hong Kong: Oxford University Press, 1984.

MALAYSIA

LEONARD Y. ANDAYA

THE Strait of Malacca has been a formative influence in the evolution of modern Malaysia. Located at the beginning and end points of the monsoon winds, and serving as the major conduit for seaborne traffic between the Indian and Pacific oceans, the strait has encouraged the development of strong maritime kingdoms based on international trade along its shores. When the Malay kingdom of Melaka (formerly Malacca) was founded by migrants from the Sumatran kingdom of Sri Vijaya at about the beginning of the 15th century, it continued the traditions of its predecessors mainly on the Sumatran side of the strait. It responded to the opportunities made possible by the monsoon winds and provided the port and storage facilities, the security, the laws and a standard of measures to attract international traders. As a major nexus in an international trade centered on spices, aromatic woods, Indian cloth and Chinese silks, Melaka became one of the busiest and wealthiest ports in the world.

In the mid-15th century, its ruler embraced Islam, and Melaka became a center of Islamic learning. From Melaka, Muslim teachers accompanied Malay and other Muslim traders throughout the Malay Archipelago, exchanging goods and ideas in the different ports. Melaka Malay became the court language of many kingdoms in the maritime world of Southeast Asia, and a more colloquial form of the language known as *pasar Melayu,* or "market Malay," was used as the language of trade even as far north as the Philippines. Melaka's life-style and fashions were imitated, and acquaintance with Melaka Malay literature became the mark of an educated and enlightened individual. When its rulers adopted Islam, that religion, too, became an essential aspect of the character and the identity of a Melaka Malay. At its height, the kingdom extended to both sides of the strait and to most of the Malay Peninsula, with the exception of the northern Malay states of Kedah, Patani, Kelantan and Terengganu, which were under the Thai kingdom of Ayudhya.

THE ARRIVAL OF THE EUROPEANS

Melaka's fame spread beyond Southeast Asia, and the Portuguese arrived in 1509 determined to seize this emporium and thereby control the lucrative spice trade. After a hard-fought battle, the Portuguese finally succeeded in conquering Melaka in 1511; but the ruling house of Melaka reestablished itself in Johor, and the traditions of Melaka were maintained until well into the 18th century. For the Portuguese, their military successes were not matched in the field of commerce, and by the end of the 16th century, they were reduced to becoming merely one of a number of others involved in the lucrative inter-Asian trade. Although the Dutch took Melaka in 1641 and gained a major share in the spice and carrying trades of the area by the end of the 17th century, they were more interested in Java than in the Malay Peninsula.

It was the British, who arrived toward the end of the 18th century, who were to leave the most lasting European impression in the Malay area. They occupied the island of Penang in 1786 and the Dutch possessions on the Malay Peninsula in 1795. But their greatest achievement was the acquisition of Singapore on January 30, 1819 as a staging post on the maritime trade route to China. With Penang and Singapore established as British ports, there was no longer the need for British traders or Chinese junks to stop at Malay harbors. Singapore outgrew all other ports in the archipelago, and the economic fortunes of the Malay states became inextricably linked with those of Singapore. The early 19th century, therefore, marked the end of a long tradition of Malay entrepôt states that extended back to the days of Sri Vijaya and Melaka and heralded the beginning of a British economic and political framework in the region.

THE FORMATION AND STRUCTURE OF BRITISH MALAYA

Modern Malaysia may have had its origins in the 15th century kingdom of Melaka, but its present form very much reflects the British colonial past. In 1824 an Anglo-Dutch treaty was signed, arbitrarily dividing the region into British and Dutch spheres of influence with little regard to previous political entities. Melaka's direct heir, the kingdom of Johor, was split into two—one part under British jurisdiction on the peninsula and the other under the Dutch in the Riau-Lingga Islands. Borneo was left unmentioned in the treaty, and it was the work of private interests that brought it under the British sphere of influence (see the article by Barbara Andaya on Brunei in this Handbook).

The British explorer James Brooke assisted the sultan of Brunei in an internal rebellion in 1841 and was rewarded with a grant of land in return for an annual payment. To this was added further cessions from the sultan in 1853 to form a sizable part of Borneo that became known as Sarawak. Under the "white raja" rule of Brooke and his successors, Sarawak introduced a philosophy of administration that associated ethnic group with economic function, creating a model for British colonial practice on the Malay Peninsula. In the area of present-day Sabah (North Borneo), two other Englishmen, William Treacher and Alfred Dent, acquired some 17 million acres/14.3 million ha. from the Brunei sultan in 1877 in return for a yearly rent. The British North Borneo Company was established and chartered in 1881 to develop the territories within the British sphere of influence.

In 1826, Singapore, Melaka, Penang and Province Wellesley (Prai, opposite Penang) were formed into the Straits Settlements and became the beachhead for British expansion (known as the "forward movement") into the Malay Peninsula. On January 20, 1874, the Pangkor Treaty was signed between the Malay state of Perak and the British. A claimant to the Perak throne obtained British recognition in return for the acceptance of a British resident whose advice had to be asked and acted upon "on all questions other than those touching upon Malay religion and custom." A similar arrangement was later made with Selangor, Negeri Sembilan and, eventually, Pahang. The cornerstone of this residential system was British indirect rule through the local rulers while continuing to preserve the customs and the traditions of the land.

In 1896, the four protected states of Perak, Selangor, Negeri Sembilan and Pahang were formed into the Federated Malay States (FMS) with a common treasury and administration and its capital in the tin-mining town of Kuala Lumpur. The incorporation of the remainder of the peninsular states into the British sphere came with Siam's relinquishing control over the northern Malay states, except for Patani, in March 1909, and with Johor's agreement to accept a British adviser in 1913. Johor, Kedah, Perlis, Kelantan and Terengganu were now governed by sultans assisted by British advisers and became known as the Unfederated Malay States (UMS).

Thus, the entire Malay Peninsula and northwest Borneo were brought under British protection by 1913. There were, however, varying degrees of control exercised by the British and differing rates of economic development. Most infrastructural and export plantation developments occurred in the west coast states and in the Straits Settlements, rather than in the east coast states of the UMS. The exception within the UMS was Johor, which benefited from its proximity to Singapore and from its enlightened Malay bureaucracy.

The British provided this loose agglomeration of states known as "British Malaya" with a "congenial political and administrative framework" to enable private enterprise to flourish. They established a colonial constabulary to maintain order, a vast communications system to link mines and plantation areas to the ports, a uniform legal and administrative system to regulate economic activity, an alien labor force for the export industries and an education system to suit the needs of a colonial economy.

Perhaps the most far-reaching of these measures was the decision to import Chinese and Indians to satisfy the labor needs of the tin mines and the rubber estates. The decision was based on the belief first enunciated by Sir Thomas Stamford Raffles, the founder of Singapore, and later put into practice by Brooke and others in Sarawak and Hugh Low in Perak, that each ethnic group should perform a specific economic function in the society. A few aristocratic English-educated Malays were to serve in the administration, while the vast majority of the Malays were to occupy their "traditional" fishing and farming roles; the Chinese were to become the petty traders and the miners; and the Indians were to staff the bureaucracy but were to be mainly the laborers in public works and the rubber estates. The different spheres of economic activity that each of the groups occupied contributed to the creation of separate social and cultural worlds. British Malaya became three distinct Asian communities, leading basically separate existences with the British overlord providing the rationale for this compartmentalization of ethnic groups.

The flow of European capital into British Malaya was facilitated by the experience and expertise offered by such prestigious Straits Settlement firms as Guthrie, Sime and Darby and Harrisons & Crosfield. They used their well-established reputations to raise capital and to float joint-stock companies in London and Shanghai. Thus it was that the tin industry, once a purely Malay activity and then dominated by the Chinese in the 19th century, became two-thirds European controlled by 1937. When rubber became an important product in the beginning of the 20th century, because of the invention of the pneumatic tire, European capital again played a role in increasing nearly fivefold the total acreage planted in rubber. This expansion occurred mainly on the west coast of the peninsula, where an infrastructure had already been created for the tin industry. Unlike tin, small rubber holdings (less than 100 acres/40 ha.) became a feature of the industry because it was possible for many Malays to plant a few trees to supplement their incomes. Rubber and tin remained the two chief export earners in Malaysia until the 1970s. Oil palm was first planted commercially in 1917, and by the 1930s, three plantation groups had large oil palm estates in Johor and in northwest Malaya. From its humble beginnings, oil palm gradually expanded until today it has become a major export earner in Malaysia, which is one of the largest producers in the world. Another lucrative export has been timber, especially from Borneo.

The extensive economic and political framework of British Malaya functioned smoothly because of the government's educational policy. A small select group of Malay aristocrats, Chinese and Indians (among whom were a large percentage of Sri Lankan Jaffna Tamils) were offered the opportunity to obtain an English education in order to play a supporting role in the colonial government and private enterprise. For the rest of the population, education was to be in the vernacular with the aim of instilling contentment by improving the quality of life of the individual within the role allotted to that person's ethnic group. Education in British Malaya was very much a servant of the colonial regime with little if any emphasis on the need to create a sense of a common bond among the various ethnic communities. The single striking exception was English-medium education that inculcated English ideas and values into students from different ethnic backgrounds. The common experience and strong bonds nurtured in the English school system created an important trust that came to characterize relations among the English-educated elite in the postcolonial period.

THE JAPANESE OCCUPATION AND THE IMMEDIATE POSTWAR YEARS

The creation of an independent Malaya was never a major priority of the British. Economic interests frequently dictated the direction of political policy, and preparation for eventual independence of Malaya was rarely, if ever, considered. It was the traumatic events of World War II and the postwar years that eventually forced the British to confront the inevitability of relinquishing control over their prosperous colony. On December 8, 1941, the Japanese invaded the Malay Peninsula, and by mid-February 1942, Singapore, the last bastion of the British and Commonwealth forces, had surrendered. Under the Japanese, a new military regional administration was created that brought together Singapore, the Straits Settlements, the FMS, the UMS and Sumatra. In August 1943, the northern Malay states of Kedah, Perlis, Kelantan and Terengganu were "returned" to Thailand, a Japanese ally. The defeat of the colonial overlords and their public humiliation and subsequent internment undermined the long-held assumption of the superiority of the white race. There now appeared little justification for the maintenance of British rule.

When, toward the end of 1943, it became apparent that the tide of the war was turning against them, the Japanese undertook to create a Malay nationalist movement to forestall the return of the British. They encouraged a radical Malay group that advocated the "Greater Indonesia" concept, and they organized a paramilitary group of young Malays known as PETA, or Defenders of the Fatherland. These efforts collapsed, however, after the sudden surrender of the Japanese on August 15, 1945.

The initial reaction of the returning British was to put a number of the sultans and other Malay leaders on trial for not having done enough to oppose the Japanese. The Malayan Peoples Anti-Japanese Army (MPAJA), a mainly Chinese wartime resistance group, took matters into their own hands and dealt harshly with those they considered to have been collaborators, many of whom were Malays. The Malays interpreted these actions as an attack on their ethnic group, and so they rallied around their village secular and religious leaders to fight the MPAJA, dominated by the "Chinese" Malayan Communist party (MCP).

This conflict highlighted the steady deterioration of relations between these two ethnic groups dating from the late 1920s, when the Chinese community began to identify openly and proudly with the burgeoning nationalism in China. Malay fears that the Chinese would one day dominate the peninsula had been further aroused by a 1931 census that showed that, for the first time in British Malaya, there were more Chinese (1,709,392) than Malays (1,644,173). In subsequent years, the Malay press began to print articles attacking the Chinese, and Malay groups were formed to safeguard Malay interests against perceived Chinese threats to Malay rights and privileges. Equally virulent anti-Malay attitudes in the Chinese press contributed to the atmosphere of distrust that encouraged inter-ethnic conflict.

On December 21, 1945, the British abandoned all pretense that they were merely advisers to the Malay rulers and forced the sultans to sign a treaty annulling all previous arrangements that had guaranteed their sovereign rights. Then, in late January 1946, a white paper was issued detailing plans for a Malayan Union, a unitary state that would comprise the FMS, the UMS, Penang and Melaka. The sultans were to retain their positions, but sovereignty was to be transferred to the British crown. Malayan citizenship was to be extended to all, each with equal rights, including admission to the administrative civil service. Opposition to the plan by the sultans, ex-Malayan civil service officers and the United Malays National Organization (UMNO), formed in March 1946 to fight the plan's implementation, had the desired effect. The Malayan Union was revoked and replaced after February 1, 1948 by the Federation of Malaya, which upheld the sovereignty of the sultans, the individuality of the states and Malay special privileges.

The most serious challenge to the survival of the Federation came from the Communists. The MCP had grown in strength during the Japanese occupation and reached its peak of activity in early September 1950. By December of that year, an emergency situation was recognized by the government, and Malaya was placed on a war footing. The British forces used a policy of isolating the MCP from its civilian support units, the Min Yuen, to contain the Communists. Eventually, the MCP was compelled to switch from military to political tactics in late 1951. This change of direction coincided with the forging of an alliance in 1952 between the UMNO and the Malayan Chinese Association (MCA) and with the British announcement of plans to grant independence to Malaya. The MCP thus lost its appeal among many Chinese and was reduced to a few hard-core guerrillas in camps along the Thai border and in a few inaccessible jungle areas. With the Communist threat largely dissipated, the state of emergency was officially ended on July 31, 1960.

INDEPENDENCE AND THE CREATION OF MALAYSIA

Preparation for independence involved the creation of a political system that could survive the conflicting demands of a multiethnic society. The union of the Malayan Indian Congress (MIC) with the other two ethnic parties, UMNO and MCA to form the Alliance party was seen as a positive sign. When the Alliance obtained 81 percent of the votes and 51 of 52 seats contested in the 1955 federal elections, it regarded this as a mandate to represent its ethnic constituencies to the British-chaired commission drafting the constitution for an independent Malaya.

In the final version of the Merdeka (Independence) constitution, there was to be a single nationality in which all persons in Malaya could qualify as equal citizens by fulfilling certain requirements. The UMNO only agreed with this in return for a guarantee of the maintenance of Malay privileges. The paramount ruler (yang di-pertuan agong) was to safeguard the special position of the Malays and the "legitimate interests" of the other communities. He was to be chosen by the Conference of Malay Rulers (Durbar) on the basis of seniority for a term of five years. There was to be a parliament composed of a wholly elected house of representatives (Dewan Rakyat) and an appointed senate (Dewan Negara). On August 15, 1957, the Merdeka constitution was ratified, and on August 31, the independence of the Federation of Malaya was proclaimed with Tengku Abdul Rahman as the first prime minister.

Under the British, each ethnic group stood in basically equal terms vis-à-vis the colonial ruler. With the ratification of the Merdeka constitution, a legal framework was created that guaranteed the special privileges of the Malays as the "indigenous" inhabitants of the land. Yet the constitution also guaranteed equal citizenship for all Malayans, an apparent conflict of intentions that became a source of bitter debate in later years. One hopeful aspect was the dominance of the Alliance party representing the three major ethnic groups. The smooth functioning of the government in the early years of independence was due primarily to the background of the leaders of these main ethnic parties who were all English-educated and imbued with common values and attitudes stemming from a similar educational experience.

Even though the Federation was still grappling with problems of creating a sense of unity among its people, in 1961 Prime Minister Rahman announced the idea of an expanded Malaya that would include Singapore, Sabah (North Borneo), Sarawak and Brunei. Singapore agreed to join once certain trade and Chinese privileges were guaranteed. Sabah and Sarawak, which had come directly under British control in 1946, also consented to join after concessions were made on certain language and religious issues. Only Brunei decided to remain outside the Federation because of fears of loss of oil revenues and the inability to resolve the question of the sultan's status. The Federation of Malaysia was officially inaugurated on September 16, 1963.

One of the most important tasks facing the Federation was the creation of loyalty among the various ethnic groups to the newly expanded nation. The Alliance government decided that language and educational policies would become the instruments in forging an integrated and united society assimilated to Malay cultural traditions. Unfortunately, these moves were regarded by the other ethnic groups as an attempt to secure the schools as yet another area for Malay special privileges. The federal elections of 1969 were fought on the language and education issues, with each communal group seeing the outcome as vital to the well-being or demise of its ethnic interests. The results saw the opposition parties winning sufficient votes to deprive the Alliance of the two-thirds majority that it had always held in parliament. The jubilant victory marches of the opposition parties in Kuala Lumpur on May 13, the day after the elections, were countered by an UMNO rally that evening. Before the night was over, violence erupted throughout the city and continued for four days before order was finally restored. Communal violence continued for two months, and during this time the constitution was suspended and a national emergency declared.

One of the first steps taken by the government after the May 13 incident was to deal directly with the problem of interethnic conflict that threatened to disrupt the country. The creation of a Malaysian identity that would be acceptable to all ethnic groups became an important priority. Toward this end, the Department of National Unity was established in July 1969 to formulate a national ideology and new social and economic programs. On Malaysia's independence day, August 31, 1970, a new ideology known as *Rukunegara* (Articles of Faith of the State) was formally proclaimed. Among the articles were those dedicated to the achievement of greater unity among

631

Malaysia's peoples, the maintenance of a democratic way of life and the creation of a just society in which the wealth of the nation would be equitably shared. To implement the *Rukunegara*, a Twenty-Year Plan for the social and economic restructuring of the country was launched, the New Economic Policy (NEP).

THE NEW ECONOMIC POLICY

Until 1970, the various Five-Year Development Plans had economic growth as their principal objective, with the elimination of economic disparity among the ethnic groups serving as a constraint. These plans were highly successful with Malaya/Malaysia achieving impressive growth since independence. But unemployment and poverty, especially in the rural areas, persisted. As a consequence of the ethnic disturbances of May 1969, the second Malaysia Plan (1971–75) altered the priorities by seeking a reduction and eventual eradication of poverty, irrespective of race and a restructuring of society so that identification of race with economic function would be reduced and ultimately eliminated. With only slight modifications, the third Malaysia Plan (1976–80) and the fourth Malaysia Plan (1981–85) continued this process.

Hopes for achieving the NEP's objectives remained high in the 1970s with Malaysia's annual growth rate averaging a remarkable 7 percent. In the early 1980s, however, the economy began to slow down. The drop in all commodity prices in 1982 was felt deeply, as rubber, tin, palm oil and crude oil made up more than 60 percent of Malaysia's foreign exchange earnings and nearly one-third of its GNP. This situation led to austerity measures in the government and the beginning of corporatization of such public services as telecommunications, railways, ports and municipal utility services. The mood was now for less reliance on a commodity-based economy and more on the development of the manufacturing sector. As part of this drive, the Industrial Master Plan revealed in 1986 had as one of its principal goals the expansion of the Malaysian economy through an increase in value-added goods. To ensure the success of this project and others planned for the last Five-Year Plan of the NEP, the government began actively encouraging multinational corporations through favorable concessions and the partial abandonment of the 30 percent restriction of foreign equity participation.

Political unrest
In the political arena, a major change occurred in 1974 when the Alliance was expanded to include most of the political parties to form the National Front (Barisan Nasional). Within the National Front, the UMNO became progressively stronger, while the MCA and the MIC were seen as having sacrificed their communities' interests "at the altar of national unity." The Democratic Action party was the most effective of the opposition parties and cultivated the image of being the only one that truly represented Chinese interests. In the 1986 elections, UMNO won 83 of the 84 seats contested in the Dewan Rakyat (parliament's lower house), 228 of 240 state assembly

seats and one-third of the total votes cast. Malaysia appeared to be heading toward a one-party state.

With official party politics incapable of challenging the dominance of the UMNO, pressure groups began to act as the watchdogs of the democratic system. One of the most effective of these groups has been the Aliran Kesedaran Rakyat (National Consciousness Movement) whose aim is to address the issues of the day through its monthly newsletters and regular public lectures. Other pressure groups that have become more outspoken with the demise of any real parliamentary opposition to the government coalition are the Association of Women Lawyers, the Institute of Social Analysis, the Consumers Association of Penang, the Environmental Protection Society of Malaysia, the Friends of the Earth, the Selangor Graduates Society and the Bar Council. These groups represent a small, urban-based, mostly English-educated, multiethnic constituency and are unlikely to mount a political challenge to the coalition. As pressure groups, however, they have been so effective that some of the more prominent leaders were among those arrested by the government in October–November 1986 as threats to the unity of the nation. Although most of them were subsequently released, the arrests highlighted the manner in which the Internal Security Act, brought into being to deal with the Communist threat, could be loosely interpreted to include any dissent regarded as a danger to the government.

Dissatisfaction with the NEP

There has been open dissatisfaction expressed at the progress of the NEP in reaching its objectives. Among the Malays, rural poverty persists, leading to the continuing flight to the cities. The presence of the Malay poor in the growing squatter settlements in Kuala Lumpur not only exacerbates the already serious problem of urban poverty among the Chinese and Indians but also accentuates the glaring discrepancy in wealth and life-style between the rural Malays and the urban-based middle-class Malays, who appear to be the chief beneficiaries of the NEP's policies. Many poor Malays in the rural areas and urban squatter settlements, as well as people of the middle-class, are beginning to question a government that has as its slogan "Clean, Capable and Trustworthy" while tolerating flagrant abuses of public trust among some of its own political and business leaders. Huge losses through fraud and bad debts were incurred by some Malaysian banks and by many of the deposit-taking cooperatives in the mid-1980s, bringing into disrepute the government's management of the economy. This disenchantment with their leaders has made Malays highly susceptible to the appeal of resurgent Islam, which is sweeping the country.

The Chinese perceive their share of the national wealth being rapidly whittled away by what they term a "reverse discrimination" of the NEP in favor of the Malays. Their acquiescence in the nation's language and educational policies instituted after the riots of May 13, 1969 has not, in their eyes, produced the promised harmony and unity among the nation's peoples. Despite the proficiency in Malay, the national language, and their attendance at national-type schools, the Chinese feel their position has deteriorated during the period of the NEP. At the MCA's Thirty-fourth Party Assembly held on July 10–12, 1987, a resolution was passed calling for the replacement of the NEP with another twenty-year blueprint to be called the Malaysian Unity Plan. It would involve all ethnic groups in the economic objectives and would guarantee basic freedoms to all Malaysians.

For the Indian community, too, the NEP has been less than successful. Now making up only 8.5 percent of Malaysia's 15.8 million people, down from 10 percent a decade ago, the Indian community's voice has often been lost in the struggles between Malays and Chinese. Their share in the equity in the commercial and industrial sector is a mere 1 percent, and there are still large numbers of Indian poor in the cities and in the rural areas, where Indians make up 38 percent of the country's 250,000 estate workers.

As the NEP enters its final years, the much vaunted general aim of creating a "new Malaysia" by 1990 appears to be an optimistic but vain hope. Ethnic interests still predominate, and the distrust engendered among the groups makes any statement by one immediately suspect by the other. Even the prime minister, Mahathir bin Mohammad, has publicly admitted a decline in the tolerance and cooperation among the National Front coalition parties. Adding to the difficulty of creating a Malaysian identity to which all ethnic groups can subscribe is the increasing strength among the Malays of a resurgent Islam known as the *dakwah* movement.

ISLAM AND THE NEW MALAYSIA

Since the days of Melaka, Islam has always been part of the Malay way of life. The form and intensity of that experience have often reflected developments in the wider Islamic world, and modern Malaysia is no exception. The resurgence of Islam in the world, which some date to the early 1970s, with the assertion of Arab control over oil prices and Arab successes against Israel, has been reinforced by the Islamic revolutions in Libya and Iran. Malaysian Muslims, especially the youth, express a fierce pride in their religion that is apparent in their life-styles. Many Malay women wear ankle-length loose dresses with long sleeves and the short head veil *(telekung)*, and increasing numbers of men sport a mustache and goatee in imitation of the Prophet Muhammad. Among the men of certain Muslim fundamental groups, the Arab flowing robe *(jubah)* and the skullcap *(serban)* are normal attire. The large attendance at mosques and at religious lectures, and the frequency with which Islamic programs are broadcast in the media, are evidence of an Islamic movement associated with *dakwah*. The word itself means literally "call" or "invitation" and was used originally to refer to the conversion of non-Muslims. But, as applied to present-day Malaysia, it refers to the religious activities that have become a prominent part of the lives of the Muslim community.

The Jamaat Tabligh (Lecture Group) and the Dural Arqam (House of Arqam) began their work in the late 1970s, spreading fundamentalist Islamic ideas throughout Malaysia. Because of their small numbers, their influence has been limited. The Islamic resurgence in Malaysia was due mainly to Malay students in the early 1970s who wished to learn more

about their religion and developed an awareness of, a pride in and an identification with the Islamic world. The Angkatan Belia Islam Malaysia (ABIM;
Malaysian Islamic Youth Movement) was formed in 1971 and seeks to generate an Islamic revival in Malaysia. Stressing that Islam must be a total
way of life, in 1975, the ABIM called upon the government and the people
of Malaysia to implement Islamic law, the *Sharia,* as the only way to create
a truly just society. It condemned corruption and poverty and the exploitation of women. At its annual conference in 1979, the ABIM urged the
government to adopt an Islamic solution to the ethnic problems besetting
the nation. It sees nationalism as responsible in the past for the disintegration of the *umma,* or world Isiamic community. The ABIM thus perceives
its role as one of convincing the other ethnic groups of the superiority of
the Islamic approach and of assuring them that the *dhimmi,* or nonbelievers
in the Islamic state, have historically always been accorded their rights,
including the right to practice their own religion.

The government's attitude toward this movement has been ambivalent.
It realizes that a strong Islamic movement can be an effective weapon in
the fight against communists, drugs and other social problems. But it also
fears that it could have a divisive effect on the fragile ethnic unity in the
country. The government has thus sought to preempt all Islamic activity
in the civil service through organizing its own *dakwah* activities. Nevertheless, the movement has continued to grow and has become more respect-
able, forcing the government to modify its concepts of national development to avoid offending Islamic sensitivities.

Although the Islamic movement has gained increasing support among
the Malays, the call for an Islamic state as a way of removing ethnocentrism
in Malaysia has not been as widely accepted. Especially among the non-
Muslim populations of Malaysia, the call has caused considerable alarm.
Few are convinced by the arguments for the establishment of an Islamic
state, and the fears that the non-Muslim population may be forced to accept it grow as the pace of Islamization increases.

In July 1983, the Bank Islam Malaysia became the first Islamic bank
established in Southeast Asia. With its subsidiary insurance system, the
Syarikat Takaful Islam, there is now an alternative system of banking and
insurance practices in accordance with Islamic ideas. The International Islamic University graduated its first 126 graduates in law and economics in
1987 and expects to have an annual intake of between 200 and 800 students. In the heart of Kuala Lumpur rises a spectacular architectural creation symbolizing the five pillars of Islam, the new Islamic Center, which
is to host Islamic seminars and exhibitions. In the state of Kelantan, the
Sharia criminal code was adopted in 1986, and in January 1987, a 21-year-
old man was sentenced by the *Sharia* court to six strokes of the cane and
fined M$1000 for drinking liquor and committing *khalwat* (close contact
with the opposite sex), and the woman fined M$1000. Five other states are
now contemplating introducing the *Sharia* criminal code. The phenomenal
political rise of Anwar Ibrahim, once the charismatic leader of ABIM and
now rumored to be Prime Minister Mahathir's choice as successor, makes
the Islamic state appear more imminent than ever.

635

The strong Islamic movement with its call on the government to establish an Islamic state is a major concern to the non-Muslim Chinese and Indians. They see such a move as the most serious threat ever mounted against their own cultures and religious beliefs. If Malaysia is to survive as a multiethnic, multicultural and multireligious society, the matter will have to be debated in private by the leaders and some compromise reached. But in order for any discussion to occur, the lines of communication among the ethnic groups must first be reopened. With Malay political dominance and the growing strength of the *dakwah* movement, Islam is the critical issue confronting Malaysia today. The future stability of the country hinges on the ability of its leaders to resolve the question of an Islamic state to the satisfaction of the major ethnic communities.

MALAYSIA AND THE ASSOCIATION OF SOUTHEAST ASIAN NATIONS (ASEAN)

As Malaysia continues to grapple with the problems of domestic stability, relations with its neighbors have steadily improved since independence. Past attempts at regional cooperation, such as the Association of Southeast Asia (Malaysia, the Philippines, Thailand) in 1960 and Maphilindo (Malaya, the Philippines and Indonesia) in 1963, failed principally because of President Sukarno's ambitions and the continuing presence and influence of the British in Malaya/Malaysia. With Sukarno's fall from power in 1965 and with Britain's announcement in January 1968 that it would end its military presence "east of Suez" by 1971, two of the major obstacles to regional cooperation were removed. The increased U.S. involvement in Vietnam after 1965 and the fear of the spread of the conflict to the rest of Southeast Asia also served to encourage a regional organization that would maintain peace and stability in the area. Thus, in August 1967, the Association of Southeast Asian Nations (ASEAN) was formed, consisting of Malaysia, the Philippines, Thailand and Singapore.

In the years since its formation, ASEAN has expanded its scope of cooperation to include not only a regional foreign policy but also a coordinated economic policy. Conflicts and disputes among the member nations (including Brunei, which joined the association soon after independence in 1984) have been avoided through procedures established by treaty, and the association has continued to urge the acceptance by the outside world of Southeast Asia as a "zone of peace, freedom and neutrality" and of a Southeast Asia nuclear-weapons-free zone, policies that Malaysia first advocated. It has acted as one in proposing resolutions in the U.N. General Assembly and in negotiating economic policies with the outside world.

For Malaysia, the creation of ASEAN proved timely and made it easier to adjust to the withdrawal of the British military presence from the area and to disengage from a heavy reliance on British economic interests. Its defense and economic and foreign policies are now closely linked with those of the other ASEAN nations, and will continue to be so in the future as long as the members maintain unified economic and political objectives.

FURTHER READING

Abdullah, Taufik, and Siddique, Sharon, eds. *Islam and Society in Southeast Asia.* Singapore: Institute of Southeast Asian Studies, 1986.

Andaya, Barbara Watson, and Andaya, Leonard Y. *A History of Malaysia,* London: Macmillan, 1982.

Arasaratnam, Sinnappah. *Indians in Malaysia and Singapore.* London and Kuala Lumpur: Oxford University Press, 1979.

Gullick, John. *Malaysia: Economic Expansion and National Unity.* Boulder, Colorado: Westview Press, 1981.

Jackson, James C. and Rudner, Martin, eds. *Issues in Malaysian Development.* Singapore: Heinemann Educational, 1979.

Lim, David, ed. *Further Readings on Malaysian Economic Development.* London and Kuala Lumpur: Oxford University Press, 1983.

Loh, Phillip Fook Seng. *Seeds of Separatism: Educational Policy in Malaya, 1874–1940.* London and Kuala Lumpur: Oxford University Press, 1975.

Milne, R. S., and Mauzy, Diane K. *Politics and Government in Malaysia.* Singapore: Federal Publications Ltd.; Vancouver: University of British Columbia Press, 1978.

Purcell, Victor. *The Chinese in Southeast Asia.* 2nd ed. London and New York: Oxford University Press, 1965.

Winstedt, R. O. *The Malays: A Cultural History.* Rev. ed. Singapore: Graham Brash, 1981.

MALDIVES

URMILA PHADNIS

LOCATED in the central Indian Ocean, Maldives' nearest neighbors are India in the north and Sri Lanka in the east, both more than 300 miles/483 km. away. Its southernmost island of Gan—a former British base—is about 240 miles/386 km. off Diego Garcia, the U.S. base in Chagos archipelago. Thus, while its geophysical setting connotes its strategic importance in the contemporary politics of the Indian Ocean, it also explains to a considerable extent its historical insularity.

On the map, Maldives appears like a garland stringing a number of islands into atolls (ring-shaped coral reefs with islands). Stretching over a vast sea expanse of about 41,000 sq. miles/106,190 sq. km., the land area of the archipelago, 1,195 islands, big and small, is barely 115 sq. miles/ 298 sq. km. Of these islands, only 202 are inhabited. About 50 others have been developed for tourism since the 1970s. Notwithstanding the dispersal of its population of 200,000, the Maldivian society has been fairly close-knit, bound by shared historical traditions, religion and language.

HISTORY AND SOCIETY

Archaeological findings indicate that until the advent of Islam, the religion of the Maldivians combined animistic worship with Buddhism, which traveled from Ceylon (now called Sri Lanka). The Indo-Iranian origins of the Maldivian language—Divehi—and its affinity with the Pali-based Sinhala also indicated the cultural impact of its neighbor. However, the Maldivian royalty, highly impressed with the miraculous powers of an Arab saint who visited Maldives in 1153, was converted to Islam. Under royal dispensation, Islam quickly became the religion of the people. The Divehi language adopted the Arabic script. Today virtually all the Maldivians are Sunni Muslims, and Islam is the official religion.

Over the centuries, Islam has provided the country with a strong national identity and distinctiveness as well as a fairly egalitarian and humane social structure. Thus, until recently, there was no capital punishment in the country; the maximum punishment accorded to offenders was banishment to one of the uninhabited islands. Also, women enjoy considerably more equality than they do in many other Islamic countries. They do not wear the veil, and they constitute a significant sector of the work force.

Along with religious homogeneity, the official language, Divehi, provides a common language base despite dialectal differences among various atolls, and operates as a national communications link.

Another unifying factor for the people of Maldives has been the historical tradition of a fairly continuous authority structure of its polity, with the monarch (sultan) at the apex. In view of the physical separation of one administrative unit from the other, the hierarchically evolved authority structure has been characterized by a fair degree of decentralization and autonomy. But due to the nature of their subsistence economy, the islands are dependent on one another and also on Male, the power center in the north and the capital of the state.

A significant part of this historical tradition has also been its assertion as a nation warding off foreign invasions. Thus in 1558 when the Portuguese, operating from Goa in India, seized the country, they were driven off by the Maldivian leadership in less than two decades. Similar was the case of the Malabari pirates from south India in 1752 who could not sustain themselves for even a year. Even when, faced with economic pressure from Ceylonese merchants, the sultan signed a treaty with the British in 1887 to become a protectorate, the British connections via the crown colony of Ceylon were infrequent and its presence was nominal.

Nonetheless, developments in Ceylon did have a spillover effect on the political framework of Maldives, as was evident from the constitutional changes in the protectorate in 1932. Reflecting a court rebellion against the autocratic rule of the monarchy, the constitution was fashioned largely on the pattern of the constitution promulgated a year earlier in the crown colony. Based on universal adult franchise, it provided for a unicameral legislature (Majlis) as well as a Council of Ministers.

POLITICS

After attaining independence in 1965, Maldives promulgated a new constitution in 1968 by which the monarchy came to an end and the country became a republic under the presidency of Ibrahim Nasir. After his two five-year terms Nasir resigned, ostensibly for health reasons, and supported the presidential candidacy of his cabinet colleague Maumoon Abdul Gayoom. In accordance with the constitutional provisions, Gayoom was nominated as the sole presidential candidate by the Majlis and sought the popular verdict through a referendum in 1978 and again in 1983. On both these occasions he won with more than 90 percent of the vote.

Since independence, the political structure of the country has been marked by continuity, stability and orderly succession. Elections for the Majlis have taken place regularly. The Majlis comprises 48 members: two elected from each of the 19 atolls and Male, along with eight members nominated by the president. The cabinet comprises the president, vice-president, if any, ministers and the attorney general.

Significantly, although the constitution provides for a power balance between the legislature, executive and judiciary, in effect there is considerable diffusion of functions as the legislators are permitted to hold administrative positions. Such a diffusion indicates an enmeshing of the initiation and implementation of public policies, which has its merits and also constraints. It can accelerate the decision-making process, but at the same time it can overburden too few people with too much work. It also underlines the lack of an adequate number of trained personnel.

In this respect, it is noteworthy that despite more than 50 years of universal adult franchise, political parties are nonexistent in Maldives. This indicates, on the one hand, the continuity of the traditional mold of consensus building, and on the other, a small elite base having a familial network. Such a situation, however, should not be viewed merely as oligarchical but also as reflecting the harsh reality of a dire lack of skilled people for a political structure in which competent critics are tolerated and those from humble origins, proving themselves, are accommodated.

In a country with expanding opportunities, until new aspirants for power can be accommodated, the process of consensus building may not get too tenuous. However, the nature and tenor of its economic development and communications network are bound to break the relative insularity of various atolls and bring in their wake a much larger number of aspirants to power to the fore than has hitherto. This is particularly so because of the demographic pattern of the country. With more than half of its population below 20 years of age, the number of those entering the labor force is bound to swell by the end of the century.

That the Maldivian leadership has been acutely aware of the challenge of the rising aspirations of the people is evident from its policies and strategies in the socioeconomic arena. Integrating the development of various atolls, building infrastructure for interaction between atolls, and encouraging maximal output of the country's meager resources have been some of its major concerns. Thus, in a conference of the least developed countries in 1981 at Paris, the country paper on Maldives summarized its manifold problems as "shortage of qualified manpower, poor health conditions, rapidly changing structure of the fishing industry, past neglect of the agricultural sector, and severe regional imbalances in economic development."[1]

ECONOMICS

In the past, with its weak agricultural structure, the economic lifeline of Maldives was closely linked with Sri Lanka, from which it imported basic foodstuffs and exported dried and salted fish. Since the 1970s, however, Maldives has made efforts to diversify exports and increase trade with more countries, while seeking assistance from the global community for economic development. Along with that from the donor countries, aid has also been sought from multilateral agencies.

The ups and downs in Maldivian economy during the last two decades indicate its vulnerability vis-à-vis its external environment on the one hand

[1] Maldives National Planning Agency, "Republic of Maldives: Programmes and Projections for 1980s: Prepared for United Nations Conference on Least Developed Countries Held in Paris," mimeographed (Male: December, 1980), 6–7.

and the externally induced economic changes of its traditional economy on the other. Thus, besides diversifying and modernizing its traditional fishing operations through mechanizing its fishing fleet, exporting fresh fish and canning fish, etc., Maldives expanded its shipping sector and developed tourism as a new industry. As foreign exchange earners, both shipping and tourism showed great potential, as did the traditional fishing industry. However, in the early 1980s the Maldivian economy had a triple blow: The slump in the international price of fish led to a decline of earnings from its fish export; the recession in the international shipping industry almost dealt a deathblow to its nascent shipping industry; and last but not least, the ethnic conflict in Sri Lanka led to a shrinking of the tourist industry since the international tourist agencies had been providing a joint package of Sri Lanka and Maldives to travelers from the West.

Fishing and tourism have survived regional problems and adverse implications of the global environment. Nonetheless, they underline the economic vulnerability of Maldives vis-à-vis external forces over which it has little control.

Besides, the economic progress that has accompanied modernization over the last decade has led to the development of a sector that, employing a minority of the labor force, has led to the emergence of a dual economy— traditional and modern—with greater income differentiation as well as concentration of capital and investment in Male and adjacent atolls. Efforts to narrow such a gap are being made by the Gayoom regime, as is clear from the national development plan for 1985–87. This plan has three major objectives: (1) improvement of the living standards of the Maldivian people, encompassing material well-being as well as quality of life, primarily social harmony and ecological balance; (2) balance of population density and social progress between Male and other atolls; and (3) attainment of self-reliance and self-sustained growth.

Herein lie the major dilemmas of the Maldivian state and society. Although the country's increasing exposure to the external environment promises a better standard of living for its people, it also entails the growing intrusion of external forces, and consequently, greater dependence on them. If such an exposure leads to the rising expectations of its people, it also impinges severely on the traditions and norms of its society. While the expanding opportunities hold promise for widening the elite base, they also bring in their wake stresses and strains on the processes of consensus building. Thus, the increasing interaction with the world beyond poses challenges as well as opportunities.

FURTHER READING

Adeney M. and Carr, W. K. "The Maldives Republic." In Ostheimer, John, ed. *The Politics of the Western Indian Ocean Islands*. New York: Praeger, 1975.

Coelho, V. H. "Constitutional and Political Developments in the Maldives." *Foreign Affairs Report* 28, no. 8 (August 1979), 134–48.

Far Eastern Economic Review. "Maldives." in *Asia Year Book*. Hong Kong: South China Morning Post. Annually since 1978.

Maldives. Department of Information and Broadcasting. *Social Development.* Male: Department of Information and Broadcasting, 1985.

Maldives. Ministry of Planning and Development. *Statistical Year Book of Maldives, 1986.* Male: Ministry of Planning and Development, 1986.

Maloney, Clarence. *People of the Maldive Islands.* Bombay: Orient Longman, 1980.

Maniku, Ahmad Hassan. *The Republic of Maldives.* Singapore: Kenwa Lithography, 1980.

Mukerjee, Dilip. "Maldives Diversifies Contact with Big Neighbours." *Pacific Community* 6, no. 4 (July 1975), 593–607.

Phadnis, Urmila, and Luithui, Ela Dutt. *Maldives: Winds of Change in an Atoll State.* New Delhi: South Asian Publishers, 1985.

Phadnis, Urmila. "Political Dynamics of the Island States: A Comparative Study of Sri Lanka and Maldives." *IDSA Journal* 12, no. 3 (January–March 1980), 305–22.

MONGOLIA

HENRY G. SCHWARZ

AREA AND POPULATION

THE term *Mongolia* has two widely different meanings, one ethnic and the other political. Ethnic Mongolia has customarily been defined as the area from Lake Baikal in the north to the Ordos bend of the Huanghe (Yellow River) in the south and from the Alta mountains in the west to the Xiao Hinggan mountains in the east. Not until the 20th century did Mongolia become divided politically, with the northern portion (excepting the area around Lake Baikal, which remained under Russian and later Soviet control) being called the Mongolian People's Republic (MPR) and the southern portion being referred to as the Inner Mongolian Autonomous Region (IMAR) of China. Later in this century, a fashion developed whereby the term *Mongolia* has been applied only to the northern portion.

Mongolia is 1,061,580 sq. miles/2,749,500 sq. km. in area, of which 604,825 sq. miles/1,566,500 sq. km. lie in the north and 456,756 sq. miles/1,183,000 sq. km. in the south. As of late 1987, the total Mongolian (excluding Chinese, Russians, et cetera) population is about 6 million, of whom 2 million live in the MPR and 4 million under Chinese jurisdiction. Although the Mongolian population in the IMAR is twice as large as that in the MPR, the net natural increase of 2.6 percent in the MPR is perhaps double that in the IMAR. This difference is almost entirely due to different governmental policies. The MPR government adovcates large families, but the Chinese government has a one-child-per-family policy, from which the Mongols and other minorities are officially exempt, though there are inducements for voluntary compliance.

HISTORY

The history of Mongolia can be said to have begun in 1206 when Genghis Khan (1162–1227) united most tribes living in the area delineated in the preceding section into a state called Mongolia. He ordered the adoption of the Uighur script (see next section), created a central government, and issued a number of regulations that later became known, collectively, as the *yasakh,* the earliest legal code of Mongolia.

Most important, Genghis Khan created a new central army, which he organized into decimal units of 10, 100, 1,000 and 10,000 soldiers; his personal bodyguard, which eventually grew to a *tümen* (Mongolian for 10,000) was placed above the army. Soon after the unification, Genghis Khan began to expand Mongol power beyond Mongolia. Between 1209 and his death in 1227, he conquered Xixia—a Tibetan state situated in the present-day Ningxia and Gansu provinces of China—and Khwarezm, a Muslim sultanate stretching from the Alta mountains in the east to the Caspian sea in the west. He also initiated the conquest of Jin, the Jurched state in northern China, a feat not completed until 1234.

Under Genghis Khan's sons and grandsons, the Mongol empire expanded tremendously and by around 1280 it had become the largest connected empire in history. It stretched from eastern Europe to the Pacific Ocean, with only India, parts of southeast Asia, western Europe and Japan beyond its control but not beyond its influence. The resulting *pax mongolica,* for the first and only time in history, enabled a person to travel from Europe to Canton without fear of mistreatment or even the inconvenience of border formalities. The empire also perfected a communications system that was swift and dependable and by far the best in the world. A third major contribution made by the Mongol empire was its religious tolerance, which allowed the flourishing of several religions within its borders. Though Europeans remained both ignorant of and hostile to the religions of the East, they carried valuable secular information from the Mongolian empire.

The Mongol world empire fell almost as swiftly as it rose. Dissension among Genghis Khan's grandsons was the single most important cause, and by 1368 China, Persia and other areas were once again independent of the Mongols. After decades of civil war, no tribal chief managed to reunify all of Mongolia. During the 17th century a divided Mongolia fell prey to a foreign power, the Manchus, who not only conquered China but also absorbed Mongolia by diplomatic means. During the more than two centuries of Manchu rule, Chinese soldiers, traders and finally immigrants moved into Mongolia. The southern portion, roughly corresponding to today's IMAR, bore the brunt of this invasion.

When in 1911 it was the Manchu empire's turn to collapse, the Mongols were quick to assert their independence on the ground that they had never submitted to China. The warlord government of Yüan Shi-kai in Beijing, the successor to Manchu rule, forced the Mongols of southern Mongolia into submission. Yüan was unable, however, to prevent northern Mongolia from forming an autonomous theocratic state under the titular leadership of the Jebtsundamba Khutukhtu, the highest-ranking official of Mongolian Lamaism. This marked the beginning of the present political division of Mongolia.

Czarist Russia acted as guarantor of autonomous Mongolia, but with the outbreak of the Russian revolution in 1917, the Anfu clique in Beijing, China's so-called national government, saw the chance to add northern Mongolia to its conquests. In 1919 it sent an army north and forced the Jebtsundamba Khutukhtu's government to sign a renunciation of autonomy. China was on the verge of consolidating its hold on northern Mongolia when the Russian civil war spilled across the border. A White Russian army under the command of Baron Ungern-Sternberg, while taking refuge in Mongolia, ousted most of the Chinese troops. In 1921, Bolshevik forces, accompanied by Mongol partisans, entered Mongolia and defeated the White Russian army. July 11, the day they entered Ikh Khüree (listed as Urga on Western maps), is now celebrated as a national holiday.

Under the leadership of Damdiny Sühbaatar, the Mongol partisans established a new, secular government while keeping the Jebtsundamba Khutukhtu as chief of state. Both men died soon afterward, Sühbaatar in 1923 and the Khutukhtu the following year. In the same year (1924), the government declared the establishment of the Mongolian People's Republic and, by the end of the 1920s, began to close down its southern border. Most foreigners, other than Russians, were encouraged to leave the MPR.

For more than two decades after its establishment in 1924, the MPR was recognized only by the Soviet Union, while the rest of the world deferred to the territorial claims of the various fractional governments of China. The fiction of Chinese sovereignty became increasingly difficult to maintain, and by the end of World War II Chiang Kai-shek agreed to abide by the outcome of a plebiscite in the MRP. When the result was a virtually unanimous vote for continued independence, Chiang Kai-shek made preparations to recognize the republic. Within a year, however, he used the resumption of his war with the Chinese Communists as an excuse to renege on his promise. Other countries did, however, recognize the MPR. India, Burma (now Myanmar), Indonesia, and all Communist countries established diplomatic relations by 1950. Great Britain was the first Western country to follow suit, in 1963, and by the 1970s virtually every major country had recognized the MPR. The MPR joined the United Nations in 1961 and the Council for Mutual Economic Aid (the economic alliance of most Communist states or Comecon) in 1962. In early 1987 even the United States of America recognized the MPR.

Meanwhile, southern Mongolia, known during the Qing dynasty as Inner Mongolia, disappeared as an administrative unit. Not only the warlord governments but the Kuomintang (Chinese Nationalist Party) under Chiang Kai-shek chopped up southern Mongolia and parceled out bits of Mongolian territory among several Chinese provinces. Small wonder, then, that many southern Mongols cooperated with the Japanese invaders when the latter set up an ostensibly independent Mongolian state in the southeastern corner of Mongolia. Although it was denounced by most Chinese and even by some Mongols as a puppet regime, this Mongolian state's very existence elicited great pride among Mongols throughout southern Mongolia.

The Communists, who also operated in Inner Mongolia during the war, emulated the Japanese by creating Mongolian political and administrative units, and in 1947, they established the IMAR, the archetype of all future autonomous areas for minorities in China. After the Communist victory in 1949, the territory of the IMAR was gradually enlarged until it extended from the Amur River in the northeast to the Alashan desert in the west. The Mongols of southern Mongolia suffered great adversities during Mao Zedong's so-called cultural revolution of 1966–76. Not only were they

645

persecuted by the Chinese, but large tracts of territory were detached from the IMAR and incorporated into Chinese provinces.[1] In 1979 these territories were restored to the IMAR, and since then Chinese policies in the region have become more lenient. The total ban on contacts with the MPR has been almost completely lifted; small groups of people in each part of Mongolia may again visit the other part, and mail service has been resumed across the frontier.

LANGUAGE AND LITERATURE

Mongolian is a member of the Mongolian language group, which, in turn, belongs to the Altaic family of languages. It is closely related to Daur, Bonan, Dongxiang, Tu, and Enger (eastern Uighur), Mongolian languages spoken in various parts of northern China. Mongolian has a number of dialects, the most important of which are Khalkha—the main dialect in the MPR—and Chakhar, Ordos, Bargu, Kharchin, Khorchin, and Ujumchin, the latter found in the IMAR. Speakers of these various dialects have no difficulty in understanding one another.

The oldest surviving sample of the Mongolian script is an inscription on a stele done about 1225. The script was adopted from the Uighur script which, in turn, had been taken from the Sogdian. As the Mongols developed their own written literature, they made some changes in the shape of letters and added new letters to express Tibetan and Sanskrit loan words. Three other scripts—called Phagspa, Galig and Soyombo—were used during the period of the Mongol world empire but fell into disuse when the empire vanished. The script adopted from Uighur, however, has survived.[2] It is still being used by the two-thirds of Mongols who live under Chinese jurisdiction, whereas the Mongols in the MPR switched to the foreign Cyrillic script at the time of World War II.

RELIGION

The earliest religion among the Mongols was the worship of nature. All natural phenomena became the objects of veneration, including fire, trees, rocks, rivers and, above all, *tenger,* "sky" or "heaven." Certain persons acting as intermediaries between these natural phenomena and humans are generally called shamans; their religion, shamanism, shares many features with religions in other parts of this planet, such as the medicine-man cult among the native American peoples.

While shamanism has to this day never been fully eliminated, it was

---

[1] The Chinese persecution of Mongols during this mad period included inane measures, such as forcing the Mongols to turn the statue of a horse atop a museum in Hohhot so that it would face south instead of north. The implication, of course, was that the horse, symbolizing the IMAR, should no longer look toward Ulaanbaatar but Beijing.

[2] When the Manchus rose to power and conquered all of China in the 17th century, they adopted the Mongol script and made certain modifications. This script fell into disuse no later than 1911, when the Manchu empire came to an end.

joined later by Buddhism, which has had a profound impact on all aspects of Mongolian society. We do not know exactly when Buddhism first appeared in Mongolia, but it is certain that by the time of the Mongol world empire, many aristocrats, most notably Kublai Khan, had become interested in the sect. During the two centuries after the empire's demise, Buddhism fell into disfavor, and shamanism once again became the predominant religion among the Mongols. In the 1570s, Altan Han, the most influential of the southern Mongolian rulers and whose capital was the modern Hohhot, made a pact with the head of the Yellow Sect of Tibetan Buddhism (also known as Northern Buddhism or Lamaism), which led to a return of Buddhism to Mongolia.

This time Buddhism penetrated every layer of Mongolian society. Hundreds of monasteries and temples were built, and between one-third and one-half of the entire male population became monks. Buddhism brought urbanization to Mongolia as well as literacy in both Tibetan, the church language, and Mongolian. These gains were purchased, however, at a steep price. Church officials came to collaborate closely with the secular aristocracy in preserving the status quo, thereby stifling innovation, social mobility and reform. In addition, the high proportion of monks, who as members of the Yellow Sect were celibate, contributed to a drastic decline in the population.[3]

Buddhism became a political as much as an economic force in Mongolia, and when in 1911 the northern part of Mongolia succeeded in liberating itself from Chinese rule, a theocratic government led by the Jebtsundamba Khutukhtu (also Bogdo Gegen), head of the Mongolian Buddhist sect, came into existence. Soon after the events of 1921 (see the section on history, above), this theocratic leadership came under pressure and in 1924 was entirely eliminated and replaced by a communist government. From about 1930 on, the Buddhist sect itself was attacked. Temples and monasteries were closed down, and the many thousands of monks put to work in secular occupations. The same fate awaited Buddhism in the southern part in the late 1940s, when the Communist Party of China assumed control there. According to official policy in both parts of Mongolia, religious belief is permissible but religious practice has been greatly curtailed. Today only the monasteries of Gandan in the MPR and Batkar Juu in the IMAR are still training small numbers of young men for monkhood.

ECONOMIC AND SOCIAL DEVELOPMENT

Until well into the 20th century Mongolia had a nomadic herding economy, with the five principal animals being the horse, sheep, goat, cow and camel. Animal husbandry is still an important part of the Mongolian economy, with the number of animals virtually unchanged between 1950 and 1985.[4] During the same period, however, agricultural production increased

---

[3] The other chief cause for a declining population was epidemic syphilis and other venereal diseases.
[4] The MPR figures are 22,702,220 in 1950 and 22,640,000 in 1985; the corresponding figures for the IMAR are 9,674,000 and 32,050,000.

647

immensely.[5] It was made possible, in part, by better irrigation[6] and by a high degree of mechanization in the MPR, where labor is still scarce. More farming has resulted in a profound change in the Mongolian diet, which traditionally consisted almost entirely of meat. Now many Mongols regularly eat grain products, vegetables and, on occasion, even fruit.

Mongolia has also undergone some measure of industrialization. The earliest factories in the MPR were built in the 1930s and processed animal products, such as wool, meat, leather, soap and sausage casings. Today they still account for about 15 percent of the MPR's industry, which is now dominated by large extractive factories processing Mongolia's great mineral resources, particularly copper, molybdenum, coal, iron ore and lime. In the MPR, entire cities, such as Daquan and Erdenet, have been built near major mineral deposits.[7] The MPR's rapid industrialization was made possible through massive aid and assistance from the Soviet Union and, since the 1950s, East European states. China rendered some help, mainly in the form of laborers, for several years in the 1950s.

Industrialization has been accompanied by major changes in society. The rapid pace of urbanization is in evidence everywhere. The MPR's capital, Ulaanbaatar, now has more than 400,000 inhabitants, which amounts to one out of every five persons in the entire country.[8] Whereas in 1950, only 10 percent of the MPR's population lived in cities and towns, by 1985 51.7 percent did so.[9] At the same time, education has become widespread. The Mongolian State University was established in 1942, and it is now joined by seven other institutes of higher learning in the MPR. Education has also grown apace in the IMAR, which has now 15 institutions of higher learning, enrolling about 12,000 students. Of these, Mongols and other minorities account for about 3,000 students. The 5,194 middle schools have about 200,000 minority students, and some 26,980 elementary schools include almost 400,000 minority students.

FURTHER READING

Bawden, Charles R. *The Modern History of Mongolia.* London: Weidenfeld & Nicolson; New York: Praeger, 1968.

Boyle, John Andrew. *The Mongol World Empire, 1206–1370.* London: Variorum Reprints, 1977.

Heissig, Walther. *Geschichte der mongolischen Literatur.* Wiesbaden, West Germany: Harrassowitz, 1972.

————. *The Religions of Mongolia.* Berkeley: University of California Press, 1980.

[5] The area under cultivation in the MPR increased from 53,400 hectares in 1950 to 756,000 hectares in 1985.

[6] As much as one-fourth of all cultivated land in the IMAR is now being irrigated.

[7] The first major industrial complex in the IMAR, the iron and steel combine in Baotou, was completed in the late 1950s.

[8] Hohhot, the capital of the IMAR, has also undergone rapid growth and now has a population of more than a half million.

[9] A similar increase occurred in the IMAR, where the urban population grew from 12.6 percent in 1950 to 43.4 percent in 1985.

Jagchid, Sechin, and Hyer Paul. *Mongolia's Culture and Society.* Boulder, Colorado: Westview Press, 1979.

Lattimore, Owen. *Nationalism and Revolution in Mongolia.* Leiden, the Netherlands: E. J. Brill; New York: Oxford University Press, 1955.

North American Conference on Mongolian Studies. *Studies on Mongolia.* Bellingham: Center for East Asian Studies, Western Washington University, 1979.

Poppe, Nicholas. *Grammar of Written Mongolian.* Wiesbaden, West Germany: Harrassowitz, 1974.

———. *Introduction to Mongolian Comparative Studies.* Helsinki: Suomalais-ugrilainen Seura, 1955.

———. *Mongolian Language Handbook.* Washington, D.C.: Center for Applied Linguistics, 1970.

Schwarz, Henry G. *Bibliotheca Mongolica.* Bellingham: Western Washington University, 1978–.

———, ed. *Mongolian Short Stories.* Bellingham: Program in East Asia Stories, Western Washington State College, 1974.

———. *The Minorities of Northern China: A Survey.* Bellingham: Western Washington University, 1984.

MYANMAR

ROBERT H. TAYLOR

SINCE 200 B.C. the core of the territory now called Myanmar (formerly Burma) has been settled by agriculturalists who developed forms of culture upon which succeeding generations have built. The first important cultural period of the Pyu ended about A.D. 900, and was succeeded by the classical period of the Pagan dynasty which founded the Buddhist capital of the same name. Pagan is now an expansive ruined city and one of the country's major tourist attractions. The glory of the Pagan period waned toward the end of the 13th century; and the next two centuries were marked by political disorganization, with the territory governed by a variety of smaller entities. The resurrection of a unified political order came in the 17th century with the powerful Restored Toungoo dynasty, which was followed in the mid-18th century by the Konbaung dynasty. This last Burmese dynasty fell to the forces of the British-Indian empire in three successive wars, starting in 1824 and ending in 1885. The country was then incorporated as a province of British India until it separated as a colony in 1937. After three years of Japanese occupation, between 1942 and 1945, Burma gained independence from Britain on January 4, 1948, following a largely peaceful but tense period of nationalist struggle which led to state sovereignty but also to four years of civil war between the government and both an internally developed Communist movement and an ethnic separatist movement. After 14 years of civilian rule, during which the military provided the props for the weak state, the army took power outright in 1962. From 1974 to 1988, Myanmar was officially a one-party socialist republic.

LAND AND PEOPLE

The original core of historic Myanmar forms only a part of the present 261,288 sq. miles/676,562 sq. km. that make up the modern country. In the precolonial period, the extent of the domain of the state was a function of the power of the center, but the modern colonial state imposed set boundaries and the country was extended to include a variety of ecological zones, marked by high mountains and deep valleys where a variety of linguistically different communities resided. Then, as now, they often practiced slash-and-burn agriculture and, in some places, cultivation of the opium poppy, which they smuggled out across the country's long borders

Table 1
POPULATION STATISTICS, 1983 CENSUS

State/Division	Population	% of Total	% Urban	Density per sq. mile
Kachin	904,000	2.56	20.13	26
Kayah	168,000	0.48	24.67	37
Karen	1,058,000	3.00	10.44	90
Chin	369,000	1.05	14.72	27
Sagaing	3,856,000	10.92	13.72	106
Tenasserim	918,000	2.60	24.12	55
Pegu	3,800,000	10.76	19.46	250
Magwe	3,241,000	9.18	15.22	187
Mandalay	4,581,000	12.97	26.49	320
Mon	1,682,000	4.76	28.15	354
Rahkine	2,046,000	5.79	14.85	144
Yangon (Rangoon)	3,974,000	11.26	67.78	1,012
Shan	3,719,000	10.53	17.66	62
Irrawaddy	4,991,000	14.14	14.89	368
TOTAL	35,314,000	100.00	23.94	

with Thailand, India, and China. From the delta of the Irrawaddy River, one of the world's great rice-growing areas, through the dry zone of the center, to the mountains of the border areas, possibly rich in minerals as well as holding the world's last remaining extensive reserves of teak, Myanmar is a society of great diversity and complexity, held together by the same ecology that makes overland communication difficult with neighboring countries. The country is penetrated by only a few roads that cross its border and by no railways. Communication flows naturally north and south along the Irrawaddy River system and the other valleys, which since the end of the 19th century have been traversed by railways. Air travel is the easiest means of communication with the northernmost reaches of the country, which are sparsely settled and in places almost inaccessible.

The approximately 38 million people who reside in Myanmar speak not only the dominant language, Burmese, but a variety of other minority languages, including Shan, and variations of Karen, Kachin or Jingphaw and Chin. The predominant religion is Theravada Buddhism, probably followed by 85 percent of the population; but there are significant communities of Muslims in the Rahkine State bordering Bangladesh and in the major cities, including the capital, Yangon (Rangoon), to which many South Asians migrated during the British colonial period. The skyline of the capital is dominated by religious structures, with the Shwe Dagon pagoda, a center of worship for all Buddhists, rising above them all.

Administratively, rulers have divided Myanmar differently. The kings developed tributary relationships with local leaders on the peripheries of their kingdoms. In the central and southern areas of the country, the British imposed a system of direct administration, penetrating down to the level of the village and township in the economic and population core of the society. They ruled the peripheral areas, including the Shan States, indirectly, bolstering the power of the local "traditional leaders," the Shan Sawbwas, Kachin Duwas and others, as their agents of control.

Not until the 1960s was a uniform system of administration imposed. Since the introduction of a new constitution in 1974, the country has been divided into 14 states and divisions, the states taking their names from the predominant linguistic group in a border area, the divisions from the place names of the core. Population is spread very unevenly among the states and divisions, as Table 1 reveals. Myanmar's low level of urbanization is a consequence of the absence of attractions to the cities, as the government has not only attempted to distribute employment opportunities and development projects throughout the country but has also operated economic structures which discourage urban immigration.

COLONIAL TRANSFORMATION

Though modern Myanmar maintains many of the religious and cultural characteristics of the precolonial periods, the colonial period shaped to a large extent the structure of the contemporary economy and society. The distribution of the labor force in the mid-1980s was little different from what it had been in the 1930s despite the efforts of governments to create a more industrialized society. Agriculture is the major occupational activity, involving over 63 percent of the population, while manufacturing accounts for a mere 8.3 percent.

The colonial period saw the transformation of an essentially subsistence economy to one that was closely tied to the economic fortunes of the rest of the world, especially the colonial power, Britain. By the 1930s, the country had become the world's largest rice exporter (at the time), and Yangon one of the busiest ports of immigration. South Asian labor flowed in and out of the country, providing the work force for the docks and export-oriented transportation system. The majority of the indigenous population remained tied to the land, having migrated southward during the previous century to open up the vast rice fields of the Irrawaddy delta. The result, however, was not prosperity for the peasants but rather their impoverishment as land was taken from their hands and placed in the hands of landlords, more than half of whom were Indian moneylenders who were often forced to foreclose on the mortgages they had extended to the cultivators when the world rice price had been high. The great depression of the 1930s led to the rise of great peasant distress and eventually widespread peasant revolt, requiring the government to import many troops from India to suppress it.

British rule not only transformed the rural economy, but also the structure of politics and social classes. The commercial emphasis of colonial policy gave rise to a class of clerks, business people, lawyers and other professionals who sought political power and were allowed to do so by the nature of British policy. Since the early 1920s—after protests at the limitations on political power for indigenous people, imposed by the colonial government—elections have taken place for a legislative council. These elections spurred the development of political parties led by members of the new middle class. However, given the economic structure of the colony, these parties were dependent on the financial support of the wealthiest segments of society, many of whom were foreigners whose fortunes had been created by the policies of the colonial state. Therefore, as the nationalist movement developed, a split became apparent between the urban, middle-class, political elite and its interests and the position of the bulk of the peasant population, which suffered most from the economic inequalities of the society.

In an attempt to bridge this gap, there emerged, in the 1930s, a new generation of nationalist youth who, through espousing an interpretation of Marxism and other current leftist ideas, sought to develop a modern nationalist ideology that appealed to the bulk of the population. In doing so, they converted many European-derived political ideas into what was essentially a Buddhist frame of reference, thus both popularizing radical Western thought while obscuring its meaning. By the time of independence, almost every successful politician advocated socialism. During the Japanese occupation of World War II there developed a Communist-led resistance movement, which drew widespread popular support and was one of the mainstays of the anti-British movement after the war.

While the rise of socialist thought was one of the key factors in the development of contemporary Myanmar, another has been the development of the armed forces. The British army largely excluded the Burmese from the core of the society and Burmese nationalist youths in the 1930s sought a means of developing their own armed force with which to drive out the British. The growing interest of Japan in establishing its hegemony over the region gave these men an opportunity. Under the auspices of the Japanese Imperial Army, 30 Burmese were trained in the early 1940s to form the officer corps of an indigenous army. Among those in this group were Gen. Aung San, normally considered the founder of independent Burma, and Gen. Ne Win, the man who led the country from 1962 to 1988. When the Japanese invaded in early 1942, these men came with them and formed the Burmese Independence Army (BIA), which is the origin of the army that now dominates the country's politics.

POLITICS AFTER INDEPENDENCE

The strains within the Burmese nationalist movement among the Communist and radical socialist left, ethnic minority political groups often with Christian or Muslim leadership, the army and others were kept in check until the British declared that they would hand over power to the Anti-Fascist People's Freedom League (AFPFL), the national front that had been formed by these groups in 1944 to resist both the Japanese and the British. However, by 1947 these strains had become too great and the AFPFL had been reduced to its conservative and urban core. Independence came six months after the assassination of Aung San, the only politician able to bridge the gap between the various groups, and civil war broke out. Even before January 1948, Muslim separatists in Rahkine had started an armed movement for unity with East Pakistan (now Bangladesh), and one faction of the Communist party had been declared illegal. But on March 28, the day after the order for their leaders' arrest, the main Communist party went into revolt, to be followed a few months later by the pro-Western Karen National Union (KNU), led by Christian Karens, who were seeking a separate state. For the next four years the country was torn by civil strife, with the government at times controlling little more than the capital.

With the restoration of order in most of the country by the early 1950s, elections were eventually held and the AFPFL continued to rule through an elected legislature. However, the government was able to do little to alleviate the causes of discontent; and the constitutional structures contained within them many contradictory principles, including a call for the construction of a nationalized socialist economy while permitting the operation of foreign firms and allowing foreign landowners. Additionally, while espousing the principle of egalitarianism, the government permitted, and in some cases increased, the powers of the hereditary leaders of the border areas. Meanwhile, the leadership of the AFPFL itself spilt over the behavior of the charismatic Buddhist prime minister, U Nu, and the Socialist party deputy prime ministers in the government. This split, which nearly led to armed conflict between the police and the army, allowed the army to assume power under Ne Win in 1958. In 1960, elections were held again and U Nu was returned to office.

In the following two years, many of the problems that had bedeviled the government in the 1950s returned. The government became even more politically isolated and relied heavily upon political symbolism to maintain its legitimacy. Nu offered to make Buddhism the national religion, which antagonized non-Buddhists, and he also offered to grant greater autonomy to peripheral states. This caused great apprehension among the leaders of the army, and on March 2, 1962, in a nearly bloodless coup, which evoked no public opposition, a revolutionary council composed of army officers seized power under Ne Win.

THE REVOLUTIONARY COUNCIL ERA

The military controlled the government from then until January 1974, when a new constitution, making Myanmar a socialist one-party state, was introduced. During this 12-year period, the army, after failing to gain the cooperation of either the underground leftists or the former civilian government leaders, set about restructuring the relationship between the state and society. All organizations other than the government-sponsored Burmese Socialist Program party (BSPP) and its affiliated mass and class organizations, were banned. Foreign economic enterprises, including joint ventures, were nationalized, and Burmese involvement in world trade progressively declined. Landlords lost control of their land by the passing of legislation making rent and loan foreclosure on farmers illegal. The press, existing under minimal censorship in the 1950s, lost its autonomy and was completely nationalized by the end of the 1960s.

Administratively, the military government installed a system of security and administration committees at the village, township, district and state levels. These bodies were usually chaired by the local military commander and were composed of local administrators. By the early 1970s their memberships were extended to include members of the local BSPP branches in preparation for the formation of elected people's councils at all levels of the administrative system. These were brought in with the 1974 constitution, which also placed judicial powers in the hands of local people's courts. These courts were composed of nonprofessional judges who were members of the relevant people's council, and who sat in rotating panels. The result of these administrative and political reforms was to impose a system of tighter central controls from the capital to the townships and villages as military personnel assumed increasingly important positions in the line of control from the top downward. Economically, however, the policies led to a decline in economic growth as productivity levels fell in the face of declining incentives for the farmers.

The centralization of control had repercussions on the border areas that were sparsely populated by individuals who had never been directly governed from the capital. Here the military government moved to undermine in practice as well as in constitutional theory the powers of the traditional leaders. Many of the latter organized revolts in the name of separatism and cultural pluralism. The government responded by reemphasizing its policies of cultural and religious liberty within the structures of the central state. The consequence was a continuation of the ethnic separatist movements of groups like the KNU as well as newer groups, formed in the late 1950s, such as the Kachin Independence Army (KIA) and the Shan United Revolutionary Army (SURA). Like the BCP, with which these groups sometimes worked but with whom they never entered into an alliance until the 1980s, these groups, now loosely grouped as the United Democratic Front, posed no threat to the government but slowed economic development as the government was denied resources from the border regions they controlled. The separatist fighters turned to smuggling to support themselves, though the KIA received a good deal of support from China during the Cultural Revolution when relations with Myanmar deteriorated. By the 1980s, the KIA, BCP and other groups, denied any external support, were supporting themselves largely by smuggling goods, including opium, from the so-called "Golden Triangle," which includes northern Thailand and Laos as well as northern Myanmar.

THE SOCIALIST REPUBLIC

The introduction of the 1974 constitution changed little at the center of the state. Many military officers retired from the army but continued on in similar roles in the government and ruling party. Gen. Ne Win became president and remained as chairman of the party. Legislative power lay in the hands of the Pyithu Hluttaw, or People's Assembly. Elected on a one-party slate every five years, the Pyithu Hluttaw met twice each year for a few days to enact legislation approved at meetings of the BSPP central committee a few days earlier. The legislature roughly reflected in its composition the ethnic and geographical diversity of the country, but, again, serving and retired army officers predominated. Younger members of the Pyithu Hluttaw tended to be civilians and over time one could see developing a greater role for civilians in the lower ranks of the party structure.

The Burmese Socialist Program party—the "party which leads the state," in the words of the constitution—had over 2,200,000 full and candidate members by January 1985. Another 1,200,000 persons were classified as "friends of the party." The party had a variety of subordinate organizations including the *Lansin* youth, veterans, peasants, workers and women's governing bodies at all levels of society. Almost all members of the armed forces are members of the party. The party's ideology—enunciated in 1962 as "the Burmese Way to Socialism" and given philosophical justification in a 1963 document entitled *The System of Correlation of Man and His Environment*—is a blending of socialist analysis and Buddhist epistemology.

The 1974 constitution—by providing for a role for elected people's councils at the village, urban ward and township levels—gave local communities a greater say in the implementation of government policies than was the case under the old order. Council members were expected to implement government policies after adjusting them to meet local conditions. They had a significant role not only in managing agricultural production but also in controlling the registration and management of the local community. The system of worker and immigration controls provided the state with a set of complex bureaucratic regulations that drew everyone into their net.

Between the center and the lowest level of political organization, the state and divisional administrative agencies served as conduits of central policy to the townships and villages. At this level there was a significant overlap of membership among the regional military command, the elected people's council, and the state and divisional BSPP organization. This system of overlap provided an intricate set of control mechanisms that ensured not only coordination of military, economic, and political policy but also the reliability of personnel.

THE POLITICAL CRISIS OF 1988

Despite attempts to restructure the polity since 1962, the chairman of the Burmese Socialist Program party, Ne Win, was forced to conclude by August 1987 that the attempt to turn Myanmar into a prosperous, one-party state had failed. By that time, the country's foreign debts had become unmanageable, farmers were not delivering their crops to the state, exports had collapsed and political malaise was widespread. In a major speech at that time, Ne Win called for a revamping of the economic and social order, perhaps even constitutional changes. Despite the partial freeing of some domestic trade, including that in grains and pulses, little reform ensued despite prodding. In the meantime, public distrust and cynicism grew, especially after the government declared a large proportion of the country's

656

currency as illegal tender without compensation. Though probably intended to drive wealth out of the hands of black marketeers and smugglers, demonetization caused the poor to suffer most.

In July 1988, Ne Win resigned as chairman of the ruling party and proposed a referendum on the restoration of multiparty democracy. The Party Central Committee rejected the reestablishment of more open politics but did endorse economic liberalization. Ne Win's successor, Gen. Sein Lwin, then faced widespread urban demonstrations, paralyzing the cities as students and others demanded a "return" to democracy and an improvement in economic conditions. After 18 days of rule during which reportedly several thousand people were killed by troops, Sein Lwin resigned and was replaced by another leader, a civilian, Dr. Maung Maung. As chairman of the BSPP, Maung Maung faced the same distrust that his predecessors faced. Despite making concessions to the demonstrators, he was unable to meet their demands for the appointment of an interim government and the holding of elections, although these were promised, and much of the structure of the one-party state was formally dismantled.

The continuing unrest led the army to respond with a military coup on September 18, 1988. The army coup group, called the Council for the Restoration of Law and Order in the State, remained loyal to Ne Win and the leadership of the old regime and were therefore no more trusted than their predecessors had been. However, their obvious display of force and their unwillingness to tolerate continued protests led to a partial return to normality in the cities. The army continued to promise that elections would be held. In the meantime, the disunity that plagued Myanmar's democratic politics in the 1950s returned. By the end of 1988, more than 200 political parties had registered with the government. While waiting for conditions to permit the holding of elections, the army government carried out a number of reforms, including the dismantling of the various government bodies set up under the 1974 constitution, and reverted to an administrative pattern similar to that of the Revolutionary Council government of 1962 to 1974. Whether or not a civilian government comes to power after any further elections, the military will remain the central political institution in Myanmar for the foreseeable future.

THE ECONOMY

Capitalism, in the minds of many older Burmese, is identified with imperialism and colonialism as well as with the Buddhist sins of greed and covetousness. Now, for many younger Burmese, socialism has an equally odious reputation. Since independence all Burmese politicians have espoused socialism in one form or another. The mixed economy of the 1950s gave way in the 1960s to direct state management and this has continued until the present. However, within this policy, there have been significant adjustments over the years. During the 1960s any foreign involvement was largely avoided and the country received little foreign economic assistance and no foreign investment. By the early 1970s the consequences of this autarkic policy had led to declining rates of growth as the state had not been able to amass sufficient capital for investment purposes. In the mid-1970s the government became more open to foreign borrowing and the receipt of foreign aid. By the mid-1980s, Myanmar had become the fourth largest recipient of Japanese development aid, West Germany had become the country's second most important bilateral aid donor and the United States had even begun a small aid program in support of rural health care, a project that the Burmese government had given high priority to since independence. The Asian Development Bank, the U.N. Development Program and other multilateral aid agencies also become involved in support for Myanmar's development effort from the mid-1970s.

The consequences of increased borrowing led to a significant debt-service problem by the mid-1980s. In 1987, Myanmar's outstanding foreign debt was insignificant by international standards, standing a little over U.S.$3 billion. However, because its international earnings were reduced as a result of declines in the world prices of its major exports (including rice, teak and minerals) and the Japanese yen and German mark had risen against the United States dollar, the country was forced to spend over 50 percent of its annual foreign earnings to pay its foreign debt. The foreign exchange left after servicing the foreign debt was devoted to the purchase of military equipment for the army in its battles with the separatists along the borders. The result was, again, declining rates of economic growth and an inability to import many necessary industrial and consumer goods. In 1987, Myanmar applied for U.N. recognized status as a "least developed country," allowing it to receive aid on the most favorable of terms. Meanwhile, the army managed to close down some of the smuggling gates along the Thai border. This led to a shortage of consumer goods fueling inflation that began to reach 25 percent or more per year by the end of 1987.

Faced with these growing economic problems, the government was forced to rethink its economic policies. In August 1987 it was announced that the state monopoly on the domestic trading of rice and other basic consumer items was to be lifted, thus allowing a legal private market to develop. This was followed in January 1988 by a decision to allow foreign trade in rice to revert to the private sector. These policies were accompanied by others which limited their liberalizing effect. Taxes were to be collected in kind rather than in cash, allowing the government to maintain a pool of rice and other commodities for its own use in distribution and trade; and in August 1987 large-denomination bank notes were demonetized, thus wiping out the savings of many who did not trust the banks. When demonetization had been conducted twice before, once as recently as 1985, individuals were given compensation but this time they were not. While demonetization had the effect of undermining the profits of black marketeers, many of whom were involved in the separatist movements, it also badly affected the financial resources of the poor.

After years of speculation as to whether Myanmar would open its economy to more foreign trade and perhaps even investment, this has now happened. One joint venture in heavy-metals work was established in the early 1980s with a state-owned German firm that had been involved with the heavy-industries ministry for some time in the production of weapons, but no other moves along these lines were announced until 1989. Many foreign firms and governments look to Myanmar as a possible area of operation, given the country's skilled population and rich and varied natural resources.

Since independence, the country has generally pursued a neutralist foreign policy. It has never allowed the location of foreign bases upon its soil, after the withdrawal of the British, and it has avoided any form of alliance with other governments, either within the region or outside. The reasons for this neutralist foreign policy can be found in both the country's geographic position and its internal politics. During the civil war in the late 1940s and early 1950s, the government was accused by its Communist opponents of being too closely allied with the so-called "Anglo-American capitalist bloc" while avoiding good relations with the Soviet Union and China. At the same time, the Karen and other separatist rebels were seeking to gain the support of Britain and other countries for their movement. Thailand, a historical rival, was becoming increasingly aligned with the United States, and facilitating the operation of antigovernment, anticommunist groups along their mutual border. Also, the civilian leaders of the government at this time were ideologically and personally attracted to the ideas of Jawaharlal Nehru, the leader of neutralist India.

At the height of the civil war, about 1949–50, Chinese Nationalist troops (KMT), escaping the Chinese Communist revolution in Yunnan Province, crossed the border into the Shan State. There they intended to set up bases from which to attack the Communist government in the hope of restoring the defeated KMT to power. They were supported in this not only by the KMT government, now located on Taiwan, but also through the auspices of the U.S. Central Intelligence Agency. The KMT intervention brought Myanmar face to face, not only with the power of Communist China, but also with the early cold-war antagonisms of the United States and China. Being unable to dislodge the KMT militarily and fearing a possible Chinese Communist attack to drive the KMT out, Myanmar turned to the United Nations in the hope of having the foreign troops removed through international pressure. This resulted in certain U.N. resolutions condemning the presence of foreign forces, and eventually some KMT troops were evacuated. The country was able to maintain good relations with China but became increasingly distrustful of Thailand and the United States as a result of the experience. In the meantime, the remaining KMT troops settled in the area and became the heart of the continuing drug smuggling operations of the region.

During the final years of civilian government under the AFPFL government of Prime Minister U Nu, the country played a reasonably active role in the Non-Aligned Movement (NAM) of which it was a founder member. At the 1955 Asian-African Conference in Bandung, and subsequently, Myanmar played a role in trying to alleviate the tensions between the East and the West in the cold war, but with little success. After the military took power in 1962, Myanmar was less active in world affairs, while continuing to rely on the United Nations as a main prop for its international position. The government has attempted to play an active role only in those international conflicts that have directly affected security. Myanmar attended the 1962 conference in Sri Lanka, which was held in an effort to end the Sino-Indian border war, as well as the 1962 Geneva conference, which attempted to end the civil war in Laos. During the various international conflicts in Vietnam and Cambodia since then, Myanmar has been willing to allow its facilities to be used as a neutral venue for international negotiations.

Myanmar's close relations with the NAM ended in 1979 when, at the Havana conference, it announced that it would withdraw from the movement if the increasingly anti-Western rhetoric of the conference, under the leadership of obviously aligned countries such as Cuba and Libya, did not cease. Drawing attention to the fact that most of the countries in the NAM—such as Cuba, the Philippines, Singapore and others—were effectively aligned with either the United States or the Soviet Union, Myanmar called for a radical restructuring of the movement. When that did not occur, the country withdrew, earning praise from various sources, including China, for its principled action.

Myanmar's neutrality is crucial to the security of its neighbors, especially China, India, and Thailand. Its borders with Laos and Bangladesh are less strategically important, though shots were fired in 1978 when the border with Bangladesh became unclear. Numerous people who had fled the civil war in Bangladesh settled in Myanmar. When local Burmese officials began to inspect their documents to see whether they were legal residents, border chaos ensued. This matter was settled when, after negotiations between the two governments, the border was redemarcated and the U.N. High Commissioner for Refugees organized a major resettlement program in Myanmar. In general, it can be said that while wooed by other governments, the country has maintained its neutrality as the quiet hub around which the serious conflicts of Asian international politics revolve.

FURTHER READING

Aung-Thwin, Michael. *Pagan: The Origins of Modern Burma.* Honolulu: University of Hawaii Press, 1985.

Butwell, Richard A. *U Nu of Burma.* 2nd ed. Stanford, California: Stanford University Press, 1969.

Cady, John Frank. *A History of Modern Burma.* Ithaca, New York, and London: Cornell University Press, 1960.

Hla Pe. *Burma: Literature, Historiography, Scholarship, Language, Life and Buddhism.* Singapore: Institute of Southeast Asian Studies, 1985.

Lieberman, Victor B. *Burmese Administrative Cycles: Anarchy and Conquest c. 1580–1760.* Princeton, New Jersey: Princeton University Press, 1984.

Maung Maung, U. *Burma and General Ne Win.* New York: Asia Publishing House, 1969.

Nu, U. *U Nu, Saturday's Son.* New Haven, Connecticut: Yale University Press, 1975.

Silverstein, Josef. *Burma: Military Rule and the Politics of Stagnation.* Ithaca, New York: Cornell University Press, 1977.

Smith, Donald Eugene. *Religion and Politics in Burma.* Princeton, New Jersey: Princeton University Press, 1965.

Steinberg, David I. *Burma's Road Toward Development: Growth and Ideology Under Military Rule.* Boulder, Colorado: Westview Press, 1981.

Taylor, Robert H. *The State in Burma.* London: C. Hurst; Honolulu: University of Hawaii Press, 1987.

NEPAL AND BHUTAN

RICHARD BURGHART

NEPAL and Bhutan are two mountainous kingdoms situated on the southern flank of the Himalaya, bordered on the east, south and west by the Republic of India and on the north by the People's Republic of China. Both kingdoms are intersected by three distinctly different ecological bands. The high Himalaya, perpetually covered by snow, rise to a height of 26,248 ft/8,000 m., deflecting east and west the northward movement of monsoon clouds, and turning the Tibetan hinterland, behind the mountains, into a rocky, arid plateau. The second ecological band is an expanse of hills and valleys, called the Mahabharat range, and the lesser Siwalik foothills, which range from 11,483 down to 3,281 ft/3,500 to 1,000 m. in altitude. This is a temperate region of terraced farming, with maize grown on the upper slopes and wet rice lower down, close to the valley floor. The third ecological zone is the Tarai, a low, flat subtropical stretch of land around 328 ft/100 m. above sea level that extends imperceptibly into the Ganges basin in the case of Nepal and to the Brahmaputra in the case of Bhutan. Each of these ecological bands has been settled by different peoples, deriving their livelihood within the constraints of their natural environment. Despite their relative smallness, there are few countries in the world that can rival Nepal and Bhutan in their cultural and natural diversity.

LAND AND PEOPLE

Although the high Himalayan peaks and ridges demarcate the northern political boundary of Nepal and Bhutan, the upper Himalayan watershed is a cultural extension of Tibet, and of its particular form of Buddhism. The Sanskrit word for Tibet is *Bhot;* the high Himalaya, on the southern periphery of Tibet, are called *Bhotant,* literally the "appendage of *Bhot.*" The name Bhutan is merely the English corruption of the Sanskrit term, which the British localized in present day Bhutan. The Tibetan-like peoples of the region, called Bhotiyas, live in clustered villages in the high alpine valleys from which they gain their names: the Dolpas (Dolpa plateau), Lopas (Mustang valley), Manangba (Marsyandi valley), Sherpas (Solu-Khumbu valley) and Lhomi (upper Arun valley). The people most known in the West are the Sherpas, at the base of Mount Everest, who claim an international reputation as guides and porters on mountaineering expeditions. The harsh ecological conditions above 9,843 ft/3,000 m. in altitude have forced the Bhotiyas to derive their livelihood by cultivating barley and root vegetables, herding yaks and goats, weaving woolen clothes and blankets, and carrying out trans-Himalayan trade. They practice polyandrous marriage, whereby a woman has several husbands, usually a man and his younger brothers. Polyandrous households are adapted to the constraints of the alpine economy, in which typically one man works the fields in the short growing season while his brother takes the yaks and goats to pasture in the upper valleys. Meanwhile another brother might engage in long-distance trade, the movement of which is defined by the seasons. The passes in the north are closed by snow in the winter and the routes in the south by fear of malaria in the summer. Given the seasonal movements of men, polyandry enables the family to organize production in such a way that there is always one man at home. The social implication of polyandry, however, is the surplus of unmarried women, obliged to live out their lives in Buddhist nunneries.

Recent political changes have affected the lives of the Bhotiyas. From the perspective of Lhasa, with its famous monasteries and libraries, the people of the high Himalaya were rustics living on the periphery of Tibet. With the Chinese administration of Tibet and the flight of the court of the Dalai Lama in 1959, the southern periphery of Tibet witnessed the arrival of Buddhist monks and the growth of local monasteries. Meanwhile security of the Sino-Nepalese frontier became a problem. The traditional trans-Himalayan trade, exchanging salt from Tibet for rice from the Himalayan foothills, was restricted. Some traders suffered from these changes; others took to smuggling, where the stakes are higher and the rewards and risks greater. For some people, like the Sherpas, whose villages are not too near the border passes, tourism has transformed the local economy. Inns, porterage services and curio shops now await the trekker and contribute to Nepal's foreign exchange.

At the lower and southernmost ecological band, the Tarai forms a 20-mile/32-km.-wide strip of land 328 to 984 ft/100 m. to 300 m. above sea level at the base of the Siwalik foothills. In the past the sloping, gravelly land, close to the hills, was forested, but about 5 miles/8 km. south from the hills the gravel turns to alluvial silt. The region is the traditional home of various Indo-Aryan peoples, speaking the same regional languages of Avadhi, Bhojpuri and Maithili as do related groups in the adjoining Indian states of Uttar Pradesh, Bihar and West Bengal. These people are largely Hindu, with smaller concentrations of Muslims, and caste is observed in the organization of commensal and connubial relations. Agriculture is the mainstay of the economy. The alluvial soil is fertile, and the Himalayan streams often bring an ample supply of water to the fields without flooding the plain with such devastating effect as occurs lower down in the Gangetic plain. Tarai people live in clustered villages, surrounded by cultivated plots of land, mango orchards and bamboo groves. The plots are separated by dikes that retain sufficient surface water for the planting and transplanting of paddy. Cultivation is by bullock-drawn plow or, on larger farms, by tractor. From many plots two crops of paddy (an early and a late one) are cultivated. Wheat is grown in the winter, with some pulses on the dikes and others between the wheat, so that after the wheat the pulses grow up between the wheat stumps and are harvested as well. Over the last several centuries the control of this fertile lowland region has been central to the political economy of both Nepal and Bhutan. Despite the fact that the Tarai comprises only 17 percent of the landmass and 31 percent of the population of Nepal, it contributes approximately 60 percent of the GNP and 75 percent of the national revenue.

The region of the Mahabharat range and the inner Himalayan valleys is home to a number of autochthonous tribes, such as the Tharu and Dhangar. More important, it has become the sociohistorical meeting place of two types of people: Hindus of Indo-Aryan origin, roughly similar in cultural background to the Hindus of the Tarai; and Buddhists of Tibeto-Burman origin, roughly similar in cultural and religious background to the peoples of the high Himalaya.

The largest ethnic group in the hills is the Indo-Aryan people, whose mother tongue is Nepali. They compromise 51 percent of the citizenry of Nepal (the Nepalese royal family is also Nepali in origin). Nepali speakers inhabit the arable land of the Mahabharat range, where they dig out terraces from the hillsides and, wherever possible, irrigate their terraces with the water drawn from mountain streams higher up the valley. Most terraced plots are inaccessible to the plow and cultivation is by hoe. Their villages, unlike the clustered ones of the Tarai and the high Himalaya, are often dispersed across a mountain ridge or down the valley side. The people are largely Hindu. Caste relations are observed, with the majority of the population being among the two highest castes—the Brahmans and the warriors (Chetri). Less numerous are the service and artisan castes—the tailors (Damai), blacksmiths (Kami) and cobblers (Sarki), all of whom are so-called Untouchables (Harijans).

Despite their linguistic homogeneity, the Nepali people are an admixture of regionally diverse groups, some claiming to have originated in western India and others to be autochthonous Hindus of the Himalaya. It is likely that some of their number are also made up of Tibeto-Burman elements fully assimilated and integrated into Indo-Aryan Nepali society. Regardless of their origins, over the last several centuries there has been a gradual movement of Nepali speakers from the west into eastern Nepal, West Bengal, Sikkim, Bhutan, Assam and Burma. The presence of migrant Nepalis, sometimes called Gorkhalis, is one of the main ethnic problems of northeastern India. From the 1970s they have been implicated in civil disturbances and constitutional rearrangements in Sikkim, and driven from Assam by the student-led nativist movement. They have agitated for separate statehood in West Bengal and have become a source of political concern for Bhutan.

In the course of this eastward movement, Nepali speakers have encountered several Tibeto-Burman peoples, many of whom trace their legendary history back to Tibet. The best-known of these are the Newars, who for many centuries made their home in the so-called Nepal valley. This valley, encircled by mountains, is an ancient lake bed dominated by the three

664

towns of Kathmandu, Patan and Bhaktapur (Bhadgaon), from which the Malla dynasty ruled between the 13th and 18th centuries. The Nepal valley, like the Kashmir valley, supported one of the great civilizations of the Himalaya. The Newars are known for their distinctive pagoda architecture, their highly skilled artisans, their urban-based agricultural caste and their merchants who worked the trans-Himalayan trade. Scattered across the southern flank of the Himalaya are other Tibeto-Burman—speaking peoples, including the Thakalis (Kali Gandaki valley), Tamangs (central Nepal), Chepang (central Nepal), Gurungs (west-central Nepal around Pokhara) and Rai and Limbu (eastern Nepal). It was from the last three Tibeto-Burman tribes, together with the Nepali people, that the British recruited soldiers into the famous Gurkha regiments of the British and Indian armies.

THE KINGDOM OF NEPAL

The history of modern Nepal conventionally begins with Prithvi Narayan Shah, king of Gorkha, who ruled from 1742 to 1774. At that time Gorkha was a small Himalayan state—situated some 50 miles/80 km. west of Kathmandu—that interacted politically in the League of Twenty-four Kingdoms in the Gandaki watershed of the central Himalaya. From Prithvi Narayan's accession to the throne in 1742 until 1814, the Shah dynasty by marriage, diplomacy and conquest succeeded in annexing to Gorkha not only the member states of the League of Twenty-four Kingdoms but also the kingdoms and tribal peoples of the southern flank of the Himalaya from Sikkim in the east to Kangra (present-day Himachal Pradesh, India) in the west. The Gorkha military organization relied upon the availability of soldiers and porters from Nepali and Tibeto-Burman peoples of the hills, and upon the income from agricultural revenue in the Tarai. Upon conquering the Nepal valley, Prithvi Narayan carried his throne across the hills from Gorkha and set it up in the palace of the deposed Newar ruler of Kathmandu. He continued, however, to refer to his territory as the Kingdom of Gorkha; it was only the East India Company, and later the government of British India, that—by virtue of the Gorkha rulers being in the Nepal valley—referred to the polity as the Kingdom of Nepal. The difference in appellation remained until the 1930s.

The geopolitical forces of the Himalayan region can be readily appreciated by considering the territorial pattern of the Shah conquests—east and west across the Mahabharat range and the adjoining Himalayan valleys and Tarai lowlands. Attempts to overstep this boundary were resisted by the Tibetans in the north and the plains rulers in the south. Eventually, even the extent of the east-west movement alarmed the East India Company, for the Gorkhalis were coming into control of all the major trans-Himalayan trade routes into Tibet, which the company saw as an important potential commercial market. The rival interests of the company and the Gorkha rulers eventually drew them into armed conflict. After a number of setbacks, the East India Company gained the upper hand, reducing the Kingdom of Gorkha (Nepal) to more or less its present-day boundaries. A cessation of hostilities was signed in 1815, and for the next several decades

665

the Shah rulers at Kathmandu—apprehensive of any relations with the East India Company—sought to preserve their political autonomy by isolating their kingdom from the world.

The next major political change in Nepal took place in 1846, with the rise of the Rana family. Mutual intrigue and suspicion between rival queens and their associated courtiers kindled a violent dispute, known as the Kot Massacre, in which 31 nobles were murdered, 26 took flight and another 26 were subsequently banished from the kingdom. The beneficiary of this turmoil was Jang Bahadur Kunwar, who, the morning after the massacre, was appointed to the posts of prime minister at the court and commander in chief of the Gorkha army. Over the next 10 years Jang Bahadur Kunwar transformed the political structure of the kingdom. In his first few months he played one faction of the court against the other in order to eliminate the influence of his rivals. He forced the abdication of King Rajendra and the succession of his son, Surendra, still a minor. In 1849 he had his caste status raised to that of Rana, equivalent in rank to the royal family. This entitled the prime minister to perpetuate his influence by arranging the marriage of his children with those of the king so that their grandchildren would sit on the throne. With his global outlook, Jang Bahadur gained the respect of the British as a "modern" ruler, and he became the first Hindu ruler to cross the Black Sea and visit Europe. In 1857 Jang Bahadur Rana forced King Surendra to renounce all civil, military and judicial authority and to invest the powers of state in the prime ministership, to be passed down by collateral succession in the Rana family. The king of Nepal became a mere head of state, the symbol of Nepalese political autonomy. Also in that year neighborly relations were established with Great Britain when Jang Bahadur offered Gurkha soldiers to the East India Company to help put down the Sepoy Mutiny in India. Thus began a period in which the Ranas sought to guarantee the political autonomy of their country and the perpetuation of their regime by being serviceable to the British, a policy that worked until the collapse of colonial rule in India.

For a 105-year period, rulership in Nepal remained a prerogative of the Rana family. Occasionally Jang Bahadur's younger brothers, cousins, sons and nephews tried to move ahead of others in the line of succession, but their disputes—the coups d'etat and attempted coups—were settled in a family manner by assassination and exile. These did not cause the Ranas to lose their collective grip on the country. By the mid-20th century, however, criticism of the Ranas had increased at home; and the British departure from India meant that the Ranas could no longer look to India for support of their system of rule. In short, Rana rule had become an anachronism, and in the winter of 1950–51 they were deposed.

Three forces contributed to the overthrow of the Ranas. First, there was considerable disunity within the Rana family itself. The principle of collateral succession to the prime ministership increased the number of potential rulers, who had to patiently await their turn. Over the generations (three since Jang Bahadur), the Rana family had become so large that distinctions were created between A, B, and C class Ranas in their right to advance to high office. Only A class Ranas could rise to the highest rank, that of prime minister. C class Ranas, the offspring of secondary Rana marriages, resented their exclusion from high office. The second force for change was the Nepalese intelligentsia. Often wealthy and of high caste, many had been educated in British India, or at least had traveled in India, where they had come under the influence of ideas similar to those that inspired the Indian freedom movement. But whereas the Indians wanted democracy and an end to foreign rule, the Nepalese wanted constitutional democracy and an end to Rana rule. They formed a political party in exile, called the Praja Panchayat party, to work toward constitutional democracy in Nepal. In 1949 in Calcutta they merged with the Nepal Prajatantrik party, founded by the C class Rana Subvarna Shamsher, to form the Nepali Congress party (NCP). The third force for change was the royal family, which had grown increasingly restive under the restrictions placed upon them by the suspicious Ranas. Discontent eventually provoked King Tribhuvan Vir Vikram Shah to flee his palace in November 1950 and seek refuge in the Indian embassy at Kathmandu. The Nepalese people were shocked by the king's plight and openly sympathized with him. A few days later the NCP crossed into Nepal and after several days of combat with the Gurkha army captured the border towns of the eastern Tarai. Meanwhile, the king fled to Delhi. Lacking both external and internal support, Mohan Shamsher—the last Rana prime minister—was obliged to travel to Delhi and negotiate with the king and the NCP a new political order for the kingdom. On January 10, 1951, an agreement was signed by the various parties calling for amnesty for all political prisoners, the appointment of an interim government supervised by the king and an election of the members of a constituent assembly no later than 1952 in order to draft a constitution for the new parliamentary government. Thus on that date, in its 105th year of rule, the Rana regime was dissolved.

The interim government comprised the members of the former Rana government and the leaders of the NCP under the general supervision of the king. During the years that followed the formation of the tripartite interim government, each participant sought as much to eliminate their comembers from the government as to direct the political future of the kingdom. Of the three competitors, the king, by playing the Ranas off against the NCP, was able to weaken the influence of his rivals and gain the upper hand in ruling the kingdom. Under the Ranas, the post of commander in chief was held by the prime minister. With the support of the NCP, the king weakened Rana power by assuming the post of commander in chief of the Gurkha army. the king felt obliged to appoint an NCP man to the prime ministership but was reluctant to appoint the party leader, B. P. Koirala, for fear that his policies might be too radical. So King Tribhuvan appointed instead another NCP member, M. P. Koirala. The appointment split the NCP into two factions, one centered around the popular party leader and the other centered around the parliamentary party leader. The message of political reform, economic development and social justice, which had inspired those who overthrew the Rana regime, became lost in the cross fire of parliamentary factional politics. The sole beneficiary of the parliamentary wrangling was the king, who claimed to be the only national leader committed wholeheartedly to the progress and welfare of the people.

Throughout the 1950s the Ranas lost power as a family, although some gained individually in support of the king's consolidation of power. Meanwhile Mahendra, who succeeded to the throne in 1955, became wary of parliamentary politicians; at times he tried to circumvent parliament; at other times he criticized it for its ineffectiveness in dealing with the country's urgent problems. The NCP, realizing that it could not outmaneuver the king under present governmental arrangements, decided to seek popular support for sovereignty to be invested in parliament. Fearful for his position, King Mahendra committed himself to holding an election in 1959. This was the first election since the overthrow of the Ranas; indeed it was Nepal's first election by popular mandate. The NCP, with 37.7 percent of the popular vote and 68 percent of seats in the parliament, won and was invited to form the government. This experiment in parliamentary democracy, however, proved to be short-lived. One year later King Mahendra accused the NCP of mismanaging the affairs of state and he dissolved the government.

Two years went by while Mahendra prepared a new constitution for Nepal whose form was both traditionally legitimate and appropriate for Nepalese conditions. Mahendra believed that political parties based on the European model though suitable for the European social conditions in which they historically developed, were unsuitable for Nepal, where they only served to promote factionalism and national disintegration. Hence the king outlawed political parties in the new constitution. Sovereignty was invested in the royal dynasty, but the king was to be advised in his rule by a partyless elected council of respected citizens. Membership in the council, called Panchayat, was by universal suffrage. Mahendra asserted that the Panchayat system was a traditional Hindu form of government and therefore appropriate for Nepalese society. Lacking legality, the members of the NCP were obliged to go underground or head for exile.

King Mahendra and his son and successor, Birendra, ruled from the throne but used the national Panchayat as a nonbinding advisory body that served to ratify royal decisions. Throughout the 1970s minor changes were made in the Panchayat system, but there was always some doubt about its legitimacy, for the king had never put it to a popular test. Meanwhile, the Communist party (including its various offshoots and factions) began to emerge as an important underground party gaining support from radical peasants and workers impatient with both Congress party and royalist policies. In a bold gamble, King Birendra in 1979 offered to put the Panchayat system to the test of a national referendum. The NCP took up the challenge and an intense campaign ensued between the advocates of partyless democracy and those of multiparty democracy. The referendum, held in May 1980, showed a narrow 54.7 percent win for the partyless model. The king had gained majority favor for panchayat democracy.

Given the illegality of much organized political activity in Nepal, it is difficult to interpret the results of the referendum. Yet local accounts suggest that the fight was even closer than this. The Communists, fearing their NCP rivals as much as the king, knew that they were less popular than the NCP and concluded that they needed another 20 years to overtake the Congress party and to challenge the king. Fearing that the referendum might be won by a popular party, they preferred to support the king, for that would forestall the NCP and yet, they believed, aggravate conditions in the country, paving the way to their coming power. Hence they encouraged their supporters to vote for the king. Even if Communist support in the kingdom had been only 5 percent of the vote (there are no firm estimates), that would have been a sufficient margin to swing the referendum. If so, that would also confirm the earlier diagnosis. In the political arena of modern Nepal as long as the king has two groups in opposition—whether it be the Ranas and the NCP in the 1950s or the Congress and Communist parties in the 1980s—he is able to perpetuate his rule.

THE KINGDOM OF BHUTAN

In contrast with Nepal, Bhutan is a Buddhist kingdom, in which the ruling family traces its origins back to Tibet. Buddhism was introduced to Bhutan as early as the middle of the 8th century A.D. with the arrival of monks from northern India, but it was not until the 12th century that the Buddhist religious traditions of modern Bhutan were established. At that time Tibetan lamas, primarily of the Red Hat sect, arrived in Bhutan and established monasteries in which their theological rivalries subsequently became enmeshed in the territorial rivalries of local chieftains. These rivalries were eventually nullified by Shabdrung Ngawang Namgyal, who entered Bhutan in 1616, subdued the local chiefs and then defended the united country from repeated Tibetan incursions.

Shabdrung Ngawang Namgyal ruled Bhutan for 35 years, setting up, in the process, a political system that lasted until the early 20th century. He took on himself the Buddhist title of dharma raja (literally, king of justice), and occupied himself with all spiritual and temporal matters, including the spiritual welfare of the realm, the organization of monasteries, command of the army, adjudication of justice and the receipt of revenue. The divine nature of the dharma raja was indicated by his particular mode of succession: reincarnation. Second in command, elected by the district governors, was the deb raja, who managed the kingdom by overseeing the collection of revenue and arranging its distribution in state expenditure. The office of dharma raja, as the ecclesiastical head of the realm, sent clear signals to the Dalai Lama of Tibet of Bhutanese political autonomy; but the division of authority between the dharma raja and the deb raja created political conflicts within Bhutan that persisted into the 20th century. At times the deb raja tried to extend his authority. By the early 18th century the dharma raja occupied himself primarily with spiritual affairs—temporal power and authority coming to reside in the deb raja. With temporal authority exercised by the deb raja, conflict surfaced between rival district governors, each trying to put his man in office. The deb raja himself eventually became a figurehead for whoever was the most powerful governor at the time of election. These internal disputes not only weakened the country; they also served as an invitation to the Tibetans, seeking any pretext to intervene.

Meanwhile, on its southern border Bhutan came into conflict with the East India Company for more or less the same reasons that Nepal did. Rivals in Cooch Behar in Bengal were subject to Bhutanese raids in the early 18th century. The ruler of Cooch Behar appealed to the East India Company to come to his aid, which the company did, thinking both to extend its influence to eastern India as well as to open trade with Tibet and China, for which Bhutan stood in the way. The company drove Bhutan from Cooch Behar and extended its influence into Assam, which it took over in 1826. In administering Assam, the British shared a frontier with Bhutan which collected revenue from the fertile lowland region, the Duars Plain, in the southern part of the realm. Part of this territory was claimed outright by Bhutan, and part was held in the name of the Assamese rulers (and now the company) on whose land the Bhutanese were merely revenue collectors. Claims and counterclaims over revenue collection led to defaults in payments and punitive raids, which culminated in the Anglo-Bhutanese war of 1864. The conflict was settled one year later with the cession of part of the Duars Plain to the British on payment of an annual allowance to the Bhutanese king. One significant clause of the peace treaty obliged Bhutan in the future to refer its disputes with neighbors to the British government.

The humiliation of the treaty sparked off a civil war in Bhutan in which one governor, Tongsa Penlop, emerged the most powerful person. In 1885 he consolidated his position by appointing his own man to the post of deb raja, but in doing so, he forced the deb raja to abdicate all powers of state in his favor. Upon the death of the deb raja in 1907, Tongsa Penlop was elected by the governors as hereditary ruler of Bhutan and was accorded precedence over the dharma raja, a constitutional change that seemed sensible to the British. Throughout this period the Penlop had also sought to establish friendly relations with India, and in 1910 the Treaty of Punakha was signed according to the terms of which the British pledged noninterference in Bhutanese internal affairs on condition that Bhutan defer to Britain's advice on external affairs.

The departure of the British from India did not change the terms of the treaty, which remain to this day. Bhutan is an independent state, yet it is bound by treaty to accede to India on matters of foreign policy. The departure of the British, together with the direct Chinese administration of Tibet, did, however, bring about further institutional changes in Bhutan. First, the post of dharma raja lapsed. The occupant of the post never fully accepted his loss of precedence to the new raja, and in 1926 he tried to intervene in the succession of Tongsa Penlop in order to regain his influence. While the hereditary ruler turned to Britain, and later India, for support, the dharma raja turned to Tibet. This, however, brought Tibet into conflict with the British, who oversaw Bhutan's external affairs. Again in 1952, two years after the death of the last dharma raja, Tibetan monks intervened, arriving in Bhutan in search of the dharma raja's reincarnation. Their arrival, however, was taken as an affront to Bhutanese autonomy, and they were dispatched from the kingdom. Since 1950 there has been no acknowledged reincarnation of the dharma raja, and for all intents and purposes the post has lapsed. The second major change has been the administrative reform of the kingdom. With the advice and cooperation of Indian lawyers and planners, an advisory National Assembly was constituted, new judicial procedures were established and administrative offices were set up to bring about the development of the country. In 1971 modern Bhutan entered the international community of states with its admission to the United Nations.

While the royal families of Nepal and Bhutan stem from lineages of considerable antiquity, both kingdoms gained their present-day form as recently as within the last two centuries in the context of changing geopolitical relations in the Himalaya. Central to this geopolitical context is the fact that for many years the Himalaya have been a border region situated between two great imperial powers: the rulers of the Ganges basin—whether they were native Indian rulers, Moghul rulers, British India or the Republic of India—and the rulers of the Tibetan plateau—the Dalai Lama of Tibet, the Chinese emperor or the People's Republic of China. Neither of these powers has ever been able to command the Himalayan region; rather, they have had to work their influence on the hill rulers. If the local rulers became overly ambitious and tried to extend their realms outward to the Gangetic plains or the Tibetan plateau, expeditionary forces were mounted to contain them within the hills. The hill rulers gained some measure of autonomy by virtue of their remoteness. More important, they have sought some measure of neutrality in their external affairs. This is particularly the case with Nepal, which exercises sovereignty in foreign affairs. Nepal's neutrality is not the Swiss form, whereby the state avoids formal political and economic ties with all superpowers; rather, neutrality is established by the state contracting nonpolitical relations with all regional and global powers. Hence Nepal accepts aid from all sources but carefully balances source and amount: Indian aid with Chinese, American aid with Soviet, and so on.

Nepal's external policy of neutrality is complemented by an internal policy designed to legitimate political autonomy with reference to its cultural uniqueness. This has entailed accentuating two aspects of Nepal's identity: first, Nepal is the world's only Hindu kingdom; and second, it is the nation-state of the Nepalese people. In this latter respect Nepal has embarked since the 1960s on a cultural policy in terms of which the language and way of life of the majority Nepali-speaking people have come to stand for the popular culture of all Nepalese citizens. All government employees, regardless of their ethnic origin, must wear Nepali dress. Nepali has been declared the national language and the medium of instruction in all public schools. The assertion of a common cultural identity is aimed at India and China, but runs the risk of exacerbating ethnic tensions within the kingdom, as minority groups find their traditional way of life deprived of public legitimacy.

Both Nepal and Bhutan are small countries, seeking to preserve their

671

independence in a subcontinent dominated by powerful neighbors. The resources of both countries are modest: Some (e.g., hydroelectric power) are underdeveloped; others are deteriorating (e.g., deforestation, soil erosion and flooding). Literacy, health and economic conditions are improving, yet the disparities are considerable when compared either with those of other nations or with those of the Nepalese and Bhutanese elites. In the past, the ability of the state to improve the condition of its subjects was not tied up with questions of its legitimacy. That, however, has changed. Underdevelopment is now a "problem," for which external aid and the internal redistribution of resources is the solution. To deal with this problem necessarily creates conflicts in which the government must balance the interests of diverse groups. To the outside world the rulers of Nepal and Bhutan appear as symbols of national sovereignty, but within their countries the two rulers are more than mere symbols; they wield all powers of state. These external and internal worlds are linked, and the perpetuation of their authority, either as symbol or fact, is very much bound up with how intelligently the two kings can deal with internal conflicts while being ever mindful that signs of internal discord may attract the unwanted attention of more powerful neighbors.

FURTHER READING

Bista, Dor Bahadur. *People of Nepal.* 2nd ed. Kathmandu: Ratna Pustak Bhandar, 1972.
Chauhan, R. S. *The Political Development in Nepal: 1950–1970.* New Delhi: Associated Publishing House, 1971.
Fürer-Haimendorf, Christoph von. *Himalayan Traders: Life in Highland Nepal.* London: John Murray, 1975.
Gaige, Frederick H. *Regionalism and National Unity in Nepal.* Berkeley: University of California Press, 1975.
Joshi, B. L. and Rose, E. *Democratic Innovations in Nepal.* Berkeley: University of California Press, 1966.
Regmi, Mahesh C. *Landownership in Nepal.* Berkeley: University of California Press, 1976.
Rose, E. *Nepal: Strategy for Survival.* Berkeley: University of California Press, 1971.
———. *The Politics of Bhutan.* Ithaca, New York: Cornell University Press, 1977.
——— and Scholz, John T. *Nepal: Profile of a Himalayan Kingdom.* Boulder, Colorado: Westview Press, 1980.
Singh, Narendra. *Bhutan: A Kingdom in the Himalayas.* 3rd ed. New Delhi: S. Chand, 1985.
Stiller, Ludwig F. *The Rise of the House of Gorkha: A Study in the Unification of Nepal, 1768–1816.* New Delhi: Manjusri, 1973.
Toffin, Gérard, ed. *L'Homme et la maison en Himalaya: Ecologie du Népal.* Paris: Editions du Centre National de la Recherche Scientifique, 1981.

NEW ZEALAND

M. J. C. TEMPLETON

A leading New Zealand journalist asserts that the country is undergoing a quiet revolution: "Society, morals, the economy and politics, are in convulsion." [1] It is true that blood has not been shed and that the constitution has not been overturned by force. It is only in that sense, however, that this revolution may fairly be described as quiet. It is still in progress, and the decibel level is rising as the extent of change becomes apparent.

Because of all this, New Zealand has become interesting, if difficult, to write about. This is something new. Until quite recently, the image of the country has been one of stability and even dullness.

THE BRITISH HERITAGE

New Zealand, an isolated group of islands in the South Pacific, became a British colony about 150 years ago. Under the Treaty of Waitangi (1840), its original Polynesian settlers were guaranteed possession of their lands and fisheries. Only now is an attempt being made to define the true extent and meaning of that guarantee, which was largely ignored in practice during more than a century of British settlement. Unlike Australia, New Zealand was not a penal colony and the native vigor of its indigenous inhabitants, after an initial decline, survived the ravages of civilization. With a more restrictive immigration policy than that of Australia, New Zealand's non-indigenous population has remained predominantly British. Thus, it is essentially a bicultural society, but with some multicultural elements added by more recent immigration.

The Maori, although enfranchised at an early date, exercised little political influence as New Zealand slowly evolved from colony to independent state. Only in part was this because they were guaranteed, but effectively restricted to, separate minority representation in the New Zealand Parliament. For the past hundred years or more of British colonization, the Maori population, after losing a fight to retain some degree of autonomy in their ancestral land, settled into rural obscurity and political impotence. The British colonists took possession of the best agricultural land, exploited the

[1] Colin James, *The Quiet Revolution: Turbulence and Transition in Contemporary New Zealand* (London: Allen and Unwin/Port Nicholson Press, 1986), p. 7.

natural resources, built the cities, controlled the country's wealth and held the reins of political power.

New Zealand became internally self-governing within a few years of its annexation as a colony, and achieved Dominion status in 1907. But until World War II, and in some minds well after that, New Zealand regarded itself as an integral part of the British Empire, and remained fiercely loyal to the crown. Not until 1947 did it formally—and hesitantly—accept the independence within the British Commonwealth conferred by the Statute of Westminster nearly two decades earlier. New Zealand has demonstrated its loyalty to British interests by its complete devotion to the Allied cause in two world wars, by maintaining its commitment to Middle East defense in the immediate postwar period, by fully supporting Britain during the Suez crisis, by sending units of its armed forces to participate with British forces in the defense of Malaysia and Singapore, and by offering military as well as diplomatic assistance to Britain in 1982 to help repel the Argentinian invasion of the Falkland Islands.

In addition, New Zealand conscientiously fulfilled its obligations as an ally of the United States, with which Australia and New Zealand had concluded a tripartite security treaty in 1951. Three years later, New Zealand joined with the United States, Australia, Britain, France, Pakistan, the Philippines and Thailand in the Southeast Asia Treaty Organization. On the basis of these commitments, New Zealand made a contribution, without notable enthusiasm, to the military efforts of the United States to prevent a Communist takeover in South Vietnam. This was the first and only occasion in which New Zealand forces participated in a military action without being part of a larger British formation.

New Zealand viewed British determination to enter the European Community (EC) in 1973 with serious misgivings, but recognized it as a fait accompli. The result for New Zealand was the loss of its assured market in Britain for the bulk of its agricultural exports. Determined diplomacy, supported by Britain, ensured that this loss has occurred gradually; some 14 years after Britain's entry into the EC, significant, although diminishing, quantities of New Zealand butter and lamb continued to enter the British market.

The shift in the weight of British interests from the Commonwealth to Europe, however, had more important consequences for New Zealand than its effect on trade. Without any noticeable diminution in the warmth of its traditional relationship with Britain, New Zealand's political leaders moved toward more independence in policy-making in all areas. A determined effort was made to diversify New Zealand's export trade, expanding markets to Australia, Japan and the United States. New Zealand's forces were withdrawn from Vietnam. It recognized the People's Republic of China and exchanged diplomatic representatives with Beijing. During the oil crisis of the 1970s, New Zealand moved to establish its own diplomatic presence in the Arab/Persian Gulf and at the same time to develop its own energy resources through major projects—the so-called think-big program. Its presence in the Middle East opened major markets for New Zealand exports. Diplomatic representation was reestablished in the Soviet Union. A closer economic-relations agreement was negotiated with Australia, looking toward the eventual establishment of a free-trade area. Friendship and trade with members of the Association of Southeast Asian Nations were actively cultivated. New Zealand became a leading proponent of regional development, both political and economic, among the island countries of the South Pacific.

All this not inconsiderable change was achieved in the decade following Britain's entry into the EC, without disturbing New Zealand's image as a safe, reliable partner in the Western alliance—albeit a minor player in the league. In appearance, and to a considerable degree in actuality, New Zealand remained the most British of Britain's fellow members in the Commonwealth. The popularity of the royal family remained undiminished. New Zealand adhered at least as resolutely as Britain itself to the Westminster system of parliamentary government, including "first past the post" elections. Its defense establishment and judicial system continued to be based on British models. Appeals from the judgments of New Zealand courts went—and still go—to the Privy Council in Britain. Its public servants remained determinedly nonpolitical.

THE WELFARE STATE AND SOCIETY

Even before the turn of the century, New Zealand had been steadily developing into one of the most comprehensive welfare states in the world. The process had been accelerated by the advent of the first Labour government in 1935, in the midst of a severe depression. It continued unimpeded, irrespective of the political coloration of the party in power, until the 1980s. The last major step, the introduction of universal superannuation, was effected by the National party (pseudoconservative) government, which attained office in 1975. Under the leadership of Robert Muldoon, the National government proved to be at least as "interventionist" in both social and economic policy-making as any of the three Labour governments that had preceded it.

Over the century leading up to the election of 1984, the New Zealand government had become all-pervasive in the lives of its citizens. Government departments provided fire insurance and life insurance; drew up wills and managed estates; and monopolized postal and telegraphic communications, the railways, internal and external air transportation, the supply of electricity, and (with minor exceptions in radio) broadcasting services. The government offered commercial and merchant banking services, owned vast forests, developed huge areas of crown-owned land, managed national parks, provided compensation for all accidents, ran its own printing office, produced its own statistics, and predicted the weather. To a considerable extent, it built its own dams, roads, bridges and government buildings. The government supported farm prices and subsidized manufacturing exports. It provided health, family, unemployment and numerous other social benefits. In the words of an economic historian, it carried the principle of

675

intervention "so far as to leave doubt over whether there was any area in which government did not have a legitimate interest."[2]

From the end of World War II until the 1980s, unemployment had not been a problem. In fact, for many years the problem had been a shortage of skilled labor. It was believed that any government that permitted significant unemployment would commit electoral suicide. Since unemployment emerged as a major social problem in the 1980s, however, the employed majority has viewed the plight of those out of work with considerable sangfroid. The growth of unemployment has proceeded hand in hand with other economic and social ills, some of which have generated more concern. There has been a steady deterioration in New Zealand's terms of trade.[3] Since 1960 New Zealand's per capita income has dropped from near the top to near the bottom of the Organization for Economic Cooperation and Development (OECD) membership table.[4] Its inflation record is one of the worst among that association's members. Its balance-of-payments deficit has had to be financed by extensive overseas borrowing.

The social ills with which New Zealand has been afflicted are shared to a greater or lesser degree with the rest of the allegedly civilized world. Violent crime has increased markedly. The use of weapons by lawbreakers, which used to be rare, is now commonplace. Drugs are an important element in crime, and New Zealand criminals have made a name for themselves as international drug runners. Racial tension provides an added dimension to New Zealand crime as it does, for example, in Britain; but whereas the racial minority in Britain consists of recent immigrants, in New Zealand it is the *tangata whenua*,[5] the indigenous Maori. Unemployment and poverty are disproportionately high among the Maori. Detribalized Maori form gangs, which are seen by the proponents of "law and order" as the principal source of violent crime. This is a grossly oversimplified picture: By no means are all gangs comprised of Maori, nor is all all violence gang inspired. But the prisons are overcrowded, and there are calls for longer sentences and more police.

New Zealanders are relatively conservative in their attitude toward moral issues—some say hypocritically so. There is a strong antiabortion lobby,

[2]G. R. Hawke, *Government in the New Zealand Economy* (New Zealand Planning Council, 1982), p. 7.
[3] Terms of Trade (1957 = 100)

1972	93	1980	82
1974	112	1982	77
1976	72	1984	74
1978	78	1986	71

Source: Department of Statistics.

[4]

1960	5th	1975	15th
1965	7th	1980	18th
1970	14th	1985	18th

Source: *OECD National Accounts 1960–85*, Paris, 1987. (The OECD has 25 members.)
[5]Literally, the people of the land.

but abortions are available under most circumstances. Although contraceptives are easily available, New Zealand has one of the highest extramarital birth rates in the Western world.[6] Smoking marijuana is a serious offense, but the plant is grown in large quantities. New Zealanders, proud of their reputation as do-it-yourselfers, have invented their own form of heroin, known as "home-bake." Only recently have homosexual acts among consenting male adults been legalized, over violent opposition in Parliament; but prosecutions in recent years had been few and far between.

Thus, the problems and questions that New Zealand had faced are shared to a greater or lesser degree (some, like AIDS, to a much greater degree) by other members of the Western community. Why, then, is a revolution—quiet or otherwise—now underway?

LABOUR'S REVOLUTION

In fact, there are really at least three revolutions, only loosely related in their nature. They are tied together by the determination of a group of youthful and energetic ministers to pursue revolutionary changes in the fields of foreign and security policy, constitutional development, and economic and social policy. These ministers are not, except in the most general sense, responding to popular demand. They *have,* however responded to a sense of malaise, an undefined feeling that "things can't go on like this." For nine years the country had been governed by the National party, led by an increasingly autocratic prime minister. Sir Robert Muldoon, minister of finance as well as prime minister, made virtually every significant decision; or, to put it another way, no significant decision was made until he had approved it. In the field of finance, he aspired to world statesmanship. At home, however, his interventionist policies and his unwillingness to accept electorally unpopular measures of austerity led to a general perception that the country was on the road to economic ruin. When in 1984, through a rare political misjudgment, he called for a snap election, his government was defeated by a substantial majority.

The Labour government that was elected in 1984 was expected by its supporters to follow traditional Labour policies designed to benefit the workers, the poor and underprivileged. Its supporters, however, were due for some surprises. Because it was a snap election, because voters were fed up with Muldoon and because the election took place in an atmosphere of financial crisis, the new government came into office with virtually a free hand. The few promises that they had made were disregarded when it was thought necessary for the greater good. Promises that were implemented proved to have unforeseen consequences. New policies, which the person in the street had neither heard of nor voted for, were introduced. New Zealand began to experience an era of radical change from the interventionist, protectionist welfare state—and this was the last thing the nation expected.

[6] 37.57 percent in 1985, per *New Zealand Official Yearbook* 1987–88.

Foreign and defense policy: prisoners of the left

New Zealanders—except for a small minority—had not expected or wanted a fundamental shift in their country's international relationships and Western alignment, and neither, it would seem, had the leaders of the parliamentary Labour party. A public inquiry in 1986 showed that a majority of New Zealanders wanted to retain the security link with the United States provided by the ANZUS Pact. At the same time, however, it showed that New Zealanders were deeply concerned about the danger of a global war, and that they wished to exclude nuclear weapons from New Zealand soil and, as far as possible, from the South Pacific. The majority, therefore, favored the exclusion of nuclear weapons and nuclear-powered ships from New Zealand ports—although, when faced with a choice between keeping the ANZUS alignment or keeping the nuclear-free ports policy, a smaller majority opted for ANZUS.[7] The government, under heavy pressure from left-wing elements in the Labour party and the parliamentary Labour caucus, had already preempted the inquiry by refusing entry to an American warship on the basis of the usual "neither confirm nor deny" policy of U.S. authorities. The United States retaliated by declaring the ANZUS Pact "inoperative" in respect to New Zealand.

The exclusion of New Zealand from the United States' commitment to come to its defense was undoubtedly something that the majority of New Zealanders had not anticipated when they voted for a nuclear-free nation. Yet, as the reelection of the Labour government in 1987 tends to confirm, they have accepted that development with apparent calm verging on indifference. It was not an issue at the forefront of their concerns during the election, despite the best efforts of the opposition to place it there.

It seems that New Zealanders, unlike Australians, do not envision a credible threat to their country's security in the foreseeable future. There has probably been a steady erosion of enthusiasm for the American alliance since Vietnam. Distaste for American policies has been reinforced by successive domestic political scandals in the United States and by the bellicose image of the Reagan administration—especially with regard to the buildup of armaments, the strategic defense initiative and that administration's determination to subvert the left-wing government of Nicaragua. Above all, antinuclear sentiment in New Zealand has grown steadily since the French government began conducting nuclear-weapons tests in the South Pacific, and it is unlikely to subside until that testing ends and the nuclear powers agree on a continuing program of reductions in their arsenals of nuclear weapons. A perceived failure by the United States to pursue such a program with vigor could only intensify New Zealanders' anti-American attitudes and lessen their desire for a reactivation of the security alliance.

In the meantime, New Zealanders seem generally content with their government's professed intention to refurbish the modest conventional equipment of its armed forces and to develop a closer defense relationship with Australia—an approach that Australia, still firmly linked through

[7] Defence Committee of Enquiry, *Defence and Security: What New Zealanders Want* (Government Printer, 1986), Annex, 70 and 76.

ANZUS to the United States, has accepted without much enthusiasm. At the same time, the New Zealand government's more active participation in efforts to promote nuclear disarmament undoubtedly has wide public support.

If New Zealanders have accepted with relative equanimity the current expulsion of their country from the inner circle of the Western system of alliances, the same cannot be said of the second revolution brought about by the fourth Labour government—an economic revolution with major social consequences. Since this economic revolution is a shift toward the right, it is sometimes said that the change in foreign and security policy was the price paid by the government for the acquiescence to these economic policies of its traditional leftward-leaning supporters. It seems increasingly unlikely that the Labour movement, and in particular the trade unions, will accept indefinitely the present direction of economic policy, especially if the promised benefits do not finally come about. It is true that in 1987 the electorate put the government on probation for a second three-year term, but it did so with the aid of affluent young voters who would not normally have been found in the Labour camp, and in the face of weakness and disarray in the principal opposition party.

Economic policy: traitors to tradition?
As with security policy, the economic policy followed by the government that took office in 1984 was far from what the electorate might have expected from a socialist party. However, a small book published four years earlier had offered important clues. Roger Douglas, a junior minister in the third Labour government, was a wealthy businessman with impeccable Labour antecedents. Regarded as a maverick by the mainstream of the party, in 1980 he produced an alternative budget that was instantly repudiated by the party leadership. Demoted from the front bench (although he was reinstated later), Douglas in 1980 wrote *There's Got to Be a Better Way!: A Practical ABC to Solving New Zealand's Major Problems.* In it he advocated a reduction in income tax for both individuals and companies; the introduction of a retail sales tax (with exemptions for food and clothing); a payroll tax as a possible substitute for personal income tax; and a tax on capital and assets. He also urged that export incentives and import licensing be abolished, that the currency be devalued, that agricultural production be doubled and further processed before export, and that national superannuation should be means tested. As to inflation, he wrote:

> we must resist the temptation of committing ourselves to huge spending programmes that cannot be financed out of revenue. . . . [Inflation] must be handled by a combination of policies including responsible fiscal and monetary measures, the encouragement of competition in domestic markets, price controls in limited areas, agreement with the trade union movement on reasonable wage fixing machinery and above all, an economic strategy which produces growth.[8]

[8] Roger Douglas, *There's Got to Be a Better Way!: A Practical ABC to Solving New Zealand's Major Problems* (Fourth Estate Books, Ltd., 1980), p. 42.

Finally, Douglas made it clear that he did not favor a gradual approach: "We can lead the world again, both in standard of living and in social justice. To do that we need to have a revolution. This doesn't mean imitating someone else's revolution: we don't have a Tsar anyway."[9]

Revolutionaries, however, tend to be no less authoritarian than the tyrants they depose. Douglas, as minister of finance in the Lange government, determined economic policy with no less strength of will than his predecessor. "Rogernomics" had a wide measure of support in the business and financial communities, and among government and moderate "more market" economists. It encountered strong criticism from the left wing of the Labour party and trade unionists for its abandonment of socialist principles, and from right-wing Friedmanites for not going far or fast enough toward freeing up the economy (including the labor market). Middle-of-the-road economists also expressed misgivings.

The government put into effect many of Douglas's 1980 proposals, but some were drastically modified and others awaited implementation. Major tax reforms were achieved. There was a shift of emphasis from direct to indirect taxation through a reduction in income tax rates and the introduction of a 10 percent goods and services tax. This was, however, a value-added tax rather than a retail sales tax, and there were no exemptions for food and clothing, so that the tax was more regressive than Douglas had envisioned. When the National party adopted his original proposal as its election policy, he did not hesitate to point out its administrative disadvantages. Company tax was not reduced and a promise to eliminate double taxation of dividends was not implemented. There was no assets tax or capital gains tax. National superannuation was subject to a surtax that effectively applied a means test.

The Labour government devalued the New Zealand dollar immediately after taking office (it had no choice because of a run on the currency) and subsequently removed all exchange controls, allowing the dollar to float freely. It instituted a policy of internal, rather than external, borrowing. Buoyed up by high interest rates, the New Zealand dollar did not fall in value, as most of the experts expected; instead it rose against the U.S. and Australian dollars. This affected the returns for New Zealand's exports, both of agricultural products and manufactured goods: Export incentives and agricultural subsidies also were abolished. The balance of payments situation remained precarious.

There was little sign of the economic growth that in theory should have resulted from deregulation and freeing up of the economy. Unemployment continued to rise, approaching levels not seen since the depression of the 1930s.[10] New Zealand continued to have one of the highest inflation rates

---

[9] Ibid., p. 75.

[10] The number of unemployed registered with the Department of Labour rose from below 5,000 in 1976 to 88,000 in October 1987 (6.6 percent of the total labor force). The quinquennial censuses give much higher figures, ranging from 9,000 in 1966 to 26,000 in 1976 and 108,000 in 1986. (Department of Labour statistics and New Zealand Official Yearbook, 1987–88.)

in the OECD; with the rate temporarily boosted by the goods and services tax, the modest goal of reducing it to a single-digit figure continued to recede.[11] (In comparison, in Britain there is concern that the inflation rate might rise into double digits.) The New Zealand government also failed to reduce the level of the national debt, even as a proportion of GDP. Official debt rose from 29.5 percent of GDP in 1983 to an estimated 40.6 percent in 1987.[12] The New Zealand stock market, which enjoyed a bull run as New Zealand entrepreneurs and financiers spread their wings in the new atmosphere of deregulation and economic freedom, showed itself especially sensitive to downward trends in the U.S. and other major financial markets. The government, meanwhile, was criticized from the right for not acting decisively enough to reduce the budget deficit by cutting government expenditure, and from the left for selling off national assets—whether to state corporations or to private enterprise—to achieve the same purpose. There was also criticism from the right that the government failed to free up the labor market along with the rest, and from the left that it went too far in that direction.

The key question, therefore, remains unanswered: Will Rogernomics work? Douglas's general approach, along lines favored by the International Monetary Fund, the OECD, and conservative governments and business interests in several of those organizations' most important member-nations, created international confidence in the direction of New Zealand's economy that, previously, was sadly lacking. For this reason, if for no other, a radical reversal in economic policy was not expected, nor was it in Douglas's character to vacillate. He was "not deflectable."[13] Changes advocated by Keynesian economists, such as a "managed float" of the exchange rate, interest rate controls, tax increases or an incomes policy aimed at full employment were unlikely to be adopted. Although the opposition's economic policy at the time of the election was obscured by internal dissension, it seemed likely that its economic policymakers would prefer to move further in the direction of "more market" rather than revert to the kind of interventionist fine-tuning associated in the public mind with the policies of the ousted Muldoon. The New Zealand electorate, which was offered no real economic choice in 1987, may in the 1990s have to decide between the same and more of the same.

Because Douglas and his colleagues saw the need for economic reform as

[11] New Zealand Consumer Price Index (1983 = 1,000)

1974	300
1976	402
1978	515
1980	686
1982	919
1984	1040
1986	1369
1987	1601 (September figure: annual rate of 16.9%)

Source: Department of Statistics.

[12] Bank of New Zealand's estimate.

[13] James. *Quiet Revolution,* p. 16.

their first priority, social reform (including the restructuring of the health and welfare systems) was effectively left for the government's second term, along with proposals for constitutional changes. To report on this, a Royal Commission on Social Policy was set up in rather leisurely fashion. The economic policy changes, however, inevitably impinged heavily on the existing "social" sector of government as well as on its administrative structure, making reform in these areas more urgent. The government, therefore, showed an increasing disposition to preempt the work of the royal commission, and set up numerous task forces to report to the Cabinet Committee on Social Equity. As a result, social issues were dealt with on a case-by-case basis—a fragmented approach that the royal commission presumably was intended to avoid.

Constitutional and administrative policy: New Zealand's innovation
The restructuring of the executive arm of government was under way. The first objective was to ensure that those government departments engaged in commercial operations (as indicated earlier, the number and range of these would amaze anyone but a New Zealander) would be obliged to operate profitably. To this end, those departments whose purpose was wholly commercial were converted into corporate bodies to be known as state-owned enterprises. They were then cut loose from the rules and regulations of the public service, placed under independent boards like other limited-liability companies, and obliged to purchase existing assets from the government and to pay dividends to their owner, the government. From the beginning, doubts were expressed as to whether corporatization went far enough to ensure maximum commercial efficiency; the opposition has espoused full privatization. The government itself made a start in that direction by selling a proportion of its shareholdings in the Bank of New Zealand and Petrocorp (which markets state-owned energy resources). As the next step, Petrocorp was to be fully sold off, followed by other commercial organizations such as Air New Zealand and the Development Finance Corporation, while private enterprise has been allotted a third television channel.

The "rump" of the public service, which has few or no commercial functions but provides the government with economic and foreign-policy advice and intelligence, gathers taxes and administers its finances, prepares for the country's defense, seeks to protect the natural environment, promotes noncommercial scientific research and cultural activities, administers justice, and controls the allocation of government finance to education, nervously awaited reform. New Zealand's public servants have traditonally sought to maintain the state services as a series of closed shops. The government proposed to loosen up the purely "Westminster" nature of the system by discouraging junior entrants from regarding public service as a lifetime career, and by facilitating easier entry and departure at all levels. Specifically, ministers wish to have a part in the selection and appointment of officials at the most senior levels (the present system of appointment by a panel of permanent heads has been unkindly described as a self-perpetuating oligarchy), and to limit their tenure through contractual agreements.

Whether such charges will improve the overall quality of the state services, and whether these changes can be achieved without the politicization of the senior appointments are questions that still have to be answered to the satisfaction of the public servants.

The principal enthusiast in the government for administrative and constitutional reform was undoubtedly the deputy prime minister, a former law professor who also served as attorney-general, minister of justice and chairman of the Cabinet Committee on Social Equity—a man of demonic energy and negative charisma. In the judicial field, Geoffrey Palmer proposed to end recourse to the Privy Council from the New Zealand courts. He also envisaged important constitutional changes. New Zealand's constitution, like that of Britain, is not embodied in a single document. A bill of rights, which would presumably reflect and formalize the obligations that New Zealand assumed in ratifying the International Covenants of Human Rights, might also give constitutional status and the force of law to the Treaty of Waitangi. There was no great enthusiasm in the legal community for a bill of rights, and the proposal to give legislative effect to the Treaty of Waitangi was also controversial because the generality of its language gave rise to widely different interpretations. In the electoral field, a commission on electoral reform recommended the introduction of proportional representation along the lines of the system employed in the Federal Republic of Germany. The government intended to conduct referenda on this proposed reform, as well as on a separate proposal for extension of Parliament's term from three to four years, during the life of the current Parliament. Not surprisingly, both the principal political parties had doubts about proportional representation, and ground swell in public opinion sufficient to carry a referendum was unlikely.

THE NEW NEW ZEALAND: WILL IT LAST?

In spite of the precarious state of the New Zealand economy, and especially the rise in unemployment, the Labour government seemed determined to remain on the course of reform that it had set for itself. However, increasing unhappiness with Rogernomics in the Labour party and the trade unions, and a quarrel over policy between Lange and Douglas, led in 1989 to the departure of both from their positions of leadership. By this time Lange's health, and his staying power, had become suspect. In the words of the journalist Colin James, "for all his bulk David Lange has a fragility about him."[14] The first Labour prime minister to have a tertiary education, Lange had a coruscating wit and a caustic tongue, took offense readily and was easily bored. In James's view, his "over-reactions under pressure continually fuel doubts that he can last the distance as Prime Minister when his government hits the inevitable rough patches."[15] This judgment proved right.

Lange was said to regard his role as prime minister as analogous to that of the chairman of a board. Geoffry Palmer, his successor, appeared to

[14] *Ibid.*, p. 190.
[15] Ibid.

confirm this: "Generally speaking the Prime Minister concentrates on the public presentation role at which he excels. I tend to concentrate on the administrative details." [16] While this description modestly understated the role of the deputy prime minister, it failed to acknowledge the leadership skills required to maintain outward harmony among a high-spirited cabinet team spanning two generations of the Labour movement and a gamut of economic and social philosophies. Lange reduced the left wing of the Parliamentary party to political impotence and saw off three leaders of the opposition in three years. But Palmer still faced a range of tensions that will undoubtedly test his statesmanship and the administrative skills of his cabinet: tension between the urban and rural sectors; tension between Maori radicalism and possible *pakeha* (New Zealander of European descent) backlash; and—most dangerous of all—tension within the Labour movement itself, between a leadership intent on completing the process of freeing up the economy and reducing the role of government, and the traditional values of a trade-union dominated political party. The success of the linked revolutions on which the government was so bravely embarked depended on the satisfactory resolution of these tensions, and on rebuilding the economy.

FURTHER READINGS

Alley, R. M., ed. *New Zealand and the Pacific.* Boulder, Colorado: Westview Press, 1984.

―――, ed. *State Servants and the Public in the 1980s.* Wellington: New Zealand Institute of Public Administration, 1980.

Jackson, William Keith. *New Zealand: Politics of Change.* Wellington: Reed Education, 1973.

Levine, Stephen, ed. *Politics in New Zealand: A Reader.* Sydney and Boston: Allen & Unwin, 1978.

McDonald, Geoff. *Shadows over New Zealand: Defence, Land Rights and Multiculturalism.* Christchurch, New Zealand: Chaston Publishers, 1985.

Mitchell, Austin Vernon. *Politics and People in New Zealand.* Christchurch, New Zealand: Whitcombe & Tombs, 1969.

Palmer, Geoffrey W. R. *Unbridled Power?: An Interpretation of New Zealand's Constitution and Government.* Wellington, New York and London: Oxford University Press, 1979.

Simpson, Tony. *A Vision Betrayed: The Decline of Democracy in New Zealand.* Auckland: Hodder & Stoughton, 1984.

Wright, Vernan. *David Lange, Prime Minister: A Profile.* Wellington and Boston: Unwin Paperbacks in association with Port Nicholson Press, 1984.

[16] Geoffrey Palmer, *Unbridled Power,* 2nd ed. (London: Oxford University Press, 1987), 65 and 68.

PACIFIC ISLAND STATES

WILLIAM NESTER

THROUGHOUT the late 1980s, the South Pacific has increasingly presented headline news through such problems as Fijian coups, guerrilla fighting in New Caledonia and Libyan intrigue in Vanuatu, creating an image in many minds of a politically unstable and dangerous region. These stories have undermined the previous image many people held of the South Pacific as a faraway region of tiny, idyllic, sun-drenched islands inhabited by friendly, sensuous people. Of course, neither the *New York Times* nor *National Geographic* image is accurate; while there are political "troubles in paradise," none of those problems is unmanageable. Fiji, New Caledonia, French Polynesia, Papua New Guinea and Vanuatu have recently experienced outbreaks of political violence and instability. Yet, these political challenges have been largely contained in all five areas by the existing political institutions. Even the most disturbing political disruptions, Fiji's two coups in 1987, failed to destroy the country's democratic foundations and the nation's parliamentary system is slowly being restored.

Both as a region and as individual countries, the Pacific remains one of the political success stories of the developing world. All of the nine independent countries, and the five states in free association with either New Zealand or the United States, are democracies with generally healthy multiparty systems. Of the five remaining foreign dependencies, all have democratic political systems. The French territories of New Caledonia and Polynesia face strong and growing independence movements, while the inhabitants of Guam, American Samoa and the Northern Marianas have chosen to remain part of the United States. These political successes are mirrored on a regional level by international organizations such as the South Pacific Commission (SPC), the South Pacific Forum and half a dozen other institutions that knit the region together and allow it to deal with a range of issues and problems.

Still, these international organizations and each country in the region face considerable problems that will strain existing political systems. Ethnic violence, "brain-drain" migration, dependence on the industrial world for aid, trade and investments, lack of economic growth and employment opportunities, corruption of various kinds, a revolution of rising mass expectations and other problems confront every Pacific region country to varying degrees.

PACIFIC REGIONALISM

A region can be considered a group of states internationally recognized as sharing a distinct geographical unit, similar values and a degree of interaction and interdependence greater than adjacent states. According to this definition, the 19 island states within the area bound by Papua New Guinea to the west, French Polynesia to the east, the Mariana Islands to the north and the Cook Islands to the south occupy a relatively distinct geographical, cultural and political region. Geographically, they are nearly all small island states in the South and Central Pacific Ocean; culturally, they share a relatively common value system expressed through the "Pacific Way"; and politically, they confront the same development challenges with similar social and political institutions. These 19 states include nine fully independent states: Western Samoa, Nauru, Tonga, Fiji, Papua New Guinea, the Solomon Islands, Tuvalu, Kiribati and Vanuatu; five self-governing states in free association with an outside power: the Cook Islands and Niue with New Zealand, and the Marshall Islands, the Federated States of Micronesia and Palau with the United States; and five islands ruled by outside powers: New Caledonia and French Polynesia by France, and Guam, American Samoa and the Northern Marianas by the United States.

Yet despite these similarities there is enough variety within this area to stimulate controversy over which states to include within the region. Why are not Australia and New Zealand included? Although both countries are island nations and members of the SPC and South Pacific Forum, they are generally not included among the Pacific island countries because of their relatively large size, industrial status, Western heritage and peripheral geographic position. Why are the American and French dependencies included within the region? Although none of these foreign-controlled territories is a member of the South Pacific Forum, and some of the American territories are actually located north of the equator, both the American and French territories are generally included within the region because they meet the geographic, cultural and development requirements for regional membership.

Another controversy involves just what to call the Pacific islands region. Delegates at the Fourteenth South Pacific Conference meeting in September 1974 were challenged to devise a new name for the SPC that was accurately descriptive of the region. Despite considerable debate, the conference was unable to reach a consensus on an appropriate name since all the suggestions suffered some deficiency. The terms "South Pacific" and "South Seas" seemed too narrow since they omitted the peoples in the Mariana, Marshall, Caroline and some of the Gilbert Islands, which are north of the equator. "Oceania" and "Pacific Islands," on the other hand, seemed too broad since Australia and New Zealand, and even conceivably countries as far away as the Philippines or Japan, could be encompassed within these terms. Although the delegates all agreed that the 21 states comprised a distinct region, they gave up the search for a more accurate label for it.[1]

[1] Richard Herr, *Regionalism in the South Seas: The Impact of the South Pacific Commission, 1947–74* (Ph.D. dissertation, Duke University, 1976), 3.

Microstate status is supposed to be another characteristic of the South Pacific countries. Yet, if that is true, why is Papua New Guinea, with a population of over 3.2 million and a land territory bigger than the rest of the islands combined, included among states that have only a fraction of that population or land size? Would it not be more appropriate to place Papua New Guinea in Southeast Asia than the South Pacific? Perhaps, but the cultural, historical and political ties of Papua New Guinea to the South Pacific seem stronger than its geographic link with Southeast Asia. Unlike most other Pacific island countries, Papua New Guinea has rich natural resources within a large land area, but it shares the development problems of other Pacific island states by being geographically remote from the rest of the world and extremely dependent on external trade and aid from its former colonial ruler.

Yet, even the assumption that the South Pacific island countries share the same development challenges is questionable. The economic development needs and potential of relatively large, richly endowed island countries such as Papua New Guinea, the Solomons, New Caledonia, and Fiji, with GNPs of around U.S.$500 million each, are very different from those of Nauru, Niue and Tuvalu, with populations of less than 8,000 and GNPs of less than $50 million each.

Another controversy swirls around the concept of the Pacific Way. The term was coined by former Fiji Prime Minister Ratu Mara in the mid-1960s to aid the island states' independence and regional development.[2] The Pacific Way is supposed to represent the traditional, precolonial values of harmony, brotherhood and courtesy among the region's inhabitants. Decisions for action are reached only after all opinions have been voiced and a consensus forged; mutual respect for one and all generally prevails. But the idea of a traditional Pacific Way has been rejected by most regional specialists. Crocombe argues that these claims exaggerate the extent of precolonial links among the Pacific islands, which he characterizes as "relatively minor" and "sporadic. Most Pacific islands had very little contact with people of other island groups . . . and the contact that occurred . . . often involved arrogant and ruthless buccaneering, oppression, and exploitation."[3] Herr agrees, saying, "There is little direct evidence extant today of intergroup identification among Pacific islanders before the advent of European intrusions into the area."[4] Kiste and Hamnett maintain that "while it is true that Pacific peoples share some common heritage and origins, there was no sense of a pan-Pacific region or Pacific unity. Indeed, there could not have been. The migrations into the area occurred over thousands of years and pre-modern systems of communications and transportation did not allow such notions to develop. Unity was lacking even within a single group as chiefs fought to enhance their own glories."[5] The South Pacific

---

[2] G. E. Fry, *South Pacific Regionalism: The Development of an Indigenous Commitment* (Canberra: Australia National University, 1979), 230.

[3] R. G. Crocombe, *The Pacific Way*, pp. 5, 12.

[4] Herr, *Regionalism*, p. 18.

[5] Robert C. Kiste and Michael Hamnett, *Information Flows in the Pacific Islands States*, p. 18.

can be roughly divided into three distinct cultural zones—Polynesia, Melanesia and Micronesia—representing different ethnic groups, languages, customs, political heritages and social structures. And within each of these broad cultural groups are myriad distinct smaller groups.

If there is little objective basis for the claim of historical unity the question arises as to why such claims are being promoted. According to Kiste and Hamnett, "Ratu Mara seems to be projecting village values onto the Pacific region as a whole; in doing so Mara is creating a modern myth. But it is a good and constructive myth that regional elites have begun to internalize."[6] These myths strengthen both individual Pacific island states and regional political development, making current attempts to cooperate politically something traditional and thus natural, rather than something arbitrarily imposed by imperialism. Instead, the colonial powers are condemned for disrupting the traditional Pacific Way and distorting regional development. By scapegoating the West for their political and economic problems, the Pacific island states have both an excuse for remaining underdeveloped and a basis for a common identity.

Fry sees the Pacific Way as part of an evolving pan-Pacific ideology including the central ideas that (1) regional organizations and their programs should be controlled by the Pacific states themselves; (2) remaining colonial influences should be opposed, controlled and eventually eliminated; (3) Pacific cultural values should be asserted over current Western values; and (4) a Pacific cultural affinity that has always existed but was interrupted by colonialism must be reborn.[7] Sione Tupounia echoes Fry's observations by maintaining that "Pacific Islanders are searching for a new way of life in which we fully accept the responsibility for creating the social, political, economic, and cultural institutions to suit our own particular needs."[8]

Although the observations of Fry and Tupounia describe the essence of political development, they fail to capture the very dynamic dialectic involved. There was no Pacific island "region" or "way" before the Western powers carved it up among themselves and labeled it as such in the late 19th century. On a superficial level, the Western institutions and values imposed by colonialism diluted and transformed each island's traditional institutions and values. Political struggles both before and after independence have forged within each Pacific island-state a hybrid political culture composed of a combination of traditional regional, Western and third world institutions and values. Village values have been asserted on not only a national but a regional level. Formal political institutions such as parliaments and bureaucracies may seem largely Western, while traditional institutions such as councils of chiefs have been given only ceremonial representation. Yet, much of the informal politics within these Western political systems remains largely traditional. Politics continues to flow along traditional patron-client lines.

Thus, each of the Pacific states experienced a similar political develop-

[6] Ibid., pp. 16–17.
[7] Fry, *South Pacific Regionalism*, pp. 214–15.
[8] Ibid., p. 180.

ment. There were no large sovereign, centralized states anywhere in the region before the South Pacific was colonized. Some of the islands, like Tonga, Fiji and the Cook Islands, had feudal systems where "kings" presiding over loose coalitions of clans battled one another for supremacy. But the rest of the South Pacific islands had no centralized authority at all; politics was centered in the clans, which constantly warred against one another.

European ships began sailing the Pacific Ocean as early as the mid-16th century, but the West made no significant impact until the 19th century when a steadily increasing stream of traders, whalers, missionaries, deserters and naval ships began exploiting the islands. The Pacific islands became yet another region for great-power rivalry, and by the end of the 19th century every archipelago had been colonized. Although imperialism ended the incessant clan and island warfare, the Pacific peoples were decimated by the impact of foreign diseases such as measles and smallpox, or the foreign "blackbirders" who enslaved tens of thousands of islanders for plantations as far away as Peru and Australia.

World War I led to a reshuffling of the imperialist order in the Pacific. Within a month after war broke out, all the German colonies were snatched by Britain, Australia, New Zealand and Japan. The Versailles Conference (1919) legitimized these seizures by designating them "mandates," with the proviso that each mandate be prepared for eventual independence. Although Japan used its mandates to strengthen its strategic position in the Pacific, the other powers began to introduce political institutions that slowly gave more administrative and policy responsibilities to native elites.

After World War II the pace of political development quickened as the appointed advisory councils were converted to elected legislative assemblies, and eventually national parliaments once independence was granted in the 1960s and 1970s. The political development of the Pacific has largely been peaceful and evolutionary. Native independence movements were few, leaders easily co-opted and followers dispersed. The nine independent states and five free association states have maintained excellent relations with their former colonial rulers.

Pacific regionalism was promoted almost two decades before the first Pacific island state achieved independence. Pacific island vulnerability, development problems and dependence became apparent to all the colonial powers during World War II. After the war, the colonial powers, led by Australia and New Zealand, committed themselves to promoting regional integration through the creation of the SPC in January 1947. The commission's purpose is to "encourage and strengthen international cooperation in promoting the economic and social welfare and advancement of the peoples of the non-self-governing territories of the South Pacific."[9] Yet, there was more to the commission than altruism; regional political, economic and social development was considered as beneficial to the Western powers as it was to the indigenous inhabitants. Before the commission's creation,

[9] Agreement Establishing the South Pacific Commission, Canberra, February 6, 1947, *Australia Treaty Series*.

there was no clearly defined South Pacific. The colonial powers set the region's boundaries, created its political institutions and gave its inhabitants an opportunity to meet for the first time. The commission's most important legacy has been the opportunity it presents for indigenous Pacific island leaders to exchange ideas. Although nonindependent Pacific island countries are not allowed to join the commission itself, each territory is allowed to send a representative to conferences held every three years to advise the commission. According to Maude, these conferences have "created a regional outlook: a sense of common interests and problems and indeed, of common destiny." [10]

This gradual evolution of Pacific island consciousness led to a transitional phase from 1965 to 1971 when an indigenous regionalism began to replace colonial regionalism. The independence movements of the Pacific islands during the 1960s attacked the commission as being merely a front for Western interests. Although newly independent Pacific island states were allowed to join the commission, many of their concerns were not addressed, since political topics were banned on both commission and conference agendas. Indigenous leaders began calling for their own regional organization in which they, and not Westerners, could set the agenda.

The first indigenous international organization was the Pacific Island Producers Association (PIPA), created at Apia in 1965 by representatives of Fiji, Tonga and Western Samoa. The Cook Islands and Niue joined later. Although PIPA was originally designed to promote regional exports and economic development, its concerns became increasingly political throughout the late 1960s. This transition period culminated at PIPA's sixth meeting in April 1971 when the member-states agreed to form the South Pacific Forum whose membership would be limited to the independent island countries plus Australia and New Zealand.

The first meeting of the forum was held in August 1971 at Wellington, and a follow-up meeting at Canberra in February 1972. A permanent secretariat for the organization—the South Pacific Bureau for Economic Cooperation (SPEC)—was then created. Through its annual meetings and the creation of a range of institutions dealing with specific development problems, the forum has become an increasingly effective regional international organization. The forum's success in promoting regional integration and development culminated with the signing of a fisheries treaty with the United States in 1985, whereby Washington recognized the jurisdiction of the Pacific islands' 200-mile economic enterprise zones over migratory tuna, and in 1986 with the signing of the South Pacific Nuclear-Free-Zone (SPNFZ) Treaty, which attempts to regulate the presence of nuclear weapons and testing in the region.

To date, the South Pacific has achieved a high degree of regional political development. Through both the commission and the forum, the South Pacific now has two institutional networks that actively and effectively deal with regional political, economic and social problems. Such regional institutions as the University of the South Pacific, the Telecommunications

[10] Maude quoted in Fry, *South Pacific Regionalism*, pp. 66–67.

Training Centre, the Pacific Forum Shipping Line, the South Pacific Regional Trade and Economic Agreement (SPARTECA), the South Pacific Regional Environmental Program (SPREP) and the Forum Fisheries Agencies (FFA) all further strengthen the efforts of the commission and the forum.

Despite these successes, regional political development may have reached a plateau. Subregional cleavages, such as between the Melanesian Spearhead Group of Papua New Guinea, the Solomons and Vanuatu, and the more loosely aligned Polynesian countries are beginning to strain forum meetings and cooperation. Fiji's traditional domination of many of the institutions and leadership positions has long been resented by other forum members. Papua New Guinea as a "giant among dwarfs" is attempting to assert more regional influence. Although the Pacific Way is considered a vital pillar of regional integration, the South Pacific in general and most of the island states in particular remain fragmented culturally, linguistically, economically and politically. Specifically, the South Pacific remains divided between independent forum members and those territories still under French and American control.

Finally, all the Pacific island states and the forum are heavily dependent on the Western powers for trade and financial aid. The island countries contribute only 3 percent and 15 percent, respectively, toward the total operating costs of the commission and forum; the rest is paid by the Western powers. Although this may sound discouraging, the island states would be even more dependent on the West without the commission or the forum.

INDEPENDENT PACIFIC ISLAND STATES

Western Samoa

In 1962 Western Samoa became the first of the Pacific island states to achieve independence, and in many ways its political structure remains among the most traditional.[11] In no other state except Tonga do clan *(aiga)* chiefs *(matai)* play such an important role in governing the country. The *matai* own all the lands and produce, and divide it among the members as the need arises. Each *aiga* selects its *matai* after forging a consensus among its members. In addition to ruling clan affairs, the *matai* of each village gather periodically (Fono) to reach a consensus on village issues.

Currently, there are about 12,000 *matai* whose collective responsibility is to vote for 45 of the 47 members of the Legislative Assembly on behalf of the 160,000 Western Samoan citizens; the other two members are elected by universal suffrage among the 1,600 remaining citizens of European ancestry. Elections are held every three years, and after each general election the legislature selects by secret ballot a prime minister who then selects eight other ministers. Every five years the legislative assembly selects the head of state *(O le Ao O le Malo)* who must be a high chief from one of the

[11] See John Carter, ed., *Pacific Islands Year Book* (New York and Sydney, Pacific Publications, 1984), and the *Pacific Islands Monthly* for further details on individual Pacific Islands states.

four royal sons *(Tam a aiga)* or families. The high chief's role is to act as supreme ratifier of all decisions made by the cabinet, such as approving all legislation, appointing the prime minister and granting pardons or suspending sentences.

Western Samoa has a long constitutional history, dating back to 1875 when King Malietopa Laupepa with Western advisers created a constitutional monarchy that included two houses of parliament and a declaration of rights for Samoans. Unfortunately, his chief adviser, American Col. A. B. Steinberger, used his power as prime minister to become a virtual dictator over the country. The Samoan government collapsed after Steinberger was arrested and deported by the British, and the country again broke up among warring clans. Delegations of Samoans petitioned both Great Britain and the United States for annexation to end the fighting and protect Samoa from other outside powers, but both countries ignored these requests.

The fighting was only temporarily interrupted in 1889 when a treaty between Germany, Britain and the United States created an independent government under King Malietopa Laupepa. Although the clans were soon warring again, the treaty did end over 30 years of struggle by the three outside powers for control over the Samoan Islands as each country attempted to assert its influence by using its traders, missionaries, commissioners and naval officers to play off different claimants to the throne against one another. A decade later, in 1899, another treaty between the three powers divided the Samoan Islands between Western Samoa, under German control, and American Samoa. Britain agreed to withdraw its claims to Western Samoa in return for Germany's surrender of its rights in Tonga, Niue and all of the Solomon Islands east and southeast of Bougainville.

But even outright colonization did not end the clans' resistance against one another and against the West. The nonviolent Mau movement harried both German and, after taking over the colony in 1914, New Zealand rule. New Zealand's rule was later "mandated" by the Versailles Conference. From then until the end of World War II, Wellington suppressed periodic Mau movements through direct rule. As on other Pacific islands, the presence of large numbers of American troops during World War II stimulated ideas of independence and democracy.

New Zealand responded to the continuing cries among Samoans for more representation by enacting a series of measures between 1947 and 1962 that prepared the country for eventual self-rule. On May 9, 1961, all adult Samoans voted on two measures, one for independence and the other for a democratic constitution. Both measures were overwelmingly approved and Western Samoa became an independent country with a democratic constitution on January 1, 1962. Western Samoa's democratic system has functioned and developed steadily since independence.

Nauru

The second Pacific island country to achieve independence, Nauru, has only a fraction of the land area and population of Western Samoa. Nauru is a single coral island of 9 sq. miles/24 sq. km., with a population of only

8,400 people. About 3,400 of the total population are temporary residents from other islands who have come to work the rich phosphate deposits that give Nauru the highest per capita income in the South Pacific. Nauru's economic viability and relative isolation have allowed it to become an independent country despite its size.

Between 1830 and 1900, however, the various beachcombers, whalers, traders, missionaries and administrators who lived on Nauru had no idea they were sitting on the world's richest concentration of phosphates. The discovery of phosphates in 1900 led to gradual exploitation by the Pacific Phosphate Company, a joint German and British venture. Shortly after war broke out in August 1914, Australian troops took over the island; the Versailles Conference granted a joint mandate to Australia, Britain and New Zealand, in which Canberra would directly administer Nauru while all three would exploit the phosphate desposits. Nauru was occupied by the Japanese during World War II. In 1947 the three countries again took over with a U.N. trust grant, with Australia again providing the administration. From 1947 to formal independence on January 31, 1968, Nauru was gradually granted greater political autonomy and economic benefits, including a rise in phosphate royalties from 37¢ a ton in 1965 to $4.50 a ton in 1967, and $11 a ton for the next three years.

Nauru has a parliament of 18 members who are elected by compulsory voting of all citizens over 20 years old. Elections are held every three years. After each election the parliament selects the president, who then chooses a cabinet of four or five ministers. The president acts as both prime minister and head of state. Nauru is the only Pacific island country in which there are no organized political parties. Despite its independent status, Nauru is an associate member of the Commonwealth of Nations and, having no military force of its own, has an unwritten understanding that Australia will take care of its defense. With its phosphate reserves estimated to run out before 2000, Nauru has successfully invested its earnings in overseas ventures in Australia and elsewhere in hopes of living off the interest. Despite these remittances, there will undoubtedly be a steady stream of immigrants from Nauru in the decades ahead.

Tonga

Tonga is the only South Pacific country that was not completely taken over by one of the Western powers and whose political system has remained relatively intact. The 90,000 people of Tonga are ruled by a constitutional monarchy in which the king wields considerable power. The king governs through a Privy Council, cabinet, Legislative Assembly and judiciary. The assembly consists of seven nobles elected by the 33 nobles of Tonga, and seven representatives elected by citizens 21 years and older. Following an election, the king appoints a prime minister and cabinet ministers; the cabinet becomes the Privy Council whenever the king presides over it, and also serves as the court of appeals.

Although a monarchy has ruled the Tongan Islands for over 1,000 years, the modern system first began to take shape in 1862 when King Tupou introduced a code of laws for his kingdom. This code allowed both chiefs and commoners to be treated equally before the law, freed commoners from forced labor and allowed commoners to control their own property. To protect these rights Tupou set up a parliament with representatives of both chiefs and commoners. He followed this in 1875 by granting a constitution that guaranteed the rights of life, liberty and property, more clearly defined the political institutions, and declared that all land belonged to the king, who would lend estates to the nobles, who would in turn lend land to commoners. These political institutions have basically remained intact.

Starting in the late 18th century, Tonga was disrupted by foreign adventurers, traders and missionaries. But because of its strong monarchy, Tonga was able to sign treaties with France (1850), Germany (1876), Great Britain (1879) and the United States (1888) that guaranteed its continued independence. Despite these treaties, Tonga feared becoming a victim of the great-power rivalry that had gobbled up the rest of the Pacific islands. In order to avoid this, Tonga agreed to a treaty with Britain in 1900 that gave Westminster control over Tonga's foreign affairs. This protectorate lasted 70 years, until June 4, 1970, when Tonga was granted complete independence.

Fiji

The two 1987 military coups that overthrew Fiji's parliament and declared Fiji a republic were a grave disappointment to most observers. Few third world countries had previously seemed to be developing, economically and politically, as successfully as Fiji. Its 750,000 inhabitants seemed to have overcome amiably the deep ethnic split between the native Fijian minority and the Indian majority. Today, Fiji is slowly recovering from the severe economic blows of a temporary loss of tourism and the sugar crop—the economy's two main pillars—and its civilian leadership seems to be succeeding in creating a new political system that will ensure continued native Fijian control while giving the Indian population representation and rights.

The roots of Fiji's current political problems go back to the late 19th century. For traders looking for sandalwood, and for deserters and missionaries who chose to settle there, Fiji was a group of islands torn by tribal warfare and presided over by King Cakobau who controlled most of the main island of Viti Levu. Faced with repeated defeats from his rivals, Cakobau decided to bolster his strength in 1854 by embracing Christianity, which by that time had converted significant numbers of Fijians. Although Cakobau beat his rivals and united many of the islands, he had gone heavily into debt to American settlers, and in 1858 petitioned Westminster for annexation in return for payment. Anticipating Fiji's imminent annexation, hundreds of Britons began arriving to take over the rich farmlands. By the time Britain finally annexed Fiji in 1874, much of the island's richest farmlands had been converted to copra, cotton and sugar crops. A measles epidemic wiped out almost one-third of all native Fijians, so the British governor began importing Indians to alleviate the severe labor shortage. From 1879 to 1916, over 2,000 Indians arrived each year, with the option of staying permanently in Fiji after working 10 years. In 1904, Fiji's Legislative Assembly, which had previously been composed of Europeans nomi-

694

nated by the governor, began to be democratized—with six elected Europeans and two Fijians nominated from the Council of Chiefs. In 1916, the first Indian representative was appointed by the governor. From then until today most of Fiji's political developments have revolved around balancing the need for equitable Indian representation with continued Fijian dominance. Reforms through independence in 1970 gradually widened the franchise and number of representatives.

The 1970 constitution created a bicameral parliament consisting of a nominated Senate and an elected House of Representative, with a cabinet presided over by a prime minister. The 52 House members included 12 Fijian, 12 Indian and three general members elected from communal rolls, and 10 Fijian, 10 Indian, and five general members elected from national rolls. The 22 senators were appointed by the governor-general, with eight members nominated by the Council of Chiefs, seven by the prime minister, six by the leader of the opposition, and one by the Council of Rotuma. The queen of England, as head of state, and Queen of Fiji, is represented by a governor-general who appoints the prime minister after each election. Each village (koro) has its own leader (turaganikoro); the koros are grouped into districts (tikina), and the districts into 14 provinces (yasana). Each province is headed by a chief who is a member of the Council of Chiefs, which forms an advisory council to parliament on all issues affecting native Fijians.

These institutions ensured continued Fijian domination over politics despite the fact that the Indian population has comprised 51 percent of Fiji's total population since 1946; native Fijians comprise only 43 percent of the population. Despite comprising the majority of the population, the Indian community owns only two percent of the land. The Europeans, Polynesians and Chinese hold six percent, and the Melanesian Fijians about 90 percent. The constitution essentially guaranteed these landholding patterns by requiring a three-quarters vote in parliament to change them, but the land issue has continued to be the most volatile issue in Fijian politics.

From the first postindependence general election in 1972 through the last election in April 1987, Fiji has impressed all observers as being a model democracy with a vigorous multiparty system and honest elections. Because of his popularity, Ratu Mara remained prime minister from 1970 to 1987. The Labor party victory over the conservative Alliance and National parties in the April 1987 election seemed to mark yet another progressive step in Fiji's political development. Although Prime Minister Bavadra was Fijian, he presided over a cabinet of both Fijians and Indians, thus breaking the domination of conservative Fijian control over politics.

The constitution insures multiracial representation, but Fiji's military force continues to be almost 95 percent native Fijian. On May 14, 1987, the military, led by Colonel Rabuka, overthrew parliament and turned over power to a council of Fijian leaders, justifying the coup on the grounds that it was necessary to safeguard Fijian land rights. On September 26, tired of the impasse over constitutional reforms, Rabuka overthrew the interim government and on October 6 declared himself head of the new republic of Fiji and the 1970 constitution void. On December 5, Rabuka again stepped down and turned over power to former Governor-General Ratu Penaia Ganilau, who became the first president of the republic. Ganilau quickly formed a cabinet of Fiji's political elite, including Ratu Mara, and the government began restoring a parliamentary system to Fiji that will balance Fijian control and Indian rights. With its relatively strong parliamentary and economic foundations, there is a good chance Fiji will overcome its present difficulties and become a democracy again.

Solomon Islands

With 248,000 inhabitants, the Solomon Islands is the third largest Pacific country in population. After independence on July 7, 1978, the Solomon Islands became a constitutional monarchy with the queen of England as head of state, represented by a governor-general appointed on the recommendation of the legislature every five years. The single-chamber parliament has 38 members, elected at most every four years. After the election, parliament chooses by secret ballot a prime minister who then selects up to 15 other ministers.

Britain declared a protectorate over the southern Solomon Islands in 1893 in an attempt to end the "blackbirding" that had carried off at least 30,000 slaves to plantations in Fiji, Queensland and elsewhere starting in 1870. The protectorate was extended to other islands in 1898 and 1899, and a 1900 treaty with Germany transferred additional islands to the Solomons in exchange for Britain agreeing to withdraw its claims in Western Samoa.

The Solomon Islands experienced no significant political development before World War II, but the presence of large numbers of U.S. troops during the war and their obvious wealth stimulated the Marching Rule movement for independence between 1946 and 1950. The movement was repressed and its leaders jailed, but reemerged briefly in 1959–60, then collapsed after its followers withdrew into the jungle to build a model community called Paradise.

In response, the British began the slow step-by-step process in preparing the Solomon Islands for nationhood. An Advisory Council was superseded by a Legislative Council and Executive Council in 1960. In 1970, these institutions were replaced by a single governing council of 17 elected members and nine appointed members, with the British high commissioner holding veto power over legislation. A new constitution was instituted in 1974 whereby the high commissioner became a governor and the governing council became the Legislative Council, with 24 elected and three appointed members.

Tuvalu

Until October 1975, the Polynesian Ellice Islands had been administered by Britain with the Micronesian Gilbert Islands (now Kiribati), but succeeded in achieving separation after a 1974 referendum overwelmingly voted in favor of secession. Independence for the 7,300 Tuvalans occurred two years later on October 1, 1978. Tuvalu is a constitutional monarchy with the queen of England as head of state, represented by a Tuvalan governor general recommended by parliament. Tuvalu's 12-member parliament is the smallest in the Pacific. It generally sits for four years; power to summon or dissolve parliament rests with the governor-general acting on the prime minister's advice. The cabinet consists of the prime minister and four other ministers.

Britain's influence in Tuvalu evolved in the pattern similar to other Pacific islands countries. A succession of beachcombers, traders, missionaries and navy ships established British interests and forced the Ellice Islands to become dependent on Britain for protection. In 1892 a visiting British warship officially asked the inhabitants if they desired protection; the Tuvalans agreed. The islands became part of the Gilbert and Ellice Islands protectorate that year; the status was changed to that of a colony in 1916.

Kiribati

Although originally scheduled for independence the same year as Tuvalu, Kiribati was forced to postpone its independence while a secession attempt by the island of Banaba was resolved by a British court. Westminster ruled against the Banabans, and the 60,000 Kiribati citizens achieved independence on July 12, 1979. Despite being lead by a "president" who serves as both head of state and head of government, Kiribati actually has a parliamentary form of government whose president is elected by a vote of the House of Assembly (Maneaba ni Maungatabu) following a general election. Kiribati's 36-member unicameral legislature must nominate either three or four presidential candidates, all of which must be assembly members. Once elected a president then chooses a vice president and an eight-member cabinet. Elections must be held at least every four years, and a president cannot serve more than two terms.

Kiribati, or the Gilbert Islands as it was known before independence, was made a British protectorate in 1892 and a colony in 1916. The Gilbert and Ellice Islands were ruled by a high commissioner appointed by Westminster, but from the early 1950s until the late 1970s Britain prepared Kiribati for eventual independence through a step-by-step process of giving the inhabitants greater autonomy. Periodic meetings of Kiribati leaders starting in 1951 gave way to the creation of an Executive Council and Advisory Council in 1963 to advise the governor-general. In 1967 the Advisory Council was replaced by a House of Representatives with no legislative powers. In 1971, the House of Representatives was replaced by a Legislative Council of 23 elected members, and the Governing Council replaced by an Executive Council. The Legislative Council was replaced by the present House of Assembly in 1974. Three years later, on January 1, 1977, Kiribati was granted full internal autonomy, followed two and a half years later by independence.

Vanuatu

Of all the Pacific island countries, none rode a rockier road to independence or has practiced more controversial policies since than Vanuatu. This is hardly surprising, since from the time Vanuatu (formerly known as the New Hebrides) came under direct foreign control in 1886 until its independence in 1980 it was governed by both Britain and France. A 1886 joint naval commission was formed after a decade of competition between Britain and France during which each scrambled to annex the islands. Although the commission brought an end to the exploitation of Vanuatu's labor by "blackbirders" and its land by foreign businessmen, it failed to administer the islands effectively since the island's rulers could not agree on a common civil code. Britain and France finally agreed to a condominium in October 1906 when Germany tried to carve out its own political economic sphere in Vanuatu.

Under the condominium there were two separate civil services—one British and one French—each with its own language, rules and procedures. Throughout the 20th century, Vanuatuns grew increasingly impatient with both systems. Following World War II a native movement arose based on a mythical figure called "John Frum" who was supposed to liberate the islanders from foreign rule and bring them tremendous wealth. The movement was inspired by the arrival of the Americans during the war with democratic ideas and obvious material riches. The condominium periodically cracked down on the movement by jailing its leaders, and repeatedly rejected its petitions for an end to foreign rule, in part because neither France nor Britain wanted to withdraw from the territory without the other.

While suppressing the John Frum movement, the condominium began preparing Vanuatu for eventual independence by creating an Advisory Council of prominent native leaders in 1957, and enlarging it to 30 members in 1969, 14 of whom were elected. In the late 1960s, a much more effective independence movement called Nagriamel under the leadership of Jimmy Stephens emerged, and by the mid-1970s, half a dozen political parties had joined the Nagriamel in battling for political power. These parties bitterly contested the 1975 municipal and Representative Assembly elections. Politically, the parties ranged from adherents of continued foreign rule to the Vanuaaku party, which campaigned for independence by 1977. Despite its popular appeal, the Vanuaaku party lost heavily in the Representative Assembly election. Alleging continued fraud, corruption and vote-buying, the Vanuaaku party then boycotted the 1977 Representative Assembly election, and declared a Provisional People's Government of its own with the power to raise taxes. The condominium did nothing to stop the Vanuaaku party, and, realizing they lacked a popular mandate, the government parties in 1978 agreed to share half the assembly seats with the Vanuaaku party in a Government of National Unity, in return for which the Vanuaaku party agreed to dissolve its Provisional People's Government.

In September 1979, the government began drafting a constitution to guide Vanuatu after independence. The constitution provides for a 39-seat unicameral legislature, presided over by a prime minister and a Council of Ministers that can include up to one-quarter of the legislature. The legislature elects the prime minister by secret ballot. A National Council of Chiefs meets at least once a year to discuss all matters relating to tradition, and recommends appropriate policies to the cabinet. In addition, there are 11 island government councils, which allow each island a certain amount of autonomy.

The Vanuaaku party won a decisive victory of 26 seats in the November

1979 general election and its leader, Father Walter Lini became chief minister. An opposition party on the northern island of Espiritu Santo, led by Jimmy Stephens, declared the election a fraud, and attempted to secede from Vanuatu in January 1980. The condominium failed to put down these rebels and when Vanuatu became independent on July 30, 1980, the northern islands remained free. Vanuatu was reunited only after the new government asked Papua New Guinea for troops, which finally captured the rebel headquarters on August 31.

With independence, Father Lini became prime minister; his Vanuaaku party has won every election since 1980. Lini's rule has recently been challenged by the Vanuaaku secretary-general, Barak Sope. Sope is said to have inspired a May 1988 riot in Port Vila, ostensibly over land rights, but actually to topple Lini's government. Although the riot was suppressed with the aid of Australian and New Zealand troops, unrest continued to simmer and Lini remained frail from a 1987 stroke.

THE NEW ZEALAND FREE ASSOCIATION STATES

Cook Islands
The Cook Islands are an internally self-governing state in free association with New Zealand. While maintaining their Polynesian culture, the 17,000 Cook Islanders and 24,000 émigrés mostly living in New Zealand are British subjects and New Zealand citizens.

Western influence in the Cook Islands began with the arrival of missionaries and traders after 1820, but New Zealand did not express an interest in the islands until fears spread that the French were considering annexing the territory in the 1880s. Instead, a British protectorate was declared in 1888 with a Westminster-appointed resident commissioner to head it. Although each island had the right of self-government, that right was superseded by Britain's ability to pass laws binding for all. Around 1900 New Zealand began to pressure the chiefs into petitioning Wellington to annex the Cook Islands, which formally became part of New Zealand in 1901. It was not until 1915, however, that New Zealand began to replace significantly Britain's administration with its own when it appointed a cabinet minister for the Cook Islands, with the resident commissioner reporting directly to him.

For the two decades following, Wellington steadily increased the Cook Islands' autonomy. In 1946 a Legislative Council representing the islands was set up with the resident commissioner as president. In 1957, the Council was transformed into a Legislative Assembly with extended powers; and in 1962, an Executive Committee of the Assembly was set up to advise Wellington on policy and budgetary matters. In November 1964, New Zealand's parliament passed legislation granting a new constitution for the Cook Islands that provided for universal suffrage and an elected Legislative Assembly of 22 members. The first general election was held in April 1965, with the Cook Islands party winning. The Legislative Assembly then voted to remain in free association with New Zealand, which assumed responsibility for defense, foreign affairs and necessary financial support.

The 1965 constitution created a unicameral parliament of 24 members

699

elected for four years. An admendment in 1981 extended the term to five years, added two constituencies in New Zealand to represent the émigrés and changed the Legislative Assembly to a parliament. The constitution can be amended by a two-thirds vote. The cabinet consists of a prime minister who appoints six other ministers. The head of state is the queen of England, who appoints a high commissioner after the advice and approval of the Cook Island parliament. There are two permanent judges, both appointed by New Zealand. Local government is dominated by village councils of chiefs *(ariki)*. The House of Ariki consists of up to 15 ariki who meet once a year to advise parliament on traditional matters. The Cook Islands has a two-party system, composed of the Cook Islands and Democratic parties. The Cook Islands party has won every election since 1965, except for 1978 when it was ousted following exposure of a corruption scandal within its ranks. The Democratic party lasted in office only a short time, when it in turn was toppled by exposure of a similar scandal.

The Cook Islands has maintained a relatively independent foreign policy despite its free association with New Zealand. President Albert Henry refused to join New Zealand's policy of denying port calls for possibly nuclear-armed U.S. warships, and was lukewarm in support of SPNFZ. President Pupuke Robati, elected in 1987, visited Paris that year to discuss with representatives of Western Samoa, American Samoa and French Polynesia the possibility of creating a "Polynesian community." Although the creation of the community remains a distant goal, Robati did succeed in returning to the Cook Islands with a $8.3 million soft loan.

Niue

Niue is a small coral island of only 3,200 people which, like the Cook Islands, was annexed by New Zealand from Britain in 1901. It agreed to form a free association with New Zealand in 1974. Under the agreement, the Polynesian Niueans are simultaneously New Zealand citizens and British subjects.

There are two distinct ethnic groups in Niue despite its small size: one originating from Samoa and the other from Tonga. These ethnic divisions are mirrored in the island's politics. Niue experienced the familiar South Pacific island pattern of occasional ship calls starting in the 18th century, followed by missionaries and settlers throughout the 19th century. In 1876, the foreign influence among the largest clans influenced the Niueans to "elect" a king. King Mataio Tuitoga then repeatedly petitioned Queen Victoria for annexation, a plea that was not granted until 1900. Originally, Niue was administered by New Zealand with the Cook Islands, but in 1904 it was given its own resident commissioner and council.

It was not until 1960 that the next significant political change occurred, when the first Niue Assembly was established with an elected representative from each village. In 1966, some of the resident commissioner's powers were delegated to the Assembly. On October 19, 1974, New Zealand granted Niue a constitution that created a Legislative Assembly of 20 members presided over by a cabinet of a prime minister and four other ministers. Each of the villages has its own council with representatives elected for three-year terms. The judicial system is topped by a High Court, but citizens can appeal to the New Zealand Supreme Court. Politics revolves around patronage and development projects. The key development issues are the continuing drain of émigrés to New Zealand and elsewhere, and the direction of the Five-Year Plans started in 1980. The economy is predominantly agricultural, with government services comprising much of the remaining work force. Almost all of Niue's trade is with New Zealand.

THE FRENCH DEPENDENCIES

French Polynesia
French Polynesia is an overseas territory of France, a status that entitles it to be represented in Paris by an elected senator and two deputies. In return, an appointed high commissioner controls all of French Polynesia's government services including the police, judicial system, television and bureaucracy. Every five years, French Polynesians elect a Territorial Assembly of 30 members, which in turn chooses the seven members of the Government Council. Since 1972, the territory has been divided into 48 communes or municipalities headed by elected councils that choose mayors.

Although French Polynesians comprise about 70 percent of the population compared to 15 percent Europeans, 8 percent mixed race and 7 percent Chinese, those favoring independence remain a minority. The multiparty system includes the Gaullist Tahoeraa Huiraatira party, led by Gaston Fosse, which dominates French Polynesian politics; the Pupu Here Aia party, which favors an independent Polynesia in association with France; and the small Socialist Ia Mana Te Nunaa party, favoring complete independence, which has the support of about 15 percent of the population.

If Westminster had been interested, the five island groups that make up French Polynesia might have been British. It was British rather than French merchantmen and missionaries who visited the islands throughout the late 18th and early 19th centuries. By 1815 most of the islands were converted to Christianity when the Tahitian chief Pomare II defeated his rivals and spread the religion with his conquests. In 1836, two French Catholic priests attempted to set up a mission in Tahiti to offset the efforts of British Protestants, but were quickly expelled. Two years later, a French warship arrived to demand and receive reparation for the priests' ill-treatment, and the next year another French warship appeared to demand permission from Queen Pomare IV for unrestricted entrance of French missionaries and settlers. The queen's pleas to Britain for protection were ignored, and in 1847 French troops landed and forced the queen to accept a French protectorate. In 1880, the French forced King Pomare V to cede Tahiti and its five island dependencies to France.

French Polynesia remained a forgotten backwater of the French empire until France's defeat in 1940, when the inhabitants overwelmingly voted to support De Gaulle's Free French government rather than that of Vichy. The introduction of U.S. troops and ideas during World War II stimulated considerable democratic and independence sentiments among Polynesians. By mid-1947, several dozen trade unions had been set up and an indepen-

701

dence committee formed under the leadership of Pouvanaa Oopa. Pouvanaa's popularity grew and his party gained a majority of seats in the 1957 Territorial Assembly; in addition, he was elected French Polynesia's representative to Paris. In April 1958, Pouvanaa announced his government's intention to secede from France and form an independent republic. The French quickly crushed the revolt by arresting Pouvanaa and 15 key followers on trumped-up charges of attempted murder, and sentenced them to prison in exile. The trial was followed by a referendum in which 64 percent of French Polynesians voted in favor of remaining an overseas French territory.

The independence issue in French Polynesian politics remained relatively dormant through the 1980s. Although proindependence parties continue to poll only about 15 percent of the vote, freedom from French rule is becoming increasingly popular among young people. With Polynesians comprising 70 percent of the population, support for independence could grow if the territory's economy continues to stagnate.

New Caledonia

New Caledonia is a French Overseas territory which, like French Polynesia, is represented in Paris by a popularly elected senator and two deputies. There is a 36-member Territorial Assembly, which is elected every five years and is allowed to debate the budget and general policy. Real power resides in the appointed high commissioner who presides over a seven-member Government Council whose members are elected by the Territorial Assembly. New Caledonia is composed of four regional councils, which are further divided into 32 communes, each with an elected mayor and municipal council. Decisions made by each mayor must be approved by the appropriate council's administrator who is appointed by Paris.

Despite its lack of power, the Territorial Assembly is fought over by a vigorous multiparty system. Two of the current parties are in favor of French administration—Calédonie dans la République (RPCR) and Fédération pour une Nouvelle Société Calédonienne (FNSC); while two other parties—Pijot-Lenormand-Uregei (PLU) and Front Indépendantiste (FI)—seek independence. In addition, there are at any time several other small parties trying to enlist political support.

The most important issue in New Caledonian politics has been independence. In 1982, Melanesians comprised 43 percent of the population, Europeans 38 percent and Polynesians 12 percent. Throughout the 1980s the Kanak Socialist National Liberation Front (FLNKS) mounted an increasingly popular campaign for independence. In 1983, the FLNKS-affiliated FI won 18 of 32 communes outside Noumea, while RPCR took all 45 commune seats in Noumea. In the 1985 commune elections RPCR won 25 of the 46 seats but only one of the four regional councils, Noumea, while FLNKS won the three other councils. This growing support, however, was undercut by an August 1987 referendum (boycotted by FLNKS), which resulted in 98 percent of those who voted—or about 60 percent of the electorate—favoring continued union with France.

FLNKS' meteorlike bid for independence is only the latest anti-European upsurge. The Melanesians have periodically revolted against Western encroachment in New Caledonia since the first hordes of merchants, deserters, escaped convicts, miners and missionaries of half a dozen nationalities began trickling into New Caledonia in the mid-19th century. Both Britain and France desired the two islands that make up New Caledonia, but it was a 1850 native attack on a French survey ship, in which the entire crew was killed and eaten, that stimulated Paris to take over the islands. By 1853 New Caledonia was being used as a dumping ground for French convicts, while its rich mineral deposits of gold and nickel were being exploited. French settlement was complicated by continued Melanesian resistance, which was finally crushed in 1917. FLNKS' 1980s independence bid is the latest in a long line of revolts against French rule.

THE AMERICAN DEPENDENCIES

Guam

Guam is a self-governing territory of the United States, supervised by the Department of the Interior. It has been a U.S. territory since 1898 when Spanish defeat in the Spanish-American War ended over 300 years of colonial rule. From then until 1950, Guam remained under the jurisdiction of the U.S. Navy. In 1917, Washington created an advisory council of 34 nominated Guamanian leaders to give the territory experience in self-government; in 1931 an elected Congress of two houses with a total of 34 members was created.

The 1950 Organic Act made Guam an unincorporated territory of the United States, gave its people U.S. citizenship and turned over its administration to the Department of the Interior. Guam was given a unicameral legislature composed of 21 senators divided among four electoral districts for two-year terms. Politically, Guam has a two-party system of Democrats and Republicans. It has a nonvoting member of the U.S. House of Representatives who is elected every two years. The Organic Act was amended in 1970 to allow an elected governor: In 1972, Guam elected its first delegate to the U.S. House of Representatives; the delegate enjoys a vote in committee but not on the floor. In September 1982, Guam's citizens voted three to one against making Guam a state. About 48 percent of Guam's 106,000 inhabitants are native Chamorro; the rest are members of other ethnic groups and 22,000 military personnel.

American Samoa

American Samoa remains an unincorporated, unorganized and non-self-governing territory of the United States. Although the national currency is the U.S. dollar, and the national anthem is "The Star-Spangled Banner," American Samoa flies both the American and American Samoan flags. As inhabitants of an American territory, the 32,000 American Samoans automatically receive resident status and can become U.S. citizens after fulfilling the necessary requirements.

While Polynesians have inhabited the Samoan Islands for well over 2,500 years, the first Western ship did not drop anchor until 1722. Ships of every

703

nationality increasingly came to trade. In 1803, escaped sailors and convicts began to settle there; and after 1830, missionaries began to preach there. Pago Pago's excellent harbor became a popular port of call for all of the Western powers throughout the 19th century.

The United States began to dominate what is now American Samoa in the late 19th century, but legal control evolved haphazardly at best. Americans succeeded in signing a treaty with the head chief of Pago Pago in 1872, which granted Washington naval base rights in return for extending protection to the Samoans; the treaty was never ratified. Thus, Americans, Germans and British continued to elbow each other for trade benefits in the islands for another quarter century until 1899 when the three powers formally agreed to divide the islands between Washington and Berlin. U.S. troops raised the flag over the islands in 1900, but the formal cession from the chiefs was not signed until 1904 and the name American Samoa was not adopted until 1911. The U.S. Department of the Navy administered American Samoa until 1951, when the responsibility was taken over by the Department of the Interior.

In 1960, after six years of negotiation, a delegation of American Samoans approved a constitution that contains a three-branch system of government and a bill of rights. The governor is the highest executive power: until 1978 he was appointed by Washington, since then he has been popularly elected. The bicameral legislature consists of a Seneate of 18 members and a House of Representatives of 20 members. The senators are elected for four-year terms by the Council of Chiefs (*matai*) whereas the representatives are popularly elected for two-year terms. There is a three-tier court system with an appointed High Court presiding over district and village courts. American Samoa has a nonvoting member in the U.S. House of Representatives. In addition to the rights guaranteed by the U.S. Constitution, the American Samoan bill of rights guarantees Samoan land rights. Ninety percent of the land is communally owned and subject to the jurisdiction of the village chiefs. The rest is either leased or individually owned, but the owner must be at least half native Samoan.

Politically, the government has been preoccupied with continuing to stimulate economic development. American Samoans voted down three referendums to grant themselves more autonomy, until they finally voted in favor of a popularly elected governor in 1978. Currently there is no strong political movement in favor of greater autonomy or independence for American Samoa.

Trust Territories
On July 18, 1947, the United States was granted a trusteeship over the 2,000 islands of three major archipelagos: the Carolines, the Marshalls and the Marianas. Since then, four constitutional governments have emerged from the trusteeship: the Republic of Palau (population 12,000), the Republic of the Marshall Islands (population 30,000), the Federated States of Micronesia (population 73,000) and the Commonwealth of the Northern Mariana Islands (population 20,000). Of the four, the Northern Marianas chose to accept commonwealth status under the continued rule of the United

States, while the other three chose to become independent republics in free association with the United States. Culturally, the islands are divided between a predominately Asian or Filipino influence in the western islands (Marianas), and a Polynesian influence in the eastern islands (Marshalls, eastern Carolines).

A plebiscite in the Northern Marianas on June 17, 1975, resulted in 79 percent of the voters supporting a measure for union with the United States. On March 24, 1976, Washington officially declared the Commonwealth of the Northern Mariana Islands, and followed this on January 9, 1978, with the implementation of a constitution that gives the Northern Marianas a three-branch system of government patterned after that of the United States, with an elected governor, a nine-member Senate, a 14-member House of Representatives and a judiciary branch headed by a federal judge presiding over a U.S. District Court.

On April 5, 1979, the United States recognized separate administrations under locally ratified constitutions in the Federated States of Micronesia, the Marshall Islands and Palau. Constitutions were subsequently installed in the Marshall Islands and Federated States of Micronesia on May 1 and 10, 1979, respectively, and Palau on January 1, 1981. All three states signed compacts of free association with the United States: the Marshall Islands on May 30, 1982; Palau on August 26, 1982; and the Federated States of Micronesia on October 1, 1982. These compacts were ratified for the Marshall Islands and the Federated States of Micronesia in 1986, and for Palau in 1987. Constitutionally, all three countries have presidential systems, with the presidents of Palau and the Marshall Islands popularly elected and the president of the Federated States of Micronesia elected by its National Congress. Under the compacts, each country has full self-government, while the United States accepts responsibility for defense: for minimal periods of 15 years for the Marshall Islands and the Federated States of Micronesia, and for 50 years for Palau. The period of free association is indefinite, but can be terminated at any time by either mutual agreement or unilateral action. In addition, Washington has agreed to provide a total of $2.2 billion over 15 years to fund aid and administrative programs in each country. According to the compacts the United States could continue to use the Kwajalein missile range in the Marshall Islands and contingency military landing rights in Palau for up to 30 years. None of the three states is allowed to admit any third country's military force without U.S. permission.

With independence, the three countries have shed foreign domination that goes back at least four centuries for some of the islands: Spain, to 1898; Germany, to 1914; Japan, to 1945; and the United States, until 1979. All four of these foreign countries had seized the islands largely for strategic rather than economic reasons. The Japanese used the islands as a springboard for the attacks on Pearl Harbor and the South Pacific. After World War II, Washington succeeded in getting the United Nations to grant it a "strategic trusteeship" over the islands. U.S. neglect of the region in the 1950s except for strategic purposes led to its being labeled the "Rust Territory." Stung by a U.N. report highly critical of the American trusteeship, the Kennedy administration began pumping in aid and created the council of Micronesia with legislative authority, although the U.S. high commissioner held veto power. In 1965, the council, renamed the Congress of Micronesia, was designed to prepare the islanders for a choice over their political future.

CONCLUSION

Overall, both as individual states and as a region, the Pacific island countries have experienced highly successful political development. All the countries and territories enjoy democratic forms of government, and these political systems have successfully overcome or contained a wide range of political and economic challenges. The nine independent states and five states in free association were carefully prepared by their respective colonial rulers for independence and democracy, while the five remaining foreign territories have used both elections and referendums to deal with independence issues. The South Pacific Forum is probably the world's most successful regional organization after the European Community. Even without its major achievement—the fisheries treaty with the United States and the SPNFZ—the forum is a model international organization due to its spectrum of relatively effective programs dealing with regional problems such as economic growth, education, transportation and communication. If the past is any guide to the future, the political institutions of the Pacific region are well prepared to deal successfully with continuing and future challenges.

FURTHER READING

Carter, John, ed. *Pacific Islands Year Book*. New York and Sydney: Pacific Publications, 1984.

Feld, Werner, Jordan, Robert S., and Hurwitz, Leon. *International Organizations: A Comparative Approach*. New York: Praeger, 1983.

Fry, G. E. *South Pacific Regionalism: The Development of an Indigenous Commitment*. Canberra: Australia National University Press, 1979.

Haas, Ernst. *The Obsolescence of Regional Integration Theory*. Berkeley: University of California Press, 1975.

Kiste, Robert C., and Herr, Richard, eds. *The Pacific Islands in the Year 2000*. Honolulu, Hawaii: East-West Center, 1985.

Krasner, Stephen, ed. *International Regimes*. Ithaca, New York and London: Cornell University Press, 1982.

Nye, Joseph, ed. *International Regionalism: Readings*. Ithaca, New York and London: Cornell University Press, 1982.

Peoples, James G. *Island in Trust: Culture Change and Dependence in a Micronesian Economy*. Boulder, Colorado: Westview Press, 1985.

Taylor, Phillip. *Nonstate Actors in International Politics: From Transregional to Substate Organizations*. Boulder, Colorado: Westview Press, 1984.

PAKISTAN

WILLIAM L. RICHTER

INTRODUCTION

PAKISTAN is in many respects an enigma, a country numbered among the world's largest but often appearing dwarfed by its even larger neighbors—India, China and the Soviet Union. Carved out of British India in 1947 as a homeland for Muslims of the subcontinent, the country has been less able to develop a sense of national identity or maintain national unity than has India, which is religiously and culturally more diverse. In 1971, less than a quarter-century after its birth, Pakistan was split by a nine-month secessionist civil war that ultimately transformed its eastern wing into the independent Republic of Bangladesh.

The "new" Pakistan (after 1971) is a country "in between": It is geographically and culturally a part of Indocentric South Asia and at the same time a part of Islamic Southwest Asia. Peripheral to both regions, it nonetheless serves as a cultural bridge between the two.

Pakistan—like India, Sri Lanka, Malaysia and other former British colonial territories—was heir to the British parliamentary and administrative tradition, but it has had an exceptionally difficult time maintaining political order and establishing a viable constitutional system. Now in its fifth decade of independence, it continues to search for workable representative institutions, legitimacy and national identity.

HISTORY

The movement to create Pakistan arose in the context of competition between the Hindu and Muslim communities in colonial India. The suggestion that Indian Muslims might merit a separate country was voiced in the late 19th century by the prominent Muslim leader Sir Syed Ahmed, but it was not until the 1930s that the concept was given the name Pakistan and gained some degree of popular support. Only in 1940, at its annual meeting in Lahore, did the Muslim League adopt the demand for Pakistan, a demand that ultimately became a reality on August 14, 1947.

The new nation was beset by problems. Its territory was designated to be the provinces of Sind, Baluchistan and North-West Frontier Province, as well as the Muslim-majority portions of Punjab and Bengal provinces, but the new boundaries of the partitioned provinces were still undetermined at the time of independence. East Bengal, which became East Pakistan, was in the Ganga delta, separated from the remaining provinces in West Pakistan by more than 900 miles/1,448 km. of Indian territory. Mass migration and communal tension, particularly in Punjab, led to widespread death and dislocation, while uncertainty over the political future of some of the former princely states led to further conflict with India and full-scale war in Kashmir.

The physical resources for starting a new government were woefully short and the human resources proved inadequate to many of the essential tasks as well. Pakistan's "founding father," Quaid-e-Azam Muhammad Ali Jinnah, died just a year after independence, and the country's second most prominent leader, Liaquat Ali Khan—who succeeded Jinnah as governor-general—was assassinated in 1951. The ensuing years were marked by political decay: endless debate over constitutional issues, including the question of what role religion should play in Pakistan; absence of national elections; deterioration of the Muslim League as a political force of even minimal effectiveness; growing alienation of East Pakistan; and frequent changes of national and provincial leaders. The country was unable to create a constitution until 1956, almost nine years after independence. That constitution lasted less than two years. In October 1958 President Iskander Mirza declared martial law and named army Commander in Chief Mohammad Ayub Khan as martial-law administrator. Three weeks later Ayub dismissed Mirza and initiated his own "revolution."[1]

In effect, Ayub's takeover constituted a second founding for Pakistan, an opportunity to start afresh. Arguing that the political instability of the previous decade had demonstrated the inappropriateness of parliamentary democracy for a new country like Pakistan, Ayub called for a system of "basic democracy" featuring indirect representation and limited popular franchise. The system was incorporated into the 1962 constitution, under which Ayub served as civilian president until his own overthrow in March 1969.

Ayub's suppression of politics and emphasis on economic development allowed him to claim, in the late 1960s, that he had provided Pakistan with a "decade of development." By that point, however, discontent was already growing over a variety of grievances. East Pakistanis objected that the basic democracy system discriminated against them and perpetuated West Pakistani domination. Non-Punjabis in West Pakistan similarly complained of Punjabi domination and West Pakistanis in general chafed at their lack of political power. Protest movements arose in both wings of the country and ultimately forced Ayub's resignation.

Ayub's successor, Gen. Agha Mohammad Yahya Khan, set about dismantling some of the more unpopular features of Ayub's system. He restored the separate provinces of West Pakistan that had been merged in 1955 into a single unit. He restored the principle of "one person one vote"

[1] Cf. Herbert Feldman, *Revolution in Pakistan: A Study of the Martial Law Administration* (London: Oxford University Press, 1967); Mohammad Ayub Khan, *Friends Not Masters: A Political Autobiography* (Lahore: Oxford University Press, 1967).

and held elections for a new parliament that would also serve as a constituent assembly for the writing of a new constitution. The elections, held December 7, 1970, were the first national popular elections in nearly a quarter-century of independence, and were generally regarded as fair and well-run.

The aftermath of the elections, however, was disastrous. The Awami League, based solely in East Pakistan and led by Sheikh Mujibur Rahman, won a clear majority of 160 seats in the 300-member assembly. Zulfikar Ali Bhutto, leader of the Pakistan People's party (PPP)—which had won approximately 60 percent of the West Pakistani seats—refused to participate in the assembly without prior negotiation with Sheikh Mujib of "ground rules" concerning the future constitution. The army and the martial-law government sided with Bhutto and, when negotiations with Mujib broke down, began a military crackdown in East Pakistan on March 25, 1971. Thus began the civil war that nine months later, aided by Indian intervention, gave East Pakistan its independence as the Republic of Bangladesh.[2]

Disgraced by their military defeat and political blunders, Yahya and his fellow generals turned over the government of what remained of Pakistan to Bhutto and the PPP. Bhutto, in effect, provided Pakistan with its third founding. He brought hope and direction to a defeated and disillusioned nation. He engineered a new constitution, adopted in 1973 with the support of all four provinces; curtailed the political power of the military and of the country's wealthiest families; and called for a system of "Islamic socialism" that would provide *Roti, Kapra aur Makaan* (food, clothing and shelter) to all. In foreign affairs, he met at Simla with Indian Prime Minister Indira Gandhi and negotiated the return of the more than 90,000 Pakistani prisoners of war held by India after the war. In 1974 he hosted an Islamic summit conference in Lahore and used the occasion to accord recognition to Bangladesh. He also forged new ties with Iran and Arab neighbors to the west.

Bhutto's political promise, however, ran afoul of his personal arrogance and high-handed tactics. The more success he enjoyed in rebuilding Pakistan, the more he appeared to regard the country as his personal fiefdom. He increasingly demeaned and alienated both opponents and allies, used state agencies to harass adversaries, controlled the media, dismissed opposition-led governments in two provinces and outlawed the major opposition political party (the National Awami party). When he attempted to hold general elections in March 1977 to confirm his ascendancy and control, he found himself faced with an unexpectedly strong and seemingly impromptu opposition coalition of nine parties, the Pakistan National Alliance (PNA).

By official count, the PPP decisively won out over the PNA in the March 7, 1977, elections, but the PNA immediately charged that the government had rigged the polling; it boycotted the provincial elections three days later

---

[2] There is an extensive literature on the Bangladesh war and the events leading up to it. Cf. G. W. Choudhury, *The Last Days of United Pakistan* (London: C. Hurst & Company, 1974); Marta R. Nicholas and Philip Oldenburg, eds., *Bangladesh: The Birth of a Nation* (Madras: M. Seshachalam & Co., 1972).

and began a protest movement calling for Bhutto's ouster. The protest spread throughout Pakistan, bringing the economy to a halt and forcing Bhutto to call upon the army to restore order in five major cities. The government agreed to negotiate with the PNA and by late June appeared to be on the verge of signing an agreement to hold fresh elections. At that point, however, the military intervened, under the leadership of army Chief of Staff Mohammad Zia ul-Haq, and declared Pakistan's third period of nationwide martial law.

General Zia promised that his martial-law regime would just be a caretaker, that through "Operation Fair Play" elections would be held within three months and power returned to civilian hands. Elections were indeed scheduled for October but were abruptly canceled without explanation two weeks before the appointed date, when it became apparent that Bhutto's popularity remained strong enough to constitute a major threat.[3] Meanwhile, the military had uncovered enough evidence to charge Bhutto with complicity in a 1974 political murder. After his prolonged trial and conviction, the refusal of the Supreme Court to overturn the verdict and Zia's negative response to widespread international appeals for clemency, Bhutto was executed by hanging on April 5, 1969.

Having eliminated his major domestic political threat, Zia again attempted to schedule elections, for November 1969, but again was forced to cancel before the event. Strict martial-law regulations were imposed, including heavy censorship and an official ban on all political parties. Although formally outlawed, parties continued to operate unofficially, and in 1981 a new anti-Zia coalition, called the Movement for the Restoration of Democracy (MRD), was created. The MRD, which included both the PPP—now led by the former prime minister's daughter Benazir Bhutto—and several components of the former anti-Bhutto PNA, demanded an end to martial law, restoration of the 1973 constitution, Zia's resignation and new elections.

In August 1983 President Zia announced a plan that may be regarded as the framework for Pakistan's fourth founding. In the plan he announced that parliamentary elections would be held, on a nonparty basis, before March 1985 and that the government would subsequently move toward restoration of civilian rule. The initial public response to the plan was negative—a massive objection to such a further prolonging of military domination. A protest movement erupted in Sind, fueled by Sindhi regional discontent and exploited by the MRD who saw it as a possible repeat of the anti-Bhutto movement of 1977 and the anti-Ayub movement of 1968–69. In this case, though, the protest failed to spread much beyond Sind, and the authorities reestablished control after several weeks.

In December 1984 Zia held, on short notice, a nationwide referendum to approve the Islamic thrust of the government's policies. With a strongly positive response in what was obviously a lopsided contest, Zia declared

[3] For an early analysis of this period, see William L. Richter, "Persistent Praetorianism: Pakistan's Third Military Regime," *Pacific Affairs* 51, no. 3 (Fall 1978): 406–26.

that the referendum constituted a mandate for him to remain in the presidency for another five years. That provision for executive continuity thus taken care of, he held the long-promised elections in February 1985. Despite a boycott by the MRD, voters turned out strongly for the elections, although not necessarily in support of Zia, who saw several of his favorite candidates defeated.

Following the elections, Zia appointed Muhammad Khan Junejo prime minister and reconvened parliament for the first time in nearly eight years. By the end of 1985 martial law was lifted and the 1973 constitution restored, though incorporating several amendments made during 1985 and earlier under martial law. In early 1986 political parties were again legalized.

Both the fragility and the vitality of Pakistani democracy were demonstrated in the dramatic events of 1988. On May 29, President Zia announced the dismissal of Prime Minister Junejo and his cabinet, the dissolution of the National Assembly, and a similar dismissal of the governments in two of Pakistan's four provinces. He promised that new elections would be held, but was himself removed from the scene before they could take place. On August 17, his military transport crashed in Bahawalpur, in central Pakistan, killing all aboard, including the American ambassador and military attaché and about thirty top Pakistani officers.

The elections were held on schedule, with the full participation of political parties. Acting President Ghulam Ishaq Khan and the new Army Chief Mirza Aslam Beg both guaranteed the fairness of the electoral process and honored the results. Benazir Bhutto, whose PPP won a strong plurality in the National Assembly, was named prime minister on December 1.

The first year of Benazir Bhutto's government was marked by several major political challenges. Bhutto clashed on more than one occasion with President Ishaq and with Mian Nawaz Sharif, chief minister of Punjab and leader of the Islami Jamhorri Ittehad (IJI), the PPP's strongest competitor nationally. In all, given the precariousness of her majority in Parliament, it was an accomplishment to survive her first year, but it was unclear how long her government—or the constitutional system—might last.

THE CURRENT POLITICAL SYSTEM

Pakistan in the late 1980s and early 1990s must be viewed as an experiment in democratic representative government. It operates within the framework of the 1973 Constitution, as modified significantly during the long period of marital law. The modifications introduced by Zia, and locked into the Constitution by the Eighth Amendment (1985), included a strengthening of the role of president vis-à-vis the prime minister. Benazir Bhutto attempted during 1989 to repeal the Eighth Amendment, but without success.

For at least the first year following the 1988 elections, the PPP managed to maintain control of the National Assembly and of the provincial assemblies of Sind and the North-West Frontier Province. The Islami Jamhoori Ittehad, a coalition of anti-PPP parties, including particularly the Pakistan

Muslim League (PML), ruled in Punjab, the country's most heavily populated province. This was the first time in Pakistan's more than four decades of independence that different parties held power in Islamabad (the national capital) and Lahore (capital of Punjab). Although this made for unprecedented strains between the two levels of government, it also carried the potential for a more meaningful system of federalism than existed at any previous time.

Although the military has played an active political role frequently and for long periods in the past, and it continues to retain a great amount of residual power, it has assiduously abstained from intervention in the political arena since Zia's death. The generals appear unlikely to return to control very soon, unless the political order should deteriorate greatly—as happened in 1958, 1969, and 1977, when previous military coups occurred.

Both the bureaucracy and the court system suffered some degree of erosion of their independence and authority during the Ali Bhutto years and Zia's martial-law period. Bhutto undermined the independence of the bureaucracy by a lateral entry program that rewarded civil service positions to the party faithful. Similarly, martial law made possible the appointment of large numbers of retired military personnel to important administrative positions. In 1981 Zia required Supreme Court and High Court judges to take an oath of loyalty to the military regime and summarily dismissed those who did not. The bureaucracy and the judiciary remain bulwarks of political order in Pakistan, but they are obviously not immune to political control.

Ethnic and regional differences have plagued Pakistan throughout its existence. Prolonged periods of ineffective government and political repression allowed Bengali nationalism to fester and grow until it exploded in the Bangladesh war and split Pakistan in two. Even after the loss of its eastern wing, Pakistan continued to encounter problems of regionalism and separatism in much of what was left of the country. During 1973–77 a longer but less publicized civil war was fought in the massive but sparsely populated province of Baluchistan. The 1983 anti-Zia protests in Sind were fueled by Sindhi regional discontent. The North-West Frontier Province, often the scene of Pathan (also called Pushtun or Pakhtun) separatism, has been relatively quiet since the Soviet occupation of Afghanistan in late 1979, but Pathan migrants to Karachi have periodically clashed violently with other ethnic groups in that city, particularly the Muhajirs, or Urdu-speaking immigrants from India. Karachi has also been the site of occasional sectarian clashes between Sunni and Shiite Muslims. While the post-1985 movement toward a more open political system might in the short run stimulate more such outbreaks, it may in the long run provide the channels for peaceful change without which a diverse country like Pakistan is doomed to repeat tragedies like the Bangladesh War.

CULTURE

Pakistan has a rich cultural heritage, from the prehistoric diggings in the Soan Valley and at Kot Diji, to the Indus Valley archaeological sites at

Mohenjo-Daro and Harappa, to relics of Aryan, Gandharan and early Islamic times. As might be expected, the dominant cultural element today is Islam, but even within that great religion is a tremendous diversity. Besides the sectarian differences between Sunnis and Shiites, doctrinal differences exist among the majority Sunni community, which are reflected in the multiplicity of religious parties. There is also a strong Sufi tradition, represented by the hundreds of tombs of Sufi saints throughout the country and by the political power and influence still exercised by the nominal caretakers of those tombs—the *pirs* and *makhdooms*—over their devotees. Still more controversial are groups like the Ahmadiyas or Qadianis, who have officially been branded as non-Muslims because of their refusal to accept the principle that Muhammad was Islam's final prophet.

The prominence of Islam as a political issue has increased greatly over the past decade and a half. This resurgence or reassertion of Islamic values has been manifested in new legal and political institutions, economic and educational reforms and other attempts to bring current Pakistani society into conformity with Islamic principles. Some moves in this direction were taken during the later Ali Bhutto years, but the main thrust came following the military takeover in 1977. General Zia established a nationwide system of welfare taxation and distribution *(zakat)*, programs of interest-free banking, *Sharia* courts to judge the Islamic legitimacy of laws and a variety of other reforms.[4] To a large extent, the Junejo government continued to voice Islamization as an ideal, but moved slowly and cautiously on this front.

The Benazir Bhutto government quietly halted the Islamization process, but did not move immediately to dismantle all of Zia's Islamic reforms. Programs like Zakat and Ushr are likely to provide political benefits to whatever party is in power, and may therefore be expected to remain for some time. The major critics of Islamization are religious groups, such as the Ahmadiyas, who feel the consequences of some of its more extreme measures, and women's groups, who object to its impact upon the role of women in the society and in the work force. Female literacy (16 percent) remains less than half that of males (35 percent), and the practice of purdah, or female seclusion, appears not only to be persisting but to be expanding, especially in urban areas. Women's groups in Pakistan, most notably the activist Women's Action Forum, have protested the declining percentages of women in the work force, the restrictions placed upon women's public participation in sports and other issues.

As in many other countries, there are major cultural differences between the predominantly rural sector of the society and the urban areas. Major cities like Karachi or Lahore display a fascinating array of the modern and the traditional, from new hotels and spacious middle-class neighborhoods to crowded hovels. Roughly a million people live, work and shop within Lahore's old walled city. Smaller cities and regional towns display less modern but still diverse cultural characteristics.

[4]Cf. Anita M. Weiss, ed., *Islamic Reassertion in Pakistan: The Application of Islamic Laws in a Modern State* (Syracuse: Syracuse University Press, 1986).

713

Rural Pakistan contains centuries-old villages in the river valleys or in the rain-fed agricultural areas of northern Punjab or North-West Frontier Province, or in the rugged tribal areas of North-West Frontier Province or Baluchistan, but also more recently established "canal colonies" in those parts of Punjab and Sind opened up to cultivation by extensive canal irrigation in the first part of this century. More than most countries, Pakistan's cultural mix has also been affected significantly by migration, particularly by the large wave of Muhajirs when Pakistan was created in 1947. Interprovincial and rural-urban migration has provided Karachi with large numbers of Pathans, Baluch and Punjabis, as well as Sindhis, Muhajirs and others. Afghan refugees have crowded into Peshawar and into temporary camps in North-West Frontier Province and Baluchistan. Finally, the out-migration of more than two million workers to jobs in the Persian Gulf has had both cultural and economic impact upon rural and urban Pakistan.

ECONOMY

Pakistan has enjoyed a period of remarkably strong economic growth since the late 1970s. Growth in GDP has averaged approximately 6 percent per year, with healthy gains in agriculture and industry.[5] Inflation has generally been kept in check, and exports have increased significantly. By World Bank estimates, Pakistan is on the threshold of graduating from the list of the world's poor countries to middle-income status. These estimates, however, are based upon such economic indicators as per capita income and growth in industrial and agricultural productivity. Other indicators, such as education, social services, female literacy, health and infant mortality, reveal a more negative picture.[6]

One of the reasons for Pakistan's impressive economic performance in recent years has been better management, especially elimination of much of the "political overhead" that characterized the Ali Bhutto period. Pakistan has also been the beneficiary of fortuitous circumstances. The late 1970s and early 1980s were a period of economic boom in the Middle East, and large numbers of Pakistani workers seeking employment migrated there. For several years their remittances—counting only those through official channels—constituted Pakistan's largest single source of foreign exchange. With the end of the oil boom, remittances dropped sharply, and Pakistan had to face the double economic bind of reduced foreign exchange receipts and massive employment needs for the returning workers.

Pakistan has also had the benefit of sizable amounts of foreign assistance from the United States and other members of the World Bank's Aid Pakistan Group, Islamic states and other donors. Although such assistance has enabled Pakistan to build its economy and its military strength, debt-ser-

---

[5] Agriculture employs about half the labor force and accounts for roughly one-quarter of GDP. Industry, with about 15 percent of the labor force, accounts for 28 percent of GDP. Ibid., pp. 33–34. *World Development Report 1987* (New York: Oxford University Press, 1987), 206.

[6] Ibid., tables 18, 23, 29–31; pp. 236, 246, 258–62.

vicing levels have also increased. Debt servicing constitutes roughly a quarter of current government expenditures, and repayment of the principal on foreign loans is equivalent to one-third of Pakistan's export earnings.

Critics have expressed concern not only over the rising foreign debt but also over the issue of the distribution of the benefits of growth. Roughly one-third of the budget is spent on defense, one of the highest proportions in the world. Privatization and the encouragement of export-oriented industry appear to have much higher priority than consumer concerns, and the examples of such newly industrialized countries as Taiwan and South Korea seem more interesting to policymakers than the dependency arguments voiced in earlier years. Women's groups question whether Pakistan can develop qualitatively as long as female illiteracy and such attendant problems as poor maternal health and high infant mortality continue.

FOREIGN AFFAIRS

Pakistan's major security concerns focus upon its immediate neighbors. From the beginning India has been regarded as Pakistan's major adversary. The prepartition conflicts between Hindus and Muslims, the slaughter that attended partition, the reluctance of prominent Indian leaders to accept the legitimacy of the new state of Pakistan and India's much greater size and military power all contributed to Pakistan's fears and insecurity.

Consequently, a major thrust of Pakistan's foreign policy throughout its existence has been a search for friends in a hostile world. Initial overtures to emergent Arab states proved generally unrewarding, because leaders like Egypt's Nasser were more attuned to the secular socialism of India's Nehru than to the Islamic raison d'être of the new Pakistan.

The United States, in its own search for anticommunist allies in Asia, proved to be more responsive. As a part of John Foster Dulles's extension of the doctrine of containment to Asia, Pakistan became a founding member of the Southeast Asia Treaty Organization and the Baghdad Pact (later, Central Treaty Organization, or CENTO). In 1959 the United States and Pakistan further formalized their military alliance by signing a mutual security agreement.

Some important changes occurred in the 1960s, however. Partially in response to the Kennedy administration's attempt to improve relations with India, including military assistance during the Sino-Indian border war of 1962, Pakistan turned to China as a new friend and ally in the region. Sino-Pakistani friendship, rooted in the ancient geopolitical doctrine (of the Indian writer Kautilya) that one's enemies' enemies make good allies, has continued to grow during the subsequent quarter-century. In fact, when American policy in Asia shifted again a decade later, it was Pakistan's good ties with both the United States and the People's Republic of China that facilitated Henry Kissinger's secret visit to Beijing in 1971.

The most prominent challenge to Pakistan during the past decade has been the Soviet occupation of Afghanistan, accompanied by the frequent intrusion of Soviet and Afghan forces into Pakistani territory. Pakistan now cares for more than three million Afghan refugees. Besides the costs of

715

defense preparation and refugee care, Pakistan has suffered major drug and domestic law-and-order problems as a partial consequence of the war.

The Soviet occupation, beginning in the closing days of December 1979, reflected both local political developments in Afghanistan and regional geopolitical changes in the late 1970s. The Afghan monarchy had been overthrown by a coup in 1973, and a second coup in April 1978 brought a Marxist government to power. At first, the two major Communist factions, the Khalq under Nur Muhammad Taraki and Parcham under Babrak Karmal, shared power to some extent, with Taraki serving as president and Karmal as vice-president. Within a few months, however, Karmal and Parcham had been dismissed, but factionalism within the Khalq remained a problem. In September 1979, apparently on advice from Moscow, Taraki attempted to remove his prime minister, Hafizullah Amin. Taraki was killed and Amin, whom the Soviets distrusted, became president. Four months later, 100,000 Soviet troops occupied the country, Amin was dead and Karmal had been installed as Moscow's man in Kabul.

The geopolitical conditions that made all this possible included a dramatic loss of American presence in the region during the period just prior to the Soviet move. Not only had the shah of Iran, the United States' major ally in Southwest Asia, fallen from power during 1979, but U.S.-Pakistani relations had also deteriorated greatly. Most American aid to Pakistan had been cut in March 1979 over the nuclear proliferation issue, both Iran and Pakistan had withdrawn from CENTO and Pakistani mobs had burned the American embassy in September.

After the Soviet occupation the United States attempted to rebuild its relationship with Pakistan. President Carter offered U.S. $400 million in security and economic assistance, but the offer was rejected by Pakistani President Zia as "peanuts," i.e., too small a commitment for Pakistan to risk provoking the Soviet Union. The Reagan administration negotiated a much more substantial agreement with Pakistan, however: a five-year program of $3.2 billion in military and economic assistance, along with $1.1 billion in direct sale of 40 F-16 aircraft. With the agreement, the United States was able to strengthen Pakistan's resolve not to accept the Soviet-directed changes in Afghanistan and to guarantee Pakistan's continued role as a conduit for arms to the Afghan Mujahideen. In 1987 the military assistance package was renewed, at the level of $4.02 billion.

Pakistan also led the diplomatic charge against the protracted Soviet occupation: It was the leading sponsor of the annual U.N. resolution calling for withdrawal, it mobilized fellow members of the Organization of the Islamic Conference in the same cause and it was a participant in the U.N.-sponsored negotiations with Afghans and Soviets at Geneva.

In April 1988 the Soviet Union signed the Geneva accords and on February 15, 1989 began a phased withdrawal of its troops from Afghanistan. The Mujahideen, who were largely excluded from the negotiating process, vowed to continue fighting until the Marxist government in Kabul, as well as the Soviet troops, was driven out of the country. Thus the prospects for peace on Pakistan's northwestern border remained somewhat unclear.

India continues to be Pakistan's greatest enduring security concern. The two neighbors have fought three major wars (1948–49, 1965, 1971) and several lesser skirmishes. The 1971 Bangladesh war truncated Pakistan and reinforced the fears of many Pakistanis that India was out to destroy their country; but it also led to a more realistic view of Indian military potential within the subcontinent.

There have been several bilateral attempts to improve Indo-Pakistani relations since then, beginning with the Simla conference between Bhutto and Indira Gandhi in July 1972. In 1981 Pakistan's President Zia proposed that the two countries sign a no-war pact, but India regarded the proposal as a trick. Later, Gandhi offered a counterproposal of a treaty of peace and friendship, a more comprehensive agreement that Pakistan viewed with similar suspicion. Although several years of intermittent negotiation of these two alternatives have not yet resolved the issue, India and Pakistan have managed to arrive at some lesser agreements, including the establishment of a Joint Commission, with subcommissions on tourism, trade and other functional concerns.

Pakistan has also established joint commissions with other South Asian countries, including Nepal and Bangladesh. South Asian regional cooperation generally has been an important foreign policy thrust of the 1980s, with the creation in 1980 of a seven-nation South Asian Regional Cooperation group which in 1985 was officially inaugurated as the South Asian Association for Regional Cooperation.

Despite these developments, relations between Pakistan and India remain charged with mutual suspicion. The dispute over the former princely state of Jammu and Kashmir remains unresolved, although both countries generally accept the post-1971 line of control as a de facto boundary. In recent years, though, renewed conflict has arisen over the massive and undemarcated Siachen Glacier, to which both countries lay claim. Ethnic tensions in either country are likely to produce accusations of outside interference from the other. Thus, Indian Prime Minister Rajiv Gandhi has frequently accused Pakistan of giving aid and support to the Sikh separatists in Indian Punjab; and Pakistan engaged in similar, though more limited, scapegoating against India during the 1983 demonstrations in Sind. Even troop movements can ignite deep-seated tensions. Early in 1987, when both armies were conducting maneuvers near their common border, misinterpretation of each other's intentions led to a rapid buildup of forces before the whole matter could be defused through hastily pursued negotiations.

Perhaps the most thorny issue for Pakistan's relations with India—as well as with the United States—concerns nuclear proliferation. India exploded a nuclear device in 1974, at which time Pakistan's Prime Minister Bhutto vowed to do likewise. India has not proceeded with the development of nuclear weapons, despite the pressures of a rather vocal pro-bomb lobby, and has raised alarms concerning Pakistan's nuclear intentions. Pakistan has apparently obtained both the plutonium-reprocessing and uranium-enrichment processes that could be utilized to develop nuclear weapons, but has not conducted a test and denies that it has any intention of acquiring nuclear-weapon capabilities. Pakistan has offered to enter into an agreement with India for mutual abandonment of the nuclear option, along with mutual inspection of facilities, but India has declined to bargain away its superior position, especially in light of its perceived threat from China.

The American policy against proliferation has been applied somewhat inconsistently. During the 1980s it has been treated as a lower priority than the war in Afghanistan. Congressional amendments prohibiting assistance to countries in the process of acquiring nuclear-weapons technology were waived in lieu of the Afghan-related military and economic assistance programs to Pakistan. During the last quarter of 1987 Congress did force postponement of assistance renewal but ultimately approved the aid. The issue is likely to continue to be one marked by both uncertainty and tension.

SUMMARY AND CONCLUSIONS

In some respects, Pakistan's future political prospects appear brighter than at any time in its history. Its solid economic growth, its movement—however gradual and sporadic—toward a more representative and open political system and its attempts to negotiate better relations with threatening neighbors all hold the promise of possible escape from the seemingly endless and tragic cycles of instability and military rule, war and internal disruption that have plagued the country since its birth.

FURTHER READING

Adams, John, and Iqbal, Sabiha. *Exports, Politics, and Economic Development: Pakistan, 1970–1982.* Boulder, Colorado: Westview Press, 1983.

Baxter, Craig, ed. *Zia's Pakistan: Politics and Stability in a Frontline State.* Boulder, Colorado: Westview Press, 1985.

Burki, Shahid Javed. *Pakistan: A Nation in the Making.* Boulder, Colorado: Westview Press, 1986.

Cohen, Stephen P. *The Pakistan Army.* Berkeley: University of California Press, 1984.

Feldman, Herbert. *Pakistan: An Introduction.* London and Lahore: Oxford University Press, 1968.

Rizvi, Hasan-Askari. *The Military and Politics in Pakistan, 1947–1986.* 3rd rev. ed. Lahore: Progressive Publishers, 1986.

Tahir-Kheli, Shirin. *The United States and Pakistan: The Evolution of an Influence Relationship.* New York: Praeger, 1982.

Weiss, Anita M., ed. *Islamic Reassertion in Pakistan: The Application of Islamic Laws in a Modern State.* Syracuse, New York: Syracuse University Press, 1986.

PAPUA NEW GUINEA

ANTHONY GOLDSTONE

PAPUA New Guinea gained its independence from Australia in September 1975 with what many regarded as a tenuous claim to nationhood. Papua New Guinea is a large but sparsely populated country. Eighty percent of its inhabitants live in small communities, separated from each other by mountains, swamp and sea. The firmest public allegiance has traditionally been to the clan, the *wantok*—literally "one talk" in Pidgin, the lingua franca that permits communication among speakers of the country's 700 languages and dialects.

Geographically, Papua New Guinea divides into three distinct regions. The coast comprises lowland malarial swamps in the east and the scarcely more hospitable lowlands of the east (which includes Papua) with their poor soils and unpredictable rainfall. In the relatively populous valleys of the highlands about 40 percent of the population lives, traditionally by raising sweet potatoes and rearing pigs, supplemented increasingly in recent times by commercial crops. The third region is comprised of the offshore islands, whose fertility and relative accessibility made them and parts of the north coast attractive to foreign commercial interests that superimposed plantations and then logging and mining on the indigenous mixed farming.

Colonialism created new divisions but its impact was limited. In 1828 the Dutch had divided the island of New Guinea by laying claim to its western half. Germany annexed the northern mainland and the islands to the north and east in 1884, and called it New Guinea. In the same year the British made Papua a protectorate; later it was made a colony, chiefly to allay Australian fears of menace from the north. Australia itself assumed responsibility for Papua in 1906. For most of its period of control Australia's main motive for planting the flag in Papua was the negative one of denying it to anyone else. The Germans, on the other hand, had clear-cut commercial motives for their presence in New Guinea, which they pursued most successfully when they set up copra and cacao plantations on the islands of the Bismarck Archipelago—on Bougainville and New Britain in particular.

When New Guinea was taken from Germany and mandated to Australia by the League of Nations at the end of World War I, the German plantations came with the territory, but the times were not propitious for new ventures. Only in the 1930s were the highlands even penetrated, and then

719

mainly by missionaries and gold prospectors. The colonial order's contact with much of the country was perfunctory, its instrument the Australian patrol officer *(kiap)*, whose effectiveness depended most on whether he could draw on the traditional authority of the local "big man."

After World War II the United Nations sanctioned the unified Australian administration of Papua and New Guinea, on the understanding that Australia would move the territory toward independence. A slightly more purposeful policy prevailed, entailing the establishment of a Legislative Council, a network of local councils and the beginnings of "localization" of the public service. These institutional changes altered little. The franchise was limited by property and education, and education was almost totally neglected. By the early 1960s less than one percent of adults had completed primary education; there were fewer than 100 Papua New Guineans with secondary schooling and not a single university graduate.

The real progress of the postwar years was economic, and took place particularly through the encouragement of smallholder cultivation of export crops. The most dramatic progress occurred in the highlands, where coffee growing took off, with output reaching 25,000 tons by independence. Important though these changes were, about 70 percent of the monetized economy was still in foreign hands in 1975. Transportation remained rudimentary, dependent almost entirely on high-cost air transport for travel over any distance. (Papua New Guinea is said to have more airstrips per capita than any other country.) The coffee industry's expansion led to the construction of what is still Papua New Guinea's only major sealed highway, linking the highlands with the port of Lae.

In the early 1960s everything suddenly changed. A U.N. report that condemned Canberra for slow progress toward self-rule, and concern about the impact of Indonesia's militant campaign to liberate the western half of New Guinea, still held by the Dutch, shook Australia; a rapid dash to independence ensued. In 1964 the first countrywide elections with universal franchise took place. Over two-thirds of the seats in the new House of Assembly were won by indigenous candidates who did not speak English, the language in which the House's business was conducted.

There was a concerted education drive, involving the foundation of the first institutions of higher education, among them the Administrative College at Waigani (founded in 1963) and the University of Papua New Guinea at Port Moresby (founded in 1967). These colleges turned out, for the first time, personnel for the upper echelons of the public service; they also created a new political consciousness. The first political party with national pretensions, the Pangu Pati, was started by students of the Administrative College in 1967—foremost among them Michael Somare, who became the country's first prime minister in 1973 when Papua New Guinea moved to self-governing status.

Other political movements emerged at this time. They were usually regionally based, and distinguished by their leaders' backgrounds (commerce, the new rural rich and the public service were the chief sources) and their attitudes to self-government. The United party, for instance, which won more seats than any other in the 1972 elections, was a highlands-based party that was happy to settle for slow progress toward self-government; it had a large nonnative business component. It regarded the Pangu Pati as "socialist" and very possibly dangerous, and viewed Pangu's predominantly island and coastal leadership with some suspicion. Later events were to suggest that this was a misreading of the impetus behind Pangu, which was as much anger among local bureaucrats at the "dual wage system"—which discriminated in favor of nonnative public servants—as attachment to the principles of the party's impeccable "Eight Aims." A more serious challenge to the world of Port Moresby politics in the years before independence came from the "micronationalists" of the provinces, principally the Tolais of east New Britain, the Papuans of the southeast and, most insistently, the people and landowners of Bougainville. This was the site of the extensive, formerly German, plantations and, since the late 1960s, of the giant Panguna copper mine (one of the world's 10 largest), and as such long exposed to unwelcome contact with Europeans and with migrant labor from other parts of Papua New Guinea. Bougainville went so far as to declare its separate independence two weeks before national independence; its secession was defused only by a pledge from the central government to create 19 provincial governments with real powers.

The rapid process of decolonization left the newly independent state with a Westminster-type political system, on to which had been grafted an unwieldy provincial apparatus intended to blunt regional aspirations. The economy was in the hands of foreigners nervous about the future. The budget was still heavily reliant on Australian support (40 percent of government revenues still came from this source in 1975–76). Australians dominated the higher reaches of the civil service. Government revenues had to finance a bloated civil service, which accounted for more than one-quarter of all jobs in the formal sector. There was also concern that land was increasingly being given over to the cultivation of vulnerable export crops, at the expense of self-sufficiency in food. Food imports increased eightfold in the 20 years up to 1975, by which point they accounted for one-fifth of all imports.

All this seemed to add up to a recipe for instability, which in the worst scenarios would end in disintegration and/or Indonesian invasion. Though Papua New Guinea's path since independence has not been smooth, the direst predictions have not been realized. Despite a period of several years soon after independence when the growth of GDP lagged behind population growth, the government made a genuine commitment to social spending, making education and health the priorities, without sacrificing fiscal responsibility. Health indicators such as child mortality have improved significantly since 1975. The number of children enrolled in primary school had shot up to nearly three-quarters of those eligible by 1987. By the late 1980s Papua New Guinea seemed to have weathered the economic storms of the previous decade and, on the basis of finds of major oil, gas and gold deposits, to be in a position to reap the benefits of a drilling and mining boom.

Since independence Papua New Guinea has also managed to loosen the grip of the former colonial power without undue acrimony. The teaching profession and the topmost slots in the civil service are now entirely the domain of Papua New Guinea citizens; although there are still many non-natives employed by the government, they are no longer only Australians. Australian budget support, though still significant, now accounts for only one-fifth of government revenues. The Australian defense role has also been cut back considerably. Yet Papua New Guinea still regards Australia as the ultimate guarantor of its security, providing some balance for Papua New Guinea in its dealings with its giant neighbor, Indonesia (with a population 60 times bigger than Papua New Guinea's and a military with 80 times more troops). Papua New Guinea has little control over border tensions with Indonesia, the source of which lies in secessionist aspirations on the Indonesian side of the border. The most serious crisis in relations was in 1984–85 when about 12,000 people fled Indonesia for Papua New Guinea. A Treaty of Mutual Respect and Friendship was ratified by the two countries in 1987, but did not prove sufficient to prevent another upsurge of border violations by Indonesian troops in 1988. To an extent, Papua New Guinea has been able to mitigate the dominance of its larger neighbors by taking a leading role among the newly independent nations of the South Pacific Forum and its Melanesian subgroup, the Melanesian Spearhead Group; among these nations Papua New Guinea is by far the largest in terms of size and population.

Papua New Guinea adapted well to the early political challenges of independence also. After 1975 the lines between the political parties grew even less distinct, blurred partly by a common interest among the different branches of the elite in doing *bisnis*. The focus of this business activity was the transfer of more of the economy into local hands. The state was engaged in this process through its Investment Corporation and the provincial governments' development associations. The political parties had their "business arms," which might also coalesce on particular deals. Members of the elite, whether traditional "big men", graduates of the Administrative College or micronationalists, also formed development associations, usually based on their communities and held up as examples of the "Melanesian Way."

The backbone of Papua New Guinea's first postindependence coalition government was formed by the Pangu Pati and the People's Progress party (PPP), the unashamed "businessman's party" of Sir Julius Chan. When that coalition broke up in 1980 it was succeeded by an even more unlikely partnership led by Chan, which brought together the PPP and the Melanesian Alliance, which had earlier split from Pangu in protest against the latter's opportunism.

By the late 1980s there were fears that the often remarked "fluidity" of Papua New Guinea politics was the first sign of entropy. The general elections of July 1987 ushered in a period of prolonged uncertainty, which still continues. More than 1,500 candidates contested the National Parliament's 109 seats. There were no easily discernible issues separating the 15 competing parties, whose candidates were far outnumbered anyway by unaffiliated independents. Independents took over 40 percent of the vote and 22 seats. One-third of the seats went to candidates who won less than 20 percent of their constituencies' votes. Half the members of the previous

National Parliament were unseated. In the face of this extreme fragmentation there followed what one commentator has termed a "bazaar." The outgoing prime minister, Paias Wingti, returned to power by putting together a coalition that relied heavily on the support of independents and Papuans. Among the Papuan bloc the most important component was the People's Action party of Ted Diro, a former commander of the Papua New Guinea Defence Forces (PNGDF). Just as the government was being formed Diro was implicated in a spectacular corruption scandal, involving allegations by an official commission of inquiry about his tenure in the forestry ministry, and an admission by Diro himself that he had taken a huge election campaign donation from the commander of the Indonesian armed forces.

The scandal did not end Ted Diro's career. He has continued to be a major influence in Papua New Guinea politics. His party's switch of allegiance was decisive in the fall of the Wingti government in July 1988 and its replacement by a Pangu coalition led by Rabbie Namaliu. The demands of coalition building have made it difficult to disavow Diro (much less to sanction his prosecution on pending perjury charges), though the seriousness of the allegations has kept him out of office.

The growing turbulence of Papua New Guinea politics has prompted proposals for constitutional and electoral reform. Since Paias Wingti's became the third of the seven governments in Papua New Guinea's short independent history to fall as a result of a no-confidence motion, there have been calls for a constitutional amendment that would extend the period during which a new government is immune from no-confidence motions—from the present six months to 30 months. Such tinkering is unlikely to work and, besides, the chances are slim of any government amassing the necessary 75 percent majority to amend the constitution. Indeed, in February 1989, in an almost exact replay of events a year before, the opposition—swelled by defectors from the Namaliu coalition—put down a no-confidence motion that was only averted by the prime minister having the National Parliament adjourned for four months.

The latest no-confidence motion had been inspired by two developments: a protracted period of violent unrest in the area around the Panguna mine on Bougainville, which the government seemed powerless to stop; and troops of the PNGDF going on a rampage on the streets of Port Moresby in protest against the nonpayment of a salary award. The two incidents were further instances of the "lawlessness" that had displaced encouragement of agricultural development as the new government's top concern. But there were also more specific fears: of a loss of foreign investor confidence and the collapse of the minerals boom; and of military intervention. Most assessments discount the possibility of a military coup, although the Australian policy of detribalizing the PNGDF has not prevented recruitment being heavily slanted toward particular *wantoks* (and Papuan ones above all), the small size of the force (only 3,200), the hostility of the police and the logistical problems of the PNGDF's securing control are thought to rule out an unassisted military takeover. But the prospect of further governmental drift preventing the implementation of policies that go to the roots of mounting discontent—whether among the rural underemployed, the urban unemployed, those with claims to resource-rich lands, or the new industrial work force—is a real one that revives all the original questions about Papua New Guinea's long-term viability.

FURTHER READING

Amarshi, Azeem, Good, Kenneth, and Mortimer, Rex. *Development and Dependency: The Political Economy of Papua New Guinea*. Melbourne and New York: Oxford University Press, 1979.

Browne, Christopher, and Scott, Douglas A. *Economic Development in Seven Pacific Island Countries*. Washington D.C.: Brookings Institution, 1989.

Cleland, Rachel. *Papua New Guinea: Pathways to Independence, Official and Family Life, 1951–1975*. Perth, Western Australia: Artlook Books, 1983.

Good, Kenneth. *Papua New Guinea: A False Economy*. London and Sydney: Oxford University Press, 1986.

Goodman, Raymond, Lepani, Charles, and Morawetz, David. *The Economy of Papua New Guinea: An Independent Review*. Canberra: Australian National University Press, 1987.

Griffin, James, Nelson, Hank, and Firth, Stewart, *Papua New Guinea: A Political History*. Richmond, Victoria: Heinemann Educational, 1979.

Hastings, Peter. *New Guinea: Problems And Prospects*. Melbourne: Cheshire, 1973.

Loffler, Ernst. *Papua New Guinea*. Melbourne: Hutchinson, 1979.

Premdas, Ralph R. *Focus Upon the South-West Pacific*. Montreal: McGill University Press, 1987.

Todd, Ian. *Papua New Guinea: Moment of Truth*. Sydney: Angus & Robertson, 1974.

Utrecht, Ernst. *Papua New Guinea: An Australian Neo-Colony*. Sydney: University of Sydney Press, 1977.

Woolford, Don. *Papua New Guinea: Initiation and Independence*. St. Lucia, Queensland: University of Queensland Press, 1976.

PHILIPPINES

NORMAN G. OWEN

THE Philippines is, and has been for nearly 20 years, in crisis, a nation whose future seems uncertain even to its own people. It now enjoys a precarious democracy, won back in 1986 after more than 13 years of "constitutional authoritarianism" and exercised since then in vigorously contested elections. Yet this democracy is tainted by violence and corruption and haunted by the suspicion that, as in the past, vested interest groups will block all meaningful reforms. The government is also threatened by an odd trio of insurgencies: a communist-led revolutionary movement, an ethnic/religious separatist rebellion and an intermittent right wing discontent that has sputtered through five military coup attempts.

The economy is just beginning to show signs of recovery after a decade of devastation that followed on two previous decades of diminishing hopes. A generation ago the Philippines was one of the richest and most promising of the second-line economies of Asia, well ahead of even South Korea and Taiwan in the effort to emulate Japanese growth. By now it has fallen far behind these newly industrializing countries and has been overtaken by such previous stragglers as Thailand. Wealth and talent have been siphoned off, population continues to grow at stupefyingly high rates, natural resources, particularly timber, have been pillaged and the pall of pollution hangs heavy over the capital, Manila.

Against this litany of ills Filipinos set their apparently inexhaustible optimism—growing in part out of a confidence in their human resources, enhanced by a relatively well-developed educational system, and in part perhaps out of their natural character and a deep faith in Divine Providence. Whatever the cause, even when the situation looks hopeless, most Filipinos remain hopeful.

BEFORE AMERICAN RULE

Many of the basic features of contemporary Philippine society had already evolved by the 18th century. Before the Spanish arrived, the archipelago was already inhabited by peoples speaking the same closely related Austronesian languages they speak today. Kinship was important and seems to have been reckoned bilaterally, in that the family of the wife was of equal importance with that of the husband (unlike the patrilineal societies of

725

many other Asian countries). The Filipinos grew rice and coconuts, they ate fruits from the forest and fish from the streams and seas and they made dwellings and utensils from wood, bamboo, rattan and palm leaves. Politically, the Philippines was fragmented, with few polities having more than 1,000 inhabitants; some would claim that even today the world of many Filipinos remains essentially parochial, not wholly at ease with whatever lies beyond the family or village. Socially, Philippine society was stratified, with a small class of chiefs (*datus,* whom the Spanish called *principales*) commanding the loyalty and labor of much larger numbers of "free" vassals and "slaves" or bondsmen.

During the first two centuries of Spanish rule, the Philippines was given Roman Catholicism and a skeletal administrative superstructure, but little more. The religious transformation was genuine, and quite remarkable. Within a generation or two the majority of Filipinos had accepted Christianity (as they understood it), and the principles of their new faith came to permeate their consciousness. The administrative apparatus, on the other hand, served chiefly to extract labor and taxes rather than to transform native society; because the colony was a distant and heavily subsidized outpost of the great Spanish-American empire, there were few serious efforts at any kind of development or systematic exploitation of resources. Although "slaves" were turned into debt-peons and corn and tobacco were added to the agricultural repertoire of the Filipinos, in much of the country the town church and the occasional tax collector remained the only visible signs of colonialism.

Sometime between 1750 and 1850 there was a major shift in the Philippine agricultural economy, from a predominantly subsistence orientation to an emphasis on cash cropping for export. Sugar was the first major commodity to find export markets, becoming even more important after it spread to the frontier island of Negros, in the western Visayas, during the latter half of the 19th century. There, local capital combined with imported technology in efficient plantations and mills; since sugar cultivation and milling lend themselves to economies of scale, wealth soon began to accumulate. In the 20th century the sugar barons would come to be the wealthiest of all Filipinos and would often convert their riches into political power, which could then be used as leverage for even greater profits. Elsewhere in the Philippines other export commodities, such as abaca (Manila hemp), tobacco, coconuts, coffee, timber and minerals, were also produced in the late colonial period.

Although each of these industries involved a different technology and organization of production and responded to different international market cycles, all had in common a profitability new to the Philippine scene. For the Spanish (and, later, the Americans), this export wealth represented the opportunity to expand their colonial superstructure. For merchants and middlemen of all nationalities—Spanish, Chinese, English, American and Filipino—it meant opportunities to develop into an urban elite. For Filipino landowners, drawn both from the *datu* class and from newcomers of part-Chinese, or mestizo, ancestry, it meant the opportunity to lift themselves out of village society and aspire to the more exalted ranks of the provincial or even national elite: *ilustrados* (literally, "enlightened ones").

726

Along with these opportunities came new tensions, most visibly between the increasingly numerous Spaniards and the increasingly ambitious Filipino elite. Not content simply with larger houses and more imported luxuries, the Filipinos who profited from the export trade also aspired to greater equality of status with Spaniards: in education, in both civil and religious offices and in polite society. At the same time the *peninsulares* (Spaniards born in Spain itself) were increasingly jealous of their own prerogatives; thus they not only blocked the upward aspirations of the *ilustrados* but also attempted to grab back earlier concessions, particularly in the church, where many Filipinos had gained advancement in the late 18th and early 19th centuries.

One response to this was the evolution of a distinctive "Filipino" consciousness, as this term took on a new meaning, referring to all who made the Philippines their home, regardless of ethnicity.[1] The first great champion of this consciousness was Father José Burgos, who contended politely but persistently for the rights of Filipino clergy. When Burgos and other priests were executed for alleged complicity in an abortive mutiny at the Cavite shipyard in 1872, it inspired a younger generation of *ilustrado* nationalists, among whom the most celebrated were José Rizal and Marcelo H. Del Pilar. As university students in Spain in the 1880s their coterie articulated a broad critique of Spanish colonialism. The Propagandists, as they were known, always stopped short of advocating actual independence, however. In this they may simply have been constrained by Spain's fierce antisubversion laws, but there remains a suspicion that some of them would in fact have been content with something less than independence.

No such ambivalence was shown by shipping clerk Andres Bonifacio, who founded the revolutionary Katipunan in 1892. Dedicated to independence at any cost, this secret society was forced into premature rebellion when Spanish authorities discovered it in 1896. Bonifacio, a better agitator than general, was soon ousted as leader (and later executed) by a young landlord named Emilio Aguinaldo, who managed to keep the revolution alive for more than a year. The Spanish, already overextended by the Cuban revolution, were willing to sign a truce with the rebels late in 1897, which brought a temporary end to the fighting. But when Admiral George Dewey sank the Spanish fleet in Manila Bay on the morning of May 1, 1898, it gave the Katipunan a new lease of life. Aguinaldo returned from exile, rallied thousands of Filipinos to his flag and proclaimed the country independent on June 12, 1898. Philippine nationalism had reached its first climax.

Meanwhile, however, there had been other profound changes in Philippine society. The commercialization of agriculture had been accompanied by the spread of legalism, the replacement of customary practices by government regulations and contracts enforceable in courts of law. At the same time, the population had started to grow rapidly, leading to pressure on existing resources in some districts. Although many benefited from all these changes, others suffered as lands were alienated or usurped, terms of ten-

---

[1] Prior to this time, the term "Filipino" referred to Spaniards born in the Philippines, while the indigenous inhabitants of the islands were referred to as "indios."

ancy were altered and the economic and social gap between rural elite and ordinary peasants widened. For some, migration was an opportunity to escape, and much of the Philippines became a frontier society, with pioneers carving new towns and provinces out of the wilderness. Others moved to Manila and the provincial ports that served as centers of expanded commerce. Migration, though, was never sufficient to release all the accumulated tensions in the rural Philippines.

Thus, beneath the rivalry between Spaniards and *ilustrados* at the top there were growing stresses within Filipino society itself, often expressed in local protests or religious movements. The former typically asked redress for grievances involving lands, debts and taxes (including compulsory labor obligations), and the latter strove to achieve a transcendent future of spiritual harmony, light and brotherhood that could be attained only through struggle and sacrifice. Although in some ways the Katipunan simply represented *ilustrado* nationalism pushed to its logical conclusion, it was also capable of crystallizing many of these social discontents as well. As Reynaldo C. Ileto has shown, its leaders spoke in an idiom that evoked the underlying tensions in Filipino society; its supporters came to include not just those whose goal was political independence but others who thought they were fighting to get rid of their landlords or to create a world "growing more radiant and beautiful, as the minds of the masses are opened." Over the long run, however, these aims proved incompatible, and with the triumph of Aguinaldo over Bonifacio and the subsequent ascendancy of the *ilustrados* at the constitutional convention of the new republic, the vision of the revolution as a transcendent experience faded, save in the hearts of a faithful few. Before Aguinaldo lost his revolution to the Americans in 1901, the original Katipuneros had already lost theirs.[2]

THE AMERICAN PERIOD

The debate over American motives for acquiring the Philippines began in 1898 and has not yet ended, with proponents of economic, strategic and altruistic or "accidental" interpretations still arguing their cases in scholarly books and journals. From a Philippine perspective, the original American motives are not terribly important, however. The fact is that by the end of 1898 the United States was present in force and had proclaimed its sovereignty over the archipelago, in defiance of the Philippine declaration of independence. This contradiction could only be resolved by war, which broke out early in 1899. The pacification of the archipelago took several years and involved both direct coercion, through force of arms and stiff sedition laws, and what the Americans referred to as their "policy of attraction." A few *ilustrados,* whether unusually farsighted or particularly self-serving, came to terms with the Americans from the start, but most Filipinos answered the call to arms and the Philippine-American War (no mere

[2] Reynaldo C. Ileto, *Pasyon and Revolution: Popular Movements in the Philippines, 1840–1910* (Quezon City: Ateneo de Manila University Press, 1979), pp. 145 and passim; cf. Milagros Camayon Guerrero, "Luzon at War: Contradictions in Philippine Society, 1898–1902" (Ph.D. dissertation, University of Michigan, 1977).

"insurrection") was a bitter and bloody one, lasting until Aguinaldo's capture in 1901 and even longer in some provinces.[3]

The United States, new at colonialism but replete with turn-of-the-century idealism and arrogance, assumed that it would soon redeem the Philippines from the backwardness to which it had been condemned by its hapless former colonial master; this was the essence of its "policy of attraction." Changes, in fact, were introduced, but not all of them were as drastic, or as successful, as William Howard Taft, the first civil governor (1901–03), implied. Only in the areas of national integration, political participation and education was a dramatic American impact visible.

The armed might of the United States not only ended the revolution but brought the non-Christian areas of the archipelago under the firm control of Manila for the first time, finishing up the Spanish campaign of conquest. Districts in the uplands of Luzon and the islands of the south that had previously been part of the Philippines in name only were now forced to accept colonial laws, pay colonial taxes and build colonial roads and schools. In view of the cultural differences and mutual animosity between these non-Christians and the Christian majority, however, the United States limited the incorporation of these areas into the Philippines, ruling them for some decades under separate regulations and administrative systems. Whether proceeding from a genuine concern for minority rights or from a cunning divide-and-rule strategy, the effect of this policy was to reinforce the sense that the Moros (as the Muslims are called) and the Igorots (inhabitants of the Luzon Cordillera) were different from the "Filipinos" that surrounded them. By enforcing political integration but failing to foster social and cultural integration, the United States bequeathed to the independent Philippines an ongoing minority problem.

In the political arena, the United States wanted collaborators to reinforce its self-image as benevolent and democratic, and it needed them to administer a new colony of nearly 8 million non-English-speaking inhabitants. Thus, compliant Filipinos not only continued to serve in municipal office, as they had under Spain, but rapidly became judges, provincial governors, minority members of the Philippine Commission and, in 1907, elected members of the Philippine Assembly, the lower house of the national legislature. This devolution of political power was later accelerated by the "Filipinization" of the bureaucracy and the establishment of an elected Senate (replacing the Commission) under the Democratic administration of Governor-General Francis B. Harrison (1913–21). Although the franchise was severely limited by property and literacy qualifications, and voting was often marred by fraud (as it was in the United States at the time), the principle and practice of democratic elections were firmly implanted in the Philippines early in the 20th century. By 1916, moreover, the United States was publicly committed to eventual Philippine independence, though no definite timetable was set until the Great Depression, when domestic

[3] The devastation was enormous, as between 1896 and 1905 the islands were also plagued by epidemic cholera, malaria, smallpox, and rinderpest (which killed most of the draft animals). Demographically, it was the most disastrous period in modern Philippine history, worse even than World War II.

interests anxious to protect themselves from Philippine competition supported independence as a means of pushing the former colony outside the tariff wall.

America's faith in democracy was exceeded only by its faith in education, exhibited first by the troops who established local school for Filipino children during the Philippine-American War. Soon after, the colonial government brought over entire boatloads of volunteer schoolteachers; like the later Peace Corps, their significance on the national scene was more symbolic than practical, as the majority of Filipinos were still taught by other Filipinos. Education was to be universal, free, secular and in English, whereas under Spain it had generally been limited in scope, controlled by the church and in vernacular languages.

By any kind of quantitative measure, the achievements of the American educational system in the Philippines were impressive. Nearly a quarter of the colonial budget went to education, as compared with less than 5 percent in the Spanish period, and the figures for school attendance, literacy and ability to speak the colonial language far exceeded those for all other colonies in Southeast Asia. At one extreme, for every university student in Indonesia—four times as populous—there were 15 in the Philippines. As a tool of social engineering, however, American education was rather less successful, though the nationalist journalist Renato Constantino continues to fulminate against the "miseducation" that, he contends, succeeded all too well in implanting pro-American (and therefore antinationalist) values in the Filipino psyche.[4] But to the extent that the colonialists saw education as a panacea for all problems from economic backwardness to political caciquism ("boss rule"), it did not fulfill their hopes.

American economic policy in the Philippines—if we can discern a "policy" in the welter of contradictory proclamations and regulations that emanated from Washington and Manila—was primarily oriented toward increasing the country's complementarity to the metropole as a producer of raw materials and a consumer of manufactured goods. (There was also some hope of developing the Philippines as a major field for American capital investment, but little came of it; domestic political considerations militated against most of the policies the "Manila Americans" thought necessary to attract investment.) The most significant measures were those that improved the infrastructure and those that brought the Philippines within the American tariff wall early in the colonial period and started to ease it out again toward the end.

Better roads, bridges and harbors helped move both people and commodities to market, and the provision of a more stable currency, expanded banking facilities and an extended communication network also enhanced commerce. Urban amenities, including improved public utilities, made city life more efficient and attractive. Improvements in sanitation helped to reduce mortality and thus increased the effective labor force (and accelerated population growth). On the other hand, desultory efforts to deal with rural

---

[4] Renato Constantino, "The Miseducation of the Filipinos" (1966), in his *The Filipinos in the Philippines and Other Essays* (Quezon City: Malaya Books, 1971), pp. 39–65.

problems were generally ineffective. The "homestead" legislation and other reforms did not change the prevailing pattern of landowning, nor did agricultural research and education significantly alter traditional farming practices.

Tariff and trade policies, which resulted in effective mutual free trade between the Philippines and the United States for a quarter of a century (1909–34), were extremely important for some sectors of the economy. Sugar and coconut products in particular benefited from access to the protected American market, and by the late 1930s, 99 percent of Philippine sugar, 95 percent of its coconut oil and nearly 80 percent of all the colony's exports went to the United States. Conversely, almost 70 percent of Philippine imports came from the United States, all duty-free, leaving the islands with no way to protect infant industries.[5] Some manufacturing for the local market developed nevertheless, especially in cheap consumer goods such as textiles, footwear, beer and ice cream, but these manufactures were unable to make serious inroads into the American market. The Philippines remained essentially a primary producer to the end of the colonial period.

Thus, after 40 years of American rule, the Philippine economy still resembled what it had been in 1898, depending on the same exports of the same primary commodities, produced by the same technology and the same system of landownership and tenancy. The fivefold increase in the total value of trade was due in part to higher prices and in part to the sheer expansion of land and labor devoted to export crops. Agricultural productivity, as best we can measure it, increased very little over the period.[6] The American connection had proved highly profitable for some industries, particularly sugar, and some social groups, particularly politicians and landlords, but this profitability was in large part built on the prosperity of the United States and the continuation of favorable access to that market, both severely tested in the 1930s. When Wall Street crashed, its echoes were heard in the dusty streets of remote abaca-growing villages; when independence (and the end of the American connection) was promised in 1934, it sent shudders throughout the entire sugar industry.

In the social sphere the United States had, by rapid devolution of political authority and promotion of export-oriented agriculture, ensured the reinforcement of the existing elite. There was a certain amount of mobility within the elite, as some families proved more adept at seizing new political and economic opportunities than others, but most "rags to riches" stories from the Philippines involve sons of the lesser gentry making it to the top of the national tree rather than peasants actually attaining elite status. From time to time Taft and other colonialists would mutter darkly about the dangers of caciquism, but they were never willing to take any action that would actually threaten the politicians through whom they ruled

---

[5] Catherine Porter, *Crisis in the Philippines* (New York: Alfred A. Knopf, 1942), pp. 150–51.
[6] Richard Hooley, "Philippine Economics: Development and Major Issues," in *Philippine Studies: Political Science, Economics and Linguistics,* ed. Donn V. Hart (DeKalb: Northern Illinois University, Center for Southeast Asian Studies, 1981), pp. 102–04.

or the landlords and businessmen with whom they enjoyed such mutually beneficial relations.

Filipino reactions to the United States, once its rule was firmly implanted, were even more ambivalent than Rizal's response to Spain had been. In the political arena there was overwhelming popular sentiment in favor of the pursuit of independence, a sentiment particularly nurtured and exploited by the Nationalist party, headed by two brilliant young politicians named Manuel Quezon and Sergio Osmeña. Starting from the first Assembly elections in 1907, in which they outpolled the previously dominant Federalist party, the Nationalists swept every election up to 1946. The culmination of their careers came in 1935, when Quezon and Osmeña were elected president and vice president, respectively, of the Commonwealth of the Philippines, the final step toward the independence for which they had so long lobbied. Quezon's public speeches represented Philippine nationalism at its most flamboyant ("I would prefer a government run like hell by Filipinos to one run like heaven by Americans"), and though recent scholarship suggests that he may have been more interested in using independence as a political issue than in actually achieving it ("Damn the Americans," he once said in private, "why don't they tyrannize us more?"), the question of his sincerity is less significant than the response his public utterances obviously provoked in the hearts of his countrymen.[7]

At the same time, Filipinos responded positively to many aspects of American life, not only taking full advantage of schooling, elections and other opportunities presented to them by the colonial government but enthusiastically adopting such unofficial institutions as basketball, Boy Scouts and beauty contests as well. Their appetite for things American was not unselective, however, as they remained cool to Protestantism, despite the efforts of many American missionaries. (Most defections from Roman Catholicism were to such distinctly Filipino alternatives as the Iglesia Filipino Independiente [Philippine Independent Church], founded in 1902, and the Iglesia ni Kristo [Church of Christ], founded in 1914.)

The Americanization of Philippine culture thus coexisted comfortably with political nationalism, a paradox that is often expressed in metaphors of kinship. Whether as parent and child or as elder sibling and "little brown brother," the relationship between the United States and the Philippines was seen by many Filipinos as essentially familial, with the younger member gradually and rightfully asserting his independence without ever losing respect and affection for the elder, who in turn was expected to allow autonomy without relinquishing responsibility. The failure of the United States to recognize its role in this family drama remains, some 40 years after independence, a source of frustration for some Filipinos.

Between Filipino and Filipino there was also friction, despite their shared hope of political independence. As in the late Spanish period, the elite

[7] Theodore Friend, *Between Two Empires: The Ordeal of the Philippines, 1929–1946* (New Haven, Conn.: Yale University Press, 1965), p. 4 and passim; see also Theodore Friend, "Manuel Quezon: Charismatic Conservative," *Philippine Historical Review* 1 (1965), 153–69.

tended to grow in wealth and power, adding now the advantages of political office and technical expertise (obtained in part from superior access to tertiary education) to their continuing control of agricultural land; the caciques were stronger than ever. With greater wealth came also the opportunity to increase their physical and social distance from ordinary peasants. The standard of living of poorer Filipinos actually improved somewhat in the early years of American rule, though it fell again during the depression. But the combination of expanding legalism and population growth continued to weaken their bargaining power with landlords and employers, and the safety valve of migration remained unable to release all the pressure. (Emigration to the United States, especially Hawaii and the West Coast, was also an option for the venturous few with the money to buy a ticket and the endurance to put up with appalling conditions and persistent discrimination.) Thus, in the interwar period, and particularly the 1930s, there was renewed agrarian unrest, especially in central Luzon. Although a few leaders were Communists, peasant grievances were often less about economic exploitation as such than about alienation and the loss of human dignity and community.

The commonwealth had been intended to provide a transition to independence, an opportunity for the economy to adjust and for officials to assume greater responsibility, but the Japanese occupation (1941–45) rudely interrupted all prewar planning. Like other Southeast Asians, Filipinos suffered abuses and great deprivation, particularly during the latter stages of the war. In part because Filipino resistance was particularly widespread and tenacious—during the original 1941–42 defense that ended in the tragic Bataan death march, during the underground years and during General Douglas MacArthur's 1944–45 campaign of "liberation"—the country actually endured more violence and greater physical destruction than any other in the region. The sense of heroism that might have redeemed this national trauma was vitiated by the fact that most of the national elite—including Jose Laurel, who served as puppet president, and Manual Roxas, who would be elected in 1946 to serve as first president of the new republic—actively collaborated with the Japanese.

INDEPENDENCE

The republic that was formally inaugurated on July 4, 1946, was a troubled one, physically devastated, emotionally ravaged and politically divided. The elite was still trying to cover its tracks and its losses—one of the first acts of the reconvened Congress in 1945 was to vote itself three years' back pay. The elite was also threatened by the left; the peasant unions of central Luzon had forged themselves into a Communist-led guerrilla army (the Huks) during the war and were not about to submit themselves to landlord despotism again. Meanwhile, the United States undercut whatever generosity underlay its grant of independence by insisting on retention of its military bases and economic prerogatives and withholding promised, and desperately needed, rehabilitation aid until the Philippines acceded to these infringements on its sovereignty.

For both Filipino leaders and their American patrons, the postwar years were a time for restoration, rather than innovation. The old political system was restored, with most of the old elite still dominating it. A two-party system developed, but as neither party had a distinctive platform, it was always easy for politicians to jump expediently from one party to the other; many, including Ramon Magsaysay and Ferdinand Marcos, did just that. The United States was allowed to retain its military bases, its investments, its position as privileged and preeminent trading partner and its assumption of the right to tell the Philippines what to do. The U.S. Central Intelligence Agency (CIA) not only sponsored Magsaysay's campaign for the presidency in 1953 but actually wrote some of his speeches. The Philippine government seemed to accept its subordinate role willingly: "In the world parliament of the United Nations," nationalist Claro M. Recto complained, "it is no more difficult to predict that the Philippines will vote with the American Union, than that the Ukraine will vote with the Soviet Union."[8]

The 1950s was a decade of relative prosperity and optimism. Thanks to extensive American aid, a successful policy of import-substitution industrialization and the windfall benefits of high commodity prices during the Korean War, the Philippine economy performed well, with net domestic product growing at over 7 percent a year, 1949–57, including manufacturing growth of over 12 percent a year.[9] With American help, Magsaysay succeeded in suppressing the Huk rebellion by 1954; one in a long series of nominal land reforms helped conceal the fact that no real solution to the agrarian problem had been achieved. For most Filipinos the advantages of capitalism, gradual reform and the "special relationship" with the United States remained almost axiomatic. In an era of economic expansion and liberal self-confidence, few dissenting voices were heard; even the "Filipino First" policy of President Carlos P. Garcia, who succeed Magsaysay on the latter's death in a plane crash in 1957, was directed more against Chinese retailers than American manufacturers.

In the 1960s, however, the economy slowed down (to around 5 percent growth a year, scarcely ahead of population growth of more than 3 percent) as manufacturing began to hit the ceiling of limited domestic demand. In

[8] Stephen Rosskamm Shalom, *The United States and the Philippines: A Study in Neocolonialism* (Philadelphia: Institute for the Study of Human Issues, 1981), chaps. 2–4; Raymond Bonner, *Waltzing with a Dictator: The Marcoses and the Making of American Policy* (New York: Times Books, 1987), chap. 2; Claro M. Recto, "Our Mendicant Foreign Policy" (1951), in Teodoro A. Agoncillo, *Filipino Nationalism, 1872–1970* (Quezon City: R. P. Garcia, 1974), p. 332. By 1986, the Philippines voted with the United States in the General Assembly less than 20 percent of the time.

[9] Economic data hereafter, except as indicated, are from Hal Hill and Sisira Jayasuriya, *The Philippines: Growth, Debt and Crisis: Economic Performance During the Marcos Era* (Canberra: Australian National University, Development Studies Centre, 1985), and Sisira Jayasuriya, "The Politics of Economic Policy in the Philippines During the Marcos Era," in *Southeast Asia in the 1980s: The Politics of Economic Crisis,* ed. Richard Robison, Kevin Hewison, and Richard Higgott (Sydney: Allen & Unwin, 1987), pp. 80–112.

some sectors real income was actually declining by mid-decade. Although various measures for tariff reform and relaxation of exchange controls, intended to promote export-oriented industrialization, were introduced, vested import-substitution interests (American as well as Filipino) limited their impact. The landed elite, which still controlled the legislature, prevented any effective rural reform, and the frontiers were closing, with those Christians who continued to migrate to Mindanao encountering increasing hostility from Muslims and other earlier inhabitants on whose lands they encroached.

Meanwhile the "special relationship" threatened to drag the Philippines into the Vietnam War, and a generation of younger Filipinos, who lacked their parents' sense of kinship and gratitude toward the United States, began to call the relationship into question. A new nationalism expressed itself in many spheres, including history, literature and the arts; it represented a rediscovery of pride in the Philippine past and a reaffirmation of the worth of Philippine culture and of Pilipino (the national language, based on Tagalog), as well as a rejection of what was characterized as the "U.S.-Marcos dictatorship." It also gave rise in 1968 to a new Communist Party of the Philippines that attempted to apply the thoughts of Chairman Mao, rather than the Moscow model, to the Philippines. On university campuses and the streets of Manila the struggles against "imperialism" and "feudalism" were rhetorically combined; in the hills and remote barrios the New People's Army began to gather. In response, Presidents Diosdado Macapagal (1961–65) and Ferdinand Marcos (1965–72) could only offer symbols: changing independence day from July 4 to June 12, asserting the Philippine claim to Sabah, building a national cultural center (which ended up featuring such shows as "The Best of Broadway") and announcing yet more land reforms.

MARCOS AND AUTHORITARIAN RULE

The crisis into which the Philippines had long been drifting finally arrived in the aftermath of the elections of 1969. Not only did the gross corruption of the campaign further discredit the political process, but the sheer volume of money that Marcos poured into his successful bid for reelection worsened the problems of runaway inflation and a declining balance of trade. As the peso collapsed in early 1970, the people of Manila took to the streets, raging against both the administration and its American sponsors; attempts to counter this new political militancy only exacerbated the economic situation. The next two years were filled with both excitement and frustration, as Filipinos looked for ways of surmounting political stalemate and economic stagnation. Some hoped that the constitutional convention assembled in 1971 would provide the answer; others sought more drastic changes.

On September 22, 1972,[10] President Marcos closed the debate by declaring martial law, locking up many of his critics and shutting down the

[10] The proclamation was backdated to September 21 because Marcos believed that multiples of seven were lucky for him.

press, until then the freest in all Asia. Shortly thereafter, he extracted a constitution of his choice from the convention, sent Congress home, bullied the judiciary into acquiescence and pushed through a national "referendum" that ratified his one-man rule. Although martial law was technically lifted in 1981, Marcos never relinquished the power to rule by decree until he fled the country on February 27, 1986, 20 years after he was first elected president.

The public justification for martial law was the threat of Communist insurgency, though it is generally conceded that in 1972 the NPA could not have presented a serious challenge to the government. Marcos partisans explained that the real purpose was to clear the decks for economic development; by dismantling the old oligarchy and giving free rein to the technocrats (mostly American-educated economists), the long-frustrated national potential for growth would be unleashed at last. In fact, although some technocrats, such as Gerardo Sicat and Cesar Virata, rose to high positions, they never really controlled economic policy, since Marcos and his family and political cronies continued to turn it to their personal advantage, replacing the old oligarchy with a new one.

Conspiracy-minded nationalists, on the other hand, saw martial law as a CIA plot, pointing in particular to Marcos's reversal of a court decision (the Quasha case) that had seemed to spell the end of American investment in the Philippines. The available evidence, however, suggests that although American officials knew of martial law in advance and did nothing to forestall it, they probably did not instigate it and certainly were not able to dictate to Marcos thereafter.[11] Finally, those whose judgments relied more on character than on complexities of state just thought that Ferdinand Marcos and his wife Imelda Romualdez Marcos were insatiably ambitious and greedy. In light of the public revelations about their wealth, this appears to have more plausibility than any other single interpretation. It still leaves open, though, the larger question of why so many others acquiesced in their grab for power.

Boosted by increased American aid and loans, a fortuitous 1973–75 boom in export prices and the success of high-yielding varieties of rice (first developed at the International Rice Research Institute, in Laguna Province, during the 1960s), the Philippine economy performed reasonably well in the 1970s. Not only did average aggregate growth exceed 6 percent a year, but manufacturing outperformed the rest of the economy and by the end of the decade accounted for nearly half of merchandise exports (though it still employed less than a tenth of the work force). These gains were achieved at the cost of growing inequality, however; real wage rates fell by almost 40 percent during the decade and the proportion of total income earned by the poorest families continued to decline. There were also other ominous signs, for those who could read them: capital flight (estimated to be in the billions of dollars), soaring debt, pollution and deforestation. The nominal rationalization of coconut and sugar marketing led not to greater efficiency but to diversion of profits into the pockets of the cronies (Eduardo Coju-

---

[11] Bonner, *Waltzing with a Dictator,* prologue and chap. 5.

angco, Jr., Juan Ponce Enrile and Roberto Benedicto) who headed the agencies that were given effective monopolies of these industries. Much the same happened in construction, where huge contracts for government projects (including a number of expensive public buildings in metropolitan Manila sponsored by Imelda Marcos, said by some to have an "edifice complex") went to a few firms owned by personal friends of the first family.

So long as foreign banks were bloated with petrodollars and the Marcos regime retained their confidence, expansion could be funded and mistakes could be buried through continued borrowing at favorable rates. But with the second oil shock of 1979 and the ensuing collapse in export prices, the shaky scaffolding started to tumble. To stave off immediate recession (and possible rebellion), the government had to borrow much more, at much worse terms; in just three years (1980–83) foreign indebtedness rose from 6.6 to 49.4 percent of the entire GNP. The World Bank and the International Monetary Fund, of course, mandated stiff measures to discipline the economy; in the short run, such measures increased unemployment and hardship among the poor, which led to more unrest, which diminished international confidence—and so the spiral led downward. Whatever performance legitimacy the regime might have earned over the first eight years of martial law was dissipated in less than half that time.

Ferdinand and Imelda Marcos had also tried to foster political legitimacy through public ostentation and through government-sponsored mass organizations, such as the New Society Movement (KBL), but they failed to create solid popular support for their "conjugal dictatorship" outside their home regions. The real foundation of the regime remained the military, which Marcos had carefully cultivated ever since he became president. He consistently promoted Ilokanos (members of his own linguistic group) ahead of their peers, and loyalty to him outweighed all other credentials, as demonstrated by the appointment in 1981 of General Fabian C. Ver, his cousin and one-time driver, as chief of staff of the armed forces. Thanks to increased American aid, the military grew both in numbers and in firepower; ironically, they faced opponents whose strength seemed to grow even faster. The economic policies of the regime and unchecked abuses by the military boosted NPA recruitment; the attempt to round up all firearms triggered a separatist rebellion among gun-loving Muslims, already deeply disturbed by Christian encroachments into their traditional territory. The result was that by the end of martial law, both insurgencies were much stronger than they had been when it began. By 1988 it was estimated that there were 20,000 to 25,000 regular NPA forces (not all of them armed), with a "mass base" of 2 to 3 million supporters, and another 11,000 to 15,000 well-armed Moro insurgents, drawing their support from among the 2.5 million Muslim Filipinos.[12]

It was the assassination of Benigno ("Ninoy") Aquino, Jr., on August 21, 1983—ordered by those close to Marcos, if not by the man himself—

[12] *Asia 1988 Yearbook* (Hong Kong: Far Eastern Economic Review, 1988); *Far Eastern Economic Review*, 18 February 1988; "A Question of Faith" [A Survey of the Philippines], *The Economist*, 7 May 1988.

that turned murmured discontent into mass resistance. Aquino had once been just a bright young politician, nearly as talented and opportunistic as Marcos, whom he challenged politically in the early 1970s. Almost eight years of imprisonment and three more of American exile had made him in Filipino eyes, and perhaps in reality, more serious, patriotic and devout. In the instant of his death he rose at once to the ranks of martyr: another Rizal, even a Christ-figure. Popular outrage was not only immediate but persistent, and the regime faced a crisis of public confidence that simply would not go away. As investors panicked and profiteers shifted their funds abroad, the economy went into a nosedive, with the GNP actually falling over the next three years. Eventually even those who refused to acknowledge that Marcos was implicated in the murder of Aquino came to believe that he should not continue to rule.

Under international pressure, Marcos allowed the press greater freedom and held more honest elections, but this only exposed further the regime's lack of popular support. His blatant attempt to steal the snap election of February 1986 from Aquino's widow precipitated the "People Power" revolution, a peaceful uprising in which nuns and street vendors, housewives and students, faced down the tanks and sent Marcos and his family scurrying into exile. Corazon ("Cory") Cojuangco Aquino came to power at the head of an extraordinarily disparate coalition, united only in their distrust of Marcos: cautiously critical clerics like Jaime Cardinal Sin, human rights activists like José Diokno, militant leftists like Leandro Alejandro, former oligarchs like Salvador Laurel, disillusioned businessmen like Jaime Ongpin and, finally, disaffected political cronies like Juan Ponce Enrile and disgruntled army officers like Fidel Ramos. Almost everyone came to the party except the Communists, who had boycotted the election as a bourgeois sham, and the Moro insurgents, still remote from Manila politics. Even the United States, after straddling the fence until the last possible moment, came down on Cory's side.[13]

The Aquino administration, backed by this extraordinarily heterogeneous coalition, found that once the initial euphoria had passed it was unable to agree on any major changes of policy. As at the end of World War II, restoration seemed more feasible than innovation, and the Philippines in the late 1980s looked in many respects very much as it did in the early 1970s. Under the 1987 constitution the new legislature, like the old, is bicameral, and the same names—often the same faces—crowd its halls. The government avidly pursues the "ill-gotten" gains of those now fallen from power, but seems rather less diligent in chasing after contemporary corruption. All the old arguments both for and against land reform and the re-

[13] Bonner, *Waltzing with a Dictator,* chaps. 16–17. Ironically, the actual trigger for the uprising was an attempted preemptive strike by Marcos against a planned military coup in favor of Enrile, not Aquino; see Lewis M. Simons, *Worth Dying For* (New York: William Morrow, 1987), chap. 16.

moval of American military bases are heard once again, with inertia and the conservative majority still tipping the balance in favor of the status quo. Although land reform has been written into the new constitution, its implementation was left to a Congress so dominated by landowners that at one point all the original sponsors of a 1988 land reform bill withdrew their support for it, claiming that it had been so amended as to become "a treacherous blow to the future of the peasant masses." With regard to the U.S. military bases, the fear that they might prove targets in any superpower war has so far been outweighed by the more than U.S. $200 million a year they bring in direct military and economic aid and the estimated $500 million more they contribute to the Philippine economy each year through on-post employment and off-post spending. Nationalist outrage is still expressed, but cynical observers suspect that much of it might be assuaged by a substantial increase in the "rent" paid for the bases (though the United States resolutely refuses to use that term).[14] Crowds still demonstrate outside the presidential palace and the American Embassy, and are still hurled back by the police. Once again genuine hope and excitement about the future mingle with frustration and even fear, as political murders remain a tragic commonplace.

There are two major differences between the Philippines today and the "Old Society" before 1972, neither boding well for the future prosperity and stability of the country. The first is massive economic deterioration. Although superficially the economy has changed very little since the early 1970s, with pockets of wealth still glittering amid surrounding squalor, there are in fact numerous slight but significant changes. On the positive side, the road network has been expanded and improved and new energy sources, particularly hydroelectric and geothermal, have been deployed, though the country still depends heavily on imported oil. There is also greater commodity and country trade diversification, as prawns, mangoes, children's clothes and computer components join more traditional exports like coconuts and minerals while the European Community, Australia and the ASEAN countries increase their share of Philippine trade. The most profitable new export, however, has been cheap labor; remittances from Filipinos overseas—nurses in North America, maids in Hong Kong, construction workers in the Middle East, "entertainers" in Japan—have actually become one of the leading sources of foreign exchange.

Against this must be set both the losses due directly to the greed and ineptitude of the Marcos regime and the structural deformities and opportunity costs of so many wasted years. The former would include not only the billions of dollars directly siphoned off by Marcos and his cronies but also the debts still owing on such disastrous projects as the $2 billion Westinghouse nuclear reactor in Bataan, which for reasons of safety could never be brought on-line. With foreign debts currently totaling more than

---

[14] *Manila Bulletin,* 26 March 1988; James Fallows, "The Bases Dilemma," *Atlantic Monthly,* February 1988, 18–30; *Far Eastern Economic Review,* 21 April 1988. By some estimates the bases account for as much as 4 to 5 percent of the entire gross domestic product of the Philippines.

$28 billion, the Philippines, even after restructuring its obligations, still has a debt-service/exports ratio estimated at 37 percent, almost double what is usually considered the danger level.[15]

Even if the crushing debt burden were lifted, however, recovery would not be quick or easy. The Philippines now faces much greater problems than it did a decade and a half ago. Though the growth rate has slowed slightly, the population, barely 18 million at independence, has now reached 60 million and is projected to reach 80 million by the turn of the century, 100 million less than a decade later. Income distribution is worse than ever, with the top 20 percent of earners now garnering well over 50 percent of all income and more than 60 percent of all families now living below the poverty line. Environmental deterioration has continued and natural resources have been seriously depleted; although definitions and estimates of deforestation vary widely, the most reliable sources suggest that if current rates of destruction—perhaps 1,482,632 acres/600,000 hectares per year—continue the Philippines, still half-forested as recently as the 1960s, will have no mature forests left by the year 2000. Commercially, the Philippines faces a more competitive international economic environment every year. Even its human resources have been depleted; the 30 to 40 percent of the work force unemployed or underemployed will not be easily retrained for productive labor, and who knows what permanent damage has been done to the minds and bodies of the millions of seriously malnourished children?[16]

The second major change is increased political mobilization, especially of groups that were relatively quiescent before. The military is the most obvious example; the adventures of Gregorio ("Gringo") Honasan, which would be ludicrous if they were not so dangerous, bear witness to the fact that a once professional army now includes officers who regard themselves as entitled not just to advise the government but also to remove it if it does not suit them. The Catholic church, too, is far more willing to take a political stance, though it remains divided between a majority that appears to support the cautious reformism and "pro-family" politics of the Aquino administration and an active minority that sides openly with the aggrieved poor and calls for more radical changes.

It is not yet clear how mobilized the poor themselves have become.

[15] *Asia 1988 Yearbook;* cf. Economist Intelligence Unit, *Country Report: Philippines,* 1986–88 passim.
[16] *Asia 1988 Yearbook;* Randolf S. David, "The Philippines, 1983–86: A Macro-Economic Picture" (mimeograph, n.p., 1987); Shalom, *The United States and the Philippines,* chap. 6; "A Question of Faith"; *IBON Facts & Figures,* nos. 157 (28 February 1985), 174 (15 November 1985), 195 (30 September 1986), 200 (15 December 1986); Norman Myers, *Conversion of Tropical Moist Forests* (Washington, D.C.: National Academy of Sciences, 1980), pp. 95–102; Delfin J. Ganapin, Jr., "Forest Resources and Timber Trade in Philippines," in *Proceedings of the Conference on "Forest Resources Crisis in the Third World,"* 6–8 September 1986 ([Kuala Lumpur?]: Sahabat Alam Malaysia, 1987), pp. 54–70; Ooi Jin Bee, *Depletion of the Forest Resources in the Philippines* (Singapore: Institute of Southeast Asian Studies, 1987).

During the Marcos years many joined local protest or action groups, often advised by clerics, Communists or other middle-class sympathizers, to defend their interests. Despite the efforts of some organizers, however, these local groups have never really coalesced into a national movement. They are up against not just elite repression but ancient ethnic prejudices and political rivalries as well as divergences of practical interests. Land reform would benefit tenants but not necessarily the 2 million landless agricultural workers, and the struggles of organized labor for decent working conditions and wages mean little to the scavengers of "Smoky Mountain," who make their homes and their livelihoods on that great heap of smoldering garbage in the slums of Tondo. Opposition to Marcos was once a common factor, though the poor were generally underrepresented in the "People Power" revolution; but now that the martyr has been avenged, will the Philippine poor revert to selling their votes to elite politicians and going about their own business? Or will they build on the class-based solidarity that began to develop under martial law? And if they do, will their movement involve a breakthrough in electoral politics, an attempt to re-create the "parliament of the streets" or armed rebellion under NPA leadership? On such questions as these may hang the ultimate fate of this battered, but still optimistic, country.

FURTHER READING

Agoncillo, Teodoro. *Filipino Nationalism, 1872–1970.* Quezon City, Philippines: R. P. Garcia, 1974.

De La Costa, Horacio. *Readings in Philippine History.* Manila: Bookmark, 1965.

Friend, Theodore A. *Between Two Empires: The Ordeal of the Philippines, 1929–1946.* New Haven, Connecticut: Yale University Press, 1965.

Ileto, Reynaldo Clemeña. *Pasyon and Revolution: Popular Movements in the Philippines, 1840–1910.* Quezon City, Philippines: Ateneo de Manila University Press, 1979.

Karnow, Stanley. *In Our Image: America's Empire in the Philippines.* New York: Random House, 1989.

Kerkvliet, Benedict J. *The Huk Rebellion: A Study of Peasant Revolt in the Philippines.* Berkeley: University of California Press, 1977.

McCoy, Alfred W., and de Jesus, Ed. C., eds. *Philippine Social History: Global Trade and Local Transformations.* Honolulu: University of Hawaii Press; Quezon City, Philippines: Ateneo de Manila University Press; Sydney: Allen & Unwin, 1982.

Owen, Norman G. *Prosperity without Progress: Manila Hemp and Material Life in the Colonial Philippines.* Berkeley: University of California Press; Quezon City: Ateneo de Manila University Press, 1984.

Shalom, Stephen Rosskamm. *The United States and the Philippines: A Study of Neocolonialism.* Philadelphia: Institute for the Study of Human Issues, 1981.

Stanley, Peter W. *A Nation in the Making: The Philippines and the United States, 1899–1921.* Cambridge, Massachusetts: Harvard University Press, 1974.

Steinberg, David Joel. *The Philippines: A Singular and a Plural Place.* Boulder, Colorado: Westview Press, 1982.

SIBERIA AND THE
SOVIET FAR EAST

ALAN WOOD

SIBERIA is not an independent political or economic entity. It is an integral part—indeed, the largest part—of the Russian Soviet Federated Socialist Republic, which in its turn is the largest of the 15 union republics that constitute the USSR. It was the early Muscovite state's astonishingly rapid military conquest and colonial settlement of Siberia in the 16th and 17th centuries that today is responsible for the Soviet Union's legitimate claim to be both a major Asian and Pacific power. Historically, the word "Siberia" has been used to identify the huge landmass of northern Asia that stretches from the Ural Mountains in the west (the traditional divide between European and Asiatic Russia) and the Pacific littoral in the east, and from the Arctic Ocean in the north down to the borders of Kazakhstan, China, Mongolia and North Korea in the south. Since the 16th century (apart from a brief hiatus during the Russian Civil War, 1918–22), the territory has always been under the direct administrative control of the metropolitan capital of Moscow or St. Petersburg. While Siberia's political center has therefore always been located in Europe, and the majority of its population is made up of ethnically and linguistically European stock, a variety of factors—geographical, historical, and cultural, as well as Siberia's contacts with Asiatic peoples both inside and outside its borders—positively substantiates an official statement made by the Soviet government in 1986 that the USSR is now "one of the most important powers in Asia and the Pacific."[1]

THE PHYSICAL ENVIRONMENT

Today Siberia is administratively divided into three major economic regions of the USSR, namely, West Siberia, East Siberia and the Far East; these are further subdivided into a number of autonomous republics (ASSRs), regions *(oblasts)*, territories *(krays)* and districts *(okrugs)*, many of them corresponding to the original homelands of Siberia's indigenous non-Russian peoples. While, therefore, there is an administrative distinction in modern

[1] *Pravda,* April 24, 1986.

Soviet usage between *Siberia* and the *Far East,* for the purposes of this chapter the latter has been subsumed under the traditional designation of *Siberia,* including the Kamchatka Peninsula, the island of Sakhalin and the Kuril archipelago. The whole territory is physically distinguished by three predominant factors—its enormous size, the extremes of its climate and the diversity of its terrain and natural features. Contrary to popular misconception, Siberia is not simply a vast frozen wilderness of ice and snow; indeed, it is inconceivable that such a large proportion of the planet's land surface (around one-twelfth) should be marked by any kind of topographical homogeneity.

Siberia and the Far East occupy a total area of some 5 million sq. miles/13 million sq. km. and cover eight different time zones. Together they are larger than either the United States or China, and the Far East alone is bigger than the continent of Australia. From Moscow to Vladivostok is a distance of over 5,592 miles/9,000 km. via the Trans-Siberian Railway, and from the Arctic shores to the southern borderlands is over 1,864 miles/3,000 km. These enormous distances and the consequent problems of transport, communication and supply have naturally had palpable effects on the human settlement and economic exploitation of the region, effects that have not yet been fully overcome by modern technological developments. As recently as the 1940s, enclaves of tiny communities are reported to have been discovered whose existence had previously been unknown and whose inhabitants were ignorant of such momentous events as the 1917 Revolution and had never before seen a European. Forest fires can, and still do, totally destroy areas of timberland larger than some European countries, and it has been estimated that an aerial photographic survey of the entire territory covering 580 sq. miles/1,500 sq. km. a day would take 15 years to complete.[2]

In the past, areas of northern Kazakhstan have been considered part of Siberia. If these are included, then—tropical rain forests apart—the whole country contains examples of almost all the world's main topographical features, from arctic region to desert, from rich arable pastureland to sterile tundra, from mosquito-ridden swamp to sheer mountain ranges. It encompasses freezing, inhospitable wastelands, active volcanoes and the picturesque "little Switzerland" of the Altay. Not all of this variety is to be found in each of the three major economic zones, but it is convenient to describe the physical environment in terms of these three administrative divisions.[3]

Though the smallest of the three regions, West Siberia nevertheless covers an area of 1 million sq. miles/2.5 million sq. km., from the Yamal Peninsula in the north to the mountainous Altay in the south and from the Urals to the Yenisey River at its eastern border. Eighty percent of this

[2] Abraham Resnik, *Siberia and the Soviet Far East: Endless Frontiers* (Moscow: Novosti, 1983), 40.

[3] Most of the geographical data, dimensions and statistics in this section are taken from the 22-volume *Sovetskii Soyuz: Geograficheskoe opisanie; Vostochnaya Sibir, Zapadnaya Sibir* and *Dalnii Vostok* (Moscow: Mysl, 1969 and 1971).

region is taken up by the great West Siberian Plain, one of the largest flatland expanses in the world, which drains into the Arctic by the mighty Ob River and its tributary the Irtysh. In the far north, the tundra belt stretches for hundreds of miles south from the Kara Sea. Vegetation here is confined to primitive lichens and mosses, and agricultural production is virtually impossible. Reindeer husbandry, hunting and fishing were the traditional pursuits of the native peoples of this region, though the discovery and exploitation of vast oil and natural gas deposits since the 1950s has now made northwestern Siberia one of the most important economic areas in the Soviet Union and has led to a massive influx of population and the growth of new urban settlements and communications networks. The oil and gas fields reach further south into the immense swamp-and-forest zone of the taiga, which covers roughly two-thirds of West Siberia. Thin top-soil, deep permafrost (permanently frozen subsoil) and consequently poor drainage have created huge areas of bogland, such as the great Vasyuganye Swamp in the Ob basin, where the establishment of drilling stations and transport and pipeline delivery networks, not to mention living conditions, are fraught with major difficulties. Apart from the principal waterways, the area is crisscrossed by thousands of small rivers and streams and dotted with countless lakes. It is prone to severe periodic flooding. Plans to divert some of West Siberia's superabundance of water southward to irrigate the arid regions of Central Asia have so far been abandoned for practical and ecological reasons, though the idea periodically resurfaces in the Soviet press and technical literature.

The southern half of the West Siberian Plain is covered by three extensive areas of fertile lowland known as the Ishim, the Baraba and the Kulunda steppes. In contrast to the grimmer northern climes, the rich black-earth soil (*chernozem*) makes this an extremely productive agricultural area, and livestock production, dairying and arable farming account for the bulk of Siberia's home-grown agricultural output. It contains, too, the bulk of West Siberia's population, mainly concentrated in the major cities and industrial centers of Novosibirsk (population in 1979, 1.3 million), Omsk (1 million), Novokuznetsk (541,500), Barnaul (533,000), Kemerovo (570,500) and Tyumen (359,000),[4] all of them lying along or within easy reach of the Trans-Siberian Railway. Two-thirds of West Siberia's population of 13 million are urban-dwellers (see Table 1).

Somewhat larger in area than West Siberia is East Siberia, lying between the Yenisey and Lena rivers and stretching eastward beyond Lake Baikal in the south (see Table 2). Before the administrative transfer of the Yakutskaya ASSR from East Siberia to the Far East in 1963 it was, in fact, the largest territorial unit in the country, comprising one-third of the entire Soviet Union. Today the region covers roughly 1.6 million sq. miles/4.2 million sq. km. and is marked by a much more rugged terrain, with more permafrost, tundra, forest and mountain than West Siberia. Its central fea-

[4] *Chislennost i sostav naseleniya SSSR: po dannym Vzesoyuznoi perepisi naseleniya 1979 goda* (Moscow: Finansy i statistika, 1985), 15–19 (figures are rounded to the nearest 500).

Table 1
ADMINISTRATIVE SUBDIVISIONS AND
POPULATION OF
WEST SIBERIA (1979)

Administrative unit	Population	Urban population (%)	Rural population (%)
Tyumenskaya *oblast*	1,887,152	61	39
including:			
Khanty Mansiyskiy			
autonomous *okrug*	(569,139)	78	22
Yamalo-Nenetskiy			
autonomous *okrug*	(157,616)	51	49
Tomskaya *oblast*	865,934	65	35
Omskaya *oblast*	1,954,663	63	37
Novosibirskaya *oblast*	2,618,024	71	29
Kemerovskaya *oblast*	2,958,066	86	14
Altayskiy *kray*	2,674,614	52	48
including:			
Gorno-Altayskaya			
autonomous *oblast*	(171,835)	28	72
TOTAL	12,958,453	66	34

Source: *Chislennost i sostav naseleniya SSSR: po dannym Vzesoyuznoi perepisi na-seleniya 1979 goda* (Moscow, 1985).

ture is the Central Siberian Plateau, a vast irregular upland averaging some 1,968 ft/600 m. in height and rising in the north to 5,577 ft/1,700 m. It is traversed by many rivers rushing through deep, steep-sided gorges and covered with the almost limitless, coniferous taiga. This gigantic central massif and its dense forest cover occupies over three-quarters of the entire territory of East Siberia and supports very little human population (averaging less than one person per square kilometer). It is, however, the home of a wide variety of fur-bearing mammals whose valuable pelts originally lured the Russian pioneers across Siberia in the 17th century.

To the north, beyond the Arctic Circle, the North Siberian Lowland presents a landscape of mixed forest and tundra that forms a broad inter-montane east-west corridor between the northern slopes of the Central Siberian Plateau and the Byrranga mountain range, which dominates the Taymyr Peninsula, the northernmost point of the Siberian landmass, thrusting out into the Arctic Ocean. The traditional nomadic occupations of the Samoyed peoples inhabiting these northern zones were hunting, fishing and reindeer herding. Since the 1930s, the area's economy has been supplemented by industrial developments connected with the intensive mining of nickel, cobalt and platinum-group metals in the region of Norilsk, now

Table 2
ADMINISTRATIVE SUBDIVISIONS AND
POPULATION OF
EAST SIBERIA (1979)

Administrative unit	Population	Urban population (%)	Rural population (%)
Krasnoyarskiy *kray* including:	4,814,835	69	31
Khakasskaya autonomous *oblast*	(500,106)	68	32
Taymyrskiy autonomous *okrug*	(44,108)	65	35
Evenkiyskiy autonomous *okrug*	(15,710)	35	65
Tuvinskaya ASSR	266,453	43	57
Irkutskaya *oblast* including:	2,559,522	78	22
Ust-Ordynskiy Buryat autonomous *okrug*	(132,732)	19	81
Buryatskaya ASSR	900,812	57	43
Chitinskaya *oblast* including:	1,233,435	63	37
Aginskiy Buryat autonomous *okrug*	(69,269)	26	74
TOTAL	9,775,057	62	38

Source: *Chislennost i sostav naseleniya* . . . (Moscow, 1985).

one of the world's largest Arctic cities with a population of over 200,000. It is served by the port of Dudinka on the Yenisey River, from where a fleet of nuclear and conventionally powered icebreakers keeps the Arctic sea route to north European Russia open all year round.

In the south, agriculture is less well developed than in West Siberia, though the valleys around Lake Baikal contain extensive grazing lands where sheep farming has for centuries been the major economic activity of the native Buryats. Some fruit, vegetable and cereal crops are also grown around the major cities of Krasnoyarsk and Irkutsk. Lake Baikal itself is the most outstanding geographical feature of southeastern Siberia and is one of the natural wonders of the world—"the pearl of Siberia." This huge inland sea, some 398 miles/640 km. long and 50 miles/80 km. wide, has a surface area in excess of 12,162 sq. miles/31,500 sq. km. It is the deepest lake in the world, plunging to 5,314 ft/1,620 m. at its lowest point and containing no less than one-fifth of the planet's entire fresh-water resources (23,000 cubic kilometers). Renowned for the purity and pellucidity of its water,

Baikal became the focus of a bitter public dispute between economic planners and Soviet environmentalists in the 1960s after industrial effluent threatened to pollute its contents irretrievably. As a result, strict conservation measures were introduced. The lake is now the center of a flourishing tourist industry.

Baikal is emptied by the great Angara River, which flows northwestward to join the Yenisey close to the city of Yeniseysk. Beginning in the 1950s, an interconnecting "cascade" of huge hydroelectric stations has been built along the Angara-Yenisey system, and by the 1980s the Siberian grid produced nearly 40 percent of the Soviet Union's hydroelectricity. The other mammoth construction project that commences its route in East Siberia is the celebrated Baikal-Amur Mainline (BAM) railroad, running parallel with but hundreds of miles north of the old Trans-Siberian line to the Pacific. After more than 10 years of construction across atrocious terrain subject to earthquakes, avalanches and mud slides, the eastern and western sectors of the railroad were linked up in October 1984 at Kuanda, in Chita *oblast*. The BAM zone is now a rapidly developing industrial region with a population of over 1 million.

East Siberia also contains the Buryat ASSR to the east of Lake Baikal and the tiny autonomous republic of Tuva, bordering on the northwest corner of Mongolia. In Kyzyl, the capital of this little-known country, stands an obelisk marking the putative geographical center of Asia.

From the north of Lake Baikal, the BAM passes from East Siberia into southern Yakutia and continues to the eastern littoral across the southern belt of the Soviet Far East, the largest of Russia's Asiatic regions (see Table 3). Despite the fact that 80 percent of its territory rests on permafrost (some of it a mile deep) and 75 percent is covered by mountains and forest, its topography nevertheless offers great diversity and contrast. From the Bering Straits in the extreme north, it stretches 2,796 miles/4,500 km. south to the paddy fields of rice on the Korean border; at its widest point it is 2,485 miles/4,000 km. The Soviet Far East, therefore, including Yakutia, includes a total land area of over 2.3 million sq. miles/6 million sq. km.—roughly one-quarter of the Soviet Union's landmass but only 2.7 percent of its population. It contains low, marshy swampland, forests where tigers roam, and the highest volcano in Eurasia, Mount Klyuchevskoy, on the Kamchatka Peninsula. From its peak 15,580 feet/4,750 meters above sea level to the bottom of the Kurilo-Kamchatka ravine in the Pacific Ocean is a vertical distance of 9.3 miles/15 km. The northernmost part of the territory is a mixture of high mountainous terrain (the Verkhoyansk and Cherskiy fold-mountains and the peaks of the Chukotskiy Peninsula) and the flat lowland tundra plains of the Kolyma-Indigirka basin and coastline.

Further south, the Aldan, Stanovoy and Dzhugdzhur ranges give way to the Amur River valley, which, together with the Zeya-Bureya lowland and the region around Lake Khanka, are the only areas in which any successful agricultural activity is possible. Traditional cereals as well as vegetables, soy beans and rice are cultivated, but despite fertile soils and a relatively long growing season, yields are often reduced by monsoon rains and widespread flooding. It seems probable that measures taken to alleviate this

Table 3
ADMINISTRATIVE SUBDIVISIONS
AND POPULATION OF
THE SOVIET FAR EAST (1983)

Administrative unit	Population	Urban population (%)*	Rural population (%)*
Yakutskaya ASSR	944,000	61	39
Kamshatskaya oblast including:	415,000	83	17
Koryakskiy autonomous okrug	(34,265)*	39	61
Magadanskaya oblast including:	510,000	78	22
Chukotskiy autonomous okrug	(132,859)*	70	30
Amurskaya oblast	1,007,000	65	35
Sakhalinskaya oblast	679,000	82	18
Primorskiy kray	2,079,000	76	24
Khabarovskiy kray including:	1,663,000	79	21
Jewish autonomous oblast of Birobidzhan	(190,219)*	68	32
TOTAL	7,297,000	75	25

*Figures for 1979
Sources: John J. Stephan and V. P. Chichkanov, eds., Soviet-American Horizons on the Pacific (University of Hawaii, 1986), 3; Chislennost i sostav naseleniya . . . (Moscow, 1985).

situation will not in the foreseeable future alter the Far East's position as a net importer of foodstuffs. On the other hand, the Far East is the Soviet Union's largest producer of fish and other seafood. The region has a 16,777 mile/27,000-km. coastline with direct access to five seas and the Pacific Ocean. It supplies 40 percent of the country's fish and other aquatic food products, including the Amur salmon, the world-famous Kamchatka crab and large quantities of kelp.

The region's agricultural deficiency is offset by its great mineral wealth and natural resources. A whole gamut of valuable deposits are hidden beneath its formidable terrain, including gold, iron, zinc, tin, copper and many other nonferrous metals, boron, oil and natural gas. The Yakut coalfields are among the largest in the USSR, while diamond mining at Mirnyy and Udachnyy has recently made the Soviet Union one of the world's most prolific diamond producers and, in fact, diamonds are considered to be the country's third-largest earner of foreign exchange after oil and natural gas.

Geological and climatic factors present awesome technical problems in the exploitation of these riches, but the construction of the BAM and its adjacent Territorial Production Complexes (TPCs) should greatly enhance the Far East's industrial and economic productivity.[5]

All three regions of Siberia are marked by extreme continentality of climate, of which the most obvious and notorious features are the long, bitter winters and the intense cold.[6] The two main reasons for this are Siberia's geographical location in the high northern latitudes, much of it beyond the Arctic Circle, and the vastness of its landmass, which means that many regions are too remote to benefit from the moderating influences of the oceans to the west, south and east. In general, the degree of continentality and the severity of the climate increase the further east and north one travels. In Yakutia, for instance, winter lasts for up to eight months a year, with an average January temperature lower than $-40°F/-40°C$. In Verkhoyansk it is almost $-58°F/-50°C$, and at Oimyakon, the northern hemisphere's "pole of cold" though well below the Arctic Circle, levels of below $-94°F/-70°C$ have been recorded, and this does not take into account the wind chill factor. Around the northern coastal areas, however, where air conditions are less stable, the freezing arctic winds can produce temperature equivalents of around $-202°F/-130°C$ in the eastern parts. Even in western Siberia, where actual temperatures are significantly higher, the effects of wind chill make living and working conditions—for instance, in the oil and gas fields—extremely unpleasant.

The difference in range between winter and summer temperatures in Siberia can be quite dramatic. Even Verkhoyansk, at a latitude beyond the Arctic Circle, has a mean July temperature of $59°-61°F/15°-16°C$, and in the southern steppelands of West Siberia, summer temperatures average around $73°F/23°C$ (on the borders of Kazakhstan, droughts are not uncommon). In some parts of Siberia the difference between the lowest winter and the highest summer temperatures can be as much as $154°F/68°C$. The greatest extremes are to be found in the Far East, where the climate differs according to elevation, latitude and the effects of Pacific Ocean currents. Annual precipitation in its coastal regions is far higher than elsewhere in the Soviet Union, mainly as a result of the heavy monsoon rains, which offset the attractiveness of the relatively mild summers. Temperatures vary from the freezing winter colds of Yakutia to the congenial summer warmth of the seaside resorts in the southern maritime regions, where even grapevines grow.

Almost all of Siberia is covered with snow from around October to April or even May, though the depth and length of cover varies from region to region; the greatest depths (over 31.5 in/80 cm.) are found in the middle

[5] Pavel G. Bunich, "Economic Impact of the BAM," in Theodore Shabad and Victor L. Mote, eds., *Gateway to Siberian Resources (the BAM)* (New York: Wiley, 1977) 135–44.
[6] Climatic data are from Paul E. Lydolph, *Climates of the Soviet Union, World Survey of Climatology,* vol. 7 (Amsterdam: Elsevier, 1977) and *Atlas SSSR,* 2nd ed. (Moscow, 1969).

Yenisey valley and the longest cover (around 280 days per year) along the Arctic coast. By contrast, Vladivostok has snow for only 80 days a year. While it remains true, therefore, that Siberia's reputation for extreme severity of climate—with its ice-bound wastes and steel-shattering frosts—is well deserved, the overall picture is not one of unrelievedly ubiquitous and perennial frigidity.

HISTORICAL DEVELOPMENT

The history of modern Siberia traditionally dates from the year 1582, when the Cossack chieftan Yermak Timofeevich crossed the Urals and defeated the tiny Tatar khanate of Sibir on the Irtysh River. During the following century, Russian fur hunters, traders, military and government personnel, fugitive peasants and exiles rapidly advanced across Siberia until, through a successful blend of state initiative and private enterprise, the whole of northern Asia came under Muscovy's sway.[7] The native tribes were subdued by superior military force and subjected to payment of the fur tribute (*yasak*); a strong network of fortified stockades (*ostrogs*) was established, and these formed the nuclei of future towns; and Siberia's forests were plundered for their wild fauna as hunters and merchants trapped and traded in the valuable pelts, which constituted the most important commodity in the Russian state's economy. The only area that escaped annexation by Moscow was the Amur-Ussuri region in the Far East, which was not incorporated into the Russian Empire until the mid-19th century (under the treaties of Aigun, 1858, and Peking, 1860). However, lucrative trading links were early established with the Chinese Manchu Empire under the treaties of Nerchinsk (1689) and Kyakhta (1727). In exchange for sable, fox and ermine fur, Russia imported precious metals, silk, porcelain and other luxury items. In the late 18th and early 19th centuries, the Kyakhta trade became more diversified and included clocks, mirrors, rhubarb, tobacco and, above all, Chinese tea, much of which was reexported to Europe. Siberia thus became a commercial landbridge between East and West very early in its history.

The systematic, scientific exploration of Siberia and the northern Pacific was inaugurated during the reign of Peter the Great (1696–1725). Throughout the 18th century, the expeditions and discoveries of Russian as well as foreign explorers greatly added to the knowledge of Siberia's geography, ethnography and natural resources. Mining industries—many of them worked by convict and exile labor—were established to exploit the country's newly found mineral wealth. There was as yet, however, no properly thought-out policy of Siberian development. Remoteness from the capital, savage physical conditions, difficulties in communication, the arbitrary and despotic rule of local military governors, and the greed and corruption

[7] Basil Dmytryshyn, E.A.P. Crownhart-Vaughan and Thomas Vaughan, eds., *Russia's Conquest of Siberia: A Documentary Record, 1558–1700* (Portland: Oregon Historical Society, 1985).

of state officials and private entrepreneurs meant that Siberia was treated as little more than a valuable source of raw materials and a usefully distant dumping ground for the criminal rejects of metropolitan Russia. The pillage of Siberia's natural and human resources by the agents of Moscow and St. Petersburg and the horrors of the exile system lay at the root of the later concept of Siberia as merely an exploited colony of European Russia, and led to the demands of 19th-century regional separatists for Siberia's political independence from czarist imperialism.[8]

On the other hand, the Russian population of Siberia steadily increased in size through a mixture of voluntary migration, flight, forcible transportation and natural procreation. Consequently, the region's economy became more diversified, as both extractive and manufacturing industries developed and as the rich agricultural belt in the south became settled by land-hungry peasants from the European provinces. Between 1815 and 1911, the total population (native and Russian) grew from 1.5 million to 9.4 million. In the early 19th century, an attempt was made to bring some order and justice to the government of Siberia by the administrative reforms of Count Mikhail Speranskiy.[9] However, despite the existence of some enclaves of sophistication and orderly civic life in a few major towns such as Tobolsk, Tomsk (where Siberia's first university was founded in 1888) and Irkutsk, Siberia remained, for the most part, a remote, wild and ungovernable territory in which banditry, mass vagrancy and violent crime were rife. Unsurprisingly, Siberia's criminal exile community, though only six percent of the total population, accounted for the vast majority of robbery, rustling, murder, arson and rape committed there, which only served to exacerbate the territory's already forbidding reputation.[10]

Toward the end of the 19th century, the government became more aware of its responsibilities and opportunities in the east and pursued a more positive, though uneven, policy toward the region's development.[11] The founding of Vladivostok and the takeover of the Amur region in 1858, the construction of the Trans-Siberian Railway (1894–1904), the reform of the exile system (1900), the encouragement of mass peasant migration to Siberia during the period of agrarian reform (1906–13), as well as the war with Japan (1904–5) were all symptomatic of St. Petersburg's more active commitment to the interests of its possessions in the Asian-Pacific region.

---

[8] The best Western study of the Siberian regionalist movement is Wolfgang Faust's *Russlands goldener Boden: Der sibirische Regionalismus in der zweiten Hälfte des 19. Jahrhunderts* (Cologne, 1980).

[9] Marc Raeff, *Siberia and the Reforms of 1822* (Seattle: University of Washington Press, 1956).

[10] Alan Wood, "Sex and Violence in Siberia: Aspects of the Tsarist Exile System," in John Massey Stewart and Alan Wood, eds., *Siberia: Two Historical Perspectives*, Great Britain-USSR Association and School of Slavonic and East European Studies (London, 1984), 23–42.

[11] Mark Bassin, "The Russian Geographical Society, the "Amur Epoch" and the Great Siberian Expedition, 1855–1863," *Annals of the Association of American Geographers* 73, no. 2 (1983): 240–56.

751

Even the sale of Russia's American territories in Alaska and the Aleutians to the United States in 1867 can be seen as part of this process.[12]

Russia's industrial revolution at the turn of the century was reflected in Siberia in an expansion of industrial production—stimulated by construction of the Trans-Siberian Railway—and the influx of foreign capital into the region's economy. Large-scale enterprises were, however, rare except in the metallurgical extractive industries, and on the eve of the 1917 Revolution, Siberia only accounted for two percent of the nation's total industrial output and contained an industrial working class of no more than half a million.

As everywhere else in the country, the revolutions of 1917 ushered in a new era in the history of Siberia, which Soviet writers refer to as the region's "third discovery."[13] During the Civil War (1918–22), Siberia and the Far East became the broad arena for a complex and bloody conflict among a variety of political, military, regional and national interests, complicated by the intervention of American, British and Japanese military forces. The whole territory was beyond Moscow's direct control, and for three to four years political power ricocheted around a bewildering number of ephemeral, regionally based regimes backed by Red, White or foreign armies.[14] This vicious internecine struggle was finally concluded with the establishment of Soviet power from the Urals to the Pacific and the Red Army's liberation of Vladivostok in 1922. In November of the same year, the short-lived semiindependent Far Eastern Republic, a "bourgeois-democratic" buffer state created by Moscow in 1920, was fully absorbed into the Soviet Union. On Sakhalin, Japan withdrew its forces from the north of the island only in 1925, and for the next 20 years it remained divided between Russia and Japan along the 50th Parallel. In 1945 Soviet troops invaded the south, and the USSR has maintained its possession, along with the Kuril Islands, ever since.[15]

Since the end of the Civil War, the major events and developments in Siberia's history have been, by and large, the same as those of the Soviet Union as a whole: Lenin's New Economic Policy in the 1920s; forced industrialization and the collectivization of agriculture; Stalin's political terror of the 1930s; World War II; the postwar policies of reconstruction; and, more recently, accelerated economic development based on the scientific assessment and exploitation of the region's fuel and mineral resources.

In the early 1920s, plans were laid for the economic development of Siberia, and these were transformed into concrete reality during the first and second Five-Year Plans (1928–37). Of particular significance were the

[12] James R. Gibson, "The Sale of Russian America to the United States," in S. Frederick Starr, ed., *Russia's American Colony* (Durham, N.C.: Duke University Press, 1987).

[13] See, for instance, "Tret'e otkrytie Sibiri," in A. Okladnikov, *Otkrytie Sibiri* (Moscow: Molodaya gvardiya, 1979), 211–22.

[14] John Albert White, *The Siberian Intervention* (New York: Greenwood Press, 1969); "Grazhdanskaya voina," in A. P. Oladnikov, et al., eds., *Istoriya Sibiri v pyati tomakh,* vol. 4 (Leningrad: Nauka, 1969), 87–171.

[15] John J. Stephan, *Sakhalin: A History* (London: Oxford University Press, 1971).

formation of the huge Urals-Kuznetsk iron and coal combine in West Siberia, which became the center of a massive new iron and steel industry, and the establishment of mineral-extracting industries at Norilsk and in the Kolyma region in the far north. During the Stalinist period, the perennial problem of manpower shortages in Siberia was met by the ruthless utilization of directed, forced and convict labor.[16] Millions of Stalin's victims were "employed" on gigantic new construction projects from Magnitogorsk to Magadan under the combined direction of Dalstroi (Far Eastern Construction Trust) and the Gulag (Main Prison Camp Administration). The latter organization, with much of its operations located in Siberia, has become an international byword for mass terror and the arbitrary and coercive practices of the police state.[17]

During World War II, Siberia's productive capacity was augmented by the wholesale shift of entire enterprises from the western battlefronts to Siberia and the Far East. Despite earlier Soviet-Japanese clashes on the Far Eastern front at Lake Khasan (1937) and Khalkhin Gol (1939), the bombing of Pearl Harbor in December 1941 lifted the immediate threat of a Japanese invasion, and Siberia's reprieve as a theater of hostilities enabled it to maintain a massive contribution in the production and supply of military matériel to the Soviet war effort. Siberian military divisions and whole armies made a distinctive impact in almost every field of battle, and the Siberian population, including the non-Russian native peoples, suffered a disproportionate share of casualties and war dead.

After Stalin's death in 1953, the ending of large-scale forced labor and the diminishing capacity of European Russia's fuel and energy supplies combined to focus attention more sharply on the need to utilize Siberia's resources more rationally and intensively. Soviet planners wisely decided that power-intensive rather than labor-intensive industries were what needed to be developed, and in the 1950s a grandiose program of hydroelectric station construction commenced that would not only feed into the national grid but also attract growth in those areas of production demanding most energy, such as aluminum. The hydroelectric program in the Angara-Yenisey basin, together with Nikita Khrushchev's Virgin Lands campaign for extensive agricultural production in West Siberia and the establishment of the Siberian branch of the USSR Academy of Sciences (1958) at Akademgorodok, near Novosibirsk, were all major symbols of the new eastward orientation in official thinking. Enormous scientific, human and financial resources were poured into Siberia in order to harness the region's huge potential.

During the 1960s, a major boost was given to Siberia's economic importance by the exploitation of the newly discovered oil and natural gas fields in the northwest. In the face of formidable odds, vast expanses of hostile

[16] David J. Dallin and Boris I. Nicolaevsky, *Forced Labour in the Soviet Union* (London: Hollis and Carter, 1948).
[17] Solzhenitsyn's concept of a "GULag archipelago" was most responsible for popularizing the term: Aleksandr Solzhenitsyn, *Arkhipelag GULag: opyt khudozhestvennogo issledovaniya,* 3 vols. (Paris: YMCA Press, 1973–75).

tundra, taiga and swampland have been transformed and are now part of the Soviet Union's largest revenue-earning industry. Apart from supplying domestic needs, oil and natural gas now account for over one-half of Soviet hard-currency earnings. The emphasis on Siberian development was maintained during the 1970s, with the construction of the BAM in the Far East and the location of new industrial complexes along its route. While strategic considerations against a background of deteriorating relations with China undoubtedly played a role in the decision to build the BAM, economic calculations based on the opening up of the Far East's natural resources and the commercial prospects for international traffic passing between Asia and Europe along the new landbridge, as well as the burgeoning potential of the Pacific region as a whole, were certainly the prime motivating factors. Siberia's whole historical experience, therefore, from Yermak to Gorbachev, has been inextricably linked with the economic development of the entire country.

ECONOMIC RESOURCES

Siberia has been described as Russia's El Dorado. Certainly, its almost inexhaustible reserves of raw materials, precious minerals, energy and timber seem to justify this image. In comparison with European Russia, however, Siberia's industrial base is still underdeveloped, and most of its output is accounted for by the extractive industries—in particular, oil, natural gas, coal, nonferrous metals and, more recently, diamonds. Despite enormous government investment during recent decades and the high priority given to prestige Siberian construction projects, a whole range of factors has militated against the creation of a more efficient, integrated industrial base. Some of these are common to the Soviet economy as a whole and are currently the subject of far-reaching transformation and restructuring under Mikhail Gorbachev's policy of *perestroika*. Others are peculiar to the region, and some are a combination of the two.

Among the all-Soviet Union problems shared by the Siberian economy are inefficient management, interministerial and intersectional rivalries, lack of cost accounting, wasteful use of raw materials and equipment, and technological lag. These defects have been identified and openly discussed by senior Soviet politicians and their economic advisors. The difficulties have been compounded in Siberia and the Far East by such chronic regional factors as the harsh environment, inaccessible locations resulting in problems of transport and communication, a poorly developed social and cultural infrastructure and consequent shortages of skilled, permanent labor. Solutions to many of these problems are impeded by conflicting sets of interests in the political and administrative hierarchy, arguments over spatial resource allocation and a recurring incongruity between micro- and macroeconomic development priorities.

These obstacles notwithstanding, and despite the current fashion of maligning Leonid Brezhnev's leadership (1964–82) as the "period of stagnation," the Siberian economy has nevertheless expanded at a tremendous rate over the past 20 years and will doubtless continue to do so well into the

21st century, though the precise nature of its role and impact in the Asian-Pacific region still remains problematical.

Coal, oil and natural gas

The Soviet Union is the world's largest producer of all three major fossil fuels, and it has been estimated that as much as 80 percent of its potential oil reserves, 90 percent of its gas and 90 percent of its coal lies within Siberia and the Far East.[18] Much of this is located in extremely remote and inaccessible parts of the region and is unlikely to be fully exploited in the immediate future. Present production levels are for the time being sufficient for the country's domestic and export requirements, though further exploration, test drilling and prospecting will obviously continue in order to prepare for increased future demand.

The three major coalfields currently in operation are situated in the Kuznetsk, Kansk-Achinsk and south Yakutian basins in the vicinity of the Trans-Siberian Railway, which is, of course, the principal mode of delivery. Of these the largest producer is the Kuznetsk basin (Kuzbas), which as early as the 1930s was fueling the iron and steel industry and local electric power stations in the Urals. In recent years, transport costs have caused Soviet planners to concentrate more attention on the Donbas coalfields in the Ukraine, which are closer to the major consuming regions in European Russia. However, under the current Five-Year Plan (1986–90), investment in the Kuznetsk mines has been increased once more and it is hoped to achieve an output of 160 million tons by 1990. Kuzbas coking coal is of very high quality, and much of it is extracted by opencast mining. Lower-grade lignite coal is produced in the Kansk-Achinsk basin further east, but because of technical difficulties with transportation caused by this coal's propensity to spontaneous combustion under certain conditions, most of it is used for local needs. Production of Kansk-Achinsk lignite was to have been enhanced under the 12th Five-Year Plan in order to fuel a series of massive new coal-fired electric power stations to be built during the late 1980s and 1990s. The electricity generated would then be transmitted westward along extremely high-voltage power lines. Recent reports suggest, however, that this project has been somewhat curtailed in scope.[19] The most recently developed major coalfield is in southern Yakutia, centered on the new town of Neryungri, which is linked to the BAM by a northern spur of the railway known as the "Little BAM." Coal from the Yakut fields is used not only for local consumption but is also exported, via the BAM, to Japan. Overall, Siberia already accounts for around 40 percent of the USSR's total coal output. And there is more to come: in

---

[18] David Wilson, "The Siberian Oil and Gas Industry," in Alan Wood, ed., *Siberia: Problems and Prospects for Regional Development* (London: Croom Helm, 1987), 96. Much of the information on energy resources and policy in this section is taken from this source. See also, by the same author, *The Demand for Energy in the Soviet Union*, (London: Croom Helm, 1983).

[19] *Sotsialisticheskaya industriya*, February 20, 1986.

1987, for instance, the Neryungri mine exceeded its planned production target by 400,000 tons.[20]

Unlike coal, Siberian oil production is largely concentrated in a single area—the marshy basin of the middle Ob in northwest Siberia. Over the last 20 years, West Siberian oil production has rocketed from 31 million tons in 1970 to an anticipated 460 million tons in 1990. Over the same period, output elsewhere in the USSR has fallen from 319 million to 172 million tons. Over 90 percent of the increase in West Siberian oil is accounted for by the enormous deposits in Tyumen *oblast*—in particular, the giant Samotlor field near Nizhnevartovsk. A fall in production levels at Samotlor between 1983 and 1985 led some American commentators to suggest that the Soviet oil boom was over and an energy crisis in the offing. However, those prognostications were soon shown to have been misplaced, and in 1986 and 1987 output once more began to soar and new world records in barrels-per-day production were established. Total Soviet oil targets have now been set at 635 million tons in 1990, and by the year 2000 deposits further north on the Yamal Peninsula and in the Kara Sea region will offset any decline in output from the middle Ob fields. East Siberia and the Far East also possess large oil reserves, possibly as large as those in West Siberia; but given the technical and geological problems involved in drilling through deep permafrost in the difficult terrain of the Central Siberian Plateau and the far northeast, and also given the continuing viability of the Tyumen fields, it is unlikely that extensive development of eastern Siberian oil will occur in the immediate future—though some small-scale expansion for local needs in Yakutia will supplement the modest output from Sakhalin (recently averaging 3 million tons per year, though planned to increase) and help to reduce the cost of transporting oil from West Siberia.[21]

Natural gas was first discovered in West Siberia in the 1960s. During the next two decades, the supergiant fields at Medvezhye and Urengoy in the far north of Tyumen *oblast* have helped to boost total Soviet production of natural gas from 254 billion cubic yards/194 billion cubic meters in 1970 to a planned 1,112 billion cubic yards/850 billion cubic meters in 1990. With an area of almost 2,317 sq. miles/6,000 sq. km., by far the largest of the gas fields is at Urengoy; their exploitation has led to the construction of the new town of Novyy Urengoy, with a projected population of 160,000. While production here continues, attention has shifted north during the period of the 12th Five-Year Plan to the Yamburg field on the Taz Peninsula and even further north to the development of deposits on the Yamal Peninsula. When these reach their full capacity, by the end of the century, West Siberian natural gas may well account for as much as 75 percent of the USSR total. Exploitation of the Siberian gas fields has been beset by the usual environmental, technical and administrative diffi-

[20]*Pravda*, December 3, 1987.
[21]David Wilson, "Exploration for Oil and Gas in Eastern Siberia," in Alan Wood and R. A. French, eds., *The Development of Siberia: People and Resources* (London: Macmillan, 1989), chap. 11.

culties, but they have nevertheless been turned into one of the country's top foreign-currency earners. Gas is supplied to the European USSR and exported to Eastern and Western Europe along extra-large-diameter steel pipelines, each capable of delivering around 33 billion cubic meters of gas per year; around 30 of these will be operational by the end of the century. As in the case of oil—and for the same reasons—it is unlikely that the large proven gas deposits in East Siberia will be subjected to any extensive development before the end of the century. The Messoyakha gas field, in the north of Krasnoyarsk *kray*, supplies the needs of the Norilsk nickel smelters, power stations and smaller industrial enterprises, and Sakhalin delivers somewhat larger quantities (around 4 billion cubic yards/3 billion cubic meters per year) by pipeline to the mainland. The export potential of natural gas in the Asian-Pacific region has so far not been developed, though the Soviet military withdrawal from Afghanistan in 1988 and a post-Moscow summit relaxation of international tensions may reopen possibilities in this area. For the time being, however, the western part of the USSR and Eastern and Western Europe will continue to be the main recipients of northern Asia's energy supplies.

Hydroelectricity

Power harnessed from Siberia's enormous rivers produces the cheapest electricity in the world. Beginning in 1950, a massive development program on the Angara-Yenisey river system resulted in the construction of a series of huge hydroelectric power stations (GES) and associated power-hungry industrial enterprises—in particular, aluminum production and cellulose- and wood-processing factories. By the early 1980s, the Siberian and Far Eastern hydroelectric stations, which include some of the largest in the world, were generating over half of Siberia's total electricity and nearly three-quarters of the hydroelectric power of the Soviet Union as a whole. The first, relatively small, station was built on the Angara River at Irkutsk and came into production in 1956, with a design capacity of 600 mW. After Irkutsk came Bratsk (4,500 mW), now the site of a thriving industrial town in the taiga with a population of a third of a million. Next came the Divnogorsk GES in Krasnoyarsk (6,000 mW), Ust Ilimsk (3,840 mW) and most recently the gigantic Sayan-Shushenskoye Dam at Sayanogorsk on the Yenisey River. This is the largest generator of hydroelectricity in the Soviet Union, with a capacity of 6,400 mW. Further stations planned or in the preliminary construction stages are the Boguchany, and Middle-Yenisey GES, at Abalakova, though the latter probably will not begin operation until the next century.[22]

Smaller stations are sited in the far north at Norilsk and at Chernyshev-skiy in the Vilyuy River basin, on the Kolyma in the extreme northeast, and on the Amur system in the Far East. Here the two major stations are the Zeya and the Bureya, with a capacity of 1,300 mW and 2,000 mW, respectively. All of these power stations are linked with local industrial

[22] Theodore Shabad, "Geographic Aspects of the New Soviet Five-Year Plan, 1986–90," *Soviet Geography* 27, no. 1 (1986): 3.

Table 4.1
OIL PRODUCTION IN THE USSR, 1970–90
(millions of tons)

	1970	1975	1980	1985	1986	1987	1990 [a]
USSR	353	491	603	595	615	624	635
of which: SIBERIA	34	151	317	375	398	415	463
Tyumenskaya *oblast*	28	143	303	359	382	398	440
Tomskaya *oblast*	3	5	11	13	13	14	20
Sakhalin	3	3	3	3	3	3	3
Rest of USSR	319	340	286	220	217	209	175

Table 4.2

GAS PRODUCTION IN THE USSR, 1970–90

(billions of cubic meters)

	1970	1975	1980	1985	1986	1987	1990[a]
USSR	194	289	436	640	686	727	850
of which: SIBERIA	11	40	158	373	424	454	
Tyumenskaya *oblast*[b]	10	38	156	369	420	450	
Yakutskaya ASSR	0	1	1	1	1	1	
Sakhalin	1	1	1	3	3	3	
Rest of USSR	187	249	277	267	262	273	

Notes: [a]Five-Year-Plan target

[b]Includes 4 billion cubic meters a year produced in Krasnoyarskiy *kray*

Source: David Wilson, "The Siberian Oil and Gas Industry," in Alan Wood, ed., *Siberia: Problems and Prospects for Regional Development* (London, 1987), 98, with additional data for 1986–87 supplied.

complexes (e.g., nickel smelting at Norilsk, gold mining in Magadan *oblast,* aluminum plants at Irkutsk, Bratsk, Krasnoyarsk and Sayanogorsk, and cellulose and other wood products at Bratsk and Ust-Ilimsk).

Siberia's mighty rivers will obviously continue to be a major source of cheap energy and play a key role in the region's future economic development.

Mineral resources

Siberia has been lavishly endowed by nature with vast subterranean resources. The BAM zone in East Siberia and the Far East alone contains almost an entire alphabet of natural riches, from alumina, boron, copper, diamonds, energy, fluorspar and gold, right through to zinc.[23] Much of it, however, is extremely difficult to retrieve and transport to the points of processing, manufacture or export, lying as it does in areas of severe environmental and geophysical hostility. Nevertheless, the Soviet Union's ever-increasing demand for essential raw materials, energy sources and strategic metals has forced the government to adopt a more purposeful program of resource development in its eastern regions in order to offset the decline in output in the traditional western zones. This is explicitly provided for in the *Basic Guidelines for the Economic and Social Development of the USSR* (up to the year 2000), a plan adopted by the 27th Congress of the Soviet Communist party in 1986 and reinforced by the announcement, in August 1987, of a 232-billion-ruble investment program for Far Eastern development until the end of the century. As a result, it is planned that the region's industrial output will double or even treble.[24]

One resource that Siberia is comparatively short of is iron ore. Local deposits in the Kuznetsk basin and at Zheleznogorsk, in Irkutsk *oblast,* have had to be supplemented by ore imports from the Urals and even the Ukraine in order to maintain full productivity of the Siberian iron and steel industry. The situation, however, will be greatly improved by the exploitation of high-quality iron deposits in the Aldan region of southern Yakutia. The Tayezhnyy deposit alone is estimated to have reserves of 1 billion tons of iron ore, which can be obtained by opencast mining. The proximity of these deposits to the Yakutian coalfields at Neryungri, together with further sources of ore in the Amur region, provide favorable conditions for the building of a new Far Eastern metallurgical base.[25] The completion of the BAM and its northern offshoots will obviously greatly facilitate this development, though at present Siberia and the Far East only account for about six percent of the Soviet Union's total iron ore production.

It is in the production of nonferrous metals that Siberia plays a more significant role in the Soviet economy. The USSR is, for instance, the world's largest producer of gold after South Africa. The major deposits are in the

[23] Oleg A. Kibal'chich, "The BAM and Its Economic Geography," in Shabad and Mote, *Gateway* 245–54.
[24] *Pravda,* August 26, 1987.
[25] Abel Aganbegyan, "Economic Development of the BAM Zone," *Social Sciences,* AN SSSR, no. 4 (1986): 66–76.

far north of Magadan *oblast*, in the Kolyma region, and the Chukotskiy Peninsula. Traditional panning, dredging and placer mining has recently been supplemented by the sinking of deep-shaft lode mines both in Siberia and in Central Asia and Armenia. There are considerable gold reserves, too, in the BAM zone and adjacent areas. It seems certain, therefore, that Siberian gold will continue to be a significant factor on the world market. Siberia likewise has a monopoly in the production of Soviet tin. For many years, the USSR was dependent on imports of tin from abroad, but since the 1960s it has risen to be the world's number-two producer (after Malaysia). Almost all of this comes from the southern tin mines at Solnechnyy and Kavalerovo, in the Far East, and further north in the inclement regions of Magadan *oblast*, where the isolated Deputatskiy mine can only be reached overland for seven months of the year. Solnechnyy ("Sunny") also produces a wide range of other minerals—including tungsten, copper, lead and zinc— though on the whole, Siberia does not contribute much to the country's total production of these particular metals. This may well change, however, especially in the output of copper, of which large deposits are to be found at Udokan in Chita *oblast*. The successful exploitation of Udokan copper could meet Soviet needs for a long time to come, though rigorous climatic and geographical conditions present enormous planning, engineering and infrastructural problems. For the time being, the Udokan project lies on the table, though again, the existence of the BAM should solve some of the problems of accessibility and transport.

Nickel is a major Siberian product, most of it located at Norilsk, in the far north of East Siberia. Extensive mining operations around Norilsk have made the Soviet Union the world's leading producer of nickel (overtaking Canada) and a major exporter to the West. Projects for sinking further and deeper mines in the 1990s mean that this position will be guaranteed for the foreseeable future. Siberia also makes a major contribution to the Soviet Union's output of nonmetallic minerals such as boron, lithium, fluorspar, mica, asbestos, apatite and, most important from a financial point of view, diamonds. Other geologically proven, but hitherto untapped, natural resources of enormous size locked within Siberia's frozen ground suggest that the region will maintain and even enhance its position as one of the world's principal mineral storehouses for a considerable time to come.

Apart from minerals, two other traditional Siberian resources also make a contribution to the Soviet economy—namely, timber and fur. Siberia contains some of the world's most extensive forestlands and timber stands. It accounts for around one-third of the total Soviet timber cut—most of it used, however, in crude, unprocessed form. Reports have appeared in the Soviet press complaining about the inferior quality of timber for export in the Far East, followed by the announcement of plans to improve the situation.[26] This is especially important in view of the large part played by timber in Soviet exports to China. More diversified and efficient use of forest resources has been made in recent years with the establishment of wood-processing industries and pulp mills producing paper, cellulose, plywood, chipboard and a range of chemical byproducts. The wood-processing

[26] *Pravda,* November 12, 1987.

complex at Bratsk, fueled by the famous local hydroelectric station, is now one of the largest factories of its kind in the world.[27]

In past centuries the Russian economy more or less depended on the Siberian fur trade, though today it makes only a minor contribution to Soviet export figures. Most of the country's fur still comes from the Siberian taiga, where sable, squirrel and fox continue to be hunted, though this is now supplemented by extensive fur farming. However, the once-paramount role of "soft gold" in the Siberian economy has long been displaced by the real gold and the "black gold" of the extractive industries.

TRANSPORT AND COMMUNICATIONS

The successful exploitation of any country's economic resources must to a large extent rest on the effectiveness and efficiency of its transport and communications network. This is especially so in the case of Siberia, with its territorial vastness and the severity of its natural conditions. Skillful use of Siberia's rivers and interfluvial portages, in fact, greatly accelerated the original military and commercial conquest of the continent by small bands of Russian trailblazers and pioneers in the 17th century. In later times, however, a number of factors have placed enormous strains on the means of communication and now pose unique problems for Soviet economic planners.[28]

Since the end of the 19th century, the backbone of the Siberian transport system has been the Trans-Siberian Railway. Built originally as a transit route between European Russia and the Far East, it soon acquired an importance of its own in the agricultural, commercial, industrial and demographic development of the areas through which it passed. Together with its subsidiaries, it has maintained this crucial role to the present day. The economic exploitation of Siberia's natural resources over the last 30 years has now made some sections of the Trans-Siberian the most densely congested tracks in the world, particularly in the agricultural and industrial tract between Omsk and Novosibirsk in West Siberia. Annual westbound shipments of raw materials out of Siberia in the early 1980s have been estimated at around 300 million tons of oil, 230 billion cubic meters of gas, 80 million tons of coal and 20 million tons of forest products.[29] Apart from natural gas, much of this—especially coal and timber—moves by rail. The east-to-west flow presents tougher problems of handling capacity than in the opposite direction, and various devices and expedients have been tried to ease the bottlenecks: increased loading, longer trains, bypass loops, extra lateral tracks, and relocation of manufacturing and processing plants closer to the sources of raw material. All of these create technical problems

[27] G. Bando, ed., *Bratskii leso-promyshlennyi kompleks* (Irkutsk, 1978).
[28] Much of the information in this section is drawn from Robert North, "Transport and Communications," in Wood, *Siberia*, 130–57, and Victor L. Mote, "The Communications Infrastructure," in Rodger Swearingen, ed., *Siberia and the Soviet Far East: Strategic Dimensions in Multinational Perspective* (Stanford, Calif.: Hoover Institution Press, 1987), 40–73.
[29] Theodore Shabad, "News Notes," *Soviet Geography* 27, no. 4 (1986): 252 and 258.

and disadvantages, and increased output in future years is bound to intensify the strain. The fame of the Trans-Siberian has tended to overshadow the importance of other eastern lines, including the South Siberian, the Central Siberian, the Turksib and more recently the northern track linking the Trans-Siberian with the oil and gas fields of northwest Siberia. The Tyumen-Surgut-Urengoy route was begun in the 1960s and reached Novyy Urengoy in 1982, its principal task being to ferry in cargoes of drilling equipment, construction materials and food supplies to the newly opened fields. It is planned to extend this line further north as far as the Yamal Peninsula across extraordinarily difficult arctic terrain.

The most celebrated recent railway construction project is the BAM. Plans for this development were first laid in the 1930s, but only in 1974 was the decision taken to drive the new artery across 1,954 miles/3,145 km. of permafrost, mountains, swamps, forests and areas of high seismicity from Ust-Kut, north of Lake Baikal, to Komsomolsk-na-Amure, near the Pacific coast. Thousands of shock workers from all over the Soviet Union and Eastern Europe contributed to this "construction of the century," and during the decade it took to build it was afforded a massive publicity treatment commensurate with the daunting and perilous nature of the enterprise. The BAM was designed not only to relieve traffic congestion on the more southerly Trans-Siberian and to provide a safer strategic link with the Far East but also, as indicated, to exploit the economic resources and boost the industrial potential of the East Siberian and Pacific regions. All along its route, a concatenation of integrated TPCs and new urban settlements has been established with fast-growing populations that need to be provided with the full range of social, educational, medical and cultural amenities. Although the BAM is not yet fully operational, it already carries around 25 million tons of freight and almost half a million passengers a year. While there is some evidence to suggest that the development of the BAM and its TPCs has received rather less priority in national terms since Gorbachev took office in 1985, nevertheless its economic, strategic and international importance as a major trade route between Europe and the Pacific cannot be gainsaid. By 1980, the Trans-Siberian landbridge already accounted for 25 percent of container traffic between Japan and Western Europe, offering strong competition in fast delivery times to commercial shipping lines.

Shipping and waterborne traffic in general continues to play an important part in the Siberian transport system, though it has not, on the whole, received the same amount of government investment as railways and pipelines. Although nationally, water transport only accounts for roughly four percent of freight and 0.7 percent of passengers carried, in Siberia—and particularly in the north, where road and rail links are less developed than in the south—the great northward-flowing rivers—the Ob, Irtysh, Yenisey and Lena—still offer a cheap, if slow-moving alternative mode, especially for the transportation of heavy bulk cargoes.[30]

[30] For an up-to-date survey of Siberian sea and river shipping, see Robert North, "The Role of Water Transport in Siberian Development," in Wood and French, *The Development of Siberia,* chap. 10.

In the south, the amount of freight carried by water is probably not much more than the national average, whereas the Lena and other north-eastern rivers take about 80 percent of all traffic in the region and serve as a vital link with the rest of the country. Until the northern extension of the "Little BAM" reaches Yakutsk around 1995, this major city of 180,000 inhabitants and the gold-, tin- and diamond-mining settlements in the north will remain to a large extent dependent on the Lena for the import of essential supplies. Similarly, the Yenisey carries goods from the south to the major river ports and wharves of Igarka and Dudinka. Both of these are accessible to sea-going ships from the north, but river vessels handle around two-thirds of the freight moved along the Yenisey. The bulk of the cargo consists of timber, sand, gravel and the mineral products of Norilsk, a proportion of which is taken via the Northern Sea Route to smelters at Murmansk on the Kola Peninsula. Further west, the Ob continues to serve as an important artery for the supply of materials to the new oil and gas fields. It faces competition from the Tyumen-Yamburg Railway, and of course almost all the gas and oil is moved out of the area by pipeline. However, the river system, including the countless tributaries and smaller waterways that crisscross the Ob basin, provides access to many areas that are virtually unapproachable by any other means of transport. It has been estimated that the energy industry in northwest Siberia requires 30 million tons of supplies per year, of which the Ob-Irtysh system accounted for two-thirds in 1986–87. River transport is relatively easy and cheap to establish in pioneer areas and is particularly useful in the conveyance of large steel pipes and prefabricated building sections, though lumber is still the main cargo. Marine transport has also played a part in the supply of equipment to the gas fields through the Ob Gulf, the first shipment of wide-diameter pipes from Japan reaching the area via the Northern Sea Route in 1984.

Despite its importance, water transport in Siberia suffers from serious disadvantages: short navigation seasons due to long winter freezing, shallowness and/or fluctuations in depth, silting and the lack of direct links between points of origin and destination, which causes problems of storage and transshipment. Port facilities, too, are often inadequate to deal with the volume of traffic, and there is an added difficulty created by the fact that ice-free periods on sea and river routes do not always coincide. Ice-breakers help to extend the navigation season to a certain extent (sometimes for only a week or two), but the size and power required of the vessels limit their usefulness in the shallow river and inshore waters. It still remains a goal, however, to achieve year-round navigation along the entire coast of the Soviet Arctic from the Kola Peninsula to, and through, the Bering Straits. Difficulties and disadvantages notwithstanding, marine and inland water transport still performs a vital function in the Siberian economy, particularly in servicing the northern regions.

When frozen over—as they are for many months each year—Siberia's rivers and lakes provide an important route for "winter roads," which are used by motor vehicles. These apart, and for obvious geographical reasons, Siberia has few motor roads in relation to the size of the territory. Other than the railway, there is still no direct overland highway route across the

USSR, and the further north and east one travels, the fewer roads there are. "Roadlessness" *(bezdorozhie)* is an age-old chronic Russian condition, but nowhere is this more apparent than in Siberia, which probably contains no more than three percent of the entire country's hard-surface road network. Most of it is in an appalling condition, which has the effect of increasing fuel consumption, reducing speeds, accelerating vehicle deterioration and shortening haulage distances. There is also an acute shortage of automobile services, such as gas stations, repair garages and availability of spare parts. According to a Soviet source, in 1982 the whole of Yakutia (an area of over 1.2 million sq. miles/3 million sq. km. traversed by the important 731 mile/1,177-km. Never-Yakutsk highway) contained only 38 service stations and three repair garages.[31] The only solution is in a massive investment program, which seems highly unlikely in view of the competing demands of railway and pipeline construction. Pipelines are, in fact, the most rapidly growing sector of the transport system, accounting for almost 100 percent of the distribution of natural gas and 90 percent of crude oil. Experimental slurry pipelines also offer an alternative mode in the transportation of low-grade coal. Oil and gas pipeline construction has recently grown at an astonishing rate in order to keep pace with rocketing production figures, and the system extends at an estimated rate of 6,214 miles/10,000 km. every year, supplying both internal and export needs.

Not surprisingly, given the enormous distances involved, air transport is used in Siberia to a greater extent than elsewhere in the USSR, accounting for 70 percent of all passenger traffic in the two eastern regions. Apart from the major airports at Omsk, Novosibirsk, Irkutsk, Khabarovsk and Vladivostok, hundreds of smaller towns and remote settlements have their own landing strips, which in some cases provide the only reliable, regular means of communication and supply with the rest of the country. However, because of the high costs involved, airplanes account for less than 10 percent of heavy freight transport in Siberia.

POPULATION, LABOR SUPPLY AND NATIVE PEOPLES

The most obvious demographic feature of Siberia is the gross imbalance between population and territory. Siberia and the Far East constitute well over half of the Soviet Union's land surface but contain only 10.7 percent of its population (30 million out of 280 million). Ever since the 17th century, Siberian officials have complained about the lack of manpower, and the problems of labor shortages, particularly skilled labor, persist to the present day. During the czarist period, population growth in Siberia from voluntary migration and natural procreation was augmented by enforced deportation and compulsory settlement, though the number of exiles never accounted for more than a small percentage of the total population.[32]

[31] *Atlas avtomobylnykh dorog SSSR*, GUGK (Moscow, 1982).
[32] A. D. Margolis, "O chislennosti i pomeshchenii ssylnykh v Sibiri v kontse XIX v.," in L. M. Goryushkin, ed., *Ssylka i katorga v Sibiri (XVIII-nachalo XX v.)* (Novosibirsk: Nauka, 1975), 223–37.

However, while most of the early settlers had not been forcibly banished, many had arrived reluctantly, as a result of military or government service. Soviet sources estimate that servants *(sluzhilie lyudi)* accounted for the vast majority of the original Russian immigrant population and were only overtaken by peasants and other voluntary colonists in the 18th and 19th centuries.[33]

In the recent era, the Siberian population has shot up from 5.6 million in 1897, through 9.3 million in 1911 and 16.6 million in 1939, to the present level of around 30 million. Despite the steady increase, manpower (and womanpower) shortage is still a perennial problem. This has become more acute since the exploitation of the region's natural resources was given priority by Soviet planners. In Stalin's time, concentration camps and forced labor were used in massive proportions, but since the dictator's death in 1953, his political heirs have had to use less draconian measures to encourage the inflow of labor to Siberia from other environmentally less forbidding areas of the Soviet Union. The so-called northern increment *(severnaya nadbavka)* in wages to compensate for geographical remoteness and climatic discomfort was introduced as early as 1932 in order to encourage migration to new construction sites, the additional amounts paid varying from region to region.[34] In 1960 these additional payments were drastically reduced, which led to a serious outflow of population at a time when the development of the Siberian economy was supposed to be receiving special attention. During the 1960s, West Siberia alone lost almost 1 million people due to migration from the region. Only Tyumen *oblast* recorded a net increase, as a result of the influx of workers into the new oil and gas fields. In order to plug the leak, substantial northern increments were reintroduced in 1967 that, in some remote areas, were twice the average for similar work elsewhere. The BAM, another pioneer area, has consistently offered a regional wage coefficient of 1.7—that is, a 70 percent addition to basic pay levels. However, apart from the oil and gas fields and premium construction projects, population growth in Siberia is less than the national average, and there is an alarmingly high rate of manpower turnover and the phenomenon known in Soviet parlance as "flight of labor." Surveys conducted by the Siberian branch of the Academy of Sciences have revealed that the much higher wages offered in Siberia are not thought to provide adequate compensation for the rigors of permanent residence in the region. Many young single workers come on short-term contracts, earn a large number of rubles and quickly return to less inclement regions. Among the reasons most often cited for reluctance to settle permanently are poor housing standards, lack of medical and educational facilities, shortage of basic foodstuffs, substandard or nonexistent cultural amenities and a generally lower standard of living than elsewhere in the country.[35]

[33] N. I. Nikitin, "Voennosluzhilie lyudi i osvoenie Sibiri v XVII veke," *Istoriya SSSR,* no. 2 (1980): 161–73.

[34] The "northern increment" is discussed in John Sallnow, "Siberia's Demand for Labour: Incentive Policies and Migration, 1960–1985," in Wood and French, *The Development of Siberia,* chap. 9.

[35] T. I. Zaslavskaya et al., "Problemy sotsialnogo razvitiya Sibiri i puti ikh reshe-

Prognostications about increased immigration in the immediate future— at a time when accelerated regional economic growth is planned—are not optimistic. Various remedies have been suggested, including the introduction of new labor-saving technologies, abolition of legal restrictions on extra earnings, better utilization of labor by improved management and organizational techniques, enhanced investment for upgrading the social-cultural infrastructure, measures to combat alcoholism and a conscious effort to ensure that living standards not simply match but actually excel those elsewhere in the USSR.[36] Vested regional interest groups will obviously press hard for such a program to be implemented, but even in the age of *perestroika* and democratization, its success will ultimately depend on political decisions about resources allocation made in Moscow.

Although Siberia is geographically part of Asia, its ethnic composition is overwhelmingly European. Russians, Ukrainians and, to a lesser extent, Byelorussians account for about 90 percent of the total population. Only in the small autonomous republic of Tuva do the indigenous people outnumber the nonnative inhabitants. The aboriginal peoples of Siberia at present account for only five percent of the population and are divided into five broad ethnolinguistic groups: Finno-Ugric, Turkic, Mongol, Tungus-Manchu and Paleo-Asiatic. These are further subdivided into around 50 separate peoples, ranging in numbers from the Yakuts of Yakutia (314,000 at the 1979 census) to the Oroks of Sakhalin, whose tiny population is not even recorded in the published census returns but which is authoritatively estimated at a mere 300.[37] At the time of the Russian conquest, many of these tribes were only at the neolithic stage of development and swiftly fell prey to the invading Slavs' policies of colonial exploitation. Though never subjected to deliberate genocide, thousands were nevertheless exterminated as a result of military conflict, forced labor and military conscription, hostage taking, abduction of native women and children, famine due to overhunting and depletion of traditional food stocks, alcohol abuse and the introduction of virulent alien diseases such as smallpox, leprosy and syphilis.[38] Hunting, fishing and animal herding were the traditional occupations of these often nomadic peoples, and they still, to a certain extent, are— though more sedentary, even urban, patterns of existence have been established.[39]

Since the 1917 Revolution, the Soviet authorities have pursued ambiguous policies toward the Siberian natives. The czarist concept of Russification has been displaced by the ideological principles of Marxist-Leninism, which emphasize class rather than nationality and look forward to the assimilation of all nationalities into a new historical community—the Soviet

niya," *Izvestiya SO AN SSSR; seriya ekonomika i prikladnaya sotsiologiya*, no. 1 (1986): 36–45.

[36] Ibid.

[37] Alfred F. Majewicz, "The Oroks: Past and Present," in Wood and French, *The Development of Siberia*, chap. 6.

[38] The example of the Yukagir people is examined in Boris Chichlo, "Yukagiry. Proshloe, nastoyashchee. A budushchee?" *SIBIRICA* 1 (1983): 18–25.

[39] S. S. Savoskul, "Urbanisation and the Minority Peoples of the Soviet North," in Wood and French, *The Development of Siberia*, chap. 5.

people. At the same time, much effort has been spent on preserving and enhancing traditional native cultures by extending educational, medical, social and cultural facilities to all nationalities, in many cases devising scripts and alphabets for those languages that previously had no written form. Most of the chronic killer diseases have been eradicated, literacy and educational levels have improved dramatically, and the social status of women has risen to the extent that standards of secondary and higher educational attainment among the minority peoples of the Soviet north are higher for women than men. Housing standards, hygiene, communication networks and social amenities have been improved, and most of the indigenous peoples now possess their own native intelligentsia, as well as professional, artistic and scientific cadres. There has also been a marked shift—even in the sparsely populated areas of the far north and Far East—in the ratio of rural to urban population, which in some ethnographers' opinion has had the beneficial effect, not of eroding, but actually raising the national consciousness of the native Siberian peoples.[40] Despite the high rate of ethnically exogamous marriages, a gradual change from "traditional" to "modern" occupations, the decreasing use of native languages in favor of Russian as the acknowledged "mother tongue" and the overriding uniformity of all-Soviet Union political and economic structures, the native peoples of Siberia and the Far East still continue to preserve their unique national identities. It is unlikely, however, that their ethnicity will express itself as forcefully and explosively as elsewhere among the Soviet Union's non-Russian peoples. Interethnic tensions and fierce regional rivalries do exist in some areas (Russo-Buryat relations in some parts of East Siberia, for example, are reportedly far from amicable[41]), but on the whole, it is difficult at present to imagine a Siberian version of the bitter Armenian-Azerbaydzhani dispute over Nagorno-Karabakh and similar nationalist demands for greater regional autonomy.

STRATEGIC FACTORS AND FOREIGN RELATIONS

The high priority recently given to the economic development of Siberia and the Far East has been matched since the mid-1960s by a similar eastward shift in Soviet strategic planning and military deployment. While it is true that the defense policies of both East and West at the end of World War II were most obviously focused on Europe and the North Atlantic, the Soviet Union has nevertheless always been highly sensitive to the vulnerability, territorial security and strategic requirements of its eastern marches. This sensitivity was most dramatically highlighted by the downing of a South Korean airliner in 1983 after it had strayed deep into Soviet airspace over the Far East. However, the assertion of some Western pundits that the USSR had militarily neglected its Asiatic front until the last two decades but has now adopted a more aggressive and threatening stance against

[40] Ibid.
[41] Caroline Humphrey, "Population Trends, Ethnicity and Religion among the Buryats," in Wood and French, *The Development of Siberia,* chap. 7.

its eastern and Pacific neighbors simply does not square with the historical record.[42] Certainly the Soviet Union has built up its military strength and effectiveness in Siberia and the Far East both quantitatively and qualitatively in recent years, but this represents only a more determined manifestation and continuing pursuit of well-established policies and defense postures in these regions. For both czarist Russia and the Soviet Union, Siberia has always been what a leading British defense expert has described as "both an outpost and a bastion, exemplifying at once both vulnerability and security."[43]

The Far Eastern outpost of Petropavlovsk, on Kamchatka, was subjected to Anglo-French naval attack during the Crimean War (in 1854), and during the 20th century the region has been the theater of extensive and bloody hostilities, principally between Russia and Japan, beginning with the war of 1904–05 and ending with the latter's defeat in 1945. During the 1930s, Stalin set up the Special Far Eastern Army to meet both Japanese and Chinese challenges, tripling the strength of its ground forces and setting up a naval command that was the forerunner of the present-day Soviet Pacific Fleet. At the outbreak of the Nazi-Soviet conflict in 1941, many Siberian divisions were tied down in the Far East and so prevented from swinging to the defense of the western front, which undoubtedly contributed to early Russian reverses. It is this continuing fear of a war on two fronts—in Europe and the Far East—that lies at the heart of the recent military build-up in Siberia, responding to what, *from the Soviet point of view*, looks like a hostile encirclement and the possibility of an aggressive anti-Soviet coalition of China, Japan and the United States.

Since the Sino-Soviet border clashes in 1969, the Soviet military presence in the Asian-Pacific region has assumed formidable proportions, and despite the 1987 INF treaty and Gorbachev's espousal of the so-called double zero option (under which intermediate-range Soviet nuclear missiles would be removed from Asia as well as Europe), it is unlikely that the USSR will substantially lower its guard in the Far East. At present it has over 50 divisions in its eastern territories, including those stationed in Central Asia and Mongolia. Its air strength has increased by one-third over the last decade, and the Pacific Fleet is now the largest and possibly the best-equipped of the Soviet Navy's four fleets, with a powerful force of the most modern surface vessels and ballistic-missile-equipped submarines.[44] It also has an important naval garrison at Cam Ranh Bay and Da Nang in Vietnam, though Soviet sources insist that Cam Ranh is merely a friendly port of call for Soviet shipping.[45] Altogether, the commander-in-chief of the Far Eastern theater of war has more than half a million men at his command.

[42] See, for example, Rodger Swearingen, "The Soviet Far East, East Asia and the Pacific—Strategic Dimensions," in Swearingen, *Siberia and the Soviet Far East,* 227–72.
[43] John Erickson, "Military and Strategic Factors," in Wood, *Siberia,* 171.
[44] Ibid., 186.
[45] Statement made by Gen. E. Ivanovskii, Commander in Chief of Soviet land forces to Thai army Commander in Chief General Chawalit. Federal Broadcast Information Service, East Asian Survey, 87/225, November 23, 1987.

However, apart from the obvious regional contingencies, the Far Eastern military build-up must be seen as part of a plan for the overall restructuring of the Soviet Union's defenses, a plan first introduced during Marshall N. Ogarkov's years as chief of the General Staff (1977–84) and aimed at the "integrated defense" of the Soviet Union as a whole.

Nevertheless, to its Far Eastern and Pacific neighbors, the USSR's heightened military profile must look ominous, and military factors play a critical role in the configuration of Soviet relations with the other major regional powers. In the case of the People's Republic of China, Beijing has insisted on three conditions that must be fulfilled if there is to be a really meaningful improvement in the two countries' uneasy relationship, which deteriorated to the point of armed conflict along the Amur-Ussuri border in 1969 and, to a more limited extent, in 1986. These conditions are: (a) a steep reduction of Soviet force levels along the Chinese border and in Mongolia, which Beijing sees as a direct military threat to itself; (b) withdrawal of Soviet troops from Afghanistan; and (c) the ending of Vietnam's Soviet-backed military intervention in Cambodia. Recent developments suggest that Mikhail Gorbachev is more serious and realistic than his predecessors about improved relations with China; and in July 1986 he made a key speech during a visit to Vladivostok in which he alluded to troop withdrawals from Mongolia and Afghanistan and also conceded for the first time that the official boundary between the two states should run along "the main channel" of the Amur River, thus implicitly abandoning Soviet claims to many of the islands closer to the Chinese shore.[46] Some reduction of troop levels in Mongolia has now been made, and the complete evacuation of Soviet forces from Afghanistan began in earnest in May 1988. Diplomatic rather than military measures are now favored by Vietnam in the settlement of Cambodia's political future, and multilateral talks by all interested parties, including China and the USSR, are now in progress. It seems reasonable to conclude, therefore, that all these initiatives, together with the implications of the 1987 INF treaty between the United States and the USSR, go a very long way toward encouraging a real rapprochement between the two major Communist powers. This is already evident in a series of economic, technical, commercial and cultural cooperation projects between the two sides, including the regular exchange of visits by senior government officials since 1984, resumption of border talks, the signing of a new consular treaty in 1987, expanding trade links, and Soviet assistance in Chinese industrial development projects. Border trade between China's northern provinces and the Soviet Far East has expanded considerably in the 1980s, and both the Chinese and the Soviet media carry regular reports of new agreements and ever-increasing volumes and values of goods exchanged. These improvements not only provide auspicious conditions for the major programs of internal *perestroika* and modernization that the two countries are individually engaged in but also reduce the level of international tension and potential military confrontation in the Far Eastern and Pacific area.

---

[46] *Pravda,* July 29, 1986.

Relations with Japan are of different order. Technically, the two countries are still in a state of declared war, there having been no formal peace treaty signed between them at the end of World War II. The chief sticking point for both parties is the territorial dispute over the so-called Northern Territories—four tiny islands at the southern end of the Kuril chain within sight of the Japanese coast. Occupied by Soviet forces in 1945, their Japanese population was deported and they are now administratively part of the Sakhalin *oblast* of the Soviet Far East. The Soviet Union doggedly persists in its refusal to consider Japanese insistence on the islands' return or even to discuss the issue as a precondition for further improvements in their mutual relations. This seemingly intractable problem has been aggravated—in the Japanese view—by the provocative deployment of Soviet military forces on the islands. Compassionate gestures allowing some Japanese to visit family graves on Shikota and Suisho should not be interpreted as a sign that the Soviet Union is "going soft" on this issue.

However, despite the entrenched positions of both sides in the territorial dispute, a number of significant cooperative ventures have been undertaken between Japan and the USSR, most importantly in the fields of trade, commerce and Japanese technological assistance in Siberian development projects. The heyday of this type of collaboration occurred during the 1960s and 1970s.[47] Japan saw Siberia, rightly, as a vast reservoir of natural resources that would benefit the country's energy-deficient economy, while Japanese businessmen eyed the territory as a huge potential market for the export of manufactured goods. On the Soviet side, the main advantage was in the import of Japanese machinery, equipment and technological know-how, which would contribute to the accelerated exploitation of Siberia's raw materials. To many it seemed that Siberia's enormous resources and Japan's technological sophistication made the two countries ideally suited trading partners, based on what one expert has described as a "complementarity of disadvantage."[48] Major collaborative projects were consequently embarked on, among which the most significant were: (a) a joint exploitation of the south Yakutia coalfields; (b) exploration for Sakhalin oil and gas; (c) cooperation in the building of new ports and container terminals on the Far Eastern littoral; (d) supply of cold-resistant steel pipes and other equipment to the West Siberian oil and gas fields; (e) the extensive use of Japanese machinery, heavy vehicles and tunneling equipment on the BAM; and (f) the establishment of a Far East trading organization (Dalintorg) in 1964 to negotiate and implement a number of import-export agreements covering such commodities as timber and wood products, fish, textiles, clothing, knitwear, ceramics, electrical goods and sundry other items. An important feature of this commerce is the so-called coastal trade *(priberezh-naya torgovlya)*, a specifically local trading arrangement between East Siberia and the Far East on the one hand and the northerly prefectures of Hokkaido on the other.

[47] Walter Joyce, "Soviet-Japanese Economic Cooperation in Siberia," *SIBIRICA* 1 (1983): 34–44.
[48] Ibid., 35.

After the initial euphoria, Japanese interest in Siberian development waned during the early 1980s and attention shifted more toward the Chinese connection. The state of Soviet-Japanese relations at the end of the 1980s is still ambiguous, though less fraught than the sometimes acrimonious (almost racist) public denunciations, complaints and criticisms of each other's policies and attitudes might suggest. The territorial issue still obtrudes; the Japanese still object to the Soviet Union's military build-up in the Far East; there are regular disputes over mutual infringements of fishing zones in Far Eastern waters, with each side occasionally detaining the other's ships and crews; the Soviet Union complains of anti-Soviet campaigns in the Japanese press and warns about the dangers of a U.S.-Seoul-Tokyo military axis directed against the Soviet Union. On the other hand, commercial, cultural and scientific exchanges still proliferate, and senior ministers and diplomats engage in regular bilateral talks aimed at an improvement in the political relations between the two countries. The anticipated visit of Mikhail Gorbachev to Japan (scheduled for January 1987 and then postponed) has not taken place. When it does it will be the first-ever visit of a Soviet leader to Japan; as such it is a sure indication that the president's respectful references to Japan in his Vladivostok speech were more than a diplomatic courtesy and evidence of the importance he attaches to a genuine Soviet-Japanese rapprochement.[49] At the present juncture, however, it seems improbable that he would be willing to pay the price for this—a Soviet surrender of the disputed Kuril islands.

Relations with other Asian-Pacific countries, including the United States, are really a matter of all-Soviet Union policy rather than being specifically centered on Siberia itself, except that the region has now unmistakenly become a forward "bastion" (rather than simply an "outpost") of Soviet military power, and the dynamic development of its resources has made it a potentially major factor in the regional economy of the Pacific basin as a whole. It remains, therefore, to consider briefly what role Siberia and the Far East will play in the future, both in the national and international contexts.

PROSPECTS AND CONCLUSIONS

Arguments among Soviet officials and planners over whether Siberian development should continue to enjoy such high priority as in recent years, at the expense of greater investment in other areas of the national economy, are mirrored in the West by differences of opinion between those observers who consider further development of the eastern regions to be still vital to the whole country's future economic and military security, and those who suggest that under Gorbachev's leadership there has been a gradual shift of emphasis away from Siberia to the more traditional industrial regions in the European USSR, where manufacturing plants and a more stable (and

[49] Hiroshi Kimura, "Soviet Focus on the Pacific," *Problems of Communism* (May–June, 1987), 7–10.

less expensive) work force are already in place.[50] The current policy of economic restructuring—with its emphasis on efficiency, cost accounting, introduction of advanced technology, computerization, development of nuclear energy (Chernobyl notwithstanding), renovation, automation,—points, according to this theory, toward a Western-oriented strategy in preference to the high costs of opening up new industries and resources in the more distant, environmentally daunting regions of Siberia and the Far East. The pro-Siberia lobby, however, continues to call for a more rounded, fully integrated development policy for the region, which will not rely exclusively on fuel production to underwrite its future. But so long as the oil continues to gush and the gas to flow, it seems clear that sustained investment in Siberia will remain high on the agenda of Soviet planning priorities.

Gorbachev is also well aware of the surging activity and burgeoning opportunities of the Asian-Pacific region, in which the Soviet Union, from its Far Eastern springboard, will certainly wish to be involved. Siberia's propinquity to the Pacific basin, the Soviet Union's expanding bilateral relations with so many nations in the region, and the government's expressed interest in becoming more fully integrated into, for example, the Pacific Economic Cooperation Committee do not argue convincingly for a declining commitment to the interests of the Soviet Union's eastern territories. So far, Siberia has played only a marginal role in the dynamic developments around the Pacific basin, and there are still many institutional, economic and political factors operating against fuller participation. The government is anxious, however, that the idea of a "Pacific Community" does not develop in such a way as to exclude the Soviet Union from membership or turn the Pacific basin into an American-Japanese-dominated lake. In his Vladivostok speech in 1986, Gorbachev stressed Soviet willingness to have the economic potential of the Soviet Far East fully included in Pacific basin developments; and even in his mammoth opening address to the (extraordinary) 19th conference of the Soviet Communist party in June 1988, he found time to refer to the "restructuring of relations in the Asian and Pacific region" as a central item on his list of Soviet foreign-policy objectives.[51] Finally, the following extract from Gorbachev's published exegis of his new thinking, *Perestroika,* provides an unequivocal statement of his own personal perspective on Siberia's future. Describing the Asian-Pacific region as "the area where world politics will most likely focus in the next century," he goes on to say that

> the East, specifically the Asian and the Pacific region, is now the place where civilization is stepping up its pace. Our economy in its development *is moving to Siberia and the Far East. . . .* In line with the concept of our country's accelerated social and economic growth we pay *special attention to the territories*

[50] Jonathan J. Schiffer, *Soviet Regional Economic Policy: The East-West Debate over Pacific Siberian Development* (London: Macmillan, 1988). See also Theodore Shabad, "The Gorbachev Economic Policy: Is the USSR Turning Away from Siberian Development?" in Wood and French, *The Development of Siberia,* chap. 12.
[51] *Pravda,* June 29, 1988.

east of the Urals whose economic potential is several times that of the European part of the USSR. We believe that joint firms and ventures set up in collaboration with the business circles of Asian-Pacific countries could take part in tapping the wealth of these areas.[52]

Apart from the rich Soviet output of scholarly materials on Siberia, a growing body of expertise has recently developed outside the USSR that focuses attention not only on the economic and strategic importance but also on the history, ecology, sociology and anthropology of Siberia. At the University of Hawaii, an ambitious program for the study of the Soviet Union in the Asian-Pacific Region (SUPAR) was inaugurated in 1986 under the directorship of Professor John Stephan. It has wide-ranging research, teaching and publication projects in hand and encourages a lively exchange program with interested scholars from all over the world, including the USSR. SUPAR publishes a regular report on its activities, as well as other useful information. In Great Britain, a study group called the British Universities Siberian Studies Seminar was established at the University of Lancaster in 1981, and it has met annually ever since. It produces an occasional journal with texts of conference papers, titled *SIBIRICA,* which has a mailing list of over 100 people worldwide. It has also published two volumes of essays written by a distinguished international team of scholars on various aspects of Siberian development. In the People's Republic of China there is the (unique) Siberian Research Institute of the Heilongjiang Academy of Social Sciences at Harbin, under the directorship of Professor Xu Jingxue. It was established in 1963, and as of 1986, it employed 30 full-time researchers engaged in the study of Siberia. There have also been major international conferences on Siberia in the United States, France, Britain, West Germany, Australia, China and Japan, and the volume of scholarly literature devoted to the region is growing each year. The prospects for this vigorous activity to flourish in the future are commensurate with Siberia's own gigantic but still problematical potential in the Soviet, the Asian-Pacific and the global context.

FURTHER READING

Conolly, Violet. *Siberia Today and Tomorrow: A Study of Economic Resources, Problems, and Achievements.* London: Collins, 1975.
Kirby, Stuart. *Siberia and the Far East.* Special Report No. 177. London: Economist Intelligence Unit, 1985.
Sansone, Vito. *Siberia: Epic of the Century.* Moscow: Progress Publishers, 1980.
Shinkaryev, Leonid. *The Land Beyond the Mountains: Siberia and its People Today.* London: Hart-Davies, 1973.
Stephan, John J., and Chichkanov, V. P., eds. *Soviet-American Horizons on the Pacific.* Honolulu: University of Hawaii Press, 1986.
Thakur, Ramesh, and Thayer, Carlyle A., eds. *The Soviet Union as an Asian Pacific Power.* London: Macmillan, 1987.
Whiting, Allen S. *Siberian Development and East Asia: Threat or Promise?* Stanford, California: Stanford University Press, 1981.

[52] Mikhail Gorbachev, *Perestroika: New Thinking for Our Country and the World* (London: Collins, 1987), 180–83 (emphasis added).

SINGAPORE

CHAN HENG CHEE

UNIQUENESS is surely the hallmark of Singapore's political and economic development. On August 9, 1965, in one of the most unusual moves in constitutional history, the island city-state became an independent political entity. After 23 months of continuous bitter and hostile disputes between Singapore and Kuala Lumpur the Malaysian prime minister (Tunku Abdul Rahman), in a federal experiment, took the decision to separate Singapore from Malaysia to avoid further bloodshed. Since then, the phenomenal transformation of Singapore, as a polity and economy, has been cited as a model strategy for small-state development. However in 1988, speaking retrospectively, Prime Minister Lee Kuan Yew assessed Singapore to have "just about made it." He ruminated: "The benefits have been seen, the long term consequences and the price that future generations will pay, I really don't know."[1]

From all perspectives, Singapore is an unlikely candidate for nationhood. That it has survived, and survived prosperously, is in no small measure due to leadership and political will. The island republic is no larger than 240.4 sq. miles/622.6 sq. km. in its total area, including its islets. It has no natural resources apart from its valuable location, at the hub of Southeast Asia, and its population of 2.6 million inhabitants, of whom 76% are Chinese, 15% Malay and 6.5% Indian. The ethnic composition of Singapore—a Chinese majority population in a Malay region with two large Malay neighbors (Malaysia and Indonesia)—is a matter of some sensitivity. The looming presence of China simply accentuates this anomaly. Thus, the constraints of size and geopolitics have been factors shaping the political and economic institutions of Singapore. The historical experience of the first-generation People's Action party (PAP) leadership, and the personality and world view of Prime Minister Lee Kuan Yew in particular, further honed the structures of state. But, as the 1980s drew to a close and a successive political leadership took over to deal with a younger electorate in a vastly different international political and economic environment, the question of change and modification in the institutions was clearly relevant; it is one that will exercise the leadership for some time to come. This is the nub of transitional politics in Singapore.

[1] *The Straits Times*, 15 November 1988.

THE POLITY

Singapore today possesses a hegemonic party system based on a Westminster parliamentary model. Singapore has also been variously described as an "administrative state," a "paternalistic corporatist state" and a "controlled democracy." These different attempts at conceptualizing the nature of its political system suggest emphases on different aspects of the political process, depending on the perspective of the author and the salient features singled out for study. Whatever the theory, all point to the fact that Singapore-style democracy has departed from the original British version.

That this should be so is perhaps to be expected in the transfer and transformation of postcolonial political models to fit different social and political contexts. In 1959 the PAP was swept into power as the leading nationalist mass-based party in the first fully elected legislature in the then semiautonomous British colony. The party was a united front coalition comprised of English-educated, non-Communist, democratic socialist moderates led by Lee Kuan Yew, a Cambridge-trained lawyer; and the Chinese-educated, Communist and pro-Communist labor union leaders. The internal party competition between the non-Communists and the Communists for ascendance in the 1950s until the mid-1960s became the principal factor conditioning the political reflexes of the moderate PAP leadership, shaping the way they viewed the political world.[2] Politics in this bitter ideological struggle was seen to be a zero-sum game. Thus, the emerging state and party institutions were restructured to defeat the Communists. The bureaucracy was expanded and strengthened to perform the tasks of delivery and to increase governmental effectiveness. In the struggle against the Communists, the PAP moderates realized their legitimacy was best anchored in producing efficient government.

It was the association with the Communists that taught Prime Minister Lee and his associates the importance of party organization and Leninist methods, and it was the association and competition with the Communists that put a premium on clean government, spartan living, party discipline and party unity. Draconian measures developed initially to deal with the Communists came to be institutionalized as part of the new political structures, and subsequently served to discourage opposition to the ruling party. The two most salient political moves that came to affect the dynamics of politics were the continuation of the Preservation of the Public Security Ordinance in 1959—which survives today as the Internal Security Act, allowing for political detention—and the reorganization of the labor movement under the rubric of the government-sponsored National Trades Union Congress. But even more enduring has been the tendency of the PAP government to centralize and monopolize political initiative, arising from the fear of resurgence of the Communists and widened later to preempt other potential opposition.

The entry into the Malaysian federation in September 1963 proved to be

[2] John Drysdale, *Singapore: Struggle for Success* (Singapore: Times Books International, 1984).

a chastening experience. It brought the PAP leadership directly into conflict with communalists and communalism. Until then Singapore's political leaders had had only a slight brush with communal extremism—the outbreak of the Maria Hertogh riots in 1950. In July and September 1964 race riots between the Malays and Chinese broke out in the island state as a consequence of the worsening Singapore-Malaysian relationship, which carried overtones of a racial conflict as well as political and economic aspects. Because of the twin experiences of dealing with Communists and then communalists, Prime Minister Lee and the PAP leaders saw politics, through Hobbesian eyes, as "nasty, brutish and short," a world in which Queensberry rules seemed inapplicable if not irrelevant.

The sudden and traumatic separation from Malaysia, and the unsolicited independence in a hostile regional environment created a crisis situation for the island state. This phase of political history has been characterized as the "politics of survival" reflecting the anxiety and urgency of the period as the new nation looked for alternative solutions to its economic and political viability.

To meet the challenge of creating a nation-state out of a city-state, Singapore's political leadership rapidly fine-tuned some of the existing institutions. The civil service, borne out of the tradition of a neutral British Civil Service, was politicized and recruited as allies in the fight against the Communists. It also gained a new prominence as the politicians turned to the bureaucrats to play a major role in the promotion of economic growth in independent Singapore. It would not be an exaggeration to say that it would be impossible to understand the development strategy of Singapore without grasping the fact that this early alliance between the politicians and the bureaucrats was fundamental to the successful implementation of the PAP's plans and policies. Bureaucrats were urged to widen their outlook, to become entrepreneurs in the absence of an industrial class in the republic. The government directly participated in the economy to provide the stimulus and leadership in development. This resulted in a public-sector dominance, with public enterprises spearheading the economic development and the emergence of the "administrative state."[3] In 1968 the Economic Development Board was reorganized, the Jurong Town Council was formed to develop Jurong and other industrial estates, and the Development Bank of Singapore was founded. These were followed by the Monetary Authority of Singapore in 1971; the Post Office Savings Bank and the Sentosa Development Corporation, for resort development, in 1972; the Industrial Training Board in 1973; and the Telecommunications Authority of Singapore and the Urban Renewal Authority in 1974. In the 1970s and 1980s the subsidiary companies of statutory boards had proliferated to an estimated 500 companies. This strong public bureaucracy became the centerpiece of the political system, with wide-ranging powers of decision making in many areas. An indication of the measure of trust it enjoys and the critical role it plays in society is the fact that the ruling

---

[3] Chan Heng Chee, *Singapore: The Politics of Survival* (Singapore: Oxford University Press, 1971).

party looks on the bureaucracy as a natural base from which to recruit potential members of parliament. The bureaucrat-turned-politician stands a good chance of being rapidly promoted to ministerial status.

From the start, the prime minister of Singapore believed that the solution to survival lay in the creation of a tightly organized and rugged society, and he was preoccupied with the fundamental limitations of an island state. This perception gave support to the belief that Singapore was a one-chance society and that there could be no let-up in its efforts and direction.[4]

This tightly organized model found expression in the establishment of an elaborate structure of grass roots institutions at the constituency level that organized and kept in contact with the population. The citizens' consultative committees, the community centers and the residents' committees formed a triad of feedback institutions that functioned as a nerve system in the body politic. This sensor system enabled the ruling party to anticipate pressures and dissatisfaction building up in the population, and to diffuse problems before they reached a critical threshold.

To support an export promotion industrialization strategy, Singapore passed the Employment Act 1968 and the Industrial Relations (Amendment) Act to discipline labor and to dispel any doubts in foreign investors' minds about labor instability. This move was counterbalanced by development of a tripartite partnership among the government, the labor unions and the employers. This approach in industrial relations, which emphasizes negotiation and consensus building, works through the National Wages Council, an advisory body to the government established in 1972 to recommend orderly wage increases and wage development. The result was a more harmonious and nonconfrontational industrial climate, and substantial economic growth. In the first seven years after 1965, before the oil shock, Singapore achieved a 13 percent growth rate, and in the decades after, from 1974 to 1984, it averaged 8 percent.

With this history and within these parameters, it is hardly surprising that the PAP established a hegemonic position, keeping political opposition down. In eight successive general elections—1959, 1963, 1968, 1972, 1976, 1980, 1984 and 1988—the ruling party reaffirmed its tight hold on the reins of government. Although 20 other political parties are registered and about seven to eight are active during the general elections, none possesses the realistic prospect of winning an election and ending the PAP dominance. This is a fact, in spite of the sizable opposition vote polled at each election. Over the years, persistent opposition support in the electorate has remained in the region of 25 percent to 30 percent. In spite of this, from 1968 to 1980, the Singapore electorate returned a one-party parliament. This situation was finally broken when J. B. Jeyaretnam of the Workers' party was elected in 1981 in the Anson by-election, thus breaking the myth of PAP invincibility. In 1984 the opposition vote increased

---

[4]Chan Heng Chee, "Politics in An Administrative State: Where Has the Politics Gone." in *Trends in Singapore,* ed. Seah Chee Meow (Singapore: Institute of South East Asian Studies, 1975).

to 35.2 percent, and in 1988, in a dramatic swing against the ruling party it reached a figure of 36.8 percent.[5] Nonetheless, under the single-member district, first-past-the-post electoral system, the odds are stacked against the opposition. In 1984 two opposition candidates managed to get elected, but in 1988 only one opposition member—Chiam See Tong of the Singapore Democratic party—was returned to parliament. The conversion of some of the electoral constituencies into multimember Group Representation Constituencies (GRCs) may in the long run improve the prospects of opposition election. The electoral reform enacted in time for the 1988 general election, was designed to encourage multiracial representation. Thirty-nine of the 81 constituencies were regrouped into 13 larger GRCs. On each GRC slate were three members of parliament and, by law, one had to be either a Malay or any minority candidate.[6]

There is, however, no doubt that Singapore in the 1980s was undergoing major political and social change. The successes of the PAP government policies brought about a fundamental transformation of society. An enlightened investment in education in the early years of PAP rule, coupled with the spread of the benefits of economic development, produced a middle-class society and the requisite foundations for functioning pluralism. Although the educational profile of Singapore compares unfavorably with other developed countries and the newly industrializing countries (NICs), within the society upward change has taken place. In 1960 some 350,000 students were enrolled in schools—mostly in primary education. The tertiary institutions had a population of only 8,000 students. In 1987 approximately 530,000 of the 2.6 million population were students enrolled in educational institutions: with 260,000 at the primary level, 200,000 at secondary level and upper secondary level, and 45,000 in institutions of higher learning, while another 24,000 were enrolled in technical and vocational institutions. Statistics indicate that five percent of the population now has received a tertiary education. The professional, technical, managerial and executive class has also expanded—from seven percent of the work force in 1960 to 17 percent in 1986, while white-collar clerical and related workers increased from 11 percent in 1960 to 16 percent in 1986.

Of greater political significance is the greening of the Singapore electorate, a demographic trend that showed its impact in 1980, when 40 percent of the voters were below the age of 40, and in 1988, when the figure reached 69 percent. The trend was expected to reverse in 1992. The existing political consensus based on the acceptance of PAP values was understood by the political leadership to be largely a compact between the first-generation leaders and the older electorate who had lived through the political crises of the 1950s and 1960s. The younger population, especially those born in independent Singapore after 1965—in an era when political stability and growing prosperity were taken for granted—held a weaker

<hr />

[5] *The Sunday Times,* 4 September 1988.
[6] *Report on the Delineation of Electoral Boundaries and the Creation of Group Representation Constituencies Cmd 7 of 1988.* (Singapore: Singapore National Printers Ltd - Government Printers, June 14, 1988.

allegiance toward the ruling party. This reality was further complicated by the self-renewal process within the PAP, which thrust forward new leaders who had yet to build a political base.

In the late 1970s, after a tenure of two decades in power and reflecting upon the generational change in the electorate, Prime Minister Lee began to deal seriously with the question of political succession, with putting in place a second generation of political leaders. The consequence of this policy was a major turnover in the leadership hierarchy. After the 1984 general election, all but three of the 14 cabinet ministers (including Prime Minister Lee Kuan Yew himself) had been recruited into politics in the 1970s. In 1988 the prime minister was the only first-generation leader contesting the election. Goh Chok Tong was the heir apparent. Before he entered politics, as the first deputy prime minister, he was a highly regarded technocrat in the civil service. With Goh was a team of younger ministers: Ong Teng Cheong, the second deputy prime minister; Dr. Tony Tan; S. Dhanabalan; Yeo Ning Hong; S. Jayakumar; Dr. Ahmad Mattar; Brigadier-General Lee Hsien Loong, the prime minister's son; and Wong Kan Seng. In spite of the fact that Lee Hsien Loong entered politics as recently as 1984, he was regarded by many as a contender for the position of prime minister. The task of the second-generation leadership was twofold: to win the confidence and support of the new electorate, and to develop ties of camaraderie and a shared purpose among themselves—qualities that produced a cohesive and effective first-generation leadership. That all this was happening under the tutelage of a strong, dominant, experienced and brilliant prime minister had both advantages and disadvantages.

It would certainly have been difficult at this time for the second-generation leaders to strike out with a distinctly different political style, for it may be argued that, for Singapore, a distinctly different political style implies a departure from the established political model, one that had worked so well in the past for this city-state. Nonetheless, there was a cautious response to pressures for the opening up of the political system. In 1985, in the wake of the massive 12.6 percent electoral swing against the PAP, and also because of a deep slide into economic recession, the second-generation leaders led by First Deputy Prime Minister Goh and Brigadier-General Lee opened up a dialogue with the strategic elites in the republic—the intelligentsia, businesspeople, and university and college students. A feedback unit was set up to invite citizen viewpoints on policies and as a complaints channel. Brigadier-General Lee formed an Economic Committee that included the broad participation of professionals, businesspeople and industrialists to work out solutions to the recession, and to develop future economic strategies. The new leadership defined its approach as a "consensus-seeking and consultative style."

Over the next few years, to introduce themselves to the population and in preparation for the 1988 general election, the second-generation undertook constituency tours to publicize and discuss the *National Agenda,* a PAP manifesto that had been turned into a document spelling out future directions for national development. With full enthusiasm, the younger ministers welcomed public debate and dialogue with different levels of Singapore society. The consensus-seeking and consultative style ushered in a trend to involve opinion makers and leaders in the professional and business world in policy making. Six advisory councils were established, each led by a minister and comprising selected leaders of the cultural, intellectual and economic fields. They were to submit policy recommendations on the aged, youth, arts, culture and heritage, sports, family and community life, and the handicapped. A Committee on the Destitute was also set up to review the position of the poor in Singapore, with the intention of helping them break out of the vicious cycle of poverty.

The announcement of the establishment of the Institute of Policy Studies (IPS), in January 1988, was presented as the creation of new intellectual space. The central objective of IPS—to encourage debate and discussion among the intellegentsia on policy-oriented issues, and to provide policy options—was an experiment without precedent in the republic. Headed by an academic and backed by the patronage of the first deputy prime minister and a board of governors, including a leading banker, the vice-chancellor of the National University of Singapore and the head of the civil service, IPS raised high expectations about its role in the policy process.

However, there were many indications that in spite of the increases in participatory channels, politics in Singapore would remain under tight control, and that the only opposition tolerated was a tame opposition. Even as the new political style of consensus seeking and consultation was introduced, the Newspapers and Printing Presses (Amendment) Act was passed to empower the government to curtail the circulation of foreign publications deemed to have "interfered" in the republic's politics. With the passage of the act, three weekly periodicals—the *Times, Asiaweek* and the *Far Eastern Economic Review*—and a regional newspaper, the *Asian Wall Street Journal*, received restriction orders. The Singapore government's battle with the foreign press, in fact, affected both domestic and international perception of the opening up of the political system. The liberalizing attempts to institute more participatory channels have often been overlooked in the evaluation of the shaping of the political system. In May and June 1986 a public exchange took place between government ministers and private citizens on the question of whether professional bodies should be allowed to comment on the political issues of the day. The government's clear position that they should not—as this would mean they had stepped beyond their "ambit of competence" and therefore should be regarded as a political body—was seen by many as the closing of political space. The discussion was occasioned by the action of Francis Seow, president of the Law Society, who issued a statement critical of the Newspaper and Printing Presses Act. The government took the position that Seow was using the Law Society for political purposes, and that the Law Society was moving on a "collision course" against the government. In the same way, when the Workers' party M.P., J. B. Jeyaretnam, was disqualified from holding his parliamentary seat, after he was convicted of making a false declaration of his party accounts (a case that began in 1982), it was taken as a sign that the political climate was hostile to the opposition. Finally, the detention of 22 young people charged with involvement in a Marxist conspiracy in 1987 confirmed for the Singapore population that the political model in Singapore had not fundamentally changed even if new leaders were in the saddle.

Ultimately the PAP leadership adhered closely to the belief that for Singapore to survive as a political and economic entity, it must be run as a tight ship. The swift turnaround of the economic recession of 1985–86 was attributed to the centralization and coordination of decision making, which enabled quick action, and the existence of a disciplined work force, which was sufficiently pragmatic to accept wage cuts to assist the economic recovery. It has also been argued that for Singapore to keep its competitive edge, it cannot afford democratic experimentation that could end in the loss of social cohesion and unity of purpose. In May and June 1988 the democratization issue received a full airing when Singapore, in a cause cèlèbre, accused some U.S. officials of interference in its domestic politics by cultivating and encouraging an opposition (led by Francis Seow) in a move to force the pace of democratization in Singapore, following developments in East Asia. A U.S. diplomat was expelled from Singapore; the United States retaliated similiarly, and relations were strained between two strategic friends. The Singapore prime minister declared in parliament: "It is best if they keep out of Singapore's domestic politics. We are a totally different category. It is not a lack of knowledge of democratic principles, constitution or law. . . . But my colleagues and I are well-versed in the theory and the practice. And we know what can work and what cannot work."[7]

With the departure of the old guard leaders and discussion of Prime Minister Lee's imminent retirement, a proposal for a popularly elected president was tabled as a white paper. The elected president was envisaged as acting as a safeguard for the official preserves and as a custodian for the integrity of the civil service.[8] The expectation that Prime Minister Lee himself would run for the post as the first elected president was less certain as he himself denied this in the election campaign of 1988.

ISSUES OF THE FUTURE

Even as Singapore grappled with the political transition, the PAP leadership reopened the issue of a cultural identity for the city-state. For multiethnic Singapore, with its unique geopolitical context, it has never been a question of benign neglect. Prime Minister Lee was for many years besieged by the problem, for a decision on the cultural identity relates to the language policy, which, in turn, carries political overtones since political, social and economic mobility is tied to the choice of language. At independence, Lee reaffirmed the relevance of the multiracial, multilingual and multicultural approach. Singaporeans at that time thought vaguely about a future national identity that would be an amalgam of the three ethnic

---

[7] *The Straits Times,* 2 June 1988.
[8] *Constitutional Amendments to Safeguard Financial Assets and the Integrity of the Public Services Cmd 10 of 1988* (Singapore: Singapore National Printers Ltd - Government Printers).

identities. The decision to emphasize the use of the English language, putting it ahead of Mandarin, Malay and Tamil, was necessitated by the recognition that Singapore needed to plug into the international economic system, and that an open economy dependent on foreign investments and multinational companies was best supported by an English-speaking population. Although teaching in the various native tongues was also given importance, to give cultural ballast to Singaporeans, the switch to English was complete. Today the only schools that exist are schools that teach in English, although selected subjects are taught in other languages. Nanyang University, a Chinese-medium university, was merged with the English-medium University of Singapore in 1980 to form the National University of Singapore.

But this major switch was to have far-reaching consequences for the society. By the 1980s Prime Minister Lee was concerned with the growing Westernization of the younger population and the erosion of traditional culture and moral values. The introduction into the schools of religious education in the five major religions—Confucianism, Islam, Hinduism, Sikhism and Christanity—and a course on world religions was aimed at strengthening the moral values of a population undergoing rapid change. The open discussion on Confucianism was received controversially. While it might have been welcomed by the Chinese-educated Chinese and the older generation of Chinese, it was viewed with suspicion by the younger Singaporeans and the English-educated Chinese who saw this as an attempt at political control. The publicity given to an ethnically specific system of ideas of the majority population was bound to have an unsettling effect on the minority population. The link between the universalization of English-language education in Singapore and the increasing pressures for democratization—as well as the link between an English education and the Christianization of the population, especially among the Chinese—was made in leadership circles. In Singapore only 12 percent of the population is Christian, but over 30 percent of the Christians are university and college graduates, and many can be counted among the economic and political elite in the republic. The trend among a minority in Roman Catholic churches to tie religion to social action, thus willy-nilly entering directly into the political arena, was also a source of disquiet for the government. These developments prompted Prime Minister Lee to say, in 1988: "I'm not at all sure that the things we set in motion as necessary for our survival—like teaching the population the English language—that that was a wise thing because we are in the process of being a different people." [9]

A lingering issue that received attention in Singapore, and one that will require several years before a solution can be realized, is the "Malay problem." By all socioeconomic measures of educational and occupational attainment, the Malay community has lagged far behind the other communities in Singapore's development. In the 1980s the PAP Government realized that not adopting an ethnic solution to the problem of the Malays simply did not help the backwardness of the community. In 1982 the government

[9] *The Straits Times,* 15 November 1988.

stepped in to fund the formation of Mendaki, a Muslim educational foundation directed at helping Malay children cope with schoolwork to achieve better grades and to complete their education. However, in the view of the political leaders the Malays still remained a community apart, with the mosque as their organizational focus rather than state community institutions, and a sense of affinity with Malaysia, a country with which they have a shared heritage and religion. This was patently demonstrated when Chaim Herzog, the Israeli president, visited the republic in October 1986. As the protests against the visit built up in Malaysia so did the negative response among Singapore Malays. The decision on the part of the government openly to discuss ethnic problems was intended to focus on the problem and to force the pace of integration. The result, however, was the opposite, with the Malay community closing in on itself.

The task of the second-generation leaders was seen to be the continuation of the nation-building process initiated more than two decades before. The foundations of the state and economy and the building of the infrastructure have been set, but the crucial test of nationhood, that of the institutionalization of the political structures and the bonding of a people to the nation, will be on the political agenda for years to come.

FURTHER READING

Barber, Noel. *The Singapore Story: From Raffles to Lee Kuan Yew*. London: Fontana, 1978.
Buchanan, Iain. *Singapore in Southeast Asia*. London: G. Bell, 1972.
Chan Heng Chee. *The Dynamics of One Party Dominance: The PAP at the Grassroots*. Singapore: Singapore University Press, 1976.
———. *Nation-building in Southeast Asia: The Singapore Case*. Singapore: Institute of Southeast Asian Studies, 1971.
———. *Singapore: The Politics of Survival, 1965–1967*. Singapore; Oxford University Press, 1971.
Hassan, Riaz, ed. *Singapore: Society in Transition*. Singapore: Oxford University Press, 1976.
Quah, Jon S. T., Chan Heng Chee and Seah Chee Meow, eds. *Government and Politics of Singapore*. Singapore and New York: Oxford University Press, 1985.
Turnbull, C. M. *A History of Singapore, 1819–1975*. Singapore: Oxford University Press, 1977.

SOVIET CENTRAL ASIA

SHIRIN AKINER

THE REGION

CENTRAL Asia is a vast landmass of no precise definition and no clearly defined boundaries. The section that lies within the Soviet Union covers an area of some 1.5 million sq. miles/4 million sq. km.—that is to say, it is well over ten times the size of France. It straddles Europe and Asia, stretching from the Caspian Sea in the west to the Tien Shan mountains in the east, from the Siberian plains in the north to the Karakum ("Black Sand") deserts in the south. It is a land of contrasts, of rolling steppes, arid deserts and towering mountain peaks. In much of the region the climate is sharply continental, with summer temperatures of 104° to 122°F/40°C to 50°C and winter temperatures of −22°F/−30°C and below. On the plains, rainfall is sparse, particularly in the south: In the lower reaches of the Amu Dar'ya, averages are as low as 1.8 in to 3.5 in/45mm. to 90 mm. per year; droughts and sandstorms are not uncommon. In the mountains of the east, however, precipitation is high, with an annual rainfall of 393.7 in/1,000 mm. and more. There are few natural sources of flowing water. In the far west, the Ural and Emba rivers empty into the Caspian Sea, and the southeast is veined by gushing, snow-fed mountain torrents; but many of these peter out in the deserts. The two largest rivers in the southern belt are the Amu Dar'ya (1,616 miles/2,600 km.) and the Syr Dar'ya (1,859 miles/2,991 km.), famous in classical times as the Oxus and Jaxartes, respectively; following roughly parallel, diagonal courses, they flow westward to the Aral Sea. A number of other great rivers rise in Central Asia but flow northward into Siberia. There are also several large lakes: In addition to the Caspian Sea (143,243 sq. miles/371,000 sq. km.), there is the Aral Sea (25,676 sq. miles/66,500 sq. km.) in the west; Lake Balkhash (7,027 sq. miles/ 18,200 sq. km) and Lake Issyk-Kul (2,425 sq. miles/6,280 sq. km.) are in the east. Wildlife in Central Asia is rich and varied; flamingos bring tropical brilliance to the margins of the Caspian Sea, while snow leopards, red wolves and wild sheep (argalis, *Ovis ammon*) roam the mountains in the east. There is an abundance, too, of mineral wealth. The region contains major deposits of ferrous and nonferrous metals, coal, oil and gas; some of the rare metals found here do not occur elsewhere in the Soviet Union.

HISTORICAL BACKGROUND

Until the 20th century, the history of Central Asia has been dominated by the division between "the steppe and the sown," the former the domain of the nomad, the latter of the settled peoples. The history of the settled belt in the south can be traced from the 4th century B.C. The earliest inhabitants were, in all probability, of eastern Iranian origin. By the 6th century B.C., this region was under the rule of the Persian Achaemenians. They were overthrown in 329 B.C. by Alexander the Great, who brought Hellenism to Central Asia. Later, in the 1st to 4th centuries A.D., the region formed part of the powerful Kushan empire. As trade routes spread across the continent, linking east with west, north with south, they passed through Transoxiana, bringing it material as well as spiritual and cultural wealth. This, the southern belt, belonged to the civilized, known world.

The lands of the north, meanwhile, were still shrouded in obscurity. Even the names of the peoples who wandered across them in an endless cycle of migration cannot be identified with certainty. Turkic peoples first appeared in the region in the 6th century A.D. They established powerful tribal confederacies that held sway over the territory between Mongolia and the Aral Sea for much of the next two centuries. At the height of their power they had diplomatic links with China, Persia and Byzantium.

The Arabs invaded southern Central Asia in the second half of the 7th century, bringing a new religion, Islam, and with it a new outlook on life, a new sense of identity. In time this led to an intellectual flowering of impressive proportions: Polymaths such as al-Ferghani and al-Khwarezmi in the 9th century and al-Farabi, Ibn Sina (Avicenna) and al-Biruni in the 10th century left a legacy without which the later scientific advances of medieval Europe would have been unthinkable. The political links with the Arab caliphate did not last long, however; by the 9th century, the local Persian governors, the Tahirids, and the Samanids were virtually independent rulers. The first Turkic dynasty to establish itself in Transoxiana was that of the Karakhanids (999–c.1165). They had been converted to Islam in the course of the 10th century, although the nomadic Turkic tribes of the steppes were still almost untouched by the religion.

The Mongols burst onto the scene in 1219; within two years they had captured Samarkand, Bukhara and all the other great cities of Central Asia. They wreaked inestimable damage on the region in the first fury of their onslaught but later succeeded in establishing the peace and stability that allowed for a revival of trade and scholarship. They themselves became Turkicized and adopted Islam. The last great ruler of this era was Tamerlane (d. 1405), whose capital was at Samarkand but whose conquests reached far beyond the confines of Central Asia. His empire did not long survive his death; his grandson Ulugh Beg (r. 1409–1449) is remembered more for his achievements in astronomy and mathematics than in statesmanship. By this time, too, the great transcontinental trade routes were shifting their course, the emphasis moving to transportation by sea rather than by land. The region gradually sank into a long period of isolation, economic stagnation and intellectual bankruptcy, the chief outlet for its energies the relentless, internecine struggles of local khans.

The Russian conquest of Central Asia dates from the 19th century, but much of the region had already fallen within their sphere of influence considerably earlier. The steppes of the north, the home of the Kazakh hordes, came under Russian control in the first half of the century, Transoxiana in the second. The three main states of the south, the khanates of Bukhara, Khiva and Kokand, put up little resistance to the intruders. Bukhara became a protectorate in 1868, Khiva in 1873; direct Russian rule was imposed on Kokand in 1876. The Turkmen fought with their customary bravery and ferocity but were decisively routed at the battle of Geok Tepe in 1881.

Unlike most other colonial regimes, the Russians did not try to change the customs and beliefs of the indigenous population. There was virtually no Christian missionary work; on the contrary, the proselytizing of Islam was encouraged, in the hope that this would have a civilizing influence on the unruly Kazakh and Kirgiz tribes, some of whom were still shamanists. Compared with other colonial regimes, there was remarkably little friction between the new administration and the local peoples. One main source of conflict, which fueled a major uprising in 1916, was the use of the steppes. Thousands of Slav peasants, set free by the abolition of serfdom in 1861, flocked to Central Asia, to the fertile expanses of the north. There they settled on the traditional pastures of the Kazakh nomads, robbing the latter of their livelihood.

The Russians' primary interest in Central Asia was its potential as a supplier of valuable raw materials. The cultivation of cotton was greatly expanded in order to satisfy the needs of the textile industry in central Russia. There was also some extraction of oil, coal and copper. Trade links were strengthened, increasing still further Central Asia's economic dependency on Russia. The construction of a rail network was an essential element in this process: The Trans-Caspian line was completed in 1899, the Tashkent-Orenburg "cotton line" in 1906. Road and telegraph communications were also developed.

The Europeans and the local peoples lived in separate enclaves and for the most part had little direct influence on each other. Improvements were introduced (mostly in the towns) in areas such as health care and community hygiene, but perhaps the most important consequence of the Russian conquest was that it brought the Central Asians into closer contact with better educated and more progressive Muslims from other parts of the empire. The Tatars in particular were very active in Central Asia, playing an important role in educational reform and the launch of the independent vernacular press.

The first years of the 20th century saw the beginnings of a political awakening in Central Asia. Rudimentary political groupings began to form, but they had no clear objectives, little sense of joint purpose and no administrative experience. The Kazakh leaders were the best organized, but even they were unprepared for the cataclysmic upheavals of 1917. Soviet power was established in Tashkent in November 1917, and the Turkmen Autonomous Soviet Socialist Republic was proclaimed in April 1918. The issue hung in the balance for several more months, however, as the Red and White armies, the foreign interventionists, the nationalists, and a variety of other dissident forces, known collectively as the *basmachi,* fought among one another. The Bolsheviks were in control by the end of 1919, but the *basmachi* continued to harry them into the mid-1920s. The Bukharan and Khivan protectorates were transformed into people's Soviet republics in 1920 and in 1924 incorporated into the rest of Central Asia; the entire region was then delimited, on ethno-linguistic principles, into the present five Central Asian republics.

THE REPUBLICS

Soviet Central Asia is divided into five "union" republics: the Kazakh, Kirgiz, Tadzhik, Turkmen and Uzbek Soviet Socialist Republics (SSRs); less formally, they are also known as Kazakhstan, Kirgiziya, Tadzhikistan, Turkmeniya or Turkmenistan, and Uzbekistan, respectively. (In Soviet sources, for historical and administrative reasons, Kazakhstan is generally not included in the definition of "Central Asia"; elsewhere it is.) These republics form part of the USSR and enjoy the same status as the other ten union republics. They are defined as "sovereign socialist states." Their rights include the right to secede from the USSR, as well as the right to enter into relations with foreign powers: No attempt has yet been made to exercise the first, but since each union republic has at least one international frontier, it would, physically speaking, be feasible; the second has only been put into practice in somewhat debatable circumstances.

All union republics have their own constitution, one that closely accords with the Soviet Constitution but reflects some of the unique characteristics of the republic in question; they have their own bodies of state authority, namely, a supreme soviet and presidium, council of ministers, and supreme court; they also other symbols of statehood such as their own national flags, anthems and emblems. Within the Soviet Union changes in territorial boundary are possible but only with the consent of any other republic (or republics) concerned. The republics do not have their own military formations. All young males are liable for military conscription, and they serve in the Soviet army in mixed, multiethnic units that are invariably based in some other part of the country. Throughout the USSR there is uniformity of legislative regulation and social and economic policy; however, each republic does have its own judicial system, and in economic and social planning there is some scope for regional decision making. All the union republics have their own Communist parties (formed shortly after they achieved union republic status); these in turn form part of the Communist party of the USSR. The first party secretaries are usually drawn from the titular ethnic group; in Kazakhstan, however, a Russian, Gennady Kolbin, has held this post since December 1986. Second party secretaries, chairmen of the KGB, regional military chiefs and similar senior posts relating to security and law and order are usually held by Slavs.

The five Soviet Central Asian republics differ considerably in size, relief, population densities, resources and other such features. The Kazakh SSR (area: 1,049,034 sq. miles/2,717,000 sq. km.) is the second-largest republic in the USSR, approximately five times the size of Texas; it is 1,243 miles/2,000 km. in length and 1,864 miles/3,000 km. in breadth. It shares a border with China. Most of its territory lies in the steppe belt in the northern and central parts of the region. The lowest spot in the USSR (433 ft/132 m. below sea level) is in the west, on the Mangyshlak Peninsula, while in the east are some of the highest mountain peaks (up to 16,400 ft./5,000 m.). The south is mostly desert. It has a population of 16.2 million, of whom 36 percent are Kazakh, 41 percent Russian, 6 percent Ukrainian, 6 percent German and 0.6 percent Korean. The capital is Alma-Ata (population: 1.1 million); in all, it has 83 towns and cities (total urban population: 54 percent). It has vast mineral reserves—including major deposits of coal, oil, natural gas, iron, lead, zinc, copper and many rare metals—and it is one of the chief grain- and meat-producing areas of the USSR.

The Kirgiz SSR (area: 76,640 sq. miles/198,500 sq. km.) also shares a border with China. Three-quarters of its territory lies in the mountains of the Tien Shan and the Pamirs. The region is prone to earthquakes (up to eleven on the Richter scale). It has many rivers, which are a valuable source of hydroelectric power. It has a population of 4.1 million, of whom 48 percent are Kirgiz, 12 percent Uzbek and 26 percent Russian. The capital is Frunze (population; 630,000); in all it has 21 towns and cities (total urban population: 39 percent). It is the USSR's main source of antimony and mercury; it also has major deposits of uranium and coal, as well as some oil, natural gas, lead, zinc and other minerals. Grain is cultivated in the valleys, and the pasture land is excellent for raising sheep.

The Tadzhik SSR (area: 55,250 sq. miles/143,100 sq. km.) is situated in the southeast corner, sharing borders with China and Afghanistan. Most of its territory lies in the Tien Shan and Pamir mountains (almost half of it more than 9,840 ft/3,000 m. above sea level), and the region is prone to earthquakes. It has a population of 4.8 million, of whom 59 percent are Tadzhik, 23 percent Uzbek and 10 percent Russian. The capital is Dushanbe (population: 582,000); the region contains 18 towns and cities (total urban population: 35 percent). It has rich deposits of a variety of minerals, including rare metals, gold, uranium, oil and natural gas, as well as precious and semiprecious stones. Its rivers provide hydroelectric power and irrigation, which is essential for farming. Cotton is the main crop, and Tadzhikistan is one of the chief sources of long-staple cotton in the USSR. It has within its boundaries the autonomous province of Gorno-Badakhshan (area: 25,985 sq. miles/67,300 sq. km.; population: 149,000).

The Turkmen SSR (area 188,455 sq. miles/488,100 sq. km.) is situated along the southern margin, between the Caspian Sea and the Amu Dar'ya river; it shares a border with Iran. Over three-quarters of its territory is in the desert belt. The region is frequently racked by earthquakes. It has a population of 3.4 million, of whom 68 percent are Turkmen, 9 percent Uzbek, and 13 percent Russian. The capital is Ashkhabad (population:

371,000); in all, it has 16 towns and cities (total urban population: 48 percent). It has enormous reserves of oil and natural gas, as well as the world's largest deposit of Glauber's salt (sodium sulphate) and common salt.

The Uzbek SSR (area; 172,741 sq. miles/447,400 sq. km.) is situated in the south, between the Amu Dar'ya and the Syr Dar'ya rivers; a border is shared with Afghanistan. Two-thirds of its territory lies in the desert and semidesert belt. It has a population of 19 million, of whom 69 percent are Uzbek, 4 percent Tatar, 4 percent Tadzhik and 11 percent Russian. The capital is Tashkent (population: 2.1 million); the region contains, in all, 123 towns and cities (total urban population: 41 percent). It has large deposits of natural gas, oil, coal and nonferrous metals, and it is a major source of high-quality gold. It is also the chief cotton-growing region of the USSR. It has within its boundaries the Kara-Kalpak ASSR (area: 63,938 sq. miles/165,600 sq. km.; population: 1.1 million).

THE PEOPLE

The indigenous population of Central Asia is composed predominantly of Turkic peoples, including (population estimates according to the 1979 census) Uzbeks (12,455,978), Kazakhs (6,556,442), Turkmen (2,027,913), Kirgiz (1,906,271), Kara-Kalpaks (303,324) and Uighurs (210,612). The Iranian group is represented mainly by the Tadzhiks (2,897,697); but there are also some Baluchis (18,997), Persians (approximately, 25,000), and the Pamiri peoples—of a number of small tribes such as the Shugnis, Rushanis and Wakhis who are now included with the Tadzhiks but themselves strongly feel that they have a separate identity (in all, about 60,000). Other small but long-established groups include the Central Asian Arabs, an ancient community of Central Asian Jews (also known as Bukharan Jews), and Central Asian gypsies (Muslims).

Slavs—mostly Russians but also large numbers of Ukrainians and some Byelorussians—have been moving into the region since the mid-19th century. After the establishment of Soviet power, the influx of Slavs increased greatly. The peak period was 1926–39, but another great wave arrived during the war years, when many industrial enterprises, as well as several branches of the Soviet Academy of Sciences, were evacuated here from the western regions of the USSR. Since the 1960s, the influx of Slavs has been decreasing and there now appears to be some emigration. The highest concentration of Slavs is in Kazakhstan (5,991,205 Russians and 897,964 Ukrainians), where they constitute almost half the population of the republic.

Other 19th-century immigrants included the Dungans (51,694), Chinese Muslims who moved to Russian-held territory in the second half of the century, and Volga Tatars, who came to the region in the wake of the colonial administration. No distinction is made in official published sources between these Tatars and the related but quite separate Crimean Tatars. The latter were deported to Central Asia in their entirety in May 1944, accused of collaborating with the Germans. They were later exonerated of this charge, but very few have as yet been allowed to return to the Crimea. There are in all over 1 million Tatars in Central Asia; an estimated 500,000 are Crimean Tatars. The Volga Germans and Soviet Koreans were also deported to Central Asia en masse, suspected of collaboration with enemy powers. Many of the Germans have been allowed to emigrate to West Germany; the Koreans appear to be content to remain in Central Asia.

The great majority of the main ethnic groups are concentrated within their own titular republics; thus, 84.9 percent of the Uzbeks are in the Uzbek SSR, 80.7 percent of the Kazakhs in the Kazakh SSR, 77.2 percent of the Tadzhiks in the Tadzhik SSR, 93.3 percent of the Turkmen in the Turkmen SSR and 88.5 percent of the Kirgiz in the Kirgiz SSR. This compactness helps greatly to develop and maintain a sense of national identity. However, all the Central Asian republics are multiethnic (in Uzbekistan alone, over 120 separate nationalities are represented). In Kazakhstan and Kirgiziya the titular ethnic groups do not even constitute the majority (36.0 percent and 47.9 percent, respectively, of the total populations of their republics); in Tadzhikistan they represent a little over half (58.8 percent) and in Turkmeniya and Uzbekistan just over two-thirds (68.4 percent and 68.7 percent, respectively). Whatever the size of their representation within the republic, however, the titular ethnic group is given priority treatment (generally unofficially) in many fields. This is one of the factors giving rise to intercommunal tension. Another is the tendency to pay off ancient scores by discriminating against those from other tribal or regional backgrounds. This has led to some unrest in Uzbekistan recently, where Tadzhiks have begun to protest the unfair treatment meted out to them by the Uzbeks; in Tadzhikistan itself, however, the Pamiri peoples complain that the Tadzhiks are treating them badly. Some resentment is felt towards the European settlers, but it is more of an impersonal, ritualized dislike of outsiders rather than the bitter rivalry shown towards other indigenous groups.

The demographic vitality of the Central Asian peoples is such that they are increasing at a rate well above the Soviet national average. The birth rate is higher (in Tadzhikistan more than double the national average) and the death rate lower than in other regions. There are several factors that contribute to this rapid expansion. One is the fact that the proportion of men and women is almost equal; among the Russians, for example, there are almost 10 percent fewer men than women (1970 estimates). Central Asian girls no longer marry at quite such an early age as formerly, but, nevertheless, younger than their European counterparts. Between 85 percent and 90 percent of the Uzbek and Tadzhik women in the 20–29-year-old age bracket, the most fertile span, are married. Large families, preferably with many sons, are the ideal for both husbands and wives. Even if married couples wanted fewer children, the disapproval of older relatives would make it difficult for them to practice any form of contraception. Abortion (forbidden by the Koran) is rare. Family life is stable, divorce uncommon, children much loved. Among educated, professional couples in the towns, the average size of the family is gradually diminishing, but this represents only a small proportion of the total number of families. In the meantime, the Central Asian population is growing steadily younger (some 70 percent are under 30 years of age), while the European population in the Soviet Union is aging. The number of nonworking dependants per family is increasing steadily in Central Asia, placing a severe strain on the household economy; the state-run social services, too, are under ever greater pressure and have fallen woefully behind the rest of the country in the provision of nursery schools, foundling homes, doctors and other such facilities.

EDUCATION

In the prerevolutionary period, educational facilities in Soviet Central Asia were very restricted. The traditional Muslim schools (*maktab*) and colleges (*madrassah*) followed a syllabus that had hardly been changed since the medieval period. After the annexation, the Russians brought their own schools to the region. Those to which the indigenous population had greatest access were the "Russo-Native" schools, which followed a program that was divided equally between Islamic subjects and "European" subjects— e.g., elementary Russian language and literature, geography and arithmetic. From the 1980s onwards, a few "new-method" (*dzhadid*) schools were opened under the influence of progressive Muslims from other parts of the Russian empire (Tatars and Azerbaydzhanis). These were still within the Islamic tradition, but they used a slightly broader curriculum and more modern teaching methods.

Throughout this period education was largely the preserve of the elite. The 1926 census records a literacy rate of 7 percent among the Kazakhs and between 1 percent and 4 percent among the other Central Asian peoples. Under Soviet rule, by contrast, mass education was promoted. In the early years there were two priorities: One was to teach adults to read and write; the other was to provide general education in the mother tongue. The literacy curve rose steadily, until by 1970 a success rate of over 99 percent was being claimed; this is surely too high if applied to the Central Asian population as a whole, but if the very young and the very old are excluded, it is probably substantially correct. This achievement has not been matched in any of the neighboring countries.

Throughout the Soviet Union education is free, and compulsory between the ages of seven and fifteen. A unified curriculum is used, but regional requirements (e.g., in language, literature and history) may be added to the syllabus, thereby prolonging the course by up to a year. The constitution guarantees mother-tongue education for all. This is indeed provided for the titular group of a republic. For minority groups, however, facilities are often far from adequate. Recent protests from the Tadzhiks in Uzbekistan (a community of some 700,000) have drawn attention to the grave lack of schools and books available to some minority groups.

There are universities and other institutes of higher education in all the Central Asian republics; Uzbekistan, the leader in this respect, has 3 universities (the first founded in 1920) and 40 other higher-educational establishments. Each republic has its own academy of science. At the tertiary level some subjects are taught in the national languages, but specialized and technical subjects are taught in Russian. Entry to higher-educational institutions is by competitive examination. For many years Central Asian students were underrepresented in the student bodies of their republics, due to a limited secondary education, a poor knowledge of Russian, and a low degree of urbanization, among other factors. Today they have achieved a level closer to their proportional representation in the population of their republics. Many Central Asian students take up subjects connected with agriculture, but efforts are being made to encourage them to opt for more industrial training. At the highest levels of research, however, it is note-worthy that Central Asian scholars are again excelling in the natural sci-ences, particularly in mathematics, a field in which they last made a sig-nificant contribution in the 15th century.

LANGUAGE AND SCRIPT

The indigenous languages of Central Asia belong to two unrelated groups, the Turkic (Altaic) and the Iranian (Indo-European). In the past, Persian was the chief administrative medium of the region, while the Turkic lit-erary language *(Chaghatai)* was used mainly for poetry. There was also a wide range of dialects that differed greatly among themselves, as well as from the literary forms. During the Soviet period, national languages have been developed for the main ethnic groups on the basis of selected dialects.

The Arabic script had been used in Central Asia from the introduction of Islam in the 7th century until the end of the 1920s, but it came under attack almost as soon as Soviet power had been established. The Latin script was adopted in 1928 (Ataturk introduced the Latin script in the Republic of Turkey at exactly the same time); in 1940 it was replaced by the Cyrillic script. All of the Central Asian languages are now written in the same graphic system as Russian, with a few additional symbols for the represen-tation of special sounds.

The new social and economic conditions ushered in by the Soviet era required a new lexicon. Many terms were acquired from western European languages through Russian (the so-called international terms). For the most part, the new words were adopted for concepts for which there were no existing terms and in fields such as specialized technology, administration and ideology. In some cases, however, they were also advocated as substi-tutes for well-established Arabic and Persian words. There is now a mani-fest reaction against this linguistic russification and a movement to replace such loans with more traditional forms has emerged.

SOCIAL CHANGE

For centuries, the traditional divide in Central Asian society was between nomads and settled peoples. The former, who constituted by far the larger group, were of Turkic origin, herders who followed a regular pattern of transhumance. The latter, predominantly Tadzhiks and Uzbeks, were farm-ers, traders and craftsmen; under the czarist administration they were generally called by the collective ethnonym *Sart* (a word of uncertain etymology meaning "merchant"). In the 1920s, as soon as Soviet power had been established, the nomads were forcibly sedentarized, and shortly afterwards, in 1929, collectivization was introduced. The life-style change was so abrupt and ill prepared that it brought terrible devastation and famine to the region. In the 1930s, among the Kazakhs alone, there was an estimated loss of some one million lives (though some of this number almost certainly survived by fleeing across the border into China). After World War II there was a gradual recovery. Farming and animal husbandry were expanded and a degree of mechanization introduced. A large proportion of the local population is still engaged in agriculture. Nomadism has been eradicated, but within the state and collective farm system there is a limited degree of migration (chiefly when animals are moved to and from the seasonal pastures).

The indigenous Central Asian peoples are still predominantly rural-based. During the Soviet period there has been a considerable growth of the urban population in each of the republics, but this has been largely the result of migration from other parts of the Soviet Union. The highest rate of urbanization has been among the Turkmen, formerly almost entirely rural dwellers (the urban population in Turkmeniya was 1.4 percent of the total in 1926 but 31.7 percent in 1970); the Kirgiz are still the least urbanized group (14.5 percent live in Kirgiziya cities in 1970). The increase in the number of urban settlements has been particularly marked in Uzbekistan (for example, in the period 1972–83, 40 percent of all new towns in the Soviet Union were sited in the Uzbek SSR) but the rate of urbanization among the Uzbeks themselves has been slower than among any of the other indigenous peoples (the urban population in Uzbekistan went from 18.3 percent in 1925 to only 23.0 percent in 1970). Of the total Uzbek urban population, 30 percent live in Tashkent, the capital of the republic. Most of the remainder are found in the smaller, older towns; almost none have been attracted to the new industrial settlements.

Among all the Central Asian peoples, the drift to the towns has been rather greater than is suggested by the present urban-rural ratios, but this fact has been obscured by the high birth rate in rural areas, which has caused the rural population to expand at a faster rate than the urban. Nevertheless, urbanization has undoubtedly been slow. One factor contributing to this is the standard of living: Food and housing are cheaper, better and far more plentiful in the countryside, and large extended families, still very common, are easier to accommodate in a village environment. Language, too, is a potential deterrent: Russian is widely used in the towns, but even if the titular language of the republic is also used, it may well represent a different dialect. Family ties and regional loyalties, as well as a simple preference for the tranquil, unhurried life of the countryside, are felt to outweigh the advantages of better amenities and job prospects in the towns. Educational qualifications play some part in determining this choice, but it is not uncommon even for those who have higher degrees to opt for less-skilled work in the village in preference to a career in the town. There are indications that the younger generation will prove more receptive to change, but this is likely to be a very long and slow process.

Traditional values are strong in almost every sphere of Central Asian society. They regulate modes of behavior at many levels, within the family as well as within the community at large. The old tribal structure has ceased to exist, but its legacy is still palpable. Among groups such as the Turkmen and the Kazakhs—among whom it was an active force up to the Soviet period—it is rare to find anybody who does not know their genealogy, with all its tribal ramifications, back to the required seventh generation; even among groups such as the Uzbeks, who lost this tradition many centuries ago, there is still a strong sense of family and clan loyalty. In contemporary society, it exhibits itself in the feeling, shared by all Central Asians, that it is a matter of honor to help, and if necessary protect, one's kin. Consequently, nepotism is endemic: At every level, political and administrative corruption is greatly facilitated, and indeed encouraged, by the existence of this network of unquestioning support. Since President Gorbachev came to power, greater attention has been focused on the issue, and wrongdoers have been more vigorously prosecuted (by outsiders). However, the phenomenon itself is not new but has existed from the very earliest years of the Soviet regime, operating, in effect, within its own alternative power structure. The problem that still faces Central Asian society today, as 70 years ago, is how to preserve the best of the old social code while adapting it to serve the needs of the present; or, as Soviet commentators express it, how to jump "from feudalism to mature socialism, bypassing capitalism."

In the domestic sphere, there has been some change but also much continuity. Traditional clothing is worn mainly by the elderly in the towns, more generally in the countryside. In urban areas, however, many young men will wear standard European dress but add some form of national headgear, such as an embroidered skullcap or the Kirgiz felt shovel hat. Most women in Turkmeniya, even in the capital, wear a version of their national dress, while in other parts of Central Asia it is reserved for the village or for informal occasions in the town. Traditional make-up (lavish use of antimony around the eyes and a heavy black line joining the brows, as in medieval miniatures) is also used mainly at home; there is a feeling that this is not "cultured" enough for multiethnic places of work or study. Food, on the other hand, is almost always in the national tradition (this is true even among recent immigrants such as the Koreans, who have some difficulty in finding the necessary ingredients for their native cuisine). Traditional styles of music and dance are also popular, though they may be enjoyed through radio or television broadcasts (almost every family possesses at least one television set and some two or three) rather than direct participation. The most popular pastimes of all are long, relaxed sessions of tea drinking and conversation, always at home for the women, sometimes in a teahouse for men (for whom the normal tea is sometimes supplemented by "cold tea"—brandy).

The performing arts and the fine arts have been heavily influenced by European models. There are ballet companies, opera companies, theaters,

795

circuses and philharmonic orchestras in all the Central Asian republics. The repertoire is wide and often up to a high standard (a young Kazakh ballerina is now one of the leading stars of the Leningrad Kirov ballet). Efforts have been made to preserve and develop the indigenous arts, but in many cases this has led to lifeless pastiche, far removed from the vigor and originality of the original inspiration. However, after a long period of apprenticeship, some promising works are beginning to appear, particularly in the fields of music and painting.

WOMEN

Before the 1917 revolution Central Asian women led severely circumscribed lives. In the towns they scarcely moved beyond the confines of their own courtyards; when they did venture out, they were heavily swathed in an all-enveloping veil *(parandzha)*, their faces hidden behind a horsehair net *(chachvan)*. In the countryside life was somewhat freer and the veil hardly ever worn, but the burden of manual labor was very great.

The movement for the emancipation of women began in the immediate aftermath of the revolution. It was led by women from outside their region, Europeans appalled at what they saw as the degradation of their Central Asian sisters. Early Soviet legislation set the minimum age for marriage at 16 years for girls, 18 years for youths; marriage without consent was prohibited, as was the payment of bride money *(kalym,* a large sum traditionally paid by the bridegroom to the bride's parents), the levirate (compulsory marriage of a widow to her dead husband's brother), and polygamy. All marriages had to be registered with the civil authorities, and divorce proceedings, which could be instigated by husband or wife, could only be heard in Soviet people's courts.

The Central Asian women were slow to respond to the opportunities offered by the new social order. Problems of communication, as well as the weight of tradition, made them reluctant to commit themselves to it wholeheartedly. However, in Uzbekistan, for example, by 1925 there were already 148 Uzbek women in the Communist Party and by 1929 over 1,000. Women were also urged to come forward for legal training, and by 1926 they accounted for over 25 percent of the people's assessors in the Tashkent courts. These developments aroused unease among the male population, but far worse was to come with the launching of the attack *(hudzhum)* against the veil in 1926–7. That year thousands of women took part in mass unveilings and ceremonial burnings of the horsehair face coverings. Men's sensibilities were outraged, and crimes of violence against women increased dramatically. Women themselves had ambivalent feelings about the matter and would often replace their veils as soon as they were out of the public eye. By 1928 the social disorders were so great that mass displays were strongly discouraged and more emphasis was placed on long-term educational measures.

Over the ensuing fifty years considerable progress has been made. Women have indeed abandoned the veil (though in rural areas they still cover their faces in the presence of strangers). They are found in all spheres of activity and some hold high administrative, professional and academic posts. However, for the great majority of women, the rate of change has been much slower. Far fewer girls than boys receive any higher education; many marry early and have large families. The responsibility of several young children, coupled with primitive household equipment, tethers women to the home, isolating them from society. This has aroused the concern of the authorities, for it not only represents a serious loss to the labor force, it also perpetuates the influence of the home and a way of life felt to be inimical to progress. Recent reports in the Soviet press have given horrifying accounts of young married women burning themselves to death because of the sheer hopeless, unremitting drudgery of their lives, made still worse by the tyranny of parents-in-law, with whom they often live. These are certainly the exceptions rather than the rule, but they are an indication that though the lot of some women in Soviet Central Asia is incomparably better than it was in the past, for others there has not been very much improvement.

ISLAM

Over the centuries, Central Asia has been home to many religions. Zoroastrianism, Buddhism, Manichaeism, Nestorian Christianity and Judaism are but some of those that flourished and left their mark on the culture and art of the region. Among the nomad tribes, vestiges of shamanism could still be found in the 20th century. For the past thousand years, however, Islam has been the dominant spiritual, cultural and political force in the region. All the Iranian and Turkic peoples were converted to it, those on the plains of Transoxiana soon after the Arab invasion in the 7th century, those in remoter areas as late as the 19th century.

The overwhelming majority of Central Asian Muslims are Sunnites, of the Hanafi school (as are the majority of Muslims elsewhere in the world). The exceptions are the 50,000 to 60,000 Pamiris (mountain Tadzhiks) who live in the Gorno-Badakhshan Autonomous Province of Tadzhikistan; most of these are Ismailis, followers of the Aga Khan (as are the other Pamiri peoples across the borders in Afghanistan, Pakistan and China). The Central Asian Muslims, numbering some 30 million, account for approximately 60 percent of all the Muslims of the Soviet Union; the remaining 40 percent are divided between the Volga region, Siberia, Daghestan and Azerbaydzhan.

The Soviet Constitution guarantees its citizens "freedom of conscience"—that is, "the right to profess any religion or to profess none, to perform religious worship or to conduct atheistic propaganda." In the first years of Soviet rule Islam was treated comparatively leniently, as a potential ally rather than an enemy. Mosques remained open, and some Islamic schools and courts continued to function until 1928. Thereafter the situation deteriorated rapidly, and a fierce antireligious campaign was launched. During the 1930s all Islamic institutions were closed, teachers and leaders of the community imprisoned and executed, and religious literature destroyed. Matters improved somewhat during the war years, but the first important step forward came in 1946, when an official Islamic administration was created in Tashkent, the Spiritual Directorate for Central Asia and Kazakhstan. Three other directorates were later established in other parts of the Soviet Union, but that of Central Asia remains the largest and most influential. It is headed by Chairman Shamsuddin Babakhanov, the son and grandson of the two previous incumbents of the post. There are official representatives *(Kazi)* in the Kazakh, Kirgiz, Tadzhik and Turkmen SSRs.

The directorates come under the Council for Religious Affairs of the Council of Ministers of the USSR. They have responsibility for such matters as the maintenance of mosques and the appointment of religious personnel. They have no legal competence but are allowed to issue opinions *(fatwa)* on religious matters. The Central Asian directorate is allowed to publish a small amount of religious literature; much of it is for foreign consumption only and not available to the general public in the Soviet Union. This directorate is also responsible for links with Muslims abroad. It organizes the annual pilgrimage to Mecca for the small number of Soviet Muslims (usually 15 to 20) who obtain permission to go on the *hajj* and makes arrangements, too, for a chosen few to go to Islamic universities in other countries (e.g., Egypt, Morocco, Libya) to study for higher degrees in Koranic law. In Central Asia itself there are now two functioning Islamic colleges *(madrassah)*, one in Bukhara, the other in Tashkent; these are the only two in the whole of the Soviet Union. Several mosques have been opened in the last few decades. No reliable information is available as to numbers, but it is generally accepted that there are about 200 open for worship in Central Asia and another 250 elsewhere in the USSR. Antireligious propaganda is still actively purveyed, and Islam receives its fair share of official censure. However, there is no evidence of actual persecution.

The majority of Central Asians do not observe Islamic precepts on prayer and fasting very closely. This is partly because work patterns do not permit it (it would be difficult as well as detrimental to career prospects to request special dispensation for religious observances). In many parts of the region religious observance has always been lax; there has also been a change in social behavior, so that formal religion now plays a less prominent role than before. The life-cycle rituals (birth, circumcision, marriage, death), however, are almost universally observed, as are the major festivals. The prohibition on pork is still very much in force, but that on alcohol is largely disregarded (though this is not a new phenomenon in Central Asia). There is a growing interest in religion among the young. It is not easy for them to obtain guidance on the subject, since so many of the links with the past have been broken; many prefer to rely on the help of unofficial "underground" teachers of Islam rather than those attached to mosques.

Influences from outside the Soviet Union have also stimulated a renewed awareness of Islam. Some religious literature and broadcasts are received from Iran; in general, however, little is known about that country, and of the information that is available, much is disconcerting to those not familiar with recent trends in Islamic societies (e.g., the veiling of women, the introduction of Islamic punishments). Developments in China are not only readily comprehensible, they also have greater bearing on the situation in

Soviet Central Asia. In that neighboring socialist country, Islam is apparently no longer seen as an obstacle to progress but as a positive asset in the struggle for economic reform; thousands of mosques are being reopened and thousands of Muslims allowed to go on the hajj. This cannot but provoke a comparison with the Soviet situation. Nevertheless, there are as yet no indications that Islam is developing into a political force in the region; it remains, for the present, a matter of private devotion.

Sufism has always played an important role in Central Asia. It was part of a powerful cult of popular religion, much of it based on pre-Islamic traditions. Some of this survives today, particularly in rural areas and among the poorer, less-educated elements in the towns. Cases are not infrequently cited in the Soviet press, often accompanied by criticism of the poor quality of local ideological work. Nothing is written about the more esoteric disciplines of mysticism. Personal communications indicate that they, too, still exist and have adherents even among the "established" administration. Unofficial religious literature, some of it based on Sufic texts, appears to be circulating in greater quantities now than ever before; technological advances make it easier to to reproduce, hence harder to control.

ENVIRONMENTAL ISSUES

Measures to protect the environment were introduced in the first years of Soviet rule. Laws were passed to regulate the use of land, water and timber resources and to protect wildlife. These were not always enforced as well as they should have been, particularly during the Stalin period; new and stricter legislation has been enacted during the last two decades.

In Central Asia, nature conservation has, on the whole, a good record in the protection of endangered species of wildlife. There have been problems with overhunting (sometimes with modern weapons of mass destruction), but on the positive side, there are several nature reserves in which rare local breeds are thriving.

The greatest environmental hazards in Central Asia are those arising from the mismanagement of water resources. The pollution of the Caspian Sea is a long-standing and well-known problem; some ameliorative measures have been introduced, but much remains to be done before an acceptable level of purity is reached. In much of Central Asia irrigation is essential for farming. There have been many schemes for bringing water to the region, and some have had disastrous consequences. One gradiose proposal required the diversion of a part of the Siberian headwaters to the south; the project found favor in official circles for many years but was widely regarded by scientists and writers as a recipe for ecological disaster. The project was abandoned in 1986. The damming of the Kara-Bogaz Gol Bay on the Caspian Sea (in northwest Turkmeniya), however, was a project that did come to fruition; it has led to an alarming increase in the desertification of the region.

The most serious problems of all are those connected with the drying up of the Aral Sea. Situated party in Kazakhstan, partly in the Kara-Kalpak ASSR, it is a shallow, tideless lake, the fourth-largest inland sea in the world. As the water retreats, the dried-up sea bed is scoured by ever-more frequent dust storms (now some thirty a year) that carry the residual salts further afield and turn yet more of the land into a desert. Already some 500,000 hectares of valuable pasture land in the Amu Dar'ya delta have been lost, making it impossible to raise the herds that were once an essential part of the local economy.

The shrinking of the Aral Sea is caused mainly by the overutilization of the two rivers that feed it, the Amu Dar'ya and the Syr Dar'ya, for irrigation. It suffers, too, from the pollution of its waters by effluent from the soil-drainage system, heavily contaminated with herbicides and pesticides. The mineral content of the sea (once noted for its low salinity) has risen to dangerously high levels. Fish stocks have been severely depleted; fishing, once an important local industry, declined sharply in the period 1958–85 and has now ceased altogether on a commercial basis. The farming of muskrats for their pelts, a thriving enterprise in the 1950s, has also had to be abandoned through lack of water. The climate has become more extreme, ranging from 113°F/45°C in the summer to −29°F/34°C in the winter. Local wildlife is threatened and some species, such as the Turan tiger, have already become extinct. The human population is also suffering. Seepage from the drainage system is contaminating the drinking water and creating a major health hazard. Once a popular holiday resort, the southern shore of the Aral Sea is now being depopulated as people move elsewhere.

There is a yet more dismal aspect to this tragedy: While the devastation caused by the systematic depletion of the natural water resources continues, there is such prodigal overirrigation in the regions that draw on this water that thousands of hectares of arable land are being turned into saline swamps. The principal fault lies with the inefficient and antiquated irrigation system. To overhaul it thoroughly—or, better still, to replace it—would require a colossal outlay of time and capital; it seems unlikely that such a commitment will be made in the near future. Until such action is taken, however, the devastation of the land will continue inexorably.

THE ECONOMY

At the beginning of the Soviet period the industrial base of the Central Asian republics was very weak. The traditional branches of the economy were animal husbandry, small-scale farming, crafts (chiefly carpet making, pottery and metalworking) and trade.

It was the first two Five-Year Plans (1928–38) that set Central Asia on the road to rapid economic development. Their aim was to achieve cultural and economic parity throughout the Soviet Union. During this period emphasis was placed on the development of the extractive industries and the improvement of the agricultural base, the creation of an indigenous workforce, and the expansion of the communications infrastructure. One of the main achievements was the construction of the Turk-Sib line (completed 1930), which linked Alma-Ata and Tashkent to the Trans-Siberian line. Large numbers of European specialists, technicians and administrators were drafted into the area to help achieve the economic targets; in the 1930s, some 85 percent of the industrial labor force was composed of immigrants from European Russia. During the war years, several industrial enterprises from the west of the country were evacuated to Central Asia, which further boosted economic development in that area.

Since the 1920s there have been several changes in the economic zoning of the USSR. For the purposes of the present Fifteen-Year Plan (1975–90), the state planning committee of the USSR (Gosplan) has divided the country into seven economic macroregions. Kazakhstan alone constitutes one such region; the four other Central Asian republics together—Kirgiziya, Tadzhikistan, Turkmeniya and Uzbekistan—comprise another. Kazakhstan has several major industrial complexes, including petrochemicals in the west, nonferrous metals and chemicals in the south and heavy industry in the center. It is one of the USSR's leading fuel and power bases. Agriculture also plays an important role in the economy. One-third of the USSR's arable land is found in Kazakhstan. There is dry-grain farming in the north, irrigated cotton and rice in the south. During the 1950s millions of hectares in the north of the republic were brought under the plough as part of Khrushchev's Virgin Lands project. Kazakhstan is now the third-largest grain-producing area in the USSR. Stock raising is also highly developed. The space center at Baykonyr and the nuclear testing ground at Semipalatinsk play a small part in the local economy.

In the other four republics, the economy is dominated by agriculture. Cotton is the most important crop; Uzbekistan alone accounts for two-thirds of the total Soviet production. Irrigation is necessary in almost all areas. Animal husbandry, a traditional occupation here, is widely practiced. The breeding of Karakul (Astrakhan) sheep, much prized for their pelts, is highly developed. Industry is largely concerned with the extracting and processing of the rich mineral resources of the region. Oil and gas production are of major importance in Turkmeniya and Uzbekistan (together they account for almost one-quarter of the total Soviet gas production); the chemical, electrical engineering and machine-building industries are also growing. Other branches of industry include textiles, silk, carpet making, food processing (canning, wine making, et cetera) and a wide range of cotton-related industries.

It is impossible to assess the performance of the economies of the Central Asian republics today with any degree of accuracy. Since the mid-1980s there have been ever-more startling revelations of corruption and fraud at every level, stretching over many years. Major embezzlement, diversion of investment funds, misappropriation of food supplies and livestock from the public sector into the private, mythical enterprises involving hundreds of thousands of rubles (most notably in connection with the cultivation of cotton) and other such fraudulent activities prompted a massive falsification of statistics. Even these, however, did not present a particularly healthy picture; thus the true state of affairs is likely to be very poor indeed. The performance in agriculture has been especially disappointing. Apart from the outright criminal misuse of resources, there has been lack of foresight and poor management in many areas. The land has been overworked, leading to a decline in productivity; in Kazakhstan, for example, only about

14 percent of the arable land is left fallow every year, and throughout the region there is a disregard for adequate crop rotation.

Scarce and costly water supplies are squandered in careless overirrigation, which in turn has led to the severe salination of arable and pasture land. Animal husbandry also has its problems; lack of appropriate fodder and slack compliance with health regulations not infrequently lead to disease and thus to major losses in production. Poor storage and transportation facilities are responsible for yet more wastage.

The effective deployment of manpower resources is an issue that urgently needs to be resolved. Central Asia's demographic explosion could be a boon for the Soviet economy, providing a young and vigorous workforce to act as a counterbalance to the aging of the population in the western regions. This, however, would require major changes in Central Asian society, and these do not as yet appear to be taking place. The indigenous population shows a marked reluctance to move within its own republic, let alone further afield to other parts of the country. Consequently, there is a rapidly growing surplus of labor in rural Central Asia, where it can no longer be absorbed effectively, and a shortage of manpower in industry, both within Central Asia and elsewhere. Some Soviet planners insist that efforts to induce the Central Asians to become more mobile must be increased; others see the solution in the provision of greater job opportunities in the countryside, where they are needed. The primary processing of local produce could well be undertaken in situ. Other branches of light industry could also be developed in rural areas. Further measures that are urged include better vocational training for Central Asians: A high proportion of the indigenous workforce still has only the most basic educational qualifications, and consequently, many take up unskilled laboring jobs. Central Asian women are still underrepresented in socialist production and it is suggested that more flexible work patterns should be introduced, including more part-time employment, in order to draw them out of the home and into industry.

Acceleration and restructuring are the key slogans in the Soviet economy today. It is by no means clear, however, how they are to be put into practice in Central Asia. The problems here are perhaps greater than anywhere else in the country. There is the inescapable question of an acceptable work ethic: Hydra-headed corruption has so far bedeviled all attempts at reform. The conservativeness of the workforce makes it difficult to inject greater flexibility into the system. More mechanization, particularly in the cotton and textile industries, could lead to increased efficiency and higher productivity, but manual labor is cheaper (for the harvesting of cotton, for example, thousands of unpaid children are employed). Also, these are the areas in which women workers predominate; if they were to be made redundant, alternative forms of employment would have to be found for them. Few such opportunities exist at present; hence there is a vicious circle that continually hinders attempts at modernization.

Since the region is of such great economic significance, it is essential that it should function well; it is possible, therefore, that the seriousness of the present situation will prompt a radical reevaluation. This could in time lead to a more sensitive appraisal of traditional local features and an attempt to build on their strengths rather than to magnify their weaknesses. Greater attention to family cooperatives and more encouragement for the native entrepreneurial spirit might be fruitful lines of development. For the present, however, these can but be matters for speculation. Little clear sense of direction has yet emerged.

CROSS-BORDER CONTACTS

Soviet Central Asia is bordered by China, Afghanistan and Iran; it is separated from Pakistan by the narrow Wakhan Corridor. These international boundaries do not follow ethnic boundaries but cut straight through them. Consequently, many groups are split among one or more countries. Moreover, the social and political upheavals of the 20th century have prompted large-scale population movements, and these in turn have divided families, leaving close blood relations separated from one another by a heavily guarded frontier.

It is mostly the Turkic peoples who are spread across the international boundaries. There are Kazakhs in China (900,000), Mongolia (40,000) and Afghanistan (3,000); Uzbeks in Afghanistan (1,000,000) and China (12,500); Turkmen in Afghanistan (400,000) and Iran (500,000); Kirgiz in China (114,000) and Afghanistan (25,000); Uighurs in China (6,000,000). (The figures for Afghanistan are based on pre-1979 estimates; the movement of refugees makes it impossible to estimate the present situation.) Among the non-Turkic peoples there are Tadzhiks (2,000,000) in Afghanistan and China (25,000); many of these are Pamiri peoples, found also in the neighboring regions of Pakistan and India. With the exception of the Uighurs and the Pamiris, the majority of all these ethnic groups live in the Soviet Union.

Policies regarding cross-border contacts are decided by the central governments of the countries concerned, not by representatives of the local communities. It is a sign of the general improvement in relations between the Soviet Union and China that the border between the two countries, firmly closed during the 1960s and 1970s, is now open for cultural exchanges and long-term family visits. Little literature appears to come from China into the Soviet Union, but Uighur and Kazakh editions of the Soviet periodical *Our Fatherland,* published in the Arabic script (still used in China but not in the USSR), are regularly dispatched the other way. The greatest cultural influence in Soviet Central Asia, on a popular level, comes not from an immediate neighbor but from India. Indian films enjoy enormous popularity and Indian goods, when available, are much in demand. The border with Iran is closed, but some religious literature and cassette recordings still find their way into the Soviet Union. Contacts with Afghanistan are strictly regulated, but illegal cross-border movements have taken place in the past and are likely to continue in the future.

The Soviet authorities are proud of the social and economic achievements represented by the Central Asian republics. Foreign visitors are encouraged to visit them, and international trade fairs, conferences and cultural festivals are often held there, particularly in Tashkent, the largest city in the region. Many students from the Indian subcontinent and the Middle East study in these republics. Relatively few Central Asians travel abroad as yet, but the number is increasing and the opportunities widening. The centuries-old isolation of the region is gradually being dispelled; this is happening, it is true, within the Soviet framework, but nevertheless it opens the way for new contacts and new influences.

FURTHER READING

Akiner, Shirin. *The Islamic Peoples of the Soviet Union*. 2nd ed. London: Kegan Paul, 1986.

Allworth, Edward, ed. *Central Asia: A Century of Russian Rule*. New York and London: Columbia University Press, 1967.

R. Kh. Aminova. *The October Revolution and Women's Liberation in Uzbekistan*. Moscow: Nauka, 1985.

Bennigsen, Alexandre, and Lemercier-Quelquejay, Chantal. *Islam in the Soviet Union*. London: Pall Mall, 1967.

Bromlei, Ju. *Present-Day Ethnic Processes in the USSR*. Moscow: Progress, 1977.

Carrère d'Encausse, Hélène. *Decline of an Empire: The Soviet Socialist Republics in Revolt*. New York: Newsweek Books, 1979.

McCagg, William O., and Silver, Brian D., eds. *Soviet Asian Ethnic Frontiers*. Oxford and New York: Pergamon, 1979.

Medlin, William K., Carpenter, Finley, and Cave, William M. *Education and Development in Central Asia: A Case Study on Social Change in Uzbekistan*. Leiden: Brill, 1971.

Rywkin, Michael. *Moscow's Muslim Challenge: Soviet Central Asia*. London: Hurst; Armonk, New York: M. E. Sharpe, 1982.

Wheeler, Geoffrey. *The Modern History of Soviet Central Asia*. London: Weidenfeld & Nicolson, 1964.

SRI LANKA

JAMES MANOR

THREE great issues have dominated Sri Lanka's history over the four decades since it achieved independence from Great Britain in 1948. The first is the character and survival of democratic politics that once flourished there; the second is the balance between market forces and the state in an economy with a strong tradition of social welfare provisions; and the third is the relationship between the majority Sinhalese linguistic group and the minority Tamils.

All three issues took on particular urgency in the decade after 1977 when the United National party led by J. R. Jayewardene swept to power at a general election. In 1982, Sri Lanka's democratic traditions, in which rival parties had peacefully alternated in power after no fewer than six elections, were abandoned at least temporarily. In that year, Jayewardene was elected to a powerful and newly created Gaullist presidency in a campaign in which the main opposition candidate, former Prime Minister Sirimavo Bandaranaike, was prevented from contesting and indeed from speaking. Then the ruling party used its huge majority in the parliament elected in 1977 to pass an amendment prolonging its own life by another six years without a general election. This change was put to the people in a referendum that was attended by so many acts of intimidation and illegality against the opposition that the "Yes" vote cannot be taken seriously.[1] It is far from clear whether free and fair elections will be revived.

The Jayewardene government also introduced striking changes in economic policy. Since the mid-1940s, Sri Lanka had developed an unusually broad range of social-welfare programs, including free education and health care, and state subsidies for food, transport and other items. One result, despite low per capita income, was an impressive record in areas such as literacy, life expectancy and infant mortality. Another, however, was a doubling of the island's population between 1949 and 1981, and this, together with economic stagnation that owed much to costly subsidies and state controls, led Jayewardene to seek rapid economic growth by allowing market forces much freer rein. This met with some limited success, but it also triggered social changes that appear to have further undermined relations between the island's linguistic groups.

[1] "Priya Samarakone," "The Conduct of the Referendum," in J. Manor, ed., *Sri Lanka in Change and Crisis* (London, 1984), pp. 84–117.

805

Table 1
POPULATION BREAKDOWN[2]

Group	Percentage of island's population
Sinhalese	72.0
Sri Lanka Tamils	11.2
Estate Tamils	9.3
Muslims	7.1
Others	0.5
TOTAL	100.0

The decade after 1977 witnessed a marked deterioration in that relationship. A severe bout of rioting by Sinhalese against Tamils living in their midst in 1977, a more modest outbreak in 1981 and a ghastly recurrence in 1983 generated profound alienation among the minority. This helped to turn what in 1977 had been a simmering secessionist movement by extremists in the mainly Tamil northern portion of the island into a full-blown civil war by 1984 that engulfed eastern areas where Tamils are also concentrated. Acts of terrorism against civilians by the overwhelmingly Sinhalese security forces and (less often) by Tamil militants became all too common after 1983. This caused major economic problems and led predictably to grotesque social polarization. As the conflict approached what could well have been a bloody climax in mid-1987, India intervened and arranged an accord with the island's government. This was in most respects productive, but it brought Indian forces into predominantly Tamil areas of the island and compromised, at least temporarily, Sri Lanka's sovereignty.

SOCIAL AND HISTORICAL BACKGROUND

Sri Lanka, known as Ceylon until 1972, is an island nation standing off the southern tip of India. At this writing, it has a population of just over 16 million.

With a degree of simplification necessary in a chapter of this brevity, Table 1 refers to the majority of Sinhalese as an undisaggregated whole.[3] They conceive of themselves as descendants of Aryans from north India who came to Sri Lanka in about the 5th century B.C., a notion that emphasizes their distinctiveness from the island's Tamil minority, which is of Dravidian or south Indian origin. The Sinhalese also see themselves as a "race," a concept that again sharpens the distinction between them and the Tamils. This latter idea is a myth, however, since very large caste groups within the so-

[2] R. N. Kearney extrapolated these figures from the 1971 census in his *Politics of Ceylon (Sri Lanka)* (Ithaca, 1973), p. 6.
[3] They are often divided into Low Country Sinhalese, who inhabit the coastal areas, and Kandyan Sinhalese, who live in the central highlands.

called "race" are clearly Dravidians who adopted Sinhala as their language.[4] The fact that that gained them admission to the "race" indicates that the Sinhalese are more accurately seen as a linguistic group of diverse origins.

The Tamils are divided into two distinct groups, the Sri Lanka Tamils who arrived many centuries ago, and the estate Tamils who came from India in the 19th century to work the tea estates in the central highlands. The latter are still concentrated on the estates and differ in caste, culture and economic position from the Sri Lanka Tamils who live in low coastal areas—in the north where they are an overwhelming majority, in the east where they coexist with concentrations of Muslims and Sinhalese, and in the southwest amid the Sinhalese who form the majority in every part of the island except the north and east. Most Sinhalese are Buddhists and most Tamils are Hindus, and although there is a significant Christian minority (7.9 percent of the island's population) within each group, the recent polarization between Sinhalese and Tamils has tended to divide the churches along linguistic lines. The other minority, the Muslims, contains many Tamil speakers, but they have carefully and successfully cultivated good relations with the Sinhalese.

The lowland areas that ring the central highlands underwent a long spell of European rule. The Portuguese ruled from 1597 until 1658, when they were succeeded by the Dutch, who in turn gave way in 1796 to the British, who conquered the highlands in 1815. Three and a half centuries of regimes that encouraged Christian evangelism and were far less accommodating to indigenous culture than were the British in India left many Sinhalese in the lowlands with problems of deculturation and perhaps a degree of self-doubt. This has helped to produce an aggressive Sinhalese Buddhist parochialism. It did not lead to violence between Sinhalese and Tamils until the postindependence period, after an upsurge of Sinhalese assertiveness, but as early as the 1930s it provided politicians with a means of cultivating popular support. This often took the form of gibes against Tamils, and when opportunistic Tamil politicians responded in kind the seeds were sown for serious conflict.

Sri Lanka is unlucky in having only two large linguistic groups since this allows people on each side to concentrate on just one set of adversaries. Neighboring India is riven by far more such divisions, but fears and resentments are rendered more diffuse and less dangerous in such a polycentric society. Sinhalese popular culture contained elements that could be manipulated for anti-Tamil purposes. Many believe that the Buddha gave the island to the Sinhalese "race" to be a citadel in which pure Buddhism might flourish. Non-Buddhist Tamils stood in the way of this ideal. Sinhalese chauvinists also exaggerated conflicts between Tamil and Sinhalese chieftains in the island's premodern history, celebrated victorious Sinhalese kings[5] and claimed that India's tens of millions of Tamils might somehow

[4] R.A.L.H. Gunawardena, "The People of the Lion," *Sri Lanka Journal of the Humanities,* v, 1–2 (1979), pp. 1–36.
[5] *Ibid.;* S. J. Tambiah, *Sri Lanka: Ethnic Fratricide and the Dismantling of Democracy* (Chicago, 1986); M. Roberts, ed., *Collective Identities, Nationalisms and Protest in Modern Sri Lanka* (Colombo, 1979).

annihilate the Sinhalese "race." It was not inevitable that these ideas would acquire enormous importance, but as we shall see, their manipulation by opportunistic politicians helped make the Sinhalese a majority with a minority complex.

Between 1931 and independence in 1948, politics was conducted largely within an elected legislature that was fragmented into six separate committees, not so much to divide and rule as to undercut Sinhalese hegemony. It largely failed at this, but the opportunities that it provided to politicians—the head of each committee was a powerful minister—and the difficulty of creating a unified Ceylonese nationalist movement amid Sinhalese-Tamil suspicions meant that British rule faced no resistance of the kind seen across the strait in India.[6] The island's legislature—uniquely within the eastern empire—was elected by universal suffrage, and this encouraged ministers to develop an unusually broad range of social-welfare programs, partly out of paternalistic altruism and partly to cultivate popular support. Some leaders, both Sinhalese and Tamils, also adopted intolerant postures toward the other linguistic group. It was with this complex legacy that the nation gained independence, with a new parliamentary system modeled loosely on that of Great Britain.

THE INITIAL POSTINDEPENDENCE PHASE: 1948 TO 1959

In 1948, power passed to the United National party (UNP), which had come into being only two years before as a broad coalition of most of the island's prominent non-Marxist Sinhalese politicians. Several Tamil leaders were also associated with it, but others remained aloof because they distrusted the Sinhalese chauvinism that certain key figures in the UNP had exhibited earlier in their careers. Their greatest suspicions were directed at the second most senior figure in the government, S.W.R.D. Bandaranaike, who had at times been energetically chauvinist, but they were also anxious about the new prime minister, D. S. Senanayake. He was far less vocal in his chauvinism than Bandaranaike, but as agriculture minister before independence, he had resettled thousands of Sinhalese in unoccupied lands in the north-central part of the island. This had turned areas that had been shared between Tamils and Sinhalese into places in which the latter predominated—a "reconquest" of those regions.[7] Tamil fears grew in 1948 when parliament passed bills disenfranchising Tamils on the tea estates, most of whom had Indian citizenship but had lived all their lives in Sri Lanka. The UNP's record through the mid-1950s, however, was otherwise relatively evenhanded.

The new government was predominantly conservative on socioeconomic

---

[6] K. M. de Silva, *A History of Sri Lanka* (Berkeley and London, 1981), chapters 28 and 31; J. Manor, *The Expedient Utopian: Bandaranaike and Ceylon* (Cambridge, 1989), chapters 3–7.

[7] D. E. Smith, "Religion, Politics and the Myth of Reconquest," in T. Fernando and R. N. Kearney, ed., *Modern Sri Lanka: A Society in Transition* (Syracuse, 1979), pp. 83–100.

issues, but there were two important exceptions to this pattern. First, a few leaders around Bandaranaike believed in an actively reformist role for the state. They found themselves outnumbered and thwarted by ministers who preferred low taxation, minimal social reform and a large role for market forces. Second, the social-welfare programs that had developed before independence were continued and modestly enhanced after 1948, and together with an expensive subsidy for rice—a staple of the islanders' diet—they placed a heavy burden on the exchequer, which was overseen by a young finance minister, J. R. Jayewardene.

In 1951, Bandaranaike resigned in frustration from a government in which he had been increasingly isolated, and formed a new center-left Sri Lanka Freedom party (SLFP), which gave more emphasis to social reform and to Sinhalese and Buddhist concerns. The new party was soundly beaten in 1952 at a general election, held amid much emotion after the death of D. S. Senanayake, by the ruling UNP led by the former premier's son, Dudley. The following year, however, the new prime minister suffered an emotional breakdown after the government mishandled protests organized by Marxist parties against a reduction in the rice subsidy. He resigned and was succeeded by his cousin, Sir John Kotelawala, a man of surpassing insensitivity to the concerns of Sinhalese Buddhist opinion.

By 1955, the government was in grave trouble amid a massive upsurge of protests from Sinhalese groups against the unresponsive, anglicized ways of the government. It emerged from among local-level Buddhist elites—schoolteachers, practitioners of indigenous medicine, small-scale entrepreneurs, students and, above all, Buddhist monks. In its initial phase, it focused mainly upon the regime's excessive use of English in the business of governance. In those days, most correspondence with officials had to be conducted in English; facilities in parliament were inadequate to allow legislators to make extensive use of the two vernaculars, and ordinary folk facing murder charges went on trial for their lives in the language of the former colonial power, which the overwhelming majority of both Sinhalese and Tamils did not understand. Resentment over such practices was shared by many Tamils who initially supported the protests of Sinhalese,[8] but by late 1955 these had begun to acquire an anti-Tamil color.

Prime Minister Kotelawala responded with ineptitude, and at the general election of 1956 the ruling UNP went down to a crushing defeat at the hands of a coalition dominated by Bandaranaike's SLFP. By the time the new government took office, Kotelawala had so inflamed Sinhalese chauvinists that they had become dangerously volatile. They believed that they had an endorsement from both the electorate and the new government to adopt harshly anti-Tamil postures. Bandaranaike treated them far too indulgently, and within weeks of the election rioting by Sinhalese against Tamils broke out—the first such violence in the island's modern history. It was soon brought under control, but it was a clear signal of the need for great care and firmness in handling anti-Tamil extremists. Bandaranaike first forged an accommodation with Tamil leaders and then reneged under

[8] Tambiah, *Sri Lanka.*

Table 2
VITAL STATISTICS AND LITERACY RATES

	Life expectancy		Infant mortalities within one year (per 1,000)		Adult literacy (%)	
	1960	*1981*	*1960*	*1981*	*1960*	*1980*
Sri Lanka	62	69	71	43	75	85
India	43	52	165	121	28	36
China	41	67	165	71	43	69
Brazil	55	64	118	75	61	76
Saudi Arabia	43	55	185	111	3	25
Portugal	63	72	82	26	63	78
Italy	69	74	44	14	91	98
Romania	65	71	77	29	89	98

pressure from extremist Buddhist monks, setting in motion a process that led to extensive and brutal anti-Tamil riots in 1958.

We see in this period an invidious pattern that has recurred at crucial junctures in the island's subsequent history. Bandaranaike, who had found it convenient while in opposition to encourage Sinhalese chauvinism in order to undermine the government, was now impelled as prime minister by his responsibilities to all the people of the island to seek accommodation with the Tamils. At the same time, UNP leaders who had sought accommodation when in office now turned chauvinistic. This tendency of those in opposition to adopt anti-Tamil postures helped to sustain Sinhalese intolerance as a potent force that in the 1980s came close to destroying democratic institutions and rending the social fabric beyond repair.[9]

The SLFP managed to establish itself as a permanent center-left alternative to the UNP and created a broad constituency among poorer people and disadvantaged castes for reformist, redistributive policies. This placed social-welfare programs, which had previously rested rather precariously upon UNP paternalism, on the firmer footing of a philosophical commitment to social justice that remained unassailable until the mid-1970s. These policies, for which both major parties can claim credit, enabled Sri Lanka to achieve very impressive results in life expectancy, infant mortality and literacy, as indicated in Table 2.

Bandaranaike was assassinated by criminal elements in his own party in September 1959, and after an indeterminate election in early 1960, his widow emerged to lead his party to victory at a further election later that year. By inflating his memory and thus her own importance as the person closest to him, and by the considerable force of her own personality, Bandaranaike managed to remain at the helm of her party for over a quarter-

[9] Manor, *Sri Lanka in Change.*

century. She survived as leader despite two severe election defeats in 1965 and 1977, and so did her principal adversary, the UNP's Dudley Senanayake. In spite of his resignation in 1953, he was allowed to resume the UNP leadership after 1956, and he retained great power in the party even after election defeats in 1960 and 1970. This is particularly surprising as his party always had available an experienced and demonstrably more intelligent alternative, J. R. Jayewardene, who was a distant relative of Senanayake. Jayewardene took command of the UNP only in 1973, after Senanayake's death. The explanation for the survival of these supreme leaders despite reverses that would have ended the careers of counterparts in many other political systems is complex. Suffice it to say that it has much to do with the highly centralized and insubstantial character of the UNP and SLFP party organizations, with the similarly centralized nature of the political system,[10] and with a tradition of inordinate deference to top leaders and families[11] that attends these features.

ECONOMIC STAGNATION AND THE GROWTH OF ILLIBERAL POLITICS: 1959 TO 1977

The period between Bandaranaike's murder in 1959 and the election of a free-market–oriented UNP government in 1977 witnessed no major violent incidents between Sinhalese and Tamils. Economic concerns preoccupied people throughout most of this phase and a centrist UNP alternated in power with a Socialist SLFP and its various Marxist allies. It appeared for a time as if the Sinhalese had become sufficiently self-confident and the Tamils sufficiently accommodating that issues of Left and Right would supersede linguistic group rivalry for good. An abortive insurrection by leftist Sinhalese youths in 1971 at first appeared to confirm this view, but the state's ferocious reaction to it undermined both the liberal political traditions of the island and Sinhalese-Tamil amity, and eventually brought both of those issues back to center stage.

The economy suffered during the 1960s. The first half of the decade, in which the SLFP held power, saw state controls stifle trade, alienate Western donors and create stagnation. Thus, for example, per capita gross national product declined in 1964. Unemployment was a particular worry, partly because the Bandaranaike government after 1956 had promised so much to the common people and the island's youth. The UNP government of the latter half of the 1960s gave greater play to market forces, but remained committed to a mixed economy and to hugely expensive subsidies for rice and certain other commodities and services. Despite an increase in Western aid and a modest revival of economic growth, trade continued to deteriorate, and unemployment remained a severe problem since growth

[10] J. Manor, "The Failure of Political Integration in Sri Lanka," *Journal of Commonwealth and Comparative Politics*, xvii, 1 (March 1979), pp. 21–46; J. Jupp, *Sri Lanka: Third World Democracy* (London, 1978), chapters 3–4.
[11] J. Jiggins, *Caste and Family in the Politics of the Sinhalese, 1947–1976* (Cambridge, 1979).

mainly occurred in rice production, which could not absorb large numbers of educated youth.

In 1971, the Guevarist Janatha Vimukthi Peramuna (JVP or People's Liberation Front) mobilized Sinhalese youth in an attempt to overthrow the government of Sirimavo Bandaranaike, which had won the general election the previous year. The insurgents were poorly armed and organized, but they still scored widespread successes because the security forces were then substantial and unprepared. An acutely traumatized prime minister encouraged fierce retribution. It is likely that 5,000 people were killed—many by summary execution—and 15,000 were interned for long periods. The insurrection caused major damage to the economy and that, plus a huge increase in spending on the security forces, the nationalization of the plantation sector and new state controls, caused yet more economic hardship during the mid-1970s.

Equally serious was the postinsurgency erosion of liberal politics and relations with the Tamil minority. In 1972, a new constitution was introduced in an illiberal manner and it soon became clear that elections that were due in 1975 would be postponed by two years on the pretext that the new constitution gave parliament a five-year term. In 1973, the government took over a major newspaper group in order to silence the main remaining critical media voice. These changes were seen as signs of Bandaranaike's mounting insecurity, and the impression gained credence from her systematic packing of high government posts with her relatives.

That same sense of insecurity impelled her to send army units into the mainly Tamil Northern Province with orders to act forcefully to maintain order, despite the fact that there were few serious threats of disruption. Many Tamils were deeply unhappy about new legislation that discriminated in favor of Sinhalese in higher education, but it was as much the brutish behavior of the overwhelmingly Sinhalese army in the Northern Province that persuaded some young Tamils during the mid-1970s to take up arms and seek a separate state.

THE DESCENT INTO CIVIL WAR: 1977 AND AFTER

The story of the island's slide into civil war after 1977 is complex and ambiguous. The UNP government that ruled in this period contained both moderates and extremists on the issues of Sinhalese-Tamil relations. The liberalization of the economy after 1977 was partly intended to give Tamil entrepreneurs a more equal chance than when the Sinhalese-dominated state machinery had controlled so much within the economy. And the new constitution of 1978 was intended to allow Tamil votes to count for something in national politics. Previously Tamils had elected a few powerless representatives to a parliament dominated by a predominantly Sinhalese party. In 1978, a new Gaullist system made the great prize in the political system a powerful executive presidency to be won by a majority of votes at a direct popular election. Under the old system Sinhalese politicians had no reason not to adopt anti-Tamil themes. Under the new system, a moderate Sinhalese candidate might win with a minority of Sinhalese votes and solid support from Tamils against an anti-Tamil candidate who attracted most Sinhalese votes. On the other hand, the constitution's liberal elements were counterbalanced by potentially draconian provisions,[12] and the extreme social polarization since 1978 has enabled extremists to manipulate the constitution for illiberal, partisan and anti-Tamil purposes.

The first major test of moderates' power came in 1981 when they steered through parliament a law to create new development councils at the district (subprovincial) level. No representative institution had ever existed below the level of the national legislature in Sri Lanka,[13] mainly because Sinhalese regarded such bodies as undesirable concessions to the Tamil desire for more autonomy. The new councils were promised modest but significant powers in the hope of reducing the alienation of Tamils, but the president failed to deliver and Tamil suspicions deepened. Jayewardene lacked the power and possibly the inclination to force potent district councils upon his ministers, who retained far more power in practice than the change to a Gaullist system might suggest.

In 1982, the government shelved—at least for the time being—Sri Lanka's democratic traditions. A presidential election was held in which the principal opposition leader, Sirimavo Bandaranaike, continued to be banned from contesting or even from speaking in public. President Jayewardene easily defeated her party's nominee, a much lesser-known figure than she. Then instead of calling for the parliamentary election that many anticipated, Jayewardene, who knew that many of his legislators were unpopular, had a constitutional amendment passed prolonging the life of the parliament elected in 1977 by another six years. This amendment was put to the people in a referendum that was attended by such widespread abuses and illegalities, including arrests and harassment of opposition activists and thuggery to break up opposition rallies, that the vote endorsing the amendment cannot be taken seriously.[14]

In mid-1983, the deaths of 13 Sinhalese soldiers in a Tamil extremist ambush in the Northern Province triggered the most serious convulsion of anti-Tamil rioting ever to occur in the Sinhalese majority areas. Between 1,000 and 2,000 Tamils were killed and tens of thousands were made homeless. Army units and other government employees sometimes assisted the rioters in some areas, and an influential minister actively fomented and coordinated attacks on Tamil homes and property. President Jayewardene felt disinclined or, more likely, too vulnerable attacks by Sinhalese bigots to speak out forcefully against the mayhem as he had done in 1977. For many Tamils, this savage episode marked the parting of the ways with the Sinhalese.[15]

The period between 1983 and 1987 witnessed something close to a full-

---

[12] A. J. Wilson, *The Gaullist System in Asia: The Constitution of Sri Lanka (1978)* (London, 1980); J. Manor, "A New Political Order for Sri Lanka," *The World Today* (September 1979), pp. 377–86.
[13] Manor, "The Failure of Political Integration."
[14] "Priya Samarakone," "The Conduct."
[15] Manor, *Sri Lanka in Change,* part II.

scale civil war in the Northern and Eastern provinces. Armed Tamil separatists with bases in south India, tolerated but seldom supported by New Delhi, proved remarkably effective against the ill-disciplined, overwhelmingly Sinhalese army of Sri Lanka. The most powerful Tamil force, the Liberation Tigers of Tamil Eelam (LTTE), used guerrilla tactics and occasional acts of terrorism—that is, attacks on unarmed noncombatants—and took de facto control of much of the Northern Province. This situation, in which neither side was able to win an outright military victory, was deeply frustrating for the security forces who had already been demoralized by political interference. That and the inexperience of new recruits and the extreme anti-Tamil stereotypes that had gained currency in the Sinhalese community led government forces to massacre Tamil noncombatants on more than 30 occasions.[16] This made the security forces the main, though not the only, source of terrorist acts.

In 1985, New Delhi's efforts to resolve this crisis led to an agreement between the Indian prime minister and Sri Lanka's President Jayewardene. India was to curtail the use of bases on its soil and Sri Lanka was to negotiate in good faith with the Tamils in Thimpu, the capital of Bhutan. As negotiations unfolded, however, the Indians, who acted as evenhanded brokers, concluded that Sri Lanka was not seeking a settlement. They seemed instead to be playing for time while they built up their weapons, supplies and forces for a major attempt at outright military victory. This eventually put them in a position to retake control of the Northern Province, but it also shattered Indian confidence in Jayewardene.

Economy

It is well known that the Jayewardene government gave market forces far freer rein, seeking to emulate the mode of development of nations farther east in capitalist Asia. But we must avoid the simplistic notion that Sri Lanka was "trying to do a Singapore." The encouragement to foreign investments and tourism, and the creation of a free-trade zone, were important aspects of the new strategy but they were not central. At the core stood an attempt to revive agriculture—especially rice production—in order to reduce or eliminate heavy food imports.

Massive irrigation projects, high-yielding grains and fertilizers and steady increases in the guaranteed price for rice all raised production. By 1986, this made the island nearly self-sufficient in rice. This crucial element of the economic strategy was therefore reasonably successful, thanks (partly and ironically) to the redistribution of land under the left-leaning government of the early 1970s which laid the basis for the small peasant capitalism of the post-1977 period.

Other aspects of the economic strategy met with difficulties, however. The free-trade zone, where it was hoped that new industries based on cheap labor would spring up, proved a disappointment in an era in which investment tended to go into machinery and high technology. Potential foreign

[16] This is based on reports in *The Hindu* (Madras) and on the BBC External Services, and on interviews with a large number of persons including eyewitnesses and a senior Sri Lanka minister between 1983 and 1988.

investors were anxious about the mounting violence between the two linguistic groups. That also took a heavy toll on the tourist industry, which had performed impressively until the riots of 1983. All of this and low world prices for Sri Lanka's three traditional exports—rubber, coconut and especially tea, where its share of the world market has been falling—created major economic difficulties. Servicing the foreign debt, which was roughly six times greater in 1986 than in 1977, was consuming more than 35 percent of all foreign exchange earnings. Amid civil war, the defense budget grew to a level in 1987 ten times higher than in 1977. This meant that the great sacrifices of many people, especially those in urban and surrounding areas, did not yield benefits over the longer term. Soaring inflation through the 1980s—over 400 percent on many essentials (the result partly of cuts in government subsidies, but mostly of market forces)—was matched by wage increases of only about 50 percent. This caused enormous stress among members of the salaried middle class and desperation among many poorer urban dwellers. As early as 1980, charities were encountering widespread destitution in urban areas and conditions deteriorated thereafter.[17]

What impact have these economic trends had upon linguistic group conflict? It is impossible to "prove" any connection,[18] but strong suspicions are unavoidable concerning a link between the liberalization of the economy and anti-Tamil rioting in 1983. It is possible that some of the urban poor who faced extreme hardships may in their panic have responded more readily to the words of leaders, including some in the government, blaming Tamils for their troubles. We also know that in this intensely status-conscious society, confusion about one's status and about how to "get ahead" in the urban sector can drive people to extreme or eccentric behavior.[19] The decade after 1977 witnessed the most severe disruption of urban status hierarchies in the history of modern Sri Lanka. White-collar government jobs, which had long carried high prestige and reasonable rewards, were suddenly hardly adequate to sustain a family, let alone middle-class pretensions. Meanwhile, unskilled persons working in more prosperous sectors made huge gains, so that the night watchman at a large hotel earned more by 1980 than the inspector-general of police. It is not unreasonable to suspect that, amid such an inversion of roles, some of those who lost out might seize irrationally upon theories that claimed that the main beneficiaries were Tamils, whom many Sinhalese had long viewed as fiendishly clever in business.

THE EVENTS OF THE LATE 1980S

At this writing, we have inadequate evidence to construct a definitive account of the momentous events of the late 1980s, but a preliminary assess-

[17] Interview with representatives of various charities in Colombo, September 1980.
[18] See, for example, M. P. Moore, "Economic Liberalism versus Political Pluralism in Sri Lanka?" (typescript).
[19] G. Obeyesekere, "Social Change and the Deities," *Man*, xii (1977), pp. 377–96.

ment can be offered. The best starting point is early June 1987, by which time an offensive by Sri Lanka's security forces had met with unprecedented success in the mainly Tamil Northern Province. This forced the leading Tamil extremist group, the LTTE, to fall back into the city of Jaffna and its environs. After making this advance, government forces paused before a final assault on a city overcrowded with refugees. The 900,000 or more noncombatants there feared the possibility of heavy casualties at the hands of security forces that had often massacred unarmed civilians. Most people on both sides expected Jaffna to fall, and although Tamil militants would thereafter have remained capable of guerrilla and terrorist attacks, many people also expected this to provide something close to a military "solution" to the linguistic conflict. This inspired euphoria among Sinhalese chauvinists and dread among Tamil extremists.

The Indian authorities knew that civilians might be massacred and they signaled both their disquiet and their massive military superiority in the region by mounting an airlift of food to the besieged city. Then on June 17, Rajiv Gandhi was provided with a compelling reason to intervene further in Sri Lanka when his party suffered a crushing election defeat in the key state of Haryana. He was near desperation for an early triumph. Available evidence strongly suggests that New Delhi confronted Colombo with something close to an ultimatum. Well-placed sources say that India informed Sri Lanka's president that it was determined to guarantee the protection of Tamils throughout the island, and that it would soon send troops into Jaffna and the Northern Province, and into the heavily Tamil Eastern Province, whether or not Sri Lanka agreed. If Sinhalese civilians launched a pogrom against Tamils elsewhere in the island, India would send troops to stop it. Sri Lanka's president could either accept this on the pretense that it was freely agreed, or see large sections of his country seized by a foreign army, much superior to his own. He chose the former alternative.

The accord of July 29, 1987, was outrageous to many Sinhalese, coming at a time when they were feeling ebullient, since a military victory over the Tamil Tigers seemed at hand for the first time. The accord dismayed them by providing for the temporary unification of the mainly Tamil Northern Province and the Eastern Province, which has only a large minority of Tamils. A referendum was to be held before the end of 1988 in the Eastern Province alone to determine whether the union with the north should be permanent. This enabled Jayewardene to argue—correctly—that the unification would not last because the non-Tamil majority in the east would reject it. But this was too subtle a point for many Sinhalese who only saw him allowing the formation of what Tamil militants claimed as their separate homeland. Many Sinhalese also balked at the sudden presence of thousands of foreign troops in the north and east. This seemed to vindicate long-standing and unfounded fears about Indian designs on Sri Lanka's territory which had been whipped up for decades by Sinhalese politicians, including those now promoting the accord. Many Sinhalese also objected to the general amnesty for thousands of detained Tamils who had long been described as terrorists by the government-controlled media.

They were further inflamed by an exchange of letters between Jayewardene and Rajiv Gandhi in which Sri Lanka effectively promised, among other things, to stop employing foreign military and intelligence personnel and to deny the use of Trincomalee and other ports to foreign naval forces in a manner prejudicial to India's interests. These concessions had little to do with linguistic group conflict in Sri Lanka. They were attempts by India to intrude upon the island's sovereignty, as President Jayewardene and close allies implicitly conceded.

India had two sets of aims in pressing for the accord, and they were incompatible. On the one hand, it sought to end the armed conflict and to promote reconciliation in Sri Lanka. On the other, it sought to enhance its formidable strategic position in South Asia. In its eagerness to accomplish the latter purpose, it wrested concessions from Jayewardene that threatened India's first aim by bringing the accord into further disrepute among the island's Sinhalese majority.[20] And despite the armed conflict between Tamil militants and the Indian army that eventually occurred, the main threat to the accord has always come from the Sinhalese side. This was apparent from the rioting by Sinhalese after the announcement of the accord, which claimed more than 20 lives before a harsh clampdown that entailed the detention without trial of several thousand Sinhalese. It was also apparent in the attack on Rajiv Gandhi by a member of the Sri Lankan honor guard after the signing of the accord in Colombo, an act that bespoke opposition to the accord in the security forces that had caused India to extend assurances to Jayewardene that it would intervene if necessary to thwart coup attempts. Sinhalese extremists then threw grenades into a UNP meeting in parliament on August 18. One minister died, several were severely injured and Jayewardene had an extremely fortunate escape. Thereafter, the insurrectionary JVP—Marxists turned communalists—continued to use anti-Tamil extremism and a campaign of bombing and assassination to seek to topple the regime.

Sinhalese extremists ignored several gains that the accord offered. India promised action to prevent its territory from being used to supply and train Tamil militants. In late 1987, after the Tamil Tigers had resumed bloodletting against Sinhalese, the Indian army mounted a major offensive that came close to breaking their military power and reduced them to guerrilla and terrorist acts. The accord also reassured major aid donors about the likelihood of reconciliation in Sri Lanka. But these and other gains did not suffice in 1987 to win popular support for the accord among the Sinhalese majority. Decades of parochialist rhetoric and years of intense polarization during a bloody civil war had created too much suspicion for that.

The intervention of India was productive since it probably averted a major massacre of Tamils[21] and led to an accord that offered Sri Lanka its first real hope of reconciliation since 1981. And yet the ability of both

---

[20] See, for example, the use made of these concessions by Anura Bandaranaike, an opposition leader.

[21] The Indian peacekeeping force has been falsely accused of atrocities against Tamil noncombatants by both the Sri Lanka government and Tamil extremists—both of whom, ironically, have reason to want to discredit the Indians.

Tamil and Sinhalese extremists to mount guerrilla and terrorist attacks was demonstrated repeatedly.

The atmosphere engendered by such violence naturally creates problems for the revival of open, representative politics—a revival that would be far from assured even in the absence of violence. Sri Lanka has now experienced two regimes that prolonged their time in power by dubious means. After Bandaranaike's government did so in 1972, Jayewardene's government failed to lift controls on the press, banned small opposition parties on spurious grounds, made heavy-handed use of the Prevention of Terrorism Act, manipulated the constitution for narrowly partisan purposes and condoned the involvement of a cabinet minister in fomenting the anti-Tamil riots of 1983. It condoned massacres of Tamil civilians by the security forces and used police harassment and systematic thuggery to intimidate the opposition to ensure a "Yes" vote in the 1982 referendum.[22]

Many people in Sri Lanka value its liberal democratic traditions and hope to see them revived. But there are compelling reasons why that may not occur. Even before the accord with India, many UNP members of parliament were patently unpopular with their constituents after abusing their authority for a decade, and the unpopularity of the accord gave them another good reason to avoid consulting the electorate. It is a cruel irony that the island's leaders may face a choice between elections and an accord that offers the only solid hope of social cohesion.

FURTHER READING

de Silva, K. M. *A History of Sri Lanka*. (London and Delhi: Oxford University Press, 1981.

————. *Sri Lanka: A Survey*. London and Delhi: Oxford University Press, 1976.

Fernando, Tissa, and Kearney, Robert N., eds. *Modern Sri Lanka: A Society in Transition*. Syracuse, New York: Syracuse University Press, 1979.

Jiggins, Janice. *Caste and Family in the Politics of the Sinhalese, 1947–1976*. Cambridge and New York: Cambridge University Press, 1979.

Jupp, James. *Sri Lanka: Third World Democracy*. London and Totowa, New Jersey: Cass, 1978.

Kearney, R. N., *Communalism and Language in the Politics of Ceylon*. Durham, North Carolina: Duke University Press, 1967.

————. *The Politics of Ceylon (Sri Lanka)*. Ithaca, New York: Cornell University Press, 1973.

————. *Trade Unions and Politics in Ceylon*. Berkeley: University of California Press, 1971.

Manor, James. ed. *Sri Lanka in Change and Crisis*. London: Croom Helm, 1984.

Moore, Mick. *The State and Peasant Politics in Sri Lanka*. Cambridge and New York: Cambridge University Press, 1985.

Phadnis, Urmila. *Sri Lanka*. New Delhi: National Bank Trust, 1973.

Roberts, Michael, ed. *Collective Identities, Nationalisms, and Protest in Modern Sri Lanka*. Colombo: Marga Institute, 1979.

[22] Manor, *Sri Lanka in Change*, especially chapters by "Priya Samarakone" and Obeyesekere.

Tambiah, S. J. *Sri Lanka: Ethnic Fratricide and the Dismantling of Democracy*. Chicago: University of Chicago Press, 1986.

Wilson, A. Jeyaratnam. *The Gaullist System in Asia: The Constitution of Sri Lanka (1978)*. London: Macmillan, 1980.

———. *Politics in Sri Lanka, 1947–1979*. London: Macmillan, 1979.

TAIWAN

YANGSUN CHOU AND ANDREW J. NATHAN

Han Chinese began moving to the island of Taiwan from the mainland more than 2,000 years ago. From the 17th century on, most of the settlers came from the nearby southeastern provinces of Fukien (Fujian) and Kwangtung (Guangdong); the Taiwanese dialect continues today to be similar to that of Fukien. The mainland authorities paid little attention to the island for centuries. During the 17th century Dutch and Spanish explorers established short-lived colonial regimes. It was from Portuguese sailors that the island acquired the other name by which it is well known—Formosa, meaning beautiful.

In the late Ming, Cheng Ch'eng-kung established a secure military base on the island. He resisted invasion by the new Manchu (Ch'ing) authorities and launched an unsuccessful counterattack on the mainland in hopes of restoring the Ming dynasty. In 1683 Ch'ing forces defeated Cheng's remnant troops and established Ch'ing rule over the island. During the next two centuries the Han residents of Taiwan rose several times in rebellion but did not succeed in throwing off Ch'ing rule.

The Japanese invasion of Taiwan in 1874 and the Sino-French War of 1884–85 made the Ch'ing rulers in Peking newly aware of the importance of the southern and southeastern portions of the empire. The government established a Naval Yamen, separated Taiwan from Fukien to make it an independent province and appointed former Huai Army commander Liu Ming-ch'uan as the province's first governor. Liu worked actively to develop the province's economy and its military forces, inviting foreign experts to help train the provincial troops.

In the 1880s the number of Han settlers in Taiwan reached approximately 2.5 million. Clashes increased between the settlers and the original natives of the island, today conventionally referred to as aborigines or "mountain people," who had been forced out of the lowland areas and into the mountains. History records 40 military clashes between Chinese troops and aborigines during Liu Ming-ch'uan's governorship (1886–90), with heavy losses on both sides. Liu was replaced in 1890 when his patron, Li Hung-chang, was out of favor. Three years after his departure the 42-mile/ 68-km. Taipei-Hsinchu railway that he had labored to establish was opened to traffic.

In 1895, Taiwan was ceded to Japanese rule in the Treaty of Shimonoseki, which ended the Sino-Japanese War. During their 50 years of rule the Japanese developed the educational and transportation infrastructures of the island and oriented its economy to the export of agricultural products and coal to Japan. They pursued a policy of full assimilation, outlawing the use of Chinese in schools and in publications. Numerous uprisings of the Taiwanese population were unsuccessful.

When Japan was defeated in 1945 Taiwan was returned to Chinese sovereignty in keeping with the commitments made by the Allied leaders at the Cairo Conference. The new governor, Ch'en Yi, and his troops were at first welcomed as liberators by the native population. But demoralized by years of war, inflation and civil war they soon proved brutal and corrupt. An uprising of the Taiwanese population that began February 28, 1947, was quickly and brutally suppressed, leaving a strong legacy of tension between Taiwanese and mainlanders that continues to influence Taiwan politics today. With the loss of the Chinese mainland to the Chinese Communists in 1949, the entire Kuomintang, or Nationalist, regime removed itself to Taiwan.

Claiming to be the legitimate government of all China under the name Republic of China, the Kuomintang regime set about consolidating its rule over the island bastion and strengthening the local economy as the basis for an eventual return to the mainland. The return to the mainland has not taken place; instead, the processes of economic and political development led in the late 1980s to a bold series of political reforms whose eventual impact on Taiwan-mainland relations is incalculable.

1950–85: LIBERALIZATION OF A LENINIST PARTY-STATE

The Kuomintang (KMT) had been shaped by its founder, Sun Yat-sen, under Comintern tutelage in the 1920s as a Leninist-style party. The basic party structure established then endures today: selective membership recruitment; a revolutionary and nationalist ideology; a centralized decision-making structure under a Central Committee; a policymaking Central Standing Committee and a policy-implementing secretariat with organization, intelligence and propaganda departments; control of the army through a political cadre system; maintenance of a youth league; leadership over the policies and personnel of the state apparatus; and—until recently—intolerance for the existence of any significant opposition party.

From the beginning, the Leninist structure stood in tension with non-Leninist strains in the party's tradition—a fact that made the KMT different from other Leninist parties. Under its ideology, Sun Yat-sen's Three Principles of the People, the KMT did not define its role in terms of the struggle between progressive and reactionary classes. Instead, it justified itself as a moral and technocratic vanguard capable of guiding national construction and gradually introducing full constitutional democracy. After its break with the Chinese Communist party (CCP) in 1927 the KMT adopted an ideology of anticommunism, with procapitalist domestic policies and a pro-West foreign policy, and all of this further opened it to the influence of non-Leninist ideas. In short, the KMT was a Leninist party without a Marxist ideology.

Sun's idea of tutelary democracy required the KMT to make progress away from party dictatorship toward constitutional democracy. In 1947, the Nationalist government promulgated a new democratic constitution, which followed the regime to Taiwan and remains in effect today. But from 1949 to 1987 some constitutional provisions were replaced by the "Temporary Provisions Effective During the Period of Communist Rebellion." Under the authority of these provisions, the regime implemented a limited regime of martial law *(chieh-yen)*. Martial-law regulations included restrictions on political organizing, demonstrations and other activities, and also publication control measures, border control measures and authorization for trials in military courts of certain defense-related and other serious charges.[1]

Starting in 1950, gradual steps were taken to implement local self-rule at the provincial level and below while maintaining the national government structure brought over from the mainland. In that year the Taiwan Provincial Assembly was established, its members indirectly elected by municipal- and county-level legislators for two-year terms. In 1954 for the first time, the provincial assemblymen were directly elected. In 1969, elections were held for Taiwan delegates to the central government's Legislative Yuan and National Assembly, and indirectly for the Control Yuan. The majority of seats in these houses, however, continued to be held by mainland delegates who had been elected in 1947. By 1986, only 1,156 of the original 4,275 delegates to these three bodies were still serving (the others had remained on the mainland or died after coming to Taiwan), and their average age exceeded 70.[2]

Local elections brought a number of non-KMT politicians into the political arena, but it was not until the rise of the nonparty opposition *(tang-wai,* hereafter TW) in the late 1970s that the KMT faced a strong, quasi-organized opposition. The one possible exception to this statement was the abortive formation of a China Democratic party (Chung-kuo min-chu tang, CDP) by Lei Chen and several other politicians in 1960. But the regime's rapid and severe response to this attempt showed that its Leninist instincts remained strong, and the CDP dissolved with Lei Chen's arrest.

By the 1970s economic growth had brought major changes to Taiwan society. The basis for rapid economic development was laid by a successful land reform in the early 1950s. Based on the lesson of its failure in mainland China, from 1949 to 1953 the KMT pushed forward a series of agricultural reforms, including rent reduction and the Land-to-the-Tiller Act,

[1] *Shih-pao chou-k'an,* No. 86 (October 18–24, 1986), pp. 8–13. Hereafter abbreviated SPCK. This is the New York edition of the popular Taiwan newsweekly, *Shih-pao hsin-wen chou-k'an.* Also see Hungdah Chiu and Jyh-pin Fa, "Law and Justice since 1966," in James C. Hsiung et al., eds., *Contemporary Republic of China: The Taiwan Experience, 1950–1980,* paperback ed. (New York: The American Association for Chinese Studies, 1981), pp. 314–30.
[2] SPCK, No. 85 (October 11–17, 1986), p. 31.

in order to solve the problem of rural inequality. By the time land reform was completed, the great landlord class had sunk into social oblivion.

At the same time, the government implemented an import substitution policy, including customs duties and import control. In 1961, the government began to carry out a series of industrial policies promoting export orientation. Beginning in 1965, export-processing zones were established in the major harbor areas in order to import foreign technical skills and industrial equipment and export manufactured products to foreign countries.

Thanks to these successful economic policies, Taiwan became a prominent model of industrial development. Average annual per capita income increased from U.S.$50 in 1941 to $3,175 in 1985 and over $6,000 in 1987 (with a population of 19.5 million in 1987.)[3] The average annual rate of economic growth was 11 percent from 1964 to 1973 and 7.7 percent from 1974 to 1984.[4] Despite increasingly severe export competition from mainland China (in terms of labor costs) and South Korea (in terms of high-technology goods), Taiwan's 1985 exports totaled almost $34 billion, with the United States taking 48 percent of the total and Japan 11 percent.[5] The egalitarian policies pursued under Sun Yat-sen's principle of "People's Livelihood" had prevented extreme polarization of wealth: the total income of the richest fifth of the population was only 4.4 times that of the poorest fifth.[6] The middle class now constitutes an estimated 30 to 50 percent of the total population. More than 46 percent of the population has attended at least junior middle school.[7]

While economic and social change created a more sophisticated public, the diplomatic and foreign-trade situations provided salient political issues. Taiwan's diplomatic isolation steadily increased after its expulsion from the United Nations in 1971, withdrawal of recognition by Japan in 1972 and the breaking of formal diplomatic relations by the United States in 1979. Except for the city-states of Singapore and Hong Kong, Taiwan's economy is the most trade-dependent in the world. Such issues as the overconcentration of export markets, lack of diplomatic relations with most countries in the world and excessive import dependency on a few suppliers played an increasingly prominent role in electoral campaigns and legislative debates.

The emergence of the TW can be dated from the 1977 election, when nonparty politicians won 22 seats in the provincial assembly and four posts as mayor or county magistrate. In the following year the term *"tang-wai"* itself came into common use when Huang Hsin-chieh, Shih Ming-teh and others organized a *"Tang-wai* campaign assistance corps" (Tang-wai chu-

---

[3] *Tai-wan ching-chi* (Taiwan Economy Monthly) (Taichung: Taiwan Provincial Government), September 25, 1987, pp. 107—19. On development policy generally, see Thomas B. Gold, *State and Society in the Taiwan Miracle* (Armonk, N.Y.: M. E. Sharpe, Inc., 1986).
[4] *Chung-kuo lun-t'an* (Taipei), No. 262 (August 25, 1986), p. 39.
[5] SPCK, No. 82 (September 20—26, 1986), p. 54.
[6] *Taiwan Statistical Data Book,* p. 60.
[7] *Chung-hua min-kuo t'ung-chi t'i-yao* (Taipei: Hsing-cheng yuan, 1983), pp. 16—18.

hsuan t'uan) to coordinate the campaigns of non-KMT candidates through-out the island. In subsequent elections held in 1980, 1981, 1983 and 1985, the KMT was generally able to get about 70 percent of the vote and TW and independent politicians about 30 percent.

Until 1986, the TW was not a party but a loosely knit movement consisting primarily of small personality-based factions absorbed in large part in local issues. What drew these factions together was dissatisfaction with the ruling party's position on the interlocked issues of Taiwan's future in the international arena and the role of the KMT in the Taiwan political system. Both the candidates and the electoral supporters of the TW consist predominantly (although not exclusively) of Taiwanese. This is not surprising since 85 percent of the island's population of approximately 19 million are conventionally counted as Taiwanese (of these, four-fifths speak the Taiwanese variant of the Fukienese dialect and one-fifth speak the Hakka dialect; the aboriginal population constitutes less than 2 percent of the population). Under Taiwan's electoral system by far the majority of the offices open for electoral competition are at the provincial level and below. Although both the KMT and the state apparatus have been heavily Taiwanized, both the highest levels of the KMT itself and the electoral offices at the national level remain mainlander-dominated.

The character of the TW as a predominantly Taiwanese political force in a mainlander-ruled polity naturally made the issue of Taiwan's relationship to the mainland central to TW politics. The KMT defines Taiwan's status as part of China as being settled beyond discussion and has always treated advocacy of Taiwan independence as a crime. Opposition politicians are ranged along a radical–moderate continuum. Few Taiwanese favor reunification with the mainland. But the moderates have been willing to forgo open challenge to the KMT's rule and to its one-China ideology, while the radicals advocated some form of Taiwan independence without KMT rule.

The radicals emerged as a strong force in the 1977 Chung-li Incident, a violent demonstration about alleged election tampering in Chung-li city. They showed still greater strength in 1979, when they mobilized a series of demonstrations that culminated on December 10 in a violent clash between demonstrators and police that became known as the Kaohsiung Incident. In response, the government arrested Shih Ming-teh, Huang Hsin-chieh and more than 60 others and closed the offices of *Mei-li-tao* (Formosa) magazine, the organization behind the demonstrations.

Beginning in 1984, TW politicians produced a series of magazines that directed strong attacks at government policies and leaders on a wide range of policy and personal issues. The government banned and closed many of the magazines but the TW evaded control by reopening them under new names and by publishing them in the disguised form of monthly or weekly book series.

Moderates continued to dominate among opposition politicians on the island (the radicals' main base is overseas), but the exigencies of Taiwanese politics imparted an increasingly militant flavor to the moderates' tactics. Despite the successes of KMT rule and the amelioration of mainlander-Taiwanese social relations, Taiwanese voters still had deep-seated feelings of having been colonized, and responded emotionally to the martyr symbolism around such jailed leaders as the Kaohsiung Eight. In this political culture, mass rallies, emotional rhetoric and confrontational demonstrations were tools of electoral survival even for policy moderates. Even while adopting such tactics to some degree, moderates like K'ang Ning-hsiang suffered constant criticism for being too soft on the KMT. The fractious Taiwanese political style alarmed many mainlanders, outside as well as inside the ruling party, who were used to a more courtly, controlled manner of maneuvering. Ample room existed in the mid-1980s for a tragic misunderstanding between the two political cultures, which might have led to a vicious circle of confrontation and repression.

1986–88: FROM LIBERALIZATION TO DEMOCRATIZING REFORM

In contrast to South Korea under Park and the Philippines under Marcos, however, where challenges to the regime were met with repression leading to further polarization, the response of the KMT to the growth and increasing militance of the opposition until late 1985 was a mix of selective repression with institutional liberalization. The regime tried to repress the radical wing of the TW while stepping up recruitment of Taiwanese into the party, army and government, including some in high posts, and gradually liberalizing electoral institutions and the media. Edwin A. Winckler has referred to this process as a movement toward "soft authoritarianism."[8] Despite opposition from the security bureaucracy and many mainlanders, President Chiang Ching-kuo had been trying to accommodate the TW as it developed. As early as 1978, he directed KMT officials to meet with TW figures under the auspices of a prominent newspaper publisher, Wu San-lien.[9] But such contacts stopped after the TW's relatively poor performance in the 1983 elections.

A bold new course of reform began in 1986. The explanation for the change of course lies in large part with President and party Chairman Chiang Ching-kuo, who occupied a position of supreme influence in the Taiwan political system similar to that of Deng Xiaoping on the mainland. Both the initiative for the reform and the power to implement it over substantial intraparty opposition lay with him.

The long-term impetus came from three factors described earlier: the KMT's ideological commitment to constitutional democracy; the economic, social and political maturation of the population; and the increasing electoral appeal of the TW. A more immediate motive was the succession problem. In 1986 Chiang was 76 years old and suffering from diabetes. Although he had a formal successor as president in Vice-President Lee Teng-hui, much of his power was personal rather than institutional, and there was no one in the senior ranks of government who appeared likely to be

[8] Edwin A. Winckler, "Institutionalization and Participation on Taiwan: From Hard to Soft Authoritarianism?" *The China Quarterly* 99 (September 1984), pp. 481–99.

[9] Interview, K'ang Ning-hsiang, Taipei, January 2, 1986.

able to replace him as the linchpin of cooperation between party conservatives and liberals and among party, state, army and security officials. The president apparently felt that difficult and controversial but necessary reforms should be undertaken before he passed from the scene rather than be left for his less well-equipped successors to handle. Moreover, reform could contribute to a smoother transition by increasing the legitimacy of the regime, reducing the motivation for the population to become involved in political disorders and setting in place improved mechanisms for long-term recruitment of new leaders at all levels.

Additional concerns motivating reform were a series of internal and foreign shocks in 1985 and 1986. These included the revelation that the 1984 assassination of U.S. businessman and writer Henry Liu (Liu Yi-liang, also known as Chiang Nan) had been carried out at the behest of the head of the Defense Ministry Intelligence Bureau; the bankruptcy of Taipei's Tenth Credit Cooperative due to mismanagement by officials with ties to KMT politicians; and the defeat suffered by the government in its policy of resistance to the "unification diplomacy" of the People's Republic of China (PRC) when officials of the state-owned airline were forced into face-to-face negotiations with PRC airline representatives in order to arrange the return of a hijacked cargo plane and crew from Guangzhou.

Such incidents suggested the need to revitalize the ruling party and government. On the international scene, in addition, political reform offered the possibility of enhancing the image of a regime that is especially vulnerable to foreign opinion because of its trade dependence and diplomatic isolation. Especially in the United States, where human rights issues exert a substantial influence on foreign policy, the maintenance of martial law had long been a public-relations embarrassment for Taiwan's supporters— a fact often brought to the president's attention by sympathetic high-level American visitors.

At the Third Plenum of the KMT's 12th Central Committee in March 1986, Chiang reminded the delegates of the party's long-standing goal of implementing constitutional democracy and said that the time had come to make further progress toward this goal. After the session he appointed a 12-man task force of Standing Committee members to suggest reform measures. This powerful temporary body became a virtual politburo above the Standing Committee, entrusted with the power to establish the party's reform strategy in line with Chiang's wishes. In June the task force reported a bold, although vague, six-point reform proposal that called, among other things, for renewing the membership of the central representative organs (the Legislative and Control Yuans and the National Assembly), simplifying the national security laws and providing a legal basis for formation of new civic associations, including political parties.

The fact that an important election was scheduled for December 1986 to fill supplementary seats in the Legislative Yuan and National Assembly meant that the reform spotlight fell first on the long-standing ban on the formation of new political parties. While the KMT's task force was still drafting detailed proposals and the party ban thus remained in legal effect, the leading TW politicians on September 28, 1986, announced the formation of a political party, which they named the Democratic Progressive party (Min-chu chin-pu tang, DPP), to contest the elections. On the key question of Taiwan's future, the new party's program called for "self-determination" by ballot of "all residents of Taiwan." As its party flag, the DPP adopted a white cross against a green background, with a silhouette of the island of Taiwan in the middle of the cross, symbols that bear no visible relationship to those of the KMT or the Republic of China. Although the term "independence" was avoided, the party's position appeared to contradict the KMT's insistence that the status of Taiwan as a part of China is already settled.

The DPP immediately came under intense pressure from the KMT to define the meaning it gave to "self-determination" and to clarify the policy and organizational relationship between itself and the Taiwan independence movement. Taiwanese organizations overseas, such as the influential, tacitly proindependence Formosan Association for Public Affairs (FAPA) in the United States, demanded that the DPP establish overseas branches. (This demand was ultimately refused.) The PRC government as well was intensely concerned with the meaning of self-determination. In keeping with its United Front policy, Beijing welcomed the formation of the new party but reiterated its opposition to Taiwan independence. For Taiwan's main trade partner and ally, the United States, the prospect of a vocal pro-independence force on the island was also unwelcome, chiefly because of the disturbance it could cause in American-PRC relations.

DPP politicians insisted for the record that these concerns were misplaced. Self-determination, they argued, meant simply that the residents of the island should be consulted in any decision concerning its future, rather than having their fate determined by the KMT, the CCP and the United States, without their participation. However, the concept contradicted the idea, dear to both the KMT and the CCP, that the status of Taiwan is already settled beyond further discussion, and left room for advocacy of independence should the party wish to do so in the future.

Although illegal, the DDP was permitted to contest the December 6 elections without government interference, while the authorities worked to draft the new civic organizations law that would legalize it retroactively. The election, which went off peacefully, confirmed both the dominance of the KMT and the strength of the DPP.[10] The results must be interpreted in light of the structure of the Taiwan political system, which places limits on campaign publicity, expenditures and access to the mass media.[11] Despite these disadvantages, the DPP won 18.90 percent of the vote in the National Assembly election, electing 11 of its 25 candidates, and 22.17 percent in the Legislative Yuan election, electing 12 of its 19 candidates.

[10] SPCK, No. 94 (December 13–19, 1986), pp. 3–25.
[11] See "Elections in Taiwan, December 6, 1986: Rules of the Game for the 'Democratic Holiday'," An Asia Watch Report, Washington, D.C.: Asia Watch, November 1986.

Counting independent and minor-party votes, the total non-KMT poll was a bit above 30 percent of the vote. [12]

The strength of militant sentiment in the electorate was shown by the overwhelming victories won by some of the more radical DPP candidates. The largest number of votes of any candidate island-wide was won by Hsu Jung-shu, wife of Chang Chün-hung, in prison because of his participation in the Kaohsiung Incident. The second heaviest vote-getter was Hung Ch'i-ch'ang, a former member of the radical Editors' and Writers' Association. The fourth largest number of votes went to Hsu Kuo-t'ai, brother of exiled radical TW leader Hsu Hsin-liang.

Some moderate DPP leaders, however, also fared well. Senior TW politician K'ang Ning-hsiang, who had suffered a surprise defeat in his run for the Legislative Yuan in the 1983 election, was resoundingly reelected from Taipei city. Other important moderate DPP victors were Huang Huang-hsiung, Ch'iu Lien-hui and You Ch'ing.

On the other hand, the strength of the KMT showing paid tribute to that party's deep organizational base and to the preference of many among Taiwan's affluent population for continuity and stability. Among KMT candidates, strong showings were made by candidates with fresh images, reform leanings or athletic, show-business or academic credentials. The outstanding example was the victory of reformist Chao Shao-k'ang, a former university professor and the top vote-getter in Taipei city.

Buoyed by its good performance in the December 1986 elections and by the favorable domestic and international response to reform, the KMT announced a further series of major reform steps in 1987, as follows:

- On July 15, 1987, the government announced the lifting of martial law. This meant, among other things, that the powers of the Garrison Command were diminished and that civilians could no longer be tried in military courts. Seven of the Kaohsiung Eight, who had been sentenced under martial law in connection with the December 10, 1979, incident, were released, leaving only Shih Ming-teh in prison. Martial law was replaced by a National Security Law that provided, among other things, police powers to patrol mountain and border areas. Despite vocal objections from the opposition, the National Security Law forbade all political activity in violation of what became known as the "three principles": support for the constitution; opposition to communism; and opposition to "splitting the national territory" (i.e., Taiwan independence).
- Although the lifting of martial law ended the legal basis for the ban on new political parties, the formation of new parties remained formally illegal pending adopting of a Civic Organizations Law. However, the government did not proceed against either the DPP or several other new parties. A draft civic organizations law was approved by the KMT and was under consideration by the Legislative Yuan in 1987. It would require all political parties to uphold the three principles—a provision to which the DPP objected because this requirement was already provided

[12] *Chung-yang jih-pao* (International Edition), December 8, 1986, p. 1.

for in the National Security Law. The government showed its resolution on the question of forbidding advocacy of Taiwan independence by rear-resting two ex-prisoners, one for advocating and the other for allowing the advocacy of Taiwan independence at a public meeting.

- The Government Information Bureau announced in September 1987 that the ban on the establishment of new newspapers would be lifted as of January 1, 1988. This gave the opposition the opportunity to publish their own newspapers.

- For years, some opposition politicians have pressed for modification of the government's no-contacts policy toward mainland China, arguing that establishment of transport, commercial, postal and other links would help counter Taiwan's diplomatic isolation. In October 1987, the KMT announced new regulations permitting civilians to go to the mainland for the purpose of visiting relatives, and it was expected that other people-to-people contacts would follow, eventually including the legitimation of the already substantial mainland-Taiwan trade and investment.

- The KMT under its new secretary-general, Lee Huan, announced reforms in its recruitment and training policies. In order to increase its popularity with workers and peasants and thus compete more effectively in elections, the KMT will emphasize its advocacy of welfare benefits for workers, peasants, veterans and aborigines. The party's internal decision-making structure is to be democratized. The policy of Taiwanization, or recruiting and promoting Taiwanese members, is to be speeded up. At bell-wether National Taiwan University the party branch headquarters were moved off campus, signaling a gradual reduction in direct political involvement in higher education.

- Although specific measures have not yet been devised, some way is being sought to solve the problem of superannuation of members of the three national representative bodies—the National Assembly, Legislative Yuan and Control Yuan. In one way or another most of the delegates elected in 1947 are expected to retire and be replaced by newly elected delegates. Intense party competition for these seats is predicted.

THE TREND TOWARD POLITICAL PLURALIZATION: PARTIES AND INTEREST GROUPS

The reforms gave impetus to the development of new political parties and interest groups. Two "friendly parties," the China Youth (CYP) and the Democratic Socialist party (DSP), have been tolerated by the KMT since the 1940s. The CYP has a membership of some 2–3,000 and has its greatest strength among local politicians in southern Taiwan. Some of its younger members have tried to form links with moderate liberal and anticommunists on the island and in overseas Chinese communities, hoping to serve as a bridge with democratic forces on the mainland and to avoid what they believe would be the disaster of Taiwan independence. The growth of the DSP has been blocked by inner-party factionalism. Its membership does not exceed 1,000.

After the establishment of the DPP in September 1986, five more new parties emerged. They were:

- The China Freedom party (CFP) a strongly anticommunist right-wing party composed largely of post-1950 refugees from the mainland. The CFP is allied with two other right-wing organizations, the All-People's Patriotic Association and the Anti-Communist Patriotic Front.
- The China Democratic Justice party, established in Kaohsiung by a dissident faction of the CYP. Most of its members are peasants and businessmen from the south of Taiwan.
- The Democratic Liberal party, organized by a small group of local politicians from Kaohsiung, most of them businessmen who were peripheral members of the moderate TW.
- The People's party, based in Taipei, established by a group of retired generals. Concerned mostly with economic policy, the party has expressed support for free trade and for social-welfare policies.
- The Labor party, established in November 1987 by some former TW leaders and socialist intellectuals. Modeled on Western European Democratic Socialist parties, it is the first party in Taiwan run internally on principles of direct democracy. It regards itself as a branch of the international labor movement and advocates welfare statism, environmentalism, feminism, minority rights and industrial democracy. It is likely to be the most serious political competitor to the KMT and the DPP among the smaller parties.

By late 1988, the DPP itself remained a loose combination of elite factions of the former TW movement. It has suffered from continuous intra-party disputes and splits. Two of the newly released Kaohsiung Eight refused to join the DPP because they disagreed with the party's position on Taiwan independence and because they were dissatisfied with the party's power structure; the Labor party was organized by a breakaway DPP member, Wang Yi-hsiung, a former law professor. In late 1987, a conflict took shape between DPP moderates and radicals calling for a revision of the party constitution to openly advocate an independent Taiwan. DPP moderates warned that this would bring the party into direct collision with both the KMT's "three principles" (upholding the constitution, opposing communism, anti-Taiwan independence) and the anti-independence stance of the PRC, with damaging consequences for the processes of domestic reform and Taiwan-PRC rapprochement. In the end, Taiwan independence was not included in the constitution, but the Second Party Congress passed a resolution defending "the freedom of the people to advocate Taiwan independence." The two factions also clashed over the election of a party chairman for 1988, finally compromising on Yao Chia-wen, a lawyer who had recently been released from prison after serving time as a member of the Kaohsiung Eight.

In addition to the formation of political parties, reform gave impetus to the growth of five social movements that had emerged during the previous decade:

- Since the 1950s, labor had been tightly controlled by the security-intelligence system of the party and state apparatus. Demonstrations and strikes were prohibited under martial law. In the December 1986 election KMT candidates who were themselves officials of the officially approved labor unions sustained a surprise defeat in the labor constituency (one of several occupational constituencies that elect delegates directly to the Legislative Yuan and National Assembly). Since the lifting of martial law, a number of independent workers' associations have been organized and a series of strikes and demonstrations have occurred. The newly established Labor party has attempted to mobilize these newly emerging labor forces, while both the KMT and the DPP have been working to forge policies attractive to labor and to recruit new party members among union officials.

- Since the mid-1970s, a growing student movement has challenged KMT control of campus life, calling for direct election of student government leaders, an end to censorship of student publications, recognition of students' rights to participate in off-campus politics, reform of the party-military-intelligence complex on campus (especially of the role of military instructors who have been overseers of student life and extracurricular activities) and faculty participation in campus decision-making. Led by students at the elite National Taiwan University, the movement became increasingly militant in 1986–87, won seats in student government and gained a number of concessions from the campus administration, including the removal of KMT branch offices from the campus, downgrading of the role of military instructors and modification of the system of censorship of student publications. A revision of the University Law was undertaken by the Legislative Yuan; the revised law was expected to give more autonomy to each university and to increase the powers of faculties in university administration. Student leaders are increasingly closely linked not only to the KMT, as in the past, but also to the DPP and Labor party.
- The Presbyterian Church is the largest Protestant denomination in Taiwan, with a membership of about 200,000, and has long been closely affiliated with the TW. In 1971, the church published a declaration to urge the government to establish a "new and independent state" on Taiwan. In the fall of 1987, over 100 Presbyterian ministers demonstrated in Taipei for the freedom to advocate Taiwan independence and for the release of the two ex-prisoners who, as mentioned above, had been rearrested for such advocacy. A second dissident church movement in Taiwan is that of the New Testament Church (Hsin-yueh chiao-hui), a radical fundamentalist Christian group with a largely lower-middle class constituency, which has branches in Singapore, Hong Kong and many Chinatowns in the United States and elsewhere. Some years ago this church claimed to have founded a Zion on a mountain in southern Taiwan. But the security authorities refused their application to establish a religious colony in this location. After the collapse of negotiations, violence occurred between the believers and the police. Although the government finally bowed to the church's demands for space on the mountain, tensions between the two continue.
- The last several years have seen a rapid proliferation of local environmental protection movements, taking advantage of political liberalization to

831

respond to pollution problems that have become increasingly severe as a consequence of rapid economic development. In 1987, after over a year of harsh struggle, a "self-help" (tzu-li chiu-chi) movement in the west-coast town of Lukang, aided by students and politicians from around the island, defeated a proposal by the DuPont Corporation to construct a chemical plant. Elsewhere, environmentalists have targeted and in some cases defeated construction projects of the state-owned China Petroleum Co. and other local and multinational firms. So far the self-help organizations have been local and nonpartisan, without strong links to either the KMT or the DPP, but they are a major target of Labor party mobilization.

- The aborigines, who comprise about one-and-a-half percent of the Taiwan population, are supposed to be the beneficiaries of a government policy to guarantee their welfare. However, their educational and living standards remain low. Most members of the younger generation have moved to the cities where they work in low-paying and low-prestige jobs. Only the Labor party has shown an interest in this constituency.

TAIWAN AFTER CHIANG CHING-KUO

President Chiang Ching-kuo died in Taipei on January 13, 1988. He was succeeded by his vice-president, Lee Teng-hui, who was also elected chairman of the Kuomintang at its 13th Congress on July 8, 1988. This congress was also noteworthy for its extension of democratizing reform into the politics of the party itself. Of 180 Central Committee members elected by the congress, 33 were candidates who had put their own names forward for election rather than being nominated by the party chairman. In a kind of intraparty popularity contest, party Secretary-General Lee Huan got the highest number of votes for the Central Committee.

President Lee Teng-hui, however, reached down to number 35 on the list to retain Chiang Ching-kuo's premier, Yü Kuo-hwa, as his own premier. One reason for this seemed to be to avoid the possibility that a more popular premier could begin to shift the balance in Taiwan's political system from one of presidential to one of cabinet dominance. The new cabinet, appointed at the end of July, also had the following characteristics:

- Most of its members held undergraduate degrees from National Taiwan University and American Ph.D. Degrees.
- For the first time, more than half the cabinet were native Taiwanese (as is President Lee).
- The cabinet included the first female minister, Minister of Finance Shirley Kuo, who was also the first Taiwanese in that sensitive post.

President Lee's extensive reorganization of the cabinet capped a successful political transition in which he managed in the face of considerable opposition to establish control over all of his predecessor's legal powers. It was unlikely, however, that he would ever command the kind of informal intraparty prestige and public charisma that had made possible Chiang Ching-kuo's era of strong-man rule.

PROSPECTS

The KMT remains by far the dominant force in Taiwan's political system. Its strengths include a nationalistic ideology with considerable appeal, much fresh blood among its membership, including many Taiwanese (constituting an estimated 70 percent of the party membership), a cadre of skilled technocrats, strong local political machines, control over the media and—through the political commissar system—control over the military. The KMT would probably perform well in elections even without the special advantages it enjoys under the current electoral system, and it is unlikely to give up all these advantages in the course of reform. Hence it is unlikely that the Taiwan political system will soon evolve into a true two-party or multiparty system. Rather, assuming that the democratic reforms continue to be carried forward, Taiwan is more likely to retain for the foreseeable future a hegemonic party system like that of Mexico, or possibly to evolve from such a system into a Japanese-style dominant-party system in which the KMT controls over half the votes while a variety of smaller parties share the remainder. Also possible, if the DPP stays together, is the development of a "one-and-a-half-party system" with a dominant KMT and a permanent minority opposition party.

The reform impetus is by no means exhausted. As of late 1988, liberals in the ruling party were pushing for further changes, especially in intraparty organization and in the area of congressional reform. Opposition parties and movements can be expected to use their new political and press freedoms to maintain pressure for even further-reaching changes, perhaps including challenges to remaining Leninist-style elements of interpenetration between party and government structures, such as the military intelligence and military political commissar systems and the system of state and party-managed enterprises.

The most unpredictable, and potentially most dangerous, element in the Taiwan political scene remains the issue of Taiwan independence. Most of the electorate is believed to realize that an open declaration of independence would not be in Taiwan's economic or political interest because of the probable strong PRC reaction. Yet the issue is an emotional one for much of the electorate. It is not clear how long moderate politicians on both sides can preserve the uneasy modus vivendi of 1986–88, which was to permit the issue to be talked about so long as it was not advocated by name.

The possibility always exists that a coalition of party conservatives, military and security personnel, and economic technocrats could call a halt to the reform process under various scenarios—for example, if the call for Taiwan independence grew too strong or if there were mass violence. However, the successful transition to a post-Chiang regime made this possibility seem more remote.

As of late 1988, the reforms appeared to have strengthened the regime both domestically and internationally. Abroad, they were praised as bold and well managed. Although the new, more open politics was more turbulent than before, it provided effective channels for the diverse ideas and interests of an increasingly plural society to be expressed and for social conflicts to be openly managed. Feeling less vulnerable at home, the government was able, beginning in 1987, to break out of the passive position in which it had long been trapped by the CCP's peaceful reunification diplomacy. Abandonment of the rigid policy of no contact with the mainland raised the prospect of mutually beneficial dealings that might not only strengthen Taiwan's hand in competition and negotiation with the mainland but might also, some observers thought, increase the island's ability to influence, by example and contact, the evolution of mainland politics and economics.

It is unlikely, however, that the Taiwan reforms can serve in any direct way as a model for the mainland. The KMT has always been an anomaly among Leninist parties because it lacks a Marxist ideology and has been, through most of its history, pro-Western and procapitalist. The applicability of its experience to other Leninist parties is thus limited. Moreover, the mainland Chinese population is far less prosperous and educated than Taiwan's, and in this sense the social conditions for pluralism there are less promising. Also in contrast to Taiwan, the PRC is not dependent on the United States economically and militarily and hence has less concern with American and other foreign public opinion. In short, the CCP leaders lack the various stimuli for fundamental party system reform that motivated Chiang Ching-kuo. Although some democrats both outside and inside the CCP have advocated a multiparty system, prospects for multipartyism on the mainland have to be counted as slight.

Nonetheless, news of Taiwan's reforms will constitute a constant and increasing source of pressure on the PRC regime for liberalization. This news was probably among the factors spurring the late 1986 student and worker demonstrations against the slow pace of political reform on the mainland. Taiwan's cancellation of the ban on travel to the mainland by its residents means that the exposure of mainland Chinese citizens to information about the Taiwan economy and political system is going to increase. Because the PRC recognizes Taiwan residents as its own citizens, their travel and social activities in China will be virtually unrestricted.

A recent body of theory argues that given permissive economic, social and international conditions, a turn toward democracy may be an attractive option for an elite facing succession problems, an economic crisis, mass unrest, international pressure or other problems. In such conditions, relatively democratic institutions offer the possibility of improving a regime's abilities to legitimate itself, regulate social conflict, recruit successors, gain access to and make use of information for policymaking and so on.[13] Since democratization in Taiwan is just beginning and still faces many problems, it is too early to say how fully the Taiwan case will confirm this functional theory of democratic transitions. But the theory seems to provide a useful perspective for understanding the reform decisions made so far. In addition, Chiang Ching-kuo's handling of the reform process provides useful lessons for reformers elsewhere in the skills of consensus building and conflict management.

FURTHER READING

Barrett, Richard, and Whyte, Martin King. "Dependency Theory and Taiwan: A Deviant Case Analysis." *American Journal of Sociology* 87 (1982), 1064–89.
Gold, Thomas B. *State and Society in the Taiwan Miracle*. Armonk, New York: M. E. Sharpe, 1986.
Gregor, A. James, and Hsia Chang, Maria. *The Republic of China and U.S. Policy: A Study in Human Rights*. Washington, D.C.: Ethics and Public Policy Center, 1983.
Haggard, Stephan, and Cheng, Tun-jen. *Economic Adjustment in the East Asian Newly Industrializing Countries*. Berkeley, California: Institute of International Studies, 1987.
Hsiung, James C. et al., eds. *Contemporary Republic of China: the Taiwan Experience, 1950–1980*. New York: American Association for Chinese Studies, 1981.
Jo, Jung-hwan. *Taiwan's Future*. Tempe: Arizona State University Press, 1974.
Kuo, Shirley. *The Taiwan Economy in Transition*. Boulder, Colorado: Westview Press, 1983.
Tien Hung-mao. *The Great Transition: Political and Social Change in the Republic of China*. Stanford, California: Hoover Institution Press, 1989.

THAILAND

ANDREW TURTON

INTRODUCTION

IN the late 20th century, Thailand ranks among the larger, better-endowed and more internationally prominent nations of the world. In terms of territory (approximately the size of France) and population (some 55 million in the late 1980s) it is one of the world's 20 or so largest countries. It has long been self-sufficient in food. It is a major exporting country, increasingly of manufactured goods, and its status as a "newly industrializing country" is growing. It is relatively well favored by natural resources and environmental conditions. Even more noteworthy, in comparison with so many countries of Asia, is the high degree of continuity, underlying stability and adaptability of its social institutions.

For many years Thailand has been known as one of the most open, indeed welcoming and hospitable, of countries—whether in terms of its wide diplomatic relations with most communist and noncommunist countries; its receptivity to foreign goods, visitors or cultural influences; or, on a more personal level, the widely admired charm and courtesy of the Thai people. At the same time, and perhaps in a deeper sense, Thailand—its people and culture—is often found by outsiders to be culturally rather impenetrable and difficult to translate and to have a unique social system that defies precise interpretation. Much of this has to do with the language. The Thai language, tonal and having a distinctive non-Roman script, is not shared with any neighboring countries (with the partial exception of Laos). Nor is English (or any other language) anything like a national second language. And relatively few foreigners become proficient in the Thai language.

A remarkable feature of Thai society is its relative homogeneity. National censuses report that over 98 percent of the population has Thai citizenship, a similar number as able to speak Thai and some 95 percent as being Buddhist. While these are in one sense facts, they are also official representations, which do not reveal important contemporary cultural variations and differences.

A similar point can be made with regard to official representations of the past—as found, for example, in school textbooks, public ceremonies and the work of the National Identity Board. In such representations, emphasis is given to a continuous linear development of the Thai nation—the Thai state from earliest times, in which external enemies and internal unity are

836

stressed, and regional, ethnic variations minimized. Much of this, some scholars argue, is the result of the imposition over the past century, of a dominant national ideology.

Originally this was part of a successful assertion of independence and a distinctive corporate identity in the face of colonial powers at the end of the 19th century and into the 20th. Arguably, Thai nationalism has been constructed from more promising and plausible materials than some others, but like others it has tended to favor the regional language and elite institutions of the political center. In other words, there have been conscious policies of centralization and homogenization. These policies have been reformulated, with differing emphasis, by successive governments. There remains a certain official unease at assertions of regional, cultural and, especially, political diversity. At times there is a sense that national unity is rather more precarious, and definitions of national culture and identity more debatable, than may at first appear. For all these reasons an account of contemporary Thailand must first examine its roots in premodern Siam as well as the impact of political, economic and social forces from the outside.

EARLY HISTORY

The early history of the territory of contemporary Thailand is not principally that of Tai-speaking peoples, but rather of Mon- and Khmer-speaking peoples of the Buddhist Dvaravati civilization (approximately A.D. 6th–9th centuries, and the predominantly Hindu Khmer empire (approximately 9th–12th centuries). Conversely, the later history (13th century to the present) of Tai-speaking peoples far exceeds the boundaries of Thailand to Laos, the Shan States of Burma (now Myanmar), the southern provinces of China, northern Vietnam and elsewhere.

Chinese records suggest that early in the first millennium (A.D.), Tai-speaking peoples were settled in southern and southwestern China, practising wet rice cultivation and several customs, such as building homes raised above the ground, that distinguished them from Chinese culture, some of which continue to this day. Toward the end of the millennium there was a slow expansion to the west and southwest into the upland valleys of what are now the border areas between China, Burma, Thailand, Laos and Vietnam. This movement of colonization and small-scale conquest was facilitated by a distinctive Tai form of social organization, the *muang,* a grouping of villages under a *chao,* chief or lord, who was capable of mobilizing manpower for both military and productive purposes. These units became established in the spaces between Chinese, Vietnamese, Burmese, Mon and Khmer kingdoms and empires, variously attracted to and forcibly drawn into them.

By the 12th century, the lowlands of northern and north central Thailand had become increasingly Tai, Buddhist and distinct from the Khmer. Strategies of intermarriage with non-Tai elites, alliances among Tai *muang,* and Tai alliances with and against neighboring powers, led to the establishment of a number of Tai kingdoms in the 13th century, notably Sukothai (from the 1240s) and Lannathai, with the foundation of Chiang Mai (New City) in 1296. But it was the kingdom of Ayudhya, founded in 1350 by the son of a Chinese merchant married to a Khmer princess, that was to establish a lasting Tai hegemony in the area and supplant the Khmer empire, especially after the capture of Angkor by the Tai in 1432. With good access to the sea, and supported by the rice-growing potential of the flood plains of the Chao Phraya River, Ayudhya was from the start an international commercial center, a port capital, with distinct advantages over the landlocked Lannathai and Lao kingdoms of the north. Ayudhya maintained extensive contact with Buddhist religious centers in South and Southeast Asia and developed a long-lasting system of administration, and civil and criminal codes of law. These developments reached a peak in the reign of King Trailok (1448–88), who codified what is known as the *sakdina* system, which in various transformations continued into the late 19th century.

Sakdina (literally, "field power") was a hierarchical ranking system, for economic, legal and political purposes, that assigned a number of units to the whole population—including women, monks and Chinese merchants—from five for a slave, to 25 for the peasant freeman, to 80 to 400 for minor officials and upward of 400 for the bureaucratic nobility. As an analytical category for a system of exploitation, *sakdina* has become the equivalent of the feudal system. The nobility was appointed to various ministries and departments, and had the task of mobilizing the unpaid labor of a specified number of freemen for public works, warfare or the delivery of tribute, which passed into the royal trading monopolies. The nobility was constantly reassigned and reappointed in attempts to prevent the formation of a hereditary, territorial aristocracy. The tension between control of manpower for personal or for bureaucratic purposes was a persistent dynamic throughout the Ayudhya period (until 1767). The resolution of this tension greatly affected success in the endemic warfare of the region, both between individual Tai states and especially between Tai and Burmese. So too did the constant building and rebuilding of personal relationships among friends, kinsmen and allies—of kings and contenders for succession. The history of the Ayudhya period is marked throughout by usurpation and regicide, treachery and rebellion, and popular uprisings. Periods of internal turmoil often contributed to major defeats, notably in the mid-16th century when the Burmese sacked all the major Tai capitals (and again in 1767 when the City and Kingdom of Ayudhya were finally destroyed by the Burmese).

Ayudhya had regained its preeminence in the late 16th century during the reign of King Naresuan (1590–1605) who defeated the Burmese in 1593. This achievement is still celebrated in Thai national history, and the dangers of disunity among the Thai remains a constantly rehearsed theme. The 17th century saw the development of a more distinctive Siamese culture in Ayudhya and divergence from its Tai neighbors. The northern Lannathai Kingdom had for two centuries been a cultural and religious center of perhaps even greater distinction, but this was followed by two centuries of virtual Burmese overrule, after which it never fully regained its importance.

The culture and outlook of the Ayudhya Kingdom, at least at the center, was remarkably international. As early as 1511 the Siamese had made a treaty with the Portuguese in Melaka, which had formerly been regarded as a dependency of Ayudhya, giving the Portuguese rights of residence and religious liberty in exchange for trading benefits, especially the procurement of guns and ammunition. Portuguese soldiers were engaged by the Siamese, and the king's bodyguard was regularly composed of Japanese, Cham and Malays. A remarkable feature of the bureaucratic structure in the 17th and 18th centuries was the appointment of foreigners—of Persian, Chinese, Indian and Greek origin—to the post of *phrakhlang,* or minister of the treasury (a virtual prime minister), in charge of foreign trade and foreign affairs. Dutch, British, French and other Europeans intermittently engaged in trade with Ayudhya in the 17th century, and there were Siamese diplomatic missions to France and Holland. These exchanges ended when an internal political crisis, fueled by foreign interventions, led, in 1688, to the virtual cessation of formal contacts with European countries for nearly a century and a half.

Within a few years of the sack of Ayudhya by the Burmese in 1767, Siam had been restored to a kingdom of even greater size under a charismatic and religiously unorthodox military leader, Taksin, who was crowned in his new capital, Thon Buri, in 1768. He was deposed and executed in 1782 by a coalition of closely knit old noble families, and succeeded by one of their number, a senior military commander generally known as King Rama I (1782–1809). The latter was the first of a dynasty of which the present King Bhumibol Adulyadej is the ninth and longest reigning monarch. The capital was moved to Bangkok, on the east bank of the Chao Phraya River, some 13 miles/20 km. from the sea.

THE RATANAKOSIN ERA

The first reign of the Bangkok, or Ratanakosin, era saw the consolidation and strengthening of the kingdom. There was mass registration of manpower, to ensure royal control and prevent princes from amassing large private followings that might threaten the monarchy. One means was the tattooing of all freemen with the name of their masters and place of residence. The Three Seals Laws of 1805 was a new code of Siamese law that was to last a century. A definitive text of the Pali-language Tripitaka, the scriptures of Theravada Buddhism, was established, and translations and adaptations were made from the literature of India, China, Persia, Sri Lanka and Java. Bangkok itself was, like Ayudhya, a highly diverse and cosmopolitan city composed of many ethnic groups, including Indian and numerous Teochiu Chinese merchants, some of whom intermarried with the Thai elite.

Trade flourished, especially the export of rice to China. Following the acquisition of Singapore in 1819, the British sent missions to Bangkok in 1821 and 1825 to seek improved conditions of trade and Siamese neutrality in Britain's war with Burma. The Burney Treaty of 1826 led to increased Western trade; but it was the Bowring Treaty with Britain in 1855 that began to open up Siam to trade with industrial and industrializing Western powers on highly unequal terms. Import duties were set at three percent ad valorem, whereas export taxes were at an average five percent. State revenues were henceforth to depend largely on excise monopolies in opium, alcoholic spirits, gambling and the lottery. In addition, British and other foreign subjects were accorded rights of extraterritoriality. These rights were not to be lifted or tariff autonomy restored until 1925.

One of the major concerns of King Mongkut (Rama IV; r. 1851–68) and his son King Chulalongkorn (Rama V; r. 1868–1910) was adjusting to the new imperialist world order. Internally, they continued to engage in military and diplomatic strategies and campaigns to control vassal states, especially in Laos and Cambodia, in the face of Vietnamese assertion and overlapping claims of suzerainty. Externally, Mongkut and his minister Suriyawong pursued a dexterous, multilateral diplomatic policy of relations with many Western nations, attempting to balance the powerful influence of Britain, and to a lesser extent that of France. But Siam paid a heavy price for maintaining its sovereignty and independence. Siam lost nearly half of the territory (over which it had claimed suzerainty in its own form of local or internal colonialism) to British Burma and Malaya, and French Indochina at the height of their imperial expansion around the turn of the century. By 1910, Siam's borders had been defined as they remain today. The economic cost was also high. On the one hand, there were the reduced revenues from import and export trade, while on the other the cost of building railways and military modernization rose.

But from the point of view of the Siamese state, it was by no means all loss, disadvantage and subordination. In the name of reform and modernization, and partly in response to Western pressures, Chulalongkorn created a more centralized kingdom, a more absolute monarchy, than Siam had ever known. Much of it was centralized in the hands of the king himself and a few senior ministers, mostly senior royal princes, the king's brothers and half-brothers. They were the first to receive modern education, frequently in European capitals. These included Prince Devawongse, minister of foreign affairs 1885–1923, and Prince Damrong, minister of the interior 1892–1915. Centralizing measures included restructuring the provincial administration and the ministerial bureaucracies, the legal system, the army, the Buddhist *sangha* (order of monkhood), public education and transport, namely the railway system. By these means, old provincial aristocracies were undermined and alternative centers of power diminished.

King Vajirawudh (Rama VI; r. 1910–25) added a cultural dimension to the absolute state. He was a creative literary writer and publicist, propagandizing the idea of the Thai nation *(chaat thai)* and the concept of "nation-religion-monarch" that remains a touchstone of conservative patriotism and is part of a still-prevailing official view of Thai national culture, which owes much to his ideas. One vehicle of this ideology was what has been called a nationwide mass paramilitary corps, the "Wild Tiger Corps", which constituted a large part of his personal following. His selective, at times quite racist, construction of a Thai tradition mixed with elements of modern nationalism poses a problem for an understanding of contemporary Thai

840

cultural identity which, as stated at the outset of this essay, is now more penetratingly debated than ever.

In addition to his literary creations, translations of European and Asian classics, studies of traditional literature, and political essays, King Vajirawudh redesigned the national flag, declared national holidays, introduced surnames, encouraged team sports, discouraged polygamy, founded the first university (Chulalongkorn University, in 1916) and instituted the beginnings of compulsory primary education.

During the reign of King Vajirawudh and his successor King Prajadhipok (Rama VII; r. 1925–35), up to the end of the absolute monarchy in 1932, there was a broadening of the bureaucratic elite beyond the royal family; but there were no major reforms of a political or democratizing nature. Indeed, in spite of what might be seen as a political watershed in 1932, slow and uncertain moves toward political reform remain characteristic of Thailand to this day, economic and cultural transformations notwithstanding.

THE MODERN PERIOD

On June 21, 1932, almost exactly 150 years after the founding of the Chakri dynasty, a group of 49 military and naval officers and 65 civilians staged a coup d'état that constrained the king to agree to submit to a constitution. The group was led by a young lawyer, Pridi Phanomyang, and an army major, Luang Phibun Songkhram (Phibun), both of whom had studied in France in the 1920s and represented a new but still small middle-class intelligentsia dissatisfied with the old royal government and impatient for a more democratic political order.

Some of the political features of the period after 1932 foreshadowed the style and stop-go momentum of subsequent political developments in the periods commencing 1946, 1957 and 1973. These include the continuously influential and usually dominant role of the military in politics; the weak development of political parties, which more than 50 years later still lack mass following; factionalism in ruling groups; recurrent abrogation and rewriting of constitutions and parliamentary structures; and recourse to military coups d'état to affect changes of regime. Broadly speaking, each of the four periods suggested started with a flurry of constitutionalism, civilian leadership and democratic, at times even somewhat socialist, rhetoric of ending absolutism, authoritarianism, corruption and so forth. And in each period there was a progression to military intervention and more authoritarian rule.

Thus from 1933 to 1938, General Phahon's government at first held the ring between the civilian faction under Pridi and the military faction under Phibun. Pridi's economic plan of 1933 was judged by the latter to be too revolutionary, even "communistic". This led to his temporary exile and the passing of the first of several anticommunist legislations, which have been a feature of most subsequent governments to this day. Pridi did, however, return from exile and was exonerated.

Phibun advocated strong personal leadership, and he admired authoritar-

841

ian and fascist regimes in Italy, Germany and especially Japan, where he was later to die in exile. When Phibun became prime minister in 1938, he initiated a new authoritarianism and cult of the leader. Eighteen elite opponents were executed. A kind of mass nationalism was propagated, more populist and racist than that of King Vajirawudh, more antiforeign yet also more Western and modern. Even more remarkable, it was antimonarchist, almost republican. King Prajadhipok had abdicated in 1935 and was succeeded by King Ananda Mahidol (Rama VIII; r. 1935–46), still at school in Switzerland and represented by regents, one of whom was Pridi. Phibun prohibited even the private display of pictures of the ex-king. And royalty was to be a virtually insignificant influence on politics for some 20 years until young King Bhumibol (Rama IX; r. 1946 to present) began to take the stage in the late 1950s.

The country's change of name from Siam to Thailand in 1939 had both anti-Chinese and irredentist pan-Tai implications. People were required to use the national (central Thai) language, salute the flag, forswear imported products (but wear Western-style clothes, especially hats) and join mass movements such as paramilitary youth groups, junior Red Cross and Boy Scouts. Economic measures were taken against the Chinese population, who were compared disparagingly in official statements to fascist views of Jews in Germany.

WORLD WAR II AND THE POSTWAR YEARS

After the outbreak of World War II, Thailand—with Japan the only fully independent state in Eastern Asia—seized the chance to restore the territories it had lost to the French and British, and permitted the Japanese army to use the country as a base from which to pursue the war in Malaya and Burma. War was declared against Britain and the United States in January 1942. An anti-Japanese "Free Thai" underground movement was established, associated with Pridi and supported by the United States, whose decision not to recognize the declaration of war was to mark postwar politics in Thailand profoundly. This signaled a special relationship between the United States and Thailand, which replaced previous British influence.

Phibun was forced to resign as the war turned against the Japanese. There followed a series of short-lived civilian governments, one headed by Pridi who was a leading figure in the relatively liberal postwar years. In November 1947, in an increasingly cold war atmosphere, the army intervened again, and by April 1948 Phibun resumed the premiership he was to hold until 1957. He resisted two coup attempts (one in 1949 and the other in 1951), the latter causing over 3,000 casualties, including 1,200 dead. These were mostly civilians who might have restored Pridi to power; Pridi was to remain in exile in China and France until his death in 1983. Internally, Phibun moved strongly against real and perceived rivals. Chinese institutions and economic activities were suppressed; northeastern (Lao) politicians were harassed and shot; and in the South, Malay and Islamic associations were banned, and a Malay insurgency was put down with massive force. Externally, Thai troops were sent to fight in Korea (1950–53), and in 1954 Thailand became the main Asian partner in the South East Asia Treaty Organization. The economy benefited from U.S. economic aid and the boom in exports stimulated by the Korean War. U.S. military aid strengthened the army and especially the police, the latter headed by General Phao Sriyanond, who also had a leading role in the illegal opium trade.

In 1957, to shore up his support, Phibun held elections. The restored freedom of press and speech exposed a series of inept, fraudulent, corrupt and coercive government practices. At the height of the crisis the army commander in chief, Sarit Thanarat, and his deputies, Gen. Thanom Kittikachorn and Police-General Praphat, resigned from the cabinet and within days staged a lightning, bloodless coup d'état. A year later Sarit—intolerant both of parliamentary in-fighting and of popular expressions of discontent, which he thought were destabilizing the country—abolished the constitution, declared martial law and instituted rule by a revolutionary council. The next 15 years were dominated by a similar style of government, first under Sarit, until his death in 1963, and subsequently under Thanom, with General Praphat as minister of the interior—until they in turn, like Phibun and Phao, were forced into exile in October 1973. For most of this period the constitution and parliament were suspended.

Sarit thought of himself as a revolutionary and popular leader. His style of rule has been called despotic paternalism. His authoritarian model of society was of three social layers: state or government; officials; and the people, who were his "children." His obsession with public order and propriety and with intellectual and religious orthodoxy manifested itself in the arrests of critical monks and intellectuals, the banning of opium trafficking and consumption, and the public executions of arsonists and other criminals, including the political opposition. In his early 30s, Sarit enhanced the public, especially the ritual, role of the Thai monarch, thereby popularizing his own legitimacy.

OUTSIDE INFLUENCES AND MODERNIZATION

Sarit's, commitment to a particular style of economic development had profound effects. At the urging of the World Bank, new policies were introduced in 1961 as part of Thailand's first Five-Year National Development Plan. Direct state involvement in running economic enterprises decreased, and private and foreign investments were promoted. There was heavy investment in infrastructural development such as roads, electric power, urban development and education. American presence and influence—political, economic and cultural—increased spectacularly. Around the country many military bases were built, from which most of the air war against Vietnam and Laos was conducted. More than 40,000 U.S. troops were stationed in Thailand, and hundreds of thousands of American servicepeople passed through Thailand on rest-and-recreation visits. The service sector of hotels, bars, brothels and massage parlors flourished. Japan became Thailand's largest trading partner. Banks and luxury hotels proliferated; new industries were established; eight-lane highways were constructed through

843

Bangkok; and other strategic highways linked outlying regions with the rapidly expanding capital.

Most neglected in this scheme of things were the vast rural areas beyond greater Bangkok. And it was in these regions, especially the northeast and the south, and in the mountains of the north, that the Beijing-oriented Communist party of Thailand met some sympathetic response. Founded in 1942, the party had for most of the time been banned and obliged to operate clandestinely. In 1965, it began to put into effect a new policy of armed opposition to the government. "Counterinsurgency" became the government's watchword; policies of national security and stability prevailed over those of rural development, though the latter was often another word for counterinsurgency. Within a few years most of the country's 73 provinces were declared "red" and "pink" zones of communist infiltration. Poor farmers were not the only people to feel dissatisfied. Expanded university and technical education had produced a large new generation of educated young people, mainly middle class, many of whom could not find jobs appropriate to their qualifications and aspirations. Many students had become critical of foreign economic and cultural influences and began to be aware of the conditions of urban and rural workers, with whom they were making contact for the first time.

A movement for the reinstatement and reform of a short-lived constitution, which had been abrogated in 1971, provided a political focus for widespread social discontent. In October 1973 there were massive street demonstrations in Bangkok. Some government troops opened fire on the crowds, causing death and casualties on a scale unprecedented in direct clashes between troops and civilians. Field Marshal Thanom and General Praphat, deprived of the support of the king and some military leaders, were forced to leave the country.

The 16-year Sarit-Thanom period was ended. A series of civilian governments followed and there were high hopes on many sides of a new democratic era. New political parties, including a small Socialist party, campaigned openly. Peasants' and workers' unions grew up rapidly; there were frequent demonstrations, and more strikes in a single year than during the whole of the Sarit-Thanom period. Students, many of them influenced by revolutionary, especially Maoist, ideas, assumed a prominent political role. There was an extraordinary blossoming of journals, newspapers and other publications of a progressive kind. Parliament began to respond to some popular demands: legislating on land reform and agricultural rents, and finally closing down American bases.

THE 1976 COUP

Old vested interests, which had by no means been dismantled following October 1973, now felt threatened by the pace and style of change, and a sometimes vicious reaction set in. A number of paramilitary groups were formed that harassed the meetings of students and farmers. There were dozens of assassinations of farmers' leaders, politicians, trade unionists and others. This reaction culminated in a military coup d'état against the elected government on October 6, 1976. This was immediately preceded by a full-scale attack by several thousand border patrol police and paramilitary groups on students at Thammasat University; over a hundred students were shot and lynched, many more wounded and thousands arrested.

The year that followed the October 1976 coup was, by Thai standards, one of extraordinary political extremism. Many intellectuals sought refuge abroad; a few thousand students and others went to the jungle to join the Communist-led guerrillas; and the antigovernment insurrection renewed its intensity. Farmers' and workers' groups were suppressed; there were political trials; books and newspapers were banned and burned. A more normal political climate was reestablished within a year, however, when a new generation of reformist army officers, known as the Young Turks, promoted first General Kriangsak and then, in 1980, another recently retired officer, the former commander-in-chief Gen. Prem Tinsulanonda. He was to remain prime minister, despite several attempted coups d'état, until 1988 when he resigned. A major feature of General Prem's premiership was the priority given to political rather than military tactics in dealing with domestic opposition. This contributed to a rapid decline in the size and influence of the Communist party of Thailand, simultaneously undermined by internal divisions and withdrawal of external support, as thousands of supporters took advantage of a government amnesty to return "from the jungle to the cities."

There is an interesting and peculiar theme in Thai political life of what one could call political forgiveness or clemency, a public show of contrition and rehabilitation that contrasts with other harsher, more violent aspects. The promoters of the 1932 coup apologized for the extremity and illegality of their act and the king issued a proclamation forgiving them. In 1976 the then king visited the former "dictator" Thanom, who had returned from three years of exile as a temporarily ordained monk. Royal pardons and regular amnesty of prisoners on the king's birthday are a related phenomenon. Leaders of failed coups have seldom been executed or even severely punished. At a lower level, however, there have been executions and assassinations of left-wing politicians, especially under Phibun and Sarit, and more recently, less formal and extra-judicial killings of peasant and trade-union leaders, investigative journalists and others who are deemed to threaten perceived public and private interests, which are frequently intertwined.

Another political theme persisting from the 1930s is what is colloquially known as Thai-style democracy (*prachatipatai baep thai thai*). There is a pervasive mistrust of popular sovereignty and a paternalistic emphasis on political tutelage and gradualism. People and institutions are thought of as "not being ready" for full political participation. The 1932 coup group envisaged a 10-year process of parliamentary development, extended to 20 years by Phibun; in 1976 the coup group, which ended the 3-year democratic interlude, announced a 16-year program of cautious restoration of democracy, though this was overtaken by events.

THE ECONOMY AND ECONOMIC TRENDS

Thailand's economy has been dramatically restructured over the past 30 years or so. In the early 1950s it was a predominantly agrarian economy with a small internal market; 88 percent of the labor force was engaged in agriculture. Rice accounted for about half of all exports by value; rice, rubber, teak and tin together some 80 percent. State monopolies and enterprises, the latter mainly inefficient and poorly managed, were preponderant in the manufacturing sector alongside small family firms employing fewer than 10 people. A major strategy of the government economic program was to prevent the industrial dominance of indigenous Chinese.

From the early 1960s, following advice from the World Bank, a policy of import-substitution industrialization and investment promotion was initiated. The 1960s saw an average annual growth of 11 percent in the manufacturing sector and a rapid accumulation of domestic capital as the state withdrew from economic entrepreneurship and concentrated on infrastructural development.

Thailand's present phase of export-oriented industrialization took off following initial legislation in 1971. The value of exports, which had been a mere US$40 million in 1970, rose to $270 million in three years. Despite political uncertainty in the mid- to late-1970s, an annual GDP growth rate of 8.9 percent was recorded. The economy was severely tested but survived the period of high energy prices from 1979 to 1985, when Thailand also met with low prices for agricultural products and raw materials, protectionist measures against its textiles and other exports, and the kind of financial pressure that bankrupted the Philippines.

Thailand's fiscal conservatism underwent some change: a government budget deficit and devaluation of the currency. For the first time in 100 years Thailand became a debtor nation, reaching a debt-service ratio of over 27 percent (back to below 20 percent in the late 1980s). The bulk of the debt and some 60 percent of state investment in industry was accounted for by electricity generating and petroleum authorities. Natural gas in the Gulf of Thailand and heavy industrial development (port facilities, and a fertilizer and petrochemical plant) on the eastern seaboard are among the main hopes for further successful industrialization.

Thailand has managed to achieve high growth rates despite oil prices, a narrow tax base and high military spending. It has managed to avoid a crippling debt burden, and to maintain a basic political stability. But perhaps the strongest feature in the equation is a large domestic capital base that has a considerable stake in the industrial future of the country. Foreign investment is commonly in the form of joint ventures with local capital. Many family and individual owners of capital are of Chinese origin. Though distinct in certain respects, Sino-Thai have become culturally and socially merged with the Thai to a considerable extent. Census figures no longer record a separate Chinese population within Thailand. The economic discrimination of the Phibun years has gone, and there is not the kind of cultural and political discrimination found in Indonesia or Malaysia. Until the 1940s, the Chinese formed a great majority of the small urban working class.

Thailand has a high proportion of its population, men and women, in the labor force (28 million out of a total population of nearly 54 million in 1987). Some 30 percent are engaged in industrial, commercial and service sectors. Most of the urban labor force is composed of first-generation workers, and many of these workers are cyclical migrants from the rural sectors, which cannot adequately support them. Rural poverty also accounts for a large number of children working in urban sweatshops under a form of indentured labor that is increasingly prevalent despite its illegality and the concern of numerous welfare rights organizations. Only a small proportion of the regularly employed work force is organized in trade unions—mainly those working in public utilities and heavy industry. In the 1980s the export of labor, mainly to Saudi Arabia and neighboring countries, became a major feature of the economy. There were 376,500 such workers in 1987; their remittances sometimes exceeded the value of rice exports. Unemployment, at approximately nine percent in 1987, was at its historically highest level. These figures underestimate the precariousness of existence in the growing "informal" sector, and they barely take into account rural underemployment.

The agricultural sector continues to be a mainstay of the national economy, accounting for over 60 percent of the labor force and 50 percent of the value of exports, though contributing only 17 percent to the GNP, compared with industry's 29 percent (1987). Most importantly, Thailand continues to be one of the highest net agricultural exporters among developing countries. At least one-third of agricultural production is exported. Rice is still the single most valuable export crop, but in the past 30 years new cash and export crops have been developed, which together have become more important than rice. These include maize, cassava (tapioca), sugar, kenaf, beans and pineapple. Thailand has become the third largest maritime fishing nation in Asia (after Japan and China), employing 350,000 people and operating 2,000 deep-sea trawlers. And yet agriculture—and the majority of the rural population—remains relatively neglected in government policy and plans. A new agribusiness sector thrives while the great majority of small farmers suffer from terms of trade that depress income and discourage increases in productivity. While volume of production is high, the rate of productivity (area yield) is one of the lowest in Asia.

There is much use of wage labor in agriculture, even by small subsistence farmers, but there is only a very small permanent agricultural wage labor force. Tenant farmers, who mostly operate on disadvantageous terms, make up some 20 percent of all farmers. The extent of small to medium land ownership can give a misleading image of well-being. The majority live in the northern and northeastern regions, while new technological inputs are highly skewed toward the central region. Access to limited credit and guaranteed price schemes (as well as many other benefits of education, health and security of well-being) is more available to a rural elite of larger landowners, who are often also engaged in machine hire, money lending, transport and construction. Many also hold official positions at the local level, and are a favored political constituency for governments, especially given the virtual absence of political party organization outside the principal towns. Official estimates suggest that there may be as many as 10 million people in rural areas living in absolute poverty. For a country self-sufficient in food, there is an avoidable degree of malnutrition and death from malnutrition, especially among rural children.

Among the most disadvantaged of the rural population are members of the various "hill peoples" (as they are collectively known in Thai) who live mainly in the northern region, and along the borders with Burma and Laos. These peoples, numbering about half a million, are of ethnic groups other than Thai, the more numerous being Karen, Hmong, Yao, Lahu, Lisu, Akha, Khmu, Htin and Lawa. Some have been represented in Thailand for centuries; others have migrated in the 19th and 20th centuries from Burma, China and Laos. They are rather misleadingly lumped together as either hill people or tribal people, since they have very varied and long histories, and are not linked in distinct tribal organizations but rather in fragmented local communities and networks of kinship and clanship. Most are numerically more substantially represented in neighboring countries but seek their future as integrated though distinct citizens in the Kingdom of Thailand, in which most have yet to be accorded full citizenship. Many practice a form of extensive agriculture land use known as swidden, or shifting cultivation, which is productive and maybe conservationist if conditions allow; most of these people, however, would prefer settled irrigated-rice cultivation if secure access to suitable land were possible. Their cultural and economic ways of life are increasingly subject to urgent, competing demands on their resources and their loyalties, which pose threats to their survival: from commercial timber companies and forestry officials; from lowland farmers; and from numerous other government agencies, both military and civilian. From a cultural point of view, these minorities confront—from a position of greater relative disadvantage—assimilationist state policies that also concern the culturally distinct Thai minorities of the large northeastern and northern regions, as well as the Muslim Thai and Malay populations of the south (numbering more than one million), and others such as the long-settled Khmer-speaking peoples of the southern part of the northeast.

ECOLOGY AND THE ENVIRONMENT

Farmers (lowlanders and especially highlanders) have been blamed in recent years for the destruction of the natural environment, most particularly the forests, which at the turn of the 20th century covered some 70 percent of the country and now cover perhaps as little as 15 percent. For more than a century the destruction of forest has been the creation of a new agricultural environment, the result of farmers' initiative in responding to market demands and limitations by extending agricultural land and production without intensification of productivity. But arguably the greatest damage to the ecological balance in recent years has been caused by commercial timber extraction—often unlicensed and uncontrolled—and the state-initiated infrastructural development. Even in the heartlands, far from the geographical peripheries, new technological developments pose new environmental and personal health dangers in the form of uncontrolled use of toxic chemicals.

A famous 13th-century inscription records that "In the water there are fish, in the fields there is rice." Peasant humor now captures a sense of decline in well-being, abundance and security with "In the water there are chemicals, in the fields there are rats." There are signs, however, that preservation and fostering of an ecologically balanced environment may become a more important political priority: In 1988 an unprecedented decision was taken to abandon a proposed hydropower plant, the Nam Choan Dam in Kanchanaburi Province northwest of Bangkok, which would have destroyed a large part of one of the finest conservation areas in mainland Asia.

CONCLUSION: THAILAND TODAY

The spectacular growth of a new middle class poses a further challenge to notions of social and cultural continuity in Thai society. In the shorter term, this admittedly multifarious part of the population may affect political changes even more than the peasantry or working class, though these too are undergoing profound transformations. Sarit's model of Thai society was both ideological and anachronistic; it now seems absurdly archaic. But at that time society comprised the monarchy, hierarchical government structures, the army, the Buddhist monkhood, the mass of the peasantry and an ethnic middle class made up of the Chinese business community. The new middle class, if it can so be called, is educated, urban, no longer differentiated primarily by ethnic criteria or largely oriented, as before, toward jobs in government service.

Paradoxically, Thailand still has a rather low proportion of its population (17 percent in 1987) living in urban areas compared with most Asian countries; certainly the proportion is the lowest of the more industrialized countries. Most urbanization is accounted for by greater Bangkok, with a population of some eight million. Bangkok remains the center of power, privilege and attraction. Regional universities, district-level branch banks and government offices may have proliferated in the provinces, but industry is still mainly located in the greater Bangkok area. Of all university applicants, 75 percent are from Bangkok as are a great majority of the country's one million graduates. In 1960, only 18,000 students were enrolled in universities, compared with 400,000 in all forms of tertiary education in 1987. Secondary education, in which only 29 percent of school-age children are engaged, is highly biased toward the middle class, and even more toward Bangkok. The same is true for health care. While there is an average of one doctor for every thousand people in Bangkok, the ratio in some provinces is as high as one for 40,000—even up to 60,000. Even within Bangkok the ratio is skewed to benefit the middle and upper classes. More than one million people live in hundreds of slum or squatter neighborhoods, in addition to those temporary workers who live on-site in makeshift shelters; their doctor-patient ratio is similar to that of the provinces.

Thailand has for centuries been open to influences from other countries and cultures. Formerly, these derived from the multi-ethnic composition of its population, its status as a trading economy and adherence to the Theravada Buddhism of South and Southeast Asia. Since the end of the 19th century there have been conscious efforts to introduce elements of Western culture in the interests, successively, of becoming more "civilized," "modern," and, recently, "developed." At the same time, attitudes to white Westerners (*farang*) and their culture are not without ambiguity or resentment. Nor have all influences been officially welcome; for example, Marxist ideas are officially condemned as being a foreign ideology, despite a long indigenous tradition of socialist thought and writing. Even here, though, there is a considerable degree of tolerance of critical debate and publishing, at least among the academic intelligentsia, which compares favorably with many neighboring countries. This same intelligentsia is strongly oriented to Western thought, and higher education is usually completed in the United States, Europe, Australia and now to some extent Japan, with many thousands of students leaving each year to study abroad.

On a more popular level there is an unchecked flow of Western commercial culture in the form of television, films, pop music, fashions and every conceivable consumer commodity. Tourism is one massive external influence whose impact has yet to be properly assessed. Some three million visitors arrive in Thailand each year, and tourism has become the top foreign-exchange earner. One aspect of this, which causes widespread concern but not official condemnation, is what is known as "sex tourism": male visitors attracted by and contributing to large-scale prostitution (also an indigenous phenomenon) in which many hundreds of thousands of women and young girls are engaged.

One of the most enduring cultural traditions is Thai popular Buddhism, whose values inform all areas of personal and social life. In addition to the everyday beliefs and practices of village Buddhism, there are other tendencies that manipulate religion in political directions. One tendency has been the creation of what has been termed "establishment Buddhism," the creation of a national religion, controlled by a unified hierarchy of the *sangha* in a bureaucratic structure. Governments have used the *sangha* directly to promote anticommunism, development programs and the assimilation of hill peoples. A more recent phenomenon is the growth of a number of sects and lay movements, some of them receiving official blessing, that seek moral reform and tend to be antiritualistic and anticonsumerist. There are lively debates about the involvement of monks in worldly activities, and of the relevance of Buddhist teachings for solving contemporary problems. But the most respected monks are those forest-dwelling, meditative monks who uphold the ideals of dispassionate detachment from the world. Most Thai, however, follow a middle path between the extremes of hedonism and asceticism.

Thailand's political leaders, too, might be said to have, by and large, followed or returned to a middle way: between consensus and coercion, narrow factional gain and wider national interest, democracy and authoritarianism, Thai and Western values, nationalism and internationalism. By most criteria and international comparisons, Thailand in the late 1980s was on the whole a materially successful and peaceful country. It was also characterized by marked inequalities of power and wealth. It must be judged a positive feature that there was also increasingly articulate criticism of the conditions that permit or give rise to rural and urban poverty, the exploitation of women and children, the disadvantaging of ethnic and religious minorities, and reckless destruction of natural environment. Such critical views may not find a place in somewhat nervous official attempts to promote a uniform national Thai identity and culture, but they are contributing to a more compassionate, decentralized and pluralistic view of society, and to a redefinition of the extremes to be avoided in the years ahead.

FURTHER READING

Anderson, Benedict R. O'G., and Mendiones, Ruchira, eds. *In the Mirror: Literature and Politics in Siam in the American era.* Bangkok: Duang Kamol, 1985.
Chatthip Nartsupha and Suthy Prasartset, eds. *The Political Economy of Siam, 1851–1910.* Bangkok: Social Science Association of Thailand, 1981.
Chatthip Nartsupha, Suthy Prasartset, and Montri Chenvidyakarn, eds. *The Political Economy of Siam, 1910–1932.* Bangkok: Social Science Association of Thailand, 1978.
Donner, Wolf. *The Five Faces of Thailand: An Economic Geography.* St. Lucia, Australia: University of Queensland Press; London: C. Hurst, 1978.
Chai-anan Samudavanija. *The Thai Young Turks.* Singapore: Institute of Southeast Asian Studies, 1982.
Girling, John L. S. *Thailand: Society and Politics.* Ithaca, New York: Cornell University Press, 1981.
Ingram, James C. *Economic Change in Thailand, 1950–1970.* Stanford, California: Stanford University Press, 1971.
Keyes, Charles F. *Thailand: Buddhist Kingdom as Modern Nation-State.* Boulder, Colorado: Westview Press, 1987.
McKinnon, John, and Wanat Bhruksasri, eds. *Highlanders of Thailand.* Kuala Lumpur and London: Oxford University Press, 1983.
Morell, David, and Chai-anan Samudavanija, *Political Conflict in Thailand: Reform, Reaction, Revolution.* Cambridge, Massachusetts: Oelgeschlager, Gunn & Hain, 1981.
Skinner, G. William. *Chinese Society in Thailand: An Analytical History.* Ithaca, New York: Cornell University Press, 1957.
Suehiro, Akira. *Capital Accumulation and Industrial Development in Thailand.* Bangkok: Chulalongkorn University Social Research Institute, 1985.
Sulak Sivaraksa. *A Buddhist Vision for Renewing Society: Collected Articles by a Concerned Thai Intellectual.* Bangkok: Thai Watana Panich, 1981.
Thak Chaloemtiarana. *Thailand: The Politics of Despotic Paternalism.* Bangkok: Social Science Association of Thailand for the Thai Khadi Institute of Thammasat University, 1979.
Turton, Andrew, Fast, Jonathan, and Caldwell, Malcolm, eds. *Thailand: Roots of Conflict.* Nottingham, United Kingdom: Spokesman Books, 1978.
Wyatt, David K. *Thailand: A Short History.* New Haven, Connecticut: Yale University Press, 1984.

VIETNAM

WILLIAM S. TURLEY

THE Socialist Republic of Vietnam (SRV) was born out of an anticolonial struggle that culminated in two wars spanning 30 years. The first war secured the independence that had been declared in 1945, but it left the country partitioned. The second war reunited the country's northern and southern halves. Since war's end in 1975, Vietnam has been thwarted in its search for peace, reconstruction and development. Thirty years of revolutionary and international conflict had left the country physically devastated and psychologically exhausted. In the north, cadres who had spent their entire careers at war lacked the skills to administer in peace. In the south, premature socialist transformation accelerated the economic decline, and many people fled abroad. Efforts to resume long-deferred socialist measures in the north depressed productivity there as well. Mismanagement and malfeasance undermined the Communist party's hard-won legitimacy. Despite significant aid from both the Soviet Union and China, by 1978 it was apparent that fundamental goals would not be met and, indeed, that the country was headed toward economic crisis.

At the same time that Vietnam most needed a peaceful international environment and broad economic support in order to address its domestic situation, the Hanoi government decided to overthrow the Khmer Rouge government of Cambodia (Kampuchea) by force. In consequence, Vietnam found itself militarily attacked by China, assailed in the United Nations, isolated from the West, shunned by its non-Communist neighbors, bogged down in Cambodia and abjectly dependent on the Soviet Union. Although the party inaugurated bold reforms in 1979–80, results were limited by continuing high military expenditures, erratic implementation and strained relations with powers outside the Soviet bloc.

To many observers, Vietnam's postwar misfortune has been a just reward for incompetence and vaulting ambition. On closer examination, however, the reality is more complex. During the war, North and South together had depended on about U.S.$2 billion per year in economic aid to keep their economies afloat, and the sudden evaporation of that sum caused a wrenching readjustment. Moreover, it was not entirely Hanoi's fault that its attempts, following the war, to diversify economic and diplomatic contacts had only limited success. In the crucial year of 1978, caught in the irreconcilable pressures of Sino-Soviet rivalry, Vietnam met indifference or hostility from most other quarters able to help. Like statesmen everywhere, Hanoi's leaders felt that the choices they made were the only rational ones in the circumstances.

By the late 1980s, Vietnam still faced an uncertain future. Stagnation implied falling farther behind more dynamic neighbors, but reform was fraught with controversy. The occupation of Cambodia was an unwanted burden, but withdrawal posed immeasurable risks. Faced with a perplexing present, Hanoi's leaders could find little guidance in their revolution's extraordinary past.

PRECOLONIAL HISTORY

Vietnam is well known for its cultural debt to China and its history of resistance to foreign rule. Claiming descent from a semimythical kingdom established in 2879 B.C., Vietnam entered written history through Chinese conquest in 111 B.C. For the next thousand years, the Chinese imparted their learning, writing and doctrines to a Vietnamese upper class while leaving village traditions largely untouched. A succession of rebellions, mostly led by Sino-Viet aristocrats, failed until one led by Ngo Quyen in A.D. 939. The Vietnamese then turned back several Chinese attempts at reconquest, including two by the Mongol Yüan dynasty in 1284 and 1287 and a brief occupation by the Ming from 1413 to 1427. Although independent, the Vietnamese state continued to borrow legal and administrative patterns from China and to disseminate Chinese cultural norms.

From their center in the Red River Delta, the Vietnamese began expanding southward in the 14th century at the expense of the Indianized kingdoms of Champa and, later, Cambodia. This expansion reached present-day Ho Chi Minh City (Saigon) about 1695 and modern Vietnam's southernmost extremity on the Ca Mau Peninsula in 1780.

Beginning in 1600, the country was divided between two rival aristocratic families, the Trinh in the north and the Nguyen in the south, both swearing allegiance to the same emperor. Division ended when a rebellion named after the village of Tay Son in central Vietnam broke out in 1774, routed the rival families and reunited the country in 1786. However, the Tay Son movement soon lost its dynamism, and a Nguyen lord named Nguyen Anh returned from refuge in Thailand to defeat the Tay Son forces. Nguyen Anh proclaimed himself Emperor Gia Long and established his capital at Hue in 1802. The Nguyen dynasty, Vietnam's last, would survive until 1945.

COLONIAL RULE

National divisions exacerbated by the southward expansion helped Roman Catholic missionaries and merchant adventurers, and later, France to gain a foothold. Although the Confucian literati, or mandarins, often demanded their expulsion, the Portuguese, Dutch and French traders and priests who began arriving in the 17th century were welcomed by aristocratic rivals who valued Western knowledge of navigation and cannon. Nguyen Anh defeated the Tay Son with military support raised for him by Pigneau de Behaine, a French bishop, in return for a promise of trade privileges and the cession of Poulo Condore (Con Son) Island and the port of Tourane (Da Nang) to France. Missionaries also found a receptive audience among poor Vietnamese who felt oppressed by the mandarins. About 10 percent of the population eventually converted to Roman Catholicism, and among this portion were individuals, who would serve as interpreters and intermediaries for France when colonial rule began.

Seizing upon the persecution of missionaries for pretext, the French navy attacked Da Nang in 1858. By 1867, France controlled Saigon and the Mekong Delta, and in 1883 it forced the Vietnamese emperor to accept a French protectorate over the remaining territory. In the northern and central parts of the country, which the French called Tonkin and Annam, respectively, a Vietnamese administration remained nominally in control of domestic affairs, while in the southern third, which the French called Cochin China, the French installed their own administration. This tripartite division conformed to, and deepened, the minor cultural differentiation among the three regions, although these regions had never been a basis of administrative organization. French economic exploitation also helped to spread plantation agriculture, increase tenancy, exacerbate inequalities of wealth and create a Westernized urban elite.

The French succeeded in consolidating their hold partly because they acted at a time when the Vietnamese court was in disarray. But resistance was tenacious. In 1885, mandarins who supported the newly installed 12-year-old Emperor Ham Nghi organized the Can Vuong (Support the King) movement that fought the French until 1896. The defeat of this traditionalist uprising led to the discrediting of Confucian doctrine and institutions in the eyes of later generations, which sought keys to independence in modern ideologies. One result of that search was the fragmentation of the political culture as movements formed around quite disparate ideas, among which was Marxism-Leninism.

ORIGINS OF VIETNAMESE COMMUNISM

The first Vietnamese Communists have been called "mandarin proletarians" because many of them were direct descendants of the scholar gentry who had participated in the Can Vuong movement. These individuals found much to attract them in Marxism's critique of capitalism, Lenin's theses on the colonial question, the Bolshevik Revolution's overthrow of a "feudal" order and the prospect of a powerful ally in the new revolutionary state. Among these individuals was Ho Chi Minh.

The 211 men and women whom Ho gathered to found the Vietnam Communist party in February 1930 (renamed the Indochinese Communist party on Comintern orders that October) were mostly like other patriotic middle-class young people who became involved in anticolonial movements at that time. However, thanks to the elimination of rivals by the colonial regime, the moderating influence of Comintern policy and the replacement of jailed or executed leaders by Moscow-trained cadres, the Communists emerged from the 1930s as the largest, best organized anticolonial group.

The organizational principles were those of a Leninist-type vanguard party. The party's vertical chain of committees was divided into six echelons, from the national to local levels. Each committee directed the work of the one below, with supreme authority vested in the Central Committee. Below the local level, the basic level of organization was the party chapter, or cell, whose members worked in the same unit, such as a factory, school or hamlet. Full-time "professional revolutionaries," or cadres, supplied leadership, while ordinary members supposedly were imbued with working-class consciousness and unconditionally obedient to the party. Outside the party core there existed, at least in theory, a network of "mass" and "front" organizations that provided links between the party and non-Communist elements.

When World War II broke out and many "nationalists" fled abroad or collaborated with the occupying Japanese, the Communists began organizing revolutionary base areas near the Chinese border under the nominal aegis of a national united front known as the Viet Nam Doc Lap Dong Minh (Vietnam Independence League), or Viet Minh for short. Although few in number, the Communists were poised to capitalize on the disarray and famine that accompanied Japan's defeat.

THE FIRST WAR

The pivotal event in modern Vietnamese history was the August Revolution of 1945. In two tumultuous weeks, the Communists rode to power on a tide of mass demonstrations that culminated, on September 2, in a declaration of independence and establishment of the Democratic Republic of Vietnam (DRV). Buoyed by patriotic fervor, the regime won broad acceptance and quickly recruited tens of thousands of young people for military service. The last Nguyen emperor, Bao Dai, abdicated in its favor.

The Communists' dominance was contested by other nationalist groups, however, and France insisted on returning to protect its interests. Against a background of furious effort by both the French and Vietnamese to strengthen their armed forces, negotiations broke down and open warfare began in December 1946. As France reasserted control over the cities, the Communists withdrew to the countryside to wage a guerrilla "people's war" of resistance. With the end of the Chinese civil war in 1949, the Communists began to receive assistance from the Chinese, while France enjoyed an even greater increase in assistance from the United States. But French efforts to create an alternative non-Communist Vietnamese administration and national army were insufficient to offset the Communists' superior legitimacy and organizational skills at the village level. In spring 1954, Communist forces laid siege to the French outpost of Dien Bien Phu, which fell on May 7, the day before the Geneva Conference opened to negotiate an end to the war. At the urging of the Soviet Union and China, the DRV reluctantly agreed to a cease-fire that left Vietnam partitioned at the 17th parallel, pending elections on reunification within two years.

NORTH AND SOUTH

Having for most of the war emphasized the primacy of national independence in its objectives, the Communist Party (renamed the Lao Dong, or Workers' Party since 1951) afterward turned to socialist transformation in the northern half of the country that it now controlled. Whereas it had welcomed participation by virtually all classes in the war against France, the party began to apply strict class criteria in recruitment, assignment and promotion in all party, state and military leadership ranks. Class criteria also determined how land was redistributed in a radical reform that equalized landholdings but also involved the execution of an estimated 3,000 to 15,000 people.[1] The land reform aroused such opposition that the party leadership felt constrained in late 1956 to admit "errors" and call for their rectification. What turned leaders against the reform was not the land redistribution but the implacable treatment of everyone, including party members, according to class criteria without regard for previous service to the revolution. The party's general secretary, Truong Chinh, and two other leaders who had direct responsibility for the reform were dismissed from their posts. However, the rectification left the new distribution of power and wealth largely intact.

With economic assistance from China and the Soviet Union, the DRV also strove to rehabilitate its modest and badly dilapidated industrial base. Production in most sectors returned to prewar levels by 1960, and the first Five-Year Plan went into effect in 1961. The establishing of agricultural cooperatives followed land reform, but output had difficulty keeping pace with population growth in this traditionally rice-deficit area. Although one of Asia's poorest regions, the North did have some political advantage in a unified leadership, an organizational structure that reached down into the villages and substantial legitimacy earned in the long war for independence.

In the southern half of the country, the State of Vietnam established its capital in Saigon with what remained of the colonial administrative structure. Weak and divided, it lacked outstanding personalities, enjoyed little popular support and exercised limited control over the countryside. Armed religious sects patrolled large parts of the Mekong Delta. The government was headed for collapse until Ngo Dinh Diem, a Catholic nationalist who took over as premier in June 1954, outmaneuvered his opposition and dispersed the sect armies. Diem proceeded to have himself elected chief of state and first president of the new republic in October 1955. With American backing, he consolidated a regime that depended heavily on his own relatives and fellow Catholics for support. Although he brought stability to Saigon, his autocratic tendencies, the excesses of his relatives and his failure to deal realistically with land and tenancy issues alienated the population. His harsh treatment of demonstrations led by Buddhist monks

[1] Edwin E. Moise, "Land Reform and Land Reform Errors in North Vietnam," *Pacific Affairs* 49 (Spring 1976): 78.

finally exasperated the United States as well as his own generals. On November 2, 1963, Diem was overthrown and executed in a military coup.

Coup followed coup until, under strong American pressure to establish a stable and nominally democratic government, General Nguyen Van Thieu was elected president in September 1967 with 34.8 percent of the votes cast. Resilient and cunning, Thieu, in 1969, began to implement long-overdue administrative and land reforms; but he was averse to sharing power, constricted opposition and never succeeded in capturing the popular imagination. He ran unopposed for reelection in 1971 and later had the constitution amended so he could run for a third term in 1975. His regime fell, however, before that election could take place.

THE SECOND WAR

War in the South evolved out of the Communist party's determination to reunify the country by force once the Saigon regime had refused to implement the Geneva agreement's provision for elections in 1956. A nucleus of party members in the South began assembling guerrilla forces, and in May 1959 the party's Political Bureau in Hanoi approved a plan for limited armed struggle. The party also organized a National Liberation Front, which was unveiled in December 1960, for the purpose of attracting non-Communist support. At that time, too, the party selected as first secretary Le Duan, a leader strongly identified with the cause of reunification. Although the party provided the leadership and strategy for the southern revolution, popular grievances against the Diem regime also were crucial in helping the party and its fronts to recruit a significant following.

Until 1964, the United States supplied only military aid and advisers to Saigon, but perception of the war as an East-West conflict and concern for the credibility of American commitments pushed the United States toward deeper involvement. American forces in South Vietnam reached a peak of 543,400 in May 1969, and American aircraft dropped more bombs on North Vietnam than were dropped in all of World War II. Hanoi, meanwhile, had substantially increased its infiltration of men, weapons and supplies into the South, partly supplanting indigenous southern forces on the revolutionary side but thwarting American strategy. The seeming endless high cost of the war without assurance of victory undermined American domestic support for intervention. Under President Richard Nixon, therefore, the United States shifted emphasis to strengthening Saigon forces in preparation for eventual American withdrawal. On March 29, 1973, in fulfillment of an agreement signed in Paris in January, the last American troops departed, leaving the Vietnamese to implement a cease-fire-in-place.

The cease-fire was never stable, and friction between the two sides expanded into maneuvers for strategic position. In October 1973, the Communists resolved to end the impasse by military means, and in March 1975, they launched coordinated attacks on Saigon's widely dispersed outposts in the central highlands. When Saigon troops fled, panic spread to the lowlands and in subsequent fighting many Saigon military units disintegrated.

By mid-April, Saigon was surrounded; on the twenty-sixth, Thieu resigned, and on the thirtieth his successor, General Duong Van "Big" Minh, surrendered.

Much attention has been focused on the failure of the United States to rescue the Thieu regime from certain defeat or even to supply the massive increase in military assistance that Thieu demanded. However, Thieu had never sufficiently overcome the political divisions and popular indifference that had weakened previous Saigon regimes. At the beginning of the Communist offensive, Saigon's armed forces were more numerous and better equipped than those under Communist command in the South. But they were also extraordinarily dependent on a high volume of American supply and psychologically dependent on American guarantees. Only American reintervention could have staved off defeat in that year and quite possibly in countless years to follow.

REUNIFICATION AND RECOVERY

In 1975, the Communists lacked the broad popular base in the south that they had enjoyed upon driving the French from the north in 1954. The south's more heterogeneous society was refractory to central authority, religious and commercial interests were quite strong and 40 percent of the population lived in cities where the Communists previously had little influence. Although the party was well entrenched among some 4 million peasants who had lived many long years in "liberated zones," it could not count on the support of other peasants who had benefited from Thieu's land reform in the early 1970s. A severe shortage of politically reliable cadres due to heavy casualties during the war further complicated the task of establishing a new administration; and a dispatch of cadres from the north to compensate for this shortage aroused southern resentment.

In fact, party leaders had not expected Saigon to fall in 1975 and were unprepared for the transition that followed. For a time the question of just how and at what pace the south should be integrated with the north was undecided. Certain southern party leaders evidently preferred to prolong the separate development of the south. But the Central Committee decided in August 1975 that reunification and socialization of the south should commence forthwith.

Elections in April 1976 created a unified National Assembly, and in July that assembly approved the formal reunification of north and south as the Socialist Republic of Vietnam (SRV). Whereas the Democratic Republic had been a "people's democratic state," the new constitution, adopted in December 1980, defined the SRV as a "proletarian dictatorship." The executive body was to be the Council of Ministers, with a chairman elected by the National Assembly, and the functions of a presidency and legislative presidium were vested in the Council of State, also elected by the National Assembly. Real power, of course, continued to reside in the Vietnam Communist party, which the 1980 constitution recognized as "the only force leading the state and society."

Along with its decision to reunify political institutions in 1976, the party resolved to hasten the development of "new relations of production" (i.e., reorganization of society along socialist lines) in combination with "new productive forces" (increased output). On this basis, the party's Fourth Congress unveiled the second Five-Year Plan (the first having been in the north in 1961–65) in December 1976. The south was to emphasize agriculture and light industry, while the north was to recentralize its economy, enlarge the scale of socialized production and develop heavy industry. The plan set goals of raising industrial output an average of 16–18 percent per year and agricultural output eight to 10 percent per year, and completing the construction of the "material and technical bases of socialism" in just 20 years.

Socializing the south proved to be more difficult than party leaders had anticipated. Attempts to bring the economy under state control made little headway, especially in Saigon, where the large, tightly knit Chinese (or Hoa) business community dominated trade and commerce. A campaign against "comprador bourgeoisie" succeeded in confiscating the largest businesses, but many smaller merchants evaded controls by bribing the party's astonishingly corruptible cadres. Finally, in March 1978, a "Communiqué on Private Trade" ordered the complete and immediate abolition of trade carried on by "bourgeois tradesmen." Although aimed against all private trade, the crackdown affected the Hoa most broadly as a group. Furthermore, the campaign came at a time of worsening relations between Vietnam and China and fueled fears of persecution among the Hoa, causing a surge in the exodus of boat people that security officials, now concerned about a possible Chinese fifth column, did little to curb and much to exploit for personal gain. Both the north and south lost many educated and talented people.

The socialization of southern agriculture also proceeded slowly. Because landholdings had been equalized by both Saigon and Hanoi during the war, a redistributive reform like the one that had preceded the establishing of cooperatives in the north was unnecessary. Serious cooperative farming did not begin until June 1977. However, the south's freeholding farmers, especially in the Mekong Delta, showed little interest in cooperatives, the Hoa Hao Buddhist sect was recalcitrant and ructions on the Cambodian border diverted the party's attention. By late 1979, only 30 percent of all peasant households in the Mekong Delta had joined any kind of "production collective." In the following year, many cooperatives dissolved as peasants reacted against forced membership and low prices paid by the state. The issue by then, however, had become not just the fate of cooperative farming in the south but the viability of the party's economic model for the entire country.

ECONOMIC PERFORMANCE AND REFORM

Vietnam's economic problems began well before its conflicts with Cambodia and China (see *The Third War* below) made matters worse. The value and tonnage of gross agricultural production were lower in 1977 and 1978 than in 1976, as was average yield of paddy per hectare (see Figure 1). The

Figure 1
FOOD GRAIN PRODUCTION, 1975–87

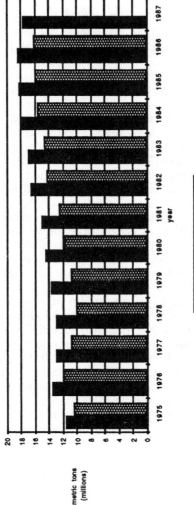

Sources: General Statistical Office, *Statistical Data 1930–1984* (Hanoi: Statistics Publishing House, 1985), 87; International Monetary Fund, *Viet Nam—Recent Economic Developments*, May 15, 1987, 8; *Far Eastern Economic Review*, April 28, 1988, 76.

food deficit swelled to 3 million metric tons in 1979. With a population growth rate of 2.4 percent a year, per capita food production decreased from 604 lb./274 kg in 1976 to 591 lb./268 kg in 1980, substantially below the 661 lb./300 kg minimum subsistence level in Vietnam.[2] Industrial production also declined; many plants operated at less than 50 percent capacity and few targets were met (see Figure 2).

In mid-1978, party leaders virtually abandoned the Five-Year Plan, pinning the blame on factors beyond their control. Indeed, natural calamities, structural problems left behind by the war, shortages of parts, supplies and energy, and China's suspension of some $300 million annual economic assistance in July 1978 all played a role. But evidence that the party's own policies also were responsible was irrefutable. In the south, peasants had fed rice to their pigs rather than sell it to the state at the low fixed price, and the constriction of the free market had weakened the incentive to earn by reducing what was available to buy. Nationwide, a tendency to push big projects and socialized distribution exceeded the capacity of technical and managerial resources. On reflection, some of the very leaders who had pressed for rigorous socialization admitted it had been a "leftist error" to abolish "nonsocialist economic sectors" at so early a stage of development, and economically unsound not to give higher priority to agriculture.

In September 1979, the sixth plenum of the Central Committee responded with one of the most fundamental revisions of policy in the party's history. Not entirely unlike Lenin's New Economic Policy, the plenum resolution rolled back controls on private production of goods that could be produced most efficiently in the private sector. Subsequent directives loosened controls on market distribution of consumer items, strengthened material incentives in both industry and agriculture, and called for a partial decentralization of planning and investment. Perhaps most significant was the introduction in 1981 of production contracts in agriculture. This reform permitted cooperatives to assign responsibility for the final stages of cultivation to family units and allowed families, after meeting the state tax and procurement quota, to sell their surplus grain on the free market. Cooperative farming continued, and in fact was accelerated in the south, with the goal of achieving "basic completion" by 1985, but on a revised format that had greater appeal. Heavy industry's share of investment declined as that of agriculture grew. These policy shifts produced significant short-term increases in output. Production of foodstuffs exceeded population growth, and in 1983 the country achieved a minimal self-sufficiency in food. With very sizable Soviet assistance,[3] gross industrial output also increased at an average annual rate of 13 percent in 1981–84.

The gains, however, were more in the nature of a rebound from the crisis of 1979–80 than the beginning of sustained rapid growth. After a spurt

---

[2] To Nhan Tri, *Socialist Vietnam's Economy, 1975–1985: An Assessment,* T.R.F. Series No. 139 (Tokyo: Institute of Developing Economies, January 1987), 31.
[3] From about $500 million annually during the 1976–80 plan, Soviet economic aid rose to over $1 billion annually in 1981–85. Based on overvalued rubles, however, these estimates may inflate the dollar value of that aid.

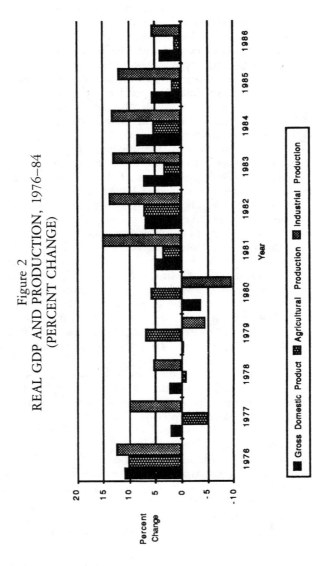

Figure 2
REAL GDP AND PRODUCTION, 1976–84
(PERCENT CHANGE)

Sources: International Monetary Fund, *Viet Nam—Recent Economic Develop-ments*, June 30, 1986, 4a; ibid., May 15, 1987, iv.

in 1982–83, growth in both agriculture and industry tapered off, and the Sixth National Party Congress in December 1986 admitted failure to achieve the objective set by the previous congress, namely, "to stabilize the socio-economic situation and the people's life." Enterprises were still operating at only half capacity, labor productivity had declined, prices had soared, expenditures still far exceeded revenues, bottlenecks choked the circulation of goods and unemployment remained high. With startling frankness, a Sixth Congress resolution acknowledged that economic deficiencies and cadre corruption "had lessened the confidence of the masses in the party leadership and the functioning of state organs." And yet a year later, agricultural production had fallen another two percent, available grain per capita had dropped from a high of 670 lb./304 kg in 1985 to 617 lb./280 kg and only 40 percent of the 1 million young people who had entered the job market had been able to find work. In spring 1988, pests and drought threatened the harvest, and the government predicted a 1.5 million ton food deficit.

Although weather and war had been factors, the reform begun in 1979 was never coherently conceived or implemented. On two separate occasions, liberalization of markets was followed by severe strictures, and an indescribably inept currency exchange accompanied by devaluation and a large budget deficit contributed to a 700 percent inflation in 1986. Contrary to declared intentions, development strategy continued to concentrate unevenly on manufacturing in heavy industry at the expense of labor-intensive sectors, and little progress was made toward terminating state subsidies and loosening administrative controls.

A major cause of the muddle was the festering dispute between leaders who would give first priority to "new releases of production" (socialist transformation) and those who would give it to "new productive forces" ("pragmatic" development). The crisis of 1979–80, by discrediting the former, made reform possible. But once the crisis had passed and inflation had undermined the earnings of low-income state cadres, conservative forces rallied. Party leaders also were constrained by their inclination—born of victory in war through organization, discipline and unanimity—to seek solutions in creating new organizations without weakening or dismantling old ones. Such was the tendency of a resolution in June 1985 on "renovating the mechanism of economic management." Last, top leaders accustomed to monopolizing all decision making, yet ignorant of economics, imposed their own confusion on weak and submissive advisory bodies.

Some hope that the political balance might shift decisively in favor of thoroughgoing reform emerged at the Sixth Congress in December 1986. Like the congress before it, this one made an apparently sincere attempt to promote younger people to positions of authority. Of 173 members of the Central Committee, 81 were new; members aged 40 to 59 accounted for 67 percent of the total; and 82 percent of the members were admitted to the party between 1945 and 1965. Three aging leaders (Truong Chinh, Pham Van Dong, Le Duc Tho) retired, and the Sixth Congress, elected as general secretary a man, Nguyen Van Linh, who was strongly identified with the reform movement. The congress also chose a Political Bureau in which known reformers were prominent, and adopted a resolution that committed the party to "major adjustments in the investment structure." But calls to "renovate the economic mechanism" on the basis of democratic centralism and to bypass the capitalist stage of development were reminders that reform, if it could be called that, rested on an unstable foundation of compromise. The death in March 1988 of Pham Hung, Pham Van Dong's successor as prime minister, removed another aging militant from the scene but had no apparent repercussions on the policy debate.

THE THIRD WAR

Although Vietnam's economic woes had mainly domestic origins, they were exacerbated by the conflict that broke into the open with Vietnam's invasion of Cambodia on December 25, 1978 and China's punitive attack on Vietnam in February–March 1979. This third major conflict since independence in 1945 was in some ways the most challenging to the nation's aspirations and the greatest test of its leaders' wits. For, unlike the first two wars, which pitted Vietnamese patriotism against distant foreign powers on Vietnamese soil, the third one involved the unfamiliar task of sending the Vietnamese army into foreign territory to overthrow a sovereign government and aroused the enmity of Vietnam's former ally and powerful neighbor, China.

The "Third Indochina War" resulted from the intersection of two separate sources of friction, the Sino-Soviet dispute and Vietnam's always uneasy relationship with the Cambodian Communist movement. For most of the second war, Hanoi had maintained a balance in its relations with Moscow and Beijing and had striven to heal the dispute because it calculated that only the support of a united bloc could deter the United States from unleasing greater, possibly unlimited, force. However, Hanoi perceived China's move to normalize relations with the United States in 1971–72 and pressure to compromise on ending the war as a strategic betrayal. As Hanoi turned increasingly to the Soviet Union, relations between Vietnam and China grew more strained. It was Vietnam's admission to the Soviet-dominated Council for Mutual Economic Assistance (CMEA, also known as COMECON) on June 29, 1978 that precipitated China's suspension of aid in July. Hanoi then proceeded to tighten its security relationship with the Soviet Union by signing a Treaty of Friendship and Cooperation with Moscow in November.[4]

Meanwhile, Hanoi had failed to reach an accommodation with Cambodian Communist leader Pol Pot, who suspected the Vietnamese of support-

---

[4] When China sent troops across the Vietnamese border in February–March 1979, the Soviet Union dispatched a naval task force to the South China Sea. On March 27, four Soviet vessels dropped anchor in Cam Ranh Bay. The Soviet Union subsequently maintained a permanent naval presence in Cam Ranh, and the number of Soviet ships operating out of that port rose to 30 in 1987. Tu-95 Bear reconnaissance aircraft and a squadron of MiG-23 Flogger fighter-interceptors also were deployed to the airfields at Cam Ranh and Da Nang.

ing a pro-Hanoi faction in his own party and harbored an atavistic fear of Vietnamese expansionism as well. China's concern about Soviet influence in Vietnam and Pol Pot's fear of the Vietnamese brought the two together, and China began supplying military and economic assistance to Cambodia. After three years of Cambodian commando raids into Vietnamese territory and Vietnamese counterthrusts into Cambodia, Hanoi concluded that its security could not afford a hostile Cambodia allied with China and moved to overthrow Pol Pot by force, preempting, Hanoi claimed, a "two-front war." China's attack on Vietnam, which devastated towns and economic installations along the border, was an attempt to show that Vietnam could not attack China's friends or align with its adversary with impunity.

Vietnam's subsequent efforts to build a Cambodian client regime and suppress Khmer resistance forces were a good deal more successful than the similar Soviet venture in Afghanistan, although not without difficulty. With an average force level of about 140,000, the Vietnamese held the major towns and lines of communication and kept most resistance forces bottled up in camps near the Thai border. Parallel efforts under Vietnamese auspices created a Cambodian army of about 30,000 men and an administrative structure that reached down into most villages. Hanoi committed itself in 1987 to withdrawing the bulk of its forces by 1990, and a troop withdrawal in 1988 brought the troop total estimated by foreign observers down to 100,000. Hanoi clearly calculated that demoralization of the Khmer resistance and disunity among its regional opponents in the Association of Southeast Asian Nations (ASEAN) would permit it to withdraw without jeopardizing its Cambodian ally or accepting a political settlement that imposed anything more than cosmetic changes on its fait accompli.

Certainly one factor motivating Hanoi to withdraw was the economic burden to itself. Although this cannot be calculated with precision, the cost involved, besides the Chinese aid suspension, the termination of economic assistance from virtually all non-Communist sources, continued high military expenditures and the diversion of educated and technically trained young people from the civilian sector. With 1 million to 1.2 million soldiers throughout the 1980s, the People's Army was the world's third or fourth largest armed force. Another factor may have been Soviet strategy to improve relations with non-Communist Southeast Asia and reduce the USSR's cost of supporting Vietnam.

But Hanoi was not about to relinquish its dominant position in Cambodia (or Laos) easily. In the Communist Vietnamese perception, Indochina comprises a strategic unity because it has been treated as such in three modern wars by Vietnam's great power adversaries. Vietnam cannot be secure if either of its weaker neighbors is susceptible to penetration by a hostile power. Because these neighbors have not been notably successful at defending their neutrality, it follows, in Vietnamese thinking, that they must be kept aligned with Hanoi. However, neither this reasoning nor ancient aspiration drives Hanoi to envision an Indochina federation, as the party's program once suggested. Not only would such a goal likely be opposed by the Soviet Union, not to mention China and the rest of the world, but the clear thrust of Hanoi's relations with both Laos and Cambodia has been to create a bloc of independent states linked by economic, security and political ties that do not require formal federate institutions to preserve them. Of course, Vietnam is the predominant partner in this bloc, as is the Soviet Union with respect to Eastern Europe.

PROSPECTS

Vietnam paid an extraordinary price for its national independence and unity, considering that by far the majority of nations to emerge from colonial rule won their independence through nonviolent struggle or had it peacefully conferred upon them. That was the price Vietnam paid for its situation on the frontlines of the cold war and then in the center of the Sino-Soviet rivalry, and, finally, for its leaders' revolutionary hubris. In addition to the carnage, the price included the massive destruction of the countryside, the redirection of almost all trade to the Soviet Union and Eastern Europe, prolonged dependency on foreign aid for economic survival, a security relationship with the Soviet Union that antagonizes almost every other state in the region and a protracted confrontation with China, the one country capable of punishing Vietnam forever.

However, Vietnam's difficulties have been symptoms of adjustment, not permanent conditions. Whatever its deficiencies, the political system is highly stable and more capable of mobilizing human resources than most countries in the Third World. The gradual succession to leadership by people for whom war lives in history not memory increases the pressure for change. Located in the world's most dynamically growing region, overlooking a strategic sea and blessed with an abundance of raw materials, Vietnam has natural advantages to help it rise from poverty and become a regional power. Whether Vietnam will begin to realize its potential depends on a combination of appropriate domestic policies, accommodation with its non-Communist neighbors and improved relations among all the major Pacific Rim nations.

FURTHER READING

Boudarel, Georges, ed. *La bureaucratie au Vietnam*. Paris: L'Harmattan, 1983.

Chanda, Nayan. *Brother Enemy: The War after the War*. San Diego, California: Harcourt Brace Jovanovich, 1986.

Duiker, William J. *Vietnam since the Fall of Saigon*. Rev. ed. Athens: Ohio University Center for International Studies, 1985.

Elliot, David W. P., ed. *The Third Indochina Conflict*. Boulder, Colorado: Westview Press, 1982.

Khanh, Huynh Kim. *Vietnamese Communism, 1925–1945*. Ithaca, New York: Cornell University Press for the Institute of Southeast Asian Studies, Singapore, 1982.

Kolko, Gabriel *Anatomy of a War: Vietnam, The United States, and the Modern Historical Experience*. New York: Pantheon, 1985.

Turley, William S.. *The Second Indochina War: A Short Political and Military History, 1954–1975*. Boulder, Colorado: Westview Press, 1986.

———., ed. *Vietnamese Communism in Comparative Perspective*. Boulder, Colorado: Westview Press, 1980.

————. "Vietnam/Indochina: Hanoi's Challenge to Southeast Asian Regional Order." In Kihl, Young Whan, and Grinter, Lawrence E., eds. *Asian-Pacific Security: Emerging Challenges and Responses.* Boulder, Colorado: Lynne Rienner, 1986.

Vietnam: Essays in History, Culture and Society. New York: The Asia Society, 1985.

White, Christine Pelzer, ed. *Postwar Vietnam: Dilemmas in Socialist Development.* Ithaca, New York: Cornell University Press, 1988.

Woodside, Alexander B. *Community and Revolution in Modern Vietnam* Boston: Houghton Mifflin, 1976.

tued from front flap)

Contributors include such authorities as Bruce Cumings and Takashi Inoguchi on the history of postwar Asia, Haruhiro Fukui on political parties, Judith Nagata on religion and politics, Christopher Howe on Japan and the world economy, Andrew Nathan on Taiwan, Mohan Rao on peasants, Anthony Rowley on banking and investment, and Edmund Leach on Asian minority groups.

Robert H. Taylor is professor of politics in the University of London and head of the Department of Economic and Political Studies at the university's School of Oriental and African Studies. Born in Ohio, he received his doctorate from Cornell University and taught previously at the University of Sydney and Wilberforce University. He is the author of *The State in Burma* and coeditor of *Context, Meaning and Power in Southeast Asia* as well as a contributing author to *In Search of Southeast Asia: A Modern History* (2nd ed.).

HANDBOOKS TO THE MODERN WORLD

Already published:

WESTERN EUROPE
edited by Richard Mayne

THE SOVIET UNION AND EASTERN
 EUROPE
edited by George Schöpflin

THE MIDDLE EAST
edited by Michael Adams

AFRICA
edited by Sean Moroney

Forthcoming:

CANADA

THE UNITED STATES